THE CONCISE
OXFORD COMPANION
TO ENGLISH
LITERATURE

THE CONCISE OXFORD COMPANION TO ENGLISH LITERATURE

EDITED BY

MARGARET DRABBLE

AND

JENNY STRINGER

Oxford   New York

OXFORD UNIVERSITY PRESS

1987

Oxford University Press, Walton Street, Oxford OX2 6DP
Oxford New York Toronto
Delhi Bombay Calcutta Madras Karachi
Petaling Jaya Singapore Hong Kong Tokyo
Nairobi Dar es Salaam Cape Town
Melbourne Auckland
and associated companies in
Beirut Berlin Ibadan Nicosia

Oxford is a trade mark of Oxford University Press

British Library Cataloguing in Publication Data
The Concise Oxford companion to English
literature.
1. English literature — Dictionaries
I. Drabble, Margaret   II. Stringer, Jenny
820'.3'21   PR19
ISBN 0–19–866140–1

Library of Congress Cataloging in Publication Data
Drabble, Margaret, 1939–
The concise Oxford companion to English
literature.
An abridgement of the 5th ed. of The Oxford
companion to English literature.
1. English literature—Dictionaries.   2. English
literature—Bio-bibliography.   3. American literature—
Dictionaries.   4. American literature—Bio-bibliography.
I. Stringer, Jenny.   II. Drabble, Margaret, 1939–   .
Oxford companion to English literature.   III. Title.
PR19.D73   1987   820'.9   87–1595
ISBN 0–19–866140–1

Set by Wyvern Typesetting Ltd
Printed in Great Britain by
Richard Clay Ltd,
Bungay, Suffolk

PREFACE

THIS work is an abridgement of the fifth edition of *The Oxford Companion to English Literature* (1985). It is hoped that the volume will provide the general reader and student with a useful and compact guide to the central matter of English literature.

There are entries for major authors born in or before 1939, not only novelists, dramatists, and poets, but also historians, philosophers, scholars, critics, editors, and journalists. Also included are plot summaries for literary works, characters from books and plays, definitions of literary and intellectual movements, literary genres, and critical theory, entries on British and Irish mythology, literary societies, and periodicals, libraries, copyright, censorship, and coffee houses, as well as printers, publishers, booksellers, and private presses.

Certain non-literary figures who have become famous in a literary context (such as actors and actresses) have been included. Our selection of American authors has been somewhat guided by British appraisals and emphasis has been placed on Anglo-American links and responses. There are individual entries for authors of other countries writing in English, including those from the Commonwealth, Africa, the Caribbean, and India, but coverage here is by no means comprehensive.

It is assumed that many of the readers of this volume will not be familiar with the parent volume, and it would therefore seem irrelevant to describe at length where cuts have been made. We have tried to prune rather than delete entries. Two areas of reference which have been almost completely omitted are music and art. Many of the entries on foreign authors have also gone, as have public schools and colleges of Oxford and Cambridge universities. However, there is a new, full entry on Foreign Influences in English Literature. Several foreign authors have individual entries but they have been treated in the context of English literature, or, in some cases, on merit alone. Classical authors are represented and their connections with English literature firmly emphasized.

As with *The Oxford Companion to English Literature*, the stress is on primary information rather than critical appreciation. Works and authors are described and characterized rather than judged. It is impossible to be consistent in coverage and we emphasize that the length of entry is not a guide to an author's importance. Some of the plot summaries have been shortened, particularly those on Restoration plays which have, in some cases, been reduced to a scene or two giving the flavour or essence of the play. But if we have been ruthless here, we have been generous with Dickens, Shakespeare, and others with such reputations, whose plot summaries remain almost entirely intact.

The editors wish to thank all the contributors to *The Oxford Companion of English Literature* whose entries have reappeared in this volume in shortened form. The editors alone are responsible for any differences between the material in this volume and that in *The Oxford Companion to English Literature*. Finally we acknowledge our particular debt to the late Sir Paul Harvey, whose original *Oxford Companion to English Literature* (1932) provided the foundation of the revised edition upon which this volume is based.

M.D.

J.S.

London
November 1986

ABBREVIATIONS

a.	*ante*, before	ff.	and following
ad fin.	*ad finem*, near the end	*fl.*	*floruit*, flourished
ASPR	Anglo-Saxon Poetic Records	Fr.	French
b.	born	Gk.	Greek
BCP	Book of Common Prayer	Lat.	Latin
Bm Cat.	British Museum Catalogue	l., ll.,	line, lines
Bk	Book	LXX	Septuagint
c.	*circa*, about	ME	Middle English
cent.	century	*MLR*	*Modern Language Review*
cf.	*confer*, compare	*N. & Q.*	*Notes and Queries*
CH	Companion of Honour	NT	New Testament
ch.	chapter	OE	Old English (Anglo-Saxon)
CHAL	Cambridge History of Ancient Literature	*OED*	*Oxford English Dictionary*
		OM	Order of Merit
CHEL	Cambridge History of English Literature	op. cit.	*opus citatum*, work quoted
		OS	Old Style dating, or calendar
d.	died	OT	Old Testament
DNB	*Dictionary of National Bigraphy*	p., pp.	page, pages
EB	*Encyclopaedia Britannica*	*PEL*	*Periods of European Literature*
ed.	editor, or edited by	PMLA	Publications of the Modern Language Association of America
edn	edition		
EETS	Early English Text Society	pron.	pronounced
OS	Original Series	Pt	Part
ES	Extra Series	*RES*	*Review of English Studies*
SS	Supplementary Series	*sc.*	*scilicet*, namely
	If no series is specified, the volume referred to is in the Original Series	STS	Scottish Text Society
		s.v.	*sub verbo*, under the word
		TLS	*Times Literary Supplement*
EML	English Men of Letters	trans.	translation, or translated by
		vol.	volume

NOTE TO THE READER

NAMES in bold capital letters are those of real people; the headwords of all other entries are in bold upper and lower case: italics for the titles of novels, plays, and other full-length works; roman in quotation marks for individual short stories, poems, essays; ordinary roman type for fictional characters, terms, places, and so on. Entries are in simple letter-by-letter alphabetical order, with spaces, hyphens, and the definite or indefinite article ignored. This applies in all languages; but where a work written in English has a title in a foreign language, the article conditions its alphabetical ordering: 'L'Allegro' and 'La Belle Dame Sans Merci' are both listed under L, while *L'Encyclopédie* appears under *Encyclopédie, L'*. Names beginning with Mc or M' are ordered as though they were spelled Mac, St as though it were Saint, Dr as Doctor; but Mr and Mrs are ordered as they are spelled. An asterisk before a name, term, or title indicates that there is a separate entry for that subject, but it has been deemed unnecessary to place an asterisk before every occurrence of the name of Shakespeare. Where a person having his or her own entry is mentioned under another heading, the surname only is given unless there are entries for more than one person of the same name, when the initial or title is shown (*Auden, F. *Bacon, Dr *Johnson): the full name appears only where this is unavoidable in the interests of clarity (Richard *Graves, Robert *Graves). Where an author and a work are mentioned together, and each has an entry, only the title of the work carries an asterisk (Pope's *Dunciad*, Fielding's *Amelia*). Old spelling has been preferred, for both titles of works and quotations, except where its use might lead to confusion. For references to the works of Shakespeare the Alexander text has been used throughout.

A

Aaron's Rod, a novel by D. H. *Lawrence, published 1922.

The biblical Aaron was the brother of Moses, appointed priest by Jehovah, whose blossoming rod (Num. 17: 43–8) was a miraculous symbol of authority. In the novel Aaron Sisson, amateur flautist, forsakes his wife and job as check-weighman at a colliery for a life of flute-playing, quest, and adventure in Bohemian and upper-class society. His flute is symbolically broken in the penultimate chapter as a result of a bomb explosion in Florence during political riots.

Aaron the Moor, in Shakespeare's *Titus Andronicus*, the lover and accomplice of Tamora.

Abbey Theatre, Dublin, opened in 1904 with three one-act plays, two by W. B. *Yeats (*On Baile's Strand* and *Cathleen ni Houlihan*) and a comedy (*Spreading the News*) by Lady *Gregory. The theatre rapidly became a focus of the *Irish revival. In 1903 Miss A. E. *Horniman decided to provide a permanent Dublin home for the Irish National Theatre Society, an amateur company led by F. J. and W. G. Fay (which had Yeats for its President). They took over the disused theatre of the Mechanics' Institute in Abbey Street, together with the old city morgue next door, and converted them into the Abbey Theatre. The company turned professional in 1906, with Yeats, Lady Gregory, and J. M. *Synge as directors, and in 1907 successfully survived the riots provoked by Synge's *The Playboy of the Western World*. In 1909 Lady Gregory, as patentee, withstood strong pressure from the lord-lieutenant to withdraw The *Shewing-up of Blanco Posnet* by G. B. *Shaw. In 1910 Miss Horniman offered the purchase of the theatre and Yeats and Lady Gregory became principal shareholders and managers. The early poetic dramas were gradually replaced by more naturalistic prose works, written by *Colum, *Ervine, L. *Robinson, *O'Casey, and others. Robinson took over the management from Yeats in 1910 and became director in 1923. In 1925 the Abbey received a grant from the new government of Eire, thus becoming the first state-subsidized theatre in the English-speaking world.

The theatre was burned down in 1951, and the company played in the Queen's Theatre until the new Abbey opened in 1966.

ABBO OF FLEURY (?945–1004), a French theologian, author of the *Epitome de Vitis Romanorum Pontificum* and of lives of the saints.

Abbot, The, a novel by Sir W. *Scott, published 1820, a sequel to *The Monastery*.

The work is concerned with the imprisonment of Mary Queen of Scots at Lochleven Castle, her escape, the rally of her supporters and their defeat at the battle of Langside, and her withdrawal across the border to England.

The novel takes its title from the abbot of Kennaquhair, Edward Glendinning (Father Ambrose), brother of Sir Halbert Glendinning, the knight of Avenel.

Abbot of Misrule, see MISRULE, ABBOT OF.

Abbotsford, Sir W. *Scott's property near Melrose on the Tweed.

À BECKETT, Gilbert Abbott (1811–56), was on the original staff of *Punch*. He wrote a large number of plays and humorous works, including a *Comic History of England* (1847–8), a *Comic History of Rome* (1852), and a *Comic Blackstone* (1846).

À BECKETT, Gilbert Arthur (1837–91), son of Gilbert Abbott *À Beckett, was, from 1879, like his father, a regular member of the staff of *Punch*. He wrote, in collaboration with W. S. *Gilbert, the successful comedy *The Happy Land* (1873).

ABELARD, Peter (1079–1142), a native of Brittany, a brilliant disputant and lecturer at the schools of Ste Geneviève and Notre Dame in Paris, where *John of Salisbury was among his pupils. He was an advocate of rational theological enquiry, and his *Sic et Non* could be regarded as the first text in scholastic theology (see SCHOLASTICISM). He was primarily a dialectician rather than a theologian, though his theological views were declared heretical by the Council of Sens (1142) where he was vigorously opposed by St *Bernard. He fell in love with Héloïse, the niece of Fulbert, a canon of Notre Dame in whose house he lodged; she was a woman of learning and Abelard's pupil. Their love ended in a tragic separation and a famous correspondence. Pope's poem *'Eloisa to Abelard' was published in 1717.

ABERCROMBIE, Lascelles (1881–1938), poet. His first volume of verse, *Interludes and*

Poems (1908), was followed by further volumes, including *Poems* (1930) and the verse play *The Sale of St Thomas* (1931). Abercrombie contributed to **Georgian Poetry* and several of his verse plays appeared in *New Numbers*.

Abessa, in Spenser's **Faerie Queene*, I. iii, the personification of superstition.

Abigail (1 Sam. 25), wife of Nabal and subsequently of David. The name came to signify a waiting-woman, from the name of the 'waiting gentlewoman' in *The Scornful Lady* by **Beaumont and Fletcher.

Abora, Mount, in Coleridge's **'Kubla Khan', is perhaps to be identified with **Milton's Mt. Amara.

'Abou Ben Adhem', a poem by L. **Hunt.

Absalom and Achitophel, a poem by **Dryden, published 1681.

An allegory based on 2 Sam. 13–19, it deals with the intrigues of the earl of Shaftesbury and the ambition of the duke of Monmouth to replace James duke of York as Charles II's heir. Various public figures are represented under biblical names, notably Monmouth (Absalom), **Shaftesbury (Achitophel), the duke of **Buckingham (Zimri), Charles II (David), **Oates (Corah), and Slingsby Bethel, sheriff of London (Shimei).

In 1682 a second part appeared, mainly written by N. **Tate. However it contains 200 lines by Dryden, in which he attacks two literary and political enemies, **Shadwell as Og and **Settle as Doeg.

ABSE, Dannie (Daniel) (1923–), doctor and poet, has published many volumes of poems, including *Tenants of the House, Poems 1951–1956* (1957); in a foreword to his *Collected Poems 1948–1976* (1977), he notes that his poems are increasingly 'rooted in actual experience', both domestic and professional. He has also published novels, plays, and volumes of autobiography.

Absentee, The, a novel by M. **Edgeworth, first published 1812 in *Tales of Fashionable Life*.

This novel, the greater part of which is in conversation, begins with the extravagant London life of the absentee Irish landlord Lord Clonbrony and his wife. The author shows Lady Clonbrony's attempts to buy her way into high society, her contempt for her Irish origins, and her treatment of her son, Lord Colambre, who refuses to marry the heiress she provides for him. He falls in love with his cousin Grace, and becomes increasingly appalled at his father's debts. He travels incognito to Ireland to visit the family estates and to see if his mother's dislike of Irish life is justified, calling himself Evans. He

finds that one of the estates, managed by the brothers Garraghty, is half-ruined, the land ill-farmed, and the tenants treated with callous indifference. Colambre discovers that both his mother and his cousin Grace are remembered with affection. He returns to London and tells his father that he will himself pay off the debts, on condition that the Garraghtys are dismissed and the Clonbrony family returns to live on its Irish estates. After the sorting out of various troubles, he and Grace become engaged, and the family leave London to live in Ireland.

Absolute, Sir Anthony, and his son Captain Absolute, characters in Sheridan's **The Rivals*.

Absurd, Theatre of the, a term used to characterize the work of a number of European and American dramatists of the 1950s and early 1960s. As the term suggests, the function of such theatre is to give dramatic expression to the philosophical notion of the 'absurd', a notion that had received widespread diffusion following the publication of Camus's essay *Le Mythe de Sisyphe* in 1942. To define the world as absurd is to recognize its fundamentally indecipherable nature, and this recognition is frequently associated with feelings of loss, purposelessness, and bewilderment. To such feelings, the Theatre of the Absurd gives ample expression, often leaving the observer baffled in the face of disjointed, meaningless, or repetitious dialogues, incomprehensible behaviour, and plots which deny all notion of logical or 'realistic' development. The recognition of the absurd nature of human existence provided dramatists with a rich source of comedy, well illustrated in two early absurd plays, Ionesco's *La Cantatrice chauve*, written in 1948 (English trans., *The Bald Prima Donna*, 1958), and **Beckett's *En attendant Godot* (1952; trans. by the author, **Waiting for Godot*, 1954). Amongst the dramatists associated with the Theatre of the Absurd are Arthur Adamov (1908–70), **Albee, Beckett, **Camus, Jean Genet (1910–86), Eugène Ionesco (1912–), Alfred Jarry (1873–1907), **Pinter, and Boris Vian (1920–59).

Academy, The, a periodical founded in 1869 as 'a monthly record of literature, learning, science, and art'. Its early contributors included M. **Arnold, T. H. **Huxley and M. **Pattison, among others. After various vicissitudes and changes of title *The Academy* disappeared in the 1920s.

ACHEBE, Chinua (1930–), Nigerian author who wrote in English. His reputation rests largely on his first four novels, which can be seen as a sequence re-creating Africa's journey from tradition to modernity. They are *Things Fall Apart* (1958), followed by *No Longer at Ease* (1960), *Arrow of God* (1964), and *A Man of the*

People (1966) in which bitterness and disillusion lie just beneath the sparkling satiric surface. The novels also display Achebe's mastery of a wide range of language, from the English of Ibo-speakers and pidgin, to various levels of formal English.

Achitophel, see ABSALOM AND ACHITOPHEL.

ACKERLEY, J(oseph) R(andolph) (1896–1967), author, and literary editor (1935–59) of *The Listener*, to which he attracted work from such distinguished contributors as E. M. *Forster and *Isherwood. *Hindoo Holiday* (1932) is based on his experiences as private secretary to an Indian maharajah; *My Dog Tulip* (1956) and his novel *We Think the World of You* (1960) concern his intense relationship with his Alsatian dog. *My Father and Myself* (1968) is an account of his discovery of his apparently respectable father's extraordinary double life.

ACKERMANN, Rudolph (1764–1834), German lithographer who settled in London and published many handsome coloured-plate books in association with Prout, A. C. Pugin, *Rowlandson, and other artists. His publications include *The Microcosm of London* (3 vols, 1808–11), an antiquarian and topographical work by W. *Combe; and the gift-book annual *Forget-me-not*, of which the first issue appeared in 1825. Combe's *The Tour of Dr Syntax in search of the Picturesque* first appeared as 'The School-master's Tour' in Ackermann's *Poetical Magazine* (1809–11).

Acrasia, in Spenser's *Faerie Queene*, II. xii, typifies Intemperance. She is captured and bound by Sir *Guyon, and her *Bower of Bliss destroyed.

Acres, Bob, a character in Sheridan's *The Rivals*.

Actes and Monuments *of these latter perillous dayes, touching matters of the Church,* popularly known as the *Book of Martyrs*, by *Foxe, first published in Latin at Strasburg 1559, printed in English 1563.

This enormous work is a history of the Christian Church from the earliest times, with special reference to the sufferings of the Christian martyrs of all ages, but more particularly of the Protestant martyrs of Mary's reign. The book is, in fact, a violent indictment of 'the persecutors of God's truth, commonly called papists'. The author is credulous in his acceptance of stories of martyrdom and partisan in their selection. The work is written in a simple, homely style and enlivened by vivid dialogues between the persecutors and their victims.

ACTON, Sir Harold Mario Mitchell (1904–   ), writer and aesthete, spent some years in the 1930s in Peking, and wrote several works on Chinese theatre and poetry. He later settled at his family home at La Pietra, near Florence. His publications include poems: *Aquarium* (1923) and *This Chaos* (1930); fiction, which includes a novel set in Peking, *Peonies and Ponies* (1941) and *Tit for Tat and other tales* (1972, short stories); and historical studies, which include *The Last Medici* (1932) and *The Bourbons of Naples* (1956). *Memoirs of an Aesthete* (1948) and *More Memoirs* (1970) are autobiographies.

ACTON, Sir John Emerich Edward Dalberg, first Baron Acton (1834–1902), was Whig MP for Carlow (1859–65) and formed a friendship with *Gladstone. He was strenuous in his opposition to the definition by the Catholic Church of the dogma of papal infallibility, and published his views in his *Letters from Rome on the Council* (1870). His literary activity was great, and took the form of contributions to the *North British Review*, the *Quarterly Review*, and the *English Historical Review* (which he helped to found), besides lectures and addresses. Lord Acton was appointed Regius professor of modern history at Cambridge in 1895, on which occasion he delivered a remarkable inaugural lecture on the study of history (reprinted in *Lectures on Modern History*, 1906). One of his principal works was the planning of the *Cambridge Modern History* (1899–1912).

ACTON BELL, see BRONTË, A.

Adam, the name given to a 12th-cent. Anglo-Norman play in octosyllabics probably written in England *c*.1140. There are three scenes: the Fall and expulsion of Adam and Eve from Paradise; Cain and Abel; and a Prophets' Play. It is regarded as important in the evolution of the medieval *Mystery Plays in England.

Adam, in Shakespeare's *As You Like It*, the faithful old servant who accompanies Orlando in exile.

Adam Bede, a novel by G. *Eliot, published 1859.

The action takes place at the close of the 18th cent. Hetty Sorrel, pretty, vain, and self-centred, niece of the genial farmer Martin Poyser, is loved by Adam Bede, the village carpenter, but is deluded by the attentions of the young squire, Arthur Donnithorne, and is seduced by him. Arthur breaks off relations with her, and Hetty, broken-hearted, agrees to marry Adam. But before the marriage she discovers she is pregnant, flies from home to seek Arthur, fails to find him, is arrested and convicted of infanticide, and saved from the gallows at the last moment. In prison she is comforted by her cousin Dinah Morris, a Methodist preacher, whose strong, serious, and calm nature is contrasted with hers throughout the novel. In the last chapters, Adam discovers that Dinah loves him; his brother Seth, who had long and hopelessly loved Dinah, resigns to him with a fine unselfishness.

Adam Bell, Clym of the Clough (or Cleugh), and William of Cloudesley, three noted outlaws, as famous for their skill in archery in Northern England as *Robin Hood and his fellows in the Midlands. Clym of the Clough is mentioned in Jonson's *The Alchemist*, I. ii; and in D'Avenant's *The Wits*, II. i. There are ballads on the three outlaws in Percy's *Reliques* (*Adam Bell*) and in *Child's collection.

Adams, Parson Abraham, a character in Fielding's *Joseph Andrews*.

ADAMS, Henry Brooks (1838–1918), American man of letters whose works include an ambitious *History of the United States During the Administrations of Thomas Jefferson and James Madison* (1889–91, 9 vols); *Mont-Saint-Michel and Chartres* (1904), an interpretation of the spiritual unity of the 13th-cent. mind; and his autobiography, *The Education of Henry Adams* (1907), which describes the multiplicity of the 20th-cent. mind.

ADCOCK, (Kareen) Fleur (1934–), poet, born in New Zealand, and educated partly in England, where she settled in 1963. Her volumes of poetry include *The Eye of the Hurricane* (1964), *High Tide in the Garden* (1971), *The Inner Harbour* (1979), and *Selected Poems* (1983). Predominantly ironic and domestic in tone, she suggests wider horizons through her evocations of travel and of varied landscapes. She edited the *Oxford Book of Contemporary New Zealand Poetry* (1983).

ADDISON, Joseph (1672–1719), was educated at Charterhouse with *Steele. He was a distinguished classical scholar and attracted the attention of *Dryden by his Latin poems. He travelled on the Continent (1699–1703), and in 1705 he published *The Campaign*, a poem in heroic couplets in celebration of the victory of Blenheim. He was appointed under-secretary of state in 1706, and was MP from 1708 till his death. In 1709 he went to Ireland as chief secretary to Lord Wharton, the lord-lieutenant. He formed a close friendship with *Swift, Steele, and other writers and was a prominent member of the *Kit-Cat Club. Addison lost office on the fall of the Whigs in 1711. Between 1709 and 1711 he contributed a number of papers to Steele's *Tatler and joined with him in the production of *The Spectator in 1711–12. His *neo-classical tragedy *Cato was produced in 1713. He contributed to *The Guardian and to the revived Spectator. On the return of the Whigs to power, Addison was again appointed chief secretary for

Ireland and started the *Freeholder* (1715–16). In 1716 he become lord commissioner of trade, and married the countess of Warwick. He retired from office in 1718.

Addison was buried in Westminster Abbey, and lamented in an elegy by *Tickell. He was satirized by Pope in the character of *'Atticus'.

Addison's prose was acclaimed by Dr *Johnson in his *Life* (1781) as 'the model of the middle style; on grave subjects not formal, on light occasions not groveling . . .'. He admired *Locke and did much to popularize his ideas. He attacked the coarseness of *Restoration literature, and introduced new, essentially middle-class, standards of taste and judgement. One of his most original and influential contributions to the history of literary taste was his reassessment of the popular ballad, previously neglected as a form, in essays in the *Spectator* on *Chevy Chase and *The Children in the Wood*.

Addison of the North, The, see MACKENZIE, H.

Adelphi, The, started in 1923 as a monthly journal under the editorship of J. M. *Murry, intended as a mouthpiece for D. H. *Lawrence and himself. From 1927 it became a quarterly entitled *The New Adelphi*. Murry's editorship ended with a D. H. Lawrence memorial number in 1930, and the periodical became *The Adelphi*, incorporating *The New Adelphi*, which ran until 1955. Contributors to the three series include W. B. *Yeats, T. S. *Eliot, A. *Bennett, H. G. *Wells, *Day-Lewis, *Orwell, and *Auden.

Admirable Crichton, The, see CRICHTON.

'Admiral Hosier's Ghost', see GLOVER, R.

ADOMNAN, St (c.625–704), abbot of Iona from 679, who *Bede says was the author of a work on 'The Holy Places', and who is also credited with writing an extant Life of St *Columba.

Adonais, an elegy on the death of *Keats, by P. B. *Shelley, written at Pisa, published 1821.

Composed in 55 Spenserian stanzas, the poem was inspired partly by the Greek elegies of *Bion and *Moschus (both of which Shelley had translated) and partly by Milton's *Lycidas. Keats is lamented under the name of Adonais, the Greek god of beauty and fertility, together with other poets who had died young, such as *Chatterton, *Sidney, and *Lucan. His deathbed is attended by various figures, both allegorical and contemporary, including *Byron 'the Pilgrim of Eternity' (st. 30). Shelley, the atheist, accepts the physical facts of death, but insists on some form of Neoplatonic resurrection in the eternal Beauty of the universe, 'a portion of the loveliness | Which once he made more lovely' (st. 43). In his Preface he attacks the Tory reviewers with a pen 'dipped in consuming fire'.

Adriana, in Shakespeare's *The Comedy of Errors,* the jealous wife of Antipholus of Ephesus.

Advancement of Learning, The, a philosophical treatise by F. *Bacon, published 1605. It appeared in English, in two books.

The first book consists of a panegyric on the dignity and profitability of learning, and a defence of it against its various detractors. The second book is an elaborate classification of the various kinds of learning, based on the relation of the three main parts of learning—history, poetry, and philosophy—to the three faculties of memory, imagination, and reason. A revised and expanded Latin translation of the *Advancement* was published in 1623 as *De Dignitate et Augmentis Scientarum.*

Adventures of a Younger Son, The, a novel by E. J. *Trelawny, published 1831.

The work, part autobiography and part fiction, tells the story of the life of a buccaneering youth who deserts from the navy and takes to a life of wandering, encountering many adventures. Episodes involving *Shelley and *Byron are of particular biographical interest.

Adventures of Master F.J., The, by G. *Gascoigne, see F.J.

Adventures of Philip, The, the last complete novel by *Thackeray, published in the *Cornhill Magazine 1861–2.

The story is told by Arthur Pendennis, now a middle-aged married man. His young friend Philip is the son of a fashionable doctor, George Firmin, who, as George Brandon, was the seducer of Caroline Gann in *A Shabby Genteel Story. After abandoning Caroline, Firmin ran away with an heiress, Philip's mother, now dead. Firmin is being blackmailed by the disreputable parson Tufton Hunt, who performed the mock marriage ceremony with Caroline Gann and threatens to prove that the marriage was in fact valid. Caroline, calling herself Mrs Brandon, is a nurse who has tended Philip through an attack of fever, and now looks on him as her own son. She refuses to give the evidence which will disinherit him. However, Dr Firmin, having lost his own money and Philip's fortune, absconds to America, and Philip's cousin Agnes Twysden breaks off her engagement to Philip. While visiting Pendennis in Boulogne, Philip comes across General Baynes, co-trustee with Dr Firmin of Philip's inheritance. Knowing that Baynes will be ruined by any financial claim on him, Philip does not pursue his legal rights. He falls in love with Baynes's daughter, Charlotte, and marries her. The couple struggle with very little to live on but a happy ending is achieved when Philip is left a large legacy.

Advocates' Library, now National Library of Scotland, see LIBRARIES.

Æ, see RUSSELL, G. W.

Aeglamour, (1) the *'Sad Shepherd' in Jonson's drama of that name; (2) a character in Shakespeare's *The Two Gentlemen of Verona.

Aeglogue, see ECLOGUE.

ÆLFRIC (*c*.955–*c*.1010), was a monk of Winchester (where he was a pupil of *Æthelwold), Cerne Abbas, and Eynsham near Oxford where he was abbot. His chief works are the *Catholic Homilies* (990–2), largely drawn from the Church Fathers, and the *Lives of the Saints* (993–8), a series of sermons also mostly translated from Latin. Several other English works of his survive; these include his Latin *Grammar*; his *Colloquy*; and a translation of the *Heptateuch*, the first seven books of the Bible. Ælfric is the most prominent known figure in Old English literature and the greatest prose writer of his time; he is celebrated not only for his stylistic excellence but also for his educational principles and the breadth of his learning as a product of the 10th-cent. Benedictine Revival in England.

Ælla, an interlude or tragedy by *Chatterton, written in 1768–9, published 1777.

It is composed mainly in ten-lined stanzas, handled with considerable assurance, and contains one of Chatterton's most admired passages, beginning 'O! synge untoe mie roundelaie'.

Aeneid, The, an epic poem in Latin hexameters by *Virgil, recounting the adventures of Aeneas after the fall of Troy.

AESCHYLUS (525–456 BC), Athenian tragic poet. He is noted for the scope and grandeur of his conceptions and style, but only seven of his many plays have survived, three of which form the famous trilogy the *Oresteia (Agamemnon, Choephoroe, Eumenides). Aeschylus was hardly known in England before Thomas Stanley's edition of the plays in 1663. Milton gave some Aeschylean traits to *Samson Agonistes (1671), but his true popularity dates from the 19th cent. when interest in Aeschylus became a feature of the *Romantic Movement. This centres initially on his play *Prometheus Bound. *Byron's 'Prometheus' (1816) was followed by Shelley's *Prometheus Unbound (1820); S. T. *Coleridge's essay *On the Prometheus of Aeschylus (1825); a translation of the play (1833) by Elizabeth Barrett (*Browning); R. *Browning's outline of the legend in 'With Gerard de Lairesse' (1887); and *Bridges's *Prometheus the Firegiver (1883). From *Landor on attention shifted to the *Oresteia and has stayed there in the 20th cent., resulting in

*O'Neill's *Mourning becomes Electra* (1930), a recasting of the *Oresteia* in terms suggested by Freudian psychology, and, less obviously, T. S. *Eliot's *The Family Reunion* (1939). See also Browning's *The Agamemnon of Aeschylus*.

AESOP (6th cent. BC), probably a legendary figure, to whom tradition attributes the authorship of the whole stock of Greek fables which became known to the West in the Renaissance through the 14th-cent. prose version compiled by the Byzantine scholar Maximus Planudes. *Erasmus produced a Latin edition in 1513.

Aesthetic Movement, a movement which blossomed during the 1880s, heavily influenced by the *Pre-Raphaelites, *Ruskin, and *Pater, in which the adoption of sentimental archaism as the ideal of beauty was carried to extravagant lengths and often accompanied by affectation of speech and manner and eccentricity of dress. It and its followers (e.g. *Wilde) were much ridiculed in *Punch, in *Gilbert and Sullivan's *Patience* (1881), etc. See also ART FOR ART'S SAKE.

ÆTHELWOLD, St (?908–84), re-established a monastic house at Abingdon, introducing the strict Benedictine Rule from Fleury, and he was appointed bishop of Winchester (963) after Edgar became king of England. He co-operated with *Dunstan and *Oswald in the Benedictine Reforms of his century. He rebuilt the church at Peterborough and built a new cathedral at Winchester. He was an important figure in the revival of learning: most significantly, he translated the *Rule* of St Benedict (*c.*960), and wrote the *Regularis Concordia*, the code of the new English rule in the 10th-cent. Revival.

Aethiopica, a Greek romance by the 3rd-cent. AD Syrian Heliodorus of Emesa. The hero and heroine are parted and there is emphasis on travel through strange lands and on maintenance of chastity in the face of temptations, as they seek each other. The intercalated stories have a 'realistic' character depicting Greek middle-class life, in contrast to the romantic adventures that dominate the main narrative. The *Aethiopica* became widely known through *Amyot's French translation (1547) and *Underdowne's English version (1569). Sidney's *Arcadia*, and J. *Barclay's *Argenis* are indebted to it.

Affectionate Shepheard, The, see BARNFIELD.

Affery, see FLINTWINCH.

Agamemnon of Aeschylus, The, a translation by R. *Browning, published 1877. It aroused controversy because of its uncompromising literalness. The translation may be taken as an attack on the Hellenism of, e.g., M. *Arnold; by making his own version 'literally' unreadable,

Browning countered Arnold's claim that the Greeks were masters of the 'grand style'.

Agape, in Spenser's *Faerie Queene, IV. ii. 41, the Fay, mother of Priamond, Diamond, and Triamond.

AGATE, James Evershed (1877–1947), wrote dramatic criticism for the *Sunday Times. He also published novels and a nine-part auto-biography, *Ego* (1935–48), in the form of a diary, recording his life in literary and theatrical London.

Agents, Literary, The role of literary agent began to develop towards the end of the 19th cent., with A(lexander) P(ollock) Watt (1834–1914) frequently cited as the founder of the profession. His clients included *Hardy, *Kipling, and *Haggard. Other major figures in the early years were James Brand Pinker (1863–1922), who represented *Conrad and Arnold *Bennett, and American-born Curtis Brown (1866–1945).

Age of Innocence, The, see WHARTON, E.

Age of Reason, The, by *Paine (1795). The work was written in Paris at the height of the Terror. In it Paine attacks Christianity and the Bible: the Old Testament consists of 'obscene stories and voluptuous debaucheries', whereas the New is inconsistent, and the account of the Virgin Birth, for example (a passage that was found particularly shocking), merely 'hearsay upon hearsay'. He concludes with a plea for religious tolerance. The work was widely attacked as blasphemous and scurrilous.

Agnes Grey, a novel by A. *Brontë, published 1847.

It is the story of a rector's daughter who takes service as a governess, first with the Bloomfield family, whose undisciplined children are described as 'tigers' cubs', and then with the Murrays, where the conduct of her eldest charge, Rosalie, a heartless coquette, is contrasted with her own modest and gentle behaviour. Rosalie marries ambitiously and unhappily, but Agnes is happily united with Mr Weston, the curate, the only one to have shown kindness in her days of servitude.

Agravain, Sir, in the Arthurian legends conspires against Launcelot and discloses to Arthur Launcelot's love for Guinevere.

AGRIPPA, Henricus Cornelius, of Nettesheim (1486–1535), a scholar and writer on the occult sciences. He wrote *De Occulta Philosophia libri tres* (1529) and *De Vanitate Scientiarum* (1530), and argued against the persecution of witches.

Aguecheek, Sir Andrew, a foolish knight in Shakespeare's *Twelfth Night.

Ahab, a character in Melville's *Moby-Dick*.

Ahasuerus, see WANDERING JEW, THE.

Aids to Reflection, a religious and philosophical treatise by S. T. *Coleridge, published 1825.

Coleridge compiled this unsystematic collection of commentaries and aphorisms on selected passages from the 17th-cent. Anglican divine Archbishop Leighton. It stresses the importance of Christianity as a 'personal revelation' and further develops his famous distinction between Reason and Understanding, originally drawn from *Kant, as the source respectively of 'Moral' and 'Prudential' action.

AIKEN, Conrad Potter (1889–1973), American author. His volumes of poetry include *Earth Triumphant* (1914); *The Jig of Forslin* (1916); *Senlin: A Biography* (1918); *John Deth* (1930); and *Preludes for Memnon* (1931). His long poems show the somewhat diffused and diffuse influence of his *Modernist contemporaries and friends. His novels, which show a debt to *Joyce and *Freud, and his own desire to explore 'the fragmented ego', include *Blue Voyage* (1927) and *A Heart for the Gods of Mexico* (1939), both concerned with actual and metaphorical journeys. *Ushant* (1952) is a psychological autobiography, with portraits of *Lowry and T. S. *Eliot. His short stories were collected in 1960, and his criticism, *A Reviewer's ABC*, in 1958. His *Selected Letters* were published in 1978.

AIKIN, Anna Laetitia, see BARBAULD.

AIKIN, John (1747–1822), physician, author, and Dissenter, and brother of Anna Laetitia *Barbauld, with whom he wrote *Evenings at Home* (6 vols, 1792–6), for children; he also wrote and collaborated with others in several volumes of memoirs and biography. He was the first editor of the *Monthly Magazine*.

Aimwell, a character in Farquhar's *The Beaux' Stratagem*.

AINGER, Alfred (1837–1904), a popular lecturer and preacher, author of a life of C. *Lamb (1882) and a life of *Crabbe (1903), and editor of Lamb's works (1883–1900).

AINSWORTH, William Harrison (1805–82), published his first novel *Rookwood*, romanticizing the career of Dick Turpin, in 1824, and followed it in 1839 with *Jack Sheppard*, exalting the life of another highwayman. These *'Newgate' novels were satirized by Thackeray in 1839–40 in *Catherine*. He edited *Bentley's Miscellany* (1840–2), *Ainsworth's Magazine* (1842–53), and finally the *New Monthly Magazine*. He wrote 39 novels, chiefly historical. They include *Guy Fawkes* (1841), *Old St Paul's* (1841), *Windsor Castle* (1843), and *The Lancashire Witches* (1848).

AKENSIDE, Mark (1721–70), author of *Pleasures of Imagination* (1744). His 'Hymn to the Naiads', written in 1746 and published in *Dodsley's *Collection of Poems* (1758), is a dazzling display of classical erudition, and other poems reveal his keen interest in the scientific theories of the *Enlightenment.

ALABASTER, William (1568–1640), an Elizabethan divine and Latin poet. Between 1588 and 1592 he produced two notable poems in Latin; an unfinished epic on Queen Elizabeth, praised by *Spenser; and the tragedy *Roxana* which Dr *Johnson thought contained the best Latin verse written in England before *Milton. In 1597 he became a Roman Catholic and was arrested and deprived of Anglican orders. His sonnets (first pub. in 1959) are among the earliest *metaphysical poems of devotion. It was as a theologian that Alabaster was chiefly known in his own day. His first major essay in mystical theology, *Apparatus in Revelationem Iesu Christi* was declared heretical by the Holy Office. By 1613–14 he was again a Protestant, later becoming a doctor of divinity at Cambridge and chaplain to the king. He devoted his later years to theological studies: *De Bestia Apocalyptica* (Delft, 1621), *Ecce Sponsus Venit* (1633), *Spiraculum Tubarum* (?1633). In 1635 he published a scholarly abridgement of Schindler's Hebrew lexicon.

Aladdin and the Wonderful Lamp, an *oriental tale generally regarded as belonging to the *Arabian Nights, but not contained in any MS of the collected tales.

Aladdin, the scapegrace son of a poor tailor in China, is employed by a Moorish sorcerer to obtain for him a magic lamp from a subterranean cavern. Aladdin keeps the lamp and, discovering its power, he acquires great wealth and marries Bedr-el-Budur, the sultan's daughter, and constructs a wonderful palace. The sorcerer, disguised as an itinerant merchant, recovers the lamp by offering 'new lamps for old', and whisks palace and princess off to Africa. Aladdin, pursuing, kills the magician, regains the lamp, and conveys palace and bride back to China.

Alastor, a visionary poem by P. B. *Shelley, published 1816. 'Alastor' is a transliteration from the Greek, meaning the 'evil spirit or demon of solitude', who pursues the Poet to his death because he will not be satisfied by domestic affections and 'human sympathy'. Composed in Miltonic blank verse, the poem reflects Shelley's early wanderings.

ALBAN, St (d. ?304), the first British martyr. While still a pagan, the story goes, he had sheltered in his house a Christian cleric by whom he was converted. Immediately after his conversion he was executed, accompanied by miracles, on a hill overlooking the Roman town of Verulamium, now St Albans.

Albany, Duke of, a character in Shakespeare's *King Lear*.

Albany, Albainn, Albin, Albania, ancient poetic names of Gaelic origin for the northern part of Britain.

ALBEE, Edward Franklin (1928–), American playwright, associated with the Theatre of the *Absurd. His works include *The American Dream* (1961), *Who's Afraid of Virginia Woolf?* (1962), *Tiny Alice* (1965), and *A Delicate Balance* (1966).

ALBERTUS MAGNUS (1193 or 1206–80), a Dominican friar and a great *scholastic philosopher. He was the first Western thinker to outline the complete philosophy of *Aristotle, whose doctrines he expounded at Cologne and Paris. *Aquinas was among his pupils. His wide learning earned for him the title 'Doctor Universalis', and his total *œuvre* (printed at Lyons, 1651) of 21 vols includes six commentaries of Aristotle and an influential *Summa Theologiae*.

Albion, an ancient poetical name for Britain, perhaps derived from its white (Latin, *albus*) cliffs, visible from the coast of Gaul.

Albions England, see WARNER, W.

Alcaics, see METRE.

Alchemist, The, a comedy by *Jonson, performed by the King's Men 1610, printed 1612, by many considered the greatest of his plays.

Lovewit, during an epidemic of the plague, leaves his house in Blackfriars in London in charge of his servant, Face. The latter, with Subtle, a fake alchemist and astrologer, and Dol Common, his consort, use the house as a place for fleecing a variety of victims. To Sir Epicure Mammon, a voluptuous knight, and Ananias and Tribulation Wholesome, fanatical Puritans, they promise the philosopher's stone, by which all metals may be turned to gold; to Dapper, a lawyer's clerk, a charm to win at gambling, bestowed by his aunt, the Queen of Fairy; to Drugger, a tobacconist, a magical way of designing his shop to improve trade; to Kastril, a country bumpkin who wants to learn the language of quarrelling, a rich marriage for his widowed sister, Dame Pliant. Surly, a gamester, sees through the fraud and attempts to expose it by presenting himself disguised as a Spaniard, but the dupes refuse to listen and drive him away. Lovewit's unexpected return puts Subtle and Dol to flight, and Face makes peace with his master by resourcefully marrying him to Dame Pliant.

Alcmena, see AMPHITRYON.

ALCOTT, Louisa M(ay) (1832–88), American author, achieved fame with *Little Women* (1868–9), which was followed by several other works in the same vein.

ALCUIN (Albinus: English name Ealhwine) (735–804), theologian, man of letters, and the principal figure in the literary and educational programme of *Charlemagne in the 'Carolingian Renaissance'. He met Charlemagne at Parma in 780, and settled on the Continent, becoming abbot of Tours in 796. He wrote liturgical, grammatical, hagiographical, and philosophical works, as well as numerous letters and poems in Latin. He was primarily an educationist rather than an original thinker. His enduring legacy was the Carolingian educational curricula and the Carolingian minuscule script developed in his writing school. (See also ANGLO-LATIN LITERATURE.)

Alcyon, in Spenser's *Daphnaïda* and *Colin Clout*, is Sir A. *Gorges, on whose wife's death the *Daphnaïda* is an elegy.

ALDHELM, St (*c*.639–709), a major figure in the intellectual movement led by *Theodore at Canterbury. He was the author of a number of Latin works which reveal a wide knowledge of Classical and Christian authors. He was abbot of Malmesbury and built churches at Malmesbury, Bruton, and Wareham and monasteries at Frome and Bradford. His major work is *De Septenario, the Letter to Acircius* (i.e. Aldfrith, king of Northumbria) which contains his own Latin riddles, the *Aenigmata*. (See also ANGLO-LATIN LITERATURE.)

Aldiborontiphoscophornio, see CHRONONHOTONTHOLOGOS.

ALDINGTON, Richard (Edward Godfree) (1892–1962), married Hilda *Doolittle (H.D.) in 1913 and they both worked as editors on the Imagist periodical *The Egoist*. In 1915 Aldington's first volume of poetry, *Images 1910–1915*, was published by the Poetry Bookshop. (See IMAGISM.) Subsequent volumes include *Images of War* (1919) and *A Fool i' the Forest* (1925), which shows perhaps an excessive debt to *The Waste Land*. Aldington achieved popular success with his first novel, *Death of a Hero* (1929, abridged; Paris, 1930, unexpurgated), based on his own war experiences. It relates the life and death of George Winterbourne, killed in action in 1918; the first two parts dwell on his youth and 'advanced' marriage, satirizing the complacency and frivolity of pre-war middle-class and Bohemian England, and Part Three is a horrifying description of life at the front in France. Of his later works the best known are his biographies, which include *Portrait of a Genius, But . . .* (1950), a controversial life of D. H. *Lawrence, and his life of T. E. *Lawrence, *Lawrence of Arabia: a biographical enquiry* (1955), which caused a furore by its attack on Lawrence as an 'impudent mythomaniac'. He also published many translations, an autobiography (*Life for Life's Sake*, 1941), and critical essays.

ALDISS, Brian Wilson (1925–), is best known for his works of *Science Fiction and his involvement with the cause of Science Fiction as a literary genre; he has written a history of the subject, *Billion Year Spree* (1973). His works include *Non-Stop* (1958), *Greybeard* (1964), and *Enemies of the System* (1978). His sense of the tradition is manifested in *Frankenstein Unbound* (1973), which pays tribute to his view of M. *Shelley's work as 'the first novel of the Scientific Revolution', and *Moreau's Other Island* (1980) which picks up the theme of H. G. Wells's *The Island of Dr Moreau* (1896). *Helliconia Spring* (1982), *Helliconia Summer* (1983), and *Helliconia Winter* (1985) form an epic trilogy describing the evolution of a whole planetary system, in which each season lasts for centuries.

ALDRICH, Thomas Bailey (1836–1907), American author. He contributed *vers de société* to various periodicals, including the *Atlantic Monthly*, which he edited from 1881 to 1890. His best-known work is his semi-autobiographical *The Story of a Bad Boy* (1870).

ALEXANDER, Sir William, earl of Stirling (?1567–1640), Scottish poet, courtier, and friend of *Drummond of Hawthornden. His chief poetical works are a collection of songs and sonnets, *Aurora* (1604), a long poem on *Doomsday* (1614), and four tragedies on Darius, Croesus, Alexander, and Caesar.

Alexander and Campaspe, see CAMPASPE.

ALEXANDER OF HALES (1170/80–1245), a native of Gloucestershire, studied at Paris where he taught theology. He held various ecclesiastical appointments in England, and returning to Paris he entered the Franciscan order and became the first member of this new order to hold the chair of theology there. He wrote glosses on the *Sententiae* of *Peter Lombard. According to R. *Bacon, the *Summa Theologica* which goes under his name was put together by other Franciscan theologians, partly drawing on his teachings. Alexander is important as evidencing a distinct Augustinian–Franciscan philosophical tradition in the first half of the 13th cent. In the later Middle Ages he was called the 'Doctor Irrefragabilis'.

Alexander's Feast, see DRYDEN, J.

ALEXANDER THE GREAT (356–323 BC), son of Philip II of Macedon and Olympias,

educated by *Aristotle, became king of Macedon in 336 BC. He caused the Greek states to nominate him to conduct the war against Persia and in 334 crossed the Hellespont. He captured the family of Darius and extended his conquests to Egypt, where he founded Alexandria; and, after completely defeating the Persians at the battle of Arbela in 331, to India. He married Roxana, and a second wife Barsine. He is said to have destroyed Persepolis, the capital of the Persian empire, at the instance of the courtesan Thais (331). He died of fever at Babylon when only 32 years old. His horse was named Bucephalus.

Alexander was made the centre of a cluster of medieval legends, comparable to the cycles concerning *Charlemagne and King *Arthur. The chief of the romances concerning him are the great French *Roman d'Alexandre* of the 12th cent., some 20,000 alexandrines, and the English *King Alisaunder* of the early 14th cent. The story of the rivalry of his two wives forms the subject of *Lee's tragedy *The Rival Queens*.

Alexandria Quartet, see DURRELL, L.

Alexandrine, an iambic line of six feet, which is the French heroic verse, and in English is used, e.g., as the last line of the Spenserian stanza or as a variant in a poem of heroic couplets. The name is derived from the fact that certain 12th- and 13th-cent. French poems on *Alexander the Great were written in this metre.

ALFRED (the Great) (848–99), king of the West Saxons from 871 to his death, important in the history of literature for the revival of letters that he effected in his southern kingdom and as the beginner of a tradition of English prose translation. He translated (before 896) the *Cura Pastoralis* of *Gregory with a view to the spiritual education of the clergy; the preface to this translation refers to the decay of learning in England and indicates Alfred's resolve to restore it. He then translated (or had translated) the *Historia Adversus Paganos* of *Orosius, inserting accounts of the celebrated voyages of the Norwegian Ohthere and of *Wulfstan. He had a translation made of *Bede's *Ecclesiastical History* and translated the *De Consolatione Philosophiae* of *Boethius. The loose West-Saxon version of *Augustine's *Soliloquia* is probably the work of Alfred. The *Anglo-Saxon Chronicle*, the systematic compilation of which began about 890, may represent in part his work or inspiration.

Alfred, a Masque, containing 'Rule, Britannia', see THOMSON, J. (1700–48).

Algarsyf, one of the two sons of King Cambuscan, in *Chaucer's 'Squire's Tale' (see CANTERBURY TALES, II).

Algrind, in Spenser's *Shepheardes Calender*, Edmund Grindal, archbishop of Canterbury, 1576–83.

Ali Baba and the Forty Thieves, an *oriental tale generally regarded as one of the *Arabian Nights, but not included in any MS of these.

Ali Baba and Kassim are two brothers in a town of Persia. Ali Baba, while collecting wood in the forest, observes forty robbers getting access to a cave by pronouncing the words, 'Open, Sesame!' Using the same password he enters the cave, finds it full of robbers' treasure, and brings home some sacks full of gold. He reveals his discovery to Kassim, who enters the cave, but forgets the password and is unable to get out. He is cut in quarters by the robbers. Ali Baba conveys the body home and, to simulate a natural death, arranges for a cobbler to sew the quarters of the body together. Through this cobbler the thieves eventually trace the house of Ali Baba, though at first their purpose is defeated by the ingenuity of Morgiana, Ali Baba's servant. At last the captain of the thieves brings his men concealed in leather oil-jars to the house of Ali Baba, but is again defeated by Morgiana, who destroys them with boiling oil; Ali Baba finally kills the captain himself.

'Alice Brand', a ballad in the 4th canto of Scott's *Lady of the Lake.

Alice's Adventures in Wonderland, a story for children by Lewis Carroll (see DODGSON), published 1865.

Originally entitled *Alice's Adventures Under Ground,* and written for his young friend Alice Liddell, it tells how Alice dreams she pursues a White Rabbit down a rabbit-hole to a world where she encounters such celebrated characters as the Duchess and the Cheshire Cat, the Mad Hatter and the March Hare, the King and Queen of Hearts, and the Mock Turtle. It contains the poems 'You are old, Father William', 'Beautiful Soup', and others, and Carroll's typographical experiment 'Fury and the Mouse', in the shape of a mouse's tail.

Alisaunder, see KING ALISAUNDER.

ALISON, Archibald (1757–1839), Scots episcopalian, father of Sir A. *Alison. He wrote *Essays on the Nature and Principles of Taste* (1790), a study of the role of the imagination and of the association of ideas in aesthetic perception.

ALISON, Sir Archibald (1792–1867), son of A. *Alison, was a frequent contributor to *Blackwood's Magazine* and author of various historical and legal works.

Allan-a-Dale, one of the companions of *Robin Hood; the subject of a song in Scott's *Rokeby.

Allegory, a figurative narrative or description, conveying a veiled moral meaning; an extended metaphor. As C. S. *Lewis argues in *The Allegory of Love,* the medieval mind tended to think naturally in allegorical terms. Allegorical works of great vitality continued to be produced, ranging from Spenser's *Faerie Queene* and Bunyan's *Pilgrim's Progress,* both of which use personifications of abstract qualities, to Dryden's political allegory *Absalom and Achitophel,* which conceals real identities.

Allegory of Love, The, see LEWIS, C. S.

Allegra, daughter of *Byron and Claire Clairmont, Mary *Shelley's half-sister.

'Allegro, L', see 'L'ALLEGRO'.

Allen, Benjamin and Arabella, characters in Dickens's *Pickwick Papers.

ALLEN, (Charles) Grant (Blairfindie) (1848–99), went to Jamaica, as professor of mental and moral philosophy, where he formulated his evolutionary system of philosophy based on the works of H. *Spencer. His *Physiological Aesthetics* (1877) introduced his name to the leaders of thought in London. He contributed articles on popular scientific and other subjects to the *Cornhill* and other journals. Next came *The Colour-sense* (1879), which won praise from A. R. *Wallace, C. *Darwin, and T. H. *Huxley. Among his works of fiction are *Strange Stories* (1884) and his best-selling *The Woman Who Did* (1895), the tale of a woman of advanced views who believes that marriage is a barbarous institution; she lives with the man she loves, bears his child, but is left alone, when he inconveniently dies, to endure the consequent social ostracism. Though intended as a protest against the subjection of women, the novel was condemned by Mrs Fawcett and other feminists.

ALLEN, Ralph (1694–1764), a man of humble origins who rose to considerable eminence and prosperity in Bath (where he was known as the 'Man of Bath'), and was generally beloved for his unobtrusive generosity, both public and private. Most notably (in the field of literature) he assisted the struggling *Fielding, who later portrayed him as Squire Allworthy in *Tom Jones* and dedicated *Amelia* to him. After the novelist's death, Allen provided for the education and support of his children. *Pope praised him as one who did good 'by stealth'; S. *Richardson, W. *Warburton, and Mrs *Delaney were among his friends.

ALLESTREE, Richard (fl. 1618–43), see ALMANACS.

ALLESTREE, Richard (1619–81), see WHOLE DUTY OF MAN, THE.

ALLEYN, Edward (1566–1626), an actor (R. *Burbage's chief rival) and partner of

*Henslowe, with whom he built the Fortune Theatre, Cripplegate. There he acted at the head of the Lord Admiral's company, playing among other parts the leading roles in Marlowe's *Tamburlaine, *Jew of Malta, and *Dr Faustus. He bought the manor of Dulwich, and built and endowed Dulwich College. His first wife was Henslowe's stepdaughter, his second the daughter of *Donne. He was a patron of *Dekker, John *Taylor, and other writers.

All for Love, or The World Well Lost, a tragedy by *Dryden (1678).
    Written in blank verse in acknowledged imitation of Shakespeare's *Antony and Cleopatra, it is Dryden's most performed and his best-known play. It concentrates on the last hours in the lives of its hero and heroine. In contrast to Shakespeare's play, it is an exemplary neo-classical tragedy, notable for its elaborately formal presentation of character, action, and theme. (See NEO-CLASSICISM and HEROIC DRAMA.)

ALLINGHAM, William (1824–89), poet, whose diary, published in 1907, contains vivid portraits of his contemporaries; his friends in the literary world included *Patmore, *Carlyle, D. G. *Rossetti, and notably *Tennyson. His first volume, Poems (1850), contains his best-known work 'The Fairies' ('Up the airy mountain'); it was followed by several others, including the long poem Laurence Bloomfield in Ireland (1864) and anthologies of verse for children.

Alliteration, the commencement of two or more words in close connection with the same sound. It was used to excess by many late 19th-cent. poets, notably *Swinburne, whose 'lilies and languors of virtue' and 'raptures and roses of vice' are characteristic examples from *'Dolores'. It is an integral part of some of the verse of G. M. *Hopkins. (See also ALLITERATIVE VERSE.)

Alliterative Prose, a tradition of Old and Middle English prose elevated in style by the employment of some of the techniques of *Alliterative Verse. Its most distinguished exponents are *Ælfric and *Wulfstan in Old English, and the writers of the *'Katherine Group' in Middle English.

Alliterative Revival, a collective term for the group of alliterative poems written in the second half of the 14th cent. in which alliteration, which had been the formal basis of Old English poetry, was again used in poetry of the first importance (such as *Piers Plowman and Sir *Gawain and the Green Knight) as a serious alternative to the continental form, syllabic rhyming verse. As well as their common formal elements, many of the poems are linked by a serious interest in contemporary politics and ethics (*Wynnere and Wastoure, Death and Liffe, The Parlement of the Three Ages, Piers Plowman).

Alliterative Verse, the native Germanic tradition of English poetry and the standard form in Old English up to the 11th cent., recurring in Middle English as a formal alternative to the syllable-counting, rhymed verse borrowed from French (see ALLITERATIVE REVIVAL). The Old English line was (normally) unrhymed, and made up of two distinct half-lines each of which contained two stressed syllables. The alliteration was always on the first stress of the second half-line, which alliterated with either, or both, of the stresses in the first half-line; e.g.

   x   x   x
  Nāp nihtscūa,   norþan snīwde (*Seafarer,
                                31)

(The shade of night grew dark,   it snowed
  from the north).

In Middle English, the alliterative rules were much less strict:

'I have lyved in londe', quod I, 'My name is Longe Wille' (*Piers Plowman B, xv 152).

Nothing after Middle English could categorically be said to be 'Alliterative Verse', despite its recurrent use as a device throughout English poetry, except perhaps for the rather self-conscious revival of the form in this century by such poets as *Auden and *Day-Lewis.

All's Lost by Lust, a tragedy by W. *Rowley, acted c.1619, printed 1633. The story is taken from a legendary episode in Spanish history. It is also the subject of Landor's *Count Julian and *Southey's Roderick (1814). Roderick, king of Spain, rapes Jacinta, daughter of his general Julianus; Jacinta and Julianus are both murdered by Roderick's Moorish successor.

All's Well that Ends Well, a comedy by *Shakespeare, first printed in the First *Folio of 1623. The Arden editor, G. K. Hunter, assigns it to 1603–4, on the grounds of its close affinity to *Measure for Measure. Both plays are generally classified as 'tragi-comedies' or 'problem comedies'.
    Its chief source is Boccaccio's *Decameron (Day 3, Tale 9), which Shakespeare may have read either in the translation by *Painter, or in the French version by Antoine le Maçon. Bertram, the young count of Rousillon, on the death of his father is summoned to the court of the king of France, leaving his mother and with her Helena, daughter of the famous physician Gerard de Narbon. The king is sick of a disease said to be incurable. Helena, who loves Bertram, goes to Paris and effects his cure by means of a prescription left by her father. As a reward she is allowed to choose her husband and names Bertram, who unwillingly obeys the king's

order to wed her. But under the influence of the worthless braggart Parolles, he at once takes service with the duke of Florence, writing to Helena that until she can get the ring from his finger 'which never shall come off', and is with child by him, she may not call him husband. Helena, passing through Florence on a pilgrimage, finds Bertram courting Diana, the daughter of her hostess there. Disclosing herself as his wife to them, she obtains permission to replace Diana at a midnight assignation with Bertram, having that day caused him to be informed that Helena is dead. Thereby she obtains from Bertram his ring, and gives him one that the king had given her. Bertram returns to his mother's house, where the king is on a visit. The latter sees on Bertram's finger the ring that he had given Helena, suspects Bertram of having destroyed her, and demands an explanation on pain of death. Helena herself now appears, explains what has passed, and claims that the conditions named in Bertram's letter have been fulfilled. Bertram, filled with remorse, accepts her as his wife. The sub-plot, concerning the braggart Parolles, has been felt by some readers, including Charles I, to dominate the play, and in performance it has often done so.

All the Year Round, see HOUSEHOLD WORDS.

Allworth, Tom and Lady, characters in Massinger's *A New Way to Pay Old Debts.*

Allworthy, Squire, and his sister Bridget, characters in Fielding's *Tom Jones.* The character of Squire Allworthy was based on Fielding's friends and benefactors R. *Allen and G. *Lyttelton.

Alma (in Italian meaning 'soul', 'spirit'), in Spenser's *Faerie Queene, II. ix, xi, represents the virgin soul.

Almanacs were, technically, tables of astronomical and astrological events of the coming year, and as such had existed since antiquity; and by the 17th cent. in England, with the advent of printing, they were the most popular literary form, containing a wide range of material. They flourished particularly strongly from 1640 to 1700, when they engaged in political, social, and religious controversy, playing an active part in the ferment of the times. Well-known publishers and compilers of almanacs included Richard Allestree (active between 1618 and 1643); *Lilly; John Gadbury (1627–1704), astrologer and physician; John Partridge (1644–1715); and Francis Moore, father of *Old Moore. In the 18th cent. growing scepticism and a declining interest in astrology led to a loss of vitality in the form. Both Old Moore and *Whitaker's Almanac* (see WHITAKER) continue today.

Almeria, the heroine of Congreve's *The Mourning Bride.*

Almeyda, a character in Dryden's *Don Sebastian.*

Alonso, the king of Naples in Shakespeare's *The Tempest* who helped Antonio depose Prospero.

Alonzo the Brave and the Fair Imogine, a ballad by M. G. Lewis, which appears in *The Monk.*

Alph, in Coleridge's *'Kubla Khan', the sacred river in Xanadu. For its connection with the river Alpheus and with the Nile, see J. L. *Lowes, *The Road to Xanadu* (1927).

Alroy, a novel by B. *Disraeli, published in 1833.
   This is the central novel of the group *Vivian Grey—Alroy—Contarini Fleming.*

Altamont, Colonel Jack, alias Amory, alias Armstrong, in Thackeray's *Pendennis*, an escaped convict, father of Blanche Amory.

'Althea, To', a poem by *Lovelace.

Alton Locke, Tailor and Poet: An Autobiography, a novel by C. *Kingsley, published 1850.
   The narrator, son of a small London tradesman and educated by a widowed Baptist mother, is apprenticed to a sweating tailor in whose workshop he experiences at first hand the miseries of the working classes and becomes imbued with the ideas of *Chartism. The novel, despite its weaknesses, is a powerful social document.

Amadis of Gaul (Amadís de Gaula), a Spanish or Portuguese romance, written in the form in which we have it by Garcia de Montalvo in the second half of the 15th cent. and printed early in the 16th cent. The romance was translated into English by *Munday (?1590), and an abridged version by *Southey appeared in 1803.

Amara, Mt., a place in Abyssinia, where the kings of that country secluded their sons, to protect themselves from sedition (*Paradise Lost, iv. 281). It figures as 'Amhara' in Johnson's *Rasselas.

Amaryllis, the name given to a shepherdess by *Theocritus, *Virgil, and *Ovid. Spenser, in *Colin Clouts come home againe, uses the name to signify Alice, one of the daughters of Sir John Spencer of Althorp. She became the countess of Derby for whom Milton wrote his *Arcades.

Amaurote, or 'shadow city', the capital of More's *Utopia.

Amazing Marriage, The, a novel by G. *Meredith, published 1895.

Ambassadors, The, a novel by H. *James, published 1903.

Chadwick Newsome, a young man of independent fortune, the son of Mrs Newsome of Woolett, Mass., a widow, has been living in Paris and is reported to have got entangled with a wicked woman. Mrs Newsome sends as ambassador the guileless Strether, to whom she is engaged, to bring home Chad. The story describes Strether's evolution in the congenial atmosphere of Paris, his desertion to the side of Chad and the bewitching comtesse de Vionnet (he is convinced that the relation between them is virtuous), and his own mild flirtation with the pleasant cosmopolitan Maria Gostrey. Meanwhile his attitude and the disquieting report of Waymarsh, Strether's stolid and conscientious American friend, have caused dismay at Woolett, and Mrs Newsome sends out a fresh ambassador in the person of her daughter, Sarah Pocock.

The attempts to bamboozle Sarah utterly fail, and she presents her ultimatum—immediate return to America—to the delinquents Chad and Strether. Chad, exhorted by Strether, refuses to abandon the lady; and Strether is accordingly notified that all is over between him and Mrs Newsome. Then, and then only, an accident throws Strether into the company of Chad and Mme de Vionnet in circumstances which leave no doubt as to the nature of their real relations. Sadly disillusioned, Strether turns his back on Paris.

AMBROSE, St (c. 340–97), born at Trèves, was a celebrated bishop of Milan (elected against his will by the people when still a catechumen), one of the Four Doctors of the Church, and a vigorous opponent of the *Arian heresy. He developed the use of music in Church services, restoring the ancient melodies and founding what is known as the Ambrosian chant (as opposed to the Gregorian chant). He composed several hymns, among which an old tradition includes the *Te Deum.

Ambrose, Father, in Scott's *The Abbot, Edward Glendinning, abbot of Kennaquhair.

Ambrose's Tavern, the scene of the *Noctes Ambrosianae, is loosely based on a real Edinburgh tavern of the same name, first described by *Lockhart in Peter's Letters to his Kinsfolk.

Ambrosio, the hero of M. G. Lewis's *The Monk.

Amelia, a novel by H. *Fielding, published 1752 (for 1751).

Set in and against a London of almost unrelieved squalor, corruption, and violence, the novel opens in the court of the 'trading Justice', Justice Thrasher, who has the innocent, penniless Captain Billy Booth thrown into Newgate. The filth and brutality of the prison provides a sombre background against which his wife Amelia's virtue shines. In prison Booth meets an old acquaintance, Miss Matthews, a courtesan who has the means to buy a clean cell and who invites Booth to share it with her. Although filled with remorse, he does so, and they exchange their stories. Booth describes his runaway marriage (in which he was assisted by the good parson Dr Harrison), his happiness with Amelia, their lives in the country, his soldiering, and Amelia's arrival in France when he was ill. There they had lived with the huge, pugnacious Colonel Bath and his sister, who had since married a Colonel James. James now bails out Booth, and takes Miss Matthews as his mistress. Booth begins a life of gambling. Amelia's life is one of poverty and distress. In the background is the kindly Dr Harrison. 'My Lord', a flamboyant and menacing character who is never given a name, begins with Colonel James to lay plans to ensnare Amelia. The Booths' friendly landlady, Mrs Ellison (who is, unknown to Amelia, a cousin of My Lord's and his procuress), arranges for Amelia to be attended at an oratorio by My Lord in disguise, and then introduces him as her cousin. My Lord becomes extremely agreeable and offers to acquire a command for Booth. Amelia then receives an invitation to a masquerade, but is sharply warned by a fellow-lodger, the learned widow Mrs Bennet (who had been seduced by My Lord after such an invitation), and she does not go. After various other dangers and complications, Dr Harrison arrives, eventually pays off Booth's debts, and arranges for him to return to the farming life he loved. Amelia discovers that she is heiress to her mother's fortune and the Booths retire to a happy and prosperous country life.

The book sold well, but was attacked by many, led by *Richardson and *Smollett, and Fielding made alterations in later editions.

American Democrat, The, see COOPER, J. F.

American Senator, The, a novel by A. *Trollope, published 1877.

Elias Gotobed, senator for the fictional state of Mickewa, comes to England on a fact-finding tour, and finds 'irrational and salutary' English manners and customs more than he can understand. In this quiet exposition of country life in and around the town of Dillsborough, two love stories are highlighted.

American Taxation, On, a speech by E. *Burke, made in 1774 on a motion for the repeal of the American Tea Duty.

American Tragedy, An, a novel by T. *Dreiser.

Amiatinus Codex, the best extant MS of the Vulgate, so called from the abbey of Monte Amiata, to which it was presented. It was written in England, early in the 8th cent., at Wearmouth or Jarrow. It is now in the Laurentian Library at Florence.

Amintor, the hero of Beaumont and Fletcher's *The Maid's Tragedy.

AMIS, Kingsley (1922–), novelist and poet, achieved popular success with his first novel, *Lucky Jim* (1954), whose hero, lower-middle-class radical lecturer Jim Dixon was hailed as an *'angry young man'. Its setting in a provincial university was also indicative of a new development in fiction (see COOPER, W., LARKIN, BRAINE), a movement that Amis confirmed in *That Uncertain Feeling* (1955) and *Take a Girl Like You* (1960). *I Like it Here* (1958), a novel set in Portugal, displays Amis's deliberate cultivation, for comic effect, of a prejudiced and Philistine pose which was to harden into an increasingly conservative and hostile view of contemporary life and manners. He is best known for satiric comedy: *One Fat Englishman* (1963), *Ending Up* (1974), *Jake's Thing* (1978), and *The Old Devils* (*Booker Prize, 1986). Amis has also successfully attempted many other genres. *The Anti-Death League* (1966), while in some respects offering the satisfaction of a conventional spy story, is a serious protest against God's inhumanity to man. *The Green Man* (1969) is a novel of the supernatural, *The Riverside Villas Murder* (1973) an imitation of a classic detective story. Amis's enthusiasm for I. *Fleming's work expressed itself in *The James Bond Dossier* (1965) and *Colonel Sun* (1968), published under the pseudonym of Robert Markham. Among other anthologies he edited *The New Oxford Book of Light Verse* (1978), and his *Collected Poems 1944–1979* appeared in 1979. (See also MOVEMENT, THE.)

Amis and Amiloun, a late 13th-cent. romance of 2,508 lines, adapted from an Anglo-Norman lay, about the virtue of friendship. *Morris and *Pater both tell the story as *Amis and Amile*. Amis and Amiloun are foster-brothers whose love withstands trial and sacrifice.

Amoret, in Spenser's *Faerie Queene, III. vi, xii and IV. vii, twin sister of Belphoebe. She is 'Of grace and beautie noble Paragone', and has been married to Sir Scudamour, but carried off immediately after by the enchanter Busirane and imprisoned by him until released by Britomart.

Amoretti, a series of 88 sonnets by *Spenser which probably illustrate his wooing of Elizabeth Boyle. His marriage to her was celebrated in *Epithalamion*, printed with the *Amoretti* (1595).

Amory, Blanche, a character in Thackeray's *Pendennis.

AMORY, Thomas (?1691–1788), author of *Memoirs containing the Lives of Several Ladies of Great Britain* (1755) and *The Life and Opinions of *John Buncle, Esq.* (1756, 1766).

Amos Barton, The Sad Fortunes of the Rev., see SCENES OF CLERICAL LIFE.

Amphibrach, a metrical foot, ∪—∪.

Amphitryon, a comedy by *Dryden, produced and published 1690.
Adapted from the comedies of *Plautus and *Molière on the same subject, it represents the story of Jupiter's seduction of Alcmena in the guise of her husband Amphitryon. The cruel abuse of mortal love by the gods is in striking contrast to the play's uninhibited eroticism. The story was adapted by Giraudoux (1929).

Amyas Leigh, the hero of C. *Kingsley's *Westward Ho!*

AMYOT, Jacques (1513–93), a French writer, whose version of *Plutarch was translated into English by Sir T. *North.

Anabasis, see XENOPHON.

Anachronism, a reference, occurring commonly in historical plays or novels, to something which could not have existed at the time described, e.g. Shakespeare's mention of clocks striking in *Julius Caesar. The concept is in some ways a modern one; the Elizabethans and later ages (e.g. the 18th-cent. stage regularly 'dressed' all plays in the costume of their own time) were not troubled by it. Anachronism can be used for humorous effect (e.g. the opening of G. B. *Shaw's *Caesar and Cleopatra*, or Mark *Twain's *Yankee at the Court of King Arthur*).

Anacoluthon (Greek, 'wanting sequence'), a sentence in which a fresh construction is adopted before the former is complete.

ANACREON (6th cent. BC), a Greek lyric poet who is supposed to have written extensively on love and wine, but only a handful of his genuine poems survive. A large collection of 'anacreontic' verse, of unknown origin, was printed for the first time in Paris in 1554. *Drayton, *Jonson, *Herrick, *Lovelace, *Cowley, all owed a debt to 'Anacreon'. In 1800 T. *Moore published a translation of the *Odes of Anacreon* in English verse.

Anacrusis, 'striking up', an additional syllable at the beginning of a line before the normal rhythm.

Analogy of Religion, Natural and Revealed, to the Constitution and Course of Nature, The, a treatise in defence of the Christian religion, by J. *Butler.

Analytical Review, The (1788–99), an important literary and radical periodical, published by J. *Johnson, which was an early influence in encouraging the growth of *Romanticism. It included *Gilpin's theories on the *picturesque, some of *Wordsworth's early poems, and the work of *Bowles, *Southey, *Lamb, and other young writers.

ANAND, Mulk Raj (1905–), Indian novelist, writing in English, made his name with the novel *Untouchable* (1935), which recounts a day in the life of a street sweeper, roused to hopes of a classless and casteless society by Gandhi. His other novels include *Coolie* (1936), a trilogy (*The Village,* 1939; *Across the Black Waters,* 1940; *The Sword and the Sickle,* 1942), and *Private Life of an Indian Prince* (1953).

Ananias, the fanatical Anabaptist in Jonson's *The Alchemist.*

Anapaest (Greek, 'reversed'), a reversed dactyl, a metrical foot, ∪∪—.

Anaphora, 'carrying back', the repetition of the same word or phrase in several successive clauses.

Anarchy, The Mask of, see MASK OF ANARCHY, THE.

Anatomie of Abuses, The, see STUBBES, P.

Anatomy of Melancholy, The, by Robert *Burton (1621; enlarged 1621–51).

In appearance the *Anatomy* is a medical work, in effect an affectionate satire on the inefficacy of human learning and endeavour. Burton finds 'Melancholy' to be universally present in mankind, 'an inbred malady in every one of us'. The book is made up of a lengthy introduction and three 'partitions'. Burton quotes and paraphrases an extraordinary range of authors, making his book a storehouse of anecdote and maxim. Its tone suits Burton's choice of pseudonym, 'Democritus Junior': *Democritus was 'the laughing philosopher'. The *Anatomy* gave Keats the story for *'Lamia'.

Ancient Mariner, The Rime of the, a poem by S. T. *Coleridge, published 1798 in *Lyrical Ballads.*

An ancient mariner meets three gallants on their way to a marriage feast, and detains one of them in order to recount his story. He tells how his ship was drawn towards the South Pole by a storm. When the ship is surrounded by ice an albatross flies through the fog and is received with joy by the crew, but is then, inexplicably, shot by the mariner. For this act of cruelty a curse falls on the ship. She is driven north to the Equator and is becalmed under burning sun in a rotting sea. The albatross is hung round the neck of the hated mariner. A skeleton ship approaches, on which Death and Life-in-Death are playing dice, and when it vanishes all the crew die except the mariner. Suddenly, watching the beauty of the watersnakes in the moonlight, he blesses them—and the albatross falls from his neck. The ship sails home and the mariner is saved, but for a penance he is condemned to travel from land to land and to teach by his example love and reverence for all God's creatures.

J. L. *Lowes, in *The Road to Xanadu* (1927), traces the sources of Coleridge's story and imagery.

Ancients and Moderns, Quarrel of the, see BATTLE OF THE BOOKS, THE.

Ancrene Wisse (often called *Ancrene Riwle*), a book of devotional advice, written for three sisters by a chaplain in about 1230. It is admired as a work of great charm and regarded as the greatest prose work of the Early Middle English period. The author is unknown. It has important linguistic and thematic connections with the *Katherine Group of texts.

ANDERSEN, Hans Christian (1805–75), Danish writer, is chiefly known in England for his fairy stories, which first appeared in Danish from 1835 onwards, and in English in 1846. See also CHILDREN'S LITERATURE.

ANDERSON, Sherwood (1876–1941), American writer, made his name as a leading naturalistic writer with *Winesburg, Ohio* (1919), a collection of short stories illustrating life in a small town. Other collections include *The Triumph of the Egg* (1921) and *Death in the Woods* (1933). His novels include *Poor White* (1920), *Dark Laughter* (1925), and the semi-autobiographical *Tar: A Midwest Childhood* (1926).

'Andrea del Sarto', a poem by R. *Browning, included in *Men and Women.*

Andrea of Hungary, Giovanna of Naples (1839), and Fra Rupert (1840), three plays forming a trilogy by W. S. *Landor.

Andreas, an Old English poem of 1,722 lines in the *Vercelli Book, based on a Latin version of the Greek Apocryphal *Acts of Andrew and Matthew amongst the Anthropophagi.* It was previously believed to be by *Cynewulf but it is now thought to have been written in the late 9th cent.

ANDREAS CAPELLANUS (*fl.* 1180s), is usually believed to have been a chaplain to

*Marie de Champagne. His book *De Arte Honeste Amandi* (also entitled *De Amore*) is a handbook of procedure in love in three sections: Book One, concerned with the nature of love and procedure in it; Book Two, on how love can be retained; and Book Three, on the rejection of love. Andreas' work corresponds very closely to the writings of *Ovid, and it has been very authoritative in the definitions of *Courtly Love from Gaston Paris to the present day.

ANDREWES, Lancelot (1555–1626), was bishop successively of Chichester, Ely, and Winchester. He was renowned for his patristic learning and was one of the divines appointed to translate the Authorized Version of the *Bible. He was a highly popular preacher, and as a writer is remembered for his sermons which are in the *metaphysical style that preceded the plainer preaching of the Puritans and *Tillotson. In T. S. *Eliot's view 'they rank with the finest English prose of their time' (*For Lancelot Andrewes*, 1928).

ANDREW OF WYNTOUN, see WYNTOUN, ANDREW OF.

Androcles and the Lion, the story used by G. B. *Shaw in the play of that name appears first in *Gellius, v. 14.

Anecdotes of Painting in England, a work by Horace *Walpole (1762–5, 3 vols) based on manuscript notebooks of the celebrated engraver George Vertue. The work surveys English art from medieval times to Walpole's own, and is a reflection of Walpole's developing aesthetic taste.

Aneirin, The Book of, the name given to a 13th-cent. manuscript which contains the poem *Y Gododdin,* attributed to the bard Aneirin (or, incorrectly, Aneurin) who lived in the second half of the 6th cent. The poem commemorates a British defeat at Catraeth (Cattrick, Yorks).

Anelida and Arcite, an incomplete poem by *Chaucer in 357 lines. The simple story tells of the faithlessness of Arcite to Queen Anelida in 210 lines of rhyme-royal, as a preface to the elaborate *Compleynt* of Anelida in 140 lines of varying and accomplished metrical patterns.

Angelica, (1) the beloved of Orlando in *Orlando Innamorato* and *Orlando Furioso*; (2) the heroine of Congreve's *Love for Love*; (3) the heroine of Thackeray's *The Rose and the Ring*.

Angel in the House, The, a sequence of poems by C. *Patmore, in four parts, published 1854–61.
   The work is a celebration of married love. Felix courts and weds Honoria, a dean's daughter; in the last two parts Frederick, a rival for Honoria's hand, marries Jane and learns to love her before her early death. It was immensely popular with the Victorian public, though its mixture of high-flown sentiment and banal details about middle-class life made it the object of much mockery from more sophisticated authors like *Swinburne and *Gosse. V. *Woolf, in a lecture on 'Professions for Women' (1931), spoke of the need for women writers to 'kill the Angel in the House'.

Angelo, the seemingly puritanical deputy to the duke in Shakespeare's *Measure for Measure*.

Anglo-Latin Literature to 1422. From *Augustine's mission in 597 until the end of the 14th cent., the language of education and culture, in England and on the Continent, was Latin, even in the *Anglo-Saxon period when English enjoyed an unusual status. The leading names of this period were *Bede, *Aldhelm, and *Alcuin; poets continued to experiment with the cryptic 'hermeneutic' style.
   From the Norman Conquest until the loss of Normandy in 1205 (the *Anglo-Norman period) English men of letters had their education as much in France as in England. *Geoffrey of Monmouth established a Trojan lineage for Britain and an Arthurian world for posterity. The reign of Henry II saw English writers of European stature: Peter of Blois (c.1135–c.1205), *Map, *John of Salisbury. By the end of the 12th cent. England (or Wales) had also produced *Geoffrey de Vinsauf, *Giraldus Cambrensis, Alexander Neckham, (d. 1217), and *Wireker. Their themes included satire against the court, personal satire, and attacks upon sin in general. Metre varied from the established classical hexameter and elegiac couplet to the new rhythms, rhymed stanzas, and rhymed hexameters. The murder of *Becket produced a large literature of its own.
   In the 13th cent. Anglo-Latin acquired a home-grown look. The arrival of the Franciscans in 1224 brought new inspiration and encouraged new poets, Walter of Wimborne (*fl.* late 12th cent.; already a prolific satirist) and John Pecham (d. 1292), later archbishop of Canterbury; although not a friar, John of Hoveden (d. 1275) was inspired by the same intense feelings for the Virgin and the Passion. Devotional literature continued in the 14th cent., with the mysticism of *Rolle and the hymns of Richard Ledrede (d. 1360). From the Wars of the Barons onwards poems on topical events were popular.
   Although *Gower wrote in Latin, French, and English, *Chaucer's choice of English alone indicated his sense that the vernacular was the language of the future.

Anglo-Norman (or Anglo-French) designates the French language as spoken and written in the

British Isles from the Norman Conquest until the 14th cent. It was a western type of French which, transplanted to Britain, developed characteristics of its own at an increasing rate. The earliest Anglo-Norman work of real literary merit, *The Voyage of St Brendan,* composed in the first half of the 12th cent., shows relatively few insular traits, whereas the French of the *Contes Moralisés* of Nicole Bozon (early 14th cent.) illustrates the disintegration of later Anglo-Norman. The French of *Gower in his *Mirour de l'Omme* is continental French, which was studied in its own right by Englishmen of the later medieval period. Anglo-Norman has many works of a moralizing nature as well as chronicles and practical works drawn from Latin sources. The *Mystère d'Adam* (see ADAM), the first French dramatic work of any moment, was almost certainly written in England. An Anglo-Norman type of French continued to be used for official documents and in English courts of law long after it had ceased to be spoken.

Anglo-Saxon. The Latin form of the word applies originally to the people and language of the Saxon race who colonized the southern parts of Britain (as distinct from the northern parts colonized by the Angles), to distinguish them from continental Saxons; hence, the 'Anglo' element is adverbial and the word does not mean the combination of Angles and Saxons: i.e. the people and language of the whole of England. For the latter the term 'Old English' is more correct. The word became applied in the erroneous way very early; *Aelfric (*c.*1000) refers to the West Saxon he spoke as 'Englisc'. The 'correct' distinction, made by the OED and enforced by modern scholars, between 'Old English' and 'Anglo-Saxon' is a somewhat pedantic one. Since the revival of such studies in the 16th cent., 'Anglo-Saxon' has been used as the general term, without a sense of geographical distinction.

Anglo-Saxon Attitudes, a novel by Sir A. *Wilson.

Anglo-Saxon Chronicle, The, an early record in English of events in England from the beginning of the Christian era to 1154, surviving in seven manuscripts in which C. Plummer descried four groups: the Parker Chronicle, named from Archbishop Parker (1504–75); the Abingdon Chronicles; the Worcester Chronicle; and the Laud Chronicle, named from Archbishop *Laud (see PETERBOROUGH CHRONICLE, THE). The most celebrated entries are those for 449 (the arrival of *Hengist and Horsa), for 755 (the story of Cynewulf and Cyneheard), for 893 to 897 (Alfred's last series of Danish wars), and for the disastrous years of Stephen's reign. Most famous of all is the poem on the Battle of *Brunanburh (937). The systematic organiza-

tion of the earlier part of the Chronicle is attributed to *Alfred in the course of his literary ventures in the 890s.

Angria and **Gondal,** imaginary kingdoms invented by the *Brontë children.

Angry Young Men, a journalistic catch-phrase loosely applied to a number of British playwrights and novelists from the mid-950s, including *Amis, J. *Osborne, *Sillitoe, and C. *Wilson, whose political views were radical or anarchic.

Animal Farm, a novel by G. *Orwell, published 1945.
　It is a satire in fable form on Revolutionary and post-Revolutionary Russia, and, by extension, on all revolutions. The animals of Mr Jones's farm revolt against their human masters and drive them out, the pigs becoming the leaders. Eventually the pigs, dominated by Napoleon, their chief, become corrupted by power and a new tyranny replaces the old. The ultimate slogan runs 'All animals are equal but some animals are more equal than others.' Napoleon, ruthless and cynical, represents *Stalin, and Snowball, the idealist whom he drives out, *Trotsky. Boxer, the noble cart-horse, stands for the strength, simplicity, and good nature of the common man.

ANNA COMNENA (1083–?1148), historian, the daughter of the Byzantine Emperor Alexius I, Comnenus. She wrote the *Alexiad,* a history in 15 books, and in the main part a panegyric about her father's life. She figures in Scott's *Count Robert of Paris.*

Annales Cambriae, a 10th-cent. series of Welsh annals, of interest for the information they offer about *Gildas and about some aspects of the *Arthur story, such as the battles of Badon and Camlan.

Annals of the Parish, a novel by J. *Galt, published 1821.
　The Revd Michael Blawhidder chronicles in some detail the social and economic changes affecting the people of the town of Dalmailing in Ayrshire during the period 1760–1810. It is the source of the term 'utilitarian' adopted by J. S. *Mill.

Anne of Geierstein, or The Maiden of the Mist, a novel by Sir W. *Scott, published 1829.
　The period of the story is the reign of Edward IV.

Annual Register, The, an annual review of events of the past year, founded by *Dodsley and *Burke in 1758, which still survives. The first volume appeared on 15 May 1759. It also published poetry, literary articles, etc.

Annus Mirabilis, a poem in quatrains by *Dryden, published 1667.

Its subjects are the Dutch War (1665–6) and the Fire of London, prefaced by 'Verses to her Highness and Dutchess' [of York].

Ann Veronica, see WELLS, H. G.

ANSELM, St (1033–1109), a native of Aosta in northern Italy and a pupil of *Lanfranc at the abbey of Bec in Normandy. William Rufus appointed him archbishop of Canterbury in 1093, in succession to Lanfranc. Anselm accepted the office with reluctance, and when the king again began to tyrannize over it he withdrew to Rome (1097), to return to England at the accession of Henry I (1100). He wrote many theological and philosophical works, the most famous of which are the *Monologion*; *Cur Deus Homo*; and *Proslogion*, in which is propounded the famous 'Ontological Argument': if God is defined as a Being than which no greater can be conceived of, then he must exist in reality since otherwise a Being of identical attributes with the further conceivable attribute of existence in reality would be greater. This argument has presented logical problems for philosophers ever since, including B. *Russell at one stage of his career.

Anselm was the cornerstone of the Augustinian tradition in the Middle Ages with its emphasis on faith in search of Reason.

ANSON, George, Baron Anson (1697–1762), made his famous voyage round the world in 1740–4; an account of it compiled, according to the title-page, by his chaplain Richard Walter appeared in 1748. It is the source of Cowper's poem *'The Castaway'.

ANSTEY, Christopher (1724–1805), author of the *New Bath Guide* (1766), later illustrated by *Cruikshank (1830), which consists of a series of letters in colloquial verse describing the adventures of squire Blunderhead and his family in Bath.

ANSTEY, F., the pseudonym of Thomas Anstey Guthrie (1856–1934), author of many novels and stories of fantasy and magic, and comic sketches. They include *Vice Versa* (1882), *Tourmalin's Time Cheques* (1891), *The Brass Bottle* (1900), and *In Brief Authority* (1915).

Anthology, The Greek, a collection of some 6,000 short elegiac poems by more than 300 writers (7th cent. BC–10th cent. AD) originated in a collection by Meleager of Gadara ('The Garland of Meleager', *c*.60 BC) which grew by successive additions. In its fullest form it is known as the 'Palatine Anthology' as it was first discovered by Salmasius in the Palatine Library at Heidelberg in 1607.

Antigonus, a Sicilian lord in Shakespeare's *The Winter's Tale*.

Anti-Jacobin, The (1797–8), a journal founded by *Canning and a group of friends to combat the Radical views supported by *The Monthly Magazine*, Coleridge's *The Watchman*, and other *Jacobin influences. It was edited by *Gifford.

Antipholus, the name of the twin brothers, sons of Egeon, in Shakespeare's *The Comedy of Errors*.

Antiquary, The, a novel by Sir W. *Scott, published 1816.

A gallant young officer, Major Neville, who is supposed to be illegitimate, falls in love in England with Isabella Wardour, who, in deference to the prejudices of her father, Sir Arthur Wardour, repulses him. Under the assumed name of Lovel, he follows her to Scotland, falling in on the way with Jonathan Oldbuck, laird of Monkbarns, a learned antiquary, and a neighbour of Sir Arthur. Lovel saves the lives of Sir Arthur and his daughter at the peril of his own. He finally turns out to be the son and heir of the earl of Glenallan, and all ends happily. The charm of the book, Scott's 'chief favourite among all his novels', lies in the character of the Antiquary, drawn according to Scott from a worthy friend of his boyish days (George Constable), but in which we may recognize a portrait or caricature of Scott himself.

Antistrophe, 'turning about', in a Greek chorus, recited as the chorus proceeded in the opposite direction to that followed in the strophe. The metre of strophe and antistrophe was the same.

Antonio, (1) the title character in Shakespeare's *The Merchant of Venice*; (2) the sea-captain in *Twelfth Night*; (3) the brother of Leonato in *Much Ado About Nothing*; (4) the father of Proteus in *The Two Gentlemen of Verona*; (5) the usurping brother of Prospero in *The Tempest*.

Antonio and Mellida, a two-part play by J. *Marston, printed 1602, probably acted two years earlier; it provided Jonson with materials for his ridicule of Marston in *The Poetaster*. Set in Italy, it is a drama of passion and revenge, in which Antonio, son of the duke of Genoa, is driven to murder Piero, duke of Venice, whose daughter Mellida he has loved and lost.

Antony and Cleopatra, a tragedy by *Shakespeare, printed in the First *Folio of 1623, probably written 1606–7. Its chief source is the *Life of Antony* by *Plutarch, as translated by Sir T. *North. Minor sources include the plays by the countess of *Pembroke and S. *Daniel.

The play presents Mark Antony, the great soldier and noble prince, at Alexandria, enthralled by the beauty of the Egyptian queen Cleopatra. Recalled by the death of his wife Fulvia and political developments, he tears himself from Cleopatra and returns to Rome, where the estrangement between him and Octavius Caesar is terminated by his marriage to Octavia, Caesar's sister, an event which provokes the intense jealousy of Cleopatra. But the reconciliation is short-lived, and Antony leaves Octavia and returns to Egypt. At the battle of Actium, the flight of the Egyptian squadron is followed by the retreat of Antony, pursued to Alexandria by Caesar. There, after a momentary success, Antony is finally defeated. On the false report of Cleopatra's death, he falls upon his sword. He is borne to the monument where Cleopatra has taken refuge and dies in her arms. Cleopatra, fallen into Caesar's power but determined not to grace his triumph, takes her own life by the bite of an asp. See also ALL FOR LOVE.

APELLES (*fl.* 330–320 BC), a celebrated Greek painter, who won the favour of *Alexander the Great. He figures in Lyly's *Campaspe.

Apemantus, the 'churlish philosopher' in Shakespeare's *Timon of Athens.

Aphorism, a term transferred from the 'Aphorisms of Hippocrates' to other sententious statements of the principles of physical science, and later to statements of principles generally. Thence it has come to mean any short pithy statement into which much thought or observation is compressed.

Apocalypse, The, from a Greek verb meaning 'to disclose', a 'revelation' or an 'unveiling', and the title given to the book of Revelation in NT. The term 'apocalyptic literature' is used in a broader sense to describe prophetic writings generally, of a range which includes many of the works of *Blake, of *Yeats (e.g. 'The Second Coming'), D. *Lessing's The Four-Gated City, the 'disaster' novels of J. G. *Ballard, and other *Science Fiction writers.

Apocrypha, The, in its special sense, those books included in the *Septuagint and *Vulgate versions of the OT which at the Reformation were excluded from the Sacred Canon by the Protestant party, as having no well-grounded claims to inspired authorship. They are 1 and 2 Esdras, Tobit, Judith, the Rest of Esther, the *Wisdom of Solomon, Ecclesiasticus, Baruch (with the Epistle of Jeremiah), the Song of the Three Holy Children, the History of Susanna, Bel and the Dragon, the Prayer of Manasses, 1 and 2 Maccabees.

The texts of the Apocryphal Gospels, Acts, Epistles, and Apocalypses are printed in The

Apocryphal New Testament, trans. M. R. *James (1924).

APOLLODORUS (2nd cent. BC), Athenian grammarian known to have written about the gods. An extant treatise on mythology, the *Bibliotheca* (first printed 1555) was attributed to him. This work, directly or indirectly, provided *Jonson and *Milton with some of their mythological material.

Apollyon, 'The Destroyer', the angel of the bottomless pit (Rev. 9: 11). He figures in Bunyan's *Pilgrim's Progress.

Apologia pro Vita Sua, see NEWMAN, J. H.

Apologue, a fable conveying a moral lesson.

Apology for Poetry, An, see DEFENCE OF POETRY, A.

Apophthegm, a fable conveying a moral lesson.

Aposiopesis, a rhetorical artifice, in which the speaker comes to a sudden halt in the middle of a sentence, as if unable or unwilling to proceed.

Apostles, The, an exclusive intellectual society formed in Cambridge in 1820, for the purpose of friendship and formal discussion. 19th-cent. members included A. *Hallam, *Tennyson, *Milnes, and R. C. *Trench, and the 20th cent. saw a new age of brilliance, largely inspired by the influence of G. E. *Moore, with members such as *Keynes, *Strachey, B. *Russell, L. *Woolf, and E. M. *Forster. Members are elected for life.

Apostrophe (from Greek, 'to turn away'), a figure of speech in which the writer rhetorically addresses a dead or absent person or abstraction.

Appius, see VIRGINIA.

Appius and Virginia, (1) a tragedy traditionally attributed to *Webster, but by some authorities to *Heywood, in whole or in part. The production date is uncertain; it was probably first printed in 1654. The plot is taken from the classical legend (see VIRGINIA) which forms one of the stories in Painter's *Palace of Pleasure; (2) a tragedy by J. *Dennis.

APULEIUS (*c.* AD 125–after 170), North African rhetorician. His best-known work is his *Metamorphoses* or *The Golden Ass. MSS of this proliferated from the 14th cent. onwards, and it became a quarry for the novella, for which its intercalated stories served as a model. *Boccaccio borrowed three and others appeared in the 15th-cent. *Cent nouvelles nouvelles.* The work is regarded as a forerunner of that *picaresque tradition which eventually produced *Tom Jones*. Special mention must be made of one story, *Cupid and Psyche*.

AQUINAS, St Thomas (*c*.1225–74), an Italian philosopher and Dominican friar, the greatest of the medieval Scholastic theologians. He represents in his writings the culmination of Scholastic philosophy, the harmony of faith and reason, and the reconciliation of Christian theology with Aristotelian philosophy (see SCHOLASTICISM). His *Summa Theologica* (unfinished) is a vast synthesis of the moral and political sciences, brought within a theological and metaphysical framework. He was called the 'Doctor Angelicus', and by his school companions 'the Dumb Ox'. His followers, called Thomists, are still an active school in contemporary philosophy, especially in France. He is a very important influence on *Dante's *Divina Commedia* whose philosophical framework is based on Aquinas. His other major works are the *Summa Contra Gentiles* and a series of commentaries on *Aristotle.

Arabia Deserta, see DOUGHTY, C. M.

Arabian Nights Entertainments, or *The Thousand and One Nights*, a collection of stories written in Arabic, made known in Europe by the translation of Antoine Galland (1646–1715), whose version appeared between 1704 and 1717. The most celebrated version in English is that of Sir Richard *Burton, published 1885–8.

The tales derive from Indian, Persian, and Arabic sources. The framework (the story of the king who killed his wives successively on the morning after the consummation of their marriage, until he married the clever *Scheherazade, who saved her life by the tales she told him) is taken from a lost book of Persian fairy-tales, called *Hazar Afsanah* (A Thousand Tales), which was translated into Arabic *c*. AD 850. Other stories of different origins were added at various dates by professional story-tellers. Burton believed that the earliest stories, including that of *Sindbad, dated back to the 8th cent., and the latest from the 16th cent.

The stories captivated the European imagination, and contributed greatly to the vogue for *oriental tales in the 18th and early 19th cents. (See also HĀRŪN AR-RASHĪD.)

Araygnement of Paris, The, a pastoral play in verse by G. *Peele, published 1584.

ARBLAY, Madame d', see BURNEY, F.

ARBUTHNOT, John (1667–1735), was MD of St Andrews and from 1705 physician to Queen Anne. In 1711 he formed a close friendship with *Swift, and was acquainted with *Pope and other literary men. His *History of *John Bull* was included in Pope and Swift's *Miscellanies* of 1727. He was a member of the *Scriblerus Club and principal author of the *Memoirs of *Martinus Scriblerus*. He also wrote on mathematics and on medical matters; his *An Essay concerning the nature of Ailments* (1731) is a farsighted account of the importance of diet.

ARC, Joan of, see JOAN OF ARC.

'**Arcades,** Part of an entertainment presented to the Countess Dowager of Darby . . .', by *Milton, written ?1630–?3 possibly at the suggestion of his friend Henry *Lawes, who wrote the music for the songs; published 1645.

This short piece consists of a song by nymphs and shepherds as they approach the seat of state of the countess, an address to them by the Genius of the Wood, and two further songs.

Arcadia, a bleak and mountainous district in the central Peloponnese which became, as a result of reference in *Virgil's *Eclogues*, the traditional and incongruous location of the idealized world of the *pastoral.

Arcadia, a series of verse eclogues connected by prose narrative, published 1504 by *Sannazar.

Arcadia, The, a prose romance by Sir P. *Sidney, including poems and pastoral eclogues in a wide variety of verse forms. It exists in two versions: the first, completed by 1581, and much of it written at *Wilton, is known as the *Old Arcadia*. Its survival as an independent work was discovered by Bertram Dobell in 1907. The second version, now known as the *New Arcadia*, was Sidney's radical revision, made about 1583–4 but never completed. It was this revised version which was first printed on its own in 1590, with chapter divisions and summaries 'not of Sir Philip Sidneis dooing', and then in 1593 and thereafter with books iii–v of the *Old Arcadia* added to make a complete-seeming but hybrid work. It was the hybrid *Arcadia* only that was available to readers until the 20th cent.

The *Old Arcadia* is in five 'Books or Acts'. The first four books are followed by pastoral eclogues on themes linked or contrasted with the main narrative. The story is of the attempts of Arcadia's ruler, the foolish old duke Basilius, to prevent the fulfilment of an oracle by withdrawing to two rustic 'lodges' with his wife Gynecia and their daughters Pamela and Philoclea. Two young princes, Musidorus and Pyrocles, gain access to the retired court by disguising themselves as, respectively, a shepherd and an Amazon. A complicated series of intrigues ensues, with Basilius and Gynecia both falling in love with the disguised Pyrocles; Musidorus meanwhile becomes enmeshed with the family of Dametas, an ill-bred herdsman who has been made Pamela's guardian, his shrewish wife Miso, and foolish daughter Mopsa. Pyrocles succeeds in seducing Philoclea and Musidorus attempts to elope with Pamela, but their schemes go awry when Basilius appears to die of a potion believed by his wife to be an aphrodisiac, and Pyrocles and Philoclea are discovered in bed by Dametas. The climax of the narrative is a trial presided over by Euarchus, the just ruler of Macedon, who sentences Gynecia to be buried alive and Pyrocles and Musidorus to be executed. Their disguises and assumed names prevent Euarchus from recognizing the young men as his own son and nephew, but even when their identities are revealed he asserts that 'If rightly I have judged, then rightly have I judged mine own children.' The day is saved by Basilius' awakening from what turns out to have been only a sleeping potion.

No new poems were added in the *New Arcadia* but the method of narration was made far more complex, both stylistically and thematically.

Shakespeare based the Gloucester plot of *King Lear* on Sidney's story of 'the *Paphlagonian* unkinde king', and *Richardson took the name of his first heroine, Pamela, from Sidney's romance.

Archer, (1) a character in Farquhar's *The Beaux' Stratagem*; (2) Isabel, the heroine of H. James's *The Portrait of a Lady*.

ARCHER, William (1856–1924), became a drama critic in London in 1879. The establishment of *Ibsen and of G. B. *Shaw owed much to his encouragement. His five-volume edition of Ibsen's prose dramas in translation (some with collaboration) appeared in 1891; the collected works of Ibsen in 1906–7. In 1919 he assisted with the establishment of the New Shakespeare Company at Stratford-upon-Avon. In *The Old Drama and the New* (1923) he pressed the merits of Ibsen, Shaw, and *Galsworthy, among others. His own play, *The Green Goddess*, was produced with great success in 1923.

Archetype, a word meaning prototype, or original pattern from which copies are made, and adapted by *Jung to mean 'a pervasive idea, image or symbol that forms part of the collective unconscious' (*OED* 1972 Supplement). Literary criticism with a Jungian slant has devoted itself to detecting archetypal figures in literature, and in myths, legends, and fairy-tales: e.g. The Divine Child, The Earth Mother, The Enchanted Prince. Jung himself described the archetypal qualities of many natural phenomena: e.g. a horse 'represents the non-human psyche, the subhuman, animal side, the unconscious', whereas the tree represents 'growth, life, unfolding of form in a physical and spiritual sense'.

Archgallo, see ARTEGAL.

Archimago, or **Archimage,** in Spenser's *Faerie Queene*, the great enchanter, symbolizing Hypocrisy, who deceives *Una by assuming the appearance of the *Redcrosse Knight (I. i). His deceits are exposed and he emerges in Bk II to seek vengeance on Sir *Guyon for what he has suffered at the hands of the Redcrosse Knight.

Arch-poet, The, the name given to the anonymous German writer of *Goliardic Latin poetry. His best-known poem is the 'Confession'. The term was used by *Pope and *Fielding as equivalent to *poet laureate.

Arcite, see PALAMON AND ARCITE.

Arden, (1) a large forest in Warwickshire often referred to in romantic literature; (2) the forest which is the setting for the pastoral parts of Shakespeare's *As You Like It, often assumed to be identical with (1) but actually based on the forest of Ardennes in what is now Belgium; (3) the surname of Shakespeare's mother Mary; (4) based on (1) and (2), the distinguishing name of a series of scholarly editions of Shakespeare's plays initiated by W. J. Craig and R. H. Case in 1899, and revised under the general editorship of Una Ellis-Fermor, H. F. Brooks, H. Jenkins, and Brian Morris from 1951 onwards.

ARDEN, John (1930–), playwright, had his first professional production at the Royal Court, of *The Waters of Babylon* (1957), a satirical play about a corrupt municipal lottery organized by a slum landlord. This was followed by *Live Like Pigs* (1958), dealing with social conflict and violence on a housing estate. *Serjeant Musgrave's Dance* (1959), set in a colliery town in the North of England in 1860–80, shows Musgrave, a deserter from the British Army, attempting to exact revenge for the death of a colleague, but finding that violence breeds violence. Arden here mixes a rich idiosyncratic, semi-historical prose with ballad and verse, as he does in *Armstrong's Last Goodnight* (1964), another play about violence. *The Workhouse Donkey* (1963) is a play about municipal corruption. Widely praised as one of the most innovatory dramatists of the 1960s, his later plays (written with his wife Margaretta D'Arcy) have been less exuberant and ambiguous, and more deliberately socialist and doctrinaire.

Arden of Feversham, *The Tragedy of Mr*, a play published 1592, author unknown, which has been attributed to Shakespeare. It deals with the persistent and eventually successful attempts of Mistress Arden and her paramour Mosby to murder Arden. The play's source is an account in *Holinshed of an actual murder committed in February 1551. *Lillo wrote a play on the same subject.

Areopagitica: a speech of Mr John Milton for the liberty of the unlicenc'd printing, to the Parliament of England, by *Milton, published in 1644. The title is derived from the Areopagus, the hills of Ares near the Acropolis in Athens where the Upper Council met. Milton, addressing the 'Lords and Commons of England', attacks their recent order (1643) 'that no book . . . shall be henceforth printed unless the same be first approved and licensed by such . . . as shall be thereto appointed'. He shows, first, that licensing has been chiefly the practice of those whom the Presbyterians most detest, the Papacy and the Inquisition. Next, that promiscuous reading, constant testing, and diversity of opinion are necessary to the growth of virtue and knowledge. And thirdly, that not only will licensing do no good but it will be a grave discouragement to learning; he quotes the case of the imprisoned *Galileo. Milton builds his rhetoric to a magnificent exhortation to the 'Lords and Commons of England' to consider 'what Nation it is whereof ye are, and whereof ye are governors: A Nation not slow and dull, but of quick, ingenious and piercing spirit . . . Methinks I see her as an eagle mewing her mighty youth . . .' Truth is stronger than falsehood, he concludes, and 'a gross conforming stupidity' more to be feared than new opinions.

Arethusa, (1) a legendary fountain in Ortygia, named after a nymph with whom the river-god Alpheus fell in love; (2) a character in Beaumont and Fletcher's *Philaster.*

Argante, (1) in the *Brut* of *Laȝamon, *Morgan le Fay, the fairy queen to whom Arthur, after the last battle, is borne to be healed of his wounds in Avalon; (2) in Spenser's *Faerie Queene* (III. vii), a mighty and licentious giantess, typifying lust, daughter of Typhoeus the Titan.

ARGYLE, Archibald Campbell, eighth earl, first marquess of (1598–1661), who took a prominent part in the events in Scotland that contributed to the downfall of Charles I, figures in Scott's *The Legend of Montrose.* He was beheaded.

ARGYLE, John Campbell, second duke of (1678–1743), distinguished military commander, figures in Scott's *The Heart of Midlothian.*

Arian heresy, named after its promulgator Arius, a Lybian who was parish priest near Alexandria c.310, declared that God the Son, because begotten by the Father, must have an origin in time and therefore is not 'consubstantial' with the Father. This breach of the doctrine of the Trinity was condemned at the Council of Nicaea, summoned by Constantine in 325, which produced the Nicene Creed as the official declaration of the Church.

Ariel, (1) an airy spirit in Shakespeare's *The Tempest;* (2) a rebel angel in Milton's *Paradise Lost* (vi. 371); (3) in Pope's *Rape of the Lock* (ii. 53 ff.) the chief of the sylphs.

Shakespeare's character (1) has inspired many later writers to identify the name 'Ariel' with poetic imagination: T. S. *Eliot called five Christmas poems (1927–54) 'Ariel poems'; the first *Penguin paperback was Maurois' life of *Shelley called *Ariel* (1935); and there have been several literary journals with 'Ariel' as title. See also PLATH, S.

Arioch, in Milton's *Paradise Lost* (vi. 371), one of the rebel angels.

ARIOSTO, Ludovico (1474–1535), Italian poet, author of *Orlando Furioso* (1532), the greatest of Italian romantic epics. He also wrote Italian and Latin and four comedies of which one, *I Suppositi* (1509), came through to Shakespeare's *The Taming of the Shrew* via Gascoigne's *Supposes.*

ARISTOPHANES (c.448–380 BC), Athenian comic dramatist whose satirical plays, the only surviving representatives of the Old Comedy, attacked individuals rather than types and are of great value for their caricatures of the leading personages of the time and their comments on current affairs. Because of the difficulties of his language and the obscurity of his contemporary references, Aristophanes did not receive much attention in England until the 19th cent., which produced translations by B. H. Kennedy (*The Birds*, 1804), Thomas Mitchell, and *Frere. These were followed by versions by B. B. Rogers (1904 onwards), by G. *Murray, Dudley Fitts, and others. The extant works of Aristophanes are *The Acharnians; The Knights; The Clouds; The Peace; The Wasps; The Birds; The Frogs; Plutus; Lysistrata* and *Ecclesiazusae,* both dealing with government by women; and *Thesmophoriazusae,* which presents the trial and conviction of *Euripides at the female festival of the Thesmophoria.

Aristophanes' Apology, a long poem in blank verse by R. *Browning, published 1875 as a sequel to *Balaustion's Adventure.*

The core of the poem is a protracted argument between Balaustion and *Aristophanes as to the moral, social, and metaphysical value of the different aesthetics they espouse; Balaustion defending the visionary humanism of *Euripides, Aristophanes his own coarse realism. The poem also contains the remarkable fragment 'Thamuris marching', which reworks some of the material of *'Childe Roland to the Dark Tower Came'.

ARISTOTLE (384–322 BC), was born at Stagira, in Macedon. He studied under *Plato for twenty years. Then after a period of travel he was appointed by Philip of Macedon to be tutor to the future *Alexander the Great in 342 and seven years later returned to Athens where he opened a school in the Lyceum, a grove outside the city. His extant works are believed to have been the notes he used for his lectures. They cover logic, ethics, metaphysics, physics, zoology, politics, rhetoric, and poetics. Transmitted through translations, they shaped the development of medieval thought first in the Arab world, then in the Latin West, where Aristotle came to be regarded as the source of all knowledge. His logical treatises won a central place in the curriculum during the 12th cent. Then after a brief struggle his ethical, metaphysical, and scientific works were harmonized with Christianity and constituted the subject-matter of higher education from the 13th to the 17th cent. They shaped the thinking of Englishmen writing in Latin from *Grosseteste to *Herbert of Cherbury, and their influence can be traced in *Spenser, *Donne, and occasionally in Sir T. *Browne. By the end of the 17th cent., however, the Aristotelian world-view had fallen out of favour except for the *Poetics, which came into prominence in the middle of the 16th cent. and contributed to the rise of *Neo-classicism. It has left its mark on the critical writings of *Sidney, *Dryden, and even Dr *Johnson.

ARLEN, Michael (1895–1956), wrote many ornate and mannered novels of fashionable London life, but is chiefly remembered for his best-seller *The Green Hat* (1924).

Armado, Don Adriano de, a 'braggart' 'fantastical' Spaniard in Shakespeare's *Love's Labour's Lost.*

Arminianism, the doctrine of James Arminius or Marmensen (d. 1609), a Dutch Protestant theologian whose views were opposed to those of *Calvin, especially on predestination.

ARMSTRONG, John (1709–79), Scottish poet and physician, is principally remembered for his didactic poem in blank verse *The Art of Preserving Health* (1744) and for a satirical epistle of literary criticism in heroic couplets, *Taste* (1753).

ARMSTRONG, William, known as Kinmont Willie (*fl.* 1596), a border moss-trooper, whose nickname is taken from his castle of Kinmont in Canonby, Dumfriesshire. He is the hero of the ballad 'Kinmont Willie', included in Scott's *Minstrelsy of the Scottish Border.*

ARNE, Thomas Augustine (1710–78), English composer, the leading musical figure of the London theatre in the mid-18th cent., producing operas, *masques, and much incidental music for plays. The masque of *Alfred* (1740) added 'Rule Britannia' to the canon of English song;

and his music for seven of Shakespeare's plays included some of the most famous of all English Shakespeare settings ('Where the bee sucks', 'When daisies pied', 'Fear no more the heat of the sun', and many others). For the Shakespeare Jubilee at Stratford-upon-Avon in 1769 he collaborated with *Garrick in an *Ode upon Dedicating a Building to Shakespeare.*

ARNOLD, Sir Edwin (1832–1904), is best remembered for his *The Light of Asia*, or *the Great Renunciation* (1879), a poem of eight books in blank verse, in which, in his own words, he attempted 'by the medium of an imaginary Buddhist votary to depict the life and character and indicate the philosophy of that noble hero and reformer, Prince Gautama of India, founder of Buddhism'.

ARNOLD, Matthew (1822–88), eldest son of Thomas *Arnold, was educated at Rugby, Winchester, and at Balliol College, Oxford, where he formed a close friendship with *Clough, and won the *Newdigate prize with a poem on Cromwell. He became a fellow of Oriel College. In 1851 he became an inspector of schools, in which capacity he served for 35 years. His first volume of poems, *The Strayed Reveller, and other Poems* (by 'A', 1849), contains 'The Forsaken Merman', 'The Sick King in Bokhara', and sonnets written at Balliol, including 'Shakespeare'. In 1851 he married Fanny Lucy Wightman; part of 'Dover Beach' (1867) dates from his honeymoon. *Empedocles on Etna, and other Poems* (1852) contained *'Tristram and Iseult' and some of the 'Marguerite' poems, including 'Yes! in the sea of life enisled'. In 1853 appeared a volume of poems containing extracts from earlier books, and *'Sohrab and Rustum', *'The Scholar-Gipsy', 'Memorial Verses to Wordsworth', and 'Stanzas in Memory of the Author of "Obermann" ', which show how profoundly Arnold had been affected by Senancour's novel. *Poems, Second Series*, including 'Balder Dead' appeared in 1855; *Merope, a Tragedy* in 1858; and *New Poems*, including *'Thyrsis', 'Rugby Chapel', and 'Heine's Grave', in 1867.

In his maturity Arnold turned increasingly to prose, writing essays on literary, educational, and social topics that established him as the leading critic of the day and which greatly influenced writers as diverse as Max Weber, T. S. *Eliot, *Leavis, and R. *Williams. His lectures on translating *Homer, with his definition of 'the grand style' (delivered in 1860, while he was professor of poetry at Oxford) were published in 1861; *Essays in Criticism (First Series)* in 1865 (*Second Series*, 1888); *On the Study of Celtic Literature* in 1867; *Culture and Anarchy* in 1869; *Friendship's Garland* in 1871; *Literature and Dogma*, a study of the interpretation of the Bible, in 1873. In these and other works, Arnold sharply criticized the provincialism, *Philistinism, sectarianism, and utilitarian materialism of English life and culture, and argued that England needed more intellectual curiosity, more ideas, and a more comparative, European outlook.

Special reference is due to Arnold's attempts to secure the improvement of education, particularly secondary education, in England. In 1859 and 1865 he visited the Continent to study educational systems, and produced reports arguing that England badly needed more educational organization and could learn much from European models.

ARNOLD, Thomas (1795–1842), is remembered principally as the headmaster (1828–42) of Rugby, which he raised to the rank of a great public school. His concept of the public school had a profound and lasting influence, and he was held in great personal veneration by his pupils, who included his son Matthew *Arnold, *Clough, A. P. *Stanley, and T. *Hughes, author of Tom Brown's Schooldays. A Broad Churchman, he wrote in favour of church reform and Catholic emancipation, and attacked the Tractarians of the *Oxford Movement. He was the author of several works on Roman history, influenced by Niebuhr, and was appointed Regius professor of modern history in 1841.

Artegal ('Archgallo' in *Geoffrey of Monmouth's Historia Regum Britanniae), legendary king of Britain. He was deposed for his crimes and replaced by his brother Elidurus the Dutiful; when he returned from exile Elidurus restored him to the throne. The story is the subject of *Wordsworth's poem 'Artegal and Elidure'.

Artegall, Sir, in Spenser's *Faerie Queene, Bk v, the champion of Justice.

Arte of English Poesie, see PUTTENHAM, G.

Arte of Rhetorique, see WILSON, T.

Art for art's sake, a phrase associated with the aesthetic doctrine that art is self-sufficient and need serve no moral or political purpose. The phrase l'art pour l'art became current in France in the first half of the 19th cent., and Gautier's formulation in his Preface to Mademoiselle de Maupin (1835), which denied that art could or should be in any way useful, was admired by *Pater, one of the leading influences on the English *'aesthetic' movement of the 1880s. (See WILDE, DOWSON, JOHNSON, L., SYMONDS, A.) Pater in his conclusion to The Renaissance (1873) spoke of 'the desire of beauty, the love of art for art's sake'.

Artful Dodger, The, a member of Fagin's gang in Dickens's *Oliver Twist.

Arthur, King. The romantic figure of King Arthur has probably some historical basis. He was probably a chieftain or general (dux bellorum) in the 5th or 6th cent. The *Annales Cambriae place the battle of Mount Badon, 'in which Arthur carried the cross of our Lord Jesus Christ on his shoulders', in 518, and the 'battle of Camlan, in which Arthur and Medraut fell' in 539. There is mention of him in certain ancient poems contained in the *Black Book of Camarthen and in the ancient Welsh romance Kilhwch and Olwen. According to the Arthur of the marquis of Bath's manuscript (1428) he died in 542 after a reign of 22 years. He was said to be the father of Modred by his half-sister Morgawse; his sister was Anna. Guinevere was the daughter of Arthur's ally Leodegan. According to *Malory, the Grail was accomplished 454 years after the passing of Christ (i.e. in 487). The legend of the return of Arthur to rule Britain again is told by Malory and in the stanzaic Le *Morte Arthur. According to the alliterative *Morte Arthure, he definitely died.

The Arthur of the cycle of legends first appears at length in the Historia Regum Britanniae of *Geoffrey of Monmouth. According to this, Arthur is the son of *Uther Pendragon and Ygaerne (Igraine), wife of Gorlois of Cornwall, whom Uther wins through Merlin's magic. Geoffrey's version was developed by the 12th-cent. Norman writer *Wace; the Round Table is first mentioned by him as a device for the settlement of disputes over precedence; and the wounded king is expected to return to rule the Britons again. Wace was the principal source of *Laȝamon's Brut, the first English version of the story which adds to both the magic and martial aspect. In Laȝamon, Arthur is borne off after the last battle at Camelford to Argante (Morgan le Fay) in Avalon in a magic boat. The story was very significantly developed in the French *'Matter of Britain', by such writers as *Marie de France, *Chrétien de Troyes, and the authors of the 13th-cent. Vulgate prose cycles. Other characters—Merlin, Launcelot, and Tristram —gradually became associated with Arthur, and he himself is the central character only in the narratives describing his early years and his final battle and death; in the intervening tales his court is merely the starting-point for the adventures of various knights. Through the history of the legends Arthur himself is exceeded in excellence by first *Gawain and then *Launcelot. Malory's *Morte D'Arthur was the most authoritative version of the legend in the English tradition. Malory gives great prominence to the exploits of the knights of the Round Table, the quest of the Holy Grail, the love of Launcelot and Guinevere, and the love of Tristram and Isoud. For other Arthurian writings, see TENNYSON, WILLIAM OF MALMESBURY, GLASTONBURY.

Arthur, Prince in Spenser's *Faerie Queene, symbolizes 'Magnificence' (?Magnanimity), in the Aristotelian sense of the perfection of all the virtues.

Arthour and of Merlin, Of, a later 13th-cent. non-alliterative romance in 9,938 lines of short rhyming couplets, possibly by the same writer as *King Alisaunder* and *Richard Cœur de Lyon*.

Art of English Poesie, *Observations in the,* an attack on the use of rhyme in English poetry by T. *Campion, to which S. Daniel replied in his *Defence of Ryme*.

Arts Council of Great Britain, The, was incorporated by royal charter in 1946 for the purpose of developing greater knowledge, understanding, and practice of the fine arts and to increase their accessibility to the public. It grew out of the war-time Council for the Encouragement of Music and the Arts, which began in 1940 with a grant of £25,000 from the Pilgrim Trust. The first chairman was Lord Macmillan; the vice-chairman and prime mover Dr Thomas Jones, CH. M. *Keynes was chairman from 1942 to 1945. See also under PATRONAGE.

Arveragus, the husband of Dorigen in Chaucer's 'Franklin's Tale'. See CANTERBURY TALES, 12.

Arviragus, the younger son of *Cymbeline, in Shakespeare's play of that name. In Spenser's *Faerie Queene* (II. x. 51), Arviragus is Cymbeline's brother.

Aryan, a term formerly applied to the large family of languages now called *Indo-European.

Asaph, in the part of *Absalom and Achitophel* written by *Tate, is *Dryden, and refers to the Asaph of 1 Chron. 16: 4–7 and 25: 1, and the hereditary choir, the 'Sons of Asaph', who conducted the musical services of the Temple.

Ascent of F6, The, a play by W. H. *Auden and C. *Isherwood, published 1936, first performed 1937.

The central character, Michael Ransom, 'scholar and man of action', succumbs to his mother's persuasions and leads a mountaineering expedition up F6, a haunted peak on the borders of disputed colonial territory; all his men die *en route* and he himself dies as he achieves his mission, destroyed by his own self-knowledge. A chorus of suburban Everyman, Mr A and Mrs A, comments in verse on his heroic exploits and their own dull lives. Ransom was in part modelled on T. E. *Lawrence, the Truly Strong Weak Man. The play is a parable about the nature of power and will and leadership, and reflects the growing apprehension of and attraction towards the 'strong man' at this period of the 1930s.

ASCHAM, Roger (1515/16–68), educated at St John's College, Cambridge, became college reader in Greek in 1540. In 1545 he published *Toxophilus,* a treatise on archery, set in the form of a dialogue between Toxophilus (lover of shooting) and Philologus (lover of books); it provided the model for many later treatises in dialogue form, including *The Compleat Angler.* In 1554 he became Latin secretary to Queen Mary, and was renewed in this office under Elizabeth. *The Scholemaster* was published posthumously in 1570. Its three most distinctive features are: Ascham's dislike of corporal punishment; the Ciceronian technique of double translation, from Latin into English and back again; and his attitude to Italy. It was an immediate influence on Sidney's *Defence of Poetry,* as well as an important landmark in later educational theory. Ascham's English works are notable for their relaxed, personal style and for considerable economy of expression. Dr *Johnson wrote an anonymous *Life of Ascham* to accompany James Bennet's edition of 1761.

Asclepiads, see METRE.

ASHFORD, Daisy (Mrs George Norman) (1881–1972), wrote *The Young Visiters* while still a young child in Lewes. It was found in a drawer in 1919 and published the same year with an introducion by J. M. *Barrie. It is a sparkling, misspelt, and unpunctuated view of High Life and the adventures of Ethel Monticue and her admirer Mr Salteena.

Ashley Library, see LIBRARIES.

ASHMOLE, Elias (1617–92), antiquarian and astrologer. His chief work was *The Institution, Laws and Ceremonies of the Order of the Garter* (1672). In 1682 he presented his collection of curiosities, bequeathed to him by *Tradescant, to Oxford University, thus founding the Ashmolean Museum.

Ashmolean Museum, see ASHMOLE, E.

'Ash Wednesday', a poem by T. S. *Eliot.

Asolando, the last volume of poems by R. *Browning, published 1889.

The poems fall into three main groups; an opening series of love lyrics; a group of anecdotal poems and longer narratives; and a concluding group of meditative or reminiscent dramatic monologues. The 'Epilogue' to the volume, containing the famous self-description 'One who never turned his back but marched breast forward' etc., stands as a traditional proof of Browning's optimism.

Aspatia, a character in Beaumont and Fletcher's *The Maid's Tragedy.

ASSER (d. 910), a monk of St David's, Pembrokeshire, who entered the household of King *Alfred. In 893 he wrote a Latin life of Alfred and a Chronicle of English History for the years 849 to 887. The authenticity of the *Life* has been questioned.

Assonance, the correspondence or rhyming of one word with another in the accented and following vowels, but not in the consonants, as e.g. in Old French versification.

Astarte, the Phoenician goddess of love. This is the name which Byron gives to his half-sister Augusta *Leigh in his drama *Manfred.

Astolat ('Ascolet' in the stanzaic Le *Morte Arthur*), the place where Launcelot meets Elaine Le Blank, is, according to Malory's *Morte D'Arthur*, Guildford in Surrey. Elaine is 'The Fair Maid of Astolat' and Tennyson's *'Lady of Shalott'.

Astraea Redux, see DRYDEN, J.

'Astrophel', a pastoral elegy, written by *Spenser in ?1591–5 on the death of Sir P. *Sidney. Spenser had previously lamented him in *'The Ruines of Time'.

Astrophel and Stella, a sequence of 108 sonnets and 11 songs by Sir P. *Sidney, written about 1582. They plot the unhappy love of Astrophel ('lover of a star') for Stella ('star'). As several sonnets make clear, e.g. 37, referring to one that 'Hath no misfortune, but that Rich she is', Stella is to be identified with Penelope *Rich; but the exact nature of Sidney's real, rather than poetic, relationship with her can never be known. Poetically the sonnets are an outstanding achievement, being written throughout in versions of the exacting Italian sonnet form, and displaying a striking range of tone, imagery, and metaphor. The best known is 31, 'With how sad steps, ô Moone, thou climb'st the skies'. There were two editions of *Astrophel and Stella* in 1591 which began a craze for sonnet sequences; from 1598 onwards it was included in editions of *The Arcadia.

As You Like It, a comedy by *Shakespeare, first printed in the *Folio of 1623, registered 1599 but perhaps written some years earlier. Shakespeare's chief source was Lodge's *Rosalynde.

Frederick has usurped the dominions of the duke his brother, who is living with his faithful followers in the forest of *Arden. Celia, Frederick's daughter, and Rosalind, the duke's daughter, living at Frederick's court, witness a wrestling match in which Orlando, son of Sir Rowland de Boys, defeats a powerful adversary, and Rosalind falls in love with Orlando and he with her. Orlando, who at his father's death has been left in the charge of his elder brother Oliver, has been driven from home by Oliver's cruelty. Frederick, learning that Orlando is the son of Sir Rowland, who was a friend of the exiled duke, has his anger against the latter revived, and banishes Rosalind from his court, and Celia accompanies her. Rosalind assumes a countryman's dress and takes the name Ganymede; Celia passes as Aliena his sister. They live in the forest of Arden, and fall in with Orlando, who has joined the banished duke. Ganymede encourages Orlando to pay suit to her as though she were his Rosalind. Oliver comes to the forest to kill Orlando, but is saved by him from a lioness, and is filled with remorse for his cruelty. He falls in love with Aliena, and their wedding is arranged for the next day. Ganymede undertakes to Orlando that she will by magic produce Rosalind at the same time to be married to him. When all are assembled in presence of the banished duke to celebrate the double nuptials, Celia and Rosalind put off their disguise and appear in their own characters. News is brought that Frederick the usurper, setting out to seize and destroy his brother and his followers, has been converted from his intention by 'an old religious man' and has made restitution of the dukedom.

Entertainment rather than plot dominates this play, however, much of it provided by the reflections of Jaques and Touchstone, and by the large number of songs, more than in any of Shakespeare's other plays, including such lyrics as 'Under the greenwood tree' (which *Hardy used as the title for a novel) and 'Blow, blow, thou winter wind' (both in II. vii).

Atalanta in Calydon, a poetic drama by *Swinburne, published 1865. It tells the story of the hunting of the wild boar sent by Artemis to ravage Calydon in revenge for its neglect of her: Meleager slays the boar, presents the spoils to the virgin athlete and huntress Atalanta, and then himself dies through the intervention of his mother Althaea. The work was highly praised for its successful imitation of Greek models. It is now chiefly remembered for the 'chorus' beginning 'When the hounds of spring are on winter's traces . . .'

Atalantis, The New, see MANLEY, MRS.

Atellan Fables were sketches depicting scenes from rustic life, presented on a crude stage with stock characters (the foolish old man, the rogue, the clown), and seem to have been the earliest form of drama to flourish in ancient Rome. It was imported from Campania where Oscan, a language akin to Latin, was spoken.

ATHANASIUS, St (*c*.296–373), bishop of Alexandria in the reign of the emperor Constantine and persecuted by him and by his successor Constantius II whose autocratic religious policies Athanasius strongly opposed. He was an uncompromising opponent of Arianism (see ARIAN HERESY). His works include the influential *De Incarnatione* and a life of St Antony of Egypt. The Athanasian Creed, which begins with the words 'Quincunque vult', has been attributed to him.

Atheism, The Necessity of, a prose pamphlet by P. B. *Shelley and his friend T. J. *Hogg, published anonymously at Oxford, 1811. Using the sceptical arguments of *Hume and *Locke, the authors smartly demolish the grounds for a rational belief in the Deity. The pamphlet ends with a flourishing 'Q.E.D.', as in a schoolboy's exercise, which caused great offence, as did its title. It is probably the first published statement of atheism in Britain.

Atheist's Tragedy, The, a tragedy by *Tourneur, printed 1611.

D'Amville, the 'atheist', seeks to marry his son Rousard to Castabella. She loves his nephew Charlemont, who is sent abroad on military service, then falsely reported dead: Castabella marries Rousard. Charlemont returns, but is urged by the ghost of his murdered father not to seek revenge. D'Amville's sons die, then he himself dies in an attempt to murder Charlemont. Charlemont and Castabella are reunited. The play is a form of 'anti-revenge' drama. (See REVENGE TRAGEDY.)

Athelstane of Coningsburgh, a character in Scott's *Ivanhoe*.

Athelston, an unhistorical but lively verse romance from about 1350 in 811 lines. It tells of the chance meeting in a forest of four messengers, one of whom, Athelston, becomes king of England, and the subsequent relations between the four. One becomes archbishop of Canterbury; one becomes earl of Dover; the fourth becomes earl of Stane and the father of Athelston's chosen successor Edmund.

Athenaeum, The (1828–1921), J. S. *Buckingham's literary review. The founder wished the journal to become the resort of thinkers, poets, orators, and other writers. *Dilke was editor 1830–46, and the list of contributors in the 19th cent. included *Lamb, *Darley, *Hogg, *Hood, *Landor, *Carlyle, R. *Browning, *Lang, and *Pater. In the 20th cent. its contributors included *Hardy, K. *Mansfield, T. S. *Eliot, R. *Graves, *Blunden, V. *Woolf, and J. M. *Murry, who became editor in 1919. In 1921 it merged with the *Nation*, ran for 10 years as *Nation and Athenaeum* and in 1931 was purchased by the *New Statesman*.

Athenaeum Club, in London, was founded in 1824 as an association of persons of literary, scientific, and artistic attainments, patrons of learning, etc.

Athenian Gazette, later the *Athenian Mercury*, a periodical published by *Dunton, a question-and-answer paper, and thus a precursor of *Notes and Queries*. It first appeared in March 1691 and flourished until 1697.

Atlantic Monthly, The, an American magazine of literature, the arts, and politics, founded in 1857. J. R. *Lowell was its first editor (1857–61) and O. W. *Holmes's contribution of *The Autocrat at the Breakfast-Table* added greatly to its early success. It continues to include many leading American men and women of letters among its contributors.

Atlantis, The New, see NEW ATLANTIS, THE.

Atom, *The History and Adventures of an*, a satire probably by T. *Smollett, published 1769.

Atossa, the wife of Darius and mother of Xerxes, appears in *The Persians* of *Aeschylus. See also MORAL ESSAYS.

ATTERBURY, Francis (1662–1732), became bishop of Rochester in 1713. He engaged in the *Phalaris controversy and in the theological and political disputes of the day, and was imprisoned in 1720 for alleged complicity in a Jacobite plot. He died in exile. He was a close friend of *Pope and *Swift, and was one of the most noted preachers of his day.

Attic, a form of Greek spoken in Athens during her period of literary pre-eminence, became later the basis of the common speech (κοινή) of the Greek-speaking East. Attic style, moulded on the great Athenian orators, aimed at a dry, grammatically correct lucidity.

Atticus, the character under which *Pope satirized *Addison in lines written in 1715, first published in 1723, and in a much altered version in Pope's *Epistle to Dr Arbuthnot* (1735), ll. 193–214. The original Atticus (109–32 BC), so called from his long residence in Athens, was a friend of Cicero.

ATWOOD, Margaret (1939–), Canadian poet and novelist. Her first volume of poetry, *The Circle Game* (1966) was followed by several others. Her novels include *The Edible Woman* (1969), *Surfacing* (1972), *Life Before Man* (1979) and *The Handmaid's Tale* (1986). She has also compiled *The New Oxford Book of Canadian Verse in English* (1983), and written a controversial study of themes in Canadian literature (*Survival*, 1972).

Aubade (Provençal, *alba*; German, *Tagelied*), a dawn song, usually describing the regret of two lovers at their imminent separation. The form (which has no strict metrical pattern) flourished with the conventions of *Courtly Love and survives in such modern examples as *Empson's 'Aubade' (1940).

AUBREY, John (1626–97), antiquary and biographer, became familiar with many of the distinguished men of his time, including *Hobbes. In 1648 he was the first to discover the ruins of Avebury, and devoted much time to archaeological research, keenly deploring the neglect of antiquities; he was one of the original fellows of the *Royal Society. His *Miscellanies* (1696; stories and folklore) was the only work completed and published in his lifetime. He is chiefly remembered for his *Lives* of eminent people. The *Lives* were much used (and in his view somewhat abused) by *A. Wood; they are a lively and heterogeneous mixture of anecdote, first-hand observation, folklore and erudition, a valuable, open-minded entertaining portrait of an age. He collected these over a period of years, depositing his manuscripts in the Ashmolean Museum in 1693. (See BIOGRAPHY.)

Auburn, see DESERTED VILLAGE, THE.

Aucassin and Nicolette, a 13th-cent. courtly story in northern French, composed in alternating prose and songs, now believed to be a loving pastiche of the excesses of courtly-love romances. The writer was probably a northern *jongleur* unfamiliar with the Provençal setting of the story. It is discussed or translated by *Swinburne, *Pater, and *Lang. The story tells of the faithful love of Aucassin, the son of Count Garins of Beaucaire, and Nicolette, a Saracen captive, and their series of adventures before they are finally married.

AUCHINLECK, see BOSWELL, J.

AUDEN, W(ystan) H(ugh) (1907–73), educated at Christ Church, Oxford. Among his contemporaries, who were to share some of his left-wing near-Marxist response to the public chaos of the thirties, were *MacNeice, *Day-Lewis, and *Spender, with whom his name is often linked. (See PYLON SCHOOL.) In 1929 he became a schoolteacher. He visited Germany regularly, staying with his friend and future collaborator *Isherwood. His first volume, *Poems* (1930; including some previously published in a private edition, 1928), established him as the most talented voice of his generation. *The Orators* followed in 1932, and *Look Stranger!* in 1936. In 1932 he became associated with Rupert Doone's Group Theatre, which produced several of his plays (*The Dance of Death*, 1933; and, with Isherwood, *The Dog Beneath the Skin*, 1935; *The Ascent of F6*, 1936; *On the Frontier*, 1938); these owe something to the early plays of *Brecht. (See also EXPRESSIONISM.) Working from 1935 with the GPO Film Unit he became friendly with *Britten, who set many of his poems to music and later used Auden's text for his opera *Paul Bunyan*. In 1935 he married Erika Mann to provide her with a British passport to escape from Nazi Germany. A visit to Iceland with MacNeice in 1936 produced their joint *Letters from Iceland* (1937); *Journey to a War* (1939, with Isherwood) records a journey to China. Meanwhile in 1937 he had visited Spain for two months, to support the Republicans; this resulted in his poem 'Spain' (1937). In January 1939 he and Isherwood left Europe for America (he became a US citizen in 1946) where he met Chester Kallman, who became his lifelong friend and companion. *Another Time* (1940), containing many of his most famous poems (including 'September 1939' and 'Lullaby'), was followed by *The Double Man* (1941, published in London as *New Year Letter*), a long transitional verse epistle describing the 'baffling crime' of 'two decades of hypocrisy', and ending with a prayer for refuge and illumination for the 'muddled heart'. From this time, Auden's poetry became increasingly Christian in tone (to such an extent that he even altered some of his earlier work to bring it in line and disowned some of his political pieces); this was perhaps not unconnected with the death in 1941 of his devout Anglo-Catholic mother, to whom he dedicated *For the Time Being: A Christmas Oratorio* (1944). This was published with *The Sea and the Mirror*, a series of dramatic monologues inspired by *The Tempest*. *The Age of Anxiety: A Baroque Eclogue* (1948) is a long dramatic poem, reflecting man's isolation, which opens in a New York bar at night, and ends with dawn on the streets.

In 1956 he was elected professor of poetry at Oxford, and in 1962 he became a Student (i.e. fellow) of Christ Church. His major later collections include *Nones* (1951, NY; 1952, London), *The Shield of Achilles* (1955), which includes 'Horae Canonicae' and 'Bucolics', and *Homage to Clio* (1960), which includes a high proportion of light verse. Auden had edited *The Oxford Book of Light Verse* in 1938, and subsequently many other anthologies, collections, etc.; his own prose criticism includes *The Enchafèd Flood* (1950, NY; 1951, London), *The Dyer's Hand* (1962, NY; 1963, London), and *Secondary Worlds* (1968, T. S. *Eliot Memorial lectures). He also wrote several librettos, notably for Stravinsky's *The Rake's Progress* (1951, with Kallman). *About the House* (1965, NY; 1966, London), one of his last volumes of verse, contains a tender evocation of his life with Kallman at their summer home in Austria.

Auden's influence on a succeeding generation of poets was incalculable. His progress from the engaged, didactic, satiric poems of his youth to the complexity of his later work offered a wide variety of models—the urbane, the pastoral, the lyrical, the erudite, the public, and the introspective mingle with great fluency. He was a master of verse form, and accommodated traditional patterns to a fresh, easy, and contemporary language.

Audrey, in Shakespeare's *As You Like It*, the country wench wooed and won by Touchstone.

Aufidius, general of the Volscians, in Shakespeare's *Coriolanus*.

Augusta Leigh, *Byron's half-sister: see LEIGH.

Augustan Age, a term derived from the period of literary eminence under the Roman emperor Augustus (27 BC–AD 14) during which *Virgil, *Horace, and *Ovid flourished. In English literature it refers generally to the early and mid-18th cent. Augustan writers (such as *Pope, *Addison, *Swift, and *Steele) greatly admired their Roman counterparts, imitated their works, and themselves frequently drew parallels between the two ages. *Goldsmith, in *The Bee*, in an 'Account of the Augustan Age in England' (1759), identifies it with the reign of Queen Anne, and the era of *Congreve, *Prior, and *Bolingbroke. See also NEO-CLASSICISM.

AUGUSTINE, St (d. 26 May, between 604 and 609), first archbishop of Canterbury, was sent by Pope *Gregory, with some forty monks, to preach the gospel in England in 597. He was favourably received by King Ethelbert of Kent who was afterwards converted and gave Augustine a see at Canterbury. Augustine was consecrated 'Bishop of the English' at Arles.

AUGUSTINE, St, of Hippo (354–430), was trained as a rhetorician and abandoned the Christianity in which he had been brought up. He was a Manichaean for some time, but was converted (387) after hearing the sermons of *Ambrose, a scene he vividly described in his *Confessions* (c.400), which contains a celebrated account of his early life. He became bishop of Hippo (396) and was engaged in constant theological controversy, combating Manichaeans, Donatists, and Pelagians. The most important of his numerous works is *De Civitate Dei*, 'The City of God' (413–27), a treatise in vindication of Christianity. His principal tenet was the immediate efficacy of grace, and his theology (which contains a significant *Neoplatonic element, probably from *Plotinus) remained an influence of profound importance in the Middle Ages, when it was often characterized as being an alternative orthodoxy to the Dominican system of *Aquinas. His views on literature became standard in the Middle Ages, particularly as they are expressed in *De Doctrina Christiana*.

'Auld Lang Syne', a song whose words were contributed by *Burns to the 5th vol. of James Johnson's *Scots Musical Museum* (1787–1803). It was not entirely of Burns's composition. The refrain, at least, had long been in print, and the first line and title appear in a poem by A. *Ramsay. Sir Robert Aytoun (1570–1638) has also been credited with the original version.

'Auld Robin Gray', see LINDSAY, A.

Aureng-Zebe, a tragedy by *Dryden, produced 1675, published 1676.

The plot is remotely based on the contemporary events by which Aureng-Zebe wrested the empire of India from his father and his brothers. The hero is a figure of exemplary rationality, virtue, and patience, whose stepmother lusts after him and whose father pursues the woman with whom Aureng-Zebe is himself in love. This last of Dryden's rhymed heroic plays evinces a deeply disturbing awareness of the anarchy and impotence which threaten every aspect of human life.

Aurora Leigh, described by its author E. B. *Browning as a 'novel in verse', published 1857, is the 11,000-line life-story of a woman writer. Her rejection of, and final reunion with, her philanthropist suitor Romney Leigh are less important than the poem's forceful and often witty speculations on the poem's mission, on social responsibilities, and on the position of women, its vivid impressionistic sketches of crowds and social groups, and its glimpses of dewy English countryside and luminous Italian landscapes.

AUSTEN, Jane (1775–1817), born in the rectory at Steventon, Hampshire, of which her father was rector. She was the sixth child in a family of seven. Her life is notable for its lack of events; she did not marry, although she had several suitors. Any references there may have been to private intimacies or griefs were excised from Jane's letters by her sister Cassandra, after Jane's death, but the letters retain flashes of sharp wit and occasional coarseness that have startled some of her admirers. Her correspondents include Cassandra, her friend Martha Lloyd, and her nieces and nephews, to whom she confided her views on the novel (to Anna Austen, 9 Sept. 1814), '3 or 4 families in a Country Village is the very thing to work on'. In 1801 the family moved to Bath, in 1806, after Mr Austen's death, to Southampton, and in 1809 to Chawton, again in Hampshire; for a few weeks before her death Jane lodged in Winchester, where she died of Addison's disease. The novels were written between the activities of family life, and the last three (*Mansfield Park*, *Emma*, and *Persuasion*) are known to have been written in the busy family parlour at Chawton.

The Juvenilia, *Love and Friendship, A History of England, A Collection of Letters,* and *Lesley Castle,* were written in her early teens and they are already incisive and elegantly expressed. *Lady Susan* is also an early work. Of the major novels, *Sense and Sensibility* was published in 1811, *Pride and Prejudice* in 1813, *Mansfield Park* in 1814, *Emma* in 1816, *Northanger Abbey* and *Persuasion* posthumously in 1818. They were, however, begun or completed in a different order. The youthful sketch *Elinor and Marianne* (1795–6) was in 1797–8 re-written as *Sense and Sensibility*; it was followed in 1797 by *First Impressions* which was later re-created and re-named *Pride and Prejudice. Northanger Abbey*, written in 1798–9, was in 1803 sold to the publishers Crosby and Sons for £10 but not published until 1818. Her unfinished novel *The Watsons*, probably begun in 1804, was abandoned in 1805, on her father's death. *Mansfield Park* was begun at Chawton in 1811, *Emma* in 1814, *Persuasion* in 1815; and in 1817, the year of her death, the unfinished *Sanditon*.

The novels were generally well received; the Prince Regent kept a set of them in each of his residences, and Sir W. *Scott praised her work in the *Quarterly Review* in 1815; he later wrote of 'that exquisite touch which renders ordinary commonplace things and characters interesting'. There were, however, dissentient voices; C. *Brontë and E. B. *Browning found her limited, and it was not until the publication of J. E. Austen Leigh's *Memoir* in 1870 that a Jane Austen cult began to develop.

AUSTIN, Alfred (1835–1913), became in 1883 joint editor with W. J. Courthope of the newly founded *National Review*, and sole editor for eight years from 1887. Between 1871 and 1908 he published twenty volumes of verse, of little merit. In 1896, to widespread mockery, Austin was made *poet laureate, shortly afterwards publishing in *The Times*, an unfortunate ode celebrating the Jameson Raid. Himself a waspish critic of his contemporaries, he was much derided and parodied as a poet. His *Autobiography* appeared in 1911.

AUSTIN, J(ohn) L(angshaw) (1911–60), became White's professor of moral philosophy in Oxford, 1952–60. He had considerable influence as an exponent of the philosophical method which takes as its starting-point the careful elucidation of ordinary, non-philosophical language. Two of his most important courses of lectures, *Sense and Sensibilia* and *How to Do Things with Words*, were published posthumously, in 1962.

Authorized Version, SEE BIBLE, THE ENGLISH.

Autobiography, the story of one's life, written by oneself. (The word does not occur before the 19th cent., though as a form of literature it occurs from the earliest period.) Autobiography has become increasingly popular in modern times. Among famous examples in English literature are *Gibbon's *Memoirs* (1796), Trelawny's *Adventures of a Younger Son* (1831), J. S. *Mill's *Autobiography* (1873), and *Gosse's *Father and Son* (1907). Samuel Butler's *The Way of All Flesh* (1903) is a good example of an autobiographical novel, in which the events of one's life slightly disguised are presented as fiction.

Autolycus, (1) in Greek mythology, a son of Hermes celebrated for his craft as a thief; (2) the roguish but charming pedlar in Shakespeare's *The Winter's Tale.*

Avalon, in the Arthurian legends, one of the Celtic 'Isles of the Blest' to which King *Arthur is carried after his death. *Glastonbury has also been identified as the burial-place of Arthur and hence with Avalon.

Avenel, Mary, a character in Scott's *The Monastery* and *The Abbot*, and Julian, her uncle, a character in the former. Roland Avenel is the hero of the latter work. The White Lady of Avenel is a supernatural being introduced in *The Monastery*.

AVERROËS (Abū 'l-Walīd Muhammad bin Ahmad bin Rushd) (1126–98), a Muslim physician and philosopher, born at Cordoba in Spain (Chaucer's Physician knows of him: *Canterbury Tales*, General Prologue, 433), the author of a famous Commentary on *Aristotle. He is placed in the Limbo of the Philosophers with *Avicenna by *Dante (*Inferno*, iv. 144). He is the inspiration for 'Latin Averroism' (1230 and afterwards), associated with Siger of Brabant. He is of immense importance as the conveyor of Aristotle back into the Western tradition.

AVICENNA (Abū-'Ali al-Husayn bin Sīna) (980–1037), a Persian physician (a capacity in which he was known to *Chaucer's Physician—General Prologue, 432—and Pardoner —CT, vi. 889) and philosopher, who made Commentaries on *Aristotle and *Galen, His views of love have been said to be influential on the ideas of *Courtly Love and he was a major influence on the development of 13th-cent. *scholasticism. *Dante places him with *Averroës in the Limbo of the Philosophers (*Inferno*, iv. 143).

Avon, the Sweet Swan of, *Shakespeare, first so called by Ben *Jonson in his commemorative poem in the First *Folio, 1623.

Awkward Age, The, a novel by H. *James.

Awntyrs of Arthure at the Terne Wathelyne, The, an alliterative poem of 715 lines in two parts, probably from the last quarter of the 14th cent.

from the region of Cumberland or the Scottish Lowlands. It seems to have borrowed from the alliterative *Morte Arthure* and from *Sir *Gawain and the Green Knight*. In the first part of the romance Gawain and Gaynor (Guinevere) are visited by an apparition, from the lake, of Gaynor's mother; the ghostly figure asks for thirty masses to be said for the relief of her suffering soul and she attacks the vices of Gawain, Arthur, and the court. In the second part, set at Arthur's court, Sir Galeron of Galway demands the return of lands which Arthur had confiscated and given to Gawain; the knight's lands are returned, and Gaynor has the masses said for her mother.

Ayala's Angel, a novel by A. *Trollope, published 1881.

AYCKBOURN, Alan (1939–   ), playwright. His first London success, *Relatively Speaking* (1967, pub. 1968), was followed by many others, including *Absurd Person Singular* (1973, pub. 1974); *The Norman Conquests* (1974, pub. 1975; a trilogy); *Absent Friends* (1975, pub. 1975); and *Joking Apart* (1979, pub. 1979). The plays are comedies of suburban and middle-class life, showing a keen sense of social nuance and of domestic misery and insensitivity, and displaying the virtuosity of Ayckbourn's stagecraft.

Ayenbite of Inwit, a devotional manual translated in 1340 by Dan Michel of Northgate, Canterbury, into English prose from the French moral treatise *Les Somme des Vices et des Vertues*, also known as *Le Somme le Roi* because it was composed for Philip III of France in 1279 by its author, the Dominican Frère Loren of Orleans.

AYER, Sir A(lfred) J(ules) (1910–   ), Wykeham professor of logic in the University of Oxford (1959–78). He is the author of *Language, Truth and Logic* (1936), which was the first exposition of logical positivism in the English language, *The Foundations of Empirical Knowledge* (1940), and *The Problem of Knowledge* (1956).

Ayesha, (1) a novel by *Morier; (2) a novel by Sir R. *Haggard.

Aylwin, a novel by W. T. *Watts-Dunton.

Aymon, The Four Sons of, a medieval French romance telling of Charlemagne's struggle with these four noblemen, the eldest of whom was *Rinaldo.

Ayrshire Legatees, The, a novel by J. *Galt, published 1821.

The book largely takes the form of letters recording the adventures of a worthy Scottish minister, Dr Zachariah Pringle, and his family, in the course of a visit to London. Their naïve comments on their experiences, and the comments of their friends in Scotland on the letters themselves, produce what is in effect a social satire, on travellers, on London society, and on the 'douce folk' at home.

AYTOUN, William Edmonstoune (1813–65), is remembered for his share of the *Bon Gaultier ballads (1845), and for his *Lays of the Scottish Cavaliers* (1849). Modelled on Sir W. *Scott and *Macaulay, these patriotic ballad-romances were based on stories of *Montrose, Dundee, and other Scottish heroes. Aytoun also wrote *Firmilian, or the Student of Badajoz* (1854), a mock-tragedy in which he parodied the poems of the *Spasmodic School; it played a decisive role in ending the vogue for such works.

B

Bab Ballads, a collection of humorous ballads by
W. S. *Gilbert, first published in *Fun*, 1866–71.
They appeared in volume form as *Bab Ballads*
(1869); *More Bab Ballads* (1873); *Fifty Bab Ballads*
(1877).

Babbitt, a novel by S. *Lewis.

BABBITT, Irving (1865–1933), American
critic and professor at Harvard. He was, with
Paul Elmer More (1864–1937), a leader of the
New Humanism, a philosophical and critical
movement of the 1920s which fiercely criticized
*Romanticism, stressing the value of reason and
restraint. His works include *The New Laokoon*
(1910), *Rousseau and Romanticism* (1919), and
Democracy and Leadership (1924).

Babes in the Wood, The, see CHILDREN IN THE
WOOD, THE.

Backbite, Sir Benjamin, one of the scandal-
mongers in Sheridan's *The School for Scandal.

Bacon, Friar, see FRIER BACON AND FRIER
BONGAY.

BACON, Francis, first baron Verulam and
viscount St Albans (1561–1626), was the son of
Sir Nicholas Bacon, lord keeper in Queen
Elizabeth's reign. He was educated at Trinity
College, Cambridge, became a barrister in 1582,
and was elected to Parliament in 1584. He was
taken up by the Queen's favourite, Essex, in
1591, but was largely responsible for Essex's
conviction after his rebellion in 1601. After
Elizabeth's death his worldly progress was
rapid. He was appointed solicitor-general in
1607, attorney-general in 1613, lord keeper in
1617, and lord chancellor in 1618. James I's
favourite, the 1st earl of *Buckingham, assisted
his rise after Burghley's death in 1612. Soon after
being created viscount St Albans in 1621, he was
charged with taking bribes as a judge. Admitting
his guilt, he was sentenced and fined by the
House of Lords. The fine was remitted and he
spent only a few days in the Tower, but his
public life was over. He occupied the last years
with energetic study and writing.

Bacon's writings are of many different kinds,
the largest and most influential body of his work
being philosophical. He saw this as all forming
part of a massive system, never to be completed,
called *The Great Instauration*. The first part, the
'division of the sciences', he carried out twice,

first in English, in *The Advancement of Learning*
(1605), and then in Latin, in *De Augmentis Scientiarum* (1623). This systematic classification of all
branches of knowledge has been the model for
all subsequent enlightened constructions of its
kind. The second part is Bacon's theory of scientific method, 'true directions, concerning the
interpretation of nature', realized in his *Novum
Organum* (1620). The third part, 'natural
history', is represented by several 'histories' of
natural phenomena, such as the winds, and a
general collection of odds and ends, the *Sylva
Sylvarum* (1627). The fourth part, the 'ladder of
the intellect', was never written, apart from a
preface, nor was the fifth part, the 'anticipations
of the new philosophy'.

In his theory of scientific classification Bacon
distinguishes knowledge of the natural world
very sharply from knowledge of the supernatural, while showing his exclusive interest in
the former. He also criticizes three prevailing
ways of seeking to gain knowledge: the abstract
disputation of the scholastics, the elegant insub-
stantiality of the humanists, and the preoccupation with marvels and monstrosities of the
Renaissance occultists. In their place he proposes
that nature's secrets should be unlocked, so that
mankind can acquire power over its circumstances, by means of a mechanical routine of
eliminative induction, making a gradual ascent
from the level of the observably particular to the
ever more general level of theory.

Many of Bacon's works lie outside the grand
project of the Great Instauration. His *New
Atlantis* (1627) describes a Utopian community;
it depends for its progress on collective scientific
research. The *Essays* (1597–1625) started as
assemblages of aphorisms, held together only by
a common subject. Bacon's *History of Henry VII*
(1622) inaugurates a new era in being a genuinely
explanatory account of its subject and not a mere
chronicle. Bacon sketched his fundamental legal
principles in *Maxims of the Law* (written in 1597).
Popular in his own time was his *De Sapientia
Veterum* of 1609 (English translation 1619), in
which rational messages are decoded from the
myths and fables of antiquity.

Bacon's prose is rich, ornate, and supple, with
a contrast between the plainness of much of his
matter and the ornamentation of his manner. He
contributed as much as anyone to the depth of
the contemporary division between art and
science, but there is no sign of it in his own
writing.

BACON, Roger (1210/14–after 1292), 'Doctor Mirabilis', philosopher, studied at Oxford and Paris, and joined the Franciscan order. He produced at the request of his friend Pope Clement IV (1265–8) Latin treatises on the sciences (grammar, logic, mathematics, physics, and modern philosophy); his great work is the *Opus Maius*; he also completed an *Opus Minus* and an *Opus Tertium*. He was in confinement for his heretical propositions *c.*1257 and again *c.*1278–92. He has been described as the founder of English philosophy. A conservative in theology, he advocated support for it from an appeal to experience rather than from the scholastic method of argument employed in the *Summa* of *Albertus Magnus and *Alexander of Hales. He begins by stating the chief causes of error to be ignorance of languages, especially Greek, bad Latin translations, and lack of knowledge of the natural sciences, especially mathematics. At the same time, his outlook remained partly mystical. He was also a practical scientist; he invented spectacles and indicated the method by which a telescope might be constructed. He was vulgarly regarded as a necromancer in the Middle Ages because of his interest in the new sciences, especially chemistry and alchemy.

Bacon and Bungay, (1) the rival publishers in Thackeray's *Pendennis*; (2) see FRIER BACON AND FRIER BONGAY.

Baconian Theory, the theory that F. *Bacon wrote the plays attributed to *Shakespeare. It was started in print in the mid-19th cent., and is based partly on (supposed) internal evidence in Shakespeare's plays (the knowledge displayed and the vocabulary), and partly on external circumstances (the obscurity of Shakespeare's own biography, and the assumption that the son of a Warwickshire husbandman was unlikely to be capable of such skilful creations). Some holders of the theory have found in the plays cryptograms in support of it, e.g. in the nonce-word 'honorificabilitudinitatibus' in *Love's Labour's Lost* (v.i), which has been rendered in Latin as 'These plays, F. Bacon's offspring, are preserved for the World'; the word, however, is found elsewhere as early as 1460. The best recent treatment of the topic is to be found in S. *Schoenbaum, *Shakespeare's Lives* (1970).

Badman, *The Life and Death of Mr*, an allegory by *Bunyan, published 1680.
   The allegory takes the form of a dialogue, in which Mr Wiseman relates the life of Mr Badman, recently deceased, and Mr Attentive comments on it. The story is entertaining as well as edifying and has a place in the evolution of the English novel.

Badon, Mount, the scene of a battle connected with *Arthur, first mentioned by *Gildas

without reference to Arthur. The *Annales Cambriae* gives the date of the battle as 518. *Geoffrey of Monmouth identifies Badon as Bath; other authorities say it was Badbury near Wimborne.

BAEDEKER, Karl (1801–59), editor and publisher of Essen, Germany, issued the famous guide-books in Koblenz; this was continued by his son, Fritz, who transferred the business to Leipzig.

BAGE, Robert (1720–1801), author of six novels, three of which *Scott included in the 'Ballantyne Novels'. *Hermsprong* (1796), the most remarkable of Bage's works, is the story of a 'natural' man, brought up without the 'civilized' conventions of morality or religion, among American Indians (see PRIMITIVISM).

BAGEHOT, Walter (1826–77), contributed articles on economic, political, historical, and literary subjects to various periodicals, became joint editor with R. H. Hutton of the *National Review* from 1855, and editor of the *Economist* from 1860 until his death. He was author of The English Constitution (1867; ed. R. H. S. Crossman, 1963), which takes the form of a philosophical discussion appraising the actual values of the elements of the constitution and has remained a classic introduction to the study of English politics, in spite of historical change. His *Lombard Street* (1873) is a lively analysis of the money market of his day. Among his other works are *Biographical Studies* (1881) and *Literary Studies* (1879–95).

Bagford Ballads, The, illustrating the last years of the Stuarts' rule and the last years of the 17th cent., were published by the Ballad Society in 1878. They were assembled by John Bagford (1651–1716).

BAGNOLD, Enid Algerine (Lady Jones) (1889–1981), novelist and playwright, moved in artistic and Bohemian circles, writing several novels, of which the best known was *National Velvet* (1935, filmed 1944 with Elizabeth Taylor as the girl who wins the Grand National). Of her plays, the most successful was *The Chalk Garden* (1955). Her *Autobiography* was published in 1969.

Bagstock, Major Joe, a character in Dickens's *Dombey and Son*.

BAILEY, Nathan or Nathaniel (d. *c.*1742), author of the *Universal Etymological Dictionary* (1721), a forerunner of Dr *Johnson's.

BAILEY, Philip James (1816–1902), author of the long poem *Festus* (1839; enlarged 1845; final edition 1889). The final edition exceeded 40,000 lines and incorporated the greater part of three volumes of poetry that had appeared in the interval (*The Angel World*, 1850; *The Mystic*, 1855; *Universal Hymn*, 1867). *Festus* is Bailey's own version of the legend of Goethe's **Faust*; it was also strongly influenced by **Paradise Lost*. At one time it was immensely popular but, like the other works of the **Spasmodic school of which Bailey was considered the father, it is now almost unreadable.

BAILLIE, Joanna (1762–1851), Scottish dramatist and poet. Her first volume of *Plays on the Passions* (1798) displays in each drama the effect of one particular passion. *Basil*, on the subject of love, and *De Montfort*, on hatred, were the most successful. The volume brought her the friendship of Sir W. **Scott. Her most successful drama, *The Family Legend*, based on a bitter Scottish feud, was produced in 1810 with a Prologue by Scott and an Epilogue by **Mackenzie. Her poems *Fugitive Verses* (1790) and *Metrical Legends* (1821) show a pleasing balance of humour and sentiment.

Bailly, Harry, in Chaucer's **Canterbury Tales* the host of the Tabard Inn where the pilgrims meet in the General Prologue. He initiates the story-telling competition which forms the basis of the work, and acts as master of ceremonies along the way.

BAINBRIDGE, Beryl (1934–), novelist, established her reputation in the 1970s with a series of original and idiosyncratic works. These include *The Dressmaker* (1973), *The Bottle Factory Outing* (1974), *Young Adolf* (1978), and *Winter Garden* (1980). Short, laconic, and rich in black comedy, they deal with the lives of characters at once deeply ordinary and highly eccentric, in a world where violence and the absurd lurk beneath the daily routine of urban domesticity, evoked in carefully observed detail: in *Injury Time* (1977), for example, a quietly illicit dinner party becomes headline news when invaded by a gang of criminals on the run who take its guests hostage.

Baines, Constance and Sophia, characters in Bennett's **The Old Wives' Tale*.

BAJAZET, or Bajayet, ruler of the Ottomans (1389–1402), figures in Marlowe's **Tamburlaine the Great* and Rowe's **Tamerlane*.

BAKER, Sir Samuel White (1821–93), traveller and big game hunter. In 1861 he undertook the exploration of the Nile tributaries, during which he discovered and named Lake Albert Nyanza (Lake Albert). He commanded an expedition to the Equatorial Nile Basin (1869–73) and later travelled to Cyprus, Syria, India, Japan, and America. His adventures are vividly described in his works, which include *The Rifle and the Hound*

in Ceylon (1854), *The Nile Tributaries of Abyssinia* (1867), and *Ismailia* (1874).

Balaam, Sir, the subject of satire in Pope's **Moral Essays* (Ep. iii. 339–402), a religious and frugal citizen who, tempted by wealth, becomes a corrupt courtier.

'Balade of Charitie, The', one of the 'Thomas Rowley' poems, see CHATTERTON.

Balan, see BALYN.

Balaustion's Adventure: Including a Transcript from Euripides, by R. **Browning, published 1871.

The story, suggested by a passage in **Plutarch's *Life of Nicias*, is set just after the defeat of the Athenian expedition against Sicily in 413 BC. A group of pro-Athenians from Rhodes, inspired by the young girl Balaustion, is intercepted on its voyage to Athens by a pirate ship and is forced to seek shelter in the harbour of Syracuse, where it is refused entry until it is discovered that Balaustion can recite a play by **Euripides. The play is *Alcestis*, a performance of which Balaustion narrates, mingling with the text her own comments and descriptions. Browning is thus able to represent Euripides' play in his own interpretation, within the framework of another speaker's consciousness, a marriage of conventional drama with dramatic monologue.

Balchristie, Jenny, in Scott's **The Heart of Midlothian*.

Balder, see DOBELL, S.

'Balder Dead', a poem by M. **Arnold.

BALDWIN, James (1924–), black American novelist. His first novel, *Go Tell it on the Mountain* (1953), set in Harlem, was followed by several on a more international scale, dealing with both homosexuality and the situation of American blacks; they include *Giovanni's Room* (1956), *Another Country* (1962), and *Just Above my Head* (1979).

BALDWIN, William, see MIRROR FOR MAGISTRATES, A.

BALE, John (1495–1563), is notable in the history of the drama as having written *King John*, the first English historical play, or at least a bridge between the **morality and the historical play proper.

BALFOUR, Arthur James, first earl of Balfour (1848–1930), philosopher and statesman, notable in a literary connection as the author of philosophic and other works. These include *A*

Defence of Philosophic Doubt (1879), *Questionings on Criticism and Beauty* (Romanes Lecture, 1909), *Decadence* (Henry *Sidgwick Memorial Lecture, 1908), *Theism and Humanism* (*Gifford Lectures, 1915), *Theism and Thought* (Gifford Lectures, 1923), and *Chapters of Autobiography* (1930, ed. Mrs Dugdale). In 1893 he was president of the *Society for Psychical Research.

Balfour, David, a character in R. L. Stevenson's *Kidnapped* and *Catriona.*

Balfour of Burley, John, a leader of the Cameronian sect, who figures in Scott's *Old Mortality.*

Balin, see BALYN.

'Balin and Balan', one of Tennyson's *Idylls of the King*, first published 1885. It is the story of two brothers who kill each other unwittingly, Balan mistaking for a demon the impassioned Balin, who is driven to frenzy by a conviction of Guinevere's adultery. (See BALYN.)

Balkan Trilogy, see MANNING, O.

BALL, John, the leader of the Peasants' Revolt of 1381. He is the subject of W. Morris's *A Dream of John Ball.*

Ballad, originally a song intended as an accompaniment to a dance; hence a light, simple song of any kind, or a popular song, often one attacking persons or institutions. Broadside ballads, such as those hawked by Autolycus in *The Winter's Tale*, were printed on one side of a single sheet (a *'broadside' or 'broadsheet') and sold in the streets or at fairs. In the relatively recent sense, now most widely used, a ballad is taken to be a single, spirited poem in short stanzas, in which some popular story is graphically narrated (e.g. *Sir Patrick Spens*), and in this sense of the word the oral tradition is an essential element. In the great collection of F. J. *Child, *English and Scottish Popular Ballads* (5 vols, 1882–98), the oldest ballad is *Judas* (c.1300), with an uncharacteristically religious theme; ballads more traditionally deal with the pagan supernatural (e.g. *Tam Lin*), with tragic love (e.g. *Barbara Allan*), or with historical or semi-historical events, e.g. the Border ballads, or the *Robin Hood ballads. There was a notable awakening of interest in the form in Britain in the 18th cent., which led to the researches and collections of *Percy (*Reliques*, 1765) and *Ritson, to the forgeries of *Chatterton and the adaptations of *Burns, and to the deliberate antiquarian imitations of *Tickell (*Lucy and Colin*), Percy himself (*The Hermit of Warkworth*), Mallet (*'William and Margaret'), Goldsmith (*'The Hermit'), and others. Scott's *Minstrelsy of the Scottish Border* is a mixture of traditional

ballads, adaptations, and imitations, whereas the *Lyrical Ballads* of *Wordsworth and *Coleridge manifests, in poems like 'The Idiot Boy' and the *Ancient Mariner*, their own interpretation and development of the term. The form has continued to inspire poets, from *Keats (*'La Belle Dame Sans Merci') to W. *Morris, *Hardy, *Yeats, and *Causley, and flourishes in a popular folk form as well as in a more literary guise. (For 'ballad stanza' see METRE.)

Ballade, strictly a poem consisting of one or more triplets of seven- or (afterwards) eight-lined stanzas, each ending with the same line as refrain, and usually an envoy addressed to a prince or his substitute; e.g. *Chaucer's *Compleynt of Venus*. It was a dominant form in 14th- and 15th-cent. French poetry. The form enjoyed a minor English revival in the late 19th cent. in the work of *Swinburne, *Henley, and *Dobson.

'Ballad of Bouillabaisse, The', a comic ballad by *Thackeray.

Ballad Opera, a theatrical and musical form, very popular in England in the 18th cent., in which the action of the play (usually comic) is carried in spoken prose, interspersed with songs. The first ballad opera is John Gay's *The Beggar's Opera* (1728).

BALLANTYNE, James (1772–1833), brother of John *Ballantyne, a printer in Kelso, printed Scott's *Minstrelsy of the Scottish Border* in 1802, and continued to print Scott's works. He was bankrupted by the crash of Constable and Co. in 1826. Scott named him 'Aldiborontiphoscophornio' from a solemn character in Henry Carey's *Chrononhotonthologos.*

BALLANTYNE, John (1774–1821), brother of James *Ballantyne, became in 1809 manager of the publishing firm started by himself and Sir W. *Scott. Scott named him 'Rigdumfunnidos', after a genial character in Carey's *Chrononhotonthologos.*

BALLANTYNE, R(obert) M(ichael) (1825–94) was a nephew of the Ballantyne brothers (above). He worked for Constable's printing firm, and in 1856 published his first adventure story, *The Young Fur Traders*. After the success of *The Coral Island* (1857) he became an extremely successful professional writer of stories for boys. Among his best-known works are *The Gorilla Hunters* (1862) and *Black Ivory* (1873).

BALLARD, J(ames) G(raham) (1930–), became known in the 1960s as the most prominent of the 'New Wave' *Science Fiction writers. He contributed to *New Worlds* during the influential editorship of *Moorcock. His first novel, *The Drowned World* (1962), a 'catastrophe' novel in which the world turns into a vast swamp, was followed by several others, including *High Rise* (1975), a grim and surreal fantasy, but he is generally more admired for the concentrated, powerful, occasionally lyrical prose and apocalyptic imagery of his short stories. His collections include *The Terminal Beach* (1964), *The Disaster Area* (1967), and *Vermilion Sands* (1971). In *Empire of the Sun* (1984) he turned away from science fiction to draw on his own war-time experiences in China.

Balor, the chief of the *Fomors of Gaelic mythology.

Balthazar ('possessor of treasure'), (1) one of the three Magi, represented as king of Chaldea; (2) the name assumed by Portia as a lawyer in Shakespeare's *The Merchant of Venice*, also that of one of her servants.

Balyn (Balin Le Savage) and Balan, are the subjects of the second Book in Malory's *Morte D'Arthur*. The two are brothers who kill each other unknowingly after a series of linked adventures. (See also BALIN AND BALAN.)

BALZAC, Honoré de (1799–1850), French novelist, author of the great series of co-ordinated and interconnected novels and stories known collectively as the *Comédie humaine*. The 91 separate completed works that make up the whole were written between 1827 and 1847. His grand design was to give an authentic and comprehensive fictional representation of French society in the latter years of the 18th cent. and the first half of the 19th. Critical analysis was an essential part of his aim, and by bold analogies between the novelist's art and that of the natural scientist and the historian he claimed for his 'studies' the orderly method, seriousness of purpose, and intellectual scope of these disciplines. A list of the masterpieces of the *Comédie humaine* would include: *La Peau de chagrin* (1831), *Illusions perdues* (1837–43), *Le Médecin de campagne* (1833), *La Rabouilleuse* (1840), *La Cousine Bette* (1846), and *Le Cousin Pons* (1847). The vitality of Balzac's creations and the breadth of his vision have led some (H. *James among them) to regard him as the greatest of novelists. His influence on later fiction has been immense, and his work is an essential reference-point in the history of the European novel.

Ban, in the Arthurian legends, king of Benwick in Brittany, the father of *Launcelot.

BANDELLO, Matteo (1485–1561), Italian short story writer, many of whose tales were translated by Belleforest into French (1564–82); 13 of these French versions were rendered into English by Geoffrey Fenton in his *Certaine tragicall discourses* (1567). Painter's *Palace of Pleasure* includes 25 of Bandello's tales, nine translated from the Italian and sixteen from Belleforest. *Turberville included two in his *Tragical Tales* (1576). Bandello is the source of plots for many English plays, including *Much Ado about Nothing*, *Twelfth Night*, and *The Duchess of Malfi*.

BANIM, John (1798–1842), Irish novelist, dramatist, and poet, is chiefly remembered for his faithful drawing of Irish life and character contained in the *Tales by the O'Hara Family* (1825, 1826, 1827), partly written with his brother Michael (1796–1874). Novels chiefly written by John include *The Nowlans* (1833), *The Boyne Water* (1836), and *John Doe* (1842). His *Damon and Pythias* (1821), a tragedy, was followed by other successful dramas.

Michael Banim's books include *The Croppy* (1828), *The Mayor of Windy Gap* (1835), and *The Town of the Cascades* (1864).

BANKS, Sir Joseph (1743–1820), eminent explorer and naturalist, accompanied *Cook round the world. He became a member of Dr Johnson's literary *Club, and was president of the *Royal Society 1778–1820.

Bannatyne Club, The, was founded in 1823, with Sir W. *Scott as president, for the publication of old Scottish documents. The club was dissolved in 1861. George Bannatyne (1545–1608), in whose honour it was named, was the compiler in 1568 of a large collection of Scottish poems.

BANNERMAN, Helen, see CHILDREN'S LITERATURE.

Bannockburn, Battle of (1314), in which the English were defeated by Robert Bruce, is described in Scott's *Lord of the Isles*, vi.

Banquo, Scottish general in Shakespeare's *Macbeth*.

Bantam, Angelo Cyrus, in Dickens's *Pickwick Papers*, Grand Master of the Ceremonies at Bath.

Barabas, the *'Jew of Malta', in Marlowe's play of that name.

Barbara Allan, a Scottish *ballad included in Percy's *Reliques*, on the subject of the death of Sir John Grehme for unrequited love of Barbara Allan, and her subsequent remorse.

BARBAULD, Mrs Anna Laetitia, *née* Aikin (1743–1824), published several popular volumes of prose for children with her brother John *Aikin. She was a friend of Mrs H. *More, Mrs

*Montagu, and a circle of dissenting radical intellectuals, and supported radical causes (*Corsica: an ode*, 1768; *Epistle to Wilberforce*, 1791). Her poem in heroic couplets, *Eighteen hundred and eleven* (1812), foretells the decline of Britain's 'Midas dream' of wealth, and the rise of prosperity and culture in America.

BARBELLION, see CUMMINGS, B. F.

BARBOUR, John (*c.*1320–95), Scottish poet, archdeacon of Aberdeen in 1357. The only poem ascribed to him with certainty is *The Bruce* (*The Actes and Life of the Most Victorious Conquerour, Robert Bruce King of Scotland*), in over 13,000 lines, which dates from 1376. The poem is a verse chronicle of the deeds of Bruce and his follower James Douglas, and it contains a celebrated, graphic account of *Bannockburn.

Barchester Towers, a novel by A. *Trollope, published in 1857, the second in the *'Barsetshire' series.

Archdeacon Grantly's hope of succeeding his father as bishop of Barchester are dashed when an ineffectual evangelical, Dr Proudie, is set over him by a new Whig government. The novel is a record of the struggle for control of the diocese. Mrs Proudie, the bishop's overbearing wife, shows her strength when she selects Mr Quiverful as the future warden of Hiram's Hospital. Despite the efforts of Mr Slope, the bishop's oily chaplain, and Grantly, to push the claims of Mr Harding, Quiverful gains the appointment. When the old Dean dies, Slope, anxious to take his place, persuades a national newspaper to advertise his own merits, and the conflict with Mrs Proudie intensifies. Slope's marital ambitions, however, start to get in his way. His designs on the fortune of Mrs Bold, Harding's widowed daughter, are handicapped by his flirtation with the fascinating but penniless Signora Vesey-Neroni, and the scandal is his undoing. The Puseyite Dr Arabin succeeds to the deanery and marries Mrs Bold, while Mrs Proudie sees to it that Slope is dismissed from his chaplaincy.

BARCLAY, Alexander (?1475–1552), poet, scholar, and divine, translated Brant's *Narrenschiff* into English verse as *The Ship of Fools* (1509) and wrote his *Eclogues* at Ely (*c.*1513–14).

BARCLAY, John (1582–1621), author of the extremely popular Latin romance *Argenis* (1621), which refers to real historical events and personages under a veil of allegory.

Bard, The, a Pindaric ode by *Gray, published 1757, based on a tradition that Edward I ordered the violent suppression of the Welsh bards.

It opens with the surviving Bard's cursing of the conqueror as he and his army return from Snowdon in 1283; he laments his slaughtered comrades, whose ghosts prophesy the fate of the Plantagenets. The Bard then foretells the return of the house of Tudor and commits triumphant suicide. Johnson's dismissal of the poem (*Lives of the English Poets*, 1781) outraged its many admirers, who regarded it as a fine example of the *Sublime, and it exerted a considerable influence on the imagination of both poets and painters (e.g. *Blake and John Martin).

Bardell, Mrs, in Dickens's *Pickwick Papers*, Mr Pickwick's landlady, who sues him for breach of promise.

Bardolph, a companion of *Falstaff in Shakespeare's 1 and 2 *Henry IV*; and in *Henry V* is hanged for robbing a French church shortly before the battle of Agincourt. In *The Merry Wives of Windsor* Falstaff finds him a post as tapster at the Garter Inn.

BARETTI, Giuseppe Marc'Antonio (1719–89), born at Turin, came to London in 1751, taught Italian, and became a friend of Dr *Johnson. Baretti's standard work, *A Dictionary of the English and Italian Languages* (1760), was clearly influenced by Johnson's dictionary. He also published *An Account of the Manners and Customs of Italy* (1768) and *A Journey from London to Genoa* (1770). In these and other works he stimulated interest in and understanding of Italian literature and culture.

BARHAM, R(ichard) H(arris) (1788–1845), a clergyman, author of *The Ingoldsby Legends: or mirth and marvels, by Thomas Ingoldsby esquire* first published from 1837 in *Bentley's Miscellany* and *The New Monthly Magazine*, and first collected in 1840. Their lively rhythms and their comic and grotesque treatment of medieval legend, made them immensely popular. One of the best known is the story of the Jackdaw of Rheims, who stole the archbishop's ring, was cursed, fell ill, but recovered when the curse was lifted, and became devout.

BARING, Maurice (1874–1945), a versatile and prolific writer. He is credited with having discovered *Chekhov's work in Moscow and helping to introduce it to the West, and his *Landmarks in Russian Literature* appeared in 1910. Of his various novels *'C'* (1924), *Cat's Cradle* (1925), *Daphne Adeane* (1926), and *The Coat without Seam* (1929), all set in his own high social world, are notable for their acute, intimate portrait of the time. His novella *The Lonely Lady of Dulwich* (1934) is often held to be the best of his works.

BARING-GOULD, Sabine (1834–1924), a prolific writer; he wrote dozens of works on travel, religion, folklore, local legend, and folksong, composed various hymns (including

'Onward Christian Soldiers') and published some 30 novels, of which the most celebrated, *Mehalah* (1880), was compared by *Swinburne to *Wuthering Heights*. He also wrote a life of R. S. *Hawker, *The Vicar of Morwenstow* (1876).

BARKER, George Granville (1913–), poet, whose volumes include *Thirty Preliminary Poems* (1933); *Poems* (1935); *Calamiterror* (1937, a semi-political poem inspired by the Spanish Civil War); *Lament and Triumph* (1940); *Eros in Dogma* (1944); and *Collected Poems 1930–1965* (1965). Barker's earlier work is characteristically rhetorical, Dionysiac, and surreal; a neo-Romantic associated with the *New Apocalypse, and a self-styled 'Augustinian anarchist', he has a marked penchant for puns, distortion, and abrupt changes of tone. His *True Confession of George Barker* (1950, augmented 1965) presents the poet as irreverent, defiant, offhand, Rabelaisian, and guilt-ridden at once. Its later stanzas, and works such as *Villa Stellar* (1978) and the long title-poem of *Anno Domini* (1983), have a more sombre, reflective, questioning tone.

BARKER, Harley Granville-, see GRANVILLE-BARKER, H.

Barkis, in Dickens's *David Copperfield*, the carrier, who sent a message by David to Clara Peggotty that 'Barkis is willin' '.

Barlaam and Josaphat, a late, 12th-cent. Anglo-Norman romance, interesting as a Christianized version of the legend of Buddha.

BARLOW, Joel (1754–1812), American poet and diplomat, born in Connecticut, who is remembered as the author of *The Columbiad* (1807, originally published as *The Vision of Columbus*, 1787), a patriotic epic in heroic couplets, and of the mock-epic, *The Hasty-Pudding* (1796). Barlow was one of the 'Hartford Wits'.

Barnaby Rudge, a novel by *Dickens published in 1841 as part of *Master Humphrey's Clock*. The earlier of Dickens's two historical novels, it is set at the period of the Gordon anti-popery riots of 1780, and Lord George Gordon himself appears as a character.

Reuben Haredale, a country gentleman, has been murdered, and the murderer never discovered. His brother Geoffrey Haredale, a Roman Catholic, and the smooth villain Sir John Chester (who models himself on Lord *Chesterfield) are enemies; Chester's son Edward is in love with Haredale's niece Emma, and the elders combine to thwart the match. The Gordon riots, secretly fomented by Chester, supervene. Haredale's house is burned and Emma carried off. Edward saves the lives of Haredale and Emma and wins Haredale's consent to his marriage with the latter. Haredale discovers the murderer of his brother, the steward Rudge, father of the half-witted Barnaby and the blackmailer of Barnaby's devoted mother Mrs Rudge. Rudge is hanged, Barnaby is reprieved from the gallows at the last moment, and Chester is killed by Haredale in a duel.

The vivid description of the riots forms the principal interest of the book, which also displays Dickens's concern with the demoralizing effect of capital punishment in the character of Dennis the Hangman and Hugh, the savage ostler who turns out to be Chester's son. Other characters involved in the plot include the upright locksmith Gabriel Varden; Simon Tappertit, his aspiring and anarchic apprentice; Miggs, his mean and treacherous servant; John Willett, host of the Maypole Inn; and Grip, Barnaby's raven.

Barnacles, The, in Dickens's *Little Dorrit*, types of government officials in the 'Circumlocution Office'.

BARNARD, Lady Anne, see LINDSAY, A.

Barnardine, in Shakespeare's *Measure for Measure*, a prisoner.

Barnavelt, Sir John van Olden, a historical tragedy, probably by J. *Fletcher and *Massinger, acted in 1619. It was discovered by A. H. Bullen among the MSS of the British Museum, and printed in his *Old English Plays* (1883, vol. ii).

The play, which deals with contemporary events in Holland, was performed within months of the execution of its real-life protagonist.

BARNES, Barnabe (?1569–1609), attempted, in 1598, to kill the recorder of Berwick with poisoned claret, but he successfully evaded sentence. He published a sonnet sequence, *Parthenophil and Parthenophe. Sonnettes, madrigals, elegies, and odes* (1593), notable as one of the first of such collections to appear after Sidney's *Astrophel and Stella*; *A divine centurie of spirituall sonnets* (1595); *Foure bookes of offices* (1606); and *The divils charter: a tragaedie conteining the Life and Death of Pope Alexander the Sixt* (1607), a vigorous Machiavellian drama which includes such melodramatic scenes as the murder of Lucrezia Borgia with poisoned face wash. Barnes's poetry is remarkable for its vigour and technical range.

BARNES, Djuna Chappell (1892–1982), American writer, is best remembered for *Nightwood* (1936), a novel which evokes, in highly wrought, high-coloured prose, a nightmare cosmopolitan world (chiefly located in Paris and New York) peopled by tormented and mutually tormenting characters, linked by the enigmatic doctor, priest of the secret brotherhood of the City of Darkness. Her *Selected Works* appeared in 1962.

BARNES, William (1801–86), West Country poet and schoolmaster, was ordained in 1848, and took up the living of Whitcombe, moving to Cambe in 1862. He waged a lifelong campaign to rid English of classical and foreign influences, suggesting many 'Saxonized' alternatives. *Orra, a Lapland Tale* appeared in 1822 and his *Poems of rural life in the Dorset Dialect* in 1844; *Hwomely Rhymes* followed in 1859 and *Poems of Rural Life*, written in standard English, in 1868. His collected dialect poems appeared as *Poems of Rural Life in the Dorset Dialect* in 1879. He wrote textbooks, a primer of Old English (*Se Gefylsta*, 1849), *Philological Grammar* (1854), a *Grammar . . . of the Dorset Dialect* (1863), and other works reflecting his interest in philology and local history.

According to his many admirers, who included *Tennyson, G. M. *Hopkins, *Hardy, and *Gosse, Barnes was a lyric poet of the first rank, but the difficulties presented by the Dorset dialect have greatly restricted his audience and contributed to the image of a quaint provincial versifier. His poems evoke the Dorset landscape, country customs (as in 'Harvest Hwome' and 'Woodcom' Feast'), and happy childhood, although his few poems of grief, such as 'Woak Hill' and 'The Wind at the Door', written after the death of his wife, are among his best. The wide variety of his verse forms much intrigued Hardy; his noun-combinations ('heart-heaven', 'sun-sweep', and 'mind-sight') foreshadow Hopkins.

Barney, in Dickens's *Oliver Twist*, a Jew, associate of Fagin.

BARNFIELD, Richard (1574–1627), published *The Affectionate Shepheard* (1594), a pastoral (based on *Virgil's second eclogue) describing the love of Daphnis for Ganymede and including a surprising digression on the 'indecencie of mens long haire'; *Cynthia, with certaine Sonnets* (1595), to Ganymede; *The encomion of lady Pecunia* (the praise of money, 1598). Two of his *Poems in divers humors* (1598) appeared also in *The Passionate Pilgrim* (1599) and were once attributed to Shakespeare, the better-known being the ode 'As it fell upon a day | In the merry month of May'. Barnfield has the distinction of being the only Elizabethan poet other than Shakespeare to have addressed love sonnets to a man.

Baroque (from Portuguese *barroco*, Spanish *barrueco*, a rough or imperfect pearl), originally a term of abuse applied to 17th-cent. Italian art and that of other countries, especially Germany, influenced by Italy. It is characterized by the unclassical use of classical forms, and by the interpenetration of architecture, sculpture, and painting to produce grandiose and emotional effects.

In a literary context the word baroque is loosely used to describe highly ornamented verse or prose, abounding in extravagant conceits; it is rarely used of English writers (with the exception of the Italianate *Crashaw), but frequently applied to *Marino, whose name became synonymous with Marinism, and to Gongora, whose name supplied the term *Gongorism.

Barrack-Room Ballads, see KIPLING, R.

BARRETT, Elizabeth, see BROWNING, E. B.

BARRIE, Sir J(ames) M(atthew) (1860–1937), began working with the *Nottinghamshire Journal*. In 1888 he began his series of *'Kailyard School' stories and novels based on the life of 'Thrums', his home town of Kirriemuir, in Scotland. These included *Auld Licht Idylls* (1888), *A Window in Thrums* (1899), and his successful *The Little Minister* (1891). His first play, *Richard Savage*, was performed in London in 1891. In 1896 he published the first of his two most revealing books, *Sentimental Tommy*, followed by *Tommy and Grizel* (1900). Meanwhile came his sentimental comedy *Quality Street*, performed in 1901, and in 1902 the enduring play *The Admirable Crichton* (see CRICHTON). *Peter Pan*, his internationally famous children's play, first performed in 1904, grew from stories he had made up for the five sons of his friends Arthur and Sylvia Llewelyn Davies, to whom he gave a home on their parents' death. It was followed by a story, *Peter Pan in Kensington Gardens* (1906) and by the play in book form in 1911. *What Every Woman Knows* was performed in 1906, *Dear Brutus* in 1917, and *Mary Rose* in 1920.

He was made a baronet, awarded the OM, and received several honorary degrees. His fame and success were considerable for the first half of this century, but his unfashionable whimsicality has come to obscure the best of his work.

BARRINGTON, Daines (1727–1800), lawyer, antiquary, and naturalist and friend of G. *White, whose *Natural History of Selborne* takes the form of letters to Barrington and *Pennant.

BARROW, Sir John (1764–1848), travelled in China and South Africa, and revived the project to explore the Arctic for a North-West Passage. He contributed to the *Quarterly Review* and published several works of history and travel, inluding *The Mutiny and Piratical Seizure of H.M.S. *Bounty* (1831); *A History of Voyages into the Arctic Region* (1846); and an *Autobiographical Memoir* (1847).

BARRY, Elizabeth (1658–1713), a celebrated actress who owed her entrance to the stage to the patronage of the earl of *Rochester. She created more than 100 roles, including Monimia in Otway's *The Orphan*. *Otway was passionately devoted to her, but she did not return his affection.

Barry Lyndon, see LUCK OF BARRY LYNDON, THE.

Barsetshire Novels, The, of A. *Trollope are the following: *The Warden*, *Barchester Towers*, *Doctor Thorne*, *Framley Parsonage*, *The Small House at Allington*, and *The Last Chronicle of Barset*.

BARSTOW, Stan(ley) (1928–), novelist. His first novel, *A Kind of Loving* (1960), is the present-tense narration of office-worker Vic Brown, trapped into marriage by his infatuation for small-minded Ingrid and harassed by his mother-in-law; it was followed by other vivid portrayals of Yorkshire life, which contributed to the development of the regional novel associated with *Sillitoe, *Waterhouse, *Braine, and others.

BARTHOLOMAEUS ANGELICUS (*fl.* 1230–50), also known as Bartholomew de Glanville, a Minorite friar, and author of *De Propietatibus rerum*, an encyclopaedia of the Middle Ages first printed *c.*1470.

Bartholomew Fair, a comedy by *Jonson, performed 1614, printed 1631.

The play is set at the fair which took place at Smithfield on 24 August, St Bartholomew's Day, and follows the fortunes of various visitors to it: Littlewit, a proctor, his wife Win-the-fight, his mother-in-law Dame Purecraft, and her mentor the ranting Puritan Zeal-of-the-land Busy, who come to eat roast pig; the rich simpleton Bartholomew Cokes, Wasp, his angry servant, and Grace Wellborn, who is unwillingly betrothed to Cokes; Justice Adam Overdo, who attends the fair in disguise in order to discover its 'enormities'; and two gallants, Quarlous and Winwife, who intend to jeer at the fair-people. Many mishaps and misunderstandings ensue. The play ends with the performance of a puppet-play written by Littlewit, in imitation of Marlowe's *Hero and Leander*.

BARTRAM, William (1739–1823), American Quaker naturalist and traveller, author of *Travels through North and South Carolina, Georgia, East and West Florida, the Cherokee Country, the Extensive Territories of the Moscogulges, or the Creek Confederacy, and the Country of the Chactaws* (1791). *Coleridge and *Wordsworth drew on its descriptions of the natural wonders of the new world.

Bas Bleu, see MORE, H.

Basilikon Doron, see JAMES I AND VI.

Basilius, (1) the foolish old duke in Sidney's *Arcadia*; (2) in *Don Quixote*, the rival of Camacho.

BASKERVILLE, John (1706–75), English printer, had established a printing office and type-foundry in Birmingham by 1754. His first book was a Latin *Virgil, 1757, followed by a *Milton in 1758. Baskerville's books are among the masterpieces of English printing; he gave his name to the roman typefaces based on his designs in current usage.

BASKETT, John (d. 1742), king's printer, was printer to the University of Oxford, 1711–42. He printed editions of the *Book of *Common Prayer*, and the *'Vinegar Bible' in two volumes (1716–17), of which it was said that it was 'a basketful of errors'.

Bassanio, in Shakespeare's *The Merchant of Venice*, the lover of Portia.

'Bastard, The', see SAVAGE, R.

Bastard, Philip the, son of Sir Robert Falconbridge in Shakespeare's *King John*.

Bates, Charley, in Dickens's *Oliver Twist*, one of the pickpockets in Fagin's gang.

BATES, Henry Walter (1825–92), naturalist, published *The Naturalist on the Amazons* in 1863.

BATES, H(erbert) E(rnest) (1905–74), novelist and short story writer. His works include volumes of stories, *The Woman Who Had Imagination* (1934), *The Flying Goat* (1939), and *The Beauty of the Dead* (1940); and novels, *The Two Sisters* (1926), *The Fallow Land* (1932), *Love for Lydia* (1952), and *The Darling Buds of May* (1958). He also published three volumes of autobiography.

Bates, Miss and Mrs, characters in Jane Austen's *Emma*.

BATESON, F(rederick Noel) W(ilse) (1901–78) edited the *Cambridge Bibliography of English Literature* (1940) and founded the periodical *Essays in Criticism*, which he edited from 1951 to 1974. His critical works include *Wordsworth: a reinterpretation* (1954) and *Essays in Critical Dissent* (1972).

Bath, in Somerset, is the site of a Roman spa, Aquae Sulis, probably built in the 1st and 2nd cents AD.

In the 18th cent. Bath was transformed into a social resort by Richard ('Beau') *Nash, who became master of ceremonies, Ralph *Allen, who promoted the development of the city, and John Wood, father and son, who designed the Palladian public buildings and houses. It is the subject of very frequent literary allusion, having been visited among many others by Smollett, Fielding, Sheridan, F. Burney, Goldsmith,

Southey, Landor, J. Austen, Wordsworth, Cowper, Scott, T. Moore, and Dickens. Its ruins seem to be the subject of the OE poem *'The Ruin'.

Bath, Wife of, see CANTERBURY TALES, 6.

Bathos (Greek, 'depth'). The current usage for 'descent from the sublime to the ridiculous' originates from *Pope's satire *Peri Bathous, or the art of sinking in poetry* (1727). The title was a travesty of *Longinus' essay *On the Sublime.*

Bathsheba Everdene, a character in Hardy's *Far from the Madding Crowd.*

Batrachomyomachia, or the *Battle of the Frogs and Mice,* a burlesque Greek epic once attributed to *Homer. It describes the battle between the mice and frogs in which Zeus and Athena join. T. *Parnell's version attacking *Dennis and *Theobald appeared in 1717.

Battle, Sarah, the subject of one of Lamb's *Essays of Elia,* 'Mrs Battle's Opinions on Whist'; a character drawn from Mrs Burney, wife of Admiral Burney and sister-in-law of F. *Burney.

Battle of Alcazar, The, a play in verse by *Peele, published 1594.

'Battle of Hohenlinden, The', a poem by T. *Campbell, describing a battle in Bavaria in 1800, in which the French defeated the Austrians.

Battle of Maldon, see MALDON, BATTLE OF.

Battle of Otterbourne, see OTTERBOURNE, THE BATTLE OF.

Battle of the Books, The, a prose satire by *Swift, written 1697, when Swift was residing with Sir W. *Temple, published 1704.

Temple had written an essay on the comparative merits of 'Ancient and Modern Learning' (the subject at that time of an animated controversy in Paris), in which by his uncritical praise of the spurious *Epistles of *Phalaris* he had drawn on himself the censure of William Wotton and *Bentley. Swift treats the whole question with satirical humour. The 'Battle' originates from a request by the moderns that the ancients shall evacuate the higher of the two peaks of Parnassus which they have hitherto occupied. Before the actual encounter a dispute arises between a spider living in the corner of the library and a bee that has got entangled in the spider's web. Aesop sums up the dispute: the spider is like the moderns who spin their scholastic lore out of their own entrails; the bee is like the ancients who go to nature for their honey. Aesop's commentary rouses the books to fury, and they join battle. The ancients, under the patronage of Pallas, are led by Homer, Pindar, Euclid, Aristotle, and Plato, with Sir W. Temple commanding the allies; the moderns by Milton, Dryden, Descartes, Hobbes, Scotus, and others, with the support of Momus and the malignant deity Criticism. The fight is conducted with great spirit. Aristotle aims an arrow at Bacon but hits Descartes. Homer overthrows Gondibert. Virgil encounters his translator Dryden, in a helmet nine times too big. Boyle transfixes Bentley and Wotton.

Battle of the Frogs and Mice, see BATRACHO-MYOMACHIA.

Baucis and Philemon, a poem by *Swift, published 1709; Baucis and Philemon were the aged couple who entertained the gods unawares, and whose cottage was transformed by Zeus into a temple. In Swift's version, the couple entertain two hermits; their cottage becomes a church and Philemon the parson, an elevation described with some irony.

Baviad, The, see GIFFORD, W.

BAXTER, Richard (1615–91), a Puritan divine who sided with Parliament and was a military chaplain during the Civil War. He was author of *The Saint's Everlasting Rest* (1650) and *Call to the Unconverted* (1657), both of which played an important part in the Evangelical tradition in England and America. He contributed powerfully to the Restoration. His numerous writings include a lengthy autobiography, *Reliquiae Baxterianae* (1696), and several well-known hymns.

Bayard, or Baiardo, the magic horse given by Charlemagne to Renaud. Bayard was formerly used as a mock-heroic allusive name for any horse, and also as a type of blind recklessness [*OED*].

Bayes, the name under which *Dryden is ridiculed in Buckingham's *The Rehearsal.*

BAYLY, Nathaniel Thomas Haynes (1797–1839), author of many well-known and much ridiculed verses, including 'I'd be a butterfly'. He wrote many pieces for the stage including *Perfection* (1836), a successful farce.

Baynes, General, Mrs, and Charlotte, characters in Thackeray's *The Adventures of Philip.*

Bayona, see NAMANCOS.

Bazzard, Mr, in Dickens's *Edwin Drood,* Mr Grewgious's clerk.

BEACONSFIELD, earl of, see DISRAELI.

Beagle, HMS, see DARWIN, C.

Bean Lean, Donald, a character in Scott's *Waverley.*

BEARDSLEY, Aubrey Vincent (1872–98), illustrator and writer, notorious in the 1890s as the outstanding artist of *fin-de-siècle* decadence. His disturbingly erotic drawings develop rapidly from the murky sensuality of *Pre-Raphaelite medievalism to rococo wit and grace. Beardsley's most important illustrations are for *Wilde's *Salome* (1894), *Pope's *The Rape of the Lock* (1896), the *Lysistrata* of *Aristophanes (1896), and *Jonson's *Volpone* (1898). He was art editor of the *Yellow Book* in 1894; the Wilde scandal led to his dismissal in 1895; he then became art editor to the *Savoy*. Beardsley's most significant achievement as a writer is *The Story of Venus and Tannhauser*, a charmingly rococo and highly cultivated erotic romance. An expurgated version entitled *Under the Hill* was published in the *Savoy*; an unexpurgated edition was privately printed in 1907; it contains a cruel caricature of Wilde as 'Priapusa, the fat manicure and fardeuse'.

Beat Generation, a phrase used to describe a group of American writers who emerged in the 1950s, and generally agreed to have been coined in this sense (with connotations of beatitude, disengagement, down-and-out 'street' language and experience, spontaneity, etc.) by *Kerouac. Leading literary exponents of the movement include Allen Ginsberg (1926–), Gregory Corso (1930–), Gary Snyder (1930–), Lawrence Ferlinghetti (1919–), W. *Burroughs, John Clellon Holmes (1926–). The beat emphasis was on escape from conventional puritanical, middle-class (termed 'square') mores, toward visionary enlightenment and artistic improvisation, approached via (Zen) Buddhism and other echoes of religious confessional, such as American Indian and Mexican Peyote cults; also through drive and accelerations charged by wheels, drugs, sex, drink, or talk. The experimental forms, metaphysical content, and provocative anti-intellectual, anti-hierarchical spirit of the movement spread across America and then beyond the English-speaking world, to be taken up by second and third generation writers (Yevtushenko, Voznesensky, Bob Dylan, the *Beatles, Wolf Biermann), evolving a 'counter-culture' which had a widespread and in many ways lasting impact. Foreshadowings of the Beat Generation have been claimed in writers as diverse as *Blake, *Whitman, Rimbaud, *Melville, T. *Wolfe, Henry *Miller, and the *'Black Mountain' poets. For its reverberations in Britain see further under UNDERGROUND POETRY and JAZZ POETRY.

Beatles, The, a group of young working-class musicians from Liverpool (George Harrison, John Lennon, Paul McCartney, and 'Ringo' Starr), whose songs and life-style, from 1962 until 1970, attracted a vast following; many of their lyrics (e.g. 'Penny Lane', 'Eleanor Rigby', 'She's Leaving Home') have been highly praised, and they had a considerable influence on the success of the *Liverpool poets and the *Underground poetry movement.

Beatrice, (1) see DANTE; (2) heroine of Shakespeare's *Much Ado about Nothing*.

BEATTIE, James (1735–1803), professor of moral philosophy at Marischal College, Aberdeen, and poet. His *Essay on the Nature and Immutability of Truth* (1770) was an attempt to refute *Hume and *Berkeley. As a poet he is remembered for *The Minstrel* (Bk I, 1771; Bk II, 1774), a poem in Spenserian stanzas tracing 'the progress of a poetical Genius, born in a rude age, from the first dawning of fancy and reason'.

Beau Brummell, see BRUMMELL.

Beauchamp's Career, by G. *Meredith, published 1876, a novel of politics, much concerned with the contemporary state of Britain.

Beau Geste, see WREN, P. C.

Beaumains ('Fair hands'), in the Arthurian legends, the nickname given to Gareth when as a probationer knight he is sent to work in the kitchens. See GARETH AND LYNETTE.

Beaumanoir, Sir Lucas, in Scott's *Ivanhoe*, Grand Master of the Knights Templars.

BEAUMONT, Sir Francis (1584–1616), collaborated with *Fletcher in dramatic works from about 1606 to 1613 (for a list of their plays, see under FLETCHER, J.). His earliest known play, *The Woman Hater*, a Jonsonian comedy of humours, was probably performed 1605, published 1607; recent linguistic analysis assigns some scenes in this to Fletcher, whereas *The Knight of the Burning Pestle* (?1607) is now generally considered to be Beaumont's alone.

Dryden, in *Of Dramatick Poesy* (1668), pays tribute to the success of the Beaumont and Fletcher plays on the Restoration stage, and comments that both writers had 'great natural gifts improved by study; Beaumont especially being so accurate a judge of plays that Ben Jonson, while he lived, submitted all his writing to his censure, and, 'tis thought, used his judgement in correcting, if not contriving, all his plots'. In the 17th cent. opinion tended to ascribe the tragic scenes in the collaborative effort to Beaumont, the comic to Fletcher, but modern critics reject this neat division, and are themselves divided about attribution. (See under FLETCHER for further details.)

Beau Nash, see NASH, R.

Beauty and the Beast, a fairy-tale of which the best-known version was adapted by Mme de

Beaumont from one of the *Contes marins* (4 vols, 1740–1) of Mme de Villeneuve.

Beauty ('la Belle') is the youngest and favourite daughter of a merchant. He sets out on a journey in the hope of restoring his shaken fortunes. Beauty asks him to bring her back only a rose. The journey proves a failure, but on his return, in the beautiful garden of an apparently uninhabited palace, he plucks a rose for Beauty. The Beast, an ugly monster to whom the palace belongs, threatens him with death as the penalty for his theft unless he gives him his youngest daughter. Beauty sacrifices herself and goes to the Beast's palace and lives there. She is gradually filled with pity and affection for the Beast and finally consents to marry him, whereupon he turns into a beautiful prince, having been released from a magic spell by her virtue and courage.

BEAUVOIR, Simone de (1908–86), French novelist and essayist whose novels reflect the major preoccupations of the *Existentialist movement. Perhaps her greatest impact on English literature was through her seminal feminist work *Le Deuxième sexe* (1949; as *The Second Sex*, 1953). See FEMINIST CRITICISM.

Beaux' Stratagem, The, a comedy by *Farquhar, produced 1707.

It describes the adventures of penniless young Aimwell and his friend Archer, who, to save money, pretends to be Aimwell's servant: much confusion follows, but all ends happily as Aimwell wins the affection of Dorinda, daughter of the wealthy Lady Bountiful, and inherits a fortune from his elder brother, and Archer is united with Mrs Sullen, newly released from her unhappy marriage to Lady Bountiful's son, a drunken sot.

BEAVERBROOK, William Maxwell ('Max') Aitken, first baron (1879–1964), newspaper proprietor, born in Canada, came to England in 1910, and embarked on a career in politics. In 1916 (the year in which he became Lord Beaverbrook) he bought the *Daily Express*, launched the *Sunday Express* in 1918, and in 1923 gained control of the *Evening Standard*, of which his friend Arnold *Bennett became the influential reviewer. He became the most powerful figure in popular journalism; he enjoyed controversy, from the 'Empire Crusade' of his early years to the anti-Common Market of his old age. His own works include *Politicians and the War* (2 vols, 1928, 1932, which provided much of the background for Bennett's novel *Lord Raingo*, 1926), and *The Decline and Fall of Lloyd George* (1963).

Beck, Madame, a character in *Villette* by C. Brontë.

Becket, a tragedy by *Tennyson, published 1884, based on the quarrel between Henry II and Thomas *Becket, interwoven with the story of Henry's love for Fair Rosamund.

BECKET, St Thomas (?1118–70). Henry II appointed him chancellor and made him his intimate friend and companion. In 1162 Thomas reluctantly became archbishop of Canterbury, an office which required him to become the champion of the rights of the Church which Henry was attempting to curtail. In particular he opposed the Constitutions of Clarendon (1164) which re-imposed the relations between Church and State that had prevailed in the time of William I. Becket was exiled on the Continent for seven years; he returned to England in 1170 and after a brief reconciliation with Henry was assassinated on the king's orders in the cathedral at Canterbury on 29 Dec. 1170. The king claimed that his orders had been misinterpreted. Becket's shrine at Canterbury became the most famous in Christendom as a place where miracles were performed, and it was the objective of *Chaucer's pilgrims 200 years later. The story of Becket has been the subject of plays by *Tennyson and T. S. *Eliot (*Murder in the Cathedral*). (See also ANGLO–LATIN LITERATURE.)

BECKETT, Samuel Barclay (1906–), was born at Foxrock, near Dublin, and educated at Trinity College, Dublin. He taught in Belfast before going to Paris as *lecteur d'anglais* at the École Normale Superieure; there in 1928 he met *Joyce, with whom he formed a lasting friendship. His first published work was an essay on Joyce (1929). His first story, 'Assumption', appeared in *transition* (1929) and in 1930 he returned as lecturer to Trinity College. He then embarked on five unsettled, solitary years in Germany, France, Ireland, and London, before settling permanently in France. *More Pricks than Kicks* (1934, stories) was followed by several full-length novels, including *Murphy* (1938), a grimly entertaining Irish evocation of London life, and *Watt* (1953), both written in English. His trilogy, *Molloy* (1951); *Malone Meurt* (1951; Beckett's own English version, *Malone Dies*, 1958); and *L'Innommable* (1953; *The Unnamable*, 1960) were all originally written in French, and all three are interior monologues or soliloquies, desolate, terminal, obsessional, irradiated with flashes of last-ditch black humour. Beckett's highly distinctive, despairing, yet curiously exhilarating voice reached a wide audience and public acclaim with the Paris performance in 1953 of *En attendant Godot* (pub. 1952; English version, *Waiting for Godot*, 1955). Beckett became widely known as a playwright associated with the Theatre of the *Absurd, whose use of the stage and of dramatic narrative and symbolism revolutionized drama in England and deeply influenced later playwrights, including *Pinter, *Fugard, and *Stoppard. Subsequent stage plays include *Fin de partie* (first performed in French at the Royal Court, 1957; English version, *End-game*, pub. 1958), a one-act drama of frustration irascibility and senility, featuring blind Hamm and his attendant Clov, and Hamm's 'accursed progenitors', who spend the action in ashcans; *Krapp's Last Tape* (1958, pub. 1959), a monologue in which the shabby and aged Krapp attempts to recapture the intensity of earlier days by listening to recordings of his own younger self; *Happy Days* (1961, pub. 1961), which portrays Winnie buried to her waist in a mound, but still attached to the carefully itemized contents of her handbag; *Breath* (1969), a 30-second play consisting only of a pile of rubbish, a breath, and a cry; and *Not I* (1973, pub. 1973), a monologue delivered by an actor of indeterminate sex of whom only the 'Mouth' is illuminated. His *Collected Poems in English and French* was published in 1977. He was awarded the *Nobel Prize in 1969.

BECKFORD, William (1759–1844), a traveller and a man of great wealth, who spent large sums in the creation and decoration of Fonthill Abbey, a Gothic extravaganza, where he lived from 1796 until 1822. He is remembered chiefly as the author of the *oriental tale *Vathek*. His other works include two books of travel, *Dreams, Waking Thoughts, and Incidents* (1783, revised 1834) and *Recollections of an Excursion to the Monastries of Alcobaça and Batalha* (1835). (See also GOTHIC NOVEL; GOTHIC REVIVAL.)

Becky, see SHARP, REBECCA.

BEDDOES, Thomas Lovell (1803–49), published in 1821 *The Improvisatore* and in 1822 *The Bride's Tragedy*. His most important work, *Death's Jest-Book, or the Fool's Tragedy* (1850), appeared after his death by suicide at Basle. It is in blank verse, heavily influenced by Elizabethan and Jacobean tragedy, and shows Beddoes's obsession with the macabre, the supernatural, and bodily decay. He is now best known for his shorter pieces, such as 'Dream Pedlary' and the lyrics which appear in *Death's Jest-Book*.

BEDE (Baeda, or 'The Venerable Bede') (673–735), historian and scholar, when young placed in charge of *Benedict Biscop, the abbot of Wearmouth. From there he went in 682 to Jarrow, where he spent most of his life. He was a diligent teacher and scholar of Latin and Greek. His *Historia Ecclesiastica Gentis Anglorum* was finished in 731, by which time he had written nearly 40 works, mostly biblical commentaries. His early treatise *De Natura Rerum*, modelled on the *Origines* of *Isidore of Seville, contains rudimentary natural science, referring phenomena to natural causes. His other influential work is the *Lives of the Abbots*, which gives an account of the earlier abbots in the Northumbrian Revival. (See also ANGLO-LATIN LITERATURE.)

BEDE, Cuthbert, see BRADLEY, E.

Bedevere, Sir, one of the most celebrated knights in the Arthurian legends. According to *Malory only he and his brother Lucan, Arthur's butler, survived with Arthur the last battle against Modred, and at Arthur's bidding Bedevere threw *Excalibur into the lake and carried the king to the barge which bore him away to *Avalon.

BEDFORD, Sybille (1911–), author, whose best-known novel, *The Legacy* (1956), is a sophisticated account of the complex matrimonial and financial affairs of a wealthy German family in the years immediately preceding the First World War. *A Favourite of the Gods* (1962) and *A Compass Error* (1968), both novels, were followed by a two-volume biography of A. *Huxley (1973, 1974).

Bedlam, a corruption of Bethlehem, applied to the Hospital of St Mary of Bethlehem, in Bishopsgate, London, founded as a priory in 1247, which became a hospital for lunatics. From Bedlam are derived such expressions as *Tom o' Bedlam and Bess o' Bedlam for wandering lunatics, or beggars posing as lunatics.

Bee, The, see GOLDSMITH, O.

Beelzebub, the name given by *Milton to one of the fallen angels, next to Satan in power (*Paradise Lost*, i. 79). Golding adopted one version of it for the title of his novel *Lord of the Flies.

BEER, Patricia (1924–), poet, the daughter of a railway clerk and a mother who was a member of the Plymouth Brethren; she describes her background vividly in her autobiographical *Mrs Beer's House* (1968). The legends and landscapes of the West Country also form the background for many of her poems (collections include *The Loss of the Magyar*, 1959; *The Estuary*, 1971; *Driving West*, 1975; *Selected Poems*, 1980), and her historical novel *Moon's Ottery* (1978) is set in Elizabethan Devon.

BEERBOHM, (Sir Henry) Max(imilian) (1872–1956), critic, essayist, and caricaturist. His one completed novel, *Zuleika Dobson* (1911), is a fantasized distillation of the Oxford atmosphere of the 1890s. His writing, like his personality, was characterized by elegance and by a light but incisive touch in applying irony and wit to society's foibles and to the idiosyncracies of writers, artists, and politicians. His first published book and collection of essays in this vein was *The Works of Max Beerbohm* (1896), followed by *More* (1899), *Yet Again* (1909), *And Even Now* (1920). *A Christmas Garland* (1912) expertly parodied the literary styles of H. *James, *Wells, *Kipling, and other leading contemporary writers. His best short stories were collected in *Seven Men* (1919). As an associate in the 1890s of *Wilde and *Beardsley, the *Rhymers Club, etc., he was well placed to comment upon avant-garde tendencies of the period. As half-brother of the actor-manager Herbert Beerbohm Tree, Max had an entrée into theatrical circles and was a brilliant dramatic critic of the *Saturday Review* from 1898 to 1910; he succeeded G. B. *Shaw, whose valedictory essay in that journal dubbed him 'the incomparable Max'. His dramatic criticism is collected in *Around Theatres* (1953) and *More Theatres* (1968). His caricatures were as elegant and as individual as his literary works. Among the best-known collections of these are *Caricatures of Twenty-Five Gentlemen* (1896), *The Poets' Corner* (1904), and *Rossetti and His Circle* (1922). In the 1930s he began a new career as broadcaster; his commentaries on England then and now are collected in *Mainly on the Air* (1957).

BEETON, Mrs, *née* Isabella Mary Mayson (1836–65), author of *Household Management* (1861), covering cookery and other branches of domestic science.

Beggar's Bush, The, a drama by J. *Fletcher and *Massinger, possibly with scenes by *Beaumont; probably performed 1622, published 1647.

The play has been admired for the intricacies of the plot, and for the realistic portrayal of its 'ragged regiment' of beggars, whose dialogue is enlivened by thieves' cant.

Beggar's Daughter of Bednall Green, The, a ballad written in the reign of Elizabeth I and included in Percy's *Reliques*.

Bessee is the fair daughter of a blind beggar, employed at the inn at Romford and courted by four suitors, a knight, a gentleman of good birth, a merchant of London, and the innkeeper's son. They all withdraw their suit on being referred by her to her father, except the knight. The old beggar gives her as dowry £3,000, two pounds for every one the knight puts down. It now appears that the beggar is Henry, son of Simon de Montfort, who has assumed the disguise of a beggar for safety.

The story forms the basis of *Chettle and *Day's *The Blind-Beggar of Bednal-Green* (1600, printed 1659). J. S. *Knowles also wrote a comedy called *The Beggar's Daughter of Bethnal Green*; and R. *Dodsley wrote a musical play, *The Blind Beggar of Bethnal Green*.

Beggar's Opera, The, a *ballad opera by J. *Gay, produced 1728.

The play arose out of *Swift's suggestion that a Newgate pastoral 'might make an odd pretty sort of thing'. The principal characters are Peachum, a receiver of stolen goods, who also makes a living by informing against his clients; his wife and his daughter Polly; Lockit, warder of Newgate, and his daughter Lucy; and Captain Macheath, a gallant highwayman. Polly falls in love with Macheath, who marries her. Peachum, infuriated by her folly, informs against Macheath who is sent to Newgate. There he makes a conquest of Lucy, who, in spite of her jealousy towards Polly, secures Macheath's release. The play, which combines burlesque of Italian opera and political satire (notably of Sir R. *Walpole) with some of Gay's most brilliant songs and scenes of genuine pathos, was an unparalleled success, and is said to have brought Gay some £800. (It was said to have made Gay rich, and *Rich—the producer—gay.) A *Brecht-Weill version, *The Threepenny Opera*, was first performed in 1928.

BEHAN, Brendan (1923–64), Irish playwright, was arrested in 1939 for his involvement with the IRA, and his subsequent period of Borstal training is described in his autobiographical *Borstal Boy* (1958). His best-known works are *The Hostage* (1958), a tragi-comedy about an English soldier held hostage in a Dublin brothel, and *The Quare Fellow* (1956), set in an Irish prison on the eve of a hanging.

BEHN, Mrs Afra or Aphra (1640–89), was employed in 1666 by Charles II as a spy in Antwerp in the Dutch war. Her first play, *The Forced Marriage* (1670) was followed by some 14 others, including her most popular, *The Rover* (in two parts, 1677–81), dealing with the adventures in Naples and Madrid of a band of English cavaliers during the exile of Charles II; *The City Heiress* (1682), a characteristic satiric comedy of London life; and *The Lucky Chance* (1686), which explores one of her favourite themes, the ill consequences of arranged and ill-matched marriages. She also wrote poems and novels. Her best remembered work is *Oroonoko, or the History of the Royal Slave* (1688), perhaps the earliest English philosophical novel. Despite her success she had even in her lifetime to contend with accusations of plagiarism and lewdness, attracted in her view by her sex. V. Woolf in *A Room of One's Own* (1928) acclaims her as the first Englishwoman to earn her living by writing, 'with all the plebeian virtues of humour, vitality and courage'.

Belarius, in Shakespeare's *Cymbeline*, the banished lord.

Belch, Sir Toby, in Shakespeare's *Twelfth Night*, a roistering humorous knight, uncle to Olivia.

Belford, John, the hero's principal correspondent in Richardson's *Clarissa*.

Belial has come to mean the spirit of evil personified, and is used from early times as a name for the Devil or one of the fiends, and by Milton (*Paradise Lost, i. 490) as the name of one of the fallen angels.

Believe As You List, a tragedy by *Massinger, acted 1631, not published until 1849. The original play was banned because it dealt with recent Spanish and Portuguese history. Massinger ingeniously transferred the story back to the safer days of the Roman empire. The play is a fine study of the recurring conflict between nationalism and imperialism.

Belinda, (1) a character in Vanbrugh's *The Provok'd Wife; (2) the heroine of Pope's *The Rape of the Lock; (3) the title of a novel by M. *Edgeworth; (4) a novel by H. *Belloc.

BELL, (Arthur) Clive (Heward) (1881–1964), art critic, educated at Cambridge where he came under the influence of G. E. *Moore and met members of what was to be the *Bloomsbury Group. In 1907 he married Vanessa Stephen. In 1910 he met R. *Fry, whose views contributed to his own theory of 'Significant Form', outlined in Art (1914). With Fry, he was a champion of the Post-Impressionists. In Civilization (1928) he argued that civilization depended on the existence of a (not necessarily hereditary) leisured élite.

BELL, Currer, Ellis, and Acton, see BRONTË, C., E., and A.

BELL, Gertrude Margaret Lowthian (1868–1926). After a dozen years of world travel and mountaineering, she began her solitary travels as a field archaeologist in Syria, Asia Minor, and Mesopotamia. Her knowledge of the desert Arabs and Middle East politics caused her recruitment to the Arab Bureau in Cairo in 1915, and later her appointment in Iraq as Oriental Secretary to the British High Commissioner. Her best-known books were Safar Nameh: Persian Pictures (1894), The Desert and the Sown (1907), and Amurath to Amurath (1911). In these, and in her brilliant Letters (1927) and diaries—largely quoted in Gertrude Bell: from her Personal Papers, ed. Elizabeth Burgoyne (1958 and 1961)—she vividly conveyed the landscapes and personalities of the desert.

Bell, Laura, a character in Thackeray's *Pendennis, who reappears as Laura Pendennis in *The Newcomes and *The Adventures of Philip.

Bellair, a character in Etherege's *The Man of Mode.

Bellamira, a comedy by Sir C. *Sedley, produced 1687, founded on *Terence's Eunuchus.

BELLAMY, Edward (1850–98), American novelist and political theorist, whose fame rests upon his popular *Utopian romance Looking Backward: 2000–1887 (1888). Its hero, Julian West, a young Bostonian, falls into a hypnotic sleep in 1887 and wakes in the year 2000 to find great changes, where the moral, social and cultural benefits of a new system are everywhere apparent. This work had an immense vogue; a Nationalist Party was formed to advocate its principles.

Bellario, (1) in Shakespeare's *The Merchant of Venice, Portia's lawyer cousin; (2) the name assumed by the heroine of Beaumont and Fletcher's *Philaster, when disguised as a page.

Bellaston, Lady, a character in Fielding's *Tom Jones.

Bella Wilfer, a character in Dickens's *Our Mutual Friend.

Belle, or Isopel, **Berners,** a character in Borrow's *Lavengro, a beautiful Amazon who acts as second to Lavengro in his fight with the Flaming Tinman.

'Belle Dame Sans Merci, La', see LA BELLE DAME SANS MERCI.

BELLENDEN, or **BALLANTYNE,** John (c. 1500–c. 1548), Scottish poet and translator into Scots of *Livy.

Bellenden, Lady Margaret, Edith, and Major, characters in Scott's *Old Mortality.

Belle's Stratagem, The, a comedy by Mrs H. *Cowley, produced 1780.
The play recounts the successful endeavours of Letitia to win the heart of her childhood friend Doricourt, who at first woos her only out of obedience to their parents.

Bell Jar, The, a novel by S. *Plath, published 1963 under the pseudonym of Victoria Lucas, and under her own name in 1966.
It opens in New York in the summer of 1953 as the narrator, Esther Greenwood, a highly ambitious intelligent college girl from Boston, spends time working on a training programme for a women's magazine and throws herself recklessly into the dangers of city life. Her story is interwoven with recollections of her boyfriend, Yale medical student Buddy Willard, who represents in part the threats of the flesh, in part the dullness of the provincial existence she fears will engulf her. She returns home, suffers a nervous breakdown, undergoes ECT, attempts suicide, is kept in psychiatric care, and in the penultimate chapter succeeds in losing her virginity to a mathematics professor. At the end

of the novel she prepares to leave the asylum and return to college. The subject matter of the novel is highly autobiographical.

BELLOC, Hilaire (Joseph Hilary Pierre) (1870–1953), born in France, of part-French Catholic ancestry. He was Liberal MP for Salford from 1906–9 and in 1910. His books of verse include *A Bad Child's Book of Beasts* (1896), *Verses and Sonnets* (1896), *Cautionary Tales* (1907), and *Sonnets and Verses* (1923). His most celebrated serious lyrics are probably 'Tarantella' ('Do you remember an inn, Miranda?') and 'Ha'nacker Hill'. He was an active journalist and literary editor of the *Morning Post* (1906–10) and founder of the *Eye-witness* (1911). His books attacking and satirizing Edwardian society (some with G. K. *Chesterton) include *Pongo and the Bull* (1910) and *The Servile State* (1912); of his books propounding Catholicism, *Europe and Faith* (1920) was well regarded. His biographies include *Danton* (1899), *Marie Antoinette* (1909), *Cromwell* (1927), and *Charles II* (1940); and his histories *The French Revolution* (1911) and a substantial *History of England* (1915). *The Cruise of the Nona* (1925) contains many of his most personal reflections. His most successful book of travel, *The Path to Rome* (1902), which was published with his own sketches and illustrations, is an account of a journey which he undertook, largely on foot, from the valley of the Moselle to Rome; other travel books include *Sussex* (1906) and *The Pyrenees* (1909). Of the novels *Mr Clutterbuck's Election* (1908), *The Girondin* (1911), *The Green Overcoat* (1912), and *Belinda* (1928) were among the most highly regarded. The last is a brief and highly individual love story, related with romantic feeling and much irony.

BELLOW, Saul (1915–), novelist, was born in Canada of Russian-Jewish parents, and educated from the age of 9 in Chicago, a city evoked in many of his works, including his first short novel *Dangling Man* (1944), a first-person account of a man waiting, unemployed, for his army draft. His subsequent works include *The Victim* (1947); *The Adventures of Augie March* (1953); *Seize the Day* (1956), a novella; *Henderson the Rain King* (1959), which records American millionaire Gene Henderson's quest for revelation and spiritual power in Africa, where he becomes rainmaker and heir to a kingdom; *Herzog* (1964), which reveals the inner life of a Jewish intellectual, Moses Herzog, driven to the verge of breakdown by his second wife's adultery with his close friend; *Dr Sammler's Planet* (1969); and *Humboldt's Gift* (1974). *The Dean's December* (1982) is a 'tale of two cities', both seen through the eyes of Albert Corde, who visits Bucharest to see his dying mother-in-law, where he reflects on the contrasts between the violence and corruption of Chicago and the bureaucratic chill of Eastern Europe; the novel

has, like much of Bellow's work, a strongly apocalyptic note. Bellow has also written short stories and a play (*The Last Analysis*, 1964). He was awarded the *Nobel Prize in 1976.

Bells, The (1871), a dramatic adaptation by L. Lewis of *Le Juif polonais* by Erckmann-Chatrian, the story of a burgomaster haunted by the consciousness of an undiscovered murder that he has committed. It provided H. *Irving with one of his most successful parts.

Bells and Pomegranates, the covering title of a series of plays and collections of shorter dramatic poems by R. *Browning, published 1841–6, comprising *Pippa Passes* (1841), *King Victor and King Charles* (1842), *Dramatic Lyrics* (1842), *The Return of the Druses* (1843), *A Blot in the 'Scutcheon* (1843), *Colombe's Birthday* (1844), *Dramatic Romances and Lyrics* (1845), and *Luria and A Soul's Tragedy* (1846).

Belmont, Portia's house in Shakespeare's *The Merchant of Venice*.

Belmont, Sir John, the heroine's father in F. Burney's *Evelina*.

Belphoebe, in Spenser's *Faerie Queene*, the chaste huntress, twin sister of *Amoret; she partly symbolizes Queen Elizabeth.

Belshazzar's Feast, the feast made by Belshazzar the son of Nebuchadnezzar and the last king of Babylonia, at which his doom was foretold by writing on the wall, as interpreted by Daniel (Dan. 5). Belshazzar was killed in the sack of Babylon by Cyrus (538 BC). He is the subject of dramas by H. *More and *Milman, of R. *Landor's *The Impious Feast*, a poem by *Byron, and an oratorio by W. *Walton.

Belton Estate, The, a novel by A. *Trollope, published 1866.

Belvidera, the heroine of Otway's *Venice Preserv'd*.

Bend in the River, A, a novel by V. S. *Naipaul, published 1979.

Benedick, in Shakespeare's *Much Ado about Nothing*, a sworn bachelor who falls in love with *Beatrice; 'Benedict' has been used subsequently to refer to a newly-married erstwhile bachelor.

BENEDICT BISCOP, St (?628–89). During visits to Rome he collected and brought back many volumes and relics. He founded (in 674) the monastery of St Peter at the mouth of the River Wear. After this he founded the sister monastery of St Paul at Jarrow. He is regarded as one of the originators of the artistic and literary development of Northumbria in the next century, celebrated by *Bede in his *Lives of the Abbots*.

BENÉT, Stephen Vincent (1898–1943), American poet, is best known for his narrative poem of the Civil War, *John Brown's Body* (1928), and for some of the poems in *Ballads and Poems* (1931), including the popular 'American Names', with its resounding last line, 'Bury my heart at Wounded Knee'.

Ben Gunn, a character in Stevenson's *Treasure Island*.

Ben-Hur: *A Tale of the Christ*, a historical novel, published 1880, about the early days of Christianity by Lew (Lewis) Wallace (1827–1905), an American novelist.

'Benito Cereno' (1856), a short story by H. *Melville.

A gothic tale of white masters and implacable black revenge, it is set off the coast of Peru in 1799.

BENLOWES, Edward (?1602–76), poet, whose principle work was *Theophila, or Love's Sacrifice* (1652), celebrating the epic progress of the soul in learned, obscure and occasionally grotesque conceits and language.

Bennett, Mr and Mrs Jane, Elizabeth, Mary, Kitty, and Lydia, characters in J. Austen's *Pride and Prejudice*.

BENNETT, Alan (1934–), dramatist and actor, made his name with the satirical review *Beyond the Fringe* (1960, pub. 1963, with Jonathan Miller and others), and his other works, most of which are satirical comedies, include *Forty Years On* (1968, pub. 1969), *Getting On* (1971, pub. 1972); and *Habeas Corpus* (1973). A more sombre work, *The Old Country* (1977, pub. 1978), deals with the theme of exile through the life of an English spy in the Soviet Union; one of his many television plays, *An Englishman Abroad* (pub. 1982, broadcast 1983) deals with the same subject.

BENNETT, (Enoch) Arnold (1867–1931), novelist, born in Hanley, Staffordshire. He went to London when he was 21 and worked as a clerk before establishing himself as a writer. His first stories were published in *Tit-Bits* (1890) and the *Yellow Book* (1895), and his first novel, *A Man from the North*, appeared in 1898. In 1902 he moved to Paris, returning to England to settle permanently in 1912. In 1926 at the suggestion of his friend *Beaverbrook he began an influential weekly article on books for the *Evening Standard*. He wrote several successful plays, notably *Milestones* (1912, with E. Knoblock, author of

Kismet), but his fame rests chiefly on his novels and short stories, the best known of which were set in the Potteries of his youth, a region he recreated as the *'Five Towns'. *Anna of the Five Towns* (1902), the story of a miser's daughter, shows clearly the influence of the French realists whom he much admired. *The Old Wives' Tale* (1908) was followed by the Clayhanger series (*Clayhanger*, 1910; *Hilda Lessways*, 1911; *These Twain*, 1916; *The Roll Call*, 1918). The novels portray the district with an ironic but affectionate detachment, describing provincial life and culture in documentary detail, and creating many memorable characters—Darius Clayhanger, the dictatorial printer who started work aged seven in a pot-bank, the monstrous but good-hearted Auntie Hamps, Edwin Clayhanger, frustrated architect, and Hilda Lessways, the independent and strong-willed young woman who marries Edwin. Two volumes of short stories, *The Grim Smile of the Five Towns* (1907) and *The Matador of the Five Towns* (1912), are set in the same region. The best novel of his later period, *Riceyman Steps* (1923), is the story of a miserly second-hand bookseller, set in drab Clerkenwell. But he also wrote many entertaining lighter works, displaying a love of luxury and fantasy, among them *The Grand Babylon Hotel* (1902), *The Card* (1911), and *Mr Prohack* (1922). His *Journal*, begun in 1896, was published in 1932–3 edited by Newman *Flower.

BENOÎT, DE SAINTE-MAURE, a 12th-cent. *trouvère* patronized by Henry II of England, for whom he composed a verse history of the dukes of Normandy. His best-known work is the *Roman de Troie*, based on the writings of *Dares Phrygius and *Dictys Cretensis; it served as a source for subsequent writers including *Boccaccio, followed by *Chaucer.

BENSON, A(rthur) C(hristopher) (1862–1925), eldest surviving son of E. W. Benson (1829–96), archbishop of Canterbury, and brother of E. F. and R. H. *Benson. He published many volumes of biography, family reminiscences, reflection, criticism, etc., and had a facility for writing public odes and verses, typified by his 'Land of Hope and Glory'. From 1897 until 1925 he kept a diary; extracts were published by *Lubbock in 1926, and David Newsome makes use of them in his biography *On the Edge of Paradise: A. C. Benson, the Diarist* (1980).

BENSON, E(dward) F(rederic) (1867–1940), brother of A. C. and R. H. *Benson, a prolific and popular novelist, whose works include *Dodo* (1893, followed by other 'Dodo' novels) and *Queen Lucia* (1920, followed by other 'Lucia' novels), and various volumes of reminiscences.

BENSON, R(obert) H(ugh) (1871–1914), younger brother of A. C. and E. F. *Benson,

49 BENWICK

and like them a prolific writer. Much of his work consists of Catholic apologia: he wrote sensational apocalyptic novels (e.g. *The Lord of the World*, 1907), melodramatic historical novels (e.g. *Come Rack! Come Rope!*, 1912), and modern novels usually involving an impossible moral conundrum (e.g. *The Average Man*, 1913), and also published sermons, poems, etc.

BENTHAM, Jeremy (1748–1832), was called to the bar at Lincoln's Inn. He published anonymously in 1776 *Fragment on Government*, in form a criticism of *Blackstone's *Commentaries*, in which he first sketched his theory of government. While in Russia, 1785–8, he wrote his *Defence of Usury* (1787) and a series of letters on a *Panopticon* (1791), a scheme for improving prison discipline. In 1789, he published *Introduction to Principles of Morals and Legislation*. Besides these he produced a number of influential works on ethics and jurisprudence, and works on logic and political economy; the vast mass of his papers were never properly prepared for publication. Bentham was greatly assisted by his devoted disciple Etienne Dumont of Geneva, who compiled several treatises based on Bentham's manuscripts which he published between 1802 and 1825 in French.

It is in the *Fragment on Government* and more fully in the *Principles* that he enunciates the political and ethical theory of Utility by which he is best remembered. 'It is the greatest happiness of the greatest number that is the measure of right and wrong.' Pain and pleasure are the 'sovereign masters' governing man's conduct; 'it is for them alone to point out what we ought to do'. The criterion of the goodness of a law is the principle of Utility, the measure in which it subserves the happiness to which every individual is equally entitled. The motive of an act always being self-interest, it is the business of law and education to make the sanctions sufficiently strong to induce the individual to subordinate his own happiness to that of the community. Bentham believed it possible that the quantitative value of pains and pleasures as motives of action could be minutely calculated, which would give scientific accuracy to morals and legislation. His democratic views are expressed in his *Constitutional Code* (1830); *Chrestomathia* (1816) is a series of papers on education. He also propounded a number of valuable reforms in the administration of English justice, which since his time have been applied. In 1824 with the assistance of J. *Mill he founded the *Westminster Review*.

BENTLEY, Edmund Clerihew (1875–1956), was called to the bar, but made his career as a journalist on the *Daily News* and *Daily Telegraph*. In *Biography for Beginners* (1905) he invented the wittily absurd verse form called *clerihew after his second name, and in *Trent's Last Case* (1913) he produced the prototype of the modern detective novel.

BENTLEY, Phyllis (1894–1977), novelist. The West Riding forms the background for many of her interconnected regional novels, which include *Carr* (1929), *Inheritance* (1932), *A Modern Tragedy* (1934), and *Manhold* (1941). She also wrote on the *Brontës, and published an autobiography, *O Dreams, O Destinations* (1962).

BENTLEY, Richard (1662–1742), made his reputation as a scholar with his *Letter to Mill* (1691), a critical letter in Latin on the Greek dramatists. He delivered in 1692 the first *Boyle lectures, printed in 1693 as *The Folly and Unreasonableness of Atheism*. He became keeper of the king's libraries in 1694, and during 1697–9 was engaged in the famous Phalaris controversy, during which he proved the *Epistles of *Phalaris to be spurious (SEE BATTLE OF THE BOOKS) and queried the antiquity of *Aesop's fables. In 1699 he was appointed master of Trinity College, Cambridge. Among his greatest critical works were his bold revisions of the texts of *Horace and Manilius; he was the last great classical scholar before the divergence of Greek and Latin studies. He was caricatured in *The Dunciad* (Bk. IV. 201 ff.) and elsewhere.

BENTLEY, Richard (1708–82), son of R. *Bentley (above), is remembered as the friend of Horace *Walpole and *Gray, and made a considerable contribution to the Gothic fantasy of *Strawberry Hill. He also illustrated Gray's poems in 1753 with designs described by *Clark as 'the most graceful monument to Gothic Rococo' (*The Gothic Revival*, 1928). Walpole quarrelled with him in 1761, and Bentley struggled on in London as a playwright and pamphleteer. (See also CHUTE.)

BENTLEY, Richard (1794–1871), publisher, who included T. *Moore, both *Disraelis, and *Dickens among his authors. In 1830 he joined with Henry *Colburn to found the firm of Colburn and Bentley, which in 1837 established *Bentley's Miscellany*. They published a popular series of 'Standard Novels'.

Bentley's Miscellany (1837–69), a successful periodical consisting of essays, stories, and poems, begun by R. Bentley (above). *Dickens was the first editor, and *Oliver Twist* appeared in its pages in 1837–8. J. H. *Reynolds, *Hook, *Maginn, *Ainsworth, *Thackeray, and *Longfellow were among its contributors. *Cruikshank and *Leech provided lively illustrations.

Benvolio, in Shakespeare's *Romeo and Juliet*, a cousin and friend of Romeo.

Benwick, Captain, a character in J. Austen's *Persuasion*.

Beowulf, an Old English poem of 3,182 lines, surviving in a 10th-cent. manuscript. It tells of two major events in the life of the Geatish hero Beowulf: the first when, in his youth, he fights and kills first Grendel, a monster who has been attacking Heorot, the hall of the Danish king Hrothgar, and then Grendel's mother who comes the next night to avenge her son; the second, 50 years later, when Beowulf, who has for a long time been king of the Geats, fights a dragon who has attacked his people, in a combat in which both Beowulf and the dragon are mortally wounded. The historical period of the poem's events can be dated in the 6th cent. from a reference to Beowulf's king Hygelac by the historian *Gregory of Tours; but much of the material of the poem is legendary and paralleled in other Germanic historical-mythological literature in Norse, Old English, and German.

The poem is generally dated in the 8th cent., when England was being won over from paganism to Christianity. This date is taken to account for the strong thread of Christian commentary which runs through the poem.

Beowulf, the more important poem in Old English and the first major poem in a European vernacular language, is remarkable for its sustained grandeur of tone and for the brilliance of its style.

Beppo: *a Venetian story,* a poem in *ottava rima* by Lord *Byron, published 1818.

This poem tells, in the mock-heroic style, with great zest and irony, the story of a Venetian carnival, at which a lady's husband, Beppo, who has been absent for many years, returns in Turkish garb, and confronts her and her *cavaliere servente.*

BERENSON, Bernard (1865–1959), art historian and philosopher. Born in Lithuania and educated in America, he settled in Europe in 1887. He published *Italian Painters of the Renaissance* (as separate essays 1894–1907) which developed the theory that the 'tactile value' of a work of art stimulated in the spectator a state of increased awareness; *Italian Pictures of the Renaissance* (1932); and works on history, aesthetics, and politics.

BERGER, John (1926–), novelist and art critic, became well known as a broadcaster and journalist holding Marxist views, and also published several novels: *A Painter of our Time* (1958), *The Foot of Clive* (1962), *Corker's Freedom* (1964), and *G.* (*Booker Prize, 1972). Works of non-fiction include *A Fortunate Man* (1967) and *Pig Earth* (1979), a study in stories, poems, and narrative of the plight of the French peasant facing the threat of migrant industrialized labour.

BERGSON, Henri (1859–1941), French philosopher who opposed scientific materialism and

positivism, and whose concept of the *'élan vital'*, or vital impulse, where the evolutionary process is directed towards new forms and increasing complexity, captured the imagination of many writers, including G. B. *Shaw. He was awarded the *Nobel Prize in 1928.

BERKELEY, George (1685–1753), philosopher, educated at Trinity College, Dublin. He visited England in 1713 and became associated with *Steele, *Addison, *Pope, *Arbuthnot, *Swift, and others.

His chief philosophical works were *An Essay towards a New Theory of Vision* (1709, 1710, 1732), *A Treatise concerning the Principles of Human Knowledge* (1710, 1734), and *Three Dialogues between Hylas and Philonous* (1713, 1725, 1734). In 1712 he published controversial sermons on 'passive obedience' and a year later contributed essays against the Whig freethinkers to *The Guardian*. Returning to the attack on the free-thinkers and the defence of his own philosophy in the 1730s, he issued his dialogue *Alciphron* (1732, 1752), and *The Theory of Vision Vindicated and Explained* (1733). In 1734 he published *The Analyst*, criticizing *Newton's theory of fluxions; and in 1735–7 *The Querist*, dealing with questions of economic and social reform.

In his works on vision, Berkeley seeks to show the mind-dependence of the ideas derived from sight, and explains their 'arbitrary' though constant connection with the more primary ideas of touch by analogy with the way in which written words 'signify' speech. His other philosophy is partly inspired by, and partly a reaction to, the work of *Locke (see ESSAY CONCERNING HUMAN UNDERSTANDING).

Berkeley was a master both of English prose and of the dialogue form; he is remarkable for his lucidity, grace, and dignity of expression.

BERKENHEAD, Sir John (1617–79), pamphleteer and the principal editor and writer of the influential royalist Oxford-based newsbook *Mercurius Aulicus* (1643–5), which was renowned for its cavalier insouciance and wit and condemned by its opponents as a 'Court Buffon'. Berkenhead also wrote polite and satiric verse. He is notable as one of the first writers to make a career in journalism. (See also NEWSPAPERS.)

BERLIN, Sir Isaiah (1909–), is best known as a political philosopher for his defence of liberalism and moral pluralism (see *Four Essays on Liberty*, 1969), views which, as historian of ideas, he has explored in his work on the recognition of the historical dimension of philosophical thought in, among others, Vico and *Herder (*Vico and Herder*, 1976). His *Russian Thinkers* (1978), a collection of essays about the intelligentsia of 19th-cent. Russia, includes 'The

Hedgehog and the Fox', a discussion of *Tolstoy focusing on the tension between monist and pluralist visions of the world and of history.

'**Bermudas**', see MARVELL, A.

BERNARD, St (1090–1153), abbot of the Cistercian foundation of Clairvaux and one of the foremost figures of the 12th-cent. monastic Reformation. He preached the Second Crusade, and opposed the dialectical theological method of *Abelard which he had condemned at Soissons and Sens. He developed and preached 'The Cistercian Programme', a progression from carnal to spiritual love which, in its literary application, became one of the most important elements in medieval poetry from the *troubadours to *Dante. In his mysticism the stress is on God's grace, according to the Augustinian school, rather than on the deliberate achievement of man's contemplative efforts which was the aspect emphasized by the *Neoplatonists and their followers in the prose mysticism of the 14th cent.

BERNARD OF MORLAIX (12th cent.), a Benedictine monk of the monastery of Cluny in Burgundy who wrote the Latin poem 'De Contemptu Mundi', c.1140. Several of his hymns were translated by J. M. *Neale.

Berners, Belle or Isopel, see BELLE BERNERS.

BERNERS, John Bourchier, second baron (1467–1533), statesman and author. He translated the *Chronicles* of Froissart (1523–5); *Huon of Bordeaux* (probably printed before 1534); Guevara's *Il Libro Aureo di Marco Aurelio* (1535); and another Spanish work, the *Castell of Love* (printed 1549).

Berners, Juliana, see BOOK OF ST ALBANS.

Bernstein, Baroness, a character in Thackeray's *The Virginians*, formerly Beatrix Esmond in *The History of Henry Esmond*.

Berowne, or Biron, one of the three lords attending the King of France in Shakespeare's *Love's Labour's Lost*.

BERRY, James (1924–), poet, born in Jamaica, who came to London in 1948. He has done much work in the field of multi-cultural education, and edited various anthologies, including *Bluefoot Traveller: An Anthology of Westindian Poets Of Britain* (1976), *Dance to a Different Drum* (1983, a Brixton Festival anthology), and *News from Babylon* (1984). His own collections include *Fractured Circles* (1979) and *Lucy's Letter and Loving* (1982). (See also JAZZ POETRY.)

BERRYMAN, John (1914–72), American poet. Much of his poetry is anguished and con-

fessional, exploring personal guilts and religious doubts. His works include *Poems* (1942), *The Dispossessed* (1948), and *Homage to Mistress Bradstreet* (1956). *77 Dream Songs* (1964), with their imaginary and protean protagonist Henry, were completed by *His Toy, His Dream, His Rest* (1968), and together form his major work.

Bertram, count of Rousillon, in Shakespeare's *All's Well that Ends Well*.

Bertram, Harry, a character in Scott's *Guy Mannering*.

Bertram, Sir Thomas and Lady, their sons Thomas and Edmund, and their daughters Julia and Maria, characters in J. Austen's *Mansfield Park*.

Bertram; or the Castle of St Aldobrand, a tragedy by C. R. *Maturin, produced 1816.

BESANT, Mrs Annie, née Wood (1847–1933), became a Fabian, a trade union organizer, and, in association with *Bradlaugh, an enthusiast for birth control. She then became a theosophist and pupil of Mme *Blavatsky, and an active supporter of the Indian nationalist movement.

BESANT, Sir Walter (1836–1901), collaborated with James Rice and together they produced several best-selling novels, including *Ready-Money Mortiboy* (1872), *The Golden Butterfly* (1876), and *The Chaplain of the Fleet* (1881). He was deeply interested in the life of the poor, especially in the East End of London, and the terrible social conditions of industrial workers and draws attention to these in *All Sorts and Conditions of Men* (1882) and *Children of Gibeon* (1886); he stimulated the foundation of the People's Palace, Mile End (1887), for intellectual improvement and rational amusement. In 1884 he founded the *Society of Authors, and became editor of *The Author* in 1890; he defined the financial position of authors in *The Pen and the Book* (1899). He also wrote historical works, histories of different parts of London, and *A Survey of London* (1902–12).

Bess of Hardwick, Elizabeth Talbot, countess of Shrewsbury (c.1520–1608), daughter and co-heir of John Hardwick of Hardwick, Derbyshire. She is described as 'a woman of a masculine understanding and conduct; proud, furious, selfish, and unfeeling' (*Lodge). To her care and to that of her husband, the 6th earl of Shrewsbury, Mary Queen of Scots was entrusted in 1569 at Tutbury. She married her daughter to Charles Stuart, younger brother of Darnley, and was imprisoned in the Tower in consequence. She built Chatsworth (not the present building) and Hardwick Hall.

Bessus, in Beaumont and Fletcher's *A King and no King*, a cowardly braggart.

Bessy, one of the stock characters, a man dressed as a woman, in the medieval *Sword-dance and in the *Mummers' Play.

Bestiaries, medieval treatises derived from the Greek *Physiologus*, which was a collection of about 50 fabulous anecdotes from natural (mostly animal) history, followed by a 'moralization' of the anecdotes for a Christian purpose. The Greek original dates from between the 2nd and 4th cents AD, and it was translated into many languages. In the 12th cent. additions began to be made to the Latin version from the popular encyclopedia of the Middle Ages, the *Etymologiae* of *Isidore of Seville. Those written in England in the 12th and 13th cents were often richly illustrated with miniatures.

BETJEMAN, Sir John (1906–84), poet, educated at Magdalen College, Oxford, where he became friendly with *Auden and *MacNiece and was encouraged by *Bowra. He began to publish poems in magazines ('Death in Leamington' appeared in the *London Mercury in 1930). His first collection of verse, *Mount Zion* (1931), was followed by other collections, including *Continental dew: a little book of bourgeois verse* (1937), *New bats in old belfries* (1945), *A few late chrysanthemums* (1954), and his extremely successful *Collected Poems* (1958, expanded 1962). His blank-verse autobiography, *Summoned by Bells* (1960), which covers his boyhood and life at Oxford, was followed by two more collections, *High and Low* (1976) and *A Nip in the Air* (1972). He was appointed poet laureate in 1972. His poetry is predominantly witty, urbane, satiric, and light of touch, a comedy of manners, place-names, and contemporary allusions. In the preface to *Old Lights for New Chancels* (1940) Betjeman writes of his own 'topographical predilection' for 'suburbs and gaslights and Pont Street and Gothic Revival churches and mineral railways, provincial towns and garden cities', a predilection also displayed in his editing and writing of Shell Guides and various works on architecture, beginning with *Ghastly Good Taste* (1933).

Betrothed, The, a novel by Sir W. *Scott, published 1825, the scene of which is laid in the Welsh Marches, in the reign of Henry II.

Betteredge, Gabriel, in Wilkie Collins's *The Moonstone*, the Verinders' steward and narrator of parts of the story.

BETTERTON, Mrs Mary (c.1637–1712), the wife of T. *Betterton, the first notable actress on the English stage (until 1660 female parts were taken by men or boys) and the first woman to act a series of Shakespeare's great female characters.

BETTERTON, Thomas (1635–1710), the greatest actor in the Restoration, joined

*D'Avenant's company at Lincoln's Inn Fields, and was associated in the management of the Dorset Garden Theatre from 1671. His dramas include the *Roman Virgin* (acted 1669), *The Prophetess* (1690), an opera; and *King Henry IV* (1700).

Between the Acts, the last novel of V. *Woolf, published shortly after her death in 1941. It has been seen as her final statement on art as the transforming and unifying principle of life.

The action takes place at a middle-sized country house, Poyntz Hall, the home of the Oliver family, and Woolf's central metaphor is the enacting of a village pageant, which aspires to portray nothing less than the sweep of English history, by means of songs, tableaux, parody, pastiche, etc.; it ends by presenting the audience its own mirror-image, in the present, as a megaphoned voice demands how civilization could be built by 'orts, scraps and fragments like ourselves?' The pageant is directed by the sexually ambiguous Miss la Trobe, who represents the ever-dissatisfied artist, and its scenes are interwoven with scenes in the lives of the audience; together, the illusion and the reality combine as a communal image of rural England, past and present—'a rambling capricious but somehow unified whole'.

Beulah, Land of, see Isaiah 62: 4. In Bunyan's *Pilgrim's Progress it lies 'beyond the valley of the Shadow of Death' where the pilgrims were in sight of the Heavenly City. Beulah is also used in a similar sense by *Blake, to represent a state of Light (often associated with the third state of vision and sexual love): its symbol is the moon.

Bevis of Hampton, a popular verse-romance from the late 13th or early 14th cent. in 4,620 lines, based on a 12th-cent. Anglo-Norman *chanson de geste* entitled *Beuves de Hanstone*.

Bevis, the Story of a Boy, a novel by R. *Jefferies, published 1882.

BEWICK, Thomas (1753–1828), wood-engraver. He engraved blocks for *Gay's *Fables* (1779), *Fables of Aesop* (1818), the poems of *Goldsmith and T. *Parnell (1795), and other books; his most celebrated and successful work was *A History of British Birds* (1797, 1804).

Bianca, (1) sister of Katharina, in Shakespeare's *The Taming of the Shrew*; (2) mistress of Cassio, in his *Othello.

Biathanatos, see DONNE, J.

Bible, The, (1) The Old Testament. The oldest surviving Hebrew text (Codex Babylonicus Petropolitanus) dates from AD 916. It is a Masoretic text, i.e. one prepared by the guild of scholars called Masoretes. Of much earlier date (5th cent. BC) is the Samaritan text of the Pentateuch. The Targums (Aramaic interpretations or paraphrases) appeared from *c.* AD 100 after Aramaic superseded Hebrew as the spoken language of the Jews. More important is the Greek *Septuagint version (3rd cent. BC): a revised text of this formed part of the 3rd-cent. AD Hexapla (see ORIGEN). An old Latin version (Vetus Itala) of an early Greek translation was superseded by the Latin *Vulgate (*c.* 404) of St Jerome.

(2) The New Testament. Manuscripts in Greek, and manuscripts of translations from the Greek into Latin, Syriac, and Coptic are extant. The most important of these are the Greek, of which the chief are the Codex Vaticanus and the Codex Sinaiticus, uncial manuscripts of the 4th cent.; the Codex Bezae, containing the Greek text on the left-hand page and the Latin on the right, probably earlier than the 6th cent.; and the Codex Alexandrinus, an uncial of the 5th cent. (See BIBLE, THE ENGLISH; POLYGLOT BIBLE; LUTHER; ULFILAS.)

Bible, The English. Apart from paraphrases attributed to *Caedmon and the translation by *Bede of part of the Gospel of St John, the earliest attempts at translation into English of the Holy Scriptures are the 9th- and 10th-cent. glosses and versions of the Psalms, followed by the 10th-cent. glosses and versions of the Gospels (the Durham Book, or *Lindisfarne Gospels, and the West-Saxon Gospels), and *Aelfric's translation of the OT at the close of the same cent. After this little was done until the time of *Wyclif, to whom and his followers we owe the two 14th-cent. versions associated with his name, the first complete renderings into English of the Scriptures.

*Tyndale was the first to translate the NT into English from the Greek text; this he probably did in Wittenberg, the translation being printed first at Cologne, and when this was interrupted, at Worms (1525–6). The Authorized Version (see below) is essentially the text of Tyndale. The complete English Bible that bears the name of *Coverdale was printed in 1535. The Prayer Book text of the Psalms is largely Coverdale's version.

The 'Great Bible', also called 'Cranmer's Bible', was brought out in 1539 under the auspices of Henry VIII; Coverdale was placed by Cromwell in charge of its preparation. The printing of it was begun in Paris and finished in London.

During Mary's reign, the reformers took refuge, some in Frankfurt am Main, some in Geneva, where in 1560 appeared the Genevan or 'Breeches' Bible. It had a marginal commentary which proved agreeable to the Puritans.

The 'Authorized Version' arose out of a conference at Hampton Court, convened by James I in 1604, between the High Church and Low Church parties. The so-called 'Authorized Version' (it was not authorized by any official pronouncement) appeared in 1611. It is practically the version of Tyndale with some admixture from Wyclif.

In 1870 the Convocation of Canterbury appointed a committee to consider the question of revision, and as a consequence of their report two companies were constituted to revise the authorized versions of the OT and NT respectively. The Revised Text was published, of the NT in 1881, of the OT in 1885. That of the NT was unfavourably received, owing to many irritating and apparently unnecessary alterations of familiar passages. The Revised Version of the OT, though not altogether free from these, was in many respects an improvement on the Authorized text. In 1922 the Revd James Moffatt produced a 'New Translation of the New Testament', and in 1924 'The Old Testament, a new Translation', both of which caused some controversy. R. *Knox published a new translation of the Bible based on the Vulgate text, the NT in 1945 and the OT in 2 vols in 1949.

In 1947 a new translation of the Bible into modern English was undertaken by a Joint Committee of all the Churches (except the Roman Catholic) in the British Isles. The work was to be carried out by panels of translators for the OT, Apocrypha, and NT, with the help of literary advisers, and published by the University Presses of Oxford and Cambridge. The New English Bible NT was published in 1961 and the OT and Apocrypha in 1970.

Bible in Spain, The, a narrative of travel by *Borrow, published 1843.

Borrow travelled in Spain as distributor of Bibles for the British and Foreign Bible Society from 1835 to 1840, and this book purports to be an account of his adventures in a country racked by civil war. It is difficult to say how far the various incidents recounted actually occurred; but the vivid picture that the author gives of Spain is unquestionably realistic, and the work is one of the finest of English travel books.

Bibliographical Society, The, founded in 1892. Its *Transactions* were first published in 1893 (merged with * *The Library* in 1920). The Society in 1926 issued the invaluable *Short-Title Catalogue of English Books, 1475–1640* (work continued by *Wing).

Bibliography, Works of, see under BOHN; BRYDGES; CAMBRIDGE BIBLIOGRAPHY; DEWEY, M.; DIBDIN, T. F.; GREG; HAZLITT, W. C.; LANG; LOWNDES; MCKERROW; QUARITCH; SADLEIR; WATT; WING; and previous entry.

Bickerstaff, Isaac, a fictitious person invented by *Swift. A cobbler, John Partridge, claiming to be an astrologer, had published predictions in the form of an *almanac. Swift in the beginning of 1708 produced a parody entitled *Predictions for the ensuing year, by Isaac Bickerstaff*, in which he foretold the death of Partridge on 29 March. On 30 March he published a letter giving an account of Partridge's end. Partridge indignantly protested that he was still alive, but Swift retorted in a *Vindication* proving that he was really dead. Other writers took up the joke, and *Steele, when he launched *The Tatler* in 1709, adopted the name of Bickerstaff for the supposed author.

BICKERSTAFFE, Isaac (1733–?1808), an Irish playwright who arrived in London in 1755 and produced many successful comedies and opera librettos including the popular comic operas *Love in a Village* (1762), with music by *Arne, which has a claim to be the first comic opera and contains the well-known song about the Miller of Dee ('There was a jolly miller once'), and *The Maid of the Mill* (1765, with music by Samuel Arnold and others), the plot of which is Richardson's *Pamela*. *The Padlock* (1768, with music by *Dibdin) provided the London stage, in the part of Mungo, with its first black-faced comedian, and the lines 'Mungo here, Mungo dere, Mungo everywhere' became a catch-phrase. *The Hypocrite* (1768, adapted from *Molière's *Tartuffe* and *Cibber's *The Non-Juror*) contains the well-known character of a hypocrite, Mawworm. Bickerstaffe also wrote adaptations of *Wycherley and Calderón.

BIERCE, Ambrose (1842–?1914), American writer, served in the Civil War, 1861–5, and afterwards became a prominent journalist. He is best known for his short stories, realistic, sardonic, and strongly influenced by *Poe. They were published in *Tales of Soldiers and Civilians* (1891), a title which was changed to *In the Midst of Life* (1892; rev. edn, 1898).

Big Brother, in Orwell's *Nineteen Eighty-four*, is the head of the Party, who never appears in person, but whose dominating portrait in every public place, with the caption 'Big Brother is watching you', is inescapable.

Bildungsroman, the term applied to novels of 'education' (in the widest sense), of which many of the best examples are German. Wieland's *Agathon* (1765–6) is usually thought of as the first example of the genre, but the best and most imitated was *Goethe's *Wilhelm Meisters Lehrjahre* (*Wilhelm Meister's Apprenticeship*, 1795–6), which became celebrated in England through *Carlyle's translation in 1824. Thomas Mann was Goethe's most distinguished successor with his philosophical novel *Der Zauberberg* (*The Magic Mountain*, 1924). The genre overlaps with the older type of the *picaresque novel, but is more philosophical. The German term *Bildungsroman* has been adopted in English

criticism as a result of the fame during the 19th cent. of *Wilhelm Meister* and Carlyle's semifictional *Sartor Resartus* (1833–4).

Billickin, Mrs, in Dickens's *Edwin Drood*, a cousin of Mr Bazzard.

BILLINGS, Josh, see SHAW, H. W.

Billingsgate, the name of one of the gates of London on the river side, and hence of the fish market established there until Jan. 1982. There are frequent references in 17th-cent. literature to the abusive language of the Billingsgate market; hence foul language is itself called 'billingsgate'.

Billy Budd, Foretopman (written 1891, published 1924), a novella by H. *Melville.

Billy, 'the handsome sailor', wrongly accused by the satanic master-at-arms Claggart and unable to defend himself verbally because of a stammer, strikes Claggart dead. After being tried by the liberal Captain Vere, Billy is hanged, his last words being 'God bless Captain Vere!' Then, in apparently Christ-like apotheosis, 'the East was shot through with a soft glory as of the fleece of the Lamb of God', and the sailors question whether Billy had actually died. *Britten's setting of *Billy Budd* (1951) has become one of the most admired operas in the modern repertoire.

Billy Liar, see WATERHOUSE, K.

Bingley, Charles, and his sister, Caroline, characters in J. Austen's *Pride and Prejudice*.

BINYON, (Robert) Laurence (1869–1943), published many works on art, chiefly English and oriental, *Painting in the Far East* (1908) being one of the best known. His dramas included *Attila* (1907) and *Arthur* (1923), the latter with music by *Elgar. His war poems include his much anthologized 'For the Fallen' ('. . . They shall grow not old, as we that are left grow old . . .'); and he wrote two long odes, *The Sirens* (1924) and *The Idols* (1928). The *Collected Poems* appeared in 1931, as did *Landscape in English Art and Poetry*.

Biographia Literaria, a work of philosophical autobiography and Romantic criticism, by S. T. *Coleridge, published 1817.

Part I is broadly autobiographical describing Coleridge's friendship with *Southey and with the *Wordsworths at Stowey, and going on to trace his struggle with the 'dynamic philosophy' of *Kant, Fichte, and *Schelling in Germany. The humorous narrative is gradually overwhelmed by Romantic metaphysics; ch. XIII contains his famous distinction between Fancy and Imagination. Part II is almost entirely critical, attacking Wordsworth's Preface to the

Lyrical Ballads and then marvellously vindicating the poetry itself. Coleridge concentrates on the psychology of the creative process, and propounds new theories of the origins of poetic language, metre, and form, as the interpenetration of 'passion and will' (chs. XV–XVIII). Other chapters discuss the poetry of Shakespeare, *Milton, *Daniel, G. *Herbert, etc., as exemplary of true 'Imagination' and the 'language of real life'.

Biography. The earliest biographies in England were written in Latin in the Middle Ages, largely to glorify saints or to commemorate and justify secular rulers. The Renaissance emphasis on man as an individual introduced a new approach, and the first biography in English, More's *The History of King *Richard the Thirde*, written about 1513, is denigratory rather than laudatory. It used more human detail and more first-hand information, and its dramatic quality served Shakespeare who used it as a source. The classic biographies of the mid-Tudor period are W. *Roper's life of *More (Paris, 1626) and G. *Cavendish's life of Cardinal Wolsey, printed 1641. The translation of *Plutarch's *Parallel Lives* (1st cent. AD) by Sir T. *North in 1579 had considerable influence, not only on Shakespeare, whose debt is well known. I. *Walton's lives of *Donne (1641), Sir Henry *Wotton (1651), Richard *Hooker (1665), George *Herbert (1670), and Bishop Sanderson (1678) show the biographer at work as a conscious artist, and *Aubrey's *Brief Lives* displays an interest in everyday details about the obscure as well as the famous. *Clarendon included valuable biographical portraits in his *History of the Rebellion and Civil Wars* (1702–4). This period also produced the first two biographies by women: Lucy *Hutchinson and Margaret Cavendish, duchess of *Newcastle, both wrote lives of their husbands. But it was in the 18th cent. that the writing of biography came of age. The great masterpiece is Boswell's *The Life of Samuel *Johnson* (1791), but *Johnson himself was also a biographer, and his *Lives of the English Poets* (1779–81) is a classic work. His *Life of Mr Richard Savage*, previously published in 1744, is notable in that it is perhaps the first full life of a very unsuccessful man. The 19th cent. produced many biographies, but their authors were inhibited by a growing stress on 'seriousness' and respectability, and most are written in a spirit of piety in order to improve rather than to inform or entertain: the moral purpose of *Smiles's *Lives of the Engineers* (1861–2), for example, is readily apparent. A distinguished exception is Mrs *Gaskell's biography of her friend Charlotte *Brontë (1857), which involved its author in some scandal despite her efforts to abide by Victorian standards of reticence. Even more exceptional for its age was *Froude's life of *Carlyle, the frankness of which caused uproar.

Biographers on the whole remained timidly unwilling to risk such opprobrium until *Strachey's *Eminent Victorians* (1918) attacked Victorianism itself through its great institutions (the Church, the Public School, the Empire). The way was paved for the psychological, analytical approach of Strachey's many imitators and successors. The last decades have witnessed what has been described as the Golden Age of biography; *Shelley's biographer, Richard Holmes, has detected what he describes as 'the rise to power of a new literary genre', a view endorsed by R. *Gittings, biographer of *Keats and *Hardy, in his *The Nature of Biography* (1978). Classics of the new genre include, notably, R. *Ellmann's *Joyce (1959), George Painter's Proust (2 vols, 1959, 1965), Leon Edel's Henry *James (5 vols, 1953–72), and M. *Holroyd's Lytton Strachey (2 vols, 1967–8).

BION (*c*.100 BC), a Greek pastoral poet who is reputed to have been born in Smyrna. His best-known work is a lament for Adonis, which was imitated by Ronsard and other continental poets and of which echoes can be found in Shakespeare's *Venus and Adonis*. Keats's *Hyperion* is indebted to its picture of Adonis and it served as one of Shelley's models for *Adonais*. *Bridges's *Achilles in Scyros* took some of its detail from Bion's idyll.

Birnam Wood, see MACBETH.

Biron, see BEROWNE.

BIRRELL, Augustine (1850–1933), chief secretary for Ireland, 1907–16, made his name as an author with a volume of lightweight essays, *Obiter Dicta* (1884), which he followed with other essays and works on *Hazlitt (1902), *Marvell (1905), and others.

Birthday Party, The, see PINTER, H.

BISHOP, Elizabeth (1911–79), American poet, educated at Vassar, where she met Marianne *Moore, with whose work her own has much affinity. The titles of some of her volumes (*North and South*, 1946; *Questions of Travel*, 1965; *Geography III*, 1976) reflect her preoccupation with place and movement, and her verse is reticent, objective, spare yet colloquial. Her *Complete Poems 1927–1979* appeared in 1983.

'Bishop Blougram's Apology', a poem by R. Browning, included in *Men and Women*.

BLACK, William (1841–98), Scottish novelist, an early member of the *'Kailyard School', whose first triumph was *A Daughter of Heth* (1871) followed by *The Strange Adventures of a Phaeton* (1872), and many others.

Blackacre, The Widow, a character in Wycherley's *The Plain Dealer*.

Black Beauty, see SEWELL, A.; also CHILDREN'S LITERATURE.

Black Book of Carmarthen, The, a 12th-cent. Welsh manuscript containing a collection of ancient Welsh poetry, interesting for references to King *Arthur.

Black British Literature, a term applied to literature produced by black British writers, who are frequently held to include writers of Afro-Caribbean descent, and also of Asian and other non-white, non-Anglo-Saxon origins.

The earliest black British writers belong to the 18th cent. *The Letters of the Late Ignatius Sancho* (1782, ed. P. Edwards, 1968), in which his correspondence with *Garrick and *Sterne shows his awareness of political issues, contribute to the debate about slavery and the status of the African; Ottobah Cugoano's autobiographical *Thoughts and Sentiments* (1787) has anti-slavery passages which may be the work of another hand, or, more probably, be largely dependent on secondary material; *The Interesting Narrative of the Life of Olaudah Equiano* (1789) is considered the most literary achievement of the three. Sake Deen Mahomed's *Travels* (Cork, 1794), depicts his life in India before his arrival in the British Isles in 1784.

Mary Seacole's *Adventures* (1857; republished in 1984 as *Wonderful Adventures of Mrs Seacole in many lands*, ed. Z. Alexander and A. Dewjee) include an account of her early life in Jamaica and of her brave and voluntary service to Britain during the Crimean War.

Black British writing has flourished in the second half of the 20th cent. in a wide variety of traditional and experimental forms. Writers include Nirad C. Chaudhuri (1897–), Bengali author and journalist, perhaps best known for *The Autobiography of an Unknown Indian* (1951); British Guiana-born novelists E. A. Mittelholzer (1909–65), R. A. K. Heath (1926–), and W. *Harris; George Lamming (1927–); V. S. *Naipaul and his novelist brother Shiva Naipaul (1945–86); novelist Samuel Selvon (1923–) from Trinidad; novelists K. *Markandaya and Salman Rushdie (1947–), both born in India; playwrights Michael Abbensetts (1938–), born in British Guiana, and Mustapha Matura (1939–) from Trinidad; Nigerian-born novelist Buchi Emecheta (1944–); and West Indian-born poets J. *Berry, E. A. Markham (1939–), and Linton Kwesi Johnson (1952–).

Black Dwarf, The, a novel by Sir W. *Scott, in *Tales of My Landlord*, 1st series, published 1816.

Blackfriars Theatre was built within the boundaries of the old Dominican monastery lying between Ludgate Hill and the river. The first theatre on the site was adapted for perform-ances by Richard Farrant in 1576; the second, adapted by J. *Burbage in 1597, reverted to his son R. *Burbage in 1608. Shakespeare had a share in the new company that performed there. The building was demolished in 1655.

BLACKMORE, R(ichard) D(odderidge) (1825–1900), published several volumes of poems and translations from *Theocritus and *Virgil, but his fame rests almost entirely on one of his novels, *Lorna Doone* (1869). He wrote 13 other novels, including *Cradock Nowell* (1866), *The Maid of Sker* (1872), *Alice Lorraine* (1875), and *Springhaven* (1887). The great excellence of these pastoral tales is the intricacy of their descriptions of lovingly-observed climate, wildlife, and vegetation.

Black Mountain Poets, a group of poets associated with Black Mountain College, an experimental liberal arts college founded in 1933 near Asheville, NC, which became in the early 1950s a centre of anti-academic poetic revolt. A leading figure was Charles Olson (1910–70), rector of the college from 1951 to 1956, whose *Projective Verse* (1950) was a form of manifesto, laying much emphasis on the dynamic energy of the spoken word and phrase and attacking the domination of syntax, rhyme, and metre. His students and followers included R. *Creeley, Robert Duncan (1919–), and Denise Levertov (1923–). The *Black Mountain Review* (1954–7; edited by Creeley) also published work by Allen Ginsberg (1926–) and *Kerouac, thus heralding the *Beat Generation.

Blackpool, Stephen, a character in Dickens's *Hard Times*.

Black Prince, The (1330–76), a name given (apparently by 16th-cent. chroniclers) to Edward, the eldest son of Edward III.

BLACKSTONE, Sir William (1723–80), became the first Vinerian professor of English law at Oxford in 1758 and lectured there until 1766; his annual lectures became the basis of his *Commentaries on the Laws of England* (4 vols, 1765–9) which exerted a powerful influence and is still regarded as a classic.

BLACKWOOD, Algernon (1869–1951), is chiefly remembered for his stories of the psychic and macabre. *The Empty House and other Ghost Stories* appeared in 1906 and more than 30 books followed, culminating in *Tales of the Uncanny and Supernatural* (1949).

BLACKWOOD, William (1776–1834), Scots publisher, founder of the firm of William Blackwood and Son, and of *Blackwood's (Edinburgh) Magazine*. He published Galt's *The Ayrshire Legatees*. His sons, in turn, became editors of *Blackwood's*.

Blackwood's Magazine (1817–1980), or 'the Maga', was an innovating monthly periodical begun by W. *Blackwood as a Tory rival to the Whiggish *Edinburgh Review*. It began in April 1817 as *The Edinburgh Monthly Magazine* and in October that year continued as *Blackwood's Edinburgh Magazine* until Dec. 1905; from Jan. 1906 onwards it became *Blackwood's Magazine*. The first editors were shortly replaced by *Lockhart, John *Wilson, and J. *Hogg, who gave the 'Maga' its forceful partisan tone. Its notoriety was early established with the publication in 1817 of the so-called *Chaldee MS*, in which many leading Edinburgh figures were pilloried; and with the beginning, also in 1817, of the long series of attacks on the *'Cockney School of Poetry', directed chiefly against Leigh *Hunt, *Keats, and *Hazlitt. *Blackwood's* gave considerable support to *Wordsworth, *Shelley, *De Quincey, *Mackenzie, *Galt, Sir W. *Scott, and others, and published the popular series *Noctes Ambrosianae*.

BLAIR, Eric, see ORWELL, G.

BLAIR, Hugh (1718–1800), Scottish divine and professor of rhetoric in Edinburgh, is remembered for his famous sermons (5 vols, 1777–1801) and his *Lectures on Rhetoric and Belles Lettres* (2 vols, 1784). He was a defender of *Macpherson; his *Critical Dissertation on the Poems of Ossian* (1763) found that *Fingal* possessed 'all the essential requisites of a true and regular epic'.

BLAIR, Robert (1699–1746), published in 1743 *The Grave*, a didactic poem of the *graveyard school, consisting of some 800 lines of blank verse. It celebrates the horrors of death, the solitude of the tomb, the pains of bereavement. It was illustrated by *Blake.

BLAKE, William (1757–1827), did not go to school, but was apprenticed to James Basire, engraver, and then became a student at the *Royal Academy. From 1779 he was employed as an engraver by the bookseller J. *Johnson. *Flaxman, a follower of *Swedenborg, deeply influenced Blake, and introduced him to the progressive intellectual circle of the Revd A. S. Mathew and his wife (which included Mrs *Barbauld, H. *More, and Mrs E. *Montagu); Mathew and Flaxman financed the publication of Blake's first volume, *Poetical Sketches* (1783). In 1784, with help from Mrs Mathew, he set up a print shop at 27 Broad Street, and at about the same period wrote the satirical *An Island in the Moon*. He engraved and published his *Songs of Innocence* in 1789, and also *The Book of Thel*, both works which manifest the early phases of his highly distinctive mystic vision, and in which he embarks on the evolution of his personal mythology; years later (in *Jerusalem*) he was to state, through the character Los, 'I must Create a System, or be enslav'd by another Man's', words which have been taken by some to apply to his own need to escape from the fetters of 18th-cent. versification, as well as from the materialist philosophy (as he conceived it) of the *Enlightenment, and a Puritanical or repressive interpretation of Christianity. The ambiguity of the much-interpreted *Book of Thel* heralds the increasing complexity of his other works which include *Tiriel* (written 1789, pub. 1874), which introduces the theme of the blind tyrannic father, 'the king of rotten wood, and of the bones of death', that reappears in different forms in many poems; *The Marriage of Heaven and Hell* (engraved *c*.1790–3), his principal prose work; and the revolutionary works *The French Revolution* (1791); *America: A Prophecy* (1793); and *Visions of the Daughters of Albion* (1793), in which he develops his attitude of revolt against authority, combining political fervour (he had met *Paine at Johnson's) and visionary ecstasy. By this time Blake had already established his poetic range; the long, flowing lines and violent energy of the verse combine with phrases of terse and aphoristic clarity, and he was once more to demonstrate his command of the lyric in *Songs of Experience* (1794) which include 'Tyger! Tyger! burning bright', 'O Rose thou art sick', and other of his more accessible pieces.

Meanwhile the Blakes had moved to Lambeth in 1790; there he evolved his mythology further in *The Book of *Urizen* (1794); *Europe, A Prophecy* (1794); *The Song of *Los* (1795); *The Book of Ahania* (1795); *The Book of Los* (1795); and *The Four Zoas* (written and revised 1797–1804). In 1800 he moved to Felpham, Sussex, where he worked for his friend and patron *Hayley, and on *Milton* (1804–8). In 1803 he returned to London, to work on *Milton* and *Jerusalem: the Emanation of the Giant Albion* (written and etched, 1804–20). In 1805 he was commissioned by R. H. Cromek to produce a set of drawings for R. *Blair's poem *The Grave*, but Cromek defaulted on the contract, and Blake earned neither the money nor the public esteem he had hoped for, and found his designs engraved and weakened by another hand. This was symptomatic of the disappointment of his later years. Both his poetry and his art had failed to find a sympathetic audience, and a lifetime of hard work had not brought him riches or even much comfort. His last years were passed in obscurity, although he continued to attract the interest and admiration of younger artists, and a commission in 1821 from the painter John Linnell produced his well known illustrations for the Book of Job, published in 1826. A later poem, 'The Everlasting Gospel', written about 1818, shows undiminished power and attack; it presents Blake's own version of Jesus, in a manner that recalls the paradoxes of *The Marriage of Heaven and Hell*, attacking the conventional 'Creeping Jesus', gentle, humble, and chaste, and stressing his rebellious nature.

At Blake's death, general opinion held that he had been, if gifted, insane. It was not until A. *Gilchrist's biography of 1863 that interest began to grow. This was followed by an appreciation by *Swinburne (1868) and by W. M. *Rossetti's edition of 1874, which added new poems to the canon and established his reputation, at least as a lyric poet; his rediscovered engravings considerably influenced the development of *Art Nouveau. In 1893 *Yeats produced with E. J. Ellis a three-vol. edition, with a memoir and an interpretation of the mythology, and the 20th cent. has seen an enormous increase in interest. The bibliographical studies and editions of G. *Keynes, culminating in *The Complete Writings of William Blake* (1966, 2nd edn), have added greatly to knowledge of both the man and his works, revealing him not only as an apocalyptic visionary but also as a writer of ribald and witty epigrams, a critic of spirit and originality, and an independent thinker who found his own way of resisting the orthodoxies of his age.

Recently, Blake has had a particularly marked influence on the *Beat Generation and the English poets of the *Underground movement, hailed by both as a liberator.

Blandamour, in Spenser's *Faerie Queene*, Bk IV, a 'jollie youthfull knight'.

Blank Verse, verse without rhyme, especially the iambic pentameter of unrhymed heroic, the regular measure of English dramatic and epic poetry, first used by *Surrey *c*.1540.

Blast, see VORTICISM.

Blatant Beast, in Spenser's *Faerie Queene*, Bk VI, a monster, the personification of the calumnious voice of the world, begotten of Envy and Detraction. Sir *Calidore pursues it, overcomes it and chains it up. But finally it breaks the chain, 'So now he raungeth through the world againe.' Cf. QUESTING BEAST.

BLATCHFORD, Robert Peel Glanville (1851–1943), journalist and socialist, was one of the founders of the Manchester Fabian Society in 1890. In 1891, with four colleagues, he started *The Clarion,* a socialist weekly which ran until 1932, in which appeared his series of articles, *Merrie England*; these appeared as a book in 1893 and made many converts to the cause of Socialism. His autobiography, *My Eighty Years,* appeared in 1931.

BLAVATSKY, Madame Helena Petrovna (1831–91), a Russian who became interested in spiritualism in New York in 1873, and in 1875 founded, with Col. H. S. Olcott and W. Q. Judge, the Theosophical Society. It aimed to promote universal brotherhood, the study of Eastern literature and religion, and research into the unfamiliar laws of nature and the latent faculties of man. Despite widespread scepticism about her powers, she had many followers, including A. *Besant and *Yeats. See SOCIETY FOR PSYCHICAL RESEARCH.

Bleak House, a novel by *Dickens, published in monthly parts 1852–3.

The book contains a vigorous satire on the abuses of the old court of Chancery, the delays and costs of which brought misery and ruin on its suitors. The tale centres in the fortunes of an uninteresting couple, Richard Carstone, a futile youth, and his amiable cousin Ada Clare. They are wards of the court in the case of Jarndyce and Jarndyce, concerned with the distribution of an estate. The wards are taken to live with their kind elderly relative John Jarndyce. They fall in love and secretly marry. The weak Richard, lured by the will-o'-the-wisp of the fortune that is to be his when the case is settled, sinks gradually to ruin and death, and the case of Jarndyce and Jarndyce comes suddenly to an end on the discovery that the costs have absorbed the whole estate in dispute.

Ada has for a companion Esther Summerson, a supposed orphan, one of Dickens's saints, and the narrative is partly supposed to be from her pen.

Sir Leicester Dedlock is devotedly attached to his beautiful wife. Lady Dedlock hides a dreadful secret: before her marriage she has loved a certain Captain Hawdon and has become the mother of a daughter, whom she believes dead. Hawdon is supposed to have perished at sea. In fact the daughter lives in the person of Esther Summerson, and Hawdon in that of a penniless scrivener. Lady Dedlock discovers the fact of his existence, and the cunning old lawyer Tulkinghorn is alerted to the existence of a mystery. Lady Dedlock's inquiries bring her, through the medium of a wretched crossing-sweeper, Jo, to the burial-ground where her former lover's miserable career has just ended. Jo's unguarded revelation of his singular experience with this veiled lady sets Tulkinghorn on the track, until he possesses all the facts and tells Lady Dedlock that he is going to expose her next day to her husband. That night Tulkinghorn is murdered. Bucket, the detective, presently reveals to the Baronet what Tulkinghorn had discovered, and arrests a former French maid of Lady Dedlock, who has committed the murder. Lady Dedlock flies from the house in despair, and is found dead near the grave of her lover.

Much of the story is occupied with Esther's devotion to John Jarndyce; her acceptance of his offer of marriage from a sense of duty and gratitude, though she loves a young doctor, Woodcourt; Jarndyce's surrender of her to Woodcourt.

There are a host of interesting minor characters, including Harold Skimpole (drawn 'in the light externals of character' from Leigh *Hunt), who disguises his utter selfishness under an assumption of childish irresponsibility; Mrs Jellyby, who sacrifices her family to her selfish addiction to professional philanthropy; Jo, the crossing-sweeper, who is chivvied by the police to his death; Chadband, the pious, eloquent humbug; Turveydrop, the model of deportment; Krook, the 'chancellor' of the rag and bone department, who dies of spontaneous combustion; Guppy, the lawyer's clerk; Guster, the poor slavey; the law-stationer Snagsby; Miss Flite, the little lunatic lady who haunts the Chancery courts; and Jarndyce's friend, the irascible and generous Boythorn (drawn from W. S. *Landor).

Blefuscu, in Swift's *Gulliver's Travels*, an island separated from Lilliput by a narrow channel.

Blenheim, Battle of (1704), at which Marlborough defeated the French and Bavarians, was celebrated in poems by *Addison (*The Campaign*, 1705) and *Southey. Southey's version ('The Battle of Blenheim', 1798) is a sharply anti-militaristic ballad in which old Kaspar describes Marlborough's victory to his grandchildren, Peterkin and Wilhelmine; in spite of the bloodshed and carnage of the battle, it was (he repeatedly and ironically assures them) 'a famous victory'.

'Blessed Damozel, The', a poem by D. G. *Rossetti, of which the first version appeared in *The Germ* (1850); many revised versions appeared subsequently.

In this poem, heavily influenced by *Dante, Rossetti describes the blessed damozel leaning out from the ramparts of Heaven, watching the worlds below and the souls mounting to God, and praying for union with her earthly lover in the shadow of the 'living mystic tree'. One of his earliest and most influential poems, it shows the *Pre-Raphaelite interest in medieval sacramental symbolism (she has three lilies in her hand, seven stars in her hair, and a white rose in her robe) and Rossetti's concept of an ideal Platonic love, which he was to develop in later works. He also painted the same subject in later years.

Blifil, Master, a character in Fielding's *Tom Jones*.

Blimber, Dr, and his daughter Cornelia, characters in Dickens's *Dombey and Son*.

Blind Beggar of Bethnal Green, The, see BEGGAR'S DAUGHTER OF BEDNALL GREEN, THE.

Blind Harry, see HENRY THE MINSTREL.

Blithedale Romance, The, a novel by *Hawthorne, published 1852, based on Hawthorne's experience at the Brook Farm *Transcendental community.

It is narrated by a poet, Miles Coverdale, who visits Blithedale Farm, near Boston, where he meets the exotic Zenobia (said to be based on Margaret *Fuller), the philanthropic, fierce social reformer Hollingsworth, and the gentle Priscilla. Coverdale broods on Fourier, *Carlyle, and *Emerson, while both the women (who turn out to be half-sisters) fall in love with Hollingsworth; Zenobia is rejected and drowns herself, Hollingsworth marries Priscilla, and Coverdale remains a sceptical, solitary observer of mankind's aspirations and its disappointments.

BLIXEN, Karen Christentze, *née* Dinesen (1885–1962), Danish writer, who wrote mainly in English, under the name of 'Isak Dinesen'. Her first major publication, *Seven Gothic Tales* (1934), was followed by several other collections which won her a considerable international reputation. *Out of Africa* (1937) is the story of her years in Kenya where she and her husband ran a coffee plantation.

BLONDEL DE NESLE, a French *trouvère of the late 12th cent. Legend makes him a friend of *Richard Cœur de Lion. Blondel sat under a window of the castle in Austria where Richard was imprisoned (1192) and sang a song in French that he and the king had composed together; half-way through he paused and Richard completed it. Blondel returned to England and told of the king's whereabouts.

Bloody Brother, The, or *Rollo, Duke of Normandy*, a play by J. *Fletcher, B. *Jonson, G. *Chapman, and P. *Massinger, performed c.1616, published 1639. It was very popular in the 17th cent. It contains the lyric 'Take, oh take those lips away', which occurs with certain changes in *Measure for Measure*.

Bloom, Leopold Paula, and his wife Molly, characters in Joyce's *Ulysses*.

BLOOMFIELD, Leonard (1887–1949), an American linguist whose book *Language* (1933) was a major influence on the development of 'Structural Linguistics', putting forward the idea that the analysis appropriate to a particular language must be inferred from its own structure, not brought to bear on it from general linguistic principles. This approach, characterized as 'Bloomfieldian', prevailed in some circles up to the 1950s; it was opposed by *Chomsky, though the origins of his analyses of grammar lie in Bloomfield's system.

BLOOMFIELD, Robert (1766–1823), worked as a farm labourer, then as a shoemaker in London, enduring extreme poverty. He is remembered as the author of the poem *The Farmer's Boy* (1800), illustrated with engravings by *Bewick, which related the life of Giles, an orphan farm labourer, throughout the seasons.

Bloomsbury Group, the name given to a group of friends who began to meet about 1905–6; its original centre was 46 Gordon Square, Bloomsbury, which became in 1904 the home of V. Bell and V. *Woolf (both then unmarried). It was to include, amongst others, *Keynes, *Strachey, D. *Garnett, D. Grant, E. M. *Forster, and R. *Fry. This informal association, based on friendship and interest in the arts, derived many of its attitudes from G. E. *Moore's *Principia Ethica*. Its members, many of whom were in conscious revolt against the artistic, social, and sexual restrictions of Victorian society, profoundly affected the development of the avant-garde in art and literature in Britain. Bloomsbury was attacked by *Leavis as dilettante and élitist, and its aims and achievements fell temporarily out of favour, but the late 1960s witnessed a great revival of interest and the publication of many critical and biographical studies (notably *Holroyd's two-volume life of Strachey, 1967–8) seeking to re-assess Bloomsbury's influence.

Blot in the 'Scutcheon, A, a tragedy in blank verse by R. *Browning, published in 1843 as no. V of *Bells and Pomegranates*. It was produced at Drury Lane in 1843, ran for three nights, and caused a final rift between Browning and *Macready; the quarrel was instrumental in Browning's decision to write no more stage plays.

Blougram, Bishop, see BISHOP BLOUGRAM'S APOLOGY.

BLOUNT, Martha (1690–1762), and her sister Teresa (b. 1688), were close friends of *Pope, who met them *c.*1705. Later he addressed his attentions more to Martha, who was rumoured to be his mistress. He dedicated his *Epistle . . . on the Characters of Women* (*Moral Essays*) to Martha, and (almost certainly) 'To a Young Lady with the Works of Voiture'; 'To the Same on her Leaving the Town after the Coronation' was probably addressed to Teresa.

Blouzelinda, a shepherdess in *The Shepherd's Week* by J. Gay.

Blue Beard, a popular tale in an oriental setting, from the French of *Perrault, translated by Robert Samber (?1729).

A man of great wealth, but disfigured by a blue beard, and of evil reputation because he has married several wives who have disappeared, asks for the hand of Fatima. She is prevailed on to marry him. Blue Beard leaves the keys of all his treasures to his young wife, but strictly enjoins her not to make use of the key of a particular room. Overcome by curiosity, she opens the room, and finds in it the bodies of Blue Beard's previous wives. Horror-struck, she drops the key, which becomes indelibly stained with blood. Blue Beard returns, discovers her disobedience and orders her death. She begs for a little delay, 'Sister Anne' sees her brothers arriving, and Blue Beard is killed before he can carry out the sentence.

*Lang, in *Perrault's Popular Tales* (1888), discusses the many parallel stories found in other countries.

Blue Lagoon, The, a novel by H. de V. *Stacpoole.

Blue Stocking Circle, Blue Stocking Ladies: an informal group of intelligent, learned, and sociable women, which flourished in London in the second half of the 18th cent. The origin of the name almost certainly lies with the stockings of Benjamin Stillingfleet, too poor to possess fine evening clothes, who came to the circle's evening receptions in his blue worsted stockings. The chief hostesses and female members were Mrs *Vesey, Mrs *Montagu, Mrs *Carter, Mrs *Chapone, Mrs *Boscawen, Mrs *Delany, and, later, H. *More. As described later by Hannah More, the sole purpose of a Blue Stocking evening was to be conversation. Learning was to be given free expression, but not be disfigured by pedantry; politics, scandal, and swearing were not allowed. The company was divided evenly between men and women; among the most famous of the men in regular attendance were *Garrick, Horace *Walpole, Dr *Johnson, *Beattie, *Boswell, Sir Joshua *Reynolds, S. *Richardson, and *Lyttelton. Hannah More wrote a poem *Bas Bleu* (1786), describing the charm of Blue Stocking society, and characterizing the chief of her friends. The expression 'Blue Stocking' seems to have been applied in the 18th cent. both affectionately and derisively, but it is now used only pejoratively to describe a pedantic, earnest woman.

Blumine, in Carlyle's *Sartor Resartus*, the lady with whom Herr *Teufelsdröckh falls in love.

BLUNDEN, Edmund Charles (1896–1974), poet and scholar. In 1914 he experienced war in the trenches and later wrote poems, such as 'Third Ypres', and 'Report on Experience', now highly regarded. In 1920 he published a small edition of MS poems of *Clare. Volumes of poems largely of rural life include *The Waggoner* (1920), *The Shepherd* (1922), and *English Poems* (1925). His best-known work, *Undertones of War* (1928), describes the double destruction of man and nature in Flanders. His first *Collected Poems* appeared in 1930, as did a biography of Leigh

*Hunt. In 1931 he produced a collected edition of the work of W. *Owen. Further volumes of his own poems were collected as *Poems 1930–1940*; a study of *Hardy appeared in 1941, and a biography of *Shelley in 1946. He published a volume of poems, *After the Bombing* (1950), more contemplative and searching than his previous work. In 1954 he produced an edition of the almost unknown I. *Gurney. He was appointed professor of poetry at Oxford in 1966.

BLUNT, Wilfred Scawen (1840–1922), poet, diplomat, traveller, anti-imperialist, and Arabist. His first volume of poetry, *Sonnets and Songs by Proteus* (1875, subsequently revised), passionately addresses various women. It was followed by several other volumes of verse, which include love lyrics, evocations of the Sussex countryside, and adaptations from the Arabic. He also wrote and agitated in support of Egyptian, Indian, and Irish independence, thus earning the approval of G. B. *Shaw; a brief spell in an Irish prison inspired his sonnet sequence *In Vinculis* (1889). *My Diaries* appeared in 2 vols, 1919–20.

BOADICEA, Bonduca, corrupt forms of the name Boudicca, queen of the Iceni in the east of Britain, who led a revolt against the Romans but was finally defeated by Suetonius Paulinus in AD 61 and killed herself.

Boar's Head Inn, celebrated in connection with *Falstaff, was in Eastcheap, and according to H. B. Wheatley (*London, Past and Present*, 1891) was 'destroyed in the Great Fire, rebuilt immediately after, and finally demolished . . . in 1831'.

Bobadill, Captain, the boastful, cowardly soldier in Jonson's *Every Man in his Humour*, a part several times acted by *Dickens in the 1840s.

Bob and Wheel, a metrical pattern used, for example, in *Sir *Gawain and the Green Knight*, at the end of the strophes of the main narrative. The 'bob' is a short tag with one stress and the following 'wheel' is a quatrain of short lines rhyming ABAB:

> . . . And al waz hol3 inwith,   nobot an olde cave
> Or a crevisse of an olde cragge,   he coupe hit no3t deme
> wiþ spelle.
> 'We! Lorde,' quoþ þe gentyle kny3t,
> Wheþer þis be þe grene chapelle?
> Here my3t aboute mydny3t
> þe dele his matynnes tell!'
>
> (*Sir Gawain*, ll. 2,182–9)

Here the words 'with spelle' form the 'bob', leading into the 'wheel' of the quatrain.

BOCCACCIO, Giovanni (1313–75), Italian writer and humanist. His chief works were *The Decameron; Filocolo*, a prose romance embodying the story of *Floris and Blanchefleour; *Filostrato*, a poem on the story of Troilus and Cressida; *Teseida*, a poem on the story of Theseus, Palamon, and Arcite, which was translated by *Chaucer in the 'Knight's Tale'; and *Fiammetta*, a psychological romance in prose. He also wrote a number of encyclopaedic works in Latin which were widely read in England.

Boccaccio is an important figure in the history of literature, particularly of narrative fiction, and among the poets who found inspiration in his works were Chaucer, *Lydgate, Shakespeare, *Dryden, *Keats, *Longfellow, and *Tennyson.

BODEL, Jean, see MATTER OF BRITAIN, FRANCE, ROME.

Bodleian Library, see BODLEY and LIBRARIES.

BODLEY, Sir Thomas (1545–1613), English diplomatic representative at The Hague (1588–96). He devoted the rest of his life to founding at Oxford the great Bodleian Library (see LIBRARIES). It was opened in 1602.

BOECE, see BOETHIUS.

BOECE, or **BOËTHIUS,** Hector (?1465–1536), published a Latin history of Scotland to the accession of James III (1526), which included many fabulous narratives, among others that of Macbeth and Duncan, which passed into *Holinshed's chronicles and thence to Shakespeare.

BOETHIUS, Anicius Manlius Severinus (c.475–525), was born at Rome and was consul in 510, in favour with the Goth Theodoric the Great who ruled over the city; but he incurred the suspicion of plotting against Gothic rule, was imprisoned and finally cruelly executed in 525 at Pavia. In prison he wrote the *De Consolatione Philosophiae*, his most celebrated work, which was translated into English in the 890s by *Alfred and in almost every generation up to the 18th cent. notably by *Chaucer (as *Boece*) and by *Elizabeth I into florid, *inkhorn language. It was translated into French by Jean de Meun, and was one of the most influential books of the Middle Ages. It is now generally believed that he was a Christian, though this is rarely explicit in the *Consolation* whose philosophy is broadly *Neoplatonic. Its form is 'Menippean Satire', i.e. alternating prose and verse. The verse often consists of a story told by *Ovid or *Horace, used to illustrate the philosophy being expounded. The influence of the book is found everywhere in the work of Chaucer and his 15th-cent. followers. Before the Middle Ages, Boethius was of most importance for his translations of and commentaries on *Aristotle which provided the main part of what was known of Aristotle before the recovery of most of his writings from Arabic scholars in the 12th cent.

Boffin, Mr and Mrs, characters in Dickens's *Our Mutual Friend*.

BOHN, Henry George (1796–1884), publisher and bookseller. His *Guinea Catalogue* (1841) is an important early bibliographical work. In 1846 he started his popular *Standard Library* (followed by the *Scientific Library*, *Classical Library*, *Antiquarian Library*, etc.). He translated several volumes for his 'Foreign Classics' series, compiled a *Dictionary of Quotations* (1867) and *A Bibliographical Account of the works of Shakespeare* (1864).

BOIARDO, Matteomaria (?1441–94), an Italian poet of the old chivalry, whose principal work was the unfinished *Orlando Innamorato*.

BOILEAU, Nicholas Despreaux (1636–1711), French critic and poet, and one of the major legislators of *neo-classical theory. His *Art Poétique* (1674), a four-canto poem, established canons of taste and defined principles of composition and criticism, and achieved international currency. *Dryden, *Pope, and *Addison regarded him as the supreme post-classical arbiter of literary judgement.

Bois-Guilbert, Sir Brian De, the fierce Templar in Scott's *Ivanhoe*.

Boke of the Duchesse, The, see BOOK OF THE DUCHESS, THE.

Bold, John, a character in Trollope's *The Warden*. Mrs Bold, his widow, figures prominently in its sequel, *Barchester Towers*, and in *The Last Chronicle of Barset*, where she is the wife of Dean Arabin.

Bold Stroke for a Wife, A, a comedy by Mrs *Centlivre, produced 1718.

Colonel Fainall, to win the consent of Obadiah Prim, the Quaker guardian of Anne Lovely, to his marriage with the latter, impersonates Simon Pure, 'a quaking preacher'. No sooner has he obtained it than the true Quaker arrives and proves himself 'the real Simon Pure', a phrase that was long in common use.

Boldwood, Farmer, a character in Hardy's *Far from the Madding Crowd*.

Bolingbroke, Henry, duke of Hereford, son of *John of Gaunt, deposes *Richard II in Shakespeare's play of that name, and becomes *Henry IV.

BOLINGBROKE, Henry St John, first Viscount (1678–1751), was elected to the House of Commons in 1701 and became a leading figure in the Tory party. He was appointed secretary of war in 1704; secretary of state in 1710; and in 1712 was made Viscount Bolingbroke. He took part in negotiating the Treaty of Utrecht in 1713. After the accession of George I, Bolingbroke fled to France and declared his allegiance to the Pretender, James Stuart; he was convicted of high treason and his peerage was withdrawn. Bolingbroke lived in exile in France for the next decade. In an attempt to justify his conduct in the eyes of his fellow Tories he wrote *A Letter to Sir William Wyndham* in 1717 (published posthumously 1753). In France, Bolingbroke wrote several philosophical essays which reflect the influence of *Locke. These writings provoked the outrage of Dr *Johnson and others when they were published, also posthumously (in 1754), because of their scepticism concerning religion. It has often been supposed that Pope's *An Essay on Man* (1734) was inspired by Bolingbroke's philosophical writings.

In 1723 Bolingbroke received a qualified pardon from the king, and he returned to England in 1725 to a life of political journalism in the company of *Pope, *Swift, *Gay, and *Lyttelton. In articles written for *The Craftsman* he attacked the policies and practices of the Walpole administration, deploring, in particular, the practice of 'influence' or 'corruption'. These articles were collected in two volumes as *A Dissertation upon Parties* (1735) and *Remarks on the History of England* (1743). He retired to France in 1735. From his retreat he addressed letters on the need for an active and united opposition to corruption (*A Letter on the Spirit of Patriotism*, written in 1736) and on the role of a monarch in a free government (*The Idea of a Patriot King*, written in 1738). These essays, like his earlier political writings, reflect the influence of *Machiavelli and the classical republican tradition.

Bolingbroke's many posthumous publications excited intense controversy in the decade which immediately followed his death. The political essays published in his lifetime had a more lasting influence: in England, in the movement for parliamentary reform in the 18th and 19th cents; and, in America, on the ideas of John Adams, Thomas Jefferson, and other publicists and statesmen of the revolutionary era.

BOLT, Robert Oxton (1924–), playwright, achieved his first West End success in 1957 with *Flowering Cherry* (pub. 1958). This was followed by *The Tiger and the Horse* (1960, pub. 1961) and *A Man for All Seasons* (1960, pub. 1960), his best-known work, based on the life of Sir T. *More. Other works include the screenplay of *Lawrence of Arabia* (1962), based on the exploits of T. E. *Lawrence.

Bolton, Fanny, a character in Thackeray's *Pendennis*.

Bombast, from 'cotton stuffing', a term used to describe verbose and exaggerated language.

BOND, (Thomas) Edward (1934–), playwright. His plays include *The Pope's Wedding* (performed 1962); his grim portrait of urban violence, *Saved* (1965); *Early Morning* (1969); *Lear* (1971, pub. 1972), a version of Shakespeare which stresses the play's physical cruelty; *The Sea* (1973), a black country-house comedy; *The Fool* (1975, published 1976), based on the life of *Clare; *Restoration* (1981), a Brechtian revolutionary historical drama with songs; and *Summer* (1982), set in a post-war Eastern European state. Bond's belief that violence occurs in 'situations of injustice' and that it therefore flourishes under capitalism, continues to arouse extreme responses from critics and audiences.

Bond, James, the debonair hero of the thrillers of I. *Fleming, and of their celluloid successors, repeatedly engaged, as '007, Licensed to Kill', in daring acts of espionage involving evil foreigners and dangerous and beautiful women, from which he invariably emerges triumphant.

Bondman, The, a tragi-comedy by *Massinger, acted 1623, published 1624.

One of the best of Massinger's tragi-comedies, with some well-developed characters and some fine satirical scenes, it is informed by his contempt for the arrogance of an effete aristocracy, which may well reflect Massinger's opinion of the ethics of the Jacobean court.

Bonduca, a tragedy by J. *Fletcher, probably performed 1613–14, published 1647.

It is based on the story of *Boadicea, as given by *Holinshed, but the principal character is her cousin, the wise, patriotic, chivalrous, Caratach (*Caractacus).

Bon Gaultier, the pseudonym (taken from *Rabelais) under which W. E. *Aytoun and T. *Martin published in 1845 *A Book of Ballads*, a collection of parodies and light poems. Among the authors parodied are *Tennyson (notably 'Locksley Hall', in 'The Lay of the Lovelorn') and E. B. *Browning (in 'The Rhyme of Sir Lancelot Bogle'). Martin also used the pseudonym in his contributions to *Tait's Magazine* and *Fraser's Magazine*.

Boniface, (1) the landlord of the inn in Farquhar's *The Beaux' Stratagem*; whence taken as the generic proper name of innkeepers; (2) in Scott's *The Monastery*, the abbot of Kennaquhair.

BONIFACE, St (680–755), 'the Apostle of Germany'. He was educated at a monastery in Exeter and at Nursling near Winchester. He went to Rome in 718 and, with authority from Pope Gregory II, proceeded to Germany where he preached, established monasteries, and organized the Church.

Bonnivard, see PRISONER OF CHILLON, THE.

Booby, Sir Thomas and Lady, and Squire Booby, characters in Fielding's *Joseph Andrews*.

Booker McConnell Prize for Fiction, a prize founded in 1969 and financed by Booker McConnell, a multinational conglomerate company, awarded annually to the best full-length novel by a British or Commonwealth citizen published in the previous 12 months.

Book of Martyrs, see ACTES AND MONUMENTS.

Book of St Albans, The, the last work issued by the press that was set up at St Albans about 1479, soon after *Caxton had begun to print at Westminster. It contains treatises on hawking and heraldry, and one on hunting by Dame Julians Barnes, probably the wife of the holder of the manor of Julians Barnes near St Albans. The book is a compilation, not all by one hand. (The name Juliana Berners, and her identity as abbess of Sopwell in Hertfordshire, are 18th-cent. inventions.)

Book of Snobs, The, a collection of papers by *Thackeray, which first appeared in *Punch in 1846–7 under the title *The Snobs of England by One of Themselves*, republished in 1848. Thackeray anatomized the various types of snobbery to be found in the society of the time, 'Military Snobs', 'Country Snobs', and so on.

Book of the Duchess, The, a dream-poem in 1,334 lines by *Chaucer, probably written in 1369, in octosyllabic couplets. It is believed to be an allegorical lament on the death of Blanche of Lancaster, the first wife of *John of Gaunt.

The love-lorn poet falls asleep reading the story of Ceix (Seys) and Alcyone and follows a hunting party. He meets a knight in black who laments the loss of his lady. The knight tells of her virtue and beauty and of their courtship, and in answer to the dreamer's question declares her dead. The hunting party reappears and a bell strikes twelve, awakening the poet who finds his book still in his hand. The poem, one of Chaucer's earliest works, has great charm and accomplishment. It is founded on the French tradition of the dream as a vehicle for love poetry.

Bookseller, The, see WHITAKER, J.

BOOTH, Charles (1840–1916), author of a monumental inquiry into the condition and occupations of the people of London, of which the earlier part appeared as *Labour and Life of the People* in 1889, and the whole as *Life and Labour of the People of London* in 17 vols (1891–1902). He was aided in the survey by Beatrice *Webb, who gives an account of him and his work in *My Apprenticeship* (1926) and credits him with the introduction of the Old Age Pensions Act 1908.

BOOTH, William (1829–1912), popularly known as 'General Booth', was the leader of the revivalist movement known from 1878 as the Salvation Army, which sprang from the Christian Mission which he founded in Whitechapel in 1865. G. B. Shaw's *Major Barbara* (perf. 1905) was based on first-hand knowledge of the Salvation Army.

Booth, William, the hero of Fielding's *Amelia*.

Boots Library, a circulating library (see LIBRARIES, CIRCULATING) established at the end of the 19th cent. by Nottingham businessman and philanthropist Jesse Boot (1850–1931). It catered largely for provincial and suburban subscribers, and by the mid-1930s was the largest of its kind.

Borderers, The, see WORDSWORTH, W.

Border Minstrelsy, see MINSTRELSY OF THE SCOTTISH BORDER.

BORGES, Jorge Luis (1899–1986), Argentinian writer whose short stories have had a great influence on European literature, and have been acclaimed as the earliest literary examples of *Magic Realism. He began to publish prose and verse in the 1920s, but it was the French edition of a collection of stories, *Labyrinths* (Paris, 1953), that established his international reputation. His stories tend to be labyrinthine, metaphysical, and dreamlike, and explore matters of identity, fictionality, and violence. Borges himself was influenced by his reading of English literature, notably of *Wilde, R. L. *Stevenson, and *Chesterton.

Born in Exile, a novel by G. *Gissing.

BORON, Robert de, a 12th–13th-cent. French poet who composed a trilogy (*Joseph d'Arimathie, Merlin,* and *Perceval*) in which he developed the early history of the Holy *Grail in Britain, linking it with the Arthurian tradition.

Borough, The, a poem by *Crabbe published 1810, in twenty-four 'letters', describing, with much penetration and accuracy of detail, the life, the characters, and the surroundings of the town of Aldeburgh, Suffolk. Two of the most successful tales, concerning *Peter Grimes and *Ellen Orford, were combined in *Britten's opera *Peter Grimes* (1945).

BORROW, George Henry (1803–81), edited *Celebrated Trials, and Remarkable Cases of Criminal Jurisprudence* (1825), an impressive piece of hack-work undertaken for a London publisher, and then travelled through England, France, Germany, Russia, Spain, and in the East, studying the languages of the countries he visited. He published a number of books based in part on his own life, experiences, and travels: *The Zincali, or an account of the Gypsies in Spain* (1841), *The Bible in Spain* (1834), *Lavengro* (1851), *The Romany Rye* (1857), and *Wild Wales* (1862). His works have a peculiar picaresque quality, and contain vivid portraits of the extraordinary personages he encountered; his own personality also emerges with much force. Though physically robust, he had suffered since his youth from bouts of manic depression that he referred to as 'the Horrors' which often temporarily frustrated him. In *Lavengro, The Romany Rye,* and *The Bible in Spain* fact is inextricably combined with fiction; and *Lavengro* he himself describes as 'a dream partly of study, partly of adventure'.

Bors de Ganys, Sir, in *Malory, king of Gannes, one of the three successful knights in the Quest of the Grail.

BOSCAWEN, Mrs Frances (1719–1805), the wife of Admiral Boscawen, who is traditionally supposed to have transformed Benjamin Stillingfleet's blue stockings into a name for his wife's learned and literary female friends. Hannah *More, in her poem *Bas Bleu* (1786), accords her, with Mrs *Vesey and Mrs *Montagu, the 'triple crown' as the most successful of the *Blue Stocking hostesses.

Bosola, a character in Webster's *The Duchess of Malfi*.

Bostonians, The, a novel by H. *James, published 1886.

Basil Ransom, a young lawyer fresh from Mississippi and the humiliations of the Civil War, has come north in search of a career. In Boston he calls on his cousin Olive Chancellor and her widowed sister Mrs Luna. Olive, a wealthy chill feminist, introduces him to a reformist group (acidly portrayed by James) at the house of the well-meaning Miss Birdseye. Selah Tarrant, a charlatan faith-healer and showman, is presenting his young daughter Verena. She is an 'inspirational' speaker, and while Basil Ransom is attracted by her prettiness Olive sees her as a valuable instrument for the cause. She removes Verena from her unacceptable parents and sets about her education. She attempts to instil in the girl her own loathing for men. Ransom, contemptuous of reform, opens a battle for possession of Verena. Olive, now passionately attached to the girl, tries to freeze him out. But Verena is now attracted by Ransom and frightened by Olive's intensity; she has begun to doubt her role. As she is about to make her first public appearance Verena, schooled to be the banner of the suffragette movement, is carried off by Ransom, who believes that women's highest achievement is to be agreeable to men.

BOSWELL, James (1740–95), the eldest son of Alexander Boswell, Lord Auchinleck (pron. Affleck), a Scottish judge. He reluctantly studied law at Edinburgh, Glasgow, and Utrecht, his ambition being directed towards literature and politics. He met Dr *Johnson in London on 16 May 1763; he then went to Holland and on through Europe to Italy. He met *Voltaire and *Rousseau, who inspired him with zeal for the cause of Corsican liberty, and he visited Corsica in 1765, establishing a lifelong friendship with General Paoli. On his return to Scotland he 'passed advocate' and was to practise there and in England for the rest of his life. His first substantial work, *An Account of Corsica* (1768), was followed in December of that year by a book of essays 'in favour of the brave Corsicans' edited by Boswell. Although his family remained in Scotland, Boswell visited London as frequently as possible. Johnson and Boswell made their celebrated tour of Scotland and the Hebrides in 1773, in which year Boswell was elected a member of the *Club. His *Journal of a Tour of the Hebrides* appeared in 1785. The rest of Boswell's life was devoted to an unsuccessful pursuit of a political career (he was recorder of Carlisle, 1788–90) and to the immense task of assembling materials for and composing his life of Johnson, a labour in which he was encouraged by *Malone. *The Life of Samuel *Johnson* appeared in 1791.

Botanic Garden, The, see DARWIN, E.

Bothie of Tober-na-Vuolich, The, see CLOUGH, A. H.

Bottom, Nick, the weaver in Shakespeare's *Midsummer Night's Dream.*

BOTTOMLEY, Gordon (1874–1948), poet. His first volume of poems, *The Mickle Drede*, appeared in 1896, and his work was included in E. *Marsh's first volume of *Georgian Poetry* in 1912. *Poems of Thirty Years* (1925) show the marked influence of *Shelley. Of his poetic plays *King Lear's Wife* (1915) and *Gruach* (1921) were the most successful.

BOUCICAULT (originally Boursiquot), Dion(ysius Lardner) (1820–90), playwright, achieved great success with his comedy *London Assurance* (1841), written under the pseudonym of Lee Morton. He subsequently wrote and adapted some 200 plays, including *The Corsican Brothers* (1852, from the French), *The Poor of New York* (1857), *The Collection Bawn; or the*

brides of Garryowen (1860), and *The Shaughraun* (1874). He was responsible for the introduction of a royalty from plays and copyright for dramatists in America. With the rise of realism and the emergence of *Ibsen and G. B. *Shaw, his work fell out of fashion, but it influenced *O'Casey.

BOUDICCA, see BOADICEA.

BOUILLON, Godefroi de (Godfrey of Bouillon) (d. 1100), duke of Lower Lorraine, leader of the First Crusade. He appears in Scott's *Count Robert of Paris.*

Bounderby, Josiah, a character in Dickens's *Hard Times.*

Bountiful, Lady, a character in Farquhar's *The Beaux' Stratagem.*

Bounty, The Mutiny and Piratical Seizure of H.M.S., by Sir J. *Barrow, published 1831.
HMS *Bounty*, which had been sent to the South Sea Islands to collect bread fruit trees, left Tahiti early in 1789. On 28 April of that year Fletcher Christian and others seized Lt Bligh, the commander, and cast him adrift in an open boat with eighteen members of the crew; they eventually reached Timor. Meanwhile the *Bounty* with twenty-five of the crew sailed to Tahiti, where sixteen were put ashore. These men were later arrested and many of them were drowned when HMS *Pandora* sank. Fletcher Christian, with eight of his companions and some Tahitians, settled on Pitcairn Island. There they founded a colony which was eventually taken under the protection of the British government. These famous events form part of Byron's poem *'The Island', and have been the subject of books and films.

BOWDLER, Thomas (1754–1825), published in 1818 his *Family Shakespeare*, an expurgated version of the text. Bowdler's admiration of Shakespeare was profound, but he believed that nothing 'can afford an excuse for profaneness or obscenity . . .' His method was to cut, not to substitute, adding almost nothing except prepositions and conjunctions. But the cutting is severe and he executed similar excisions on Gibbon's *Decline and Fall. His work gave rise to the verb 'to bowdlerize'.

BOWEN, Elizabeth Dorothea Cole (1899–1973), Anglo-Irish novelist and short story writer. Her novels include *The Hotel* (1927), *The House in Paris* (1935), *A World of Love* (1955), and *Eva Trout* (1969). The best-known are probably *The Death of the Heart* (1938), and *The Heat of the Day* (1949). The first is the story of Portia, a 16-year-old orphan whose dangerous innocence threatens the precarious, sophisticated London lives of her half-brother Thomas and his wife

Anna, and who is herself threatened by her love for the glamorously despairing young Eddy, a young admirer of Anna; the second centres on the tragic war-time love affair of Stella Rodney and Robert Kelway, and their reactions to the revelation, through the sinister Harrison, that the latter is a spy. The war inspired many of Elizabeth Bowen's best short stories, including 'Mysterious Kôr' (*Penguin *New Writing*, 1944); her *Collected Stories* appeared in 1980. She writes most confidently of the upper class and middle classes, but within that social range her perceptions of change are acute.

BOWEN, Marjorie, the best-known pseudonym of Gabrielle Margaret Vere Campbell (1886–1952), prolific writer of historical novels, children's stories, etc.

Bower of Bliss, The, in Spenser's *Faerie Queene* (II. xii), the home of *Acrasia, demolished by Sir *Guyon.

Bowge of Courte, The, an allegorical poem in seven-lined stanzas by *Skelton, satirizing court life (c.1498).

BOWLES, William Lisle (1762–1850), is remembered chiefly for his *Fourteen Sonnets* (1789). His work was greatly admired by *Coleridge, *Lamb, and *Southey. *Byron, however, describes him as 'the maudlin prince of mournful sonneteers', and was roused to further anger by the strictures on *Pope in Bowles's edition of 1806.

Bowling, Tom, (1) a character in Smollett's *Roderick Random*; (2) see DIBDIN, C.

BOWRA, (Sir Cecil) Maurice (1898–1971), scholar and critic, from 1922 a fellow and from 1938 until 1970 warden of Wadham College, Oxford, where his wit, hospitality, and energy made him a legendary figure. Bowra published various works on and translations of Greek literature, notably *Pindar, and edited *The Oxford Book of Greek Verse in Translation* (1938) and two books of Russian verse in translation (1943, 1948).

Bows, Mr, a character in Thackeray's *Pendennis*.

Bowzybeus, a drunken swain, the subject of the last pastoral in *The Shepherd's Week* by J. Gay.

Box and Cox, a farce by J. M. *Morton, adapted from two French vaudevilles, published 1847. Box is a journeyman printer, Cox a journeyman hatter. Mrs Bouncer, a lodging-house keeper, has let the same room to both, taking advantage of the fact that Box is out all night and Cox out all day to conceal from each the existence of the other. Discovery comes when Cox unexpectedly gets a holiday. Indignation follows, and complications connected with a widow to whom both have proposed marriage; and finally a general reconciliation.

BOYLE, Charles, see PHALARIS, EPISTLES OF.

BOYLE, John, fifth earl of Orrery (1707–62), son of Charles Boyle (1676–1731), was an intimate friend of *Swift, *Pope, and Dr *Johnson. His *Remarks on the Life and Writings of Dr Jonathan Swift* (1751) were written in a series of letters to his son Hamilton at Christ Church, Oxford; they give a critical account of Swift's character, his life, his relations with Stella and Vanessa and his friendship with Pope and others, and discuss his works.

BOYLE, Robert (1627–91), became the dominant figure in English science between F. *Bacon and I. *Newton. His experiments on air led to the formulation of 'Boyle's Law'. Boyle's 'corpuscularianism', a rendering of the mechanical philosophy, exercised great influence throughout Europe. Among his more popular scientific writings *The Sceptical Chymist* (1661) is the best known and *The Origin of Forms and Qualities* (1666) anticipates much of the philosophy of *Locke. His *Occasional Reflections* (1665) supplied Swift with one of the central story-lines in *Gulliver's Travels*. In his Will he made provision for the foundation of a series of annual lectures in defence of natural and revealed religion. The first series of Boyle Lectures was delivered by Richard *Bentley in 1692. The influence of these lectures was at its peak during the first 20 years.

BOYLE, Roger, first earl of Orrery (1621–79), author of *Parthenissa* (1654–65), the first English romance in the style of La Calprenède and M. de Scudéry, which deals with the prowess and vicissitudes of Artabanes, a Median prince, and his rivalry with Surena, an Arabian prince, for the love of Parthenissa. His heroic play *Mustapha* (1665) is based on Mlle de Scudéry's *Ibrahim* and the history of *Knolles.

Boyle Lectures, see BOYLE, ROBERT.

'Boy stood on the burning deck, The', see HEMANS, F. D.

Boythorn, a character in Dickens's *Bleak House*.

BOZ, the pseudonym used by *Dickens in his contributions to the *Morning Chronicle* and in the *Pickwick Papers*.

Brabantio, in Shakespeare's *Othello*, the father of Desdemona.

BRACEGIRDLE, Anne (?1673/4–1748), a famous actress, the friend of *Congreve, to the success of whose comedies on stage she largely contributed. She was finally eclipsed by Mrs *Oldfield in 1707 and retired from the stage.

Brachiano, a character in Webster's *The White Devil*.

BRACTON, BRATTON, or **BRETTON,** Henry de (d. 1268), a judge and ecclesiastic, was author of *De Legibus et Consuetudinibus Angliae*, the first attempt at a complete treatise on the laws and customs of England.

Bradamante, in *Orlando Innamorato* and *Orlando Furioso*, a maiden warrior, sister of Rinaldo. *Spenser owed much to Bradamante in fashioning his Britomart in *The Faerie Queene*.

BRADBURY, Malcolm Stanley (1932–), critic and novelist, became professor of American studies at the University of East Anglia in 1970. His critical works include *Possibilities: essays on the state of the novel* (1973) and (with J. W. McFarlane) *Modernism* (1976), and studies of E. *Waugh (1962) and *Bellow (1982). His first three novels are satirical *Campus novels: *Eating People is Wrong* (1959) is set in a second-rate redbrick provincial university; *Stepping Westward* (1965) is set in the mid-west of America; and *The History Man* (1975) is set in the new plate-glass university of Watermouth, where the ambivalent figure of the ambitious Dr Howard Kirk manipulates wife, colleagues, students, lovers, and academic politics with a fine sense of the historical moment. *Rates of Exchange* (1983) is a witty and satiric commentary on cultural exchange.

BRADDON, Mary Elizabeth (1837–1915), won fame and fortune with her sensational novel, *Lady Audley's Secret* (1862). The bigamous pretty blonde heroine, who deserts her child, murders her husband, and contemplates poisoning her second husband, shocked Mrs *Oliphant who credited Miss Braddon as 'the inventor of the fair-haired demon of modern fiction'. The novel has been dramatized, filmed, and translated. She published a further 74 inventive, lurid novels including the successful *Aurora Floyd* (1863), and edited several magazines including *Belgravia* and *Temple Bar*. (See SENSATION, NOVEL OF.)

BRADLAUGH, Charles (1833–91), social reformer and advocate of free thought. His voice was to be heard on platforms throughout the country and in the *National Reformer* (of which he became proprietor) which was a chief outlet for his friend James *Thomson's poems. He was elected MP for Northampton in 1880, but was unseated having been refused the right to make affirmation of allegiance instead of taking the parliamentary oath; he was re-elected in 1881, but it was not until 1886 that he took his seat, having agreed finally to take the oath. He was engaged in several lawsuits to maintain freedom of the press. In association with Mrs *Besant, he republished a pamphlet *The Fruits of Philosophy* advocating birth control, which led to a six-month prison sentence and a £200 fine; the conviction was quashed on appeal.

BRADLEY, A(ndrew) C(ecil) (1851–1935), brother of F. H. *Bradley, was professor of poetry at Oxford from 1901 to 1906. He is particularly remembered for his contributions to Shakespearian scholarship; his best-known works are *Shakespearean Tragedy* (1904) and *Oxford lectures on poetry* (1909).

BRADLEY, Edward (1827–89), wrote under the pseudonym 'Cuthbert Bede'. He is remembered as the author of *The Adventures of Mr Verdant Green* (1853–7), a novel which traces the Oxford career of a gullible young undergraduate, fresh from Warwickshire, from his freshman days to graduation and marriage.

BRADLEY, F(rancis) H(erbert) (1846–1924), brother of A. C. *Bradley, published *Ethical Studies* (1876), notable for its essay on 'My Station and its Duties'; and *Principles of Logic* (1883). His *Appearance and Reality* (1893) was considered an important philosophical discussion of contemporary metaphysical thought; Bradley endeavoured to draw attention in England to continental philosophy, and particularly to Hegelianism. *Essay on Truth and Reality* appeared in 1914.

BRADLEY, Dr Henry (1845–1923), philologist, is principally remembered for his work on the *Oxford English Dictionary* with which he was associated for forty years, from 1884. He became second editor in 1887 and succeeded James *Murray as senior editor on Murray's death in 1915. Among Bradley's works may be mentioned the successful *The Making of English* (1904, rev. 1968).

Bradshaw's Railway Guide was first published in 1839 in the form of Railway Time Tables by George Bradshaw (1801–53), a Quaker engraver and printer. These developed into *Bradshaw's Monthly Railway Guide* in 1841 and it continued to be published until May 1961.

BRADSTREET, Anne (c. 1612–72), American poet, born in England, emigrated to Massachusetts. Her volume of poems *The Tenth Muse Lately Sprung Up in America* was published in London in 1650 without her knowledge. Her work was highly praised in her own time and she has received much attention both as a woman writer and as the first poet of the New World.

Bradwardine, The Baron of, and Rose, characters in Scott's *Waverley*.

BRADWARDINE, Thomas (*c.*1280–1349), Oxford theologian appointed archbishop of Canterbury immediately before his death. His *De Causa Dei* reasserted the primacy of faith and divine grace in opposition to the rationalist sceptics (whom he characterized as New Pelagians) of the tradition of *Ockham and *Holcot.

Braggadochio, in Spenser's *Faerie Queene*, the typical braggart. His adventures and final exposure and humiliation occurs in Bks. ii. iii; iii. viii, x; iv. iv, v, ix; v. iii.

BRAINE, John Gerard (1922–86), novelist, won fame with his first novel, *Room at the Top* (1957), set in a small Yorkshire town; its hero, Joe Lampton, was hailed as another of the provincial *'angry young men' of the 1950s. Lampton, a ruthless opportunist working at the Town Hall, seduces and marries the wealthy young Susan Browne, despite his love for an unhappily married older woman. *Life at the Top* (1962) continues the story of his success and disillusion. Braine's later novels express his increasing hostility to the radical views with which he was once identified.

Brainworm, the wily, high-spirited servant in Jonson's *Every Man in his Humour*.

Bramble, Matthew and Tabitha, characters in Smollet's *Humphry Clinker*.

Brandon, (1) Colonel, a character in J. Austen's *Sense and Sensibility*; (2) George, the assumed name of George Firmin in Thackeray's *A Shabby Genteel Story*; (3) Mrs, a character in Thackeray's *The Adventures of Philip*.

Brangwane (Bragwaine, Bregwaine), the maid-servant of Isoud (Isolde); see TRISTRAM AND ISOUD.

Branwen, see MABINOGION.

Brass, (1) a character in Vanbrugh's *The Confederacy*; (2) Sampson and his sister Sally, characters in Dickens's *The Old Curiosity Shop*.

BRATHWAITE, Edward Kamau (1930–), poet, born in Barbados, has written works on West Indian history and culture, and his volumes of poetry include *The Arrivants, A New World Trilogy* (1973), which consists of *Rights of Passage* (1967), *Masks* (1968), and *Islands* (1969). The poem explores the complex Caribbean heritage and search for identity, using (but not exclusively) vernacular rhythms and diction. *Mother Poem* (1977) and *Sun Poem* (1982) are the first two parts of a trilogy about Barbados.

Brave New World, a novel by A. *Huxley, published 1932.

It is a fable about a world state in the 7th cent. AF (after Ford), where social stability is based on a scientific caste system. Human beings, graded from highest intellectuals to lowest manual workers, hatched from incubators and brought up in communal nurseries, learn by methodical conditioning to accept their social destiny. The action of the story develops round Bernard Marx, an unorthodox and therefore unhappy Alpha-Plus (something had presumably gone wrong with his antenatal treatment), who visits a New Mexican Reservation and brings a Savage back to London. The Savage is at first fascinated by the new world, but finally revolted, and his argument with Mustapha Mond, World Controller, demonstrates the incompatibility of individual freedom and a scientifically trouble-free society.

In *Brave New World Revisited* (1958) Huxley reconsiders his prophecies and fears that some of these may be coming true much sooner than he thought.

BRAWNE, Fanny (1800–65), the young woman with whom *Keats fell in love in 1818. To what extent she returned or understood his passion for her (expressed in many of his letters and several poems) is not clear. His letters to her were published in 1878 and in the collected edition of 1937; hers to his sister, also called Fanny, were published in 1937.

Bray, Madeline, a character in Dickens's *Nicholas Nickleby*.

Bray, Vicar of, see VICAR OF BRAY.

BRECHT, Bertolt (1898–1956), German dramatist and poet who emigrated to the US during the Fascist period, then settled in 1949 in East Berlin. His early plays show kinship with *Expressionism. *Die Dreigroschenoper* (*The Threepenny Opera*, 1928, from *The Beggar's Opera*) was an immense success. His development of the 'alienation effect' (which discouraged empathy with the characters on stage) and of 'epic theatre' (which used short, loosely connected scenes linked by songs, rather than a carefully constructed climactic drama) had an immense influence on succeeding generations of playwrights, as did his radical politics and subject matter. Major works include *The Life of Galileo* (1937–9); *Mother Courage* (1941); *The Caucasian Chalk Circle* (1948).

Breck, Alan, a character in R. L. Stevenson's *Kidnapped* and *Catriona*.

BRENDAN, St (?484–?577), of the monastery of Clonfert in Ireland, about whom grew up a tradition of legendary voyages as a Christianized version of the Old Irish genre *imram*, describing sea-adventures; other examples are 'The Voyage of Bran' and 'The Voyage of Maeldune' of which the latter too was Christianized. The *Navigatio Sancti Brandani* is one of the earliest substantial texts in *Anglo-Norman, but there are earlier Latin versions, none from before the 10th cent. The legends of Brendan have been revived in popularity at various times, for example by M. *Arnold. The most familiar stories are those of the meeting with Judas cooling himself on a rock on Christmas night, a privilege allowed him once a year; and of the landing on a whale, mistaking it for an island, and its being aroused by the lighting of a fire.

Brer Fox and **Brer Rabbit,** the chief characters in *Uncle Remus*. See HARRIS, J. C.

BRETON, Nicholas (?1555–1626), author of a miscellaneous collection of satirical, religious, romantic, and political writings in verse and prose. His best poetry is to be found among his short lyrics in *Englands Helicon* (1600) and in his volume of pastoral poetry *The Passionate Shepheard* (1604).

Breton Lays, in English literature of the Middle English period, are short stories in rhyme like those of *Marie de France. English examples include *Emaré, Sir *Orfeo, and Chaucer's 'The Franklin's Tale' (*Canterbury Tales* 12).

Bretton, John, a character in *Villette* by C. Brontë.

Brewer's Dictionary of Phrase and Fable, by the Revd Ebenezer Cobham Brewer (1810–97), first published 1870. It contains explanations and origins of the familiar and unfamiliar in English phrase and fable, embracing archaeology, history, religion, the arts, science, mythology, fictitious characters and titles, etc.

Briana, in Spenser's *Faerie Queene* (VI. i), the mistress of a castle who takes a toll of ladies' locks and knights' beards to make a mantle for her lover Crudor.

Bridal of Triermain, The, a poem by Sir W. *Scott, published 1813.

Bridehead, Sue, a character in Hardy's *Jude the Obscure.*

Bride of Abydos, The, a poem by Lord *Byron, published 1813, 'a Turkish tale', as Byron called it, in which the beautiful Zuleika, daughter of the Pasha Giaffir, is destined, by her father's order, to marry the rich, elderly Bey of Carasman, whom she has never seen.

Bride of Lammermoor, The, a novel by Sir W. *Scott, published 1819 in *Tales of My Landlord, 3rd series.

Brideshead Revisited, a novel by E. *Waugh, published 1945.

Narrated by Charles Ryder, it describes his emotional involvement with an ancient aristocratic Roman Catholic family, which grows from his meeting as an undergraduate at Oxford the handsome, whimsical younger son, Sebastian Flyte, already an incipient alcoholic. Charles meets his mother, the devout Lady Marchmain, who refuses to divorce Lord Marchmain, exiled to Venice with his mistress; the heir, Lord Brideshead; and the sisters Julia and Cordelia. Lady Marchmain attempts to enlist Charles's support in preventing Sebastian's drinking, but Sebastian finally escapes to North Africa, where, after his mother's death, he becomes some kind of saintly down-and-out. Meanwhile Charles, now an unhappily married but successful artist, falls in love with Julia, also unhappily married; they both plan to divorce, but the power of the Church reclaims Julia, and they part forever. The narrative is set in a war-time framework of prologue and epilogue, in which Charles is billeted in Brideshead, the great country house which had once dominated his imagination.

Bridgenorth, Major and Alice, characters in Scott's *Peveril of the Peak.

'Bridge of Sighs, The', a poem by T. *Hood, published 1843. It is a morbid and ostensibly compassionate elegy on the suicide by drowning of a 'Fallen Woman'.

BRIDGES, Robert (1844–1930), studied medicine and continued to practise until 1881. At Oxford he met G. M. *Hopkins, who became a close and influential friend, and whose complete poems Bridges eventually published in 1918. Bridges' early volumes include *The Growth of Love* (1876), a sonnet sequence; *Prometheus the Firegiver* (1883); and *Eros and Psyche* (1885). Between 1885 and 1894 he wrote eight plays. He wrote two influential essays, *Milton's Prosody* (1893) and *John Keats* (1895); and between 1895 and 1908 wrote the words for four works by H. Parry. He was much interested in the musical settings of words, and edited several editions of the *Yattendon Hymnal* from 1895 onwards. In 1898 appeared the first of the six volumes of his *Poetical Works* (1898–1905). His poetry appeared in one volume in 1912. The following year he was appointed poet laureate, and became a founder of the *Society for Pure English. For many years he was closely connected with the Oxford University Press. His successful anthology of prose and verse, *The Spirit of Man* (1916), included six poems by Hopkins, little of whose work had yet been published. *October and other Poems* appeared in 1920, *New Verse* in 1925, and in 1929 *The Testament of Beauty* a long poem, in four books, on his spiritual philosophy, which he regarded as the culmination of his work as a poet. Bridges' general reputation does not stand as high as it once did, but the simplicity of his diction and his adventurous experiments in metre and prosody are still respected.

BRIDIE, James, pseudonym of Osborne Henry Mavor (1888–1951), playwright, established his reputation with *The Anatomist* (1930), a comedy on the grave-robbers Burke and Hare. His plays fall roughly into four groups: those on biblical themes, such as *Tobias and the Angel* (1930), *Jonah and the Whale* (1932), and *Susannah and the Elders* (1937); those with medical themes, such as *A Sleeping Clergyman* (1933); portrait plays, including *Mr Bolfrey* (1943); and experimental, symbolist, and partly poetic plays such as *Daphne Laureola* (1949) and his last play, the dark, foreboding *The Baikie Charivari* (1952). Many of Bridie's dramas, with their bold characterization, lively debate, and humour, are reminiscent of *Morality plays. Bridie assisted in the establishment of the Glasgow Citizen's Theatre in 1943, and founded the first College of Drama in Scotland in 1950.

Brigadore, in Spenser's *Faerie Queene*, the horse of Sir *Guyon.

Briggs, (1) a character in Fanny Burney's *Cecilia*, drawn in some respects from the sculptor Nollekens; (2) Miss, a character in Thackeray's *Vanity Fair*, companion first to Miss Crawley and then to Becky.

BRIGHOUSE, H., see HOBSON'S CHOICE.

Brighton Rock, a novel by G. *Greene, published 1938.

Set in Brighton in the criminal underworld of gang warfare and protection rackets, it describes the brief and tragic career of 17-year-old Pinkie, 'The Boy', whose ambition is to run a gang to rival that of the wealthy and established Colleoni. He murders a journalist called Hale, marries a 16-year-old girl, the downtrodden Rose (like himself a Roman Catholic), to prevent her giving evidence in court against him, and is driven to further crimes and eventual death by the almost casual pursuit of Ida, a justice-seeking acquaintance of Hale.

BRINK, André Philippus (1935–), South African novelist and playwright, who writes in both English and Afrikaans. His novels, which have encountered troubles with the censor in South Africa because of their open criticism of apartheid, include *Looking on Darkness* (1974; in Afrikaans, 1973, *Kennis van die aand*), *Rumour of Rain* (1978), *A Dry White Season* (1979), and *A Chain of Voices* (1982).

Brisk, Fastidious, a foppish courtier in Jonson's *Every Man out of his Humour*.

Britannia, by W. *Camden, published in Latin 1586, the sixth (much enlarged) edition appearing in 1607. It was translated in 1610 by *Holland. It is in effect a guide-book of the country, county by county, replete with archaeological, historical, physical, and other information.

Britannia's Pastorals, see BROWNE, W.

British Academy, a society, incorporated in 1902, for the promotion of the study of the moral and political sciences. Its first secretary was Sir I. *Gollancz.

British Museum, Bloomsbury, occupies the site of the old Montagu House, which was acquired in 1753 to house the library and collection of curiosities of Sir H. *Sloane. These were enormously increased, notably by the purchase of the *Harleian MSS, the gift by George II and George IV of royal libraries, the purchase of the Elgin Marbles, and the acquisition of Egyptian antiquities. The new buildings were erected in 1823–47, and the great reading-room, designed by *Panizzi, the librarian, was opened in 1857.

Britomart, the heroine of Bk III of Spenser's *Faerie Queene*, the daughter of King Ryence of Britain and the female knight of chastity. She has fallen in love with *Artegall, whose image she has seen in a magic mirror. She is the most powerful of several types of Queen Elizabeth in the poem.

BRITTAIN, Vera Mary (1893–1970), writer, pacifist, and feminist. Her *Testament of Youth* (1933) is a moving account of her girlhood and struggle for education and of her war experiences. She formed a close friendship with Winifred *Holtby, recorded in *Testament of Friendship* (1940). She also published various volumes of poetry, fiction, essays, etc.

BRITTEN, (Edward) Benjamin (1913–76), English composer who set many English poems to music, ranging from *Spenser, *Jonson, and *Herrick, to *Blake, *Keats, *Tennyson, and *Auden (who wrote the libretto of Britten's first opera *Paul Bunyan*, 1941). Britten's second opera, *Peter Grimes* (1945), was drawn from *Crabbe; *Billy Budd* (1951) from *Melville's story adapted by E. M. *Forster; *The Turn of the Screw* (1954) and *Owen Wingrave* (1970) were both from H. *James; *Plomer provided the text for Britten's 'coronation' opera *Gloriana* (1953); the libretto of *A Midsummer Night's Dream* (1960) was compiled from Shakespeare's text. Britten made solo settings of individual poets, including *The Holy Sonnets of John Donne* (1945), *Winter Words* (*Hardy, 1953), five *Canticles* with texts from *Quarles, the Chester Miracle Play, E. *Sitwell, and two from T. S. *Eliot. His *War Requiem* (1962), to celebrate the dedication of the new cathedral at Coventry, includes settings of poems by W. *Owen.

Broad Church, a popular term especially current in the latter half of the 19th cent. for those in the Church of England who sought to interpret the creeds in a broad and liberal manner. The existence of the Broad Church school owes much to the influence of T. *Arnold and to Romantic philosophy as interpreted by *Coleridge, who earned the title of 'Father of the Broad Church Movement'. Other characteristic representatives of the school were T. *Hughes, *Jowett, *Pattison, and most of the other writers for *Essays and Reviews.

Broadside, a sheet of paper printed on one side only, forming one large page; a term generally used of *ballads, etc., so printed.

Brobdingnag, see GULLIVER'S TRAVELS.

Broceliande, a legendary region adjoining Brittany, in the Arthurian legends, where *Merlin lies.

Broken Heart, The, a tragedy by J. *Ford, printed 1633.
  The scene is Sparta. Penthea, who was betrothed to Orgilus whom she loved, has been forced by her brother Ithocles to marry the jealous and contemptible Bassanes, who makes her life so miserable that presently she goes mad and dies. Ithocles returns, a successful general, and is honourably received by the king. He falls in love with Calantha, the king's daughter, and she with him, and their marriage is sanctioned by the king. Orgilus, to avenge the fate of Penthea, of which he has been the witness, entraps Ithocles and kills him. During a feast, Calantha hears, in close succession, of the deaths of Penthea, of her father, and of Ithocles. She dances on, apparently unmoved. When the feast is done, she sentences Orgilus to death, and herself dies broken-hearted.
  Spartan values (courage, endurance, self-control) dominate the action, and the characters represent abstractions rather than individuals. The grave, formal, stately language, and emblematic imagery make it Ford's finest dramatic achievement.

BROME, Richard (c. 1590–1652/3) was servant or perhaps secretary to *Jonson, whose friendship he afterwards enjoyed and whose influence is clear in his works, as is that of *Dekker. Among the best of his fifteen surviving plays are his comedy The Northern Lass (printed 1632), his earliest exant play; The Sparagus Garden (acted 1635), a comedy of manners; The City Witt (a comedy, printed 1653) which tells of the comic revenge taken by easy-going young Crasy, who disguises himself and punishes his virago

mother-in-law and his wife's suitors, and others who have taken advantage of his past generosity; and his masterpiece *The Joviall Crew (acted 1641), a romantic comedy.

BRONTË, Anne (1820–49), sister of Charlotte and Emily *Brontë, was educated largely at home, where, as the youngest of the motherless family, she was much under the Wesleyan influence of her Aunt Branwell, who is thought to have encouraged her tendency to religious melancholy. Emily and Anne invented the imaginary world of Gondal, the setting of many of their dramatic poems. Anne became a governess in 1839 and her experiences with the over-indulged young children and the worldly older children of the two households where she was employed are vividly portrayed in *Agnes Grey (1847). The novel appeared under the pseudonym Acton Bell, as did a selection of her poems, together with those of her sisters, in 1846. Her second novel, *The Tenant of Wildfell Hall (1848), portrays in Arthur Huntingdon a violent drunkard clearly to some extent drawn from her brother Branwell.

BRONTË, Charlotte (1816–55), daughter of Patrick Brontë, an Irishman, perpetual curate of Haworth, Yorkshire. Charlotte's mother died in 1821, leaving five daughters and a son, Branwell, to the care of their aunt, Elizabeth Branwell. Four of the daughters were sent to a Clergy Daughters' School at Cowan Bridge (which Charlotte portrayed as Lowood in *Jane Eyre), an unfortunate step which Charlotte believed to have hastened the death in 1825 of her two elder sisters and to have permanently impaired her own health. The surviving children pursued their education at home; they became involved in a rich fantasy life that owes much to their admiration of *Byron, Sir W. *Scott, the *Arabian Nights and Tales of the Genii. They began to write stories, and Charlotte and Branwell collaborated in the elaborate invention of the imaginary kingdom of Angria, Emily and Anne in the invention of Gondal. In 1831–2 Charlotte was at Miss Wooler's school at Roe Head, whither she returned as a teacher in 1835–8. She was subsequently a governess and in 1842 she and Emily went to study languages at the Pensionnat Heger in Brussels. Charlotte fell deeply in love with M. Heger, who failed to respond to the letters she wrote to him after her return to Haworth. In 1845 she 'discovered' (or so she alleged) the poems of Emily, and projected a joint publication; a volume of verse entitled Poems by Currer, Ellis and Acton Bell (the pseudonyms of Charlotte, Emily, and Anne) appeared in 1846. Charlotte's first novel, *The Professor, never found a publisher in her lifetime, but Jane Eyre, published in 1847 by Smith, Elder, achieved immediate success, arousing much speculation about its authorship. To quell the suspicion that the Bell pseudonyms concealed but one author, Charlotte and Anne visited Smith, Elder in July 1848 and made themselves known.

She was not able to enjoy her success and a tragic period of her life followed. Branwell, whose wildness and intemperance had caused the sisters much distress, died in Sept. 1848, Emily in Dec. of that year, and Anne the following summer. Charlotte nevertheless persevered with the composition of *Shirley (1849). The loneliness of her later years was alleviated by friendship with Mrs *Gaskell, whom she met in 1850 and who was to write her biography (1857). *Villette, founded on her memories of Brussels, appeared in 1853. Although her identity was by this time well known in the literary world, she continued to publish as Currer Bell. In 1854 she married her father's curate, A. B. Nicholls, but died a few months later of an illness probably associated with pregnancy. 'Emma', a fragment, was published in 1860 in the *Cornhill Magazine with an introduction by *Thackeray, and many of her juvenile works have subsequently been published, adding to our knowledge of the intense creativity of her early years. In her lifetime, Charlotte was the most admired of the Brontë sisters, although she came in for some criticism (which deeply wounded her) on the grounds of alleged 'grossness' and emotionalism, considered particularly unbecoming in a clergyman's daughter. More widespread was praise for her depth of feeling and her courageous realism.

BRONTË, Emily Jane (1818–48), sister of Charlotte and Anne *Brontë, briefly attended the school at Cowan Bridge with Charlotte in 1824–5, and was then educated largely at home, where she was particularly close to Anne, with whom she created the imaginary world of Gondal, the setting for many of her finest dramatic poems. She was even more intensely attached than her sisters to the moorland scenery of home. She was for a time in 1837 governess at Law Hill, near Halifax, and in 1842 went to Brussels with Charlotte to study languages, but returned on her aunt's death at the end of the year to Haworth, where she spent the rest of her brief life. In 1845 Charlotte 'discovered' Emily's poems, and projected a joint publication, *Poems, by Currer, Ellis and Acton Bell* (1846). *Wuthering Heights was written between Oct. 1845 and June 1846, and published by T. C. Newby in Dec. 1847. Unlike Charlotte's *Jane Eyre, it met with more incomprehension than recognition, and it was only after Emily's death (of consumption) that it became widely acknowledged as a masterpiece. The vein of violence, of stoicism, and of mysticism in Emily's personality have given rise to many legends but few certainties. She is now established as much the most considerable poet of the three sisters, and one of the most original poets of the century, remembered for her lyrics (e.g. 'The night is darkening round me'), for her passionate invocations from the world of Gondal ('Remembrance', 'The Prisoner'), and her apparently more personal visionary moments ('No coward soul is mine').

Brooke, Mr, and his nieces Dorothea and Celia, characters in G. Eliot's *Middlemarch*.

BROOKE, Frances (1724–89), published in 1760 *Letters from Juliet Lady Catesby*, translated from Riccoboni, in which intricate currents of feeling are carefully traced. The highly successful *History of Lady Julia Mandeville* (1763) is a book of considerable pessimism. *The History of Emily Montague* (1769) is set in Quebec. Her other works include *The Excursion* (1777), several works of history and translation, and various dramatic works, including the tragedies *Virginia* (1756) and the *Siege of Sinope* (1781) and a musical play, *Rosina* (1783).

BROOKE, Henry (1703–83), published *Universal Beauty* (1735), a poem which was thought to have greatly influenced E. *Darwin's *The Botanic Garden*. Encouraged by *Garrick, he wrote several plays. His highly successful novel *The Fool of Quality* (1765–70) and *Juliet Grenville* (1774) are notable for their looseness of structure and for a sustained tone of high sensibility.

BROOKE, Rupert Chawner (1887–1915), won a scholarship to King's College, Cambridge, where he spent five years as a leader of the literary world. He settled at Granchester in 1909. *Poems 1911* was well received, as was his work in the first and second volumes of *Georgian Poetry*. In 1912 he won a fellowship to King's; wrote a stark one-act play, *Lithuania*; and suffered a serious breakdown which led him in 1913 to travel in the US, Canada, and the Pacific, where, in Tahiti, he wrote 'Tiara Tahiti' and other poems. In 1914 he joined the RNVR and took part in the Antwerp expedition; he died on the way to the Dardanelles of blood-poisoning and was buried on Scyros. His five 'War Sonnets', which included 'The Soldier' ('If I should die'), appeared in *New Numbers* early in 1915. The ecstatic reception they received made him the nation's poet of war, a reputation further enhanced by the posthumous publication of *1914 and Other Poems* in 1915. He is now chiefly valued for his lighter verse, such as 'The Old Vicarage, Granchester' and 'Heaven'; for the Tahiti poems; for a few sonnets (other than the war sequence); and for an intriguing last fragment 'I strayed about the deck'. His *Collected Poems*, with a memoir by E. *Marsh, appeared in 1918, and further poems were added in the *Poetical Works* edited by G. *Keynes in 1946.

Brook Farm Institute, see TRANSCENDENTAL CLUB.

BROPHY, Brigid Antonia (1929–), novelist. Her novels include *Hackenfeller's Ape* (1953), *Flesh* (1962), *The Snow Ball* (1962), and *In Transit* (1969). Her non-fiction works (which, like her fiction, express her interest in opera and the visual arts) include *Black and White: a portrait of Aubrey Beardsley* (1968) and a life of *Firbank, *Prancing Novelist* (1973).

Brothers, The, a comedy by R. *Cumberland, produced 1769.

BROUGHAM, Henry Peter, Baron Brougham and Vaux (1778–1868), rose to be lord chancellor. His distinguished legal career included the defence of Queen Caroline in 1820. He played an important part in the founding of London University. In the history of literature he is remembered principally as one of the founders, with *Jeffrey and Sydney *Smith, of the *Edinburgh Review* in 1802. He is said to have been the author of the disparaging article on *Hours of Idleness* in the *Edinburgh Review* of Jan. 1808, which provoked Byron into writing *English Bards and Scotch Reviewers*.

The brougham, a one-horse closed carriage, with two or four wheels, is named after him.

'Brougham Castle, Song at the Feast of', a poem by *Wordsworth, composed in 1807. See under SHEPHERD, LORD CLIFFORD, THE.

BROUGHTON, Rhoda (1840–1920), author of many light, witty novels of country-house and town life, with lively and articulate heroines, which gained her a reputation for audacity. She began her career with the three- and two-decker novels that were still popular (*Not wisely, but too well*, 1867; *Cometh up as a flower*, 1867; *Nancy*, 1873), but was possibly more at home with the form of her later short, sharp, observant one-volume novels, which include *Mrs Bligh* (1892), *Dear Faustina* (1897), *Lavinia* (1902, which boldly presents an anti-Boer War hero, fond of old lace), and *A Waif's Progress* (1905).

Browdie, John, in Dickens's *Nicholas Nickleby*, a bluff, kind-hearted Yorkshireman.

Brown, Father, in G. K. *Chesterton's detective stories, a Roman Catholic priest, highly successful in the detection of crime by intuitive methods.

BROWN, Charles Brockden (1771–1810), acclaimed as the first professional American author, is remembered for his four *Gothic novels *Wieland* (1798), *Arthur Mervyn* (1799), *Ormond* (1799), and *Edgar Huntly* (1799). Although obviously indebted to *Godwin and A. *Radcliffe, these were pioneer works which gave Gothic romance an American setting, and

Brown's psychological interest in obsession, seduction, madness, and cruelty made him a precursor of *Poe.

BROWN, George Douglas, see DOUGLAS, GEORGE.

BROWN, George Mackay (1921–), Scottish writer. His volumes of poetry include *Loaves and Fishes* (1959), *The Year of the Whale* (1969), and *Selected Poems* (1977); he has also published several collections of short stories, two novels (*Greenvoe*, 1972; *Magnus*, 1973), and other works including *An Orkney Tapestry* (1969), a medley of prose and verse, history, legend, and anecdote. His work springs from a deep local source, and is rooted in Norse saga, island folklore, and the cycle of rural life.

BROWN, Dr John (1810–82), Edinburgh physician and essayist, most of whose writings are contained in his three volumes of *Horae Subsecivae* (1858–82), including *Marjorie Fleming* and the memorable dog story *Rab and his Friends*.

BROWN, Lancelot (1716–83), landscape architect, known as 'Capability' Brown because he was reputed to tell patrons that their estates had 'great capabilities'. His creations include the lake at Blenheim and the park at Chatsworth. He was a key figure in the development of the *Picturesque and his landscapes were deliberately fashioned to evoke the landscapes of Claude.

BROWN, Thomas (1663–1704), satirist, wrote the famous lines beginning 'I do not love you, Dr Fell' (see FELL). He settled in London as Tory pamphleteer, translator, and hack writer.

BROWN, T(homas) E(dward) (1830–97), published *Betsy Lee*, *A Foc's'le Yarn* (1873), *Foc's'le Yarns* (1881), and other books of verse, most of it in the Manx dialect, and dealing with Manx life.

BROWNE, Charles Farrar (1834–67), American humorous moralist, wrote under pseudonym 'Artemus Ward'. He purported to describe the experiences of a travelling showman, using, like 'Josh Billings' (H. W. *Shaw), his own comic phonetic spelling. He became a contributor to *Punch* and died in England.

BROWNE, Hablot Knight (1815–82), under the pseudonym 'Phiz', illustrated some of the works of *Dickens, *Surtees, *Smedley, etc.

BROWNE, Robert, see BROWNISTS.

BROWNE, Sir Thomas (1605–82), studied medicine at Montpellier and Padua, received a doctorate from Leiden, and settled in Norwich c.1637 to practise medicine. *Religio Medici*

(1642), first published without his consent, quickly made him famous by its distinctive wit and style. His most ambitious work, *Pseudodoxia Epidemica* (1646; commonly known as *Vulgar Errors*), established him as a man of learning. In the 1650s he wrote for friends the shorter tracts *Hydriotaphia* or *Urn Burial*, *The Garden of Cyrus*, and *A Letter to a Friend* (published 1690); the latter overlapping in content with *Christian Morals* (1716), a sententious piece which was re-edited in 1756 by Dr *Johnson, who prefaced it with a substantial 'Life'. He was knighted in 1671 by Charles II.

BROWNE, William (?1590–1645), published *Britannia's Pastorals* (Bks I and II, 1613, 1616), a narrative poem dealing with the loves and woes of Marina, Celia, etc., in couplets interspersed with lyrics; Bk III, unfinished, remained in manuscript until 1852. Among various epitaphs he wrote the well-known lines on the dowager countess of Pembroke, 'Sidney's sister, Pembroke's mother'. His poetry, which displays genuine love and observation of nature, influenced *Keats, and Milton's *'L'Allegro' and *Lycidas* contain echoes and imitations.

BROWNING, Elizabeth Barrett (1806–61), eldest child of Edward Moulton Barrett. She was largely self-educated at home and became deeply versed in the classics and in prosodic theory. In 1838 she became seriously ill as a result of a broken blood-vessel and was sent to Torquay, where two years later her eldest brother Edward was drowned, to her lifelong grief. She returned to London, still an invalid, in 1841. In 1845 Robert *Browning began a correspondence with her which led to their meeting and to an engagement, necessarily secret since the tyrannical Mr Barrett forbade his adult sons and daughters to marry. In Sept. 1846 Browning and Elizabeth Barrett were secretly married and left for Italy. Florence became their base for the rest of Mrs Browning's life. Their only child, Robert Wiedemann, was born in 1849.

The Seraphim, and Other Poems (1838) was her first work to gain critical and public attention. Her next set of *Poems* (1844) was so highly regarded that she was widely canvassed as *Wordsworth's successor as poet laureate. Throughout her married life her poetic reputation stood higher than Browning's in general contemporary opinion, though her progressive social ideas and her audacious prosodic experiments—perhaps the most appealing aspects of her work to many 20th-cent. readers—were considered alarming by readers in her own day. Her *Sonnets from the Portuguese* first appeared in a collected edition of her poems in 1850; *Casa Guidi Windows*, on the theme of Italian liberation, in 1851; and her magnum opus, *Aurora Leigh*, in 1857. The stridently political *Poems Before Congress* (1860) injured her

popularity. *Last Poems*, issued posthumously in 1862, contained some of her best-known lyrics. Since her death many volumes of her spirited and engaging letters, including her exchange of love letters with Browning and her correspondence with such friends as M. R. *Mitford and *Haydon, have been published.

BROWNING, Oscar (1837–1923), became a history lecturer at King's College, Cambridge, where he was known as a legendary figure: fat, vain, snobbish, and quarrelsome, he nevertheless commanded considerable loyalty from his favoured pupils, and enjoyed his own somewhat ridiculous reputation and the anecdotes he inspired. He published various historical and biographical works, including a life of G. *Eliot (1890).

BROWNING, Robert (1812–89), received his education mainly in his father's large and eclectic library. The contrasting influences of his boyhood were those of his reading (particularly of *Shelley, *Byron, and *Keats) and of his mother's strong Nonconformist piety. His first published poem, *Pauline* (1833), attracted little notice. Browning travelled to Russia in 1834 and made his first trip to Italy in 1838. *Paracelsus* (1835) was a critical success and Browning formed several important friendships, notably with J. *Forster and *Macready, who persuaded him to write for the stage. In 1837 his play *Strafford* was produced at Covent Garden. He next published *Sordello* (1840), whose hostile reception eclipsed his reputation for over twenty years, and *Bells and Pomegranates* (1841–6). He began corresponding with Elizabeth Barrett (see BROWNING, E.B.) in Jan. 1845, after reading and admiring her 1844 *Poems*. He met her first in 1845; their relationship had to be kept a secret from her father, and they finally married and eloped to Italy in Sept. 1846. They lived mainly in Italy until Elizabeth's death in 1861. They had one child, Robert Wiedemann Barrett Browning ('Pen', 1849–1913). In 1850 Browning published *Christmas-Eve and Easter Day* and in 1855 the masterpiece of his middle period, *Men and Women*, which, together with *Dramatis Personae* (1864), began to revive his reputation; the revival was completed by the triumph of *The Ring and the Book* (1868–9). Meanwhile he had returned to England. He was awarded an honorary fellowship by Balliol College, Oxford, whose master *Jowett was a close friend. The Browning Society was founded in 1881. Browning's publications after *The Ring and the Book* were: *Balaustion's Adventure* (1871), *Prince Hohenstiel-Schwangau* (1871), *Fifine at the Fair* (1872), *Red Cotton Night-Cap Country* (1873), *Aristophanes' Apology* (1875), *The Inn Album* (1875), *Pacchiarotto . . . with Other Poems* (1876), *The Agamemnon of Aeschylus* (1877), *La Saisiaz* and *The Two Poets of Croisic* (1878), *Dramatic

Idyls (1879), **Dramatic Idyls, Second Series* (1880), *Jocoseria (1883), *Ferishtah's Fancies* (1884), **Parleyings with Certain People of Importance in their Day* (1887) and *Asolando (1889). Browning issued collections of his work in 1849, 1863, 1868, and 1888–9. The most recent collected edition (1981) contains his fugitive pieces, of which the most notable are the fine unfinished poem known as 'Aeschylus' Soliloquy', the sonnet 'Helen's Tower', 'Gerousios Oinos', the sonnet 'Why I am a Liberal', and the sonnet 'To Edward FitzGerald' (a savage attack after Browning read a disparaging reference to his wife in one of *FitzGerald's posthumously published letters). Browning's only prose works of importance are two 'essays' on *Chatterton (1842) and *Shelley (1852). His correspondence with Elizabeth Barrett has been published, along with other separate volumes of letters. Browning died in Venice and is buried in Westminster Abbey.

Brownists, adherents of the ecclesiastical principles of Robert Browne (?1550–?1633), who preached *c.*1578 denouncing the parochial system and ordination, whether by bishops or by presbytery. He is regarded as the founder of Congregationalism.

BROWNJOHN, Alan Charles (1931–   ), poet, whose volumes of verse include *The Railings* (1961) and *Collected Poems 1952–83* (1983). Brownjohn's poetry is, characteristically, good-humoured, ironic, and urbane, and, in P. *Porter's phrase, it unites 'wit and civic responsibility' in its survey of contemporary social, domestic, and literary life. He has also written for children (*Brownjohn's Beasts*, 1970) and edited several anthologies.

Brownlow, Mr, a character in Dickens's *Oliver Twist.

BRUCE, James (1730–94), African traveller, educated at Harrow, was author of an interesting narrative of his *Travels to discover the source of the Nile* (he discovered that of the Blue Nile), and of his visit to Abyssinia, published in 1790.

Bruce, The, see BARBOUR, J.

BRUMMELL, George Bryan (1778–1840), generally called Beau Brummell, a friend of the prince regent (George IV) and leader of fashion in London. He died in poverty at Caen.

Brunanburh, a poem in Old English, included in four manuscripts of the **Anglo-Saxon Chronicle* under the year 937, dealing with the battle fought in that year at Brunanburh between the English under Athelstan, the grandson of Alfred, and the Danes under Anlaf from Dublin, supported by the Scots led by Constantine II and

the Welsh. The poem is a triumphant celebration of the deeds of Athelstan and his brother and successor Edmund. *Tennyson wrote a verse translation (*Ballads and Other Poems*, 1880).

Brunhild, see BRYNHILD.

Brut, or **Brutus,** legendary founder of the British race. *Geoffrey of Monmouth states that Walter, archdeacon of Oxford, gave him an ancient book containing an account of the kings of Britain from Brutus to Cadwallader. This Brutus was son of Sylvius, grandson of Ascanius and great-grandson of Aeneas. He collected a remnant of the Trojan race and brought them to England (uninhabited at the time 'except by a few giants'), landing at Totnes. He founded Troynovant or New Troy (later known as London) and was the progenitor of a line of British kings including Bladud, *Gorboduc, Ferrex and Porrex, *Lud, *Cymbeline, *Coel, *Vortigern, and *Arthur. Drayton, in his *Poly-Olbion (i. 312), relates the legend.

His name came to be used to mean 'chronicle of the Britons', by Geoffrey of Monmouth's followers such as *Wace and *Laȝamon after Geoffrey began his history of the kings of Britain with him.

Brute, The Prose, a long English version of the Anglo-Norman prose *Brut* which extends up to 1333, translated between 1350 and 1380. Over 100 copies of the English version are extant. It has a strong Lancastrian bias, unlike the pro-York 15th-cent. *Brut* composed in London *c.*1461.

Brutus: in Shakespeare's *Julius Caesar, Decius Brutus is one of the conspirators. Marcus Brutus is the idealistic friend of Caesar who is persuaded by *Cassius to join the conspiracy. Caesar receives his wound from Brutus with the legendary words '*Et tu, Brute?*—Then fall, Caesar!' (III. i. 76). Antony's tribute to Brutus after his death as 'the noblest Roman of them all' (v. v. 68) is well known. The internal deliberations of Brutus have been seen as precursors of those of *Hamlet, hero of what was probably Shakespeare's next play.

BRYANT, William Cullen (1794–1878), American poet, was for 50 years editor of the New York *Evening Post*. He received attention as a poet with his Wordsworthian blank verse meditation 'Thanatopsis', published 1817 in the **North American Review*, and confirmed his reputation with *Poems* (1821), which contains his well-known 'To a Waterfowl', 'The Yellow Violet', and 'Green River'. His *Poems* (1832) contains 'The Death of the Flowers' and 'To the Fringed Gentian'. Although limited in range, his poetry has simplicity and dignity, and some delicate observations of the natural world.

BRYCE, James, Viscount (1838–1922), Regius professor of civil law at Oxford (1870–93), chief secretary for Ireland (1905–6), and ambassador to the USA (1907–13). Bryce published works on various subjects, including the two notable volumes *The Holy Roman Empire* (1864) and *The American Commonwealth* (1888).

Brynhild, or **Brunhild,** one of the principal characters in the *Vǫlunga saga* and the *Nibelungenlied.* (See RING DES NIBELUNGEN, DER.)

BUCHAN, John, first Baron Tweedsmuir (1875–1940), combined a literary career with a career in public life, culminating with the post of governor-general of Canada, 1935–40. He wrote many non-fiction works, including lives of *Montrose (1913) and *Scott (1932), but is remembered for his adventure stories, most of which feature a recurring group of heroes (Richard Hannay, Sandy Arbuthnot, Peter Pienaaer, Edward Leithen, etc.); favoured settings include Scotland, the Cotswolds, and South Africa, although the last, *Sick Heart River* (1941), prefiguring his own death, is set in the icy wastes of Canada. The stories, packed with action, often involving elaborate cross-country chases, include *The Thirty-Nine Steps* (1915; filmed by Hitchcock, 1935), *Greenmantle* (1916), *Mr Standfast* (1918), and *John Macnab* (1925).

BUCHANAN, George (1506–82), satirized the Franciscans and was imprisoned at St Andrews. Escaping, he went to the Continent, became a professor at Bordeaux, where he had *Montaigne among his pupils, and in 1547 was invited to teach in the university of Coimbra, but was imprisoned by the Inquisition, 1549–51. He returned to Scotland and professed himself a Protestant. He became a bitter enemy of *Mary Queen of Scots, in consequence of the murder of Darnley, and vouched that the *Casket Letters were in her handwriting. He wrote his *Detectio Mariae Reginae* in 1571. He was tutor to James VI and I during 1570–8. Chief among his many writings are his Latin poem *De Sphaera,* an exposition of the Ptolemaic system as against that advocated by *Copernicus, and his Latin *Rerum Scoticarum Historia* (1582).

BUCHANAN, Robert Williams (1841–1901), published many novels, poems, and plays (most of which are now forgotten). He is remembered largely for his attacks on *Swinburne (whom he satirized in a poem 'The Session of the Poets' in the *Spectator,* 1866) and on the *Pre-Raphaelites, principally D. G. *Rossetti, whom he attacked in 'The Fleshly School of Poetry' in the *Contemporary Review* (1871) under the pseudonym 'Thomas Maitland'. After Rossetti's death he recanted in an essay in *A Look Round Literature* (1887).

Bucket, Inspector, the detective in Dickens's *Bleak House.*

BUCKHURST, Lord, see SACKVILLE, T. and C.

BUCKINGHAM, George Villiers, first duke of (1592–1628), the favourite of James I, figures in Scott's *The Fortunes of Nigel.* He was assassinated by John Felton.

BUCKINGHAM, George Villiers, second duke of (1628–87), a prominent figure in the reign of Charles II, famed for his debauchery, his amorous adventures, and the vicissitudes of his public life. He was the author of verses, satires, and the burlesque *The Rehearsal* (printed 1672). He was the Zimri of Dryden's *Absalom and Achitophel* and figures in Scott's *Peveril of the Peak.*

BUCKINGHAM, James Silk (1786–1855), author and traveller, and founder of the *Athenaeum.*

Buckingham, Complaint of, see COMPLAINT OF BUCKINGHAM.

Buckingham, duke of, in Shakespeare's *Richard III,* acts as Richard's ally in murdering Lord *Hastings but defects to the support of Richmond. The line 'Off with his head! So much for Buckingham' occurs in C. *Cibber's adaptation (1700).

BUCKLE, Henry Thomas (1821–62), received no school or college training, but through travelling on the Continent acquired several languages and became a radical free-thinker. He published two volumes of a *History of Civilization in England* (1857; 1861). These were only to be introductory portions of a far larger work, but he died prematurely of typhoid in Damascus. Buckle criticized the methods of previous historians and sought to establish a scientific basis, arguing that changing phenomena have unchanging laws and that the growth of civilization in various countries depended on the interrelated factors of climate, food production, population, and wealth. The work achieved great success, and was much admired by C. *Darwin.

Bucolic, see ECLOGUE.

Buffone, Carlo, in Jonson's *Every Man out of his Humour,* 'a public scurrilous profane jester', from the Italian *buffone,* 'jester', the origin of the English 'buffoon'.

Bufo, a character in *Pope's *Epistle to Dr Arbuthnot* (ll. 230–48), a patron of the arts 'fed with soft Dedication all day long'.

Bull, John, see JOHN BULL.

Bull-dog Drummond, see SAPPER.

Bulstrode, Mr, a character in G. Eliot's *Middlemarch.*

BULWER-LYTTON, Edward George Earle Lytton, first Baron Lytton (1803–73). Educated at Trinity Hall, Cambridge, he embarked on a career in politics as MP for St Ives in 1831; he was subsequently MP for Lincoln and in 1858–9 secretary for the colonies. He financed his extravagant life as a man of fashion by a versatile and prolific literary output, publishing either anonymously or under the name of Bulwer Lytton. His first success *Pelham: or the adventures of a gentleman* (1828), of the *Fashionable school, brought him considerable acclaim and established his reputation as a wit and dandy. His *'Newgate' novels were more in the 'reforming' manner of *Godwin, e.g. *Paul Clifford* (1830), about a philanthropic highwayman, and *Eugene Aram* (1832), about a repentant murderer. He also wrote novels of domestic life; many popular *historic novels, including *The Last Days of Pompeii* (1834), *Rienzi, the last of the Roman Tribunes* (1835), and *The Last of the Barons* (1843); tales of the occult, including *Zanoni* (1842) and *A Strange Story* (1862); and a *science fiction fantasy, *The Coming Race* (1871). Other novels include *Falkland* (1827), *Godolphin* (1833), *Ernest Maltravers* (1837), *Harold, the last of the Saxons* (1848), *Kenelm Chillingly* (1873), and *The Parisians* (1873, unfinished). He was also editor of the *New Monthly Magazine*, 1831–3, and the author of three plays, *The Lady of Lyons, or Love and Pride*, a romantic comedy first performed in 1838; *Richelieu, or the Conspiracy*, a historical play in blank verse performed in 1839; and *Money*, a comedy performed in 1840, all of which have been successfully revived. He published several volumes of verse, including his earliest *Byronic tale, *Ismael* (1820); *The New Timon* (1846), an anonymous satirical poem in which he attacked *Tennyson as 'School-Miss Alfred', thus aggravating previous criticisms and stinging Tennyson into a bitter response in verse, mocking Lytton as a rouged and padded fop; and an epic, *King Arthur* (1848–9). Bulwer-Lytton made many enemies in his career but he nevertheless had powerful admirers, including *Disraeli and *Dickens. His works, though now little read, span many of the changes in 19th-cent. fiction and are thus of considerable social interest.

Bumble, the beadle in Dickens's *Oliver Twist*.

Bumby, Mother, a fortune-teller frequently alluded to by the Elizabethan dramatists. *Lyly wrote a Terentian comedy entitled *Mother Bombie* (1594), which is, says *Hazlitt, 'very much what its name would import, old, quaint, and vulgar'.

Bumppo, Natty, see COOPER, J. F.

Bunbury, an imaginary character introduced by Wilde in *The Importance of being Earnest*.

Buncle Esq., John, see JOHN BUNCLE.

BUNGAY, Thomas, known as 'Friar Bungay' (*fl.* 1290), a Franciscan who was divinity lecturer of his order in Oxford and Cambridge. He was vulgarly accounted a magician. (See FRIER BACON AND FRIER BONGAY.)

Bunsby, Captain John, a character in Dickens's *Dombey and Son*, a friend of Captain Cuttle.

Bunthorne, Reginald, the principal male character in Gilbert and Sullivan's opera *Patience*, a 'fleshly poet', in whose person the *Aesthetic Movement of the 1880s was caricatured.

BUNTING, Basil (1900–85), born in Northumberland. Although he had been published abroad (*Redimiculum Matellarum*, Milan, 1930; *Poems*, Texas, 1950) and had a considerable reputation among younger American poets as an important figure in the modernist movement, he was virtually unknown in England until the appearance of his long, semi-autobiographical, and deeply Northumbrian poem *Briggflatts* (1966). His *Collected Poems* (1968) includes translations ('Overdrafts') from Latin and Persian.

BUNYAN, John (1628–88), the son of a brazier, was early set to his father's trade. He was drafted into the parliamentary army 1644–6, an experience perhaps reflected in *The Holy War*. His first wife (who died *c.*1656 leaving four children) introduced him to two religious works, Dent's *Plain Man's Pathway to Heaven* and Bayly's *Practice of Piety*; these, the Bible, the Prayer Book, and Foxe's *Actes and Monumentes* (or *Book of Martyrs*) were his principal reading matter. In 1653 he joined a Nonconformist church in Bedford, preached there, and came into conflict with the Quakers, against whom he published his first writings. He married his second wife Elizabeth *c.*1659. He was arrested in Nov. 1660 for preaching without a licence, and spent most of the next twelve years in Bedford Gaol. During the first half of this period he wrote nine books, the principal of which was *Grace Abounding to the Chief of Sinners* (1666). In 1665 appeared *The Holy City, or the New Jerusalem*, inspired by a passage in the book of Revelation. After his release in 1672 he was appointed pastor at the same church, but was again imprisoned for a short period in 1676, during which he probably finished the first part of *The Pilgrim's Progress* which was published in 1678; the second, together with the whole work, appeared in 1684. His other principal works are *The Life and Death of Mr *Badman* (1680) and *The Holy War* (1682).

Burana, Carmina, see CARMINA BURANA.

BURBAGE, James (*c.*1530–97), actor, was one of the earl of Leicester's players in 1572. He leased land in Shoreditch (1576), on which he erected, of wood, the first building in England specially intended for plays. In 1596 he acquired a house in Blackfriars, and converted it into the *Blackfriars Theatre. The first English play-house is mentioned in an order of council, Aug. 1577, and was known as 'The Theatre'; the fabric was removed, *c*. Dec. 1598, to the Bankside and set up as the *Globe Theatre.

BURBAGE, Richard (?1567–1619), actor, the son of James *Burbage, acted major roles in plays by Shakespeare, *Jonson, and *Beaumont and *Fletcher, and excelled in tragedy.

BURCHFIELD, Robert William (1923–), born in New Zealand, editor from 1957 of *A Supplement to the *Oxford English Dictionary*, published 1972–86.

Burden, the refrain or chorus of a song, a set of words recurring at the end of each verse, or the dominant theme of a song or poem.

BURGESS, Anthony (John Anthony Burgess Wilson) (1917–), novelist, whose varied early career included some years (1954–60) in the colonial service in Malaya and Borneo. During this time he wrote his first three novels, set in the Far East: *Time for a Tiger* (1956), *The Enemy in the Blanket* (1958), and *Beds in the East* (1959; published together as *The Malayan Trilogy* in 1972). *A Clockwork Orange* (1962), an alarming vision of violence, high technology, and authoritarianism, appeared in a film version by Stanley Kubrick in 1971. His comic trilogy about the gross and fitfully inspired poet Enderby (*Inside Mr Enderby*, 1963, under the pseudonym 'Joseph Kell'; *Enderby Outside*, 1968; *The Clockwork Testament*, 1974), displays a fine flair for pastiche, satiric social comment, and verbal invention. *Earthly Powers* (1980) is a long and ambitious first-person novel, narrated by a successful octogenarian homosexual writer, Kenneth Toomey, in which real and fictitious characters mingle to produce an international panorama of the 20th cent. Burgess has also written critical works, notably on *Joyce; composed orchestral works; written film and television scripts, innumerable reviews, and a biography of Shakespeare (1970).

BURGON, John William (1813–88), is remem-bered as the author of the poem 'Petra' (1845), which contains the well-known line 'A rose-red city—"half as old as time" '.

BURGOYNE, Sir John (1722–92), nicknamed 'Gentleman Johnny', remembered principally as the general who was forced to capitulate to the Americans at Saratoga in 1777, was the author of a clever and successful comedy *The Heiress* (1786), in which the vulgarity of the rich Alscrip family is contrasted with the native good breed-ing of Clifford, Lord Gayville, and his sister; while the temporary humiliation of the virtuous heroine Miss Alton, who is driven to take service in the Alscrip family until she is discovered to be an heiress and Clifford's sister, provides a sen-timental interest. He figures in G. B. *Shaw's play *The Devil's Disciple* (1900).

Burgundy, duke of, the 'wat'rish' suitor of *Cordelia in Shakespeare's *King Lear*.

'Burial of Sir John Moore, The', see WOLFE, C.

BURKE, Edmund (1729–97), educated at Trinity College, Dublin, entered the Middle Temple in 1750. He was more interested in literature than in law: Dr *Johnson (of whose *Club he was a founding member) was among his many eminent literary friends. In 1758 with *Dodsley he founded the *Annual Register to which he contributed until 1788. He was elected MP for Wendover in 1765 and first spoke in the House in 1766 on the American question. Dur-ing the following years he vehemently attacked the Tory government. He published his *Observa-tions on a late Publication on the *Present State of the Nation* in 1769, and his *Thoughts on the Cause of the *Present Discontents* in 1770. In 1774 he became MP for Bristol, and made his speeches *On American Taxation* (1774) and *On *Concili-ation with America* (1775). His *Letter to the Sheriffs of Bristol* was written 1777. His cham-pionship of free trade with Ireland and Catholic emancipation lost him his seat in Bristol in 1780; he became MP for Malton in 1781. His attacks on the conduct of the American war contributed to North's resignation in 1783. Burke opened the case for the impeachment of Warren Hast-ings in 1788 and supported *Wilberforce in advocating abolition of the slave trade. The French Revolution prompted his *Reflections on the *Revolution in France* (1790) and other import-ant works, including *Letters on a *Regicide Peace* (1795–7). He retired in 1794 and received a pension from the ministry, for which he was criticized; he defended himself in his *A Letter to a Noble Lord* (1796).

Burke's political life was devoted to five 'great, just and honourable causes': the eman-cipation of the House of Commons from the control of George III and the 'King's friends'; the emancipation of the American colonies; the emancipation of Ireland; the emancipation of India from the misgovernment of the East India Company; and opposition to the atheistical Jacobinism displayed in the French Revolution. As a writer and orator he won admiration from all sides. *Macaulay declared him the 'greatest man since Milton'. (See also SUBLIME AND BEAUTIFUL, A PHILOSOPHICAL ENQUIRY INTO THE; VINDICATION OF A NATURAL SOCIETY, A.)

Burlesque, from the Italian *burla*, ridicule, mockery, a literary composition or dramatic representation which aims at exciting laughter by the comical treatment of a serious subject or the caricature of the spirit of a serious work. Notable examples of burlesque in English literature are Butler's *Hudibras* and Buckingham's *The Rehearsal*.

BURNABY, Frederick Gustavus (1842–85), cavalry officer and traveller. His ride across the Russian steppes resulted in his best-selling *A Ride to Khiva* (1876) and warned Gladstone of Russia's expansionist aims. It was followed by *On Horseback through Asia Minor* (1877). *A Ride across the Channel* (1882) was written after a perilous flight to Normandy in a balloon.

BURNAND, Sir Francis Cowley (1836–1917), was a regular contributor to *Punch*. He wrote many burlesques and adaptations of French farces, and his operatta *Cox and Box*, with music by *Sullivan, adapted from J. M. Morton's *Box and Cox*, was performed in 1867.

Burnell the Ass, the hero of the *Speculum Stultorum* by *Wireker. Burnell, who represents the monk who is dissatisfied with his lot, is an ass who wants a longer tail. He goes to Salerno and Paris to study, and finally loses his tail altogether. In the course of his travels he hears the tale that Chaucer alludes to in 'The Nun's Priest's Tale' (see CANTERBURY TALES, 20).

BURNET, Gilbert (1643–1715), was a popular preacher, a latitudinarian, and a Whig. He went to The Hague in 1686, where he became an adviser of William of Orange. In 1689 he became bishop of Salisbury. He published an account of the death-bed repentance of *Rochester (1680) and *A History of the Reformation in England* (3 vols, 1679, 1681, 1715). His best-known work, *The History of My Own Times* (2 vols, 1724, 1734), is a mixture of history, autobiography, and anecdote.

BURNET, Thomas (?1635–1715), was the author of *The Theory of the Earth* (2 vols, 1684–90), an imaginative and romantic cosmogony, containing sonorous and magniloquent descriptive passages.

BURNETT, Frances (Eliza) Hodgson (1849–1924), is remembered for her books for children, notably *Little Lord Fauntleroy* (1886), whose character was based on her second son, Vivian, and whose velvet suit began a fashion; and *The Secret Garden* (1911), a children's classic about a spoilt, ill-tempered orphan, Mary, who finds an abandoned garden. While trying to revive it she encounters Colin, her sickly and hysterical cousin; as they work in the garden together he achieves health and she happiness. (See CHILDREN'S LITERATURE.)

BURNEY, Dr Charles (1726–1814), organist, musical historian, and minor composer, was the father of Fanny *Burney and friend of *Garrick, Joshua *Reynolds, and Dr *Johnson. He wrote a *History of Music* (4 vols, 1776–89).

BURNEY, Charles (1757–1817), son of Dr *Burney, a classical scholar. After his death the British Museum bought his library of over 13,000 volumes, which included the largest extant collection of early English newspapers.

BURNEY, Fanny (Frances, Mme d'Arblay) (1752–1840), daughter of Dr *Burney, lived in her youth in the midst of that London society which included Dr *Johnson, *Burke, *Reynolds, *Garrick, and the *Blue Stocking Circle. In 1778 she published anonymously her first novel *Evelina*, and the revelation of its authorship brought her immediate fame. She published *Cecilia* in 1782, and in 1786 was appointed second keeper of the robes to Queen Charlotte. In 1793 she married General d'Arblay, a French refugee in England. *Camilla* was published in 1796. She and her husband were interned by Napoleon and lived in France from 1802 to 1812. In 1832 she edited the *Memoirs* of her father. She was a prodigious writer of lively letters and journals: her *Early Diary 1768–1778* (1889) includes sketches of Johnson, Garrick, and others; her later *Diary and Letters . . . 1778–1840* (1842–6) has a vivid account of her life at court.

Her three major novels take as their theme the entry into the world of a young girl of beauty and understanding but no experience, and expose her to circumstances and events that develop her character; they display, with a satirical eye and a sharp ear for dialogue, the varied company in which she finds herself.

'Burning Babe, The', see SOUTHWELL, R.

BURNS, Robert (1759–96), was one of seven children born to a cotter near Alloway in Ayrshire. His spare time was fully employed on the ailing farm as labourer and ploughman. The experience of poverty and injustice as a youth no doubt increased his belief in the equality of men, which led him to become an ardent supporter of the early days of the French Revolution. In 1784, after the death of his father, he and his brother continued to farm, now at Mossgiel. To this period belong 'The Cotter's Saturday Night', 'To a Mouse', 'To a Mountain Daisy', 'Holy Willie's Prayer', the Epistles to Labraik, 'The Holy Fair', and many others.

His Kilmarnock edition of *Poems, chiefly in the Scottish Dialect* (1786) was an immediate success and Burns found himself fêted by the literary and aristocratic society of Edinburgh. His attractive appearance and his gregarious temperament led him into a life of dissipation and amorous complexity. He was encouraged to write in the rhetorical and sentimental fashion of the day, and in this mode he wrote 'The Lament', 'Despondency', and 'Address to Edinburgh', but his own characteristic voice was not subdued. He collected, amended, and wrote some 200 songs for *The Scots Musical Museum* which includes many of his best-known lyrics, such as *'Auld Lang Syne', 'O my luve's like a red, red rose', 'Ye Banks and Braes', and 'Scots wha hae'. He contributed in 1792 to *Select Scottish Airs*. In 1788 he married Jean Armour, and settled on a poor farm at Ellisland, near Dumfries. A year later he secured a post as an Excise officer, and in 1791 relinquished his farming life and moved to Dumfries. Also in 1791 he published his last major poem *'Tam O'Shanter'. Turning against the French at last, he joined the Dumfries Volunteers in 1795, dying the following year of rheumatic heart disease.

Burns wrote with equal facility in correct 18th-cent. English and in his native Scots. The Scottish poems owe much to Scottish song, to the early Scottish poets (such as *Ramsay), and to the 18th-cent. poet *Fergusson. His popularity with his fellow-countrymen is reflected in celebrations held all over the world on 'Burns Night', 25 Jan., his birthday.

BURROUGHS, Edgar Rice (1875–1950), American novelist and writer of *Science Fiction, remembered principally for his adventure stories about Tarzan, who first appeared in *Tarzan of the Apes* (1914).

BURROUGHS, William Seward (1914–), American novelist, best known for his frank accounts of life as a drug addict (*Junkie*, 1953; *The Naked Lunch*, 1959), for his experiments with collage technique, and for his obsession with the underworld and homosexual fantasy (*Nova Express*, 1964; *The Wild Boys*, 1971). See also under BEAT GENERATION.

BURTON, Sir Richard Francis (1821–90), joined the Indian army in 1842. He left India in 1849, and subsequent travels took him to the forbidden city of Mecca, to Africa on several expeditions, to the Crimea, to Salt Lake City (where he studied the Mormons), and as consul to Brazil, Damascus (1869–71), and Trieste (1871) where he died. He published over 40 volumes of travel, including his *Personal Narrative of a Pilgrimage to El-Medinah and Meccah* (1855–6) and *The Lake Regions of Central Africa* (1860). He is best remembered for his unexpurgated versions of the *Arabian Nights* (1885–8), *The Kama Sutra* (1883), *The Perfumed Garden* (1886, from the French), and other works of Arabian erotology. His interest in sexual behaviour and deviance (which he shared with his friends *Milnes and *Swinburne) and his detailed, frank, and valuable ethnographical

notes led him to risk prosecution many times under the Obscene Publications Act of 1857.

BURTON, Robert (1577–1640), author of *The Anatomy of Melancholy*.

BUSBY, Richard (1606–95), was a famous headmaster of Westminster School from 1638 to 1695 whose pupils included *Dryden, *Locke, *Atterbury, and *Prior.

Busie Body, The, a comedy by S. *Centlivre, produced 1709.

The devices by which Sir Francis Gripe's intentions to marry his ward Miranda are defeated, and those by which his son Charles secures the hand of Isabinda, occupy the play. Marplot, whose well-meant but misdirected interference constantly endangers the course of true love, has enriched the language with a name for the blundering busybody.

Busirane, in Spenser's *Faerie Queene* (III. ix and xii) the 'vile Enchaunter' symbolizing unlawful love.

Buskin, a word existing in many European languages, whose ultimate derivation is unknown. It is the word used for the high thick-soled boot (*cothurnus*) worn by actors in ancient Athenian tragedy, hence applied figuratively to the style or spirit of tragedy.

Bussy D'Ambois, a tragedy by *Chapman, written ?1604, published 1607. The most famous of Chapman's plays.

Bussy D'Ambois (in real life Louis de Bussy-d'Ambois), a man of insolence and fiery courage, is raised from poverty and introduced to the court of Henri III of France by Monsieur, brother of the king, his protector. He quarrels with the king's courtiers, of whom he kills three in an encounter, and even with the duc de Guise. He wins the favour of Tamyra, wife of Montsurry (Montsoreau); Monsieur, who also desires Tamyra, betrays Bussy to Montsurry. Montsurry by torture forces Tamyra to lure Bussy into a trap; he is overpowered and killed, dying defiantly on his feet. ('Here like a Roman statue I will stand | Till death hath made me marble.') Chapman's sequel is *The Revenge of Bussy D'Ambois*.

BUTLER, Lady Eleanor, see LLANGOLLEN, THE LADIES OF.

BUTLER, Joseph (1692–1752), was appointed bishop of Bristol in 1738, from which he was translated to Durham in 1750. His reputation stemmed from the publication in 1726 of *Fifteen Sermons* preached at the Rolls Chapel, in which he defines his moral philosophy, affirming an intuitional theory of virtue. In 1736 appeared his

Analogy of Religion, a defence of the Christian religion against the Deists, in which Butler argues that belief in immortality, revelation, and miracles is as reasonable as the beliefs upon which natural religion is founded.

Butler, The Revd Reuben, marries Jeanie Deans in Scott's *The Heart of Midlothian*.

BUTLER, Samuel ('Hudibras') (1613–80), was probably secretary to the countess of Kent, and by 1661 he was steward at Ludlow Castle to Richard Vaughan, earl of Carbery. The most significant event in an otherwise obscure life was the publication of his *Hudibras* (1663), which instantly became the most popular poem of its time. It was probably as a result of its success that he became secretary to the second duke of *Buckingham. In 1677 he was awarded an annual pension of £100 by Charles II, but by then he himself appears to have given currency to the complaint that, though a loyal satirist, he had been left to endure his old age in poverty. He wrote a number of shorter satirical poems, including 'The Elephant in the Moon', an attack on the *Royal Society, and a great many prose 'Characters'.

BUTLER, Samuel (1835–1902), grandson of Dr Samuel Butler, headmaster of Shrewsbury School and bishop of Lichfield. He went to New Zealand, where he achieved success as a sheep-farmer. *A First Year in Canterbury Settlement* (1863) was compiled by his father from Samuel's letters and became the core of *Erewhon*. He returned to England in 1864 and settled in Clifford's Inn, where he began to study painting. *Erewhon* (1872), published anonymously, enjoyed a brilliant but brief success. *The Fair Haven* (1873), an elaborate and ironic attack on the Resurrection, brought him encouragement from C. *Darwin and L. *Stephen. A journey to Canada in 1874–5 inspired his well-known poem 'A Psalm of Montreal', first printed in the *Spectator* in May 1878.

Butler produced a series of works of scientific controversy, many of them directed against certain aspects of Darwinism, in particular C. Darwin's theory of natural selection: they include *Evolution, Old and New* (1879), *Unconscious Memory* (1880), and three articles on 'The Deadlock in Darwinism' (*The Universal Review*, 1890). Butler's espousal of the cause of Lamarck and creative evolution won him the praise of G. B. *Shaw in his preface to *Back to Methuselah* (1921); Shaw also praised Butler's outspoken views on religion and the 'importance of money' in his preface to *Major Barbara* (1907).

Butler published *Alps and Sanctuaries of Piedmont and the Canton Ticino* (1881), the first of several animated works on art and travel. He experimented with musical composition,

including a comic pastoral oratorio, *Narcissus* (1888), written in collaboration with his great friend Festing Jones. In 1896 appeared his *The Life and Letters of Dr Samuel Butler*, his revered grandfather. A long interest in *Homer led to his theory of the feminine authorship of the *Odyssey* and its origin at Trapini in Sicily. *The Authoress of the 'Odyssey'* appeared in 1897, and translations of the *Iliad* and the *Odyssey* into vigorous colloquial prose in 1898 and 1900. A quirky study, *Shakespeare's Sonnets Reconsidered*, appeared in 1899, and *Erewhon Revisited* in 1901. Butler's most revealing work was his semi-autobiographical novel, *The Way of All Flesh* (1903). He left six large Notebooks, full of incident, self-revelation, and ideas; selections of these were published by Festing Jones in 1912.

Button's Coffee House, the rival of *Will's, stood in Russell Street, Covent Garden, and was frequented by *Dryden, *Addison, *Steele, and *Pope.

Buzfuz, Mr Serjeant, in Dickens's *Pickwick Papers*, counsel for the plaintiff in Bardell v. Pickwick.

BYATT, A(ntonia) S(usan) (1936–   ), novelist and critic. Her novels include *Shadow of a Sun* (1964) and *The Game* (1967). *The Virgin in the Garden* (1978), set largely in the coronation year of 1953, is rich in complex allegorical allusions to *Spenser, *Ralegh, *Shakespeare, and many others, and provides a vivid portrait of provincial life in the 1950s. It was followed by a sequel, *Still Life* (1985).

By-Ends, Mr, in Bunyan's *Pilgrim's Progress*, 'a very arch fellow, a downright hypocrite'.

BYROM, John (1692–1763), had many varied literary, linguistic, religious, and scientific interests, and was from 1724 a fellow of the *Royal Society; his varied acquaintance included *Hartley, the *Wesleys, J. *Butler, and, notably, *Law, of whom he left interesting accounts in his *Private Journals and literary remains* (1854–7). Bryom had Jacobite sympathies and was, like Law, a non-juror; he was the author of the ambiguously loyal toast, beginning 'God bless the King! I mean the Faith's Defender . . .' His *Miscellaneous Poems* (1773) include some curious versifications of Law's *Serious Call* and the well-known hymn 'Christians, awake! Salute the happy morn'.

BYRON, George Gordon, sixth baron (1788–1824), son of Captain John Byron and Catherine Gordon of Gight. Byron was born with a club-foot, which (it is generally supposed) had a profound effect on his future temperament. He inherited the baronetcy, and Newstead Abbey in Nottinghamshire, in 1798. He was educated at

Harrow and Trinity College, Cambridge. His first published collection of poems, *Hours of Idleness*, appeared in 1807, and was bitterly attacked by *Brougham in the *Edinburgh Review*. Byron avenged himself in 1809 with his satire *English Bards and Scotch Reviewers*. In 1808 he returned to Newstead, in 1809 took his seat in the House of Lords, and during 1809–11 visited Portugal, Spain, Malta, Greece, and the Levant. He swam the Hellespont, wrote his famous lyric *'Maid of Athens' (1810), and became fired with the wish that Greece be freed from the Turks.

His first great literary triumph came with the publication of the first two cantos of *Childe Harold's Pilgrimage* in March 1812. He was lionized by aristocratic and literary London, survived a hectic love-affair with Lady Caroline *Lamb, and became the constant companion of his half-sister Augusta. In 1813 appeared *The Bride of Abydos* and *The Giaour*; in 1814, *The Corsair* and *Lara*. In the same year Augusta gave birth to a daughter (generally supposed to be Byron's). In 1815 Byron married Annabella Milbanke; in this year their daughter Ada was born, and *Hebrew Melodies* appeared. By now his debts were accumulating and public horror at the rumours of his incest was rising. Annabella left Byron and a legal separation was eventually arranged.

Byron travelled to Geneva in 1816 where the *Shelleys and Claire Claremont had rented a villa. Here he wrote *The Prisoner of Chillon* (1816) and Canto III of *Childe Harold*. After four months he left for Italy, and his daughter by Claire, Allegra, was born in Jan. 1817 in England. While living a riotous life in Venice he completed *Manfred* (1817). While travelling to Rome he passed Tasso's cell, which inspired his *Lament of Tasso* (1817). He returned to Venice and there wrote *Beppo* (1818). Newstead Abbey was sold and Byron was at last free from financial worries. In 1819 he published *Mazeppa*, and the first two Cantos of *Don Juan*. In this year he met Teresa, Countess Guiccioli, to whom he became deeply attached. They lived first in Venice, then he followed her and her household to Ravenna, where he wrote *The Prophecy of Dante*. In 1820 he became deeply involved with the cause of the Italian patriots. In 1821 Teresa left her husband for Byron and *Marino Faliero* was published. At this time Byron became interested in drama, and wrote *The Two Foscari*, *Sardanapalus*, *Cain*, the unfinished *Heaven and Earth*, and the unfinished *The Deformed Transformed*. In 1822 *Werner* and *The Vision of Judgement* were published and in that year his daughter Allegra died. Byron, with Teresa and her family, left for Leghorn, where Leigh *Hunt joined them. Hunt and Byron co-operated in the production of *The Liberal* magazine. In 1823 he published *The Age of Bronze*, a satirical poem on the Congress of Verona, and *The Island*. In Jan. 1824, after

various mishaps and escapes, he arrived at Missolonghi. He formed the 'Byron Brigade' and gave large sums of money, and great inspiration, to the insurgent Greeks; but before he saw any serious military action he died of fever in April.

Byron's poetry, although widely condemned on moral grounds, and frequently attacked by critics, was immensely popular. Much of his poetry and drama exerted great influence on *Romanticism. His legacy of inspiration in European poetry, music, the novel, opera, and painting, has been immense. B. *Russell wrote that 'As a myth his importance, especially on the continent, was enormous.'

Byron, Harriet, the heroine of Richardson's *Sir Charles Grandison*.

BYRON, John (1723–86), as a midshipman on one of the ships of Anson's squadron, was wrecked on an island off the coast of Chile in 1741. His 'Narrative' of the shipwreck, published 1768, was used by his grandson Lord *Byron in his description of the storm and wreck in *Don Juan*.

BYRON, Robert (1905–41), travel writer, Byzantinist, and aesthete. His works include *The Station* (1928), *The Byzantine Achievement* (1929), and *The Appreciation of Architecture* (1932), but he is chiefly remembered for his classic study *The Road to Oxiana* (1937), a record in the form of diary jottings of a journey from Venice through the Middle East and Afghanistan to India in search of the origins of Islamic architecture and culture.

Byron, *The Conspiracy and Tragedy of Charles Duke of*, a two-part play by *Chapman, published 1608.

Byronic, characteristic of or resembling *Byron or his poetry; that is, contemptuous of and rebelling against conventional morality, or defying fate, or possessing the characteristics of Byron's romantic heroes, or imitating his dress and appearance.

BYWATER, Ingram (1840–1914), eminent Greek scholar. He succeeded *Jowett as Regius professor of Greek at Oxford in 1893. His major works were an edition (1877) of the Fragments of *Heraclitus and a monumental edition of the Poetics of *Aristotle (1909).

Byzantine, the word used to designate the art, and especially the architecture, developed in the eastern division of the Roman Empire. This eastern division endured from the partition of the Empire between the two sons of Theodosius in AD 395 to the capture of Constantinople, its capital, formerly known as Byzantium, by the Turks in 1453. Byzantine architecture is distinguished by its use of the round arch, cross, circle, dome, and rich mosaic ornament. St Mark's at Venice is a prominent example. Byzantium stands as an important symbol in the poems of *Yeats ('Sailing to Byzantium', 'Byzantium') where it appears to represent the undying world of art, contrasted with the 'fury and the mire of human veins'; but the word 'byzantine' is also sometimes used (with reference to history rather than art) to convey a sinister sense of oriental intrigue.

C

Cade, Jack, Rebellion of, a popular revolt by the men of Kent in 1450, Yorkist in sympathy, against the misrule of Henry VI. Its leader Jack Cade, who is said to have been Irish, took the name Mortimer and marched triumphantly into London where his followers beheaded Say, the lord treasurer. After a fight on London Bridge, Cade retreated into Sussex where he was killed. He appears as a character in Shakespeare's *Henry VI*.

Cadenus and Vanessa, a poem by *Swift, written in 1713 for Esther Vanhomrigh ('Vanessa'). It is the narrative, in mock classical form, of the author's relations with 'Vanessa' and an apology for his conduct. 'Cadenus' is an obvious anagram of 'Decanus', dean. Miss Vanhomrigh evidently took no exception to his statement of the facts, since she preserved the poem and desired it to be published. It appeared in 1726, three years after her death.

Cadwal, in Shakespeare's *Cymbeline*, the name of *Arviragus during his childhood in Wales.

CADWALLADER, (1) the last of the British kings of England; he died in 689 according to *Geoffrey of Monmouth; (2) a character in Smollett's *Peregrine Pickle*; (3) a Mrs Cadwallader figures in George Eliot's *Middlemarch*.

CAEDMON (*fl.* 670), entered the monastery of Streaneshalch (Whitby) between 658 and 680, when already an elderly man. He is said by *Bede to have been an unlearned herdsman who received suddenly, in a vision, the power of song. In 1655 François Dujon (Franciscus Junius) published at Amsterdam from the unique Bodleian MS Junius II (*c*.1000) long scriptural poems, which he took to be those of Caedmon. These are *Genesis*, *Exodus*, *Daniel*, and *Christ and Satan*, but modern scholarship denies attribution to Caedmon. The only work which can be attributed to him is the short 'Hymn of Creation', quoted by Bede.

Caelia, in Spenser's *Faerie Queene* (I. x) the Lady of the House of Holiness.

Caerleon, see CARLIOUN.

CAESAR, Gaius Julius (102/100–44 BC), Roman general and politician. Victor in the factional struggles that destroyed the Republic, and eventually dictator, he prepared the ground for six centuries of imperial rule. He was also a writer of exceptional ability and has left a lucid account of his campaigns in his *Commentaries*. The *Commentaries on the Gallic War* were translated in part by A. *Golding (1565) and C. Edmundes (1600). Mentions of Caesar abound in English literature. *Dryden for example cites his opinions repeatedly. But the true signposts to the nature of his reputation are Shakespeare's *Julius Caesar* (*c*.1600) and *Shaw's *Caesar and Cleopatra* (1901). It is in these that we have the time-honoured Caesarian legend.

Caesar and Pompey, a Roman tragedy by *Chapman, published 1631.
It deals with the contention of Caesar and Pompey, the events leading to the battle of Pharsalus (48 BC), the murder of Pompey and the suicide of Cato of Utica. The motto of the play is 'Only a just man is a free man'.

Caesura, in Greek and Latin prosody, the division of a metrical foot between two words, especially in certain recognized places near the middle of the line; in English prosody, a pause about the middle of a metrical line, generally indicated by a pause in the sense.

Café Royal, a French-style café-restaurant at 68 Regent Street, which was for several decades from the 1880s onwards the haunt of artists and writers. Its habitués included *Wilde, *Dowson, A. *Symons, *Beerbohm, and G. B. *Shaw; it appeared in the novels of D. H. *Lawrence, *Maugham, Arnold *Bennett, E. *Waugh, and others.

Cain: a Mystery, a poetic drama by *Byron published 1821.
Cain, revolting against the heavy toil imposed upon him because of another's fault and bewildered how to reconcile the world he knows with the goodness of an omnipotent God, becomes a willing pupil of Lucifer and questions him about the problems of existence. The audacity of the poem aroused intense indignation, and the publisher, John *Murray, was threatened with prosecution. Byron strongly denied that the views of either Cain or Lucifer represented his own.

CAINE, (Sir Thomas Henry) Hall (1853–1931), novelist, was befriended by D. G. *Rossetti, and spent the last few months of Rossetti's life as his housemate: see Caine's *Recollections of Dante Gabriel Rossetti* (1882). He edited an anthology, *Sonnets of Three Centuries* (1882), in which all three Rossettis and W. B. *Scott were well represented. He wrote many novels of wide popularity and a somewhat sensational reputation, many of them centred in the Isle of Man; they include *The Shadow of a Crime* (1885), *The Bondman* (1890), *The Manxman* (1894), *The Eternal City* (1901), *The Prodigal Son* (1904), *The White Prophet* (1909).

Caius, Dr, a French physician in Shakespeare's *The Merry Wives of Windsor*.

Calantha, the heroine of Ford's *The Broken Heart*.

Caleb Williams (*Things as they are: or The Adventures of Caleb Williams*), a novel by W. *Godwin, published 1794. This work is remarkable as an early example of the propagandist novel, as a novel of pursuit, crime, and detection, and as a psychological study. A provocative preface to the original edition was withdrawn.

It is related in the first person to its eponymous hero. The first part of the book deals with the misdeeds of Tyrrel, an arrogant and tyrannical country squire, who ruins a tenant on his estate, Hawkins, for refusing to yield to one of his whims, and drives to the grave his niece Miss Melville for refusing to marry a boor of his selection. In the course of these events he comes into conflict with the idealistic and benevolent Falkland, a neighbouring squire, knocks him down in public, and is shortly after found murdered. Suspicion falls on Falkland but is diverted to Hawkins and his son, who are tried and executed. From this time Falkland becomes eccentric and solitary. Caleb Williams, the self-educated son of humble parents, is appointed his secretary, and convinces himself that Falkland is in fact Tyrrel's murderer. The remainder of the book concerns Falkland's unrelenting persecution of Williams, despite William's devotion to his employer and refusal to betray his secret. Williams is imprisoned on a false charge of robbing his employer, escapes, but is tracked by Falkland's agents until, in despair, he lays a charge of murder against Falkland, is confronted with him, and, although he has no proof to offer, through his generosity and sincerity wins from the murderer a confession of guilt. Godwin's original ending was radically different.

Caledonia, the Roman name for the northern part of Britain, hence used poetically for Scotland.

Calendar, the system according to which the beginning and length of the year are fixed.

The Julian Calendar is that introduced by Julius Caesar in 46 BC, in which the ordinary year has 365 days and every fourth year is a leap year of 366 days. This was known as 'Old Style' when the Gregorian Calendar was introduced.

The Gregorian Calendar is the modification of the preceding, introduced by Pope Gregory XIII in 1582, and adopted in Great Britain in 1752. It was known as 'New Style'. The error, due to the fact that the Julian year of 365¼ days (allowing for leap years) was 11 minutes 10 seconds too long, amounted in 1752 to 11 days, and in order to correct this, 2 Sept. was in that year followed by 14 Sept., while century years were to be leap years only when divisible by 400 (e.g. 1600, 2000).

Calendar of Modern Letters, The (1925–7), a literary periodical, first a monthly, then a quarterly, edited by E. *Rickword and Douglas Garman. It published fiction by D. H. *Lawrence, *Pirandello, A. E. *Coppard, *Gerhardi, and others; in its critical articles it condemned the 'non-combatant' and uncommitted critical attitudes of *Gosse and the grossness of Arnold *Bennett, found the products of *Bloomsbury to be on the whole frivolous and sentimental, and praised the critical approach of I. A. *Richards. *Towards Standards of Criticism: Selections from the Calendar of Modern Letters* was published in 1933 with an introduction by *Leavis, who credited the periodical with having established 'the critical basis for appreciating Mr Eliot, Mr Pound and their successors'. *Scrutiny* upheld many of its attitudes.

CALENIUS, Walter, see GEOFFREY OF MONMOUTH.

Caliban, in Shakespeare's *The Tempest*, is described in the *Folio 'Names of the Actors' as 'a salvage and deformed slave'.

'Caliban upon Setebos', a poem by R. Browning, included in *Dramatis Personae*.

Caliburn, see EXCALIBUR.

Calidore, Sir, the Knight of Courtesy, the hero of Bk VI of Spenser's *Faerie Queene*. He pursues and chains the *Blatant Beast.

Calista, the heroine of Rowe's *The Fair Penitent*, in which the 'gay Lothario' figures as her lover.

Calisto and Melibea, see CELESTINA.

CALLIMACHUS (*c.*310–after 246 BC), perhaps the finest of Hellenistic poets and a scholar who worked in the library of Alexandria. Many of his works were lost in the upheavals of the 13th cent., and only six hymns, sixty epigrams, and a number of fragments have survived. Callimachus found few readers until the end of the 17th cent. He was imitated by *Akenside in his 'Hymn to the Naiads'. One of his epigrams served as a model for W. J. *Cory's 'They told me Heraclitus . . .' (1845), and mythological material drawn from his hymns can be found in Tennyson's *'Tiresias' and *Bridges' *Prometheus the Firegiver* (1883).

Callista, a religious novel by J. H. *Newman.

CALVERLEY, Charles Stuart (1831–84), became known under the initials C.S.C. as a writer of light verse, parodies, and translations. His *Verses and Translations* appeared in 1862, *Fly Leaves* in 1872.

CALVIN (from Calvinus, the Latinized form of Cauvin), Jean (1509–64), French theologian and reformer. In 1536 he published in Basle the first (Latin) edition of his *Institution de la religion chrétienne* which was conceived as a defence of the Reformed Faith. It repudiated scholastic methods of argument in favour of deductions from biblical authority and the moral nature of man, and it advocated the doctrines of sin and grace—with the attendant doctrine of predestination derived from St Paul—at the expense of salvation by works. Calvin was an unswerving opponent of episcopacy. The influence of his ideas in 16th- and 17th-cent. England can scarcely be exaggerated.

Cambalo, one of the two sons of King Cambuscan, in Chaucer's 'Squire's Tale': see CANTERBURY TALES, II; see also Cambell (below) for the continuation of his story in Spenser's *Faerie Queene.*

Cambell, or Cambello, the name given by Spenser in *The Faerie Queene,* IV. iii, to *Cambalo, whose tale he borrows from 'Dan *Chaucer,* well of English undefyled', and completes. Cambell is brother of *Canacee, for whom there are many suitors. It is arranged that the strongest of these, three brothers, shall fight with Cambell and the lady be awarded to the victor. Two of the brothers are defeated: the contest between the third, Triamond, and Cambell is undecided, each wounding the other. They are reconciled by Cambina, Triamond's sister; Canacee is awarded to Triamond and Cambell marries Cambina. The magic ring of Canacee in the 'Squire's Tale' reappears in the *Faerie Queene,* with the power of healing wounds.

Camber (Kamber), according to legend one of the sons of Brutus (see BRUT). Camber is supposed to have given his name to Cambria (Wales) which is a Latinized derivative of Cymry (Welshmen).

CAMBRENSIS, Giraldus, see GIRALDUS CAMBRENSIS.

Cambridge Bibliography of English Literature, an invaluable reference work in four volumes, edited by F. W. *Bateson, published 1940, with a supplement, edited by George Watson, 1957. It was succeeded by the *New Cambridge Bibliography of English Literature* (1969–77; 5 vols).

Cambridge Platonists, a group of Anglican divines who had close connections with Cambridge University and tried to promote a rational form of Christianity in the tradition of *Hooker and *Erasmus. The group included Benjamin Whichcote (1609–83), whose writings, mostly sermons and letters, were published posthumously; John Smith (1618–52), a pupil of Whichcote and author of *Select Discourses* (1660); Henry More (1614–87), whose early poetry *Psychodia Platonica* (1642) has some remarkable passages, and whose prose works are profound and complex; Ralph Cudworth (1617–88), whose major work, *The True Intellectual System of the Universe* (1678), must be regarded as the group's most detailed manifesto. Nathaniel Culverwell (d. 1651) is often included in the group, but his outlook differed from that of the rest, being more Calvinist and Aristotelian.

The aims of the group were to combat materialism, which was finding a forceful exponent in T. *Hobbes, and to reform religion by freeing it from fantacism and controversy. Drawing inspiration from *Plato and *Plotinus, they maintained that Sense reveals only appearances, Reality consists in 'intelligible forms' which are 'ideas vitally protended or actively exerted from within itself'. They held furthermore that Revelation, the Rational Order of the Universe and human Reason were all in harmony, so that to search for Truth was to search for God. They rejected the Calvinist doctrine that human nature was deeply corrupt, capable of salvation only through the action of a Divine Grace granted to some and withheld from others, and saw Man as 'deiform', able to advance towards perfection through Reason and the imitation of Christ.

These doctrines were presented in a rhetorical, often verbose manner which has masked their revolutionary character, but it is evident that they prepared the way for the *Deism of the 18th cent.

Cambridge University Press. Books were first printed at Cambridge in 1521–2 by John Siberch (John Lair of Siegburg), a friend of *Erasmus. A charter was granted to the University by Henry VIII in 1534 authorizing the printing of books there, but not until 1583 was the first university Printer, Thomas Thomas, appointed. The activity of the Press was developed under the influence of R. *Bentley (1662–1742) when the present system of control by a Syndicate, or committee of senior academics, was instituted. With a history of continuous activity since 1584, the Press claims to be the oldest printer-publisher in England, perhaps in the world. The Press has been a notable scientific publisher from I. *Newton and *Ray to the present day, and its wide range of publications include editions of classical authors, works by C. S. *Lewis and F. R. *Leavis and the great range of collaborative histories first planned by *Acton. The principle of large-scale collaborative history has also been applied to English literature, and a history of American literature is planned.

Cambuscan, in Chaucer's 'Squire's Tale' (see CANTERBURY TALES, II), a king of Tartary.

Cambyses, King, subject of a tragedy (1569) by T. *Preston, which illustrates the transition from the morality play to the historical tragedy. It is founded on the story of Cambyses (king of Persia) in Herodotus; its bombastic grandiloquence became proverbial and is referred to in *1 *Henry IV*, II. iv.

CAMDEN, William (1551–1623), antiquary and historian, was appointed headmaster of Westminster School in 1593; one of his pupils was *Jonson, who said that he owed Camden 'All that I am in arts, all that I know'. He made tours of antiquarian research up and down England. He published his *Britannia* (1586) and his *Annales . . . regnante Elizabetha . . . ad annum 1589* (1615; pt. II, 1629), a civic history, and founded a chair of ancient history in Oxford. Camden wrote principally in Latin.

Camden Society, founded in 1838 in honour of W. *Camden, for the purpose of publishing documents relating to the early history and literature of the British empire. In 1897 it was amalgamated with the *Royal Historical Society.

Camelot, the seat of King Arthur's court, is said by *Malory to be Winchester. It may be Camelford in Cornwall, the name actually given it by *Laȝamon; following Drayton's *Poly-Olbion*, it is identified as South Cadbury in Somerset, and *Leland says he found traces of Arthur in Queen's Camel in Somerset which was previously called Camelot. Colchester has also claimed it.

CAMERON, (John) Norman (1905–53), poet. His poems were published in periodicals during the 1930s, principally in *New Verse*; his collections include *The Winter House* (1935) and *Forgive me, Sire* (1950). His *Collected Poems* were published posthumously in 1957 with an introduction by Robert *Graves. His poems are brief, lucid, and concentrated, built usually on a single image or parable.

Camilla, or a Picture of Youth, a novel by F. *Burney, published 1796.

The book relates the stories of a group of young people, the lively and beautiful Camilla Tyrold, her sisters, and her exotic, selfish cousin Indiana Lynmere; and centres on the love affair of Camilla herself and her eligible, but cool and judicious, suitor Edgar Mandlebert. Its happy consummation is delayed over five volumes by intrigues, contretemps, and misunderstandings, many of them designed to exhibit the virtues and failings of Camilla, or to test and improve her character.

Camillo, in Shakespeare's *The Winter's Tale*, a Sicilian lord.

Camiola, the heroine of Massinger's *The Maid of Honour*.

Camlann, according to the 9th–10th-cent. *Annales Cambriae* the place of the battle in 537 in which *Arthur and Medraut (Modred) fell. It may possibly be Slaughter or Bloody Bridge on the River Camel, in Cornwall.

CAMOËNS (or CAMÕES), Luis de (1524–80), a Portuguese poet, is remembered outside his own country for his great epic poem *Os Luciadas* (1572), the *Lusiads*, in ten cantos of eight-lined stanzas. Its subject is the history of Portugal, and it celebrates the descendants of Lusus, the legendary founder of Lusitania, or Portugal, and more particularly the exploits of Vasco da Gama, the Portuguese navigator. Sir Richard *Burton translated much of Camoëns' work.

Campaspe, a prose comedy by *Lyly, published 1584 under the title *Alexander, Campaspe and Diogenes*. Alexander the Great engages Apelles to paint the portrait of his Theban captive Campaspe. Apelles and Campaspe fall in love; when the portrait is finished he spoils it to occasion further sittings. Alexander becomes suspicious and by a trick makes Apelles reveal it. He surrenders Campaspe to Apelles and returns to his wars. The story is told in *Pliny's *Natural History*, XXXV. 10.

CAMPBELL, Joseph (1879–1944), Irish poet, who published some of his works under the Irish version of his name, Seosamh MacCathmhaoil. Most of his lyrics and ballads are based on Irish legend and folklore; his collections include *The Garden of Bees* (1905), *The Gilly of Christ* (1907), and *Earth of Cualann* (1917). His *Collected Poems*, with an introduction by A. *Clarke, was published in 1963.

CAMPBELL, (Ignatius) Roy(ston Dunnachie) (1901–57), poet, born in Natal, came to England in 1918. His works include *The Flaming Terrapin* (1924); *The Wayzgoose* (1928), a satire on South African life; *Adamastor* (1930); *The Georgiad*

(1931), a long, biting attack on the *Bloomsbury Group; *Flowering Reeds* (1933), lyrics; *Mithraic Emblems* (1936); *Flowering Rifle* (1939), a pro-Fascist work which brought him much opprobrium; and *Sons of the Mistral* (1941), a selection of his best poems. His *Collected Poems* appeared in 1950. He published two autobiographical works, *Broken Record* (1934), a narrative of adventure and Fascist opinions, and *Light on a Dark Horse* (1951), propagating his legend. He did much translation and in 1952 published an important study and translation of García Lorca.

CAMPBELL, Thomas (1777–1844), was closely associated with the founding of the University of London in the late 1820s. He published *The Pleasures of Hope* (1799), *Gertrude of Wyoming* (1809), *Theodric, and other poems* (1824) and *The Pilgrim of Glencoe, and other poems* (1842). He is now chiefly remembered for his war-songs, *'The Battle of Hohenlinden', 'The Battle of the Baltic', and 'Ye Mariners of England'; and his ballads, such as 'The Soldier's Dream' and 'Lord Ullin's Daughter'.

CAMPION, Thomas (1567–1620), poet, musician, and doctor. In 1595 he published his Latin *Poemata* and between 1601 and 1617 four *Bookes of Ayres*, with many settings composed by himself, and his *Songs of Mourning* for Prince Henry. His *Observations in the Art of English Poesie* (1602) defended classical metres against 'the vulgar and unarteficiall custome of riming'. In the early years of James I's reign he wrote a number of court masques.

Campo-Basso, count of, an Italian captain in the army of Charles the Bold of Burgundy, who figures in Scott's *Quentin Durward* and *Anne of Geierstein*.

Campus Novel, a novel set on a university campus. Notable English examples include *Amis's Lucky Jim* (1954), D. *Lodge's Changing Places* (1975), and *Bradbury's The History Man* (1975).

CAMUS, Albert (1913–60), French novelist, dramatist and essayist, whose works defined and contributed to the philosophical concept of the 'absurd' (see ABSURD, THEATRE OF THE).

Canacee, the daughter of King Cambuscan in Chaucer's 'Squire's Tale' (see CANTERBURY TALES, II) and in Spenser's *Faerie Queene*, Bk IV.

Candour, Mrs, one of the scandal-mongers in Sheridan's *The School for Scandal*.

CANNING, George (1770–1827), Tory statesman, became prime minister in 1827. Apart from his political speeches (published 1828), he

is remembered in a literary connection as founder of and contributor to *The Anti-Jacobin*. His *Poems* were published in 1823.

Canongate, Chronicles of the, see CHRONICLES OF THE CANONGATE.

'Canon's Yeoman's Tale, The', see CANTERBURY TALES, 22.

Canterbury Tales, The, *Chaucer's most celebrated work probably designed about 1387 and extending to 17,000 lines in prose and verse of various metres, but predominantly in rhyming couplets. The General Prologue describes the meeting of 29 pilgrims in the Tabard Inn in Southwark (in fact they add up to 31; it has been suggested that the prioress's 'preestes three' in line 164 may be an error since only one 'Nun's Priest' is mentioned in the body of the work). Detailed pen-pictures are given of 21 of them, vividly described but perhaps corresponding to traditional lists of the orders of society, clerical and lay. The host (see BAILLY, HARRY) proposes that the pilgrims should shorten the road by telling four stories each, two on the way to Canterbury and two on the way back; he will accompany them and award a free supper on their return to the teller of the best story. The work is incomplete; only 23 pilgrims tell stories, and there are only 24 stories told altogether (Chaucer tells two). In the scheme the stories are linked by narrative exchanges between the pilgrims and by prologues and epilogues to the tales; but this aspect of the work is also very incomplete. It is uncertain in what order the stories are meant to come. The order that follows is that of the Ellesmere MS, followed in the best complete edition of Chaucer, F. N. Robinson's (2nd edn, 1957, currently under revision).

(1) 'The Knight's Tale', a shortened version of the *Teseida* of *Boccaccio, the story of the love of Palamon and Arcite, prisoners of Theseus king of Athens, for Emelye, sister of Hippolyta queen of the Amazons, whom Theseus has married. The rivals compete for her in a tournament. Palamon is defeated, but Arcite, the favourite of Mars, at the moment of his triumph is thrown and injured by his horse through the intervention of Venus and Saturn, and dies. Palamon and Emelye, after prolonged mourning for Arcite, are united.

(2) 'The Miller's Tale', a ribald story of the deception, first of a husband (a carpenter) through the prediction of a second flood, and secondly of a lover who expects to kiss the lady's lips but kisses instead her 'nether eye'. He avenges himself on her lover for this humiliation with a red-hot ploughshare. The Tale has been said to be a parody of a courtly-love story.

(3) 'The Reeve's Tale' is a *fabliau about two clerks who are robbed by a miller of some of the meal which they take to his mill to be ground,

and who take their vengeance by sleeping with the miller's wife and daughter. In Chaucer's context, it is an obvious rejoinder to the miller's tale of the duping of a carpenter, the reeve's profession.

(4) 'The Cook's Tale' of Perkyn Revelour only extends to 58 lines before it breaks off. It is another ribald fabliau which ends with the introduction of a prostitute, and it has been suggested that Chaucer may have decided that the occurrence of three indecent tales together was unbalanced.

(5) 'The Man of Law's Tale' is the story of Constance, daughter of a Christian emperor of Rome, who marries the Sultan of Syria on condition that he become a Christian and who is cast adrift in a boat because of the machinations of the Sultan's jealous mother. It is a frequently told medieval story, paralleled by the romance *Emaré* and by *Gower's Constance story in Confessio Amantis.

(6) 'The Wife of Bath's Tale' is preceded by an 856-line prologue in which she condemns celibacy by describing her life with her five late husbands, in the course of which Chaucer draws widely on the medieval anti-feminist tradition, especially on Jean de Meun's La Vielle (the Duenna) in the *Roman de la rose. After this vigorous, learned, and colourful narrative, the following tale, though appropriate, seems rather flat. It is the story of 'the loathly lady' (paralleled by Gower's 'Tale of Florent' in Confessio Amantis), in which a knight is asked to answer the question, 'what do women most desire?' The correct answer, 'sovereignty', is told him by a hideous old witch on condition that he marry her; when he does she is restored to youth and beauty.

(7) 'The Friar's Tale' tells how a summoner meets the devil dressed as a yeoman and they agree to share out what they are given. They come upon a carter who curses his horse, commending it to the devil; the summoner asks the devil why he does not take the horse thus committed to him and the devil replies that it is because the commendation does not come from the heart. Later they visit an old woman from whom the summoner attempts to extort twelve pence, whereupon she commends *him* to the devil. The devil carries him off to Hell because her curse was from the heart. Chaucer's exact source is not known, but it is clear that the friar tells it to enrage the summoner on the pilgrimage, who interrupts the narrative and rejoins with a scurrilous and discreditable story about a friar.

(8) 'The Summoner's Tale' tells of a greedy friar who undertakes to divide a deathbed legacy amongst his community; he receives a fart and has to devise an ingenious stratagem to divide it with perfect justice.

(9) 'The Clerk's Tale', which the poet tells us he took from *Petrarch, was translated into Latin by the latter from the Italian version of Boccaccio in *The Decameron. (It is clear, however, that Chaucer's version is rather more dependent on a French prose version than on Petrarch's Latin). The story tells of patient Griselda and her trials by her husband, the Marquis Walter.

(10) 'The Merchant's Tale', in which the Merchant, prompted by the tale of Griselda's extreme obedience, tells his 'Tale' of January and May, the old husband with his young wife, and the problems with obedient fidelity involved in this relationship. After a lengthy review of the pros and cons of taking a young wife, January ignores the good advice of Justinus in favour of the time-serving opinion of Placebo and marries May. When he goes blind she makes love to her suitor Damyan in a pear-tree round which January wraps his arms. Pluto mischievously restores January's sight at this point, but Proserpine inspires May to explain that the restoration of his sight was brought about by her activities in the pear-tree and that this had been their purpose. There are parallels to the various sections of the story in French, Latin, Italian, and German.

(11) 'The Squire's Tale', of Cambuscan, king of Tartary, to whom on his birthday an envoy from the king of Arabia brings magic gifts, including a ring for the king's daughter Canacee, which enables her to understand the language of birds. A female falcon tells Canacee the story of her own desertion by a tercelet. The tale is incomplete but it seems likely that Chaucer meant to finish it.

(12) 'The Franklin's Tale', of Dorigen, wife of Arveragus, who to escape the assiduity of her lover, the squire Aurelius, makes her consent depend on an impossible condition, that all the rocks on the coast of Brittany be removed. When this condition is realized by the aid of a magician, the lover, from a generous remorse, releases her from her promise. Chaucer states that the tale is taken from a *'Breton Lay', but that this is lost. There are a number of parallels in medieval literature, of which the closest is Boccaccio's Il Filocolo, Question 4.

(13) 'The Physician's Tale' tells of Virginia who, at her own request, is killed by her father to escape the designs of the corrupt judge Apius. The original source is *Livy's History, and this is what Chaucer cites, though his version seems to rely principally on the Roman de la rose by Jean de Meun.

(14) 'The Pardoner's Tale' follows a prologue in which he declares his own covetousness, and takes covetousness as its theme, relating it to other sins: drunkenness, gluttony, gambling, and swearing. Three rioters set out to find Death who has killed their companion; a mysterious old man tells them they will find him under a particular tree, but when they get there they find instead a heap of gold. By aiming to cheat each

other in possessing the gold they kill each other. The character of the Pardoner in the prologue here is related to Faus-Semblant (False-Seeming) in Jean de Meun's part of the *Roman de la rose*.

(15) 'The Shipman's Tale'. There is a similar story in *The Decameron* (Day 8, Tale 1). The wife of a niggardly merchant asks the loan of a hundred francs from a priest to buy finery. The priest borrows the sum from the merchant and hands it to the wife, and the wife grants him her favours. On the merchant's return from a journey the priest tells him that he has repaid the sum to the wife, who cannot deny receiving it.

(16) 'The Prioress's Tale' tells of the murder of a child by Jews because he sings a Marian hymn while passing through their quarter and of the discovery of his body because of its continued singing of the hymn after death. There are a great many parallels for the story. Some critics see the bland story as a comment on the uncritical nature of the prioress.

(17) 'Chaucer's Tale of Sir Thopas' is a witty and elegant parody of the contemporary romance, both in its subject and in the unsubstantiality of its *tail-rhyme form. Its butts are no doubt general; but it can perhaps be taken to have special reference to the heroes it catalogues (VII. 898–900): Horn Child, the legend of Ypotys, Bevis of Hampton, *Guy of Warwick, the unidentified Pleyndamour, and *Libeaus Desconsus.

(18) When the Host interrupts the tale of Sir Thopas, Chaucer moves to the opposite extreme with a heavy prose homily, 'The Tale of Melibeus'. The story of the impetuous Melibeus and his wise wife Prudence dates from Italy in the 1240s, when the story was written in Latin prose for his third son by Albertano of Brescia. Chaucer's immediate source was the 1336 version in French prose by Renaud de Louens.

(19) 'The Monk's Tale' is composed of a number of 'tragedies' of persons fallen from high estate, taken from different authors and arranged on the model of Boccaccio's *De casibus virorum illustrium*. The tale is in eight-lined stanzas.

(20) 'The Nun's Priest's Tale' is related to the French cycle of Renart (see REYNARD), telling of a fox that beguiled a cock by praising his father's singing and was in turn beguiled by him into losing him by pausing to boast at his victory. The mock-heroic story is full of rhetoric and *exempla*, and it is one of the most admired of the Tales, regarded as the most typically 'Chaucerian' in tone and content. The famous ending of the tale invites the reader to 'take the morality' of the Tale in spite of its apparent lightness of substance, on the grounds that St Paul says everything has *some* moral.

(21) 'The Second Nun's Tale', in rhyme-royal, is perhaps translated from the life of St Cecilia in the *Golden Legend of Jacobus de Voragine. It describes the miracles and martyrdom of the noble Roman maiden Cecilia and her husband Valerian.

(22) 'The Canon's Yeoman's Tale' is told by a character who joins the pilgrims at this late stage (VIII. 554 ff.) with his master, the suspicious Canon whose alchemical skills the yeoman praises. The first 200 lines of the Tale tells of the Alchemist's arcane practice and its futility, before proceeding to the tale proper which tells of how an alchemical canon tricks a priest out of £40 by pretending to teach him the art of making precious metals.

(23) 'The Manciple's Tale' is the fable of the tell-tale crow, told by many authors from *Ovid in *Metamorphoses* (ii. 531–62) onwards. Phebus (Phoebus) has a crow which is white and can speak. It reveals to Phebus the infidelity of his wife and Phebus kills her in a rage. Then, in remorse, he plucks out the crow's white feathers, deprives it of speech and throws it 'unto the devel', which is why crows are now black. A very similar version of the story is told in Gower's *Confessio Amantis* (iii. 768–835).

(24) 'The Parson's Tale' which concludes the work is a long prose treatise, ostensibly on Penitence but dealing at most length with the *Seven Deadly Sins. The two principal sources are Raymund de Pennaforte's *Summa* (dating from the 1220s) and Guilielmus Peraldus' *Summa Vitiorum* (probably from the 1250s) for the Seven Deadly Sins.

Most manuscripts have 'The Parson's Tale' leading straight into Chaucer's closing 'Retracciouns' in which he takes leave of his book. He asks forgiveness of God for his 'translacions and enditynges of worldly vanities', including 'The Tales of Caunterbury, thilke that sownen into (i.e. tend towards) synne'. But this rhetorical conclusion need not be read as a revocation of his work by the poet.

Canto, a subdivision of a long narrative or epic poem, employed in the works of *Dante, *Ariosto, *Tasso, and others; *Spenser was the first to employ the term in English.

CANUTE (Cnutr), a Dane who was king of England 1016–35. The old legend of his failing to repel the sea is told by Holinshed, after *Henry of Huntingdon (who may have invented it) and *Gaimar.

Canute, The Song of, a famous early English poetic fragment stated to have been composed and sung by the king as he rowed past Ely, and recorded by a monk of Ely in 1166.

Can you Forgive Her?, a novel by A. *Trollope, published 1864–5, the first in the *'Palliser' series.

Alice Vavasor, a girl of independent spirit and means, is engaged to the 'paragon' John Grey, but she jilts him in favour of her less reputable cousin George Vavasor. Alice uses her means to help George to a political career. George, disinherited by his grandfather and having lost his parliamentary seat, takes ship for America, pausing only to make a murderous attack on Mr Grey. When, after a suitable interval, John Grey proposes again to Alice, he is accepted.

Interwoven with this story is the account of the early married life of Alice's friend Lady Glencora who has made a splendid match with Plantagenet Palliser, nephew and heir of the old duke of Omnium, but remains in love with the handsome wastrel Burgo Fitzgerald. Palliser decides to take his wife out of harm's way, and arranges an extensive foreign tour.

Capability Brown, see BROWN, L.

ČAPEK, Karel, see ROBOT.

CAPELL, Edward (1713–81), Shakespearian commentator. His edition of Shakespeare in 10 vols (1768) was the first to be based on complete and careful collations of all the old copies, and it is his arrangement of the lines that is now usually followed. His *Commentary, Notes and Various Readings to Shakespeare*, was published in 3 vols in 1783. Capell was responsible for the first full scholarly discussion of Shakespeare's sources, and for the first attempt to establish the relationship between the *Folios and Quartos.

CAPGRAVE, John (1393–1464), an Augustinian friar who wrote a number of theological and historical works in Latin. In English he wrote lives of St Gilbert of Sempringham and St Catharine of Alexandria. His most significant English work is his *Chronicle* of English history up to AD 1417, which is marked by simplicity and lucidity of style.

CAPOTE, Truman (1924–84), American author, whose work ranges from the light-hearted story of playgirl Holly Golightly in *Breakfast at Tiffany's* (1958) to the grim investigation *In Cold Blood* (1966), in which Capote re-created the brutal multiple murder of a whole Kansas family and traces the lives of the murderers to the moment of their execution.

Captain Singleton, Adventures of, see SINGLETON.

Capulets, in Shakespeare's *Romeo and Juliet*, the noble, Veronese house (the Cappelletti) to which Juliet belongs, hostile to the family of the Montagues (the Montecchi).

Carabas, Marquess of, a character in (1) the fairy tale of *Puss in Boots*; (2) Disraeli's *Vivian Grey*; (3) Thackeray's *Book of Snobs*.

CARACTACUS, or **CARADOC,** king of the Silures in the west of Britain during the reign of Claudius, was defeated by the Romans and fled

to Cartimandua, queen of the Brigantes, who betrayed him. He was taken a prisoner to Rome in AD 51, where his noble spirit so pleased the emperor that he pardoned and released him. He figures as Caratach in Fletcher's *Bonduca*. W. *Mason wrote a play *Caractacus*.

CARADOC, see CARACTACUS.

Carbonek, see CORBENIC.

Cardenio, a lost play by Shakespeare, probably in collaboration with *Fletcher, acted at Court in 1613. *Theobald in his play *Double Fals'hood* (1728) claimed to have made use of an old prompt copy of *Cardenio*, but this has never been seen since and Theobald's version lacks Shakespearian touches. It may be assumed, however, that Shakespeare's play, like Theobald's, was based on the story of Cardenio and Lucinda in *Don Quixote* (Part 1, ch. 24–8).

Cardinal, The, a tragedy by J. *Shirley, acted 1641, printed 1652.

This play, which Shirley and his contemporaries thought his best work, describes the intrigues of the diabolical Cardinal in his efforts to marry the Duchess Rosaura, a young widow, to his nephew Columbo, despite her love for Alvarez. All ends badly with assassinations, attempted rape, and poisonings.

Carduel, see CARLIOUN.

Careless Husband, The, a comedy by C. *Cibber, performed and published 1704 (imprint 1705).

Sir Charles Easy, who neglects his wife and carries on an intrigue with her maid Edging and with Lady Graveairs, is eventually moved to reconciliation by her toleration.

Caretaker, The, a play by H. *Pinter, performed and published in 1960.

One of Pinter's characteristically enigmatic dramas, it is built on the interaction of three characters, the tramp Davies and the brothers Aston and Mick. Aston has rescued Davies from a brawl and brought him back to a junk-filled room, in which he offers Davies a bed and, eventually, an ill-defined post as caretaker, although it emerges that the flat actually belongs to his brother. The characters reveal themselves in inconsequential dialogue and obsessional monologue. In the end both brothers turn on Davies, after he has tried to play the one off against the other, and evict him.

CAREW (pron. Carey), Thomas (1594/5–1640), one of the best-known of the *Cavalier poets. He won the favour of Charles I, was appointed to an office at court, and received an estate from him. He was much influenced by

*Jonson and by *Donne; his elegy for Donne was published with Donne's poems in 1633. His works include the masque *Coelum Britannicum* (1634), many graceful, witty, and often cynical songs and lyrics, and several longer poems including the erotic 'A Rapture'. Carew's *Poems* appeared in 1640.

CAREY, Henry (?1687–1743), is remembered as the author of *Chrononhotonthologos*, as the inventor of the nick-name 'Namby-Pamby' for Ambrose *Philips, and as the author of the words and music of 'Sally in our Alley'. His burlesque opera *The Dragon of Wantley* was performed with much success in 1737.

CARKER, James, a character in Dickens's *Dombey and Son*.

Carleton, Memoirs of Captain, see MEMOIRS OF CAPTAIN CARLETON.

CARLETON, William (1794–1869), author of many stories of Irish peasant life, both melancholy and humorous, including *Traits and Stories of the Irish Peasantry* (1830–5), and *Tales of Ireland* (1834). His novels include *Fardorougha, the Miser* (1839) and *Black Prophet* (1847), a bleak story of the potato famine.

Carlioun (sometimes Carduel), in Malory's *Morte D'Arthur*, the city where Arthur was crowned and held his court, probably Caerleon-upon-Usk, though in places Carlisle appears to be meant.

Carlos, Don, the deformed son of Philip II of Spain. The marriage of the latter with Elizabeth of France, who had been affianced to Don Carlos, forms the subject of Otway's tragedy *Don Carlos* and of Verdi's opera.

CARLYLE, Jane Baillie Welsh (1801–66), married Thomas *Carlyle in 1826, and is remembered as one of the best letter-writers in the English language, witty, caustic, and observant, and as a literary hostess who impressed all who met her. Her vast circle of friends, acquaintances, and correspondents included Mazzini, R. *Browning, *Tennyson, J. *Forster, and G. *Jewsbury, but many of her best letters were written to her relatives in Edinburgh and Liverpool and, most notably, to Thomas himself. Various collections and selections of her letters have been published, including editions by J. A. *Froude (1883), Leonard Huxley (1924), and T. Scudder (1931).

CARLYLE, Thomas (1795–1881), was born in Dumfriesshire, the son of a stonemason. He was educated at Annan Academy and at the University of Edinburgh. He became a teacher but soon took to literary work, tutoring and reviewing.

He studied German literature; his life of Schiller appeared in the *London Magazine* in 1823–4 and was separately published in 1825. This was followed by translations of *Goethe's *Wilhelm Meister's Apprenticeship* (1824) and *Wilhelm Meister's Travels* (1827), the latter being included in his anthology of selections from German authors, *German Romance* (4 vols, 1827). In 1826 he married Jane Welsh (see above) and after two years in Edinburgh they moved to her farm at Craigenputtock. 'Signs of the Times', an attack on *Utilitarianism, appeared in 1829 in the *Edinburgh Review*; *Sartor Resartus* followed in *Fraser's Magazine* in 1833–4. In 1834 the Carlyles moved to Cheyne Walk, Chelsea, where he worked on his *History of the *French Revolution*, which appeared in 1837; the manuscript of the first volume was accidentally used to light a fire while on loan to J. S. *Mill, but Carlyle rewrote it. This work established Carlyle's reputation, and he from this time onward strengthened the position that made him known as 'the Sage of Chelsea'. His series of lectures, *On *Heroes, Hero-Worship and the Heroic in History*, delivered in 1840 and published in 1841, attracted glittering and fashionable audiences, and taught him to distrust (and indeed to abandon) his own blend of 'prophecy and play-acting'. In *Chartism* (1839) and *Past and Present* (1843) Carlyle applied himself to what he called 'the Condition-of-England question', attacking both *laissez-faire* and the dangers of revolution it encouraged, and manifesting with more passion than consistency a sympathy with the industrial poor which heralded the new novels of social consciousness of the 1840s (see GASKELL, E. and DISRAELI, B.). His evocation in *Past and Present* of medieval conditions at the time of Abbot Samson (see JOCELIN DE BRAKELOND) provided a new perspective on machinery and craftsmanship that was pursued by *Ruskin and W. *Morris, but Carlyle, unlike some of his followers, turned increasingly away from democracy towards the kind of feudalism which he saw expressed in the rule of the 'Strong Just Man'. His 'Occasional discourse on the nigger question' (1849) and *Latter-day Pamphlets* (1850) express his anti-democratic views in an exaggerated form. His admiration for *Cromwell was expressed in his edition of *Oliver Cromwell's letters and speeches* (2 vols, 1845), and for *Frederick the Great of Prussia in a lengthy biography (6 vols, 1858–65). A more modest and, to 20th-cent. tastes, more readable work, a life of his friend *Sterling (with some remarkable reminiscences of *Coleridge) appeared in 1851.

Jane Carlyle died in 1866, a blow which he said 'shattered my whole existence into immeasurable ruin'. He gave her papers and letters in 1871, with ambiguous instructions, to his friend and disciple J. A. *Froude, who published them after Carlyle's death, in 1883; Froude also published Carlyle's *Reminiscences* (1881) and a four-vol.

biography (1882–4). These posthumous publications caused much controversy, largely by breaking the conventions of Victorian *biography (against which Carlyle had himself fulminated) to suggest marital discord and sexual inadequacy on Carlyle's part.

Carlyle's influence as social prophet and critic, and his prestige as historian, were enormous during his lifetime. In the 20th cent. his reputation waned, partly because his trust in authority and admiration of strong leaders were interpreted as foreshadowings of Fascism. His prose, which had always presented difficulties, became more obscure with the lapse of time; his violent exclamatory rhetoric, his italics and Teutonic coinages, and his eccentric archaisms and strange punctuation were already known by the late 1850s as 'Carlylese'.

Carmarthen, *The Black Book of,* see BLACK BOOK OF CARMARTHEN, THE.

Carmelide (Camylyard in *Malory), the realm of King Leodegan (Lodegraunce in Malory), the father of Guinevere.

Carmina Burana, a compilation of 228 Latin and German poems, discovered in the monastery of Benediktbeuern in 1803, whence it is also known as the 'Benediktbeuern manuscript'. It was probably written c. 1230, and is the work of three compilers. It contains works corresponding to three categories of poetry written by the 12th-cent. troubadours: moral-satirical poems; love poems; and poems of camaraderie, many of them drinking-songs. It is the most important collection of *Goliardic Latin poetry. Carl Orff used a selection for his scenic cantata *Carmina Burana* (1935–6).

CARNEGIE, Andrew (1835–1919), one of the foremost ironmasters of the United States. In 1900 he published *The Gospel of Wealth*, maintaining that a 'man who dies rich dies disgraced'; the most important of his many benefactions was his provision of public libraries in Great Britain and the United States, on condition that the local authorities provided site and maintenance. (See LIBRARIES, PUBLIC.)

Carol, a word whose etymology is obscure, and of which the earliest meaning appears to be a round dance; thence a song, originally the song of joy sung at Christmas time in celebration of the Nativity. The first known collection of Christmas carols was printed by *Wynkyn de Worde in 1521.

CAROLINE, Queen, (1) consort of George II, figures in Scott's *The Heart of Midlothian* and is prominent in the memoirs of the time; (2) consort of George IV, figures in *Byron's poems, etc.

CARPENTER, Edward (1844–1929), became fellow of Trinity Hall, Cambridge and curate to F. D. *Maurice. In 1874 he abandoned fellowship and orders and moved north, eventually settling at Millthorpe, near Chesterfield, where he pursued, by precept and example, his own concept of Socialism and communal fellowship, in a manner much influenced by *Thoreau and also by *Ruskin and W. *Morris. He wrote and lectured in support of varied progressive causes and his own life-style and revolt against middle-class convention (expressed by sandals, vegetarianism, overt homosexuality, praise of manual labour and the working man) became an important symbol of liberation for many, including E. M. *Forster. Of his many writings the best remembered is probably his long poem *Towards Democracy* (published in 4 parts, 1883–1902), in which he expresses his millenarian sense of the cosmic consciousness and 'spiritual democracy', and of the march of humanity towards 'freedom and joy', much influenced by *Whitman and the *Bhagavadgita*. His autobiography, *My Days and Dreams*, was published in 1916.

CARPENTER, John (?1370–?1441), town clerk of London, 1417–38, a generous patron and a friend of *Whittington and of *Pecock. He compiled the *Liber Albus*, a valuable collection of records of the City of London, and he left lands for educational purposes, from which the City of London School was founded.

CARROLL, Lewis, see DODGSON, C. L.

CARTER, Angela, see MAGIC REALISM.

CARTER, Mrs Elizabeth (1717–1806), a noted member of the *Blue Stocking Circle; she learned Latin, Greek, and Hebrew in childhood. Dr *Johnson thought her one of the best Greek scholars he had known. In 1738 she published her early poems, and Johnson, as a high honour, invited her to contribute to *The Rambler*. Her translation of *Epictetus (1758) gained her a European reputation.

Carton, Sydney, a character in Dickens's *A Tale of Two Cities*.

CARTWRIGHT, William (1611–43), preacher, poet, and dramatist, one of the 'sons' of *Jonson. His most successful play was *The Royal Slave* (perf. 1636).

CARY, Henry Francis (1772–1844), translated Dante's *Divina Commedia*, producing with his translation the first Italian text of Dante to be printed in England. The *Inferno* appeared in 1805, and together with the *Purgatorio* and the *Paradiso* in 1814.

CARY, (Arthur) Joyce (Lunel) (1888–1957), novelist, born in Londonderry. He joined the

Nigerian political service in 1913, and served with the Nigerian regiment in the Cameroons campaign, 1915–16. His early 'African' novels, *Aissa Saved* (1932), *An American Visitor* (1933), *The African Witch* (1936), and *Mister Johnson* (1939), show with shrewd sympathy the relations between Africans and their British administrators. His major work consists of two trilogies; *Herself Surprised* (1941), *To Be a Pilgrim* (1942), and *The Horse's Mouth* (1944), chiefly concerned with the life of the artist Gulley Jimson; and *Prisoner of Grace* (1952), *Except the Lord* (1953), and *Not Honour More* (1955), a study of politics. Two further novels are studies of childhood: *Charley is my Darling* (1940) and the semi-autobiographical *A House of Children* (1941). Cary also wrote political studies, such as *Power in Men* (1939) and *The Case for African Freedom* (1941); poetry, including *Marching Soldier* (1945) and *The Drunken Sailor* (1947); a study in aesthetics, *Art and Reality* (1958); short stories, such as *Spring Song and Other Stories* (1960); and an unfinished novel with a religious theme, *The Captive and the Free* (1959).

CARY, Lucius, see FALKLAND.

CARYLL, John (1625–1711), author of a tragedy, *The English Princess: or the death of Richard III* (1667), and a comedy, *Sir Salomon* (1670). His nephew, also John Caryll (?1666–1736), was a friend and correspondent of Pope, to whom he suggested the subject of *The Rape of the Lock*.

Casaubon, Mr, a leading character in G. Eliot's *Middlemarch*.

CASAUBON, Isaac (1559–1614), French classical scholar, born in Geneva of Huguenot refugee parents. From 1610 until his death he lived in London, receiving a pension from James I and becoming naturalized in 1611. Casaubon published critical editions and commentaries on the works of a number of ancient authors, chiefly Greek, including *Theophrastus (1592).

Casby, Christopher and Flora, characters in Dickens's *Little Dorrit*.

Casca, one of the conspirators in Shakespeare's *Julius Caesar*.

Case is Altered, The, a comedy by *Jonson performed c.1597–8, printed 1609.

Casket Letters, letters supposed to have passed between *Mary Queen of Scots and Bothwell, and to have established her complicity in the murder of Darnley. They were repudiated by the queen as forgeries. They disappeared before the end of the 16th cent.

CASLON, William (1692–1766), the first English typefounder to make a complete range of Roman and Italic types of his own design, besides cutting Greek and exotic scripts. His types are still in use.

Cassio, Michael, in Shakespeare's *Othello*, a sophisticated Florentine who has been appointed as Othello's lieutenant.

Cassius, in Shakespeare's *Julius Caesar*, friend of *Brutus and leader of the conspiracy against Caesar.

Cassivelaunus ('Cassibelan' in Shakespeare's *Cymbeline), according to *Geoffrey of Monmouth's *History*, the brother and successor of *Lud as King of Britain.

Castalio, a character in Otway's *The Orphan*.

'Castaway, The', a poem by *Cowper, written 1799, published 1803. It is based on an incident from *Anson's *Voyage Round the World*. Cowper depicts with tragic power the suffering of a seaman swept overboard and awaiting death by drowning.

CASTELVETRO, Ludovico (1505–71), Italian scholar and critic known for his commentary on Aristotle's *Poetics* (1750, 1756). His views on the *Unities, more rigid than Aristotle's own, had considerable influence on the development of neo-classical theory.

CASTIGLIONE, Baldassare (1478–1529), Italian humanist, chiefly known for his prose dialogues *Il libro del cortegiano* (1528), translated into English as *The Courtyer* (1561) by *Hoby. In these dialogues, which take place at the court of Urbino and are presided over by the duchess, nineteen men and four women (all historical characters) discuss the qualifications for the ideal courtier, who should unite ethical and intellectual virtues, military and sporting prowess, and yet display his talents with an easy grace and nonchalance. The book ends with a discussion of love by Bembo, describing the 'ladder' whereby the lover ascends from love of one person to love of the abstract good. The work had much influence on the literature of England, e.g. on *Surrey, *Wyatt, *Sydney, *Spenser, and Shakespeare.

Castle Dangerous, a novel by Sir W. *Scott, published 1831 in *Tales of My Landlord*, 4th series.

Castle of Indolence, The, a poem in Spenserian stanzas by J. *Thomson published 1748.
    It consists of two cantos, of which the first describes the castle of the wizard Indolence, into which he entices weary pilgrims who sink into torpor amidst luxurious ease; the inmates, becoming diseased, are thrown into a dungeon

to languish. The second canto describes the conquest of the castle by the knight of Arts and Industry.

Castle of Otranto, The, a Gothic Story, by Horace *Walpole, published 1765.

The first of the true *'Gothic' novels, this was an immediate success, and has run to over 150 editions since its original publication. Walpole wrote of its composition, 'I gave rein to my imagination; visions and passions choked me.' The narrative is filled with ghosts, vaults, giants, living statues, mysterious appearances and violent emotions of terror, anguish, and love. Walpole's fear of ridicule led him to publish the first edition anonymously, with an elaborate preface describing the author as 'Onuphrio Muralto', an Italian canon of Otranto, writing somewhere between the 11th and 13th cents. The principal characters are Manfred, the tyrant of Otranto; his devoted wife Hippolita; his son Conrad (who is crushed to death by a black-plumed helmet); and Isabella, first betrothed to Conrad, then wooed by Manfred, and finally won by Theodore, a mysterious stranger who is eventually revealed as the rightful Prince of Vicenza.

Castle of Perseverance, The, the earliest surviving complete *morality play, in 3,700 lines, dating from the first quarter of the 15th cent., one of the group (the others are *Mankind and *Wisdom) known as Macro plays from their 18th-cent. owner. In four parts, it is of interest as an exhaustive compendium of such morality features as a battle between vices and virtues, a mixture of allegorical (Backbiter) and diabolical (Belyal) figures, and the enactment of Death and Judgement; but it is also highly significant in the history of English theatre, largely because of a diagrammatic representation of the Castle-mound as 'Theatre in the Round' which its staging requires.

Castle Perilous, in Malory's *Morte D'Arthur, the castle of the lady Lyonesse. (See GARETH AND LYNETTE.)

Castle Rackrent, a novel by M. *Edgeworth, published 1800.

This work may be regarded as the first fully developed *historical novel and the first true *regional novel in English. Set in Ireland before 1782, it is narrated by the elderly Thady Quirk, steward to three generations of Rackrents. The narrative begins with the wild life of the hard-drinking Sir Patrick, 'inventor of raspberry whisky', who lived before Thady's time. He was succeeded by the litigious and debt-ridden Sir Murtagh, a skinflint who died of a fury. His brother Sir Kit, who inherits, brings to the castle his unfortunate English Jewish wife, who, after many arguments over sausages, diamonds, and

other matters, is shut up in the Castle for seven years, until her gambling husband is killed in a duel. Meanwhile the cunning young lawyer Jason Quirk, Thady's son, is gathering more and more of the family's affairs into his hands. The next heir, Sir Condy, is an ardent, extravagant politician, who tosses a coin to decide whether to marry the rich Isabella Moneygawl or the pretty Judy M'Quirk (Thady's grandniece). He marries Isabella and, keeping lavish open house in their tumbledown castle, they finally exhaust the last resources of the Rackrents. When the bailiffs arrive Isabella flees and Jason Quirk is found to own almost everything. The Castle is sold and Condy amuses himself by feigning death at his own wake. When he eventually dies Isabella contests the property, but Jason emerges as a 'high gentleman with estates and a fortune'.

CASTLEREAGH, Robert Stewart, Viscount Castlereagh (1769–1822) was foreign secretary (1812–22) and took a leading part in the European settlement at the Congress of Vienna and after Waterloo, restraining the Allies from retaliation on France. He was greatly disliked by many of the young writers of his day, who felt that he opposed the cause of liberty. Shelley, in *The Mask of Anarchy (which was provoked by the massacre of Peterloo, 1819), wrote:

I met Murder on the way—
He had a mask like Castlereagh.

Castlewood, Thomas, third Viscount, and his wife Isabel; Francis, fourth Viscount, his wife Rachel, his daughter Beatrix, and his son Frank, characters in Thackeray's *The History of Henry Esmond. Also Eugene, earl of Castlewood, in Thackeray's *The Virginians.

Catcher in the Rye, The, see SALINGER, J. D.

Catch-22, a comic, satirical, surreal, and apocalyptic novel by J. *Heller, published in 1961, which describes the ordeals and exploits of a group of American airmen based on a small Mediterranean island during the Italian campaign of the Second World War, and in particular the reactions of Captain Yossarian, the protagonist. The title of the novel has passed into the language to describe a situation of deadlock, composed of two mutually exclusive sets of conditions: the original instance in the novel of 'Catch-22', defined in ch. 5, concerns pilot Orr, Yossarian's room-mate. According to Doc Daneeka, 'Orr was crazy and could be grounded. All he had to do was ask; and as soon as he did, he would no longer be crazy and would have to fly more missions. Orr would be crazy to fly more missions and sane if he didn't, but if he was sane he had to fly them. If he flew them he was crazy and didn't have to; but if he didn't want to he was sane and had to.'

Catharsis, a much-disputed term used by Aristotle in his *Poetics, where he speaks of the function of tragedy which should succeed in 'arousing pity and fear in such a way as to accomplish a catharsis (i.e. purgation) of such emotions'. The concept has been redefined by generations of critics and Milton gives his own interpretation in his preface to *Samson Agonistes*: 'Tragedy . . . said by Aristotle to be of power by raising pity and fear, or terror, to purge the mind of those and such like passions, that is to temper and reduce them to just measure with a kind of delight, stirr'd up by reading or seeing those passions well imitated.'

CATHER, Willa Sibert (1876–1947), American novelist. Her many works include *My Antonía* (1918), the story of an immigrant girl from Bohemia, settled in Nebraska; *A Lost Lady* (1923); *The Professor's House* (1925), a rich and suggestive work which contrasts the middle-aged disillusion of Professor St Peter with his memories of his favourite student, the brilliant explorer and inventor Tom Outland; *Death Comes for the Archbishop* (1927), a historical novel, set in New Mexico, based on the French Catholic mission of Father Latour, and his years of work with the peasant population. The dual impulse towards exploration and cultivation, towards art and domesticity, towards excitement and safety, is a constant theme in Miss Cather's work; she was a pioneer not only in her treatment of the frontiers of the West, but also in her development of the American novel. She records her own debt to another pioneer, S. O. *Jewett, in *Not Under Forty* (1936).

Catherine, a novel by *Thackeray, published serially in *Fraser's Magazine*, 1839–40.
Thackeray took the outline of the story of the murderess Catherine Hayes from the *Newgate Calendar, and deliberately made his novel as grim and sordid as possible, in reaction against the popular 'Newgate novels' of *Bulwer-Lytton, *Ainsworth, and others.

Catiline, a Roman tragedy by *Jonson, performed 1611, based principally on *Sallust's *Catiline* and *Cicero's orations.
The play concerns the events of the year 63 BC, when Catiline organized a conspiracy to overthrow the existing government and to renew with the aid of Sulla's veterans the scenes of bloodshed which Rome had recently seen. Cicero and Antonius were elected consuls, and Catiline, secretly encouraged by Caesar and Crassus, prepared for a rising. Cicero, warned by Fulvia, the mistress of one of the conspirators, of the intention to assassinate him as a first step in the movement, summons the senate and accuses Catiline, who leaves Rome and joins the troops raised by his adherents at Faesulae. Cicero obtains evidence of the guilt of the conspirators through the ambassadors of the Allobroges, and submits it to the senate, which condemns them

to death. Catiline falls in the decisive engagement between his troops and those of the government commanded by Petreius.

Cato, a tragedy by *Addison, produced 1713.
It deals with the death of Cato the republican, who commits suicide rather than submit to the dictator Caesar. Dr *Johnson described it as 'rather a poem in dialogue than a drama'. It owed its success partly to the political intentions imputed to it.

Cat on a Hot Tin Roof, a play by T. *Williams.

Catriona, see KIDNAPPED.

CATULLUS, Gaius Valerius (*c*.84–*c*.54 BC), was one of the most versatile of Roman poets, writing love poems, elegies, and satirical epigrams. His work remained virtually unknown during the Middle Ages until a manuscript of his poems came to light at Verona in the 14th cent. He left his mark on *Campion's *Bookes of Ayres*, on *Jonson's songs, and generally on *Herrick and *Lovelace. Leigh *Hunt translated his *Attis* (1810) and *Tennyson, visiting Sirmione where Catullus once had a house, wrote his pathetic 'Frater Ave atque Vale'.

CAUDWELL, Christopher, pseudonym of Christopher St John Sprigg (1907–37), Marxist literary critic. He published poems, novels and many books on aircraft, but is known for his critical works *Illusion and Reality* (1937) and *Studies in a Dying Culture* (1938). These attempted to define a Marxist theory of art and called on writers of the thirties to commit themselves to the culture of the revolutionary proletariat. He was killed in the Spanish Civil War. (See MARXIST LITERARY CRITICISM.)

CAUSLEY, Charles (1917–), poet, born in Launceston, Cornwall. His volumes of verse include *Farewell, Aggie Weston* (1951), *Survivor's Leave* (1953), *Union Street* (1957), *Johnny Alleluia* (1961), *Underneath the Water* (1968), and *Figgie Hobbin* (1970). He has published various collections of children's stories and anthologies of verse. His poetry is marked by a powerful simplicity of diction and rhythm, and shows the influence of popular songs and the ballad tradition. Innocence is a recurrent theme, and his admiration for *Clare is the direct inspiration of several poems. Religious and seafaring images, often interwoven, are also characteristic. His own selection of *Collected Poems 1951–75* appeared in 1975.

Cavalier, Memoirs of a, see MEMOIRS OF A CAVALIER.

Cavaliers, a name given to supporters of Charles I in the Civil War, derived from the

Italian for horseman or knight and carrying overtones of courtly gallantry. 'Cavalier lyrics' is the term applied to lyrics by *Carew, *Lovelace, *Suckling, and *Herrick (the last of whom was not a courtier) and to work similar in tone and style. These poets were not a formal group, but all were influenced by *Jonson and like him paid little attention to the sonnet; their lyrics on the whole are distinguished by short lines, precise but idiomatic diction, and an urbane and graceful wit.

CAVE, Edward (1691–1754), who called himself 'Sylvanus Urban', became a London printer and publisher, chiefly remembered as the founder of *The Gentleman's Magazine*, to which his friend Dr *Johnson contributed extensively.

CAVENDISH, George (?1499–?1561), a gentleman of Thomas Wolsey's household, and author of *The Life and Death of Cardinal Wolsey* (1641), in which with much art he contrasts the magnificence of the cardinal's life with his subsequent disgrace.

CAVENDISH, Margaret, see NEWCASTLE.

Cave of Mammon, see MAMMON, THE CAVE OF.

Cawdor, Thane of, see MACBETH.

CAXTON, William (c.1422–91), the first English printer, and a prominent merchant. After apprenticeship in London he spent 30 years in the Low Countries. From 1465 to 1469 he was governor of the English merchants at Bruges, and he successfully negotiated commercial treaties with the dukes of Burgundy. In 1469 he became secretary to the household of Margaret of Burgundy, the sister of Edward IV. After his return to Bruges from Cologne (where he probably worked in a printing house) he presented Margaret with his *Recuyell of the Historyes of Troye* (printed in Bruges, 1473–4). He next printed, with the calligrapher Colard Mansion, *The Game and Playe of the Chesse*. He set up a press at Westminster in 1476—his first dated book printed there is *The Dictes or Sayengis of the Philosophres* (1477)—and printed about 100 books, a number of them his own translations from French. He used eight founts of type, and he began to use woodcut illustrations c.1480. His translations contributed to the development of the 15th-cent. prose style. It was his modified version of *Malory that appeared as Malory's work before the discovery of the Winchester manuscript by W. F. Oakeshott in 1934.

Cecilia, or Memoirs of an Heiress, a novel by F. *Burney, published 1782.
Cecilia Beverley has inherited a large fortune on the condition that her future husband takes her name. Until she comes of age she is required to live with one of her three guardians. The first is Harrel, a gambler, who failing in his attempt to exploit his ward, kills himself, the second is the vulgar and avaricious Briggs, the third, the Hon. Compton Delvile. Cecilia and Delvile's son, Mortimer, fall in love and a marriage is arranged on the basis that Cecilia will renounce her fortune and Delvile keep his name. But the plan is defeated by the crafty Monckton, who hopes to win both her and her fortune when his wife dies. Monckton's treachery is exposed; Cecilia marries Mortimer.

Ceix and Alceone, see GOWER, J., and BOOK OF THE DUCHESS, THE.

Celestial City, in Bunyan's *Pilgrim's Progress*, signifying Heaven.

Celestina, or the Tragi-Comedy of Calisto and Melibea, a Spanish novel in dialogue which has had several stage adaptations. The first known edition appeared about 1499, in 16 acts, and a later version, in 1502, in 21 acts. It is reasonably certain that Acts II–XVI were written by Fernando de Rojas (c.1465–1541). The work is essentially dramatic, and marks an important stage in the literary history of Spain and of Europe.
Calisto, a gentleman of fortune, casually meeting Melibea falls violently in love with her, but is, from her modesty, sharply repulsed. On the advice of one of his servants he calls in the aid of Celestina, a crafty wise old bawd, who deflects Melibea from the path of virtue and brings about a general catastrophe. Celestina is murdered by Parmeno and Sempronio (the braggart servants of Calisto), for a share in the reward that she has received, and they are punished with death for their crime. Calisto is killed in one of his secret meetings with Melibea, and she in despair kills herself.
An excellent translation into English prose, *The Spanish Bawd* (1631), was made by *Mabbe. The early part of *Celestina* was translated into English verse by *Rastell, provided with a happy ending, and published, about 1530, as 'A new comody in englyshe in maner of an interlude', better known as 'An Interlude of Calisto and Melebea'. It is one of the first English dramatic works that approach true comedy. There are modern translations by P. Hartnoll (1959) and by J. M. Cohen (1964).

Celia, in Shakespeare's *As You Like It*, daughter to Duke Frederick.

Celtic Twilight, The, a collection of stories by *Yeats, published 1893, illustrating the mysticism of the Irish and their belief in fairies, ghosts, and spirits. It has since become a generic phrase (slightly ironical) for the whole *Irish revival in literature.

Cenci, The, a verse tragedy by P. B. *Shelley, published 1819 and 1821.

The melodramatic plot is taken from the true story of Beatrice Cenci, who was tried and executed for the murder of her father, count Francesco Cenci, at Rome in 1599. Shelley was attracted by the themes of incest and atheism: the play concentrates on the Iago-like evil of the count and the inner sufferings of Beatrice. Beatrice's great speech on the prospect of death, 'So young to go | Under the obscure, cold, rotting, wormy ground!' (v. 4) is based on Claudio's in *Measure for Measure* (III. i).

Censorship. Proclamations against the publishing of seditious and heretical books were made in the reign of Henry VIII soon after the introduction of printing; in 1538 licensing by the Privy Council or other royal nominees was made a necessary requirement. When the *Stationers' Company obtained a charter for incorporation in 1557 (see also COPYRIGHT), only members of the Company might print any work for sale in England. Further efforts to enforce State control were made in the time of Elizabeth, notably by Archbishop Whitgift, in an attempt to suppress Puritan pamphlets (see MARTIN MARPRELATE). The abolition by the Long Parliament in 1641 of the Court of Star Chamber (one of whose last measures was a stringent decree in 1637) did not bring any greater freedom. Milton's *Areopagitica* is a noble appeal for a free press which was not, however, granted. Under the Restoration the control and licensing of the press continued, although there was greater liberty in practice. The licensing system came finally to an end in 1694, although prosecutions for seditious or other obnoxious publications were frequent in the 18th cent. The unsuccessful prosecution of *Wilkes in 1763 brought a greater measure of freedom, which was increased by the responsibility of determining a libel being given to the jury and not to the judge (Fox's Libel Act, 1792). Executive interference with the press had on the whole declined throughout the 18th cent. and governments had come to rely on presenting their own case in rival publications. This freedom of the press has not been questioned in Great Britain in recent years—except perhaps by the rulers of totalitarian states anxious to remove sources of foreign criticism. The following are the chief heads under which the law today punishes the publication of illegal matter: (1) *Libel as a civil injury*, the publication of matter defamatory to the plaintiff. (2) *Libel as a criminal offence*, i.e., as calculated to provoke a breach of the peace or to outrage public feeling or morality, or to endanger the State. Under the Obscene Publications Act 1959 a book 'is deemed to be obscene if its effect . . . taken as a whole, is such as to tend to deprave and corrupt persons who are likely . . . to read . . . the matter contained . . . in it', but 'A person shall

not be convicted of an offence [of publishing an obscene article] if it is proved that publication of the article in question is justified as being for the public good on the ground that it is in the interests of science, literature, art, or learning, or of other subjects of general concern.' Since 1959, for the first time, defendants have been allowed to bring witnesses to give evidence on the literary and moral qualities of a publication, and in 1960 in the case of *Regina* v. *Penguin Books Limited* Penguin Books were acquitted of an offence in publishing *Lady Chatterley's Lover* after the hearing of such evidence.

In 1977 the crime of blasphemous libel was deployed for the first time since 1922 by a private prosecutor to obtain the conviction of the editor of *Gay News* for publishing a poem by J. *Kirkup: the opinions of experts on the poem's literary merits were in this case ruled inadmissible.

Control of the drama was exercised in Elizabethan times by the Master of the Revels, from Restoration times onwards by the Lord Chamberlain. This control, which became more concerned with questions of public morality than with political matters, lasted until 1968, when the Lord Chamberlain's responsibility for licensing plays ceased. An attempt to prosecute a play by Howard Brenton, performed at the National Theatre in 1982, under Section 13 of the Sexual Offences Act, collapsed on technical grounds.

CENTLIVRE, Susannah (1669–1723), actress and dramatist, married in 1706 Joseph Centlivre, cook to Queen Anne. She wrote 19 plays, chiefly comedies, between 1700 and 1722, the best being comedies of intrigue and manners. They include *The Gamester* (1705), *The Wonder: A Woman Keeps a Secret* (1714), *The Busie Body* (1709), and *A Bold Stroke for a Wife* (1718).

Cent nouvelles nouvelles, Les, a collection of French tales, loosely modelled on Boccaccio's *Decameron*, and written down probably between 1464 and 1467. The tales, predominantly licentious in character, were related at the court of Philip, duke of Burgundy.

Certain Sonnets, 32 sonnets and poems by Sir P. *Sidney appended to editions of the *Arcadia* from 1598 onwards.

CERVANTES SAAVEDRA, Miguel de (1547–1616), the great Spanish novelist and dramatist. La Galatea (1585), a pastoral novel, was followed by his masterpiece *Don Quixote* (Pt I 1605; Pt II 1613), a satirical romance. He wrote several plays (16 of which survive), a collection of short stories (*Novelas ejemplares*, 1613) and a tale of adventure, *Persiles y Sigismunda* (1617). J. *Fletcher drew largely on the last two of these for his plots.

Chabot, The Tragedy of, a tragedy by *Chapman, probably revised and added to by *Shirley, published 1639.

Chadband, a character in Dickens's *Bleak House.*

Chaffanbrass, Mr, a character in Trollope's novels *The Three Clerks,* *Orley Farm,* and *Phineas Redux.*

Chainmail, Mr, a character in Peacock's *Crotchet Castle.* He believes the 12th cent. to be the best period in 'English History'.

CHALKHILL, John (d. 1642), author of a pastoral *Thealma and Clearchus* (1683), with a preface by I. *Walton, and of other verse included in *The Compleat Angler.*

Challenger, Professor George Edward, hero of *The Lost World* and other stories of Sir A. C. *Doyle, a distinguished zoologist and anthropologist of great vitality and violent temper.

CHALMERS, Thomas (1780–1847), was known as one of the most formidable orators of the Scottish pulpit. He was the leader of the movement which led to the disruption of the Scottish Established Church and the founding of the Free Church of Scotland in 1843; he became its first moderator. His many works, mainly on natural theology and social economy, included 'The Adaptation of External Nature to the Moral and Intellectual Constitution of Man' (1833, the first of the *Bridgewater Treatises*).

CHAMBERLAYNE, Edward (1616–1703), author of *Angliae Notitia, or the Present State of England* (1669), a successful handbook of social and political conditions.

CHAMBERLAYNE, William (1619–89), remembered for his *Pharonnida* (1659), a heroic romance in five books of rhymed couplets, recounting the adventures of the knight Argalia, his beloved Pharonnida, and the villainous Almanzor.

CHAMBERS, Sir E(dmund) K(erchever) (1866–1954), Shakespearian scholar and dramatic historian, served in the education department of the civil service, 1892–1926. His major works of dramatic history are *The Medieval Stage* (2 vols, 1903), *The Elizabethan Stage* (4 vols, 1923), and *William Shakespeare: A Study of the Facts and Problems* (2 vols, 1930). As well as editions of all Shakespeare's plays for the Red Letter Shakespeare and an important lecture on 'The Disintegration of Shakespeare' (1924) he published *Arthur of Britain* (1927), a synthesis and reassessment based on available evidence; editions of *Donne, *Milton, *Beaumont and *Fletcher, among others; and the *Oxford Book of Sixteenth Century Verse* (1932).

CHAMBERS, Ephraim (d. 1740), published his *Cyclopaedia,* the first true English encyclopaedia (which has no connection with the current *Chambers's Encyclopaedia*) in 1728.

CHAMBERS, R(aymond) W(ilson) (1874–1942), was Quain professor at University College, London (1922–41). The range of his scholarly interests extended from Old English to the Renaissance; his most celebrated works are *Widsith* (1912); *Beowulf: an Introduction to the Study of the Poem* (1921); *On the Continuity of English Prose from Alfred to More* (1932); *Thomas More* (1935); and *Man's Unconquerable Mind* (1939), a collection of essays of which the most striking are on *Langland, *More, and the Philologists of UCL. He became president of the *Philological Society in 1933.

CHAMBERS, Robert (1802–71), founded with his brother the publishing firm of W. and R. Chambers, Edinburgh. He established *Chambers's Journal* in 1832, and his firm issued *Chambers's Encyclopaedia* (1859–68), which has been through many subsequent editions. He wrote and published anonymously in 1844 *Vestiges of the Natural History of Creation* in which he maintained a theory of biological evolution produced by the action of universal and progressive natural law; this work was very influential in popularizing an evolutionary view of nature.

Chambers's Encyclopaedia, see CHAMBERS, R.

Chambers's Journal (originally *Chambers's Edinburgh Journal*), one of the most popular of the 19th-cent. journals of literature, science, and the arts, founded by R. *Chambers in 1832. It changed its name in 1854, and survived until 1938.

Chamont, one of the principal characters in Otway's *The Orphan.*

Champion, The, (1739–41), an anti-Jacobite, opposition journal written largely by H. *Fielding.

Chance, a novel by J. *Conrad.

Chances, The, a play by J. *Fletcher, almost certainly his unaided work, printed 1647. The 'chances' are the coincidences by which the eloping couple, Constantia and the duke of Ferrara, are brought into a number of complications, from which they are eventually extracted. It is based on one of the *Novelas ejemplares* of *Cervantes. It was adapted by *Buckingham (1682) whose version was successfully adapted by *Garrick.

CHANDLER, Raymond (1888–1959), American writer of thrillers and detective stories. His first novel, *The Big Sleep* (1939), introduced his detective narrator, cool, attractive, wise-cracking, lonely tough-guy, Philip Marlowe. Later works include *Farewell, my Lovely* (1940), *The High Window* (1942), *The Lady in the Lake* (1943), and *The Long Goodbye* (1953), all of which were filmed.

Changeling, The, a tragedy by T. *Middleton and W. *Rowley, acted 1622, printed 1653.

Beatrice-Joanna, daughter of the governor of Alicante, is ordered by her father to marry Alonzo de Piracquo. She falls in love with Alsemero, and in order to avoid the marriage employs the ill-favoured villain De Flores, whom she detests but who cherishes a passion for her, to murder Alonzo. To the horror of Beatrice, De Flores exacts the reward he had lusted for. Beatrice is now to marry Alsemero. To escape detection she arranges that her maid Diaphanta shall take her place on the wedding night; and to remove a dangerous witness, De Flores then kills the maid. The guilt of Beatrice and De Flores is revealed to Alsemero, and they are both brought before the governor, whereupon they take their own lives. The title of the play is taken from the sub-plot, in which Antonio disguises himself as a crazy changeling in order to get access to Isabella, wife of the keeper of a madhouse. The main plot is taken from John Reynolds's *God's revenge against Murther* (1621).

CHANNING, William Ellery (1780–1842), an American Unitarian clergyman, exercised a marked influence on American intellectual life, and is considered a forerunner of the Transcendentalists. His *Remarks on American Literature* (1830) calls for a Literary Declaration of Independence.

His nephew, also William Ellery Channing (1818–1901), poet and Transcendentalist, is remembered largely as the friend of *Emerson and of *Thoreau, whose biography Channing wrote.

Chanson de Roland, see ROLAND and CHANSONS DE GESTE.

Chansons de geste, epic poems in Old French embodying legends which had grown up about earlier historical figures. The earliest extant versions are from the 12th cent. and use the legends to embody problems and difficulties of feudal society: either the stresses within the feudal system itself caused by conflicting loyalties, as in *Raoul de Cambrai* and *Girart de Roussillon*; or those caused by the impact of the Crusades on feudalism, as in the *Chanson de Guillaume* and, above all, in the *Chanson de Roland* (see ROLAND). These epics gradually grew into three cycles, first delineated by Bertran de Bar-sur-Aube, a writer of two such poems in the early 13th cent.: firstly, the *geste du roi*, those dealing with the *Charlemagne of legend and his knights; secondly, those dealing with Charlemagne's rebellious vassals, the *geste de Doon de Mayence*; and thirdly, the William of Orange cycle, the *geste de Garin de Monglane*. The genre followed the usual development of narrative literature during the Old French period: the earliest poems, the *Roland* and *Gormont and Isembart*, are heroic; the 12th-cent. poems, with William of Orange as their hero, are more realistic; the later poems have courtly and marvellous elements in them, and lose the tragic seriousness of the earlier works. Similarly, the later ones become more elaborate in style, while the early poems were written in a simple, formulaic style of great dramatic force. The only parallel English poems are those concerned with Charlemagne, such as the fragmentary Middle English *Song of Roland* (see FERUMBRAS and OTUEL).

Chanticleer, the cock in *Reynard the Fox*, and in Chaucer's 'The Nun's Priest's Tale' (see CANTERBURY TALES, 20) as Chauntecleer.

Chapbook, a modern name applied by book-collectors and others to specimens of the popular literature which was formerly circulated by itinerant dealers or chapmen, consisting chiefly of small pamphlets of popular tales, ballads, tracts, etc. They reproduced old romances, stories, nursery rhymes, and fairy-tales. They were issued in great numbers throughout the 18th cent.

Chapel, Children of the, see PAUL'S, CHILDREN OF.

CHAPMAN, George (?1559–1634). After more than a decade as a professional playwright he turned to his major work of translating Homer, completed in 1616. Chapman's earliest published works include non-dramatic poems: *The Shadow of Night* (1594); a pair of complex Neoplatonic poems; and his completion of Marlowe's *Hero and Leander* (1598). Seven comedies are extant: *The Blind Beggar of Alexandria* (1598), *An Humorous Day's Mirth* (1599), *All Fools* (1605), *The Gentleman Usher* and *Monsieur D'Olive* (1606), *May-Day* (1611), and *The Widow's Tears* (1612). He collaborated with *Jonson and John *Marston on a further comedy, *Eastward hoe*, in 1605, which led to a short period of imprisonment for Jonson and Chapman because of its anti-Scottish satire. The tragedies consist of two two-part plays, *Bussy D'Ambois* (1607) and *The Revenge of Bussy D'Ambois* (1613), *The Conspiracy of Charles, Duke of Byron* and *The Tragedy of Byron* (1608), and one single play, *Caesar and Pompey* (1631). *The Tragedy of Chabot* (1639) appears to be a

Chapman tragedy revised by James *Shirley. Chapman also collaborated with *Fletcher, Jonson, and *Massinger in writing The Bloody Brother (c.1616, pub. 1639). The hasty publication of the first of his Homeric translations, Seven Books of the Iliads (1598), marked the earl of Essex's embarkation for Ireland; the complete Iliad and Odyssey were published together as The Whole Works of Homer; Prince of Poetts (1616). Jonson praised Chapman as second only to himself as a writer of *masques. Chapman was long the favourite candidate for the 'rival poet' referred to in Shakespeare's Sonnets. In more recent times Chapman has been seen as a crucial figure in a secret society of freethinkers called the *School of Night, of which *Marlowe, *Harriot, and Matthew Roydon were also members. Though there are links between Chapman and all these figures, it is not now thought that they took such a formal shape. As poet and dramatist, Chapman is most often seen as a genius manqué, whose learning and energy were never sufficiently disciplined. Perhaps the only lines of Chapman's poetry that are still well known are these from Bussy D'Ambois:

Man is a torch borne in the wind; a dream
But of a shadow, summ'd with all his
    substance.

CHAPMAN, John (1821–94), publisher and editor (from 1851) of the *Westminster Review.

Chapman and Hall, a publishing company founded in 1830 at 186 Strand, London, by Edward Chapman and William Hall. It owed much of its success to its early association with *Dickens (*Pickwick Papers having originated in a suggestion from Hall) and published many distinguished authors, including *Carlyle, *Kingsley, Mrs *Gaskell, and *Trollope. G. *Meredith was for a time literary director. The firm was sold to Methuen in 1938.

CHAPONE, Mrs (Hester) (1721–1801), a famous member of the *Blue Stocking circle, published her verse tales in 1750–3, her essays in 1773–7; and her Letters on the Improvement of the Mind (1773), addressed to Mrs *Montagu, was much admired as a work on education. Dr *Johnson invited her to contribute to *The Rambler. She was a particular friend of S. *Richardson, who called her 'little spit-fire' and with whom she discussed his female characters. Her Works and Posthumous Works appeared in 1807.

Characters of Shakespeare's Plays, essays by W. *Hazlitt, published 1817.

Character-writing. Books of 'characters' were popular in the 17th cent., and many were based, though some loosely, on *Theophrastus translated by *Casaubon in 1592 and by Healey (printed 1616, but previously circulated). The first was published in 1608 by J. *Hall, followed by *Overbury in 1614, the Satirical Essays, Characters and Others of J. *Stephens in 1615, Geffray Mynshul's Certain Characters and Essays of Prison and Prisoners in 1618, *Earle's Microcosmographie (1628), Richard Brathwaite's Whimzies (1631), and others. The 'characters' gave generalized but detailed descriptions of the behaviour and appearance of a class or type; they were on the whole short, succinct, pointed, and less discursive than the essay, also a popular literary form of the period.

Charalois, the hero of Massinger's *The Fatal Dowry.

'Charge of the Light Brigade, The', a poem by *Tennyson, first published in the Examiner in 1854 only weeks after the famous charge (25 Oct. 1854) at Balaclava, near Sebastopol, during which, owing to a misunderstood order, 247 officers and men out of 637 were killed or wounded. The line 'Someone had blundered', suggested by a phrase in a report in *The Times, was omitted from the version published in 1855 (*Maud, and Other Poems) but later reinstated.

CHARLEMAGNE (742–814), king of the Franks (768), Emperor of the West (800). He and his *Paladins are the subject of numerous *chansons de geste, of which the Chanson de Roland is the most famous (see ROLAND). Of the three groups of French chansons de geste concerned with Charlemagne, only the first, the geste du roi, is represented in English, in such romances as *Otuel and Sir *Ferumbras. Charlemagne is of significance in English literature for the tradition of learning he established at his court (led by the Northumbrian *Alcuin) which King *Alfred copied a century later.

CHARLES, duc d'Orléans (1394–1465), French poet, and a member of the French royal family. He fought at the battle of Agincourt in 1415, was captured, and held prisoner in England until 1440. On his return to France he established his court at Blois, where he received many literary figures. He is often considered to be the last important poet in the French courtly tradition; he wrote numerous ballades, chansons, complaintes, and rondeaux. A large number of English poems, many of which are versions of Charles's French lyrics, are also probably to be attributed to him.

Charley's Aunt, a highly popular farce by (Walter) Brandon Thomas (1856–1914), produced in 1892 and still performed.

Charmian, in Shakespeare's *Antony and Cleopatra and Dryden's *All for Love, Cleopatra's chief waiting woman.

Charmond, Felice, a character in Hardy's *The Woodlanders*.

Chartist Movement, a chiefly working-class political movement between 1837 and 1848, arose as a result of the *Reform Bill of 1832. Their six-point 'People Charter' consisted of: Universal Suffrage, Vote by Ballot, Annually Elected Parliaments, Payment for Members of Parliament, Abolition of the Property Qualification, and Equal Electoral Districts. The movement was alluded to by novelists of the mid-19th cent. who were concerned with the Condition of the People question, in particular B. Disraeli in *Sybil*, and C. Kingsley in *Alton Locke*; and also by *Carlyle in his essay 'Chartism'.

Chaste Mayd in Cheap-side, A, a comedy by T. *Middleton, written 1613, printed 1630.

The play centres on the attempt of the dissolute Sir Walter Whorehound to pass off his mistress as his niece (the 'Chaste Maid') and to marry her to the foolish pedantic son of Yellowhammer, a rich goldsmith; while Whorehound himself is to marry Yellowhammer's daughter Moll. The second part of the plot fails; Moll and the resourceful young Touchwood are in love and their attempts to get married, though repeatedly foiled, are finally successful.

CHATTERTON, Thomas (1752–70), left school aged 14 and was apprenticed to an attorney. In 1768 he published in *Felix Farley's Bristol Journey* a passage of pseudo-archaic prose, of which he claimed to have discovered the original in a chest in St Mary Redcliffe, Bristol. This attracted the attention of local antiquaries, for whom he provided fake documents, pedigrees, deeds, etc. He had by this time already written some of his 'Rowley' poems, including his 'Bristowe Tragedie'; these purported to be the work of an imaginary 15th-cent. Bristol poet, Thomas Rowley, a monk and friend of William Canynge, a historical Bristol merchant. He offered some of the poems (without success) to *Dodsley in Dec. 1768. In March 1769 Chatterton sent to Horace *Walpole a short treatise on painting 'bie T. Rowleie', which Walpole temporarily accepted as authentic. In the same month he published in the *Town and Country Magazine* the first of seven Ossianic pieces in poetic prose, 'Ethelgar. A Saxon poem', though he took care in this and similar pieces to avoid using the Scottish background of *Macpherson. The only Rowleian piece published in Chatterton's life was 'Elinoure and Juga', which appeared in the same periodical in May 1769. In April 1770 he went to London, but within four months he committed suicide by taking arsenic, apparently reduced to despair by poverty. In these last months he wrote a burletta, *The Revenge*; the satirical 'Kew Gardens', modelled on the satires of Charles

*Churchill; and one of his finest Rowleian pieces, 'An Excelente Balade of Charitie'. The Rowley poems were first published in 1777 by Thomas Tyrwhitt, and a year later Thomas *Warton publicly raised doubts of their authenticity; the controversy raged for decades, and Rowley continued to find champions until *Skeat's edition of 1871.

Chatterton's life, work, and tragic death had a powerful effect on the *Romantic imagination; *Wordsworth wrote of him as 'the marvellous Boy, | The sleepless Soul that perished in his pride', and *Keats, who dedicated *Endymion to his memory, described him in a letter as 'the purest writer in the English Language . . .' In his Rowley poems Chatterton employs a variety of verse forms, including Spenserian stanzas, rhyme-royal, and the ballad; notable among them are his *Pindaric 'Songe to Ella' in which Ella (or, as often, Ælla) makes his first appearance, and 'Ælla' itself, 'a tragycal enterlude'.

CHAUCER, Geoffrey (c.1343–1400), was the son of John Chaucer (c.1312–68), a London vintner. In 1357 he served with Lionel, afterwards duke of Clarence. In 1359 he was in France with Edward III's invading army, was taken prisoner, and ransomed. He married, c.1366, Philippa, the daughter of Sir Paon Roet of Hainault and the sister of *John of Gaunt's third wife, Katherine Swynford. Philippa died in 1387 and Chaucer enjoyed Gaunt's patronage throughout his life. He held a number of positions at court and in the king's service, and he travelled abroad on numerous occasions on diplomatic missions; as well as missions to France, he made a journey to Genoa and Florence in 1372–3 in the course of which he could theoretically have met *Boccaccio and *Petrarch. In 1374 he was appointed controller of customs in the port of London and leased his house over Aldgate. He was knight of the shire for Kent in 1386. His last official position was deputy forester in the King's Forest at Petherton in Somerset (1391–8 at least). He was buried in the Poets' Corner of Westminster Abbey where a monument was erected to him in 1555. His writings develop through his career from a period of French influence in the late 1360s (of which the culmination was *The Book of the Duchess* in about 1370), through his 'middle period' of both French and Italian influences (including *The House of Fame* in the 1370s and the mature Italian-influenced works of which the most important is *Troilus and Criseyde, c.1385), to the last period of most of *The Canterbury Tales* and his short lyrics. His prose works include a translation of *Boethius (Boece) and the complicated *A Treatise on the Astrolabe*, written to 'little Lewis', probably the poet's son. Portraits of Chaucer occur in three places: in the Ellesmere MSS (now in the Huntington Library and the basis of most modern editions); in the manuscript of *Troilus and Criseyde* in Corpus Christi College, Cambridge; and in *Hoccleve's *The Regement of Princes*, beside lines 4,995–6.

For a good brief selection of the immense bibliography on Chaucer (up to 1972), see 'Chaucer: a Select Bibliography' by L. D. Benson in *Geoffrey Chaucer*, ed. D. S. Brewer (1974), pp. 352–72.

Chaucerians, Scottish, the name traditionally given to a very diverse group of 15th- and 16th-cent. Scottish writers who show some influence from *Chaucer, although the debt is now regarded as negligible or indirect in most cases. See JAMES I (of Scotland); KINGIS QUAIR, THE; HENRYSON; DUNBAR; DOUGLAS, GAWIN.

Chauntecleer, see CHANTICLEER.

Cheeryble Brothers, Ned and Charles, characters in Dickens's *Nicholas Nickleby*.

CHEKE, Sir John (1514–57), scholar and tutor to Edward VI, and subsequently the first Regius professor of Greek at Cambridge. He wrote many Latin translations from the Greek and was influential in promoting a simple style of English prose. He is referred to in *Milton's Sonnet XI, 'A Book was writ of late'.

CHEKHOV, Anton Pavlovich (1860–1904), Russian dramatist and short story writer. Among the greatest of his mature stories are 'A Dreary Story' (1889), 'Ward No. Six' (1892), 'My Life' (1896), 'Ionych' and the trilogy 'The Man in a Case', 'Gooseberries', and 'About Love' (all 1898), and 'The Lady with the Little Dog' (1899). Chekhov's first successful play was *Ivanov* (1887), but his status as a dramatist rests on his four late plays: *The Seagull* (1895), *Uncle Vanya* (1900), *Three Sisters* (1901), and *The Cherry Orchard* (1904).

Chekhov's success and influence in England has been immense. Since 1903 most of his work has been translated. The first major translation is that by C. *Garnett, *The Tales of Tchehov* (1916–22) and *The Plays of Tchehov* (1923–4). The major modern translation is that by Ronald Hingley, *The Oxford Chekhov* (9 vols, 1964–80). The Incorporated Stage Society's 1911 London production of *The Cherry Orchard* was much admired by Arnold *Bennett, E. M. *Forster, V. *Woolf, *Gerhardie, J. M. *Murry (who placed him above *Joyce and Proust), and especially K. *Mansfield, whose stories are held to be the main channel through which his work influenced England. G. B. *Shaw declared that reading Chekhov's plays made him want to tear up his own, and he went on to write *Heartbreak House* as a tribute to him. He is also held to have influenced E. *Bowen, *O'Faolain, *Maugham, H. E. *Bates, Rodney Ackland, and others.

Chekhov's work is characterized by its subtle blending of naturalism and symbolism; by its sympathetic, humane, but acutely observed portraits of a threatened upper class stifled by inactivity and ennui; and above all by its unique combination of comedy, tragedy, and pathos, and the sensitivity of its movement from one mode to another.

Cherry, and Merry, in Dickens's *Martin Chuzzlewit*, Pecksniff's daughters, Charity and Mercy.

Cherry and the Slae, The, see MONTGOMERIE, A.

Cheshire Cheese, The, 'an ancient eating-house in Fleet Street' where the *Rhymers Club met for some years in the 1880s and 90s.

Chester, Sir John, and Edward his son, characters in Dickens's *Barnaby Rudge*.

CHESTERFIELD, Philip Dormer Stanhope, fourth earl of (1694–1773), was a distinguished statesman and diplomatist, wrote political tracts, contributed to the weekly journal *The World* and was responsible for securing the adoption of the New Style Gregorian *calendar in 1751. He is chiefly remembered for his 'Letters' to his natural son Philip Stanhope (1732–68), which were written (not for publication) almost daily from 1737 onwards. These consist largely of instruction in etiquette and the worldly arts, and became after publication (by the son's widow in 1774) a handbook of good manners. Although widely admired, the letters increasingly attracted criticism, as the century became less cynical and more sentimental. *Johnson addressed the *Plan* of his *Dictionary* to Chesterfield, but it was received with neglect; on publication of the *Dictionary*, Chesterfield wrote two papers in *The World* commending it. Thereupon, on 7 Feb. 1755, Johnson addressed to him the famous letter in which he bitterly rejected a notice which 'had it been early, had been kind; but it has been delayed till I am indifferent, and cannot enjoy it; till I am solitary, and cannot impart it; till I am known, and do not want it.'

Chester Plays, see MYSTERY PLAYS.

CHESTERTON, G(ilbert) K(eith) (1874–1936), made his name in journalism writing (with *Belloc) for *The Speaker*, in which both took a controversial, anti-Imperial, pro-Boer line on the Boer war; his friendship with Belloc earned them from G. B. *Shaw, the twin nickname of 'Chesterbelloc'. His first novel, *The Napoleon of Notting Hill* (1904), a fantasy set in a future in which London is plunged into a strange mixture of medieval nostalgia and street warfare, develops his political attitudes, glorifying the little man, the colour and romance of 'Merry England', and attacking big business, technology, and the monolithic state. These themes echo through his fiction, which includes *The Man who was Thursday: a nightmare* (1908), and his many volumes of short stories, of which the best known are those which feature Father Brown, an unassuming East Anglian Roman Catholic priest, highly successful in the detection of crime by intuitive methods, who first appears in *The Innocence of Father Brown* (1911); Chesterton himself became a Roman Catholic in 1922. He published several volumes of verse; his most characteristic poems (with some exceptions, such as 'The Donkey' from *The Wild Knight*, 1900, and 'Lepanto', from *Poems*, 1915) celebrate the Englishness of England, the nation of Beef and Beer, e.g. 'The Secret People' (1915) and 'The Rolling English Road' (1914).

Chesterton also wrote literary criticism, including works on R. *Browning (1903), *Dickens (1906), and Shaw (1910), and many volumes of political, social, and religious essays. Much of his vast output has proved ephemeral, but Chesterton's vigour, idiosyncrasies, optimism, puns, and paradoxes celebrate the oddity of life and the diversity of people and places with a peculiar and at times exhilarating violence.

CHESTRE, Thomas, see SIR LAUNFAL.

CHETTLE, Henry (c. 1560–?1607), is reputedly the author of about 13 plays and the joint author of considerably more (including *The Blind Beggar of Bednal-Green* with J. *Day). The only extant play attributed to him alone is *The Tragedy of Hoffman* (c. 1603). He edited *Greenes Groats-Worth of Witte* (1592), which, like his own satirical pamphlet *Kind Harts Dreame* (?1592), is noteworthy for its allusion to Shakespeare. He also published *Englandes Mourning Garment* (1603), an elegy on Queen Elizabeth.

Chevy Chase, *The Ballad of*, one of the oldest of the English ballads, included in Percy's *Reliques*, probably dates in its primitive form from the 15th cent. Its subject is the rivalry of the neighbouring families of Percy and Douglas. The two parties meet and fight, there is a great slaughter on both sides, and both Percy and Douglas are killed.

Chiasmus, a figure of speech by which the order of the words in the first of two parallel clauses is reversed in the second, e.g. 'He saved others; himself he cannot save.'

CHICHELE, or **CHICHELEY,** Henry (?1362–1443), became archbishop of Canterbury in 1414. He founded the Chichele chest in Oxford University for the relief of poor students, built a house for Cistercians in Oxford, and was co-founder with Henry VI of All Souls College.

Chicken Soup with Barley, see WESKER TRILOGY.

CHILD, Francis James (1825–96), American scholar, edited *Spenser (5 vols, 1855) and wrote a pioneering study of *Chaucer (1863), but is most widely known for his great collection of *English and Scottish Popular Ballads* (5 vols, 1882–98). (See BALLAD.)

Childe, in 'Childe Harold', 'Childe Roland', etc., signifies a youth of gentle birth, and is used as a kind of title.

Childe Harold's Pilgrimage, a poem by *Byron, of which the first two cantos appeared in 1812, Canto III in 1816, and Canto IV in 1818.

The poem describes the travels, experiences, and reflections of a pilgrim who, sated with his past life of sin and pleasure, finds distraction in his travels through Portugal, Spain, the Ionian Islands, and Albania. In Canto III the pilgrim travels to Belgium, the Rhine, the Alps, and the Jura; this section contains Byron's famous evocation of the Battle of Waterloo. In Canto IV the device of the pilgrim is abandoned and the poet speaks directly, in a long meditation on time and history, on Venice, *Petrarch and Arqua, *Tasso and Ferrara, *Boccaccio and Florence, Rome and her great men, ending with a passage on the eternal symbol of the sea. The pilgrim is the first of the truly *Byronic heroes in the author's work.

Childe Roland, in an old Scottish ballad, a son of King Arthur. His sister, Burd Ellen, is carried away by the fairies to the castle of the king of Elfland. Aided by the instructions of Merlin, Childe Roland makes his way into the castle and rescues his sister.

> Child Rowland to the dark tower came,
> His word was still 'Fie, foh, and fum,
> I smell the blood of a British man.'
>
> (Shakespeare, *King Lear*, III. iv)

*Hallwell (*Nursery Rhymes*) thinks that Shakespeare is here quoting from two different compositions, the first line from a ballad on Roland, the second and third from the story of *Jack the Giant-killer.

'Childe Roland to the Dark Tower Came', a poem by R. *Browning, published in *Men and Women*. The title derives from a snatch of song recited by Edgar in *King Lear* (see above).

A knight errant crosses a nightmare landscape in search of the Dark Tower; he eventually reaches the Tower and blows his horn defiantly at its foot. The poem ends with the title phrase, and there is no indication of what happened next. Browning consistently refused to explain the poem, saying simply that it had come upon him as a dream. The intensity of the poem's language remained unsurpassed in Browning's work until the fragment known as 'Thamuris marching' appeared in *Aristophanes' Apology*.

CHILDERS, (Robert) Erskine (1870–1922), writer and political activist, was a clerk in the House of Commons (1895–1910), served in the Boer War, and in 1921 was appointed director of publicity for the Irish republicans. In 1922 he was court-martialled and shot by a firing squad. As a writer he is remembered for his novel *The Riddle of the Sands* (1903), a sea story about two amateur British yachtsmen who discover German preparations for an invasion of England.

Childe Waters, one of the most beautiful of the old ballads, celebrating the constancy of Ellen to Childe Waters, her heartless lover. The ballad is in Percy's *Reliques*.

Child of the Jago, A, see MORRISON, A.

Children in the Wood, The, popularly known as the story of the Babes in the Wood, is the subject of an old ballad, included in *Percy's and *Ritson's collections.

A Norfolk gentleman leaves his property to his infant son and daughter and gives the children into his brother's charge; the wicked uncle hires two ruffians to slay them in a wood. One of these repents and kills his fellow, then abandons the children in the wood. The children perish, and a robin covers them with leaves.

Children of the Chapel of Paul's, see PAUL'S, CHILDREN OF.

Children's Literature. In the 15th cent. 'courtesy books', such as *The Babees' Book*, provided children with instruction on behaviour; but for entertainment they had to turn to adult books such as *Aesop or collections of legends. It was not until the 17th cent. that books were specifically written for children, and then the stories (such as James Janeway's *A Token for Children* in 1671) were sternly moralistic. Children read Bunyan's *Pilgrim's Progress (1678–84). Defoe's *Robinson Crusoe (1719), Swift's *Gulliver's Travels (1726), and other works primarily written for adults; not until the 18th cent., when (largely under the influence of *Locke and *Rousseau) education became more humane, did the first books appear designed to attract and please children. In 1745 *Newbery opened a children's bookshop (described in *The Vicar of Wakefield*) and wrote many of the volumes he sold; Thomas Boreman produced, from 1740, booklets called *Gigantick Histories*. Crude *chapbooks of alphabets, rhymes, and fairy-tales began to abound, as did more serious didactic works, such as T. *Day's *The History of Sandford and Merton* (1783–9) and M. *Edgeworth's *Moral Tales* (1801). With the publication in 1814 of J. D. Wyss's *The Swiss Family Robinson* and in 1818–47 of Mrs *Sherwood's *History of the Fairchild Family*, the demand for children's books of quality was firmly established, and the

various categories (adventure, school stories, family sagas, animal stories, fantasy, etc.) became distinguished. The perennial argument as to whether children should read fairy-tales was stimulated by the publication of *German Popular Stories* by the brothers *Grimm in 1823, and the stories of *Andersen in 1846; Thackeray's *The Rose and the Ring* (1855) is a gentle satire of fairy-story conventions. Adventure stories for boys were produced from the 1840s onwards by *Marryat, R. M. *Ballantyne, *Henty, and others. School stories were established by Thomas *Hughes's *Tom Brown's Schooldays* (1857) and F. W. *Farrar's *Eric, or Little by Little* (1858); family sagas by C. M. *Yonge's *The Daisy Chain* (1856) and by the American L. M. Alcott, with *Little Women* (1868); and animal stories by A. *Sewell's *Black Beauty* (1877). During the rest of the century many classics of children's literature appeared: Kingsley's *The Water Babies* (1863); Lewis Carroll's *Alice's Adventures in Wonderland* (1865); Mrs *Molesworth's *The Tapestry Room* (1879); R. *Jefferies's *Bevis* (1882); R. L. *Stevenson's *Treasure Island* (1883), one of the first adventure stories with no obvious didactic purpose; F. H. *Burnett's *Little Lord Fauntleroy* (1886); Stevenson's *Kidnapped* (1886) and *Catriona* (1893); *Haggard's *King Solomon's Mines* (1885); *Kipling's *Jungle Books* (1894–5); and the first of E. *Nesbit's long line of successes, *The Story of the Treasure-Seekers* (1899). In 1899 appeared *Little Black Sambo*, the first of a popular and vividly illustrated series by Helen Bannerman (1862/3–1946); she, with Beatrix *Potter (whose *Peter Rabbit* appeared in 1902), did much to establish the book in which pictures and text are of equal importance. The increasing demand for children's fiction was manifested not only in a vast amount of work of lesser quality, but also in Kipling's *Puck of Pook's Hill* (1906), *Grahame's *The Wind in the Willows* (1908), F. H. Burnett's *The Secret Garden* (1911); the first of the 'Dr Dolittle' books by Hugh Lofting (1886–1947) which appeared in 1920; E. *Farjeon's *Martin Pippin in the Apple Orchard* (1921); A. A. *Milne's *Winnie-the-Pooh* (1926); and the first of A. *Uttley's 'Little Grey Rabbit' books in 1929. The first of *Ransome's 'Swallows and Amazons' series appeared in 1930, and Noel Streatfeild (1895–1986) established the 'career' novel with *Ballet Shoes* in 1936. *Tolkien restimulated the tradition of fantasy with *The Hobbit* (1937).

Since about 1950 the publishing of fiction for children has been a vast industry, with specialist guides and reviewers and many annual prizes and medals. In the flourishing field of fantasy, work of a high standard has been produced by C. S. *Lewis, Alan Garner (1934–), and Philippa Pearce (1920–). The historical novels of Rosemary Sutcliff (1920–) and Leon Garfield (1921–), and the daily-life novels of Nina

Bawden (1925–), should also be mentioned.

The history of verse written for children is much briefer. The first identifiable children's poet was probably *Watts, whose memorable jingles, *Divine Songs for Children*, were popular from 1715. At about this time collections of nursery rhymes began to appear. Ann and Jane *Taylor, whose first book, *Original Poems for Infant Minds*, included 'Twinkle, twinkle little star', were extremely successful in 1804 and thereafter. *The Butterfly's Ball and the Grasshopper's Feast* (1806), a *jeu d'esprit* by *Roscoe, produced scores of imitations. R. *Browning's 'The Pied Piper of Hamelin' was published in 1842, *Lear's *Book of Nonsense* (followed by many other verses) in 1846, and R. L. Stevenson's *A Child's Garden of Verses* in 1885. Verse in this century has included distinguished work by *Belloc, *De La Mare, A. A. Milne, Robert *Graves, Ted *Hughes, and *Causley, among others.

CHILLINGWORTH, William (1602–44), one of the literary coterie that gathered round *Falkland at Great Tew, and author of the controversial work *The Religion of the Protestants a safe Way to Salvation* (1637).

Chillip, Dr, in Dickens's *David Copperfield*, the physician who attended Mrs Copperfield at the hero's birth.

Chillon, The Prisoner of, see PRISONER OF CHILLON, THE.

Chimes, The, a Christmas book by *Dickens, published 1845.

It is the story of a nightmare or vision in which Toby Veck, porter and runner of errands, under the influence of the goblins of the church bells and a dish of tripe, witnesses awful misfortunes befalling his daughter, a vision happily dissipated at the end.

Chingachgook, the Indian chief in the 'Leatherstocking' series of tales of Indian life of J. F. *Cooper.

Chips with Everything, see WESKER, A.

Chivery, Mr and 'Young John', characters in Dickens's *Little Dorrit*.

Chloe, the name under which Pope satirizes Lady Suffolk, mistress of George II (*Moral Essays*, ii. 157).

The 'Chloe' or 'Cloe' in Horace *Walpole's letters was the duke of Newcastle's French cook Clouet.

Choice, The, see POMFRET, J.

CHOMSKY, Noam (1928–), professor of modern languages and linguistics at Massachu-

setts Institute of Technology, after *Saussure the most important figure in modern linguistics. Two of his books, in particular, proposed a radically new view of the nature and analysis of language: *Syntactic Structures* (1957) and *Aspects of the Theory of Syntax* (1965). Following on from the systems of grammatical analysis developed by L. *Bloomfield and Chomsky's teacher Zellig Harris, Chomsky's 'generative grammar' proposes a set of 'deep structure' grammatical rules which produce a set of sentences at the 'surface structure' of language. A grammar of a language would be a set of rules which generates 'all and only the correct sentences of the language'. The significance of his emphasis is that it brings linguistic analysis closer to analyses of mental operations such as are conducted by psychologists and logicians.

CHOPIN, Kate, *née* O'Flaherty (1850–1904), American writer, married Oscar Chopin, a Creole. She has won posthumous recognition principally for *The Awakening* (1899), set in Grand Isle and New Orleans, the story of Edna Pontellier, married to a successful Creole businessman. She defies convention by committing adultery with a young man; on the last page she swims out to sea and presumably drowns, thus ambiguously asserting the individual's right to freedom. The novel was greeted as scandalous and morbid. Discouraged from writing more full-length fiction, Kate Chopin turned to poems, essays, and short stories. Interest in her largely neglected work increased from the late 1940s.

Choriamb, a metrical foot of four syllables, —◡◡—. A choree is a *trochee.

CHRÉTIEN DE TROYES (*fl.* 1170–90), regarded as the greatest of the writers of courtly romances (see COURTLY LOVE), which he wrote in French. Four complete romances survive, all written in octosyllabic rhyming couplets: *Erec and Enide* (c.1170); *Cligés* (c.1176); *Yvain* (c.1177–81); and *Lancelot*, or *Le Chevalier de la Charrette* (c.1177–81): the last 1,000 lines of the latter were written by Godefroy de Lagny. He left incomplete the lengthy *Perceval*, or *Le Conte de Graal* (1181–90). He lived and worked for some time at the court of *Marie de Champagne, but little else of his life is known. His influence on all subsequent Arthurian literature, including English, is general rather than particular, but the English romance *Iwain and Gawain* is a loose translation of his *Yvain*.

'Christabel', a poem by S. T. *Coleridge, published 1816.

The poem, which is unfinished, is written in what is sometimes referred to as 'Christabel metre', that is, in four-foot couplets, mostly iambic and anapaestic, used with immense variety, so that the line length varies from seven syllables to ten or eleven.

Christabel, praying at night in a wood for her betrothed lover, discovers the fair Geraldine in distress and takes her to the castle of her father, Sir Leoline. Geraldine claims to be the daughter of Sir Leoline's estranged friend Sir Roland of Vaux. She shares Christabel's chamber for the night, and bewitches her as they lie in one another's arms. In the morning she meets Sir Leoline, who vows reconciliation with her father and vengeance on the 'reptile souls' of her abductors. Christabel, who has seen Geraldine's true malignant serpent nature, is at first silenced by the spell placed upon her, but manages to implore her father to send Geraldine away. Sir Leoline, offended by his daughter's insult to a guest, turns from her to Geraldine, and so the poem ends.

Christ and Satan, an Old English poem of 733 lines found in the *Junius manuscript. It has been suggested that the work dates from 790–830 and is of Anglian origin. The subjects of the three sections are: Satan's lament for his fall; the *Harrowing of Hell; and the temptation of Christ by Satan.

Christian and **Christiana,** the hero of Bunyan's *The Pilgrim's Progress* and his wife.

Christian Hero, The. *An Argument proving that no Principles but those of Religion are Sufficient to make a great Man,* a treatise by *Steele, published 1701.

Finding, as the author tells us, military life 'exposed to much Irregularity', he wrote this 'little work'. In it he stresses the value of the Bible as a moral guide and the failure of Stoic philosophy. The work is important as one of the first signs of a change in tone in the English literature of the period. (See also STOICISM.)

Christian Morals, see BROWNE, T.

Christian Year, The, see KEBLE, J.

CHRISTIE, Dame Agatha, *née* Miller (1890–1976), writer of *detective fiction. During the First World War she worked as a hospital dispenser, which gave her a knowledge of poisons which was to be useful in her fiction. Her first detective novel, *The Mysterious Affair at Styles* (1920), introduced Hercule Poirot, the Belgian detective who appeared in many subsequent novels (her other main detective being the elderly spinster Miss Marple). In the next 56 years she wrote 66 detective novels, among the best of which are *The Murder of Roger Ackroyd* (1926), *Murder on the Orient Express* (1934), *Death on the Nile* (1937), and *Ten Little Niggers* (1939). She also wrote six novels under the pseudonym Mary Westmacott, two self-portraits (*Come Tell Me How You Live*, 1946; *An Autobiography*, 1977), and several plays, including *The Mousetrap*, which has run continuously in London for more than 30 years. Her prodigious international success seems due to her matchless ingenuity in contriving plots, sustaining suspense, and misdirecting the reader, to her ear for dialogue, and brisk, unsentimental common sense and humour.

Christis Kirk on the Green, an old Scottish poem, doubtfully attributed to James I or James V of Scotland, in nine-lined stanzas with a 'bob' after the eighth line, descriptive of the rough fun, dancing, and love-making of a village festival or 'wappinshaw'. Two additional cantos were composed by *Ramsay.

Christmas Carol, A, a Christmas book by *Dickens, published 1843.

Scrooge, an old curmudgeon, receives on Christmas Eve a visit from the ghost of Marley, his late partner in business, and beholds a series of visions, including one of what his own death will be like unless he is quick to amend his ways. As a result of this he wakes up on Christmas morning an altered man.

Christmas-Eve and Easter-Day, a poem by R. *Browning, published 1850. The poem is in two parts, in octosyllabic metre, with an irregular rhyme-scheme. 'Christmas-Eve', in narrative form, combining realistic and visionary elements, accepts that denominational religion is an imperfect medium for divine truth, but emphasizes the need to choose the best method of worship according to one's lights. 'Easter-Day', in the form of an imagined dialogue, examines the difficulties of holding to the Christian faith at all, and argues that the condition of doubt is, in fact, essential to the existence of human faith.

Christs Teares over Jerusalem, a tract by T. *Nashe, published 1593. Nashe here figures as a religious reformer and analyses with his usual vigour the vices and abuses of contemporary society.

Chronicle Play, a type of drama popular in the 1590s and the early 17th cent., in which scenes from the life of a monarch or famous historical character were depicted. Examples are Shakespeare's *Henry V and *Henry VIII, the Sir Thomas *More play, and *Dekker and *Webster's Sir Thomas Wyat.

Chronicles, see under ANGLO-SAXON CHRONICLE, ANNALES CAMBRIAE, ASSER, BEDE, CAMDEN, CAPGRAVE, EADMER, FABYAN, GEOFFREY OF MONMOUTH, GILDAS, GIRALDUS CAMBRENSIS, HALL, E., HARRISON, W., HOLINSHED, HOVEDEN, JOCELIN DE BRAKELOND, NENNIUS, PETERBOROUGH

CHRONICLE, RICHARD THE THIRDE, ROBERT OF GLOUCESTER, SPEED, STOW, VERGIL, WACE, WILLIAM OF MALMESBURY, WILLIAM OF NEWBURGH, WYNTOUN, A.

Chronicles of the Canongate, The, an inclusive title for Sir W. Scott's novels *The Highland Widow*, *The Two Drovers*, and *The Fair Maid of Perth*.

Chrononhotonthologos, a burlesque of contemporary drama by H. *Carey, acted 1734.

Chrononhotonthologos is king of Queerum-mania, and two of the characters are Aldiborontiphoscophornia and Rigdum-Funnidos, names which Sir W. *Scott gave to James and John *Ballantyne, on account of the pomposity of the one and the fun and cheerfulness of the other.

Chrysal, or the Adventures of a Guinea, see JOHNSTONE, C.

Chrysaor, in Spenser's *Faerie Queene* (v. i. 9 and v. xii. 40), the sword of Justice, wielded by Sir *Artegall.

CHRYSOSTOM, St John (c. 345–407), a Greek father of the Church. His name means 'Golden-mouth', in tribute to his eloquent preaching; in his writings he stressed the ascetical element in religion and the need for personal study of the Scriptures. The most celebrated of his many works are his Commentaries on the Gospel of St Matthew and on the Epistles to the Romans and Corinthians.

Chuffey, in Dickens's *Martin Chuzzlewit*, Anthony Chuzzlewit's old clerk.

CHURCH, Richard Thomas (1893–1972), poet, novelist, and essayist, published many volumes of verse from 1917 onwards, mainly of a Georgian tone, and also both adult and children's fiction. He also published three volumes of autobiography, 1956–64.

CHURCH, Richard William (1815–90), dean of St Paul's, fellow of Oriel College, Oxford, where he met *Newman and became a supporter of the *Oxford Movement. He wrote lives of St *Anselm (1870), *Spenser (1879), *Bacon (1884) and *The Oxford Movement, Twelve Years, 1833–1845* (1891), a notable interpretation of the history of the movement.

CHURCHILL, Caryl (1938–), playwright. Her plays, predominantly radical and feminist in tone, include *Owners* (1972, pub. 1973), a satire on property and capitalism; *Light Shining in Buckinghamshire* (1976, pub. 1978); *Cloud Nine* (1979, pub. 1979); *Top Girls* (1982, with an all-female cast); and *Softcops* (1984, with an all-male cast). She has also written radio and television plays.

CHURCHILL, Charles (1732–64), curate at St John's, Westminster, was oppressed by poverty until the publication of *The Rosciad* and *The Apology* (both 1761), which brought him fame and fortune. He increasingly abandoned the church, leading a worldly and dissipated life, and by 1762 was a close friend of *Wilkes, writing for his paper *The North Briton* and attacking his opponents in satiric verse. *The Prophecy of Famine* (1763) is a mock-pastoral and a powerful satiric attack on Bute, J. *Home, and other Scots. *Gotham* (1764) describes Churchill as Patriot King (see BOLINGBROKE) of an ideal state. Its heroic couplets mark the transition to the softer usages of the later 18th cent. (Gotham, a village near Nottingham, was traditionally famed for the simplicity of its inhabitants.) Churchill died young at Boulogne on his way to visit Wilkes in France.

Churchill, Frank, a character in J. Austen's *Emma.

CHURCHILL, Rt Hon. Sir Winston Leonard Spencer (1874–1965), eldest son of Lord Randolph Churchill (third son of the 7th duke of Marlborough), first lord of the Admiralty, 1911–15; secretary of state for war, 1918–21; for the colonies, 1921–2; chancellor of the exchequer, 1924–9; prime minister, 1940–5, and 1951–5. Among his publications are: *London to Ladysmith via Pretoria* (1900), *Lord Randolph Churchill* (1906–7), *My African Journey* (1908), *Liberalism and the Social Problem* (1909), *The World Crisis* (4 vols, 1923–9), *My Early Life* (1930), *Marlborough* (1933–8), *War Speeches 1940–5* (1946), *The Second World War* (6 vols, 1948–54), and *A History of the English-speaking Peoples* (4 vols, 1956–8). He was awarded the *Nobel Prize in 1953.

CHURCHYARD, Thomas (?1520–1604), published, before 1553, *A myrrour for man*. Between 1560 and 1603 he issued a multitude of broadsheets and small volumes in verse and prose. His best-known works are *Shores Wife* (1563), in the *Mirror for Magistrates*, and the *Generall Rehearsall of Warres* (1579). Spenser in his *Colin Clout* refers to Churchyard as 'old Palemon . . . That sung so long untill quite hoarse he grew'.

CHUTE, John (1701–76), friend and correspondent of Horace *Walpole. He contributed greatly to the creation of *Strawberry Hill. Walpole referred to him as 'my oracle in taste . . .'. He has been credited with more fidelity to antiquity than his fellow connoisseur, the more fantastic Richard *Bentley.

CIBBER, Colley (1671–1757), became an actor in 1690. His first play, *Love's Last Shift* (1696), introduced the character of Sir Novelty Fashion, who was transformed into Lord Foppington in Vanbrugh's *The Relapse. Cibber wrote in his varied theatrical career many plays and adaptations, notably She Would and She Would Not (1702), *The Careless Husband (1704), both comedies, and a successful adaptation of Shakespeare's *Richard III (1700). The Non-Juror (1717), a comedy based on *Molière's Tartuffe, was ridiculed by *Pope in a pamphlet, and Cibber became the hero of Pope's *Dunciad in its final edition, after becoming poet laureate in 1730. He attracted many enemies by his rudeness and vanity, and as a writer was more concerned with theatrical effect than with literary merit, but nevertheless made a significant contribution to 18th-cent. drama, particularly to the genre of *sentimental comedy. In 1740 Cibber published his autobiography, An Apology for the Life of Mr Colley Cibber, Comedian, which gives a vivid picture of the theatrical life of the time.

CICERO, Marcus Tullius (106–43 BC), referred to sometimes as Tully, was the most influential of Roman prose writers. He became consul in 63 BC when he suppressed the conspiracy of Catiline. He supported the senatorial party against Julius *Caesar, and after Caesar's assassination he attacked Mark Antony in his Philippic orations. On the formation of the triumvirate he was put to death. His writings left their mark on ethics, epistemology, and political thought, on men's ideals of conduct, on the development of oratory and letter-writing, on literary style, the popularity of paradox, and the viability of Latin as an international language. During the Middle Ages Cicero figures primarily as a master of rhetoric. The textbook De Inventione remained the best-known of his works and was imitated by *Alcuin. De Amicitia served Aelred of Rievaulx and others as a model for disquisitions on Christian love. His works contributed substantially to the late 16th-cent. revival of *Stoicism and Scepticism. Cicero stood behind *Hume's systematic doubt as he stood behind the half-hearted republicanism that led up to the French revolution.

Cid, The, (c.1030–99), the favourite hero of Spain in whose story history and myth are difficult to disentangle. Rodrigo Díaz de Bivar, el Cid Campeador, of a noble Castilian family, rose to fame by his prowess in the war between Sancho of Castile and Sancho of Navarre, and in conflicts with the Moors. Having incurred the jealousy of Alphonso, king of Castile, he was banished and became a soldier of fortune, fighting at times for the Christians, at others for the Moors. His principal feat was the capture of Valencia from the Moors after a siege of nine months. He died of grief at the defeat of his force.

In myth, his character has been glorified into a type of knightly and Christian virtue and patri-

otic zeal. His achievements are narrated in the Poema del Cid of the 12th cent., in the Spanish Chronicle of the 13th cent., and in numerous ballads. The chronicles relating to him were translated by R. *Southey (1808). The Cid is the subject of the most famous drama of *Corneille, Le Cid (1637).

Cider with Rosie, see LEE, L.

Cinderella, a fairy-tale, from the French of *Perrault, translated by Robert Samber (?1729).

The gentle Cinderella is cruelly used by her stepmother and two stepsisters, and when her household drudgery is done, sits at the corner of the hearth in the cinders. Her stepsisters having gone to a ball, she is left crying at home. Her fairy godmother arrives, provides her with beautiful clothes, a coach made out of a pumpkin, and six horses transformed from mice, and sends her to the ball, on condition that she returns before the stroke of twelve. The prince falls in love with her. She hurries away at midnight, losing one of her tiny glass slippers. The prince has a search made for her and announces that he will marry her whom the slipper fits. To the discomfiture of the stepsisters the slipper is found to fit only Cinderella, who marries the prince.

*Lang, in Perrault's Popular Tales (1888), discusses the analogous stories which exist in the folklore of various countries. Various operas have been based on this fairy-tale, including Rossini's La Cenerentola (1817), and it is one of the most popular subjects for Christmas pantomimes.

Circulating Libraries, see LIBRARIES, CIRCULATING.

Circumlocution Office, the type of a government department, satirized in Dickens's *Little Dorrit.

Citizen Comedy, an early 17th-cent. type of play, usually set in contemporary London and dealing with the common life of the middle classes. Jonson's *Bartholomew Fair and Middleton's *A Chaste Mayd in Cheap-side are examples of the genre.

Citizen of the World, The, by *Goldsmith, a collection of 119 letters purporting to be written by or to an imaginary philosophic Chinaman, Lien Chi Altangi, residing in London. They first appeared as Chinese Letters in *Newbery's Public Ledger (1760–1) and were republished under the above title in 1762.

They are a series of whimsical or satirical comments on English life and manners, with character sketches and episodes strung on a slender thread of narrative. The best-known character sketches are those of the 'Man in

Black', a covert philanthropist, and 'Beau' Tibbs, an affected nonentity who claims acquaintance with the great.

City Heiress, The, a comedy by A. *Behn.

City Madam, The, a comedy by *Massinger, acted 1632, printed 1658.

The play deals with the efforts of Sir John Frugal to curb the extravagance of his wife and daughters, by pretending to retire to a monastery, and leaving them to the mercy of his prodigal brother Luke. Luke treats them so harshly that Frugal is welcomed home, with promises of reform.

City of Destruction, in Bunyan's *Pilgrim's Progress, typifies the state of the worldly and irreligious.

'City of Dreadful Night, The', see under THOMSON, J. (1834–82).

City Witt, The, or the Woman Wears the Breeches, see BROME, R.

'Civil Disobedience', see THOREAU, H. D.

Civil Wars between the two Houses of York and Lancaster, The, an epic poem by S. *Daniel in eight books, published 1595–1609. It contains some 900 eight-lined stanzas, of a grave and philosophical cast and marked by strong patriotism.

CLAIRMONT, Claire (1798–1879), daughter of Mary Clairmont, who became William *Godwin's second wife. She accompanied Mary Godwin on her elopement with *Shelley, and in spite of pursuit remained with them on the Continent. She returned to London with the Shelleys in 1816, fell in love with *Byron, and when he went to Switzerland she induced the Shelleys to follow him with her. Byron's daughter Allegra was born to her in 1817. In 1818 Claire surrendered the child to Byron who, in 1821, placed Allegra in a convent near Ravenna, where she died of a fever in 1822.

Clandestine Marriage, The, a comedy by *Colman the elder and *Garrick, performed 1766; it caused a rift between the two collaborators when Garrick refused to take the role of Lord Ogleby.

Lovewell has secretly married his employer's younger daughter Fanny. Her father, Sir Sterling, a wealthy London merchant, has arranged a marriage between his elder daughter and Sir John Melvil, nephew of Lord Ogleby, who accepts the alliance for mercenary reasons. Melvil suddenly reveals his aversion to the proposed match and his passion for Fanny, who repels his advances. Melvil induces Mr Sterling, for a financial consideration, to allow him to

transfer his suit to Fanny. But now Mrs Heidelberg, Mr Sterling's wealthy sister (whose eccentric speech foreshadows that of Mrs *Malaprop), intervenes, and orders Fanny from the house. Fanny in despair applies to old Ogleby who, mistaking her inarticulate confession for a declaration of love for himself, announces that he himself will marry her, thereby increasing the confusion. Finally a lover is discovered in Fanny's bedroom. When he turns out to be Lovewell, Lord Ogleby good-naturedly intervenes on behalf of the guilty couple and all ends well.

CLANVOWE, Sir John (d. 1391), one of the Lollard Knights, and the author of the pacifist and puritanical work The Two Ways. He was a friend of *Chaucer, and he may also have been the author of The Cuckoo and the Nightingale or The Boke of Cupide, an elegant debate-poem in 290 lines which *Wordsworth translated.

Clapham Sect, the name given by Sydney *Smith to a group of Evangelical and anti-slave-trade philanthropists, centred on Clapham, whose members included *Wilberforce, Zachary Macaulay (father of T. B. *Macaulay), the scholar and pamphleteer Granville Sharp, and the Thornton family, ancestors of E. M. *Forster.

Clare, Angel, a character in Hardy's *Tess of the D'Urbervilles.

CLARE, John (1793–1864), poet, the son of a labourer, was born in Helpstone, Northamptonshire, where he worked as a hedge-setter and day labourer. In 1820 he married Martha Turner, having parted from his first love, Mary Joyce, a sorrow which troubled him throughout his life. His successful first volume, Poems Descriptive of Rural Life and Scenery (1820), was followed by The Village Minstrel (1821), The Shepherd's Calendar (1827), and The Rural Muse (1835). In 1832 he left his native cottage for Northborough, only four miles away, but the move, to one so deeply attached to place, was disturbing, and reinforced the theme of loss in his work. In 1837 he was admitted as insane to an asylum in High Beach, Epping, whence he escaped in 1841, walking home to Northamptonshire in the delusion that he would there be reunited with Mary, to whom he thought himself married. He was once more certified insane, and spent the rest of his life in Northampton General Asylum where he was allowed much freedom. By the 1830s the vogue for rural poetry and 'ploughman' poets such as *Burns and R. *Bloomfield was passing; and Clare's work remained little read until this century. Clare is now recognized as a poet of great truth and power; his much anthologized asylum poems have perhaps tended to obscure the real nature of his gifts, and recently more attention has been paid to his highly personal evocations of landscape and place. His best poems ('Remembrances', 'The Flitting', 'Decay') demonstrate a complex sensibility and fine organization, and have been variously read as laments for lost love and talent, for the death of rural England, or for lost innocence. Unlike many poets from a similar background, he insisted to his publisher John *Taylor that he would continue to write in his own language, dialect, and idiosyncratic grammar. His *Poems* (1935), *Prose* (1951), and *Letters* (1951) were edited by J. W. and A. Tibble; *The Shepherd's Calendar*, ed. E. Robinson and G. Summerfield, appeared in 1964; and his *Later Poems* (ed. E. Robinson and D. Powell, with M. Grainger) in 1984.

CLARENDON, Edward Hyde, earl of (1609–74), entered Parliament in 1640 and at first sided with the popular party, but as a strong Anglican he was from 1641 onwards one of the chief supporters and advisers of the king. He followed Prince Charles into exile. At the Restoration he returned as lord chancellor but fell out of favour. He was impeached in 1667 and fled to France where he wrote his autobiography, *The Life of Edward, Earl of Clarendon* (1759), and completed his History, *The True Historical Narrative of the Rebellion and Civil Wars in England* (first printed from a transcript under the supervision of Clarendon's son, 1702–4; the first true text was edited by W. D. Macray, 6 vols, 1888). It is composed from material written at different periods and in widely differing circumstances and it remains a classic work. It is also an important contribution to the art of *biography and autobiography, and memorable for its portraits of figures as varied as *Falkland, *Godolphin, *Laud, and *Strafford. Clarendon's daughter Anne Hyde married the future James II. His works were presented to the University of Oxford by his heirs, and from the profits of the History a new printing-house, which bears his name, was built for the *Oxford University Press.

Clarendon Press, see OXFORD UNIVERSITY PRESS.

Clarion, The, see BLATCHFORD, R.

Clarissa: or The History of a Young Lady, an *epistolary novel by S. *Richardson, published 1748 (for 1747)–1749, in 8 vols. About one-third of the work (which is in all over a million words) consists of the letters of Clarissa Harlowe and Lovelace, mainly written to Anna Howe and John Belford respectively, but there are over 20 correspondents in all.

Clarissa, a young lady of good family, is wooed by Lovelace, an unscrupulous man of fashion. Her family oppose the match, intending her for the wealthy Solmes, whom she detests. Lovelace, representing himself as her deliverer, carries her off to London, where she resists his advances, although fascinated by his charm and wit. He, increasingly enraged and attracted by her intransigence, continues to press his suit by trickery and violence, and eventually drugs and rapes her. Clarissa initially loses her reason, but recovers her sanity and makes a lengthy preparation for an exemplary Christian death. Lovelace, overcome with remorse, is killed by her cousin Colonel Morden in a duel.

CLARK, Kenneth Mackenzie, Lord (1903–83), art historian. He was director of the National Gallery (1934–45). His first book, *The Gothic Revival* (1928), was hailed as original and audacious; his approach, derived from *Ruskin and also from *Berenson (with whom he studied), was interpretative rather than pedantic. Other publications include a study of Leonardo da Vinci (1939), *Landscape into Art* (1949), and his major work, *The Nude: A Study of Ideal Art* (1953); also two volumes of autobiography, *Another Part of the Wood* (1974) and *The Other Half* (1977). His television series *Civilization* appeared in book form in 1969.

CLARKE, Arthur C(harles) (1917–   ), writer of *Science Fiction, whose great technical expertise in the realm of aeronautics and astronautics is manifested both in his fiction, which includes *Childhood's End* (1953), *The City and the Stars* (1956), *The Nine Billion Names of God* (1967), and *2001: A space odyssey* (1968), and in his many non-fiction works on space travel.

CLARKE, Austin (1896–1974), Irish poet and verse dramatist. He published some 18 volumes of poetry, from his first, *The Vengeance of Fionn* (1917) to his *Collected Poems* of 1974. His early work is influenced by *Yeats and the *Celtic Twilight, but much of his later work is sharply satiric and highly critical of his own nation's attitudes; in form it is subtle and complex, with an unobtrusive technical expertise. Clarke was also greatly interested in verse drama; he founded the Dublin Verse-Speaking Society in 1938, which developed into the Lyric Theatre Company and performed many of his own plays as well as those of *Bottomley, T. S. *Eliot, and others. Clarke's plays are rooted in medieval Irish legend, but many have pantomime or farcical elements. His *Collected Plays* were published in 1963.

CLARKE, Charles Cowden- (1787–1877), the son of *Keats's schoolmaster and a friend of the poet. With his wife, Mary Victoria Cowden-Clark (1809–98), author of *The Complete Concordance to Shakespeare*, 1844–5), he produced editions of Shakespeare, G. *Herbert and other poets, and they wrote *Recollections of Writers*

(1878), a collection of reminiscences of their close friends Keats, *Lamb, Mary *Lamb, Leigh *Hunt, Douglas *Jerrold, and *Dickens.

CLARKE, Marcus Andrew Hislop (1846–81), emigrated to Australia in 1863. He is remembered for his celebrated novel *For the Term of his Natural Life* (1874), a powerful and sympathetic portrayal of an Australian penal settlement, and his shorter stories of Australian life.

CLARKSON, Laurence (1615–67), a pamphleteer whose spiritual autobiography *The Lost Sheep Found* (1660) charts his progress through many religious affiliations; from his Church of England boyhood in Lancashire he became Anabaptist, Seeker, Ranter, and finally *Muggletonian, suffering imprisonment for his views. His tracts shed an interesting light on the adventurous and speculative ideas of the age.

Classicism, Classic, are terms used in several different and at times overlapping senses. A 'literary classic' is a work considered excellent of its kind, and therefore standard, fit to be used as a model or imitated. More narrowly, 'classicism' may be taken to denote the deliberate imitation of the works of antiquity, and in this sense is often qualified as *'Neo-classicism', which flourished in England in the late 17th and 18th cents. An elaboration of this concept leads to a distinction between Classicism and *Romanticism; the Romantic movement, which dominated the early 19th cent., and which saw itself in part as a revolt against Classicism, led in turn to a reaction at the beginning of the 20th cent. from writers such as T. S. *Eliot and T. E. *Hulme, whose concern was to stress man's limitations rather than his perfectibility and illimitable aspirations, and who emphasized the virtues of formal restraint in literature rather than the virtues of inspiration and exuberance.

The shades of meaning which the term have acquired lead at times to apparent confusion: when one speaks of the drama of *Racine and *Corneille as 'classical', and the drama of *Shakespeare or *Hugo as 'romantic', one is not depriving Shakespeare or Hugo of classic status, nor suggesting that Shakespeare himself had any sense of such a contrast; whereas Hugo wrote as a conscious rebel against classicism. *Auden and Dylan *Thomas, near-contemporaries, are frequently described as exemplars of, respectively, the classical and the romantic in modern poetry, and both are widely considered classics of their own period and aesthetic approach.

CLAUDIAN (Claudius Claudianus) (*fl. c.* AD 395–404), the last great Latin poet to be a pagan, was born in Alexandria and wrote in Rome. His short epic *De raptu Proserpinae* influenced Spenser's account of the garden of Proserpina (*Faerie Queene*, II. vii. 52).

Claudio, (1) the lover of Hero in Shakespeare's *Much Ado about Nothing*; (2) the brother of Isabella and betrothed husband of Julietta in his *Measure for Measure*.

Claudius, in Shakespeare's *Hamlet*, brother of old Hamlet and husband of his widow *Gertrude.

CLAVERHOUSE, Graham of, see GRAHAM OF CLAVERHOUSE.

Clavering, Sir Francis and Lady, characters in Thackeray's *Pendennis*.

Claverings, The, a novel by A. *Trollope, published 1867.

Clayhanger, see BENNETT, ARNOLD.

Claypole, Noah, in Dickens's *Oliver Twist*, a fellow apprentice of the hero and subsequently one of Fagin's gang of thieves.

Cleanness (or *Purity*), an alliterative poem in 1,812 lines from the second half of the 14th cent., the only manuscript of which is the famous Cotton Nero A x which is also the sole manuscript of *Pearl*, *Patience*, and *Sir *Gawain and the Green Knight* (see PEARL). It deals with three subjects from the Scriptures: the Flood, the destruction of Sodom and Gomorrah, and the fall of Belshazzar.

Cleishbotham, Jedediah, see TALES OF MY LANDLORD.

CLELAND, John (1709–89), journalist and novelist. Although *Memoirs of a Woman of Pleasure* (often known as *Fanny Hill*), published 1748–9, had an enormous sale, and brought his publisher £10,000, it brought him only 20 guineas. He was summoned before the Privy Council for indecency, but discharged. In 1751 he published the *Memoirs of a Coxcomb*, and in 1764 *The Surprises of Love*.

CLEMENS, S. L., see TWAIN, M.

Clementine Vulgate, see VULGATE.

CLEMENT OF ALEXANDRIA (b. *c.* AD 160), a Greek Father of the Church, the first to apply Greek culture and philosophy to the exposition of Christianity. Of his four surviving works, the *Exhortation to the Greeks* is an attempt to convert the Greeks to Christianity.

Clennam, Arthur and Mrs, characters in Dickens's *Little Dorrit*.

CLEMO, Jack (Reginald John) (1916–), poet, published a novel, *Wilding Graft* (1948), an autobiography, *Confession of Rebel* (1949), and several volumes of poetry, including *The Clay Verge* (1951) and *The Echoing Tip* (1971), which evoke with a kind of visionary grimness the tormented landscapes of the clay pits of Cornwall, and express his own Calvinist faith.

Cleon, (1) governor of Tarsus in Shakespeare's *Pericles*; (2) title of a poem by R. Browning, included in *Men and Women*.

Cleopatra, a tragedy in blank verse by S. *Daniel, published 1594.

It is on the Senecan model, and deals with the story of Cleopatra after the death of Antony.

Clerihew, an epigrammatic verse-form invented by Edmund Clerihew *Bentley, consisting of two rhymed couplets, usually dealing with the character or career of a well-known person, e.g.:

Sir James Jeans
Always says what he means;
He is really perfectly serious
About the Universe being Mysterious.

'Clerk's Tale, The', see CANTERBURY TALES, 9.

CLEVELAND, John (1613–58), *Cavalier poet, joined the king's camp in Oxford during the civil war as an active royalist; he wrote there one of his best-known satires, 'The Rebel Scot'. Although criticized during his life as an academic and coterie poet, his works were highly popular. *Dryden's opinion of him as one 'who gives us common thoughts in abstruse words' eventually prevailed, but the 20th-cent. revival of interest in the *Metaphysicals and in political satire has led to more serious consideration.

Cliché, French, 'a stereotype block', a stock expression which by constant use has become hackneyed and lost its sharp edge.

CLIFFORD, Martin, see HAMILTON, C.

CLIVE, Mrs Caroline Archer (1801–73), wrote chiefly under the initial 'V'. She was lame from an early age. Her first volume of poems, *IX Poems by V* (1840), attracted high praise, but her reputation rests on her powerful novel *Paul Ferroll* (1855); the hero murders his wife, escapes suspicion, and marries his true love, who, after 18 years of happy marriage, dies of shock when Paul Ferroll voluntarily confesses his crime. By substituting villain for hero, this novel was a forerunner of the purely sensational novel (see SENSATION, NOVEL OF).

CLIVE, Kitty (Catherine) (1711–85), the celebrated comic actress, was a close friend of Horace *Walpole, and his neighbour at *Strawberry Hill, where he gave her for life a small house called Little Strawberry Hill, later known as Cliveden.

Cloddipole, one of the rustics in Gay's *The Shepherd's Week*.

Cloister and the Hearth, The, a novel by C. *Reade, published 1861.

The story is set in the 15th cent. Gerard, the son of a mercer living in Tergou in Holland, is destined to enter the Church, but falls in love with Margaret Brand. Family opposition forces him to leave Margaret and flee Holland; in Italy he hears a false report of Margaret's death, and, after a period of reckless dissolution, he becomes a Dominican monk. Eventually he returns to Holland, where he finds Margaret has borne him a son: he returns to her and is accepted as vicar of Gouda. The son, the conclusion indicates, is to be *Erasmus. The novel arose from Reade's discovery of the story of Erasmus' father, an obscure cleric.

Clorin, the central character in *The Faithful Shepherdess* by J. Fletcher.

Cloten, the clownish son of the queen in Shakespeare's *Cymbeline*.

Cloud-cuckoo-land (Nephelococcygia), an imaginary city built in the air in *The Birds* of *Aristophanes.

Cloud of Unknowing, The, a mystical prose work, probably from the North-East Midlands, dating from the second half of the 14th cent. and one of the most admired products of the Middle English mystical tradition. The author was presumably a priest, though no more certain identification can be made: several other lesser works are attributed to the same writer.

CLOUGH, Arthur Hugh (1819–61), was a pupil at T. *Arnold's Rugby. He became a fellow of Oriel, but resigned; he became principal of University Hall, London, then an examiner in the Education Office. His career was inconclusive, and he was tormented by doubt when the Rugby indoctrination was challenged by the religious ferment of Oxford. Yet out of religious doubt and minutely-analysed uncertainties Clough wrote lasting poetry. M. Arnold's *'Thyrsis' was written to commemorate his death.

The Bothie of Tober-na-Vuolich (1848) originally published as *The Bothie of Toper-na-fuosich*, is a poem in hexameters about a student reading party in Scotland. Philip falls in love with Elspie, a peasant who represents 'work, mother earth, and the objects of living'. There is no place for them in English society, so 'they rounded the globe to New Zealand'.

'Amours de Voyage' (first published in the

Atlantic Monthly, 1858) is similar in form, but *epistolary. Clough is also remembered for 'Dipsychus' (1865), a Faustian dialogue set in Venice, and for some of his shorter poems, such as the satirical 'The Latest Decalogue' (*Poems*, 1862).

Club, The (sometimes known later as the Literary Club), was an informal group founded by Dr *Johnson at the suggestion of Joshua *Reynolds in the winter of 1763–4. The nine original members included *Goldsmith and *Burke; those elected later included *Percy, *Garrick and *Boswell, C. J. *Fox and *Steevens, Adam *Smith, *Banks, and *Malone.

Clumsy, Sir Tunbelly, a character in Vanbrugh's *The Relapse* and Sheridan's *A Trip to Scarborough*.

Clutterbuck, Captain Cuthbert, a fictitious personage supposed to be concerned with the publication of some of Sir W. Scott's novels.

Clym of the Clough, see ADAM BELL.

CNUT, CNUTR, see CANUTE.

Coart, Couwaert, or Cuwaert, the name of the hare in *Reynard the Fox*.

Coavinses, in Dickens's *Bleak House*, see NECKETT.

COBBETT, William (1763–1835), enlisted as a soldier and served in New Brunswick from 1784 to 1791. He brought an accusation of peculation against some of his former officers, and in 1792 retired, first to France then to America, to avoid prosecution. There he published *The Life and Adventures of Peter Porcupine* (1796), a provocatively pro-British work, and his *Works* (1801), critical of America. He returned to England in 1800, and became an anti-Radical journalist, founding and writing Cobbett's *Political Register* in 1802. Soon his views began to change, and from about 1804 he wrote in the Radical interest, suffering two years' imprisonment for his attack on flogging in the army. He published *Parliamentary Debates*, afterwards taken over by *Hansard, and *State Trials*. The reflections assembled in 1830 as *Rural Rides* began to appear in the *Political Register* from 1821. His *History of the Protestant "Reformation" in England and Ireland* appeared in 1824; his *Advice to Young Men* in 1829. He became MP for Oldham in 1832.

COCKBURN, Alison, *née* Rutherford (c.1712–94), Scots poet and song-writer, whose lively soirées brought together most of the literary talent of 18th-cent. Edinburgh. She was friendly with *Hume and Sir W. *Scott, and was admired by *Burns. She wrote one of the well-known versions of 'The Flowers of the Forest'. (See also ELLIOT, J.)

COCKBURN, Catharine, *née* Trotter (1679–1749), had her first tragedy, *Agnes de Castro*, performed at the Theatre Royal, Drury Lane, when she was 15 and published a year later. She wrote four other stage works, occasional poetry, and published several works in explication and defence of the writings of *Locke.

Cocke Lorells Bote, a popular verse satire of the early 16th cent. in which types of the various tradesfolk take ship and sail through England. The captain of the 'Bote' is Cocke Lorell, a tinker and probably a historical personage.

Cockney School, a term apparently first used in *Blackwood's Magazine* in Oct. 1817, when *Lockhart and his associates began a series of attacks 'On the Cockney School of Poetry'. Leigh *Hunt was the chief target, but *Hazlitt and *Keats were also objects of frequent derision. The Londoners, all of humble origin, were contrasted with the great writers, all of whom 'have been men of some rank'. The virulence of the attacks, which described the writers as 'the vilest vermin' and of 'extreme moral depravity', was sustained over several years.

Cocktail Party, The, a comedy by T. S. *Eliot.

Cock Lane Ghost, a supposed ghost to which were attributed mysterious noises heard at 33 Cock Lane, Smithfield, in 1762. They were discovered to be due to the imposture of one William Parsons and his daughter. Dr *Johnson took part in the investigation of the mystery, and wrote a brief 'Account of the Detection of the Imposture in Cock-Lane', published in *The Gentleman's Magazine* (Feb. 1762).

Codex, a manuscript volume e.g. of one of the ancient manuscripts of the Scriptures, or of the ancient classics [*OED*]. See entries under AMIATINUS CODEX and BIBLE (*Codex Bezae, Codex Vaticanus, Codex Alexandrinus*, etc.).

Codlin and Short, in Dickens's *The Old Curiosity Shop*, travel about the country with a Punch and Judy show.

COEL (King Cole of the nursery rhyme) was duke of Colchester who (according to *Geoffrey of Monmouth's *History*) became king of Britain for a short time.

Coelebs in Search of a Wife, a novel by H. *More, published 1809. The book consists of a collection of social sketches and moral precepts, strung together by the hero's search for a wife, who must possess the qualities stipulated by his departed parents.

Coffee Houses were first introduced in the time of the Commonwealth; the first recorded in England was in Oxford in 1650 (mentioned by A. *Wood), and the first in London was in 1652, in St Michael's Alley, off Cornhill, at the Sign of Pasqua Rosee. They were much frequented in the 17th and 18th cents for political and literary discussions, circulation of news, etc. Their decline during the 18th cent. has been in part attributed to the increased popularity of clubs. For individual coffee houses see BUTTON'S, DON SALTERO'S, GARRAWAY'S, GRECIAN, TOM'S, WHITE'S, WILL'S.

COKE, Sir Edward (1552–1634), through Burghley's influence, was advanced to be attorney-general, to the disappointment of F. *Bacon, whose lifelong rival he was. Coke's fame as a legal author rests on his eleven volumes of *Reports* (1600–15), and his *Institutes* (1628–44) in which he recast, explained, and defended the common law rules.

Cokes, Bartholomew, the simpleton in Jonson's *Bartholomew Fair*.

'Colbeck, The Dancers of', see HANDLYNG SYNNE.

Colbrand, see GUY OF WARWICK.

COLBURN, Henry (d. 1855), publisher who founded the *New Monthly Magazine* in 1814 and the *Literary Gazette* in 1817. He published the fashionable novels of T. *Hook; *Evelyn's Diary* (1818); and *Pepys's newly-deciphered *Diaries* (1825). In 1830 he went into partnership with Richard *Bentley and together they published a successful series of Standard Novelists (1835–41).

Cold Comfort Farm (1932), the first novel of Stella Gibbons (1902–   ), a witty and highly successful parody of the earthy primitive school of regional fiction popular at the beginning of the century (by e.g. Sheila Kaye-Smith, M. *Webb, and D. H. *Lawrence).

Flora Poste visits her relatives the Starkadders in Sussex, and finds herself in a household of seething emotion, gloom, and rural intrigue, which she proceeds to reform. The descriptive 'purple passages' common to the genre are obligingly marked with asterisks by the author, after the method 'perfected by the late Herr *Baedeker'.

Cole, King, see COEL.

COLE, G(eorge) D(ouglas) H(oward) (1889–1959), Fabian economist, held important academic posts at Oxford. He became prominent immediately before the First World War as a leading exponent of guild socialism and

published his first major work, *The World of Labour*, in 1913. During the 1930s he was acknowledged as the most prolific writer on the intellectual history of British Socialism in articles in the *New Statesman* and in his works, which included *A History of Socialist Thought* (1953–8). He was married to Margaret Postgate (sister of Raymond Postgate) with whom he collaborated in detective fiction.

COLENSO, John William (1814–83), a mathematician who became bishop of Natal. He was denounced for his strong views on Zulu polygamy in relation to Christian conversion and for applying the Christian ethic to the problem of race relations in southern Africa. His commentary on *St Paul's Epistle to the Romans* (1861) aroused a storm of controversy by its repudiation of much orthodox sacramental theology and its denial of everlasting punishment; *The Pentateuch and the Book of Joshua Critically Examined* (1862–79) challenged the traditional historical accuracy and authorship of these books.

COLERIDGE, Hartley (1796–1849), eldest son of S. T. *Coleridge. He lost his Oxford fellowship for intemperance. In 1833 he published *Poems, Songs and Sonnets* and his unfinished *Biographia Borealis*, retitled *Worthies of Yorkshire and Lancashire* in 1836. He contributed to *Blackwood's Magazine*, the *London Magazine*, and other journals. His *Essays and Marginalia* (1851) were edited by his brother Derwent. He is the subject of two important poems by his father, *'Frost at Midnight' and 'The Nightingale'.

COLERIDGE, Mary (1861–1907), the great-great-niece of S. T. *Coleridge, published *Fancy's Following* (1896) and *Fancy's Guerdon* (1897). Two sonnets, 'True to myself am I' and 'Go in the deepest, darkest dead of night' have been much anthologized. Her first novel, *The Seven Sleepers of Ephesus* (1893), was praised by R. L. *Stevenson but achieved little success; her second, *The King with Two Faces* (1897), a historical romance centring on Gustavus III of Sweden, was well received.

COLERIDGE, Samuel Taylor (1772–1834), youngest son of the vicar of Ottery St Mary, Devon, was destined for the church. He was educated at Christ's Hospital school, London, where he attracted a circle of young admirers including Leigh *Hunt and *Lamb. At Jesus College, Cambridge (1792–4), a brilliant career in classics was diverted by French revolutionary politics, heavy drinking, and an unhappy love affair, which led Coleridge to enlist in desperation in the 15th Light Dragoons under the name of Comberbache. He met *Southey in 1794 and together they invented Pantisocracy, a scheme to set up a commune in New England.

Coleridge now published his first poetry in the *Morning Chronicle*, a series of sonnets to eminent radicals including *Godwin and J. *Priestley. To finance Pantisocracy, he and Southey gave political lecturers in Bristol and collaborated on a verse-drama, *The Fall of Robespierre* (1794); they also simultaneously courted and married two sisters, Sara and Edith Fricker. After quarrelling with Southey, Coleridge retired with Sara to a cottage at Clevedon where their first son Hartley (above), named after the philosopher David *Hartley, was born. Here Coleridge edited a radical Christian journal, *The Watchman*, and published *Poems on Various Subjects* (1796).

In June 1797 Coleridge met *Wordsworth and his sister Dorothy. The intense friendship that sprang up between the three shaped their lives for the next 14 years and proved one of the most creative partnerships in English *Romanticism. Between July 1797 and Sept. 1798 they lived and worked intimately together; the Coleridges at Nether Stowey, Somerset, and the Wordsworths two miles away at Alfoxden. Here Coleridge wrote a moving series of blank verse 'conversation' poems, addressed to his friends: 'Fears in Solitude', 'This Lime Tree Bower My Prison', 'The Nightingale', and *'Frost at Midnight'. He also composed *'Kubla Khan', and at Wordsworth's suggestion wrote 'The Rime of the *Ancient Mariner', and started three other ballads including *'Christabel'. A selection from their work appeared as the *Lyrical Ballads* (1798), intended as an 'experiment' in English poetry, which achieved a revolution in literary taste and sensibility.

Disenchanted with political developments ('France: an Ode'), Coleridge now turned towards Germany, where he spent ten months (1798–9), partly in the company of the Wordsworths, studying *Kant, *Schiller, and *Schelling. Returned to London, he translated Schiller's verse play *Wallenstein* and engaged in journalism for D. *Stuart of *The Morning Post*. In 1800 he moved to the Lake District with the Wordsworths, but his marriage was increasingly unhappy and he had fallen in love with Wordsworth's future sister-in-law Sara Hutchinson, as recorded in 'Love' (1799) and other 'Asra' poems. His use of opium now became a crippling addiction. Many of these difficulties are examined in *'Dejection: an Ode' (1802). During these years he also began to compile his *Notebooks*, daily meditations on his life, writing, and dreams, which have proved among his most enduring and moving works. In 1804 Coleridge went abroad; he worked for two years as secretary to the governor of wartime Malta, and later travelled through Sicily and Italy. In 1807 he separated from his wife and went to live again with the Wordsworths and Sara Hutchinson at Coleorton, Leicestershire. In 1808, though ill, Coleridge began his series of Lectures on Poetry

and Drama, which as his *Shakespearian Criticism* introduced new concepts of 'organic' form and dramatic psychology. In 1809–10 he wrote and edited with Sara Hutchinson's help a second periodical, *The Friend*. The intellectual effort, combined with the struggle against opium, shattered his circle of friends: Sara left for Wales, Dorothy grew estranged, he quarrelled irrevocably with Wordsworth. Coleridge fled to London, where between 1811 and 1814 he was on the verge of suicide, sustained only by his friends the Morgans, who took him to live in Calne, Wiltshire. His play *Remorse* had a *succès d'estime* at Drury Lane (1813). After a physical and spiritual crisis in the winter of 1813–14, Coleridge achieved a rebirth of his Christian beliefs, submitted himself to a series of medical regimes, and began slowly to write again. To this period belong his essay 'on the Principles of Genial Criticism', adapted from Kant, and his *Biographia Literaria* (1817).

In the spring of 1816 Coleridge found permanent harbour in the household of Dr James Gillman. *Christabel and Other Poems*, which included 'Kubla Khan' and 'The Pains of Sleep', was published in 1816; *Sibylline Leaves*, the first edition of his collected poems, in 1817 (expanded 1828 and 1834); *Zapolya* in 1817. His *Aids to Reflection* (1825) had a fruitful influence on *Sterling, *Kingsley, and the young Christian Socialists; while his *Church and State* (1830), a short monograph on the concept of a national 'Culture' and the 'clerisy' responsible for it, was taken up by M. *Arnold and *Newman. Coleridge also gave lectures on general literature and philosophy, which have survived in the form of notes and shorthand reports.

These later works develop Coleridge's leading critical ideas, concerning Imagination and Fancy; Reason and Understanding; Symbolism and Allegory; Organic and Mechanical Form; Culture and Civilization. The dialectical way he expresses them is one of his clearest debts to German Romantic philosophy; his final position is that of a Romantic conservative and Christian radical. He also wrote some haunting late poems, 'Youth and Age', 'Limbo', 'Work Without Hope', and 'Constancy to an Ideal Object'. He died of heart failure at 3, The Grove, Highgate. The last echoes of his inspired conversation were captured in *Table Talk* (1836).

Coleridge has been variously criticized as a political turncoat, a drug addict, a plagiarist, and a mystic humbug, whose wrecked career left nothing but a handful of magical early poems. But the shaping influence of his highly imaginative criticism is now generally accepted, and his position (with Wordsworth) as one of the two great progenitors of the English Romantic spirit is assured.

COLERIDGE, Sara (1802–52), daughter of S. T. *Coleridge, grew up largely in the company of *Southey and his family and of the *Wordsworths. She edited and annotated her father's papers with such skill that much of her work still stands. Her *Pretty Lessons for Good Children* appeared in 1834, and her long prose narrative 'Phantasmion' in 1837. The lively and engaging *Memoir and Letters*, published by her daughter in 1873, provides much information on the literary and personal lives of the Coleridges, the Wordsworths, and the Southeys.

COLET, John (1466–1519), one of the principal Christian Humanists of his day in England. He lectured at Oxford on the New Testament from 1496 to 1504, *Erasmus being among his audience. As dean of St Paul's (1505) he founded and endowed St Paul's School, writing for it a Latin Grammar for which *Lily wrote the Syntax; from this work and others is derived the grammar authorized by Henry VIII, which was known from 1758 as the Eton Latin Grammar. He was a famous preacher and lecturer, a pioneer of the Reformation in England. He first came to notice in 1497–8 with his lectures at Oxford on the Epistles of St Paul which draw on *Neoplatonism from *Plotinus to Pseudo-*Dionysius to *Pico della Mirandola. He was a vitriolic and powerful opponent of *Scholasticism, of ecclesiastical abuses, and of foreign wars.

Colin Clout, the name adopted by *Spenser in *The Shepheardes Calendar* and *Colin Clouts come home againe*. Colin Clout is also the name of a rustic in Gay's *The Shepherd's Week*. See also COLLYN CLOUTE.

Colin Clouts come home againe, an allegorical pastoral written by *Spenser on his return to Kilcolman after his visit to London of 1589–91, published 1595. It was dedicated to *Ralegh. The poem describes in allegorical form how Ralegh visited Spenser in Ireland and induced him to come to England 'his *Cynthia* to see'—i.e. the queen. The poet tells of the glories of the queen and her court and the beauty of the ladies who frequent it. Then follows a bitter attack on the envies and intrigues of the court. The poem ends with a definition of true love and a tribute to Colin's proud mistress *Rosalind.

Colkitto, 'or Macdonnel or Galasp', in Milton's first *Tetrachordon* sonnet, was the lieutenant-general of the marquis of Montrose in his campaign on behalf of Charles I. He figures in Scott's *A Legend of Montrose*.

Collegiate, Ladies, in Jonson's *Epicene*, a coterie of domineering women 'who live from their husbands and give entertainment to all the wits and braveries [beaux] of the time'. Wycherley copied them for Lady Fidget and her cronies in *The Country Wife*.

COLLIER, Jeremy (1650–1726), became a non-juring bishop in 1713. He is chiefly remembered for his *Short View of the Immorality and Profaneness of the English Stage* (1698), in which he attacked *Dryden, *Wycherley, *Congreve, *Vanbrugh, *D'Urfey, and *Otway, complaining particularly of profanity in stage dialogue and mockery of the clergy. The work created a great impact; Congreve and D'Urfey were prosecuted, *Betterton and Mrs *Bracegirdle were fined, and several of the poets replied, though not very effectively. Collier contributed towards the climate that produced the 'reformed' drama of C. *Cibber and his successors. (See also RESTORATION.)

COLLIER, John (1901–80), was a poetry editor of *Time and Tide* during the 1920s and 1930s, but is remembered as a writer of fantastic stories combining satire with the macabre and the supernatural. His best-known novel is *His Monkey Wife* (1930), describing the marriage between a repatriated explorer and his pet chimpanzee. In 1935 he moved to the US and made his living as a screenwriter in Hollywood.

COLLIER, John Payne (1789–1883), antiquarian, whose *The History of English dramatic poetry to the time of Shakespeare: and Annals of the Stage to the Restoration* (1831) contained valuable new documentary information but was contaminated with his own fabrications, the first of his insidious literary frauds. In 1840 he founded the Shakespeare Society for which he published many rare works including *The Memoirs of Edward Alleyn* (1841). It was the falsification of the marginal corrections of the so-called Perkins Folio (a Second *Folio of Shakespeare's plays dated 1632, with a possibly forged signature of Tho. Perkins on its cover) that finally brought him discredit.

Doubt was cast on the nature and extent of Collier's frauds by D. Ganzel in a biography, *Fortune and Men's Eyes* (1982).

COLLINS, Anthony (1676–1729), a leading freethinker, became intimate with *Locke. His best-known work, the boldly insinuating *Discourse of Free-thinking* (1713), drew angry replies from Richard *Bentley, *Berkeley, *Steele, *Hoadley, and *Swift. A *Philosophical Inquiry* (1717) is his classic defence of determinism. Collins attacked nearly every part of Christian theology; T. H. *Huxley described him as 'the Goliath of Freethinking'.

COLLINS, John Churton (1848–1908), lecturer and critic, was known in literary circles for his long pursuit of the academic recognition of English in the university curriculum, and for his arguments in favour of the conjunct study of English and classical literature, which drew support from M. *Arnold, T. H. *Huxley, and

*Swinburne. His efforts were rewarded when in 1893 a final honours school was established at Oxford. He edited the works of *Tourneur (1878), of R. *Greene (1905), and Lord *Herbert of Cherbury's poems (1881); his critical works included *Ephemera Critica* (1891).

COLLINS, (William) Wilkie (1824–89), elder son of the landscape painter William Collins. His first book, a biography of his father, was published in 1848, and he later wrote numerous articles and short stories for *Household Words*, *All the Year Round*, and other journals. His reputation rests on his novels which began with *Antonina* (1850), a historical novel about the fall of Rome; and with *Basil* (1852) he found his true *métier* as an expert in mystery, suspense, and crime. His finest work in this genre, the Novel of *Sensation, was written in the 1860s, when he produced *The Woman in White* (1860), *No Name* (1862), *Armadale* (1866), and *The Moonstone* (1868). Between 1870 and his death he produced 15 more novels of deteriorating quality. The falling-off was possibly due to ill-health and to his addiction to opium for the last 27 years of his life. He was a close friend and collaborator of Dickens from 1851.

Collins wrote the first full-length detective story in English (see DETECTIVE FICTION), and set a mould for the genre which has lasted for well over a century. He excelled at constructing ingenious and meticulous plots, and made interesting experiments in narrative technique. Many of his novels contain vivid and sympathetic portraits of physically abnormal individuals —the blind, deaf, crippled, deformed, and obese.

COLLINS, William (1721–59), published his *Persian Eclogues* (1742) while an undergraduate at Oxford. His *Odes on Several Descriptive and Allegoric Subjects* (1746, dated 1747) was to have considerable influence; the volume includes his well-known 'Ode to Evening' and 'How sleep the Brave', and odes to Pity, Fear, Simplicity, and other abstractions. The last work published in his lifetime was an ode on the death of *Thomson (1749), and in 1750 he presented an unfinished draft of his *Ode on the Popular Superstitions of the Highlands* (published 1788) to J. *Home. Thereafter he suffered increasingly from severe melancholia, and died in Chichester. Johnson in his *Lives of the English Poets* commented on his wildness and extravagance, which produced harshness and obscurity as well as 'sublimity and splendour', but later poets responded more eagerly to his lyrical intensity and to his conception of poetry as visionary and sacred (see SUBLIME); with *Gray he was one of the dominant influences of the later 18th cent.

Collins, William, in J. Austen's *Pride and Prejudice*, a pompous and self-satisfied young clergyman. The fulsome letter of thanks that he addressed to Mr Bennet (ch. xxiii, though the text is not given) after his stay with the family has led to his name being colloquially associated with such 'bread-and-butter' letters.

Collyn Clout, a satirical poem by *Skelton, directed against ecclesiastical abuses, written about 1521. See also COLIN CLOUT.

COLMAN, George, the elder (1732–94), edited *The Connoisseur* (1754–6) with Bonnell Thornton (1724–68) and collaborated with *Garrick in writing *The Clandestine Marriage* (1766). He was manager of Covent Garden, 1767–74, and of the Haymarket, 1777–89. He wrote many plays, adapted Shakespeare and *Beaumont and *Fletcher for the stage, and translated the comedies of *Terence (1765). He was elected to Dr Johnson's literary *Club in 1768.

COLMAN, George, the younger (1762–1836), son of the above, made his name with the musical romantic comedy *Inkle and Yarico* (1787). Among many other dramatic works, *The Iron Chest* (1796) is a dramatization of Godwin's *Caleb Williams*. Colman's comedy of contemporary life, *The Heir-at-Law* (1797), became famous for the character of Dr Pangloss, a greedy, pompous pedant. *John Bull* (1803) contains a sketch of the supposed British character in Job Thornberry.

Colombe's Birthday, a play in blank verse by R. *Browning, published in 1844 as no. VI of *Bells and Pomegranates*.

Colonel Jack, The History and Remarkable Life of Colonel Jacque, Commonly Call'd, a romance of adventure by *Defoe, published 1722.

Colophon, from Gk. κολοφών, summit, 'finishing touch', the inscription or device, sometimes pictorial or emblematic, placed at the end of a book or manuscript, and containing the title, the scribe's or printer's name, the date and place of printing, etc.; now the publisher's imprint, or logotype, usually found on the title-page and often on the spine of a book.

COLUM, Padraic (1881–1972), Irish poet and playwright. Prominent among the younger members of the *Irish Revival, he wrote several gloomily realistic plays for the *Abbey Theatre. His first collection of poems, *Wild Earth* (1907), was followed by many others (*Collected Poems*, 1953) and by works on Irish and Hawaiian folklore. He and his wife Mary wrote a memoir, *Our Friend James Joyce* (1958).

COLUMBA, or **COLUMCILLE,** St (521–97), a recluse of Glasnevin, near Dublin. He went to Scotland in 563 and founded the monastery of Iona, from which the conversion of Scotland and Northumbria by the Celtic Church proceeded. The book of his miracles was written by *Adomnan of Iona.

Columbine, a character in Italian *commedia dell'arte*, the daughter of *Pantaloon and mistress of *Harlequin, which has been transferred to our pantomime or harlequinade.

COLVIN, Sir Sidney (1845–1927), critic of art and literature. He published several volumes including lives of W. S. *Landor (1881) and *Keats (1887). He moved in artistic and literary circles, and corresponded with some of the most eminent intellectuals of his day. He edited the Edinburgh edition of R. L. *Stevenson's works (1894–7) and *The Letters of R. L. Stevenson* (1899 and 1911) and in 1895 published the *Vailima Letters* written to him by Stevenson, 1890–4.

COMBE, William (1741–1823), published many works in prose and verse, including *The Devil upon Two Sticks in England* (1790) and *The Microcosm of London* (1808). He is particularly remembered for his verses written to accompany Rowlandson's coloured plates and drawings of the adventures of 'Dr Syntax'. The first of these works, *The Tour of Dr Syntax in search of the Picturesque*, a parody of the popular books of picturesque travels of the day, and particularly of the works of *Gilpin, appeared in *Ackermann's *Poetical Magazine* in 1809, and in 1812 as a book. Dr Syntax is the grotesque figure of a clergyman and schoolmaster, who sets out on his tour and meets with a series of absurd misfortunes. This was followed by two further volumes of Dr Syntax (1820, 1821); the three Tours were collected in 1826.

Comedy, a stage play of a light and amusing character with a happy conclusion to its plot [OED]. In Greece it originated in the festivals of Dionysus, celebrated with song and merriment at the vintage; the Roman comedy of Plautus and Terence was imitated, with some native elements, from the Greek comedy of Menander and other dramatists of his period. Latin comedy continued to exercise an influence throughout the Middle Ages, particularly on the 'Saints Plays' which were often written to celebrate some merry saint and were largely comic with a concluding serious scene. The Miracle Plays of the later Middle Ages were also conducive to comedy rather than to tragedy, and as with the *Morality Plays were most independent in their comic parts, which were often separated from the main theme of the play. In Morality Plays the gradual rise of a humorous element is noticeable and the Vice in particular came to be recognized as a stock comic character.

With the recovery in the 15th cent. of twelve lost plays of Plautus and a renewed study of Terence, comedies on classical models came to be written. The plays of John *Heywood and *Rastell retain more of the elements of the Morality, but Nicholas Udall's *Ralph Roister Doister* (perf. *c*.1552) and *Gammer Gurtons Nedle* (acted 1566) are clearly based on classical models. These two plays are the first recognizable examples of modern English comedy. Throughout the 16th cent. this type of college or university play became gradually more popular, while the Morality passed out of fashion. Elizabethan comedy was lightened by a romantic element, as exemplified by *Lyly and *Greene, drawn from Italian and French romances. Lyly in particular explored the possibilities of prose dialogue and Greene showed great skill in his blending of plot and sub-plot. Shakespeare's comedies, which were nearly all written before 1600, owed much to these two predecessors. His comedies make no great attempt at moralizing or satirizing: their main essentials are a delightful story, in some romantic setting, arriving at a fortunate issue. The comedies of Ben *Jonson, which are written almost entirely in prose, have a definite moral and satirical vein running through them, but *Beaumont and *Fletcher preserved the more romantic and less realistic tradition.

With the revival of drama after the Restoration, the influence of French comedy, and particularly of *Molière, was predominant, while Jonson was regarded as the greatest English model. The characteristics of Restoration comedy, as exemplified in the plays of *Wycherley, *Etherege, *Dryden, etc., are wit—rather than humour—a great measure of licentiousness, but at the same time considerable polish and elegance. Prose was by this time recognized as the natural vehicle for comedy. The Restoration comedy reached its greatest heights in the works of *Congreve at the end of the century, while *Vanbrugh and *Farquhar continued the same tradition, though with less wit and originality. After these, *Steele, deprecating the immoral tone of contemporary plays, popularized what is known as the 'sentimental comedy'. In such plays as his *The Conscious Lovers* (1722), the rewards attendant on virtuous behaviour are stressed and vices such as drinking and duelling are condemned. This type of play came to be dominant throughout the 18th cent. Steele and his followers had no doubt a salutary influence on the morals of their generation, but their plays on the whole lacked realism and dramatic intensity. Goldsmith in *She Stoops to Conquer* (1773) and Sheridan in *The School for Scandal* (1777) and *The Critic* (1779) deliberately and successfully recaptured the best features of Restoration comedy. Their plays were successful, but they found no followers of any distinction and, in general, few comedies of the 18th and 19th cent. have any place in literary history. **Examples** from the end of the 19th cent. include Wilde's *The Importance of being Earnest*, *Lady Windermere's Fan*, and *A Woman of No Importance*, the lighter plays of *Shaw (*You Never Can Tell*), and the better plays of *Pinero.

The 20th cent. has seen various developments in comedy, including the Theatre of the *Absurd, the drawing-room comedies of *Coward and *Rattigan, and the reaction against these in the *Kitchen Sink School, and the black comedies of *Orton, *Pinter, *Beckett, and others. (See also SENTIMENTAL COMEDY.)

Comedy of Errors, The, a comedy by *Shakespeare, first printed in the First *Folio of 1623, acted 1594.

Syracuse and Ephesus being at enmity, any Syracusan found in Ephesus is put to death unless he can pay a ransom of 1,000 marks. Egeon, an old Syracusan merchant, has been arrested in Ephesus and on the duke's order explains how he came there. He and his wife Emilia had twin sons, exactly alike and each named Antipholus; the parents had purchased twin slaves, also exactly alike, each named Dromio, who attended on their sons. Having in a shipwreck been separated, with the younger son and one Dromio, from his wife and the other son and slave, Egeon had never seen them since. The younger son (Antipholus of Syracuse) on reaching manhood had gone (with his Dromio) in search of his brother and mother and had no more been heard of though Egeon had now sought him for five years over the world, coming at last to Ephesus.

The duke, moved by this tale, gives Egeon till evening to find the ransom. Now, the elder Antipholus (Antipholus of Ephesus), with one of the Dromios, has been living in Ephesus since his rescue from shipwreck and is married. Antipholus of Syracuse and the other Dromio have arrived there that very morning. Each twin retains the same confusing resemblance to his brother as in childhood. From this the comedy of errors results. Antipholus of Syracuse is summoned home to dinner by Dromio of Ephesus; he is claimed as husband by the wife of Antipholus of Ephesus, the latter being refused admittance to his own house, because he is supposed to be already within; and Antipholus of Syracuse falls in love with Luciana, his brother's wife's sister. Finally Antipholus of Ephesus is confined as a lunatic, and Antipholus of Syracuse takes refuge from his brother's jealous wife in a convent.

Meanwhile evening has come and Egeon is led to execution. As the duke proceeds to the place of execution, Antipholus of Ephesus appeals to him for redress. Then the abbess of the convent presents Antipholus of Syracuse, also claiming redress. The simultaneous presence of the two brothers explains the numerous misunderstandings. Egeon recovers his two sons and his liberty, and the abbess turns out to be his lost wife Emilia.

COMENIUS, John Amos (Jan Komenský) (1592–1670), Moravian educational reformer, chiliast, and pansophist. He gained European fame in 1633 with the publication of *Janua linguarum reserata*, published in England as *The Gates of Tongues unlocked and opened*. His last great work, *De rerum humanorum emendatione consultatio catholica*, much of which was presumed lost until 1934, was published in its entirety in 1966. His *Orbis Sensualium pictus* (1658; published in English, 1659, as *Comenius's Visible World*) was the first school-book consistently to use pictures in the learning of languages.

COMESTOR, Petrus (d. 1179), from Troyes in Champagne, was the author of a *Historia Scholastica*, a collection of scriptural narratives with commentary. He was one of the first of the many commentators of the *Sententiae* of *Peter Lombard. His work was familiar to *Chaucer and *Dante.

Comical Revenge, The, or *Love in a Tub*, a comedy by *Etherege, acted 1664.

The serious part of the plot, in heroic couplets, deals with the rivalry of Lord Beaufort and Colonel Bruce for the hand of Graciana. The comic and farcical part, in prose, centres on the French valet Dufoy, who for his impudence is confined by his fellow servants in a tub. His master Sir Frederick Frolick, a debonair libertine, is courted by a rich widow; he cajoles her out of £200 and finally marries her.

Comics, Comic Strips, flourished from the end of the 19th cent. with *Ally Sloper's Half-Holiday* (1884–1923), widely acknowledged as the publication that established the form, although comic strips had appeared earlier in papers such as *The Graphic* (1869–1932); and Edwin John Brett's *The Boys of England* (1866–99). Ally Sloper was a sharp, gin-drinking, working-class anti-hero, the first regular character in the comic world. The growing boom continued with such publications as *Comic Cuts* (1890–1953) and *Chips* (1890–1953); *The Gem* (1907–39) and *The Magnet* (1908–40; see HAMILTON, C.); with boys' adventure comics such as *Adventure* (1921–61), *Wizard* (1922–63) and *Hotspur* (1933–59); and with *Beano* (1938–) and *Dandy* (1937–), both still flourishing with many of their original characters. *Rainbow* (1914–56), with its hero Tiger Tim, was the first coloured comic designed exclusively for children, and described itself as 'The Children's Paper Parents Approve of', whereas *Chips* less loftily called itself 'The "Kid" 's Quietener, Father's Comfort, and Mother's Joy'. The battle between the subversively entertaining and the morally improving continued; Rupert Bear, who first appeared in the *Daily Express* on 8 Nov. 1920 (the creation of Mary Tourtel, distinguished by being written in rhyming couplets) was on the side of the angels, as was Dan Dare in *Eagle*. The founding of *Eagle* in 1950 by Lancashire vicar Marcus Morris was directly prompted by the growing infiltration of American horror comics, and it aimed to combine high moral values with the thrills of space adventure; the original series came to an end in 1969, but Dan Dare himself survives in *2000 AD*.

'Coming of Arthur, The', one of Tennyson's *Idylls of the King* published 1869. It describes the newly-crowned Arthur's first meeting with Guinevere, and their marriage.

Coming Race, The, a novel by *Bulwer-Lytton, published 1871.

The narrator describes his visit to a subterranean race of superior beings that long ago took refuge in the depths of the earth. There they have evolved a highly sophisticated civilization, with the aid of a form of energy called Vril, which has great powers of destruction as well as great utility. Much of the novel is devoted to a satiric account of the narrator's own democratic society, of which he is initially proud, and to praise of the underground society, which has no war, no crime, and no inequality, and where women are stronger than men and free to choose their own mates.

Commedia dell'arte, Italian popular character comedy, in which masked professional actors improvised on a traditional plot. It developed in the 16th cent., but some critics postulate an even earlier origin in the mime of the popular Latin *Atellan fables. Its main characters came to be fixed into farcical types (e.g. Harlequin, Pulcinella, Pantaloon, Columbine).

Common, Dol, one of the cheaters in Jonson's *The Alchemist.*

Common Prayer, *The Book of,* was evolved in the 16th cent. to meet the popular need for aids to devotion and the demand for the use of the vernacular in church services. The reading in churches of a chapter of the Bible in English, and the Litany in English (probably the work of *Cranmer), were introduced in 1544, and an English communion service in 1548. About the same time the Primers were revised, and the King's Primer issued in 1545 in the interest of uniformity; it included the English Litany. Cranmer and a commission each drafted a scheme for a prayer book, and these were discussed in Edward VI's reign, leading to the successive issue of the Prayer Books of 1549 and 1552. In the latter the form of the *Book of Common Prayer* was practically settled, though a revision was made under Elizabeth (1559),

minor changes under James I, and the final text is that of 1662. As it stands the Prayer Book represents largely the work of Cranmer; N. *Ridley may perhaps claim some share.

Alternative forms of service in contemporary language were published in 1980 and recommended for general use in church services in preference to the 1662 Prayer Book. This gave rise to vigorous argument as to the respective merits of attempting to improve the congregation's understanding of the liturgy and of preserving its traditions and literary qualities.

Common Reader, The, the title of two collections of essays by V. *Woolf, taken from Dr Johnson's life of Gray in *Lives of the English Poets*, which concludes with a famous paragraph in praise of the *Elegy*: 'In the character of his Elegy I rejoice to concur with the common reader ... The *Church-yard* abounds with images which find a mirrour in every mind, and with sentiments to which every bosom returns an echo.'

Commonwealth of Oceana, The, a political work by J. *Harrington (1656) dedicated to *Cromwell; in form it is part historical analysis, part *Utopia, and part a written constitution.

Harrington analyses the events leading to the Civil War, using both historical and fictional names. Oceana is England, the Normans became the Neustrians, Henry VII becomes Panurgus, etc. He then draws up a plan for an ideal republic, under the leadership of the Archon, Olphaus Megaletor, an idealized Cromwell figure. He expresses his admiration for the republics of Greece and Rome and for the Venetian republic, and frequently invokes *Machiavelli as 'the only politician of later ages'. His own proposals include the dividing of the great estates, a two-chamber system, indirect election by ballot, rotation in office, a popularly elected poet laureate, and a National Theatre. Overall, he proposes a carefully worked-out system of checks and balances which *Hume was to describe as 'the only valuable model of a commonwealth that has yet been offered to the public'. Harrington's *Oceana* is an intended contrast to Hobbes's *Leviathan*.

COMNENA and **COMNENUS**, see ANNA COMNENA.

Complaint, a poetic form derived from the Latin *planctus*, bewailing the vicissitudes of life (as in *Hoccleve's *Complaint*) or addressed to a more particular end (such as *Chaucer's 'Complaint to his Purse'). The form is particularly common in poems up to the Renaissance; thereafter the terms *'elegy' and 'lament' were used.

Complaint, The, or *Night Thoughts on Life, Death and Immortality*, see NIGHT THOUGHTS.

Complaint of Buckingham, The, a poem by T. *Sackville, contributed by him to *A Mirror for Magistrates.

Complaynt to the King, see LINDSAY, D.

Compleat Angler, The, or the Contemplative Man's Recreation, a discourse on fishing by I. *Walton, first published 1653, the second much enlarged edition 1655, 5th edn. with a continuation by C. *Cotton, 1676.

It takes the form of a dialogue, at first between the author Piscator (a fisherman), Auceps (a fowler), and Venator (a hunter), each commending his own recreation, in which Auceps is silenced and Venator becomes a pupil of the angle; then between Piscator and Venator alone. The author instructs his pupils in the art of catching various kinds of freshwater fish, with directions for dressing some of them for the table. The five days' fishing expedition along the river Lea also contains interludes of verse and song, angling anecdotes, moral reflections, and snatches of mythology and folklore. In Cotton's continuation Piscator and Viator (who turns out to be Venator) fish along the river Dove which divides Derbyshire and Staffordshire; there are fuller instructions for making of artificial flies (Walton was not an experienced fly-fisher) and descriptions of the picturesque scenery of the district.

COMPTON-BURNETT, Dame Ivy (1884–1969), novelist. Her highly condensed and abstracted novels were composed almost entirely in dialogue. They are all dated round about the turn of the century and set in large, gloomy, generally dilapidated houses full of servants, children, and dependent relatives. Each family is ruled in almost complete isolation from the outside world by a more or less tyrannical parent or grandparent: hence the consistently high rate of domestic crime ranging from adultery, incest, and child abuse to murder and fraud. Her inward-looking, self-contained, and heavily monitored high Victorian households provided her with an ideal environment in which to examine the misuse of power together with the violence and misery that follow. Her chief formative influences were G. *Eliot, the Greek tragic dramatists, and S. *Butler. She embarked on a serious career as a writer in 1925 with Pastors and Masters. Many more novels followed, including Brother and Sisters (1929) and More Women than Men (1933). Her most outstanding are perhaps A House and its Head (1935), A Family and a Fortune (1939), and Manservant and Maidservant (1947). Her achievement has been well summed up by A. *Wilson: 'In the age of the concentration camp, when, from 1935 or so to 1947, she wrote her very best novels, no writer did more to illuminate the springs of human cruelty, suffering and bravery.'

COMTE, Auguste (1798–1857), French philosopher and positivist, regarded by many as the founding father of sociology. His principal works (Cours de philosophie positive, 1830–42; Système de politique positive, 1851–4) develop a general system of knowledge and attempt to prepare the way for the new science of social phenomena, Sociology. Comte argues that human knowledge passes through 'Three States', the theological, the metaphysical, and the positive: this 'Law' applies both to the historical progress of the mind and the development of the individual mind. He rejects metaphysics and revealed religion, substituting a cult of Humanity and altruism, based on the motto 'Live for Others'. Comte's principal English followers were F. *Harrison, E. S. Beesley, J. H. Bridges, and Richard Congreve: his ideas were expounded by G. H. *Lewes (Comte's Philosophy of the Sciences, 1853) and influenced J. S. *Mill (Auguste Comte and Positivism, 1865).

Comus, A Maske presented at Ludlow Castle, 1634: on Michaelmasse night, before the Right Honorable John Earl of Bridgewater, Lord President of Wales, by *Milton, first printed, anonymously and untitled, 1637.

This work was written at the suggestion of Milton's friend H. *Lawes to celebrate the earl of Bridgewater's entry on the presidency of Wales and the Marches. Although described as a 'masque', Comus depends little on spectacle and has been better defined as a *pastoral drama. Comus himself is a pagan god invented by Milton, son of Bacchus and Circe, who waylays travellers and transforms their faces to those of wild beasts by means of a magic liquor. The Lady, benighted in a forest and separated from her brothers, comes across Comus in the guise of a shepherd; he leads her off to his cottage, offering protection. The brothers appear and are told what has happened by the Attendant Spirit Thyrsis, also disguised as a shepherd; he warns them of the magic power of Comus and gives them a root of the plant Haemony as protection. The scene changes to 'a stately Palace', where Comus with his rabble tempts the Lady to drink his magic potion. She defends herself and Chastity with such spirit that even Comus feels her possessed of 'some superior power'. At this point the brothers burst in. Unfortunately they have not secured the wand of Comus and are unable to release the Lady from her enchanted chair, which provides an opportunity for Thyrsis to invoke *Sabrina, goddess of the neighbouring river Severn, in the lovely song 'Sabrina Fair, | Listen where thou art sitting'. She arrives, the Lady is freed, and the Lady and her brothers are returned to Ludlow.

CONAN DOYLE, Arthur, see DOYLE, A. C.

Conceit, an elaborate metaphor comparing two apparently dissimilar objects or emotions, often with an effect of shock or surprise. The *Petrarchan conceit, much imitated by Elizabethan sonneteers and both used and parodied by Shakespeare, usually evoked the qualities of the disdainful mistress and the devoted lover, often in highly exaggerated terms; the *Metaphysical conceit, as used by *Donne and his followers, applied wit and ingenuity to, in the words of Dr *Johnson, 'a combination of dissimilar images, or discovery of occult resemblances in things apparently unlike' e.g. Donne's famous comparison of two lovers to a pair of compasses.

Conchubar, or **Conchobar** (pron. Conachoor), in the Ulster cycle of Irish mythology, king of Ulster, see CUCHULAIN and DEIRDRE.

Conciliation with America, On, by *Burke, speech made in the House of Commons on 22 March 1775.
    This, one of Burke's greatest speeches, was a last effort to find a peaceful solution of the difference with the American colonies.

Concrete Poetry, a term used to describe a kind of experimental poetry developed in the 1950s and flourishing in the 1960s, which dwells primarily on the visual aspects of the poem. Concrete poets experiment with typography, graphics, the 'ideogram concept', computer poems, collages, etc., and acknowledge influence from *Dada, Hans Arp, Schwitters, Malevich, and other visual artists. Ian Hamilton Finlay (1925–), one of the leading Scottish exponents, expressed his own affinity with 17th-cent. *emblems and poems such as G. *Herbert's 'Easter Wings', which use the shape as well as the sense of a poem to convey meaning. E. *Morgan, also a Scot, has written a variety of concrete poems. Mary Ellen Solt in 'A World Look at Concrete Poetry' (*Hispanic Arts*, Vol. I, Nos 3 and 4, 1968) declares that 'the concrete poet seeks to relieve the poem of its centuries-old burden of ideas, symbolic reference, allusion and repetitious emotional content'. Others claim a less radical role, pointing to Herbert, *Blake, Carroll (C. L. *Dodgson), *Pound's use of Chinese characters, and E. E. *Cummings as evidence of a long tradition of typographical experiment.

CONDELL, Henry, see HEMING, J.

Condition of England, see CARLYLE, T.

Coney-Catching, see ROGUE LITERATURE.

Confederacy, The, a comedy by *Vanbrugh, produced 1705, adapted from Dancourt's *Les Bourgeoises à la mode*.
    The play concerns the intrigues whereby the wives of two rich but niggardly husbands, Gripe and Moneytrap, attempt to settle their debts: a pawned necklace leads to many confusions and recriminations, but all ends well.

Confessio Amantis, see GOWER, J.

Confessions, see AUGUSTINE, ST (OF HIPPO) and ROUSSEAU.

Confessions of a Justified Sinner, see PRIVATE MEMOIRS AND CONFESSIONS OF A JUSTIFIED SINNER by J. Hogg.

Confessions of an English Opium Eater, by *De Quincey, published 1822 (enlarged version 1856).
    De Quincey's study of his own opium addiction and its psychological effects traces how childhood and youthful experiences were transformed under the influence of opium, into symbolical and revealing dreams. The central experience for subsequent dream-formations was his childhood loss of his sister, duplicated by the disappearance of the 15-year-old prostitute Ann, who befriended him during his months of homeless near-starvation in London. The euphoric reveries of the early stages of his addiction and the appalling nightmares of the later stages are described in sonorous and haunting prose.

Confidence-Man: His Masquerade, The (1857), a novel by H. *Melville.

Confidential Clerk, The, a comedy by T. S. *Eliot.

CONGREVE, William (1670–1729), educated at Kilkenny school and Trinity College, Dublin, at both of which he was a fellow student of *Swift. He entered the Middle Temple, but soon gave up law for literature, published a novel of intrigue, *Incognita* (1691), and in 1693 suddenly achieved fame with his comedy *The Old Bachelor*. Of his other comedies, *The Double Dealer* was published in 1694 (first performed 1693), *Love for Love* in 1695, and *The Way of the World* in 1700. In these Congreve shows himself the master of *Restoration comedy, studying the social pressures on love and marriage with wit and subtlety. His one tragedy, *The Mourning Bride*, was produced in 1697. After 1700 he wrote comparatively little for the stage; he was by then in comfortable circumstances, holding more than one government post, and enjoying general admiration and the friendship of men like Swift, *Steele, and *Pope. He was visited by *Voltaire, and had an affair with the duchess of Marlborough, who bore him a daughter. He was throughout the friend of

Mrs *Bracegirdle. He was buried at Westminster Abbey.

Coningsby, a political novel by B. *Disraeli, published 1844. Disraeli declares that his purpose in the trilogy Coningsby— *Sybil—*Tancred was to describe the influence of the main political parties on the condition of the people, and to indicate how those conditions might be improved. Coningsby celebrates the new Tories of the 'Young England' set, whose opposition to Whiggery and whose concern at the treatment of the poor and the injustice of the franchise is strongly reflected in the narrative.

The high-spirited and generous Coningsby, whose parents both die, is sent to Eton by his wealthy grandfather, Lord Monmouth, who represents the old type of oppressive Tory aristocrat. There Coningsby saves the life of his friend Oswald Millbank, the son of a Lancashire manufacturer, detested by Monmouth. At Cambridge and thereafter Coningsby develops political and social ideals and meanwhile falls in love with Oswald's sister Edith. His behaviour angers Monmouth. When he dies Coningsby finds he has been disinherited and has to work in the Inns of Court. Gradually Millbank, who had opposed Coningsby's marriage to his daughter, realizes the young man's worth; he helps him to stand for Parliament and sees him returned. Edith and Coningsby are married and Coningsby's fortunes are restored.

Connoisseur, The, a periodical edited by G. *Colman the elder, and journalist and wit Bonnell Thornton (1724–68). It ran from Jan. 1754 to Sept. 1756, and *Cowper was among its contributors.

CONNOLLY, Cyril Vernon (1903–74), was for many years a weekly reviewer for the *Sunday Times. In 1939, with *Spender, he founded *Horizon. His only novel, The Rock Pool (Paris, 1936; London, 1947), is a satiric extravaganza describing the adventures of an artistic expatriate colony on the French Riviera. His works include Enemies of Promise (1938), critical essays; The Unquiet Grave (1944), published under the pseudonym of Palinurus, which consists of aphorisms, reflections, etc.; and various collections of essays. Connolly's favourite themes include the dangers of early success and the hazardous lure of literary immortality, but he also celebrated the ephemeral pleasure of food, wine, and travel.

CONQUEST, (George) Robert (Acworth) (1917–), poet, historian, and critic, edited the important and controversial anthology *New Lines (1956). His publications include Poems (1955), Between Mars and Venus (1962), Arias from a Love Opera (1969), and several works on the USSR.

CONRAD, Joseph (Teodor Josef Konrad Korzeniowski) (1857–1924), novelist and short story writer, born of Polish parents in the Russian-dominated Ukraine. From an early age he longed to go to sea and in 1874 he went to Marseilles, embarked on a French vessel, and began the career as a sailor which was to supply so much material for his writing. In 1886 he became a British subject and a master mariner and in 1894 he settled in England and devoted himself to writing. He published his first novel at the age of 38, writing in English, his third language.

Almayer's Folly (1895) was followed by An Outcast of the Islands (1896), *The Nigger of the 'Narcissus' (1897), and *Lord Jim (1900). The sea continued to supply the setting for most of his novels and short stories. His narrative technique is characterized by a skilful use of breaks in time-sequence and he uses a narrator, Marlow, who provides a commentary on the action not unlike that of a Greek chorus. Conrad has been called an Impressionist, and the movement of the stories, of the images and emotions, are portrayed through each character's private vision of reality. He collaborated with F. M. *Ford on The Inheritors (1900) and Romance (1903). *Typhoon (1902) was followed by a major work, *Nostromo (1904), a novel which explores one of Conrad's chief preoccupations—man's vulnerability and corruptibility. In his short story *'Heart of Darkness' (1902) Conrad had carried this issue to a terrifying conclusion. *The Secret Agent (1907) and Under Western Eyes (1911) are both novels with political themes, the latter set in Switzerland and Russia and centred on the tragedy of student Razumov, caught up in the treachery and violence of revolution. Conrad's work was at first ill-received by critics and public alike, and it was the novel Chance (1913) that brought him his first popular and financial success; it is the story of Flora de Barral, lonely daughter of a crooked financier, and combines the attractions of a sea background with the theme of Romantic love and more female interest than is usual with Conrad. His other major works include Youth (1902), The Mirror of the Sea (1906), Victory (1915), The Shadow Line (1917), The Rescue (1920), and The Rover (1923). Conrad's autobiography, A Personal Record, appeared in book form in 1912 and his unfinished novel Suspense was published in 1925.

By the time of his death, Conrad was well established in the literary world as one of the leading *Modernists; a decline of interest in the 1930s was followed by increasing scholarly and critical attention, pioneered in part by a study in 1941 by M. C. Bradbrook, and by an essay in the same year by *Leavis in *Scrutiny (later reprinted in The Great Tradition) in which Conrad is placed 'among the very great novelists in the language'. The first volume of his *Collected Letters 1861–1897*, ed. F. Karl and L. Davis, was published in 1983.

Conscience, Mr, in Bunyan's *The Holy War*, the Recorder of the city of Mansoul, deposed from his office during the tyranny of Diabolus.

Conscious Lovers, The the last comedy of *Steele, based on the *Andria* of *Terence, performed 1722.

The play, with its high moral tone, considerably influenced the drift towards *sentimental comedy in England and in France.

CONSTABLE, Archibald (1774–1827), a Scots publisher who published most of Scott's early work. He established the *Edinburgh Review* in 1802, and bought the *Encyclopaedia Britannica* in 1812. Yet in 1826 he went bankrupt, heavily involving Scott in his debts. In 1827 he established Constable's Miscellany, a series of volumes of literature, art, and science.

CONSTABLE, Henry (1562–1613), published *Diana*, a volume of sonnets, in 1592; it was republished in 1594 with additions by other poets. Verses by him were embodied in various collections, among others in *Englands Helicon*.

Constance, (1) the heroine of 'The Man of Law's Tale' in Chaucer's *Canterbury Tales*, 5; (2) in Shakespeare's *King John*, the mother of Arthur, the king's nephew.

Constant, a character in Vanbrugh's *The Provok'd Wife*.

Constant Couple, The, or a Trip to the Jubilee, a farcical comedy by *Farquhar, produced 1699, which was very successful owing chiefly to the amusing character of Sir Harry Wildair, 'an airy gentleman, affecting humorous gaiety and freedom in his behaviour'. It had a less successful sequel in *Sir Harry Wildair* (1701).

Contarini Fleming; a Psychological Romance, a novel by B. *Disraeli, published 1832.

This novel was the last in the group *Vivian Grey—Alroy—Fleming*.

Contemporary Review, The, founded in 1866, covered religious, political and literary subjects; in 1955 it incorporated *The Fortnightly*, and now deals largely with current affairs.

Conversation, A complete Collection of polite and ingenious, by *Swift, published 1738.

In this entertaining work Swift good-humouredly satirizes the stupidity, coarseness, and attempted wit of the conversation of fashionable people. In three dialogues he puts into the mouths of various characters samples of questions and answers, proverbial sayings, and repartees, fitted 'to adorn every kind of discourse that an assembly of English ladies and gentlemen, met together for their mutual entertainment, can possibly want'. The work was published under the pseudonym of 'Simon Wagstaff, Esq.'

COOK, Eliza (1818–89), largely self-educated. Her first volume, *Lays of a Wild Harp* (1835), appeared when she was 17. Her most popular poem 'The Old Armchair' first appeared in the *Weekly Dispatch* in 1837. Her poems were characterized by an unaffected domestic sentiment which appealed strictly to popular uncultured tastes. She conducted *Eliza Cook's Journal* from 1849 until 1854. Her complete poetical works were published in 1870.

COOK, James (1728–79), celebrated circumnavigator, left records of his three principal voyages in *An Account of a Voyage round the World 1768–71* (1773), compiled by J. Hawkesworth from the journals of Cook and his botanist *Banks; *A Voyage towards the South Pole . . . 1772–3* (1777); *A Voyage to the Pacific Ocean . . . 1776–1780* (1784, the third vol. by Capt. T. King). Passages from Cook's second volume provided sources for the story and imagery of Coleridge's *'Ancient Mariner' (see J. L. *Lowes, *The Road to Xanadu*, 1927). Cook was murdered by natives in Hawaii.

'Cook's Tale, The', see CANTERBURY TALES, 4.

Coole Park, Co. Galway, home of Lady *Gregory, famous as the headquarters of the *Irish Revival. Summer home of W. B. *Yeats for nearly 20 years, it was the subject of many of his poems. Guests who carved their names on its famous autograph tree (a copper beech) included G. B. *Shaw, J. M. *Synge, W. B. Yeats. The house was pulled down in 1941.

COOPER, James Fenimore (1789–1851), American novelist, came into prominence with his second book *The Spy* (1821), a stirring tale of the American revolution. *The Pioneers* (1823) was the first of his best-known group of novels, *Leather-Stocking Tales*, called after the deerskin leggings of their hero, pioneer scout Natty Bumppo (alias 'Deerslayer', 'Pathfinder' or 'Hawkeye'); the sequels were *The Last of the Mohicans* (1826), *The Prairie* (1827), *The Pathfinder* (1840), and *The Deerslayer* (1841). They deal with adventures of the frontier and give a vivid picture of American Indian and pioneer life.

From 1826 to 1833 Cooper travelled in Europe, and on his return appeared several highly critical accounts of European society, including *England, with Sketches of Society in the*

Metropolis (1837) which was violently attacked in Britain, notably by *Lockhart. Cooper was also deeply critical of American democracy, and expressed his conservative opinions directly in *The American Democrat* (1838) and fictionally in *Homeward Bound* and *Home as Found* (both 1838). Among his many other works are the scholarly *The History of the Navy of the United States* (1839); *Satanstoe* (1845), a historical novel of manners; and *The Crater* (1848), a Utopian social allegory.

COOPER, William, pseudonym of Harry Summerfield Hoff (1910–), novelist. He embarked on a career in government service after the war; the civil service features in much of his work. His most influential novel, *Scenes from Provincial Life* (1950), was hailed as seminal by *Braine and other writers of the 1950s, who also chose provincial, anarchic, but ambitious, lower-middle-class heroes, and a low-key realist tone, in what some have seen as a reaction against *Modernism. (See also ANGRY YOUNG MEN.) It was followed by *Scenes from Married Life* (1961) and *Scenes from Metropolitan Life* (1982). In these novels Joe Lunn narrates with comic irony his own story, from his schoolmaster days in a nameless provincial city when his mistress, Myrtle, is trying to marry him, through the immediate post-war years in London when he is trying to marry Myrtle, to his successful marriage to schoolmistress Elspeth; his affairs and career are contrasted with those of his colleague, confidant, and fellow novelist, Robert. A sequel, *Scenes from Later Life*, appeared in 1983.

Cooper's Hill, see DENHAM, J.

COPERNICUS, Latinized form of the surname of Nicolas KOPPERNIK (1473–1543), astronomer, native of Torun, Poland, who propounded in his *De Revolutionibus* (1543) the theory that the planets, including the earth, move in orbits round the sun as centre, in opposition to *Ptolemy's earlier geocentric theory.

Cophetua, King, a legendary king in Africa, who cared nothing for women until he saw a beggar maid 'all in gray', with whom he fell in love. The tale is told in one of the ballads included in Percy's *Reliques*, where the maid's name is given as Penelophon. Shakespeare in *Love's Labour's Lost* (IV. i) gives it as Zenelophon. There are other references to the story in Shakespeare's *Romeo and Juliet* (II. i) and *2 Henry IV* (V. iii), in Jonson's *Every Man in his Humour* (III. iv), and in *Tennyson's 'The Beggar Maid'* (1842).

COPPARD, A(lfred) E(dgar) (1878–1957), poet and short story writer. His first collection of short stories, *Adam and Eve and Pinch Me* (1921), established his name. *Hips and Haws* (1922) was his first collection of verse, and thereafter he produced a book almost every year until the early 1950s. The deceptive simplicity of Coppard's stories conceals a widely admired technical skill; many of his tales are set in robust country backgrounds, and display a deep sympathy for the oddity and misfit.

COPPE, Abiezer (1619–72), a Ranter, preacher, mystic, and pamphleteer, famed for his eccentric behaviour (he preached naked in the streets of London, denouncing the rich); his two *Fiery Flying Rolls* (1649) are charged with fervour and compassion, and are written in a highly original poetic prose.

Copper, Lord, the domineering newspaper magnate in E. Waugh's *Scoop*.

Copyright. The protection of literary property in some measure was ensured in early times either by a royal grant of privilege to publish or else by the activity of the *Stationers' Company. (It should be noted that the ownership of the copyright in unpublished manuscripts, including letters, has always been assumed in English common law to rest with the author.) The Stationers' Company, incorporated in 1557, protected the rights of its different members to print particular books by domestic measures, fines, etc. It often gave only little protection to authors (as witness the piracy of Elizabethan plays), but defended the rights of publishers in works to which they may or may not have had good title. The prerogative of the Crown remained—and remains to this day—in the granting of the right to publish Bibles, prayer books, etc., which is reserved for the Queen's Printers and for the Oxford and Cambridge university presses.

The Act of 1709 gave to authors, and their assignees for the future, the sole right of publishing a book for a term of fourteen years, renewable for a further fourteen years if the author was alive at the end of the first term. The question whether or not the title to a perpetual literary property (e.g. *Tonson and his descendants' ownership of *Paradise Lost*) had survived this Act was debated throughout the 18th cent. and finally settled against the publishers and authors. The author's period was in 1814 increased to 28 years or the term of his life and, with *Macaulay's intervention, to 42 years or 7 years after death, whichever might be the longer, by the Act of 1842.

The Act of 1911 extended the period of copyright to the life of the author and 50 years after his death; made registration at Stationers' Hall no longer necessary; and included in the definition of 'copyright' the right to publish a hitherto unpublished work, the right thus becoming part of the personal property of the deceased author. The provisions of the Act of

1911 were incorporated and to some extent modified in the Act of 1956, which also recognized that scope should be given to certain libraries to make research and private study easier by providing students with copies of articles in periodicals, and copies of parts of published works. But the Act has subsequently become seriously out of date, due in particular to the 1971 Paris revision of the Berne Convention of 1885, and also to problems created by rapid advance of technology (photocopiers, audio and video recording equipment, computers, etc.). These problems were considered by the Whitford Report, 1977, and a Government Green Paper, 1981, but no comprehensive new legislation has yet been introduced.

International copyright has been obtained by a series of Conventions following the Berne Convention. A step forward in the sphere of international relations was taken with the passing of the Universal Copyright Convention, the product of UNESCO, in 1952. It brought in not only the USA but also a large number of states which had hitherto not entered into copyright relations with the European countries, e.g. most of the South American republics, and, in 1973, the USSR.

Copyright Libraries may, under the Copyright Act, 1911, claim a free copy of any book published in Britain. There are six: the British Library, London; the Bodleian, Oxford; the University Library, Cambridge; the National Library of Wales, Aberystwyth; the National Library of Scotland, Edinburgh; and Trinity College, Dublin: see under LIBRARIES.

Corah, name for Titus *Oates in Dryden's *Absalom and Achitophel.

Coral Island, The, see BALLANTYNE, R. M.

Coranto, or current of news, the name applied to periodical news-pamphlets issued between 1621 and 1641 (their publication was interrupted 1632–8) containing foreign intelligence taken from foreign papers. They were one of the earliest forms of English journalism, and were followed by the *newsbook. See also NEWSPAPERS, ORIGINS OF.

Corbaccio, the deaf old miser in Jonson's *Volpone.

Corbenic, the castle where the *Grail is found in the Arthurian legends.

CORBETT, or **CORBET,** Richard (1582–1635), became chaplain to James I and later bishop of Oxford, then Norwich. His poetry —Certain Elegant Poems (1647) and Poetica Stromata (1648)—ranges from the entertaining traveller's story of 'Iter Boreale' and the ironical

verses on 'The Distracted Puritane' to the charming little poem 'To his son, Vincent Corbet' on his third birthday. His best-known poem is probably 'A Proper New Ballad, entitled The Fairies Farewell' which begins 'Farewell, rewards and fairies'.

Corceca, in Spenser's *Faerie Queene (I. iii. 18), 'blindness of heart', an old blind woman, mother of Abessa (Superstition).

Cordelia, in Shakespeare's *King Lear, the youngest of the king's three daughters.

CORELLI, Marie, pseudonym of Mary Mackay (1855–1924), novelist. Her first novel, A Romance of Two Worlds (1886), was followed by many more romantic melodramas. She hypnotized her public with her exuberant imagination and her far-fetched theories on anything from morality to radioactive vibrations. But her popularity turned to ridicule long before her death. Her other novels include Barabbas (1893), The Sorrows of Satan (1895), and The Mighty Atom (1896).

Corflambo, in Spenser's *Faerie Queene (IV. vii and viii), symbolizes lust. He carries off *Amoret, who is released from him by Timias and *Belphoebe. He is slain by Prince *Arthur.

CORIAT, Thomas, see CORYATE.

Coriolanus, a play by *Shakespeare first printed in the *Folio of 1623. In order of composition, however, it was probably Shakespeare's last tragedy, written about 1608. Its source is *North's version of *Plutarch's 'Life of Caius Martius Coriolanus'.

Caius Marcius, a proud Roman general, performs wonders of valour in a war against the Volscians, and captures the town Corioli, receiving in consequence the surname Coriolanus. On his return it is proposed to make him consul, but his arrogant and outspoken contempt of the Roman rabble makes him unpopular with the fickle crowd, and the tribunes of the people have no difficulty in securing his banishment. He goes to the Volscian general, Aufidius, his enemy of long standing, is received with delight, and leads the Volscians against Rome to effect his revenge. He reaches the walls of the city, and the Romans, to save it from destruction, send emissaries, old friends of Coriolanus, to propose terms, but in vain. Finally his mother Volumnia, his meek wife Virgilia, and his son come to beseech him to spare the city and he yields to the eloquence of his mother, suspecting that by so doing he has signed his own death warrant: makes a treaty favourable to the Volscians, and returns with them to Antium, a Volscian town. Here Aufidius turns against him, accusing him of betraying the Volscian interests, and with the assistance of conspirators of his faction, publicly kills Coriolanus.

CORNEILLE, Pierre (1606–84), French dramatist, best known as the creator of French classical tragedy. He exerted a powerful influence on the English dramatists of the Restoration, particularly on *Dryden, and on *Neo-classical theory in general. His most important works are *Le Cid* (1637), *Horace* (1640), and *Polyeucte* (1643).

Cornelia, a tragedy translated by T. *Kyd from a Senecan play by Robert Garnier, published 1594. It appeared in the following year under the title *Pompey the Great, his faire Corneliaes Tragedie.*

It deals with the story of Cornelia, daughter of Metellus Scipio and wife of Pompey the Great, and her lamentations for her misfortunes.

Cornelia, a character in Webster's *The White Devil.*

CORNFORD, Frances (1886–1960), poet, mother of John *Cornford. She is best known for her triolet 'To a Fat Lady Seen from a Train', with its curiously memorable though undistinguished lines 'O why do you walk through the fields in gloves, | Missing so much and so much? | O fat white woman whom nobody loves'. Her *Collected Poems* appeared in 1954.

CORNFORD, John (1915–36), poet, son of Frances *Cornford. He became heavily involved with radical politics and Communism. In 1936 he was the first Englishman to enlist against Franco in the Spanish Civil War, and was killed in action. His poems had been published in various periodicals including *New Writing, and were collected with various prose pieces, mainly political, in *John Cornford: A Memoir,* ed. Pat Sloan, 1938.

Cornhill Magazine, The (1860–1975), a literary periodical, began with *Thackeray as editor and specialized in the serialization of novels. Trollope's *Framley Parsonage* was succeeded by the novels of, among others, Mrs *Gaskell, *Reade, G. *Eliot, and *Hardy; many poems of *Tennyson, R. *Browning, and *Swinburne first appeared in it, as well as work by *Ruskin, *MacDonald, and another of its editors, L. *Stephen.

Corn Law Rhymer, see ELLIOTT, E.

Corno di Bassetto, the name under which G. B. *Shaw wrote his music criticism.

CORNWALL, Barry, pseudonym of Brian Waller Procter (1787–1874), enjoyed success as a writer of songs and lyrics. His works include *Dramatic Scenes* (1819); *Marcian Collona* (1820); *Mirandola* (1821), a dramatic work; and *English Songs* (1832). He also wrote biographies of *Lamb and *Kean.

Corridors of Power, The, see SNOW, C. P.

Corsair, The, a poem by Lord *Byron, published 1814.

Conrad, a pirate chief, is warned that the Turkish Pacha is about to descend upon his island. He leaves his beloved Medora, arrives at the Pacha's rallying-point, and introduces himself as a dervish escaped from the pirates. His plans go amiss. He is wounded and taken prisoner, but he has rescued Gulnare, the chief slave in the Pacha's harem, from imminent death. She falls in love with him and brings him a dagger with which he may kill the Pacha in his sleep. Conrad resists, whereupon she kills the Pacha. They escape and arrive at the pirate island to find Medora dead from grief. Conrad disappears and is never heard of again: but see LARA.

Corvino, one of Volpone's would-be heirs in Jonson's *Volpone.*

CORVO, Baron, see ROLFE, F. W.

CORY, William Johnson (1823–92), is best remembered for his volume of poems *Ionica* (1858), and in particular for the translation that it contains of the epigram of Heraclitus of Halicarnassus by *Callimachus, 'They told me Heraclitus, they told me you were dead.' He also wrote the 'Eton Boating Song', published 1865.

CORYATE, Thomas (?1577–1617), travelled in 1608 through France, Italy, Switzerland, Germany, and Holland, mainly on foot. His fame as a traveller was legendary in his lifetime. His *Coryats Crudities* (1611) is a long narrative of his travels. In 1612 he set out overland to India, travelling through Constantinople, Palestine, Mesopotamia, and reaching Agra in 1616. He died at Surat. A letter of his from the court of the Great Mogul is printed by *Purchas, and is included in the compilation *Thomas Coriate Traveller for the English Wits: Greeting.* Coryate wrote in an extravagant and euphuistic style ('He is a great and bold carpenter of words', said *Jonson), and was well known as an eccentric; there are many references to him in 17th-cent. literature.

Corydon, a shepherd who figures in the *Idylls* of *Theocritus and the *Eclogues* of *Virgil, and whose name has become conventional in pastoral poetry.

Coryphaeus, the leader of a chorus in the Attic drama.

Costard, a clown in Shakespeare's *Love's Labour's Lost.*

Costigan, Captain and Emily (Miss Fotheringay), characters in Thackeray's *Pendennis.*

COTGRAVE, Randle (d. ?1634), author of a famous French-English dictionary published 1611. *Urquhart relied largely upon his dictionary for the translation of *Rabelais.

Cotswold Olimpick Games, yearly celebrations held during Whit week on the hillside above Chipping Campden in Gloucestershire, organized in 1612 by Robert Dover (1582–1652), using traditional pastimes and customs such as horse-racing, coursing, wrestling, backsword fighting, leaping, and dancing; they were commemorated in *Annalia Dubrensia* (1636), a collection of poems by 34 writers including *Drayton, *Jonson, T. *Randolph, and T. *Heywood. Suspended during the Civil War, the games were later continued as Dover's Meeting until 1852. They were again revived in 1963 and are held annually on the Friday of Spring Bank Holiday week on Dover's Hill.

'Cotter's Saturday Night, The', a poem by *Burns, published 1786.

COTTLE, Joseph (1770–1853), a bookseller of Bristol, who published the *Lyrical Ballads* and other works by *Wordsworth, *Coleridge, and *Southey. He edited, with Southey, the works of *Chatterton in 1803.

COTTON, Charles (1630–87), wrote the dialogue between Piscator and Viator which forms the second part in the 5th edn of *The Compleat Angler* (1676). He also published *Scarronides* (1664), a burlesque of *Virgil, and in 1665 a burlesque of *Lucian. His *topographical poem *The Wonders of the Peake* (1681) celebrates the beauties and curiosities of the Peak District. Cotton's love of his native landscapes and particularly of 'fair Dove, princess of rivers', is also expressed in many of his *Poems on Several Occasions* (1689). *Wordsworth and *Coleridge both admired his work.

COTTON, Sir Robert Bruce (1571–1631), gave the free use of his library to *Bacon, *Camden, *Ralegh, *Selden, *Speed, *Ussher, and other scholars, and sent a gift of manuscripts to the Bodleian Library on its foundation. He joined the parliamentary party and published various political tracts. The Cottonian Library, largely composed of works rescued from the dissolved monasteries, was left to the nation by his grandson Sir John Cotton (1621–1701); it suffered severely from fire in 1731 and was removed to the British Museum in 1753. It includes such treasures as the *Lindisfarne Gospels and biblical MSS such as the Codex Purpureus, the MS of *Beowulf, and the famous MS that includes *Pearl and Sir *Gawain and the Green Knight.

Count Alarcos, The Tragedy of, a verse play by B. *Disraeli, published 1839.
The play is set in 13th-cent. Burgos and based on a Spanish ballad.

Countess Cathleen, The, a play in blank verse by *Yeats, published 1892. It is based on the story of Countess Kathleen O'Shea told in Yeats's compilation *Fairy and Folk Tales of the Irish Peasantry* (1888). The scene is laid 'in Ireland in old times' at a period of famine. The people sell their souls to the demons for food. The countess does all she can to relieve their needs, till the demons steal her wealth. Finally she sells her own soul to the demons for a great sum, sacrificing her hope of salvation for the people. But at the end she is forgiven, for her intention was good. The play was first performed in Dublin in 1899, and marked the beginning of the *Irish Revival in the theatre.

Count Julian, a tragedy by W. S. *Landor, published 1812. The drama relates the vengeance taken by Count Julian, a Spanish nobleman, on Roderigo the king, who has seduced Julian's daughter. The subject is also treated in *Southey's *Roderick* and in a different form by Rowley in *All's Lost by Lust.

Count Robert of Paris, a novel by Sir W. *Scott, published 1831. This was one of the *Tales of my Landlord,* 4th series, the last of the Waverley Novels. It was written in ill health and betrays the decline of his powers.
The scene is Constantinople in the days of the Emperor Alexius Comnenus (1081–1118), and the story centres in the arrival there of the first crusaders. *Anna Comnena figures largely in the novel and provides some of its best pages.

Country Wife, The, a comedy by *Wycherley, published and probably first performed 1675. It is now considered by many to be his finest play, a sharp satiric attack on social and sexual hypocrisy and greed and on the corruption of town manners, but even in the author's time was attacked for its alleged obscenity. *Garrick's version, *The Country Girl* (1766), aimed to remove the original's 'immorality' and 'obscenity'.
The main plot concerns Mr Pinchwife, who comes to London for the marriage of his sister Alithea, bringing with him his artless young wife Margery; his excessive warnings against wrongdoing put ideas into her head, and she is eventually seduced by Horner, innocently protesting the while that she is merely behaving as town ladies do. Alithea's suitor Sparkish loses

her to a new lover, Harcourt, through the opposite fault of excessive credulity. Pinchwife's conclusion, as he apparently accepts the excuse of Horner's impotence, is 'Cuckolds like Lovers shou'd themselves deceive.'

Coup de théâtre, an unexpected and sensational turn in a play.

Courcy, Lord and Lady de, and their sons and daughters, characters in A. *Trollope's *Barsetshire series of novels.

Courier, The, an evening newspaper published in the early part of the 19th cent., under the management of D. *Stuart. *Coleridge, *Wordsworth, *Lamb, and *Southey were among its contributors, and *Galt was at one time its editor.

Courtesy Literature, as a distinct literary genre teaching courtiers and others good manners and morals, was imported into England through works such as *Il Cortegiano* of *Castiglione (translated by *Hoby in 1561). One of the most popular native examples of this type of writing was H. *Peacham's *The Compleat Gentleman* (1622).

Courtier, The (*Il Cortegiano*), see CASTIGLIONE.

Courtly Love. The term 'amour courtois' was coined by Gaston Paris in 1883 in the course of an essay on the *Lancelot* of *Chrétien de Troyes, to describe the conception of love developed by the Provençal troubadours in the 12th cent. Its relation of lover to adored lady is modelled on the dependence of feudal follower on his lord; the love itself was a religious passion, ennobling and ever increasing and unfulfilled, which meant that the love was usually pre-marital or extramarital. A code of practice for courtly lovers, *De Arte Honeste Amandi* (*c.*1185) was written by *Andreas Capellanus. From its beginnings in Provence the writing of this kind of poetry had spread to northern France and to the German *Minnesingers and epic by 1200; the most influential works in the 13th cent. were the *Roman de la rose (Guillaume de Lorris, *c.*1230, and Jean de Meun, *c.*1275), and the lyric poems of the *dolce stil nuovo* in Italy at the end of the century such as those in *Dante's *Vita Nuova*. Though the elements of courtly love are found in many places in medieval and Renaissance English literature, it is never the central theme of medieval English poetry, probably because it only reached England in the period of its decadence, after the mid-13th cent. and mostly as presented through the sceptical satire of writers such as Jean de Meun.

Court of Love, The, an early 15th-cent. allegorical poem in 1,442 lines of rhyme-royal. It des-

cribes the visit of the poet to the court of Venus and the love scenes he saw portrayed there, and ends with a May-day concert of birds when they sing descants on the opening words of psalms. It claims to be the work of 'Philogenet of Cambridge, clerk'. It was once doubtfully attributed to *Chaucer.

Covent Garden, in London, the old Convent Garden of Westminster. Covent Garden is frequently mentioned in 17th- and 18th-cent. literature, generally as a centre of dissipation. It remained the principal wholesale market in London for vegetables, fruit, and flowers until the 1970s, and was then rebuilt as a shopping centre.

The first Covent Garden Theatre was opened by J. *Rich in 1732. It was burnt down in 1808, and its successor in 1856. In these, many famous actors were seen, including *Garrick, the *Kembles, Mrs *Siddons, and *Macready. The new theatre (by Barry) opened in 1858 has been the principal home in England of grand opera.

Covent-Garden Journal, The, a periodical issued twice a week during 1752 by H. *Fielding, in which under the name of Sir Alexander Drawcansir, Censor of Great Britain, Fielding attacks political abuses, scandal, hypocrisy, meanness, sexual morality, fashion, etc.

COVENTRY, Francis (1725–54), the author of *The History of Pompey the Little: or the Life and adventures of a Lap-Dog* (1751), a satire in the form of a life of a dog 'born A.D. 1735 at Bologna in Italy, a Place famous for Lap-Dogs and Sausages'.

Coventry Miracle Plays, or *Ludus Coventriae*, see MYSTERY PLAYS.

COVERDALE, Miles (1488–1568), was ordained priest in 1514, and adopted Lutheran views. He translated at Antwerp the *Bible and *Apocrypha from German and Latin versions with the aid of *Tyndale's New Testament; a modified version was issued in 1537. Coverdale also superintended the printing of the Great Bible of 1539 (see under BIBLE, THE ENGLISH). He was bishop of Exeter, 1551–3. He published his last book, *Letters of Saintes*, in 1564. If he was (which has been questioned) the translator of the version of the Bible attributed to him, he is entitled to the credit for much of the noble language of the Authorized Version, and in particular for the Prayer-Book version of the Psalter.

Coverdale, Miles, the narrator of Hawthorne's novel *The Blithedale Romance*.

Coverley, Sir Roger de, a character described in *The Spectator*, a member of the Spectator Club, 'a gentleman of Worcestershire, of ancient descent, a baronet. His great-grandfather was inventor of that famous country-dance which is called after him. He is a gentleman that is very singular in his behaviour, but his singularities proceeded from his good sense . . . It is said he keeps himself a batchelor, by reason he was crossed in love by a perverse beautiful widow of the next county to him.' (No. 2, by *Steele.) He figures in a number of *Spectator* papers by both *Addison and Steele. His death is reported in No. 517, by Addison.

COWARD, Noël (1899–1973), actor, dramatist, and composer. He achieved fame with his play *The Vortex* (1924) in which a young drug-addict is tormented by his mother's adulteries. More characteristic of his talent were his comedies *Fallen Angels* (1925), *Hay Fever* (1925), *Private Lives* (1933, about two disastrous interconnected second marriages), *Design for Living* (1933, about a successful *ménage à trois*), and *Blithe Spirit* (1941), which features the hearty medium, Madame Arcati, and Elvira, a predatory ghost. The smart sophistication, technical accomplishment, and convention-defying morality (or amorality) of these pieces captured the public of the day. His patriotic works (*Cavalcade*, 1931) and wartime screenplays (*Brief Encounter*, 1944, and *This Happy Breed*, 1942) reveal Coward's more sentimental side. He was knighted in 1970. He also published volumes of verse, short stories, a novel (*Pomp and Circumstance*, 1960), and two volumes of autobiography. *The Noel Coward Diaries* appeared in 1982, ed. G. Payn and Sheridan Morley.

COWLEY, Abraham (1618–67), scholar and fellow of Trinity College, Cambridge. His precocity is shown by 'Pyramus and Thisbe', a verse romance written when he was 10 years old, and 'Constantia and Philetus', written two years later (both included in *Poetical Blossomes*, 1633). *Loves Riddle*, a pastoral drama, and *Naufragium Joculare*, a Latin comedy, appeared in 1638. On the outbreak of the Civil War Cowley left Cambridge for Oxford where he contributed to the Royalist cause by writing a satire. *The Puritan and the Papist* (1643), and a political epic, *The Civil War*. (Bk I was published in 1679; the two other books were presumed lost until recently discovered and edited.) In 1644 he left Oxford for Paris, where he served at the court of Henrietta Maria. Returning to England, apparently as a Royalist spy, he was imprisoned briefly in 1655. At the Restoration the earl of St Albans and the duke of Buckingham combined to provide him with a competence. On his death Charles II bestowed on him the epitaph, 'That Mr Cowley had not left a better man behind him in England.' He is buried in Westminster Abbey.

His other principal works include *The Mistress* (1647), love poems; 'Miscellanies' in *Poems*

(1656); also in the same collection 'Davideis', an epic on the biblical history of David, and 'Pindarique Odes' (see PINDAR), in which he introduces the irregular ode imitated by *Dryden and others. His prose works, marked by grace and simplicity of style, include some 'Essays', notably one 'Of My Self' containing interesting particulars of his early life, first published in *The Works* (1668) to which was prefixed a life by his friend *Sprat.

COWLEY, Hannah, *née* Parkhouse (1743–1809), wrote a number of comedies including *The Runaway* (1776), *A Bold Stroke for a Husband* (1783), and her most successful, *The Belle's Stratagem*, performed 1780. They tend to preach the importance of marriage and the domestic virtues. She also wrote long narrative romances, and corresponded as 'Anna Matilda' in poetry in *The World* with Robert Merry (see DELLA CRUSCANS), a correspondence satirized by *Gifford.

COWPER, William (1731–1800), was educated at a private school (where he was bullied) and at Westminster. He was subject to periods of depression and he attempted suicide. His melancholia took a religious form; he felt himself cast out of God's mercy, and wrote later in his *Memoir* (*c.*1767, pub. 1816), 'conviction of sin and expectation of instant judgement never left me.' In 1765 he became a boarder (in his own words, 'a sort of adopted son') in the home of the Revd Morley Unwin at Huntingdon, and on Morley's death moved with Mary, his widow, to Olney and came under the influence of J. *Newton, with whom he wrote *Olney Hymns* (1779); his contributions include 'God moves in a mysterious way' and 'Oh, for a closer walk with God'. He became engaged to Mrs Unwin, but suffered another bout of depression and made another suicide attempt; he spent a year with the Newtons before returning to Mrs Unwin's home. During a calmer period he wrote, at Mrs Unwin's suggestion, his satires ('Table Talk', 'The Progress of Error', 'Truth', 'Expostulation', 'Hope', 'Charity', 'Conversation', and 'Retirement') published in 1782 with several shorter poems (including 'Verses supposed to be written by Alexander Selkirk'; see SELKIRK, A.); in the same year he wrote *John Gilpin* and in 1783–4 his best-known long poem *The Task* (1785), both subjects suggested by his new friend and neighbour Lady Austen. The volume in which these appeared also contained 'Tirocinium', a vigorous attack on public schools. In 1786 he moved with Mrs Unwin to Weston Underwood, where he wrote various poems published after his death, including the unfinished 'Yardley-Oak' (admired by *Wordsworth), the verses 'On the Loss of the Royal George' ('Toll for the brave . . .'), 'To Mary', and 'The Poplar-Field'. Mrs Unwin died in

1796, leaving Cowper in severe depression from which he never fully recovered.

He wrote *'The Castaway' shortly before his death; like many of his poems it deals with man's isolation and helplessness. Storms and shipwrecks recur in his work as images of the mysterious ways of God. Yet his poems and his much-admired letters (published posthumously) have been highly valued for their intimate portrait of tranquillity and for their playful and delicate wit. His sympathetic feelings for nature presage *Romanticism and his use of blank verse links that of James *Thomson with that of *Wordsworth. He was a champion of the oppressed and wrote verses on *Wilberforce and the slave trade.

Cox and Box, see BURNAND, F.

Crab, in Shakespeare's *Two Gentlemen of Verona, Launce's dog.

CRABBE, George (1754–1832), was born in Aldeburgh, Suffolk, where his father was a collector of salt-duties. He was apprenticed to a doctor and during that time he published *Inebriety* (1775) and met Sarah Elmy (the 'Mira' of his poems and journals), whom he married in 1783. He subsequently practised medicine in Aldeburgh. In 1780 he went to London, where he was generously befriended by *Burke. He published *The Library* (1781), a poem in the manner of *Pope containing the author's reflections on books and reading. Burke encouraged him to take orders and in 1781 he became curate at Aldeburgh, then from 1782 to 1785 was chaplain to the duke of Rutland at Belvoir. In 1783, after revision from Burke and *Johnson, he published *The Village, which established his reputation and made plain his revulsion from the conventions of the *pastoral and the myth of the Golden Age, painting instead a grim, detailed picture of rural poverty and of a blighted, infertile landscape described with a botanist's precision.

In 1785 he published a satirical work, *The Newspaper*. A long interval followed during which he held a living at Muston, Leicestershire, and lived in Suffolk. In 1807 appeared a volume containing among other poems *'The Parish Register' (which revealed his gift as a narrative poet), and another atypical narrative in 55 eight-line stanzas, 'Sir Eustace Grey', set in a mad-house in which Sir Eustace relates the tale of his guilt and his subsequent demented hallucinations.

In 1810 he published *The Borough, a poem in 24 'letters' which includes the tales of *'Peter Grimes' and *'Ellen Orford'. This was followed in 1812 by *Tales in Verse*. In 1814 he was appointed vicar of Trowbridge, and in 1819 published *Tales of the Hall*, a series of varied stories. He visited Sir W. *Scott in Edinburgh in 1822 and became his friend. He died in Trowbridge and much unpublished work was found, some of which (for instance 'The Equal Marriage' and 'Silford Hall') was published in a collected edition in 1834; later discoveries appeared in *New Poems* (1960), ed. A. Pollard.

Throughout the upheaval represented by the *Romantic movement, Crabbe persisted in his precise, closely observed, realistic portraits of rural life and landscape, writing mainly in the heroic couplets of the *Augustan age.

Craftsman, The, a periodical started in Dec. 1726 to which *Bolingbroke contributed his 'Remarks upon the History of England' (1730–1) and his 'Dissertation upon Parties' (1733). Its title was intended to indicate Sir R. *Walpole as a 'man of craft'.

CRAIG, (Edward Henry) Gordon (1872–1966), artist, actor, wood-engraver, writer, and stage-designer, the son of Edward William Godwin and Ellen *Terry. He began his career as an actor. His first book, *The Art of the Theatre* (1905), which was further expanded as *On the Art of the Theatre* (1911), was followed by several other works on the same subject *Towards a New Theatre* (1913). In 1908 in Florence he founded a theatre magazine, *The Mask*, which he edited (with a wartime interlude) until 1929. His radical ideas on design and stagecraft had considerable influence in both Europe and America.

CRAIGIE, Sir William Alexander (1867–1957), lexicographer and philologist, co-editor of the *Oxford English Dictionary* and its first Supplement, co-editor (1925–44) of the *Dictionary of American English*, editor (1919–55) of the *Dictionary of the Older Scottish Tongue*, and a notable contributor to Anglo-Norman, Frisian, and Icelandic philology.

CRAIK, Mrs (Dinah Maria Mulock) (1826–87), a prolific writer of novels, poems, children's books, fairy-tales, essays, and short stories. She is remembered for her highly successful novel, *John Halifax, Gentleman* (1856). Her short stories were collected in *Avillion* (1853) and her *Collected Poems* appeared in 1881.

Crambo poem, one designed to exhaust the possible rhymes with someone's name.

CRANE, (Harold) Hart (1899–1932), American poet, published two volumes of verse, *White Buildings* (1926) and *The Bridge* (1930), the latter an obscure but powerful work which explores the 'Myth of America', with many echoes of *Whitman; its national symbols include Brooklyn Bridge itself, invoked in its Proem, and such historical and legendary characters as Columbus, *Rip Van Winkle, and *Pocahontas.

His *Complete Poems and Selected Letters and Prose*, ed. B. Weber, appeared in 1960.

CRANE, Stephen (1871–1900), American writer. His first novel, *Maggie: A Girl of the Streets* (1893), was too grim to find a readership. His next work, *The Red Badge of Courage* (1895), a study of an inexperienced soldier (Henry Fleming) and his reactions to the ordeal of battle during the American Civil War, was hailed as a masterpiece of psychological realism. His other works include two volumes of free verse, volumes of short stories (notably 'The Open Boat', 1898), and sketches.

Cranford, a novel by Mrs *Gaskell, published serially in *Household Words*, 1851–3.
   Cranford, a series of linked sketches of life among the ladies of a quiet country village in the 1830s, is based on Knutsford in Cheshire where Mrs Gaskell spent her childhood. It centres on the formidable Miss Deborah Jenkyns and her gentle sister Miss Matty, daughters of the former rector. Moments of drama are provided by the death of the genial Captain Brown, run over by a train when saving the life of a child; by the panic caused in the village by rumours of burglars; by the surprising marriage of the widowed Lady Glenmire with the vulgar Mr Hoggins, the village surgeon; by the failure of a bank which ruins Miss Matty, and her rescue by the fortunate return from India of her long-lost brother Peter. But the greatest charm of *Cranford*, which has kept it unfailingly popular, is its amused but loving portrayal of the old-fashioned customs and 'elegant economy' of a delicately observed group of middle-aged figures in a landscape.

CRANMER, Thomas (1489–1556), archbishop of Canterbury. He propounded views in favour of the divorce of Henry VIII from Catherine of Aragon, was appointed to the archbishopric in 1533, and maintained the king's claim to be the supreme head of the Church of England. He supervised the production of the first prayer book of Edward VI, 1549; prepared the revised prayer book of 1552; and promulgated the 42 articles of religion (afterwards reduced to 39) in the same year. To meet the need for suitable sermons, he contributed to and probably edited the first book of *Homilies* issued in 1547. In Queen Mary's reign he was condemned for heresy by Cardinal Pole, and degraded in 1556. He signed six documents admitting the truth of all Roman Catholic doctrine except transubstantiation, in vain; he was burned at the stake, repudiating these admissions, on 21 March 1556 at Oxford, holding his right hand (which had written his recantation) steadily in the flames, that it might be the first burnt. His chief title to fame is that of being the principal author of the English liturgy.

CRASHAW, Richard (1612/13–49), poet, became a Catholic convert *c.*1645 and fled to Paris, where his friend *Cowley persuaded Queen Henrietta Maria to interest herself on his behalf. Through her influence he moved to Italy, first as attendant on Cardinal Palotta, then in 1649 in a minor post at the Santa Casa of Loreto, where he died. His principal work was the *Steps to the Temple* (1646), a collection of religious poems influenced by *Marino and the Spanish mystics, which has been acclaimed as the height of baroque in English poetry. To this was attached a secular section, the *Delights of the Muses*, containing 'Music's Duel', a paraphrase of the Latin of Strada, in which nightingale and lute-player contend until the former fails and dies. His best-known poems are those addressed to St Theresa, the 'Hymn' and 'The Flaming Hart'. Both celebrate the bliss of martyrdom in characteristically baroque imagery of doves, darts, hearts, and 'delicious wounds'. The extravagant conceits of 'The Weeper', addressed to Mary Magdalen, were much ridiculed in subsequent periods.

Cratchit, Bob, a character in Dickens's *A Christmas Carol*.

Crawford, Henry and Mary, characters in J. Austen's *Mansfield Park*.

Crawley, (1) the Revd Josiah, one of the most memorable characters in A. Trollope's 'Barsetshire' novels, figuring most prominently in *The Last Chronicle of Barset* and also in *Framley Parsonage*; (2) Sir Pitt, his sister Miss Crawley, his sons Pitt and Rawdon, characters in Thackeray's *Vanity Fair*.

CRAYON, Geoffrey, pseudonym of W. *Irving.

Creakle, in Dickens's *David Copperfield*, the bullying headmaster of the hero's first school.

CREELEY, Robert (1926–), American poet and lecturer, and one of the *Black Mountain group; he edited (1954–7) the *Black Mountain Review*. His *Collected Poems 1945–1975* was published in 1983.

CREEVEY, Thomas (1768–1838), was Whig MP successively for Thetford and Appleby. *The Creevey Papers* (ed. Sir H. Maxwell), published 1903, are interesting for the light they throw on the characters of prominent persons and on the society of the later Georgian era. He was in Brussels for some years from 1814 and left a classic first-hand account of the city at the time of Waterloo.

Cresseid, see TESTAMENT OF CRESSEID, THE; **Cressida,** see TROILUS AND CRESSIDA; see also TROILUS AND CRISEYDE.

Cretic, see METRE.

Crewler, the Revd Horace and Mrs, characters in Dickens's *David Copperfield*, the parents of Sophy, whom Traddles marries.

CRICHTON, James, 'The Admirable' (1560–82), Scots adventurer, scholar, linguist, and poet, who served in the French army, travelled in Italy, and died in a brawl in Mantua. His colourful career is recounted by *Urquhart. *Barrie's play *The Admirable Crichton* concerns a polymath manservant cast away with his employers on a desert island.

Cricket on the Hearth, The, a Christmas book by *Dickens, published 1846.

John Peerybingle, carrier, and his much younger wife, Dot, are as happy a couple as possible, although the venomous old Tackleton, who himself is about to marry the young May Fielding, throws suspicion on Dot's sincerity. This suspicion appears to be disastrously verified when an eccentric old stranger takes up his abode with the Peerybingles and is discovered one day by John, metamorphosed into a bright young man by the removal of his wig, in intimate conversation with Dot. By the fairy influence of the Cricket on the Hearth John is brought to the decision to pardon her offence, which he attributes to the incompatibility of their ages and temperaments. But there turns out to be no occasion for forgiveness, for the bright young man is an old friend, the lover of May Fielding, believed dead, who has turned up just in time to prevent her marrying Tackleton.

Crimsworth, William, the hero of C. Brontë's *The Professor*.

Criseyde, see TROILUS AND CRISEYDE.

Crisparkle, the Revd Septimus, a character in Dickens's *Edwin Drood*.

Crispinus, a false poet in Jonson's *The Poetaster*, in part a caricature of J. *Marston.

Criterion, The (1922–39), an influential literary periodical launched as a quarterly and edited by T. S. *Eliot; *The Waste Land appeared in its first issue. It became the *New Criterion* in 1926, and in 1927, briefly, *The Monthly Criterion*, but then reverted to its original title. It included work by *Pound, *Empson, *Auden, *Spender, *Grigson, etc.; it also introduced the work of Proust, Valéry, Cocteau, and other European writers.

Critic, The, or a Tragedy Rehearsed, a comedy by R. B. *Sheridan, produced 1779.

Based on Buckingham's *The Rehearsal*, *The Critic* is an exuberant burlesque on the problems of producing a play. The work under rehearsal by its distraught producer is 'The Spanish Armada', a ludicrous parody of the modish tragic drama of the day (see, for example, CUMBERLAND, R.; COLMAN, G.). Mr Puff, the author, has invited to the rehearsal Dangle and Sneer, two savage and inept theatre critics, and Sir Fretful Plagiary (a caricature of Cumberland). His absurd historical drama, written in both the bombastic and the sentimental styles, introduces Sir Walter Ralegh, Sir Christopher Hatton, the earl of Leicester, Lord Burleigh, and others, at the time when the armada is approaching. Meanwhile Tilburina, the daughter of the governor of Tilbury Fort, complicates the plot with her love for Don Ferolo Whiskerandos, a Spanish prisoner. The action of the main play, including the solemn discussions by the author and his guests, their confused involvement with the rehearsal, and continual interruptions by producer, actors, and stage hands, continues with undiminished vivacity to the end.

Critical Quarterly, The, a literary review founded in 1959 and edited by C. B. Cox and A. E. Dyson. It publishes essays, reviews, and poetry, and contributors have included A. *Wilson, P. *Larkin, D. *Davie, D. J. *Enright, W. *Empson, S. *Heaney.

Critical Review, The, (1756–90), a Tory and Church journal founded in opposition to the liberal *Monthly Review*. It was edited by *Smollett (1756–9). Dr *Johnson and *Goldsmith were among its contributors.

Criticism, Schools of, see under FEMINIST CRITICISM; FREUDIAN CRITICISM; MARXIST LITERARY CRITICISM; NEW CRITICISM; PRACTICAL CRITICISM; and STRUCTURALISM. See also JUNG, C. G., ARCHETYPE.

Croaker, a character in Goldsmith's *The Good-Natur'd Man*.

CROCKETT, S. R., see KAILYARD SCHOOL.

Crockford, Crockford's Clerical Directory, first published 1857. A book of reference for facts relating to the clergy and the Church of England.

Croft, Admiral and Mrs, characters in J. Austen's *Persuasion*.

CROKER, John Wilson (1780–1857), secretary to the admiralty, and a prominent Tory politician. He was a regular contributor to the *Quarterly Review*, in which he made plain his Tory and Anglican stance. He became notorious for his criticism of Keat's *Endymion* in 1818. *Shelley (in his Preface to *Adonais) and *Byron (in his jingle 'Who killed John Keats?') established the belief that Croker's review hastened the death of the poet. Croker was an expert on the 18th cent. His books include *An Intercepted Letter from Canton* (1804), a satire on Dublin society; a reliable edition of Boswell's *Life of Samuel *Johnson* (1831); *Military Events of the French Revolution of 1830* (1831); and *Essays on the Early Period of the French Revolution* (1857). He was a much hated man, caricatured in Peacock's *Melincourt* (1817) and Disraeli's *Coningsby* (1844). *Macaulay detested him 'more than cold boiled veal'. *The Croker Papers* (1884) cover Croker's political life.

CROKER, Thomas Crofton (1798–1854), an Irish antiquary, probably the first collector to regard national and folk stories as a literary art. His *Researches in the South of Ireland* (1824), *Fairy Legends and Traditions in the South of Ireland* (1825–8), *Legends of the Lakes* (1829), and *Popular Songs of Ireland* (1839) provide a rich source of information on Irish folklore.

CROLY, George (1780–1860), author of *Paris in 1815* (1817); *Catiline* (1822), a tragedy; *May Fair* (1827), a satire; *Salathiel* (1829), a romance of the *Wandering Jew, Rome under Nero, and the siege of Jerusalem by Titus; *Marston* (1846), a romance to which the French Revolution and the Napoleonic wars provide the background; and numerous other works.

Crome Yellow, see HUXLEY, A.

CROMWELL, Oliver (1599–1658), soldier, politician, general, and from 1653 to 1658 Lord Protector, was the subject of innumerable contemporary pamphlets, satires, odes, and panegyrics. *Marvell's 'An Horatian Ode upon Cromwell's Return from Ireland', written in 1650, and his *The First Anniversary of the Government under his Highness the Lord Protector* (1655) are notable expressions of balanced admiration for Cromwell's 'active star'; 'If these the times, then this must be the man.' *Milton appealed to him in the sonnet 'Cromwell, our chief of men' as the defender of conscience and liberty. After his death Cromwell was variously depicted by writers and historians as honest patriot, 'frantic enthusiast' (*Hume), corrupt hypocrite, and true Englishman: *Carlyle in his lecture on the 'Hero as King' (1840) and his *Letters and Speeches of Oliver Cromwell* (1845) praised him as a Puritan hero, God-sent to save England.

CROMWELL, Thomas, earl of Essex (?1485–1540), secretary to Cardinal Wolsey and subsequently to Henry VIII, the principal promoter of the dissolution of the monasteries. He negotiated Henry's marriage with Anne of Cleves, and the failure of this match and of the policy that underlay it led to his downfall. A bill of attainder was passed and Cromwell was executed.

Cromwell, The True Chronicle Historie of the whole life and death of Thomas Lord, a play

published in 1602 and stated in the title to have been 'written by W.S.' It was included in the 3rd and 4th Shakespeare Folios (1663 and 1685). The play has little merit and is certainly not by Shakespeare.

CRONIN, A(rchibald) J(oseph) (1896–1981), practised as a doctor for some years before devoting himself to an extremely successful career as a middle-brow novelist. His best-known novels (e.g. *The Stars Look Down*, 1935; *The Citadel*, 1937) combine in their subject-matter the appeal of medicine and of mining, reflecting his own early experiences as a doctor in South Wales.

Crosbie, Adolphus, a character in A. *Trollope's *The Small House at Allington*.

'Crossing the Bar', a poem in four stanzas by Lord *Tennyson, published 1889.

Crotchet Castle, a satire by *Peacock, published 1831.

The story assembles a group of theorists at a country house, such as Mr Skionar (who resembles *Coleridge), Mr MacQuedy (a Scottish economist), Mr Chainmail (who wants to revive the Middle Ages), and others. The Revd Dr Folliott is mocked for his bigoted conservatism. The dinner-table conversations at Crotchet Castle turn on the clash between Folliott's Toryism and MacQuedy's progressivism. In Lady Clarinda, Peacock supplies the most spirited and cynical of his heroines. The book ends with an assault by the mob on Mr Chainmail's 12-cent. castle, an ironic comment on the more visionary schemes to solve the troubles of the age of reform.

Crow, a volume of poetry by Ted *Hughes.

CROWE, William, see LEWESDON HILL.

CROWLEY, 'Aleister' (really Edward Alexander) (1875–1947), a diabolist and a bad but prolific poet who claimed to be the Beast from the Book of Revelation. He joined the Order of the Golden Dawn, a group of theosophists involved in Cabbalistic magic, of which *Yeats was a member.

CROWNE, John (?1640–?1703). His first comedy *The Country Wit* (1675), contained the character of Sir Mannerly Shallow, subsequently developed into *Sir Courtly Nice in the play of that name (1685). He wrote several other comedies, a court masque, *Calisto* (1675), and eleven tragedies, including the two-part rhymed *The Destruction of Jerusalem* (1677), *Thyestes* (1681), and *Caligula* (1698). The success of the tragedies is said to have owed much to expensive and elaborate scenery.

Croyland, or *Crowland, History, The,* a chronicle of the 14th or 15th cent., printed in 1596 and for long erroneously attributed to Ingulf, abbot of Croyland (d. 1109). It was shown by Sir Francis Palgrave and others to be a forgery of the 15th cent.

CRUDEN, Alexander (1701–70), a bookseller who in 1737 published his *Biblical Concordance.*

CRUIKSHANK, George (1792–1878), illustrator and caricaturist, son of Isaac Cruikshank, also a caricaturist, illustrated a large amount of literary works including *Sketches by Boz* in 1836, which began a long association with Dickens including the illustrations to *Oliver Twist* in 1837.

Crummles, Mr Vincent, Mrs, and Ninetta ('the infant phenomenon'), characters in Dickens's *Nicholas Nickleby.*

Cruncher, Jerry, a character in Dickens's *A Tale of Two Cities.*

Crusoe, Robinson, see ROBINSON CRUSOE.

Cry, the Beloved Country, a novel by Alan Paton published 1948. Paton (1903–   ) was educated at the University of Natal, and was National President of the South African Liberal Party until it was declared illegal in 1968.

The Revd Stephen Kumalo sets off from his impoverished homeland at Ndotasheni, Natal, for Johannesburg, in search of his sister Gertrude and his son Absalom. He finds Gertrude has turned to prostitution, and Absalom has murdered the son of a white farmer, James Jarvis. Absalom is convicted and condemned to death, and Kumalo returns home with Gertrude's son and Absalom's pregnant wife. The novel ends with the reconciliation of Jarvis and Kumalo, and Jarvis's determination to rise above tragedy by helping the poor black community.

C.S.C., see CALVERLEY, C. S.

Cuala Press, a *private press founded in 1902 at Dundrum, Co. Dublin, by Elizabeth and Lily Yeats, sisters of W. B. *Yeats. It was originally called the Dun Emer Press. From 1908 until the late 1940s it flourished as the Cuala Press, publishing works by Yeats, *Synge, *Gogarty, Lady *Gregory, etc.

Cuchulain (pron. Cuhoolin), one of the principal heroes of the Ulster cycle of Irish mythology, the nephew or ward of Conchubar, king of Ulster. He is supposed to have lived in the 1st cent. AD. Of his numerous feats of valour, which won him the love of many women, the chief was his defence of Ulster, single-handed,

against Medb (pron. Maeve), queen of Connaught. Cuchulain was killed, aged 27, by Lugaid, son of a king of Ulster, and the daughters of Calatin the wizard, in vengeance for their fathers whom Cuchulain had slain.

A series of the legends about him have been translated by Lady *Gregory (*Cuchulain of Muirthemne*). He figures in *Macpherson's Ossianic poems as 'Cuthullin'.

Cuddy, a herdsman or shepherd in *The Shepheardes Calender* of Spenser and *The Shepherd's Week* of Gay.

CUDWORTH, Ralph (1617–88), see CAMBRIDGE PLATONISTS.

Cuff, Sergeant, the detective in W. Collins's *The Moonstone.*

CULPEPER, Nicholas (1616–54), apothecary, conducted a campaign against the monopoly of the College of Physicians, and published an English translation of the college's *Pharmacopoeia* (1649), making its contents available for the first time to the poor. This work and his *The English Physician Enlarged, or the Herbal* (1653) sold in vast quantities, but his infringement of the monopoly made him many enemies.

Culture and Anarchy, a collection of essays by M. *Arnold, published 1869. This work contains many of Arnold's central critical arguments.

The first chapter is devoted to his concept of culture as 'sweetness and light', a phrase adopted from Swift's *The Battle of the Books*; Arnold presents culture as the classical ideal of human perfection, rather than 'a smattering of Greek and Latin'. Subsequent chapters set forward his definitions of Barbarians, *Philistines, and the Populace, and contrast the spirit of Hebraism (as manifested in primitive Christianity and Protestantism) with that of Hellenism, with its aim of seeing 'things as they really are'; both are important contributions to human development and should not be mutually exclusive.

CULVERWEL, Nathaniel (d. 1651), see CAMBRIDGE PLATONISTS.

CUMBERLAND, Richard (1732–1811), author of a number of *sentimental comedies, of which *The Brothers* (1769) and *The West Indian* (1771) are the most interesting. He also wrote tragedies; two novels, *Arundel* (1789) and *Henry* (1795); a translation of the *Clouds* of *Aristophanes; and an autobiography. Cumberland is caricatured by *Sheridan as Sir Fretful Plagiary in *The Critic.*

CUMMINGS, Bruce Frederick (1889–1919), diarist and biologist, known under his pseudonym of W. N. P. Barbellion as the author of a diary covering the years 1903–17, *The Journal of a Disappointed Man* (1919), with an introduction by H. G. *Wells. It is largely an account of the author's struggle with an illness (diagnosed as disseminated sclerosis) that made him increasingly introspective; he alternates between moods of elation, egotism, self-disgust, and physical nausea, leading more and more of a substitute existence through his diaries. His *A Last Diary* (1920, ed. A. J. and H. R. Cummings) covers the last two years of his life.

CUMMINGS, E(dward) E(stlin) (1894–1962), American poet. His first book, *The Enormous Room* (1922), an account of his three-month internment in a French detention camp in 1917, won him an immediate international reputation. *Tulips and Chimneys* (1923) was the first of 12 volumes of poetry. Strongly influenced by the English Romantic poets, by *Swinburne, and by *Pound, and marked by *Dada and the jazz age, the early poems attracted attention more for their experimental typography and technical skill than for their considerable lyric power. In *Eimi* (1933), a typographically difficult but enthralling journal of a trip to Russia, he broke in disillusion from his earlier socialist leanings, and thenceforth his work reflected his increasingly reactionary social and political views. His *Complete Poems: 1910–1962* was published in 1980.

CUNNINGHAM, Allan (1784–1842), born in Dumfriesshire, profited from the vogue for *primitivism by disguising his own poems as old Scottish songs, many of which Robert Hartley Cromek (1720–1812) then published as *Remains of Nithsdale and Galloway Song* (1810). He was a frequent contributor to the *London Magazine* and to *Blackwood's. He published *Traditional Tales of the English and Scottish Peasantry* (1822); *The Songs of Scotland* (1825); various romantic tales; *Lives of the most eminent British Painters, Sculptors, and Architects* (1829–33); and an edition of Burns (1834). Several of his poems and ballads, such as 'A wet sheet and a flowing sea' and 'Hame, hame, hame', which were very popular in his lifetime, are still remembered.

CUNNINGHAME GRAHAM, Robert Bontine (1852–1936). During a flamboyant and varied career he was a rancher in Argentina, an outspoken MP, and a traveller in remote parts of the world, particulrly in Spanish America where he gained an intimate knowledge of gaucho life and of the older civilization surviving from the period of Spanish rule. His many stories, books, and articles include remarkable and exotic tales of travel. *Mogreb-el-Acksa* (1898) recounts his attempt to reach the forbidden city of Tarudant in Morocco. Other titles include *Thirteen Stories*

(1900), *Success* (1902), *Scottish Stories* (1914), and *The Horses of the Conquest* (1930); he also wrote several volumes of Latin-American history.

CUNOBELIN (Cymbeline), a king of Britain in the early years of the Christian era, and father of *Caractacus.

Cupid and Psyche, the allegorical centrepiece of the *Golden Ass* of Apuleius, in which the author blends a familiar folk-tale depicting an enchanted suitor and his abandoned bride with a Hellenistic epyllion about the god of love. Psyche, daughter of a king, is beloved by Cupid, who visits her nightly, but remains invisible, forbidding her to attempt to see him: one night she takes a lamp and looks at him as he sleeps, and agitated by his beauty lets fall a drop of hot oil on his shoulder. He departs in wrath, leaving her solitary and remorseful. Like the hero of the novel in which her tale is set, Psyche has forfeited her happiness through misplaced curiosity, and has to regain it through painful wanderings. Apuleius' story has been retold by W. *Browne (*Britannia's Pastorals* Bk 3), by S. *Marmion (*Cupid and Psyche*), by W. *Morris (*The Earthly Paradise*), and by *Bridges (*Eros and Psyche*). Pater's *Marius the Epicurean* provides a prose version. Milton's *Comus* (1,003–11), contains a reference to Apuleius' story and *Keats's 'Ode to Psyche' owes a debt to it.

Cure for a Cuckold, A, a comedy by J. *Webster and W. *Rowley, possibly with T. *Heywood, brought out in 1661.

CURLL, Edmund (1683–1747), a bookseller and pamphleteer who specialized in scandalous biographies, seditious pamphlets, pirated works, and pornography; he was imprisoned in 1724 for publishing *Venus in the Cloister: or the Nun in her Smock* (a characteristic title), but denied that it was his. *Pope, who pilloried him in *The Dunciad, was involved in various manoeuvres to encourage Curll to publish an unauthorized edition of his letters (which he did, in 1735).

CURRER BELL, see BRONTË, C.

Curse of Kehama, The, a narrative poem by R. *Southey, published 1810.

Cursor Mundi, a northern poem dating from about 1300 surviving in seven manuscripts of about 24,000 short lines, supplemented in most of them by another 6,000 or so lines of devotional material. It is founded on the works of late 12th-cent. Latin writers and covers mankind's spiritual history from the Creation to the Last Judgement.

Custance, the widow in Udall's *Ralph Roister Doister*.

Custom of the Country, The, (1) a tragi-comedy by J. *Fletcher and P. *Massinger, composed between 1619 and 1622, derived from the *Persiles y Sigismunda* of *Cervantes. Famed for its obscenity, it was described by *Dryden as containing more bawdry than any Restoration play. (2) a witty and satiric novel by E. *Wharton published in 1913.

Cute, Alderman, a character in Dickens's *The Chimes*, said to be intended for Sir Peter Laurie, the City magistrate.

CUTHBERT, St (d. 687), entered the monastery of Melrose, of which he became prior. He was sent to fill the post of abbot of Lindisfarne, on which the monastery of Melrose then depended; and after several years, feeling himself called to a life of perfect solitude, he returned to the small island of Farne. In 684, at a synod held under St Theodore, archbishop of Canterbury, he was selected for the see of Lindisfarne. After two years, feeling death approaching, he retired to the solitude of his island and died in his cell on 20 March (his feast day).

Cuttle, Captain Edward, a character in Dickens's *Dombey and Son*. His favourite expression is, 'When found, make a note of.' (See NOTES AND QUERIES).

Cyder, see PHILIPS, J.

Cymbeline, a play by *Shakespeare, first published in the Folio of 1623. It may have been written in 1609/10, probably first performed 1611. Its sources are *Holinshed, *A Mirror for Magistrates*, and perhaps Boccaccio's *Decameron* (see also PHILASTER). Though included among the tragedies in the First *Folio, the play is now generally classified as a 'romance'. The play was much loved in the 19th cent.; *Tennyson died with a copy of it on the coverlet of his bed. G. B. *Shaw wrote an emended version of the long fifth act, published in 1938 under the title *Cymbeline Refinished*.

Imogen, daughter of Cymbeline, King of Britain, has secretly married Leonatus Posthumus, a 'poor but worthy gentleman'. The queen, Imogen's stepmother, determined that her clownish son Cloten shall marry Imogen, reveals the secret marriage to the king, who banishes Posthumus. In Rome Posthumus boasts of Imogen's virtue and makes a wager with Iachimo that if he can seduce Imogen he shall have a diamond ring that Imogen had given him. Iachimo is repulsed by Imogen, but by hiding in her bedchamber he observes details of Imogen's room and her body which persuade Posthumus of her infidelity, and he receives the ring. Posthumus writes to his servant Pisanio directing him to kill Imogen; but Pisanio instead provides her with male disguise, sending a bloody cloth to Posthumus to deceive him that the deed is done. Under the name Fidele Imogen becomes a page to Bellarius and the two lost sons of Cymbeline, Guiderius and Arviragus, living in a cave in Wales. Fidele sickens and is found as dead by the brothers, who speak the dirge 'Fear no more the heat o' th' sun'. Left alone she revives, only to discover at her side the headless corpse of Cloten which she believes, because of his borrowed garments, to be that of her husband Posthumus. A Roman army invades Britain; Imogen falls into the hands of the general Lucius and becomes his page. The Britons defeat the Romans, thanks to the super-human valour in a narrow lane of Bellarius and his two sons aided by the disguised Posthumus. However Posthumus, pretending to be a Roman, is subsequently taken prisoner and has a vision in gaol of his family and Jupiter, who leaves a prophetic document with him. Lucius pleads with Cymbeline for the life of Fidele/Imogen: moved by something familiar in her appearance, he spares her life and grants her a favour. She asks that Iachimo be forced to tell how he came by the ring he wears. Posthumus learning from this confession that his wife is innocent but believing her dead is in despair till Imogen reveals herself. The king's joy at recovering his daughter is intensified when Bellarius restores to him his two lost sons, and the scene ends in a general reconciliation. Posthumus's words to Imogen on being reconciled with her, 'Hang there like fruit, my soul, | Till the tree die!' were described by Tennyson as 'the tenderest lines in Shakespeare'.

Cymochles, in Spenser's *Faerie Queene* (II. v, vi, and viii), 'a man of rare redoubted might', 'given all to lust and loose living', the husband of *Acrasia and brother of *Pyrochles. He is finally slain by Prince *Arthur.

Cymodoce, one of the Nereids. Cymodoce is the name of the mother of Marinell in Spenser's *Faerie Queene* (IV. xii). *Swinburne's 'Garden of Cymodoce' in *Songs of the Springtides* is the island of Sark.

CYNEWULF, probably a Northumbrian or Mercian poet of the late 8th or 9th century. At one time a great number of Old English poems were attributed to him, but modern scholarship restricts attribution to the four poems in the *Exeter Book and the *Vercelli Book which end with his name in runes. The poems are *Juliana*, *Elene*, *The Fates of the Apostles*, and *Christ II* (the last is a poem on the Ascension in the Exeter Book placed between poems on the Incarnation and on the Last Judgement, the three together being taken as a composite poem, *Christ*). *Elene* is the story of the finding of the Cross by St Helena, the mother of the emperor Constantine.

Cynthia, (1) a name for Artemis or Diana, from Mount Cynthus in Delos, where Artemis was born, and used poetically to denote the Moon; (2) the name given by the Roman poet *Propertius to his mistress; (3) deriving from (1), a name used by *Spenser (in *Colin Clouts come home againe), *Ralegh, and others to denote Elizabeth I as virgin moon-goddess; (4) in Congreve's *The Double Dealer, the daughter of Sir Paul Plyant, affianced to Mellefont; (5) in Mrs Gaskell's *Wives and Daughters, Cynthia Kirkpatrick, stepsister of Molly Gibson.

Cynthia, Oceans Love to, a poem by *Ralegh reflecting on his shifting relationship with Elizabeth I.

Cynthia's Revels, an allegorical comedy by *Jonson, performed 1600, printed 1601.

The play satirizes various court vices represented by characters whose names typify their failings. The song of Hesperus in Act V, 'Queen and huntress, chaste and fair', is one of Jonson's most beautiful lyrics.

Cypress, Mr, a character in Peacock's *Nightmare Abbey, a caricature of *Byron.

Cypresse Grove, A, see DRUMMOND OF HAWTHORNDEN.

D

Dacier, the Hon. Percy, a character in Meredith's *Diana of the Crossways*.

Dactyl, a metrical foot consisting of one long followed by two short syllables, or of one accented followed by two unaccented. See METRE.

Dada (Fr. 'hobby-horse' a name chosen at random from a dictionary), a movement in art and literature founded *c.*1916 in Zurich and more or less simultaneously in New York. The movement's aim was nihilistic, a denial of sense or order; it lasted until the mid-1920s, with Paris as its centre from 1920. Writers connected with Dada included Tristan Tzara, who appears as a character in Stoppard's *Travesties*. Notable among Dada artists were Hans Arp, Marcel Duchamp, and Man Ray.

'Daffodils' ('I wandered lonely as a cloud'), an untitled poem by *Wordsworth, written 1804, published 1807, possibly the most popular and anthologized of all Wordsworth's poems.

Dagon, the national deity of the ancient Philistines, represented as half man, half fish (Judges 16: 23; 1 Sam, 5: 1–5; Milton, *Paradise Lost*, i. 462 and *Samson Agonistes*).

DAICHES, David (1912–), scholar and author, whose works include studies of R. L. *Stevenson (1947), *Burns (1950), and Sir W. *Scott (1971); a *Critical History of English Literature* (4 vols, 1960); and two vivid autobiographies, *Two Worlds* (1957) and *Was* (1975).

Daily Courant, The, (1702–35) the first English daily newspaper. It contained foreign intelligence, translated from foreign newspapers. (See NEWSPAPERS, ORIGINS OF.)

Daily News, The, founded by *Dickens in 1845 as a Liberal rival to the *Morning Chronicle*; the first issue appeared on 21 Jan. 1846. Dickens edited the paper for 17 numbers only, then handed over to John *Forster. Among notable contributors and members of its staff at various times may be mentioned H. *Martineau, *Lang, G. B. *Shaw, *Wells, Arnold *Bennett. It became the *News Chronicle* in 1930, having absorbed the *Daily Chronicle*, and survived under this title until 1960.

Daily Telegraph, The, founded in 1855, was the first daily paper to be issued in London at a penny. It enjoyed a larger circulation than any other English newspaper, and in its early days, with T. *Hunt as assistant editor, its political views were Radical. After a period of decline in the early 20th cent., circulation recovered in the 1930s; in 1937 the *Morning Post* was amalgamated. The *Sunday Telegraph* was added in 1961. Among famous members of its staff have been G. A. *Sala, Sir E. *Arnold, and Edward Dicey (1832–1911).

Daisy Miller, a story by H. *James published in 1879, dramatized by James 1883.

Daisy Miller travels to Europe with her wealthy, commonplace mother, and in her innocence and audacity offends convention and seems to compromise her reputation. She dies in Rome of malaria. She is one of the most notable and charming of James's portrayals of 'the American girl'.

Dale, (1) Laetitia, a character in Meredith's *The Egoist*; (2) Lily, the heroine of A. *Trollope's novel *The Small House at Allington*, and an important character in *The Last Chronicle of Barset*.

Dalila, see DELILAH.

Damoetas, (1) a shepherd in the *Idylls* of *Theocritus and the *Eclogues* of *Virgil; (2) a character in Sidney's *Arcadia*, a base herdsman who has become a royal favourite; (3) an old shepherd (representing a Cambridge academic?) in Milton's *Lycidas*.

Damon, a shepherd singer in *Virgil's eighth *Eclogue*; a name adopted by poets for a rustic swain. Cf. *Epitaphium Damonis*, *Milton's Latin elegy on his friend *Diodati.

Damon and Pithias, a rhymed play by R. *Edwards, acted probably 1564, printed 1571.

Damon and Pythias, Pythagorean Greeks, visit Syracuse; Damon is arrested on a baseless charge of spying and conspiring against the tyrant Dionysius who orders his execution. Damon obtains a respite of two months to return home and settle his affairs, Pythias offering himself as security for his return. Damon is delayed, but arrives just as Pythias is about to be put to death and they contend which shall be executed. Dionysius, impressed with their mutual loyalty, pardons Damon and asks to be admitted to their brotherhood.

DAMPIER, William (1652–1715), navigator, explorer, and buccaneer, who travelled to South America, Yucatan, the Pacific, Australia, and the East Indies. His accounts of his travels (*New Voyage round the World*, 1697; *Voyages and Descriptions*, 1698; *A Voyage to New Holland*, 1703–9; edited by J. *Masefield in 2 vols, 1906), written in a lively and straightforward style and showing precise scientific observation, heralded an era of great interest in travel and voyage literature. (See also SELKIRK, A.)

D'Amville, the 'atheist' in Tourneur's *The Atheist's Tragedy*.

Dance of Death, or *danse macabre* (or *danse macabré*), gave expression to the sense especially prominent in the 15th cent. (perhaps as a consequence of the plague and the preaching of the mendicant friars) of the ubiquity of Death the leveller. The Dance appears to have first taken shape in France, as a mimed sermon in which figures typical of various orders of society were seized and haled away each by its own corpse. The earliest known painting of the Dance, accompanied by versified dialogues between living and dead, was made in 1424 in the cemetery of the Innocents in Paris, and the German artists (including Holbein) who later depicted it appear to have drawn inspiration from French sources.

Dance to the Music of Time, A, see POWELL, A.

Dandie Dinmont, in Scott's *Guy Mannering*, a sturdy Liddesdale farmer.

DANE, Clemence, the pseudonym of Winifred Ashton (1888–1965), playwright and novelist, whose first play, *A Bill of Divorcement* (1921), had a success never quite matched by her later works. Her novels include *Regiment of Women* (1917) and *Legend* (1919).

Dangerfield, a character in (1) Sedley's *Bellamira*; (2) Scott's *Peveril of the Peak*; (3) *The Ginger Man* by *Donleavy.

Dangle, a character in Sheridan's *The Critic*.

'Daniel', an Old English poem of 764 lines found in the *Junius manuscript, paraphrasing the Old Testament Book of Daniel.

DANIEL, Samuel (1563–1619), became tutor of William Herbert, third earl of Pembroke, and later to Lady Anne Clifford, daughter of the countess of Cumberland. In 1592 he published *Delia*, a collection of sonnets inspired by *Tasso and Desportes, to which was appended the 'Complaint of Rosamund'. Spenser mentioned him by name in *Colin Clouts come home againe.

Daniel made the transition to tragedy with *Cleopatra* (1594), a Senecan tragedy; *'Muso-philus: Containing a generall defence of learning' appeared in 1599. In 1603 he published his verse 'Epistles' and *A Defence of Ryme*, the last being a reply to T. *Campion's *Observations in the Art of English Poesie*. His career as a court poet developed with his masques and plays. He was licenser for the Children of the Queen's Revels from 1604 to 1605. His tragedy *Philotas*, performed in 1604, caused a row for its close and sympathetic allusion to the rebellion of the earl of *Essex in 1600 and the play was suppressed. Daniel affixed an 'Apology' when the play was published in 1605. His weightiest work was his *Civil Wars* (1595–1609). *Jonson called Daniel 'a good honest Man, . . . but no poet'; other contemporaries esteemed him, such as W. *Browne who called him 'Well-languag'd Danyel'. In later times his greatest admirers have been in the Romantic period including *Lamb, *Wordsworth, and *Coleridge.

Daniel Deronda, a novel by G. *Eliot, published 1876, the last of her novels.

Gwendolen Harleth, high-spirited, self-confident, and self-centred, marries the arrogant, cold-hearted Henleigh Grandcourt for his money and his position, to save her mother, sisters, and herself from destitution and in spite of the fact that she knows of the existence of Lydia Glasher, who has had a long-standing affair with Grandcourt, and children by him. She suffers in consequence from guilt and a sense of her husband's increasing power over her. In her misery she comes increasingly under the influence of the idealistic young Daniel Deronda, who becomes her spiritual adviser. It is gradually revealed that he is not, as he had assumed, an illegitimate cousin of Grandcourt's but the son of a Jewish singer of international renown. This discovery strengthens his bonds with Mirah, a young Jewish singer whom he has saved from drowning, and her brother Mordecai, an intellectual Jewish nationalist. Gwendolen's husband is drowned at Genoa, in a manner that leaves her feeling partly guilty for his death; she confesses to Deronda, but shortly discovers to her initial despair that he is to marry Mirah and devote himself to the Jewish cause. Notable among the minor characters is Klesmer, the musician, who persuades Gwendolen that her talent as a singer, though acceptable in an amateur, would not repay training, thus unwittingly pushing her towards her disastrous marriage.

Dannisburgh, Lord, a character in Meredith's *Diana of the Crossways*, drawn from Lord Melbourne.

DANTE ALIGHIERI (1265–1321), the great Italian poet, was born at Florence of a Guelf family. During the early period of his life he fell in love with the girl whom he celebrates under

the name of Beatrice in his masterpiece, the
Divina Commedia. When she died, in 1290,
Dante was grief-stricken and sought consolation
in the study of philosophy.

In the *Vita nuova*, written in the period 1290–
4, Dante brings together 31 poems, most of
them relating to his love for Beatrice. There is a
translation by D. G. *Rossetti (1861).

Daphnaïda, an elegy by *Spenser closely modelled on Chaucer's *Book of the Duchess*. See
ALCYON.

Daphnis and Chloe, is the finest of Greek
romances and the only one that has a purely
pastoral character. Written by an otherwise
unknown Longus it belongs probably to the end
of the 2nd cent. AD and describes how two
young people waken to sexual desire, fall in
love, and eventually marry. G. *Moore produced a modern translation in 1924.

Dapper, the clerk in Jonson's *The Alchemist*
who is gagged and locked in the privy for most
of the play.

d'ARBLAY, Mme, see BURNEY, F.

Darcy, Fitzwilliam and his sister Georgiana,
characters in J. Austen's *Pride and Prejudice*.

Dares Phrygius, a Trojan priest mentioned by
*Homer (*Iliad*, v. 9). He was supposed to have
been the author of *De excidio Troiae*, an account
of the fall of Troy dating probably from the 5th
cent. AD. This work, together with the comp-
lementary history of *Dictys Cretensis, provided the only detailed account of the Trojan
War available in the medieval West.

Dark as the Grave Wherein my Friend is Laid, a
novel by M. *Lowry, based on a journey to
Mexico taken in 1945–6, published 1968. The
title is taken from *Cowley's elegy 'On the
Death of Mr William Harvey'.

Darkness at Noon, a novel by A. *Koestler,
published 1940, translated from German.

It deals with the arrest, imprisonment, trial,
and execution of N. S. Rubashov in an unnamed
dictatorship over which 'No. 1' presides. The
novel did much to draw attention to the nature
of Stalin's regime.

DARLEY, George (1795–1846), born in
Dublin, settled in London in 1821, and earned
his living by writing textbooks on mathematics
and as dramatic critic for *The London Magazine*
and later as art critic for *The Athenaeum*. His
first published poem was *The Errors of Ecstasie*
(1822). *Sylvia* (1827), a pastoral drama, was the
most successful of his works in his own lifetime.
Many of his lyrics were published in magazines,

the best known being *Syren Songs*, 'Serenade of a
Loyal Martyr', and 'It is not Beauty I demand',
a 17th-cent. pastiche which F. T. *Palgrave
included in his *Golden Treasury* under the
impression that it was a genuine Caroline poem.
Darley also published two historical plays,
Thomas à Becket and *Ethelstan*. His finest work
was his unfinished *Nepenthe*, privately printed
1835, an allegory of the imagination in excesses
of joy or melancholy, partly inspired by
*Milton, *Shelley, and *Keats, but containing
some remarkable lyrics and passages of wild
fantasy and highly skilled versification.

Darnay, Charles, a character in Dickens's *A
Tale of Two Cities*.

Dartle, Rosa, a character in Dickens's *David
Copperfield*.

DARWIN, Charles Robert (1809–82), educated
at Edinburgh University and Christ's College,
Cambridge. He embarked in 1831 with *Fitzroy
as naturalist on the *Beagle*, bound for South
America, returned in 1836, and published *Journal
of Researches into the Geology and Natural History of
the various countries visited by H.M.S. Beagle*
(1839). His great work *On the Origin of Species by
means of Natural Selection* appeared in 1859.
Darwin had received from A. R. *Wallace a
manuscript containing a sketch of his theory.
Building upon the Uniformitarian geology of
Charles Lyell (1797–1875), which supposed a
very great antiquity for the earth and slow,
regular change, Darwin argued for a natural, not
divine, origin of species. In the competitive
struggle for existence, creatures possessing
advantageous mutations would be favoured,
eventually evolving into new species. In the
'survival of the fittest' (a phrase coined by H.
*Spencer, but accepted by Darwin) organic
descent was achieved by natural selection, by
analogy with the artificial selection of the stock-
breeder. An agnostic, Darwin saw no higher
moral or religious ends in evolution. Darwin's
book gave rise to intense opposition, but found
distinguished supporters in T. H. *Huxley,
Lyell, and Sir Joseph Hooker (1817–1911); the
reverberation of his ideas can be seen throughout
the literature of the second half of the 19th cent.
In *The Descent of Man* (1871) Darwin discussed
sexual selection, and argued that man too had
evolved, from the higher primates. A dedicated
naturalist, Darwin also wrote extensively on
barnacles, earthworms, and orchids, and was a
pioneer observer of animal behaviour. *The Life
and Letters of Darwin*, edited by his son Francis
Darwin, appeared 1887–8.

DARWIN, Erasmus (1731–1802), embodied
the botanical system of *Linnaeus in his long
poem *The Loves of the Plants* (1789). The work
reappeared as Part II of *The Botanic Garden*

(1791), of which Part I was 'The Economy of Vegetation'. The poem is in heroic couplets, in imitation of *Pope. The work contains an interesting embryonic theory of evolution, similar in many ways to that developed by the poet's grandson, C. *Darwin. The poem was ridiculed by *Canning and *Frere in 'The Loves of the Triangles'. In his prose *Zoonomia* (1794–6), Darwin further describes the laws of organic life, both plant and animal, on an evolutionary principle. His heretical views on creation brought him into some disrepute.

DASENT, Sir George Webbe (1817–96), became professor of English literature at King's College, London, in 1853. He devoted much of his life to the popularization of Scandinavian literature and the interpretation of Icelandic sagas. Among his publications are *Prose, or the Younger Edda* (1842), dedicated to *Carlyle, who had encouraged him, the *Grammar of the Icelandic or Old Norse Tongue* (1843), *Popular Tales from the Norse* (1859), and *The Story of Burnt Njal* (1861).

Dashwood, Mrs, her daughters Elinor, Marianne, and Margaret, and their stepbrother John, characters in J. Austen's *Sense and Sensibility*.

Datchery, Dick, the name assumed by one of the characters in Dickens's *Edwin Drood*.

Dauphine Eugenie, Sir, the hero of Jonson's *Epicene*.

D'AVENANT, Sir William (1606–68), was rumoured to be the natural son of Shakespeare. In 1630–2 he was gravely ill with syphilis, a subject referred to in his own works and in the jests of others; his first play on his recovery was probably his comic masterpiece *The Wits*, performed 1633, printed 1636. In 1638 he succeeded to *Jonson's pension as unofficial *poet laureate, then actively supported Charles I in the Civil War and was knighted by him in 1643 at the siege of Gloucester. In 1645 he visited Paris, where he met *Hobbes, to whom he addressed his *Preface* (1650) to *Gondibert* (1651). He was imprisoned in the Tower, 1650–2, and is said to have been saved by *Milton. With *The Siege of Rhodes* (1656) he simultaneously evaded the ban on stage-plays and produced one of the earliest English operas (but see also FLECKNOE). After the Restoration he and T. *Killigrew the elder obtained patents from Charles II giving them the monopoly of acting in London. Among the innovations of the period were movable scenery and the use of actresses. In conjunction with *Dryden, D'Avenant adapted various of Shakespeare's plays including *The Tempest* (1667); he is satirized with Dryden in Buckingham's *The Rehearsal*. (See also HEROIC DRAMA.)

DAVID, Elizabeth, *née* Gwynne (1913–), writer on food and cookery, whose early works (*A Book of Mediterranean Food*, 1950; *French Country Cooking*, 1951; *Italian Food*, 1954) were read avidly by a generation brought up on a wartime diet. She has become respected for her serious, indeed scholarly, approach to the history of gastronomy.

David, *Song to*, see SMART.

David and Fair Bethsabe, *The Love of King*, a play in blank verse by *Peele, printed 1599.

David Copperfield, a novel by *Dickens, published 1849–50. 'Of all my books,' wrote Dickens, 'I like this the best.' It is (in some of its details) Dickens's veiled autobiography.

David Copperfield is born at Blunderstone in Suffolk, soon after the death of his father. His mother, a gentle, weak woman, marries again, and her second husband Mr Murdstone, by cruelty disguised as firmness and abetted by Miss Murdstone his sister, drives her to an early grave. Young Copperfield, who has proved recalcitrant, is sent to school, where he is bullied by the tyrannical headmaster Creakle, but makes two friends in the brilliant and fascinating Steerforth and the good-humoured plodding Traddles. Thence he is sent to menial employment in London, where he lives a life of poverty and misery, enlivened by his acquaintance with the mercurial and impecunious Mr Micawber and his family. He runs away and walks penniless to Dover to throw himself on the mercy of his aunt Betsey Trotwood, an eccentric old lady. He is kindly received and given a new home, which he shares with an amiable lunatic, Mr Dick. Copperfield continues his education at Canterbury living in the house of Miss Trotwood's lawyer Mr Wickfield, whose daughter exercises a powerful influence on the rest of his life. He then enters Doctors' Commons, being articled to Mr Spenlow, of the firm Spenlow and Jorkins. Meanwhile he has come again into touch with Steerforth, whom he introduces to the family of his old nurse Clara Peggotty, married to Barkis the carrier. The family consists of Mr Peggotty, a Yarmouth fisherman, his nephew Ham, and the latter's cousin Little Em'ly, a pretty, simple girl whom Ham is about to marry. The remaining inmate of Mr Peggotty's hospitable home is Mrs Gummidge, another dependant and a widow. Steerforth induces Em'ly to run away with him. Mr Peggotty sets out to find her, following her through many countries, and finally recovering her after she had been cast off by Steerforth. The latter's crime also brings unhappiness to his mother and to her protégée Rosa Dartle, who has long loved Steerforth. The tragedy finds its culmination in the shipwreck and drowning of Steerforth, and the death of Ham in trying to save him.

Meanwhile Copperfield marries Dora Spenlow, a pretty empty-headed child, and becomes famous as an author. Dora dies after a few years of married life and Copperfield, at first disconsolate, awakens to a growing appreciation and love of Agnes Wickfield. Her father has fallen into the toils of a villainous and cunning clerk, Uriah Heep, who under the cloak of fawning humility has obtained complete control over him and nearly ruined him. Uriah also aspires to marry Agnes. But his misdeeds, which include forgery and theft, are exposed by Micawber, employed as his clerk, with the assistance of Traddles, now a barrister. Uriah is last seen in prison, under a life sentence. Copperfield marries Agnes. Mr Peggotty, with Em'ly and Mrs Gummidge, is found prospering in Australia, where Mr Micawber, relieved of his debts, appears finally as a much-esteemed colonial magistrate.

'Davideis', see COWLEY, A.

David Simple, The Adventures of, in Search of a Real Friend, a novel by S. *Fielding, published 1744, and described by the author as 'a Moral Romance'. This was one of the earliest novels to examine minutely what the author's brother, Henry *Fielding, described in his Preface to her book as 'the Mazes, Windings, and Labyrinths' of the heart.

DAVIDSON, John (1857–1909), was a schoolmaster in Scotland before settling in London in 1899, having already published several plays. He contributed to the *Yellow Book, and his collection of verse, Fleet Street Eclogues (1893), showed a genuine poetic gift. Between 1901 and 1908 he wrote a series of 'Testaments' expounding in blank verse a materialistic and rebellious philosophy, described very fully in the introduction to The Theatrocrat God and Mammon, an intended trilogy of which the first two parts were published in 1907. T. S. *Eliot expressed his debt to Davidson's use of 'dingy urban images' and colloquial idiom, singling out for particular praise his best-known ballad, the defiant and satiric 'Thirty Bob a Week'.

DAVIE, Donald Alfred (1922–   ), poet and critic, educated at Cambridge where he was much influenced by the ethos of F. R. *Leavis and the Cambridge English school. His critical work Purity of Diction in English Verse (1952) expressed many of the anti-Romantic, anti-Bohemian ideals of the *Movement and of his fellow contributors to *New Lines. His volumes of poetry include Bridges of Reason (1955), A Winter Talent (1957), Essex Poems (1969), and In the Stopping Train (1977); collected poems appeared in 1972 and 1983. His poems are philosophical, speculative, and erudite, manifesting a mind that (in his own phrase) 'moves most easily and happily among abstractions', yet they also vividly evoke the various landscapes of his travels and academic appointments in different parts of the world.

DAVIES, John (?1565–1618), poet and writing-master, published Microcosmos (1603), The Muse's Sacrifice, containing the famous 'Picture of an Happy Man' (1612), and Wits Bedlam (1617). Some of his epigrams, most of which are contained in The Scourge of Folly (?1611), are valuable for their notices of *Jonson, *Fletcher, and other contemporary poets.

DAVIES, Sir John (1569–1626), was appointed Lord Chief Justice of the King's Bench but died before taking office. His Orchestra Or a Poeme of Dauncing (1596) describes the attempts of the suitor Antinous to persuade Penelope to dance with him, giving a long account of the antiquity and universality of dancing. His other works include The Hymnes of Astraea (1599) and Nosce Teipsum (1599), written in quatrains, a philosophical poem on the nature of man and the nature and immortality of the soul. His Epigrammes and Gullinge Sonnets reflect his keen and satirical interest in the contemporary scene.

DAVIES, W(illiam) H(enry) (1871–1940), poet, spent several years wandering in America; on his second visit he lost a leg in an accident, an experience recounted in a few laconic paragraphs in his The Autobiography of a Super-Tramp (1908); it had a preface by G. B. *Shaw, who did much to encourage the young poet and interested himself in Davies's first volume, The Soul's Destroyer and other poems (1905). This was followed by several other volumes. His best-known poems record his sharp and intense response to the natural world. In 1923 he married a girl much younger than himself, and he tells the story of his extraordinary courtship in Young Emma, posthumously published in 1980. His Complete Poems, with an introduction by O. *Sitwell, appeared in 1963.

DAVISON, Francis, see POETICAL RHAPSODY, A.

DAVY, Sir Humphry (1778–1829), professor of chemistry at the Royal Institution, who greatly advanced knowledge of chemistry and magnetism and invented the miner's safety-lamp. His collected works, prose and verse, with a memoir by his brother, were published in 1839–40. Among these is a brief dialogue, Salmonia, or Days of Fly-fishing, by an Angler (1828).

Day, Fancy, a character in Hardy's *Under the Greenwood Tree.

DAY, DAYE, or **DAIE,** John (1522–84), the foremost English printer of the reign of

Elizabeth I. He published Protestant devotional books under Edward VI and was imprisoned by Queen Mary. He printed the first church music book in English (1560), and the first English edition of Foxe's *Actes and Monuments (or Book of Martyrs) (1563). He was the first to print Old English, having type made for it.

DAY, John (c.1574–c.1640), playwright, collaborated with *Dekker and others in a number of plays. His best work, *The Parliament of Bees*, a dramatic allegory or masque, appeared perhaps in 1607, although the earliest extant copy is of 1641. It is a charming and inventive piece containing a series of 'characters' of different bees with their virtues and vices, and ending with Oberon's Star Chamber, where he pronounces penalties on the offenders, the wasp, the drone, and the humble bee. The *Parnassus Plays have been doubtfully attributed to Day.

DAY, Thomas (1748–89), an admirer of *Rousseau, was keenly interested in educational theory and natural upbringing. He was the author of the celebrated children's book *The History of Sandford and Merton* (3 vols, 1783–9), which was intended to illustrate the doctrine that many may be made good by instruction and by an appeal to reason; in a series of episodes the rich and objectionable Tommy Merton is contrasted with the upright and tender-hearted Harry Sandford, a farmer's son. Day also wrote *The History of Little Jack* (1787), the story of a young wild boy suckled by goats.

DAY-LEWIS, Cecil (1904–72) (who wrote as C. Day Lewis), was educated at Wadham College, Oxford, where he was befriended by *Bowra and became associated with a group of young left-wing poets of which *Auden was the acknowledged leader, and with whom he edited *Oxford Poetry* (1927). (The nickname 'MacSpaunday' was coined by R. *Campbell: see also PYLON SCHOOL.) He joined the Communist Party in 1936 and edited a socialist symposium, *The Mind in Chains* (1937), with contributions from *Upward, *Madge, R. *Warner, and others. These preoccupations are not reflected in his earliest verse (e.g. *Beechen Vigil*, 1925), but became apparent in *Transitional Poem* (1929), *From Feathers to Iron* (1931), and *The Magnetic Mountain* (1933), which have a strong revolutionary flavour. The title poem of *A Time to Dance* (1935) more ambiguously celebrates the heroic flight of Parer and M'Intosh to Australia. After the poor reception of *Noah and the Waters* (1936), a verse morality play about the class struggle, his poetry became more pastoral and personal. During the thirties he also embarked, under the pseudonym of 'Nicholas Blake', on a career as a writer of *detective fiction; his first book in this genre, *A Question of Proof* (1935), introducing his Audenesque detec-

tive Nigel Strangeways, was followed by some twenty others. *The Friendly Tree* (1936) was the first of three largely autobiographical novels.

In 1938 he moved to Musbury, Devon; his poetry of this period (*Overtures to Death*, 1938; *Poems in Wartime*, 1940) reflect its obvious concerns. He also published in 1940 the first of his translations, a version of *Virgil's *Georgics*. From this time he became an increasingly establishment figure, meanwhile consolidating his literary reputation with a translation of Valéry (1946), further translations of Virgil (*The Aeneid*, 1952; *The Eclogues*, 1963), and collections of original verse, including *An Italian Visit* (1953), recording a journey with R. *Lehmann. He was professor of poetry at Oxford from 1951 to 1956.

Dead Sea Scrolls, the popular name for the remains of the once considerable collection of Hebrew and Aramaic MSS discovered in caves at the NW end of the Dead Sea between 1947 and 1956. Although no one MS is intact, nearly all the books of the canonical OT are represented, as well as apocryphal books and some works not previously known. The Scrolls belonged to the library of the Jewish community at Qumran and it is probable that most of them were written there between 20 BC and AD 70. The Scrolls are important in being almost the only surviving MS material in Hebrew and Aramaic from this period and have a valuable bearing on the study of OT texts.

Deane, Mr and Lucy, characters in G. Eliot's *The Mill on the Floss.

Deans, David, and his daughters Jeanie and Effie, the principal characters in Scott's *The Heart of Midlothian*.

'Death and Dr Hornbook', a satirical poem by *Burns, published 1786.

Death of a Hero, see ALDINGTON, R.

Death's Jest-Book, see BEDDOES, T. L.

De Bourgh, Lady Catherine, a character in J. Austen's *Pride and Prejudice.

Decameron, The, a collection of tales from many sources by *Boccaccio, assembled in their definitive form between 1349 and 1351.

Florence being visited by the plague in 1348, seven young ladies and three young men leave the city for neighbouring villas, and spend part of each of ten days (whence the title) in amusing one another with stories, each person telling one tale on each day, so that there are 100 tales in all. The work had much influence on English literature, notably on *Chaucer, and many of the tales were incorporated in Painter's *Palace of Pleasure*.

Decline and Fall, the first novel of E. *Waugh, published with great success in 1928.

It recounts the chequered career of Paul Pennyfeather, sent down from Scone College, Oxford, for 'indecent behaviour', as the innocent victim of a drunken orgy. Thus forced to abandon a career in the church, he becomes a schoolmaster at Llanabba Castle, where he encounters headmaster Fagan and his daughters, the dubious, bigamous, and reappearing Captain Grimes, and young Beste-Chetwynde, whose glamorous mother Margot carries him off to the dangerous delight of high society. They are about to be married when Paul is arrested at the Ritz, and subsequently imprisoned for Margot's activities in the white slave trade; however, Margot (now Margot Metroland) arranges his escape, and he returns incognito, but under his own name, to resume his theological studies at Scone.

Decline and Fall of the Roman Empire, The History of the, a work by *Gibbon, vol. i of the first (quarto) edition published 1776, vols ii and iii 1781, and the last three vols 1788.

This, the most celebrated historical work in English literature, falls into three divisions, as defined by the author in the preface, according to a plan that expanded during composition: from the age of Trajan and the Antonines to the subversion of the western Empire; from the reign of Justinian in the East to the establishment of the second or German Empire of the West, under *Charlemagne; from the revival of the western Empire to the taking of Constantinople by the Turks. It thus covers a period of about 13 centuries, and comprehends such vast subjects as the establishment of Christianity, the movements and settlements of the Teutonic tribes, the conquests of the Muslims, and the crusades. It traces in fact the connection of the ancient world with the modern.

Gibbon's great erudition, breadth of treatment, and powerful organization render this a lasting monument, of substantial accuracy as well as elegance. The work is enlivened by ironic wit, much of it aimed at the early Church and the credulity and barbarism that overwhelmed the noble Roman virtues he so much admired.

Dedalus, Stephen, a character in J. Joyce's *A Portrait of the Artist as a Young Man and *Ulysses.

Dedlock, Sir Leicester, Lady, and Volumnia, characters in Dickens's *Bleak House.

DEE, Dr John (1527–1608), mathematician and astrologer, became a fellow of Trinity College, Cambridge, where the stage effects he introduced into a performance of the Peace of *Aristophanes procured him his lifelong reputation of being a magician, which was confirmed by his erudition and practice of crystallomancy

and astrology. His works include Monas Hieroglyphica (1564), and General and Rare Memorials pertayning to the perfect Art of Navigation (1577). He was a profoundly learned scholar and hermeticist, but also a sham.

DEEPING, (George) Warwick (1877–1950), prolific novelist, who caught the popular imagination with Sorrell and Son (1925), the story of a wounded ex-officer who takes a job as under-porter in a hotel to earn money to ensure an appropriate private education for his son Christopher, where he will not be exposed to 'class hatred'.

Deerslayer, The, a novel by J. F. *Cooper.

Defarge, M. and Mme, characters in Dickens's *A Tale of Two Cities.

Defence of All Learning, see MUSOPHILUS.

Defence of Poetry, A, an essay by P. *Sidney written in 1579–80. Sidney's chief aim was probably to write an English vindication of literature to match the many recently written on the Continent. Two editions of the work appeared posthumously in 1595; one bore the title The Defence of Poesie and the other An Apologie for Poetrie.

Sidney expounds the antiquity of poetry in all cultures. He demonstrates its superiority to philosophy or history as a means of teaching virtue. After defining and distinguishing the 'parts, kinds, or species' of poetry, vindicating each in turn, he digresses to England: he sees contemporary poetry as having reached a low ebb, with little to be admired since *Chaucer, but affirms with prophetic confidence that major poetry in every genre, including drama, can be written in the English language. A Defence of Poetry is remarkable for the lightness of Sidney's style and the catholicity of his examples, often drawn from experience. The poetic qualities of the essay in themselves illustrate the power of imaginative writing.

Defence of Poetry, an essay by P. B. *Shelley, published 1840. It was begun as a light-hearted reply to his friend Peacock's magazine article *'The Four Ages of Poetry'. In vindicating the role of poetry in a progressive society, and defending the whole notion of imaginative literature and thinking within an industrial culture, Shelley came to write his own poetic credo with passionate force and conviction. Against a background of classical and European literature, he discusses in some detail the nature of poetic thought and inspiration; the problems of translation; the value of erotic writing; the connections between poetry and politics; and the essentially moral nature of the imagination—an emphasis he drew from *Coleridge.

Throughout, Shelley associates poetry with

social freedom and love. He argues that the 'poetry of life' provides the one sure response to the destructive 'accumulating and calculating processes' of modern civilization. It contains the famous peroration, ending 'Poets are the unacknowledged legislators of the world.'

Defence of Ryme, a treatise by S. *Daniel written in reply to T. *Campion's *Observations in the Art of English Poesie.*

DEFOE, Daniel (1660–1731), born in London, the son of James Foe, a butcher. He changed his name to Defoe from *c.*1695. He attended Morton's academy for Dissenters at Newington Green with a view to the ministry, but by the time he married Mary Tuffley in 1683/4 he was established as a hosiery merchant in Cornhill, having travelled to Europe. He took part in Monmouth's rebellion, and in 1688 joined the advancing forces of William III. His first important signed work was *An Essay upon Projects* (1697), followed by *The True-Born Englishman* (1701), an immensely popular satirical poem attacking the prejudice against a king of foreign birth and his Dutch friends. In 1702 appeared *The Shortest Way with Dissenters,* a notorious pamphlet in which Defoe, himself a Dissenter, ironically demanded the total and savage suppression of dissent; for this he was fined, imprisoned (May–Nov. 1703), and pilloried. While in prison he wrote his mock-Pindaric ode *Hymn to the Pillory.* *Harley employed him as a secret agent; between 1703 and 1714 Defoe travelled around the country for Harley and Godolphin, gathering information and testing the political climate. Defoe wrote many pamphlets for Harley, and in 1704 began *The Review,* and in 1706 appeared his *True Relation of the Apparition of one Mrs Veal,* a vivid report of a current ghost story. Certain anti-Jacobite pamphlets in 1712–13 led to his prosecution by the Whigs and to a brief imprisonment. He now started a new trade journal, *Mercator,* in place of *The Review.*

Defoe produced some 560 books, pamphlets, and journals, but the works for which he is best known belong to his later years. *Robinson Crusoe* appeared in 1719, the *Farther Adventures* following a few months later. The next five years saw the appearance of his most important works of fiction: *Adventures of Captain Singleton* (1720); *Moll Flanders, A Journal of the *Plague Year,* and *Colonel Jack* in 1722; *Roxana,* the *Memoirs of a Cavalier* (now considered to be certainly by Defoe), and his tracts on Jack *Sheppard in 1724. The *Memoirs of Captain George Carleton* (1728) were probably largely by his hand. His *Tour through the Whole Island of Great Britain,* a guide-book in 3 vols (1724–6), is a vivid first-hand account of the state of the country. Defoe's influence on the evolution of the English novel was enormous, and many regard him as the first true novelist. He was a master of plain prose and powerful narrative, with a journalist's curiosity and love of realistic detail; his peculiar gifts made him one of the greatest reporters of his time, as well as a great imaginative writer who in *Robinson Crusoe* created one of the most familiar and resonant myths of modern literature.

Deformed Transformed, The, an unfinished poetic drama by Lord *Byron, published 1824.

Degaré, Sir, a metrical romance in 1,073 lines of short couplets from the early 14th cent. in a south Midland dialect, one of the Middle English Breton lays.

Degaré, the son of a princess of Brittany who has been raped by a knight, is abandoned in a forest with a purse of money, a letter of directions, and a pair of gloves which are to fit the lady that he is to marry. The poem recounts Degaré's prowess in the course of his searches for his parents. The lady that the gloves fit is, in the event, his own mother who recognizes him with joy as her son immediately after their wedding ceremony and before its consummation.

Deirdre, the heroine of the tale of 'The Sons of Usnach' (pron. 'Usna'), one of the 'Three Sorrowful Stories of Erin'. King Conchubar destined her for his wife and had her brought up in solitude. But she fell in love with Naoise the son of Usnach, who with his brothers carried her off to Scotland. They were lured back by Conchubar and treacherously slain, and Deirdre took her own life. See Lady *Gregory, *Cuchulain of Muirthemne,* and the dramas on Deirdre by G. W. *Russell (Æ), *Synge, and *Yeats.

Deism, or 'natural religion', the belief in a Supreme Being as the source of finite existence, with rejection of revelation and the supernatural doctrines of Christianity.

The Deists, who came into prominence at the end of the 17th and during the 18th cent. were much influenced by the views of Lord *Herbert of Cherbury, often known as 'the father of Deism'. They include Charles Blount (1654–93), *Toland, Matthew Tindal (1657–1733), Anthony *Collins, Thomas Chubb (1679–1747), and the third earl of *Shaftesbury. *Locke, who rejected the label of Deist, nevertheless contributed significantly to the movement with his *Reasonableness of Christianity* (1695).

'Dejection: An Ode', an autobiographical poem by S. T. *Coleridge, first published in the *Morning Post,* 1802.

The poem describes the loss of his poetical powers, the dulling of his response to Nature, the breakdown of his marriage, and the paralysing effect of metaphysics (or opium). Paradoxically this is achieved in verse of great emotional intensity and metrical brilliance. *Wordsworth partly answered it in his *'Intimations of Immortality' ode.

DEKKER, Thomas (?1570–1632), was born and mainly lived in London. He suffered from poverty and was several times imprisoned for debt. He was engaged by *Henslowe about 1595 to write plays (over 40 of which are now lost) in collaboration with *Drayton, *Jonson, J. *Webster, and many others.

He published *The Shoemaker's Holiday and *Old Fortunatus, comedies, in 1600. Having been ridiculed, jointly with J. *Marston, by Jonson in *The Poetaster, he retorted in *Satiromastix (presumably in collaboration with Marston), a play produced in 1601. His other principal plays are *The Honest Whore, written 1604–5 (Part I in collaboration with *Middleton, 1604; Part II, 1630); *Patient Grissil (1603), in collaboration with *Chettle and Haughton; *The Witch of Edmonton, written in collaboration with *Ford and *Rowley in 1621, first published 1658. He also collaborated with Webster in Westward Hoe (1607), written in 1604; with Middleton in *The Roaring Girle (1611), written 1604–10; and with Massinger in *The Virgin Martyr (1622), written in 1620. Dekker also wrote pageants, tracts, and pamphlets. His pamphlet The Wonderfull yeare (1603), a poignant description of London during the plague of that year, was used by Defoe for his Journal of the *Plague Year. Newes from Hell (1606) is an imitation of *Nashe; *The Guls Hornebooke (1609) is a satirical book of manners.

Dekker's work is noted for its realistic and vivid portrayal of daily London life, both domestic and commercial, for its sympathy with the poor and oppressed, including animals tortured for man's amusement, and for its prevailing cheerfulness.

DELAFIELD, E. M., the pen-name of Edmée Elizabeth Monica Dashwood, née De La Pasture (1890–1943), whose many popular novels include The Diary of a Provincial Lady (1930), a gentle satire of a middle-class life of laundry lists, cooks, and visits from the vicar.

DE LA MARE, Walter (1873–1956), poet, published many volumes of verse for both adults and children including, for adults, The Listeners (1912); The Veil (1921); various volumes of Collected Poems; The Burning Glass (1945); and two long visionary poems, 'The Traveller' (1946) and 'The Winged Chariot' (1951). Among many volumes for children were Peacock Pie (1913), Tom Tiddler's Ground (1932), and Bells and Grass (1941). Several collections were amalgamated in Collected Rhymes and Verses (1970) and Collected Poems (1979). De la Mare's highly individual prose works include the novels Henry Brocken (1904); The Return (1910); the children's story The Three Mulla-Mulgars (1910, later The Three Royal Monkeys); 'The Almond Tree' (in The Riddle, 1923); and the celebrated Memoirs of a Midget (1921). Many volumes of short stories, often arresting or bizarre, for both adults and children, include Broomsticks (1925), The Lord Fish (1933), and The Scarecrow (1945). De la Mare's anthologies include Come Hither (1923), a widely admired collection for children; Behold this Dreamer (1939); and Love (1943). Essays and critical work include studies of R. *Brooke (1919) and Lewis Carroll—C. L. *Dodgson—(1932), and an edition of C. *Rossetti in 1930.

De la Mare was fluent, highly inventive, technically skilful, and unaffected by fashion. In his favourite themes of childhood, commonplace objects and events are invested with mystery, and often with an undercurrent of melancholy.

DELANE, John Thaddeus (1817–79), famous editor of *The Times, 1841–77, was caricatured by Trollope in *The Warden as 'Tom Towers'.

DELANEY, Shelagh (1939–), playwright, is known for A Taste of Honey, written when she was 17. It was presented by Joan Littlewood in 1958 and was hailed as a landmark in the new school of *'kitchen sink' realism, a movement partly inspired by reaction against the drawing-room drama of *Rattigan and *Coward.

DELANY, Mrs Mary, née Granville (1700–88), a member of the *Blue Stocking circle, who became a friend and correspondent of *Swift, and married his friend Patrick *Delany in 1743. Her Autobiography and Correspondence (1861–2, 6 vols, ed. Lady Llanover) gives a spirited account of 18th-cent. court, literary, and social life.

DELANY, Patrick (?1685–1768), Irish divine, friend of *Swift, husband of Mary *Delany. He was the author of Observations upon Lord Orrery's Remarks on the Life and Writings of Dr Jonathan Swift (1754), a series of letters, signed 'J.R.', written in an attempt to correct what he describes as 'the very mistaken and erroneous accounts [of Swift] that have been published'. See BOYLE, J.

DE LA RAMÉE, Marie Louise, see OUIDA.

Delectable Mountains, in Bunyan's *Pilgrim's Progress. 'Emmanuel's Land', within sight of the Celestial City.

Delia, a collection of sonnets by S. *Daniel.

Delilah (Dalila in Milton's *Samson Agonistes), in Judges 16, a woman of the valley of Sorek, loved by Samson; she persuaded him to tell her the secret of his strength and (by cutting off his hair) betrayed him to the Philistines. In Milton's version she is Samson's wife.

Della Crusca, the name of a literary academy established in Florence in 1582, with the principal object of purifying the Italian language. The first edition of its dictionary appeared in 1612.

Della Cruscans, a band of poets, led by Robert Merry (1755–98), who produced affected, sentimental, and highly ornamented verse towards the end of the 18th cent. Merry lived in Florence from 1784 to 1787 as a member of the *Della Crusca academy. With Mrs Piozzi (see THRALE) and others he produced in 1785 a *Miscellany* in which he signed his work 'Della Crusca'. 'Anna Matilda' (H. *Cowley) was another copious writer of the school who contributed with Merry and others to the *British Album* in 1790, a volume which proved very successful until the publication in 1791 of *Gifford's *The Baviad*, a savage satire on the Della Cruscans.

DELONEY, Thomas (?1560–1600), wrote broadside ballads on popular subjects. He is now best known for his four works of prose fiction, originally published between 1597 and 1600: *Jack of Newberie*; *The gentle craft*, which includes the story of Simon *Eyre adapted by Dekker in *The Shoemaker's Holiday*; *The gentle craft. The second part*; and *Thomas of Reading*. His fiction celebrates the virtues and self-advancement of hard-working craftsmen, especially in the cloth trade, and has been much admired in modern times for its effective use of dialogue.

Delvile, Mortimer, the hero of F. Burney's *Cecilia*.

Demetrius, (1) a character in Shakespeare's *Titus Andronicus*; (2) one of the young lovers in his *A Midsummer Night's Dream*; (3) Demetrius Fannius in Jonson's *The Poetaster*, a satirical portrait of *Dekker.

DEMOCRITUS (b. *c*.460 BC), a celebrated Greek philosopher, born at Abdera. He advanced (with Leucippus) the theory that the world was formed by the concourse of atoms, the theory subsequently expounded by *Lucretius and confirmed and developed by recent scientific discovery. *Juvenal speaks of him as ever laughing at the follies of mankind, and he is sometimes known as the 'laughing philosopher'.

DEMOCRITUS JUNIOR, the pseudonym of Robert Burton. (See ANATOMY OF MELANCHOLY.)

Demogorgon, the name of a mysterious and terrible infernal deity described in the *Genealogia Deorum* of *Boccaccio as the primeval god of ancient mythology, and this appears to be the sense of the word in modern literature (*Spenser, *Milton, *Shelley, etc.).

DE MORGAN, William Frend (1839–1917), at first devoted his attention to art and in particular to the production of stained glass and glazed pottery, working for a time in association with his friend W. *Morris. He embarked on the writing of fiction at the age of 67; his first and best novel, *Joseph Vance* (1906), is the rambling but entertaining tale of a drunken builder's son befriended by a middle-class family, who graduates from Oxford and becomes an engineer and inventor. This was followed by several others; the last two, *The Old Madhouse* (1919) and *The Old Man's Youth* (1921), left unfinished on his death, were skilfully completed by his widow, the artist Evelyn de Morgan.

DEMOSTHENES (*c*.383–322 BC), Athenian orator and prose writer whose reputation rested on the excellence of his style. His ideals were lofty, his policies statesmanlike. His orations roused his countrymen to the danger of the subjugation of Greece by Philip of Macedon (hence the word 'philippic'). T. *Wilson's translation of the *Philippics* appeared in 1570.

Dempster, Mr and Janet, characters in G. Eliot's 'Janet's Repentance' (see SCENES OF CLERICAL LIFE).

DENHAM, Sir John (1615–69), born in Dublin, is chiefly known for his *topographical poem *Cooper's Hill* (piratically published 1642), an early and influential example of what was to become a very popular genre. It combines descriptions of scenery with moral, historical, and political reflections, and contains the well-known address to the Thames, 'O, could I flow like thee', praised by Dr *Johnson for its economy of language, smoothness, and sweetness. His poetry (and notably his use of the heroic couplet) played an important part in the transition from what were seen as the rugged eccentricities of the *Metaphysicals to the neo-classicism of the *Augustan age. (See also WALLER.)

Denis Duval, *Thackeray's last, unfinished, novel, published in the *Cornhill Magazine 1864.

Dennis, in Dickens's *Barnaby Rudge*, the hangman and one of the leaders of the no-Popery riots.

DENNIS, John (1657–1734), poet and dramatist, but best known for his criticism, which combines a respect for *neo-classical theory with a passion for the *Sublime (particularly as manifested by *Milton), and with a dislike for the new *sentimental comedy. His critical works include *The Advancement and Reformation of Modern Poetry* (1701), *The Grounds of Criticism in Poetry* (1704), and *An Essay on the Genius and Writings of Shakespeare* (1712). His tragedies include *Appius and Virginia*, unsuccessfully produced in 1709, which was mocked by Pope in his *Essay on Criticism*; this started a feud between the two writers. But Pope accepted and acted upon some of his critical comments, and shortly before Dennis's poverty-stricken death wrote a prologue for his benefit performance.

DENNIS, Nigel Forbes (1912–), novelist, playwright, journalist, and critic. His best-known work is *Cards of Identity* (1955), a satiric fantasy set in an English country house, which comments harshly but with much incidental comedy on post-war social change and insecurity and the ease with which the human personality can be controlled. *A House In Order* (1966) is a more abstract, Kafkaesque treatment of the problem of identity. Dennis also published three plays and several critical works.

Denouement, the unravelling of the plot, the final solution, in a drama or novel; *Aristotle's λύσις.

DENT, J. M., see EVERYMAN'S LIBRARY.

De Nugis Curialium, see MAP; also the subtitle of the *Policraticus* of *John of Salisbury.

Deor, an Old English poem from the 9th or 10th cent., of 42 lines divided into seven sections and containing the refrain 'that passed; so can this'. Deor seems to be a minstrel who has fallen out of favour and consoles himself by considering the past misfortunes of others such as Wayland the Smith, Theodoric, and Hermanric. It is one of the group of poems in the *Exeter Book referred to as 'elegies'.

De Profundis, 'Out of the depths', the first two words of the Latin version of Psalm 130. It is the title of the prose apologia of *Wilde.

'Deputy', in Dickens's *Edwin Drood*, the nearest thing to a name acknowledged for the imp who attends on Durdles.

DE QUINCEY, Thomas (1785–1859), ran away from Manchester Grammar School to the homeless wanderings in Wales and London which he was to describe in *Confessions of an English Opium Eater* (1822). He afterwards went to Worcester College, Oxford, and—having made the acquaintance of *Coleridge and *Wordsworth—settled at Grasmere. In 1804, while at Oxford, he had begun to take opium, and from 1812 he became an addict. He earned a precarious living, mainly in Edinburgh, by tales, articles, and reviews, mostly in *Blackwood's and Tait's, including *Klosterheim* (1832), *Recollections of the Lake Poets* (1834–9), 'Sketches . . . from the Autobiography of an English Opium Eater' (1834–41, later entitled *Autobiographic Sketches*).

Since nearly all De Quincey's work was journalism, written under pressure to support his family, it is more remarkable for brilliant *tours de force* such as 'On the Knocking on the Gate in "Macbeth" ', 'On Murder Considered as One of the Fine Arts', and 'The Revolt of the Tartars', than for sustained coherence. Eclectic learning, pungent black humour sometimes degenerating into facetiousness, a stately but singular style, distinguish all his writings. His impressionistic reminiscences both of his own childhood and of his literary contemporaries are memorably vivid. His greatest, though never completed, achievement was his psychological study of the faculty of dreaming in 'Suspiria de Profundis' (1845) and 'The English Mail Coach' (1849) in which he traced—twenty-five years before Freud was born—how childhood experiences and sufferings are crystallized in dreams into symbols which can form and educate the dreamer's personality, and can also give birth to literature, either as poetry or as 'impassioned prose'. His influence, both on writers such as *Poe and Baudelaire and on ordinary readers tempted to experiment with opium, has been immense.

Derriman, Festus, a character in Hardy's *The Trumpet Major*.

DESAI, Anita (1937–), novelist and short story writer, born in India; her father was Bengali, her mother German. Her novels, which vividly evoke the atmosphere, society, and landscapes of India, include *Fire on the Mountain* (1977) and *Clear Light of Day* (1980). *Games at Twilight* (1978) is a collection of short stories, and her works for children include *The Village by the Sea* (1982).

DESANI, G. V. (1909–), Indian writer, born in Nairobi, Kenya; he lived in Britain during the Second World War. His prose-poem *Hali* (1950) was published with a preface by E. M. *Forster, but he is known principally for his eccentric and inventive novel, *All about H. Hatterr* (1948). This was revised and republished in 1972 with an introduction by A. *Burgess.

DESCARTES, René (1596–1650), French philosopher and mathematician. His main works are: *Discours de la méthode* (printed as an introduction to the conclusions of his scientific research in 1637), *Méditations philosophiques* (originally published in Latin in 1641), *Principia philosophiae* (1644), and *Traité des passions de l'âme* (1649). They have exerted a unique influence on European thought. Philosophically his starting point is the problem of certainty posed by *Montaigne's radical scepticism. Rejecting the accumulated preconceptions of the past ('systematic doubt'), he proposes to reconstruct the whole of philosophy on the basis of a few self-evident intuitions, such as the existence of the self in consciousness ('cogito ergo sum') and of elementary logical truths, such as the principle of non-contradiction. From these premisses he attempts to deduce the existence of God as guarantor of the reliability of the perceptible world, and thus of its susceptibility to scientific analysis. As a mathematician he considered mathematical reasoning to be applicable to the whole of science. His reduction of matter to the quantifiable has remained fundamental to science. In epistemology and ethics, his rigorous dualism (between mind and body) has been immensely influential. He is generally regarded as the founder of modern philosophy.

DESCHAMPS, Eustache (*c.*1346–*c.*1406), French poet, a disciple of *Guillaume de Machaut, influential in the development of the *ballade,* and the writer of the first treatise on poetry in French. He addressed one of his 'Balades de moralitez' to *Chaucer, whom he styled 'grand translateur'.

Desdemona, the heroine of Shakespeare's *Othello.*

Deserted Village, The, a poem by *Goldsmith, published 1770, in which he evokes the idyllic pastoral life of Auburn, 'loveliest village of the plain', in its days of prosperous peace, now over; the poet laments the growth of trade, the demand for luxuries, and the mercantile spirit which have depopulated such villages and driven 'a bold peasantry, their country's pride' to emigration. *Boswell attributes the last four lines to Dr *Johnson.

Despair, Giant, in Bunyan's *Pilgrim's Progress, imprisons Christian and Hopeful in *Doubting Castle.

Desperate Remedies, a novel by *Hardy, published 1871.

Cytherea Gray, who loves and is loved by Edward Springrove, becomes lady's maid to Miss Aldclyffe. The contrivances of Miss Aldclyffe, the discovery that Edward is already engaged, and the need to support a sick brother, drive Cytherea to marry Aeneas Manston, Miss Aldclyffe's villainous and illegitimate son, whose first wife is supposed to have perished in a fire. As soon as she is married Cytherea discovers that Edward is free from his engagement and that Aeneas's wife is probably still alive. Ingenious investigations reveal that Aeneas murdered his first wife in order to gain Cytherea. He hangs himself in his cell and the lovers are united.

Destiny, a novel by S. *Ferrier, published 1831.

The story relates, in a complex plot, the fortunes of the various members of the Malcolm family.

Detective Fiction. In the detective story, or 'whodunit' a crime (generally, though not necessarily, murder) is committed by one of a group of people; the puzzle of the criminal's identity is finally solved, through a process of investigation, observation, and deduction, by an expert detective, who may be either police or private.

Although crime novels such as Godwin's *Caleb Williams and hidden secret novels such as Dickens's *Bleak House have been allocated to the British ancestry of the detective story, its real progenitor is generally agreed to have been *Poe's 'Chevalier Dupin' stories. In England Wilkie Collins's *The Moonstone (1868) was the prototype for the full-length detective novel. Detective fiction, and the image of the super-humanly intelligent detective Sherlock Holmes and his auxiliary Watson, reached world-wide popularity in the novels and short stories of A. C. *Doyle. Short detective stories, of which G. K. *Chesterton's 'Father Brown' stories were the other outstanding example, remained in the ascendant until E. C. *Bentley, in Trent's Last Case (1913), introduced in a full length novel more spacious characterization and the gentle-manly amateur detective, setting the pattern for the next quarter-century, generally regarded as the Golden Age of the genre.

During this period rules of fair play between author and reader in the game of puzzle-solving were formulated, and generally adhered to; law and order were always finally vindicated, and crime punished. Scientific and technical expertise (as in R. Austin Freeman and Freeman Wills Croft), locked room puzzles (in which John Dickson Carr specialized), ingeniously recondite murder weapons such as daggers of ice or trained killer bees, and murder by the least likely suspect were the characteristics of Golden Age detective novels. Leading authors were D. L. *Sayers, A. *Christie, H. C. Bailey, and Anthony Berkeley (who as Francis Iles also pioneered the crime novel genre), and, in the 1930s, Margery Allingham, Michael Innes (pseudonym of J. I. M. *Stewart), Ngaio *Marsh, and Nicholas Blake (pseudonym of C. *Day-Lewis).

After the Second World War, the American school of tough detective fiction began to erode the classic British genre, and some of the younger writers—disapproving of what were seen as the snobbery, nostalgia, and lack of social concern in the Golden Age detective story—turned to writing crime and spy stories, in which the conflict between justice and the criminal was no longer seen entirely from one side. Those, including Michael Gilbert, Elizabeth Ferrars, H. R. F. Keating, Ellis Peters, and P. D. James, who have remained faithful to the classic formula, have mostly abandoned the amateur detective and rely less on ingenious murder methods and more on realistic characterization. Exotic settings in the distant past, in remote countries, or in specialized milieux such as Dick Francis's racing world, are often deployed. A new sub-genre is the 'police procedural', whose chief English exponent is J. J. Marric (pseudonym of John Creasey), in which a complete police unit investigates concurrently a series of separate crimes.

Deus ex machina, 'God from the machine', an unexpected event or intervention in a play or novel, which resolves a difficult situation. When a god was introduced in the ancient Greek drama, he was brought on to the stage by some mechanical means (μηχανή). *Euripides was particularly fond of the device.

DE VERE, Aubrey Thomas (1814–1902), born in Co. Limerick, the son of Sir Aubrey de Vere (1788–1846, himself a poet), came early under the influence of *Wordsworth and *Coleridge. His voluminous works include *The Waldenses, or the Fall of Rora, with other Poems* (1842); *English Misrule and Irish Misdeeds* (1848), which displays Irish sympathies; and *Recollections* (1897).

DE VERE, Edward, see OXFORD.

DEVEREUX, Robert, see ESSEX.

De Veritate, see HERBERT OF CHERBURY.

Devil is an Ass, The, a comedy by *Jonson, acted 1616, printed 1631, ridiculing the 'projectors' or monopolists, and exposing the pretended demoniacs and witchfinders of the day.

Devils, The, a play by J. *Whiting, based on A. *Huxley's *The Devils of Loudon*.

'Devil's Thoughts, The', a satirical poem by S. T. *Coleridge and R. *Southey, published 1799, describing the Devil going walking and enjoying the sight of the vices of men. The poem was imitated by *Byron in his 'Devil's Drive', and by *Shelley in his 'Devil's Walk'.

Devil upon Two Sticks in England, The, a continuation by W. *Combe, published 1790, of *Lesage's *Le Diable boiteux*. S. *Foote also wrote a farce called *The Devil upon Two Sticks*, produced 1768.

DEWEY, John (1859–1952), American philosopher, one of the leaders of the Pragmatist school.

DEWEY, Melvil (1851–1931), American librarian, invented the Dewey decimal system of library cataloguing.

Dewy, Dick, a character in Hardy's *Under the Greenwood Tree*.

Dial, The, (1) (1840–4), the literary organ of the American Transcendental movement (see TRANSCENDENTAL CLUB), of which M. *Fuller was editor; she was succeeded by *Emerson. It contained contributions by *Thoreau. (2) (1889–97) (Nos 1–5), a literary and artistic periodical edited by *Ricketts and Charles Shannon. The 'Dial Group' also included T. S. *Moore and Lucien Pissarro (1863–1944). (3) (1880–1929), a literary monthly founded in Chicago, which moved in 1918 to New York. In its last decade it was one of the most important international periodicals, publishing work by T. S. *Eliot, *Yeats, D. H. *Lawrence, *Pound, *Cummings, *Aiken, and many others.

Diall of Princes, the title of the translation by Sir T. *North of Guevara's *El Relox de Principes*, published 1557.

Dialogues concerning Natural Religion, a treatise on natural theology by *Hume, written in the 1750s and published posthumously 1779. The work is modelled on *Cicero's *De Natura Deorum*. It portrays in 18th-cent. terms the conflict between scientific theism and philosophical scepticism, on the question of whether the human mind is capable of inferring the nature of the source of order in the universe.

Dialogues of the Dead, Four, by *Prior, written 1721, imaginary conversations on the model set by *Lucian. The first is between 'Charles the Emperor and Clenard the Grammarian' on the subject of greatness; the second is between 'Mr John Lock and Seigneur de Montaigne'; the third between 'The Vicar of Bray and Sir Thomas More'; and the fourth between 'Oliver Cromwell and his Porter'.
    *Lyttelton also wrote *Dialogues of the Dead* (1760).

Dialogus de Scaccario, or *Dialogue of the Exchequer,* is the work of Richard Fitz-Nigel, treasurer of England (c.1195–8), bishop of London (1189–98). It takes the form of a dialogue in Latin between teacher and pupil, and is one of the principal sources of our knowledge of the Norman administration in England before Magna Carta.

Diana, a character in Shakespeare's *All's Well that Ends Well*.

Diana of the Crossways, a novel by G. *Meredith, published 1885.
    Diana Merion is based on Caroline Norton, whose husband unsuccessfully cited Lord Melbourne in a divorce case, and who was later accused of giving *The Times* information about the repeal of the Corn Laws, gleaned from Sidney Herbert.
    Diana marries Mr Warwick, a man incapable

of understanding the remarkable qualities of his wife. Her innocent indiscretions arouse his jealousy and he brings an action for divorce, citing Lord Dannisburgh (drawn from Melbourne), which he loses. Percy Dacier, a rising young politician, falls in love with Diana, but when she is about to live with him the dangerous illness of her friend Lady Dunstane recalls her sense of duty and propriety. Dacier perseveres but he discovers that an important political secret which he had confided to her has been passed to a London newspaper, and after much pain they part. Diana's husband dies, and after a time she becomes the wife of her steady and faithful adorer Thomas Redworth.

DIAPER, William (1685–1717), poet, born in Somerset, wrote *Nereides: or, Sea-Eclogues* (1712), in which the speakers are mermen and mermaids and the landscapes subaqueous. He also wrote *Dryades* (1712) and a *topographical poem, 'Brent' (printed 1754).

Diarmid, or **Diarmait O'Duibhne,** in the legends relating to the Irish hero *Finn, the lover of *Grainne.

Diary of a Country Parson, The, see WOOD-FORDE, J.

Diary of a Nobody, The, by G. and W. *Grossmith, published 1892.

The diary covers fifteen months of the life of Charles Pooter in the early 1890s. His entries describing the events of his life with his wife Carrie in Brickfield Terrace, Holloway, reveal in cumulative detail the society of anxious gentility in which he lives. Pooter emerges as worthy, deferential, and acutely sensitive to minor humiliations. Text and illustrations reveal much precise contemporary background.

DIBDIN, Charles (1745–1814), actor, dramatist, and song-writer, is best remembered for his sea songs, including 'The Lass that Loved a Sailor' and 'Tom Bowling'. He wrote many musical entertainments (including *The Waterman*, 1774) and dramatic monologues; also an autobiography, *The Professional Life of Mr Dibdin . . . with the words of six hundred songs* (4 vols, 1803), in which he describes his relations with *Garrick and others.

DIBDIN, Thomas Frognall (1776–1847), a renowned bibliographer and librarian to Lord Spencer at Althorp. He published his *Introduction to the Knowledge of Rare and Valuable Editions of the Greek and Latin Classics* (1802) and other bibliographical works. His *Bibliomania* ('a bibliographical romance', 1809) did much to stimulate interest in old books and rare editions.

Dick, Mr, the amiable lunatic in Dickens's *David Copperfield.

DICKENS, Charles John Huffham (1812–70), the son of a clerk in the Navy pay office. His father was imprisoned for debt in the Marshalsea and he himself (aged 12) worked in a blacking warehouse. Memories of this painful period inspired much of his fiction, notably the early chapters of *David Copperfield. He became reporter of debates in the Commons for the *Morning Chronicle and contributed to periodicals the articles subsequently republished as *Sketches by 'Boz', Illustrative of Every-Day Life and Every-Day People* (1836–7); these led to an approach from *Chapman and Hall which resulted in the creation of Mr Pickwick, and the publication in 20 monthly numbers of *The Posthumous Papers of the Pickwick Club* (1836–7). (See PICKWICK PAPERS.) The series achieved immense popularity, and Dickens, with his young wife Catherine Hogarth, embarked on a promising future. On Christmas Day 1836 he met John *Forster, who became his close friend and biographer.

*Oliver Twist (1837–8) appeared in monthly numbers in *Bentley's Miscellany, a new periodical of which Dickens was the first editor. His next novel was *Nicholas Nickleby (1838–9), also in monthly numbers. In 1840 Dickens launched a new weekly, *Master Humphrey's Clock, in which appeared *The Old Curiosity Shop (1840–1) and his long-deliberated *Barnaby Rudge (1841), but the novels proved so popular that the linking by 'Master Humphrey' was dropped. In 1842 he and his wife visited America, where he was rapturously received. His first impressions were favourable, but disillusion followed and his *American Notes (1842) caused much offence in America, as did his portrayal of American stereotypes in *Martin Chuzzlewit (1843–4). While in America he advocated international copyright and the abolition of slavery.

*A Christmas Carol (1843) was the first of a series of Christmas books (*The Chimes, *The Cricket on the Hearth, The Battle of Life, and *The Haunted Man). In 1844 he paid a long visit to Italy, which produced 'Pictures from Italy' contributed to the *Daily News, a new Radical paper founded by Dickens in 1846. He began *Dombey and Son (1848) during a visit to Switzerland in 1846. In 1850 he started the weekly periodical *Household Words; in 1859 it was incorporated into All the Year Round, which he continued to edit until his death. In this he published much of his later writings. David Copperfield appeared in monthly numbers in 1849–50; *Bleak House in 1852–3; and A Child's History of England appeared irregularly, 1851–3. *Hard Times appeared in 1854, *Little Dorrit in 1855–7, *A Tale of Two Cities in 1859, *Great Expectations in 1860–1, and *Our Mutual Friend in 1864–5.

During these years of intense productivity he also found time for his large family, for a vast circle of friends, and for philanthropic enterprises, at times combined with his passion for amateur theatricals. His admiration for the young actress Ellen Ternan further strained his deteriorating marriage and he and Catherine separated in 1858. He defied scandal, protesting his own innocence and distracting himself from domestic sorrow by throwing his restless energy into public readings of his own works. He revisited America in 1867–8, delivered a series of readings there, and on his return continued to tour the provinces. He died leaving unfinished his last novel, *The Mystery of *Edwin Drood*.

Dickens captured the popular imagination as no other novelist had done and, despite some murmurs against his sensationalism and sentimentality and his inability to portray women other than as innocents or grotesques, he was also held in high critical esteem. But it was not until this century that he began to attract serious academic attention. Later criticism has tended to praise the complexity of the sombre late works at the expense of the high-spirited humour and genius for caricature traditionally labelled 'Dickensian'. Several distinguished illustrators are inseparably connected with his work, including H. K. *Browne ('Phiz'), *Leech, and *Cruikshank. Dickens collaborated with Wilkie *Collins in various stories which appeared in *Household Words*.

DICKINSON, Emily Elizabeth (1830–86), American poet, who gradually withdrew into an inner world, eventually, in her forties, refusing to leave her home, although she maintained intimate correspondence with people she never saw face to face. Only seven poems out of nearly 2,000 are known to have been published during her lifetime. From *c.*1858 she assembled many of her poems in packets or 'fascicles', which were discovered after her death; a selection, arranged and edited by Mabel Loomis Todd and T. W. Higginson, appeared in 1890; eventually other editions and volumes of letters appeared, restoring her individual punctuation and presentation. Her work presents recurrent themes—a mystic apprehension of the natural world, a preoccupation with poetic vocation, fame, death, and immortality—and is expressed in a rhetoric and language of her own, cryptic, elliptical, and at times self-dramatizing and hyperbolic. Her imagery reflects an intense and painful inner struggle over many years, and her verse is full of allusions to volcanoes, shipwrecks, funerals, storms, imprisonments, and other manifestations of natural and human violence.

Dictionary. The origins of the English dictionary are found in the late 16th cent. when people became aware of the two levels of English ('learned', 'literary', *'inkhorn', distinct from 'spoken', 'popular') to an extent that made it desirable to gloss one in the other's terms. Cawdrey's *Table Alphabeticall of Hard Words* (1604), containing about 3,000 words, might be called the first English dictionary; Henry Cockeram's *English Dictionarie* (1623) translates hard words to easy as well as easy to hard. The first major English dictionary was N. *Bailey's *Universal Etymological English Dictionary* (1721). Dr *Johnson's Dictionary (1755) is one of the two great landmarks in English lexicographical history; Johnson illustrates his words in practice, and attempts to indicate the connotations of words, as well as offering their exact meaning. The second great landmark is the greatest dictionary of any modern language, *The Oxford English Dictionary* (1884–1928), edited by J. A. H. *Murray, H. *Bradley, W. A. *Craigie, and C. T. *Onions. The *OED* attempts to give a full history of the development of all English words since the 12th cent., with full illustrative quotations, ordered according to the principal distinct senses of the word. It has been updated by a series of supplements under the editorship of R. W. *Burchfield. The possibility of a dictionary organized on synchronic, rather than historical, principles was brought closer when in 1984 the *OED* files began to be converted into a computerized database. The other major English language dictionary is N. *Webster's dictionary of American English (1828; *Third New International Dictionary*, 1961), the Third being controversial on its appearance for its omission of indications of inferior usage in categories such as 'slang', 'obscene', etc.

Dictionary of National Biography, The, designed and published by George *Smith, was begun in 1882 with Sir L. *Stephen as editor. It included in its original form biographies of all national notabilities from earliest times to 1900. The work has been continued by the publishing of decennial supplements. Stephen was succeeded in the editorship by Sir Sidney *Lee. In 1917 the Dictionary was transferred to the *Oxford University Press. The *Concise DNB* is in two parts: Part I, epitome of the *DNB* from earliest times to 1900, and Part 2, epitome of the supplements, 1901–70.

Dictionary of the English Language, A, see JOHNSON'S DICTIONARY.

DICTYS CRETENSIS is the supposed author of a diary of the Trojan War which we possess in Latin. In the preface, written in the 4th cent. AD, Lucius Septimius claims that he translated the work from a Greek version prepared for Nero from a Phoenician original. Dictys claims to have been present at the siege of Troy. Like the narratives of *Dares Phrygius his diary is probably a fabrication, but the two were the chief sources of medieval Trojan legends.

Diddler, Jeremy, the chief character in James Kenney's farce *Raising the Wind* (1803). Jeremy's habit of borrowing money which he does not pay back probably gave rise to the present sense of the verb 'diddle'—to cheat or deceive.

DIDEROT, Denis (1713–84), French philosopher and man of letters; a leading member of the *Enlightenment, and from 1746 editor of the *Encyclopédie. His works demonstrated close links with English literature: he translated *Shaftesbury, wrote on *Richardson, adapted E. *Moore, and wrote plays influenced by *Lillo.

Dido Queene of Carthage, The Tragedie of, written by *Marlowe and *Nashe, published in 1594. It is closely based on Virgil's *Aeneid (Bks I, II, and IV), depicting Dido's failure to persuade Aeneas to stay with her in Carthage and her subsequent suicide.

Dies Irae, 'Day of wrath', the first words of one of the greatest medieval Latin hymns, which is attributed to Thomas of Celano (d. c.1255).

Dietrich of Bern, the name given in the *Nibelungenlied to Theodoric, a great king of the Ostrogoths (c.454–526). He was the hero of the German epics of the 13th cent. and of the Teutonic race in general, and the centre round which clustered many legends.

DIGBY, Sir Kenelm (1603–65), was author, diplomatist, naval commander, and one of the first members of the *Royal Society; he discovered the necessity of oxygen for the life of plants. In 1625 he secretly married the celebrated beauty Venetia Stanley, and gives an account, under disguised names, of his wooing in his *Private Memoirs* (published 1827). His criticism of Browne's *Religio Medici, 'Of Bodies', and 'Of the Immortality of Man's Soul' all appeared in 1643.

Digby Plays, The, three late Mystery plays from East Anglia, probably dating from the early 16th cent., bearing on them the name or initials of Myles Blomefeld (1525–1603). They are *Mary Magdalen, The Conversion of St Paul,* and *The Killing of the Children of Israel.*

Dilettanti, Society of the, originally founded about 1732 as a dining society by some gentlemen of wealth and position who had travelled in Italy, soon devoted itself to the patronage of the fine arts. It has chiefly encouraged the study of classical archaeology.

DILKE, Sir Charles Wentworth (1843–1911), radical statesman, held offices under *Gladstone. On his father's death in 1869 he inherited the baronetcy and the proprietorship of the *Athenaeum and *Notes and Queries. He was the author of *Greater Britain* (1868); *Problems of Greater Britain* (1890); and *The Fall of Prince Florestan of*

Monaco (1874), a political satire. In 1885, he married the widow of Mark *Pattison (née Emilia Francis Strong). It has been suggested that Dilke might have succeeded Gladstone but for his connections with a divorce scandal (*Crawford* v. *Crawford and Dilke*) which led to his defeat and temporary retirement in 1886.

Dimmesdale, the Revd Arthur, a character in Hawthorne's *The Scarlet Letter.*

DINESEN, Isak, see BLIXEN, K.

Dinmont, see DANDIE DINMONT.

DIODATI, Charles (d. 1638), close friend of *Milton, and son of an Italian Protestant settled in London. Milton addressed to him two Latin elegies and mourned him in the pastoral *Epitaphium Damonis* (?1640).

DIODORUS SICULUS, a Greek historian of the latter half of the 1st cent. BC. The surviving portion of his history of the world was translated into Latin by Poggio. *Skelton produced a translation into English, and there are references to it in D. *Lindsay, *Kirke, *Milton, and even W. *Morris.

DIOGENES LAERTIUS, a Greek historian of philosophy of the early 3rd cent. AD. He presented philosophers as heroic figures, so that his lives, like *Plutarch's, served as an admirable source of moral examples.

DIONYSIUS THE AREOPAGITE, (1) a disciple of St Paul (Acts 17:34); (2) more importantly, a 5th-cent. Neoplatonic writer (now known as Pseudo-Dionysius) claimed to be his disciple, in an attempt to give canonical authority to elements of mysticism and *Neoplatonism which he attempted to introduce, with considerable success. His works, the most important of which was *The Divine Names*, first appeared in 532. This work, and the Commentary on it by Maximus the Confessor (580–662), was very influential on *Scotus Erigena and on the whole medieval mystical tradition.

Dionyza, in Shakespeare's *Pericles, wife of Cleon.

'Dipsychus', a poem by *Clough.

Discoverie of Witchcraft, The, see SCOT, R.

Discoveries made upon Men and Matter, see TIMBER.

DISRAELI, Benjamin (1804–81), first earl of Beaconsfield, politician, prime minister, novelist, eldest son of I. *D'israeli. He was to attempt an ambitious variety of literary forms before he settled on the novel. His first novel, *Vivian Grey* (1826), published anonymously, achieved considerable success. In 1827 he published a Swiftian satire, *Popanilla*. Between 1828 and 1831 he travelled in Spain and Italy, and made much use of these, and of subsequent travels in Albania, the Levant, and Egypt, in future novels. In 1831 he published *The Young Duke* followed by *Contarini Fleming* (1832) and *Alroy* (1833), which, together with *Vivian Grey* (in the order *Grey—Alroy—Fleming*), formed his first trilogy. In 1833 appeared the burlesque *Ixion in Heaven* and in 1834 another burlesque, *The Infernal Marriage*, his one long, serious but unsuccessful attempt at poetry, *The Revolutionary Epic*, in blank verse, and *A Year at Hartlebury*, written with his sister Sarah, whose authorship he never admitted. *A Vindication of the English Constitution* appeared in 1835; the *Junius-inspired Letters of Runnymede*, together with *The Spirit of Whiggism*, in 1836.

By 1834 Disraeli had established himself in the highest social and political society, which was vividly reflected in his next two novels, *Henrietta Temple* and *Venetia*, both love stories and both published in 1837. A verse play, *The Tragedy of Count Alarcos*, appeared in 1839. The trilogy for which Disraeli is most renowned, *Coningsby* (1844), *Sybil* (1845), and *Tancred* (1847) may be regarded as the first truly political novels in English. He published no more novels until *Lothair* in 1870. *Endymion* (1880), his last completed novel, was set in the period of his youth. He left *Falconet* unfinished at his death.

Many of the characters in his novels were intended as portraits of prominent men and women of the time. A combination of fascination and amused contempt for high society, both social and political; a clever vein of irony; shrewd observation of personal and political manoeuvre; an apparently genuine sympathy for poverty and oppression; and a brisk readability characterized his novels.

D'ISRAELI, Isaac (1766–1848), father of B. *Disraeli, was the author of several discursive collections of literary history including *Curiosities of Literature* (1791–1834). His most remarkable and original work was *The Literary Character* (1795), in which he attempts to identify the qualities of temperament common to creative writers. *Calamities of Authors* followed in 1813, *Quarrels of Authors* in 1814. His study in five vols of *The Life and Reign of Charles I* appeared in 1828–30, and *Amenities of Literature* in 1840. He also published several novels and essays.

Dissertation upon Parties, A, see BOLINGBROKE, H. ST J.

Dissociation of Sensibility, a phrase coined by T. S. *Eliot in an essay entitled 'The Metaphysical Poets' (1921), to describe the 'something

which happened to the mind of England between the time of Donne or Lord Herbert of Cherbury and the time of Tennyson and Browning; it is the difference between the intellectual poet and the reflective poet.' Eliot suggests that by an increasing refinement of language, accompanied by an increasing crudity of feeling (*Gray is cruder than *Marvell), thought became separated from feeling. The phrase has given rise to much discussion; it is now more generally regarded as a comment on Eliot's own creative problems and innovations than as an objective historical analysis.

Dithyramb, a lyric poem in a lofty style with a flute accompaniment in the Phrygian mode originally antistrophic and sung in honour of Bacchus. Later dithyrambs were monostrophic and could be addressed to other gods.

Diurnalls, see NEWSBOOKS.

Diversions of Purley, Ἔπεα πτερόεντα *or*, see TOOKE, J.

Divina Commedia, the great work of *Dante, comprising the *Inferno*, the *Purgatorio*, and the *Paradiso*, in *terza rima.

The *Inferno* is a description of Hell, conceived as a graduated conical funnel, to the successive circles of which the various categories of sinners are assigned. The *Purgatorio* is a description of Purgatory, a mountain rising in circular ledges, on which are the various groups of repentant sinners. At the top of the mountain is the Earthly Paradise, where Dante encounters Beatrice. In his visit to Hell and Purgatory, Dante has for guide the poet *Virgil, and there he sees and converses with his lost friends or former foes. The *Paradiso* is a vision of a world of beauty, light, and song, where the Poet's guide is Beatrice. The poem is not only an exposition of the future life, but a work of moral edification, replete with symbolism and allusions based on Dante's wide knowledge of philosophy, astronomy, natural science, and history.

Dante's name first occurs in English in *Chaucer, and that of Beatrice in *Sidney; Dante was read and admired in the 17th cent. by *Milton, Jeremy *Taylor, and Sir T. *Browne, among others. The first acknowledged translation was by the artist Jonathan Richardson in 1719, a blank verse version of the famous Ugolino episode (*Inferno*, Canto 33), which remained a favourite with translators including T. *Gray; it was also the subject of one of *Blake's illustrations. His reputation rose in the 19th cent. with the admiration of *Byron, *Shelley, *Carlyle, and others. In the 20th cent. he profoundly influenced T. S. *Eliot; his essay *Dante* (1929) and the many references and quotations in his poetry brought Dante to the attention of a new readership.

Among well-known translations are those of H. F. *Cary (1805–14, blank verse); *Longfellow (1867, blank terzine); P. H. Wicksteed (1899, prose); H. F. Tozer (1904, prose); G. L. Bickersteth (1932–55, *terza rima*); L. *Binyon (1933–43, *terza rima*); J. D. Sinclair (1939–46, prose); D. L. *Sayers (1949–62, *terza rima*); and C. H. *Sisson (1980, unrhymed verse).

Divorce, *The Doctrine and Discipline of,* the first of *Milton's Divorce Tracts.

DIXON, Richard Watson (1833–1900), the intimate friend of Burne-Jones and W. *Morris. He was closely involved in the *Pre-Raphaelite movement before marriage and various preferments distanced him from his early life. He published an important *History of the Church of England from the abolition of the Roman jurisdiction* (1878–1902). His original and striking poetry found few but discriminating admirers, including *Bridges and G. M. *Hopkins; his correspondence with Hopkins (ed. C. C. Abbott, 1935), covering the years 1878–88, is of great interest. His long narrative poem *Mano* (1883), set in the year AD 999 as the world awaits the Millennium, recounts in *terza rima* the adventures of Mano, a Norman knight. Dixon is now better remembered for his shorter pieces ('Dream', 'The Wizard's Funeral'), reprinted with a memoir by Bridges in a selection in 1909.

DNB, see DICTIONARY OF NATIONAL BIOGRAPHY.

Dobbin, Colonel William, a character in Thackeray's *Vanity Fair.*

DOBELL, Sydney Thompson (1824–74), published *The Roman* (1850), a dramatic poem inspired by sympathy with oppressed Italy, and *Balder* (1854), one of the most extreme productions of the *Spasmodic school. This lengthy dramatic poem, of which only the first part was completed, describes the inner turmoil and aspirations of a young poet, who has taken his bride and baby daughter to live in 'a tower gloomy and ruinous' while he plans his great work. His search for the ultimate experience of death is rewarded by the death of his baby in mysterious circumstances; his wife Amy goes mad; and finally, unable to witness her sufferings, Balder kills her. Balder's destructive egoism so shocked readers that Dobell prefaced a second edition with an explanation claiming that his hero was not held up for admiration. In 1855 Dobell published (jointly with Alexander *Smith) *Sonnets on the War* and in 1856 *England in Time of War,* which contains the ballad with the refrain 'O Keith of Ravelston' ('A Nuptial Eve').

DOBSON, Henry Austin (1840–1921), an accomplished writer of verse of the lighter kind, with a particular fondness for French forms;

many of his best-known poems evoke the courtly elegance of French society of the 18th cent. His collections include *Vignettes in Rhyme* (1873), *Proverbs in Porcelain* (1877), and *At the Sign of the Lyre* (1885). His knowledge of the 18th cent. was also displayed in prose biographies of *Hogarth (1879), *Steele (1886), *Goldsmith (1888), Horace *Walpole (1890), S. *Richardson (1902), and F. *Burney (1903). He also published three series of *Eighteenth Century Vignettes* (1892–4–6), besides several volumes of collected essays.

Doctor, etc., The, a miscellany by R. *Southey, published 1834–47 (7 vols), chiefly renowned for containing the nursery story of 'The Three Bears'.

Doctor Angelicus, *Aquinas; **Invincibilis,** *Ockham; **Irrefragabilis,** *Alexander of Hales; **Mirabilis,** Roger *Bacon; **Subtilis,** *Duns Scotus; **Universalis,** *Albertus Magnus.

Dr Faustus, *The tragical history of,* a drama in blank verse and prose by *Marlowe, published 1604 and, in a radically different version known as the 'B-text', 1616. The earliest known performance was by the Lord Admiral's men in 1594. It is perhaps the first dramatization of the medieval legend of a man who sold his soul to the Devil, and who became identified with a Dr Faustus, a necromancer of the 16th cent. The legend appeared in the *Faustbuch,* first published at Frankfurt in 1587, and was translated into English as *The Historie of the damnable life, and deserved death of Doctor John Faustus.* Marlowe's play follows this translation in the general outline of the story, though not in the conception of the principal character, who from a mere magician becomes, under the poet's hand, a man athirst for infinite power, ambitious to be 'great Emperor of the world'.

Faustus, weary of the sciences, turns to magic and calls up Mephistopheles, with whom he makes a compact to surrender his soul to the Devil in return for 24 years of life; during these Mephistopheles shall attend on him and give him whatsoever he demands. Then follows a number of scenes in which the compact is executed, notable among them the calling up of Helen of Troy, where Faustus addresses Helen in the well-known line: 'Was this the face that launched a thousand ships . . .' The anguish of mind of Faustus as the hour for the surrender of his soul draws near is poignantly depicted. Both in its end and in the general conception of the character of Faustus, the play thus differs greatly from the *Faust* of *Goethe.

Doctor Fell, see FELL.

Dr Syntax, see COMBE, W.

Doctor Thorne, a novel by *A. Trollope, published 1858, the third of the *'Barsetshire' series.

DODD, William (1729–77), a popular preacher and the king's chaplain who forged a bond in the name of his former pupil, the 5th Lord Chesterfield. Despite the efforts of Dr *Johnson and others, he was convicted and hanged. His many works inlude *The Beauties of Shakespeare* (1752) and *Thoughts in Prison* (1777).

DODDRIDGE, Philip (1702–51), a Non-conformist divine, celebrated hymn-writer, and author of *The Rise and Progress of Religion in the Soul* (1745), a much reprinted work notable for its literary as well as its devotional quality. He published a life of Col. James Gardiner (1747), who figures in Scott's *Waverley*.

DODGSON, Charles Lutwidge (1832–98), celebrated under his pseudonym Lewis Carroll. He was educated at Rugby and Christ Church, Oxford, where he became a lecturer in mathematics in 1855. His most famous work *Alice's Adventures in Wonderland* (1865) originated in a boat trip with the young daughters of H. G. *Liddell, Lorina, Alice, and Edith; it was for Alice that he expanded an impromptu story into book form. *Through the Looking-Glass and What Alice Found There* followed in 1871; both volumes were illustrated by *Tenniel. One reviewer attributed the success of these works to the fact that, unlike most children's books of the period, they had no moral and did not teach anything. Dodgson's other works include *Phantasmagoria and other poems* (1869), *The Hunting of the Snark* (1876), and *Sylvie and Bruno* (1889, vol. 2, 1893). The most valuable of his various mathematical treatises is his light-hearted defence of Euclid, *Euclid and His Modern Rivals* (1879). Dodgson was also a keen amateur photographer, with a particular interest in photographing little girls, whose friendship he valued highly. His diaries were edited by R. L. Green (2 vols, 1953), his letters by M. N. Cohen with R. L. Green (2 vols, 1979).

DODINGTON, George Bubb (1691–1762), a time-serving politician who attained high office and a peerage (as Baron Melcombe) was author of a *Diary*, published posthumously in 1784, which throws much light on the venal politics of his day. It was edited in 1965 in 2 vols by J. Carswell and L. A. Dralle as *The Political Journal of George Bubb Dodington*. Dodington was also a patron of the arts, and in particular of James *Thomson, E. *Young, and H. *Fielding, who dedicated *Jonathan Wild* to him.

DODSLEY, Robert (1703–64), wrote several poems while a footman in the service of the Hon. Mrs Lowther, including *Servitude* (anon., 1729). He set up as a bookseller and wrote several plays, including a musical play, *The Blind Beggar of Bethnal Green* (1741). He is chiefly remembered as the publisher of works by *Pope, Dr *Johnson, E. *Young, *Goldsmith, T. *Gray, *Akenside, and *Shenstone and *A Collection of poems, by several hands* (1748–58, revised and continued by Pearch, 1775) was a classic and influential statement of mid-18th-cent. taste. In 1758 he founded, in conjunction with *Burke, *The Annual Register*. He also has the credit of having suggested the compiling of a dictionary to Dr Johnson.

Dodson and Fogg, in Dickens's *Pickwick Papers*, Mrs Bardell's attorneys.

Dogberry and Verges, in Shakespeare's *Much Ado about Nothing*, constables. Dogberry is a precursor of Mrs *Malaprop in his gift for misapplying words.

Doggerel, comic or burlesque, or trivial, mean, or irregular verse. The derivation is unknown, but cf. DOG-LATIN [OED].

Dog-Latin, bad unidiomatic Latin. ' "Nescio quid est materia cum me", Sterne writes to one of his friends (in dog-Latin, and very sad dog-Latin too)'; *Thackeray, *The English Humorists of the Eighteenth Century*, vi. Cf. DOGGEREL.

Dolabella, a character in Shakespeare's *Antony and Cleopatra*, and in Dryden's *All for Love*.

Dol Common, one of the cheaters in Jonson's *The Alchemist*.

Doll Tearsheet, Falstaff's tavern mistress in Shakespeare's *2 *Henry IV*.

Dolon, in Spenser's *Faerie Queene* (v. vi), 'A man of subtill wit and wicked minde', who tries to entrap *Britomart.

'Dolores', a poem in anapaests by *Swinburne, included in *Poems and Ballads* (1866).
  One of his most notorious works, it addresses Dolores, 'Our Lady of Pain', in a profane hymn to perverse and cruel sensual delights, and contains some of his most parodied lines, e.g. 'the lilies and languors of virtue' and 'the raptures and roses of vice'. It clearly shows Swinburne's obsession with erotic pain and the image of a 'splendid and sterile' *femme fatale*.

Dolorous Stroke, The, the stroke dealt by *Balyn to King Pellam in Bk II of Malory's *Morte D'Arthur*. The story is the starting point of the anthropological investigation in J. L. Weston's *From Ritual to Romance* (1920).

Dombey and Son, Dealings with the Firm of, a novel by *Dickens, published 1847–8.
  When the story opens Mr Dombey, the rich, proud, frigid head of the shipping house of Dombey and Son, has just been presented with a

son and heir, Paul, and his wife dies. The father's love and ambition are centred in the boy, a delicate, prematurely old child, who is sent to Dr Blimber's school, under whose strenuous discipline he sickens and dies. Dombey neglects his devoted daughter Florence, and the estrangement is increased by the death of her brother. Walter Gay, a good-hearted youth in Dombey's employment, falls in love with her, but is sent to the West Indies by Dombey, who disapproves of their relationship. He is shipwrecked and believed drowned. Dombey marries again—a proud and penniless young widow, Edith Granger, but his arrogant treatment drives her into the arms of his villainous manager Carker, with whom she flies to France. They are pursued, Carker meets Dombey in a railway station, falls in front of a train, and is killed. The house of Dombey fails; Dombey has lost his fortune, his son, and his wife; Florence has been driven by ill-treatment to fly from him, and has married Walter Gay, who has survived his shipwreck. Thoroughly humbled, Dombey lives in desolate solitude till Florence returns to him, and at last finds the way to his heart.

Among the other notable characters are Solomon Gills, the nautical instrument-maker and uncle of Gay, and his friend Cuttle, the genial old sea-captain; Susan Nipper, Florence's devoted servant; Toots, the innocent and humble admirer of Florence; Joe Bagstock, the gouty retired Major; and 'Cousin Feenix', the good-natured aristocrat.

Domesday Book, 'the Book of the day of assessment', is the name applied since the 12th cent. to the record of the great inquest or survey of the lands of England made by order of William the Conqueror in 1086. It contains a record of the ownership, area, and value of lands, and of the numbers of tenants, livestock, etc.

Dominic, Father, a character in Dryden's *The Spanish Fryar*.

Don, Arabella, a character in Hardy's *Jude the Obscure*.

Don Carlos, a tragedy by *Otway, in rhymed verse, produced 1676.

Philip II, king of Spain, having married Elizabeth of Valois, who had been affianced to his son Don Carlos, is stirred by jealousy by their mutual affection. This jealousy is inflamed by the machinations of Ruy Gomez and his wife the duchess of Eboli, till he believes in their guilty relations; he causes the queen to be poisoned and Don Carlos takes his own life, the king discovering too late their innocence.

Don Juan, according to a Spanish story apparently first dramatized by Gabriel Téllez (who wrote under the name 'Tirso da Molina')

in *El burlador de Sevilla*, and subsequently by Molière in *Le Festin de pierre* and in Mozart's *Don Giovanni*, was Don Juan Tenorio, of Seville. Having attempted to ravish Doña Anna, the daughter of the commander of Seville, he is surprised by the father, whom he kills in a duel. A statue of the commander is erected over his tomb. Juan and his cowardly servant Leporello visit the tomb, when the statue is seen to move its head. Juan jestingly invites it to a banquet. The statue comes, seizes Juan, and delivers him to devils. Don Juan is the proverbial heartless and impious seducer. His injured wife is Elvira.

Don Juan is also the subject of plays by *Shadwell (*The Libertine*), Goldoni, *Pushkin, and Montherlant, and of a poem by *Byron (see below). For R. *Browning's Don Juan see FIFINE AT THE FAIR, and for *Shaw's see MAN AND SUPERMAN. *Molière's version was translated by Christopher Hampton (pub. 1974). *The Joker of Seville* (pub. 1978) by *Walcott is an adaptation of *El Burlador de Sevilla*, based on R. *Campbell's blank verse translation.

Don Juan, an unfinished epic satire in *ottava rima* by Lord *Byron, published 1819-24.

Don Juan, a young gentleman of Seville, in consequence of an intrigue with Donna Julia, is sent abroad by his mother at the age of 16. His ship is wrecked and the passengers take to the long-boat. After many tribulations, Juan is cast up on a Greek island. He is restored to life by Haidée, the daughter of a Greek pirate, and the pair fall in love. The father, who is supposed dead, returns, finds the lovers together, and captures the fighting Juan, who is put in chains in one of the pirate's ships. He is then sold as a slave in Constantinople to a sultana who has fallen in love with him. He arouses her jealousy and is threatened with death, but escapes to the Russian army, which is besieging Ismail. Because of his gallant conduct he is sent with dispatches to St Petersburg, where he attracts the favour of the Empress Catherine, who sends him on a political mission to England. The last cantos (the 'English cantos') are taken up with a satirical description of social conditions in England and with the love affairs of Juan. The outspoken wit and satire are especially directed at hypocrisy in all its forms, at social and sexual conventions, and at sentimentality. There are many attacks on the objects of Byron's scorn: *Southey, *Coleridge, *Wordsworth, *Wellington, Lord Londonderry, and many others.

Don Juan himself is a charming, handsome young man, who delights in succumbing to beautiful women, but his character is little more than the connecting thread in a long social comedy.

DONLEAVY, J(ames) P(atrick) (1926–), novelist, born in Brooklyn of Irish parents, an Irish citizen since 1967. He is best known for *The*

Ginger Man (1955), a comic and bawdy account, much influenced by *Joyce, of Sebastian Dangerfield's adventures as a law student in Dublin. His other works include *A Singular Man* (1964), *The Beastly Beatitudes of Balthazar B* (1968), and *The Destinies of Darcy Dancer, Gentleman* (1977), all novels, and several plays, including *Fairy Tales of New York* (1960).

DONNE, John (1572–1631), related on his mother's side to Sir T. *More, was born into a devout Catholic family. Donne apparently renounced his faith in his early twenties. He sailed with *Essex to sack Cadiz (1596) and with *Ralegh to hunt the Spanish treasure ships off the Azores (1597). His poems 'The Storm' and 'The Calm' commemorate these voyages. He became secretary to Sir T. Egerton, Lord Keeper of the Great Seal, and in 1601 was elected MP for Brackley, Northants. However, late in 1601 he secretly married Ann More, Lady Egerton's niece, and was dismissed from Egerton's service and briefly imprisoned. Donne spent the next 14 years trying to live down his disgrace and find responsible employment. At first he lived on the charity of his friends and patrons. Among these were Sir Robert Drury of Hawstead, Suffolk, whom he had accompanied on his continental travels: he wrote his extravagant *Anniversaries* in honour of Sir Robert's dead child Elizabeth. Others included Sir Walter Chute, Sir Henry Goodyer (to whom many of Donne's letters are addressed), Lucy, countess of Bedford, Magdalen Herbert (mother of G. *Herbert), and Sir Robert Ker, Viscount Rochester (later earl of Somerset). Despite Ker's good offices, James I considered Donne unfit for confidential employment and urged him to enter the Church. James made him chaplain ordinary and forced Cambridge to grant him a DD. In the church Donne became a pluralist, being presented by influential friends to livings at Keyston, Sevenoaks, and Blunham, and in addition holding the divinity readership at Lincoln's Inn. After the death of his wife in 1617 (after giving birth to their twelfth child) Donne went to Germany as chaplain to the earl of Doncaster. His 'Hymn to Christ at the Author's last going into Germany', full of apprehension of death, was written before this journey. He won the favour of the duke of Buckingham and procured the deanery of St Paul's. Donne was one of the most celebrated preachers of his age and its greatest non-dramatic poet. He is regarded as the founder of the *Metaphysical group of poets.

Donne's earliest poems, his Satires and Elegies, belong to the 1590s. His unfinished satirical epic, 'The Progress of the Soul' is dated 1601 and some of his Holy Sonnets were probably written in 1610–11. His 'Songs and Sonnets' are largely impossible to date. His poems were collected by his son John (1633; enlarged edn 1635). His prose works include *Pseudo-Martyr* (1610), an attack on

Catholics who had died for their faith and an attempt to gain royal favour by encouraging surviving Catholics to take the oath of allegiance to James; *Ignatius His Conclave* (1611), a scurrilous onslaught on the Jesuits; *Biathanatos*, a defence of suicide which was unpublishable until after his death; *Essays in Divinity* (1651), composed in preparation for his ordination; and the *Devotions* (1924). His sermons, edited by his son John, appeared posthumously in 3 vols (1640, 1649, 1660). Before his death, I. *Walton (his earliest biographer) records, Donne had his portrait drawn wearing his shroud and standing on a funeral urn, as he would appear when rising from the grave at the Last Judgment.

Donnithorne, Arthur, a character in G. Eliot's *Adam Bede.

Don Quixote de la Mancha, a satirical romance by *Cervantes, published 1605, a second part appearing 1615. Cervantes gave to his work initially the form of a burlesque of the ballads and romances of chivalry (see AMADIS OF GAUL and PALMERIN OF ENGLAND). But the character of his hero developed and deepened and his work acquired the richness and profundity that have made it one of the most popular classics ever written.

Don Quixote, a poor gentleman of La Mancha, a man of amiable disposition, has had his wits disordered by inordinate devotion to the tales of chivalry, and imagines himself called upon to roam the world in search of adventures on his old horse, Rosinante, and accoutred in rusty armour, accompanied by his squire Sancho Panza, a curious mixture of shrewdness and credulity. Quixote conforms to chivalric tradition by electing a girl of the neighbouring village as the mistress of his heart, under the style of Dulcinea del Toboso, an honour of which she is entirely unaware. He is consequently involved in the most absurd adventures, as in the famous episode (Part I, ch. viii) when he tilts at windmills, imagining them to be giants. Finally one of his friends, the bachelor Samson Carrasco, in order to force him to return home, disguises himself as a knight, overthrows Don Quixote, and requires him to abstain for a year from chivalrous exploits. This period Don Quixote resolves to spend as a shepherd, living a pastoral life, but, falling sick on his return to his village, after a few days he dies. The plot also contains several lengthy digressions, including the story of the Curious Impertinent, and the story of *Cardenio and Lucinda.

The book was translated into English in 1616, by Thomas Shelton, and in 1700–3 by *Motteux; J. M. Cohen's Penguin classic version first appeared in 1950. *Don Quixote* supplied the plots of several 17th-cent. English plays, and inspired and continues to inspire innumerable imitations. Don Quixote and Quixotism have been described as the genius of the Spanish nation, but he has also been adopted by many other countries.

Don Saltero's Coffee House, founded by John Salter, one-time servant of Sir H. *Sloane about 1690; it stood in Cheyne Walk, Chelsea, and Salter (encouraged by Sloane) turned it into a museum of curios. It was still in existence when *Carlyle moved into Cheyne Walk in 1834.

Don Sebastian, a tragi-comedy by *Dryden, produced 1689, published 1691.

The play is based on the legend that King Sebastian of Portugal survived the battle of Alcazar. He and the princess Almeyda, with whom he is in love, are captured by Muley Moloch, who spares their lives until he discovers that they have secretly married. In love with Almeyda himself, he orders Dorax, a renegade Portuguese nobleman, to execute Sebastian, but Dorax, once Sebastian's favourite, refuses to do so. Muley Moloch is killed in a revolt, but Sebastian and Almeyda then discover that their marriage is incestuous, and they renounce each other and their thrones. The play is Dryden's most complex dramatic treatment of a number of important political, sexual, and religious themes.

Doolittle, Eliza, the flower seller in Shaw's *Pygmalion.

DOOLITTLE, Hilda (1886–1961), American poet, who wrote as 'H.D.', followed her friend *Pound to Europe, where both became leading members of the Imagist movement (see IMAGISM). She married *Aldington in 1913, but the marriage was not a success. Her several volumes of poetry, from her first, *Sea Garden* (1916), to her last, the quasi-epic *Helen in Egypt* (1961), show a deep involvement with classical mythology, a sharp, spare use of natural imagery, and interesting experiments with *vers libre*. She also published several novels, including *Bid Me to Live* (1960), a roman-à-clef about her *Bloomsbury years, and *Tribute to Freud* (1965), an account of her analysis by *Freud in 1933.

Doomsday Book, see DOMESDAY BOOK.

Dora Spenlow, in Dickens's *David Copperfield*, the hero's 'child-wife'.

Dorax, a character in Dryden's *Don Sebastian.

Doric, an adjective from Doris, a small district south of Thessaly from which the Dorians were conventionally supposed to have emigrated to the Peloponnese about the 12th cent. BC. The Dorian dialect was dominant in southern and western Greece in historical times. Since the Dorians were regarded as uncivilized by the Athenians, 'Doric' came to mean 'rustic' in English and was applied particularly to the language of Northumbria and the Lowlands of Scotland, and also to the simplest of the three orders in architecture.

Dorigen, the heroine of 'The Franklin's Tale' in Chaucer's *Canterbury Tales*, 12.

Dorimant, a character in Etherege's *The Man of Mode* based on *Rochester.

Dorothea, St, a Christian martyr who suffered in the persecution under Diocletian (303). Her story forms the subject of *The Virgin Martyr* by Massinger and Dekker.

Dorothea Brooke, the heroine of G. Eliot's *Middlemarch.

DORSET, earl of, see SACKVILLE, C., and SACKVILLE, T.

DOS PASSOS, John Roderigo (1896–1970), American novelist. His first important novel, *Three Soldiers* (1921), which has war as its subject, was followed by many others including *Manhattan Transfer* (1925) and *U.S.A.* (1938), a trilogy composed of *The 42nd Parallel* (1930), *1919* (1932), and *The Big Money* (1936). He also wrote poetry, plays, essays, travel books, and memoirs.

DOSTOEVSKY, Fyodor Mikhailovich (1821–81), Russian prose writer. The series of brilliant works on which his reputation is based are *Notes from Underground* (1864), *Crime and Punishment* (1866), *The Idiot* (1868), *The Devils* (1872), *An Adolescent* (*A Raw Youth*, 1875), and *The Brothers Karamazov* (1880). In these Dostoevsky reveals extraordinary powers of character analysis, considers profound religious and political ideas, and develops the Russian novel, both through the use of urban settings and by his gift for narrative tension. Many of Dostoevsky's novels appeared in English in the 1880s. R. L. *Stevenson was an early admirer, and the influence of *Crime and Punishment* on Stevenson's *Dr *Jekyll and Mr Hyde* (1886) is apparent. The main impact of his work in England followed the appearance of *Baring's *Landmarks in Russian Literature* (1910), *Murry's *Fyodor Dostoevsky* (1916), and above all the translations by C. *Garnett (1912–20). Opposition to Dostoevsky remained strong, however, led by H. *James, *Galsworthy, *Conrad, and D. H. *Lawrence. During the 20th cent. Dostoevsky has become the Russian writer most widely read and influential in England.

Dotheboys Hall, in Dickens's *Nicholas Nickleby*, the school conducted by Mr Squeers.

Double Dealer, The, a comedy by *Congreve, produced 1693, published 1694.

The promiscuous Lady Touchwood is in love with Mellefont, nephew and heir of Lord Touchwood. He rejects her advances, and she attempts to ruin his reputation, with the help of her one-time lover, Maskwell, the Double Dealer, whose intrigues are finally exposed.

Double Deceit, The, or *The Cure for Jealousy*, a comedy by W. *Popple.

Doubting Castle, in Bunyan's *Pilgrim's Progress*, the castle of Giant Despair.

DOUCE, Francis (1757–1834), antiquary and book-collector. His *Illustrations of Shakespeare* (1807) was a pioneering assemblage of sources and analogues. He bequeathed his personal collection of books, manuscripts (including the famous illuminated 'Douce Apocalypse'), and coins to the Bodleian Library, Oxford.

DOUGHTY, Charles Montagu (1843–1926), is principally remembered for his remarkable record of *Travels in Arabia Deserta* (1888) carried out in 1876–8, republished 1921 with an introduction by T. E. *Lawrence. It is notable for its extraordinary and eccentric style: Doughty mingled his own prose with Chaucerian and Elizabethan English and Arabic. His volumes of verse include the epic *The Dawn in Britain* (6 vols, 1906), *Adam Cast Forth* (a sacred drama, 1908), and *Mansoul, or the Riddle of the World* (1920).

Douglas, a romantic tragedy by J. *Home, based on a Scottish ballad, and first performed in Edinburgh in 1756.
  Old Norval, a shepherd, brings up the infant son of Douglas, supposed dead by his mother, now Lady Randolph. Young Norval saves Lord Randolph's life, and is reunited with his mother, only to be slain through the machinations of Randolph's heir, Glenalvon.

DOUGLAS, Lord Alfred Bruce (1870–1945), poet, and friend of *Wilde, who addressed to him his letter from prison *De Profundis*. Douglas translated Wilde's *Salome* from French to English (1894), and published several volumes of verse. He also wrote various defensive accounts of his relationship with Wilde, including *Oscar Wilde and myself* (1914) and the less extreme *Oscar Wilde: a summing up* (1940); his autobiography appeared in 1929.

Douglas, Ellen, heroine of Scott's *Lady of the Lake*.

DOUGLAS, Gawin, or Gavin (?1475–1522), Scottish poet and bishop of Dunkeld. He wrote an allegorical poem, *The Palice of Honour* (?1553), and *King Hart*, a homiletic allegory (1786), has also been attributed to him. He was best known for his translation of the *Aeneid* (*Eneados*, with prologues, 1553), the earliest translation of the classics into English; or rather, as he commented, into 'Scottis'. He was one of the first to draw the distinction between *Scots and 'Inglis' and, unlike many of his contemporaries, he wrote only in the vernacular.

DOUGLAS, George, the pseudonym of George Douglas Brown (1869–1902), the son of an Ayrshire farmer, published *The House with the Green Shutters* (1901) which was described as 'a masterpiece' by J. B. *Priestley. The work, in contrast with the sentimental view of Scotland depicted by the *'Kailyard School', is set in the village of Barbie and describes the rise of the tyrannical, dull-minded John Gourlay who builds his business on his feckless wife's dowry. His house, which becomes the 'passion of his life', gives him a sense of triumph over the village, but his world finally collapses with the failure of his business and the disgrace of his son, and retribution falls. Brown died suddenly the year after the novel's publication, leaving other works unfinished.

DOUGLAS, (George) Norman (1868–1952), novelist and essayist, is chiefly remembered for his travel books about Capri, Tunisia, and Calabria, published as *Siren Land* (1911), *Fountains in the Sand* (1912), and *Old Calabria* (1915); and for his novel *South Wind* (1917), which celebrates the pleasures of the hedonistic life on the island of Nepenthe.

DOUGLAS, Keith Castellain (1920–44), poet. He was killed in Normandy, and inevitably is remembered largely as a war poet, whose descriptions of wartime Cairo and desert fighting and whose contemplations of death show a rapidly maturing energy and simplicity of diction. His *Selected Poems* (1943) was the only volume published in his lifetime; *Alamein to Zem Zem* (1946) is a vivid experimental narrative of desert warfare; his *Collected Poems* appeared in 1951. A selection with an introduction by Ted *Hughes appeared in 1964 and the *Complete Poems* in 1979.

Douglas Tragedy, The, a ballad included in Sir W. Scott's *Minstrelsy of the Scottish Border*, the story of the carrying off of Lady Margaret by Lord William Douglas. They are pursued by her father and seven brothers, who fall in the ensuing fight. Douglas dies of his wounds and she does not survive him.

Dousterswivel, Herman, a character in Scott's *The Antiquary*.

Dove Cottage, near the north-east shore of Grasmere, occupied by *Wordsworth and his sister (1799–1807).

'**Dover Beach**', a poem by M. *Arnold.

DOWDEN, Edward (1843–1913), became professor of English literature at Trinity College, Dublin, in 1867. He was a noted Shakespearian scholar and published *Shakspere: A Critical Study of His Mind and Art* (1875) which influenced future approaches to Shakespearian biography; *Shakspere* (1877), a primer; and editions of single plays. He wrote other volumes of criticism, a life of *Shelley (1887), short biographies of *Southey, R. *Browning, and *Montaigne, and published editions of *Spenser and other English poets.

Dowel (Dobet, Dobest), see PIERS PLOWMAN.

DOWLAND, John (1563–1626), English composer and lutenist, generally considered the greatest of all English song-writers. His *The First Booke of Songs or Ayres of Foure Partes with Tableture for the Lute* (1597) is the earliest and most popular work of its kind. It was followed by *The Second Booke of Songs or Ayres* (1600), *The Third and Last Booke of Songs* (1603), and *A Pilgrimes Solace* (1612). A few of the texts set by Dowland are by courtly amateurs (Sir F. *Greville, Sir E. *Dyer, the earls of *Essex), but many more (e.g. 'In darknesse let mee dwell'; 'Flow, my teares') are by unknown authors.

Down with Knavery, see HEY FOR HONESTY.

DOWSON, Ernest Christopher (1867–1900) established himself in the London society of *Beardsley, *Le Gallienne, *Wilde, and their friends. He contributed poems to the *Yellow Book*, the *Savoy*, and the anthologies published by the *Rhymers' Club. He was received into the Roman Catholic Church in 1891. Dowson's stories *Dilemmas* appeared in 1895. The first of his two books of poetry, *Verses* (containing his celebrated 'Non Sum Qualis Eram', better known as 'Cynara'), appeared in 1896, and *Decorations* in 1899. His one-act verse play *The Pierrot of the Minute* was published in 1897. The poems, which display much variety in stanza and prosody, group themselves chiefly into love poetry, including 'Cynara'; devotional poems; poems of the natural world; and above all poems of ennui and world-weariness, such as the well-known 'Vitae Summa Brevis' ('They are not long, the days of wine and roses'), 'To One in Bedlam', and several translations and adaptations of Verlaine. See also ART FOR ART'S SAKE.

DOYLE, Arthur Conan (1859–1930), is chiefly remembered for his creation of the amateur detective Sherlock Holmes, whose brilliant solutions to a wide variety of crimes began in *A Study in Scarlet* (1887) and continued through a long line of stories, collected in *The Adventures of Sherlock Holmes* (1892), *The Memoirs of Sherlock Holmes* (1894), *The Hound of the Baskervilles* (1902), and other works. His friend and foil Dr Watson, with whom he shares rooms in Baker Street, attends him throughout most of his adventures. Doyle also wrote a long series of historical and other romances, notably *Micah Clarke* (1889); *The White Company* (1891); *The Exploits of Brigadier Gerard* (1896), the first of many 'Gerard' tales; *Rodney Stone* (1896); and *The Lost World* (1912), the first of a series of stories dominated by Professor Challenger. Doyle later wrote many books on public themes. He published a *History of Spiritualism* (1926), a subject in which he was greatly interested.

DOYLE, Richard (1824–83), illustrator, designed the cover of *Punch (with Mr Punch, Toby, and a margin of nymphs, goblins, and satyrs) that lasted from 1844 to 1956. He illustrated chiefly fairy stories, including *Ruskin's *The King of the Golden River* (1851) and W. *Allingham's *In Fairyland* (1870), and also some of *Dickens's Christmas Books; and published books of annotated drawings, including *The Foreign Tour of Brown, Jones and Robinson* (1854), whose comic adventures he had depicted in *Punch*.

Drab, term used first by C. S. *Lewis (*English Literature in the Sixteenth Century*, Introduction) to denote poetry and prose of the later medieval period until the early Renaissance: 'a period in which, for good or ill, poetry has little richness either of sound or images'. The term has generally been used, by Lewis and by later critics, to characterize works of the Tudor period which are unappealing to a modern ear. Typically, 'Drab' poets wrote in strongly rhythmical verse forms such as *poulter's measure, making use of alliteration and of poetic 'fillers' such as 'eke', and employed few Latinate words. Yet many so-called 'Drab' writers, such as *Wyatt, have been much admired in modern times. The Tudor translators of *Seneca's plays were highly regarded by T. S. *Eliot, and many other 'Drab' translations were of crucial importance for the later Renaissance in England, such as Sir T. *Hoby's version of *Castiglione's *Il Cortegiano* (1561) and A. *Golding's of *Ovid's *Metamorphoses* (1567).

DRABBLE, Margaret (1939–), novelist, born in Sheffield. Her first novel, *A Summer Birdcage* (1962), was followed by several others, including *The Millstone* (1966), which were associated with the new feminism of the 1960s: her later novels (*The Needle's Eye*, 1972; *The Ice Age*, 1977) have had a broader social range, although women's issues continue to play a significant part.

Dracula, a novel by B. *Stoker, published 1897, the most famous of all tales of vampirism.

The story is told through the diaries of a young solicitor, Jonathan Harker, his fiancée Mina, her friend Lucy Westenra, and Dr John Seward, the superintendent of a large lunatic asylum at Purfleet, in Essex. It begins with Harker's journey to Count Dracula's eerie castle in Transylvania. After various horrifying experiences as an inmate of the castle, Jonathan goes to a ruined chapel, where he finds 50 great wooden boxes filled with earth recently dug from the graveyard of the Draculas, in one of which the Un-Dead Count is lying, gorged with blood. The boxes are shipped to Whitby and thence to Carfax. Dracula disembarks at Whitby in the shape of a wolf, having dispatched the entire ship's crew *en route*, and proceeds to vampirize Lucy who despite multiple blood transfusions and the occult precautions of Dr Seward's old teacher Professor Van Helsing dies drained of blood but remains Un-Dead until staked through the heart. The rest of the book tells of the attempt to save Mina from Dracula's insidious advances and of the search for the boxes of earth, his only refuge between sunrise and sunset. All but one of these are neutralized with fragments of the Host. The last, with Dracula in it, is followed by Van Helsing and the others back to Transylvania where, after a thrilling chase, the Count is beheaded and stabbed through the heart, at which his body crumbles to dust.

Dracula—tall and thin, with his beaky nose, pointed ears, cruel and sensual features, and 'peculiarly shaped white teeth' protruding over his lips—has been the subject of many films.

Dragon of Wantley, The, a humorous ballad, probably of the 17th cent., satirizing the old verse romances. It tells of a Yorkshire dragon that devoured children and cattle, and was killed by Moore of Moore Hall. It was included in Percy's *Reliques*. *Carey's opera The Dragon of Wantley* was performed in 1737.

DRAKE, Sir Francis (?1540–96), circumnavigator and admiral. In 1577 he set out in the *Pelican* (afterwards renamed the *Golden Hind*) for the river Plate, sailed through the Straits of Magellan, plundered Valparaiso, rounded the Cape of Good Hope, and completed the circumnavigation of the world. He was knighted by Elizabeth on his return in 1581. In 1587 he destroyed a Spanish armament in the harbour of Cadiz. Drake, as vice-admiral, commanded one of the divisions of the English fleet against the Armada. The narratives of some of his expeditions figure in *Hakluyt and *Purchas, and he became the hero of many legends. *Newbolt assimilated Drake's achievements into the public school ideal in his popular poem 'Drake's Drum' (1895).

Dramatic Idyls, a volume of six poems, by R. *Browning, published in 1879. After the publication of a sequel (below), the collection was called 'Dramatic Idyls, First Series'. The poems are among the finest of Browning's later period, particularly 'Ivàn Ivànovitch', a story based on a Russian folk-tale of a woman who threw her children to the wolves in order to save her own life. The collection focuses on human behaviour in conditions of extreme stress.

Dramatic Idyls, *Second Series,* a volume of six poems by R. *Browning, published 1880. The collection demonstrates Browning's continuing interest and vitality in the dramatic monologue form, notably 'Clive'.

Dramatic irony, or Tragic irony, a figure of speech in which what is said by the characters in a play has a different and more serious meaning to the audience who are more aware than are the characters concerned of the catastrophe which is either impending or has occurred. As, for example, Duncan's speech in *Macbeth on arriving at Macbeth's castle, where his murder has already been planned, or Macbeth's 'Fail not our feast' to Banquo when he has arranged Banquo's murder for that same evening.

Dramatic Lyrics, a collection of poems by R. *Browning, published in 1842 as no. III of *Bells and Pomegranates. The collection included some of Browning's best-known poems such as 'My Last Duchess', 'Porphyria's Lover', and 'The Pied Piper of Hamelin'.

Dramatic monologue, generally, a poem delivered as though by a single imagined person, frequently but not always to an imagined auditor: the speaker is not to be identified with the poet, but is dramatized, usually ironically, through his or her own words. One of its most accomplished exponents was R. *Browning ('My Last Duchess', 1842; 'Caliban upon Setebos', 1864). The form was employed by many 19th- and 20th-cent. poets, including *Tennyson, *Hardy, *Kipling, *Frost, *Pound, and T. S. *Eliot.

Dramatic Romances and Lyrics, a collection of poems by R. *Browning, published 1845 as no. VII of *Bells and Pomegranates. The collection included some of Browning's best-known poems, such as 'How They Brought the Good News from Ghent to Aix', 'The Lost Leader', and 'The Flight of the Duchess'.

Dramatis Personae, a collection of poems by R. *Browning, published 1864. They were marked by Browning's grief after the death of his wife (see BROWNING, E. B.) in 1861, and by his searching examination of the relation of human to divine love, especially as it concerns the nature of belief. Several of the poems are anthology favourites—notably 'Rabbi Ben Ezra' and 'Prospice'—but the heart of the collection are the long dramatic monologues such as 'A Death in the Desert', 'Caliban upon Setebos', and 'Mr Sludge, "the Medium" '.

DRAPER, Mrs Elizabeth (1744–78), the wife of Daniel Draper (an official of the East India Company), with whom *Sterne fell in love in 1767 and to whom he wrote the *Journal to* Eliza* and *Letters of Yorick to Eliza.*

Drapier's Letters, The, a series of pamphlets published by *Swift in 1724. The word 'Drapier'='Draper'.

A patent had been granted to the duchess of Kendal for supplying copper coins for use in Ireland, and by her had been sold to a certain William Wood for £10,000. In 1723 the Irish Houses of Parliament voted addresses protesting against the transaction, and Swift, writing in the character of a Dublin draper, published a series of four letters in which he prophesied ruin to the Irish if 'Wood's half-pence' were admitted into circulation; a fifth letter of protest, also signed Drapier, was addressed to *Molesworth. The letters produced an immense effect and the government was forced to abandon the project and compensate Wood. Swift thus became an Irish national hero.

Drawcansir, a character in Buckingham's *The Rehearsal,* parodying Almanzor in *Dryden's *The Conquest of Granada.*

DRAWCANSIR, Sir Alexander, pseudonym of H. *Fielding, under which he contributed to the *Covent Garden Journal.*

DRAYTON, Michael (1563–1631), of whose personal life little is known. He died in comparative poverty, but was buried in Westminster Abbey.

He was an extremely prolific writer, producing historical, *topographical, and religious verse, as well as odes, sonnets, and satires. He published *Idea. The Shepheards Garland* (1593), eclogues in the Spenserian manner including praise of Queen Elizabeth and lament for the death of *Sidney; *Ideas Mirrour* (1594), a sonnet sequence, which in its final version, entitled *Idea* (1619), included the famous sonnet 'Since there's no help, come let us kiss and part'. His poems on legendary and historical figures began *c.*1593 with *Peirs Gaveston,* followed by *Matilda* (1594), *Robert, Duke of Normandy* (1596), and *Mortimeriados* (1596), later revised as *The Barrons Warres* (1603). *Englands Heroicall Epistles* (1597) was modelled on *Ovid's *Heroides*; it consists of twelve pairs of verse letters exchanged by lovers from English history. Among later works are *The Owle* (1604), an obscure satire; and *Odes* (1606). This innovatory collection included his 'Ballad of Agincourt', which opens with the lines:

> Fayre stood the winde for *France*
> When we our sailes advaunce.

He later wrote a narrative poem on the same subject, *The Battaile of Agincourt* (1627); the same volume also included *The Miseries of Queene Margarite,* *Nimphidia, The Court of Fayrie,* and the interesting epistle to Henry Reynolds 'Of Poets and Poesie'. Drayton's largest project is his great topographical poem on England, *The Poly-Olbion,* written 1598–1622.

'Dream, The', a poem by Lord *Byron, written 1816, describing his long love for his cousin Mary Chaworth and the disaster of his marriage to Annabella Milbanke.

Dream of Gerontius, The, see NEWMAN, J. H.

Dream of John Ball, A, a historical socialist fantasy by W. *Morris, published in 1888. It takes the form of a dream in which the narrator is carried back to the early stages of the peasants' revolt in 1381; he encounters the 'hedge-priest' John Ball, and in their final night-long dialogue Morris both satirizes the 19th-cent. present and offers hope for a future.

Dream of the Rood, an Old English poem of 156 lines, in the *Vercelli Book, in three parts: a description of the poet's vision of the cross and the address to him by the cross describing the Crucifixion (paralleled in part by the inscriptions on *Ruthwell Cross); a homiletic address to the dreamer by the cross; and a declaration of faith and confidence in Heaven by the dreamer himself.

DREISER, Theodore Herman Albert (1871–1945), American novelist. His first novel, *Sister Carrie* (1900), is a powerful account of a working girl's rise to worldly success, and of the slow decline of her lover and protector Hurstwood. It was withheld from circulation by its publishers, who were apprehensive about Dreiser's frank and amoral treatment of Carrie's sexuality and ambition. Other novels include *Jennie Gerhardt* (1911) and a trilogy about an unscrupulous business magnate, Frank Cowperwood (*The Financier,* 1912; *The Titan,* 1914; *The Stoic,* 1947). *An American Tragedy* (1925) is the story of Clyde Griffiths, who escapes from his evangelist parents to the exciting and colourful life of a bell-boy in a Kansas City hotel; he moves to New York State to work in a collar factory, and when his girl-friend Roberta becomes pregnant he drowns her, possibly accidentally, and is tried and condemned to death. Dreiser's many other works include *Dreiser Looks at Russia* (1928) and *America is Worth Saving* (1941), which express the growing faith in Socialism that replaced the nihilistic naturalism and pessimism of his earlier works.

'Dreme, The', see LINDSAY, D.

DRINKWATER, John (1882–1937), a prolific poet, dramatist, critic, and actor. His work appeared in all five volumes of *Georgian Poetry*, and was collected in 1933 in *Summer Harvest*. He wrote many plays, including *Abraham Lincoln* (1918), *Oliver Cromwell* (1921), *Mary Stuart* (1922), and a successful comedy *Bird in Hand* (1927). He also wrote stories and plays for children, and many critical works.

DROESHOUT, Martin (1601–c.1650), engraver of the portrait of Shakespeare on the title-page of the First *Folio (1623).

Drolls, or **Droll-Humours**, in Commonwealth days when stage plays were forbidden, were farces or comic scenes adapted from existing plays or invented by the actors, produced generally at fairs or in taverns. Most were published after the Restoration by Francis Kirkman in *The Wits, or Sport upon Sport* (two parts, 1662, 1673).

Dromio, the name of the twin slaves in Shakespeare's *The Comedy of Errors*.

Drugger, Abel, the credulous tobacconist of Jonson's *The Alchemist*. The character was one of *Garrick's most famous parts.

Druidism, see STUKELEY, W.

DRUMMOND OF HAWTHORNDEN, William (1585–1649), was a correspondent of *Drayton, and in 1618/19 was visited by *Jonson, an event recorded in his Conversations; Jonson found Drummond's own poetry 'smelled too much of the schools', but some of his shorter pieces show originality and power. Drummond's poems were edited by E. *Phillips in 1656. His works include pamphlets and verses in the Royalist cause, laments for the early death of his betrothed, satires and hymns, and a history of Scotland 1423–1524 (1655). His best-known prose work was *A Cypresse Grove* (1623), a meditation on death.

Drury Lane, London, named after the Drury family. The Theatre Royal, Drury Lane, was originally a cock-pit, converted into a theatre in the times of James I. It was rebuilt by T. *Killigrew (1612–83), again by Sir C. *Wren in 1674, and again in 1812. *Garrick, Mrs *Siddons, J. P. *Kemble, and *Kean are among the famous actors who have appeared there. In the 19th cent. it was the great house of Christmas pantomimes, and after the Second World War many successful American musicals were staged there.

Dryasdust, Dr Jonas, a fictitious character, a prosy antiquarian, to whom Sir W. *Scott addresses the prefaces of some of his novels.

DRYDEN, John (1631–1700), was educated at Westminster School under *Busby and at Trinity College, Cambridge. His first major poem was the *Heroique Stanza's* (1658) on the death of Cromwell; he later celebrated the king's return with *Astraea Redux* and *To His Sacred Majesty*. Other poems were addressed to Sir Robert Howard (whose sister, Lady Elizabeth, Dryden married in 1663), the earl of *Clarendon, Charleton, and Lady Castlemaine. He also published a long poem in quatrains, *Annus Mirabilis* (1667), but most of his early writing was for the theatre and included several rhymed heroic plays: *The Indian Queen* (1664), *The Indian Emperour* (1665), *Tyrannick Love* (1669), and *The Conquest of Granada* (1670, in two parts). He also wrote comedies, including *The Wild Gallant* (1663), *The Rival Ladies* (1664), and *An Evening's Love* (1668). He was most original with his tragi-comedies, *Secret Love* (1667), *Marriage à-la-Mode* (1672), and *The Assignation* (1672). All these plays, together with adaptations of *Paradise Lost (The State of Innocence, and the Fall of Man, 1667), *The Tempest* (1667), and *Troilus and Cressida* (1679), reveal Dryden's considerable interest in philosophical and political questions. He became poet laureate in 1668, and historiographer royal in 1670.

Dryden constantly defended his own literary practice. His first major critical work was *Of Dramatick Poesie* (1668). However *Aureng-Zebe* (1675), his best heroic play, has a prologue denouncing rhyme in serious drama, and his next play, *All for Love* (1678), was in blank verse. At the same time he reverted to an earlier high evaluation of *Jonson. This flexibility as critic and dramatist left him vulnerable to attack. He was represented as Bayes in *The Rehearsal* (1671) by *Buckingham, and physically assaulted in 1679, possibly at the instigation of *Rochester. But his principal opponent was *Shadwell, whom Dryden ridiculed in *Mac-Flecknoe* (1682). He develops his critical principles in many notably fluent prologues and epilogues, and poems about, or addressed to, fellow-writers and artists.

The constitutional crisis of the late 1670s troubled Dryden greatly. Three plays, *The Duke of Guise* (1679, written with Lee), *Mr Limberham* (1679), and *The Spanish Fryar* (1681), and his prologues and epilogues, testify to this. His interest in religion also heightened at this time. He produced his most celebrated satires in the early 1680s, *Absalom and Achitophel* (1681), *The Medall* (1682), and 200 lines for N. *Tate's *The Second Part of Absalom and Achitophel* (1682), as well as *Religio Laici* (1682), a defence of the Anglican *via media*. However, following the accession of James II Dryden became a Catholic and wrote *The Hind and the Panther* (1687) in support of his new co-religionists. At the death of Charles II he attempted a pindaric ode (see PINDAR), *Threnodia Augustalis* (1685), the first of several poems in this form, notably *To the Pious Memory . . . of Mrs Ann Killigrew* (1686), and *Alexander's Feast* (1697), which was later incorporated into *Fables Ancient and Modern* (1700).

In 1688 he lost both his court offices and returned to the theatre. Two of his late plays, *Don Sebastian* (1689) and *Amphitryon* (1690), are excellent, but Dryden was tired of the theatre and turned to translating. His immense and splendid achievements in this field include translations of small pieces from *Theocritus and *Horace, and more substantial passages from *Homer, *Lucretius, *Persius, *Juvenal, *Ovid, *Boccaccio, and *Chaucer, as well as the whole of *Virgil. His version of the *Georgics* is especially magnificent. He also returned to criticism, notably in 'A Discourse concerning the Original and Progress of Satire' (1693). His culminating and most impressive achievement both as critic and translator was *Fables Ancient and Modern* (1700), with its famous coda, 'The Secular Masque'. He was buried in Westminster Abbey. (See also RESTORATION.)

DU BARTAS, Guillaume de Salluste, Seigneur (1544–90), French poet. His most famous work was the creation epic *La Semaine* (1578, complete English trans. by *Sylvester, 1605). Partly because of his Protestant convictions, he was more influential in England than in France; *Spenser, *Sidney, and *Milton were familiar with his work.

DU BELLAY, Joachim (1522–60), French poet, some of whose sonnets were translated by *Spenser as *The Visions of Bellay*, appended to the *Complaints* of 1591.

DUBRIC, or **DUBRICIUS, St** (d. 612), the reputed founder of the bishopric of Llandaff, said by *Geoffrey of Monmouth to have crowned *Arthur king of Britain at Silchester. He is mentioned in Tennyson's *'The Coming of Arthur'.

Duchess of Malfi, The (*The Tragedy of the Dutchesse of Malfy*), by *Webster, written 1612/13, printed 1623.

The duchess, a high-spirited and high-minded widow, reveals her love for the honest Antonio, steward at her court, and secretly marries him, despite the warnings of her brothers, Ferdinand, duke of Calabria, and the Cardinal, and immediately after informing them that she has no intention of remarrying. Their resistance appears to be induced by consideration for their high blood, and by, as Ferdinand later asserts, a desire to inherit her property; there is also a strong suggestion of Ferdinand's repressed incestuous desire for her. The brothers place in her employment as a spy the cynical ex-galley-slave Bosola, who betrays her to them; she and Antonio fly

and separate. She is captured and is subjected by Ferdinand and Bosola to fearful mental tortures, including the sight of the feigned corpse of her husband and the attendance of a group of madmen; finally she is strangled with her two children and Cariola, her waiting woman. Retribution overtakes the murderers: Ferdinand goes mad, imagining himself a wolf; the Cardinal is killed by the now remorseful Bosola, and Bosola by Ferdinand. Bosola has already killed Antonio, mistaking him for the Cardinal. The humanity and tenderness of the scenes betweeen the Duchess, Antonio, and their children; the pride and dignity of the Duchess in her suffering; and individual lines such as the celebrated 'Cover her face: Mine eyes dazell: she di'd yong' have long been admired.

DUCK, Stephen (1705–56), began his working life as a farm labourer. Almost entirely self-educated, he took to writing verse, and came to the notice of Queen Caroline, who gave him a pension and made him a yeoman of the guard in 1733. In 1746 he took Holy Orders but drowned himself four years later in a fit of despondency. His best-known poem, *The thresher's labour* (in heroic couplets), is a vividly realistic portrayal of the unremitting toil of the labourer's life. (See also PRIMITIVISM.)

DUDLEY, Robert, earl of Leicester (?1532–88), courtier and favourite of Queen Elizabeth I. Uncle of Sir P. *Sidney he was a notable patron of writers and poets, including *Spenser. His personal power and ambitions provoked many literary attacks, notably by Scott in *Kenilworth* in which Dudley's unfortunate wife Amy Robsart also figures.

Duenna, The, a comic opera-play by R. B. *Sheridan, produced 1775. The play contains much music, a great deal of which consists of pleasant airs familiar to the audiences of the time.

Duessa, in Spenser's *Faerie Queene*, the daughter of Deceit and Shame, Falsehood in general, in Bk I signifies in particular the Roman Catholic Church, and in Bk v. ix, Mary Queen of Scots.

DUFFY, Maureen Patricia (1933–   ), writer, has published plays, poetry, and non-fiction (including a life of A. *Behn, *The Passionate Shepherdess*, 1977), but is perhaps best known for her novels which include *That's How It Was* (1962), a moving autobiographical account of her childhood and of her relationship with her mother, who died of tuberculosis when she was 14; and several others, some of which deal with the subject of homosexuality frankly and with dignity. They include *The Paradox Players* (1967), *Wounds* (1969), *Capital* (1975), and *Londoners* (1983), a sardonic view of the writer's lot in the bedsitter London of Earl's Court; the sex of the narrator, Al, is left intentionally ambiguous.

DUGDALE, Sir William (1605–86), author of *The Antiquities of Warwickshire* (1656), a topographical history that set new standards of fullness and accuracy for the genre and inspired, amongst others, A. *Wood. His *Monasticon Anglicanum* (3 vols, 1655–73; in collaboration with Roger Dodsworth) is an account of the English monastic houses.

Duke of Milan, The, a tragedy by *Massinger, printed 1623. It is based on the story of Herod and Marianne as told by Josephus. The play relates the unsuccessful efforts of Francisco, the favourite of Lodovico Sforza, duke of Milan, to corrupt Sforza's wife Marcelia in revenge for Sforza's dishonouring of Francisco's sister: a plot of intrigue and jealousy ends with the death of the three principal characters.

Duke's Children, The, a novel by A. *Trollope, published 1880, the last novel in the *'Palliser' series.

Dulcinea del Toboso, the name given by *Don Quixote to his chosen mistress; hence the English use of the name Dulcinea for a sweetheart.

Dumaine, in Shakespeare's *Love's Labour's Lost*, one of the three lords attending the king of Navarre.

DU MAURIER, Dame Daphne (1907–), novelist and granddaughter of George *du Maurier. Many of her popular novels and period romances, including her most famous, *Rebecca* (1938), are set in the West Country where she spent much of her life.

DU MAURIER, George Louis Palmella Busson (1834–96), artist and writer. He contributed to *Punch and other periodicals, and illustrated editions of *Mrs Gaskell, *Meredith, *Hardy, and H. *James. He wrote humorous verse, including 'The History of the Jack Sprats', and a parody of W. *Morris's ballads, 'The Legend of Camelot', with mock *Pre-Raphaelite illustrations. In 1891 he published his first novel, *Peter Ibbetson*, and in 1894, *Trilby, for which he is still remembered. *The Martian*, a story based on school life, appeared posthumously in 1897.

Dumbello, Lady, in A. Trollope's *Barsetshire series of novels, the married name of Griselda, daughter of Archdeacon Grantly.

Dumbiedikes, The Laird of, in Scott's *The Heart of Midlothian*, (1) the grasping landlord of the widow Butler and Davie Deans; (2) Jock Dumbie, his son, Jeanie Deans's silent suitor.

Dumb Show, a piece of silent action or stage business, especially in the Elizabethan and Jacobean theatre. These shows, such as the one before the play scene in *Hamlet, suggest by mime and symbolism what is shortly to take place and its meaning.

DUNBAR, William (?1456–?1513), Scottish poet and priest. In 1503 he wrote 'The Thrissill and the Rois', a political allegory in rhyme-royal, the Rose representing Margaret Tudor, married to James IV, the Thistle, and in 1507, 'The Dance of the Sevin Deidly Synnis', in which the poet in a trance sees the fiend Mahoun call a dance of unshriven outcasts. At about the same time he wrote 'The Tretis of the Tua Mariit Wemen and the Wedo', a visionary dialogue in which the three interlocutors relate their experiences of marriage; and 'The Goldyn Targe', an allegory in which the poet, appearing in a dream before the court of Venus, is wounded by the arrows of Beauty in spite of the shield ('targe') of Reason. The 'Lament for the Makaris' is a powerful elegy for the transitoriness of things, with its refrain *Timor mortis conturbat me*', in which the poet bewails the deaths of his fellow poets including *Chaucer, *Gower, and *Henryson. Dunbar's satirical energy and Rabelaisian humour are particularly well displayed in 'The Flyting of Dunbar and Kennedie'.

Duncan, king of Scotland in Shakespeare's *Macbeth; murdered by Macbeth.

Dunciad, The, a mock-heroic satire by *Pope, of which three books were published anonymously in 1728. Its authorship was acknowledged in 1735. The *New Dunciad* was published in 1742, and forms the fourth book of the complete work as it appeared in 1743. The poem had been under preparation for some years and its issue was determined by the criticisms of Pope's edition of Shakespeare contained in *Theobald's *Shakespeare Restored*. Theobald was made the hero of the poem in its earlier form, but in the final edition of 1743 C. *Cibber was enthroned in his stead. The satire is directed against 'Dulness' in general, and in the course of it all the authors who have earned Pope's condemnation are held up to ridicule. But the work is not confined to personal abuse, for literary vices receive their share of exposure. The argument of the poem is as follows.

Bk I. The reign of Dulness is described. Bayes (i.e. Cibber) is carried off by the goddess and anointed king in the place of *Eusden, the poet laureate, who has died.

Bk II. This solemnity is graced by games, in which poets, critics, and booksellers contend.

Bk III. The king is transported to the Elysian shades, where, under the guidance of *Settle, he sees visions of the past and future triumphs of the empire of Dulness, how this shall extend to the theatres and the court, the arts and the sciences.

Bk IV. The realization of these prophecies is described, and the subjugation of the sciences and universities to Dulness, the growth of indolence, the corruption of education, and the consummation of all in the restoration of night and chaos.

Dun Cow, Book of the, an Irish manuscript of the 11th cent. containing mythological romances. A fragment of it survives, containing in particular many of the feats of *Cuchulain.

Dun in the Mire, where 'Dun' (originally a dun horse) is a quasi-proper name for any horse, an old Christmas game (also called 'drawing Dun out of the mire'), in which the horse in the mire is represented by a heavy log, and the players compete to lift and carry it off.

> If thou art Dun, we'll draw thee from the mire.

> (Shakespeare, *Romeo and Juliet, I. iv. 41)

Dunmow Flitch, according to an ancient custom of the manor of Dunmow in Essex, a side of bacon given to any married couple who after twelve months of marriage could swear that they had maintained perfect harmony and fidelity. There is reference to it in the Prologue to Chaucer's 'Wife of Bath's Tale' (*Canterbury Tales, 6). The custom is said to have been instituted by Robert Fitz-Walter in 1244 and is still observed.

DUNN, Nell (1936–), novelist and playwright, whose early novels Up the Junction (1963) and Poor Cow (1967) showed a sensitive ear for working-class dialogue and an uninhibited approach to female sexuality. Her other works include The Only Child (1978, a tale of the rich) and Steaming (perf. 1981), a comedy with an all-female cast set in a Turkish bath.

DUNNE, J(ohn) W(illiam) (1875–1949), pioneer aircraft designer and author of the widely-read An Experiment with Time (1927) and The Serial Universe (1934), in which he outlined a theory of time to account for such phenomena as precognition, previsional dreaming, etc. Dunne's concept proved a useful dramatic device to J. B. *Priestley in his 'Time' plays.

DUNSANY, Edward John Moreton Drax Plunkett, 18th Baron (1878–1957), of Anglo-Irish parentage, was associated with the *Irish revival, and a friend of *Yeats, *Gogarty, and Lady *Gregory. His first book of (non-Celtic) mythological tales, The Gods of Pegana (1905), was illustrated by S. H. Sime, whose weird fin-de-siècle drawings were to accompany many subsequent fantasies, including The Book of Wonder (1912) and The Blessing of Pan (1927). Dunsany's first play, The Glittering Gate, was performed at the *Abbey Theatre in 1909; this and many later plays show the influence of Maeterlinck's not dissimilar vein of fantasy. If (an *oriental tale) was a success in London in 1921. Dunsany wrote the popular 'Jorkens' stories, beginning with The Travel Tales of Mr Joseph Jorkens (1931).

DUNS SCOTUS, John (c. 1266 or 1270–1308), the 'Doctor Subtilis', a Scottish Franciscan. He lectured on the Sentantiae of *Peter Lombard at Oxford (c. 1300–4) and at Paris (c. 1304–5). His principal works were his two series of commentaries on the Sentantiae, the Reportata Parisiensia (?1306) and the Opus Oxoniense (?1297). He wrote many other works, though many of those attributed to him are of disputed authorship (such as the De Anima and the important, advanced Theoremata). His principal significance in the history of *Scholasticism is that he drove the first wedge between theology and philosophy with his emphasis on the separation ' tween God as necessary Being from all con-...igent Beings, and the impossibility of arguing from the latter to the former. Although this emphasis, together with his associated Augustinian–Franciscan stress on faith and will rather than reason, distinguishes him from the synthesis of *Aquinas, he resembles him in the employment of an emphatically *Realist metaphysics in the theory of Essences, and in his incorporation of a good deal of *Aristotle into his metaphysics. He was much influenced too by Arabic philosophers, especially *Avicenna. His great significance is that he straddles the dividing-line between 13th-cent. system-building and 14th-cent. scepticism. The word 'dunce', first in the sense of 'a maker of impossibly ingenious distinctions', derives from him.

DUNSTAN, St (c. 910–88), became a favourite with King Athelstan, but withdrew from the court in disfavour. He was restored to favour by King Edmund who appointed him abbot of Glastonbury (939). He made it a famous school, restoring it spiritually and materially. He was one of the chief advisers of kings Edmund and Eadred; but when King Eadwig succeeded Eadred, he incurred his disfavour and retired to Flanders in disgrace in 956. Edgar recalled him and appointed him bishop of Worcester (957), London (959), and Canterbury (960). Dunstan set about restoring and reforming English monasteries (as *Ælfric says) and making the Danes an integral part of the nation.

DUNTON, John (1659–1733), a publisher and bookseller who between 1691 and 1697 issued the *Athenian Gazette (afterwards Athenian Mercury), dealing with philosophical and scientific matters. He also wrote many political pamphlets.

Dupin, the detective in the detective tales of *Poe.

D'Urberville, Alec, a character in Hardy's *Tess of the D'Urbervilles.*

Durdles, the stonemason in Dickens's *Edwin Drood.*

D'URFEY, Thomas (1653–1723), familiarly known as Tom Durfey, wrote a large number of songs, tales, satires, melodramas, farces, and many adaptions. A friend of Charles II and James II, he was still writing in the reign of Queen Anne, and was one of the most familiar figures of the day, given to singing his own songs in public. His *Wit and Mirth, or Pills to purge Melancholy* (6 vols, 1719–20) is an interesting collection of songs and ballads.

Durham, Constantia, a character in Meredith's *The Egoist.*

Durindana, or Durandal, the sword of *Roland or *Orlando.

DURRELL, Lawrence George (1912–), poet, novelist, and travel writer, was first recognized as a poet: his collections include *A private country* (1943); *Cities, plains and people* (1946); *On seeming to presume* (1948); *The Tree of Idleness* (1955); and *Collected Poems* (1960). His first novel of interest, *The Black Book: an Agon* (Paris, 1938; London, 1973) is a mildly pornographic fantasia, peopled by prostitutes and failed artists. He achieved fame with the publication of *Justine* (1957), the first volume of his *Alexandria Quartet; Balthazar* and *Mountolive* followed in 1958, and *Clea* in 1960. Set in Alexandria during the period just before the Second World War, the first three novels cover roughly the same period of time and the same events, while *Clea* advances the action in time; the central topic, according to Durrell, is 'an investigation of modern love'. Principal characters include the narrator L. G. Darley, his Greek mistress Melissa, the British ambassador Mountolive, the British intelligence agent Pursewarden, the artist Clea, and Justine (who is Jewish) and her wealthy Coptic husband Nessim. The style is ornate, lyrical, and sensual, perhaps too much so for English tastes, as the *Quartet* tends to be more highly regarded abroad than in Britain. Durrell's later novels include *Tunc* (1968), *Nunquam* (1970), *Monsieur* (1974), and *Constance* (1982). His best-known travel books are *Prospero's Cell* (1945), based on his prewar years in Corfu; *Reflections on a Marine Venus* (1953), based on his experiences as Information Officer in Rhodes, 1945–6; and *Bitter Lemons* (1957), on Cyprus.

Lawrence Durrell's brother, the zoologist Gerald Malcolm Durrell (1925–), is also a writer, well known for his popular accounts of animal life and his own zoo on Jersey: titles include *The Overloaded Ark* (1953), *My Family and Other Animals* (1956), *Island Zoo* (1961).

Dutch Courtezan, The, a comedy by *Marston, printed 1605.

DYCE, Alexander (1798–1869), scholar. His editions include the works of G. *Peele (1828–39), T. *Middleton (1840), *Beaumont and *Fletcher (1843–6). *Marlowe (1850), J. *Ford (1869), R. *Greene (1831, 1861), and J. *Webster (1830, 1857). He produced a full edition of Shakespeare's works (1857, 1864–7) and was the first editor of *Sir Thomas *More (1844). He left his valuable collection of books and manuscripts to the Victoria and Albert Museum.

DYER, Sir Edward (1543–1607), poet, was introduced at court by the earl of *Leicester, and took part in the queen's entertainment at Woodstock in 1575. The most famous poem attributed to him, *'My mind to me a kingdom is', is probably not his work. One of the best of his surviving poems is his elegy on his close friend Sir P. *Sidney, which begins 'Silence augmenteth griefe', printed in *The Phoenix Nest (1593).

DYER, George (1755–1841), published *Poems* (1792), and various critical essays. He is principally remembered as a friend of *Lamb, who writes of him as a gentle and kindly eccentric. He is the subject of Lamb's essay 'Amicus Redivivus' in *The Last Essays of Elia.*

DYER, John (1699–1757), Welsh poet, is remembered chiefly for his *topographical poem in tetrameter couplets, *Grongar Hill* (1726), which describes the scenery of the river Towy. He also wrote *The Ruins of Rome* (1740) and *The Fleece* (1757), a poem about the wool trade, which contains fine early industrial and pastoral landscapes.

Dynasts, The; an epic-drama of the War with Napoleon, in three Parts, nineteen Acts and one hundred and thirty scenes, by T. *Hardy, published in three parts, 1904, 1906, 1908.

This great work is written partly in blank verse, partly in a variety of other metres, and partly in prose. The events of history with which it deals are recounted in the descriptive passages and stage directions. The work centres on the tragic figure of Napoleon. Part I opens with the year 1805, and Napoleon's threat of invasion.

Part II covers the defeat of the Prussians at Jena, the meeting of Napoleon and Alexander at Tilsit, the battle of Wagram, the fall of Godoy and the abdication of the king of Spain, war in Spain, the divorce of Josephine, and Napoleon's marriage with Marie Louise.

Part III presents the Russian expedition of 1812, the British victories in the Pyrenees, the battle of Leipzig, Napoleon's abdication, his return from Elba, the ball in Brussels, Quatre-Bras, and Waterloo. Accompanying the major scenes are small vignettes, seen at close quarters, showing how these great events affected English rustics in Wessex, private soldiers, camp followers, and other ordinary people. Above them all, supernatural spectators of the terrestrial action, are impersonated abstractions, or Intelligences; the Ancient Spirit of the Years, the Spirit of the Pities, the Spirits Sinister and Ironic, and the Spirit of Rumour, with their attendant choruses, the Shade of the Earth, and the Recording Angels. Above all is the Immanent Will, the force, unconscious and heedless, that moves the world. They are introduced not, as the author is careful to point out in his Preface, 'as a systematized philosophy' but to give by their comments a universal significance to the particular events recounted.

E

EADMER (d. ?1124), a monk of Canterbury who wrote a Latin chronicle of the events of his own time down to 1122, *Historia Novorum in Anglia*, a biography of his friend and leader *Anselm, and an early Marian work, the *Liber de Excellentia Beatae Mariae*.

EAGLETON, Terry, see MARXIST LITERARY CRITICISM.

Eames, Johnny, a character in A. *Trollope's novels *The Small House at Allington* and *The Last Chronicle of Barset*.

Earine, the shepherdess loved by Aeglamour in Jonson's *The Sad Shepherd*.

EARLE, John (?1601–65), a member of *Falkland's circle at Great Tew. After the Restoration he became bishop of Worcester, then Salisbury. *Microcosmographie* (1628) was a collection of character sketches, chiefly by his hand, based on the model of *Theophrastus. He analyses varied social and moral types, ranging from the plain country fellow to the pot poet, with wit, sympathy, and insight. (See CHARACTER-WRITING.)

Early English Text Society, founded in 1864 by *Furnivall for the publication of Early and Middle English texts.

Earnshaw, Catherine, Hindley, and Hareton, characters in Emily Brontë's *Wuthering Heights*.

Earthly Paradise, The, a poem by W. *Morris, published 1868–70, consisting of a prologue and 24 tales, in Chaucerian metres.

The prologue tells how a company of Norsemen, fleeing from the pestilence, set sail in search of the fabled Earthly Paradise 'across the western sea where none grow old'. They are disappointed in their quest and return after long wanderings, 'shrivelled, bent and grey', to a 'nameless city in a distant sea' where the ancient Greek gods are still worshipped. Twice in each month they meet their hosts at a feast and a tale is told, alternately by one of the elders of the city and one of the wanderers. The tales of the former are on classical subjects, those of the latter from Norse and other medieval subjects. Between the tales are interpolated lyrics describing the changing seasons, and the whole work is prefaced by an Apology which contains some of Morris's best-known (and in a sense most misleading) lines, in which he describes himself as 'the idle singer of an empty day', 'born out of my due time'.

Earwicker, Humphrey Chimpden, a character in Joyce's *Finnegans Wake*.

Eastern, see ORIENTAL.

East Lynne, see WOOD, E.

Eastward hoe, a comedy by G. *Chapman, *Jonson, and J. *Marston, printed 1605. A passage derogatory to the Scots (III. iii. 40–7) gave offence at court, and Chapman and Jonson were imprisoned, but released on the intercession of powerful friends. The play is particularly interesting for the light it throws on London life of the time. Like Dekker's *Shoemaker's Holiday*, it gives a sympathetic picture of a tradesman.

The plot contrasts the careers of the virtuous and idle apprentices, Golding and Quicksilver, of the goldsmith Touchstone; and the fates of his two daughters, the modest Mildred, who marries the industrious Golding, and the immodest Gertrude who, in order to ride in her own coach, marries the penniless adventurer Sir Petronel Flash. Golding prospers and becomes deputy alderman, in which capacity he is able to intercede on behalf of the imprisoned and delinquent Quicksilver and Sir Petronel.

Eatanswill, the scene of the parliamentary elections in Dickens's *Pickwick Papers*.

Ecclesiastical History of Bede, see HISTORIA ECCLESIASTICA.

Ecclesiastical Politie, Of the Laws of, see LAWS OF ECCLESIASTICAL POLITIE.

Echidna, in Spenser's *Faerie Queene* (VI. vi), is the mother of the *Blatant Beast. In Greek mythology, a monster, half woman and half snake.

ECKHARD, Johannes (?1260–1327), known as 'Meister Eckhard', a German Dominican, regarded as the founder and one of the greatest exponents of German Mysticism.

Eclogue, the term for a short pastoral poem, comes from ἐκλογή (a choice), the title given in

Greek to collections of elegant extracts. The Latinized form *ecloga* was used, however, for any short poem and attached itself particularly to *Virgil's pastorals which their author had called *bucolica*. The terms eclogue, bucolic, and idyll have been widely used as synonyms, except that grammarians have made an effort to confine 'eclogue' to poems in dialogue form. The alternative spelling 'aeglogue' was prompted by a mistaken derivation from the Greek αἴξ, a goat.

Eclogues, The, of A. *Barclay, written *c.*1513–14, are interesting as the earliest English *pastorals, anticipating *Spenser. They are moral and satirical in character and are modelled upon *Mantuan and the *Miseriae Curialium* of *Piccolomini.

Economist, The, a weekly financial and commercial review founded in 1843. James Wilson was its first editor. It advocated free trade and the repeal of the corn laws. Among its later editors was *Bagehot, Wilson's son-in-law.

It was considerably modernized under the successful editorship of Alastair Burnet (1965–74). The contributions remain anonymous.

Ector, Sir, in Malory's *Morte D'Arthur*, the knight to whom the infant King Arthur was entrusted.

Ector de Marys, Sir, in Malory's *Morte D'Arthur*, the illegitimate son of King Ban of Benwick and half-brother of *Launcelot. It is he who finds Launcelot dead and utters his great lament over him.

Edda, an Old Norse name of uncertain meaning given to a 13th-cent. poetic manual written by *Snorri Sturluson, known as the Prose, Younger, or Snorra Edda. The same name was applied in the 17th cent. to a manuscript collection of poems, the Poetic or Elder Edda. The Prose Edda is divided into a Prologue and three parts: the 'Gylfaginning', or Deluding of Gylfi, a series of mythological stories in the form of a dialogue between one Gylfi and the Norse gods; the 'Skáldskaparmál', or Poetic Diction, in which Snorri illustrates the elaborate diction of *Skaldic Verse, retelling many myths and legends; and the 'Háttatal', or List of Metres, a long poem each strophe of which exemplifies a different Norse metre. The Poetic Edda was compiled *c.*1270. The poems fall into two groups: heroic lays about legendary Germanic heroes and mythological lays, such as the Vǫluspá, a history of the Norse gods from creation to apocalypse, and the Hávamál, the words of the High One, Oðinn. *Auden wrote free translations of many Eddaic lays.

EDEN, Emily (1797–1869), accompanied her brother to India in 1835, when he became governor-general. She published *Portraits of the People and Princes of India* (1844), *Up the Country* (1866), and *Letters from India* (1872). Her two novels *The Semi-detached House* (1859, anon.) and *The Semi-attached Couple* (1860, by 'E.E.') are a valuable record of social life, shedding a revealing light on attitudes to marriage, politics, and manners.

Edgar, in Shakespeare's *King Lear*, the legitimate son of Gloucester.

Edge-hill, see JAGO, R.

EDGEWORTH, Maria (1768–1849), was the eldest daughter of the first wife of Richard Lovell Edgeworth (1744–1817), a wealthy Irish landlord. He was an eccentric, radical, and inventive man, deeply interested in the practical applications of science and in education. His influence on Maria was profound; he frequently 'edited' her work, managed her career, and imparted to her many of his own enthusiasms. They wrote together *Practical Education* (1798), a treatise which owes much to *Rousseau.

Maria spent most of her life with her family in Ireland. Her first publication was *Letters to Literary Ladies* (1795), a plea for women's education. Sir W. *Scott acknowledged his debt to her Irish novels in the Preface to his 'Waverley' edition of 1829.

Miss Edgeworth appears to have initiated, in *Castle Rackrent*, both the first fully developed *regional novel and the first true *historical novel in English, pointing the way to the historical/regional novels of Scott. Her writings fall into three groups: those based on Irish life (considered her finest), *Castle Rackrent* (1800) and *The Absentee* (first published in *Tales of Fashionable Life* in 1812) together with the lesser *Ormond* (1817); those depicting contemporary English society, such as *Belinda* (1801), *Leonora* (1806), *Patronage* (1814), and *Helen* (1834); and her many popular lessons and stories for and about children, including *The Parent's Assistant* (1796–1800), *Moral Tales* (1801), *Popular Tales* (1804), and *Harry and Lucy Concluded* (1825).

Edinburgh Review, The, (1802–1929), a quarterly periodical, established by F. *Jeffrey, Sydney *Smith, and H. *Brougham, and originally published by A. *Constable. It succeeded immediately in establishing a prestige and authority which lasted for over a century. Under the influence of Jeffrey, its politics became emphatically Whig. Although Jeffrey perceived the genius of *Keats, his veneration for 18th-cent. literature led him to notorious and scathing denouncements of *Wordsworth, *Coleridge, and *Southey as the 'Lake School'. Between Jeffrey's resignation in 1829 and the demise of the *Review* in 1929 contributions were published from almost all the major writers and critics of the 19th and early 20th cents.

Edith of Lorn, the heroine of Scott's *The Lord of the Isles*.

Edmund, in Shakespeare's *King Lear*, the bastard son of the earl of Gloucester.

Edward II, a tragedy in blank verse by *Marlowe probably first performed 1592, published 1594.

It deals with the recall by Edward II, on his accession, of his favourite, Piers Gaveston; the revolt of the barons and the capture and execution of Gaveston; the estrangement of Queen Isabella from her husband; her rebellion, supported by her paramour Mortimer, against the king; the capture of the latter, his abdication of the crown, and his murder in Berkeley Castle. The play was an important influence on Shakespeare's *Richard II*.

Edward III, *The Raigne of King*, a historical play, published 1596, of uncertain authorship, attributed by some, at least in part, to Shakespeare.

Edwardian, strictly, of the reign of Edward VII, but the term is commonly used (in contrast with 'Victorian') of the years 1900–14. H. G. *Wells wrote that Queen Victoria sat on England like a great paper-weight, and that after her death things blew all over the place. This expresses well the excitement, the new sense of freedom, and the lack of direction, in Wells himself and in Arnold *Bennett, *Galsworthy, E. M. *Forster, and other liberal writers of the period. It was an era of outstanding achievement in the theatre (with G. B. *Shaw and *Granville-Barker) and, especially, in the novel, notably in the great works of H. *James's last phase and the radical experiments of *Conrad (and his collaborator F. M. *Ford). At the same time strongly traditional themes in the writing of the period—the Empire as a source of national pride, the countryside as the custodian of national values, the upper-class house-party representing the whole of English life—support the still current alternative sense of the word 'Edwardian', referring to a period of sunlit prosperity and opulent confidence preceding the cataclysm of the Great War.

EDWARDS, Jonathan (1703–58), American philosopher, ardent divine, and formidable preacher who provoked the fervent religious revival in New England known as the 'Great Awakening'. His principal philosophical work *A Careful and Strict Enquiry into the Modern Prevailing Notions of . . . Freedom of Will* (1754), in which he attacked from a predestinarian standpoint the *Arminian view of liberty, occasioned Dr *Johnson's aphorism, 'All theory is against the freedom of the will; all experience for it.'

EDWARDS, Richard (?1523–66), was master of the children of the Chapel Royal, 1561. *The Excellent Comedie of . . . *Damon and Pithias* (printed 1571) is his only extant play. He was the compiler of the *Paradyse of Dainty Devises* (1576).

'Edwin and Angelina', see HERMIT, THE.

Edwin Drood, *The mystery of*, an unfinished novel by *Dickens, published 1870.

The fathers of Edwin Drood and Rosa Bud, both widowers, have before their deaths betrothed their young children to one another. The orphan Rosa has been brought up in Miss Twinkleton's school at Cloisterham (Rochester), where Edwin, also an orphan, has an uncle, John Jasper, the precentor of the cathedral, to whom he is devoted and who appears to return the devotion. Jasper, a sinister and hypocritical character, gives Rosa music lessons and loves her passionately, but inspires her with terror and disgust. There now come upon the scene two other orphans, Neville and Helena Landless. Neville admires Rosa and is disgusted at Edwin's unappreciative treatment of her. This enmity is secretly fomented by Jasper and there is a violent quarrel between the young men. On the last of Edwin's periodical visits to Cloisterham Rosa and he recognize that marriage will not be for their happiness and break off the engagement. That same night Edwin disappears under circumstances pointing to foul play and suggesting that he has been murdered by Neville Landless, a theory actively supported by Jasper. But Jasper receives with uncontrollable symptoms of dismay the intelligence that the engagement of Edwin and Rosa had been broken off before Edwin's disappearance, and this betrayal of himself is noted by Mr Grewgious, Rosa's eccentric, good-hearted guardian. Neville is arrested but, as the body of Edwin is not found, is released untried. He is ostracized by public opinion and is obliged to hide himself as a student in London. The remainder of the fragment of the novel is occupied with the continued machinations of Jasper against Neville and his pursuit of Rosa, who in terror of him flies to her guardian in London; with the countermoves prepared by Mr Grewgious, assisted by the amiable minor canon Mr Crisparkle and a new ally, the retired naval officer Mr Tartar; also with the proceedings of the mysterious Mr Datchery, directed against Jasper.

Other notable characters include the fatuous Mr Sapsea, auctioneer and mayor; Mr Honeythunder, the bullying 'philanthropist'; the grim stonemason Durdles; and his attendant imp 'Deputy'.

EGAN, Pierce, the elder (1772–1849), the author of *Life in London; or the Day and Night Scenes of Jerry Hawthorn Esq. and Corinthian Tom*

(1821), issued in monthly numbers from 1820, illustrated by George and Robert *Cruikshank. The book is interesting for the light it throws on the manners of the period and for the many slang phrases it introduces. His son, also Pierce Egan (1814–80), was associated with him in several of his works, and wrote a vast number of novels.

Egeon, in Shakespeare's *The Comedy of Errors* the Syracusan merchant, father of the Antipholus twins.

EGERTON, George, the pen-name of Mary Chavelita Dunne (1859–1945), short story writer. Her first volume of short stories, *Keynotes* (1893), published by John *Lane with a cover by *Beardsley, created something of a sensation with its echoes of Scandinavian realism and portraits of the *New Woman. Other works include *Discords* (1894) and *The Wheel of God* (1898).

EGERTON, Sir Thomas, Baron Ellesmere and Viscount Brackley (?1540–1617), was lord chancellor from 1603 till his death. He befriended F. *Bacon. *Donne was his secretary (1597–1602) and S. *Daniel addressed poems to him. It was to his third wife that Milton's *Arcades* was addressed.

Eglantine, or **Eglentyne,** Madame, the Prioress in Chaucer's *Canterbury Tales.*

Egoist, The, a novel by G. *Meredith, published 1879.

The central character, the Egoist himself, is Sir Willoughby Patterne, rich and handsome, with a high position in the county. Laetitia Dale, an intelligent young women but past her first bloom, has loved him for many years. But the dashing Constantia Durham is a greater prize, and she accepts his proposal. She soon discerns the true Sir Willoughby and elopes with Harry Oxford, an officer in the hussars, thus bringing Willoughby his first humiliation. Soon he discovers the qualities he requires in Clara Middleton, the daughter of an elderly scholar (said to be a sketch of Meredith's first father-in-law, *Peacock) with a passion for wine. Clara becomes engaged to him, but soon perceives his intention of directing and moulding her; her attempts to free herself from the entanglements of the engagement form the main theme of the book. Clara envies but cannot emulate Constantia, and Willoughby struggles frantically against an incredible second jilting. Clara is meanwhile seeing more and more of Vernon Whitford, a poor and earnest young scholar (based on L. *Stephen), who lives at Patterne and is tutor to young Crossjay, son of a poor relation, an officer of the marines. The spirited Crossjay is finally the means of Clara's release, for he unintentionally overhears Willoughby proposing to Laetitia Dale, a proposal which she refuses. Willoughby finds himself trebly humiliated. In the end his persistence achieves the reluctant Laetitia, and Clara marries Vernon Whitford.

Egoist, The (1914–19), originally *The New Freewoman: An Individualist Review*, founded by Harriet Shaw Weaver and Dora Marsden. It published articles on modern poetry and the arts, and from being a feminist paper became, under the influence of *Pound and others, a mouthpiece for the Imagist poets (see IMAGISM). It was first a fortnightly, then a monthly, with *Aldington as assistant editor, followed by T. S. *Eliot in 1917. Joyce's *Portrait of the Artist as a Young Man* was published serially in the magazine in 1914–15.

Egotistical Sublime, a phrase coined by *Keats to describe his version of *Wordsworth's distinctive genius. See under NEGATIVE CAPABILITY, and see also ROMANTICISM.

Eikon Basilike, *the Pourtraicture of His Sacred Majestie in His Solitudes and Sufferings,* a book of which Dr John Gauden (1605–62), bishop of Worcester, claimed authorship. It purported to be mediations by Charles I, and was long so regarded; it was published about the date of his execution, 30 Jan. 1649 (1648 OS), and appealed so strongly to popular sentiment that 47 editions of it were published, and Parliament thought it necessary to issue a reply, *Milton's *Eikonoklastes* (1649). ('Eikon Basilike' means 'royal image' and 'Eikonoklastes' 'image breaker'.) *Eikonoklastes* takes the *Eikon* paragraph by paragraph in an effort to refute it: it also attacks the 'miserable, credulous and deluded' public with much vigour.

Eikonoklastes, see EIKON BASILIKE.

Eisteddfod, a Welsh word meaning 'session', the annual congress of Welsh bards.

E.K., see KIRKE, E.

Elaine, (variously spelt), in Malory's *Morte D'Arthur,* is the name of several ladies whose identities sometimes overlap: (1) Elaine Le Blank, the Fair Maid of Astolat (*Tennyson's Lady of Shalott) who falls in love with Launcelot and dies for love of him (see LAUNCELOT OF THE LAKE); (2) Elayne the Fair or Sans Pere (Peerless), the daughter of King Pelles and the mother, by Launcelot, of *Galahad; (3) Elayne the sister of Morgawse and *Morgan le Fay; (4) Elayne the wife of King *Ban and mother of Launcelot; (5) Elayne the daughter of King Pellinore.

Élan vital, a phrase coined by *Bergson to describe the vital impulse which he believed directed evolutionary growth. See also under MAN AND SUPERMAN.

Elayne, see ELAINE.

Elder Brother, The, a drama by J. *Fletcher, written *c*.1625, probably with *Massinger, who completed it about 1635.

Elder Statesman, The, a comedy by T. S. *Eliot.

ELEANOR OF AQUITAINE (1122–1204), the granddaughter of the first troubadour whose work survives, Guilhem IX of Aquitaine, and inheritor of the kingdom of Aquitaine, married for her inheritance by Louis VII of France in 1137. After their divorce in 1152 she was immediately remarried to Henry Plantagenet of Anjou, the future Henry II of England, to whom she bore eight children including the future *Richard I and the future King John. After the death of Henry II in 1189 she was regent of England until 1199. She was an immensely influential patron of the arts, particularly in her patronage of the development of courtly poetry in Poitiers, a function carried on by her daughter *Marie de Champagne.

Eleatic, the name used to describe the philosophy of Parmenides (d. *c*.450 BC) and Zeno (*fl. c*.460 BC), who lived or were born at Elea, an ancient Greek city on the west coast of south Italy. They held that the real universe is a single, indivisible, eternal, unchanging whole; what is mutable and perishable, and phenomena, are illusions.

Elegiac, (1) in prosody, the metre consisting of a dactylic *hexameter and *pentameter, as being the metre appropriate to elegies; (2) generally, of the nature of an *elegy.

Elegy, from the Greek, the word has been variously used with reference to different periods of English. In Old English a group of short poems in the *Exeter Book whose subject is the transience of the world, are called elegies (see WANDERER; SEAFARER; DEOR; RUIN). From the 16th cent. onwards the term was used for a reflective poem by poets such as *Donne; later it was applied particularly to poems of mourning, and the general reflective poem, as written by *Coleridge and *Yeats, is sometimes called 'reverie'. The great English mourning elegies are Milton's *Lycidas (for E. *King), Shelley's *Adonais (for *Keats), Tennyson's *In Memoriam (for A. H. *Hallam), M. Arnold's *Thyrsis (for *Clough); and *Hopkins's Wreck of the Deutschland.

'Elegy on the Death of a Mad Dog', a poem by Goldsmith, from *The Vicar of Wakefield.

Elegy Written in a Country Church-Yard, a meditative poem in quatrains by T. *Gray, published in 1751, but begun some years earlier. The churchyard is perhaps that of Stoke Poges, where Gray often visited members of his family. The poem, which contains some of the best-known lines in English literature, reflects on the obscure destinies of the villagers who lie buried ('Full many a flower is born to blush unseen') and then describes the supposed death of the melancholy and unknown author. Critics have related the closing stanzas both to Gray's fears about his own poetic destiny, and to the early death of his friend Richard *West in 1742.

Elene, see CYNEWULF.

'Elephant in the Moon, The', see BUTLER, S. (1613–80).

ELGAR, Sir Edward William (1857–1934), English composer. His great oratorio The Dream of Gerontius (1900) is a setting from *Newman's poem. His Symphonic Study Falstaff (1913) is inspired by Shakespeare's Henry IV and V. His works Fringes of the Fleet (poems by *Kipling), The Spirit of England (*Binyon), and 'Land of Hope and Glory' (words by A. C. *Benson), belong to the period of the First World War. He was a friend of and encouraged by G. B. *Shaw.

Elia, see ESSAYS OF ELIA.

Elidure, see ARTEGAL.

ELIOT, George (Mary Ann, later Marian, Evans) (1819–80), daughter of Robert Evans, agent for a Warwickshire estate. She became a convert to Evangelicalism when she was at school; she was freed from this by the influence of Charles Bray, a freethinking Coventry manufacturer, but remained strongly influenced by religious concepts of love and duty; her works contain many affectionate portraits of Dissenters and clergymen. She translated *Strauss's Life of Jesus which appeared without her name in 1846. In 1850 she met J. *Chapman, contributed to the *Westminster Review and became assistant editor in 1851. In this year she became a paying guest in Chapman's house, where her emotional attachment to him proved an embarrassment; she subsequently met *Spencer, for whom she also developed strong feelings which were not reciprocated. In 1854 she published a translation of *Feuerbach's Essence of Christianity; she endorsed his view that religious belief is an imaginative necessity for man and a projection of his interest in his own species, a heterodoxy of which the readers of her novels only gradually became aware. At about the same time she joined G. H. *Lewes in a union without legal form (he was already married) that lasted until his death. 'The Sad Fortunes of the Rev. Amos Barton', the first of the *Scenes of Clerical Life, appeared in *Blackwoods Magazine in 1857, followed by 'Mr Gilfil's Love-Story' and 'Janet's Repentance'; these at once attracted praise for their domestic realism, pathos, and humour, and speculation about the identity of 'George Eliot'. *Adam Bede* (1859), which established her as a leading novelist, was followed by *The Mill on the Floss* (1860) and *Silas Marner* (1861). *Romola* was published in the *Cornhill* in 1862–3; *Felix Holt, The Radical* appeared in 1866. She travelled in Spain in 1867, and her dramatic poem *The Spanish Gypsy* appeared in 1868. *Middlemarch* was published in instalments in 1871–2, and *Daniel Deronda*, also in instalments, in 1874–6. She was by now recognized as the greatest living English novelist, by readers as diverse as *Turgenev, H. *James, and Queen *Victoria. In 1878 Lewes died. Her *Impressions of Theophrastus Such* appeared in 1879, and in 1880 she married the 40-year-old John Walter Cross who had become her financial adviser. She died seven months later. After her death her reputation declined somewhat, and L. *Stephen indicated much of the growing reaction in an obituary notice (1881) which praised the 'charm' and autobiographical elements of the early works, but found the later novels painful and excessively reflective. In the late 1940s a new generation of critics, led by *Leavis (*The Great Tradition*, 1948), introduced a new respect for and understanding of her mature works; Leavis praises her 'traditional moral sensibility', her 'luminous intelligence'.

George Eliot also wrote various poems and short stories; her letters and journals were edited by Cross (3 vols, 1885); her complete letters were edited by G. S. Haight (9 vols, 1954–78), who also wrote a life (1968).

ELIOT, T(homas) S(tearns) (1888–1965), a major figure in English literature since the 1920s. He was born at St Louis, Missouri, and educated at Harvard, the Sorbonne, and Merton College, Oxford. In 1914 he met *Pound, who encouraged him to settle in England. In 1915 his poem 'The Love Song of J. Alfred Prufrock' appeared in *Poetry*. Eliot began to work for Lloyds Bank in 1917 when he also became assistant editor of *The Egoist*. His first volume of verse, *Prufock and other Observations* (1917), was followed by *Poems* (1919), hand-printed by L. and V. *Woolf at the *Hogarth Press; these struck a new note in modern poetry, satiric, allusive, cosmopolitan, at times lyric and elegiac. In 1922 Eliot founded a new quarterly, *The Criterion*; in the first issue appeared, with much éclat, *The Waste Land*, which established him decisively as the voice of a disillusioned generation. In 1925 he left Lloyds and became a director of Faber and Faber, where he built up a list of poets (*Auden, G. *Barker, Pound, *Spender, etc.; see also FABER BOOK OF MODERN VERSE) which represented the mainstream of the modern movement in poetry in England: from this time he was regarded as a figure of great cultural authority, whose influence was more or less inescapable.

In 1927 he became a British subject and a member of the Anglican church; his pilgrimage towards his own particular brand of High Anglicanism may be charted in his poetry through 'The Hollow Men' (1925), with its broken asseverations of faith, through 'The Journey of the Magi' (1927) and 'Ash-Wednesday' (1930), to its culminating vision in *Four Quartets* (1935–42). His prose also shows the same movement; for example, in the preface to *For Lancelot Andrewes* (1928) he describes himself as 'classical in literature, royalist in politics, and Anglo-Catholic in religion'. The same preoccupation with tradition continued to express itself in his critical works, and developed in part from the concept of *'dissociation of sensibility' which he had formulated in 1921. (See HULME, whose views influenced Eliot.)

In the 1930s Eliot began his attempt to revive poetic drama. *Sweeney Agonistes* (1932), an 'Aristophanic fragment' which gives, in syncopated rhythms, a satiric impression of the sterility of proletarian life, was followed by a pageant play, *The Rock* (1934), *Murder in the Cathedral* (1935), *The Family Reunion* (1939), and three 'comedies': *The Cocktail Party* (1950), *The Confidential Clerk* (1954), and *The Elder Statesman* (1959). Eliot's classic book of verse for children, *Old Possum's Book of Practical Cats* (1939), reveals the aspect of his character that claimed the influence of *Lear.

Eliot was equally influential as critic and poet, and in his combination of literary and social criticism may be called the M. *Arnold of the 20th cent. Among his critical works may be mentioned: *The Sacred Wood: Essays on Poetry and Criticism* (1920) (which contains the essay on *Hamlet*, coining the phrase *'objective correlative'); *The Use of Poetry and the Use of Criticism* (1933); *Elizabethan Essays* (1934); *The Idea of a Christian Society* (1940); *Notes Towards the Definition of Culture* (1948); *Poetry and Drama* (1951); *On Poets and Poetry* (1957). *Leavis, himself much influenced by Eliot, has pointed out the vital connections between Eliot's creative work and critical attitude (in, e.g., his revaluation of *Donne, *Marvell, Elizabethan and Jacobean verse drama, *Milton, *Dryden, and his praise of *Dante, *Laforgue, and the French Symbolists). He was awarded the *Nobel Prize for literature and the Order of Merit in 1948.

Elision, the suppression of a vowel or syllable in pronouncing.

Elissa, (1) a name borne by Dido; (2) in Spenser's *Faerie Queene* (II. ii.), one of the two 'froward sisters' of the sober *Medina.

Eliza (Mrs Elizabeth Draper), see DRAPER.

Eliza, The Journal to, by L. *Sterne, written 1767, first published 1904.

The *Journal*, also called by Sterne the *Bramine's Journal*, was kept intermittently between mid-April and Nov. of 1767, and describes with fulsome pathos, often in the persona of Yorick, sometimes as 'Bramin' to 'Bramine', his love for the young Mrs Elizabeth *Draper and his torment at their separation.

ELIZABETH I (1533–1603), a daughter of *Henry VIII, and queen of England from 1558 to 1603. She was celebrated by the greatest poets of her age, including *Spenser, *Ralegh, and *Shakespeare, under such names as *Cynthia and *Gloriana (with many allusions to her semi-mythological role as Virgin Queen) and has been the subject of innumerable plays, novels, romances, and biographies. She was famed for her ready wit and stirring eloquence. She also wrote poetry, which was highly praised by her courtiers and by *Puttenham, who used one of her undisputed works ('The doubt of future foes', on the conspiracies of *Mary Queen of Scots) as an example of rhetoric in his *Art of English Poesy*.

Elizabeth and her German Garden, see VON ARNIM, E.

Elizabethan Literature, a name often applied vaguely to the literature produced in the reigns of Elizabeth I and the first Stuarts. See under DRAB and GOLDEN.

'Ellen Alleyn', the pseudonym under which C. *Rossetti produced her earlier poems.

Ellen Douglas, the 'Lady of the Lake' in *Scott's poem of that name.

'Ellen Orford', one of the tales in Crabbe's *The Borough*.

ELLIOT, Jean (1727–1805), author of the most popular version of the old lament for Flodden, 'The Flowers of the Forest', beginning 'I've heard them lilting at our ewe-milking', written c.1763, and published in 1776. Another popular version was written by A. *Cockburn.

Elliot, Sir Walter, his daughters Elizabeth, Anne, and Mary, and his heir William Walter Elliot, characters in J. Austen's *Persuasion*.

ELLIOTT, Ebenezer (1781–1849), became a master-founder in Sheffield, and is remembered as the 'Corn Law Rhymer'. He published *The Village Patriarch* (1829) and *Corn Law Rhymes* (1830), a collection of simple poems which employ both satire and pathos in fiercely condemning the Bread Tax. Some of Elliott's poems are of genuine quality, and his themes of poverty and oppression are deeply felt. His collected works were published in 1846.

Elliott, Kirstie, Robert, Gilbert, Clement, and Andrew, characters in R. L. Stevenson's *Weir of Hermiston*.

Ellipsis, the leaving out from a sentence words necessary to express the sense completely.

ELLIS, George (1753–1815), was one of the talented group who, with *Canning and *Frere, founded and contributed to *The Anti-Jacobin* in 1797. His contributions to the Whig *Rolliad* appeared in 1784; his most important works were his translations and selections from Middle English verse: *Early English Poets* (1801) and *Specimens of Early English Romances in Metre* (1805).

ELLIS, Henry Havelock (1859–1939), qualified as a physician, although much distracted by his literary pursuits. He edited the unexpurgated *Mermaid Series of Elizabethan dramatists (1887–9). In 1884 he met Olive *Schreiner, who became an intimate friend and who shared his interest in progressive thought, particularly in the realm of sexuality, the subject with which he is most closely identified. An energetic pioneer in the field of sexology, his works (which include *The New Spirit*, 1890; *Sexual Inversion*, 1897, with J. A. *Symonds; *Affirmations*, 1898; *The Dance of Life*, 1923; and his autobiographical *My Life*, 1939, as well as many other volumes on the psychology of sex, marriage, censorship, social hygiene, etc.) had a considerable and liberating influence. He had many followers, although the scientific accuracy of his investigations has been questioned, and he damaged his own reputation by indiscriminate publication and by his apparent misunderstandings of *Freud.

ELLIS BELL, see BRONTË, E.

ELLISON, R. W., see INVISIBLE MAN.

ELLMANN, Richard (1918–), American scholar and biographer. In 1970 he became Goldsmiths' professor of English literature at Oxford. His publications include *Yeats: The Man and the Mask* (1948, rev. 1979) and several works on *Joyce, including his biography, *James Joyce* (1959, rev. 1982), which made a highly influential contribution to the new conception of the art of *biography that developed at this period. He also edited the *New Oxford Book of American Verse* (1976).

'Eloisa to Abelard', a heroic epistle by *Pope, published 1717. Pope's version of the tragic love of Héloïse and *Abelard; it portrays Héloïse, in a Gothic seclusion of 'grots and caverns', still tormented by passionate love, unable to renounce for God the memory of the 'unholy joy'.

ELSTOB, Elizabeth (1683–1756), a pioneer in Anglo-Saxon studies, as was her brother William (1673–1715). Her publications include *An English-Saxon homily on the birthday of St Gregory* (1709) and *The rudiments of grammar for the English-Saxon tongue . . .* (1715).

Elton, the Revd Philip, a character in J. Austen's *Emma.*

Elvira, (1) the wife of *Don Juan; (2) the heroine of *Dryden's *The Spanish Fryar*; (3) the mistress of Pizarro in *Sheridan's play *Pizarro.*

ELYOT, Sir Thomas (c.1490–1546), author of the *Boke named the Governour*, published in 1531, a treatise on education and politics. His other works include *The Doctrinall of Princis* (c.1533), translated from Isocrates, *The Image of Governance* (1540), *The Castel of Helth* (c.1536), an important manual of health, and Platonic dialogues and compilations from the Fathers. His translations did much to popularize the classics in England. His *Dictionary* (Latin and English, 1538) was the first book published in England to bear this title.

Emaré, a mid-14th-cent. verse romance of 1,035 lines in a north-east Midland dialect, written in twelve-line tail-rhyme stanzas. It is a Breton lay on the model of the repeatedly told Constance story.

Emblem book. An emblem usually refers to a genre of verbal–pictorial art which is particularly associated with the Renaissance.

The first emblem book, the *Emblematum liber* of Alciati (or Alciato), was published in 1531. Each emblem consists of a motto, a symbolic picture, and an explanatory set of verses called an epigram. All three parts of an emblem contribute to its meaning. Writers often borrowed one another's pictures and wrote new verses which reinterpreted them. The earliest emblem book to contain illustrations as well as verses was Geoffrey Whitney's (?1548–?1601) *A Choice of Emblemes* (1586), which distinguished three categories: natural, historical, and moral. The 17th cent. produced many religious emblem books, of which the most famous English example was the *Emblems* of Quarles (1635). The children's figures of these emblem books represent Divine Love (God) and Earthly Love (Man); they have been derived from the Cupid figures of earlier love emblems. A *Collection of Emblemes*, also illustrated, was published by G. *Wither, 1634–5.

*Bunyan wrote an emblem book without pictures (*A Book for Boys and Girls*, 1686). By then the form had already gone out of fashion; it enjoyed something of a revival in the Victorian period.

Emblems, a book of short devotional poems by *Quarles, published 1635, in various metres, each based on some scriptural text, and some in the form of dialogues. The engravings are mostly by William Marshall (fl. 1630–50).

Emelye, the lady loved by Palamon and Arcite in Chaucer's 'The Knight's Tale' (see CANTERBURY TALES, 1). She figures as Emilia in *The Two Noble Kinsmen.*

EMERSON, Ralph Waldo (1803–82), American philosopher and poet, was ordained and became a pastor in Boston, but resigned his charge feeling unable to believe in the sacrament of the Lord's Supper. He visited England in 1833, where he met *Coleridge and *Wordsworth, and notably *Carlyle, who became a lifelong friend and correspondent. On his return to America Emerson embarked on a career as lecturer, evolving the new quasi-religious concept of *Transcendentalism, which found written expression in his essay *Nature* (1836). This form of mystic idealism and Wordsworthian reverence for nature was immensely influential in American life and thought. His 1837 Harvard address, 'The American Scholar', urged America to assert its intellectual independence. *The Dial*, founded in 1840, was edited by Emerson from 1842 to 1844, and published many of his gnomic, rough-hewn, but frequently striking poems, including 'The Problem' and 'Woodnotes'. His first volume of essays appeared in 1841, the second in 1844.

In 1845 Emerson delivered the lectures later published in 1850 as *Representative Men*. In 1847 he revisited England on a lecture tour, and his *English Traits* (1865), a perceptive study of the English national character, won him great admiration.

Emilia, (1) in Shakespeare's *Othello, the plain-spoken wife of *Iago; (2) the lady loved by Palamon and Arcite in Chaucer's 'The Knight's Tale' (see EMELYE), who also figures in *The Two Noble Kinsmen*; (3) Peregrine's love in Smollett's *Peregrine Pickle.*

Emilia in England, see SANDRA BELLONI.

Emilia Viviani, see EPIPSYCHIDION.

Eminent Victorians, a biographical work by L. *Strachey.

Em'ly, Little, a character in Dickens's *David Copperfield.*

Emma, a novel by J. Austen, begun 1814, published 1816.

Emma, a clever, pretty, and self-satisfied young woman, is the daughter, and mistress of the house, of Mr Woodhouse, an amiable old valetudinarian. Her former governess and companion, Anne Taylor, has just left to marry Mr

Weston. Emma takes under her wing Harriet Smith, a pretty, pliant girl of 17, daughter of unknown parents, who is parlour-boarder at the school in the neighbouring village of Highbury. Emma schemes for Harriet's advancement. She first prevents Harriet from accepting an offer of marriage from Robert Martin, an eligible young farmer, as being beneath her. This tampering greatly annoys Mr Knightley, the bachelor owner of Donwell Abbey, who is Emma's brother-in-law. Emma hopes to arrange a match between Harriet and Mr Elton, the young vicar, only to find that he aspires to Emma's own hand. Frank Churchill, the son of Mr Weston by a former marriage, now visits Highbury. Emma first supposes him in love with herself, but presently thinks that Harriet might attract him, and encourages her not to despair. This encouragement, however, is misunderstood by Harriet, who assumes it is directed at the great Mr Knightley himself, with whom Emma is half unwittingly in love. Emma then suffers the double mortification of discovering, first that Frank Churchill is already engaged to Jane Fairfax, niece of the garrulous old maid Miss Bates; and second, that Harriet has hopes of supplanting her in Mr Knightley's affections. In the end Knightley proposes to the humbled Emma, and Harriet is happily consoled with Robert Martin.

EMPEDOCLES (*c.*484–*c.*424 BC), a Greek scientist, philosopher, and democratic politician of Agrigentum in Sicily. He was responsible for demonstrating the existence of air, and taught that the universe was in a state of unending change thanks to the contrary action of Love, which united the four elements, and Strife, which drove them apart. He was supposed to have met his death plunging into the crater of Etna. The opposition of Love and Strife is mentioned by Spenser (*Faerie Queene*, IV. x). The legend of Empedocles' death is referred to in *Paradise Lost* (iii. 471), by *Lamb in 'All Fools Day', and by *Meredith in *Empedocles*; but the finest work it inspired is M. Arnold's *Empedocles on Etna* (1852).

Empedocles on Etna, a dramatic poem by M. *Arnold, published anonymously 1852.

Arnold portrays the philosopher *Empedocles, who committed suicide by throwing himself into the crater of Etna, on the verge of his last act. Empedocles expresses his intellectual doubts, dismissing the reassuring platitudes of religion and philosophy; man's yearning for joy, calm, and enlightenment is in itself no proof that these things exist or can be attained. He grieves over his own 'dwindling faculty of joy', and finally, in a kind of triumph, concluding that at least he has been ever honest in his doubts, hurls himself to his death.

EMPSON, Sir William (1906–84), poet and critic, became professor of English at Sheffield.

He published two volumes of verse, *Poems* (1935) and *The Gathering Storm* (1940): *Collected Poems* (revised) appeared in 1955. His criticism includes *Seven Types of Ambiguity* (1930), *Some Versions of Pastoral* (1935), *The Structure of Complex Words* (1951), and *Milton's God* (1961). Empson's poetry is extremely difficult, making use of analytical argument and imagery drawn from modern physics and mathematics; a technical virtuoso, he employed metaphysical conceits and linguistic, metrical, and syntactical complexities. *Using Biography* (1984), a posthumous collection of essays, 1958–82, constitutes a spirited attack on the *New Criticism's neglect of the biographical element in literary interpretation.

Encounter, a political, cultural, and literary review, founded in 1953, originally edited by S. *Spender and Irving Kristol. It was the vehicle for N. *Mitford's celebrated formulation of the 'U' and 'Non-U' concept (1955), and C. P. *Snow pursued the *Two Cultures controversy in its pages (1959–60). It has also published poetry by R. *Lowell, *Plath, *Roethke, *Auden, *Larkin, *Amis, and many others, and articles by *Koestler, *Popper, *Naipaul, etc.

Encyclopaedia Britannica. It was first issued by a 'Society of Gentlemen in Scotland' in numbers (1768–71), edited by William Smellie, a printer, afterwards secretary of the Society of Scottish Antiquaries. It was a dictionary of the arts and sciences. The second edition (1777–84), in ten vols, added history and biography. The third edition, in 15 vols, appeared in 1788–97; and the fourth edition, in 20 vols, in 1801–10. The undertaking was taken over by Constable in 1812, and the copyright sold after the failure of that house in 1826. It passed to Cambridge University for the publication in 1910–11 of the eleventh edition in 28 vols [*EB*]. The fourteenth edition, under the editorship-in-chief of J. L. Garvin, was published in London and New York in 1929. Since then a system of continuous revision has replaced the making of new editions. (See also CHAMBERS'S ENCYCLOPAEDIA.)

Encyclopaedists, the collaborators in the *Encyclopédie* of *Diderot and D'Alembert.

Encyclopédie, L', a dictionary of universal knowledge published 1751–76 in 35 vols under the editorship of *Diderot, with (until 1758) D'Alembert as his chief assistant, and with the leading intellectuals of the age, including *Voltaire, Montesquieu, *Rousseau, Buffon, and Turgot, as contributors. It can be regarded as the most representative monument of the *Enlightenment. Its attack on superstition and credulity attracted the hostility of church and state.

Endimion, The Man in the Moone, an allegorical prose play by *Lyly, published 1591.

End of the Affair, The, a novel by G. *Greene.

Endymion, a poem in four books, by *Keats, written 1817, published 1818.

The poem tells, with a wealth of epithet and invention, the story of Endymion, 'the brainsick shepherd-prince' of Mount Latmos, who falls in love with Cynthia, the moon, and descends to the depths of the earth to find her. There he encounters a real woman, Phoebe, and falls in love with her. She turns out to be none other than Cynthia, who, after luring him, weary and perplexed, through 'cloudy phantasms', bears him away to eternal life. With the main story are woven the legends of Venus and Adonis, of Glaucus and Scylla, and of Arethusa. The poem includes in Bk I the well-known 'Hymn to Pan', and in Bk IV the roundelay 'O sorrow'.

The allegory appears to represent the poet pursuing ideal perfection, and distracted from his quest by human beauty. The work was violently attacked in the *Quarterly Review and in *Blackwood's.

Endymion, a novel by B. *Disraeli, published 1880.

The novel is set in the period between 1830 and the early 1850s and describes the political and social scene of that time; the antagonism between Whig and Tory; the power of the great political hostesses; the Tractarians; railwaymania; the Chartists; and the story of Louis Napoleon as 'Florestan'. There are many other identifications: Lord Palmerston appears as the engaging Lord Roehampton; Bismark as Ferroll; *Cobbett and Cobden combine in Job Thornberry; *Thackeray (in revenge for his *Codlingsby*) is satirized as St Barbe.

ENGELS, Friedrich (1820–95), German philosopher, the son of a factory owner who supervised his father's business in Manchester. He wrote influential essays on the social and political conditions in Britain in the 1840s, including *The Condition of the Working Class in England* (1845), in which he praised *Carlyle as the only British writer to take account (in *Past and Present*, 1843) of the atrocious working conditions of the urban poor. Engels collaborated with *Marx, whom he helped to support when the latter settled in London in 1849, in writing *The German Ideology* (1845–6, but not published until 1932), a critique of German philosophy as lacking in social application; the *Manifesto of the Communist Party* (1848); and their great work, *Das Kapital*, the third volume of which Engels completed after Marx's death.

Englands Helicon, a miscellany of Elizabethan verse, published in 1600, with additions in 1614. It is the best collection of lyrical and pastoral poetry of the Elizabethan age, and includes pieces by *Sidney, *Spenser, *Drayton, R.

*Greene, T. *Lodge, *Ralegh, *Marlowe, and others.

England's Parnassus, a collection of extracts from contemporary poets, by R. Allott, published in 1600.

English, the Germanic language spoken in England which takes its name from the Angles (who first committed their dialect to writing) and was extended to refer to all the dialects of the vernacular, Saxon and Jutish too. Old English (formerly *Anglo-Saxon) is the English language of the period ending soon after the Norman Conquest (c. 1100–50); Middle English is used to describe the language from then to about 1500; Modern English, founded on the dialect of the East Midlands in Middle English, extends from 1500 to the present day.

English Bards and Scotch Reviewers, a satirical poem by Lord *Byron, published 1809.

Angered by contemptuous criticism of his *Hours of Idleness*, by *Brougham in the *Edinburgh Review*, Byron wrote this vigorous satire, in which he attacks not only *Jeffrey, the editor of the *Review*, but *Southey, Sir W. *Scott, *Wordsworth, *Coleridge, and other poets and poetasters of *Romanticism, at the same time holding up to admiration *Dryden, *Pope, *Burns, *Crabbe, *Campbell, *Rogers, and others who wrote in the classical tradition of the 18th cent.

English Comic Writers, The, essays by W. *Hazlitt, published 1819.

Englishman's Magazine, The (1831–3), an original and ambitious literary monthly, edited by E. *Moxon. It published the work of the unknown young *Tennyson, as well as that of *Hood, *Lamb, Leigh *Hunt, *Clare, A. H. *Hallam, and others. It vigorously supported *Wordsworth and the *'Cockney School', defending them against *Blackwood's, the *Quarterly, and similar journals.

English Review, The, a periodical founded in 1908 through the inspiration of a group of writers including *Conrad, H. G. *Wells, and E. *Garnett, with the purpose, in the words of its first editor F. M. *Ford (then Hueffer) of 'giving imaginative literature a chance in England'. Ford published work by established writers such as Arnold *Bennett, *Galsworthy, H. *James, *Hardy, and Wells, and by newcomers such as D. H. *Lawrence and W. *Lewis. He was replaced by Austin Harrison, who remained editor until 1923. It was eventually merged with the *National Review*.

English Stage Company, an organization founded in 1956 by George Devine (1910–66) to present modern plays and encourage new dramatists; its home is the Royal Court Theatre, London. It has produced important work by *Osborne, *Wesker, *Arden, *Bond, *Beckett, and many others. (See also KITCHEN SINK DRAMA.)

English Traveller, The, a romantic drama by T. *Heywood, written c.1624, printed 1633.

The play concerns the disappointed love of returned traveller Geraldine for the wife of his elderly friend Wincot; she proves faithless to Geraldine's old passion and to her husband, and dies of remorse when challenged with her adultery.

'Enid', see IDYLLS OF THE KING, THE.

Enitharmon, in the mystical books of *Blake, the female counterpart and emanation of *Los, who represents Time, as she represents Space. She also represents Inspiration. She is the mother of the rebellious *Orc. See under URIZEN, THE BOOK OF, and EUROPE: A PROPHECY.

Enjambment, a technical term in verse, signifying the carrying on of the sense of a line or couplet into the next.

Enlightenment, a term (originally taken from the German *Aufklärung*) generally used to describe the philosophic, scientific, and rational spirit, the freedom from superstition, the scepticism and faith in religious tolerance of much 18th-cent. Europe. The ancestors of the movement were *Descartes, *Locke, *Shaftesbury, and *Newton. *Voltaire, *Rousseau, Condorcet, and Buffon were associated with the Enlightenment in the minds of English readers, as was one of its great monuments, *L'*Encyclopédie. In England many writers and poets echo or develop the educational and political ideas of the Enlightenment, including *Godwin, *Shelley, E. *Darwin, *Akenside, and the *Edgeworths. *Blake subscribed to the politics of the Enlightenment, but not to what he saw as the 'single vision' of Newtonian materialism. *Paine was much influenced by the politics of the French Enlightenment and his *The Rights of Man and the American Declaration of Independence were also characteristic products. On a more literary level, some have seen a connection between the philosophy of the Enlightenment, the growth of literary realism, and the rise of the novel: *Romanticism was in part a reaction. (See also SCOTTISH ENLIGHTENMENT.)

ENNIUS, Quintus (239–169 BC), the father of Roman poetry, an Italian from Calabria. His *Annals*, of which 550 survive, show him to have achieved a rugged grandeur. *Dryden mentions him in his critical essays, stressing

*Virgil's debt to him and comparing him to *Chaucer.

Enobarbus (Domitius Ahenobarbus), friend of Antony in Shakespeare's *Antony and Cleopatra.

Enoch Arden, a narrative poem by *Tennyson, published 1864.

Enoch Arden, Philip Ray, and Annie Lee are children together in a little seaport town; both boys love Annie, but Enoch wins and marries her. They live happily for some years, until Enoch is compelled through temporary adversity to go as boatswain in a merchantman. He is shipwrecked, and for more than ten years nothing is heard of him; Annie, consulting her Bible for a sign, puts her finger on the text 'Under the palm tree', which, after a dream, she interprets to mean that he is in heaven. She marries Philip, who has long watched over her. Tennyson then turns to Enoch on his desert island, which is described in a fine, clear, bright Parnassian passage, and contrasted with the 'dewy meadowy morning-breath of England' for which he yearns. He is rescued and returns home, but when he discovers that Annie has remarried does not reveal himself, resolving that she shall not know of his return until after his death.

Enquiry concerning Human Understanding, see HUME, D.

Enquiry into the Present State of Polite Learning, An, a treatise by *Goldsmith, published 1759.

Goldsmith examines the causes of the decline of 'polite learning' from ancient times, through the dark ages, to its present state in Italy, Germany, Holland, France, and England, with perfunctory references to Spain and the Scandinavian countries. He attributes the alleged decay in England to the low status of the writer, driven to hack-work for the booksellers through lack of patronage—'We keep him poor, and yet revile his poverty'; also to the 'disgusting solemnity' and lack of comic spirit among poets, the restrictive conditions of the theatre, and the carping of critics.

ENRIGHT, D(ennis) J(oseph) (1920–), poet. Many of his poems are set on Japan, Egypt, Singapore, and Germany, and concern cultural differences and misunderstandings, themes which he also explores in various critical essays and in his autobiographical *Memoirs of a Mendicant Professor* (1969). His collections of verse include *The Laughing Hyena and other poems* (1953), *Bread rather than Blossoms* (1956), *Addictions* (1962), *Sad Ires* (1975), *A Faust Book* (1979), and *Collected Poems* (1981). He has also published novels for children (*The Joke Shop*, 1976; *Wild Ghost Chase*, 1978; *Beyond Land's End*, 1979) and various other prose works, including *The World of Dew: Aspects of Living Japan* (1955), *Insufficient Poppy* (1960, a novel), and works of criticism, including *Man is an Onion* (1972, collected reviews and essays). His anthologies include *Poets of the 1950s* (1955), which brought together many of the poets to appear in R. Conquest's **New Verse*; and *The Oxford Book of Contemporary Verse 1945–1980* (1980).

Entail, The, a novel by J. *Galt, published 1823, a satire on the corrupting effects of greed.

Eōthen, see KINGLAKE, A.W.

Epic, a poem that celebrates in the form of a continuous narrative the achievements of one or more heroic personages of history or tradition. Among the great epics of the world may be mentioned **The Iliad*, **The Odyssey*, and *The Aeneid* (see VIRGIL) of classical, and the *Mahābhārata and Rāmāyaṇa* of Hindu literature; the *Chanson de Roland* (see ROLAND and CHANSONS DE GESTE); **The Cid*; Boiardo's **Orlando Innamorato*; Ariosto's **Orlando Furioso*; Tasso's **Jerusalem Delivered*; and **Camoëns's Lusiads*.

In English literature, the Anglo-Saxon poem **Beowulf* is perhaps the only genuine epic, if an epic is defined as a long poem of a heroic age, based on anonymous lays and being impersonal and objective in its narrative.

Of 'literary epics', Spenser's **The Faerie Queene* and Milton's **Paradise Lost* are most famous. There was much speculation among critics in the 17th cent. on the theory of epic poetry, and several attempts were made to write an epic in English comparable to *The Iliad*. (Famous examples, both poor and unfinished, are **Cowley's Davideis* and D'Avenant's **Gondibert*.) Wordsworth's **Prelude* has been termed an 'epic of the mind', and Byron's **Don Juan* ranks as epic poetry. Some critics have claimed the same rank for Browning's **The Ring and the Book*; it is perhaps more accurately classed as a 'novel in verse'.

Epicene, or *The Silent Woman*, a comedy by *Jonson, acted 1609, printed 1616.

Morose, an egotistic old bachelor with a pathological aversion to noise, proposes to disinherit his nephew Sir Dauphine Eugenie, by marrying and producing children, provided he can find a silent woman. Cutbeard, his barber, has found such a one in Epicene. Immediately after the wedding Epicene proceeds to torment her husband by turning into a loquacious shrew, and his agony is increased when Dauphine and his friends Truewit and Clerimont arrive with a rowdy party of guests and musicians to celebrate the marriage. Among the guests are a henpecked bearward, Captain Otter, and his Amazonian wife, the *Collegiate Ladies, and two boastful knights, Amorous La Foole and John Daw.

Morose accepts Dauphine's offer to rid him of Epicene for £500 a year and the reversion of his property. Whereupon Dauphine pulls off Epicene's wig and reveals that, unknown to everyone else, including the audience, she is a boy whom he has trained for the part.

Epic Simile, an extended simile which compares one composite action with another, often with a digressive effect; it originates in *Homer, and was imitated by *Virgil, *Dante, and, in English, notably by *Milton. It is frequently parodied by *Fielding.

EPICTETUS (*c.* AD 60–after 100), a *Stoic philosopher. He wrote nothing himself; the *Encheiridion*, or collection of his principles, was complied by his disciple Arrian. Epictetus held health, pleasure, possessions to be of no account. Virtue resided in the will which should direct man to abstain and endure. The *Encheiridion* influenced *Chapman and was praised by *Dryden and M. *Arnold.

EPICURUS (341–270 BC), the founder of the school of philosophy that bears his name, after teaching in various places settled finally in Athens. Some fragments of his writings survive, but his ideas are perhaps best studied in the *De rerum natura* of *Lucretius. Epicurus adopted the atomic theory of *Democritus but postulated an indeterminacy in the movement of his atoms which allowed him to believe in free will. In ethics he regarded the absence of pain—ἀταραξα or peace of mind—as the greatest good. Conventional moralists tended to describe him as a contemptible pleasure-seeker, but Sir T. *Browne defends his reputation (*Pseudodoxia*, 7. 17).

Epigram, originally an inscription, usually in verse, e.g. on a tomb; hence a short poem ending in a witty turn of thought; hence a pointed or antithetical saying.

Epigrams, The, a collection of poems by *Jonson, printed 1616, including 'Inviting a Friend to Supper', 'On My First Son', 'The Famous Voyage', and addresses to *Donne and King James.

Epiphany, 'manifestation', usually used in a Christian context to refer to the festival commemorating the manifestations of Christ to the Gentiles in the persons of the Magi (celebrated on 6 Jan., or Twelfth Night); but adapted by *Joyce to describe the sudden 'revelation of the whatness of a thing', the moment in which 'the soul of the commonest object seems to us radiant'. He uses the word in this sense in *Stephen Hero*, an early draft of **A Portrait of the Artist as a Young Man*; these 'sudden spiritual manifestations' bear some similarity to the 'spots of time' described by Wordsworth in *The Prelude* (see Bk XI, ll. 208 ff.).

Epipsychidion, an autobiographical poem by P. B. *Shelley, published 1821.

Composed in couplets of breathless energy, the poem celebrates Shelley's lifelong search for the eternal image of Beauty, in the earthly form of his various wives, mistresses, and female friends: notably Harriet Westbrook, Mary *Shelley, Claire *Clairmont, and Emilia Viviani—to whom the work is addressed. Though drawing on the courtly love and planetary imagery of *Petrarch and *Dante, the work is passionately sexual as well as Platonic: it ends with an invitation to Emilia to elope to 'an isle under Ionian skies, | Beautiful as a wreck of Paradise'. There is an attack on conventional marriage, 'the dreariest and longest journey', and praise of 'Free' or 'True' Love (ll. 148–73). The poem is also a study of the creative process itself.

Epistolae Obscurorum Virorum (*Epistles of Obscure Men*), published 1515–17, an anonymous collection of letters in medieval Latin in support of the new learning. The letters are attributed principally to Ulrich von Hutten (1488–1523), soldier, humanist, and supporter of *Luther.

Epistolary novel, a story written in the form of letters, or letters with journals, and usually presented by an anonymous author masquerading as 'editor'. The first notable example in English was a translation from the French in 1678, *Letters of a Portugese Nun*. In 1683, A. *Behn published *Love-letters between a Nobleman and his Sister*, and many similar tales of illicit love and love-manuals followed. Thus when *Richardson, the first and perhaps greatest master of the form, came to write *Pamela* (1741) he felt a duty to rescue the novel from its tainted reputation. Between the 1740s and about 1800 the form flourished; it was employed by Richardson, *Smollett, *Bage, J. *Moore (the elder), and F. *Burney, among many others. After 1800 M. *Edgeworth, J. *Austen, *Swinburne, H. *James, and others experimented with the form but it is now rarely adopted. W. *Golding's *Rites of Passage* (1980) provides an interesting variation in the form of an epistolary journal. (See also NOVEL, RISE OF THE.)

Epithalamion, a hymn by *Spenser (perhaps in celebration of his marriage with Elizabeth Boyle in 1594) printed with the *Amoretti in 1595. Its beauty of composition has always been much admired.

Epithalamium, or **Epithalamion,** a poem or song written to celebrate a marriage. The form flourished in the Renaissance, one of the most notable examples being Spenser's *Epithalamion.

Eponymous, that gives his name to anything, used for example of the mythical personages from whose names the names of places or peoples are reputed to be derived. It is now most frequently used in the phrase, 'the eponymous hero/heroine' of a work: e.g. *Tom Jones or *Clarissa.

Eppie, in G. Eliot's *Silas Marner*, the daughter of Cass and adopted child of Silas.

ERASMUS, Desiderius (c.1467–1536), the great Dutch humanist, came more than once to England, where he was welcomed by the great scholars of the day, *More, *Colet, and *Grocyn, and was induced by *Fisher to lecture at Cambridge on Greek from 1511 to 1514. His principal works include a new edition of the Greek New Testament (1516), followed by Latin paraphrases (1517–24); *Encomium Moriae* (*The Praise of Folly*, 1511, a satire written at the suggestion of More, principally directed against theologians and Church dignitaries); *Institutio Christiani Principis* (*Education of a Christian Prince*); the vivid and entertaining *Colloquia* and letters furnishing autobiographical detail and pictures of contemporary life, which were drawn upon by C. Reade in *The Cloister and the Hearth* and by Sir W. *Scott in *Anne of Geierstein*. His many editions and translations of the Bible, early Christian authors, and the classics revolutionized European literary culture. Erasmus prepared the way for the Reformation by his writings. With the movement itself he sympathized at first, but he refused to intervene either for or against *Luther at the time of the Diet of Worms, although invoked by both sides. He urged moderation on both and disclaimed sympathy with Luther's violence and extreme conclusions, and at a later stage (1524, in his tract on 'Free Will') entered into controversy with him.

ERCELDOUNE, Thomas of, called also the Rhymer and Learmont (fl. ?1220–?97), seer and poet, is said to have predicted the death of Alexander III, king of Scotland, and the battle of Bannockburn, and is the traditional source of many (fabricated) oracles. He is the reputed author of a poem on the *Tristram story, which Sir W. *Scott considered genuine.

Erewhon (e-re-whon, an anagram of 'nowhere'), a satirical novel by S. *Butler, published anonymously 1872.

The narrator (whose name is revealed in *Erewhon Revisited* as Higgs) crosses a range of mountains and comes upon the undiscovered country of Erewhon. He is first thrown into gaol, where he is helped by his beautiful girl gaoler, Yram. On his release he is lodged with Mr Nosnibor (Robinson) and his family. In this society morality is equated with health and beauty, and crime with illness. The Unborn select their parents, who have to endure their selection. The Musical Banks produce a currency which is venerated but not used. The development of machinery, which had at one stage threatened to usurp human supremacy, had led to a civil war and is now forbidden. The country is ruled by so-called philosophers and prophets, whom Higgs sees to be merely faddists and fanatics. When he is threatened with prosecution for contracting measles, Higgs announces that he will visit the air-god and end the terrible drought; with Nosnibor's daughter Arowhena, he escapes in a balloon to England, where they marry.

Erewhon Revisited, a sequel to *Erewhon*, by S. *Butler, published 1901.

After 20 years Higgs finds that his ascent in the balloon has become that of a god, the Sunchild, in a sun-chariot, his conversation has become the basis of sacred texts, a temple has been built to him at Sunchildston, and that the new religion is organized by two cynical exploiters, professors Hanky and Panky. Once again Higgs's life is threatened, but again he escapes and, after further bewildered wanderings in Erewhon, returns, half unhinged, to England.

ERIGENA, see SCOTUS ERIGENA.

Erin, the ancient name of Ireland.

Eros, in Shakespeare's *Antony and Cleopatra*, is the faithful attendant of Antony, who kills himself to avoid killing his master.

Erse, a term formerly used for Irish Gaelic (i.e. Irish) or occasionally (and inaccurately, since the term is the Lowland Scots word for Irish) for Scots Gaelic.

ERVINE, St John Greer (1883–1971), playwright and novelist, born in Belfast. Many of his early plays (including *Mixed Marriage*, 1911; *The Magnanimous Lover*, 1912; and *John Ferguson*, 1915) were performed at the *Abbey Theatre in its realist phase, and dealt with themes of religious violence and conflict in Northern Ireland. Ervine later moved to England, where he wrote as drama critic for the *Morning Post and the *Observer*, and achieved his first West End success with *The First Mrs Fraser* (1929).

Esmond, see HISTORY OF HENRY ESMOND, THE.

Esmond, Beatrix, a character in Thackeray's *The History of Henry Esmond* and, as Baroness Bernstein, in *The Virginians*.

Esoteric, a word used by *Lucian, who attributes to *Aristotle a classification of his own works into 'esoteric', i.e. designed for, or appropriate to, an inner circle of advanced or privileged disciples, and 'exoteric', i.e. popular, untechnical. Later writers use the word to designate the secret doctrines said to have been taught by *Pythagoras to a select few of his disciples; it has come to denote any work restricted to a narrow, informed audience.

Esperanto, an artificial language for universal use invented (c.1887) by a Polish physician, Dr L. L. Zamenhof.

Essay concerning Human Understanding, a philosophical treatise by *Locke, published 1690 (2nd edn, 1694; 4th, 1700; 5th, 1706; all with large additions).

The Essay is an examination of the nature of the human mind and its powers of understanding. Locke begins in Bk I by rejecting the doctrine of 'innate ideas', maintaining that all knowledge is based on experience. The objects of understanding are termed by him *ideas*, and Bk II provides an account of the origin, sorts, and extent of our ideas. The source of ideas is *experience*, the observation of external objects or of the internal operations of the mind, i.e. sensation or reflection.

In Bk III Locke discusses language. He holds that words have meaning in so far as they stand for ideas in the mind; distinguishing between 'real' and 'nominal' essence, he argues that terms for natural kinds (e.g. 'gold', 'horse') can express only nominal essences or sets of ideas.

Bk IV defines knowledge as the perception of the agreement or disagreement of ideas. It is either intuitive and direct, demonstrative (through the interposition of a third idea), or 'sensitive', i.e. based upon perception. Knowledge in matters of real existence is limited to two certainties, of our own existence, by intuition and of the existence of God, by demonstration. We have a lesser degree of certainty of the existence of finite beings without us, for which we must rely on sensitive knowledge. The faculty that God has given us in place of clear knowledge is judgement, whereby the mind takes a proposition to be true or false without demonstration. Locke discusses the relations of faith and reason. Unlike F. *Bacon and *Hobbes, he holds that faith is nothing but the firm assent of the mind, which should not be accorded to anything except for good reason. Revelation must be judged by reason. But the field of knowledge being so limited, it must be supplemented by faith, and this is the basis of his *Reasonableness of Christianity* (1695).

Essay on Criticism, a didactic poem in heroic couplets by *Pope, published anonymously 1711. It begins with an exposition of the rules of taste and the authority to be attributed to the ancient writers on the subject. The laws by which a critic should be guided are then discussed, and instances are given of critics who have departed from them. The work is remarkable as having been written when Pope was only 21.

Essay on Man, a philosophical poem in heroic couplets by *Pope, published 1732–4.

It consists of four epistles addressed to *Bolingbroke, and perhaps to some extent inspired by his fragmentary philosophical writings. Its objective is to vindicate the ways of God to man; to prove that the scheme of the universe is the best of all possible schemes, in spite of appearances of evil, and that our failure to see the perfection of the whole is due to our limited vision.

Essays, The, or Counsels, Civill and Morall, of F. *Bacon, are collections of reflections and generalizations, and extracts from previous authors, woven together, for the most part, into counsels for the successful conduct of life and the management of men.

Three editions of the essays were published in Bacon's lifetime (1597, 1612, 1625). Of these some deal with questions of state policy, such as the essay on 'Greatness of Kingdoms'; some with personal conduct, such as those on 'Wisdom for a Man's Self' and 'Cunning'; some on abstract subjects, such as 'Truth', 'Death', and 'Unity'; while some reveal Bacon's delight in Nature, such as the pleasant essay on 'Gardens'.

Essays and Reviews, a collection of essays on religious subjects from a *Broad Church standpoint, published 1860. The essayists were the Revd H. B. Wilson (editor), M. *Pattison, *Jowett, Frederick Temple, Rowland Williams, Baden Powell, and C. W. Goodwin. A meeting of the bishops, urged on by Samuel Wilberforce, in 1861 denounced the book for its liberalism. Williams and Wilson were condemned to deprivation for a year, but were acquitted on appeal. The Essays were finally synodically condemned in 1864.

Essays Contributed to the Edinburgh Review, Critical and Historical, by T. B. *Macaulay, a collection published in 1843 and later editions. The essays deal with literary and historical subjects, taking the form not so much of a review as of a general survey of the subject of the book discussed; topics include *Milton, *Machiavelli, *Croker's edition of Boswell, Horace *Walpole, Sir F. *Bacon, Sir W. *Temple, W. Hastings, and *Addison.

Essays in Criticism, three series of essays by M. *Arnold (1865, 1888, 1910).

Essays of Elia, The, miscellaneous essays by C. *Lamb. The first series appeared in the *London Magazine, 1820–23, and as a separate volume 1823. The Last Essays of Elia were published in 1833. Lamb adopted the name Elia, which was that of a former Italian clerk at the South Sea House, ostensibly to save the embarrassment of his brother John, who worked at that same place. The essays are not reliably autobiographical. The fanciful, old-fashioned character of the narrator is, in Lamb's words, 'a bundle of prejudices' with a strong liking for the whimsical, the quaint, and the eccentric. The tone is never didactic or seriously philosophical, and all the more disturbing aspects of life are avoided. The style is very literary, filled with archaisms and with echoes of Lamb's master *Sterne. Some of the best-known essays were: 'Some of the Old Benchers of the Inner Temple'; 'Christ's Hospital'; 'The South Sea House'; 'Mrs Battle's Opinions on Whist'; 'Dream Children'; and 'A Dissertation on Roast Pig'.

ESSEX, Robert Devereux, second earl of (1566–1601). He was regarded as the natural successor to *Sidney, whose widow he married in 1590. He was despatched to Ireland in March 1599 to suppress Tyrone's rebellion. Shakespeare referred optimistically in *Henry V (v. Prologue 29–34) to the successful return of 'the General of our gracious Empress', but in fact Essex's return was sudden and ignominious. A special performance of Shakespeare's *Richard II, showing a monarch willingly abdicating an unpopular rule, had been among the activities by which Essex and his friends fomented discontent. Essex was executed on 25 Feb., the episode casting a dark shadow over the last 18 months of Elizabeth's reign. He was a literary patron of some discernment, and himself wrote poems. L. *Strachey's Elizabeth and Essex (1928) is a highly coloured and highly readable fictionalization.

Estella, a character in Dickens's *Great Expectations.

Esther Lyon (or **Bycliffe**), the heroine of G. Eliot's *Felix Holt.

Esther Summerson, a character in Dickens's *Bleak House, and narrator of part of the story.

Esther Waters, a novel by G. *Moore, published in 1894.

It is the story of the life of a religiously minded girl, a Plymouth sister, driven from home into service at 17 by a drunken stepfather. She obtains a situation at Woodview, the house of the Barfields, where a racing-stable is kept, and all above- and below-stairs (except Mrs Barfield, a Plymouth Sister like Esther) are wrapped up in gambling on races. She is seduced by a fellow servant and has to leave. Poverty, hardship, and humiliation follow: the lying-in hospital, service as wet-nurse, even the workhouse, in her struggle to rear her child. Her seducer re-enters her life and marries her. But he is a bookmaker and publican; exposure to weather at the races ruins his health and trouble with the authorities over betting at his public house causes the latter to be closed. He dies, and leaves his wife and son penniless. Finally Esther returns to Woodview, where she finds peace at last with Mrs Barfield, now a widow, living alone and impoverished in a corner of the old house.

Estrildis, a German princess captured and brought to England by King *Humber (according to *Geoffrey of Monmouth's *History*).
*Locrine, king of Britain, fell in love with her and they had a daughter Habren (*Sabrina). Locrine put aside his wife Gwendolen for her, but she exacted vengeance on him by pursuing and slaying him in battle and having Estrildis and her daughter drowned in the river Severn, thereafter named from the daughter. The story is treated in *Lodge's 'The Complaynt of Elstred' (1593), in Spenser's *Faerie Queene* (II. x), and in *Swinburne's drama *Locrine* (1887).

ETHEREGE, or **ETHEREDGE,** Sir George (?1634–91). His first comedy, *The Comical Revenge, or Love in a Tub*, was performed in 1664. The serious portions are in rhymed heroics, setting a fashion that was followed for some years, while the lively and realistic comic underplot, in prose, was the foundation of the English comedy of manners of *Congreve and *Goldsmith; Etherege drew his inspiration in part from *Molière's farces and from Italian mime. In 1668 *She wou'd if she cou'd was performed. His best play, *The Man of Mode, was performed in 1676. He was knighted, c.1680, and was an envoy of James II in Ratisbon, 1685–9; his *Letterbook*, recording his stay and his non-chalant attitude to his duties was edited in 1928 by S. Rosenfeld. His polished and fashionable comedies were savagely attacked as immoral and coarse by the more genteel generation of *Steele, and the 19th cent. found them formless and plotless, but they now enjoy a high reputation.

Ettrick Shepherd, The, a name given to James *Hogg.

Eugene Aram, a novel by *Bulwer-Lytton, published 1832. It is the story of a schoolmaster, driven to crime by poverty, who is later tormented by remorse. The same subject suggested T. *Hood's poem 'The Dream of Eugene Aram'.

Eugenius, a minor character in *Tristram Shandy*, and *A Sentimental Journey*, by L. Sterne, thought to be based on Sterne's friend, *Hall-Stevenson.

EULENSPIEGEL, Till, a German born according to tradition about 1300, the son of a peasant, and the subject of a collection of satirical tales, German or Flemish in origin, published in 1519 (Flemish version 1520–1). He is a scapegrace whose knaveries and escapades are carried on under a pretence of simplicity and stupidity, and are directed against noblemen, priests, tradesmen, and innkeepers. One of these incidents figures in Chaucer's 'Summoner's Tale' (*Canterbury Tales*, 8). The book was translated into many languages, among others into English in an abridged form by William Copland, under the title of *A merye jest of a man that was called Howleglas* (?1555, ?1560).

Euphues, a prose romance by *Lyly, of which the first part, *Euphues. The Anatomy of Wit*, was published in 1578, and the second, *Euphues and his England*, 1580. The plot of each is very slender and little but a peg on which to hang discourses, conversations, and letters, mainly on the subject of love. The work is largely based on North's *Diall of Princes*.
Euphues is famous for its peculiar style, to which it has given the name 'Euphuism'. Its principal characteristics are the excessive use of antithesis, which is pursued regardless of sense, and emphasized by alliteration and other devices; and of allusions to historical and mythological personages and to natural history drawn from such writers as *Plutarch, *Pliny, and *Erasmus. Sir W. *Scott satirized Euphuism in the character of Sir Piercie Shafton in *The Monastery* and C. *Kingsley defended *Euphues* in *Westward Ho!*

Euphues Golden Legacie, see ROSALYNDE.

Euphuism, see EUPHUES.

EURIPIDES (480–406 BC), the youngest of the great Attic tragedians. The strength of Euripides lay in his ability to represent ordinary human beings, especially women, with impassioned sympathy. Nineteen of his plays have survived. Milton's *Samson Agonistes* was the first English tragedy to show his influence. *Dryden praised his depiction of human behaviour, and *Shelley translated his satyr play *Cyclops*. But it was at the end of the 19th cent. that Euripides truly made his mark. W. *Morris sentimentalized the *Medea* in *The Life and Death of Jason* (1867) and the *Alcestis* in *The Earthly Paradise* (1868–70). R. *Browning, commenting on the *Alcestis*, arraigned Admetus in *Balaustion's Adventure* (1871) and defended Euripides in *Aristophanes' Apology* (1875).

Europe: A Prophecy, a poem by W. *Blake, printed 1794 at Lambeth, in which Blake portrays the oppression of Albion during the 1,800-year sleep of *Enitharmon, the female principle, and the approach of the French Revolution, symbolized by her son, the terrible

*Orc, spirit of revolt. The frontispiece of *Europe* portrays *Urizen as the Creator with his measuring instruments, and I. *Newton appears in the poem as an ambiguous herald of change.

EUSDEN, Laurence (1688–1730), poet laureate from 1718 until his death. He had celebrated the marriage of the duke of Newcastle, who gave him the laureateship. Pope refers to his notorious drinking habits in *The Dunciad* (Bk i. 293):

Know, Eusden thirsts no more for sack or praise;
He sleeps among the dull of ancient days.

EUSEBIUS of Caesarea, in Palestine (AD 265–340), a celebrated historian and theologian. His *Chronicle* in Greek (known in a Latin version by St *Jerome) is the basis of our knowledge of the dates of events in Greek and Roman history. He was involved in the *Arian controversy, was one of the leaders at the Council of Nicaea, and voted for the 'Nicene formula'. He was a voluminous writer and a valuable authority on the early church.

Eustace Diamonds, The, a novel by A. *Trollope, published 1873, the third in the *'Palliser' series.
Lizzie Eustace marries for money and, when Sir Florian Eustace dies, she not only inherits the family estates at Portray, but pockets the family diamonds as well, despite the demands of the Eustace lawyers that they be returned. She looks for support to her cousin and legal adviser Frank Greystock, but when his engagement to the demure governess Lucy Morris proves too durable, she sets her cap at the stuffy Lord Fawn. Fawn proposes, but stipulates that the necklace must be returned to the Eustace estate. Lizzie retires to Portray, and assembles a curious collection of house-guests, including dashing Lord George de Bruce Carruthers, who becomes her third suitor, and the fashionable preacher Mr Emilius, who becomes her fourth. When Lizzie and her entourage set off southwards, Lizzie's bedroom is robbed at Carlisle. The thieves get away with the casket but not the jewels, which Lizzie has extracted for safe keeping. The police begin to be suspicious, and when Lizzie is robbed a second time she is unable to conceal her trickery. Lord Fawn drops her immediately, Frank Greystock stops procrastinating and marries Lucy Morris, Lord George disappears, and Lizzie has no alternative but to marry Mr Emilius—without, as it will turn out, sufficiently enquiring into his shady past.

Eva, Little, see LITTLE EVA.

Evadne, a character in Beaumont and Fletcher's *The Maid's Tragedy*.

Evandale, Lord, a character in Scott's *Old Mortality*.

Evangeline, a narrative poem by *Longfellow.

Evan Harrington, a novel by G. *Meredith, published 1861.
The hero Evan is, like the author, a tailor's son, and the novel is a comedy of social class in which Evan is torn between the desire of his successfully married sisters to conceal their humble origins and arrange a grand marriage for him, and his mother's determination that he shall carry on the family business.

EVANS, Sir Arthur John (1851–1941), devoted much energy to transforming the Ashmolean Museum into the centre of archaeology in Oxford. From 1893 his archaeological investigations in Crete, which centred on the excavations of the palace at Knossos, resulted in the discovery of the pre-Phoenician script and an entire new Bronze Age civilization which he named 'Minoan'. His most important publications were *Scripta Minoa* (1909–52) and *The Palace of Minos at Knossos* (1922–35).

Evans, Sir Hugh, Welsh parson in Shakespeare's *The Merry Wives of Windsor*.

EVANS, Mary Ann, see ELIOT, G.

Evans's, in the NW corner of the Piazza, Covent Garden, became famous for its musical parties and suppers. *Thackeray's 'Cave of Harmony' is partly drawn from it.

Evelina, *or a Young Lady's Entrance into the World*, an *epistolary novel by F. Burney, published anonymously 1778.
Sir John Belmont, disappointed of the fortune he expected to receive with his wife, abandons her and their child Evelina, who is brought up in seclusion by a guardian, Mr Villars. Evelina, goes to visit a friend, Mrs Mirvan, in London, where she is introduced into society and falls in love with the handsome Lord Orville. But she is much mortified by her vulgar grandmother, Mme Duval, her ill-bred relatives, and the pursuit of her persistent lover, Sir Clement Willoughby. Sir John Belmont is asked to recognize Evelina as his daughter, but he insists that his daughter has been in his care since infancy. It is now discovered that Lady Belmont's nurse had passed her own child off on Sir John. Evelina is recognized as his heir, and marries Lord Orville.

EVELYN, John (1620–1706), a member of the *Royal Society, and a man of varied cultural interests, including gardening; among his friends were Jeremy *Taylor and *Pepys. His works include *Sculptura* (1662) on engraving; *Sylva* (1664), an influential work on practical arboriculture; and translations from the French on architecture, gardening, etc. He is remembered principally for his *Memoirs* or *Diary*, first published in 1818 and in a full and authoritative edition by E. S. de Beer in 1955 (6 vols). It covers most of his life, describing his travels abroad, his contemporaries, and his public and domestic concerns, and is an invaluable record of the period. His *Life of Mrs Godolphin* was first printed in 1847.

'Evening, Ode to', see COLLINS, W.

Evening's Love, An, or *The Mock Astrologer,* a comedy by *Dryden produced 1668, published 1671.

The Preface to this play is among the most attractive of Dryden's critical essays.

'Eve of St Agnes, The', a narrative poem in Spenserian stanzas by *Keats, written 1819, published 1820.

Madeline has been told the legend that on St Agnes's Eve maidens may have visions of their lovers. Madeline's love, Porphyro, comes from a family hostile to her own, and she is herself surrounded by 'hyena foemen, and hot-blooded lords'. Yet he steals into the house on St Agnes's Eve. When she wakes from dreams of him, aroused by his soft singing, she finds him by her bedside. Silently they escape from the house, and fly 'away into the storm'.

Everdene, Bathsheba, a character in Hardy's *Far from the Madding Crowd.*

Ever Green, The, see RAMSAY, A.

'Everlasting Gospel, The', a poem by W. *Blake.

Everyman, a popular morality play in 921 lines (*c.*1509–19), almost certainly derived from its Dutch close counterpart *Elckerlijc.* Everyman is summoned by death and, in the last hour of his life, he discovers that his friends Fellowship, Kindred, Cousin, and Goods will not go with him. He is dependent on the support of Good Deeds whom he has previously neglected. It is the most admired of the English *Morality Plays and it has had a revival of popularity in the 20th cent.

Every Man in his Humour, a comedy by *Jonson, performed by the Lord Chamberlain's Men 1598, with Shakespeare in the cast, printed 1601. In his folio of 1616 Jonson published an extensively revised version, with the setting changed from Florence to London and the characters given English names.

In the latter version Kitely, a merchant, is the husband of a young wife, and his 'humour' is irrational jealousy. His house is resorted to by his brother-in-law Wellbred with a crowd of riotous but harmless gallants, and these he suspects of designs both on his wife and on his

sister Bridget. One of these young men is Edward Knowell, whose father's 'humour' is excessive concern for his son's morals. Bobadill, one of Jonson's greatest creations, a 'Paul's man', is a boastful cowardly soldier, who associates with the young men and is admired by Matthew, a 'town gull' and poetaster, and Edward's cousin Stephen, a 'country gull'. Out of these elements, by the aid of the devices and disguises of the mischievous Brainworm, Knowell's servant, an imbroglio is produced in which Kitely and his wife are brought face to face at the house of a water-bearer to which each thinks the other has gone for an amorous assignation; Bobadill is exposed and beaten; Edward Knowell is married to Bridget; and Matthew and Stephen are held up to ridicule. The misunderstandings are cleared up by the shrewd and kindly Justice Clement.

Every Man out of his Humour, a comedy by *Jonson, acted by the Lord Chamberlain's Men at the newly built Globe theatre 1599, printed 1600.

The play parades a variety of characters dominated by particular 'humours', or obsessive quirks of disposition; Macilente, a venomous malcontent; Carlo Buffone, a cynical jester; the uxorious Deliro and his domineering wife Fallace; Fastidious Brisk, an affected courtier devoted to fashion; Sordido, a miserly farmer, and his son Fungoso, who longs to be a courtier; Sogliardo, 'an essential clown, enamoured of the name of a gentleman'; and Puntarvolo, a fantastic, vainglorious knight, who wagers that he, his dog, and his cat can travel to Constantinople and back. By means of various episodes, each character is eventually driven 'out of his humour'. Two judicious onlookers, Mitis and Cordatus, provide a moral commentary.

Everyman's Library, a series of reprints of the world's masterpieces in literature, and some original reference works, founded in 1906 by publisher Joseph Malaby Dent (1849–1926) and first edited by Ernest Rhys (1859–1946).

Evidences of Christianity, see PALEY, W.

EWART, Gavin Buchanan (1916–), poet, contributed to G. Grigson's *New Verse* when he was seventeen; his first volume, *Poems and Songs* (1939) was followed, after a long interval, by *Londoners* (1964) and he has since published several volumes of poetry, mainly of light, comic, satiric, and erotic verse, which shows the influence of *Auden: these include *Pleasures of the Flesh* (1966), *Or Where a Young Penguin Lies Screaming* (1977), *All my Little Ones* (1978), *More Little Ones* (1982). *The Collected Ewart 1933–1980* (1980) was followed by *The new Ewart: Poems 1980–1982* (1982). He has also edited the *Penguin Book of Light Verse* (1980) and *Other People's*

Clerihews (1983), and is himself a master of the
*limerick, the *clerihew, and the occasional
verse.

EWING, Mrs (Juliana Horatia) (1841–85),
writer of books for children. These include *The
Land of the Lost Toys* (1869), *Jackanapes* (1879),
A Flat Iron for a Farthing (1872), and *Lob-lie-by-
the-Fire* (1873).

***Examination of Sir William Hamilton's Philo-
sophy,*** a treatise by J. S. *Mill, in which he
attacks *Hamilton's epistemology and his logic,
published 1865, amplified in subsequent
editions.

Examiner, The, (1) a Tory periodical started by
*Bolingbroke in Aug. 1710; *Swift briefly took
charge in Oct. (Nos 14–46), and was succeeded
by Mrs *Manley in 1711. It engaged in controversy with Steele's *Guardian and *Addison's
Whig Examiner. It lasted with interruptions until
1716. (2) (1808–81), a Radical weekly periodical,
established by John and Leigh *Hunt. Its first 20
years were of particular interest because of Leigh
Hunt's support for the work of *Shelley, *Keats,
*Lamb, and *Hazlitt, whose writing was often
bitterly attacked by the *Quarterly and *Blackwood's (see also COCKNEY SCHOOL). The political
section supported reform, and the Hunts were
fined £500 and sentenced to two years' imprisonment for a libel on the Prince of Wales.

Excalibur, a corrupt form of 'Caliburn' (the
name used in *Geoffrey of Monmouth), was
King Arthur's sword, which he drew out of a
stone when no one else could move it or which
was given to him by the Lady of the Lake
(*Malory, Bk I). When Arthur was mortally
wounded in the last battle, he ordered Sir
Bedevere to throw Excalibur into the lake. A
hand rose from the water, took the sword, and
vanished.

Excursion, The, a poem in nine books by
W. *Wordsworth, published 1814. This is the
middle section of a projected three-part poem
'on man, on nature and on human life', of which
this part alone was completed. The whole work
was to have been entitled 'The Recluse', 'as
having for its principal subject the sensations and
opinions of a poet living in retirement'. It was
planned in 1798, when Wordsworth was living
near *Coleridge at Alfoxden.

The story is very slight. The poet, travelling
with the Wanderer, a philosophic pedlar, meets
with the pedlar's friend, the sad and pessimistic
Solitary. The source of the Solitary's despondency is found in his want of religious
faith and of confidence in the virtue of man, and
he is reproved with gentle and persuasive argument. The Pastor is then introduced, who
illustrates the harmonizing effects of virtue and

religion through narratives of people interred in
his churchyard. They visit the Pastor's house,
and the Wanderer draws his general and philosophic conclusions from the discussions that
have passed. The last two books deal in particular with the industrial expansion of the early part
of the century, and the degradation that followed in its train. The poem ends with the
Pastor's prayer that man may be given grace to
conquer guilt and sin, and with praise for the
beauty of the world about them. Bk I contains
'The Story of Margaret' or *'The Ruined Cottage', originally written as a separate poem.

Exeter Book, The, one of the most important
manuscripts containing Old English poetry,
copied about 940, given by Bishop Leofric
(d. 1072) to Exeter Cathedral, where it still
remains. It contains many of the most admired
shorter poems, such as *The Wanderer, *The
Seafarer, *Deor, *Widsith, *The Ruin, *'Wulf and
Eadwacer', and *The Husband's Message, most of
which are grouped together as 'The Exeter Book
Elegies', as well as a famous collection of Riddles
and some longer religious poems, notably
*Guthlac, *The Phoenix, and *Cynewulf's
Juliana.

Existentialism, the name commonly given to
a group of somewhat loosely associated
philosophical doctrines and ideas which have
found contemporary expression in the work of
such men as *Sartre, Heidegger, Marcel,
*Camus, and Jaspers. Though the theories
advanced by different existentialist writers
diverge widely in many important respects,
certain underlying themes can be singled out as
characteristic. Existentialists tend, for example,
to emphasize the unique and particular in human
experience; they place the individual person at
the centre of their pictures of the world, and are
suspicious of philosophical or psychological
doctrines that obscure this essential individuality
by speaking as if there were some abstract
'human nature', some set of general laws or
principles, to which men are determined or
required, by their common humanity, to conform. Each man is what he chooses to be or
make himself. Sartre, in particular, insists upon
the notion of the individual as the source of all
value, and as being obliged to choose for himself
what to do and what standards to adopt or reject:
consciousness of such freedom is a condition of
'authentic' existence. Thus existentialists typically give priority to sincerity and creativity in the
moral life, and sometimes appear to regard any
decision as justified if it is made in perfect
honesty and with absolute inner conviction. In
their psychological explorations they have often
shown an impressive insight and introduced
interpretative concepts which have greatly
extended the area of moral self-knowledge and
self-awareness. This, perhaps more than anything, explains the wide appeal of their writings.

Exodus, a 590-line poem in Old English, based on the biblical story, contained in the *Junius manuscript probably dating from the early 8th cent. It used to be attributed to *Caedmon, and it contains a vigorous description of the destruction of the Egyptians in the Red Sea.

Exoteric, see ESOTERIC.

Experience, Songs of, see SONGS OF INNOCENCE.

Expressionism, a term coined in the early 20th cent. to describe a movement in art, then in literature, the theatre, and the cinema, characterized by boldness, distortion, and forceful representation of the emotions. One of its earliest manifestations was in the group of German painters, *Die Brücke* ('the Bridge'), formed in Dresden in 1905 and influenced by Van Gogh and Munch. In the theatre the term has been associated with the works of Toller, *Strindberg, Wedekind, and early *Brecht, and embraces a wide variety of moods—satirical, grotesque, visionary, exclamatory, violent, but always anti-naturalistic. The epitome of Expressionism in German cinema was Robert Wiene's *The Cabinet of Dr Caligari* (1919). Expressionism flourished principally in Germany, and took little root in Britain, though W. *Lewis and *Vorticism have some affinities with it, and traces of its influence can be found in the verse dramas of *Auden and *Isherwood, and later in the cinema (e.g. G. *Greene's *The Third Man,* directed by Carol Reed, 1949).

Extravaganza, a composition, literary, musical, or dramatic, of an extravagant or fantastic character.

Eyeless in Gaza, a novel by A. *Huxley, published 1936. The title is a quotation from Milton's *Samson Agonistes.*

It traces the career of Anthony Beavis from the death of his mother in his early boyhood in 1902, through various emotional entanglements and intellectual quests, to his involvement with a pacifist movement in 1935. At preparatory school Beavis is acquainted with three characters whose lives deeply affect his own: his closest friend, the sensitive intellectual Brian Foxe (modelled on Huxley's brother Trevenen) who later, like Trevenen, commits suicide; Hugh Ledwidge, pompous victim, with whose wife Helen he has an affair; and Mark Staithes, who becomes a Marxist and leads Beavis to a revolution in Mexico where he loses a leg and Beavis finds a faith. The main theatre of the novel is a sophisticated, iconoclastic, intellectual, middle-class English world, rich in references to Pavlov and Krafft-Ebing, anthropology and sociology, masturbation and Proust. Much of the novel is clearly autobiographical. It is rich in portraits, ranging from that of Beavis's pedantic and uxorious philologist father, to Mary Amberley, Helen's mother, who turns from lovers to morphia, and the possessive, high-minded, destructive Mrs Foxe.

EYRE, Simon (d. 1459), according to *Stow, a draper who became mayor of London, was a generous benefactor of the city, and built Leadenhall as a public granary and market. He figures in Dekker's *The Shoemaker's Holiday.*

F

FABER, Frederick William (1814–63), under the influence of *Newman, was received into the Roman Catholic Church in 1845. He was the author of many devotional books, and hymns, including 'My God, how wonderful Thou art'.

Faber Book of Modern Verse, The, an anthology published in 1936, edited by M. *Roberts, which did much to influence taste and establish the reputations of a rising generation of poets, including *Auden, *MacNeice, *Empson, *Graves, Dylan *Thomas. In his introduction, Roberts traces the influences of *Clough, G. M. *Hopkins (himself well represented), the French *Symbolists, etc. on modern poetry, defines the 'European' sensibility of such writers as T. S. *Eliot, *Pound, and *Yeats, and offers a persuasive apologia for various aspects of *Modernism.

FABIAN, Robert, see FABYAN.

Fabian Society, The, a society founded in 1884 consisting of Socialists who advocate a 'Fabian' policy, as opposed to immediate revolutionary action, and named after Quintus Fabius Maximus (below). One of its instigators was Thomas Davidson (1840–1900). The Fabians aimed to influence government and affect policy by permeation rather than by direct power. The first two Fabian tracts were *Why are the Many Poor* (1884) by W. L. Phillips, a house painter and one of the few working-class members, and *A Manifesto* (1884) by G. B. *Shaw, who also edited *Fabian Essays in Socialism* (1889), with contributions by S. *Webb, Sydney Olivier, and A. *Besant. The Society itself continued to attract a distinguished membership of politicians, intellectuals, artists, and writers, ranging from Keir Hardie, Ramsay Macdonald, and G. D. H. *Cole to E. *Carpenter, E. *Nesbit, R. *Brooke, and the painter Walter Crane.

FABIUS (Quintus Fabius Maximus) (d. 203 BC), nicknamed *Cunctator* (the man who delays taking action), was appointed dictator after Hannibal's victory at Trasimene (217 BC). He carried on a defensive campaign, avoiding direct engagements and harassing the enemy. Hence the expression 'Fabian tactics' and the name of the *Fabian Society (1884), dedicated to the gradual introduction of Socialism.

Fable, a term most commonly used in the sense of a short story devised to convey some useful moral lesson, but often carrying with it associations of the marvellous or the mythical, and frequently employing animals as characters. *Aesop's fables and the *'Reynard the Fox' series were well known and imitated in Britain by *Chaucer, *Henryson, and others, and La Fontaine, the greatest of modern fable writers, was imitated by *Gay.

Fable of the Bees, The, see MANDEVILLE, B. DE.

Fables, *Ancient and Modern,* by *Dryden, published 1700.
Verse paraphrases of tales by *Ovid, *Boccaccio, and *Chaucer are interspersed with Dryden's own poems. They compose themselves into an Ovidian and Catholic meditation on the place of nature, sex, and violence in the flux of history. The Preface is one of the most important examples of Dryden's criticism.

Fabliau, a short tale in verse, almost invariably in octosyllabic couplets, dealing for the most part from a comic point of view with incidents of ordinary life. The fabliau was an important element in French poetry in the 12th–13th cents., and was imitated by *Chaucer.

FABYAN, Robert (d. 1513), chronicler, was sheriff of London in 1493. His chronicles are of importance with respect to the history of London.

Face, one of the rogues in Jonson's *The Alchemist.*

Faction, a term coined c. 1970 to describe fiction based on and mingled with fact, applied particularly to American works of fiction such as *In Cold Blood* (1966) by *Capote and *The Armies of the Night* (1968) by *Mailer.

Factotum, see JOHANNES FACTOTUM.

Faerie Queene, The, the greatest work of *Spenser, of which the first three books were published 1590, and the second three 1596.
The general scheme of the work is proposed in the author's introductory letter addressed to *Ralegh. By the Faerie Queene the poet signifies Glory in the abstract and *Elizabeth I in particular (who also figures under the names of *Britomart, *Belphoebe, *Mercilla, and *Gloriana). Twelve of her knights, the 'patrons'

or examples of twelve different virtues, each undertake an adventure, on the twelve successive days of the queen's annual festival. Prince Arthur symbolizes 'magnificence', in the Aristotelian sense of the perfection of all the other virtues (Spenser must have meant 'magnanimity' or 'gentlemanliness'). Arthur has a vision of the Faerie Queene and, determining to seek her out, is brought into the adventures of the several knights and carries them to a successful issue. This explanation, given in the introduction, does not appear from the poem itself, for the author starts at once with the adventures of the knights. Of the six books Spenser published, the subjects are:

I, the adventures of the *Redcrosse Knight of Holiness (the Anglican Church), the protector of the Virgin *Una (truth, or the true religion), and the wiles of *Archimago and *Duessa;

II, the adventures of Sir *Guyon, the Knight of Temperance, his encounters with *Pyrochles and *Cymochles, his visit to the cave of *Mammon and the House of Temperance, and his destruction of *Acrasia and her *Bower of Bliss. Canto x of this Book contains a chronicle of British rulers from *Brut to Elizabeth;

III, the legend of Chastity, exemplified by *Britomart and *Belphoebe;

IV, the legend of *Triamond and *Cambell, exemplifying Friendship; together with the story of *Scudamour and *Amoret;

V, the adventures of *Artegall, the Knight of Justice, in which allegorical reference is made to various historical events of the reign of Queen Elizabeth: the defeat of the Spaniards in the Netherlands, the recantation of Henry IV of France, the execution of *Mary Queen of Scots, and the administration of Ireland by Lord Grey de Wilton;

VI, the adventures of Sir *Calidore, exemplifying Courtesy.

There is also a fragment on *Mutabilitie, being the sixth and seventh cantos of the legend of Constancie, which was to have formed the seventh Book. This fragment contains a charming description of the seasons and the months.

The work as a whole, modelled to some extent on the *Orlando Furioso of Ariosto, suffers from a certain monotony, and its chief beauties lie in the particular episodes with which the allegory is varied and in descriptions, such as those of the Cave of Mammon. The poem is written in the stanza invented by Spenser (see SPENSERIAN STANZA) and since utilized by James *Thomson, *Keats, *Shelley, and *Byron.

Fagin, a character in Dickens's *Oliver Twist.

Fainall and Mrs Fainall, characters in Congreve's *The Way of the World.

Fairchild Family, The, see SHERWOOD, M.

Fair Maid of Perth, Saint Valentine's Day, or the, a novel by Sir W. *Scott, published 1828, as the second of the *Chronicles of the Canongate.

The scene is Perth in the turbulent times at the close of the 14th cent. when the mild Robert III was king of Scotland.

Fair Maid of the West, The, or A Girl worth Gold, a comedy of adventure by *Heywood, in two parts, Pt I c.1600, Pt II c.1630, both printed 1631.

The 'fair maid' is Bess Bridges, the 'flower of Plymouth', who is beloved by the gallant Spencer: he kills a man while protecting her from insult, and flees the country. Subsequent escapades take them as far afield as Morocco before they are finally reunited. The second part is marred by extreme coincidences, bed-tricks, etc.

Fair Penitent, The, a tragedy in blank verse by N. *Rowe, produced 1703.

The plot of the play is that of Massinger and Field's *The Fatal Dowry, shortened and somewhat modified at the end. The 'haughty, gallant gay Lothario' (taken from Novall in the earlier play) has become proverbial, and was the model on which Richardson drew Lovelace in *Clarissa.

Fair Quarrel, A, a comedy by J. *Middleton and W. *Rowley, published 1617.

Fair Rosamond, see ROSAMOND.

Fairservice, Andrew, in Scott's *Rob Roy, a gardener at Osbaldistone Hall.

Faithful, in Bunyan's *Pilgrim's Progress, the companion of *Christian put to death at *Vanity Fair.

Faithful Shepherdess, The, a pastoral tragicomedy by J. *Fletcher, printed not later than 1610.

The action takes place at night in the woods of Thessaly, and revolves around the central figure of the faithful shepherdess herself, Clorin, who has dedicated herself to a life of chastity in memory of her dead love. The play, though without much dramatic interest, ranks as a *pastoral with Jonson's *The Sad Shepherd, and Milton's *Comus.

FALCONER, William (1732–69), author of The Shipwreck (1762, rev. 1764, 1769), a poem in three cantos recounting the wreck of a ship on the coast of Greece, which had considerable vogue in its day. Falconer was drowned at sea.

Falkland, one of the principal characters in Godwin's *Caleb Williams.

FALKLAND, Lucius Cary, second Viscount (1610–43), a famous royalist, 'a man learned and accomplished, the centre of a circle which embraced the most liberal thinkers of his day' (J. R. *Green). The circle at Great Tew, near Oxford, included *Jonson, *Suckling, *Sandys, *Earle, *Godolphin, and *Chillingworth; also *Clarendon, who draws a memorable portrait of him. Falkland wrote verses and theological works (*Discourses of Infallibility* and a *Reply*, 1660).

FALKNER, J(ohn) Meade (1858–1932), is remembered for his three novels: *The Lost Stradivarius* (1895), a tale of the supernatural set largely in Oxford and Naples; *Moonfleet* (1898), a romance involving smuggling; and *The Nebuly Coat* (1903), an antiquarian romance dealing with a church threatened by collapse, in which Falkner was able to display his love and knowledge of ecclesiastical history and architecture, heraldry, etc. He also published a volume of *Poems* (*c*.1933); three of his poems appear in *Larkin's *The Oxford Book of Twentieth Century English Verse* (1973).

Fall of Robespierre, The, a drama written in 1794 by *Coleridge, who wrote Act I, and R. *Southey, who wrote Acts II and III.

'Fall of the House of Usher, The', see POE, E. A.

False One, The, a drama attributed to J. *Fletcher, in which *Massinger may also have had a share, performed ?*c*.1620, printed 1647.

Falstaff, Sir John, a character in Shakespeare's *1* and *2* *Henry IV* and *The Merry Wives of Windsor*. His remote historical origin seems to have been the Wycliffite Sir John *Oldcastle, but his more important literary foundations lie in the stock figure of the *Vice, together with some elements of the Plautine *Miles gloriosus. He is fat, witty, a lover of sack and jests, and skilful at turning jokes on him to his own advantage—'I am not only witty in myself, but the cause that wit is in other men': 2 Henry IV, i. ii. 8–9). The Falstaff of *The Merry Wives of Windsor* is a diminished figure, whose attempts to mend his fortunes by wooing two citizens' wives simultaneously end in his discomfiture in Windsor Forest. It is this Falstaff who is the subject of at least nine operas, including Verdi's *Falstaff* (1893).

Family Reunion, The, a play by T. S. *Eliot.

Fanny, Lord, see HERVEY, JOHN.

Fanny Hill, see MEMOIRS OF A WOMAN OF PLEASURE.

FANSHAWE, Anne, Lady (1625–80), wife of Sir Richard Fanshawe, who was ambassador to

Portugal, then to Spain. She shared her husband's travels and her interesting *Memoirs* were first printed in 1829.

Farce (from a metaphorical use of the word *farce*, stuffing), was originally applied to explanatory or additional matter introduced into the liturgy; thence to the impromptu buffoonery which the actors were wont to insert in the text of religious dramas. It now means a dramatic work designed solely to excite laughter. It should be distinguished from *extravaganza, with which it is sometimes confused.

Farewell to Arms, A, a novel by E. *Hemingway.

Farfrae, Donald, a character in Hardy's *The Mayor of Casterbridge*.

Far from the Madding Crowd, a novel by T. *Hardy, published 1874. The title is a quotation from Gray's *Elegy . . . in a Country Churchyard*.

The shepherd Gabriel Oak serves the young and spirited Bathsheba Everdene, owner of the farm, with unselfish devotion. The dashing Sergeant Troy loves one of Bathsheba's servants, Fanny Robin, but after a fatal misunderstanding deserts her and she eventually dies in childbirth in the workhouse. Troy has meanwhile married Bathsheba, but soon begins to ill-treat her. When he hears of Fanny's death he disappears and is deemed to have been drowned. Farmer Boldwood, now obsessed with Bathsheba, gives a party at which he pledges Bathsheba to marry him some time in the future. Troy reappears at the party and Boldwood shoots him. Boldwood is tried and pronounced insane. Gabriel and Bathsheba are at last married.

FARJEON, Eleanor (1881–1965), became well known as a children's writer after the success of *Martin Pippin in the Apple-Orchard* (1921); she followed it with many volumes of poems, fantasies, stories, etc.

Farmer's Boy, The, see BLOOMFIELD, R.

FARNOL, (John) Jeffery (1878–1952), historical novelist, whose popular tales of adventure and the open road, many of them set in the Regency period (*The Broad Highway*, 1910; *The Amateur Gentleman*, 1913; and many others) show a debt both to *Borrow and to *Weyman.

FARQUHAR, George (?1677–1707), at first an actor, gave up the stage and took to writing comedies. He produced *Love and a Bottle* in 1698, *The Constant Couple, or a Trip to the Jubilee* in 1699, *Sir Harry Wildair* in 1701, *The Inconstant* and *The Twin Rivals* in 1702, *The Stage Coach*

(with *Motteux) in 1704, *The Recruiting Officer* in 1706, and *The Beaux' Stratagem* in 1707. The last two are the best of his plays and are marked by an atmosphere of reality and good humour. He died in poverty. (See RESTORATION.)

FARRAR, F(rederic) W(illiam) (1831–1903), philosopher and theologian, who, when a master at Harrow, published *Eric, or, Little by Little* (1858), an edifying story of school life. As well as many works of theology, he also wrote *Julian Home; a tale of College life* (1859) and *St Winifred's, or the World of School* (1862). (See also CHILDREN'S LITERATURE.)

FARRELL, J(ames) G(ordon) (1935–79), novelist, educated at Oxford, where, in his first term, he contracted poliomyelitis. He later travelled widely in America, Europe, and the East. *A Man from Elsewhere* (1963) was followed by *The Lung* (1965) and *A Girl in the Head* (1967). His first substantial novel, *Troubles* (1970), is set in Ireland, in the decaying Majestic Hotel, just after the First World War. *The Siege of Krishnapur* (1973, *Booker Prize) deals with the events of the Indian Mutiny, in a characteristically ironic and comic vein. *The Singapore Grip* (1978) moves closer to the epic, blending real and fictitious characters and describing the fall of Singapore to the Japanese. His last three novels reflect a sense of the end of the Empire and the stubborn refusal of his characters to recognize the course of history. *The Hill Station* (1981) was left unfinished when Farrell was accidentally drowned.

FARRELL, J(ames) T(homas) (1904–79), American naturalist novelist, best known in Britain for his trilogy about Studs Lonigan, a young Chicago Catholic of Irish descent: *Young Lonigan* (1932), *The Young Manhood of Studs Lonigan* (1934), and *Judgement Day* (1935).

Fashion, Sir Novelty and Young, characters in Vanbrugh's *The Relapse,* who reappear in Sheridan's adaptation *A Trip to Scarborough.*

Fashionable novel, or 'silver-fork school', a class of novel, popular c.1825–50, which held up for admiration the lives of the wealthy and fashionable. *Hook was one of the leaders of this highly successful school of writing. *Hazlitt, in his essay on 'The Dandy School' (*The Examiner,* 1827), castigates the narrow superficiality of such novels. *Bulwer-Lytton (whose own *Pelham* was a celebrated example) held that the genre was influential in the paradoxical sense that its effect was ultimately to expose 'the falsehood, the hypocrisy, the arrogant and vulgar insolence of patrician life'. M. W. Rosa, in *The Silver-Fork School* (1936), discusses the work of S. *Ferrier, T. H. *Lister, *Disraeli, P. *Ward, Mrs *Gore, and others, and argues that

the school 'culminated in a single great book —*Vanity Fair*'. (See also NOVEL, RISE OF THE.)

FASTOLF, Sir John (1380–1459), a successful soldier in the French wars of Henry IV and Henry V, who contributed towards the building of philosophy schools at Cambridge. He figures prominently in the *Paston Letters. In Shakespeare's 1 *Henry VI he is presented as a coward. The *Folio text calls him *'Falstaff', but from *Theobald onwards it has become traditional to call him 'Fastolfe' to distinguish him from his fictitious namesake.

Fatal Curiosity, The, a tragedy in blank verse by *Lillo, first produced in 1736. It is based on an old story of a Cornish murder, but its plot is archetypal and appears in many literatures; Lillo's version influenced the German 'fate-drama'.

Old Wilmot, under stress of poverty and urged by his wife, murders a stranger who has deposited a casket with them, only to find the victim is his son, supposed lost in a shipwreck.

Fatal Dowry, The, a tragedy by *Massinger and *Field, acted c.1617–19, printed 1632. The play is based on one of the *controversiae* (or imaginary legal disputes) of Seneca the elder. The 'dowry' is Beaumelle, the bride presented to Charalois by her father Rochfort: Charalois kills Beaumelle's lover Novall, stabs Beaumelle in accordance with Rochfort's condemnation, then is himself killed by a friend of Novall.

Rowe's *The Fair Penitent is founded on this play.

Fatal Marriage, The, or the Innocent Adultery, a tragedy by *Southerne, performed 1694.

The play is founded on A. *Behn's novel *The Nun or the Perjur'd Beauty* and describes the sufferings of Isabella, who marries Villeroy after the assumed death of her husband Biron. Biron reappears, is killed, and Isabella takes her own life.

Fata Morgana, see MORGAN LE FAY. (The word *fata* in Italian means 'fairy'.)

Fat Boy, The, Joe, Mr Wardle's servant, in Dickens's *Pickwick Papers.*

Father and Son, see GOSSE, E.

Father Brown, see BROWN, FATHER.

'Father O'Flynn', a popular Irish song by A. P. *Graves.

Fathers of the Church, the early Christian writers, a term usually applied to those of the first five cents. Sometimes the Greek and Latin fathers are distinguished, the former including *Clement of Alexandria, *Origen, Cyprian,

*Athanasius, Basil the Great, Gregory Nazianzen, and *Chrysostom; the latter *Tertullian, *Jerome, *Ambrose, *Augustine of Hippo, *Gregory (Pope Gregory I), and Bernard.

Fathom, see FERDINAND COUNT FATHOM.

Faulconbridge, Robert and Philip, the legitimate and illegitimate sons of Sir Robert Faulconbridge in Shakespeare's *King John*.

Faulkland, a character in Sheridan's *The Rivals*.

FAULKNER (originally Falkner), William Harrison (1897–1962), American novelist. His first novel, *Soldier's Pay* (1926), was followed by others, including *Sartoris* (1929), the first of the series describing the decline of the Compson and Sartoris families, representative of the Old South, and the rise of the crude and unscrupulous Snopes family. The principal setting of these novels is 'Jefferson'—a composite picture of several Mississippi towns—in the mythical Yoknapatawpha County. *The Sound and the Fury* (1929) is a narrative *tour de force* in which Faulkner views the decline of the South through several eyes, most remarkably those of Benjy Compson, a 33-year-old 'idiot'. *As I Lay Dying* (1930) demonstrates Faulkner's comic as well as his tragic vision, in his account of the death and burial of poor white Addie Bundren. He made his name, however, with *Sanctuary* (1931), a more sensational work written to attract sales. *Light in August* (1932) and *Absalom, Absalom!* (1936) confirmed his reputation as one of the finest of modern novelists. He was awarded the *Nobel Prize in 1949.

Faust, the subject of the great dramas of *Marlowe and *Goethe, was a wandering conjuror, who lived in Germany about 1488–1541 and is mentioned in various documents of the period. For Marlowe's play see DR FAUSTUS.
   Goethe's *Faust* (Pt I, 1808; Pt II, 1832) begins with a Prologue in Heaven, in which Mephistopheles obtains permission to try to effect the ruin of the soul of Faust. The play itself opens with a soliloquy by Faust, disillusioned with the world. Mephistopheles having presented himself, Faust enters into a compact to become his servant if Faust should exclaim, of any moment of delight procured for him, 'Stay, thou art so fair.' Then follow the attempts of Mephistopheles to satisfy Faust, culminating in the incident of Gretchen (Margaret), whom Faust, at the Devil's instigation, seduces, bringing about her miserable death. This is the end of Part I, Faust being left remorseful and dissatisfied.
   The story of Part II is extremely complex and its symbolism obscure. It consists in the main of two portions, of which the first is the incident of Helen (symbolizing perfect beauty). She is ardently pursued by Faust, but finally reft from him. Euphorion, their son, personifying poetry and the union of the classical and the romantic, and at the end representing Lord *Byron, vanishes in a flame. In the second portion (Acts IV and V) the purified Faust, pursuing the service of man, reclaims from the sea, with the help of Mephistopheles, a stretch of submerged land. But Care attacks and blinds him. Finally satisfied in the consciousness of good work done, he cries to the fleeting moment, 'Ah, stay, thou art so fair', and falls dead. Hell tries to seize his soul, but it is borne away by angels.

Faustus, Doctor, see DR FAUSTUS.

FAWCETT, Millicent Garrett, see WOMEN'S SUFFRAGE.

Fawn, The, see PARASITASTER.

Feathernest, Mr, in Peacock's *Melincourt*, a caricature of *Southey.

Feeble, in Shakespeare's 2 *Henry IV* (III. ii), one of the recruits brought before *Falstaff.

Feenix, Cousin, a character in Dickens's *Dombey and Son*, the nephew of Mrs Skewton, and cousin of Edith, Dombey's second wife.

Felix Holt, The Radical, a novel by G. *Eliot, published 1866, set in 1832 in Loamshire.
   Harold Transome arrives from the East to inherit the family estate, and startles his family by standing as a Radical candidate. His political convictions are not incompatible with 'treating' the local workers, and his character is strongly contrasted with that of Felix Holt, austere, idealistic, and passionate, who has deliberately chosen the life of an artisan, and who aims to stir his fellow workers to a sense of their own worth and destiny. The heroine, Esther, who supposes herself to be the daughter of old Lyon, the Independent minister, has an innate love of refinement, and when Felix chastises her for her frivolity she gains a new consciousness, and gradually falls in love with him. A complex chain of events reveals that Esther is the heir to the Transome estate; Harold woos her, and Esther is forced to choose between his wordly attractions, and poverty with Felix. She renounces her claim to the estate and chooses Felix. It is revealed to Harold at the end of the novel that he is not his father's son, but the son of the hated lawyer Jermyn; the account of the years of suffering of the proud and lonely Mrs Transome, subjected in secrecy to a man she no longer respects, ever fearful of her son's discovery, befriended only by her faithful servant Denner, forms, in the view of *Leavis, the most successful part of the book.

FELL, Dr John (1625–86), dean of Christ Church, Oxford, and bishop of Oxford, remembered in a literary connection as the promoter of the *Oxford University Press. He procured for it the matrices and punches of the best types that could be found, and arranged every year for the publication of some classical author. He is the subject of the well-known epigram beginning 'I do not love you, Dr Fell', a translation by T. *Brown of *Martial, *Epigrams,* i. 32.

Female Quixote, The, or the Adventures of Arabella, a novel by C. *Lennox, published 1752.

This vivacious and ironical work was probably the most consistent of the various attempts to reproduce the spirit of *Cervantes in English.

Female, or **Feminine, Rhymes,** see RHYME.

Feminist Criticism, a critical approach to be detected retrospectively in e.g. the early reviewing of Rebecca *West and V. Woolf's *A Room of One's Own (1929), but which acquired a distinct identity in the late 1960s and 1970s with the publication of such works as Mary Ellmann's *Thinking about Women* (1968), Eva *Figes's *Patriarchal Attitudes* (1970), Elizabeth Hardwick's *Seduction and Betrayal* (1974), *Literary Women* (1976) by Ellen Moers, *A Literature of their Own* (1977) by Elaine Showalter, and *The Mad Woman in the Attic* (1978) by Sandra Gilbert and Susan Gubar. The influence of S. de *Beauvoir's *The Second Sex* (1949, translated) is evident in many of these studies. Feminist criticism, which ranges from the scholarly to the political and prescriptive, seeks to re-examine women's literature of the past and present with the aid of a new feminist awareness ('raised consciousness') of female and male stereotypes, women's economic situation as authors, the supposed prejudice of male critics and publishers, the relationship between writing and gender, etc. Women's Studies as a separate subject grew in popularity greatly during the 1970s, particularly in the United States; the same period also saw the founding in Britain of feminist publishing houses, notably Virago (which published its first independent title in 1977) and The Women's Press (1978). Feminist criticism may thus be associated with the rediscovery and reprinting of many works by women writers of the past, and with the encouragement of new feminist writing both scholarly and creative.

Fenians, originally a semi-mythical, semi-historical military body said to have been raised for the defence of Ireland against Norse raids. *Finn, in his day, was its chief. The Fenians of modern times were an association formed among the Irish in the United States and in Ireland in the middle of the 19th cent. for promoting the overthrow of the English government in Ireland.

Fenton, a spendthrift young gentleman in Shakespeare's *The Merry Wives of Windsor.

Ferdinand, (1) in Shakespeare's *Love's Labour's Lost, the king of Navarre; (2) in his *The Tempest, son of *Alonso, king of Naples; (3) in Webster's *The Duchess of Malfi, the brother of the duchess.

Ferdinand Count Fathom, The Adventures of, a novel by T. *Smollett, published 1753.

FERGUSON, Adam (1723–1816), was professor in turn of natural philosophy, moral philosophy, and mathematics at Edinburgh after 1764, and was a member of the *Select Society and co-founder of the *Royal Society of Edinburgh. His writings include The Morality of Stage-Plays Seriously Considered (1757), written in defence of J. Home's *Douglas; An Essay on the History of the Civil Society (1767), a pioneer work in political sociology; The History of the Progress and Termination of the Roman Republic (3 vols, 1783); and Principles of Moral and Political Science (2 vols, 1792). In the *Essay* he has a discussion 'Of the History of Literature', in which he argues that poetry is a more original and natural form of literary expression than prose, and that all literature develops better in periods and contexts of great social activity than in leisure and solitude.

FERGUSON, Sir Samuel (1810–86), an important figure in the *Irish revival. Among many translations and works based on Gaelic legend, he published a widely praised elegy on Thomas Davis, a nationalist leader, in 1845; Lays of the Western Gael (1865); Congal (1872), an epic on the last stand of Irish paganism against Christianity; and Ogham Inscriptions in Ireland, Wales, and Scotland (1887), his most important antiquarian work.

FERGUSSON, Robert (1750–74), published his first poems in Ruddiman's *Weekly Magazine* (1771), in imitation of English models, and his first *Scots poem, 'The Daft Days', appeared in 1772. A volume appeared in 1773 which was to have a profound influence on *Burns, who found himself inspired to 'emulating vigour'. Fergusson's 'The Farmer's Ingle', a vernacular description of homely rustic life, is a clear foreshadowing of Burns's 'The Cotter's Saturday Night'. Fergusson vividly evokes the street life, taverns, and amusements of Edinburgh, and mocks the established literary world in satirical attacks on Dr *Johnson and *Mackenzie ('The Sow of Feeling').

Ferishtah's Fancies, a volume of poems by R. *Browning, published 1884.

FERRAR, Nicholas (1592–1637), established in 1625 at *Little Gidding, with his brother, his brother-in-law John Collett, and their families, a religious community based on Anglican principles. Ferrar was a close friend of G. *Herbert, who on his death-bed entrusted to him the manuscript of his poems *The Temple* (1633).

Ferrars, (1) Mrs, and her sons Edward and Robert, in *Sense and Sensibility* by J. Austen; (2) William, and his children Endymion and Myra, in *Endymion* by B. Disraeli.

FERRERS, George, see MIRROR FOR MAGISTRATES, A.

Ferrex and Porrex, see GORBODUC.

FERRIER, James Frederick (1808–64), nephew of Susan *Ferrier, studied German philosophy at Heidelberg and was successively professor of civil history at Edinburgh (1842–5) and of moral philosophy and political economy at St Andrews (1845–64).

His idealistic philosophy, connected with that of *Berkeley, is set forth in *The Institutes of Metaphysic* (1854) and *Lectures on Greek Philosophy and other Philosophical Remains* (1866). In substance, Ferrier's conclusions closely resemble those of *Hegel, though reached independently and from a different starting point.

FERRIER, Susan Edmonstone (1782–1854), a friend of Sir W. *Scott, was the successful authoress of three good novels of Scottish life: *Marriage* (1818), *The Inheritance* (1824), and *Destiny* (1831). Her object was avowedly to instruct, particularly on the subject of marriage, but her method lies in shrewd observation and comedy.

Ferumbras (or *Firumbras*), *Sir,* a Middle English metrical romance of 10,540 short lines related to the French Charlemagne romances *Fierabras* and the *Destruccion de Rome.* It is one of the more artistic of the English romances of 'The Matter of France'. The story tells of the capture by Ferumbras, the son of the Sultan of Babylon, of Rome and the Holy Relics, of his combat with Oliver, and of the conversion to Christianity of Ferumbras and his sister Floripas. The two become friends of Roland, Oliver, and Charlemagne. The same story is told in *The Sowdone of Babylon,* a version from about 1400 of a lost French romance.

Feste, in Shakespeare's *Twelfth Night,* *Olivia's jester.

Festus, see BAILEY, P. J.

FEUERBACH, Ludwig (1804–72), German philosopher and critic of the Bible, whose most influential work, *Das Wesen des Christentums (The Essence of Christianity,* 1841), had a great influence on European thought. It was translated by G. *Eliot.

Fezziwig, Mr and Mrs, characters in Dickens's *A Christmas Carol.*

Fiammetta, the name given by *Boccaccio to the lady he loved, and the title of one of his works.

FICINO, Marsilio (1433–99), Italian humanist and philosopher, whose Neoplatonic views influenced Reuchlin and *Colet and were an inspiration to many English poets, including *Sidney and *Milton.

Fidele, in Shakespeare's *Cymbeline,* the name assumed by *Imogen when disguised as a boy.

Fidessa, in Spenser's *Faerie Queene* (I. ii), the name assumed by the fair companion of *Sansfoy, whom the *Redcrosse Knight takes under his protection. She turns out to be the false *Duessa.

FIELD, Michael, the pseudonym of Katherine Bradley (1846–1914) and her niece Edith Cooper (1862–1913), who together published many verse dramas, including *Callirrhoe* (1884) and *Canute the Great* (1887).

FIELD, Nathan (1587–1619/20), actor and dramatist, sometimes called Nathaniel by confusion with his brother, a printer. He probably succeeded to Shakespeare's place as actor and shareholder in the King's Men, c.1616. He wrote two comedies, *A Woman is a Weathercock* (1609) and *Amends for Ladies* (1610). He is best known for his share of Massinger's *The Fatal Dowry.*

FIELDING, Henry (1707–54), was educated at Eton where he made lifelong friends of *Lyttelton, who later became a patron, and of *Pitt the elder. In 1728 he became a student of letters at Leyden and later read for the bar at the Middle Temple. He settled in London determined to support himself as a dramatist, and between 1729 and 1737 wrote some 25 assorted dramas, largely in the form of farce and satire, including the most successful of all his dramas, *Tom Thumb.* In 1734 he married Charlotte Cradock who became his model for Sophia in *Tom Jones and the heroine of *Amelia.* Fielding suffered long periods of poverty but was greatly assisted by Ralph *Allen. In 1736 Fielding took over the management of the New Theatre, for the opening of which he wrote the successful satirical comedy *Pasquin,* which aimed at various religious and political targets, including electioneering abuses. But *The Historical Register for 1736* was fiercer political satire than *Walpole's government would tolerate, and the Licensing Act of 1737, introducing *censorship by the Lord Chamberlain, brought Fielding's career in the theatre to an end.

In 1739–40 he wrote most of the columns of *The Champion*. In 1740 Richardson's *Pamela* appeared and enjoyed great popular success; Fielding expressed his contempt in his pseudonymous parody, *An apology for the life of Mrs *Shamela Andrews* (1741). Meanwhile, increasing illness prevented Fielding from pursuing his legal career with any consistency. Instead he produced *The Adventures of *Joseph Andrews and his Friend, Mr Abraham Adams* (1742). In 1743 Fielding published three volumes of *Miscellanies*, which included *A Journey from this World to the Next* and a ferocious satire, *The Life and Death of *Jonathan Wild the Great*. His wife died in 1744 and in 1747 Fielding caused some scandal by marrying his wife's maid and friend Mary Daniel. With the aid of Lyttelton, he was appointed JP for Westminster in 1748 and, in 1749 (the year in which *Tom Jones* appeared), his legal jurisdiction was extended to the whole county of Middlesex; he was made chairman of the quarter sessions of Westminster. From his court in Bow Street he continued his struggle against corruption and lawlessness and, with his blind half-brother and fellow magistrate Sir John Fielding, strove to establish new standards of honesty on the bench. He wrote various influential legal enquiries and pamphlets, including a proposal for the abolition of public hanging. He published *Amelia* (1751) and returned to journalism in 1752 with *The Covent-Garden Journal*. He organized and saw successfully implemented a plan for breaking up the criminal gangs who were then flourishing in London. In 1754, in the hope of improving his health, he left for Portugal. He died in Lisbon and his *The Journal of a Voyage to Lisbon* was published posthumously in 1755.

Fielding is generally agreed to be an innovating master of the highest originality. He himself believed he was 'the founder of a new province of writing'. His three acknowledged masters were *Lucian, *Swift, and *Cervantes. In breaking away from the epistolary methods of his contemporary Richardson and others, he devised what he described as 'comic epics in prose', which are in effect the first modern novels in English, leading straight to the works of *Dickens and *Thackeray.

FIELDING, Sarah (1710–68), sister of H. *Fielding, published in 1744 her best-known work, *The Adventures of *David Simple*, a 'Moral Romance' with (in its second edition of that year) a Preface by her brother Henry; it was followed by *Familiar Letters between the Principal Characters in David Simple* (1747), and *Volume the Last* (1753), completing the story of Simple. With Jane Collier she published *The Cry* (1754),

a clever dialogue between Portia (the Solo) representing integrity, and an audience (the Chorus) representing malice and ignorance. Her other works include *The Lives of Cleopatra and Octavia* (1757), *The History of the Countess of Dellwyn* (1759), and the light-hearted *History of Ophelia* (1760). Her translations of *Xenophon's *Memorabilia* and *Apologia* appeared in 1762.

Sarah Fielding was one of the earliest of the English novelists to explore with close attention varying states of feeling and the roots of motive.

FIENNES, Celia (1662–1741), travelled, between 1685 and 1703, into every county of England, and her Journal provided the first comprehensive survey of the country since *Harrison and *Camden. An incomplete version appeared in 1888 under the title *Through England on a Side Saddle in the Time of William and Mary* (definitive edition, *The Journeys of Celia Fiennes*, ed. Christopher Morris, 1947). Her style is breathless and her spelling erratic, but she communicates a lively enthusiasm.

Fierabras, or **Fierebras,** see FERUMBRAS.

Fifine at the Fair, a poem in alexandrine couplets by R. *Browning, published 1872.

The speaker is Don Juan, who is strolling with his wife Elvire near Pornic in Britanny, where a fair is being held. Don Juan, attracted by the gipsy dancer Fifine, dissertates to Elvire on the nature of his feelings, contrasting the intense ephemerality of desire with the dull permanence of love, this initial theme then giving rise to a series of brilliant variations on the interconnected topics of knowledge, identity, and truth in life and art.

FIGES, Eva (1932–), novelist and feminist, born in Berlin; she came to England in 1939. Her novels include *Winter Journey* (1967), *B* (1972), *Days* (1974), *Nelly's Version* (1977), and *Waking* (1981). Her non-fiction works include *Patriarchal Attitudes* (1970), a seminal work of *Feminist social and literary criticism.

Filostrato, a poem in *ottava rima* on the story of Troilus and Cressida, by *Boccaccio, of special interest as the source of Chaucer's *Troilus and Criseyde*.

FINCH, Anne, see WINCHILSEA.

Fingal, an Ancient Epic Poem, in Six Books: together with several other Poems, composed by Ossian, the son of Fingal. Translated from the Galic language, 1762, and *Temora*, an ancient epic poem, in Eight Books (1763).

These epics, which purported to be translated from an ancient Gaelic original were in fact largely the work of J. *Macpherson; the first was based loosely on various old ballads and fragments, the second was entirely invented. Macpherson transforms the legendary Irish hero *Finn or Fionn into the Scottish Fingal, ignores various episodes and characters in the original Fenian and Ossianic stories and brings together Fingal and Cuthullin (the Irish Cuchulain) who according to legend were divided by centuries. Morven, Fingal's kingdom in the north-west of Scotland, is Macpherson's invention. The original Finn MacCoul, whether historical or mythical, is usually assigned to the 3rd cent. AD; he was the son of Comhal, and the father of Ossian the warrior bard; he was also leader of the Fianna or *Fenians. Fingal is pictured by Macpherson as fighting both the Norwegians and the Romans under Caracalla—'Caracul, King of the World'. The astonishing sway of Macpherson's version is indicated by the fact that even *Gibbon took the trouble to discuss it; he writes (though with some irony) of 'the tenderness, the elegant genius of Ossian'. The appeal of *Fingal* lay in its *primitivism, its qualities of the *sublime, and its sentiment.

FINLAY, Ian Hamilton, see CONCRETE POETRY.

Finn, or **Fionn**, the principal hero of the southern or later cycle of Irish legends, also called the Fenian or Ossianic cycle. Finn MacCoul has been thought a historical personage by some modern authorities; others regard him as mythical. He was the son of Cumal (Comhal) and father of Ossian, and is supposed to have lived in the 3rd cent. AD, a contemporary of King Cormac. The king appointed him chief of the Fianna (pron. Fēna) or *Fenians, of whose heroic or romantic deeds there are endless tales. Finn was chosen their leader for his wisdom and generosity. He is said to have perished in an affray with mutinous Fenians in AD 283.

Finn, Phineas, hero of A. Trollope's novels *Phineas Finn* and *Phineas Redux*.

Finnegans Wake, a prose work by J. *Joyce, published 1939. It is written in a unique and extremely difficult style, making use of puns and portmanteau words, and a very wide range of allusion. The central theme of the work is a cyclical pattern of fall and resurrection.

This is presented in the story of Humphrey Chimpden Earwicker, a Dublin tavern-keeper, and the book is apparently a dream-sequence representing the stream of his unconscious mind through the course of one night. Other characters are his wife Anna Livia Plurabelle, their sons Shem and Shaun, and their daughter Isabel. In spite of its obscurity it contains passages of great lyrical beauty, and also much humour.

Finnsburh, *The Fight at,* a 48-line fragmentary poem in Old English dealing with part of the tragic tale of Finn and Hildeburh, a later part of

which is sung by the *scôp* in *Beowulf,* ll. 1,063–1,159. The fragment is included by F. Klaeber in his edition of *Beowulf* (1922, etc.) and in other editions.

FIONA MACLEOD, see SHARP, W.

FIRBANK, (Arthur Annesley) Ronald (1886–1926), novelist, received little encouragement as a writer during his lifetime. His novels include *Vainglory* (1915); *Inclinations* (1916); *Caprice* (1917); *Valmouth* (1919, set in a watering place dominated by the erotic and manipulating black masseuse Mrs Yajñavalkya); *Santal* (1921, set in North Africa); and *The Flower beneath the Foot* (1923). A play, *The Princess Zoubaroff*, was published in 1920. The first of his novels to be financed by a publisher, not by himself, was *Prancing Nigger* (1924; published as *Sorrow in Sunlight* in Britain); set in the West Indies, it describes the social aspirations and adventures of a Negro family. His last finished work, *Concerning the eccentricities of Cardinal Pirelli* (1926), appeared shortly after his death; other posthumous publications include *The Artificial Princess* (1934) and *The New Rhythum and Other Pieces* (1962); the latter includes a very early work, *Lady Appledore's Mésalliance*.

Dandy, aesthete, exotic, homosexual, and *habitué* of the *Café Royal, Firbank succeeded in creating a distinctive 'Firbankian' style, in both life and works. His use of dialogue, his oblique narration, his highly coloured fantasies, and his intense concentration of language and image are now seen as truly innovative, and some writers have claimed that he did more to liberate the novel from 19th cent. concepts of realism than *Joyce himself. Those who show traces of his influence include E. *Waugh, I. *Compton-Burnett, *Gerhardi, and M. *Spark.

Fir Bolgs, legendary early invaders of Ireland, according to tradition of an Iberian tribe, who were driven into Arran, Islay, and the Hebrides by the *Milesians.

FIRDAUSI, Abul Kasim Mansur (*c.*950–1020), Persian poet, and author of the *Shahnama* (or *Shanameh*), the great epic which recounts the legendary history of the ancient kings and heroes of Persia. It is known to English readers principally through M. *Arnold's version of one of its main incidents, *'Sohrab and Rustum'.

Firmilian, see AYTOUN, W. E.

Firmin, Dr George Brand and Philip, characters in Thackeray's *The Adventures of Philip.

Firumbras, Sir, see FERUMBRAS.

FISHER, St John (1469–1535), became chancellor of Cambridge University and bishop of

Rochester, 1504, and was president of Queen's College, Cambridge, 1505–8. He was a patron of *Erasmus. He wrote three treatises against the Lutheran reformation and was deprived, attainted, and beheaded for refusing to acknowledge *Henry VIII as supreme head of the Church. His Latin theological works were issued in 1597 (republished 1967); his English works, edited by J. E. B. Mayor, appeared in 1876. His English prose style showed a great advance, in point of rhetorical artifice and effect, on that of his predecessors. He was canonized in 1935 and is commemorated on 22 June.

FitzBoodle, George Savage, one of *Thackeray's pseudonyms. As the narrator of the FitzBoodle Papers, published in *Fraser's Magazine 1842–3, FitzBoodle, a bachelor clubman, tells the story of his own amorous misadventures.

FITZGERALD, Edward (1809–83), educated at Trinity College, Cambridge. His quirky but engaging personality made him much beloved by many close friends, who included *Thackeray, Alfred and Frederick *Tennyson, and *Carlyle. In 1851 he published Euphranor, a Dialogue on Youth and later he produced translations of plays by Calderón, *Aeschylus, and *Sophocles, a collection of aphorisms, and a selection of *Crabbe's poetry. His only celebrated work is his free translation of The Rubáiyát of *Omar Khayyám (1859). He was a prolific and delightful letter-writer, whose anecdotes of his literary friends have been a gold-mine to biographers. His Collected Letters was published in 1980.

FITZGERALD, F(rancis) Scott (Key) (1896–1940), American novelist. His first novel, This Side of Paradise (1920), made him instantly famous; shortly after its publication he married Zelda Sayre, and together they embarked on a life of high living, big spending, and party going. His short stories, first published in fashionable periodicals, were collected as Flappers and Philosophers (1920) and Tales of the Jazz Age (1922), the latter including his child's-eye fantasy of extravagance, 'The Diamond as Big as the Ritz'. The Beautiful and Damned (1922), a novel about a doomed marriage, was followed by The Great Gatsby (1925), the story of shady, mysterious financier Jay Gatsby's romantic and destructive passion for Daisy Buchanan. More short stories followed (All the Sad Young Men, 1926; Taps at Reveille, 1935), but by this time Zelda was suffering from mental breakdown, Scott from the effects of their violent lives, and Tender is the Night (1934) records, through the story of American psychiatrist Dick Diver and his schizophrenic wife Nicole, his own sense of impending disaster. Fitzgerald's own 'crack-up' accelerated, as Zelda failed to recover: he died in

Hollywood, of a heart attack, after working as a screenwriter, leaving his last novel, The Last Tycoon (1941), unfinished.

Fitzpiers, Edred, a character in Hardy's *The Woodlanders.

FITZRALPH, Richard (d. 1360), frequently referred to as 'Armachanus', was chancellor of Oxford (1333) and archbishop of Armagh (1347). He was regarded as the official spokesman of the secular clergy against the friars, and he wrote a treatise against the friar's doctrine of obligatory poverty, De Pauperie Salvatoris, in which he discussed 'dominion' or 'lordship', taking a view on the subject similar to that later adopted by *Wyclif.

Fitzrovia, a term coined to describe the 'artists' quarter' north of Oxford Street, London, which centred first on the Fitzroy Tavern, on the corner of Charlotte Street. Its focus then moved, according to Julian Maclaren-Ross (Memoirs of the Forties, 1965) to the Wheatsheaf. Dylan *Thomas, W. *Empson, Tambimuttu of *Poetry London, W. *Lewis, G. *Orwell, and many of the characters observed by A. *Powell were among its habitués.

FITZROY, Vice-Admiral Robert (1805–65), commanded the Beagle in the surveying expedition to Patagonia and the Straits of Magellan (1823–36), having C. *Darwin as naturalist for the last five years; like Darwin, he wrote a narrative of the voyage. He suggested the plan of the Fitzroy barometer, and instituted a system of storm warnings, the first British weather forecasts.

FITZSTEPHEN, William, author of a Latin life of *Becket (c.1180), which contains a valuable account of early London first printed in *Stow's Survey of London (1598).

Five Towns, The, in the novels of A. *Bennett, Tunstall, Burslem, Hanley, Stoke-on-Trent, and Longton, now forming the federated borough of Stoke-on-Trent. These are represented in the novels by Turnhill, Bursley, Hanbridge, Knype, and Longshaw.

Fizkin, Horatio, in Dickens's *Pickwick Papers, the Buff candidate in the Eatanswill election.

F.J., The pleasant Fable of Ferdinando Jeronimi and Leonora de Valasco, normally referred to as The Adventures of Master F.J.; a novella by G. *Gascoigne, supposedly translated 'out of the Italian riding tales of Bartello', but probably his own invention.

It concerns the love affair between F.J., a Venetian, and the lady of the house where he is staying in Lombardy. The novella exists in two versions: the first, printed in *A Hundreth Sundrie Flowres* in 1573, is set in the north of England and is erotic. The second, printed in *The Posies of George Gascoigne* (1575), is more fully Italianate and has been to some extent expurgated.

FLACCUS, see HORACE.

Flamineo, a character in Webster's *The White Devil*.

Flaming Tinman, The, a character in Borrow's *Lavengro*.

Flanders, Moll, see MOLL FLANDERS.

Flashman, a character in *Tom Brown's Schooldays* by T. *Hughes and revived in a series of humorous novels by George Macdonald Fraser.

FLAUBERT, Gustave (1821–80), French novelist. His first and best-known novel, *Madame Bovary* (1857), is one of the landmarks of 19th-cent. fiction, distinguished for its psychological insight, impersonal narrative method, and harmonious style: other works include *Salammbô* (1862), *L'Éducation sentimentale* (1869), and *Trois Contes* (1877). Flaubert was claimed both by the *Realists and the *Naturalists, and the objectivity of his method and authenticity of his detail, contrasting with the sentimentality and melodrama of much 19th-cent. English fiction, had a great influence on late 19th-cent. British writers, including A. *Bennett and G. A. *Moore.

Flavius, in Shakespeare's *Timon of Athens*, the faithful steward of Timon.

FLAXMAN, John (1755–1826), English neoclassical sculptor and draughtsman. He illustrated *Pope's translation of the *Iliad* and the *Odyssey*. He was a lifelong friend of *Blake.

Fleance, son of *Banquo in Shakespeare's *Macbeth*.

FLECKER, James (Herman) Elroy (1884–1915), educated at Trinity College, Oxford, where he was influenced by the last flowering of the *Aesthetic movement. In the course of a career in the consular service he produced several volumes of lyrical romantic verse (some of which was included in *Georgian Poetry*) including *The Bridge of Fire* (1907), *Forty-Two Poems* (1911), and *The Golden Journey to Samarkand* (1913). He also published an experimental, highly individual novel, *The King of Alsander* (1914). The work for which he is best remembered is the posthumously published poetic Eastern play *Hassan* (1922).

FLECKNOE, Richard (d. ?1678), a writer with an interest in experimental forms. His *Miscel-*

lanea (1653) includes a defence of the stage and a lament for the theatres silenced under the Commonwealth. His *Ariadne* (1654) has a claim to be the first English opera, though the music (which he composed himself) is lost. His *Love's Dominion* (1654), a pastoral with songs, was acted after the Restoration under the title *Love's Kingdom*. Its reputation for insipidity, and *Marvell's earlier satire ('Flecknoe, an English priest at Rome', ?1645) suggested to Dryden his attack on *Shadwell, *MacFlecknoe.

Fledgeby, in Dickens's *Our Mutual Friend*, a cowardly villain.

Fleet Prison, in the neighbourhood of the present Farringdon Street, London, was built in the time of Richard I. From 1640 it served mainly as a debtors' prison, until demolished in 1848, and it figures as such in Dickens's novels, notably *Pickwick Papers*.

Fleet Street, traditionally the headquarters of London journalism.

Fleet Street Eclogues, see DAVIDSON, J.

FLEMING, Ian Lancaster (1908–64), journalist and thriller writer. His first novel, *Casino Royale* (1953), introduced his handsome, tough, romantic hero James Bond, who subsequently appeared in many other adventures with exotic settings, including *Live and Let Die* (1954), *Diamonds are Forever* (1956), and *On Her Majesty's Secret Service* (1963). Bond also appeared in many highly popular films, which mingle wit, sex, and violence. These include *Dr No* (1962), *From Russia With Love* (1963), and *Goldfinger* (1964).

FLEMING, (Robert) Peter (1907–71), journalist and travel writer, brother of Ian *Fleming, is remembered largely for his travel books, which include *Brazilian Adventure* (1933) and *News from Tartary* (1936), an account of an overland journey from Peking to Kashmir.

Fleming, (1) Rose and Agnes, characters in Dickens's *Oliver Twist*; (2) Archdeacon, in Scott's *The Heart of Midlothian*; (3) Lady Mary, in his *The Abbot*.

Fleshly School of Poetry, see ROSSETTI, D. G., and BUCHANAN, R.

FLETCHER, Giles, the elder (1546–1611), was sent as an envoy to Russia in 1588. He published *Of the Russe Commonwealth* (1591), a pioneering account of Russian government. His *Licia, or Poemes of Love* (1593) is one of the first sonnet sequences to follow the publication of *Astrophel and Stella* (1591). He was the uncle of John *Fletcher and father of Giles and Phineas *Fletcher.

FLETCHER, Giles, the younger (?1585–1623), the younger son of Giles *Fletcher the elder, a poet of the Spenserian school whose allegorical treatment of religious themes is said to have influenced *Milton. His principal work was *Christs Victorie and Triumph in Heaven and Earth* (1610).

FLETCHER, John (1579–1625), nephew of Giles *Fletcher the elder and cousin of Giles the younger and Phineas *Fletcher. From about 1605 he wrote some 15 plays in collaboration with Sir F. *Beaumont, and some 16 of which he was sole author. He also collaborated with *Massinger, *Rowley, *Middleton, *Jonson, *Chapman, and others in the writing of many other works.

Among the principal plays of which Fletcher was probably sole author are: *The Faithful Shepherdess* (printed not later than 1610); *Valentinian* (perf. 1610–14); *The Loyal Subject* (perf. 1618); *The Humorous Lieutenant* (perf. 1619); *The Wilde Goose Chase* (perf. 1621); *The Woman's Prize*, written 1604–17; *Rule a Wife and Have a Wife* (perf. 1624); *The Chances*, written c.1617.

Among plays certainly or probably by Beaumont and Fletcher are: *Philaster*, written 1609; *The Maid's Tragedy*, written 1610–11; *A King and No King* (perf. 1611); *Bonduca* (perf. 1613–14); *Thierry King of France* (printed 1621; with Beaumont and Massinger).

Among plays probably by Fletcher and some other dramatist are: *Sir John Van Olden *Barnavelt* (perf. 1619); *The False One* (perf. c.1620); *The Custom of the Country* (printed 1647); *The Spanish Curate* and *The Beggar's Bush* (both perf. 1622). In all the above Fletcher certainly or probably collaborated with Massinger. The romantic drama *The Lover's Progress* (perf. 1623) was later revised by Massinger. *The Elder Brother* (printed 1637) is thought to have been written by Fletcher and revised by Massinger. *The Bloody Brother, or Rollo, Duke of Normandy* (perf. c.1616) is by Fletcher, Jonson, Chapman, and Massinger. Fletcher also collaborated with Shakespeare in *The Two Noble Kinsmen* and *Henry VIII.

FLETCHER, Phineas (1582–1650), the elder son of Giles *Fletcher the elder. Like his brother Giles (above), he was a poet of the Spenserian school. His chief work, *The Purple Island* (1633), is an allegory of the human body and mind. *Britain's Ida* (1628), attributed to *Spenser, appears to be his.

Flintwinch, a character in Dickens's *Little Dorrit*. His wife was known as Affery.

Flite, Miss, a character in Dickens's *Bleak House*.

Flodden, or **Floddon Field**, the battle of Flodden, in Northumberland, fought on 9 Sept.

1513, when the earl of Surrey on behalf of Henry VIII (then in France) defeated James IV of Scotland, the latter being killed on the field. It was made the subject of poems, of rejoicing or lament, on both sides of the border. *Skelton's 'Agaynst the Scottes' is a rude song of exultation of the English victory. On the Scottish side there is the beautiful lament 'The Flowers o' the Forest', of which the most popular version is by J. *Elliot. The battle is described in the 6th canto of Scott's *Marmion: A Tale of Flodden Field*.

Florac, comte de, his wife, son, and daughter-in-law, characters in Thackeray's *The Newcomes*. The comte also appears as a young French officer in *The Virginians*.

Flore et Zephyr, a series of ballet caricatures drawn by *Thackeray, published 1836.

Florent, see GOWER, J., and CANTERBURY TALES, 6.

Flores and Blancheflour, see FLORIS AND BLANCHEFLOUR.

Florestan, a character in *Endymion* by B. Disraeli.

Florimell, in Spenser's *Faerie Queene*, Bks III and IV, the type of chastity and virtue in woman. She is in love with the knight Marinell.

FLORIO, John (c.1553–1625), son of an Italian Protestant refugee, was reader in Italian to Anne of Denmark, wife of James I (1603), and groom of the privy chamber from 1604. His interesting collections of Italian–English dialogues, *Firste* and *Second Frutes*, were followed in 1598 by an Italian dictionary entitled *A Worlde of Wordes*; it was revised and augmented as *Queen Anna's New World of Words* (1611). His most important work was his translation from *Montaigne: *Essayes, Or Morall, Politike and Millitarie Discourses* (1603, 1613). Not only did Florio make Montaigne's work available in English, but he displayed great resourcefulness and ingenuity in the process of translation.

Floris and Blancheflour, a Middle English metrical romance in 1,083 lines from the first half of the 13th cent., based on a 12th cent. French original.

Floris and Blancheflour are brought up together; he is the son of a Saracen king and she the daughter of a Christian lady who has been captured and brought to the king's court. They fall in love and Blancheflour is banished. Floris finds her, with the aid of a precious cup and a magic ring, and they are ultimately married. The story is the subject of *Boccaccio's *Filocolo*.

Florizel, in Shakespeare's *The Winter's Tale*, the lover of *Perdita.

Flosky, Mr, a character in Peacock's *Nightmare Abbey,* who illustrates the transcendentalism of *Coleridge.

Floure and the Leaf, The, a 15th-cent. allegory in 595 lines of rhyme-royal, formerly attributed to *Chaucer and included by Skeat in *Chaucerian and Other Pieces,* appended as vol. 7 to his edition of Chaucer. The poet, wandering in a grove, sees the white company of knights and ladies of the leaf (Diana, goddess of chastity) and the green company of the flower (Flora), 'folk that loved idleness' and had delight 'of no business but for to hunt and hauke and pley in medes'.

FLOWER, Sir Newman Walter (1879–1964), publisher and author, who became the proprietor of Cassell's publishing company in 1927. He published biographies of *Handel (1923), *Sullivan (1927), and Schubert (1928), and edited the journals of Arnold *Bennett.

'Flowers of the Forest, The', see ELLIOT, J., and COCKBURN, A.

FLUDD, Robert (1574–1637), physician and Neoplatonist, entered the debate on the authenticity of the *Rosicrucian texts with his defence, *Apologia* (1616). His views on the universe as macrocosm–microcosm attracted much controversy, but despite his own mystical views on the circulation of the blood, he was the first to defend W. *Harvey's *De Motu Cordis.*

Fluellen, in Shakespeare's *Henry V,* a pedantic but courageous Welsh captain.

Flute, in Shakespeare's *A Midsummer Night's Dream,* a bellows-mender, who takes the part of Thisbe in the play of 'Pyramus and Thisbe'.

Flyting, derived from the Old English word *flitan,* to quarrel or dispute, was a verse contest in obloquy, practised in particular by the Scottish poets of the early 16th cent. The most famous example is the *Flyting of Dunbar and Kennedy.*

Foedera, Conventiones et Cujuscunque generis Acta Publica, a collection of public records in 20 vols, by *Rymer and Robert Sanderson, published 1704–35, which extend down to 1654, and provide for the first time a scientific basis for the writing of history.

Foker, Harry, a character in Thackeray's *Pendennis.*

Folios and Quartos, Shakespearian. *Shakespeare's earliest published plays are referred to as folios or quartos according to the folding of the printed sheets and therefore the size of the book: folios being large, tall volumes and the quartos smaller and squarer.

Of about 1,200 copies of the First Folio printed between Feb. 1622 and Nov. 1623, some 230 survive. A second Folio was issued in 1632, containing 'An Epitaph on . . . Shakespeare' by *Milton, which was his first published poem; a third Folio was issued in 1663, whose second impression of 1664 contained *Pericles* and six apocryphal plays; the fourth and last Folio was published in 1685. Except for the text of *Pericles* none of the Folios later than the first has any textual integrity.

Thirty-six plays, eighteen printed for the first time, were arranged by *Heming and Condell into sections of comedies, histories, and tragedies for F1. It was dedicated to William Herbert, earl of Pembroke, and Philip Herbert, earl of Montgomery, and contains the *Droeshout portrait and a list of 'the Principall Actors in all these Playes', together with commendatory verses by contemporaries including *Jonson.

During his lifetime 18 of Shakespeare's plays were published in quartos: *Othello* appeared in 1622. Following A. W. *Pollard's analysis, it is now established that over half of those quartos are 'bad' ones. Their texts are extremely corrupt as a result of their reconstruction from memory by a member, or members, of their cast.

Textual criticism and bibliography have largely been concerned with establishing relationships between the 'good' quartos (and in some cases the 'bad' ones as well) and their versions in the Folio, to determine on which text an editor is to base his edition. Scholars have mainly sought to determine the nature of the copy of which the printers made use. The chief types of copy which have been distinguished are: (1) foul papers, that is an original authorial draft; (2) a fair scribal copy; (3) a prompt copy from the theatre; (4) a memorial text, as discussed above, and (5) a reconstructed text, that is one based on an early quarto but where some kind of manuscript copy has also been used.

The fullest accounts of F1 are W. W. *Greg's *The Shakespeare First Folio* (1955) and C. Hinman's *The Printing and Proof-reading of the First Folio of Shakespeare* (1963).

Folklore, the traditional beliefs, legends, and customs current among the common people; and the study of them. The term was first introduced by W. J. *Thoms in the *Athenaeum* (1846).

Folk-song, a song, origin usually unknown, that is handed down orally from generation to generation and often exists in different forms in different parts of the country. In England the first person to make any systematic attempt at recording the material in this field was *Percy in the middle of the 18th cent. The end of the 19th and the beginning of the 20th cents. saw an immense increase of activity in the collection, transpiration, and publication of folk-songs (see SHARP, C.).

Folliott, The Revd Doctor, a character in Peacock's *Crotchet Castle*.

Fomors, the sea-giants of Gaelic mythology. They are represented as more ancient than the gods (the *Tuatha Dé Danann).

Fondlewife, one of the characters in Congreve's *The Old Bachelor*.

Fonthill Abbey, see BECKFORD, W.

Fool of Quality, The, a novel in 5 vols by H. *Brooke, published in Dublin 1765–70 and in London 1766–70.

The narrative follows the education, growth, and manhood of Harry Clinton, the Fool of Quality, the second son of the earl of Moreland. The most important adult in his world is not his decadent father but his merchant uncle, Mr Clinton (sometimes Fenton), whose enlightened views on Harry's education (much influenced by *Rousseau's *Émile* and *Locke's *On Education*) guide the boy's growth into a wise and generous adult.

The book appealed greatly to *Wesley and to *Kingsley (who drew on it for his own novel *Yeast*). (See also SENTIMENTAL NOVEL and BILDUNGSROMAN.)

FOOTE, Samuel (1720–77), actor and dramatist, was particularly successful in comic mimicry; acting in his own plays, he caricatured his fellow actors and other well-known persons, often savagely. *The Minor* (1760), a satire directed against the Methodists in which Foote mimicked *Whitefield as 'Dr Squintum', was his most powerful work. In *The Maid of Bath* (1771) Foote pilloried Squire Long, the unscrupulous sexagenarian lover of Miss Elizabeth Linley, who was to marry *Sheridan. *The Nabob* (1772) was aimed at the directors of the East India Company and *Piety in Patterns* (1773) ridiculed *sentimental comedy and Richardson's *Pamela. He was known to his contemporaries as 'the English Aristophanes'.

Fopling Flutter, Sir, a character in Etherege's *The Man of Mode*.

Foppington, Lord, a character in Vanbrugh's comedy *The Relapse* and Sheridan's *A Trip to Scarborough*; also in C. Cibber's *The Careless Husband*.

FORD, Ford Madox (formerly Ford Hermann Hueffer) (1873–1939), spent much of his childhood in *Pre-Raphaelite circles, an inheritance which deeply affected him. His first published works were fairy-stories (*The Brown Owl*, 1892, etc.) In 1894 he eloped with and married Elsie Martindale. In 1898 he met *Conrad and they collaborated in various works including the novels *The Inheritors* (1901) and *Romance* (1903); but from 1901 their relationship deteriorated. During a diverse and productive literary career Ford published over 80 books, both fiction and non-fiction, and developed his own theory of 'Impressionism' in the novel. His *Fifth Queen* trilogy (1907, 1907, 1908) describes in ornate and colourful prose the fate of Catherine Howard, wife of *Henry VIII, portrayed as an earnest, innocent Catholic idealist. In 1908 Ford embarked on two significant enterprises, an affair with the glamorous and emancipated novelist Violet *Hunt, which was to involve him in scandal and in complex, unsuccessful divorce proceedings; and the founding of the *English Review*, which he edited for 15 months.

In 1915 Ford published what he himself regarded as his finest achievement, *The Good Soldier*, and in the same year enlisted in the army. The war inspired his other major work of fiction, *Parade's End*, which was published in four parts between 1924 and 1928. Ford moved to Paris in 1922 where he founded in 1924 the *Transatlantic Review*. During his last years, which were spent in France and America, he published several volumes of autobiography and reminiscence (including *Return to Yesterday*, 1931, and *It was the nightingale*, 1933) and a volume of criticism, *The March of Literature* (1938). As an editor, he has long been regarded as a highly influential figure whose devotion to literature and ready appreciation of originality and quality in others (see MODERNISM) did much to shape the course of 20th-cent. writing.

FORD, John (1586–after 1639), wrote all or a substantial part of 18 plays, of which seven have been lost. Between 1621 and 1625 he collaborated with *Dekker and others in at least five plays including *The Witch of Edmonton*. After 1625 Ford probably worked alone. His chief plays are *The Lover's Melancholy* (1629), *Love's Sacrifice* (1633), *'Tis Pity She's a Whore* (1633), *The Broken Heart* (1633), *Perkin Warbeck* (1634), *The Lady's Trial* (1639). Ford's plays are predominantly concerned with human dignity, courage, and endurance in suffering. He explores melancholy, torture, incest, delusion, but always seriously and objectively, through 'the distinct personal rhythm in blank verse which could be no one's but his alone' (T. S. *Eliot).

Ford, and Mrs Ford, characters in Shakespeare's *The Merry Wives of Windsor*.

Foreign influences. In the earlier periods covered by this volume, national and linguistic distinctions had not yet settled into their now familiar forms: the language of culture and education in England from 597 until the end of the 14th cent. was Latin, and from the Norman Conquest until the loss of Normandy in 1205 many English writers were educated in France. (See ANGLO-LATIN and ANGLO-NORMAN LITERATURE.) By the time of *Chaucer it becomes possible to distinguish different strands of influence: Chaucer himself was indebted to the *Roman de la Rose and to *Guillaume de Machaut, and his sources include *Breton lays, French *fabliaux, and *Boccaccio's *Decameron. His great contemporary *Gower, who wrote in Latin, Anglo-Norman, and English, drew both from the classics and from popular French romances. *Lydgate translated Boccaccio's De Casibus Virorum Illustrium, and his version in turn inspired *A Mirror for Magistrates. The Sicilian author *Guido delle Colonne provided much material for *Chaucer, *Henryson, and *Lydgate, but as he wrote in Latin cannot perhaps be described as a foreign influence.

More distinctively Italian were the vernacular writings of *Petrarch, which were known to Chaucer, although their main influence was on a succeeding generation of poets, including *Surrey, *Wyatt, and *Sidney, all of whom imitated and translated him; the vogue for the Petrarchan sonnet lasted into the 17th cent., when it began to wane. Another major influence on the English sonnet was the French group known as the *Pléiade (notably Pierre de Ronsard, 1524–85, and *du Bellay): *Spenser translated both Petrarch and du Bellay. Spenser was also much influenced in his great work *The Faerie Queene by the famous Italian epic, the *Orlando Furioso of *Ariosto. The Latin eclogues of the Italian *Mantuan had a vogue in England, and influenced the pastorals of *Barclay and Spenser: *Piccolomini's work also provided a model for Barclay.

Among Italian prose writers, Cinthio and *Bandello succeeded the greater Boccaccio as story tellers and providers of plot for Shakespeare, *Fletcher, *Shirley and others, although their tales often reached England indirectly (see under PALACE OF PLEASURE.)

On a more philosophical level, English writers of this and of later periods were much affected by the revival of *Neoplatonic thought in 15th-cent. Italy: *Ficino and *Pico della Mirandola inspired, among others, *Colet, *Sidney, and *Milton, as well as Sir Thomas *More, who translated Pico's life. Giordano Bruno (?1548–1600), the heretical philosopher, dedicated work to Sidney, and visited Oxford under his auspices. One of the most important books of the period was *Castiglione's Il libro del cortegiano (1528) translated as The Courtyer (1561) by *Hoby, which presented the concept of the ideal man, soldier, poet, and statesman, and developed the notion of Platonic love. In sharp contrast, another great prose work which deeply influenced English thought was *Machiavelli's Il Principe (The Prince, 1513), which circulated widely in manuscript and in conversation before its official English translation in 1640:

Machiavellian villains abounded upon the Elizabethan and Jacobean stage, and more authentic, subtle versions of Machiavelli's arguments appeared in works and acts of statesmanship and politics. Towards the end of the 16th cent., and in the 17th cent., Italian influence expresseed itself in imitations of the pastorals of *Guarini and *Tasso: Fairfax's translation of Tasso's epic *Jerusalem Delivered (1600) had an influence on English versification, according to *Dryden, in its own right.

To speak of 'foreign influences' at this period, however, remains problematic: one of the features of Renaissance humanism was its internationalism, and a figure like the scholar *Erasmus, although Dutch by nationality, was a citizen of Europe, who visited England frequently and was a friend of Sir Thomas *More.

The works and thoughts of *Montaigne reached England fairly easily, through the translations of *Florio, and his challenging essays were read by F. *Bacon, Shakespeare, Robert *Burton, and many others. A more 'foreign' figure may be detected in *Rabelais, whose extraordinary creations, *Gargantua and *Pantagruel, although known to some readers in their original version, took a century to reach Britain in the famous version of *Urquhart: thenceforth their influence on a later generation of satirists (*Butler, *Swift, *Sterne) was immense. The impact of the greatest Spanish prose writer of the epoch was less delayed: *Don Quixote, by *Cervantes, published in Spain in two parts, 1605, 1615, first appeared in English in 1616, and thereafter in various versions, supplying (along with the prose tales of Cervantes) the plots of innumerable 17th-cent. plays by *Fletcher, *Middleton, and others. Don Quixote kept alive through affectionate parody the earlier influence of *Amadis of Gaul and *Palmerin of England, Spanish–Portuguese romances that were immensely popular with the Elizabethan middle classes. The Palmerin cycle was translated by *Mabbe, who also translated the Spanish novel *Celestina as The Spanish Bawd (1631): an early part of Celestina had also been translated (into verse) by *Rastell (c.1530), a version that has been described as one of the first English comedies. Spanish elements also reached Britain through the *picaresque novels of the 16th cent.: they appear in many 17th-cent. prose romances and, more enduringly, in the great 18th-cent. novels of *Fielding, *Smollett, and *Defoe. The great Spanish dramatists of the period, Lope de Vega (1562–1635) and Calderón de la Barca (1600–81), had a less obvious direct impact on English writing. The French picaresque writer *Lesage also had a great influence on 18th-cent. comic fiction.

In the 17th cent. Italian influence was no longer dominant, except in odd instances, as in that of *Marino's influence upon *Crashaw: the

English tended towards their own version of the *Metaphysical rather than towards Italianate *baroque. But, as the century progressed, French influence increased. The popular pastoral romance, *L'Astrée* (1607–19) of Honoré D'Urfé (1567–1625), which influenced playwrights at the court of Charles I, was followed by the works of Madeleine de Scudéry (1607–91) and La Calprenède (1614–63): their lengthy, implausible, sentimental romances were much admired in England during the Restoration period and inspired much *heroic drama. A more lasting French influence arrived through the theories of *Neo-classicism and the practice of its great writers—*Corneille, *Racine, *Boileau, *Molière, *Dryden, *Addison, *Pope—and many succeeding writers and critics explained and expounded the new aesthetics, although some authors (notably Racine) remained stubbornly untranslatable. The Augustan period was permeated with French theory. There were some notably happy results of the new cross-currents, as, for example, in Pope's *The Rape of the Lock* (1712–14): other products, such as Dr Johnson's frigid tragedy *Irene*, were less fortunate. The 18th cent. also saw a considerable interest in oriental or exotic subjects: the plot of *Irene* is taken from *Knolles, but Johnson's interest in the east expresses itself more felicitously in *Rasselas*. For an account of these influences, see under ORIENTAL NOVEL.

Neo-classicism gradually evolved into the *Enlightenment, an international movement with national components: French writers of the Enlightenment include *Voltaire, *Rousseau, Condorcet (1743–94), and *Diderot, and German writers (who began at this stage to impinge on English consciousness) include *Leibniz and G. E. Lessing (1729–81), whose play *Nathan der Weise* (1779) was an important plea for religious tolerance, and whose treatise on aesthetics *Laokoon* (1766) had a lasting influence. The *Laokoon* was a reply to the theories of J. J. Winckelmann (1717–68), whose studies of Greek art had made a decisive contribution to Neo-classical taste. Towards the end of the 18th cent. with the rise of *Romanticism, German influence became more and more marked in Britain: *Goethe and *Schiller were hailed by *Coleridge, *Hazlitt, and *Wordsworth, and German critics (*Herder, the *Schlegels) and philosophers (*Hegel, Johann Gottlieb, 1762–1814, Fichte) were read with admiration and enthusiasm. Their works were translated by eminent scholars, including *Lockhart and *Carlyle. Sir Walter *Scott was much influenced by German romanticism, and his versions of the ballads of the German poet, G. A. Burger (1747–94) (see LENORE) added to the vogue for German culture. George *Eliot was much affected by German philosophy, notably by the German scholar *Feuerbach, whose works she translated.

The most influential of the French romantics was *Rousseau: his follower Bernadin de Saint-Pierre (1737–1814) also had an international success with his *primitivist novel, *Paul et Virginie* (1788). Constantin François de Chasseboeuf, comte de Volnay (1757–1820), had a following in Britain, particularly among rationalists and freethinkers (including the *Shelleys): his *Les Ruines* (1791), meditations on the ruins of Palmyra, was translated in 1795. Later French romanticism produced some outstanding figures (Victor *Hugo; François-René de Chateaubriand, 1768–1848; Charles Baudelaire, 1821–67) who were widely admired throughout Europe, but perhaps less directly influential. One of the movements that reacted against Romanticism had a more discernible impact. *Realism, and its successor *Naturalism, as expressed in the works of *Balzac, *Flaubert, and the brothers Edmond and Jules de Goncourt (1822–96 and 1830–70), de Maupassant (1850–93), *Zola, and, more indirectly, Stendhal (Henri Beyle, 1783–1842), permanently affected the course of the novel in Britain, despite initial resistance, largely on the grounds of the 'immorality' of the new fiction. The theories of realism were intimately connected with the positivist philosophy of *Comte (who also influenced *Mill, George *Eliot, and many other English writers and thinkers).

French realism joined with Russian influences in British fiction of the late 19th and early 20th cents. The works of *Tolstoy, *Dostoevsky, and *Turgenev began to reach English readers, partly through the versions of Constance *Garnett: *Chekhov influenced both the short story (notably in the works of K. *Mansfield) and the drama. Strong Scandinavian influences also began to influence British drama, through the works of *Ibsen and *Strindberg; German *Expressionism took less root in British theatre.

Towards the end of the century, the phenomenon of *fin-de-siècle* decadence and aestheticism (SEE ART FOR ART'S SAKE) was common to both France and England: the works of Joris-Karl Huysmans (1848–1907), and in particular his novel *A Rebours* (1884), were much admired by *Wilde. The *Symbolist movement, which claimed Baudelaire, Paul Verlaine (1844–96), Stephane Mallarmé (1842–98), and the Belgian playwright Maurice Macterlinck (1862–1949), overlaps to some extent with the aesthetic movement: it too had a pervasive influence. Jules *Laforgue is well known as one of the inspirations behind the early work of T. S. *Eliot and *Pound. Another major French figure of the period, the novelist Marcel Proust (1871–1922), was to be imitated in Britain by writers as diverse as A. *Powell and C. P. *Snow: his master-work, *A la recherche du temps perdu*, appeared in English between 1922 and 1931 in a celebrated translation by C. K. Scott-Moncrieff.

The late 19th and early 20th cents gave rise to

various literary and artistic movements, most of which had a strong international flavour, as well as national elements: these include *Surrealism, *Dada, *Futurism, and *Modernism, *Brecht and *Pirandello were both strong influences on 20th-cent. British drama. The somewhat isolated figure of the novelist Franz *Kafka (born in Prague) produced an *œuvre* that crosses all national barriers: the dilemma of the Kafkaesque hero was recognized throughout Europe. *Existentialism, which many have seen as a development of the philosophy of the Danish writer *Kierkegaard, reached Britain principally through the writings of *Sartre, and became a fashionable pose in the 1950s, in life and literature: see Colin *Wilson's *The Outsider* (1956). The Theatre of the *Absurd influenced *Pinter and others: *Beckett remains a major figure in both English and French literature and theatre. There has also been a certain amount of influence from French critical theory pertaining to the *nouveau roman*, and from continental literary theory in general, arising from the spread of *Structuralism and Post-structuralism. *Marxist critical theory, and the views of Hungarian critic Georg *Lukács, have influenced critical thinking more than creative writing. A more creative encounter, perhaps, has been between the *Magic Realism of Latin American writers such as *Borges and *García Márquez and the younger generation of British writers, some of whom are also indebted to the German novelist Gunter Grass (1927–), whose long, humorous, experimental novels have been widely admired in Britain. The experimental works of the Italian Italo Calvino (1923–85) are also now widely read, and have elements of Magic Realism.

The above-listed influences are necessarily only an incomplete summary: space does not permit more than a mention of the influence of the Norse and Icelandic literatures on W. *Morris and W. H. *Auden (see SAGA, EDDA, SNORRI STURLUSON), of the Japanese *Nōh plays on *Yeats and Pound, of Provençal poetry on Pound, of *Dante upon T. S. Eliot, or of the quite different popularity of international classics such as the works of French *science fiction writer Jules *Verne or the adventures of *Baron Munchausen* (1785) by Rudolph Erich Raspe. Collections of fairy stories and children's tales that have crossed all frontiers include *Perrault's, the *Arabian Nights*, the stories of the brothers *Grimm and Hans Christian *Andersen, and the Sanskrit *Fables of Bidpai*.

Forest, The, a collection of miscellaneous short poems, odes, epistles, and songs by *Jonson, printed in the folio of 1616, including 'To Penshurst' and the song 'Drink to me only with thine eyes'.

FORESTER, C(ecil) S(cott) (Cecil Lewis Troughton Smith) (1899–1966), is principally

remembered for his seafaring novels set during the Napoleonic wars, featuring Horatio Hornblower, introduced in 1937 in *The Happy Return*. His other works include *Brown on Resolution* (1929), *The African Queen* (1935), and *The Hornblower Companion* (1964).

Forester, Sylvan, a character in Peacock's *Melincourt*, partly based on Peacock's friend *Shelley.

***Fors Clavigera;** Letters to the Workmen and Labourers of Great Britain*, by *Ruskin, was issued monthly in 1871–8, then at irregular intervals until 1884.

Fors Clavigera was a continual challenge, deliberate and serious, to the supporters of and apologists for a capitalist economy. The obscurity of the title suggests how little he wished to ingratiate himself with the working classes. He delivers lessons in 'the principles and plans of political economy' by setting events from contemporary history and his own immediate experience against the nobler human possibilities expressed in literature and art. *Fors Clavigera* became the mouthpiece of Ruskin's Guild of St George.

FORSTER, E(dward) M(organ) (1879–1970), educated at Tonbridge School (which he disliked) and King's College, Cambridge, where the atmosphere of free intellectual discussion and a stress on the importance of personal relationships inspired partly by G. E. *Moore was to have a profound influence on his work. In 1901 he was elected to the *Apostles. A year of travel in Italy with his mother and a cruise to Greece followed, providing material for his early novels, which satirize the attitude of English tourists abroad. On his return he wrote for the *Independent Review*, launched in 1903 by a group of Cambridge friends, led by G. M. *Trevelyan; in 1904 it published his first story, 'The Story of a Panic'. In 1905 he published *Where Angels Fear to Tread*, and spent some months in Germany as tutor to the children of the Countess *von Arnim. In 1906 he became tutor to Syed Ross Masood, a striking and colourful Indian Muslim patriot. He then published *The Longest Journey* (1907), *A Room with a View* (1908), and *Howard's End* (1910). *The Celestial Omnibus* (1911) was a collection of short stories. In 1912–13 he visited India and travelled with Masood. In 1913 a significant visit to the home of E. *Carpenter resulted in his writing *Maurice*, a novel with a homosexual theme which he circulated privately; it was published posthumously in 1971. He went to Alexandria in 1915 for the Red Cross; his *Alexandria: A History and a Guide* was published in 1922. In Alexandria he met Constantine Cavafy, whose works he helped to introduce; an essay on Cavafy appears in *Pharos and Pharillon* (1923). In 1921–2 he revisited India, and worked as personal secretary for the maharajah of the native state of Dewas Senior. *A Passage to India (1922–4), which he had begun before the war, was his last novel. The remainder of his life was devoted to a wide range of literary activities; he took a firm stand against censorship, involving himself in the work of PEN and the NCCL, campaigning in 1928 against the suppression of R. *Hall's The Well of Loneliness, and appearing in 1960 as witness for the defence in the trial of the publishers of *Lady Chatterley's Lover. In 1927 he delivered the Clark lectures at Cambridge, printed as Aspects of the Novel (1927). King's College offered him in 1946 an honorary fellowship and a permanent home. Forster's other publications include The Eternal Moment (1928), a volume of pre-1914 short stories; two biographies, Goldsworthy Lowes Dickinson (1934) and Marianne Thornton (1956); Abinger Harvest (1936), essays; Two Cheers for Democracy (1951), essays; and The Hill of Devi (1953), a portrait of India. He worked with Eric Crozier on the libretto for *Britten's opera Billy Budd (1951). Maurice was followed by another posthumous publication, The Life to Come (1972), a collection of short stories, many with homosexual themes.

FORSTER, John (1812–76), was editor of Foreign Quarterly Review, 1842–3, the Daily News, 1846, and the Examiner, 1847–55. He was the literary associate and close friend of Leigh *Hunt, C. *Lamb, W. S. *Landor, *Bulwer-Lytton, and *Dickens: from 1837 on he read in MS or proof everything Dickens wrote. His earliest biographical work, Lives of Eminent British Statesmen (1836–9) in Lardner's Cyclopedia, was followed by various political lives partly reprinted as Historical and Biographical Essays (1858). His popular literary biographies include Life and Adventures of Oliver Goldsmith (1848; rev. 2 vols, 1854), Landor (2 vols, 1869), Dickens (3 vols, 1872–4), and the first volume of a scholarly life of *Swift (1875). He is recognized as the first professional biographer of 19th-cent. England. Landor, Dickens, and *Carlyle appointed him their literary executor.

Forsyte Saga, The, a sequence by J. *Galsworthy, published 1922.

The three novels containing the story, The Man of Property (1906), In Chancery (1920), and To Let (1921, with two interludes, 'Indian Summer of a Forsyte', 1918, and Awakening, 1920), appeared together in 1922 as The Forsyte Saga, tracing the fortunes of three generations of the Forsyte family.

Soames Forsyte, a successful solicitor, the nephew of 'old Jolyon', lives in London surrounded by his prosperous old uncles and their families. He marries the penniless Irene and builds a country house for her, Robin Hill; when she falls in love with its architect, Bosinney,

Soames asserts his rights over his property and rapes her. Bosinney is killed in a street accident and Irene returns to Soames. In Chancery describes the growing love of young Jolyon, Soames's cousin, for Irene; Irene's divorce from Soames and her happy marriage with Jolyon; and the birth of their son Jon. Meanwhile Soames marries Annette Lamotte and they have a daughter, Fleur. In To Let Fleur and Jon fall in love; Jon's father feels compelled to reveal the past of Irene and Soames, and the agonized Jon, in spite of Fleur's Forsyte determination, rejects her. She marries Michael Mont, the heir to a baronetcy, and when young Jolyon dies Irene leaves to join Jon in America. The desolate Soames learns that his wife is having an affair with a Frenchman, and discovers that Irene's house, Robin Hill, is empty and to let.

FORTESCUE, Sir John (?1394–?1476), chief justice of the king's bench under Henry VI, and the earliest English constitutional lawyer. His principal works were a Latin treatise, De Natura Legis Naturae (1461–3), distinguishing absolute from constitutional monarchy; an English treatise on the same subject (Monarchia or The Difference between an Absolute and a Limited Monarchy); a Latin treatise, De Laudibus Legum Angliae (1471); and an English work, On the Governance of England (1470s, ed. C. Plummer, 1885). His recantation of his Lancastrian views is contained in A Declaration upon Certain Wrytinges (1471–3).

Fortinbras, prince of Norway in Shakespeare's *Hamlet.

Fortnightly Review, The, (1865–1934), a positivist and anti-orthodox literary periodical. G. H. *Lewes, the first editor, was succeeded by John *Morley. Almost all numbers ran a serialized novel; the first contained a chapter of Trollope's *The Belton Estate and a part of *Bagehot's The English Constitution. The Review published work by *Thackeray, G. *Eliot, M. *Arnold, T. H. *Huxley, *Meredith, D. G. *Rossetti, L. *Stephen, *Pater, and *Hardy, among others. In this century work published included that of H. *James, *Gissing, *Kipling, H. G. *Wells, *Joyce, and *Pound. In 1934 it became The Fortnightly, under which title it survived until 1954. It was then incorporated in the *Contemporary Review.

Fortunate Mistress, The, see ROXANA.

Fortunatus's purse, the subject of a European 15th-cent. romance, translated into many languages and dramatized by *Dekker. For the story see OLD FORTUNATUS.

Fortunes of Nigel, The, a novel by Sir W. *Scott, published 1822.

The young Nigel Olifaunt, Lord Glenvarloch, threatened with the loss of his ancestral estate if he is unable promptly to redeem a heavy mortgage, comes to London to endeavour to recover from James I a sum of 40,000 marks lent to him at a crisis in his fortunes by Nigel's father. The story concerns his adventures in London, their successful issue, and his marriage to Margaret Ramsay, the clockmaker's daughter.

The novel contains a number of interesting characters, including the pedantic freakish James I; Richard Moniplies, Nigel's conceited servant; Dame Ursula Suddlechop, milliner and secret agent; the miser Trapbois and his austere daughter; the rattling Templar Lowestoffe; and the embittered courtier Sir Mungo Malagrowther.

For Whom the Bell Tolls, a novel by E. *Hemingway.

Foscari, The Two, see TWO FOSCARI, THE.

Fosco, Count, a character in Wilkie Collins's *The Woman in White*.

Fotheringay, Miss, the stage name of Emily Costigan, a character in Thackeray's *Pendennis*.

FOULIS, Robert (1707–76), with his brother Andrew, visited Oxford and France in 1738–40, collecting rare books, and started as bookseller and printer in Glasgow. He printed for the university their first Greek book (1743) and the 'immaculate' *Horace (1744) and issued a number of other remarkable books.

Foul Play, a novel by C. *Reade.

'Four Ages of Poetry, The', a literary essay by *Peacock, published 1820. It makes ironic use of the argument advanced by 18th-cent. cultural historians such as J. J. Winckelmann (1717–68), that as society progresses, poetry deteriorates in inevitable stages. Shelley replied in his *Defence of Poetry*.

Four Quartets, a poem in four parts by T. S. *Eliot, published as a whole in New York in 1943. It comprises 'Burnt Norton', 'East Coker', 'The Dry Salvages', and 'Little Gidding', all of which appeared previously in other volumes.

The four quartets represent the four seasons and the four elements; the imagery of the first centres on a Cotswold garden; that of the second round a Somerset village; the third mingles the landscape of Missouri and New England, the landscapes of Eliot's youth; and the fourth uses as a symbol 'Little Gidding. But all are concerned with time past and time present, with the wartime London of the blitz as well as the England of *Julian of Norwich and Sir T.

*Elyot. These were the first of Eliot's poems to reach a wide public and they succeeded in communicating in modern idiom the fundamentals of Christian faith and experiences.

Four Sons of Aymon, see AYMON.

Four Zoas, The, a symbolic poem by *Blake, originally entitled *Vala*, written and revised 1795–1804, described by John Beer (*Blake's Humanism*, 1968) as 'a heroic attempt to write the first psychological epic'. It presents characters familiar from Blake's earlier symbolic works (*Urizen, *Los, *Enitharmon, *Orc, and others), elaborating his cosmic mythology in a framework of a 'Dream of Nine Nights'. The Four Zoas appear to represent the four human faculties, once united, but then at war with one another until the final radiant vision of joy and peace when the eyes of the Eternal Man 'behold the depths of wondrous worlds' and around his tent 'the little children play among the wooly flocks'.

FOWLER, Henry Watson (1858–1933), and Francis George (1870–1918), lexicographers and grammarians; joint authors of *The King's English* (1906), *The Concise Oxford Dictionary* (1911), and *The Pocket Oxford Dictionary* (1924). *A Dictionary of Modern English Usage* (1926; 2nd edn. 1965, ed. Sir E. Gowers) is the work of H. W. Fowler.

FOWLES, John Robert (1926–), novelist, educated at New College, Oxford. His first novel *The Collector* (1963), a psychological thriller, was followed by *The Aristos* (1965), an idiosyncratic collection of notes and aphorisms, and *The Magus* (1966, revised version 1977), a novel set largely on the Greek island of 'Phraxos', where British schoolmaster Nicholas D'Urfe is subjected to a series of mysterious apparitions which give the novel a narrative complexity and mythological dimension faintly suggestive of *Magic Realism. *The French Lieutenant's Woman* (1969) is a semi-historical novel, set largely in Lyme Regis in 1867; wealthy amateur palaeontologist Charles Smithson, engaged to conventional Ernestina Freeman, falls under the spell of Sarah Woodruff, a lady's companion, who is believed to have been deserted by the French lover of the title. His pursuit of Sarah breaks his engagement, but Sarah eludes him, and when he finds her again she has become a *New Woman. *The Ebony Tower* (1974) is a collection of novellas; *Daniel Martin* (1977) is a long, self-searching semi-naturalistic work about a screenwriter. *Mantissa* (1982) consists largely of extended erotic fantasy on the subject of *la femme inspiratrice*.

FOX, Charles James (1749–1806), a great Whig statesman and orator, who first made his mark by speeches against *Wilkes in 1769. He was one of the managers of the proceedings against Warren Hastings, and a constant opponent of the policy of Pitt. He was a man of great personal charm, noted for his scholarship but also for his gambling and drinking and the bad influence he exercised over the prince of Wales. He was elected a member of Dr Johnson's *Club (1774).

FOX, George (1624–91), founder of the Society of *Friends, or Quakers. He was a magnetic preacher and travelled widely in the British Isles and to the New World and Holland. His *Journal* (1694), revised by a committee under the superintendence of *Penn, describes in simple, direct but powerful prose his visions, his teaching, and the frequent imprisonments and persecutions to which he and other Friends were exposed.

FOXE, John (1516–87), the martyrologist, became a fellow of Magdalen College, Oxford, but resigned his fellowship in 1545, being unwilling to conform to the statutes in religious matters. In 1554 he retired to the Continent and issued at Strasburg his *Commentarii* (the earliest draft of his *Actes and Monuments*). On his return to England he was ordained priest by Grindal in 1560, and in 1564 joined John *Day, the printer, who in 1563 had issued the English version of the *Rerum in ecclesia gestarum . . . commentarii* as *Actes and Monuments*, popularly known as the *Book of Martyrs*. He preached at Paul's Cross a famous sermon 'Of Christ Crucified', in 1570. His edition of the canon laws *Reformatio Legum* appeared in 1571.

Fradubio, in Spenser's *Faerie Queene* (I. ii. 32 *et seq.*), 'the doubter', the lover of Fraelissa.

'Fra Lippo Lippi', a poem by R. Browning, included in *Men and Women*.

Framley Parsonage, a novel by A. *Trollope first published 1861, the fourth in the *'Barsetshire' series.

Mark Robarts is an ambitious young clergyman. At the age of 26 Lady Lufton helped him to the comfortable living at Framley, but he has now become involved with the unreliable Mr Sowerby and hopes for further preferment from the duke of Omnium. Sowerby promises Robarts a prebendal stall at Barchester and Robarts rashly guarantees some bills in return. He becomes liable for the full amount of the debts and has to appeal to his original patron, Lady Lufton.

This is doubly embarrassing for the Luftons, as young Lord Lufton has fallen in love with Robarts's sister, Lucy. At first Lady Lufton vehemently opposes the match, and hopes to interest her son in Griselda Grantly, daughter of the archdeacon. Griselda, however, marries the wealthy Lord Dumbello, and Lady Lufton and

Lucy are thrown together by the illness of Mrs Crawley, wife of a neighbouring clergyman. In nursing her Lucy shows her true worth, and Lady Lufton removes her opposition to the match; Mark Robarts's debts are paid as a gesture of goodwill. The novel is remarkable for the first appearance of the proud, impoverished curate Mr Crawley.

Francesca da Rimini, see PAOLO AND FRANCESCA.

FRANCIS, Sir Philip (1740–1818). From 1762 to 1772 he was a clerk in the War Office, and became one of the four newly appointed councillors of the governor-general of India in 1774. He left India in 1780 and assisted *Burke in preparing the charges against Warren Hastings. Recent research confirms the long-standing identification of Francis as *Junius.

FRANCIS OF ASSISI, St, Giovanni Francesco Bernardone (1181/2–1226), experienced as a young man two serious illnesses and a spiritual crisis on a military expedition, in consequence of which he lived for a time in solitude and prayer and devoted himself to the relief of the poor, the sick, and the lepers. He was joined by disciples, the first members of the Franciscan order for which he drew up the rule in 1209, the principal characteristic of which was humility, in token of which they called themselves 'Friari Minori'. The special notes of his teaching were poverty and love of nature (St Francis preaching to the birds is a favourite painter's subject). Two years before his death, after a period of fasting on Mount Alverno, he is said to have discovered on his body the stigmata, the marks made by the nails of Christ's Crucifixion. The *Fioretti de San Francisco (Little flowers of St Francis)* is a 14th-cent. Italian narrative, partly legendary, of the doings of St Francis and his first disciples. His own Italian poem *Cantico di Frate Sole* (Canticle of Brother Sun) is a song or psalm in praise of God and his creations.

Frankenstein, or the *Modern Prometheus*, a *Gothic tale of terror by M. *Shelley, published 1818.

Technically an *epistolary novel, told through the letters of Walton, an English explorer in the Arctic, the tale relates the exploits of Frankenstein, an idealistic Genevan student of natural philosophy, who discovers at the university of Ingolstadt the secret of imparting life to inanimate matter. Collecting bones from charnel-houses, he constructs the semblance of a human being and gives it life. The creature, endowed with supernatural strength and size and terrible in appearance, inspires loathing in whoever sees it. Lonely and miserable (and educated in human emotion by studies of *Goethe, *Plutarch, and *Paradise Lost*), it turns upon its creator, and, failing to persuade him to provide a female counterpart, eventually murders his brother, his friend Clerval, and his bride Elizabeth. Frankenstein pursues it to the Arctic to destroy it, but dies in the pursuit, after relating his story to Walton. The monster declares that Frankenstein will be its last victim, and disappears to end its own life. This tale inspired many film versions, and has been regarded as the origin of modern *science fiction, though it is also a version of the myth of the Noble Savage (see PRIMITIVISM), in which a nature essentially good is corrupted by ill treatment. It is also remarkable for its description of nature, which owes much to the Shelleys' admiration for *Wordsworth, *Coleridge, and in particular the *Ancient Mariner.

FRANKLIN, Benjamin (1706–90), born in Boston, Massachusetts, was largely self-educated. After working in a London printing house, 1724–5, he returned to Philadelphia and set up his own press, from which he issued The Pennsylvania Gazette. He acquired a wide reputation by his occasional writings, especially Poor Richard's Almanack (1733–58), and was active as a public figure, founding the American Philosophical Society and the academy that became the University of Pennsylvania. In 1757 he travelled to England as agent for the colonies, where he mixed widely in intellectual society (his friends including *Burke, *Hume, Adam *Smith, William Strahan, and J. *Priestley) and contributed greatly to the controversies that caused the breach with England; he returned home in 1774 and, after helping to draft the Declaration of Independence, travelled to France as ambassador. Upon his return in 1785 he signed the Constitution as a member of the Federal Constitutional Convention. His Autobiography was published in England in 1793 (translated from the French), in America in 1818. Franklin's prose was much admired in England. *Lecky (History of England in the Eighteenth Century) described it as 'always terse, luminous, simple, pregnant with meaning, eminently persuasive'.

FRANKLIN, Sir John (1786–1847), Arctic explorer, author of two Narratives (1823 and 1828) of voyages to the Polar Sea. His final voyage of discovery in Erebus and Terror in search of the North-West Passage, began in 1845, and resulted in disaster. One relief expediton, organized by his widow, found a record of the expedition proving that Franklin had discovered the North-West Passage.

'Franklin's Tale, The', see CANTERBURY TALES, 12.

FRASER, George Sutherland, see NEW APOCALYPSE.

Fraser's Magazine (1830–82), a general and literary Tory journal founded by *Maginn and Hugh Fraser. Among contributors were J. *Hogg, *Coleridge, *Southey, *Peacock, *Carlyle, *Ainsworth, *Thackeray, and *Ruskin. J. A. *Froude was editor, 1860–74.

FRAYN, Michael (1933–), novelist and playwright. His novels include Towards the End of the Morning (1967), a comedy of Fleet Street Life, and A Very Private Life (1968), a satiric anti-Utopian fantasy. His stage comedies include Alphabetical Order (1975, pub. 1976), with a background of journalism; Donkeys' Years (1976, pub. 1977), based on a college reunion; and Noises Off (1982), a farce of theatre life.

FRAZER, Sir James George (1854–1941), fellow of Trinity College, Cambridge, from 1879. He held the chair of anthropology in Liverpool from 1907. He is often regarded as one of the founders of modern anthropology. The Golden Bough (12 vols, 1890–1915; followed by Aftermath, a supplement in 1936) is a vast and enterprising comparative study of the beliefs and institutions of mankind, offering the thesis that man progresses from magical through religious to scientific thought. Its discussion of fertility rites, the sacrificial killing of kings, the dying god, the scapegoat, etc., and its analysis of the primitive mind, caught the literary imagination, and its influence may perhaps be seen most lastingly in the works of D. H. *Lawrence, T. S. *Eliot, and *Pound. Frazer's many other works include Totemism and Exogamy (1910) and Folklore in the Old Testament (1918).

Frederick, in Shakespeare's *As You Like It, the usurping duke.

FREDERICK THE GREAT, of Prussia (1712–86), military genius, able administrator, and man of considerable culture, who established the nationhood of Prussia; he was the subject of a biography by T. *Carlyle, entitled The History of Frederick II of Prussia called Frederick the Great (6 vols, 1858–65), in which he is described as 'a questionable hero' who nevertheless was able to emerge from a 'century opulent in accumulated falsities'. The work was a labour of many years.

FREEMAN, E(dward) A(ugustus) (1823–92), historian and controversialist, was appointed Regius professor of modern history at Oxford in 1884. His best-known work is his History of the Norman Conquest (5 vols, 1867–79), and its sequel on The Reign of William Rufus (2 vols, 1882). Here his firm Whig belief in the excellence of the British Constitution as it had developed from the Conquest was at odds with his deep affection and respect for Anglo-Saxon culture, which also led him to write in a curiously archaic style, eschewing Latin derivations wherever possible. In his hands, therefore, the events of 1066 emerge as a happy tragedy. He was capable of close friendships (for instance with W. *Stubbs and J. R. *Green), but guilty of almost paranoid hatreds, particularly for C. *Kingsley and J. H. *Froude, whom he pursued with venom, and all his work exhibits anti-Semitism and xenophobia.

French Lieutenant's Woman, The, see FOWLES, J.

French Revolution, The: A History, by T. *Carlyle, published 1837.

It is in three volumes, 'The Bastille', 'The Constitution', and 'The Guillotine'; it opens with the death of Louis XV in 1774, covers the reign of Louis XVI, the period which included the assembly of the States General, the fall of the Bastille, the Constituent and Legislative Assemblies, the flight of the king to Varennes, the Convention, the trial and execution of the king and queen, the reign of terror, the fall of Robespierre, and extends to 5 Oct. 1795, when Bonaparte quelled the insurrection of the Vendémiaire, the title of the last chapter being 'The Whiff of Grapeshot'. It is a work of great narrative and descriptive power, with a notable gallery of portraits (Mirabeau, Lafayette, Danton, Robespierre).

French Revolution, Reflections on the, by E. Burke, see REVOLUTION IN FRANCE.

FRENEAU, Philip Morin (1752–1832), the 'poet of the American Revolution', and miscellaneous writer, editor, and journalist, was born in New York. In 1780 during the Revolutionary War he was captured by the British, an experience which prompted the bitter satire of his poem *The British Prison-Ship* (1781), one of his many attacks on the British. His first collection of verse, *Poems* (1786), was followed by various volumes of essays, poems, etc. His verse ranged from the satirical and patriotic to works such as 'The Wild Honey Suckle' (1786), a nature poem of delicacy and sensitivity which heralds *Romanticism.

FRERE, John Hookham (1769–1846), friend of *Canning, an MP, and an official of the Foreign Office. While at Eton Frere wrote a translation of *Brunanburh, and was one of the founders of *The Microcosm* periodical (1786–7). He contributed humorous verse to *The Anti-Jacobin, including most of 'The Loves of the Triangles' (a parody of E. *Darwin). He collaborated in *Ellis's *Specimens of the Early English Poets* (1801), and in *Southey's *Chronicle of the Cid. He was one of the founders of *The Quarterly Review* in 1809, and an adviser to John *Murray the publisher. He is chiefly remembered as the inspirer of the style, stanza, and idiom of *Beppo* and *Don Juan, which Byron adapted from Frere's mock-

epic on King Arthur (1817). Frere also published lively metrical versions of *Aristophanes: *Frogs* (1839); *Acharnians, Knights,* and *Birds* in 1840; and *Theognis Restitutus* (1842).

FREUD, Sigmund (1856–1939), born at Freiberg in Moravia, and known as the creator of psychoanalysis, a science (or, as some claim, a mythology) which has had an incalculable effect both on literature and on literary theory. Freud practised for many years in Vienna, until Hitler's invasion of Austria drove him to London, where he died. His theories of the normal and abnormal mind, were evolved originally from his study of neurotic ailments. His many contributions to knowledge include his studies of the development of the sexual instinct in children, his descriptions of the workings of the unconscious mind and of the nature of repression, and his examinations and interpretations of dreams. Many of his concepts have become universally familiar in a vulgarized form, e.g. the Oedipus complex, the death wish, the family romance, penis envy, phallic symbolism, and the formulation of the divisions between the 'Id, the Ego and the Superego'. Such phrases rapidly acquired a currency even among those who had not read the works of Freud, and direct or indirect influence is frequently hard to ascertain. A characteristic case is that of D. H. Lawrence's *Sons and Lovers* (1913), considered by many a classic example of a novel about the Oedipus complex. L. *Strachey, in *Elizabeth and Essex* (1928), produced what is possibly the first consciously Freud-oriented biography; its many successors include Leon Edel's life of H. *James. The significance for both biographers and novelists of Freud's stress on the formative experiences of childhood is obvious; equally obvious is the importance to poets and prose-writers such as *Joyce of Freud's theories of word association, although Joyce always indignantly repudiated the influence of Freud. Freud's works were made available in English by James Strachey, Lytton's brother, who was responsible for the *Standard Edition of the Complete Psychological Works of Sigmund Freud* (24 vols, 1953–73). The works reveal Freud himself as a writer of great distinction. (See FREUDIAN CRITICISM.)

Freudian Criticism and Artistic Theory. The view that, in Freudian terms, artistic creativity is a form of sublimation, and that both art and the artist are pathological phenomena, has been argued in many works, including E. *Wilson's *The Wound and the Bow* (1941), a study of the biographical relationship between painful childhood experience and artistic creation. *Trilling summarized the position thus: 'the poet is a poet by reason of his sickness as well as by reason of his power' ('Neurosis and the Health of the Artist', 1947). A separate issue is the use of works of art and literature as subjects of analysis. This Freud himself did, notably in his studies of *Hamlet and Oedipus (*The Interpretation of Dreams*, 1900) and of *Richard III, Lady Macbeth, and *Ibsen's Rebecca West ('Some Character-Types met with in Psychoanalytic Work', 1915). Freudian criticism may thus direct itself to detecting connections between the biography of the artist and its product in art or artefact, or to the analysis of fictional characters; it may also direct itself to the analysis of 'Freudian' imagery, either deliberate or unintentional within a work. The influence of Freud, both on literature and its interpretation, has been vast: *Auden wrote in his eloquent elegy, 'to us he is no more a person | now but a whole climate of opinion | under whom we conduct our different lives . . .' ('In Memory of Sigmund Freud', 1939).

Friar Bacon and Friar Bungay, see FRIER BACON AND FRIER BONGAY.

FRIAR BUNGAY, see BUNGAY, T.

'Friar's Tale, The', see CANTERBURY TALES, 7.

Friar Tuck, one of the principal characters in the legend of *Robin Hood; the fat, jovial, and pugnacious father confessor of the outlaw chief. He figures in Scott's *Ivanhoe* and in Peacock's *Maid Marian*. (See also BALLAD.)

Friday, Man, see ROBINSON CRUSOE.

Friend, The, a weekly periodical edited and largely written by S. T. *Coleridge in the Lake District, 1809–10.

It was the first to publish early sections of Wordsworth's *Prelude*. In its final 3-vol. book form of 1818, Coleridge transformed it into a substantial series of interlinked essays 'to aid in the formation of fixed principles in politics, morals, and religion, with literary amusements interspersed'.

Friends, Society of, a religious society founded in 1648–50 by G. *Fox, distinguished by pacifist principles, plainness of dress and manners, refusal to take oaths, faith in the Inner Light, and the absence of clergy or ministers; the Society is also now noted for its involvement with social and educational reform. Members of the Society are also known as Quakers.

Friendship's Garland, a collection of essays in letter form by M. *Arnold, published 1871.

The principal imaginary correspondent is a Prussian, Arminius, Baron von Thunderten-Tronckh, and through him Arnold expresses his mockery of the English *Philistine, of narrow Liberal reform, of the *Daily Telegraph* and its naïve patriotism, and of English foreign and educational policy.

Frier Bacon, and Frier Bongay, The Honorable Historie of, a comedy in verse and prose by R. *Greene, acted 1594. The play is partially based on a prose pamphlet *The famous historie of Fryar Bacon*, embodying legends relating to R. *Bacon and T. *Bungay.

Bacon with the help of Friar Bungay makes a head of brass, and, conjuring up the Devil, learns how to give it speech. After watching day and night for three weeks, Bacon hands over the duty to his servant Miles and falls asleep. The head speaks two words, 'Time is'. Miles, thinking his master would be angry if waked for so little, lets him sleep. The head presently speaks again, 'Time was'; and finally, 'Time is past', when it falls down and breaks. Bacon awakes, and heaps curses on Miles's head. The tale is diversified with the pleasant story of the loves of Edward prince of Wales (afterwards Edward I) and Lord Lacy for the fair Margaret, the keeper's daughter of Fressingfield, and the prince's surrender of her to Lacy.

FROISSART, Jean (*c.*1337–*c.*1410), French historian, chronicler, and poet whose chronicles record the chivalric exploits of the nobles of England and France from 1325 to 1400. They were translated into English by John Bourchier in 1523–5. As author of lively personal *lais* and *ballades* he had some influence on *Chaucer.

FROST, Robert Lee (1874–1963), American poet. In 1912 he came to England where he published his first volumes of poems, *A Boy's Will* (1913) and *North of Boston* (1914), which contains 'Mending Wall' and 'The Death of the Hired Man'; he formed a close friendship with E. *Thomas. Upon his return to New England in 1915 he settled in New Hampshire. His volumes include *Mountain Interval* (1916); *New Hampshire* (1923); *Collected Poems* (1930); *A Witness Tree* (1942); and *In The Clearing* (1962). He established himself as one of the most popular of 20th-cent. American poets, admired for the blend of colloquial and traditional in his verse. But beneath the country lore and wisdom lay a more troubled, combative, at times destructive spirit, both in his life and work, expressed in such poems as 'Fire and Ice' (1923) and 'Bereft' (1928).

'Frost at Midnight', a blank verse poem by S. T. *Coleridge, written in 1798. Addressed to his sleeping child Hartley *Coleridge, it meditates on the poet's own boyhood, and magically evokes the countryside, ending on a note of rare and thrilling happiness.

Froth, Lord and Lady, characters in Congreve's *The Double Dealer*.

FROUDE, J(ames) A(nthony) (1818–94), historian. Educated at Oriel College, Oxford, he was an early casualty of the *Oxford Movement, who lost his faith when his leader J. H. *Newman reneged on the Church of England in 1845. Out of his religious agonies and his sexual frustrations he wrote a bad but spectacular novel, *The Nemesis of Faith* (1849), which obliged him to resign his fellowship at Exeter College and leave for London, where he maintained himself by journalism; he edited *Fraser's Magazine*, 1860–74. He now fell under the influence of *Carlyle; he was also a friend of A. H. *Clough and C. *Kingsley (later his brother-in-law). His *History of England from the Death of Cardinal Wolsey to the defeat of the Spanish Armada* (12 vols, 1856–70), was a distinguished work of scholarship. He was the first to glorify the deeds of the Elizabethan seamen, a topic to which he returned in his Oxford lectures on *English Seamen in the Sixteenth Century* (1892–4, published 1895). All his books were highly successful, even his collected essays, *Short Studies in Great Subjects* (4 vols, 1867–83; but in later life he seemed to attract public controversy and caused an uproar with his *Reminiscences* of Carlyle (1881) and his *Letters and Memorials* of Jane Welsh *Carlyle (1883), which were distinguished by their shattering frankness. He was appointed Regius professor of modern history at Oxford in 1892.

FROUDE, R(ichard) H(urrell) (1803–36), Tractarian, brother of J. A. *Froude, educated at Oriel College, Oxford, where he became a fellow. He collaborated with *Newman in the early stages of the *Oxford Movement. He contributed three of the *Tracts for the Times* and wrote poems contained in *Lyra Apostolica*. His *Remains* (1838–9), including strictures on the Reformers, aroused public hostility against the Movement.

FRY, Christopher (Harris) (1907–), playwright, made his name with works that were hailed in the late 1940s as a sign of a renaissance of poetic drama; his mystical and religious plays (*The Boy with a Cart*, 1939; *The Firstborn*, 1946; *Thor with Angels*, 1949; *A Sleep of Prisoners*, 1951) were frequently compared to those of T. S. *Eliot. His audiences tended to prefer the ebullient optimism and exuberant word-play of his comedies, e.g. *A Phoenix too Frequent* (1946, based on *Petronius), *The Lady's not for Burning* (1949, set in the Middle Ages), and *Venus Observed* (1950, a romantic château comedy). The vogue for poetic drama proved short-lived, giving way to the *kitchen sink school and Fry's later plays were less successful. Fry also wrote several screenplays, and successful translations and adaptations of Anouilh.

FRY, Roger Eliot (1866–1934), art critic and painter, educated at King's College, Cambridge, where he became a member of the *Apostles. He

became art critic of the *Athenaeum* in 1901, helped to establish the *Burlington Magazine* in 1903, and was employed at the Metropolitan Museum of Art in New York (1905–10). He organized two highly influential and controversial exhibitions of Post-Impressionist paintings (a term he coined himself) at the Grafton Galleries in 1910 and 1912, and his collected essays (*Vision and Design*, 1920; *Transformations*, 1926) were also instrumental in spreading his enthusiasm for modern French painting. He was closely associated with the *Bloomsbury Group, and his biography was written by V. *Woolf (1940).

FRYE, Northrop Herman (1912–), Canadian critic, and from 1967 professor of English at the University of Toronto. His works include an important study of *Blake, *Fearful Symmetry* (1947); *Anatomy of Criticism* (1957); *Fools of Time: studies in Shakespeare Tragedy* (1967); and *Literature and the Bible* (2 vols, 1982, 1986), and are remarkable for their exploration of the Jungian *archetype in literature, for their concern with mythology and anthropology, and for their wide-ranging and imaginative insights.

Fudge Family in Paris, The, verses by T. *Moore published 1818.

These light verses take the form of letters written by or to various members of the Fudge family when visiting Paris in 1817, shortly after the restoration of the Bourbons. They include inane descriptions by the mindless Fudges, and pompous, sycophantic letters from Mr Fudge to *Castlereagh.

FUGARD, Athol (1932–), South African playwright. Racial tension and inequality are the subject of much of his drama. His plays include *The Blood Knot* (1961, pub. 1963), about the fraught relationship of two coloured brothers; *Boesman and Lena* (1968, pub. 1969); *Sizwe Bansi is Dead* (1972, pub. 1974, written with John Kani and Winston Ntshona); *A Lesson from Aloes* (1980, pub. 1981), which contrasts the political attitudes, ranging from stoicism to defeat of an Afrikaner, his wife, and their Coloured friends; and *'Master Harold' . . . and the boys* (1982, pub. 1983), portraying the relationship between a white South African teenager and two black family servants, 'the boys'.

Fulgens and Lucrece, a late 15th-cent. *interlude by Henry Medwall (fl. 1486), regarded as the earliest known purely secular play in English.

FULLER, John Leopold (1937–), poet and novelist, son of Roy *Fuller. His several volumes of poetry include *Fairground Music* (1961), *Cannibals and Missionaries* (1972), *Lies and Secrets* (1979), and *The Illusionists* (1980), a satiric narrative in stanza form of contemporary life.

His poems range from lyrics to pastiche verse epistles, from sonnets to long unrhymed monologues. His novel *Flying to Nowhere* (1983) is a fantasy about a 16th-cent. abbot who thinks he has discovered, through surgical dissection, the seat of the soul.

FULLER, (Sarah) Margaret (1810–50), American author and feminist whose name is associated with the New England Transcendentalists; she helped to found * *The Dial*, which she edited (1840–2), and conducted a series of conversations or seminars for educated women in Boston (1839–44). One of the products of these discussions was her influential feminist tract *Women in the Nineteenth Century* (1845). Her *Memoirs* (1852) were edited by *Emerson, W. H. Channing, and J. F. Clarke. She is said to have suggested the character of the magnetic and passionate Zenobia in Hawthorne's * *The Blithedale Romance*.

FULLER, Roy Broadbent (1912–), poet and novelist, contributed to left-wing literary magazines, including * *New Verse*, and his first volume, *Poems* (1939), shows the influence of *Auden and *Spender. This was followed by several collections of poetry: *Collected Poems 1936–1961* (1962) forms a link between the poets of the thirties and the poets of the *Movement, in its lucid, ironic, detached tone, and its formal accomplishment. His later volumes, which include *From the Joke Shop* (1975) and *The Reign of Sparrows* (1980), frequently strike a more personal note, particularly in the many sardonic reflections on old age and the ageing process. His novels include *Image of a Society* (1956), which is a portrait of personal and professional conflicts in a northern provincial building society. He was professor of poetry at Oxford, 1968–73, and *Owls and Artificers* (1971) and *Professors and Gods* (1973) are collections of his Oxford lectures. He has also published three volumes of memoirs, *Souvenirs* (1980), *Vamp till ready* (1982), and *Home and Dry* (1984).

FULLER, Thomas (1608–61), became, after the Restoration, 'chaplain in extraordinary' to the king. He published *The History of the Holy Warre* (i.e. of the crusades) in 1639; * *The Holy State and the Profane State* (1642); *Good Thoughts in Bad Times* (1645); *A Pisgah of Palestine* (1650), a topographical and historical work; and *The church-history of Britain; with the history of the University of Cambridge* (1655). *The History of the * *Worthies of England* (1662) is his best-known and most characteristic work. His writings are marked by a lively and eccentric curiosity, by 'fantastic caprices' (L. *Stephen), and by a fondness for aphorisms.

Funeral, The, or *Grief à-la-Mode*, a comedy by R. *Steele, produced 1701.

The play is notable as marking a change of moral tone in the drama after the licentiousness of the *Restoration.

Fungoso, a foolish law student in Jonson's * *Every Man out of his Humour*.

FURNIVALL, Frederick James (1825–1910), was secretary to the *Philological Society; in 1861 he became editor of the proposed New English Dictionary which developed into the *Oxford English Dictionary. He founded the *Early English Text Society, the Chaucer Society, the Ballad Society, and the New Shakespeare Society, the Wyclif, the Browning, and the Shelley societies, and himself edited many texts. He was also a leader in the move for popular education, and taught grammar at the Working Men's College founded in 1854.

FUSELI, Henry (1741–1825), Swiss artist who came to England in 1764; after studying in Rome (1770–8) he settled in London. His fascination with the *sublime and the supernatural expressed itself in many paintings taken from Shakespeare, *Milton, *Dante, *Macpherson's Ossian, and others. He was a learned artist who shone in the literary society of London, and his essays and lectures illumine the intellectual life of his times. He was a friend and admirer of *Blake. Blake engraved some of Fuseli's designs and Fuseli wrote the preface to Blake's edition of *Blair's *The Grave*.

FUST, Johann (d. 1467), German goldsmith. He financed *Gutenberg's experiments in printing, but their partnership was dissolved probably in 1455 and Fust carried on with his son-in-law Peter Schöffer. Their Latin Psalter of 1457 is the first to bear a printer's imprint and date.

Futhorc, the runic alphabet, named from its first six letters (th=þ, 'thorn'). (See RUNE.)

Futurism, a 20th-cent. avant-garde movement in Italian art, literature, and music, promoted by Filippo Tommaso Marinetti (1876–1944) and others. Its programme, outlined in the *Futurist Manifesto* (1909), was to break with the past and its academic culture and to celebrate technology, dynamism, and power. In language and in poetry it advocated the destruction of traditional syntax, metre, and punctuation in the name of the 'free word'.

The movement petered out during the 1930s after Marinetti's incorporation into Fascist academic culture. The principal founder of Russian Futurism was Vladimir Mayakovsky (1893–1930): the Russian manifesto was published in 1912 but the movement found little favour with Lenin and the Communist authorities, and it also dwindled away, although Mayakovsky himself was later reinstated (posthumously) by Stalin.

G

Gabriel, the name of one of the archangels (Dan. 9: 21 and Luke 1: 19, 26). Milton makes him 'Chief of the angelic guards' (*Paradise Lost*, iv. 550).

Gadshill, near Rochester, the scene of Prince *Hal's joke robbery of *Falstaff in Shakespeare's *1 *Henry IV* (II. ii); also the name of one of Falstaff's companions. Gadshill was the home of *Dickens in his later years.

Gahagan, Major, see TREMENDOUS ADVENTURES OF MAJOR GAHAGAN, THE.

Gaheris, in Malory's *Morte D'Arthur*, the youngest son of King Lot of Orkney and Arthur's sister Morgawse. He was accidentally killed by Launcelot. Variant forms of his name are confusable with variants of Gareth (Gaheret) his brother.

GAIMAR, Geoffrei (*fl. c.*1140), probably a secular monk of Norman blood, author of *L'Estoire des Engleis*, an Anglo-Norman romance history in octosyllabic rhymed couplets covering the period from the Anglo-Saxon settlements to the death of William Rufus.

Gai saber, the title of a 13th-cent. society in Toulouse devoted to the consideration and cultivation of the courtly troubadour idea of 'jois', 'exaltation'.

Galahad (The Haute Prince), in Malory's *Morte D'Arthur*, is (by enchantment) the son of *Launcelot and *Elaine, daughter of King *Pelles. He is predestined by his immaculate purity to achieve the Siege Perilous (see ROUND TABLE) and the *Grail.

Galehaut (or **Galehault**) of Surluse and the Long Isles, a highly significant character in the story of the love of Launcelot and Guinevere as described in the early 13th-cent. French prose 'Vulgate' cycle. He was a close friend of Launcelot and first introduced the lovers. He is most famous as the Galeotto in *Dante's reference to this story (*Inferno*, v. 137). *Malory wrongly calls him 'the Haute Prince' through a confusion with the similar name *Galahad.

GALEN (Claudius Galenus) (*c.*AD 129–99), a celebrated physician reputed to have written some 500 treatises in Greek, a number of which have survived. Translated into Latin during the 11th and 12th cents, his writings dominated the development of medieval medicine. *Linacre translated six of his works and there are references to him in *Chaucer, F. *Bacon, and Sir T. *Browne.

Galeotto, see GALEHAUT.

GALILEO GALILEI (1564–1642), Italian astronomer and physicist, he made important discoveries (the isochronism of the pendulum, Jupiter's satellites, the libration of the moon) and experiments, proving, e.g., that unequal weights drop with equal velocity, by, it is said, making the experiment from the leaning tower of Pisa. His observations brought him into conflict with the Inquisition, and in 1633 he was compelled to repudiate the Copernican theory. His principal works were the dialogues *Delle nuove scienze* and *Ai due massimi sistemi*. *Milton records his conversation with Galileo on his visit to Florence in *Areopagitica*.

Galliambic, the metre of the *Attis* of *Catullus, so called because it was the metre used by the Galli, or priests of Cybele, in their songs. It was imitated by *Tennyson in his 'Boadicea'.

GALSWORTHY, John (1867–1933), trained for the law then turned to literature. The first appearance of the Forsyte family was in one of the stories in *Man of Devon* (1901). His novel *The Island Pharisees* (1904), revealing his interest in the effects of poverty and the constraints of convention, was followed by other novels including *Fraternity* (1909) and *The Dark Flower* (1913). The first of the Forsyte novels, *The Man of Property* (1906), was followed by *In Chancery* (1920) and *To Let* (1921) which, together with two interludes, appeared collectively as *The Forsyte Saga* (1922). The second part of the Forsyte chronicles, containing *The White Monkey* (1924), *The Silver Spoon* (1926), *Swan Song* (1928), and the two interludes 'A Silent Wooing' and 'Passers By', was published as *A Modern Comedy* in 1929. Galsworthy followed their immense success with a further collection of stories, *On Forsyte Change* (1931).

Galsworthy began his playwriting career with *The Silver Box* (1906)—a play about theft in which he employed a favourite device of 'parallel' families, one rich, one poor. This was the first of a long line of plays on social and moral themes, including *Strife* (1909), an examination of men and managers in industry, and *Justice* (1910), in which a minor felon is ground down by the cruel majesty of the law; the play was part of Galsworthy's long campaign against the practice of solitary confinement, which strongly influenced the Home Office. His later plays include *The Skin Game* (1920), *Loyalties* (1922), and *Old English* (1924).

Posthumous publications included *Collected Poems* (1934) and in 1935 *The End of the Chapter*, consisting of *Maid in Waiting* (1931), *The Flowering Wilderness* (1932), and *Over the River* (1933), relating the family history of the Charwells, cousins of the younger Forsytes. Galsworthy received the *Nobel Prize for literature in 1932.

GALT, John (1779–1839), born in Ayrshire, was employed for some time in the customs-house at Greenock. While travelling on the Continent he made the acquaintance of *Byron (of whom he published a life in 1830) and later of *Carlyle, who admired his work. He was secretary of the Canada Company, and between 1825 and 1829 he visited Canada as a member of a Government commission to evaluate the price of land. Galt produced poems, dramas, historical novels, and travel books, but is chiefly remembered for his studies of country life in Scotland: *The Ayrshire Legatees* (1821), *Annals of the Parish* (1821), *The Provost* (1822), *The Entail* (1823), and *The Member* (1832). Galt made a unique contribution to fiction with the subtlety and irony of his writing in the first person, and he was an acute observer of social change.

Gama, King, the father of Princess Ida in Tennyson's *The Princess.

Game and Playe of the Chesse, The, a translation by *Caxton from Vignay's French version of the *Liber de ludo scacchorum* of Jacobus de Cessolis, probably the second book printed at Caxton's press in Bruges, c.1475.

Game at Chesse, A, a comedy by T. *Middleton, produced 1624, when it successfully ran for nine nights at the Globe until suppressed by the authorities.

It deals allegorically with the rivalry of England and Spain and the project of the 'Spanish Marriage' (1623). It places on the stage the sovereigns of the two countries, Charles, prince of Wales, Buckingham, and the Spanish ambassador Gondomar. The play, reflecting the popular aversion to the Spanish match, gave great offence to the Spanish ambassador and to King James.

Gamelyn, The Tale of, a verse romance of the mid-14th cent. from the East Midlands, in 902 lines of long couplets. It is found in a number of manuscripts of *The Canterbury Tales*, usually assigned to the Cook, and Chaucer possibly intended to write a version of it for use as the Cook's tale.

The story, which recounts Gamelyn's flight to the forest and attempts to recover his stolen birthright, has affinities with Shakespeare's *As You Like It* and with the legends of *Robin Hood.

Gamester, The, a comedy by J. *Shirley, acted 1633, printed 1637.

This was one of Shirley's most popular plays, adapted (and sentimentalized) by Charles Johnson (1679–1748) in 1712 as *The Wife's Relief* and by *Garrick in 1758 as *The Gamesters*. Its main plot is taken from the *Heptameron of Marguerite of Navarre, and turns on an elaborate double 'bed-trick' in which Wilding, the title character, manages to cheat himself twice in his unsuccessful efforts to seduce his ward Penelope.

The Gamester is also the title of a play by Mrs *Centlivre and of a tragedy by E. *Moore.

Gammer Gurtons Nedle, the second English comedy in verse (the first being *Ralph Roister Doister*), published 1575, having been acted in 1566 at Christ's College, Cambridge. Its authorship has been attributed either to J. Still, or to William Stevenson, both fellows of the college.

It is written in rhymed long doggerel, and deals farcically with the losing and finding of the needle used to mend the garments of Hodge, Gammer Gurton's man, who becomes acutely aware that the needle is in the seat of his breeches. The play includes the famous old drinking song with the refrain:

> Back and syde go bare, go bare,
> booth foote and hande go colde:
> But Bellye god sende thee good ale ynoughe,
> whether it be newe or olde.

Gamp, Sarah, a character in Dickens's *Martin Chuzzlewit*. Her large cotton umbrella has given rise to the expression 'a gamp' for an umbrella, especially an untidy one; also for a midwife.

Gandercleugh, the imaginary place of residence of Jedediah Cleishbotham in Scott's *Tales of my Landlord.

Ganelon, or **Gano,** in the *Charlemagne romances, the villain and traitor who schemes for the defeat of the rearguard at Roncesvalles (see ROLAND). He figures in *Dante's *Inferno* (xxxii. 122) and in *Chaucer's 'Nun's Priest's Tale' (see CANTERBURY TALES, 20).

Gann, Mr, Mrs, and Caroline, characters in Thackeray's *A Shabby Genteel Story.

GARCÍA MÁRQUEZ, Gabriel (1928–   ), Colombian novelist, whose *Magic Realist works, including his most famous novel *Cien* años de soledad (1967; *One Hundred Years of Solitude*, 1970), have greatly influenced the younger generation of English novelists.

'Garden, The', a poem by *Marvell.

Garden of Cyrus, The (1658) by Sir T. *Browne, the companion piece to *Hydriotaphia*; it treats of the occurrence of the quincunx (∴) or lozenge and the number five in man-made objects, primarily the plantations of the ancients, and then their buildings, other artefacts, and customs, in plants, in animals, and in traditional philosophy and theology. By intertwining many heterogeneous observations he playfully demonstrates his ability to elaborate and digress.

GARDINER, Colonel James (1688–1745), a historical character introduced in Scott's *Waverley*. He was killed at the battle of Prestonpans. (See also DODDRIDGE.)

GARDINER, Samuel Rawson (1829–1902), became professor of modern history at King's College, London. The first instalment of his great *History* of the first Stuarts and Cromwell appeared in 1863; successive instalments followed, and in 1883–4 appeared a second edition of all these, entitled a *History of England from the Accession of James I to the Outbreak of the Civil War, 1603–42*. Subsequent volumes carried the record down to the year 1656. Gardiner's historical writing shows minute accuracy and impartiality but is, perhaps necessarily, lacking in picturesque quality.

'Gareth and Lynette', one of Tennyson's *Idylls of the King*, published 1872. It describes Gareth's disguise as a scullion at court, and his winning of Lynette through his rescue of her besieged sister Lyonors.

Gareth of Orkney (or **Gaheret**), Sir, in Malory's *Morte D'Arthur*, the third son of King Lot of Orkney and Arthur's sister Morgawse who is made to work in the kitchen and nicknamed by Kay 'Beaumains'. See GARETH AND LYNETTE.

Gargantua, originally the name of a beneficent giant of French folklore, connected with the Arthurian cycle. It is probably to this folklore giant that Shakespeare refers in *As You Like It* (III. ii. 239). In Rabelais' *La Vie très horrificque du Grand Gargantua* (1534), a preliminary volume to *Pantagruel*, which had appeared in 1532, Gargantua is presented as a prince of gigantic stature and appetite, but also as studious, athletic, good-humoured, and peace-loving. (See PANTAGRUEL.)

Gargery, Joe, a character in Dickens's *Great Expectations*.

GARIOCH, Robert, the pen-name of Robert Garioch Sutherland (1909–81), Scottish poet, known principally for his witty and satiric poems in *Scots. His works include *17 poems for 6d. In Gaelic, Lowland Scots and English* (1940; in collaboration with S. *Maclean); *The Masque of Edinburgh* (1954); and *Collected Poems* (1977). He also translated into Scots *Pindar, G. *Buchanan, Belli, Apollinaire, and others. His *Complete Poetical Works*, ed. R. Fulton, was published in 1983.

Garland, (1) Mr and Mrs, characters in Dickens's *The Old Curiosity Shop*; (2) Anne, a character in Hardy's *The Trumpet Major* .

GARNER, Alan, see CHILDREN'S LITERATURE.

GARNETT, Constance (1862–1946), mother of D. *Garnett, was responsible for introducing many of the great Russian classics to English readers. She translated *Turgenev, *Tolstoy, *Dostoevsky, *Chekhov, Gogol, and Herzen; her versions, although now superseded, had enormous impact and influence in their day.

GARNETT, David (1892–1981), novelist and critic, son of E. and C. *Garnett, and friend and associate of the *Bloomsbury Group. His first short novel, *Lady into Fox* (1922), an enigmatic fable about a young wife transformed into a vixen, had a considerable success, and was followed by *A man in the zoo* (1924), about a thwarted lover who donates himself as a specimen of *Homo sapiens* for exhibition in the zoo; *The sailor's return* (1925); *Pocahontas: or the nonpareil of Virginia* (1933), a biography; the semi-fictional *Beany-eye* (1935); and three volumes of autobiography. Garnett also edited the letters of T. E. *Lawrence (1938), the novels of *Peacock (1948), and his own correspondence with T. H. *White (1968).

GARNETT, Edward (1868–1936), son of R. *Garnett and husband of C. *Garnett, is chiefly remembered as publisher's reader and influential advocate of the work of *Conrad, D. H. *Lawrence, D. *Richardson, and others.

GARNETT, Richard (1835–1906), was superintendent of the Reading Room of the British Museum (1875–84), then became chief editor of the library's first printed catalogue. He published several volumes of original and translated verse, several biographies, and edited many works, including *Relics of Shelley* (1862). He is best remembered as a writer for his collection of pagan tales, *The Twilight of the Gods* (1888), some of which originally appeared in *The Yellow Book.

Garraway's, a celebrated coffee-house in Cornhill. It was a meeting-place of dealers in stocks and shares, notably in the days of the *South Sea Company. It is mentioned in the works of *Addison, *Pope, *Swift, and *Gay.

GARRICK, David (1717–79), of Huguenot descent, became a pupil of Dr *Johnson at Edial. He accompanied Johnson to London. In 1741 he appeared as an actor at Ipswich in Southerne's *Oroonoko. Later that year he made his London début as Richard III and subsequently proved his versatility by many successes in both comic and tragic parts. He wrote a number of lively farces, including Bon Ton, or High Life above Stairs (1775), and collaborated with *Colman in writing *The Clandestine Marriage (1766). In 1747 he joined Lacy in the management of Drury Lane, where he produced many of Shakespeare's dramas; he made his last appearance in 1776, when he sold his share of the patent to *Sheridan and two others for £35,000. In 1773 he was elected a member of Johnson's *Club; his interesting correspondence with many of the most distinguished men of his day was published in 1831–2 and in a greatly enlarged collection in 1963. Garrick's fame as an actor was unsurpassed. He was painted by many of his celebrated contemporaries, including *Reynolds, *Hogarth, and Gainsborough.

Garrick Club, founded in 1831 as a club in which 'actors and men of education and refinement might meet on equal terms'. It was much frequented by *Thackeray, and possesses a famous collection of portraits of actors and actresses.

Garsington Manor, the Oxfordshire home of Ottoline *Morrell from 1915 to 1927, where she and her husband entertained many distinguished guests from the political and artistic worlds.

GARTH, Sir Samuel (1661–1719), a physician, free-thinker, and member of the *Kit-Cat Club, is remembered as the author of The Dispensary (1699), a burlesque poem in which he ridiculed the opposition of apothecaries to the supply of medicines to out-patients' dispensaries. *Pope described him as 'the best good Christian without knowing it'. See TOPOGRAPHICAL POETRY.

GASCOIGNE, George (c.1534–77), soldier and poet. Many of his works were contained in The Posies of George Gascoigne (1575), a variety of secular and devotional verse, including 'The delectable history of Dan Bartholmew of Bathe'; a verse account of his adventures as a soldier in the Netherlands, 'The fruites of Warre'; two plays written for performance at Gray's Inn in 1566, *Supposes, a prose comedy based on *Ariosto's I Suppositi, and Jocasta, a blank verse tragedy; a strange Chaucerian novella of sexual intrigue, The Adventures of Master *F.J.; and

Certayne notes of Instruction concerning the making of verse or ryme in English, a pithy but pioneering account of English versification. Gascoigne's other works include The Glasse of Governement. A tragicall Comedie (1575), The Droomme of Doomes day (1576), and *The Steele Glas. A Satyre (1576). Gascoigne's achievement has been overshadowed by the later Elizabethan poets, but he was an innovator in a wide variety of literary forms.

GASCOIGNE, Sir William (?1350–1419), appointed lord chief justice of the king's bench in 1400 by Henry IV, he figures in that capacity in Shakespeare's *Henry IV. Shakespeare follows *Holinshed's apparently apocryphal story (told in *Elyot's Governour) that Prince Hal struck Gascoigne for attempting to arrest one of the prince's unruly followers, whereupon Gascoigne arrested the prince himself.

GASCOYNE, David (1916–), poet, published A Short Survey of Surrealism (1935), which established him as a champion of *surrealism and a writer unusually aware of European literature. He translated many of the French surrealists. His work includes Man's Life is His Meat (1936), Hölderlin's Madness (1938), Poems 1937–1942 (1943), and Night Thoughts, a long poem commissioned by the BBC, broadcast 1955, published 1956.

Gashford, a character in Dickens's *Barnaby Rudge .

GASKELL, Mrs Elizabeth Cleghorn (1810–65) was brought up by her aunt in Knutsford, Cheshire (the original of 'Cranford' and of 'Hollingford' in Wives and Daughters). In 1832 she married William Gaskell, minister at the Cross Street Unitarian Chapel in Manchester; they had four daughters and a son who died in infancy. As a distraction from her sorrow at his death she wrote her first novel, *Mary Barton (1848). It won the attention of *Dickens, at whose invitation much of her work was first published in *Household Words and All the Year Round. Her other full-length novels were *Cranford (1853), *Ruth (1853), *North and South (1855), *Sylvia's Lovers (1863), and *Wives and Daughters (1866), which was left unfinished at her death. She also wrote the first and most celebrated biography of C. *Brontë—which caused a furore because it contained some allegedly libellous statements which had to be withdrawn—and many vivid and warm-hearted short stories and novellas, of which the finest was Cousin Phillis (1864).

Mrs Gaskell was an active humanitarian and the message of several of her novels was the need for social reconciliation, for better understanding between employers and workers. She was a keen observer of human behaviour and speech, among both industrial workers in Manchester and farming and country-town communities, and a careful researcher of the background and technicalities of her novels. She had many friends, including *Ruskin, *Milnes, the *Carlyles, *Kingsley, and C. E. *Norton. Her contemporaries classed her as a novelist with the Brontës and G. *Eliot, but although *Cranford* has always remained a favourite her other novels were underrated in critical esteem for a full century after her death.

GAUDEN, Dr J., see EIKON BASILIKE.

GAUNT, John of, see JOHN OF GAUNT.

Gawain (Walwain), the eldest of the four sons of King Lot of Orkney and Arthur's sister Morgawse. In the Arthurian legends he is prominent from the first 12th-cent. stories in which he is the leading knight, courageous, pure, and courteous. In later versions his excellence was surpassed by that of Launcelot. In *Geoffrey of Monmouth he is Arthur's ambassador to Rome; in *Malory he becomes at the end the bitter enemy of Launcelot who has accidentally killed Gawain's beloved youngest brother Gaheris and who also killed Gareth. Gawain is killed when Arthur lands at Dover before the final battle with Mordred. The most celebrated single adventure of Gawain is the one described in Sir *Gawain and the Green Knight.

Gawain and the Green Knight, Sir, an alliterative poem from the north-west midlands, dating from the second half of the 14th cent., the only manuscript of which is the famous Cotton Nero A x which is also the sole manuscript of *Pearl, *Patience, and *Cleanness. The poem is in 2,530 lines in long-lined alliterative stanzas of varying length, each ending with a *'bob and wheel'. Most modern critics regard the four poems in the manuscript as the work of a single poet.

The story of the poem is as follows (under the headings of its four 'fitts', narrative divisions). *Fitt 1*: Arthur and his court are seated at a New Year's feast in Camelot waiting for a marvel when a huge green man enters, bearing an axe and a holly bough. He challenges a knight to cut his head off on condition that the knight agrees to have his head cut off a year hence. Gawain accepts the challenge and cuts the green knight's head off; the knight picks it up and rides away. *Fitt 2*: A year later Gawain sets off to keep his side of the bargain. He comes upon a beautiful castle where he is graciously received. The lord of the castle makes an agreement with Gawain that each day he himself will hunt in the fields and Gawain in the castle; at the end of the day they will exchange spoils. *Fitt 3*: For three consecutive days, the lord hunts and Gawain is amorously approached by the beautiful lady of the castle, who gives him one kiss on the first

day, two on the second, and on the third day three kisses and a girdle which has magic properties that will save his life. Each evening Gawain exchanges the kisses with his host for the animals slain in the hunt; but on the third evening he keeps the girdle (thus breaking his bargain), to protect him in the imminent meeting with the green knight. *Fitt 4*: Gawain is directed to the green knight's chapel where he kneels to receive his blow. Twice the knight feints at him, and the third time he makes a slight cut in Gawain's neck. Then he explains that he is the knight of the castle in a different form, and that the cut in the neck was sustained because of Gawain's infidelity in keeping the girdle. Gawain bitterly curses his failing and the snares of women; but the green knight applauds him and, on Gawain's return to Arthur's court, they declare that they will all wear a green girdle in honour of his achievement. The poem may be connected with the founding of the Order of the Garter. This is agreed to be one of the greatest poems in Middle English.

GAY, John (1685–1732), published *Rural Sports* (1713), on the model of his friend Pope's *Windsor Forest*, and *The Fan*, which is in the mock-heroic style of *The Rape of the Lock. *The Shepherd's Week* (1714) was the first poem to show his real ability. His first play, *The What d'ye Call it*, a satirical farce, was produced in 1715, and *Trivia* appeared in 1716. With *Pope and *Arbuthnot he wrote a comedy, *Three Hours after Marriage*, acted in 1717. He became an inmate of the household of the duke of Queensberry, who was to be his literary executor. The first series of his popular *Fables* appeared in 1727, but real success came with *The Beggar's Opera* (1728) and its sequel *Polly* (1729). These two plays contain many of Gay's best-known ballads, but 'Sweet William's Farewell to Black-Eyed Susan' was published in *Poems* (1720) and 'Twas when the seas were roaring' is from his first play. He also wrote, c.1718, the librettos of *Handel's *Acis and Galatea* (pub. 1732) and *Achilles*, an opera produced at Covent Garden in 1733. His poem in *ottava rima* 'Mr Pope's Welcome from Greece' (1776) was written to celebrate his friend's finishing his translation of *The Iliad*; it gives a vivid picture of the members of the *Scriblerus Club. He was buried in Westminster Abbey, accompanied by his own epitaph:

Life is a jest, and all things show it;
I thought so once, and now I know it.

Gay, Walter, a character in Dickens's *Dombey and Son*.

Gazette, from It. *gazzetta,* a news-sheet first published in Venice about the middle of the 16th cent., and similar news-sheets (see CORANTO, and NEWSPAPERS, ORIGINS OF) appeared in England from the 17th cent., giving news from foreign parts.

Gazetteer, a geographical index or dictionary.

Gebir, an epic poem by W. S. *Landor in seven books, published 1798.

Gellatley, Davie, a character in Scott's *Waverley,* in whose mouth the author places some of his finest lyrics.

GELLIUS, Aulus (2nd cent. AD), Roman man of letters, author of *Noctes Atticae,* a miscellany containing extracts from many authors, anecdotes, and short discussions on various topics. Twelve of the stories in Painter's *Palace of Pleasure* are taken from Gellius.

Gem, The, (1) a literary annual, edited by T. *Hood, 1829–32; (2) a weekly paper for boys, largely written by C. *Hamilton under the penname Martin Clifford, 1907–39.

General, Mrs, in Dickens's *Little Dorrit,* the lady companion to Mr Dorrit's daughters, and inventor of the formula 'prunes and prism'.

Generydes, a late Middle English romance perhaps from the first part of the 15th cent. It tells of the love of Generydes and Clarionas who, after his exile, cures and marries him.

Genesis, meaning 'origin', 'creation', is the first in order of the books of the Bible, containing the account of the creation of the world.

Genesis, an Old English poem of 2,396 lines in the *Junius manuscript and previously attributed hypothetically to *Caedmon. Lines 235–851 are an interpolated section (usually called 'Genesis B') translated from a continental Saxon original which deals in a dramatic and vivid manner with the Fall of the Angels.

Genesis and Exodus, a Middle English poem in just over 4,000 lines of rhyming couplets, written about the middle of the 13th cent. in Norfolk. It relates scriptural history from the Creation to the death of Moses in popular form.

GENEST, John (1764–1839), author of *Some Account of the English Stage from the Restoration in 1660 to 1830* (10 vols, 1832).

Geneva Bible, see BIBLE, THE ENGLISH.

Genevieve, the heroine of S. T. *Coleridge's poem 'Love', first published in the *Morning Star* (1799) and included in the second edition of *Lyrical Ballads.*

Gentleman Dancing-Master, The, a comedy by *Wycherley, probably performed 1671,

published 1673. It is loosely based on Calderón's *El maestro de danzar,* and describes the wooing of young Hippolita by Gerrard, in the disguise of a dancing master. The moral of the play appears to be contained in the final verse of Act II:

Our Parents who restrain our liberty
But take the course to make us sooner free,
Though all we gain be but new slavery;
We leave our Fathers, and to Husbands fly.

Gentleman's Journal, The, a periodical edited by *Motteux (1692–4) containing the news of the month and miscellaneous prose and poetry. It was the germ of the modern magazine.

Gentleman's Magazine, The, (1731–1914), a periodical founded by *Cave (under the pseudonym Sylvanus Urban) originally to reproduce from news-sheets and journals, interesting news, essays, anecdotes, and information. Cave's appears to be the first use of the word 'magazine' to describe a journal. By about 1739 original contributions had largely replaced news-digests, and the magazine began to include serious works of criticism, essays, a record of publications, and parliamentary reports. Dr *Johnson, a friend of Cave, was a regular contributor and had a great influence on the management of the *Magazine;* with Cave he devised a means of evading the official ban on parliamentary reporting by pretending his reports were from 'Lilliput'. J. *Nichols was an effective editor from 1792 to 1826.

Gentleman Usher, The, a tragi-comedy, by *Chapman, probably acted *c.*1602, printed 1606.

Gentle Shepherd, The, see RAMSAY, A.

GEOFFREY DE VINSAUF (*fl. c.*1200), an English rhetorician, author of *Nova Poetria* and *Summa de Coloribus Rhetoricis,* which were the standard and much-cited textbooks of poetic rhetoric in the later Middle Ages. (See also ANGLO-LATIN LITERATURE.)

GEOFFREY OF MONMOUTH (Gaufridus Monemutensis) (d. 1155), probably a Benedictine monk of Monmouth, studied and worked at Oxford and was attached to *Robert, earl of Gloucester. He is said to have been archdeacon of Llandaff, and he was appointed bishop of St Asaph in 1152. In his *Historia Regum Britanniae* (*c.*1136) he purports to give an account of the kings who dwelt in Britain since before the Incarnation of Christ, extending from Brutus (see BRUT), to Cadwallader (AD 689), 'and especially of Arthur and the many others who succeeded him'. For this purpose he states that he drew upon a 'most ancient book in the British tongue' handed to him by Walter, archdeacon of Oxford (also known as Calenius); but this book is unknown to any chronicler of the time. It is possible that this alleged work is an invention. He drew on *Bede and *Nennius, on British traditions, perhaps on Welsh documents now lost, and probably for the rest on a romantic imagination. The life and clarity of his writing contributed substantially to the popularity of the Arthurian legends.

George-a'-Green, the merry pinner or pinder (pound-keeper) of Wakefield. The story is given in W. C. *Hazlitt's *Tales and Legends*. He is the subject of a play (licensed for publication, 1595) probably by R. *Greene.

George Barnwell, *The History of, or The London Merchant*, a domestic tragedy in prose by *Lillo, produced 1731. In this play, for the first time, everyday commercial life is made the theme of tragedy. Based on an old ballad, it tells the story of an innocent young apprentice, Barnwell, who is seduced by a heartless courtesan, Millwood. She encourages him to rob his employer, Thorowgood, and to murder his uncle, for which crime both are brought to execution, he profoundly penitent and she defiant.

Georgian, a term applied in a literary sense to the writers of the reign of George V (1910–36), and usually indicating poetry of a pastoral or, as later critics asserted, an escapist nature. (See GEORGIAN POETRY.)

Georgian Poetry, a series of five volumes of verse planned by R. *Brooke, H. *Monro, and E. *Marsh which appeared between 1912 and 1922, edited by Marsh and published by Monro at the Poetry Bookshop. The early volumes brought a fresh vision and manner into the tired poetry of the time. Writers represented in the first volume included Brooke, W. H. *Davies, *Masefield, D. H. *Lawrence, *de la Mare, *Abercrombie, *Bottomley, and *Drinkwater. Later volumes contained the work of *Blunden, R. *Hodgson, *Sassoon, Robert *Graves, and *Rosenberg. The poems of quality were fewer in the volumes of 1919 and 1922; several poets (including Graves, Sassoon, and Blunden) objected to being identified as 'Georgian', in the company of J. C. *Squire, *Baring, and other traditionalists; and the term began to acquire its present strong pejorative sense. *Pound, T. S. *Eliot, and the *Sitwells attacked the entire series, though about half of the poets represented are now of high repute.

Georgics, The, see VIRGIL.

'Geraint and Enid', one of Tennyson's *Idylls of the King, first published under this title 1886. It originally formed with 'The Marriage of Geraint' a single idyll, published in 1859 as 'Enid' and divided in 1873. Geraint, suspecting his wife's virtue, subjects her to various trials, from which she emerges patient and triumphant.

Geraldine, the enchantress in Coleridge's *'Christabel'; see also SURREY.

Gerard, the hero of Reade's *The Cloister and the Hearth*.

GERARD, Alexander (1728–95), theological and philosophical writer, published two analytical studies which contributed to the development of aesthetics in Britain: 'An Essay on Taste' (1759, augmented 1780) and 'An Essay on Genius' (1774).

GERARD, John (1545–1612), a herbalist, was author of the celebrated *Herball or Generall Historie of Plantes* (1597), in a large measure adapted from the *Pemptades* of Rembert Dodoens.

GERHARDIE (originally GERHARDI), William Alexander (1895–1977), was born of English parents in St Petersburg. He then attended Worcester College, Oxford, where he wrote the first English book on *Chekhov, *Anton Chehov* (1923). His first novel, *Futility: A Novel on Russian Themes* (1922), was followed by many others, including *The Polyglots* (1925), the narrative of a wildly egocentric young officer, George Hamlet Alexander Diabologh, who on a military mission in the Far East comes into contact with a highly eccentric Belgian family, the Vanderflints; the intermingling of events of historical significance and the utmost human triviality, of Belgians, British, Russians, and Japanese, of love and war, create an oblique, lyrical, inconsequential world which is characteristic of Gerhardie. Other novels include *Pending Heaven* (1930), *Resurrection* (1934), and *Of Mortal Love* (1936). His autobiography *Memoirs of a Polyglot* appeared in 1931, and in 1940 a historical study, *The Romanovs*.

Germ, The, *Thoughts towards Nature in Poetry, Literature and Art*, a periodical edited by W. M. *Rossetti; it was the organ of the *Pre-Raphaelite Brotherhood, and ran for four issues (Jan.–Apr. 1850). The last two were renamed *Art and Poetry, being Thoughts towards Nature*. It contained work by D. G. *Rossetti, C. *Rossetti, *Patmore, F. M. Brown, W. B. *Scott, and others.

Gerontius, *The Dream of*, see NEWMAN, J. H.

Gertrude, in Shakespeare's *Hamlet*, mother of Hamlet and married to her late husband's brother *Claudius.

Gertrude of Wyoming, a poem by T. *Campbell, in Spenserian stanzas, published 1809.

Gerusalemme Liberata, see JERUSALEM DELIVERED.

Geryoneo, in Spenser's *Faerie Queene* (v. x and xi), a three-bodied giant who represents Philip II's power which controlled Spain, Portugal, and the Low Countries.

Gesta Francorum, a chronicle in medieval Latin, the first known to have been written by a layman. It gives the story of the First Crusade. Its actual author is unknown.

Gesta Romanorum, a collection of fictitious stories and fables in Latin, probably compiled in England in the late 13th cent.; they have an attached moralization, like the *bestiaries and *allegories. The popularity of the work is shown by the existence of 15th-cent. versions in many European languages and by its influence on later medieval writers such as *Boccaccio, *Hoccleve, and *Lydgate.

Ghost-words, a term used by *Skeat to signify words which have no real existence, 'coinages due to the blunders of printers or scribes, or to the perfervid imaginations of ignorant or blundering editors'.

Giafar, see JAFFAR.

Giaffir, in Byron's *Bride of Abydos*, the father of Zuleika.

Giant Pope, in Bunyan's *Pilgrim's Progress* a giant by whose power and tyranny many men were cruelly put to death in the past, but who is 'grown so crazy and stiff in his joints that he can now do little more than sit in his cave's mouth, grinning at pilgrims as they go by, and biting his nails, because he cannot come at them'.

Giaour, The, a poem by Lord *Byron, published 1813.

The story is of a female slave, Leila, who loves the Giaour, a true *'Byronic' hero, and is in consequence bound and thrown in a sack into the sea by her Turkish lord, Hassan. The Giaour avenges her by killing Hassan, then in grief and remorse banishes himself to a monastery.

GIBBON, Edward (1737–94), was educated at Westminster and at Magdalen College, Oxford; in his posthumously published *Memoirs* he paints a vivid portrait of the 'narrow, lazy and oppressive' spirit of Oxford, and of the 'idle and unprofitable' time he spent there. He became a Catholic convert at the age of 16, and was sent off to Lausanne by his father, where he was reconverted to Protestantism. He returned to England in 1758 after an absence of nearly 5 years. In 1761 he published his *Essai sur l'étude de la littérature*. He left again for the Continent in 1763; it was in Italy, while 'musing amid the ruins of the Capitol', that he formed the plan of his *The History of the *Decline and Fall of the Roman Empire*.

He entered Parliament in 1774, voted steadily for Lord North, and was made a commissioner of trade and plantations. He was elected to Dr Johnson's *Club in 1774. In 1776 appeared the first volume of the *History* which was very favourably received, although his chapters on the growth of Christianity provoked criticisms from *Porson and others. Gibbon replied in 1779 in *A Vindication of some Passages in the XVth and XVIth Chapters*. The second and third volumes appeared in 1781, but were less warmly received. He retired to Lausanne in 1783 where he completed the work. The last three volumes were published in 1788. He returned to England and spent most of his remaining days in the home of his friend the earl of Sheffied (John Baker Holroyd), who published his remarkable *Memoirs* with his *Miscellaneous Works* (1796). The memoirs reveal Gibbon's sense of vocation as a historian, and record on several occasions his gratitude at having been born 'in a free and enlightened country'; he was in many ways a representative product of the *Enlightenment, anticlerical, rational, and one of the last of the great Augustans.

GIBBON, Lewis Grassic, the pen-name of James Leslie Mitchell (1901–35), joined the Royal Army Service Corps in 1919 and from 1923 to 1929 he was a clerk in the RAF. The army offered him opportunities to travel which resulted in various works written under his own name, including *The Calends of Cairo* (1931). He also published fiction under the same name, including *Stained Radiance* (1930), his first novel. He is now remembered principally for his trilogy *A Scots Quair* (1946). It consists of *Sunset Song* (1932), *Cloud Howe* (1933), and *Grey Granite* (1934), novels which relate the life of Chris Guthrie from girlhood on her father's farm, through three marriages, the First World War, the Depression, her son's commitment to the Communist Party, etc. They were written in a powerful, idiosyncratic, lyrical prose, with a highly personal use of Scottish dialect and archaisms, and the plot abounds in lurid and violent incident. *Sunset Song* was hailed as the first really Scottish novel since *Galt.

GIBBONS, Stella, see COLD COMFORT FARM.

Gibson, Dr, Mrs, and Molly, characters in Mrs Gaskell's *Wives and Daughters*.

GIBSON, Wilfrid Wilson (1878–1962), poet, contributed to *Georgian Poetry*. He published many volumes of verse and verse drama, much of it dealing somewhat conventionally with Northern rural themes; his experiences in the

First World War inspired several shorter, sharper battle pieces, such as 'Breakfast'. His *Collected Poems 1905–25* appeared in 1926.

GIFFORD, William (1756–1826), published two satires, *The Baviad* (1791) and *The Maeviad* (1795), the first directed against the *Della Cruscan school of poetry, and the second divided between the Della Cruscans and the contemporary drama. In 1797–8 he was editor of *The Anti-Jacobin* and in 1809 the first editor of the *Quarterly Review. He bitterly attacked most of the young innovating writers of the time; e.g. he wholly altered the warm tone of *Lamb's essay on Wordsworth's *The Excursion* and published J. W. *Croker's virulent attack on Keats's *Endymion. His character and inadequacies are mercilessly exposed by Hazlitt in *The Spirit of the Age. He translated the satires of *Juvenal (1802) and of *Persius (1821), and edited the works of *Massinger, *Jonson, *Ford, and *Shirley.

Gifford Lectures, on natural theology, founded in the universities of Edinburgh, Glasgow, Aberdeen, and St Andrews by Adam, Lord Gifford (1820–87).

GILBERT, William (1540–1603), physician to *Elizabeth I and James I. He declared the earth to be a magnet in his *De Magnete* (1600), the first great scientific book to be published in England.

GILBERT, Sir William Schwenck (1836–1911), began in 1861 contributing regular columns of comic verse, with his own illustrations, to the magazine *Fun*; this was the beginning of the *Bab Ballads (collected in 1869). In these he showed his ingenious metrical skill and sketched out his fantasy world, turning the odd into the ordinary, calling it 'Topsy-Turvydom'. The ballads became the favourite literature of sailors, soldiers, lawyers, doctors, and other non-literary people, though Gilbert had a low opinion of his ballads: 'I am a doggerel bard', runs the refrain in one of them. Encouraged by T. W. *Robertson he produced his first dramatic work, *Dulcamara* (1866), a burlesque based on Donizetti's opera *L'elisir d'amore*. His second period, which began with *The Palace of Truth* (1870), a poetical fantasy, included the verse plays *Pygmalion and Galatea* (1871); *The Wicked World* (1873) and a burlesque version, *The Happy Land* (1873), in collaboration with Gilbert Arthur *À Beckett; and *The Princess* (1870), a 'respectful perversion' of *Tennyson's poem. Gilbert was a great verbal rhythmist and in his third period he found his true genius in comic opera. He met *Sullivan in 1869 and in 1874 D'Oyly Carte. For him Gilbert and Sullivan wrote *Trial by Jury* (1875), which began the series of light operas which was permanently to link the names of Gilbert and Sullivan (see GILBERT AND SULLIVAN

OPERAS). D'Oyly Carte built the Savoy Theatre especially for the D'Oyly Carte company. The collaboration lasted for over 20 years, though after *The Gondoliers* (1889) there was a rift resulting from a business transaction in which Sullivan sided with D'Oyly Carte. *Utopia Limited* (1893) healed the breach. Gilbert continued writing plays and operas without Sullivan; among them *Rosencrantz and Guildenstern* (1891), *Fallen Fairies* (1909), and *The Hooligans* (1911). He was knighted in 1907. He used the profits from his plays to build the Garrick Theatre.

Gilbert and Sullivan Operas, comic operas containing much social satire; the librettos were written by Sir W. S. *Gilbert, the music by Sir A. *Sullivan, for D'Oyly Carte. The operas are: *Trial by Jury* (1875); *The Sorcerer* (1877); *H.M.S. Pinafore* (1878); *The Pirates of Penzance* (1879, NY; 1880, London); *Patience* (1881); *Iolanthe* (1882); *Princess Ida* (1884), a satire on feminism suggested by Tennyson's *The Princess; The Mikado* (1885); *Ruddigore* (1887); *The Yeomen of the Guard* (1888); *The Gondoliers* (1889); *Utopia, Limited* (1893); and *The Grand Duke* (1896). They are sometimes known as the 'Savoy Operas' because from *Iolanthe* onwards they were produced at the Savoy Theatre.

Gilbert Markham, in A. Brontë's *The Tenant of Wildfell Hall*, the narrator.

Gil Blas, see LESAGE, A.-R.

GILCHRIST, Anne, *née* Burrow (1828–85), was the wife of Alexander Gilchrist (1828–61), author of a *Life of Etty* (1855) and a life of *Blake which he left unfinished at his death. The work was completed by Anne Gilchrist and published 1863. It made a considerable contribution to the awakening of interest in Blake's work in the late 19th cent. Mrs Gilchrist corresponded passionately with *Whitman (who occasionally replied), wrote appreciations of his work, and visited him in America in 1876–9. She also wrote a life of Mary *Lamb (1883) and various articles, sketches, etc.

GILDAS (d. 570), a British historian who wrote shortly before 547 a Latin sketch of the history of Britain, *De Excidio et Conquestu Britanniae*, followed by a castigation of the degraded rulers and priests of his day. He says nothing of Arthur, but refers to the victory of Mount *Badon. He is the first writer of history in Britain. He was an important source for later historians from *Bede onwards.

Gilfil, The Revd Maynard, see SCENES OF CLERICAL LIFE.

GILFILLAN, George (1813–78), a Scottish Dissenting minister, literary critic, and editor, who for a brief period in the mid-19th cent. exercised considerable influence, particularly as the champion of the *Spasmodic school. His *A Gallery of Literary Portraits* ran to three series, 1845, 1850, 1854, with essays on the Spasmodics, *Macaulay, *Carlyle, etc.

GILL, (Arthur) Eric (Rowton) (1882–1940), stone-carver, engraver, and typographer, who cut lettering and designed types, among them Perpetua and Gill Sans-serif. He settled in Ditchling in 1907, where a community of craftsmen and artists began to gather round him including D. *Jones. He worked for some years from 1914 on a commission to carve the Stations of the Cross for Westminster Cathedral. From 1924 he was associated with the *Golden Cockerel Press, for which he illustrated many books, including *The Four Gospels* and Chaucer's *Troilus and Criseyde*. In his writings Gill proclaimed the religious basis of art, the validity of craftsmanship in the machine age, and the holiness of the body (many of his early works were erotic); his works include *Art-Nonsense and other essays* (1929), *The Necessity of Belief* (1936), and an *Autobiography* (1940).

Gills, Solomon, a character in Dickens's *Dombey and Son*.

Gilpin, John, see JOHN GILPIN.

GILPIN, William (1724–1804), is remembered for his influential writings on the *Picturesque, which did much to form the taste in landscape, art, and the literary treatment of nature in the later 18th cent. and which some have seen as heralds of *Romanticism. From 1768 onwards he embarked on various travels in search of the picturesque, visiting many parts of the British Isles, and produced the series of illustrated tours parodied by *Combe in his *Dr Syntax*. His theoretical principles are set out in his *Three Essays: On Picturesque Beauty; On Picturesque Travel; and on Sketching Landscape* (1792).

Gipsies Metamorphosed, The, a masque by *Jonson, performed before James I 1621, printed 1640. The masque is unique in its assigning of speaking parts to members of the court. The chief event is the telling of the king's fortune by the gypsy captain, a part taken by the duke of *Buckingham.

GIRALDUS CAMBRENSIS (de Barri) (?1146–?1220), a native of Pembrokeshire. He studied at Paris and became archdeacon of Brecon, but as a churchman he had a stormy career. His most important work is the *Itinerarium Cambriae*, a description of the topography of Wales. Among his other works are *Topographia Hibernica*, an account of the geography, fauna, marvels, and early history of Ireland; *Expugnatio*

Hibernica, a narrative of the partial conquest of Ireland (1169–85); and *Gemma Ecclesiastica*, a charge to the clergy of his district, affording interesting information as to the conditions then prevailing. (See also ANGLO-LATIN LITERATURE.)

GISBORNE, Maria, *née* James (1770–1836), a friend of *Shelley. She refused *Godwin and married John Gisborne in 1800. Shelley published his buoyant 'Letter to Maria Gisborne' in 1820.

Gismond of Salerne, see TANCRED AND GISMUND.

GISSING, George Robert (1857–1903). His education in Manchester was cut short and he went to America in 1876, wandering for a year, and in 1877 moved to London. He had few friends apart from H. G. *Wells, who came from a similar background; he was twice married, unhappily, to proletarian girls. Although Gissing wrote about poverty and failure, he was a successful writer though not a rich one. His first novel, *Workers in the Dawn* (1880), was followed by *The Unclassed* (1884); *Isabel Clarendon* and *Demos* (1886); *Thyrza* (1887); *A Life's Morning* (1888); *The Nether World* (1889); *The Emancipated* (1890); and his best-known work, *New Grub Street* (1891). His other works include *Born in Exile* (1892); *The Odd Women* (1893); *Sleeping Fires* (1895); *The Whirlpool* (1897); *Human Odds and Ends* (short stories, 1897); a critique, *Charles Dickens* (1898); *The Town Traveller* (1898); *The Crown of Life* (1899); *Our Friend the Charlatan* (1901); and *By the Ionian Sea* (1901), impressions of Italy. *The Private Papers of Henry Ryecroft* (1903) reflected in part the time Gissing spent in seclusion in Devon. Respected in his own time as a naturalistic novelist in the continental style, Gissing went out of fashion for half a century, but interest in England and America steadily revived from the 1960s onwards, manifesting itself in many new editions of his works and in the publication of previously unpublished works, including volumes of correspondence, *George Gissing's Commonplace Book* (1962), *The Diary of George Gissing, Novelist* (1978), and other items.

GITTINGS, Robert William Victor (1911–), poet and biographer. His first volume of poetry, *The Roman Road and other poems* (1932), was followed by several volumes of poems and plays, and a *Collected Poems* (1976). His biographical works include *John Keats* (1968), a 2-vol. life of *Hardy (1975, 1978), and *Dorothy Wordsworth* (1985, with his wife Jo Manton).

GLADSTONE, William Ewart (1809–98), the great Liberal statesman, was educated at Eton (where one of his close friends was A. H. *Hallam) and at Oxford, where he distinguished himself as an orator. His is remembered in literary history for his *Studies on Homer and the Homeric Age* (1858), a subject further dealt with in his *Juventus Mundi* (1869) and *Homeric Synchronism* (1876). His political writings include *The State in its Relations with the Church* (1838) and his impassioned *Bulgarian Horrors and the Question of the East* (1876). His minor political writings and contributions to periodicals were republished as *Gleanings of Past Years* (7 vols, 1879, with a supplementary vol. 1890). *The Gladstone Diaries* (1968– ; vol. 8, 1982), ed. M. R. D. Foot and H. C. G. Matthew, shed new light on his complex personality, particularly on his interest in prostitutes, which expressed itself in a zeal for 'rescuing' them, dutifully recorded in what Matthew describes as 'a classic of mid-Victorian self-analysis of guilt'. The journalistic nickname 'G.O.M.' ('Grand Old Man'), current from 1882, is said to have been coined by Lord Rosebery.

GLANVILL, Joseph (1636–80), rector of the Abbey Church at Bath. He attacked the scholastic philosophy in *The Vanity of Dogmatizing* (1661), a work that contains the story of *'The Scholar-Gipsy'.

GLANVILLE, Ranulf de (d. 1190), chief justiciar of England. The authorship of the first great treatise on the laws of England, *Tractatus de Legibus et Consuetudinibus Angliae*, has been doubtfully ascribed to him on the evidence of *Hoveden.

GLASGOW, Ellen Anderson Gholson (1873–1945), American novelist, born in Richmond, Virginia. She was a woman of advanced views, a supporter of *Women's Suffrage, attracted by *Fabianism. Her novels, which show the social and political conflicts of her native region, include *Virginia* (1913); *Barren Ground* (1925); *They Stooped to Folly* (1929); *The Sheltered Life* (1932); *Vein of Iron* (1935); and *In This Our Life* (1941). *The Woman Within* (1954) is a posthumously published autobiography.

Glass Menagerie, The, a play by T. *Williams.

Glastonbury, in Somerset, the abbey of which was said to have been founded by Joseph of Arimathea, according to the *Grail legends. *William of Malmesbury suggests that it may have been one of the first Christianized areas in England, founded by French monks. *Giraldus Cambrensis tells the story of the discovery there by the monks of the bodies of Arthur and Guinevere in the 1180s, confirming the story of 'a certain Breton poet' who, according to Henry II, said they were buried there. This led to the identification of Glastonbury with *Avalon.

Glastonbury Romance, A, a novel by J. C. *Powys.

Glatysaunt Beast, The, the creature in Malory's *Morte D'Arthur* which is the original of *Spenser's blatant beast'. (see BLATANT BEAST; QUESTING BEAST.)

Glaucé, in Spenser's *Faerie Queene* (III. ii. 30, etc.), the nurse of *Britomart.

Glegg, Mr and Mrs, characters in G. Eliot's *The Mill on the Floss.

Glenallan, earl of, a character in Scott's *The Antiquary.

Glendinning, Halbert and Edward, characters in Scott's *The Monastery* and *The Abbot.

GLENDOWER, Owen (?1359–?1416), Welsh rebel leader who in Shakespeare's 1 *Henry IV* allies himself with *Hotspur and Mortimer to divide the kingdom between them.

Glennaquoich, the seat of Fergus Mac-Ivor, in Scott's *Waverley.

Glenvarloch, Lord, the title borne by Nigel Olifaunt in Scott's *The Fortunes of Nigel.

Globe Theatre, the *Burbages' theatre on Bankside in Southwark, erected in 1599. It was a large circular building, thatched, with the centre open to the sky. The thatch caught fire in 1613 during a performance of *Henry VIII. It was rebuilt in 1614 and demolished in 1644. Shakespeare had a share in the theatre and acted there.

Gloriana, one of the names under which Queen *Elizabeth I is indicated in Spenser's *Faerie Queene.

Glossin, Gilbert, a character in Scott's *Guy Mannering.

Gloucester, earl of, in Shakespeare's *King Lear, father of *Edgar and the bastard *Edmund.

GLOVER, Richard (1712–85), published much blank verse including *Leonidas* (9 books, 1737) and *The Athenaid* (30 books, 1788), but is remembered as the author of the ballad 'Admiral Hosier's Ghost' (1740) which was included in Percy's *Reliques.

Glowry, Scythrop, see SCYTHROP.

Glumdalclitch, in *Gulliver's Travels, the farmer's daughter who attended on Gulliver during his visit to Brobdingnag.

GLYN, Elinor, *née* Sutherland (1864–1943), author of many sensational and romantic novels, of which the best known is *Three Weeks* (1907), a *succès de scandale*, which features illicit passion in Venice on a tiger skin. Adaptations of her works achieved great success in Hollywood during the silent movie era.

Gnomic, from Gr. γνώμη, consisting of gnomes or general maxims, sententious.

Gnosticism, a religious movement of oriental origin which penetrated early Christianity, giving rise to a great variety of sects, prominent in the 2nd cent. AD, who claimed special knowledge. They held the material world to be the work, not of the supreme Deity, but of an inferior Demiurge, antagonistic to what was truly spiritual. Gnosticism was allied to *Manichaeism. It has been claimed that later writers such as *Comenius, the *Cambridge Platonists, and *Blake were familiar with Gnostic thought, through patristic sources: genuine Gnostic treatises were translated from the Coptic in the late 19th cent. and recent discoveries of documents in Egypt (in 1945, at Nag Hammadi) have much enlarged our knowledge.

Gobbo, Launcelot, the 'clown' and servant to *Shylock in Shakespeare's *The Merchant of Venice*; his father is Old Gobbo.

Go-Between, The, a novel by L. P. *Hartley.

Goblin Market, a poem by C. *Rossetti, published 1862. It is a fairy-tale which has been subjected to many interpretations, some seeing it as religious allegory, others as sexual symbolism, and tells the story of two sisters, tempted by goblins with forbidden fruit.

GODFREY OF BOUILLON, see BOUILLON, GODEFROI DE.

GODIVA, the wife of Leofric, ealdorman of Mercia, one of Edward the Confessor's great earls. According to legend, her husband imposed a tax on the inhabitants of Coventry, which he jestingly promised to remit if she would ride naked through the streets at noonday. She directed the people to stay indoors and shut their windows, and complied with his condition. Peeping Tom, who looked out, was struck blind.

The story is told by Drayton in his *Polyolbion*, xiii; by Leigh *Hunt; and by *Tennyson in 'Godiva'.

GODOLPHIN, Sidney (1610–43), poet and Royalist, a friend of *Falkland. His poems, not collected during his life, were edited by W. Dighton (1931).

God That Failed, The, Six Studies in Communism, published 1950, edited by R. H. S. Crossman. It marked a significant point in the reaction against the pro-Communist mood of the 1930s. It contained contributions by three ex-Communists, *Koestler, Ignazio Silone, and R. *Wright, and by three sympathizers, André Gide, Louis Fischer, and *Spender.

GODWIN, William (1756–1836), was at first a Dissenting minister, but became an atheist and philosopher of anarchical view. He believed that men acted according to reason and that rational creatures could live in harmony without laws or institutions. He married Mary *Wollstonecraft in 1797; she died at the birth of their daughter Mary, the future wife of *Shelley, and Godwin subsequently married Mrs Clairmont, whose daughter by her first marriage, Claire *Clairmont, bore a daughter, Allegra, to Lord *Byron.

Godwin produced in 1793 his *Enquiry concerning Political Justice*, in which he proclaimed that 'Truth is omnipotent . . . Man is perfectible, or in other words susceptible of perpetual improvement'. In 1794 he published *The Adventures of *Caleb Williams*. His life of Mary Wollstonecraft, *Memoirs of the author of a Vindication of the Rights of Woman*, appeared in 1798; and there is a portrait of her in his novel *St Leon* (1799). He wrote several other novels (*Fleetwood*, 1805; *Mandeville*, 1817; *Cloudesley*, 1830; *Deloraine*, 1833) and a life of *Chaucer (1803–4).

Göemot, the name under which *Gogmagog figures in Spenser's *Faerie Queene*.

Goesler, Madame Marie Max, a character of importance in the *'Palliser' novels of A. Trollope.

GOETHE, Johann Wolfgang von (1749–1832), spent most of his life in Weimar, occupying positions of increasing importance in the government until 1786. In 1791 he was appointed director of the Weimar court theatre, a post he held for many years.

In the field of literature his most famous work was the poetic drama in two parts, *Faust. His first important work was *Götz von Berlichingen mit der eisernen Hand* (1773), a rough, exuberant play which excited Sir W. *Scott, who translated it in 1799, and it was adapted for the English stage by J. *Arden under the title *Iron Hand* (1965). *Die Leiden des jungen Werthers* (*The Sorrows of Young Werther*, 1774) is a semi-autobiographical *epistolary novel. Werther is a sensitive artist, ill at ease in society and hopelessly in love with Charlotte, who is engaged to someone else. This novel, with the eventual suicide of the hero, caused a sensation throughout Europe (see WERTHERISM). In 1786 Goethe visited Italy and returned with his ideas about art radically changed in favour of 'classicism' and cured of the *Sturm und Drang* tendencies of his early works.

In 1787 appeared his drama *Iphigenie auf Tauris* based on *Euripides, and in 1795 his *Roman Elegies*. *Die Wahlverwandtschaften* (*Elective Affinities*, 1809) is a remarkable exploration of love, marriage, and friendship, and the famous 'Wilhelm Meister' novels written between 1777 and 1829 are the prototype of the German *Bildungsroman*. In the first part, *Wilhelm Meister's Apprenticeship* (1795–6), translated into English by *Carlyle in 1824, Goethe describes the disillusioning experiences of a stage-struck youth as he travels the country. The sequel *Wilhelm Meisters Wanderjahre* (*Wilhelm Meister's Travels*), also translated by Carlyle, completes Wilhelm's education. Many of Goethe's poems, as well as the songs from 'Wilhelm Meister', were set to music by German Romantic composers.

Goethe's achievement in literature covers an astonishing range of forms. In Britain, Goethe exercised an enormous influence on Carlyle, who elevated him to the status of 'the Wisest of our Time' (*Sartor Resartus*). Through Carlyle a whole generation of Victorians turned their attention to Goethe, and eminent authors like G. *Eliot and M. *Arnold paid tribute to his genius both in essays on Goethe and in their creative works. G. H. *Lewes wrote the first full biography of Goethe in any language (1855), a book he researched, with George Eliot's help, in Weimar in 1854. This biography is still one of the best introductions to Goethe for English readers.

GOGARTY, Oliver Joseph St John (1878–1957), poet and surgeon, published several novels and volumes of verse, but is better remembered as the original of 'stately, plump Buck Mulligan' in *Ulysses*.

Gogmagog, according to *Geoffrey of Monmouth's *History*, a twelve-foot member of the tribe of giants who occupied Britain before the coming of Brutus (*Brut). He attacked Brutus and the settlers, killing many of them. Brutus told the avenging Britons to spare Gogmagog so that he could wrestle with Brutus's ally Corineus; Corineus defeats the giant, throwing him to his death far out in the sea.

Golagros and Gawain, a 15th-cent. Scottish poem of 1,362 lines in 13-line alliterative stanzas, printed in a pamphlet in Edinburgh in 1508, and having some similarities to *The Awntyrs of Arthure*. It is loosely based on the French prose *Perceval* and is concerned with a journey of Arthur and his knights to the Holy Land. The stress throughout is on chivalry, especially that of Gawain.

Golden, a term used by C. S. *Lewis (*English Literature in the Sixteenth Century*, Introduction) to distinguish the literature of the later Elizabethan period from its predecessors in the *'Drab' age. The 'Golden' period may be seen as running roughly from Lyly's *Euphues* (1579) to the death of Queen *Elizabeth in 1603. All the major works of *Spenser, *Sidney, and *Marlowe fall within this period, as does two-thirds of the work of Shakespeare. The term suggests a certain bright, innocent, repetitive beauty, which one might see exemplified in, for example, the poems of T. *Campion. But the limited applicability of the term will be realized when we remember that *Hamlet, *Dr Faustus, and much of the poetry of *Donne were among the works written within the period of so-called 'Golden' poetry.

Golden Age, The, see GRAHAME, K.

Golden Ass, The, a satire by *Apuleius. It takes the form of the supposed autobiography of the author, who is transformed into an ass by the mistake of the servant of an enchantress. He passes from master to master, observing the vices and follies of men, and finally recovers human form. The story includes a number of episodes of which the best known is the beautiful fable of *Cupid and Psyche.

Golden Bough, The, see FRAZER, J. G.

Golden Bowl, The, the last completed novel of H. *James, published 1904.

The widowed American Adam Verver is in Europe with his daughter Maggie, who has all the innocent charm of so many of James's young American heroines. She is engaged to Amerigo, an impoverished Italian prince who must marry into money. The golden bowl, first seen in a London curio shop, is symbolic of the relationship between the main characters and of the world in which they move; its perfect surface conceals a flaw.

Also in Europe is an old friend of Maggie's, Charlotte Stant, and Maggie is blindly ignorant of the fact that she and the prince are lovers. Maggie and Amerigo are married and have a son, but Maggie remains dependent for real intimacy on her father, and she and Amerigo grow increasingly apart. Maggie decides to find her father a wife and her choice falls on Charlotte. The affair with the prince continues and Adam Verver seems to Charlotte to be a convenient match. When Maggie finally comes into possession of the golden bowl the flaw is revealed to her, and, inadvertently, the truth about Amerigo and Charlotte. Fanny Ashingham (an older woman, aware of the truth from the beginning) deliberately breaks the bowl, and this marks the end of Maggie's 'innocence'. Abstaining from outcry and outrage, she takes the reins and manoeuvres people and events. She realizes that to be a wife she must cease to be a daughter. Adam Verver and the unhappy Charlotte are banished forever to

America, and the new Maggie will establish a real marriage with Amerigo.

Golden Cockerel Press, a *private press founded in 1920 at Waltham St Lawrence, Berkshire, by Harold Taylor, and taken over in 1924 by Robert Gibbings (1889–1958), woodengraver, illustrator, and writer of travel books. Eric *Gill, who designed the Golden Cockerel type, was associated with the press from 1924 and designed *The Four Gospels* (1941).

Golden Grove, The, see TAYLOR, JEREMY.

Golden Legend, The, a medieval manual of ecclesiastical lore: lives of saints, commentary on church services, homilies for saints' days, and so on. An English version from various sources was published by *Caxton (1483) and was his most popular production. One of its most important sources was the *Legenda Aurea* in Latin by Jacobus de Voragine (1230–98), an Italian Dominican friar who became archbishop of Genoa.

Golden Notebook, The, a novel by D. *Lessing.

Golden Treasury, see PALGRAVE, F. T.

GOLDING, Arthur (?1536–?1605), translator of Latin and French works, including *Ovid's *Metamorphoses* (1565–7), and *Caesar's *Gallic War* (1565).

GOLDING, William (1911–), novelist, who worked for many years as a teacher before achieving an instant success with his first novel, *Lord of the Flies* (1954). *The Inheritors* (1955) tells of man's brutal extermination of his gentler ancestors; the intrinsic cruelty of man is at the heart of many of Golding's novels. *Pincher Martin* (1956), *The Brass Butterfly* (a play, 1958), *Free Fall* (1959), *The Spire* (1964), were followed by a collection of essays, *The Hot Gates* (1965). His other novels are *The Pyramid* (1967), *The Scorpion God* (three novellas, 1971), *Darkness Visible* (1979), *Rites of Passage* (1980, *Booker Prize), and *Paper Men* (1984). Golding often presents isolated individuals or small groups in extreme situations dealing with man in his basic condition, creating a quality of a fable. He was awarded the *Nobel Prize in 1983.

GOLDSMITH, Oliver (?1730–74), the second son of an Anglo-Irish clergyman, educated at Trinity College, Dublin. He presented himself for ordination, was rejected, and went to Edinburgh, where he studied medicine. He studied in Leyden, and during 1755–6 wandered about France, Switzerland, and Italy, reaching London destitute in 1756, where he supported himself with difficulty as a physician, an usher, reviewer and hack-writer for Griffith's *Monthly

Review. In 1758 he published, under the pseudonym 'James Willington', his translation of *The Memoirs of a Protestant condemned to the Galleys of France for his Religion* (by Jean Marteilhe of Bergerac, a victim of the Edict of Nantes), and in 1759 *An Enquiry into the Present State of Polite Learning in Europe*. It was at this period he met *Percy, who was to become a loyal friend and also his biographer. During 1759 he published his own periodical, *The Bee*, in which appeared his 'Elegy on Mrs Mary Blaize' (a pawnbroker) and 'A City Night-Piece'. He contributed to *Smollett's *British Magazine,* started in 1760, and was also employed by *Newbery, for whose new *Public Ledger* he wrote his 'Chinese Letters', subsequently republished as *The Citizen of the World* in 1762; he is also said to have written the nursery tale *Goody Two-Shoes*. In 1761 he met Dr *Johnson and became one of the original members of Johnson's *Club. Goldsmith wrote lives of Voltaire (1761) and Beau *Nash (1762), an abridgement of *Plutarch (1762), a *History of England in a series of letters from a nobleman to his son* (1764), a *Roman History* (1769), a *Grecian History* (1774), lives of T. *Parnell and *Bolingbroke (1770), etc.—in all more than 40 volumes. But he first achieved literary distinction with his poem *The Traveller* (1764) which also introduced him to his only patron, Lord Clare. His *The Vicar of Wakefield* (1766) became one of the most popular works of fiction in the language.

Goldsmith's first comedy, *The Good-Natur'd Man* was produced at Covent Garden in 1768; *She Stoops to Conquer* followed in 1773. His best-known poem, *The Deserted Village*, was published in 1770; his lighter verses include *Retaliation* (1774) and *The Haunch of Venison* (1776). His *An History of the Earth and Animated Nature* (8 vols, 1774), inventively portrays 'tygers' in Canada, and squirrels migrating on bark boats in Lapland, fanning themselves along with their tails.

There are many anecdotes about Goldsmith in Boswell's *Life of *Johnson*. He never married, and his relationship with Mary Horneck, his 'Jessamy bride', remains mysterious. He was introduced to the Horneck family by Sir Joshua Reynolds in 1766, when Mary was 14, and accompanied Mrs Horneck, Mary, and her other daughter Catherine ('Little Comedy') to Paris in 1770.

Goliard, Goliardic, see GOLIAS.

Golias, or **Goliardus,** the name found attached in English MSS of the 12th and 13th cents to Latin poems of a satirical and profane kind, the most famous of these being the so-called 'Apocalypse of Golias', of uncertain authorship. According to F. J. E. Raby (*A History of Secular Latin Poetry in the Middle Ages*), the conception of Golias as 'Bishop' or 'Arch-poet' is a myth. The

'Goliards' are, it seems, to be linked with Golias, Goliath of Gath, the symbol of lawlessness and of evil, though the original derivation may have been from 'gula', on account of their gluttony. The famous 'Goliardic' measure or 'Vagantenstrophe' appears to have passed from secular into religious verse. See CARMINA BURANA.

GOLLANCZ, Israel (1864–1930), professor of English at King's College, London (1905–30). He followed *Furnivall as director of the Early English Text Society, and he was one of the founders and original fellows of the *British Academy (1902). As well as editing several texts in Old and Middle English, he was the general editor of the Temple Shakespeare and of Temple Classics.

GOLLANCZ, Sir Victor (1893–1967), nephew of Sir I. *Gollancz, publisher; he founded his own firm in 1928, and in 1936 the *Left Book Club. He was well known for his progressive views and his resistance to Fascism.

G.O.M., see GLADSTONE.

GOMBRICH, Sir Ernst (1909–), distinguished British art historian, was long associated with the Warburg Institute in the University of London, as director and as professor of the history of the classical tradition. He has written extensively on the theory of art and on the psychology of pictorial representation. His works include The Story of Art (1950) and Studies in the Art of the Renaissance (1966, 1972, 1976).

Gondal, see ANGRIA AND GONDAL.

Gondibert, an uncompleted romantic epic by *D'Avenant, published 1651, consisting of some 1,700 quatrains.
It is a tale of chivalry, set in Lombardy. Duke Gondibert loves Birtha, and is therefore impervious to the love of Rhodalind, the king's daughter, who is in turn loved by Oswald, but before these issues are resolved the author declares himself bored with the poem.

Goneril, in Shakespeare's *King Lear, the king's eldest daughter.

Gone with the Wind, see MITCHELL, M.

Gongorism, an affected type of diction and style introduced into Spanish literature in the 16th cent. by the poet Luis de Góngora y Argote (1561–1627), a style akin to Euphuism in England and Marinism in Italy (see EUPHUES and MARINO).

Gonzalo, 'an honest old Councellor' loyal to *Prospero and part of Antonio's company in Shakespeare's *The Tempest.

Goodbye to Berlin, see ISHERWOOD, C.

Good Companions, The, a novel by J. B. *Priestley.

Good-Natur'd Man, The, a comedy by *Goldsmith, produced 1768.
It describes the testing and education of the open-hearted and open-handed young Honeywood, who suffers from excessive generosity, and is cured by the experience of being arrested for debt.

Good Soldier, The, A Tale of Passion, a novel by F. M. *Ford, published 1915; an earlier version of the first part of the novel appeared in Blast, 20 June 1914, as 'The saddest story'.
The novel consists of the first-person narration of American John Dowell who relates the history of relationships that begin in 1904, when he and his wife Florence meet Edward and Leonora Ashburnham in a hotel in Nauheim. The two couples form a foursome, a 'round table', and meet regularly. In August 1913 the Ashburnhams take their young ward Nancy Rufford to Nauheim with them, and Florence commits suicide. Later that year the Ashburnhams send Nancy to India (where she goes mad) and Edward also commits suicide. Dowell becomes Nancy's 'male sick nurse'; Leonora remarries. The substance of the novel lies in Dowell's growing understanding of the intrigues and passions that lay behind the orderly Edwardian façade both couples had presented to the world. The novel remains, through its ironies, ambiguities, and inconsistencies, an interpreter's delight.

Good Thoughts in Bad Times, a collection of reflections by T. *Fuller (1645). It was followed by Good Thoughts in Worse Times (1647), and by Mixt Contemplations in Better Times (1660).

Goody Two-Shoes, a moralistic nursery tale, said to have been written by *Goldsmith, published by *Newbery.

GOOGE, Barnabe (1540–94), published Eglogs, Epytaphes, and Sonnetes (1563, reprinted 1871), which are of interest as being, with those of *Barclay, the earliest examples of pastorals in English.

Gorboduc, or Ferrex and Porrex, one of the earliest of English tragedies, of which the first three acts are by Thomas Norton (1532–84) and the last two by T. *Sackville. It was acted in the Inner Temple Hall on Twelfth Night 1561. The play is constructed on the model of a Senecan tragedy, and the subject is taken from the legendary chronicles of Britain.
Gorboduc and Videna are king and queen, Ferrex and Porrex are their two sons, and the

dukes of Cornwall, Albany, Logres, and Cumberland are the other chief characters. Ferrex and Porrex quarrel over the division of the kingdom. Ferrex is killed by Porrex, and Porrex is murdered in revenge by his mother. The duke of Albany tries to seize the kingdom and civil war breaks out. There is no action on the stage, the events being narrated in blank verse.

The legend of Gorboduc is told by *Geoffrey of Monmouth, and figures in Spenser's *Faerie Queene* (II. x. 34 and 35), where Gorboduc is called Gorbogud.

GORDIMER, Nadine (1923–   ), South African novelist and short story writer, most of whose work is concerned with the political situation in her native land; her protests against apartheid and censorship have been outspoken. Her collections of stories include *The Soft Voice of the Serpent* (1953); *Friday's Footprint* (1960); and *Livingstone's Companions* (1972); her novels include *A Guest of Honour* (1970); *The Conservationist* (1974, joint winner of the *Booker Prize); *Burger's Daughter* (1979); and *July's People* (1981), a novella.

GORE, Mrs Catherine Grace Frances, *née* Moody (1799–1861), author of *Fashionable novels, of which she published about 70; they include *Mothers and Daughters* (1830) and *Mrs Armytage: or female domination* (1836). She also wrote plays and many short stories. Her novels, with their marked predilection for titled ladies and fashionable life, were parodied by *Thackeray in 'Lords and Liveries', one of *Mr Punch's Prize Novelists*.

GORGES, Sir Arthur (1557–1625), courtier and poet, was a close friend of *Ralegh. His love poems *Vannetyes and toyes of youth* were not published until 1953; other works include *The Olympian Catastrophe* (1612), an elegy on Prince Henry; *Lucans Pharsalia* (1614), a powerful rendering of *Lucan's epic into rhyming tetrameters; and a translation of F. *Bacon's *Wisedome of the Ancients* in 1619.

Gorlois, in the Arthurian legend, duke of Cornwall and husband of *Igraine.

GOSSE, Sir Edmund William (1849–1928), the son of Philip Henry Gosse (1810–88), eminent zoologist and fanatical fundamentalist Christian, his relations with whom he describes in *Father and Son* (1907), his masterpiece. This is in Gosse's own words 'the record of a struggle between two temperaments, two consciences and almost two epochs'.

Gosse was a transcriber at the British Museum and in 1875 became a translator at the Board of Trade. He made early acquaintance with the *Pre-Raphaelites. Much of his early critical work was devoted to Scandinavian literature and he was the first to introduce *Ibsen's name to England. A successful lecture tour of America in 1884–5 was followed by Churton *Collins's attack on his published lectures *From Shakespeare to Pope*, an indictment of his carelessness which shadowed the rest of his life.

His books include lives of *Gray (1882), *Congreve (1888), P. H. Gosse (1890), *Donne (1899), Jeremy *Taylor (1904), *Patmore (1905), Ibsen (1907), and *Swinburne (1917), as well as collections of poems and critical essays. His close friends included Swinburne, R. L. *Stevenson, H. *James, and *Hardy. From 1904 he was librarian of the House of Lords and exercised considerable power and influence.

GOSSON, Stephen (1554–1624). His plays are not now extant, but were ranked by *Meres among 'the best for pastorall': however, he soon became a leader of the Puritan attacks on plays and players. His *School of Abuse* (1579), dedicated to *Sidney, helped to stimulate Sidney to write his *Defence of Poetry*. T. *Lodge replied more directly to Gosson in *A Defence of Stage Plays*, provoking a reply from Gosson in *Playes confuted in Five Actions* (1582).

Gotham, see CHURCHILL, CHARLES.

Gothic Novel, tales of the macabre, fantastic, and supernatural, usually set amid haunted castles, graveyards, ruins, and wild *picturesque landscapes. They reached the height of their fashion in the 1790s and the early years of the 19th cent. The word 'Gothic' originally implied 'medieval', as in Walpole's *The Castle of Otranto: A Gothic Story* (1764), generally accepted to be the first of the true Gothic novels. In the later 18th cent. its meaning altered until its emphasis lay on the macabre, and the original medieval element was sometimes wholly disregarded. Many of the best works in the genre (e.g. by M. G. *Lewis, C. R. *Maturin, W. *Beckford, and Mrs *Radcliffe) show an exuberance of invention and produce moments of horror far greater than the mere *frisson* conveyed by less skilful imitators. *Peacock mocks the form vigorously, notably in *Nightmare Abbey* and *Gryll Grange*, as does J. *Austen in *Northanger Abbey*. The leading American exponent of the early period was Charles Brockden *Brown. Later practitioners include Mary *Shelley, *Poe, and *Le Fanu. In the 20th cent. the genre flourishes notably in popular horror fiction and films, and in the Neo-Gothic of younger writers such as J. C. *Oates, Emma Tennant (1938–   ), Angela Carter (1940–   ), and Clive Sinclair (1948–   ).

Gothic Revival, a revival of the Gothic style of architecture which began in the late 18th cent. with a new romantic interest in the medieval, and produced Walpole's *Strawberry Hill and

*Beckford's Fonthill. This was followed in the 19th cent. by a more scholarly study of Gothic, expressed in the works of *Pugin and the writings of *Ruskin. The widespread adoption of the Gothic style transformed the appearance of English towns and cities.

Governour, The, a treatise on politics and education by *Elyot.

Gower, (1) in Shakespeare's *Henry V, a Welsh captain; (2) the poet Gower (below) who acts as Chorus and narrator in his *Pericles.

GOWER, John (?1330–1408), lived at the priory of St Mary Overie's in Southwark, from about 1377 to his death, devoted to his writing. He was a friend of Chaucer and (jointly with Ralph Strode) the dedicatee of *Troilus and Criseyde (see V. 1856).

Gower's considerable learning is attested by his writing with accomplishment in three languages. In French he wrote his *Cinkante Balades* (written in *Anglo-Norman before 1374) and his first large-scale work, the *Mirour de l'Omme (Speculum Meditantis)*, an allegory written c.1376–8, in octosyllabics, concerned with fallen man, his virtues and vices. His second major work was the Latin *Vox Clamantis* (c.1379–81), an apocalyptic poem of seven books in 10,265 lines of elegiac couplets, containing reflections on the disturbances of the early years of Richard II and the Peasants' Revolt of 1381. In English he wrote the poem 'In Praise of Peace' in 55 stanzas of rhyme-royal, as well as his principal work, the *Confessio Amantis*, which exists in three manuscript versions. The first of these (published 1390), and the most commonly attested, contains 141 stories in octosyllabic couplets which are handled with a metrical sophistication and skill unsurpassed in English. The framework of the poem is the confession of a lover, Amans, to Genius, a priest of Venus; the confessor tells him exemplary stories of behaviour and fortune in love, organized under the headings of the *Seven Deadly Sins and drawing widely on classical story (most prominently *Ovid) and medieval romance. There are eight books: one for each of the sins, and one (Book VII) which gives an encyclopedic account of philosophy and morals. This work is as interesting for its Prologue and admirable Epilogue, and for its exchanges between the priest and lover, as it is for the narratives themselves.

Several of the exemplary tales are paralleled by stories in *The Canterbury Tales and other works of Chaucer: for example, the story of Florent (I. 1,407–1,861) corresponds to 'The Wife of Bath's Tale' (CT, 6); Ceix and Alceone (IV. 2,927–3,123) to *The Book of the Duchess (62–220). Up to the 17th cent. almost every writer who praised Chaucer coupled his name with Gower's; he has more examples than any other

writer in *Jonson's *Grammar*, and he speaks the Prologue to Shakespeare's *Pericles, part of the story of which is taken from Gower's 'Apollonius of Tyre'. Perhaps his significance as an English writer is to have brought into the mainstream of the canon of the literature the disparate narratives of the classics and the popular romances. (See also ANGLO-LATIN LITERATURE.)

Graal, Holy, see GRAIL.

Grace Abounding to the Chief of Sinners, or the brief Relation of the exceeding Mercy of God in Christ to his poor Servant John Bunyan, a homiletic narrative by *Bunyan (1666).

The author relates his tormented spiritual history, from his mean birth to his awakening to religion and call to the ministry. The book is written with intense, neurotic fervour in powerful and impassioned prose.

Gradgrind, Mr, Louisa, and Tom, leading characters in Dickens's *Hard Times.

GRAHAM, James, see MONTROSE.

GRAHAM, R. B. Cunninghame, see CUNNINGHAME GRAHAM, R. B.

GRAHAM, William Sydney (1918–86), Scottish poet, settled in Cornwall, which provides the landscape for many of his later poems. His first volume, *Cage without Grievance* (1942), shows considerable verbal energy and a debt to Dylan *Thomas; his own voice emerges more clearly by *The White Threshold* (1949), through which the image of drowning and the seascapes of his youth resound. The poems in *The Nightfishing* (1955) range from its long and complex title poem, which uses the metaphor of a herring fishing expedition to explore the poet's struggle with language and vocation, to the grim but lively ballad 'The Broad Close'. Later collections, *Malcolm Mooney's Land* (1970) and *Implements in Their Places* (1977), continue the same preoccupations. Graham's *Collected Poems 1942–1977* were published in 1979.

GRAHAME, Kenneth (1859–1932), contributed to *The Yellow Book and was encouraged by W. E. *Henley, who published many of the essays which later appeared in *Pagan Papers* in 1893. Six of the 'papers' described the life of a family of five orphans, whose activities then filled the chapters of *The Golden Age* (1895) and its continuation, *Dream Days* (1898). The reception of *The Wind in the Willows* (1908; based largely on bedtime stories and letters to his son) was muted, and it was not for some years that the story of Rat, Mole, Badger, and Toad, and their life by the river, became established as a children's classic. The book was dramatized by A. A. *Milne in 1929.

GRAHAM OF CLAVERHOUSE, John (?1649–89), first viscount Dundee, a royalist officer employed by the Scottish Privy Council in executing the severities of the government in Scotland during the reigns of Charles II and James II. He was killed at the battle of Killiecrankie. He figures prominently in Scott's *Old Mortality*; see also *Wordsworth's sonnet 'In the Pass of Killiecranky', published 1807.

Grail, The Holy, in Arthurian legend, a symbol of perfection sought by the knights of the *Round Table. In the latest development of the legend it is identified as the cup of the Last Supper in which Joseph of Arimathea caught the blood of the crucified Christ and which, in some versions, he brought to north Wales at the end of his lengthy wanderings. The legend is most familiar in English in the version of *Malory, which is mostly an abridgement of the stories contained in three of the romances of the early 13th-cent. French prose 'Vulgate' cycle. The ten principal versions of the legend were written between 1180 and 1230. As well as *Chrétien de Troyes' *Perceval* or *Conte del Graal* and the Vulgate versions, there is a third major version in that period, the *Parzival* of *Wolfram von Eschenbach (c.1205) which was the inspiration for *Wagner's *Parsifal*. Von Eschenbach's and Chrétien's story, in which Perceval is the successful quester, may be regarded as related to the original and more 'authentic' Grail myth which was joined by accretions and euhemerization of a Christian kind until, by Malory's time, it was very far removed from its archetype.

In Malory's *Tale of the Sankgreal*, Launcelot fathers Galahad on *Elaine, the daughter of the Grail King *Pelles. On the feast of Pentecost Galahad is brought to the Round Table and seated at the Siege Perilous; the Grail appears, accompanied by lightning, but the knights cannot see it. Led by Gawain they set off in search of it. Launcelot fails in the Quest, despite several glimpses, because of the sin of his amour with Guinevere; Gawain gives up the quest. Three knights distinguished by great purity, Galahad, Bors, and Perceval, come to the castle of *Corbenic where they have a vision of Christ and receive the Eucharist from him; they take the Grail from him and carry it to Sarras. Galahad dies in ecstasy; Perceval becomes a monk and dies two months later; Bors returns to Logrus and reports their adventures in Camelot, in particular telling Launcelot of the eminence of his son Galahad.

The origins and motivation of the Grail have been explained in three principal ways: (1) as a Christian legend from the first, which altered only in detail through its history; (2) as a pagan fertility ritual, 'the horn of plenty', related to the devastation of the land of King Pellam and its redemption; (3) as a Celtic story, already mythological in its origins in Irish, transmitted through Welsh (see MABINOGION) and Breton to the French romance tradition and gradually christianized.

Grainne, in the legends relating to the Irish hero *Finn, the daughter of King Cormac. Finn sought to marry Grainne, but she fell in love with Finn's nephew Diarmait O'Duibhne and eloped with him. Finn finally caused the death of Diarmait.

Grammar of Assent, The, a work by J. H. *Newman.

Gramont, *Mémoires de la Vie du Comte de*, published anonymously at Cologne 1713, was written by Anthony Hamilton (?1646–1720), brother-in-law of the Comte de Gramont, who married Elizabeth Hamilton in 1663. The memoirs were edited (in French) by Horace *Walpole and translated into English (with many errors) by Abel Boyer in 1714; and this translation, revised and annotated by Sir W. *Scott, was reissued in 1811. A new translation was made in 1930 by *Quennell, with an introduction and commentary by C. H. Hartmann.

The first part of the memoirs, dealing with Gramont's life on the Continent down to the time of his banishment from the French court, was probably dictated by Gramont to Hamilton. The second part, relating to the English court, appears to be Hamilton's own work. It is an important source of information, but its trustworthiness on details is doubtful.

GRAND, Sarah (1854–1943), the pseudonym of novelist Frances Elizabeth Bellenden McFall, *née* Clarke. She achieved sensational success with *The Heavenly Twins* (1893), which attacked the sexual double standard in marriage and dealt frankly with the dangers of syphilis and the immorality of the Contagious Diseases Act. This novel launched her on a public career as a *New Woman (a phrase she is said to have coined in 1894). *The Beth Book* (1897), a semi-autobiographical novel, describes with much spirit the girlhood, disillusioning marriage, literary aspirations, and eventual independence of its heroine.

Grandison, *Sir Charles*, see SIR CHARLES GRANDISON.

Grand Tour, The, which began in the 16th cent. and became a fashion in 18th-cent. England, was a leisurely journey through Europe, during which the sons of the aristocracy enriched their knowledge of the classical past and developed the socially desirable skills of the connoisseur. By the mid-1760s the educated middle classes were also travelling, and a colony of British painters and architects was studying in

Rome. Travellers followed a well-established route, musing on the sublime landscape of the Alps, with the glories of ancient Rome and Naples as their main aim. In England the Palladian villa and Claudian garden suggest an English nostalgia for Italian grace. Guide-book writing flourished; among these may be mentioned *Addison's *Remarks on several parts of Italy* (1705); J. *Richardson's (father and son) *An Account of the Statues, Bas-reliefs, Drawings and Pictures in Italy, France, etc.* (1722); *Letters from Italy* of Mariana Starke (?1762–1838; written in 1797 and 1815), a forerunner of *Baedeker and the *Guide Bleu*. The letters of *Gray and Horace *Walpole describe the Grand Tour that they made together in 1739–41; among very many repetitive travel writings, accounts by *Boswell, *Gibbon, and *Beckford stand out. *Smollett's *Travels through France and Italy* (1766) is a cross, original account (his dislike of the Medici Venus was notorious) which was satirized in Sterne's *A Sentimental Journey through France and Italy* (1768).

GRANGE, John (c.1557–1611), author of *The Golden Aphroditis* (1577), a novel of romantic intrigue, largely made up of speeches, moral discourses, letters, and poems, which concerns the courting of Lady A.O. (who turns out to be the daughter of Diana and Endymion) by Sir N.O.

Granger, Edith, in Dickens's *Dombey and Son*, the daughter of the Hon. Mrs Skewton, and Dombey's second wife.

Grangerize, to, to illustrate a book by the addition of prints, engravings, etc., especially such as have been cut out of other books. In 1769 James Granger (1723–76) published a *Biographical History of England*, with blank pages for the reception of engraved portraits or other pictorial illustrations of the text. The filling up of the 'Granger' became a favourite hobby, and afterwards other books were treated in the same manner [OED].

Grania, see GRAINNE.

Granta, The, a Cambridge University undergraduate periodical started in 1889. It went through various transformations, and in the 1950s and 60s was edited as a literary magazine devoted to publishing poetry and fiction by promising young students (who included S. *Plath and Ted *Hughes). After some years' disappearance it re-emerged in 1979 as an avant-garde literary periodical, publishing work by G. *Steiner, A. *Sillitoe, Angela Carter, Emma Tennant, Salman Rushdie, and others. In 1983 appeared Granta No. 7, *Best of Young British Novelists*, its first in association with *Penguin Books, with work by Martin Amis, Ian McEwan, A. N. Wilson, and others.

Grantly, The Revd Theophilus, Mrs, and their daughter Griselda, in the *'Barsetshire' novels of A. Trollope.

Grantorto, in Spenser's *Faerie Queene* (v. xii), the tyrant from whom Sir *Artegall rescues Irena (Ireland). He probably represents the spirit of rebellion.

GRANVILLE-BARKER, Harley (1877–1946), became director at the Royal Court Theatre, producing Shakespeare, many classics, the work of modern dramatists, and his own *The Voysey Inheritance* (1905), and above all establishing the reputation of G. B. *Shaw. At the Savoy he produced in 1910 his *The Madras House* and in 1912 two productions, *A Winter's Tale* and *Twelfth Night*, which revolutionized the presentation of Shakespeare. An apron stage, simple settings, an authentic text, and swift continuity of action were new to critics and public. Barker produced five series of Prefaces (1927–47) covering twelve of Shakespeare's plays. These studies broke new ground in presenting the producer's rather than the scholar's point of view. Among much other writing, lectures, and broadcasts he published *On Dramatic Method* (1931), *On Poetry in Drama* (1937), and *The Use of Drama* (1946).

Grapes of Wrath, The, a novel by J. *Steinbeck.

Gratiano, in Shakespeare's *The Merchant of Venice*, one of Antonio's friends.

Grave, The, see BLAIR, R.

GRAVES, Alfred Perceval (1846–1931), born in Dublin, an inspector of schools, 1875–1910, published many volumes of Irish songs and ballads, including 'Father O'Flynn', and an autobiography, *To Return to All That* (1930).

GRAVES, Richard (1715–1804), wrote successful novels, verses, and articles, and is now chiefly remembered for his lively novel *The Spiritual Quixote, or the Summer's Ramble of Mr Geoffry Wildgoose* (1773). The eccentric Methodist Wildgoose travels, with many ludicrous adventures, through the West Country and to the Peak District, encountering (and refuting) everywhere the 'enthusiasm' of the new Methodists. His other works include *Columella* (1779), a novel based on his friend *Shenstone.

GRAVES, Robert von Ranke (1895–1985), son of A. P. *Graves. His first poetry appeared (with the encouragement of E. *Marsh) while he was serving in the First World War (*Over the Brazier*, 1916; *Fairies and Fusiliers*, 1917); his poems also appeared in *Georgian Poetry*. In 1926, accompanied by his wife and Laura *Riding, he went briefly to Egypt as professor of literature.

He was to live and work with Laura Riding in Majorca, then Brittany, until 1939, publishing various works in collaboration with her, including *A Survey of Modernist Poetry* (1927). He spent the Second World War in England, then returned to Majorca in 1946 with his second wife Beryl Hodge, and settled there permanently.

Graves's output was prodigious; he wrote many volumes of poetry, essays, fiction, biography, and works for children, and published many free translations from various languages. His powerful autobiography, *Goodbye to All That* (1929), is an outstanding example of the new freedom and passionate disillusion of the post-war generation. He wrote many novels, most of them with a historical basis; they include *I, Claudius* and *Claudius the God* (both 1934), narrated in the imaginatively and idiosyncratically conceived persona of the Emperor Claudius; and the controversial *The story of Mary Powell, Wife to Mr Milton* (1943). Notable amongst his non-fiction works is *The White Goddess: a historical grammar of poetic myth* (1948), which argues that true poets derive their gifts from the Muse, the primitive, matriarchal Moon Goddess, the female principle, once dominant but now disastrously dispossessed by male values of reason and logic. Graves's often unorthodox interpretation of myth may also be seen in his *The Greek Myths* (1955), *The Hebrew Myths* (1963, with R. Patai), and other works.

His *Collected Poems* (1955) confirmed a worldwide reputation. Graves avoided identification with any school or movement, speaking increasingly with a highly individual yet ordered voice in which lucidity and intensity combined to a remarkable degree. His love poetry, some of his best-known and most distinctive work, is at once cynical and passionate, romantic and erotic, personal and universal.

Graves was professor of poetry at Oxford from 1961 to 1966, and various of his essays and lectures have been published in *Poetic craft and principle* (1967), *The Crane Bag and other disputed subjects* (1969), and other works.

Graveyard poets, a term applied to 18th-cent. poets who wrote melancholy, reflective works, often set in graveyards, on the theme of human mortality. Examples include T. *Parnell's 'Night-Piece on Death' (1721), E. Young's *Night Thoughts* (1742), R. *Blair's *The Grave* (1743), and Gray's *Elegy written in a Country Church-Yard* (1751), the best-known product of this kind of sensibility.

GRAY, John Henry (1866–1934), poet, spent many years as rector of St Peter's in Edinburgh. He was a friend of *Wilde, who urged on the publication of his first volume of poetry, *Silverpoints* (1893). He published other volumes of poetry, booklets of devotional verse, and a surreal novel, *Park: A Fantastic Story* (1932), set in the future. His best long poem, 'The Flying Fish', first appeared in *The Dial* in 1896, and was republished in *The Long Road* (1926).

GRAY, Simon James Holliday (1936–), playwright, is best known for his plays about the problems and contradictions of middle-class and academic life: these include *Butley* (1971) and *Otherwise Engaged* (1975).

GRAY, Thomas (1716–71), educated at Eton, with Horace *Walpole, and at Peterhouse, Cambridge. He accompanied Walpole on a tour of France and Italy in 1739–41, but they quarrelled and returned home separately. In 1742 Gray moved to Cambridge, where he was to live, apart from travels and visits, for the rest of his life. In 1741–2 he began to write English rather than Latin poetry, producing a fragment of a Racinian tragedy, *Agrippina*, and his first odes, including *Ode on a Distant Prospect of Eton College* (1747), the first of his works to appear in print. In June 1742 his other Etonian friend Richard *West died, just after Gray had sent him his 'Ode on the Spring' (1748); Gray paid tribute in 'Sonnet on the Death of West' (1775). In 1745 he was reconciled with Walpole, to whom he showed his 'Ode on the Death of a Favourite Cat' (1748) and his highly successful *Elegy written in a Country Church-Yard* (1751).

In 1754 Gray finished his Pindaric ode on *The Progress of Poesy*, and in 1757 a second Pindaric ode, *The Bard*, both remarkably ambitious and intense, and marking a clear shift from *neoclassical lucidity towards the obscure and the *Sublime; both were published by Walpole in 1757, the first works printed by the *Strawberry Hill Press. On the death of *Cibber (1757) he was offered the laureateship, which he declined. He was deeply interested in new discoveries of Old Norse and Welsh poetry (including *Macpherson's) and produced various imitations, including 'The Fatal Sisters' and 'The Descent of Odin' (1768). One of the best of his later poems is the satiric 'On Lord Holland's Seat near Margate, Kent' (1769). His *Journal* (1775) is an account of his visit to the Lakes, and his letters (3 vols, 1935, ed. P. Toynbee and L. Whibley) are an interesting mixture of erudition, affectionate informality, and enthusiasm for nature and literature.

Great Expectations, a novel by *Dickens, which first appeared in *All the Year Round* 1860–1, published in book form 1861.

It recounts the development of the character of the narrator, Philip Pirrip, commonly known as 'Pip', a village boy brought up by his termagant sister, the wife of the gentle, humorous, kindly blacksmith Joe Gargery. He is introduced to the house of Miss Havisham, a lady half-crazed by the desertion of her lover on her bridal night, who, in a spirit of revenge, has brought up the girl Estella to use her beauty as a means of torturing men. Pip falls in love with Estella, and aspires to become a gentleman. Money and expectations of more wealth come to him from a mysterious source. He goes to London, and meanly abandons the devoted Joe Gargery. Misfortunes come upon him. His benefactor proves to be an escaped convict, Abel Magwitch, whom he, as a boy, had helped; his great expectations fade away and he is penniless. Estella marries his sulky enemy Bentley Drummle, by whom she is cruelly ill-treated. Taught by adversity, Pip returns to Joe Gargery and honest labour, and is finally reunited to Estella who has also learnt her lesson. Other notable characters in the book are Joe's uncle, the impudent old impostor Pumblechook; Jaggers, the skilful Old Bailey lawyer, and his good-hearted clerk Wemmick; and Pip's friend in London, Herbert Pocket.

Great Gatsby, The, a novel by F. S. *Fitzgerald.

Great-heart, in the second part of Bunyan's *Pilgrim's Progress,* the escort of Christiana and her children on their pilgrimage.

Great Hoggarty Diamond, The, a story by *Thackeray, published in *Fraser's Magazine* in 1841.
  The Hoggarty diamond, given to an obscure young clerk, Samuel Titmarsh, by his aunt, at first brings him prosperity. But misfortune follows and only when he gets rid of the diamond do his fortunes take a turn for the better.

Great Tew, see FALKLAND.

Grecian Coffee-House, stood in Devereux Court, Essex Street, Strand, and was frequented by *Addison, *Steele and *Goldsmith, and by many fellows of the *Royal Society, which gave it a reputation for learning. It was announced in No. 1 of *The Tatler* that all learned articles would proceed from the Grecian.

'Grecian Urn', see ODE ON A GRECIAN URN.

GREELEY, Horace (1811–72), founder of the *New York Tribune* (1841), and one of the prominent figures in the history of American journalism, who did much to raise its political and literary standards.

GREEN, Henry (1905–73), novelist and industrialist, was born Henry Vincent Yorke. His first novel, *Blindness* (1926), was published while he was an undergraduate at Magdalen College, Oxford, when, in his aesthete phase, he was a contemporary of E. *Waugh and H. *Acton. *Living* (1929) describes life on the factory floor in Birmingham, and is based on his own experiences working for the family firm,

H. Pontifex and Sons. It manifests the idiosyncracies of prose—dropped articles, sentences without verbs, a highly individual use of colloquial language in both narrative and dialogue—which contribute to his work's distinctive quality. His other works include *Party Going* (1939); *Caught* (1943); *Loving* (1945), which describes life above and below stairs in an Irish country house during wartime; *Back* (1946); *Concluding* (1948); *Nothing* (1950); and *Doting* (1952).

GREEN, John Richard (1837–83), is best known for his *Short History of the English People* (1874), which was remarkable for its broad approach, simple style, generosity of outlook, and attention to the social, economic, and intellectual aspects of national history. It was enlarged in *The History of the English People* (1877–80).

GREEN, Matthew (1697–1737), is remembered for his poem *The Spleen* (1737), which praises in fluent octosyllabics the simple life and describes his dream of 'a farm some twenty miles from town' where he could live on 'two hundred pounds half-yearly paid'.

GREEN, Thomas Hill (1836–82), whose philosophical publications began with a criticism of *Locke, *Hume, and *Berkeley in the form of two very full introductions to a new edition of Hume's *Treatise.* His philosophical views as set forth in his *Prolegomena to ethics* (1883) and his collected *Works* (1885–8) show a qualified acceptance of the doctrines of *Hegel as speculatively true but requiring to be supplemented for practical purposes.

GREENAWAY, Kate (1846–1901), writer and illustrator of children's picture books. Her drawings suggest an idyllic world, where quaintly dressed children play and sing amid flowery meadows and trim gardens. Her works include *Under the Window* (1878) and *Marigold Garden* (1885), collections of rhymes for children; and an illustrated edition of *The Pied Piper of Hamelin* (1888) by R. *Browning.

GREENE, (Henry) Graham (1904–   ), novelist and playwright, educated at Balliol College, Oxford; he joined the Roman Catholic Church in 1926, married in 1927, and was from 1926 to 1930 on the staff of *The Times.* His novel *Stamboul Train* (1932) was followed by many increasingly successful novels, short stories, books of reportage and travel, plays, children's books, etc. Greene describes his own early years in *A Sort of Life* (1971). His pursuit of danger (despite quieter interludes, e.g. as literary editor on the *Spectator* and *Night and Day)* dominated much of his life and travels, as described in his second volume of autobiography, *Ways of Escape*

(1980). His novels include *England Made Me* (1935); *The Power and the Glory* (1940); *The Heart of the Matter* (1948); *The End of the Affair* (1951; a wartime love affair with strong religious supernatural touches modified by Greene himself in a later version); *The Quiet American* (1955, set in Vietnam); *A Burnt-Out Case* (1961, set in a leper colony in the Congo); *The Honorary Consul* (1973, set in Argentina); and *The Human Factor* (1978, a Secret Service novel). Other works of fiction he classed as 'entertainments': these include *Brighton Rock* (1938, paradoxically the first novel in which critics detected a strong Catholic message); *The Confidential Agent* (1939); *Loser Takes All* (1955); and *Our Man in Havana* (1958). *The Third Man* (1950) was originally written as a screenplay and filmed (1949) by Carol Reed. (See EXPRESSIONISM.) Greene's plays include *The Living Room* (1953), *The Potting Shed* (1957), and *The Complaisant Lover* (1959). He also published several travel books, describing journeys in Liberia (*Journey without Maps*, 1936), Mexico (*The Lawless Roads*, 1939), and Africa (*In search of a character: two African journals*, 1961). His *Collected Essays* appeared in 1969. His preoccupations with moral dilemma (personal, religious, and political), his attempts to distinguish 'good-or-evil' from 'right-or-wrong', and his persistent choice of 'seedy' locations give his work a highly distinctive and recognizable quality.

GREENE, Robert (1558–92), was attacked at length by G. *Harvey in *Foure Letters* (1592) as the 'Ape of Euphues' and 'Patriarch of shifters'; *Nashe defended him in *Strange Newes* in the same year, claiming that 'Hee inherited more vertues than vices.' Greene's 37 publications, progressing from moral dialogues to prose romances, romantic plays, and finally realistic accounts of underworld life, bear out Nashe's assertion that printers were only too glad 'to pay him deare for the very dregs of his wit'.

Among the more attractive of his romances are the Lylyan sequel *Euphues his Censure to Philautus* (1587); *Pandosto. The Triumph of Time* and *Perimedes the Blacke-Smith* (1588); *Menaphon* (1589). Among his 'repentance' pamphlets are *Greenes Mourning Garment* and *Greenes Never too late* (1590) and *Greenes Groats-Worth of Witte* (1592). *Greenes Vision* (1592) is a fictionalized account of his death-bed repentance in which he receives advice from *Chaucer, *Gower, and King Solomon. The low-life pamphlets include *A Notable Discovery of Coosnage* (1592) and three 'conny-catching' pamphlets in the same year. The best-known of his eight plays are *Orlando Furioso* (1594), *Frier Bacon, and Frier Bongay* (1594), and *James the Fourth* (1598). Greene is now best known for his connections with Shakespeare. His attack on him in the *Groats-Worth of Witte* (below) is the first reference to Shakespeare as a London dramatist; and his

Pandosto provided Shakespeare with the source for *The Winter's Tale*.

Greenes Groats-Worth of Witte, bought with a Million of Repentance, an autobiographical prose tract by R. *Greene, published 1592.

It begins with the death of the miser Gorinius, who leaves the bulk of his large fortune to his elder son, Lucanio, and only 'an old groat' to the younger, Roberto (i.e. the author), 'wherewith I wish him to buy a groats-worth of wit'. The tract ends with the curious 'Address' to his fellow playwrights *Marlowe, *Lodge, and *Peele, urging them to spend their wits to better purpose than the making of plays. It contains the well-known passage about the 'upstart Crow, beautified with our feathers', the *'Johannes fac totum', who 'is in his owne conceit the onely Shake-scene in a countrey', which probably refers to Shakespeare as a non-graduate dramatist newly arrived in London.

Green Knight, see GAWAIN AND THE GREEN KNIGHT, SIR.

Green Mansions, a novel by W. H. *Hudson, published 1904.

The young hero, Abel, fleeing from persecution in Venezuela, travels into the vast jungle (the 'green mansions'), where he falls in love with Rima, a wild and beautiful girl of the woods. The story ends tragically, with the death of Rima at the hands of an Indian tribe, and with Abel's revenge. The book's animistic overtones made a deep impression in its day.

Green-sleeves, the name of an inconstant lady-love, who is the subject of a ballad published in 1580; both the ballad and its tune have remained popular and are mentioned by Shakespeare (*The Merry Wives of Windsor*, II. i and v. v).

GREENWOOD, Walter (1903–74), novelist, is remembered for his classic novel of life in a northern town during the depression, *Love on the Dole* (1933; dramatized 1934; filmed 1941).

GREG, Sir Walter Wilson (1875–1959), scholar and bibliographer, author of *A Bibliography of the English Printed Drama to the Restoration* (1939–59). In 1906 he founded, and was general editor (1906–39) of, the *Malone Society. His edition of *Henslowe's Diary and Papers (1904–8) is an outstanding example of his skill in palaeography and his knowledge of Elizabethan theatrical history, and in subsequent works (notably his edition of *Sir Thomas *More*, 1911) he continued to raise the standards of bibliography and textual criticism.

Gregorian Calendar, see CALENDAR.

GREGORY I, St (Gregory the Great) (540–604), one of the greatest of the early popes (from

590), a reformer of monastic discipline and a prolific writer whose works include the *Cura Pastoralis* (see ALFRED), the *Dialogues*, and famous collections of letters and sermons. He sent *Augustine to England. The story that he delivered the emperor Trajan from Hell by his prayers is mentioned by *Aquinas, by *Dante, and by *Langland.

GREGORY (Isabella) Augusta, Lady, *née* Persse (1852–1932), married Sir William Gregory of *Coole Park in 1880 and was widowed in 1892. A leading figure in the *Irish Revival, she assisted *Yeats and *Martyn in the foundation of the *Irish Literary Theatre, forerunner of the *Abbey Theatre, for which she became playwright, director, and patent holder. She helped popularize Irish legends with her translations *Cuchulain of Muirthemne* (1902) and *Gods and Fighting Men* (1904), and Irish folklore with *Poets and Dreamers* (1903), *A Book of Saints and Wonders* (1906, enl. 1907), and *Visions and Beliefs in the West of Ireland* (1920). She collaborated with Yeats on several plays including *Cathleen ni Houlihan* (1902) and *The Unicorn from the Stars* (1908). Excelling in the one-act form, with plays such as *Spreading the News*, *The Workhouse Ward*, *The Rising of the Moon*, and *The Gaol Gate*, Lady Gregory wrote or translated over 40 plays. Her defence of Synge's *Playboy of the Western World*, G. B. *Shaw's *The Shewing up of Blanco Posnet*, and *O'Casey's *The Plough and the Stars* typify her tenacious work. Her collected works are published in the Coole Edition (1970–82), ed. Colin Smythe.

GREGORY OF TOURS (*c.*540–94), bishop of Tours, whose *Historia Francorum* is the chief authority for the early Merovingian period of French history.

Gregynog Press (1923–40), a *private press founded at Gregynog Hall, near Newtown, Montgomeryshire, and endowed by Miss Gwendoline and Miss Margaret Davies. It excelled in the fineness of its bindings. It was revived in 1974.

Grendel, SEE BEOWULF.

GRENFELL, Julian (1888–1915), was killed in the First World War. His celebrated poem, 'Into Battle', appeared in *The Times* in 1915 and has been much anthologized.

GREVILLE, Charles Cavendish Fulke, see GREVILLE MEMOIRS.

GREVILLE, Sir Fulke, first Baron Brooke (1554–1628), was from the mid-1560s at court, where he had a long career, culminating in his peerage in 1621, when he was granted Warwick Castle and Knowle Park by James I.

Greville began to write poetry during *Sidney's lifetime and was intimately concerned with the first plans for posthumous publication of his friend's works. Poems written after Sidney's death, in his sequence *Caelica,* show him moving away from secular love towards broader political and religious themes. His neo-Stoic *Letter to an Honourable Lady* belongs to 1589; his two Senecan tragedies *Mustapha* (published 1609) and *Alaham,* in the earliest versions, before the fall of *Essex in February 1601; the verse *Treatise of Monarchy* about 1600. His major prose work, the *Life of Sir Philip Sidney,* is as much about Greville's own political ideals and disappointments as about his friend's career, and in its published version (1652) it incorporates judgements of *Elizabeth I and her reign which he had originally hoped to include in a life of the monarch. C. S. *Lewis saw him as a writer of 'genuinely didactic verse, verse utterly unadorned and dependent for interest almost exclusively on its intellectual content'.

Greville Memoirs, The (1874–87), the memoirs of Charles Greville (1794–1865), politician, who was for many years clerk to the Privy Council. He was the trusted confidant of both Whigs and Tories, and includes in his *Memoirs* many lively portraits of friends and colleagues, such as the duke of *Wellington and Lord Palmerston.

Grewgious, Mr, a character in Dickens's *Edwin Drood.*

Gride, Arthur, a character in Dickens's *Nicholas Nickleby.*

GRIERSON, Sir Herbert John Clifford (1866–1960), scholar, who advanced the study of *Donne and the *Metaphysical poets in his pioneering, well-annotated edition of Donne's poems (1912) and in *Metaphysical Lyrics and Poems of the Seventeenth Century* (1921). He also edited (with G. Bullough) *The Oxford Book of Seventeenth Century Verse* (1934), was co-editor of a 12-vol. edition of Sir W. *Scott's letters (1932–7), and published a biography of Scott (1938).

GRIEVE, C. M., see MACDIARMID, H.

GRIFFIN, Gerald (1803–40), Irish dramatist, novelist, and poet, remembered chiefly for his novel *The Collegians* (1829), in which young Cregan, allured by wealth and beauty, permits the murder of his humble country wife; *Boucicault made it the basis of a play, *The Colleen Bawn* (1860).

Griffith Gaunt, or *Jealousy,* a novel by C. *Reade, published 1866.

The novel, set in the 18th cent., is based on a story by Wilkie *Collins. It was unusually frank for its time and Reade was prosecuted in a case in which *Dickens ('as a husband and father') refused to help defend him. Reade's interest lay clearly not only in the theme of jealousy, both male and female, but in the sexual nature of the heroine Kate, an ardent young woman who is attracted to one suitor, marries another (Griffith Gaunt), and then falls in love with her spiritual director, unleashing a trail of violence which eventually ends in reconciliation with her husband.

GRIGSON, Geoffrey Edward Harvey (1905–85), poet, critic, and editor of the influential *New Verse* (1933–9) which he founded. His volumes of verse include *Several Observations* (1939), *Under the Cliff* (1943), *The Isles of Scilly* (1946), *Collected Poems 1924–1962* (1963), *Angels and Circles* (1974), and *History of Him* (1980). Much of his prose and verse celebrates his native Cornwall. His collections of essays, many of them fiercely polemical, include *The Harp of Aeolus* (1947) and *The Contrary View* (1974). He also edited selections of work by W. *Barnes (1950), J. *Clare (1950), and others.

Grim, see HAVELOK THE DANE.

GRIMALD, Nicholas (c.1519–c.1562), contributed 40 poems to *Tottel's *Miscellany* and assisted in its compilation. He made translations from *Virgil and *Cicero, and wrote two Latin plays.

GRIMALDI, Joseph (1779–1837), a celebrated clown and pantomimist, whose *Memoirs* were edited by *Dickens, with illustrations by *Cruikshank (2 vols, 1838).

GRIMBALD, or GRIMBOLD (?820–903), a native of Flanders and a monk who was summoned to England by King *Alfred for the promotion of learning; Alfred appointed him abbot of the new minster at Winchester.

Grimes, (1) Peter, see PETER GRIMES; (2) Thomas, chimney-sweep, Tom's employer in C. Kingsley's *The Water-Babies*.

GRIMM, Jacob Ludwig Carl (1785–1863), and Wilhelm Carl (1786–1859), German brothers who pioneered the study of German philology, law, mythology, and folklore. They are chiefly known in England for their collection of fairy-tales, *Kinder- und Hausmärchen* (1812–15), of which an English translation by Edgar Taylor, illustrated by *Cruikshank, was published in 1823 under the title *German Popular Stories*. The brothers also began the German etymological dictionary *Deutsches Wörterbuch*.

Grimwig, Mr, a character in Dickens's *Oliver Twist*.

Gringolet, or **Gryngolet,** Gawain's horse, in *Sir *Gawain and the Green Knight*, etc. Speght, in his 1598 edition of Chaucer, gives it as the name of *Wade's infamous boat.

Grip, in Dickens's *Barnaby Rudge*, Barnaby's raven.

Griselda, the type of long-suffering fortitude; see PATIENT GRISELDA.

Groats-Worth of Witte, see GREENES GROATS-WORTH OF WITTE.

GROCYN, William (1449–1519), studied in Italy with *Linacre under *Poliziano and Chalcondyles, and was instrumental in introducing the study of Greek at Oxford.

Grongar Hill, see DYER, J.

GROSART, Alexander Balloch (1827–99), editor remembered for his reprints of rare Elizabethan and Jacobean literature.

GROSSETESTE, Robert (1175–1253), bishop of Lincoln and first chancellor of Oxford University. He was the author of translations from the Greek, including *Aristotle's *Ethics* and the works of Pseudo-Dionysius (see DIONYSIUS THE AREOPAGITE). He was a major figure in the development of the Augustinian philosophical tradition, and he was largely responsible for the Oxford emphasis on the development of the natural sciences; it is likely that he passed on to his pupil R. *Bacon his knowledge of and interest in experimental science. In his work *De Luce* he identifies a form of corporaneity as the most important of forms and makes the individual the essence of the form.

GROSSMITH, George (1847–1912) and Weedon (1852–1919), brothers, and authors of *The Diary of a Nobody* which first appeared in *Punch from 1892 with illustrations by Weedon.

GROTE, George (1794–1871), was MP for the City of London, 1832–41, and took an active part in favour of the reform movement. His outlook was much influenced by James *Mill and *Utilitarianism. He retired from Parliament in order to devote himself to his famous *History of Greece* (8 vols, 1846–56). Grote's other works include studies of *Plato (1865) and *Aristotle (1872).

Group, The, an informal association of writers, mostly poets, set up in London by Philip *Hobsbaum in 1955. Membership was by invitation of the chairman. The key figures included *Redgrove, P. *Porter, *Lucie-Smith, and G. *MacBeth. Lucie-Smith became chairman in 1959, and the group expanded to include F.

*Adcock, B. S. *Johnson, and others. An anthology of the Group's writings, edited by Hobsbaum and Lucie-Smith, appeared in 1963 (*A Group Anthology*). In 1965 the Group was restructured into a more formal organization called the Writers' Workshop, but its basic purpose, to expose the work of young writers to their peers, remained constant.

Grubbinol, a shepherd in Gay's *The Shepherd's Week*.

Grub Street, London, according to Dr *Johnson was 'originally the name of a street near Moorfields in London, much inhabited by writers of small histories, dictionaries, and temporary poems, whence any mean production is called *grubstreet*' (*Dictionary*). The name of the street was changed in the 19th cent. to Milton Street (Cripplegate). 'Grub Street' is current in modern usage as an epithet meaning 'of the nature of literary hack-work'.

Grub Street Journal, The (1730–37), a weekly literary newspaper, highly satirical in tone; its targets included the *Gentleman's Magazine and The Bee, *Theobald, *Cibber, *Eusden, and *Curll. *Pope (whose enemies were reviled as 'Knights of the Bathos') is thought to have had a hand in it.

Grueby, John, a character in Dickens's *Barnaby Rudge*.

Grundy, Mrs, see MORTON, T.

Gryll, in Spenser's *Faerie Queene* (II. xii. 86), the hog in the Bower of *Acrasia who repined greatly at being changed back into a man.

Gryll Grange, the last satirical novel of T. L. *Peacock, serialized 1860, issued as a book 1861.
   The main plot concerns Mr Falconer, idealist, ascetic, and classicist, who lives in a tower attended by seven virgins, but is persuaded to join a convivial house party at Gryll Grange, where he woos and wins its presiding genius, Morgana Gryll. Notable characters include the Revd Dr Opimian, an agreeable gourmet with conservative views. Perhaps the most urbane and polished of Peacock's books, *Gryll Grange* upholds civilization, harmony, and completeness against both technology and religious asceticism, two dominant strands of mid-Victorian thought.

Guardian, The, (1) a periodical started by *Steele in March 1713. It professed to abstain from political questions, and *Addison contributed 51 papers to it. It included also among its contributors *Berkeley, *Pope, and *Gay. But Steele soon launched into political controversy and owing to some disagreement with

*Tonson, the publisher, *The Guardian* came to an abrupt end in Oct. 1713 and was succeeded by *The Englishman*; (2) a national daily paper originally published as *The Manchester Guardian*.

GUARINI, Giovanni Battista (1538–1612), author of the pastoral drama *Il pastor fido* (1589), which had a considerable vogue in England in the 17th cent., where it was translated many times; notably by Sir Richard *Fanshawe in 1647 as *The Faithful Shepherd*.

Gudrun, (1) in the *Volsunga saga and in W. Morris's *Sigurd the Volsung, the daughter of the king of the Niblungs; (2) the heroine of the *Laxdaela saga* (see SAGA), who appears in Morris's version, 'The Lovers of Gudrun', in *The Earthly Paradise*.

Guest, Stephen, a character in G. Eliot's *The Mill on the Floss*.

Guiderius, in Shakespeare's *Cymbeline*, elder son of the king.

GUIDO DELLE COLONNE, a 13th-cent. Sicilian writer of Latin romances, author of the *Historia Destructionis Troiae* which was in fact a prose version of a poem by *Benoît de Sainte-Maure. His romance was used as a source in poems attributed to *Barbour and *Huchown, and by *Lydgate in his *Troy Book*. The story of Troilus and Cressida, taken by Guido from Benoît, was in turn developed by *Boccaccio, *Chaucer, *Henryson, and Shakespeare.

Guignol, the chief character in the popular French puppet-show of that name, similar to the English Punch and Judy show. Grand Guignol is a term applied to a theatre presenting plays of a gruesome character.

Guildenstern, see ROSENCRANTZ.

Guild of St George, see RUSKIN, J.

GUILLAUME DE LORRIS, see ROMAN DE LA ROSE.

GUILLAUME DE MACHAUT (c. 1300–77), French musician and poet, was prominent in the development of the *ballade and the *rondeau. His poetry influenced Chaucer, particularly in *The Book of the Duchess*.

Guinea, Chrysal, or the Adventures of a, see JOHNSTONE, C.

Guinevere, the wife of King *Arthur in the Arthurian legend. In *Geoffrey of Monmouth she is 'Guanhamara', brought up in the household of Cador, duke of Cornwall. In the *Brut of *Laȝamon she is 'Wenhaver', a relative of

Cador; in *Sir *Gawain and the Green Knight* she is Wenore, Guenore, Gwenore, and Gaynor (the form also in *The Awntyrs of Arthure*). The most prevailing form both of her name and her story developed in the French tradition, in *Chrétien's *Lancelot* (1170s) and the related early 13th-cent. prose *Lancelot* of the Vulgate cycle, where the queen Guênièvre is the lover of Lancelot, with disastrous consequences. (See LAUNCELOT OF THE LAKE.) In the main tradition, the tragic love of Guinevere and Lancelot is one of the classics of *Courtly Love.

'Guinevere', one of Tennyson's *Idylls of the King*, published 1859. It describes Guinevere's growing repentance, her parting with Launcelot, her last meeting with Arthur, and her death as abbess of the nunnery of Almesbury.

Gulley Jimson, in *The Horse's Mouth* by J. *Cary.

Gulliver's Travels, a satire by *Swift, published 1726.

Swift probably conceived the idea of a satire in the form of a narrative of travels at the meetings of the *Scriblerus Club, and intended it to form part of the 'Memoirs of Scriblerus'.

In the first part Lemuel Gulliver, a surgeon on a merchant ship, relates his shipwreck on the island of Lilliput, the inhabitants of which are six inches high. Owing to this diminutive scale, the pomp of the emperor, the civil feuds of the inhabitants, and the war with their neighbours across the channel, are made to look ridiculous. The English political parties and religious dissensions are satirized in the description of the wearers of high heels and low heels, and of the controversy on the question whether eggs should be broken at the big or small end.

In the second part Gulliver is accidentally left ashore on Brobdingnag, where the inhabitants are as tall as steeples, and everything else is in proportion.

The third part is occupied with a visit to the flying island of Laputa, and its neighbouring continent and capital Lagado. Here the satire is directed against philosophers, men of science, historians, and projectors, with special reference to the *South Sea Company. Gulliver is enabled to call up the great men of old, and discovers the deceptions of history. The Struldbrugs, a race endowed with immortality, turn out to be the most miserable of mankind.

In the fourth part Swift describes the country of the Houyhnhnms, who are horses endowed with reason; their rational, clean, and simple society is contrasted with the filthiness and brutality of the Yahoos, beasts in human shape whose human vices Gulliver is reluctantly forced to recognize.

Guls Hornebooke, The, a satirical book of manners by *Dekker, published 1609.

It is an attack on the fops and gallants of the day under the guise of ironical instructions how they may make themselves conspicuous in places of public resort by their offensive conduct. It is a parody of the *courtesy-books of the period, and was suggested by a German original, a burlesque by F. Dedekind (1549).

Gummidge, Mrs, a character in Dickens's *David Copperfield*.

GUNN, Thom(son William) (1929–), poet. Shortly after publishing his first volume of poems, *Fighting Terms* (1954), he took up a fellowship at Stanford University, California (where he came under the influence of *Winters), and in 1960 he settled permanently in San Francisco. His collections include *The Sense of Movement* (1957), *My Sad Captains* (1961), *Moly* (1971), and *Jack Straw's Castle* (1976). His celebration of men of action (soldiers, motorcyclists, tough boys), his fascination with violence, his gallery of heroes (who range from Elvis Presley to Caravaggio), together with his predominantly low-key, rational, laconic, colloquial manner, provide an interesting synthesis of the English *Movement and the romantic elements of American *Beat poetry.

Guppy, a character in Dickens's *Bleak House*.

GURDJIEFF, Georgei Ivanovitch (?1874–1949), esoteric thinker and teacher, born in Russia. In 1922 he founded the Institute for the Harmonious Development of Man at Fontainebleau, where K. *Mansfield died. His ideas influenced A. *Huxley, *Isherwood, and *Orage: his principal disciple was *Ouspensky.

GURNEY, Ivor (Bertie) (1890–1937), poet and composer, published two volumes of verse, *Severn and Somme* (1917) and *War's Embers* (1919). During the First World War he served on the Western Front and was wounded and gassed. After the war he became increasingly unsettled and was committed to a mental institution in 1922, spending the rest of his life in care. In these later years he composed poetry of growing individuality. *Blunden made a selection of his post-1919 poems, published 1954, and Leonard Clark published a larger selection in 1973. Interest in his verse—with its memories of the war, its evocations of Gloucestershire, and descriptions of his own mental state—continued to grow, and his *Collected Poems,* edited and with an introduction by P. J. *Kavanagh, appeared in 1982.

Gurth, the Saxon swineherd in Scott's *Ivanhoe*.

Guster, a character in Dickens's *Bleak House*.

GUTENBERG, Johann (c.1400–?68), traditionally considered the inventor of printing with movable types. He developed his invention in partnership with *Fust, who provided the capital but dissolved the partnership in 1455. The 42-line Bible (sometimes called the 'Gutenberg Bible', printed at Mainz 1453–5) has been attributed to him.

GUTHLAC, St (d. 714/15), a young nobleman of Mercia who reacted against his military life and became a hermit at Crowland (or Croyland) in Lincolnshire. Æthelbald, king of Mercia, had a church built over his tomb, which later became the abbey of Crowland. Not long after his death was written the Latin *Vita Sancti Guthlaci* (*c*.740) by Felix of Croyland. There are two adjacent poems in Old English, in the *Exeter Book known as *Guthlac A* and *Guthlac B,* which used to be attributed to *Cynewulf.

Guy Mannering, a novel by Sir W. *Scott, published 1815.

The story, laid in the 18th cent., centres in the fortunes of young Harry Bertram, son of the laird of Ellangowan, who is kidnapped by smugglers when a child, and carried to Holland. This is done at the instigation of a rascally lawyer, Glossin, who has hopes of acquiring on easy terms the Ellangowan estate, in default of an heir male. Bertram, ignorant of his parentage and bearing the name of Brown, goes to India, joins the army, and serves with distinction under Colonel Guy Mannering. Bertram (or Brown) is suspected by Mannering of paying attentions to his wife, and is wounded by him in a duel and left for dead. In reality Bertram is in love with Julia, Mannering's daughter. Recovering from his wound, he follows her to England and the neighbourhood of Ellangowan. Glossin, now in possession of the Ellangowan estate, plots with Dirk Hatteraick, the smuggler who had orig-inally kidnapped the child, to carry him off once more. But an old gypsy, Meg Merrilies, also recognizes Harry and devotes all her energies to secure his restoration. She frustrates the plot with the help of Bertram and Dandie Dinmont, a sturdy Lowland farmer, but at the sacrifice of her own life. Hatteraick and Glossin are captured, and Hatteraick, after murdering Glossin in prison as the author of his misfortunes, takes his own life. Bertram is acknowledged and restored to his property and to Mannering's favour, and marries Julia. The novel includes the notable character of Dominie Sampson, the uncouth simple-minded tutor of the little Harry Bertram.

Guy of Warwick, a popular verse romance of about 1300, based on an Anglo-Norman original occurring in four manuscripts ranging from 7,000 to 12,000 lines.

Guy is the son of Siward, steward of Rohand, earl of Warwick, and the romance tells of the exploits he performs in order to win the hand of the earl's daughter, Fenice.

Guyon, Sir, in Spenser's *Faerie Queene,* the knight of Temperance. His various exploits, the conquest of *Pyrochles, the visit to the cave of *Mammon, the capture of *Acrasia, and the destruction of her *Bower of Bliss, are related in Bk II. v–xii.

Guzman de Alfarache, see PICARESQUE.

Gwendolen, in *Geoffrey of Monmouth's *History,* the daughter of Corineus and wife of King *Locrine.

GWYN, Eleanor ('Nell') (1650–87), orange-sel-ler, actress, and mistress of Charles II; her best role seems to have been the 'breeches part' of Florimel in *Dryden's *Secret Love.* One of her sons was created duke of St Albans in 1684.

H

Habbakkuk Hilding, the name given to *Fielding in a scurrilous pamphlet of 1752, possibly by *Smollett.

HABINGTON, William (1605–54), married Lucy Herbert, and celebrated her in *Castara* (1634, anon.), a collection of love poems. A later edition (1635) contained in addition some elegies on a friend, and the edition of 1640 a number of sacred poems. He also wrote a tragi-comedy, *The Queene of Arragon* (1640).

Hadrian the Seventh, see ROLFE, F. W.

HĀFIZ, Shams ud-din Muhammad (d. *c.* 1390), a famous Persian poet and philosopher, born at Shiraz, whose poems sing of love and flowers and wine and nightingales. His principal work is the *Divan*, a collection of short lyrics called *ghazals*, or *ghasels*, in which some commentators see a mystical meaning.

HAGGARD, Sir H(enry) Rider (1856–1925), author of 34 adventure novels that made him famous. Their varied settings include Iceland, Mexico, Constantinople, and Ancient Egypt; but his best novels—of which *King Solomon's Mines* (1886) and *She* (1887) are the most celebrated—were set in Africa, and vividly conveyed the fascination he found in its landscape, wild-life, tribal society, and mysterious past. He had a world-wide readership which included *Jung, who used *She* as a striking example of the anima concept. *The Days of My Life: an Autobiography* appeared in 1926.

Haidée, a character in Byron's *Don Juan.*

Haiku, a Japanese lyric form of 17 syllables in lines of 5, 7, 5 syllables. It emerged in the 16th cent. and flourished from the 17th to the 19th cent., and dealt traditionally with images of the natural world; in this century it has been much imitated in Western literature.

HAKLUYT (pron. Haklit), Richard (1552–1616), was chaplain to Sir Edward Stafford, ambassador at Paris, 1583–8. Here he learnt much of the maritime enterprises of other nations, and decided to devote himself to collecting and publishing the accounts of English explorations; to this purpose he gave the remainder of his life. In 1582 he published *Divers voyages touching the discoverie of America*, and in 1587 appeared his *A notable historie, containing four Voyages made by certain French Captains into Florida*, a translation of Réné de Laudonnière. His *Principall Navigations, Voiages, and Discoveries of the English Nation* was issued in 1589 and, much enlarged in three vols, 1598–1600. He thus brought to light the hitherto obscure achievements of English navigators, and gave a great impetus to discovery and colonization. He left unpublished a number of papers which came into the hands of *Purchas.

The Hakluyt Society was founded in 1846 as an offshoot of the (Royal) Geographical Society to publish voyages and travels, which it has done at the rate of at least two volumes a year since then.

Hal, Prince, in Shakespeare's 1 and 2 *Henry IV,* the prince of Wales who later becomes Henry V.

HALDANE, J(ohn) B(urdon) S(anderson) (1892–1964), geneticist and brother of N. *Mitchison. He became known as a witty popularizer of science with such works as *Daedalus* (1924), *Possible Worlds* (1927), *Animal Biology* (with J. *Huxley, 1927), and a collection of children's stories, *My Friend Mr Leakey* (1937).

Hale, Mr, Mrs, Margaret, and Frederick, characters in E. Gaskell's *North and South.*

HALES, Alexander of, see ALEXANDER OF HALES.

HALIBURTON, Thomas Chandler (1796–1865), born at Windsor, Nova Scotia. As a writer he became known for his *The Clockmaker; or, the Sayings and Doings of Samuel Slick, of Slickville* (1836; London, 1837), a satirical and humorous work of fiction. It was followed by other works in the same series designed to stimulate political reform through the satirical observations of the character of Sam Slick, a Yankee from Ohio.

HALIFAX, George Savile, marquess of (1633–95), a powerful influence in the court of Charles II, is chiefly remembered for his *Character of a Trimmer* (1688), in which he urged the king to free himself from his brother's influence and advocated compromise and moderation. His political tracts (which include his subtle piece of argument *The Anatomy of an Equivalent*, 1688) were reprinted in 1898. He also wrote some much-reprinted essays, *A Lady's New Year's Gift, or Advice to a Daughter* (1688). He saved the throne by his resolute opposition to the Exclusion Bill. He is the 'Jotham' of Dryden's *Absalom and Achitophel*.

Hali Meiðhad (Holy Maidenhood), a prose treatise on virginity from the West Midlands, written 1190–1225. It occurs in two manuscripts which also contain *Sawles Warde* and one or more members of the group of saints' lives known as the *Katherine Group.

HALL, Edward (d. 1547), was the author of a chronicle glorifying the House of Tudor entitled *The Union of the two Noble and Illustre Families of Lancastre and York*, which is interesting for the account it gives of the times of Henry VIII. It was used by Shakespeare as a source in his early history plays.

HALL, Joseph (1574–1656), was successively bishop of Exeter (1627) and of Norwich (1641), where, in 1643, he was sequestered, his revenues and bishop's palace seized, his cathedral desecrated. He published two volumes of satires, *Virgidemiarum, Sex Libri*; a semi-bawdy satirical novel in Latin, *Mundus Alter et Idem*; and, very probably, the last play in the St John's College *Parnassus Plays*. He is famous for his plain Senecan prose style and is responsible for initiating several literary genres: the first to publish his epistles in English (1608–10); the beginner of the mode of *character-writing (1608); the introducer of Juvenalian satire. He was employed as a controversialist by King James and later by *Laud against *Smectymnuus.

HALL, (Marguerite) Radclyffe (1883–1943), published four volumes of verse and eight novels, but is chiefly remembered for her novel *The Well of Loneliness* (1928). Its open treatment of lesbianism occasioned a trial for obscenity; it was banned and an appeal refused, despite the support of many eminent writers including E. M. *Forster, L. and V. *Woolf, and Arnold *Bennett. It was republished in 1949.

HALL, Willis (1929–), playwright, whose successful play *The Long and the Short and the Tall* (1958, pub. 1959), set in 1942 in the Malayan jungle during the Japanese advance on Singapore, was followed by many other works for stage, screen, and television, many written in collaboration with K. *Waterhouse.

HALLAM, Arthur Henry (1811–33), became a close friend of *Tennyson, and after his early death, the subject of Tennyson's poem *In Memoriam*. His *Remains*, edited by his father Henry *Hallam in 1834, contain work of distinction in poetry, philosophy, and criticism.

HALLAM, Henry (1777–1859), historian, and the father of Arthur *Hallam. His first published work was *A View of the State of Europe during the Middle Ages* (1818). His *Constitutional History of England* (1827) became a work of great and prolonged influence; it was continued by Sir T. E. May. His last great work was *An Introduction to the Literature of Europe during the Fifteenth, Sixteenth, and Seventeenth Centuries* (1837–9).

HALLIWELL, afterwards **HALLIWELL-PHILLIPPS,** James Orchard (1820–89), a noted Shakespearian scholar. In 1842 he married Henrietta, daughter of Sir Thomas Phillipps. His published works include *The Life of William Shakespeare* (1848), *Observations on the Shakespearean Forgeries at Bridgewater House* (1853), on the J. P. *Collier controversy, *A Dictionary of Old English Plays* (1860), *Outlines of the Life of Shakespeare* (1881–7), which became a primary source for subsequent 19th-cent. Shakespeare biographies. He edited the *Works* of Shakespeare (16 vols, 1853–65) and some 150 volumes, mainly of 17th cent. literature, and did much work for the *Percy Society, notably *The Nursery Rhymes of England* (1842–6) a pioneering study which remained standard until that of the *Opies.

HALL-STEVENSON, John (1718–85), the friend of *Sterne, traditionally said to be the original of Eugenius in *Tristram Shandy* and *A Sentimental Journey*. He was squire of Skelton Castle, near Saltburn-by-the-Sea, Yorkshire, where he was host to a circle of literary friends, 'the Demoniacs', which included Sterne. He published *Fables for Grown Gentlemen* (1761), *Crazy Tales* (1762), and other coarse, sometimes indecent, verse satires.

Hamartia, see POETICS, THE.

HAMBURGER, Michael Peter Leopold (1924–), poet and translator, born in Berlin of a German family which emigrated to England in 1933. His collections of poetry include *Flowering Cactus* (1950), *Weather and Season* (1963), and *Collected Poems* (1984). His many distinguished translations include versions of Hofmannsthal (1961), Grass (1966), and, notably, the *Poems and Fragments* of Hölderlin (1966).

HAMILTON, Anthony, see GRAMONT.

HAMILTON, Charles Harold St John (1876–1961), for half a century the world's most prolific author for boys. He was most renowned as 'Frank Richards' of the *Magnet* (1908–40) and 'Martin Clifford' of the *Gem* (1907–39). The *Magnet*'s Greyfriars School included Billy Bunter, who survived with his friends after the *Magnet*'s closure, in book form, on television, and in the theatre.

HAMILTON, Ian, see REVIEW, THE (2).

HAMILTON, (Anthony Walter) Patrick (1904–62), wrote several successful plays, including *Rope* (1929) and *Gas Light* (1939), both thrillers. His novels include a trilogy (*The Midnight Bell*, 1929; *The Siege of Pleasure*, 1932; *The Plains of Cement*, 1934) published in 1935 as *Twenty Thousand Streets Under the Sky*, which deals respectively with the interlocking lives of Bob, a waiter, Jenny, a prostitute, and Ella, a barmaid; *Hangover Square* (1941), a thriller set in Earls Court; and *The Slaves of Solitude* (1947), a novel of boarding-house life in wartime. All the novels show a preoccupation with the perils and pleasures of drinking, and Hamilton's Marxism is expressed in his compassion for the hopelessness of his characters' lives.

HAMILTON, Sir William (1730–1803), diplomat, archaeologist, collector, and husband of Emma, who achieved notoriety as Nelson's mistress. Hamilton corresponded with *Beckford and Horace *Walpole and his collections exerted a wide influence on British *neo-classical taste.

HAMILTON, Sir William (1788–1856). His philosophical reputation was made by a number of articles which appeared in the *Edinburgh Review*, 1829–36 (republished in 1852 as *Discussions on Philosophy and Literature, Education and University Reform*). He was elected to the chair of logic and metaphysics at Edinburgh in 1836. His *Lectures on Metaphysics and Logic* appeared in 1859–60.

A man of great philosophical erudition rather than a great philosophical thinker, Hamilton represents the influence of *Kant upon the commonsense philosophy of the Scottish school set forth by T. *Reid.

In logic, Hamilton introduced a modification of the traditional doctrine, known as the 'Quantification of the Predicate'. His philosophical views were vigorously attacked by J. S. *Mill in his *Examination of Sir William Hamilton's Philosophy*.

HAMILTON, William Gerard (1729–96), known as 'Single-Speech Hamilton' from his celebrated 3-hour maiden speech in 1755 as MP for Petersfield. Some of his contemporaries claimed he was *'Junius'. His works were published after his death by *Malone under the title *Parliamentary Logick*.

HAMILTON, Sir William Rowan (1805–65), mathematician, whose fame rests principally on his discovery of the science of quaternions, a higher branch of calculus. He was also an amateur poet, and friend and correspondent of *Wordsworth, *Coleridge, and M. *Edgeworth.

HAMILTON, William, of Bangour (1704–54), Scottish Jacobite patriot and poet, is chiefly remembered for his song 'The Braes of Yarrow' ('Busk ye, busk ye, my bony bony bride'), published in *Ramsay's *Miscellany*.

Hamlet, a tragedy by *Shakespeare, registered as 'latelie Acted' in July 1602. A short, 'bad' Quarto was published 1603 and another text, almost twice as long, 1604–5. The *Folio text (1623) adds some passages not in the Second Quarto, and omits others. His chief nondramatic source was *Saxo Grammaticus's narrative in his *Historiae Danicae*, as retold by Belleforest in his *Histoires Tragiques*.

Old Hamlet, king of Denmark, is recently dead, and his brother Claudius has assumed the throne and married his widow Gertrude. Young Hamlet, returning from university at Wittenberg, learns from the ghost of his father that Claudius murdered him by pouring poison into his ear, and is commanded to avenge the murder without injuring Gertrude. Hamlet warns his friend Horatio and the guard (who have also seen the apparition) that he intends to feign madness, and swears them to secrecy. Immediately after his famous speech of deliberation beginning 'To be, or not to be' (III. i) he repudiates Ophelia, whom he has loved, while spied on by Claudius and by Ophelia's father Polonius. He welcomes a troupe of visiting players, and arranges a performance of a play ('the Mouse-trap') about fratricide, which Claudius breaks off, in apparently guilty and fearful fury, when the player Lucianus appears to murder his uncle by pouring poison into his ear. Hamlet refrains from killing Claudius while he is at prayer, but stabs through the arras in his mother's bedroom, killing the old counsellor Polonius, before reprimanding his mother for her affection for Claudius. Claudius sends Hamlet to England with sealed orders that he should be killed on arrival. Hamlet outwits him, however, returning to Denmark, having arranged the deaths of his old friends Rosencrantz and Guildenstern, who were his uncle's agents. During Hamlet's absence Ophelia has gone mad with grief from Hamlet's rejection of her and her father's death, and is found drowned. Her brother Laertes returns from France intent on avenging his sister's death. Hamlet and Laertes meet in the graveyard where Ophelia is to be buried, and fight in her grave. Claudius arranges a fencing match between Hamlet and Laertes, giving the latter a poisoned foil; an exchange of weapons results in the deaths of both combatants, not before Gertrude has drunk a poisoned cup intended for her son, and the dying Hamlet has succeeded in killing Claudius. Fortinbras, prince of Norway, whose resolute military heroism has been alluded to throughout the play, appears fresh from wars with Poland

and gives Hamlet a military funeral. (See also OBJECTIVE CORRELATIVE.)

Hamley, Squire, Mrs, and their sons Osborne and Roger, in *Wives and Daughters* by E. Gaskell.

HAMMETT, (Samuel) Dashiell (1894–1961), American writer of detective fiction, whose tough, realistic works (*Red Harvest,* 1929; *The Maltese Falcon,* 1930; *The Glass Key,* 1931; *The Thin Man,* 1932; etc.), based in part on his own experiences as a detective in San Francisco, created a vogue for a new kind of hard-boiled hero and seedy locale.

HANDEL, George Frideric (1685–1759), German-born composer who settled in England, aged 27. He became court composer in 1727. His great contribution to English music was the English oratorio. Among these are the *Messiah* (1742; from biblical sources selected by Charles Jennens); *Samson* (1743), with a text from Milton's *Samson Agonistes*; and the secular oratorio *Semele* (1743), a setting of a *Congreve text adapted for Handel by *Pope. *Gay wrote the libretto of Handel's masque *Acis and Galatea* (1718), and *Alexander's Feast* (1736) is Handel's setting of *Dryden's Cecilian Ode.

Handful of Dust, A, a novel by E. *Waugh, published 1934.

It describes the infatuation of Lady Brenda Last with an idle parasite, John Beaver, and the disastrous consequences for her husband Tony, who at the end of the novel is condemned to read Dickens aloud forever in the Amazonian jungle.

Handlyng Synne, by *Mannyng of Brunne, written in rough octosyllabics and begun in 1303. It is based on the French *Manuel des Pechez,* by William of Wadington. It deals with sin under various headings: the Ten Commandments, the Seven Deadly Sins, Sacrilege and the Sacraments, culminating with Penance. Each sin is illustrated by a story and the value of the work lies in Mannyng's narrative vigour. His most familiar and often anthologized story is 'The Dancers of Colbeck' which tells of some churchyard revellers, including the priest's daughter, who would not stop dancing when the priest bade them do so and whom he cursed, condemning them to dance incessantly for a year. They do this, and at the end of the year the priest's daughter drops dead.

Hand of Ethelberta, The, a novel by T. *Hardy, published 1876.

Ethelberta is one of the numerous family of Chickerel, a butler. She marries the son of the house where she is governess, and is soon left a widow at 21. Her spirited efforts to maintain her social position, while concealing her relationship to the butler, account for most of the story. She finally secures a wicked old peer for a husband, while her faithful admirer, the musician Christopher Julian, is left to marry her sister Picotee.

Hansard, an established familiar title of the official reports of the proceedings of the Houses of Parliament, colloquially so called because they were for a long period compiled by Messrs Hansard. Luke Hansard (1752–1828) commenced printing the *Journal of the House of Commons* in 1774. They are now a regular publication of HM Stationery Office.

Harapha, in Milton's *Samson Agonistes,* the giant of Gath who comes to mock the blind Samson in prison.

Hard Cash, a novel by C. *Reade.

Hardcastle, Squire, Mrs and Miss, characters in Goldsmith's *She Stoops to Conquer.*

Harding, The Revd Septimus, a character in the *'Barsetshire' novels of A. Trollope.

Hard Times, a novel by *Dickens, published 1854.

Thomas Gradgrind, a citizen of Coketown, a northern industrial city, is a misguided exponent of Utilitarianism, who believes in facts and statistics and brings up his children Louisa and Tom accordingly. He marries Louisa to Josiah Bounderby, a manufacturer 30 years older than herself. Louisa consents partly from the indifference and cynicism engendered by her father's treatment, partly from a desire to help her brother, who is employed by Bounderby. James Harthouse, a young politician without heart or principles, taking advantage of her unhappy life with Bounderby, attempts to seduce her. The better side of her nature is awakened at this experience, and she flees for protection to her father, who in turn is awakened to the folly of his system. He shelters her from Bounderby and the couple are permanently separated. But Tom has robbed the bank of his employer, and though he contrives for a time to throw suspicion on a blameless artisan, Stephen Blackpool, is finally detected and hustled out of the country. Among the notable minor characters are Sleary, the proprietor of a circus, and Cissy Jupe, whose father had been a performer in his troupe; also Mrs Sparsit, Bounderby's venomous and intriguing housekeeper.

HARDY, G(odfrey) H(arold) (1877–1947), distinguished mathematician, whose Oxford lectures drew audiences from beyond the confines of his subject. His review of his career and vocation, *A Mathematician's Apology* (1940), was reprinted in 1967 with a foreword by C. P. *Snow.

HARDY, Thomas (1840–1928), born at Upper Bockhampton, near Dorchester in Dorset, son of a stonemason. At the age of 16 he was articled to a local architect and when he was 22 he went to London to continue his architectural work, returning home in 1867. During this time he lost his religious faith. In 1874 he gave up architecture for writing, and married Emma Gifford. He and his wife travelled in Europe and Hardy spent several months of nearly every year in London. He greatly enjoyed the admiration of London's literary and aristocratic society, but resented the constant carping of reviewers on his 'pessimism' and 'immorality'; the hostile reception of his last two major novels led him to abandon fiction and devote himself to poetry, always his first love. In 1912 Emma died and in 1914 Hardy married Florence Dugdale.

The underlying theme of many of Hardy's novels, the short poems, and the epic drama *The Dynasts* is the struggle of man against the indifferent force that rules the world and inflicts on him the sufferings and ironies of life and love. Hardy's sharp sense of the humorous and absurd finds expression largely in the affectionate presentation of the rustic characters in the novels. Most of the poems and novels reveal Hardy's love and observation of the natural world, often with strong symbolic effect.

Hardy's novels and short stories, according to his own classification, fall into three groups: Novels of Character and Environment: *Under the Greenwood Tree* (1872); *Far from the Madding Crowd* (1874); *The Return of the Native* (1878); *The Mayor of Casterbridge* (1886); *The Woodlanders* (1887); *Tess of the D'Urbervilles* (1891); *Jude the Obscure* (1896, in the edition of the *Works* that year).

Romances and Fantasies: *A Pair of Blue Eyes* (1873); *The Trumpet Major* (1880); *Two on a Tower* (1882); *The Well-Beloved* (published serially 1892, revised and reissued 1897).

Novels of Ingenuity: *Desperate Remedies* (1891); *The Hand of Ethelberta* (1876); *A Laodicean* (1881).

Hardy published eight volumes of poetry: *Wessex Poems* (1898); *Poems of the Past and Present* (1902); *Time's Laughingstocks* (1909); *Satires of Circumstance* (1914); *Moments of Vision* (1917); *Late Lyrics and Earlier* (1922); *Human Shows* (1925); *Winter Words* (1928). The *Collected Poems* (1930), published posthumously, contain over 900 poems of great variety and individuality, yet consistent over more than 60 years in their attitudes to life and fate. Probably the most remarkable are in the group of poems written in recollection of his first wife ('Poems of 1912–13' in *Satires of Circumstance*). Hardy followed *Wordsworth and R. *Browning in his endeavour to write in a language close to that of speech. He experimented constantly with rhythms and stresses and verse forms, disliking and avoiding any facile flow.

He published over 40 short stories, most of which were collected in *Wessex Tales* (1888); *A Group of Noble Dames* (1891); *Life's Little Ironies* (1894); and *A Changed Man* (1913).

Hardy wrote two dramas: *The Dynasts* (3 vols, 1904–8) in blank verse and prose; and *The Famous Tragedy of the Queen of Cornwall* (1923).

HARDYNG, John (1378–c.1465), author of *The Chronicle of John Hardyng* in verse written 1440–57, covering the period from Brutus (see BRUT) to 1437 and arguing the claims of English kings (in the interests of Henry V and Henry VI) to overlordship of Scotland. A second version revises the work in the Yorkist interest.

HARE, Julius Charles (1795–1855), an intimate companion of *Whewell. He became rector of Hurstmonceaux in 1832. He was author, with his brother Augustus William Hare (1792–1834, biographer and compiler of travel books), of the popular *Guesses at Truth* (1827), a collection of observations on philosophy, religion, literature, language, and related subjects. With *Thirlwall he was joint editor of the *Philological Museum* (1832–3), which made some effort to introduce the much neglected new continental philology of *Grimm. He edited *Sterling's *Essays and Tales* (1848) with a memoir, to which *Carlyle replied with his *Life of John Sterling* (1851).

Haredale, Geoffrey and Emma, characters in Dickens's *Barnaby Rudge.

HARINGTON, James, see HARRINGTON.

HARINGTON, Sir John (c.1561–1612), godson of Queen *Elizabeth I. Supposedly at the command of the queen, he translated Ariosto's *Orlando Furioso* (1591), retaining the *ottava rima* of the original and providing *A Preface or Briefe Apologie of Poetrie,* closely modelled on Sidney's *Defence of Poetry. Harington's next work, *A new discourse of a Stale Subject, called the Metamorphosis of Ajax* (1596) (a proposal for the introduction of water closets), was an ill-judged bid for royal favour; together with other satires and epigrams it led to a period of exile from court. In 1599 Harington accompanied *Essex to Ireland, and was deputed by him to appease the queen's anger on his return, without success. His letters and miscellaneous writings were collected in Henry Harington's *Nugae Antiquae* (1769–75). The lasting interest of Harington's writings lies in his lively personality and ability to record detailed impressions of his world.

HARLAND, Henry (1861–1905), American author, became editor of *The Yellow Book. He published several romances including the popular *The Cardinal's Snuff-Box* (1900).

Harleian Miscellany, The, a reprint of a selection of tracts from the Harleian MSS, edited by

*Oldys and Dr *Johnson, published 1744–6 by Thomas Osborne.

Harleian MSS, The, a collection of manuscripts made by R. *Harley, first earl of Oxford, and augmented by his son Edward, the second earl (1689–1741). It consisted of some 50,000 books, 350,000 pamphlets, and over 7,000 volumes of manuscripts, including early biblical texts in Greek, Latin, and Hebrew, texts of classical authors and church fathers, papal bulls and registers, deeds, charters, state papers, etc. The manuscripts were bought by Parliament in 1753 and placed in the British Museum.

Harlequin, from the Italian *arlecchino,* via French Arlequin, originally a character in Italian comedy (*commedia dell'arte);* in English pantomime a mute character supposed to be invisible to the clown and the pantaloon, the rival of the clown in the affections of Columbine.

Harleth, Gwendoline, the heroine of G. Eliot's *Daniel Deronda.*

Harley, (1) the principal character in *The Man of Feeling* by H. Mackenzie; (2) Adrian Harley, in Meredith's *The Ordeal of Richard Feverel,* the cynical 'wise youth' and tutor of Richard, drawn from Meredith's friend Maurice Fitz-Gerald.

HARLEY, Robert, first earl of Oxford (1661–1724), Tory statesman and bibliophile. He frequented the *Scriblerus Club, and acquired a great library of books and manuscripts, which his son inherited. (See HARLEIAN MSS.)

Harley Lyrics, a collection of 32 Middle English lyrics occurring with other material in the manuscript Harley 2253, from the West Midlands, dated *c.*1314–25. Among the most celebrated poems in the collection are 'Alysoun', 'Lenten ys come with love to toune', 'Blow, Northerne Wynd', 'Wynter wakeneth al my care', and 'The Man in the Moon'. They have been edited by G. L. Brook (1956).

Harlowe, Clarissa, see CLARISSA.

Harmon, John, alias John Rokesmith, alias Julius Handford, the hero of Dickens's *Our Mutual Friend.*

HARMSWORTH, Alfred Charles William, 1st viscount Northcliffe (1865–1922). In 1887 he formed, with his brother Harold, a publishing business which issued a growing number of periodicals including the popular *Answers* (1888), which laid the foundations of his career. In 1894 the brothers acquired the *Evening News* and in 1896 Alfred started the *Daily Mail,* which changed the course of English journalism. In 1903 he added to his empire the *Daily Mirror,* and

in 1908 he became chief proprietor of *The Times.* In 1917 Lloyd George appointed him to lead a war mission to the USA and in 1918 he directed British propaganda in enemy countries. He was created baronet in 1903, baron in 1905, and viscount in 1917.

Harold, a historical drama by *Tennyson, published 1876, based on the brief reign of Harold II who died in 1066.

Harold, Childe, see CHILDE HAROLD'S PILGRIMAGE.

Harold the Dauntless, a poem by Sir W. *Scott, published 1817.

Harold, the Last of the Saxon Kings, a historical romance by *Bulwer-Lytton.

HAROUN-AL-RASCHID, see HĀRŪN AR-RASHĪD.

Harper's Monthly Magazine, an American periodical founded in 1850 originally for the avowed purpose of reproducing in America the work of distinguished English contributors (including *Dickens, *Thackeray, and *Bulwer-Lytton). It subsequently became more American in character, publishing work by *Melville, *Howells, S. O. *Jewett, and others. From 1900 to 1925 it was known as *Harper's New Monthly Magazine,* and subsequently as *Harper's Magazine.*

Harper's Weekly (1857–1916), an illustrated political and literary journal, published in New York, best known for its engravings and woodcuts. It also serialized novels by *Dickens, Mrs *Gaskell, and others, and published work by *Kipling, H. *James, A. C. *Doyle, etc.

HARPSFIELD, Nicholas (*c.*1519–75). As well as controversial works and a history of the English church, he wrote (*c.*1557) and important life of Sir T. *More, first published in full in 1932.

Harriet Smith, a character in J. Austen's *Emma.*

HARRINGTON, or **HARINGTON,** James (1611–77), published his great republican work *The Commonwealth of Oceana* in 1656 and wrote several tracts in defence of this work, and other political works (*The Prerogative of Popular Government,* 1657–8; *The Art of Law-giving,* 1659; *Aphorisms Political,* 1659). In all these he expounds his concept of a republic or commonwealth, advocates the ballot, rotation of officers, indirect elections, etc. He was the founder of the *Rota. In 1661 he was arrested and imprisoned on a charge of treason, defended himself ably, and was later released. Harrington has never been considered a great stylist but he had many admirers, including *Wordsworth and *Coleridge, and his shrewd historical analysis and political projections have increasingly attracted attention.

HARRINGTON, John, see HARINGTON.

HARRIOT, or **HARIOT,** Thomas (1560–1621), mathematician and astronomer. In 1585 he went on *Ralegh's expedition to Virginia. His *A Brief and True Report of the new found land of Virginia* (1588) is one of the earliest examples of a large-scale economic and statistical survey. His name was popularly associated with atheism and necromancy. He was thought by some to have been the leading spirit of the so-called *'School of Night', but appears to have been a faithful believer.

HARRIS, Frank (really James Thomas) (1856–1931), edited the *Evening News* (1882–6), the *Fortnightly Review* (1886–94), and the *Saturday Review* (1894–8), in which he published, among others, G. B. *Shaw (as dramatic critic), H. G. *Wells, and *Beerbohm, all of whom left vivid recollections of him. A scandalous reputation gathered round him, occasioned by his fight against Victorian prudery, by his decreasingly respectable role as editor (of such periodicals as *The Candid Friend, Vanity Fair,* and *Hearth and Home*), by his championship of Germany while in America during the First World War, and by his sexually boastful, explicit (and unreliable) memoirs, *My Life and Loves* (4 vols, 1922–7). His other publications include volumes of short stories, a novel (*The Bomb,* 1908, set in Chicago), two plays, one of them (*Mr and Mrs Daventry,* 1900, pub. 1956) based on a scenario by his friend *Wilde, and lives of Shakespeare, Wilde (1916), and Shaw (1931). His *The man Shakespeare and his tragic life story* (1909), though derided by scholars, had a considerable impact. His real achievements tend to be obscured by his persistent and self-destructive self-aggrandisement.

HARRIS, Joel Chandler (1848–1908), American author of the famous 'Uncle Remus' series. These contain a great number of folklore tales, relating to a variety of animals, with the rabbit as hero and the fox next in importance (i.e., Brer Fox and Brer Rabbit) told by a Negro to a little boy and interspersed with comments on many other subjects.

HARRIS, (Theodore) Wilson (1921–), Guyanese-born novelist, came to England in 1959. His 'Guiana Quartet' consists of *Palace of the Peacock* (1960), *The Far Journey of Oudin* (1961), *The Whole Armour* (1962), and *The Secret Ladder* (1963), and his later works include *The*

Waiting Room (1967), *The Age of the Rainmakers* (1971), and *The Tree of the Sun* (1978). His fiction is experimentatl in form, built on a complex, poetic structure.

HARRISON, Frederic (1831–1923), professor of jurisprudence and international law to the Inns of Court (1877–89), and from 1880 to 1905 president of the English Positivist Committee, formed to disseminate the doctrines of *Comte. He was the author of many works on historical, policital, and literary subjects, and attracted the censure of M. Arnold in *Culture and Anarchy* for his challenging remarks on culture.

HARRISON, Tony (1937–), poet and translator, born in Leeds. Memories of his working-class childhood and family life provide the material for much of his poetry. His volumes include *The Loiners* (1970), *From 'The School of Eloquence' and other poems* (1978), and *Continuous* (1981), and he has also written translations of *Molière's *The Misanthrope* (1973), *Racine's *Phèdre* (*Phaedra Britannica,* 1975), and the *Oresteia* (1981), collected in his *Dramatic Verse 1973–85* (1985). His works and his translations show a great facility in rhyme and a skilful adapation of colloquial speech.

HARRISON, William (1535–93), was the author of the admirable *Description of England* and translator of *Bellenden's Scottish version of *Boece's *Description of Scotland,* both included in the *Chronicles* of *Holinshed.

Harrowing of Hell, a semi-dramatic poem of 250 lines in octosyllabic couplets from about 1250, based on the legend that Christ descended into Hell to lead out the souls of the just condemned there by the closing of the gates of Heaven by Adam's sin. Christ reproves Satan and claims Adam; Satan replies that he will win one of mankind on Earth for every soul released. But Christ breaks down the door, binds Satan, and frees his servants.

Harry Richmond, The Adventures of, a novel by G. *Meredith, published 1871.

HARRY THE MINSTREL, see HENRY THE MINSTREL.

HARTE, (Francis) Bret (1836–1902), born at Albany, New York, is remembered for his short stories, notably 'The Luck of Roaring Camp' (1868), and 'Tennessee's Partner' and 'The Outcasts of Poker Flat', which were included in *The Luck of Roaring Camp and Other Sketches* (1870). His humorous–pathetic verse includes 'Plain Language from Truthful James' (1870), often referred to as 'The Heathen Chinee'. He spent his later years in England.

Harthouse, James, a character in Dickens's *Hard Times.*

HARTLEY, David (1705–57), practised as a physician. In his *Observations on Man, his Frame, his Duty, and his Expectations* (1749), he repudiated the view of *Shaftesbury and *Hutcheson that the 'moral sense' is instinctively innate in us, and attributed it to the association of ideas. From this association of the ideas of pain and pleasure with certain actions, he traces the evolution of the higher pleasures out of the lower, until the mind is carried to 'the pure love of God, as our highest and ultimate perfection'. With this psychological doctrine he combined a physical theory of 'vibrations' or 'vibratiuncles' in the 'medullary substance' of the brain. This theory was popularized by Joseph *Priestley in *Lectures on Oratory and Criticism* and influenced the development of critical theory up to the time of *Coleridge, who named his first son Hartley in honour of the philosopher, and many of whose poems show that he took the theory of association in a touchingly literal sense; indeed, it considerably influenced the Romantic view of man's relationship with the natural world. (See ROMANTICISM.)

HARTLEY, L(eslie) P(oles) (1895–1972), novelist, began his literary career as a writer of short stories and as a fiction reviewer; his stories were published as *Night Fears* (1924) and *The Killing Bottle* (1932). His first full-length novel, *The Shrimp and the Anemone* (1944), was followed by *The Sixth Heaven* (1946) and *Eustace and Hilda* (1947), the last being the title by which the trilogy is known. Hartley's best-known novel is *The Go-Between* (1953), narrated in the first person by an elderly man recalling in 1952 the events of the hot summer of 1900, when, staying with a schoolfriend in a Norfolk country house, he innocently carried letters between the friend's sister and the local farmer with whom she was having an affair. As the story progresses, it becomes clear that this distant holiday has marked him for life. Hartley's other novels include *A Perfect Woman* (1955); *The Hireling* (1957), which takes up the recurrent theme of dangerous inter-class sexual relationships; *The Brickfield* (1964); and *The Love-adept* (1969).

HĀRŪN AR-RASHĪD (763–809), caliph of Baghdad, who figures in many tales of the *Arabian Nights*, together with *Jaffar, his vizier, and Mesrour, his executioner.

HARVEY, Gabriel (c. 1550–1631), became the friend of *Spenser and was probably his tutor. He commemorated Sir Thomas Smith, his patron, in a series of Latin elegies, *Smithus* (1578), which may have influenced the form of Spenser's 'Tears of the Muses'. After a brilliant but troubled academic career, he turned his interests towards the court and the vernacular. In his exchange of *Letters* with Spenser (1580) he sensibly indicated the difficulties and limitations

of writing English verse in classical metres, but also delivered his famous judgement of *The Faerie Queene*, as it then existed, as 'Hobgoblin runne away with the Garland from Apollo'. His attack on the dying *Greene in *Foure Letters* (1592) provoked *Nashe's stinging replies which Harvey's *Pierces Supererogation* (1593) did not mitigate. With his old-fashioned humanist values and often awkward prose style Harvey came off worse in the controversy.

HARVEY, Sir (Henry) Paul (1869–1948), scholar and diplomat, was the compiler of *The Oxford Companion to English Literature* (1932), the first of the *Oxford Companions*, the idea for which originated in a suggestion from Kenneth Sisam at the *Oxford University Press in 1927–8. Harvey went on to compile the *Oxford Companions* to *Classical Literature* (1937) and *French Literature*, completed by Janet E. Heseltine (1959).

HARVEY, William (1578–1657), practised medicine in London and became influential in the College of Physicians. Harvey's discovery of the circulation of blood was announced in *De motu cordis* (1628; English trans. 1653). He then worked on a major embryological treatise which was left incomplete. Despite its innovatory nature, Harvey's work was rapidly accepted by the medical establishment. Metaphysical poets such as H. *Vaughan and Henry More made use of the imagery of Harveian circulation.

Hastings, a character in Goldsmith's *She Stoops to Conquer*.

Hatchway, Lieutenant, a character in Smollett's *Peregrine Pickle*.

HATHAWAY, Anne (1555/6–1623), married *Shakespeare in Nov. 1582. Her family home, 'Anne Hathaway's cottage', is still to be seen in Shottery, on the edge of Stratford-upon-Avon.

Hatteraick, Dirk, the smuggler captain in Scott's *Guy Mannering*.

HATTON, Sir Christopher (1540–91), became the favourite of Queen *Elizabeth I because of his graceful dancing (alluded to by Sheridan, *The Critic*, II. ii). Hatton was lord chancellor, 1587–91, and chancellor of Oxford University, 1588. He was the friend and patron of *Spenser and *Churchyard, and wrote Act IV of *Tancred and Gismund*.

Haunch of Venison, The, a poetical epistle to Lord Clare by *Goldsmith, written about 1770, published 1776.

Haunted Man and the Ghost's Bargain, The, a Christmas book by *Dickens, published 1848.

Redlaw, a learned man in chemistry, is haunted by the memories of a life blighted by sorrow and wrong. His Evil Genius tempts him to think that these memories are his curse, and makes a bargain with him by which he shall forget them; but on condition that he communicates this power of oblivion to all with whom he comes in contact. He discovers with horror that he blots out from his own life and the lives of those about him (in particular the delightful Tetterbys) gratitude, repentance, compassion, and forebearance. He prays to be released from his bargain, which is effected by the influence of the good angel Milly Swidger.

Haut-ton, Sir Oran, the orang-utan in Peacock's *Melincourt*, in which Peacock makes satiric use of *Monboddo's claim that the higher primates have most of the essential qualities of human beings, except speech.

Havelok the Dane, The Lay of, a 13th-cent. romance (before 1272) from Lincolnshire, in 3,000 lines of rhyming octosyllables. The story tells of the dispossessed Havelok, prince of Denmark, and his marriage to Goldborough, the dispossessed daughter of King Athelwold of England. Havelok is brought up at Grimsby by the eponymous fisherman Grim and becomes kitchen-boy in the household of Godrich, the treacherous guardian of Goldborough. His noble origins are twice declared, once to Grim and once to Goldborough, by a mystical light that shines over his head. At the end all three return to Denmark, defeat and hang Havelok's usurping guardian Godard, and reclaim the throne. The story has parallels with events in English and Norwegian history, but most of its material and themes are legendary.

Havisham, Miss, a character in Dickens's *Great Expectations.*

HAWES, Stephen (*c.*1475–1511), a poet of the school of *Chaucer and *Lydgate, was groom of the chamber to Henry VII. His *Passetyme of Pleasure* or *The Historie of Graunde Amoure and La Bell Pucel* (1509) and his *Example of Vertu* (1512), both allegorical poems in rhyme-royal, were printed by *Wynkyn de Worde.

Hawk, Sir Mulberry, a character in Dickens's *Nicholas Nickleby.*

HAWKER, R(obert) S(tephen) (1803–75), was from 1834 the eccentric vicar of Morwenstow in Cornwall; much of his poetry was inspired by Cornish landscape and legend, and by the frequent shipwrecks off the dangerous coast of his parish. He was the author of 'The Song of the Western Men' (1825); based on an Old Cornish ballad, it has the refrain: 'And shall Trelawney die?' He published various volumes of poetry,

including in 1864 part of the projected long blank verse Arthurian poem, *The Quest of the Sangraal.*

HAWKESWORTH, John (1715–73), conducted, with assistance from Dr *Johnson and *Wharton, the *Adventurer,* a bi-weekly successor to the *Rambler,* 1752–4. He produced a reliable edition of *Swift, with a biography, in 1754–5, and in 1766 an edition of Swift's letters. His *Almoran and Hamet* (1761) is an exotic *Oriental tale concerning Almoran's ability to change into any shape to pursue his strange, and often supernatural, adventures. Hawkesworth edited and annotated various journals, including *Cook's and Carteret's, for his *Account of the Voyages . . . in the Southern Hemisphere* (1773).

Hawkeye, see COOPER, J. F.

HAWKINS, Sir Anthony Hope (1863–1933), author of *The Prisoner of Zenda* (1894), published under the pseudonym 'Anthony Hope'. A sequel, *Rupert of Hentzau,* followed in 1898. Hawkins also published several other novels and plays, and *The Dolly Dialogues* (1894), a series of light-hearted conversations featuring a flirtation between Samuel Carter, a bachelor, and Dolly Foster, who in ch. 5 marries Lord Mickleham.

Hawkins, Jim, the narrator and hero of R. L. Stevenson's *Treasure Island.*

HAWKINS, Sir John (1532–95), naval commander, who led expeditions in 1562, 1564, and 1567 to the West African and Spanish-American coasts, slave-trading and fighting the Spaniards, and published an account of his voyages in 1569.

HAWKINS, Sir John (1719–89), a lawyer and magistrate who devoted much of his life to music and literature. He was a friend of Dr *Johnson, who made him an executor. Hawkins wrote a life (later overshadowed by *Boswell's), published 1787: he also edited Johnson's works in 15 vols, 1787–8. His scholarly *General History of the Science and Practice of Music* (5 vols, 1776) was seen as the rival of Dr *Burney's history: these were the first two histories of music in England of their kind.

HAWTHORNE, Nathaniel (1804–64), American novelist and short story writer. His stories were collected in *Twice-Told Tales* (1837), *Mosses from an Old Manse* (1846), and *The Snow-Image and Other Twice-Told Tales* (1851); he also wrote some lasting works for children, including *A Wonder Book* and *Tanglewood Tales* (1852 and 1853, stories from Greek mythology).

He spent in 1841 several months at Brook Farm, an experience on which he based *The Blithedale Romance* (1852), a novel which conveys his mixed response to the *Transcendentalists. He married in 1842 and settled in Concord; from 1846 to 1849 he was Surveyor of the port of Salem. He wrote *The Scarlet Letter* (1850), a classic enquiry into the nature of American Puritanism and the New England conscience, and *The House of the Seven Gables* (1851), a study in ancestral guilt and expiation, also deeply rooted in New England and his own family history. From 1853 to 1857 Hawthorne was in England, as American consul at Liverpool; he then spent two years in Italy, which provided the setting and inspiration for *The Marble Faun* (1860), returning in 1860 to Concord, where he spent his last years. *Our Old Home*, sketches of his life in England, appeared in 1863.

Hawthorne has long been recognized as one of the greatest of American writers, a moralist and allegorist much preoccupied with the mystery of sin, the paradox of its occasionally regenerative power, and the compensation for unmerited suffering and crime.

HAYDON, Benjamin Robert (1786–1846), a historical painter but best known for his posthumously published *Autobiography and Journals* (selections ed. Tom *Taylor, 1853; complete text in 5 vols, ed. W. B. Pope, 1960, 1963). His vigorous advocacy helped to secure the Elgin Marbles for the British Museum, and his pioneering theories on art education, industrial design, and state patronage of the arts, expressed in his *Lectures on Painting and Design* (1846), had much influence. He was a friend of *Keats, *Wordsworth, *Hazlitt, Leigh *Hunt, M. R. *Mitford, and Elizabeth Barrett (*Browning). His outrageous personality has interested many novelists, notably Dickens who used him (combined with Leigh Hunt) as the model for Harold Skimpole in *Bleak House*.

HAYLEY, William (1745–1820), a prolific poet, whose most ambitious works, *The Triumphs of Temper* (1781) and *The Triumphs of Music* (1804), were ridiculed by *Byron. In 1805 his *Ballads on . . . Animals* was illustrated by his protégé *Blake. He published a life of his friend *Cowper (1803) and was offered the laureateship in 1790, but declined it.

Haymarket, The, London, so called from the Hay Market established there in 1664, and maintained until 1830. Her Majesty's Theatre, Haymarket (called also the Opera House), was the first opera house in London (1705). The Haymarket Theatre, on the opposite side of the street, also built at the beginning of the 18th cent., was *Foote's theatre from 1747, and later that of the Bancrofts.

HAYWARD, Abraham (1801–84), barrister, was author of *The Art of Dining* (1852); his gastronomic dinners in his chambers were famous for their distinguished company which included *Lockhart and *Macaulay. His articles appeared in the leading periodicals of his day and many were collected in 5 vols of *Biographical and Critical Essays* (1858–74).

HAYWARD, Sir John (?1564–1627), was the author of various historical works, in which he emulated the style of the great Roman historians. His *First Part of the Life and Raigne of Henrie the IIII* (1599), dedicated to *Essex, gave offence to *Elizabeth I and led to his imprisonment.

HAYWOOD, Eliza (?1693–1756), an actress and author of several plays and many novels. She conducted a periodical, *The Female Spectator*, 1744–6, and in 1751 published the most memorable of her novels, *The History of Miss Betty Thoughtless*, followed in 1753 by *Jenny and Jemmy Jessamy*.

HAZLITT, William (1778–1830), the son of a Unitarian minister. Most of his youth was spent in the village of Wem, near Shrewsbury. He began to train for the ministry, relinquished his training in the hope of becoming a painter, then (under the powerful influence of *Coleridge), decided on writing as his career. In London he became the friend of C. *Lamb, and he began a long career as a prolific journalist, parliamentary reporter, dramatic and literary critic, essayist, and lecturer. He was an ardent supporter of the French revolution and of Napoleon, and was deeply concerned about the social ills of his own country. In 1808 he married Sarah Stoddard, from whom he was divorced in 1822. From about 1812 he wrote abundantly for various periodicals, including the *Edinburgh Review*. He published *Lectures on English Philosophy* (1812); *Characters of Shakespeare's Plays* (1817); a book of essays, *The Round Table* (1817), with Leigh *Hunt; *A View of the English Stage* (1818); and *Lectures on the English Poets* (1818). In 1818 he was violently attacked by *Lockhart, the editor of *Blackwood's Magazine*, who called him a 'mere quack', and derided him as one of the members of the *'Cockney school of poetry'. In 1819 he produced *Lectures on the English Comic Writers* and his *Political Essays* concerning the distresses of the poor, and essays entitled *Table Talk* appeared in 1821–2.

In 1823 he was arrested for debt, and he became the subject of public obloquy with the publication of *Liber Amoris*, an agonized account of his love for Sarah Walker. In 1824 he married Isabella Bridgewater, who left him in 1827. In 1825 he published *The Spirt of the Age*, and in 1826 *The Plain Speaker* and *Notes of a Journey through France and Italy*. His *Boswell Redivivus*, a conversational portrait of the painter Northcote, appeared in 1827. His *Life of

Napoleon (1828–30) has never been greatly esteemed.

His merits as a critic are not always agreed, yet even his detractors concede the great range of his reading and his achievement as a critical historian at a time when no history of English literature existed.

HAZLITT, William Carew (1834–1913), bibliographer, grandson of William *Hazlitt. His works include a *Hand-book to the popular poetical and dramatic literature of Great Britain . . . to the Restoration* (1867), *Bibliographical Collections and Notes* (1876–89, 3 series), memoirs of his grandfather (1867), an edition of *English Proverbs and Proverbial phrases collected from the most authentic sources* (1869, for which H. G. *Bohn accused him of plagiarism), *Letters of Charles Lamb* (1886). His *Confessions of a Collector* appeared in 1897. *Schoenbaum describes him as 'unreliable' and 'an antiquarian bumbler'.

H.D., see DOOLITTLE, H.

Headlong Hall, a satire by T. L. *Peacock, published 1816, the first of the series of books in which Peacock adapts the Socratic dialogue as a tool for satirizing contemporary culture.

Mr Foster the optimist, Mr Escot the pessimist, Mr Jenkinson the status-quo-ite, Dr Gaster, a gluttonous cleric, Mr Milestone, a landscape gardener, and many others gather at the Welsh country house of Squire Headlong to eat, drink, and discuss the arts. See also PICTURESQUE.

Headrigg, Cuddie, in Scott's *Old Mortality*, ploughman to Lady Margaret Bellenden, and Mause, his old Covenanting mother.

Headstone, Bradley, a character in Dickens's *Our Mutual Friend*.

HEANEY, Seamus Justin (1939–), Irish poet. His early poetry is rooted in the farmland of his youth, and communicates a strong physical sense of environment with subtlety and economy of words, as in *Eleven Poems* (1965), *Death of a Naturalist* (1966), and *Door into the Dark* (1969). His later work, densely written and often poignant, as in *Wintering Out* (1972), *North* (1975), and *Field Work* (1979), broods on the cultural and historical implications of words and explores their use in wider social and political contexts. His later volumes include *Selected Poems, 1965–1975* (1980); *Preoccupations* (1980), a collection of essays and lectures; and *Station Island* (1984).

HEARD, Gerald, see HUXLEY, A.

HEARN, Lafcadio (1850–1904), born in Santa Maura (Levkas) of Irish-Greek parentage, educated in England. He worked as a journalist in Cincinnati and incurred scandal by living openly with a mulatto woman. He then lived in Martinique, an experience which produced *Two Years in the French West Indies* (1890) and a novel, *Youma* (1890). In 1890 he went to Japan, where he married a Japanese wife and spent the rest of his life. He published several works which vividly evoke the landscapes, mythology, and customs of his adopted country, including *Glimpses of Unfamiliar Japan* (1894), *Out of the East* (1895), and *Japan: an attempt at interpretation* (1904).

HEARNE, Thomas (1678–1735), historical antiquary, author of *Reliquiae Bodleianae* (1703) and editor of a valuable collection of early English chronicles, of *Leland's *Itinerary*, *Camden's *Annales*, and other works. He was the 'Wormius' of Pope's *Dunciad.

Heartbreak House: *A Fantasia in the Russian manner on English themes*, a play by Bernard *Shaw, first performed in New York 1920, published there 1919.

It describes the impact of Ellie Dunn, daughter of the idealistic and unworldly Mazzini Dunn, upon the 'horribly Bohemian' household of 88-year-old Captain Shotover, with whom she strikes up an alliance: the inmates include beautiful, dominating Hesione Hushabye (determined Ellie shall not marry the ageing business magnate Boss Mangan); her husband, the fantasist Hector Hushabye; her sister, the apparently conventional Lady Utterword; and Lady Utterword's devoted brother-in-law Randall, prototype of the useless artist. Shaw appears to be portraying an aspect of British (or European) civilization (suggested in part by the *Bloomsbury Group, in part by the society portrayed by *Chekhov), about to run on the rocks or blow itself up through lack of direction and lack of grasp of economic reality, but, after various Shavian debates on money, marriage, and morality, the play ends in deep ambiguity: an air raid destroys Boss Mangan, the practical man, who takes refuge in a gravel pit where the Captain stores dynamite, and is greeted with exhilarated rapture by Hesione and Ellie, who with the rest of the household refuse to take shelter, and survive.

Heartfree, (1) a character in Vanbrugh's *The Provok'd Wife*; (2) Heartfree and Mrs Heartfree, characters in Fielding's *Jonathan Wild*.

'Heart of Darkness', a tale by J. *Conrad, published 1902. On board a boat anchored peacefully in the Thames the narrator, Marlow, tells the story of his journey on another river.

Travelling in Africa to join a cargo boat, Marlow grows disgusted by what he sees of the greed of the ivory traders and their brutal exploitation of the natives. At a company station he hears of the remarkable agent Mr Kurtz who is stationed in the very heart of the ivory country. Marlow makes a long and arduous cross-country trek to join the steamboat which he will command on an ivory collecting journey into the interior, but at the Central Station he finds that his boat has been mysteriously wrecked. He learns that Kurtz has dismissed his assistant and is seriously ill. With repairs completed Marlow sets off on the two-month journey towards Kurtz. The river passage through the heavy motionless forest fills Marlow with a growing sense of dread. Nearing its destination the boat is attacked by tribesmen and a helmsman is killed. At the Inner Station Marlow is met by a naïve young Russian sailor who tells Marlow of Kurtz's brilliance and the semi-divine power he exercises over the natives. A row of severed heads on stakes round the hut give an intimation of the barbaric rites by which Kurtz has achieved his ascendancy. While Marlow attempts to get Kurtz back down the river Kurtz tries to justify his actions and his motives: he has seen into the very heart of things. But dying his last words are: 'The horror! The horror!' Marlow is left with two packages to deliver, Kurtz's report for the Society for Suppression of Savage Customs, and some letters for his girlfriend.

Heart of Midlothian, The, a novel by Sir W. *Scott, published 1818, as the 2nd series of *Tales of My Landlord.

The novel takes its name from the old Edinburgh Tolbooth, or prison, known as the 'Heart of Midlothian', and opens with the Porteous riot of 1736. Captain John Porteous, commander of the City Guard, had, without sufficient justification, caused the death of a number of citizens by ordering his force to fire, and had himself fired, on the crowd on the occasion of the hanging of a convicted robber, Wilson. He had been sentenced to death but reprieved; whereupon a body of the incensed citizens, headed by Robertson, the associate of Wilson, broke into the Tolbooth, carried Porteous out, and hanged him. With these substantially historical events, Scott links the story of Jeanie and Effie Deans, which also has some basis in fact. Robertson, whose real name is George Staunton, a reckless young man of good family, is the lover of Effie Deans, who is imprisoned in the Tolbooth on a charge of child-murder, and the attack on the Tolbooth is partly designed by him to free Effie. But Effie refuses to escape. She is tried, and as her devoted half-sister Jeanie, in a poignant scene, refuses to give the false evidence which would secure her acquittal, is sentenced to death. Jeanie sets out on foot for London, through the influence of the duke of Argyle obtains an interview with Queen Caroline, and obtains her sister's pardon. By the duke's favour she is also enabled to marry her lover, the Presbyterian minister Reuben Butler. Effie mar-

ries her lover, and becomes Lady Staunton, and it comes to light that her child, whom she was accused of having murdered, is in fact alive. He had been sold to a vagrant woman by Meg Murdockson (who had charge of Effie during her confinement) presumably in revenge against Robertson (alias Staunton) for having seduced her daughter 'Madge Wildfire'. Staunton, in his efforts to recover his son, encounters a band of ruffians and is killed by a boy who turns out to be his own son.

Among the notable minor characters are the officious Bartoline Saddletree, the law-loving harness-maker; and the Laird of Dumbiedikes, Jeanie's taciturn suitor. Beautiful lyrics are placed in the mouth of Madge Wildfire, in particular 'Proud Maisie', which she sings on her deathbed.

Heart of the Matter, The, a novel by G. *Greene, published 1948.

Set in West Africa, 'the white man's grave', during the Second World War, the novel vividly evokes an area of 'Greeneland' characterized by intense heat, vultures, cockroaches, rats, heavy drinking, corruption, and a painful struggle to maintain faith, in a hostile environment, with concepts of justice and religion.

Heartwell, the title role in Congreve's comedy *The Old Bachelor.

Heathcliff, the central figure in E. Brontë's *Wuthering Heights.

HEATH-STUBBS, John Francis Alexander (1918–), poet and critic, whose inspiration comes chiefly from Ancient Greece, Rome, Alexandria, classical myth, Christian legend, and works of art and scholarship. But he is also a poet of contemporary urban society, and in *A Charm Against the Toothache* (1954) the megalopolis is modern London. His principal works include poetry: *Wounded Thammuz* (1942), *Beauty and the Beast* (1943), *The Divided Ways* (1946), *The Swarming of the Bees* (1950), *The Blue-Fly in his Head* (1962), *Artorius* (an epic poem on Arthurian legend, 1972), and *Naming the Beasts* (a collection, 1982); and criticism: *The Darkling Plain* (a study of Victorian romantic poetry, 1950) and *Charles Williams* (a monograph, 1955).

Heaven and Earth, a poetic drama by Lord *Byron, published in *The Liberal, 1822.

Heavenly Twins, The, see GRAND, S.

HEBER, Reginald (1783–1826), became in 1822 bishop of Calcutta. His published works include an edition of the works of Jeremy *Taylor (1822), and his *Life* (1824); various hymns of his own authorship, including 'Hark, the herald angels sing', 'From Greenland's icy mountains', and 'Holy, holy, holy' in 1827; and his *Poetical Works* (1841).

HEBER, Richard (1773–1833), half-brother of Reginald *Heber, travelled widely to collect his library of 150,000 volumes, and edited *Persius and other classical authors. He is the 'Atticus' of T. F. *Dibdin's *Bibliomania*.

Hebrew Melodies, a collection of short poems by Lord *Byron, published 1815.

Most of the poems are on scriptural subjects, and some were arranged to traditional Hebrew melodies by I. Nathan. The collection also contains love-songs, including 'She walks in beauty'; and the much anthologized 'The Destruction of Sennacherib' ('The Assyrian came down like the wolf on the fold . . .').

Hebrides, *The Journal of a Tour to the*, see JOURNAL OF A TOUR TO THE HEBRIDES. See also JOURNEY TO THE WESTERN ISLANDS OF SCOTLAND.

Hector, Sir, see ECTOR.

Heep, Uriah, a character in Dickens's *David Copperfield*.

HEGEL, Georg Wilhelm Friedrich (1770–1831), German philosopher.

Hegel's central idea is the dialectic of thesis–antithesis–synthesis, which he applied to the problem of historical evolution as represented by the *Weltgeist* or World Spirit. His dialectical method was adopted by political thinkers of both right and left, those who supported authoritarian rule in Prussia in the 19th cent. and those, like *Feuerbach, *Marx, and *Engels, who advocated reform and revolution. As Engels said, his doctrine was large enough to give shelter to the ideas of the most varied groups. Hegel enjoyed a vogue in philosophical circles in England, particularly at Oxford, in the 1880s and 1890s.

Heidelberg, Mrs, a character in Colman and Garrick's *The Clandestine Marriage*. Her illiteracy and mispronunciations foreshadow Mrs *Malaprop.

Heimskringla, a series of short sagas making up a history of the kings of Norway from mythical times to the year 1177, written by *Snorri Sturluson. It has a bearing on English history, covering as it does the reign of the Danish king *Canute (Knútr) and describing Viking expeditions to England.

Heir-at-Law, The, a comedy by G. *Colman the younger.

Heiress, The, a comedy by *Burgoyne.

Heir of Redclyffe, The, a novel by C. M. *Yonge, published 1853.

Guy Morville, the heir of a baronetcy and an ancient house, is hot-tempered but generous. His priggish cousin Philip, by passing on ill-founded suspicions about Guy, at first succeeds in thwarting Guy's marriage to his guardian's daughter Amy. Guy's character is eventually vindicated and he marries Amy. On their honeymoon they find Philip severely ill with fever; Guy nurses him through the fever, catches it himself, and dies, whereby the now repentant Philip inherits Redclyffe.

He Knew He Was Right, a novel by A. *Trollope, published 1869.

Helena, (1) the taller of the two young heroines in Shakespeare's *A Midsummer Night's Dream*; (2) the heroine of his *All's Well that Ends Well*; (3) Helen of Troy in Goethe's *Faust*.

Helen of Kirkconnell, the subject of an old ballad (included in Sir W. Scott's *Minstrelsy of the Scottish Border* and F. T. *Palgrave's *Golden Treasury*), who dies to save her lover. The story is the subject of *Wordsworth's 'Ellen Irwin'.

Heliand, The, an Old Saxon paraphrase in alliterative verse of the NT, dating from the 9th cent.

HELIODORUS, see AETHIOPICA.

Hellas, a lyrical drama by P. B. *Shelley published 1822. Based in form on the *Persians* of *Aeschylus, it was inspired by news of the Greek War of Independence against the Turkish empire, and dedicated to their national leader, Prince Mavrocordato, whom Shelley had known as Pisa.

The action, 'a series of lyric pictures', is set at Constantinople, where the Turkish Sultan Mahmud receives a number of messengers reporting the insurrection, and prophesying Greek victory. Shelley uses visionary figures —Christ, Mahomet, Ahasuerus the Wandering Jew, and the phantom of Mahomet II—to explore a cyclical philosophy of history. But the main interest lies in the choruses, composed like songs for opera, and concluding with the celebrated poem, 'The world's great age begins anew'. Shelley's Preface, his last great appeal for political liberty in Europe, remains a classic statement of English philhellenism: 'We are all Greeks.'

Hellenistic, a term that has come to replace during the present century the earlier adjective 'Alexandrian', applied to the civilization, language, art, and literature of the Graecized lands of the eastern Mediterranean from the death of *Alexander (323 BC) to that of Cleopatra (31 BC). Hellenistic literature displayed a mandarin artificiality full of recondite, learned allusions and a lively, realistic interest in everyday life. Its treatment of the gods of Greece showed at times genuine religious feeling, but was often playful and mocking, marked by a preoccupation with the excitements of sex that bordered on the pornographic. The Hellenistic tradition had a marked influence on the Latin poets of the late Republic and the *Augustan age and so exercised a far-reaching, if indirect, influence.

Hellenore, in Spenser's *Faerie Queene* (III. x), the wife of *Malbecco, who elopes with *Paridell.

HELLER, Joseph (1923–   ), novelist born in New York, served as a bombardier in the air force during the Second World War, an experience which resurfaced in his first novel, *Catch-22 (1961), which brought him instant fame. His second novel, *Something Happened* (1974), is the domestic tragi-comedy of a middle-aged New York executive, and *Good as Gold* (1979) a surreal and comic satire about Jewish New York and Washington politics.

Hell-fire Clubs, associations of reckless and profligate young ruffians who were a nuisance to London chiefly in the early 18th cent. There was a later and more famous Hell-fire Club, founded about 1745, at *Medmenham Abbey.

Héloïse, or Eloisa, see ABELARD.

HEMANS, Mrs Felicia Dorothea, *née* Browne (1793–1835), poet, published her first volume of *Poems* when she was 15. *Domestic Affections* appeared in 1812 and *Translations from Camoens and other Poets* in 1818. Her works were very popular, especially in America. The most famous of her poems, 'Casabianca', beginning 'The boy stood on the burning deck', appeared in *The Forest Sanctuary* (1829).

HEMING, or **HEMINGES,** John (1556–1630), and CONDELL, Henry (d. 1627), were fellow actors of Shakespeare and joint editors of the First *Folio of his plays (1623). Heming is said to have been the first player of *Falstaff.

HEMINGWAY, Ernest Miller (1899–1961), American short story writer and novelist. He worked as a reporter and served in 1918 as a volunteer with an ambulance unit on the Italian front, before settling in Paris among the American expatriate literary group, where he met *Pound, G. *Stein, F. M. *Ford, and others described in his posthumously published *A Moveable Feast* (1964). He made his name with *The Sun Also Rises* (1926; in England, as *Fiesta*, 1927), a novel which catches the post-war mood of disillusion of the so-called 'lost generation'. *A Farewell to Arms* (1929), the story of a love affair

between an American lieutenant and an English nurse during the war on the Italian front, confirmed his position as one of the most influential writers of the time. His collections of short stories *Men without Women* (1927) and *Winner Take Nothing* (1933) are especially notable. His growing dissatisfaction with contemporary culture was shown by his deliberate cultivation of the brutal and the primitive; he celebrated bullfighting in *Death in the Afternoon* (1932) and big-game hunting in *The Green Hills of Africa* (1935). He actively supported the Republicans during the Spanish Civil War, and *For Whom the Bell Tolls* (1940) is set against its background. In his later years he lived mostly in Cuba, where his passion for deep-sea fishing provided the setting for *The Old Man and the Sea* (1952). He was awarded the *Nobel Prize in 1954.

Hemlock and After, a novel by Sir A. *Wilson.

Henchard, Michael, the mayor in Hardy's *The Mayor of Casterbridge*.

Hendecasyllabic, a verse line of eleven syllables (– – – ◡◡ – ◡ – ◡ – –), used by *Catullus and imitated by *Tennyson:

> O you chorus of indolent reviewers.

(See METRE.)

Hendiadys, from the Greek words meaning 'one by means of two', a figure of speech by which a single complex idea is expressed by two words joined by a conjunction, e.g. 'Such as sit in darkness and in the shadow of death, being fast bound in misery and iron' (Ps. 107: 10).

HENGIST and **HORSA,** the traditional leaders of the Jutes who, according to *Bede (*Ecclesiastical History*), landed at Ebbsfleet in 449 and were given by *Vortigern the Isle of Thanet for a dwelling-place.

HENLEY, John (1692–1756), an eccentric preacher, generally known as 'Orator' Henley, who published works on oratory, theology, and grammar. He was caricatured by *Hogarth and ridiculed by *Pope.

HENLEY, W(illiam) E(rnest) (1849–1903), a pupil of T. E. *Brown, suffered from boyhood from tubercular arthritis and had a foot amputated. His 'Hospital Sketches', poems first published in the *Cornhill in 1875, record this grim ordeal; his best-known poem, the defiant and stoic 'Invictus' ('Out of the night that covers me') was written in 1875. While in hospital he was introduced by L. *Stephen to R. L. *Stevenson, who became a close friend and with whom he collaborated in several plays. He did a great deal of miscellaneous literary work, much of it as editor of the *Magazine of Art* (1881–6), *The Scots Observer*, continued as the *National Observer*

(1888–94), and the *New Review (1895–8); he was a courageous and independent editor, publishing important work by *Hardy, *Kipling, Stevenson, *Yeats, H. *James, and H. G. *Wells, among many others. He also compiled anthologies, and edited *Slang and its Analogues* (7 vols, 1890–1904). He had considerable influence on his contemporaries, particularly in his defence of realism and activism. His volumes of poetry include *A Book of Verses* (1888), *The Song of the Sword and other verses* (1892), *London Voluntaries* (1893), and *For England's Sake* (1900), some of which, notably the last, expound his jingoistic patriotism. Stevenson acknowledged him as the inspiration behind the creation of Long John Silver in *Treasure Island*.

HENRI, Adrian Maurice (1932–), poet and painter, settled in Liverpool in 1957, and during the 1960s was known (with Roger McGough and Brian Patten) as one of the *'Liverpool Poets'. His collections of poetry include *Tonight at Noon* (1968), *City* (1969), and *From the Loveless Motel* (1980).

Henrietta Temple: *a Love Story,* a novel by B. *Disraeli, published 1837. The novel was begun in 1834, during Disraeli's open love affair with Lady Henrietta Sykes.

HENRY II, king of England 1154–89. His literary occurrences tend to be related to his order (traditionally regarded as misinterpreted) to kill *Becket.

Henry IV, King, Parts *1* and *2*, historical plays by *Shakespeare, written and performed about 1597. Part 1 was printed in quarto 1598, Part 2 1600. The chief sources are the chronicles of *Hall and *Holinshed, and *Daniel's historical poem *The Civil Wars*.

The subject of Pt 1 is the rebellion of the Percys, assisted by Douglas and in concert with Mortimer and Glendower; and its defeat by the king and Prince Hal, the prince of Wales, at Shrewsbury (1403). *Falstaff first appears in this play. The prince of Wales associates with him and his boon companions, Poins, Bardolph, and Peto, in their riotous life. Poins and the prince contrive that the others shall set on some travellers at Gadshill and rob them, and be robbed in their turn by themselves. The plot succeeds, and leads to Falstaff's well-known fabrication to explain the loss of the booty, and his exposure. At the battle of Shrewsbury, Prince Hal kills *Hotspur in a heroic single combat, and then discovers Falstaff feigning death, whom he mourns with the words, 'I could have better spar'd a better man.'

Pt 2 deals with the rebellion of Archbishop Scroop, Mowbray, and Hastings; while in the comic under-plot the story of Falstaff's doings is continued, with those of the prince, *Pistol,

Poins, Mistress *Quickly, and Doll Tearsheet. Falstaff, summoned to the army for the repression of the rebellion, falls in with Justices Shallow and Silence in the course of his recruiting, makes a butt of them, and extracts £1,000 from the former. Henry IV dies, reconciled to his son, and Falstaff hastens from Gloucestershire to London to greet the newly crowned king, who rejects him in the speech beginning 'I know thee not, old man. Fall to thy prayers', banishing him from his presence but allowing him 'competence of life'.

Henry V, King, a historical drama by *Shakespeare, written in 1599, printed in 1600 from a memorial reconstruction; the First *Folio text (1623) is based on Shakespeare's own papers. Its chief sources are the chronicles of *Hall and *Holinshed.

The play opens with the newly ascended Henry astonishing clergy and courtiers by his piety and statecraft (cf. Prince *Hal). The archbishop of Canterbury demonstrates, in the long 'Salic Law' speech, Henry's claim to the throne of France, and the Dauphin's jesting gift of tennis balls gives him an immediate pretext for invasion. Henry unmasks the three traitors, Scrope, Grey, and Cambridge, and sets out for France; he besieges and captures Harfleur, and achieves a resounding victory at Agincourt (1415), a battle for which he prepares his soldiers in the 'Crispin Crispian' speech. Comic relief is provided by the old tavern companions of *Falstaff, who have fallen on hard times, and by some of Henry's soldiers, especially the pedantic but courageous Welsh captain Fluellen. The new, patriotic, comic characters symbolically defeat the old when Fluellen compels the braggart Pistol to eat a leek (v. i). The last act is given to Henry's wooing of Katherine of France.

Henry VI, King, Parts *1, 2,* and *3,* sections of a historical tetralogy (completed by *Richard III*) by *Shakespeare written between 1590 and 1592. Part 1 was first published in the First *Folio (1623), but Part 2 was published anonymously in 1594 under the title 'The First part of the Contention betwixt the two famous Houses of Yorke and Lancaster . . .', and Part 3 in 1595 as 'The true Tragedie of Richard Duke of Yorke, and the death of good King Henrie the Sixt'. Shakespeare's authorship of the play was doubted throughout the 18th and 19th cents. In the 20th cent. scholars have made increasingly confident claims for his sole authorship. Reference to 'an upstart Crow' in *Greenes Groats-Worth of Witte* used to be taken as evidence of plagiarism, but is now generally read as merely the malice of a rival dramatist. The plays' chief sources are the chronicles of *Hall and *Holinshed.

Pt 1, opening with the funeral of Henry V, deals with wars in France in which the gallant Talbot is a powerful leader on the English side, and the witch-like *Joan of Arc, 'La Pucelle', on the French. After a series of encounters Talbot, together with his valiant son John Talbot, are killed near Bordeaux (IV. vii). A crucial scene (II. iv) is that in the Temple garden, in which the plucking of red and white roses establishes the opposition of Plantagenet and York in the subsequent wars. In the fifth act the earl of Suffolk arranges a marriage between the young Henry VI and *Margaret of Anjou, daughter of the king of Naples, vowing ominously to rule both king, queen, and kingdom.

Pt 2 presents the marriage of Henry to Margaret of Anjou, the intrigues of the Yorkist faction, and other chief historical events, including Jack Cade's rebellion. The final act concerns the battle of St Albans (1455), in which Somerset is killed, a victory for the Yorkists.

Pt 3 opens with Henry's attempt to buy peace by making the duke of York his heir, thus disinheriting his son by Margaret. She, enraged and eloquent, instigates the murder of the boy Rutland, York's youngest son, by Clifford, and the mock-coronation and murder of York himself. Clifford is killed at the battle of Towton. Henry VI is captured and Edward (IV) declared king; he marries the dowerless widow Elizabeth Grey, though previously promised to Bona, the French king's sister. Richard, duke of Gloucester (later Richard III), emerges as an ambitious *Machiavelli. Warwick, a powerful contriver on the Lancastrian side, is killed at Barnet by King Edward; the battle of Tewkesbury is a decisive victory for Edward, and Margaret's young son (also an Edward) is killed in cold blood by Edward, Richard, duke of Gloucester, and George, duke of Clarence. King Henry, imprisoned in the Tower, is murdered by Richard.

HENRY VIII (1491–1547), king of England, from 1509. His life was written by Lord *Herbert of Cherbury. His book *A defence of the Seven Sacraments*, directed against *Luther's teaching, was printed in 1521 and presented to Leo X, who thereupon conferred on Henry the title 'Defender of the Faith'. Henry was also an accomplished musician and poet. His lyrics deal with courtly and chivalric themes, with one known exception, the sacred composition 'Quam pulcra es'. Henry's private life became the subject of many dramas and he remains legendary on account of his six wives, who were, successively, Catherine of Aragon (m. 1509), Anne Boleyn, mother of *Elizabeth I (m. 1533), Jane Seymour (m. 1536), Anne of Cleves (m. 1539), Catherine Howard (m. 1540), and Catherine Parr (m. 1543).

Henry VIII, a historical drama. Shakespeare has been claimed as its sole author, but it is usually held that he was responsible for less than half of the play, the remainder being written by J.

*Fletcher. Its performance in June 1613 resulted in the burning down of the *Globe Theatre.

It deals with the fall and execution of the duke of Buckingham; the question of the royal divorce (vividly depicting the dignity and resignation of Queen Catherine); the pride and fall of Cardinal Wolsey and his death; the advancement and coronation of Anne Boleyn; the triumph of Cranmer over his enemies; and the christening of the Princess Elizabeth.

The chief sources of the play are *Holinshed's *Chronicles* and Foxe's *Actes and Monuments* (or *Book of Martyrs*).

HENRY, O., pseudonym of William Sydney Porter (1862–1910), American short story writer. He had a chequered early career, which included a term in prison for embezzlement (1896). He began to write short stories in prison, and published the first of his many collections, *Cabbages and Kings,* in 1904.

HENRY OF HUNTINGDON (?1084–1155), archdeacon of Huntingdon, compiled a *Historia Anglorum,* which in its latest form extends to 1154.

HENRYSON, Robert (?1424–?1506), a Scottish poet of the school known until recently as 'Scottish *Chaucerians'. His most important poems are *The Testament of Cresseid,* written as a moralizing but sympathetic sequel to Chaucer's *Troilus and Criseyde* and printed with editions of Chaucer as its Book VI until the 18th cent., *Robene and Makyne,* a pastoral, and his *Morall Fabillis of Esope.* Henryson's distinctive virtue is the combination of stern morality with humane sympathy.

HENRY THE MINSTREL, or **BLIND HARRY** or **HARY** (?1440–?92), a half-legendary Scottish poet, who wrote *The Wallace,* one of the most famous of all *Scots poems, of about 12,000 lines in heroic couplets, which concerns the martial feats of Wallace, who was executed by the English in 1305. The earliest text is a manuscript written in 1488 by John Ramsay, the scribe of *Barbour's *The Bruce.* A popular version of the poem was a rewriting in 1722 by William Hamilton of Gilbertfield.

HENSLOWE, Philip (d. *c.* 1616), built the Rose Theatre on Bankside in 1587, and thereafter was involved in theatrical affairs (as financier, manager, and owner) and, with *Alleyn, in the affairs of several important companies of actors, notably the Lord Admiral's Men, and in the building of the Fortune and Hope theatres. Most of the dramatists of the period, apart from Shakespeare, at some time wrote for his companies. His *Diary* (ed. R. A. Foakes and R. T. Rickert, 1961) contains a mass of information about theatrical life, and about dramatists and their methods of writing plays.

HENTY, G(eorge) A(lfred) (1832–1902), was war correspondent in the Crimea, Italy, Abyssinia, Ashanti, Spain, India, and in Paris during the Commune. He wrote some dozen novels for adults, including *Colonel Thorndyke's Secret* (1898), but was very successful as the author of stories for boys, mainly based on military history. Among the best-remembered are *Out in the Pampas* (1868), *The Young Buglers* (1880), *Under Drake's Flag* (1883), *With Clive in India* (1884), and *The Lion of St Mark's* (1889).

Heorot, see BEOWULF.

Heptameron, The, a collection of tales of love, composed by Marguerite, sister of Francis I and queen of Navarre (1492–1549). Only 72 of the intended 100 tales were completed. The name 'Heptameron', 'seven days', was first given to the collection in 1559, on the analogy of Boccaccio's *Decameron*.

HERACLITUS of Ephesus (*fl. c.*500 BC), a philosopher who maintained that all things are in a state of flux. F. *Bacon calls him 'the profound', but more generally he was called 'the weeping philosopher' because of his conviction that nothing lasts.

HERBERT, A(lan) P(atrick) (1890–1971), a writer of great versatility and humour, contributed to *Punch* for many years. His works include *The Secret Battle* (1919), *Misleading Cases in the Common Law* (1929), *A Book of Ballads* (1949), and *Independent Member* (1950), describing his experiences as MP for Oxford University (1935–50). Herbert campaigned for several causes, including the improving of authors' rights and changes in the obscenity laws. He was knighted in 1945. His autobiography, *My Life and Times*, appeared in 1970.

HERBERT, George (1593–1633), younger brother of Lord *Herbert of Cherbury, published his first poems (two sets of memorial verses in Latin) in a volume mourning prince Henry's death in 1612. But he had already, according to his earliest biographer, I. *Walton, sent his mother, in 1610, a New Year's letter dedicating his poetic powers to God and enclosing two sonnets. In 1616 he was elected a major fellow of Trinity, and in 1618 appointed reader in rhetoric. He was public orator at Cambridge from 1620 to 1628. He was ordained deacon, probably in 1624, and installed in 1626 as a canon of Lincoln cathedral and prebendary of Leighton Bromswold in Huntingdonshire, near *Little Gidding, where *Ferrar, whom Herbert had known at Cambridge, had established a religious community. Herbert set about restoring the ruined church at Leighton. His mother, whom he greatly loved, died in 1627, and his *Memoriae matris sacrum* was published in the volume containing *Donne's commemoration sermon. He became rector of Bemerton, near Salisbury, in April 1630, being ordained priest the following September. He died of consumption. Shortly before his death he consigned his poems to Ferrar, to publish or to burn as he saw fit. *The Temple*, containing nearly all his surviving English poems, was published in 1633, and Herbert's prose picture of the model country parson, *A Priest to the Temple*, in 1652, as part of *Herbert's Remains*. He told Ferrar that his poems represented 'a picture of the many spiritual conflicts that have passed betwixt God and my soul, before I could subject mine to the will of Jesus my Master'. Their simple piety was much admired in the 17th cent. but in the 18th cent. Herbert went out of fashion, though J. *Wesley adapted some of his poems. The Romantic age saw a revival, and the appreciative notice in Coleridge's *Biographia Literaria* (1817) enhanced Herbert's reputation. Modern critics have noted the subtlety rather than the simplicity of his poems, seeing them as an attempt to express the ultimately ineffable complications of the spiritual life. (See also METAPHYSICAL POETS.)

HERBERT, Mary, see PEMBROKE.

HERBERT of Cherbury, Edward, Lord (1582–1648), elder brother of G. *Herbert, was created knight of the Bath in 1603. His adventures, from birth to 1624, are recounted by Herbert in his *Life*, a remarkable document, not least for its unabashed presentation of its author's martial valour, success with women, truthfulness, sweetness of breath, and other virtues. Herbert aspired to a career in public service and spent much of the time from 1608 to 1618 in France, getting to know the French aristocracy and court. He also travelled in Italy and the Low Countries, fighting at the siege of Juliers (1610).

He was from 1619 to 1624 ambassador to France, on *Buckingham's recommendation. There he completed his most famous philosophical work, *De Veritate* (1624), which postulates that religion is common to all men and that, stripped of superfluous priestly accretions, it can be reduced to five universal innate ideas: that there is a God; that he should be worshipped; that virtue and piety are essential to worship; that man should repent of his sins; and that there are rewards and punishments after this life. *De Veritate* gained Herbert the title of father of English *Deism. He joined Charles's council of war in 1629, and became Baron Herbert of Cherbury. In 1632 he began a detailed 'official' history of *Henry VIII's reign, assisted by Thomas Masters, published 1649. From 1644 Herbert dedicated himself to the study of philosophy, supplementing his *De Veritate* with *De Causis Errorum* and *De Religione Laici*, both published in 1645, and writing besides *De Reli-

gione Gentilum and his autobiography (begun in 1643). In 1647 he visited Gassendi in Paris. When archbishop *Ussher offered him the last sacrament Herbert replied, according to *Aubrey, 'If it did no good 'twould doe no hurt', whereupon Ussher refused it. Herbert also wrote poetry which is obscure and metrically contorted, evidently influenced by his friend *Donne. (See also METAPHYSICAL POETS.)

HERDER, Johann Gottfried (1744–1803), German philosopher and critic, who decisively influenced *Goethe during the latter's *Sturm and Drang* period. He was an ardent collector of folksong, and also an admirer of *Macpherson's 'Ossian'.

HEREWARD THE WAKE (*fl.* 1070), a Lincolnshire outlaw, a legendary account of whose exploits is given by the 15th-cent. forger who calls himself Ingulf of Croyland in his *Gesta Herewardi*. He headed a rising of the English, aided by a Danish fleet, against William the Conqueror in 1070. He is said to have been pardoned by William and (according to *Gaimar) killed by Normans at Maine. C. *Kingsley tells a legendary version of the story of Hereward and his wife Torfrida (1866). His mare was Swallow.

Hergest, Red Book of, see MABINOGION.

Hermes Trismegistus, the 'thrice great Hermes' of Milton's *'Il Penseroso', the name given by the *Neoplatonists and the devotees of mysticism and alchemy to the Egyptian god Thoth. From the 3rd cent. onwards the name was applied to the author of various Neoplatonic writings, some of which have survived, notably the Ποιμάνδρης, a word of uncertain derivation used to signify the Divine Intelligence. This work made a notable impact on 16th- and 17th-cent. minds, but its influence cannot be isolated from the general one exercised by the Neoplatonist, cabbalistic, and occultist tradition which had such a marked effect on writers like G. *Chapman, H. *Vaughan, Sir T. *Browne, *Comenius, and the *Cambridge Platonists.

Hermia, the smaller of the two young heroines in Shakespeare's *A Midsummer Night's Dream*

Hermione, (1) daughter of Menelaus and Helen, the wife first of Neoptolemus, then of Orestes; (2) in Shakespeare's *The Winter's Tale*, the wife of Leontes.

'Hermit, The, or Edwin and Angelina', a ballad by *Goldsmith, written 1764 and included in *The Vicar of Wakefield*. (See BALLAD.)
'The Hermit' is also the title of a poem by T. *Parnell.

Hermit of Hampole, see ROLLE, R.

Hermsprong, or Man as He is not, a novel by R. *Bage (1796).

Herne the Hunter, a spectral hunter said to have been in medieval times a keeper in Windsor Forest, who hanged himself from the tree known as Herne's (or, later, Falstaff's) oak. The story bears some resemblance to the tale of the *Wild Huntsman, and a version of it is related by Mrs Page in *The Merry Wives of Windsor* (IV. iv). Herne also appears in *Ainsworth's historical romance *Windsor Castle* (1843).

Hero, the beloved of Claudio in Shakespeare's *Much Ado about Nothing*.

Hero and Leander, in the tragic story of Leander's love for Hero, the priestess of Aphrodite: he is drowned while swimming to her at night across the Hellespont, and she then in despair throws herself into the sea. This story has been made the subject of poems by *Marlowe and T. *Hood, and of a burlesque by T. *Nashe in his *Lenten Stuffe*.

HERODOTUS (*c.*480–*c.*425 BC), a Greek historian, often known as the 'father of history' since he was the first to collect his materials systematically, test their accuracy as far as he was able, and arrange them agreeably. His work, the first masterpiece of Greek prose, takes as its main theme the struggle between Asia and Europe which culminated in the Persian invasions of Greece. His 'fabulosities', as Sir T. *Browne called them, provided material for miscellanists like *Painter (1567–8), *Landor, *Beddoes in *Death's Jest Book*, and for M. *Arnold's 'Mycerinus' (1849).

Heroes, Hero-worship and the Heroic in History, On, a course of six lectures by T. *Carlyle, delivered 1840, published 1841. In this series Carlyle elaborates his view that 'Universal History, the history of what man has accomplished in this world, is at bottom the History of . . . Great Men', and chooses for his examples The Hero as Divinity (e.g. Odin, the 'Type Norseman'); The Hero as Prophet (e.g. Muhammad); The Hero of Poet (e.g. *Dante, Shakespeare); The Hero as Priest (e.g. *Luther, *Knox); The Hero as Man of Letters (e.g. Dr *Johnson, *Rousseau, *Burns); and The Hero as King (e.g. *Cromwell, Napoleon).

Heroic Couplet, a pair of rhymed lines of iambic pentameter. The form was introduced into English by *Chaucer, and widely used subsequently, reaching a height of popularity and sophistication in the works of *Dryden and *Pope.

Heroic drama, a term applied to the tragedies of the Restoration period. They were usually written in rhymed heroic couplets, but this was not essential to the concept: Dryden's *All for Love* and Otway's *Venice Preserv'd* are examples of blank verse tragedies which preserved nearly all the ingredients of the 'heroic play'.

The essentials of this type of play were that it should present in dramatic form all the qualities of the heroic poem or epic. 'The work of an heroic poem', wrote *Hobbes, 'is to raise admiration, principally for three virtues, valour, beauty, and love.' The characters were exaggerated and spoke habitually in terms of bombast and rant; plays were produced—following *D'Avenant's lead—with a lavish regard to spectacle and splendour; the plots were simple but involved usually the actions of kings and queens, a background of war, love, and jealousy, and more often than not, after certain preliminary slaughter, a happy ending for the hero and heroine. In this last respect the plays were not strictly tragedies: the Restoration audience on the whole preferred to avoid the spectacle of ultimate disaster; Elizabethan tragedies were often emended to give them a happy ending, e.g. Waller's version of Beaumont and Fletcher's *The Maid's Tragedy*.

The heroic drama was parodied, notably in *The Rehearsal* and later in Fielding's *Tom Thumb*.

Heroic Poetry, the same as *Epic.

Heroic Verse, that used in *epic poetry: in Greek and Latin poetry, the hexameter; in English, the iambic of five feet or ten syllables; in French, the alexandrine of twelve syllables.

HERRICK, Robert (1591–1674), seventh child of Nicholas Herrick, a prosperous goldsmith. Herrick's earliest datable poem was written about 1610 to his brother Thomas on his leaving London to farm in Leicestershire ('A Country Life: To his Brother M. Tho. Herrick'). 'To my dearest Sister M. Mercie Herrick' must also have been written before 1612.

In 1613 he entered St John's College, Cambridge, as a fellow commoner, and later moved to Trinity Hall. College friends included Clipsby Crew, to whom he addressed the outstanding 'Nuptiall Song'. In 1623 he was ordained priest. He evidently mixed with literary circles in London, particularly the group around *Jonson, and by 1625 he was well known as a poet. In 1627 he was one of the army chaplains on the duke of *Buckingham's disastrous expedition to the Isle of Rhé. In reward for his services he received in 1630 the living of Dean Prior in Devon.

Repelled by the barren isolation of rural life at first, he developed, as his poems show, a feeling for folk customs and festivals like May Day and Harvest Home. He left Dean Prior for a period without permission from his bishop, and lived in Westminster with Tomasin Parsons, 27 years younger than Herrick. An ardent loyalist, Herrick was ejected from his living by Parliament in

1647 and returned to London, where the following year his poems *Hesperides*, together with his religious poems *Noble Numbers*, were published. In 1660 he was reinstated at Dean Prior where he remained until his death. As late as 1810 villagers there could repeat some of his verses.

Herrick's secular poems are mostly exercises in miniature, very highly polished and employing meticulous displacements of syntax and word order so as to give diminutive aesthetic grace to the great chaotic subjects—sex, transience, death—that obsess him. He is one of the finest English lyric poets, and has a faultless ear. *Swinburne called him 'the greatest song-writer ever born of English race'.

HERVEY, James (1714–58), was prominent in the early Methodist movements. His prose poems *Meditations among the Tombs, Reflections on a Flower Garden*, etc. (1746–7) bear some affinity to the works of the *Graveyard school.

HERVEY, John, Baron Hervey of Ickworth (1696–1743), as vice-chamberlain exercised great influence over Queen Caroline. He was a close friend of Lady M. W. *Montagu. He was satirized by *Pope in various works from 1732 onwards, at first with mildness, as 'Lord Fanny', an idle versifier, and then with increasing bitterness in *The Dunciad* and as *'Sporus' in the *Epistle to Dr Arbuthnot* ('this painted child of dirt, that stinks and stinks'). His *Memoirs of the Reign of George II* (first pub. 1848) gave a vivid satirical picture of the court.

HERZEN, Alexander Ivanovich (1812–70), leading Russian revolutionary thinker, who settled in London in 1852, where he established the first Free Russian Press (1853) and wrote various works which, smuggled into Russia, were a major influence on Radical opinion there.

HESIOD (8th cent. BC), an early Greek epic poet, the reputed author of two important poems. The *Theogony* contains an account of the origins of the world and the genealogy of the gods. *Works and Days* gives an account of a farmer's life that was to serve *Virgil for a model in the *Georgics*. Both *Spenser and *Milton made use of Hesiod.

Hesperides, see HERRICK, R.

Hetty Sorrel, a character in G. Eliot's *Adam Bede*.

HEWLETT, Maurice Henry (1861–1923), novelist, poet, and essayist, became known for his romantic novel of the Middle Ages, *The Forest Lovers* (1898), which was followed by other historical novels and various volumes of poetry including *The Song of the Plow* (1916), a long poem which recounts the history of the 'governed race' in England and particularly of Hodge, the agricultural labourer, from the Norman conquest.

Hexameter, a verse of six metrical feet, which in the typical form consists of five dactyls and a trochee or spondee; for any of the dactyls a spondee may be substituted, except in the fifth foot, where a spondee is rare. It is not frequently used in English, but has sometimes been employed, as in *Clough's *The Bothie of Tober-na-Vuolich*, to considerable effect. (See METRE.)

HEYER, Georgette (1902–74), writer of detective stories and *historical novels; she was best known for her Regency romances.

Hey for Honesty, Down with Knavery, a comedy by T. *Randolph, printed 1651. The play is a free adaptation of *Aristophanes' *Plutus*, and contains interesting allusions to current events and recent plays, including mentions of *Falstaff, *Hamlet's ghost, and Shakespeare himself.

HEYWOOD, John (?1497–?1580), married Elizabeth Rastell, niece of Sir T. *More. Under Henry VIII he was a singer and player on the virginals. He was much favoured by Queen Mary. He published *interludes, substituting the human comedy of contemporary types for the allegory and instructive purpose of the *morality; but he did this in the form of narrative and debate rather than of plot and action. His principal works were *The Four P's* (?1545); *The Play of the Wether* (1533); and *A Play of Love* (1533). He may also have been the author of *The Pardoner and the Frere* and *Johan Johan the husbande, Tyb his wyfe & syr Jhān the preest*, comedies of a wider scope. Heywood also wrote a dialogue called *Witty and Witless*, collections of proverbs and epigrams, and a long satirical poem, *The Spider and the Flie* (1556).

HEYWOOD, Thomas (?1574–1641), was writing for *Henslowe's Admiral's Men in 1596, and later became a leading dramatist of Queen Anne's and Lady Elizabeth's Men. He claimed to have written over 200 plays, many of which are lost; his chief strength lay in domestic drama. His best plays are *A Woman Killed with Kindness* (acted 1603, printed 1607), *The Fair Maid of the West* (printed 1631), and *The English Traveller* (printed 1633). His *An Apology for Actors* (1612) is the best Jacobean summary of traditional arguments in defence of the stage. He also published poems (including *The Hierarchy of the Blessed Angels*, 1635), translations, and pageants for seven Lord Mayor's shows.

Hiawatha, The Song of, a narrative poem in unrhymed trochaic tetrameter, by *Longfellow, published 1855, reproducing American Indian stories which centre in the life and death of Hiawatha. He marries Minnehaha ('laughing water'), the Dacotah maiden, and after various adventures departs for the Isles of the Blest to rule the kingdom of the North-west Wind. Longfellow took nothing but the name from the historical figure of Hiawatha (*fl. c.*1570), an Indian statesman, probably a Mohawk.

Hibernia, one of the Latin names for Ireland.

HICKES, George (1642–1715), was the acknowledged leader of the first great generation of Anglo-Saxon scholars which included the *Elstobs and *Wanley. The climax of his work was the *Linguarum Veterum Septentrionalium Thesaurus* (1703–5), a comparative grammar of Old English and the related Germanic tongues. Its examination of the manuscript sources of Anglo-Saxon history had a deep influence upon the study of the whole Old English past.

HICKEY, William (?1749–1830), author of entertaining *Memoirs*, 1749–1809 (first pub. 1913–25), in which he describes his numerous voyages, his chequered career as an attorney, and his weakness for women and claret.

Hieronimo, the principal character in Kyd's *The Spanish Tragedy*.

HIERONYMUS, see JEROME, ST.

Higden, Mrs Betty, a character in Dickens's *Our Mutual Friend*.

HIGDEN, Ranulf (d. 1364), a Benedictine of St Werburg's, Chester, credited by popular tradition with the composition of the Chester Cycle of *Mystery Plays. He wrote in Latin prose *Polychronicon*, a universal history extending down to 1327, which was translated by John of *Trevisa in 1387 and printed by *Caxton in 1482.

Higgins, Henry, the phonetician in Shaw's *Pygmalion*, modelled on H. *Sweet.

Highland Widow, The, a short, tragic tale by Sir W. *Scott, one of the stories in *The Chronicles of the Canongate*, published 1827.

High Life below Stairs, a comedy by the Revd J. *Townley, produced 1759.
  Lovel, a rich young West Indian merchant, receives warning that he is being outrageously robbed by his servants. He assumes the character of a country lad, and obtains employment under his own butler. The servants ape the vices and follies of their masters until, the iniquities of most of his staff having been revealed to him, Lovel reveals himself and packs them off.

HIGHSMITH, Patricia (1921–), writer, whose stylish crime novels have a distinctively black humour: the best-known (*The Talented Mr Ripley*, 1956; *Ripley Under Ground*, 1971; *Ripley's Game*, 1974, etc.) feature her amoral anti-hero, the leisure-loving amateur villain Tom Ripley.

Hildebrandslied, a 68-line fragment of an alliterative poem in Old High German, thought to date from about 800, consisting of a dialogue between Hildebrand, a follower of Theodoric, who is returning home after many years' absence, and a young knight who challenges him. The text is in Klaeber's *Beowulf* (App. 4, pp. 290–2).

HILL, Aaron (1685–1750), wrote the libretto for *Handel's *Rinaldo* (1711). He was satirized by Pope in *The Dunciad*, and responded in *The Progress of Wit* (1730). He was responsible for launching *The Plain Dealer* (1724), a bi-weekly. His *A Collection of letters between Mr Aaron Hill, Pope and Others* (1751) is an interesting record of the period.

HILL, (John Edward) Christopher (1912–), Marxist historian, master of Balliol College, Oxford (1965–78). His many works on the period of the Civil War include *The World Turned Upside Down; Radical Ideas during the English Revolution* (1972), which introduces the prose of many of the lesser-known and radical writers of the period. He also edited the works of *Winstanley, and has written studies of *Cromwell (*God's Englishman*, 1970) and *Milton (*Milton and the English Revolution*, 1977).

HILL, Geoffrey (1932–), poet. His first volume of poetry was *For the Unfallen* (1959), followed by *King Log* (1968), *Mercian Hymns* (1971), and *Tenebrae* (1978). His early works show the influence of *Blake and A. E. *Housman; his language is rich and complex, and his themes predominantly historical and religious. His long poem *The Mystery of the Charity of Charles Péguy* (1983) is a densely allusive meditation on the life, faith, and death of the French poet Péguy.

HILL, G(eorge) B(irkbeck Norman) (1835–1903) is chiefly remembered as the editor of Dr *Johnson. *Dr Johnson, his Friends and Critics* appeared in 1878. His six-vol. edition of Boswell's *Life of *Johnson* (1887) is generally regarded as a masterpiece of editing. He also edited the letters of Johnson and *Swift, wrote a memoir of *Gibbon, and produced editions of the works of *Goldsmith and *Chesterfield.

HILLIARD, Nicholas (*c.*1547–1619), miniaturist, patronized by *Elizabeth I and later by James I. He wrote an interesting treatise, the *Art of Limning* (1603), which records discussions with Sir P. *Sidney and Elizabeth I. He was eulogized by contemporary poets, including *Constable and *Donne.

HILTON, James (1900–54), novelist and Hollywood scriptwriter, remembered principally for *Lost Horizon* (1933), set in the Tibetan lamasery of Shangri-La where the inmates enjoy extended youth, and *Good-bye Mr Chips* (1934), a novella about an old schoolmaster.

HILTON, Walter (d. 1396), an Augustinian canon, the mystical author of *The Scale of Perfection* which is addressed to a single woman recluse. It is the most approachable and least esoteric of the celebrated 14th-cent. English mystical texts.

Hind and the Panther, The, a poem by *Dryden published 1687.

Dryden became a Catholic in 1685, and the poem represents an attempt to reconcile Anglican and Catholic political interests, while at the same time defending Catholic doctrine. The first part describes various religious sects under the guise of different beasts and in particular the Catholic Church and the Church of England as the Hind and the Panther respectively. The second part is occupied with arguments about Church authority and transubstantiation. The third part is designed to recommend a political alliance between both Churches and the Crown against Whigs and Dissenters. It contains two celebrated fables, that of the swallows and that of the doves.

HIPPOCRATES, (*c.*460–357 BC), the most celebrated physician of antiquity. Of the *Corpus Hippocraticum*, or collection of Greek medical works of various dates which have come down to us, only a small portion can be attributed to Hippocrates himself. It contains the ethical doctrine of the medical profession, the 'Hippocratic Oath'.

Hippolyta, a queen of the Amazons given in marriage to *Theseus by Hercules, who had conquered her and taken away her girdle, the achievement being one of his twelve labours. She had a son by Theseus called *Hippolytus. According to another version she was slain by Hercules, and it was his sister Antiope that was the wife of Theseus. She and Theseus frame the action in Shakespeare's *A Midsummer Night's Dream*.

Hippolytus, a son of *Theseus and *Hippolyta. The fatal passion of Phaedra for her stepson Hippolytus is the subject of one of *Racine's dramas, *Phèdre*.

Historia Britonum, see NENNIUS.

Historia Ecclesiastica Gentis Anglorum, the most famous work of *Bede, completed in 731. It is a Latin history of the English people, in five books, from the invasion of Julius Caesar, beginning with a description of Britain and ending with an account of the state of the country in 731. The author draws on *Pliny and other Latin authors, and on *Gildas and probably the *Historia Britonum* of *Nennius. It was translated into Old English in the 890s, in the course of the programme of translations inaugurated by *Alfred.

Historical Novel, a novel set in a period before the birth of the author, and often containing not only fictional but historical people and/or events. In England the form developed largely from La Fayette's *Princesse de Clèves* (1678) through the *Gothic novel to M. Edgeworth's *Castle Rackrent* (1800) and *Adelaide* (1806), and J. *Porter's *The Scottish Chiefs* (1810), culminating in Sir W. Scott's *Waverley* (1814). Scott established the form, so emphatically that its influence spread throughout Europe, and it continued to flourish for the rest of the century in England, in the works of *Thackeray, *Dickens, *Bulwer-Lytton, *Reade, *Kingsley, G. * Eliot, *Hardy, and many others. The attraction of the form has now greatly declined, except in the popular market, where G. *Heyer succeeded such writers as *Orczy, *Weyman, and *Hewlett; but the form has also been successfully used by writers as diverse as M. *Renault, N. *Mitchison, W. *Golding, and J. G. *Farrell.

Historic Doubts on ... Richard III, see WALPOLE, HORACE.

History of Henry Esmond, Esquire, The, a novel by *Thackeray, published 1852.

Henry Esmond, who narrates his own story, is the (supposed illegitimate) son of the third Viscount Castlewood, who dies at the battle of the Boyne. Henry comes under the protection of the fourth viscount, and his young wife Rachel. The couple have two children, Frank, the heir, and Beatrix. The Castlewoods become estranged after Lady Castlewood catches smallpox. The wicked Lord Mohun takes advantage of Castlewood's neglect of his wife to attempt to seduce her. There is a duel and Castlewood is killed. On his deathbed he reveals to Henry that he is in fact legitimate and the rightful heir, but Henry keeps silent for the sake of Lady Castlewood and her son. He is imprisoned for a year for having acted as Castlewood's second in the duel, for which Lady Castlewood bitterly reproaches him, and on his release joins the army and fights in the war of the Spanish Succession. On a visit to England he is reconciled to Lady Castlewood, who is secretly in love with him, and falls in love with Beatrix. But Beatrix is too ambitious to consider a man who has no fortune or position in society. Henry goes back to the wars and fights in Marlborough's Flemish campaign. The wayward Beatrix becomes engaged, first to Lord Ashburnham, then to the

much older duke of Hamilton, who fights a duel with Lord Mohun, in which both are killed. Beatrix and her brother Frank, now the fifth viscount, are ardent Jacobites, and Esmond becomes involved with them in a plot to restore James Edward Stuart, the Old Pretender, to the throne on the death of Queen Anne. The plot fails because Beatrix is carrying on an intrigue with the Pretender, and at the moment when he should be in London he is at Castlewood, 'dangling after Trix'. Esmond, disillusioned with Beatrix and the Jacobite cause, marries her mother Rachel and they emigrate to Virginia. The later history of the family in America and England is told in *The Virginians*.

History of the Decline and Fall of the Roman Empire, The, see DECLINE AND FALL OF THE ROMAN EMPIRE.

Histriomastix, see PRYNNE, W.

HOADLY, Benjamin (1676–1761), bishop successively of Bangor, Hereford, Salisbury, and Winchester, much in favour with the Whigs and Queen Caroline, whose famous sermon 'The Nature of the Kingdom or Church of Christ' (1717) initiated the Bangorian Controversy.

HOADLY, Dr Benjamin (1706–57), son of Bishop Hoadly (above). He was a physician and (with his brother) the author of one comedy, *The Suspicious Husband* (1747).

HOBBES, Thomas (1588–1679), philosopher, was for a great part of his life in the service of the Cavendish family, and in 1647 was appointed mathematical tutor to the prince of Wales. At some time he was in contact with F. *Bacon, translated some of his essays into Latin, and took down his thoughts from his dictation. On three occasions he travelled on the Continent with a pupil, and met *Galileo, Gassendi, *Descartes, and the French mathematician Mersenne. On his return to England he submitted to the Council of State in 1652, and was pensioned after the Restoration. He was intimate with G. *Harvey, *Jonson, *Cowley, and *Godolphin.

As a philosopher Hobbes resembles Bacon in the practical or utilitarian importance that he attaches to knowledge. Nature and man are the objects of his enquiry. Hobbes has been generally described as a nominalist. The basis of all knowledge, according to him, is sensation, and the causes of all sensations are the several motions of matter. Motion is the one universal cause, and our appetites are our reactions, in the direction of self-preservation, to external motions. Accordingly man is essentially a selfish unit. Upon this theory Hobbes bases the political philosophy expounded, most notably in *Leviathan*.

Hobbes's philosophical works, founded on a

comprehensive plan in which matter, human nature, and society were successively to be dealt with, include *Human Nature* (1650), *De Corpore* (Latin 1655, English 1656), and *De Homine* (1658). He published a translation of *Thucydides in 1629 and of *Homer in quatrains (1674–5); also a sketch of the Civil Wars, *Behemoth, or the Long Parliament* (1680), which was suppressed. His reply to *D'Avenant's dedication of *Gondibert* expresses his literary theory. His prose is masterly, distinguished by economy, directness, a highly effective use of metaphor, and passages of sustained and inventive irony. The aphorism which expresses a central tenet of his philosophy, that the life of man in a state of nature is 'solitary, poore, nasty, brutish and short', has had an incalculable influence on later writers.

Hobbinol, in *Spenser's writings, the poet's friend G. *Harvey.

Hobbit, The, see TOLKIEN, J. R. R.

HOBHOUSE, John Cam (1786–1869), a politician, and close friend of Lord *Byron, one of whose executors he became. His *Journey through Albania* (1813) describes the same journey that appears in Byron's *Childe Harold*. In 1818 he produced the 'Historical Illustrations' to Canto IV of that poem. In 1865 appeared his *Recollections of a Long Life*, which contains much material relating to Byron.

HOBSBAUM, Philip Dennis (1932–), poet and lecturer, was the founder of the *Group.

HOBSON, a Cambridge carrier, who died in Jan. 1630–1. *Milton wrote two epitaphs on him, and his name survives in the phrase 'Hobson's choice', which refers to his custom of letting out his horses in rotation, and not allowing his customers to choose among them. (See *Spectator*, No. 509.)

Hobson's Choice (1916), by Harold Brighouse (1882–1958), the most successful and often revived play of the *Manchester School.

HOBY, Sir Thomas (1530–66), made frequent visits to the Continent and his notebook covering the years 1547–64, with interesting accounts of Italy, was published by the *Camden Society (1902). He translated *Castiglione's *Il Cortegiano* (*The Courtyer*, 1561) which was an important influence on such writers as *Spenser, *Jonson, and Shakespeare.

HOCCLEVE, or **OCCLEVE,** Thomas (?1369–1426), apart from *Lydgate the most significant named English poet of the 15th cent. He was a clerk in the office of the Privy Seal. Most of his small corpus is taken up with moral

writings, but a significant part of his output describes the events of his own life, in 'La Male Regle de Thomas Hoccleve', the prologue to *The Regiment of Princes* (1411–12), and in a number of his 'Series Poems', such as 'The Complaint' and 'The Dialogue with a Friend'. Of his 'autobiographical' writings, the most interesting deal with his mental breakdown. Traditionally he has been regarded as a poor imitator of *Chaucer; more sympathetic recent accounts examine him in his own right and find him less wanting.

Hock-Tuesday Play, an early English mimetic performance, perhaps of ritual origin, representing the defeat of the Danes by the English. It was revived during the festival given to *Elizabeth I at Kenilworth in 1575. Hock Tuesday, or Hocktide, is the second Tuesday after Easter Sunday.

Hodge, a familiar adaptation of Roger, used as a typical name for the English rustic. Also the name of Dr *Johnson's cat.

HODGSON, Ralph Edwin (1871–1962), poet. His first collection of poems was *The Last Blackbird* (1907). He established his reputation with *Poems* (1917), a volume which contains one of his most ambitious visionary works, 'A Song of Honour'. Some of his work was published in *Georgian Poetry*. *The Skylark and Other Poems* (1958) contained, among many shorter works, two important long poems: 'To Deck a Woman', a passionate protest against man's cruelty to the animal world, and 'The Muse and the Mastiff'. The *Collected Poems* were published in 1961.

HOFF, Harry Summerfield, see COOPER, W.

HOGARTH, David George (1862–1927), archaeologist and authority on Near Eastern affairs. He was keeper of the Ashmolean Museum (1908–27). His publications include *A Wandering Scholar in the Levant* (1896) and *The Life of C. M. Doughty* (1928). One of his disciples at Oxford was T. E. *Lawrence, who came very much under his influence.

HOGARTH, William (1697–1764), British painter and engraver. In 1726 he designed 12 large engravings for Butler's *Hudibras*. In 1732 *The Harlot's Progress* introduced his 'modern moral subjects'; it was followed by *The Rake's Progress* (1733–5) and *Marriage à la Mode* (1743–5; London, National Gallery). This highly original genre consisted of a series of paintings, popularized through engravings, which tell a story that is topical, erotic, spiced with contemporary portraits, and yet comments with humanity and passion on social and political vices and corruption. Hogarth also published a work on aesthetics, *The Analysis of Beauty*

(1753). His series of engravings inspired numerous plays and novels. *Fielding, and later *Smollett, compared characters and scenes in their novels to the prints of Hogarth. His popularity soared in the early 19th cent., with essays by *Hazlitt and *Lamb that emphasized his literary qualities. He influenced *Thackeray and Dickens, who, in the preface to *Oliver Twist, writes that he had never met 'the miserable reality' of low-life London except in Hogarth. Hogarth's Portrait of the Painter and his Pug (1745, London, Tate Gallery) shows his aggressive image resting on volumes of Shakespeare, *Milton, and *Swift and lays claim to his place within a British artistic tradition.

Hogarth Press, The, was founded in 1917 by L. and V. *Woolf at their home, Hogarth House, Richmond, and their earliest publications included K. *Mansfield's Prelude (1918), V. Woolf's Kew Gardens (1919, illustrated with woodcuts by Vanessa Bell), and T. S. *Eliot's Poems (1919). Their policy was to publish new and experimental work; they also published translations of Gorky, *Chekhov, *Tolstoy, *Dostoevsky, Bunin, Rilke, and Svevo. In 1924 they moved to Tavistock Square, where J. *Lehmann became part-owner (1938–46). The present Hogarth Press has been an allied company of Chatto and Windus since 1947.

HOGG, James (1770–1835), the 'Ettrick Shepherd', was born in Ettrick Forest and became a shepherd. His poetic gift was discovered by Sir W. *Scott, to whom he had sent poems for *Minstrelsy of the Scottish Border. His early ballads were published as The Mountain Bard (1807). He made his reputation as a poet with *The Queen's Wake (1813). He became the friend of *Byron, *Wordsworth, *Southey, and John *Murray. He was on the editorial board of *Blackwood's Edinburgh Magazine, to which he frequently contributed, notably to the 'Noctes Ambrosianae'; and he conceived the idea of the notorious 'Chaldee MS' of 1819. His chief prose works are The Three Perils of Man (1822), *The Private Memoirs and Confessions of a Justified Sinner (1824), and The Domestic Manners and Private Life of Sir Walter Scott (1834). Wordsworth wrote a poem 'Upon the Death of James Hogg'.

HOGG, Thomas Jefferson (1792–1862), educated at Oxford with *Shelley and sent down with his friend on the publication of the latter's Necessity of *Atheism. His Life of Shelley appeared in 1858. *Peacock, in his Memorials of Shelley, felt obliged to question and revise many of Hogg's observations.

HOGGART, Richard (1918–), scholar and writer. His interest in literature, education, and the means of communication was expressed in his influential work The Uses of Literacy (1957),

which has been followed by many other works of literary criticism and sociology.

HOLBEIN, Hans, the younger (1497/8–1543), German painter who on the recommendation of *Erasmus spent the years 1526–8 in England, probably in the household of Sir T. *More: he settled in England in 1532, and, as court painter, was responsible for many portraits of the period, including those of Sir T. *Wyatt, *Surrey, More, and *Henry VIII.

HOLCOT, Robert (d. 1349), a Dominican who was theologically a follower of *Ockham in his insistence on human free will, in opposition to his contemporary *Bradwardine. The canon of his works is large but uncertain; his most important work is his Moralitates Historiarum, a series of metaphorical stories which influenced the *Gesta Romanorum. Throughout his work he alluded to and used 'pictures', metaphorical representations of abstract phenomena, in a lively and literary way.

HOLCROFT, Thomas (1745–1809), successively stable-boy, shoemaker, actor, and author. His varied and energetic life is described in his Memoirs (edited and completed by his friend *Hazlitt), which contain early reminiscences of *Foote and the aged *Macklin, and later accounts of radical associates such as *Godwin and *Tooke. He was indicted for high treason in 1794, and spent eight weeks in Newgate before being discharged. He wrote a number of sentimental plays, of which the best-known was The Road to Ruin (1792): also several novels, including Anna St Ives (1792) and The Adventures of Hugh Trevor (1794), both of them influenced by Godwin's radical philosophy.

HOLINSHED, Raphael (d. ?1580), was employed as a translator by Reyner *Wolfe, the printer and publisher. While in his employ he planned the Chronicles (1577) which are known by his name and are by several hands. They form the first authoritative vernacular and continuous account of the whole of English history. The Historie of England was written by Holinshed himself. The Description of England, a vivid account of English towns, villages, crops, customs, etc. of the day, was written by W. *Harrison. The Chronicle was reissued, with continuation, edited by John Hooker, alias Vowell, in 1587, and politically offensive passages again taken out. This edition was widely used by Shakespeare and other dramatists.

HOLLAND, Philemon (1552–1637), celebrated for his translations of *Livy (1600), *Pliny's Natural History (1601), *Plutarch's Moralia (1603), *Suetonius (1606), Ammianus Marcellinus (1609). Camden's *Britannia (1610), and *Xenophon's Cyropaedia (1632). His know-

ledge of Greek and Latin was accurate and profound, and his renderings are made in a vivid,
familiar, and somewhat ornamented English.

Holland House, Kensington, London, built at
the beginning of the 17th cent. In 1767 it was
acquired by Henry Fox, 1st baron Holland, who
entertained Horace *Walpole and George
Selwyn there. In the time of his grandson, the
3rd baron (1773–1840), Holland House became a
great political, literary, and artistic centre, and
many eminent authors, such as *Sheridan,
T. *Moore, T. *Campbell, S. *Rogers,
*Macaulay, *Grote, *Dickens, and *Thackeray,
were received there.

'Hollow Men, The', a poem by T. S. *Eliot.

HOLME, Constance (1881–1955), novelist,
born in Westmorland, where her successful
*Regional novels were set; they include *The
Lonely Plough* (1914), *The Splendid Fairing*
(1919), and *The Trumpet in the Dust* (1921),
written in the genre satirized by Stella Gibbons
in *Cold Comfort Farm*.

HOLMES, Oliver Wendell (1809–94), American writer, was professor of anatomy and
physiology at Harvard University (1847–82).
His *Autocrat of the Breakfast-Table* appeared in the
Atlantic Monthly in 1857–8, *The Professor at the
Breakfast-Table* in 1860, *The Poet at the Breakfast-
Table* in 1872, and *Over the Tea-cups* in 1891. His
essays in the *Breakfast-Table* series are notable for
their kindly humour and width of erudition;
they take the form of discourses by the author,
the other characters being listeners, who inter-
pose occasional remarks. He also wrote novels,
essays, and memoirs of *Emerson and *Motley,
and a considerable quantity of mainly light and
occasional verse.

Holmes, Sherlock, the private detective who
appears in *The Adventures of Sherlock Holmes* and
other books by A. C. *Doyle.

Holofernes, (1) Nebuchadnezzar's general,
who was decapitated by Judith (Judith, ch. 4), a
subject often treated by Renaissance painters; (2)
the great doctor in theology (Tubal Holofernes)
who instructed the youthful Gargantua
(*Rabelais, I. xiv); (3) the pedantic schoolmaster
in Shakespeare's *Love's Labour's Lost*.

HOLROYD, Michael de Courcy Fraser (1935–
), author and biographer, wrote a critical biography of *Kingsmill, a two-vol. life of L.
*Strachey (*The Unknown Years*, 1967; *The Years
of Achievement*, 1968), a work which greatly
contributed to a revival of interest in the
*Bloomsbury Group and to a new interest in the
art of *biography, and a life of Augustus John
(1974, 1975).

Holt, Father, a character in Thackeray's *The
History of Henry Esmond*, a Jesuit priest and
Jacobite spy.

HOLTBY, Winifred (1898–1935), writer,
published several novels, the best-known of
which is her last, *South Riding* (1936), set in
Yorkshire, which is at once the story of enterprising headmistress Sarah Burton and a portrait
of a whole community. Her other novels include
Anderby Wold (1923), *The Crowded Street* (1924),
The Land of Green Ginger (1927), and *Mandoa,
Mandoa!* (1933). She was also a prolific journalist.

Holy Grail, see GRAIL.

'Holy Grail, The' one of Tennyson's *Idylls of
the King*, published 1869, in which Sir Percivale,
now a monk, describes the quest of the Holy
Grail, and the differing degrees of failure of
himself, Bors, Gawain, and Launcelot.

Holy Living and **Holy Dying,** see TAYLOR,
JEREMY.

Holy State and the Profane State, The, by T.
*Fuller (1942) was the most popular of his works
during his life, a mixture of *character-writing,
essays, and 30 short biographies.

Holy War, The, an allegory by *Bunyan (1682).
The author narrates how Diabolus gets possession by his wiles of the city Mansoul (i.e. soul
of man), the metropolis of the universe.
Thereupon King Shaddai, the builder of the city,
sends Boanerges and three other captains to
recover it, and finally his own son Emmanuel to
lead the besieging army. It is an allegory both of
the progress of the Christian soul and of the
history of the Christian church.

'Holy Willie's Prayer', a satirical poem by
*Burns, published 1799.

Homage to Catalonia, see ORWELL, G.

HOME, Henry, Lord Kames (1696–1782),
Scottish judge and landowner, keenly interested
in agricultural improvement and philosophy, a
representative figure of the *Scottish Enlightenment. His works include *Elements of Criticism*
(1762) and *Sketches of the History of Man* (1774).

HOME, John (1722–1808), Scottish minister,
later became secretary to Bute and tutor to the
prince of Wales. His friends included *Hume,
Adam *Smith, W. *Collins, and W. *Robertson. His romantic tragedy *Douglas was performed with much success at Edinburgh in 1756
where it caused violent controversy from those
who believed it improper for a minister to write
for the stage.

Homecoming, The, a play by H. *Pinter, performed and published 1965.

A black Freudian family drama, the play presents the return to his North London home and ostentatiously womanless family of Teddy, an academic, and his wife of six years, Ruth, once a photographic model. The patriarch, Mac, a butcher, is alternately violent and cringing in manner, and the other two sons, Lenny and Joey, in a very short time make sexual overtures to Ruth, who calmly accepts them; by the end of the play Teddy has decided to leave her with the family, who intend to establish her as a professional prostitute.

HOMER, the supposed author of two famous early Greek epics, *The Iliad* and *The Odyssey*, of whom nothing is known. It is now considered unlikely that both epics are the work of a single poet. U. von Wilamowitz's theory (1916) that a poet, 'Homer', living in the 8th cent. BC combined and remodelled earlier poems, and that his work was in its turn enlarged and remodelled by others, seems the most plausible account of the genesis of *The Iliad*, while *The Odyssey* is generally held to consist of a substantial kernel poem with some later additions. Homer occupied in the culture of ancient Greece a position even more central than Shakespeare's in England, since his works provided everyone's elementary education, and his reputation survived in the Middle Ages even in the Latin West where his works were unknown. When the humanists began to learn Greek in the 14th cent. they turned eagerly to *The Iliad*, but found its directness and realism disappointing. The study of Homer stagnated, and a serious interest in his work did not show itself, in spite of G. *Chapman's heroic versions (*Il.* 1611, *Od.* 1614–15), until *Hobbes's and *Dryden's attempts at translation towards the end of the century. During the 18th cent. there was the natural wish to make an ancient masterpiece available to contemporary readers which produced *Pope's *Iliad* (1715–20); there was the new view of poetic inspiration fostered by *'Longinus', which justified the 'fire' Pope found in Homer, and a new cult of *Primitivism which prepared the ground for F. A. Wolf's theory (1795) that the *Iliad* consisted of bardic lays roughly woven together. In the 19th cent. some poets like *Tennyson (in 'The Lotos-Eaters') made use of a Homeric story for unhomeric purposes, but it is M. *Arnold's lectures 'On Translating Homer' that indicate most forcefully the almost extravagant worship that the poet inspired in cultivated Englishmen of the Victorian age.

In the 20th cent. the most widely read English translations are those of E. V. Rieu.

Homeric Hymns, of unknown authorship and various dates, are preludes to epic poems, addressed to various deities and recounting legends relating to them. *Shelley, *Peacock, *Tennyson, *Swinburne, and *Bridges are all indebted to them in particular poems.

Homilies, Books of, in the Church of England, two books of Homilies, published 1547 and 1563, appointed to be read in the churches.

HONE, William (1780–1842), author and bookseller, who published numerous political satires, some illustrated by *Cruikshank. He was prosecuted for his *Political Litany* (1817). His *Every-Day Book* (1826–7) was dedicated to *Lamb and praised by Sir W. *Scott and *Southey.

Honest Whore, The, a play by *Dekker in two parts, of which the first was printed 1604, the second 1630. It appears from *Henslowe's diary that *Middleton collaborated in writing the first part.

In Pt I Count Hippolito, making the acquaintance of Bellafront, a harlot, upbraids her bitterly and converts her to honesty. She falls in love with Hippolito, who repels her and marries Infelice, daughter of the duke of Milan. Bellafront is married to Matheo, who had caused her downfall.

In Pt II we find the converted Bellafront as the devoted wife of the worthless Matheo, who, to get money for his vices, is prepared to see her return to her old way of life. Hippolito, now falling in love with her, tries to seduce her. She stoutly resists temptation and is finally rescued from misery by her father, Orlando Friscobaldo. The painful character of the play, one of the great dramas of the age, heightened by Dekker's powerful treatment and by scenes in Bedlam and Bridewell, is somewhat alleviated by the admirable character Orlando Friscobaldo, and by the comic underplot, dealing with the eccentricities of the patient husband Candido, the linendraper.

Honeychurch, Lucy, a character in E. M. Forster's *A Room with a View*.

Honeycomb, Will, in *The Spectator*, introduced in No. 2 as an expert in 'the female world' of fashion and conversation.

Honeyman, the Revd Charles and Miss Martha, characters in Thackeray's *The Newcomes*.

Honeythunder, Luke, a character in Dickens's *Edwin Drood*.

Honorificabilitudinitatibus, the long word in Shakespeare's *Love's Labour's Lost* (v. i), in which Baconians see a cryptogram indicating that Bacon was the author of the works attributed to Shakespeare. (See BACONIAN THEORY.)

HOOD, Thomas (1799–1845), the friend of *Lamb, *Hazlitt, *de Quincey, and other literary men. He edited various periodicals: *The Gem* (1829), the *Comic Annual* (1830), *The

New Monthly Magazine (1841–3), and *Hood's Magazine* (1843). He wrote much humorous and satirical verse, often making use of his remarkable skill with puns. His serious poems include *'The Song of the Shirt'; *'The Bridge of Sighs'; 'The Dream of Eugene Aram', about a murder; 'The Last Man'; 'The Plea of the Mid-summer Fairies' (which includes 'I remember, I remember'); and shorter pieces, such as 'The Death-bed'.

HOOD, Thomas, the younger (1835–74), a humorous writer and artist, known as Tom Hood, was the son of Thomas *Hood. *Pen and Pencil Pictures* (1857) was the first of his illustrated books. His most successful novel was *Captain Master's Children* (1865). He became editor of *Fun* in 1865, and in 1867 he founded *Tom Hood's Comic Annual*. He wrote and illustrated many children's books; his collected verse, *Favourite Poems*, was published in 1877.

Hood, Robin, see ROBIN HOOD.

Hook, Captain, the pirate captain in J. M. *Barrie's *Peter Pan*.

HOOK, Theodore Edward (1788–1841), is remembered as a wit, a writer of light verses and dramas, and a successful editor of the Tory *John Bull*. He was the most successful of the writers of the *'Fashionable Novel'. As a friend of the prince of Wales Hook knew the fashionable world. Among his novels are *Sayings and Doings* (1824–8), *Maxwell* (1830), *Gilbert Gurney* (1836), *Jack Brag* (1837), and *Gurney Married* (1838).

HOOKER, Sir Joseph, see DARWIN, C.

HOOKER, Richard (?1554–1600), theologian. Of his great prose classic, the defence of the Church of England as established in Queen Elizabeth's reign entitled *Of the *Laws of Ecclesiastical Politie*, four books appeared in 1593, the fifth in 1597. A biography of Hooker was written by I. *Walton and published with the 1666 edition of his *Works*. There is some reason to credit Hooker with the first steps towards making known in England the theory of 'original contract' as a basis of sovereignty.

HOPE, Anthony, see HAWKINS, A. H.

HOPE, Thomas (?1770–1831), author of the once popular novel *Anastasius* (1819), at first attributed to Lord *Byron. It is the story of a brave but unscrupulous Greek who, in the 18th cent., travels in the Middle East and becomes involved in a variety of escapades. It is possible that the story influenced the later cantos of *Don Juan*.

Hope Theatre, on Bankside, Southwark, built in 1613 by *Henslowe as a bear-garden, with a movable stage on which plays could be performed. Jonson's *Bartholomew Fair* was acted there in 1614.

HOPKINS, Gerald Manley (1844–89). In 1863 he went to Balliol College, Oxford, where he wrote much poetry, including 'Heaven-Haven' and 'The Habit of Perfection'. He came under the influence of the *Oxford Movement and *Newman, and in 1866 was received into the Roman Catholic Church. In 1868 he resolved to become a Jesuit and symbolically burned his poems, though he sent some copies to his friend *Bridges for safekeeping. He was professor of rhetoric at Roehampton 1873–4, then studied theology at St Beuno's in North Wales (1874–7), where he also learned Welsh.

A new phase of creativity began in 1876. Inspired by the loss of the *Deutschland* in December 1875, which had among its passengers five Franciscan nuns exiled for their faith, Hopkins wrote his most ambitious poem, 'The Wreck of the Deutschland'. In 1877 he composed some of his best-known poems, including 'The Windhover' and 'Pied Beauty'. After ordination he was sent to Chesterfield, then London, then Oxford, where he wrote 'Henry Purcell'. Work in various industrial parishes followed, including an exhausting spell in Liverpool (1880–1) where he was oppressed by a sense of his own failure as a preacher.

In 1884 he was appointed to the chair of Greek and Latin at University College, Dublin. There he became ill and deeply depressed, and wrote (mainly in 1885) a number of 'Dark Sonnets', powerfully expressing his sense of exile and frustration; these include 'Carrion Comfort' and 'No worst, there is none'. He also managed to produce in these last years less desperate poems, including 'Harry Ploughman' and 'That Nature is a Heraclitean Fire'. He died of typhoid.

Apart from work in anthologies (including *Poets . . . of the Century*, 1893, and Bridges's own *The Spirit of Man*, 1916), nothing was published until 1918, when Bridges produced his *Poems*; Bridges had judged the public not ready to receive Hopkins's 'oddity', but initial bewilderment was followed by steadily rising admiration. His poems, letters, and journals reflect his sense of vocation (sometimes conflicting) as priest and poet, his technical interest in prosody, and his search for a unifying sacramental view of creation. His concepts of 'inscape', 'instress', and 'sprung rhythm' have given rise to a large body of aesthetic theory. By 'inscape' he seems to have meant 'the individual or essential quality of the thing'; 'instress' refers to the energy which sustains an inscape, and flows into the mind of the observer. Both words were coined by Hopkins. *'Sprung rhythm' he considered less an innovation than a return to the rhythms of speech and of earlier forms of verse. But the great (though delayed) impact of Hopkins's work may be seen less in terms of technical innovation than as a renewal of poetic energy, seriousness, and originality, after a period marked by much undistinguished and derivative verse.

HOPKINS, Matthew (d. 1647), the witch-finder, who initiated many prosecutions, and procured a special judicial commission under which 60 women were hanged in Essex in one year, and many in Norfolk and Huntingdon-shire. His *The Discovery of Witches* was published in 1647.

HORACE (Quintus Horatius Flaccus) (65–8 BC), Latin poet. Like his friend *Virgil, he joined in celebrating the restoration of order after the civil wars and worked to lift Latin literature to the level of Greek. In his *Odes* he imitated the lyric poets of early Greece. His *Satires* and *Epistles* were characterized by percep-tive realism and by an ironical approach in that the persona of the satirist was mocked as well as his ostensible victims. His critical works, notably the *Ars Poetica*, supplemented and in some cases distorted the teachings of *Aristotle. English satire from *Wyatt to Dr *Johnson derives much of its manner and aims from Horace. The writers of formal odes, *Marvell and *Dryden in particular, are also indebted to him and the critical writings of Dryden and the *Augustans plainly reveal the influence of his *Ars Poetica.* Horace's poems formed during the 17th and 18th cents an essential element in the pattern of English culture.

Horatio, in Shakespeare's *Hamlet, the univer-sity friend of Hamlet.

Horizon (1940–50), a literary magazine founded in 1939 by *Connolly, *Spender, and Peter Watson, edited throughout by Connolly; it published works by *Orwell, *Waugh, Angus *Wilson, L. *Lee, *Auden, and *Grigson, amongst others.

HORMAN, William (c. 1458–1535), head-master of Winchester and Eton, of which he became vice-provost, author of *Vulgaria* (1519), a remarkable book of Latin aphorisms for boys to learn.

Hornblower, Horatio, see FORESTER, C. S.

Horn-book, a leaf of paper containing the alphabet (often with the addition of the ten digits, some elements of spelling, and the Lord's Prayer) protected by a thin plate of translucent horn, and mounted on a tablet of wood with a projecting piece for a handle, used for teaching children to read. A simpler and later form of this, consisting of the tablet without the horn cover-ing, or a piece of stiff cardboard varnished, was also called a battledore.

Horn Childe, a northern verse-romance from the period 1290–1340 of 1,136 lines in tail-rhyme stanza. The plot is broadly similar to that of *King Horn though different in some details. It is believed that *Horn Childe* is the version of the romance referred to in 'Sir Thopas' (*Canterbury Tales,* 17).

HORNE, Richard Henry or Hengist (1802–84), made his name with *Orion,* an allegorical epic which he published in 1843 at a farthing 'to mark the public contempt into which epic poetry had fallen'. The poem deals with the myth of Orion, portrayed as 'a Worker and a Builder for his fellow men', and contrasted with Akinetos, the 'Great Unmoved', or Apathy. Horne wrote several blank verse tragedies, influenced by *Webster, and adapted various plays for the stage; contributed many articles to Dickens's *Daily News* and *Household Words*; and published other volumes of verse. In 1852, in the midst of the gold fever, he went to Australia and stayed until 1869. E. B. *Browning collaborated with him in his *A New Spirit of the Age* (1844) and Horne published two volumes of her letters to him (1877).

HORNECK, see GOLDSMITH, O.

Horner, a character in Wycherley's *The Country Wife.*

HORNIMAN, Annie Elizabeth Fredericka (1860–1937), a pioneer supporter of the modern English drama, founder of the Manchester Repertory Theatre. By her generous assistance the Irish National Theatre Society was provided with a permanent home in the *Abbey Theatre, Dublin.

HORNUNG, E(rnest) W(illiam) (1866–1921), novelist, is remembered as the creator of Raffles, the gentleman burglar, public-school man, and cricketer, who first appeared in *The Amateur Cracksman* (1899), narrated by his admiring assistant and ex-fag Bunny.

Hortensio, friend to Petruchio and suitor of Bianca in Shakespeare's *The Taming of the Shrew.*

'Hosier's Ghost, Admiral', see GLOVER, R.

HOTSPUR, nickname of Sir Henry Percy (1364–1403), eldest son of the first earl of Nor-thumberland. He figures in Shakespeare's *Richard II and 1 *Henry IV.

HOUGHTON, Baron, see MILNES, R. M.

HOUGHTON, William Stanley (1881–1913), playwright and drama critic. His plays include *The Dear Departed* (1908), *Independent Means*

(1909), *The Younger Generation* (1910), *Master of the House* (1910), *Fancy-Free* (1911), and *Hindle Wakes* (1912). Most of his plays centre, with sympathy and insight, on problems of homely Lancashire life, and are strongly influenced by *Ibsen. (See MANCHESTER SCHOOL.)

'Hound of Heaven, The', a poem by Francis *Thompson.

Hours of Idleness, a collection of poems by Lord *Byron, published 1807.
It was bitterly attacked by *Brougham in *The Edinburgh Review* as 'so much stagnant water', an attack which led to Byron's reply *English Bards and Scotch Reviewers*.

House for Mr Biswas, A, see NAIPAUL, V. S.

HOUSEHOLD, Geoffrey (Edward West) (1900–   ), author of many successful adventure stories. The most characteristic (including his best-known, *Rogue Male*, 1939, and its sequel *Rogue Justice*, 1982) pit a sporting, well-bred, lonely adventurer against the forces of darkness in the modern world.

Household Words, a weekly periodical started in 1850 by *Dickens, and incorporated in 1859 into *All the Year Round*, which he edited until his death. It published much of Dickens's own work and other writers such as Mrs *Gaskell, *Reade, and *Bulwer-Lytton, established the reputation of Wilkie *Collins, and published poems by the young *Meredith and *Patmore.

House of Fame, The, an unfinished dream-poem by *Chaucer, composed between 1374 and 1385. There are three books, in 2,158 lines of octosyllabics.
After the Prologue on Dreams and the Invocation to the god of sleep, Bk I says the poet fell asleep and dreamt that he was in a Temple of Glass where he saw depicted Aeneas and Dido; the dream moves on to deal more briefly with other parts of the *Aeneid*. The poet sees an eagle who alights by him and is his guide through the House of Fame. The eagle explains, philosophically and at length, how Fame works in its arbitrary ways. The eagle departs and Chaucer enters the Palace of Fame (Rumour) where he sees the famous of both classical and biblical lore. Eolus blows a trumpet to summon up the various celebrities who introduce themselves in categories reminiscent of the souls in Dante's *Divina Commedia*. Towards the end of the poem comes a vision of bearers of false tidings: shipmen, pilgrims, pardoners, and messengers, whose confusion seems to be about to be resolved by the appearance of 'A man of gret auctorite . . .'; but there the poem ends.

'House of Life, The', a sonnet sequence by D. G. *Rossetti, published in two parts in

Poems (1870) and *Ballads and Sonnets* (1881).
Rossetti described these sonnets as an evocation of 'life representative, as associated with love and death, with aspiration and foreboding, or with ideal art and beauty'.

House of Mirth, The, see WHARTON, E.

House of the Seven Gables, The, a novel by N. *Hawthorne, published 1851.
It deals with the problem of hereditary guilt, unmerited misfortune, and unexpiated crime, through the story of the Pyncheon family, suffering from generation to generation from the curse of old Maule, the dispossessed owner of the Pyncheon property. Pyncheon's descendant Hepzibah Pyncheon, an old spinster inhabiting the decayed paternal mansion, is obliged to do violence to the family pride by opening a small shop. Her brother Clifford Pyncheon, who has spent years in prison for a crime of which he has been unjustly convicted by the machinations of his cousin Judge Pyncheon, returns home. A young country cousin, Phoebe, arrives to lighten the gloom. Judge Pyncheon continues his persecution of Clifford until the judge's sudden death. With the help of Holgrave, a descendant of 'old Wizard Maule', Clifford is rehabilitated; Holgrave marries Phoebe, and the curse appears to be lifted.

House that Jack Built, The, a nursery accumulative tale of great antiquity, possibly based on an old Hebrew original.

House with the Green Shutters, The, see DOUGLAS, G.

HOUSMAN, A(lfred) E(dward) (1859–1936), educated at St John's College, Oxford. Housman was for ten years a clerk in the Patent Office in London, during which time he worked on *Propertius, *Ovid, *Juvenal, and other classical authors; he produced a definitive edition of Manilius (5 vols; 1902–30). He published, at his own expense, *A Shropshire Lad* (1896), a series of 63 spare and nostalgic verses, based largely on ballad-forms, and mainly set in a half-imaginary Shropshire, a 'land of lost content', and often addressed to, or spoken by, a farm-boy or a soldier: it became hugely popular during the First World War. In 1911 Housman was appointed professor of Latin at Cambridge. *Last Poems* (1922) met with great acclaim. *Praefanda* (1931) is a collection of bawdy and obscene passages from Latin authors. His lecture 'The Name and Nature of Poetry' (1933) provides illuminating comments on the process of poetic creation. *Collected Poems* appeared in 1939.

HOUSMAN, Laurence (1865–1959), brother of A. E. *Housman, illustrator, art critic, writer, and dramatist. Among his works were volumes of poems, including *Green Arras* (1896) and *Spikenard* (1898); *An Englishwomen's Loveletters* (1900); and several successful novels, among them *Trimblerigg* (1924), directed against Lloyd George, and *The Duke of Flamborough* (1928). His dramatic works include *Bethlehem*, which was banned in 1902, as were many later plays on religious or royal figures; and *Angels and Ministers* (1921), consisting of gently mocking scenes laid in the court of Queen Victoria, which were collected with further royal playlets into *Victoria Regina* (1934). He also published an autobiography, *The Unexpected Years* (1937), and *A. E. Housman* (1937), which contained poems, letters, and a valuable *Memoir* of his brother.

Houyhnhnms, the talking horses in *Gulliver's Travels* by Swift.

HOVEDON, or **HOWDEN,** Roger of (d. ?1201), a Yorkshireman and a chronicler. He was the author of both the main chronicles of the reigns of Henry II and Richard I, the *Gesta Regis Henrici* and the *Chronica*.

HOWARD, Henry, see SURREY.

Howards End, a novel by E. M. *Forster, published 1910, deals with personal relationships and conflicting values.
    The Schlegel sisters, Margaret and Helen, and their brother Tibby, care about civilized living, music, literature, and conversation. The Wilcoxes, Henry and his children Charles, Paul, and Evie, are concerned with the business side of life and distrust emotions and imagination. Helen Schlegel is drawn to the Wilcox family, falls briefly in and out of love with Paul Wilcox, and thereafter reacts away from them. Margaret is stimulated by the very differences of their way of life. She marries Henry Wilcox, to the consternation of both families. Her marriage cracks but does not break. In the end, torn between her sister and her husband, she succeeds to bridging the mistrust that divides them. Howards End, where the story begins and ends, is the house that belonged to Henry Wilcox's first wife, and is a symbol of human dignity and endurance.

Howe, Anna, the heroine's principal correspondent in Richardson's *Clarissa.

HOWELL, James (?1593–1666), held diplomatic and administrative posts under Charles I and was imprisoned in the Fleet as a royalist, 1643–51; at the Restoration he became Historiographer Royal. He wrote a number of political and historical pamphlets and other works but is chiefly remembered for his *Epistolae Ho-Elianae: familiar letters domestic and forren* (1645–55). These letters to correspondents, most of whom are imaginary, were written largely during his imprisonment; their intimate 'back-stairs' view of history had a lasting appeal.

HOWELLS, William Dean (1837–1920), American novelist and friend of H. *James. He was editor of the *Atlantic Monthly* (1871–81) and associte editor of *Harper's Magazine* (1886–91), to which periodicals he contributed many articles. His numerous romances include *The Undiscovered Country* (1880), *The Rise of Silas Lapham* (1885), *Indian Summer* (1886), and *A Hazard of New Fortunes* (1890), which shows the effect of his political and critical moves towards socialism and realism. He also wrote works of travel, criticism, and reminiscence, and several dramas.

'How many children had Lady Macbeth?', see KNIGHTS, L. C.

Hoyden, Miss, a character in Vanbrugh's *The Relapse* and in Sheridan's *A Trip to Scarborough.

Hrothgar, see BEOWULF.

HROTSVITHA, or **ROSWITHA** (*fl.* 10th cent.), a Benedictine abbess of Gandersheim in Saxony, who adapted the comedies of *Terence for the use of her convent, an example of the survival of classical influence in the Middle Ages.

Hubbard, Mother, see MOTHER HUBBARD and MOTHER HUBBERDS TALE.

Hubris, see POETICS, THE.

HUCHOWN (*fl.* 14th cent.), apparently a northern alliterative poet. Andrew of *Wyntoun, *c.*1400, claims that 'He made the gret Gest of Arthure | And the Anteris of Gawane, | The Epistill als of Suete Susane.' These poems have been tentatively identified as respectively the alliterative *Morte Arthure*, *The Awntyrs of Arthure*, and *The Pistyll of Susan*. He is perhaps to be identified with the Scot Sir Hew of Eglinton.

Huckleberry Finn, The Adventures of, a novel by Mark *Twain, published 1884, as a sequel to *Tom Sawyer.
    Huck Finn, the narrator, recounts his adventures after being taken away from the Widow Douglas's by his drunken and brutal father. He escapes from his father, faking his own death, and joins up with a runaway slave, Jim, and together they make their own way down the Mississippi on a raft. Huck becomes a witness of the blood feud between the Grangerford and Shepherdson families; he and Jim are joined by two villainous confidence men, the 'Duke' and the 'Dauphin', who sell Jim into captivity again, but at the end of the book Tom reappears in time to help Huck to rescue him in a characteristically romantic and quixotic manner (unnecessarily, as it turns out, for Jim had earlier and unknowingly

been given his freedom). The novel is a profound moral commentary on the nature of the 'American experience' and the institution of slavery, and a vital contribution to the myth of the frontier. The flexibility and power of Twain's narrative is in no way impeded by his brilliant use of various dialects.

Hudibras, a satire in three parts, each containing three cantos, by Samuel *Butler (1613–80). Part I, dated 1663, appeared in Dec. 1662, Part II, dated 1664, was published in 1663, and a revised version of both parts appeared in 1674. Part III was published 1680.

Its narrative form is that of a mock romance, derived from *Don Quixote, in which a grotesque Presbyterian knight, Sir Hudibras, and his sectarian squire Ralpho set out on horseback and encounter a bear-baiting mob who, after a comic skirmish, imprison them in the stocks. In Pt II a widow, whom Hudibras hopes to marry for the sake of her jointure, agrees to release them on condition that the knight undergoes a whipping for her sake. They visit Sidrophel, a charlatan posing as an astrologer, whom Hudibras assaults and leaves for dead. In Pt III Hudibras returns to the widow and claims that he has fulfilled his promise to whip himself, but is interrupted by a gang which he mistakes for Sidrophel's supernatural agents. They cudgel him and force him to confess to his iniquities. He consults a lawyer, who advises him to write love-letters to the widow in order to inveigle her in her replies.

The digressions from the loose narrative framework of the poem deal with academic pedantry, the theological differences between the Presbyterians and independent sectarians, Aristotelian logic, the hermetic philosophy, the politics of the civil war period, the ethics of oath-breaking, witchcraft, alchemy, astrology, and the nature of marriage. *Hudibras* is the most learnedly allusive poem in English; Butler's most powerful satirical weapon is his style, the deliberately cumbersome octosyllabic metre and comic rhymes of which render absurd every subject to which they are applied.

Hudibras, or **Huddibras,** in Spenser's *Faerie Queene* (II. ii. 17), the lover of *Elissa. Another Huddibras, in II. x. 25 of the same poem, is a legendary king of Britain.

Hudibrastic, in the style of Butler's *Hudibras; in octosyllabic couplets and with comic rhymes.

HUDSON, W(illiam) H(enry) (1841–1922), was born near Buenos Aires. He came to London in 1874 where he remained, often in poverty, for the rest of his life. His novel *Green Mansions* (1904) is probably his best-known book. His remarkable *A Shepherd's Life* (1910) describes Caleb Bawcombe, a Wiltshire

shepherd, who lives night and day, through all the seasons, with his sheep and his dogs among the people and the wild life of the downs. His other works include *The Purple Land* (1885), a series of strange and vivid stories set in South America; *The Crystal Age* (1887), an account of a Utopian land where the sex impulse has burned out and society is therefore at last stable and at peace; *Argentine Ornithology* (1888), a standard work of which Hudson was part-author; *The Naturalist in La Plata* (1892); *British Birds* (1895); *Adventures among Birds* (1913); *Far Away and Long Ago* (1918); and *Birds of La Plata* (1920), another standard work.

Hugh, in Dickens's *Barnaby Rudge, the ostler of the Maypole Inn.

HUGHES, Richard Arthur Warren (1900–76), educated at Oriel College, Oxford. While at Oxford, he published a volume of poems, *Gipsy Night* (1922). His dramatic works include *The Sister's Tragedy* (1922), *A Comedy of Good and Evil* (1924), both performed at the Royal Court, London, and *Danger* (1924), the first original radio play (commissioned by the BBC). He gained fame with his first novel, *A High Wind in Jamaica* (1929), the story of the adventures of a family of children bound for England and captured by pirates. *In Hazard* (1938) is a seafaring novel. He produced three volumes of short stories, *A Moment of Time* (1926), *The Spider's Palace* (1931), and *Don't Blame Me* (1940), the last two for children. He worked for the Admiralty during the war, and in 1961 broke a long silence with *The Fox in the Attic*, the first volume of an ambitious new project, 'The Human Predicament'; opening in Wales just after the First World War, it mingles real and fictional characters, both German and British, ending with Hitler's Munich *putsch*. The second volume, *The Wooden Shepherdess* (1973), ends with the murder of Röhm.

HUGHES, Ted (Edward James) (1930–), poet, educated at Pembroke College, Cambridge, where he met Sylvia *Plath, whom he married in 1956. His obsession with animals and his sense of the beauty and violence of the natural world appear in his first volume, *The Hawk in the Rain* (1957). This was followed by *Lupercal* (1960), *Wodwo* (1967, prose and verse), and several books of children's verse. *Crow* (1970) is a sequence of poems introducing the central symbol of the crow. Hughes retells the legends of creation and birth through the dark vision of predatory, mocking, indestructible crow. Later volumes include *Cave Birds* (1975), *Season Songs* (1976), and *Moortown* (1979). He has also published plays for children, a version of *Seneca's *Oedipus* (1968), and edited various anthologies. *Remains of Elmet* (1979) celebrates the landscape of his youth in the Calder valley; *River*

(1983) is a sequence of poems invoking riverside and river life. Together these volumes constitute interesting examples of the renewed vogue for *topographical poetry. He was appointed poet laureate in 1984.

HUGHES, Thomas (1822–96), educated at Oriel College, Oxford, was a barrister and Liberal MP and, under the influence of F. D. *Maurice, devoted much energy to Working Men's Education, the Co-operative movement, etc. He is remembered as the author of *Tom Brown's Schooldays* (1857, by 'An Old Boy'), which evokes the Rugby of his youth and his veneration for its headmaster, Dr T. *Arnold. Hughes condemned, in the character of the tyrannical Flashman, the bullying prevalent in public schools of the day, and advocated a form of what came to be known as 'muscular Christianity', which attempted to combine Christian principles with physical courage, self-reliance, love of sport, school loyalty, and patriotism, a mixture that had much impact on the public school ethos. Hughes wrote several biographies, memoirs, one other novel, and various sermons and addresses.

HUGH OF LINCOLN, St (?1246–55), a child supposed to have been crucified by a Jew named Copin or Joppin at Lincoln, after having been starved and tortured. The body is said to have been discovered in a well and buried near that of *Grosseteste in the cathedral, and to have been the cause of several miracles. The story, a frequent theme for poets, is referred to by Chaucer ('The Prioress's Tale', *Canterbury Tales*, 16) and by Marlowe in *The Jew of Malta*.

HUGH OF ORLEANS, see PRIMAS.

Hugh Selwyn Mauberley, see POUND, E.

HUGO, Victor(-Marie) (1802–85), poet, novelist, and dramatist, the central figure of the Romantic movement in France.

HULME, T(homas) E(rnest) (1883–1917), poet, essayist, and (in his own phrase) 'philosophic amateur', whose reaction against *Romanticism and advocacy of the 'hard dry image' influenced *Imagism. His essay 'Romanticism and Classicism' defines Romanticism as 'spilt religion', and predicts a new 'cheerful, dry and sophisticated' poetry. Only six of his poems were published in his lifetime, five in *Orage's *The New Age*, 1912, as 'The Complete Poetical Works of T. E. Hulme'. Hulme also contributed to the *New Age* his essays on *Bergson, whom he also translated. He was killed in action, and much of his work survived only in notebooks. *Speculations: essays on humanism and the philosophy of art* (1924) and *Notes on language and style* (1929) were edited by *Read. Hulme's double role as

conservative and Modernist had considerable influence on the development of 20th-cent. taste; T. S. *Eliot described him in 1924 as 'classical, reactionary and revolutionary'.

Human Understanding, *Enquiry concerning*, see HUME, D.

Humber, in *Geoffrey of Monmouth's *History* (ii. 1–2), a king of the Huns who invaded northern Britain. He was defeated by *Locrine, who drowned him in the river Albus which afterwards bore his name. The story is told in Spenser's *Faerie Queene* (II. x. 15–16).

HUME, David (1711–76), born and educated at Edinburgh, developed early in life a passion for philosophy. He spent three years (1734–7) in private study in France, and in 1739 published anonymously his *Treatise of Human Nature* in two volumes, a third volume and a promotional *Abstract* appearing in 1740. During his lifetime it was generally received with hostility, but its doctrines had an important impact on H. *Home and Adam *Smith. Hume's *Essays Moral and Political* (1741–2) was more successful. His *Enquiry concerning Human Understanding* (originally entitled *Philosophical Essays*) appeared in 1748 and his *Enquiry concerning the Principles of Morals* in 1751. In 1752 he published his *Political Discourses*, which was translated into French and made Hume famous on the Continent. In 1754 appeared the first volume of his *History of Great Britain*, devoted to the early Stuarts, followed by further volumes in 1757, 1759, and 1762. From 1763 to 1765 Hume was secretary to the embassy in Paris. He brought back *Rousseau to England and befriended him, but Rousseau's suspicious nature presently led to a quarrel. Hume was under-secretary of state in 1767–8, and after this finally settled in Edinburgh. After his death, his friend Adam Smith published his autobiography with a eulogy (1777). Hume's *Dialogues concerning Natural Religion* was published in 1779 by his nephew.

For Hume's philosophical views, see TREATISE OF HUMAN NATURE. His views on religion are contained, (a) in sections X–XI of *An Enquiry concerning Human Understanding*; (b) in the dissertation entitled *The Natural History of Religion*, in which he investigates its origin in human nature and traces its development from polytheism to monotheism and its inevitable degeneration; (c) in the *Dialogues concerning Natural Religion*, of which the cautious and ambiguous conclusion is 'that the cause or causes of order in the universe probably bear some remote analogy to human intelligence'.

Hume's writings on politics and history show a strong interest in human character and motivation. Though a believer in civil liberties (except freedom of divorce), and an opponent of 'divine right', he also defended the characters of the

Stuart kings; and he rejected the social contract theory of society and social obligation as historically unrealistic, tracing these instead to custom and convenience. By deliberately steering between the extremes of prevailing Whig and Tory philosophies he incurred the complaints of both sides. As a political economist Hume attacked the mercantile system, and in general anticipated the views of later economists in the tradition of Adam Smith.

Humorous Lieutenant, The, a comedy by J. *Fletcher, produced about 1619.

Humours, Comedy of, a term applied especially to the type of comic drama written by *Jonson, where a 'humour' is the embodiment of some dominating individual passion or propensity. The cardinal humours were blood, phlegm, choler, and melancholy or black choler.

HUMPHREY, duke of Gloucester (1391–1447), youngest son of Henry IV, 'the Good Duke Humphrey'. He was appointed Protector on the death of Henry V in 1422 and acted as regent, 1420–1 and periodically until 1431, in place of his brother, the duke of Bedford. He owes the epithet 'Good' only to his patronage of men of letters, including *Lydgate and *Capgrave. He promoted Renaissance humanism in England and gave the first books for a library at Oxford; still named after him is the oldest part of the Bodleian which was built to house his bequest in the 15th cent.

Humphry Clinker, The Expedition of, a novel by T. *Smollett, published 1771.

The mellowest and most accomplished of Smollett's works. It is *epistolary in form, and relates the adventures of Matthew Bramble's family party as they travel through England and Scotland. The party consists of Bramble himself, an outwardly misanthropical but really kind-hearted old valetudinarian bachelor; his sister Tabitha, a virago bent on matrimony; his nephew Jery, an amiable young spark, and his sister Lydia; Mrs Winifred Jenkins, the maid; and Humphry Clinker, a ragged ostler whom they pick up *en route* as postilion, and who turns out a creature of much resource and devotion.

Huncamunca, a character in Fielding's *Tom Thumb*. (See also SOPHONISBA.)

Hundreth Good Pointes of Husbandrie, see TUSSER, T.

HUNT, (William) Holman (1827–1910), painter and founder member of the *Pre-Raphaelite Brotherhood. His autobiographical *Pre-Raphaelitism and the Pre-Raphaelite Brotherhood* (1905) is a full but personal history of the movement.

HUNT, John (1775–1848), the brother of Leigh *Hunt, an enterprising publisher who was prosecuted, threatened with legal actions, and fined many times. In 1808 he and Leigh established the *Examiner*; in 1810 he started a quarterly, the *Reflector* (with Leigh as editor). Both John and Leigh were in 1813 sentenced to two years' imprisonment in separate gaols and fined £500 apiece for a libel on the prince regent. In 1815–17 John published those essays of his brother and of *Hazlitt which were collected as *The Round Table* (1817). He was the publisher and Leigh the editor of the short-lived *Liberal* founded in 1822.

HUNT, (James Henry) Leigh (1784–1859), was educated at Christ's Hospital. His first collection of poems appeared in 1807. In 1808 he founded and edited, with his brother John (above), the *Examiner*, and in 1810 he edited the *Reflector*, in which he published *Lamb's essays on Shakespeare and *Hogarth. In 1813 he and his brother were fined £500 and sentenced to two years' imprisonment for a libel in the *Examiner* on the prince regent. While in jail he continued to write and edit the *Examiner*, and received visits from *Byron, *Moore, the *Lambs, *Bentham, James *Mill, and *Brougham. In 1816 he printed *Keats's sonnet 'O Solitude' in the *Examiner*, and began his lifelong support of Keats, *Shelley, and the *Romantic poets; his name was linked with that of Keats and Hazlitt in attacks on the so-called *Cockney school. Hunt's influential poem *The Story of Rimini appeared in 1816; his verse collection *Foliage* in 1818; and in 1819 his poems *Hero and Leander* and *Bacchus and Ariadne*. In his journal the *Indicator he published in 1821 Keats's *'La Belle Dame sans Merci', and in the *Liberal*, founded jointly with Byron, appeared *The Vision of Judgement (1822). 'Abou Ben Adhem' (probably, with 'Jenny kissed me', Hunt's best-known poem) was published in an anthology, the *Book of Gems* (1838). His many other works include plays, *Poetical Works* (1844), a lively *Autobiography* (1850), and *Table Talk* (1851).

Hunt's essays, although much influenced by the essayists of the previous century, were not moral in intent. His aim was to convey appreciation and enjoyment. His gift for detecting talent, from Keats to *Tennyson, and his determined support for it, made him an invaluable editor. His sunny, optimistic nature is sketched in the early character of Skimpole in *Bleak House*.

HUNT, (Isobel) Violet (1866–1942), novelist, was for some years the companion of F. M. *Ford. A flamboyant feminist, a supporter of *Women's Suffrage, and a friend of H. G. *Wells and H. *James, she published several novels (including *The Maiden's Progress*, 1894, and *White Rose of Weary Leaf*, 1908), an autobiography, *The Flurried Years* (1926), and the macabre *Tales of the Uneasy* (1911).

HUNTER, Sir William Wilson (1840–1900), entered the Indian civil service in 1862. He was author of several notable volumes mainly on Indian historical subjects including *Annals of Rural Bengal* (1868), *Orissa* (1872), *The Imperial Gazetteer of India* (1881), *The Old Missionary* (1895), and *The Thackerays in India* (1897). He had completed only two volumes of his *History of British India* (1899–1900) at his death.

Huntingdon, Arthur and Helen (Graham), leading characters in A. Brontë's *The Tenant of Wildfell Hall*.

HUNTINGDON, Robert, Earl of, see ROBIN HOOD.

HUNTINGDON, Selina Hastings, countess of (1707–91), founder of the group of Calvinistic Methodists known as 'Lady Huntingdon's Connection'.

Hunting of the Snark, The, a mock-heroic nonsense poem by Lewis Carroll (C. L. *Dodgson), published 1867.

Huon of Bordeaux, the hero of a French 13th-cent. *chanson de geste*. He has the misfortune to kill Charlot, son of *Charlemagne, in an affray, not knowing who his assailant is. He is thereupon condemned to death by the emperor, but reprieved on condition that he will go to the court of Gaudisse, amir of Babylon, bring back a handful of his hair and four of his teeth, kill his doughtiest knight, and kiss Esclarmonde his daughter. By the help of the fairy Oberon, Huon achieves the adventure. The work was translated by Lord Berners and printed by *Wynkyn de Worde in 1534. Huon's adventure is the theme of Weber's opera *Oberon*.

HURD, Richard (1720–1808), bishop successively of Lichfield and Worcester. His *Moral and Political Dialogues* appeared in 1759. *Letters on Chivalry and Romance* (1762) is an important reassessment of Elizabethan literature: Hurd was notably sympathetic to *Spenser, argued that the 'Gothic' was more poetic than the 'Grecian', and that *neo-classical rules were inappropriately applied to chivalric romances, which were composed on different but no less artistic principles.

Hurlothrumbo (1729), a popular burlesque by Samuel Johnson (1691–1773), a Manchester dancing master.

Husbandrie, *Hundreth Good Pointes of,* see TUSSER, T.

Husband's Message, The, an Old English poem of 53 lines in the *Exeter Book. Its ostensible form

is a message to a woman from her husband who has had to leave his own country because of a feud, telling her of his prosperity in another land and asking her to join him.

HUTCHESON, Francis (1694–1746), professor of moral philosophy at Glasgow from 1729 until his death. Before this he had published aesthetic, moral, and political essays in the Dublin and London press, and two books, *An Inquiry into the Original of our Ideas of Beauty and Virtue* (1725) and *An Essay on the Nature and Conduct of the Passions and Affections with Illustrations on the Moral Sense* (1728), both subsequently revised. His posthumous *System of Moral Philosophy* was published in 1755.

A protégé of *Molesworth, Hutcheson introduced the civic humanist tradition into higher education: he trained a whole generation of students, among them Adam *Smith, in the Whig philosophy of personal liberty and government restraint, and his progressive views were influential among Scots *émigrés* to America. In ethics he developed the ideas of *Shaftesbury on the moral sense into a fully-fledged system. He saw a close relation between aesthetic and moral perception, by which we come to be aware of providentially designed order. Virtue is identical with benevolence in so far as it gives disinterested pleasure, that action being best which aims at the greatest happiness of the greatest number. This view anticipates Utilitarianism.

HUTCHINSON, Mrs Lucy (b. 1620), the author of *Memoirs of the Life of Colonel Hutchinson* (first published 1806), which she wrote after the death of her husband, John Hutchinson (1615–64). It is a vivid and valuable account of the state of the country at the outbreak of civil war and of the conflict in the vicinity of Nottingham, told from the Puritan point of view.

HUTCHINSON, R(ay) C(oryton) (1907–75), novelist. His works include *The Unforgotten Prisoner* (1933), a powerful portrayal of revenge and conciliation in the aftermath of the First World War; *Testament* (1938), set in Russia at the time of the revolution; *The Stepmother* (1955); and *Rising* (1976), a historical novel set in South America.

HUTH, Henry (1815–78), merchant banker and bibliophile. His library contained narratives of voyages, Shakespearian and early English literature, early Spanish and German books, and valuable editions of the Bible.

HUTTEN, Ulrich von, see EPISTOLAE OBSCURORUM VIRORUM.

HUXLEY, Aldous Leonard (1894–1963), grandson of T. H. *Huxley and brother of Julian

*Huxley. By 1919, when he began to write for *Murry in *The Athenaeum*, he had already published three volumes of verse; a volume of stories, *Limbo* (1920), was followed by *Crome Yellow* (1921), a country-house satire which earned him a reputation for precocious brilliance and cynicism, and which much offended Lady Ottoline *Morrell whom Huxley had frequently visited at Garsington. During the 1920s and 1930s Huxley lived in Italy, then France; in this period he wrote much fiction, including *Mortal Coils* (1922, stories; includes 'The Gioconda Smile'); *Antic Hay* (1923, set in post-war London's nihilistic Bohemia); *Those Barren Leaves* (1925, set in Italy); and *Point Counter Point* (1928), in which were recognized portraits of his friend D. H. *Lawrence as Rampion and Murry as Burlap. *Brave New World* (1932), his most popular work, was followed by *Eyeless in Gaza* (1936). Huxley left for California in 1937, partly in search (with his friend Gerald Heard, 1889–   ) of new spiritual direction. He continued to write in many genres: novels include *After Many a Summer* (1939), in which Heard appears as the mystic Propter, and *Island* (1962), an optimistic Utopia; and other works include essays, historical studies, travel works, and *The Devils of Loudun* (1952), a study in sexual hysteria which became the basis of *Whiting's play *The Devils*. He became deeply interested in mysticism and parapsychology; *The Doors of Perception* (1954) and *Heaven and Hell* (1956) describe his experiments with mescalin and LSD.

Huxley's novels with their mixture of satire and earnestness, of apparent brutality and humanity, have led some to dismiss them as smart and superficial, a symptom rather than an interpretation of a hollow age; others have seen them as brilliant and provocative 'novels of ideas' written by a man who was not by nature a novelist.

HUXLEY, Sir Julian Sorell (1887–1975), biologist and writer, brother of Aldous *Huxley. He published a small collection of verse, *The Captive Shrew and other poems of a biologist* (1932), which shows, though less vividly than some of his scientific works, his keen interest in and love of the natural world, particularly of birds. He was professor of zoology at King's College, London, 1925–7, professor of physiology in the Royal Institution, 1926–9, and secretary of the Zoological Society, 1935–42. Like his grandfather T. H. *Huxley, he had a gift for popular exposition which did not impede the rigours of his scientific work.

HUXLEY, T(homas) H(enry) (1825–95), was assistant surgeon on HMS *Rattlesnake*, 1846–50. His surveys of marine life on the Australian Barrier Reef appeared as papers for the *Royal and Linnean Societies (see LINNAEUS), he was elected FRS in 1851, and in 1854 became pro-fessor of Natural History at the Royal School of Mines. He wrote extensively on specialist subjects, but also became widely known and admired as a lecturer to lay audiences. His views on religion, education, philosophy and evolution, and on man's newly conceived place in the universe (e.g. in *Evidence as to man's place in nature*, 1863, *Evolution and Ethics*, 1893, and other essays) had a profound impact on 19th cent. thought. He was a friend of *Darwin, and an influential though discriminating supporter of his theories. He coined the word 'agnostic' to describe his own philosophical position, which he expounded at the *Metaphysical Society and in the *Nineteenth Century*. His *Collected Essays* were published in 1893–4, his *Scientific Memoirs* in 1898–1903, and his *Life and Letters*, edited by his son Leonard, in 1900–3.

HYDE, Douglas (1860–1949), Irish writer and pioneer in the *Irish Revival, became the first professor of Irish at the National University in 1908. Several of his writings, including *Love Songs of Connacht* (1893) and *A Literary History of Ireland* (1892), together with several volumes of verse translations from the Gaelic, were highly influential. He became a vice-president of the *Abbey Theatre company. He was the first president of Eire (1938–45).

HYDE, Edward, see CLARENDON.

Hyde Park, a comedy by J. *Shirley, acted 1632, printed 1637.

Hydriotaphia, or *Urn Burial* (1658), by Sir T. *Browne, the companion piece to *The Garden of Cyrus*, has been called the first archaeological treatise in English. He takes the discovery of some burial urns in a Norfolk field as the occasion for a wide-ranging meditation on the funeral procedures of many nations. The fragility of all relics and monuments prompts him to turn to the Christian doctrine of resurrection as the only lasting hope. Browne achieves the 'high style' demanded by his subject with a richness of diction and rhythmical power seldom if ever equalled in English prose.

Hymenaei, a marriage masque by *Jonson, performed and printed in 1606.

Hymns Ancient and Modern, a collection promoted and edited by the Revd Sir H. W. Baker (1821–77), vicar of Monkland, near Leominster, who contributed to it many original hymns and translations from the Latin. The collection first appeared in 1861 and various supplements and revised editions have since been published.

'Hymn to the Naiads', see AKENSIDE, M.

Hypallage, from a Greek word meaning 'exchange', a transference of epithet, as

'Sansfoy's dead dowry' for 'dead Sansfoy's dowry' (*Spenser).

Hyperbole, the use of exaggerated terms to emphasize the importance or extent of something. *Puttenham translated it as 'the over reacher'. Marlowe was particularly addicted to this figure of speech: e.g. 'Was this the face that launched a thousand ships? | And burnt the topless towers of Ilium?' (*Dr Faustus).

Hyperion: a fragment and *The Fall of Hyperion,* fragments of epic poems by *Keats, written 1818–19. *Hyperion* was published 1820, *The Fall of Hyperion,* 1856.

In the first version, written as direct narrative, Saturn, conquered by Jove, mourns the loss of his kingdom and debates with his fallen fellow-Titans how he may regain it. They conclude that only the magnificent Hyperion, who is still unfallen, will be able to help them. In Bk III the golden Apollo, god of music, poetry, and knowledge, speaks to the goddess Mnemosyne of this inexplicable anguish; then, at the moment of his deification, the fragment ends. In the second version, where he drinks an elixir which induces a vision. He finds himself in a vast domed monument, then proceeds to climb the stair to the shrine of the priestess Moneta. Together they find the agonized fallen Saturn, and with Mnemosyne and Thea they speak to him of his pain and loss. In despair he leaves with Thea to comfort his fellow-Titans, while the poet and Moneta watch the magnificent, but much troubled, Hyperion blaze into the west.

Hysteron Proteron, in grammar and rhetoric, a figure of speech in which the word or phrase that should properly come last is put first; in general, 'putting the cart before the horse'.

Hythloday, Raphael, in More's *Utopia,* the traveller in whose mouth the author places the criticisms of English institutions, etc.

I

Iachimo, the villain in Shakespeare's *Cymbeline*.

Iago, the villainous ensign in Shakespeare's *Othello*.

Iamb, Iambic trimeter, Iambic pentameter, see METRE.

IBSEN, Henrik (1828–1906), Norwegian dramatist, generally acknowledged as the founder of modern prose drama. All his great dramas are now in the standard English repertoire. His first successes, *Brand* (1866) and *Peer Gynt* (1867), created his name in Scandinavia, but it was over 20 years before the work of *Gosse and *Archer, and later the support of *Hardy, W. *James, G. B. *Shaw (whose *The Quintessence of Ibsenism*, 1891, reveals his debt to Ibsen), and others, established him as a major dramatist in England. Ibsen's other great plays include *A Doll's House* (1879), *Ghosts* (1881), *An Enemy of the People* (1882), *Rosmersholm* (1886), *Lady from the Sea* (1888), *Hedda Gabler* (1890), *The Master Builder* (1892), *Little Eyof* (1894), and *When We Dead Awaken* (1900). Ibsen created new attitudes to drama, and is credited with being the first major dramatist to write tragedy about ordinary people in prose. The quality of his dialogue, and his discarding of traditional theatrical effects, demanded and achieved a new style of performance.

Iceman Cometh, The, see O'NEILL, E.

Icon Basilike, see EIKON BASILIKE.

Ida, Princess, the heroine of Tennyson's *The Princess*, which is the basis of the *Gilbert and Sullivan opera *Princess Ida*.

Idea, a sonnet sequence by M. *Drayton, first published as *Ideas Mirrour* in 1594, much revised and expanded, reaching its final form of 63 sonnets in 1619.

Idealism, in philosophy, the view that minds or spirits are the only, or the fundamental, entities in the world, material things being unreal or in some way parasitical upon the mental. There are several varieties of idealist philosophy, and their most notable exponents include *Berkeley, *Kant, and *Hegel.

Idea of a University, The, see NEWMAN, J. H.

Ideas Mirrour, see IDEA.

Idea, the Shepheards Garland, see DRAYTON, M.

'Idiot Boy, The', a ballad by *Wordsworth, first published in *Lyrical Ballads* (1798). One of the most characteristic and controversial of the poet's early works, it takes as hero the idiot son of a poor countrywoman, Betty Foy. The boy's descriptions of his night-time adventures,

'The cocks did crow to-whoo, to-whoo, And the sun did shine so cold',

fittingly illustrate Wordsworth's intention of 'giving the charm of novelty to things of everyday'.

Idler, The, (1) a series of papers contributed by Dr *Johnson to the *Universal Chronicle: or Weekly Gazette* between 15 April 1758 and 5 April 1760. These papers are shorter and lighter than those of *The Rambler*, but their general character is the same. They include the weil-known sketches of Dick Minim, the critic, of Mr Sober (the author himself), Jack Whirler (*Newbery the publisher), and Tom Restless. (2) a monthly journal edited by J. K. *Jerome and Robert Barr, 1892–1911.

Idylls, see ECLOGUE.

Idylls of the King, a series of 12 connected poems by *Tennyson, of which *Morte d'Arthur', subsequently incorporated in 'The Passing of Arthur', was composed in 1833 after A. H. *Hallam's death and published in 1842. In 1855–6 he began writing the first Idyll, which was to become 'Merlin and Vivien', which he followed with 'Enid', later divided into 'The Marriage of Geraint' and 'Geraint and Enid'. The first four were published in 1859 as 'Enid', 'Vivien', 'Elaine', and 'Guinevere' and constituted, though with many revisions, roughly half of the final version. In 1869 followed 'The Coming of Arthur', 'The Holy Grail', 'Pelleas and Ettarre', and 'The Passing of Arthur'. 'The Last Tournament' was published in the *Contemporary Review* in 1871, then, with 'Gareth and Lynette', in 1872. 'Balin and Balan', written 1872–4, did not appear until 1885. The sequence as now printed first appeared in 1891.

The poems present the story of *Arthur, from

his first meeting with Guinevere to the ruin of his kingdom and his death in the 'last, dim, weird battle of the west'. The protagonists are Arthur and Guinevere, Launcelot and Elaine, but the design embraces the fates of various minor characters. The adultery of Guinevere and Launcelot is seen as one of the forces that destroys the idealism and bright hopes of the Round Table, and the scene in which the guilty Guinevere 'grovelled with her face against the floor' before Arthur to listen to his long denunciatory speech was received with great enthusiasm; his forgiveness of her ('Lo! I forgive thee, as Eternal God | Forgives') moved the poet himself to tears.

Ignatius His Conclave, see DONNE, J.

Ignoge, in *Geoffrey of Monmouth's History,* married Brutus (*Brut) and was the mother of *Locrine, *Camber, and Albanactus. Spenser (*Faerie Queene) calls her Inogene of Italy.

Ignoramus, a famous university farcical play by George Ruggle (1575–1622), produced in 1615 before James I, an adaptation of an Italian comedy by Della Porta. The title part is a burlesque of the recorder of Cambridge, Brackyn, who is subjected to various humiliations.

Igraine, in Arthurian legend, the wife of Gorlois of Cornwall, taken as his wife by *Uther Pendragon who assumed the likeness of Gorlois by Merlin's magic. *Arthur was the child of this union.

Iliad, The, a Greek epic poem attributed to *Homer, describing the war waged by Achaean princes against Troy for the purpose of recovering Helen, wife of Menelaus, whom Paris, son of King Priam of Troy, had carried off. In particular it deals with the wrath of Achilles, the special hero of the poem, at the slight put upon him by Agamemnon, leader of the host, and his final return to the field and slaying of Hector.

'Il Penseroso', a poem by *Milton, written ?1631, printed 1645. The poem is an invocation to the goddess Melancholy, bidding her bring Peace, Quiet, Leisure, and Contemplation. It describes the pleasures of the studious, meditative life, of tragedy, epic poetry, and music. It is a companion piece to *'L'Allegro'.

Imaginary Conversations of Literary Men and Statesmen, by W. S. *Landor, published 1824–9, followed by Imaginary Conversations of Greeks and Romans, published 1853.

These represent the bulk of Landor's prose work. The conversations are between characters from classical times to the 19th cent.; some are dramatic, some idyllic, some satirical. There are some 150 dialogues and the quality is uneven, for Landor's own passionate views tend to obtrude.

Imagism, a movement of English and American poets in revolt from *Romanticism, which flourished c.1910–17, and derived in part from the aesthetic philosophy of T. E. *Hulme. Its first anthology, *Des Imagistes* (1914), edited by *Pound, had eleven contributors: R. *Aldington, H. *Doolittle, F. S. Flint, Skipwith Cannell, A. *Lowell, W. C. *Williams, *Joyce, Pound, F. M. Hueffer (*Ford), Allen Upward, and John Cournos. Some of D. H. *Lawrence's poems of this period may also be described as Imagist. The characteristic products of the movement are more easily recognized than its theories defined: they tend to be short, composed of short lines of musical cadence rather than metrical regularity, to avoid abstraction, and to treat the image with a hard, clear precision rather than with overt symbolic intent. The influence of Japanese forms (tanka and *haiku) is obvious in many. Amy Lowell succeeded Pound as spokesperson of the group, and was responsible for severage Imagist anthologies.

Imitation of Christ, or De Imitatione Christi, see THOMAS À KEMPIS.

Imitations of Horace, see POPE, A.

Imlac, a character in Dr Johnson's *Rasselas.

Imogen, the heroine of Shakespeare's *Cymbeline.

Importance of Being Earnest, The: A Trivial Comedy for Serious People, a play by O. *Wilde, first performed 1895.

John Worthing (Jack) and Algernon (Algy) Moncrieff are in pursuit respectively of Gwendolen Fairfax (Algy's cousin) and Jack's ward, Cecily Cardew. Both young men lead double lives, in that Jack is known in town as Ernest, while representing to his ward Cecily in the country that he has a wicked brother Ernest; Algy has created a fictitious character, the sickly Bunbury, whose ill health requires a visit whenever engagements in town (particularly those with his formidable aunt Lady Bracknell) render his absence desirable. After many confusions of identity, during which it transpires that Cecily's governess, Miss Prism, had once mislaid Jack as a baby in a handbag at Victoria Station, it is revealed that Jack and Algy are in fact brothers, and that Jack's name is indeed Ernest. All objections to both matches are thus overcome, and Gwendolen's addiction to the very name of 'Ernest' is satisfied.

Impressionism, the name given in derision (from a painting by Monet called *Impression, soleil levant*) to the work of a group of French painters who held their first exhibition in 1874. Their aim was to render the effects of light on objects rather than the objects themselves.

Claude Monet (1840–1926), Alfred Sisley (1839–99), and Camille Pissarro (1831–1903) carried out their aims most completely. The term is used by transference in literature and music.

Impressions of Theophrastus Such, The, a volume of essays by G. *Eliot, published 1879. Most of the 18 essays are character studies loosely based on the model of *Theophrastus.

Imprimatur, 'let it be printed', the formula signed by an official licenser authorizing the printing of a book.

In a Glass Darkly, a collection of stories by J. S. *Le Fanu, published 1872. They purport to be cases from the papers of 'Dr Martin Hesselius, the German Physician'—the first of a long line of psychic investigators in English literature. Of the five stories the best-known are 'Green Tea', featuring an apparition in the form of a malignant monkey, and 'Carmilla', an extremely powerful tale of a female vampire which antedates Stoker's *Dracula* by 25 years and was adapted by Carl Dreyer in his film *Vampyr* (1932).

INCHBALD, Mrs Elizabeth, *née* Simpson (1753–1821), novelist, dramatist, and actress. She is chiefly remembered for her two prose romances, *A Simple Story* (1791) and *Nature and Art* (1796), both of which display some skill in character and narration and illustrate her faith in natural upbringing (see PRIMITIVISM); and her play *Lovers' Vows* (1798), the drama enacted by the Bertram family in J. Austen's *Mansfield Park*.

'Inchcape Rock, The', a ballad by R. *Southey, written 1796–8, published 1802. Because the rock, off the Firth of Tay, was dangerous to mariners, the abbot of Arbroath, or Aberbrothock, fixed a warning bell upon it. A piratical character, Sir Ralph the Rover, in order to plague the abbot, cuts the bell from its float and later, on his homeward way, is wrecked upon the rock.

Incunabula, Incunables, books printed before the 16th cent., from the Latin word for 'swaddling clothes', hence 'infancy'.

Index Expurgatorius, strictly, an authoritative specification of the passages to be expunged or altered in works otherwise permitted to be read by Roman Catholics. The term is frequently used in England to cover the 'Index Librorum Prohibitorum', or list of forbidden books (not authors, as sometimes thought). The 'Index Expurgatorius' and the 'Index Librorum Prohibitorum' were abrogated in 1966.

Index on Censorship, a periodical founded in 1972 by Writers and Scholars International, a group concerned with the promotion of intellectual freedom, formed largely at the instigation of the Soviet dissident Pavel Litvinov and S. *Spender. It contains reports on cases of censorship and imprisonment of writers throughout the world, and also publishes original poetry and prose by authors many of whom are suppressed in their own countries.

Indicator, The (1819–21), a periodical established and edited by Leigh *Hunt devoted to literary matters. It published the work of young poets, including Keats's *'La Belle Dame sans Merci', and introduced much foreign literature.

Indo-European, the name applied to the great family of cognate languages (formerly called Indo-Germanic and Aryan) spoken over most of Europe and extending into Asia as far as northern India.

Infernal Marriage, The, a burlesque by B. *Disraeli, published 1834.

Inferno, The, of Dante, see DIVINA COMMEDIA.

INGE, William Ralph (1860–1954), dean of St Paul's 1911–34, dubbed 'the gloomy dean' for his pessimistic views on democracy, progress, education, etc. published in articles for the *Evening Standard*. He also published diaries, memoirs, and many volumes on religion, politics, and philosophy.

INGELOW, Jean (1820–97), poet, published several volumes of verse and some stories for children; her best-known poems are 'Divided' and 'The High Tide on the Coast of Lincolnshire, 1571', both in *Poems* (1863).

Ingoldsby Legends, The, see BARHAM, R. H.

Inheritance, The, a novel by S. *Ferrier, published 1824. The novel relates, in an improbably complex plot, but with much humour, the fortunes of Gertrude St Clair, grand-daughter of the earl of Rossville and heiress presumptive to his estate.

Inkhorn, a term originating in the 16th cent., applied to excessively literary, bookish, or pedantic language.

Inkle and Yarico, a romantic musical comedy by G. *Colman the younger, performed 1787.
The young Londoner, Inkle, saved from cannibals on a voyage to Barbados by the beautiful native girl Yarico, has to decide between fidelity to her and a wealthy marriage to Narcissa, the Governor's daughter; he chooses the latter and is punished for his ingratitude. (See PRIMITIVISM.)

'Inklings, The', a group of friends who gathered round C. S. *Lewis at Oxford from the

1930s to the 1960s, and read aloud their original compositions. Members included J. R. R. *Tolkien and C. *Williams.

In Memoriam A.H.H., a poem by *Tennyson, written between 1833 and 1850 and published anonymously in the latter year. The poem was written in memory of A. H. *Hallam. It is written in stanzas of four octosyllabic lines rhyming a b b a, and is divided into 132 sections of varying length.

It is not so much a single elegy as a series of poems written over a considerable period, inspired by the changing moods of the author's regret for his lost friend, and expressing his own anxieties about change, evolution, and immortality, the last a subject which continued to perturb him deeply. The epilogue is a marriage-song on the occasion of the wedding of the poet's sister Cecilia to Edward Lushington; Hallam had himself been engaged to his sister Emily.

Inn Album, The, a poem in blank verse, by R. *Browning, published 1875.

INNES, Michael, the pseudonym of J. I. M. *Stewart.

Innisfail, a poetic name for Ireland.

Innocence, Songs of, see SONGS OF INNOCENCE.

Innocents Abroad, The, a satirical account by Mark *Twain, published 1869 (in England, 1870, as *The New Pilgrim's Progress*), of a cruise on the *Quaker City* to the Mediterranean with a company of Americans in 1867.

Inogene, see IGNOGE.

Inscape, Instress, see HOPKINS, G. M.

Intelligent Woman's Guide to Socialism and Capitalism, The (1928), by G. B. *Shaw. This closely argued and passionately felt political testament treats women as the have-nots of a male culture and traces specific social evils to inequality of income.

Interior Monologue, see STREAM OF CONSCIOUSNESS.

Interludes were plays performed at Court, in the halls of the nobles, at the Inns of Court, and in colleges, generally but not exclusively by professional actors, dealing with a short episode and involving a limited number of characters. That interludes were sometimes performed by villagers we know from 'Pyramus and Thisbe' in *A Midsummer Night's Dream*. Their vogue was chiefly in the 15th and 16th cents. They succeeded *Morality Plays in the history of the drama, and are not always clearly distinguishable from them. The characters are still frequently allegorical, but the comic or farcical element is more prevalent, the versification tends to doggerel, and they are shorter than the moralities. The origin of the name is obscure. There are good examples by *Heywood, Henry Medwall (see FULGENS AND LUCRECE), and *Rastell.

'Intimations of Immortality from Recollections of Early Childhood', an ode by *Wordsworth, composed 1802–4/6, published 1807.

It is Wordsworth's most profound and memorable exploration of the significance of the intensity of childhood experience of the natural world (which suggests to him a state of pre-existence). The poem ends with a moving affirmation of the poet's faith in the powers of the philosophic mind and the human heart.

Invisible Man, The, (1) a science fiction romance by H. G. *Wells, published 1897, about a scientist who fatally stumbles upon the secret of invisibility; (2) *Invisible Man*, a Kafkaesque and claustrophobic novel by the American writer Ralph Waldo Ellison (1914–), published 1952, which describes the life of a young black man in New York City.

IONESCO, Eugène, see ABSURD, THEATRE OF THE.

Ionic a Minore, see METRE.

Ipomadon, a Middle English romance, taken from the French of Huon de Rotelande (c.1190). Of the three English versions the most famous is in 8,890 lines of twelve-line tail-rhyme stanzas of the mid-14th cent. possibly from Lancashire. Ipomadon is a prince of Apulia who wins by his exploits (mostly in disguise) the love of La Fière, the disdainful duchess of Calabria.

Iras, in Shakespeare's *Antony and Cleopatra*, one of Cleopatra's attendants.

IRELAND, William Henry (1777–1835), is remembered chiefly as a forger of Shakespeare manuscripts. When working in a lawyer's office he had easy access to old parchment, deeds, and antiquated forms of writing. An exhibition of his forgeries of poems and deeds wholly deceived the general public, and *Boswell kissed the parchments. A facsimile edition of the 'works' was published in 1795, and other works, including the plays *Vortigern and Rowena* and *Henry II*, made their appearance. Ireland subsequently admitted to the forgeries. He published two volumes of poems; *The Fisher Boy* (1808); *The Sailor Boy* (1809); and *Scribbleomania* (1815).

'**I remember, I remember**', the first line of a well-known work by T. *Hood.

Irena, in Spenser's *Faerie Queene* (Bk V), personifies Ireland, oppressed by *Grantorto and righted by Sir *Artegall.

Irene, a blank verse tragedy by Dr *Johnson, written 1736, performed 1749, without much success. The story, taken from *Knolles's history of the Turks, concerns the fate of Irene, a Greek slave loved by the emperor Mahomet.

Irish Literary Theatre was founed by W. B *Yeats, Lady *Gregory, and E. *Martyn in 1899. It became the Irish National Theatre Society in 1903, with Yeats as president, and moved into the new *Abbey Theatre in 1904.

Irish Revival, a resurgence of Irish nationalism and culture which began in the last quarter of the 19th cent. and flourished until the 1920s. The revival was fostered by translations and re-tellings of Irish legend, folklore, and poetry, such as S. *Ferguson's *Lays of the Western Gael* (1865) and D. *Hyde's *Love Songs of Connacht* (1893). The *Irish Literary Theatre, founded by W. B. *Yeats and others in 1899, developed into the important *Abbey Theatre company. Plays by Yeats, *Synge, G. B. *Shaw, and *O'Casey made the Abbey renowned. Meanwhile the poetry of Yeats and the prose work of G. *Moore, *Joyce, and many others established the new literary stature of Irish writing.

Irish R.M., see SOME EXPERIENCES OF AN IRISH R.M.

IRON, Ralph, pseudonym of O. *Schreiner.

IRVING, Sir Henry (1838–1905), originally John Henry Brodribb, achieved fame as an actor for his performance in *The Bells* (1871–2), and afterwards scored successes in a large number of Shakespearian and other parts, his impersonation of *Tennyson's Becket being one of his chief triumphs. His management of the Lyceum Theatre in association with Ellen *Terry, 1878–1902, was distinguished, and he revived popular interest in Shakespeare.

IRVING, Washington (1783–1859), born in New York, the son of an Englishman. He published (with his brother William Irving and J. K. Paulding) a series of satirical essays and poems collected in *Salmagundi: or, the Whim-Whams and Opinions of Launcelot Langstaff, Esq. and others* (1808). This was followed by his highly successful burlesque *A History of New York from the Beginning of the World to the End of the Dutch Dynasty*, by 'Diedrich Knickerbocker', a pseudonym chosen to represent the solid, phlegmatic Dutch burgher created by Irving.

Irving visited England and met Sir W. *Scott, T. *Moore, T. *Campbell, John *Murray, and others; on his return, he wrote *The Sketch Book* (1820), essays and tales under the pseudonym 'Geoffrey Crayon, Gent.', which contains sketches of English life, essays on American subjects, and American adaptations of German folk-tales (including *'Rip Van Winkle' and 'The Legend of Sleepy Hollow'). It was followed by other popular works, including *Bracebridge Hall* (1822), which features Squire Bracebridge, a sort of 19th-cent. de *Coverley. Some of his subsequent works were inspired by his period as diplomatic attaché in Spain (1826–9), including *Legends of the Alhambra* (1832). He was hailed in his own country as the first American author to have achieved international fame.

Irvingites, members of the Catholic Apostolic Church, a religious body founded about 1835, which developed from a revivalist circle that had gathered round H. Drummond (1851–97), and was partly inspired by the teachings of Edward Irving (1792–1834), a Scottish minister, who was a friend and encourager of *Carlyle. They believed in the near approach of the second coming of Christ and sought the re-establishment of the primitive offices of the Church (viz. the apostles, prophets, evangelists, etc.).

Isaac of York, in Scott's *Ivanhoe*, the father of Rebecca.

Isabella, (1) in *Orlando Furioso*, daughter of a Saracen king of Spain; (2) in Kyd's *Spanish Tragedy*, wife to Hieronimo; (3) queen to Marlowe's *Edward II*; (4) the heroine of Shakespeare's *Measure for Measure*.

'**Isabella, or The Pot of Basil**', a narrative poem by *Keats, written 1818, published 1820.
   The poem is based on a story in Boccaccio's *Decameron*. The worldly, ambitious brothers of Isabella intend that she shall marry a nobleman. When they discover her love for the humble Lorenzo they lure him away, murder him, and bury his body in a forest. His ghost then appears to Isabella and tells her where he is buried. She finds his body, severs the head, and places it in a pot with a plant of basil over it. Her brothers, observing how she cherishes the plant, steal the pot, discover the mouldering head, and fly, conscience-striken, into banishment. Isabella mourns her loss, pines away, and dies.

Isengrym, or **Isengrin,** the wolf in *Reynard the Fox*.

Iseult the Fair (also Isolde, Isoud, Isode, Ysoude), the daughter of the king of Ireland in Arthurian legend. She is the lover of *Tristram (Tristan) who has been sent by his uncle King Mark of Cornwall to bring Iseult as his wife. The story of Tristram and Iseult is the great classic of doomed love; Tristram is the slayer of her uncle Marhaus and they are fated to love each other by drinking in error the potion which was meant to have been shared by Mark and Iseult on their wedding night, binding them in everlasting love. Her mother is also called Iseult (even sometimes Iseult the Fair).

Iseult of the White Hands, in Arthurian legend, daughter of the ruler of Brittany, with whom *Tristram falls in love and marries after his banishment by King Mark. But Iseult of Brittany does not succeed in erasing the memory of *Iseult the Fair; when Tristram is dying, he sends for his first Iseult by ship; if she is on the ship on its return from Ireland she is to fly a white flag; if not a black one. The white flag is flown; but Iseult of the White Hands tells Tristram it is black, whereupon he dies.

ISHERWOOD, Christopher William Bradshaw (1904–86), novelist. His first novels, *All the Conspirators* (1928) and *The Memorial* (1932), show the influence of E. M. *Forster and V. *Woolf; his own voice appears distinctly in *Mr Norris Changes Trains* (1935) and *Goodbye to Berlin* (1939), works which reflect his experiences of living in Berlin, 1929–33. Both novels are largely autobiographical and give a vivid portrait of Germany on the eve of Hitler's rise to power; the first is about a con-man and double agent, the corrupt, seedy, emotional, and engaging Arthur Norris, and his adventures in the criminal and political underworld; the second is a series of sketches, of which the best-known is the section 'Sally Bowles' (published independently in 1937). Sally is a cabaret artist and her Bohemian enterprises were later successfully dramatized in 1951 by John Van Druten as *I am a Camera*, and turned into a stage musical in 1968 as *Cabaret*. Isherwood travelled widely in Europe after leaving Berlin, went to China with Auden in 1938, and in 1939 went with him to America; he became an American citizen in 1946.

He collaborated with Auden in the writing of *The Ascent of F6* and several other works (see under AUDEN), translated some of *Brecht, and wrote the semi-autobiographical *Lions and Shadows* (1938), in which his friends (Auden, *Spender, *Upward, V. *Watkins, and others) appear under fictitious names. After settling near Hollywood, he became interested in Hindu philosophy and Vedanta and edited various works on the subject. Novels written in America include *Down there on a Visit* (1962) and *A Single Man* (1964); *Christopher and His Kind* (1977) is a frank account of the homosexual affairs of his young manhood.

ISIDORE OF SEVILLE (570–636), archbishop of Seville, an encyclopaedic writer; author of *Origenes* or *Etymologiae*. Much of this is fantastic, but it can be seen as one of the first texts in the encyclopaedic tradition in medieval literature.

Island, The, a poem by Lord *Byron, published in 1823. The poem is based on the story of the mutiny on HMS *Bounty*. The mutineers' island is depicted as an earthly paradise, which forms the background to the idyllic love of Torquil and Neuha, children of nature.

Island in the Moon, An, an untitled burlesque fragment by W. *Blake, written c.1784–5, first printed (though inaccurately) in 1907 by E. J. Ellis in *The Real Blake*. It is a satirical portrait of scientific and cultural dilettantism and pretension, interspersed with songs (some of them bawdy).

Island of Dr Moreau, The, a *science fiction tale by H. G. *Wells, published 1896. It is an evolutionary fantasy about a shipwrecked naturalist who becomes involved in an experiment to 'humanize' animals by surgery. The theme was developed by *Aldiss.

Isumbras, Sir, a verse-romance in 804 lines of twelve-line tail-rhyme stanzas, from the North-East Midlands, popular before 1320. Its theme is that of 'the man tried by fate' of which the model is St Eustace, of Eastern origin. Isumbras is strong, handsome, and prosperous, but also proud and arrogant. A bird sent by God offers him the choice of suffering in youth or old age, and he chooses the former. He loses his wife, children, and possessions, and suffers for 21 years among the Saracens. At the end of that period an angel tells him that his sins are expiated and he is restored to his family and possessions.

It is Never too Late to Mend, a novel by C. *Reade.

Iuliene, St, see KATHERINE GROUP, THE.

Ivanhoe, a novel by Sir W. *Scott, published 1819. This was the first of the author's novels in which he adopted a purely English subject.

Wilfred of Ivanhoe, son of Cedric, of noble Saxon birth, loves his father's ward, the lady Rowena, who traces her descent to King Alfred, and who returns his love. Cedric, who is passionately devoted to the restoration of the Saxon line to the throne of England and sees the best chance of effecting this in the marriage of Rowena to Athelstane of Coningsburgh, also of the Saxon blood royal, has in anger banished his son. Ivanhoe has joined Richard Cœur de Lion at the crusade and there won the king's affection. In Richard's absence, his brother John has found support among the lawless and dissolute Norman nobles for his plan to depose Richard, a design favoured by Richard's imprisonment in Austria on his return from Palestine.

The story centres in two chief events: a great tournament at Ashby de la Zouch, where Ivanhoe aided by Richard, who unknown to all has returned to England with Ivanhoe, defeats all the knights of John's party, including the fierce Templar Sir Brian de Bois-Guilbert and Sir Reginald Front-de-Bœuf; and the siege of Front-de-Bœuf's castle of Torquilstone, whither Cedric and Rowena, with the wounded Ivanhoe, Athelstane, the Jew Isaac, and his beautiful and courageous daughter Rebecca, have been carried captives by the Norman nobles. After an exciting fight, the castle is carried by a force of outlaws and Saxons, led by Locksley (otherwise *Robin Hood) and King Richard himself. The prisoners are rescued, with the exception of Rebecca whom the Templar carries off to the Preceptory of Templestowe. Here the unexpec-

ted arrival of the Grant Master of the order, while relieving Rebecca from the dishonourable advances of Bois-Guilbert, exposes her to the charge of witchcraft, and she escapes sentence of death only by demanding trial by combat. Ivanhoe appears as her champion, and in the encounter between him and Bois-Guilbert the latter falls dead, untouched by his opponent's lance, the victim of his own contending passions. Ivanhoe and Rowena are united; Rebecca, suppressing her love for Ivanhoe, leaves England with her father.

Among the many characters in the story, besides Robin Hood and Friar Tuck, are the poor fool Wamba, who imperils his life to save that of his master Cedric; Gurth, the swineherd; and Isaac the Jew, divided between love of his shekels and love of his daughter. Thackeray's *Rebecca and Rowena* is an amusing sequel to, and critical reinterpretation of, Scott's tale.

J

Jabberwock, a fictitious monster, the subject of the poem 'Jabberwocky' in Lewis Carroll's *Through the Looking-Glass*. The story, told in an invented vocabulary, begins: ' 'Twas brillig and the slithy toves'.

Jack, Colonel, see COLONEL JACK.

'Jack and Jill', a nursery rhyme, involving perhaps originally some political allusion now lost. *Baring-Gould (*Curious Myths*) finds the origin of Jack and Jill in the Hjuki and Bil of Scandinavian mythology, two children who had been drawing water and were stolen by the moon.

Jack and the Bean-stalk, a nursery tale based on a world-wide myth, found e.g. among the North American Indians and the native tribes of S. Africa. The bean-stalk is said to be derived from the ash tree Yggdrasil, the world-tree of northern mythology.

'Jackdaw of Rheims, The', see BARHAM, R. H.

Jacke Wilton, *The Life of*, see UNFORTUNATE TRAVELLER, THE.

Jack Horner, the subject of a nursery rhyme ('Little Jack Horner sat in a corner', etc.), which occurs in an 18th-cent. chapbook. The origin of the rhyme is dubiously attributed to Jack Horner who was steward to the abbot of Glastonbury in the reign of Henry VIII and by a trick acquired the deeds of the manor of Mells at the dissolution of the monasteries; the Horner family still holds the manor.

Jack of Dover, in Prologue to Chaucer's 'Cook's Tale' (see CANTERBURY TALES, 8); refers probably to a pie (or, less probably, fish) that has been reheated.

Jack of Newbery, or **Newbury,** John Winchcombe, alias Smallwood (d. 1520), a clothier of Newbury, whose wealth inspired the authors of numerous chapbook stories.

Jack Straw, the leader of a party of insurgents from Essex in the Peasant's Revolt of 1381.

Jack the Giant-Killer, a nursery tale of Northern origin, known in England from very early times.

Jack the Ripper, the name given to a murderer who, between 1888 and 1891, killed several prostitutes in the Whitechapel area of London. Attempts to guess his identity have included a Harley Street surgeon, a mad midwife, a Russian anarchist, the duke of Clarence (1864–92), and J. K. *Stephen.

Jacobin, originally a name of the French friars of the order of St Dominic, so called because the church of St Jacques in Paris was given to them and they built their first convent near by. From them the name was transferred to the members of a French political club established in 1789, in Paris, in the old convent, to maintain the principles of extreme democracy and absolute equality. It was applied about 1800 as a nickname for any political reformer.

JACOBS, W(illiam) W(ymark) (1863–1943), is chiefly remembered as a writer of short stories. These fall roughly into two groups: those dealing humorously with the escapades of sailors and of country characters and rogues, as in the 'Claybury' stories; and tales of the macabre, such as the celebrated 'The Monkey's Paw', which was dramatized. His collections include *Many Cargoes* (1896), *Light Freights* (1901), *The Lady of the Barge* (1902), and *Night Watches* (1914).

Jacob's Room, see WOOLF, V.

Jacobus de Voragine, see GOLDEN LEGEND, THE.

Jaffar the Barmecide (Ja'far al-Barmeki), in the *Arabian Nights*, the vizier of *Hārūn ar-Rashīd.

Jaffeir, one of the principal characters in Otway's *Venice Preserv'd*.

JAGGARD, William (*fl.* 1594–1623), and Isaac (*fl.* 1613–27), London printers and principal publishers of the Shakespeare First Folio (see FOLIOS AND QUARTOS, SHAKESPEARIAN).

Jaggers, Mr, a character in Dickens's *Great Expectations*.

JAGO, Richard (1715–81), was the author of *Edge-hill* (1767), a *topographical poem in four books describing, with many digressions, the views seen at morning, noon, afternoon, and evening, as he looks from that famous spot over his favourite country.

Jakin, Bob, a character in G. Eliot's *The Mill on the Floss.*

JAKOBSON, Roman (1896–1982), a Russian-born linguist who was one of the most celebrated members of the school of criticism known as 'Russian formalism' and principal member of the 'Prague School' of linguistics; in 1939 he settled in America. His principal linguistic contribution was to apply to phonetics the idea of *Saussure that linguistic systems are characterized by *oppositions* which define various units, developing the notion of 'distinctive features' in phonology. Latterly he has become more celebrated for his influence on literary criticism, partly through the medium of Roland Barthes; his work laid the foundation for a *Structuralist approach to literary theory.

JAMES I (1394–1437), king of Scotland, was captured while on his way to France by an English ship, probably in 1406. He was detained in England for 19 years and well educated. While in England he composed his famous poem *The Kingis Quair,* the authorship of which has been doubted, but there seems no good reason to deny it to James. One or two other poems have been doubtfully attributed to him: 'The Ballad of Good Counsel', *'Christis Kirk on the Green', and 'Peblis to the Play'.

JAMES I (James VI of Scotland) (1566–1625), king of England 1603–25. He is reputedly the author of *True Law of Free Monarchies* (1598). His works include *Basilikon Doron* (1599, precepts on the art of government, addressed to his son), theological works, poetry in Scots, Latin, and English, metrical versions of 30 psalms, and a short treatise on the rules for writing *Scots poetry.

James the Fourth, *The Scottish Historie of,* a play by R. *Greene, published posthumously 1598. In spite of the title, this is a fictionalized romantic comedy, framed by the comments of Oberon, king of fairies.

JAMES, George Payne Rainsford (1799–1860), was appointed historiographer royal by William IV. Influenced by Sir W. *Scott he wrote numerous romantic novels, biographies, and popular historical works, including *Richelieu* (1829), *Darnley* (1830), *Life of Edward the Black Prince* (1836). *Thackeray parodied him as 'the solitary horseman' in his burlesque *Barbazure, by G. P. R. Jeames, esq.* for the two horsemen who were a frequent beginning to his romances.

JAMES, Henry (1843–1916), born in New York, the son of Henry James senior, writer on questions of theology and a follower of *Swedenborg, and brother of William *James. After a desultory education in New York,

London, Paris, and Geneva, Henry James entered the law school at Harvard in 1862. He settled in Europe in 1875. From 1865 he was a regular contributor of reviews and short stories to American periodicals and owed much to his friendship with W. D. *Howells. For more than 20 years he lived in London, and in 1898 moved to Lamb House, Rye, where his later novels were written. He at first chiefly concerned himself with the impact of the older civilization of Europe upon American life, and to this period belong his novels *Roderick Hudson* (1876), *The American* (1877), *Daisy Miller* (1879), and *Portrait of a Lady* (1881). He next turned to a more exclusively English stage in *The Tragic Muse* (1890), *The Spoils of Poynton* (1897), and *The Awkward Age* (1899), in which he analysed English character with extreme subtlety. *What Maisie Knew* appeared in 1897. In his last three great novels, *The Wings of the Dove* (1902), *The Ambassadors* (1903), and *The Golden Bowl* (1904), he returned to the 'international' theme of the contrast of American and European character. *The Ivory Tower* and *The Sense of the Past* remained unfinished at his death and were published in fragments in 1917. For the revised collection of his fiction, which began in 1907, James wrote a series of prefaces of high interest. In his critical essays James concentrated on the 19th-cent. novel.

Besides more than 100 short stories (including the well-known ghost story *The Turn of the Screw,* 1898), James wrote several volumes of sketches of travel (*Portraits of Places,* 1883; *A Little Tour in France,* 1884), several plays, and a life of *Hawthorne. A short story called 'The Middle Years' appeared in the volume *Terminations* in 1895. The autobiographical work of the same title is a fragment (published posthumously, 1917).

His other works include *Madonna of the Future* (1879), *Washington Square* (1881), *The Siege of London* (1883), *The Bostonians* (1886), *The Princess Casamassima* (1886), *The Reverberator* (1888), *The Aspern Papers* (1888), *The Real Thing* (1893), *Embarrassments* (1896), *The Other House* (1896), *In the Cage* (1898), *The Two Magics* (1898), *The Better Sort* (1903).

JAMES, M(ontague) R(hodes) (1862–1936), a brilliant linguist, palaeographer, medievalist, and biblical scholar, was successively provost of King's College, Cambridge, and of Eton. He edited works by *Le Fanu, wrote several volumes of distinguished ghost stories, many with East Anglian settings, including 'Oh Whistle, and I'll Come to You, My Lad', which appeared in *Ghost Stories of an Antiquary* (1904). *More Ghost Stories of an Antiquary* appeared in 1911, and his collected stories in 1931.

JAMES, William (1842–1910), American philosopher, elder brother of Henry *James. His views are embodied in his *Principles of Psychology* (1890), and show a tendency to subordinate logical proof to intuitive conviction. He was a vigorous antagonist of the idealist school of *Kant and *Hegel, and an empiricist who made empiricism more radical by treating pure experience as the very substance of the world. Pragmatism, for which he is best remembered by philosophers, was his method of approach to metaphysics. James's other principal works were *Varieties of Religious Experience* (1902), *Pragmatism* (1907), *The Meaning of Truth* (1909), a *Pluralistic Universe* (1909), *Essays in Radical Empiricism* (1912). The conclusions of his *Varieties of Religious Experience* are notable: 'the visible world is part of a more spiritual universe from which it draws its chief significance . . . spiritual energy flows in and produces effects within the phenomenal world.' He coined the phrase *'stream of consciousness' now widely used as a literary term.

JAMESON, Anna Brownell (1794–1860), first attracted attention in 1826 with *A Lady's Diary* (later re-titled *The Diary of an Ennuyée*), describing a visit to Italy. The work for which she is now chiefly remembered is *Characteristics of Women* (1832, later known as *Shakespeare's Heroines*), dedicated to Fanny *Kemble. Shakespeare she saw as 'the Poet of Womankind', whose heroines display all the aspects and complexities of womanhood. She was a close friend of the *Brownings and of M. R. *Mitford.

JAMESON, (Margaret) Storm (1891–1986), novelist; her first novel, *The Pot Boils* (1919), was followed by many other works of fiction, including *Women Against Men* (1933, stories), *Company Parade* (1934), *Love in Winter* (1935), and *None turn Back* (1936), the last three forming a trilogy. She also published poems, essays, and biographies, and several volumes of autobiography, including *Journey from the North* (1969), describing her time during the Second World War as president of *PEN.

Jane Eyre, a novel by C. *Brontë, published 1847.
   The heroine, a penniless orphan, has been left to the care of her aunt Mrs Reed. Harsh and unsympathetic treatment rouses her defiant spirit, and Mrs Reed consigns her to Lowood Institution. There, consoled by the kindness of the superintendent Miss Temple, she spends some miserable years, eventually becoming a teacher. She then becomes a governess at Thornfield Hall to Adèle, the illegitimate daughter of Mr Rochester, a *Byronic hero of grim aspect and sardonic temper. Rochester, despite Jane's plainness, is fascinated by her sharp wit and independence, and they fall in love. After much resistance she agrees to marry him, but on the eve of their wedding her wedding veil is rent by an intruder who is the next day revealed to be his mad Creole wife Bertha, confined to the upper regions of the Hall for years, whose unseen presence has long disturbed Jane. Despite Rochester's full confession, Jane flees. After nearly perishing on the moors, she is taken in and cared for by the Revd St John Rivers and his sisters Mary and Diana. It emerges that they are her cousins, and that Jane has inherited money from an uncle. Under pressure from the dedicated Rivers, she nearly consents to marry him and share his missionary vocation in India, but is prevented by a telepathic appeal from Rochester. She returns to Thornfield Hall to find the building burned, and Rochester blinded and maimed from his attempt to save his wife from the flames. She marries him, and in the last chapter we learn that his sight is partially restored.

JANE SHORE, see SHORE.

'Janet's Repentance', see SCENES OF CLERICAL LIFE.

'January and May', a version by *Pope of Chaucer's 'Merchant's Tale' (see CANTERBURY TALES, 10).

Jaquenetta, in Shakespeare's *Love's Labour's Lost*, a country wench loved by Armado.

Jaques, a discontented lord attending the banished duke in Shakespeare's *As You Like It*. Many of the play's most memorable lines are his, including the speech beginning 'All the world's a stage' (II. vii).

Jarley, Mrs, in Dickens's *The Old Curiosity Shop*, the proprietor of a travelling waxworks show.

Jarndyce, John, a character in Dickens's *Bleak House*.

JARRELL, Randall (1914–65), American poet and critic. His one novel, *Pictures from an Institution* (1954), is a satire on life in a progressive women's college and an early example of a *campus novel. He published several volumes of poetry, from his first, *Blood for a Stranger* (1942), to *The Lost World* (1966).

Jazz Poetry, a genre presaged in the US by (Nicholas) Vachel Lindsay (1879–1931) with his incantatory ballads, and then by (James) Langston Hughes (1902–67), who was probably the first to pitch his verse in conjunction with musicians in the late 1930s. The fusion was developed in the 1950s by Kenneth Patchen (1911–72), Kenneth Rexroth (1905–82), Amiri Baraka (adopted name of black militant writer Everett Le Roi Jones, 1934–), Ted Joans (1928–), and the poets of the American *Beat Generation; and in Britain from the mid-1950s to the 1980s by Christopher Logue (1926–), Roy Fisher (1930–), Michael Horovitz (1935–), Pete Brown (1940–), Spike Hawkins (1942–), and others. Various permutations of primarily non-academic, often regional, entertainers and singer-songwriters have proliferated since, including the Rastafarian and reggae-cadenced contributions of Anglo-Jamaican poets such as James *Berry, E. K. *Brathwaite, Linton Kwesi Johnson, and Benjamin Zephaniah. See also UNDERGROUND POETRY.

Jean de Meun, see ROMAN DE LA ROSE.

JEBB, Richard Claverhouse (1841–1905), professor of Greek at Glasgow University 1874, regius professor at Cambridge 1889. His first major work, *The Attic Orators* (1876) and subsequent critical editions, translations of Sophocles (1883–96), and other works on classical subjects show his voluminous and precise knowledge of ancient Greece. He became MP for his university (1891) and received the OM and a knighthood in 1900.

Jeeves, in many of P. G. *Wodehouse's stories, the omniscient and resourceful valet.

JEFFERIES, Richard (1848–87), writer and naturalist, the son of a Wiltshire farmer. He first attracted attention with *The Gamekeeper at Home: Sketches of Natural History and Rural Life* (1878). This, together with *Hodge and his Masters* (1880), appears to have influenced *Hardy's article of 1883, 'The Dorsetshire Labourer'. Jefferies relied greatly on 'field notebooks', where he entered his meticulous observations on the life of the countryside. His other works include *Wild Life in a Southern County* (1879); *The Amateur Poacher* (1879); *Wood Magic* (1881), in which a solitary boy lives in a magical world of speaking wild animals; *Bevis, The Story of a Boy* (1882), an evocation (for both adults and children) of his country childhood (see CHILDREN'S LITERATURE). The book for which he is probably best known, *The Story of my Heart* (1883), tracing the growth of his unorthodox beliefs, caused some scandal; *After London* (1885) is a savage vision of the future, in which London is a poisonous swamp inhabited by cruel dwarfs; *The Open Air* (1885) is a collection of essays. *Amaryllis at the Fair* (1887) contains in Iden an impressive portrait of Jefferies's father.

JEFFERS, (John) Robinson (1887–1962), American poet. The scenery of the redwood and seashore of California inspires much of his works, and one of his dominant themes is what he called 'Inhumanism'—the insignificance of man, contrasted with the vast, merciless, enduring processes of nature. He made his name with *Tamar and Other Poems* (1924), of which the title poem is a tragic narrative of family passion and incest in a wild Californian setting. Other volumes include *The Women at Point Sur* (1927), *Cawdor and Other Poems* (1928), *Thurso's Landing and Other poems* (1932), *Selected Poetry* (1938), and *Hungerfield and Other Poems* (1954).

JEFFREY, Francis (1773–1850), a Whig who became a Scottish judge and an MP. He is remembered in a literary connection as the founder, with Sydney *Smith, of *The Edinburgh Review* in 1802, as its editor until 1829, and as a stern but judicious critic of the writers of his day. Although he wrote appreciatively of many writers, including *Crabbe, Sir W. *Scott, *Byron, and *Keats, his inability to understand *Wordsworth led to a series of attacks on *'The Lake Poets'.

Jekyll and Mr Hyde, *The Strange Case of Dr,* a novel by R. L. *Stevenson, published 1886.

Dr Jekyll, a physician, discovers a drug by means of which he can create for himself a separate personality that absorbs all his evil instincts. This personality, repulsive in appearance, he assumes from time to time and calls Mr Hyde, and in it he gives rein to his evil impulses. It gradually gains the greater ascendancy, and Hyde commits a horrible murder. Jekyll now finds himself from time to time involuntarily transformed to Hyde, while the drug loses its efficacy in restoring his original form and character. On the point of discovery and arrest he takes his own life.

JELLICOE, (Patricia) Ann (1927–), playwright and director, associated for some years with the *English Stage Company, which in 1958 put on the play that made her name, *The Sport of My Mad Mother*, an experimental drama about a London street gang. This was followed by *The Knack* (1962) and *Shelley* (1965).

Jellyby, Mrs, a character in Dickens's *Bleak House.*

Jenkins, (1) Nicholas, the narrator of A. *Powell's *A Dance to the Music of Time*; (2) Mrs Winifred, a character in Smollett's *Humphry Clinker.*

Jenkyns, Deborah, Matilda, and Peter, characters in Mrs Gaskell's *Cranford.*

Jennings, Mrs, (1) a character in J. Austen's *Sense and Sensibility*; (2) the mother of *Keats, as she became by her second marriage.

JENNINGS, Elizabeth (1926–), poet; her early poems appeared in several collections and in Robert Conquest's *New Lines* (1956). Her subsequent volumes of verse (e.g. *Recoveries,*

1964; *The Mind has Mountains*, 1966) are highly personal and confessional accounts of mental breakdown and hospital treatment. Her *Collected Poems* (1967) were followed by several more volumes, including *Lucidities* (1970) and *Moments of Grace* (1979), which manifest her quiet and sensitive control of experiences of suffering, loneliness, friendship, and religious faith.

'**Jenny**', a poem by D. G. *Rossetti, first published 1870. It was one of the poems buried with his wife Lizzie in 1862. The poet describes a night spent in the chamber of a prostitute, golden-haired Jenny; she falls asleep against his knees and at dawn he leaves her, after much meditation on her thoughtless gaiety, shame, and beauty, and on the toad Lust which has ruined her.

Jenny Wren, see WREN.

JENYNS, Soame (1704–87), is chiefly remembered for his *A Free Enquiry into the Nature and Origin of Evil* (1757), which elicited a brilliant and scathing attack from Dr *Johnson in *The Literary Magazine*. Jenyns's work is a classic statement of the more facile elements of 18th-cent. optimism, justifying evil and suffering by their place in the 'scale of being' and ignorance as the 'opiate' of the poor: 'the sufferings of individuals are absolutely necessary to universal happiness.'

Jeremiad, a doleful complaint, in allusion to the *Lamentations of Jeremiah* in the OT.

JEROME, St (Hieronymus) (*c*. 342–420), one of the four 'Doctors of the Church', born at Strido near Dalmatia, educated at Rome. He visited Gaul and Asia Minor, and after a period of dissipation he practised asceticism. He lived as a hermit near Chalcis (south-east of Antioch), spent the years 382–5 at Rome, and in 386 settled at Bethlehem. His principal works were a translation and continuation of the chronicles of *Eusebius and the Latin version of the scriptures which came to be known as the *Vulgate.

JEROME, Jerome K(lapka) (1859–1927), achieved lasting fame with *Three Men in a Boat* (1889), the story of three young men and their dog who take a rowing holiday on the Thames. In 1892 Jerome and some friends founded *The Idler*, a humorous magazine which published work by *Harte, *Twain, and W. W. *Jacobs, among others. His other works include *On the Stage and Off* (1885) and *Idle Thoughts of an Idle Fellow* (1886), both collections of light essays; *Three Men on the Bummel* (1900); *Paul Klever* (1902), an autobiographical novel; and many plays, in the manner of his friend *Barrie, including *The Passing of the Third Floor Back* (1907).

Jeronimo, or Hieronimo, the chief character in Kyd's *The Spanish Tragedy*.

JERROLD, Douglas William (1803–57), made his name in the theatre with *Black-Ey'd Susan* (1829), founded on *Gay's ballad. He was a friend of *Dickens and was associated with *Punch from its beginnings, for which he wrote several serial works, including social political articles signed 'Q' and *Mrs Caudle's Curtain Lectures* (issued as a book in 1846). From 1845, he ran *Douglas Jerrold's Shilling Magazine* and from 1846 *Douglas Jerrold's Weekly Newspaper*. He wrote several successful plays, novels, and studies of *Men of Character* (1838) which were illustrated by *Thackeray. His son, William Blanchard Jerrold (1826–84), was also a prolific and miscellaneous writer.

Jerusalem: The Emanation of the Giant Albion, a prophetic poem by *Blake, written and etched, with 100 plates, 1804–20. (It is not to be confused with the short poem beginning 'And did those feet . . .', commonly known as 'Jerusalem', which appears at the beginning of Blake's *Milton.) After a Preface in which he defends his use of free verse, Blake proceeds to personify England as the fallen giant *Albion, and to summon him to the 'awakening of Eternal Life' which lies beyond the Vegetable Universe, and to reunion with his banished emanation, the lovely Jerusalem. Blake mingles prophecy with social criticism, and biblical legend with legends of druids and Gog and Magog (see GOGMAGOG).

Jerusalem Delivered (*Gerusalemme Liberata*), a poem by *Tasso, published without his consent 1580, in authorized form 1581.

The poem is an epic of the First Crusade, with the addition of romantic and fabulous elements. By the side of Godfrey of Bouillon, the leader of the Christian host besieging Jerusalem, and other historical characters, we have the romantic figures of Sofronia and her lover Olindo, who are prepared to face martyrdom to save the Christians in the beleaguered city; the warlike Clorinda, who is beloved by Tancred the Norman, and killed by him unwittingly; and Armida, the niece of the king of Damascus, who lures away the Christians to her enchanted gardens. Rinaldo, prince of Este, rescues the prisoners of Armida, and Armida falls in love with him. By her enchantments they live happily together until Rinaldo is summoned away to help the army by slaying the devil-enchanted wood. He takes part in the capture of Jerusalem, and at last marries a repentant Armida.

The poem was translated into English in 1594 by R. Carew (1555–1620), and in 1600 by Edward Fairfax (d. 1635) as *Godfrey of Bulloigne*. Spenser's description of Acrasia's Bower of Bliss (*Faerie Queene*, II. xii) was modelled on the gardens of Armida, and the poem considerably influenced *Milton and others (see TASSO).

Jessamy Bride, The, the name given by *Goldsmith to the younger Miss Horneck, with whom he is supposed to have been in love.

Jessica, in Shakespeare's *The Merchant of Venice*, Shylock's daughter.

Jessica's First Prayer, see STRETTON, H.

Jest Book Literature, collections of 'merie Tales', 'quicke answeres', and 'pleasant conceites' popular throughout the 16th and 17th cents and later. Their authorship was often ascribed to witty writers such as *Skelton and *Peele or to famous jesters such as J. *Scogan and R. Armin.

Jesuits, members of the Society of Jesus founded by St Ignatius Loyola (1491–1556), in Paris in 1534. They were bound by vows of chastity, poverty, obedience, and submission to the holy see, and authorized by papal bull in 1540. The Society's principal activities were preaching, instruction, and confession, and it formed a spiritual army bound by obedience. The object of the Society was to support the Roman Church in its conflict with the 16th-cent. reformers and to propagate its faith among the heathen. Francis Xavier and other missionaries carried out the latter work in distant parts of the world. The secret power of the organization brought it into collision with the civil authorities even in Roman Catholic countries, whence its members have at times been expelled.

Jew, The Wandering, see WANDERING JEW.

Jewel in the Crown, The, see SCOTT, P.

JEWETT, Sarah Orne (1849–1909), American novelist and short story writer. Her volumes include *Deephaven* (1877), *A Country Doctor* (1884), *A White Heron* (1886; short stories), and *The Country of the Pointed Firs* (1896). Her precise, realistic, subdued portraits of ordinary New England people and her sense of community have won her an enduring reputation.

Jew of Malta, The, a drama in blank verse by *Marlowe, performed about 1592, not published until 1633.

The Grand Seignior of Turkey having demanded the tribute of Malta, the governor of Malta decides that it shall be paid by the Jews of the island. Barabas, a rich Jew who resists the edict, has all his wealth impounded and his house turned into a nunnery. In revenge he indulges in an orgy of slaughter, procuring the death of his daughter Abigail's lover among others and poisoning Abigail herself, and finally is killed in one of his own traps. The Prologue to the play is spoken by 'Machevil', and Barabas is one of the prototypes for unscrupulous *Machiavellian villains in later Elizabethan and Jacobean drama. His praise of gold and precious stones as 'Infinite riches in a little roome' is often quoted.

JEWSBURY, Geraldine Endsor (1812–80), an intimate friend of the *Carlyles. Besides contributing to the *Athenaeum*, the *Westminster Review*, and other journals, she wrote six novels, including *Zöe* (1845), *The Half Sisters* (1848), and *Marian Withers* (1851), and two stories for children. *A Selection from the Letters of Geraldine Jewsbury to Jane Carlyle* (1892), edited with a memoir by Mrs A. Ireland), gave undue emphasis to the emotional element of the friendship between the two women and was the subject of an interesting article by V. *Woolf ('Geraldine and Jane', *TLS*, 28 Feb. 1929).

JHABVALA, Ruth Prawer (1927–), novelist, the daughter of a Polish Jewish solicitor; she came to England in 1939 and was educated in London. In 1951 she married an Indian architect, and subsequently lived for 24 years in India, where she wrote several novels including *Esmond in India* (1958), *A New Dominion* (1973), and *Heat and Dust* (1975, *Booker Prize), all of which reflect her mingled affection for and impatience with her adopted country. She published volumes of short stories and wrote several original screenplays, including *Shakespeare-Wallah* (1965). In 1975 she moved to New York, where her novel *In Search of Love and Beauty* (1983) is set.

Jig, 'an afterpiece in the form of a brief farce which was sung and accompanied by dancing', popular in the Elizabethan and Jacobean theatre, but few have survived.

Jimson, Gulley, the Bohemian artist hero of J. *Cary's novel *The Horse's Mouth*.

Jingle, Alfred, a character in Dickens's *Pickwick Papers*.

Jiniwin, Mrs, in Dickens's *The Old Curiosity Shop*, the mother of Mrs Quilp.

Jo, the crossing-sweeper in Dickens's *Bleak House*.

JOAN OF ARC, St (1412–31), Jeanne D'Arc, or more correctly Jeanne Darc, an illiterate girl who contributed powerfully to liberate France from the English in the reign of Charles VII. Inspired, she claimed, by the voices of Sts Michael, Catherine, and Margaret, her mission was a double one, to raise the siege of Orléans, and to conduct Charles to his coronation at Rheims. She accomplished both these tasks and then wished to return home; but she yielded to the demands of the French patriots and was taken prisoner by the Burgundians, who handed her over to the English. But it was a French court of ecclesiastics (with the help of the Inquisition) who sentenced her as a heretic, and the English who burned her at Rouen. She was canonized in 1920. She is the subject of *Voltaire's *La Pucelle*, of a tragedy by *Schiller, of a poem by *Southey, and of dramas by G. B. *Shaw and Anouilh.

Job Trotter, a character in Dickens's *Pickwick Papers*.

Jocasta, a tragedy in blank verse, supposedly based on *Euripides but actually translated from Lodovico Dolce, included in *Gascoigne's *Posies* (1575).

JOCELIN DE BRAKELOND (*fl.* 1200), a monk of Bury St Edmunds, whose chronicle of his abbey (1173–1202) inspired *Carlyle's *Past and Present*.

Jocoseria, a volume of ten poems by R. *Browning, published 1883. The volume contains the much-parodied lyric 'Wanting is—what?', an exquisite miniature of Browning's whole philosophy of art as a mode of desire.

'Jock o' Hazeldean', a ballad, of which one stanza is ancient, the rest by Sir W. *Scott.

Joe, 'the fat boy' in Dickens's *Pickwick Papers*.

Joe Gargery, a character in Dickens's *Great Expectations*.

Joe Miller's Jests: or the wit's vade-mecum (1739), a *jest-book by J. *Mottley. The name is taken from Joseph Miller (1684–1738), an actor in the Drury Lane company, and a reputed humorist.

Johannes Factotum, 'John Do-everything', a Jack of all trades, a would-be universal genius. The phrase is found in the 16th cent. It occurs in *Greenes Groats-Worth of Witte, bought with a Million of Repentance*.

John, Little, see LITTLE JOHN.

'John Anderson, my Jo', a lyric by *Burns, suggested to him by an older song.

John Bull, The History of, a collection of pamphlets by *Arbuthnot, issued 1712, re-arranged and republished in *Pope and *Swift's *Miscellanies* of 1727.
    The pamphlets were designed to advocate the cessation of war with France, and introduced the allegorical character John Bull, who represents England; he is 'an honest plain-dealing fellow, choleric, bold, and of a very inconstant temper . . . very apt to quarrel with his best friends, especially if they pretend to govern him . . . a

boon companion, loving his bottle and his diversion'. Other characters are Nicholas Frog (the Dutch), Lord Strutt (Philip of Spain), and Lewis Baboon (Louis XIV of France).
    John Bull is also the title of a play by G. *Colman the younger.

John Buncle Esq, The Life and Opinions of, a novel by T. *Amory (2 vols, 1756, 1766).
    Buncle, a man of passionate temperament and a highly original turn of mind, sets out on a journey through the more magnificent and dangerous landscapes of northern England. He comes upon small centres of civilized elegance and culture, in many of which he encounters beautiful and learned women, seven of whom (with the intervention of successive deaths) he marries. The bulk of the book is taken up with eloquent discussion and digression on religious, scientific, and literary subjects, descriptions of awesome scenery, and much eating and drinking.

'John Gilpin, The Diverting History of', a poem by *Cowper, first published anonymously in *The Public Advertiser*, reprinted in chapbook form, and included in the same volume as *The Task* (1785).
    John Gilpin, a 'linen-draper bold' of Cheapside, and his wife decide to celebrate their 20th wedding anniversary by a trip to the Bell at Edmonton, he on a borrowed horse, she, her sister, and the children in a chaise and pair. But John loses control of his horse, and the poem describes his headlong career to Edmonton, ten miles beyond it to Ware, and then back again.

John Halifax, Gentleman, a novel by Mrs *Craik published 1856.
    The story tells of the poor honest orphan John, who finds employment with the tanner Abel Fletcher and is befriended by Abel's weakling son Phineas, improves his position, and marries the book's heroine, Ursula March. John's status as 'gentleman' is earned not by birth and wealth but by his own integrity and worth.

John Inglesant, see SHORTHOUSE, J. H.

JOHN OF GAUNT (1340–99), duke of Lancaster, the fourth son of Edward III and father of Henry IV, named from his birthplace Ghent (Gaunt). He was the dominant figure in English politics during much of the reign of Richard II, the employer of *Wyclif, and the patron of *Chaucer. He is a major figure in Shakespeare's *Richard II*.

JOHN OF HOVEDEN, see ANGLO-LATIN LITERATURE.

JOHN OF SALISBURY (*fl.* 1120–80), studied at Paris under *Abelard and at Chartres, returning to England 1154. He was secretary to *Becket with whom he was exiled when he fell into disfavour with Henry II. He wrote a life of Becket and of *Anselm. He became bishop of Chartres in 1176. The most learned classical writer of his time, he was often seen as the principal humanist inspiration in 'the twelfth-century Renaissance'. Among his works are the *Polycraticus* (or *De nugis Curialium*), on the vanities of the court and miscellaneous questions of philosophy; the *Metalogicon*, a treatise on logic and an account of Aristotle's treatment of the subject; and *Historia Pontificalis*. (See also ANGLO-LATIN LITERATURE.)

JOHNSON, B(ryan) S(tanley William) (1933–73), London-born novelist whose works include *Albert Angelo* (1964), *Trawl* (1966), *The Unfortunates* (1969, consisting of 27 unbound sections in a box), *House Mother Normal* (1971), and *Christy Malry's Own Double-Entry* (1973). Johnson was an admirer of *Joyce and *Beckett, and his works combine verbal inventiveness with typographical innovations that resemble the techniques of *concrete poetry.

JOHNSON, Joseph (1738–1809), a radical bookseller and publisher of St Paul's Churchyard, who held literary dinners over the shop, where his guests included *Blake, *Fuseli, *Godwin, J. *Priestley, and *Paine. From 1788 to 1799 he published the scientific and literary monthly *The Analytical Review*.

JOHNSON, Lionel Pigot (1867–1902), became an influential man of letters, and one of the notable Catholic converts of his day. His *The Art of Thomas Hardy* (1894) was one of the first full-length studies of *Hardy to appear. His *Poems* appeared in 1895, *Ireland and other poems* in 1897, and *Post liminium*, a posthumous collection of essays, in 1911. There is an account of his personality and decline into alcoholism in Yeats's *Autobiographies*. See also ART FOR ART'S SAKE.

JOHNSON, Pamela Hansford (1912–81), critic and novelist. In 1950 she married C. P. *Snow. She is perhaps most widely known for her comic 'Dorothy Merlin' trilogy, a satire on the pretensions of literary life, which consists of *The Unspeakable Skipton* (1959), *Night and Silence, Who is Here* (1962), and *Cork Street, Next to the Hatter's* (1965).

JOHNSON, Richard (1573–?1659), the author of *The Famous History of the Seven Champions of Christendom* (c.1597), a widely read romance of chivalric legend, which influenced *Spenser and, among other works, *The Nine Worthies of London* (1592).

JOHNSON, Samuel (1709–84), born at Lichfield, the son of a bookseller. He was educated at Lichfield Grammar School and Pembroke College, Oxford, where he spent 14 months, 1728–9, but took no degree; his college days were marred by poverty. During the scantily documented period between leaving Oxford and his father's death in 1731 he appears to have suffered acute mental stress; bouts of melancholia were to recur in later life. He translated and abridged from the French an account of Father Lobo's *Voyage to Abyssinia*, published anonymously in 1735. In the same year he married Mrs Elizabeth Porter, a widow considerably older than himself, and started a private school at Edial, near Lichfield. This was not a success and in 1737 he set off with one of his few pupils, *Garrick, to try his fortune in London. He entered the service of Edward Cave, the founder of *The Gentleman's Magazine*, to which he contributed essays, poems, Latin verses, biographies, and, most notably, his *Parliamentary Debates*. In 1738 he published his poem *London*. In 1744 appeared his *Life of Mr Richard Savage*, a vivid evocation of *Grub Street. In 1747 he issued the 'Plan' of his Dictionary (see JOHNSON'S DICTIONARY), which he dedicated to *Chesterfield, with results recorded under the latter's name. In 1749 he published *The Vanity of Human Wishes*, the first work to bear his own name, and in the same year Garrick produced his tragedy *Irene*. In 1750 he started *The Rambler*, a periodical written almost entirely by himself. His wife died in 1752, a loss which caused him prolonged grief. From March 1753 to March 1754 Johnson contributed regularly to *Hawkesworth's *The Adventurer*. His *Dictionary* was published in 1755, after nine years of labour; it firmly established his reputation, and also brought him, just before publication and through the support of Francis Wise and T. *Warton, the Oxford degree he had failed to achieve earlier. During 1758–60 he contributed the *Idler* series of papers to the *Universal Chronicle*. In 1759 appeared *Rasselas, Prince of Abyssinia*. In 1762 Johnson received a crown pension of £300 a year, and the following year he met his biographer, *Boswell, in the bookshop of his friend Thomas Davies.

From this period onwards we have Boswell's account of Johnson's life as one of the most eminent literary figures of his day, and also vivid portraits of his contemporaries, notably of the members of the *Club (later known as the 'Literary Club'), founded in 1764. In January 1765 he met the *Thrales, in whose town and country houses he found much comfort and companionship. Later that year appeared his edition of Shakespeare. Although superseded by later scholarship, it contained valuable notes and emendations, and its Preface is regarded as one of his finest works of critical prose. In 1773 he travelled with Boswell to Scotland and the Hebrides, a journey recorded in his *A Journey to the Western Islands of Scotland* (1775) and

Boswell's *Journal of a Tour to the Hebrides* (1785). In 1777 he undertook, at the request of a number of booksellers, to write *The Lives of the English Poets*, the crowning work of his old age (1779–81). In 1784, saddened by the deaths of his friend Robert Levet and Thrale and by his estrangement from Mrs Thrale, he died at his house in Bolt Court and was buried in Westminster Abbey.

Johnson's reputation rests not only on his works but also on Boswell's evocation of his brilliant conversation, his eccentricities and opinionated outbursts (against Scots, Whigs, Americans, players, etc.), his interest in the supernatural (see COCK LANE GHOST), his generosity and humanity, and many other aspects of his large personality. His profound but melancholy religious faith is revealed also in his diaries and meditations, and in his attacks on the facile optimism of mid-18th-cent. thought (see JENYNS, S.). Two useful accounts appeared before Boswell's: *Anecdotes of the Late Samuel Johnson* (1786) by Mrs Piozzi, formerly Mrs Thrale, and a *Life* by Sir John *Hawkins (1787). For a 20th-cent. assessment of Johnson, see T. S. *Eliot's essay, 'Johnson as Critic and Poet' (1944).

Johnson, *The Life of Samuel*, by *Boswell, published 1791.

Boswell informed Dr *Johnson in 1772 of his intention to write his life, and had been collecting materials for this purpose since their first meeting in 1763. After Johnson's death in 1784 he set to work arranging and adding to the 'prodigious multiplicity of materials', a task which, he writes in 1789, involved him in great labour, perplexity, and vexation. The result was the most celebrated biography in the English language. His portrait is vivid and intimate, in his own words a 'Flemish picture' made up of trifling incidents as well as significant events. The final edition, after Boswell's death, was revised by *Malone. The standard edition (G. B. *Hill, 6 vols, 1887) has been revised by L. F. Powell (1934–50; 1964). See also BIOGRAPHY.

'Johnson's Dictionary', *A Dictionary of the English Language*, by S. *Johnson, published 1755.

Johnson entered into an agreement in 1746 with *Dodsley and others to write a dictionary, the first of its kind in English. A *Plan* and dedication to *Chesterfield followed in 1747. Johnson said his object was to produce 'a dictionary by which the pronunciation of our language may be fixed, and its attainment facilitated; by which its purity may be preserved, its use ascertained, and its duration lengthened'. He wrote the definitions of over 40,000 words, illustrating them with about 114,000 quotations drawn from every field of learning and literature from the time of *Sidney onwards; his deriva-

tions suffer from the scantiness of etymological knowledge in his day, but the work as a whole remained without rival until the creation of the *Oxford English Dictionary*. His well-known playful definitions (e.g. *lexicographer*, 'a writer of dictionaries, a harmless drudge') represent a mere handful in the body of his enormous achievement. (See also DICTIONARY.)

JOHNSTON, (William) Denis (1901–84), playwright, critic, and mystical philosopher, is best known for his plays, which include *The Old Lady Says 'No!'* (1929), *The Moon in the Yellow River* (1931), *A Bride for the Unicorn* (1933), and *The Scythe and the Sunset* (1958). His daughter Jennifer Johnston (1930–   ) is well known as a novelist.

JOHNSTONE, Charles (?1719–1800), travelled in 1782 to Calcutta, where he remained as a journalist and later as a prosperous newspaper proprietor. His best-known work is *Chrysal, or the Adventures of a Guinea* (1760–5). 'Chrysal' is the articulate spirit of gold in the guinea, whose progress from hand to hand, through some six different countries, serves to link various inventive and satirical episodes, including a section on the *Hell-fire Club at *Medmenham Abbey. His other works include *The History of Arsaces, Prince of Betlis* (1774), an *Oriental tale, *The Pilgrim* (1775), and *John Juniper* (1781).

'Jolly Beggars, The', a poem by *Burns, written 1786.

Jonathan Wild the Great, *The Life of*, a short novel by H. *Fielding, published as the third volume of his *Miscellanies*, 1743, based on the life of a notorious thief-taker, Jonathan *Wild, who was hanged in 1725.

Fielding's hatred of hypocrisy here finds its most mordant expression. The quality Wild most values in himself and in others is 'that of hypocrisy'. His own position as the Great Man among thieves, cheats, and bullies is constantly compared, directly and by implication, with that of the Great Man among public figures of power (with Sir Robert *Walpole as a particular target), whose palaces are no more than 'Newgate with the mask on'. The life of Fielding's Wild is traced from his birth to his death on the gallows, through a series of episodes involving thieves, highwaymen, whores, cheats, murderers, and the corrupt and brutal officers of Newgate.

JONES, David Michael (1895–1974), poet and artist. He served in the trenches throughout the First World War, which left him with a lifelong interest in warfare and soldiers. In 1921 he became a Roman Catholic and in 1922 began a long association with *Gill. He preferred that his work in engraving, water-colour, and drawing should be intimately combined with his own writing, or the writing of others. The Welsh *Mabinogion*, the *'matter of Britain' (centring on King *Arthur), and the Bible provided much of the material and the background for his poetry. In *Parenthesis* (1937) was an epic work of mixed poetry and prose on the subject of war. *The Anathemata* (1952) is a long, complex work of poetry and prose, celebrating in richly allusive language the ancient 'matter of Britain'; *The Sleeping Lord* (1974) is a collection of complete fragments of a projected work centred on the Crucifixion, and the lives of Roman soldiers at the time.

JONES, Henry Arthur (1851–1929), dramatist, achieved success with *The Silver King* (1882). A friend and contemporary of *Pinero, Jones did much to re-establish serious themes in the theatre. As a young man he was greatly encouraged by G. B. *Shaw and *Beerbohm. Although he wrote many comedies (including *The Liars*, 1897; *Dolly Reforming Herself*, 1908; *Mary Goes First*, 1913), his most influential plays treated social themes, often the double standards of behaviour expected of men and of women; *The Dancing Girl* (1891), *The Case of Rebellious Susan* (1894), *Mrs Dane's Defence* (1900), and *The Lie* (1923) were considered among the most effective.

JONES, Inigo (1573–1652), architect, stage designer, painter, mathematician, and man of letters, whose depth of knowledge of Roman and Italian art and of Renaissance theory was new in England, and whose revolutionary buildings brought the classical style to this country. He travelled abroad and developed a deep admiration for Palladio, met Scamozzi, and copied ancient Roman monuments. In 1615 he became surveyor of the King's Works; his most famous buildings are the Queen's House, Greenwich, and the Banqueting Hall, Whitehall, which mark a turning-point in English architecture. Jones's career as a designer of *masques opened in 1605 and a stormy but fruitful collaboration with *Jonson began with *The Masque of Blacknesse*, and lasted until 1630/1; their quarrel about the rival claims of the visual arts and literature was also long standing, and became notorious. Later Jones worked with other poets, producing with T. *Carew, in *Coelum Britannicum* (1634), perhaps the most brilliant of later Caroline masques. Jones's fame in England soared between 1710 and 1760, when, with Palladio, he became one of the heroes of the Palladian movement.

JONES, Sir William (1746–94), a distinguished orientalist and brilliant jurist. A master of Sanskrit and a pioneer in the science of comparative philology, he did much to make Indian literature and learning known to Europe, and is remembered for his translations (including *The Moallakat*, 1782, from the Arabic, and *Sacontala, or the Fatal Ring: an Indian Drama*, 1789), and for the well-known 'A Persian Song of Hafiz' (*Poems consisting chiefly of translations from the Asiatic languages*, 1772). He had considerable influence on the Oriental themes of the Romantic poets such as *Byron, *Southey, and T. *Moore.

JONSON, Ben(jamin) (1572/3–1637), born in London of Border descent. He was educated at Westminster School under *Camden. During the early 1590s he worked as a bricklayer in his stepfather's employ, and saw military service in Flanders. In 1597 he began to work for *Henslowe's companies. His first important play, *Every Man in his Humour*, with Shakespeare in the cast, was performed by the Lord Chamberlain's company in 1598, and *Every Man out of his Humour* at the Globe in 1599. *Cynthia's Revels* (1600) and *Poetaster* (1600–1, attacking *Dekker and *Marston), were performed by the Children of the Queen's Chapel. His first extant tragedy, *Sejanus*, was given at the Globe by Shakespeare's company, 1603; his first court masque, *The Masque of Blacknesse*, written to accommodate Queen Anne's desire to appear as a Negress, was given on Twelfth Night, 1605. In that year he was imprisoned for his share in *Eastward hoe*, and gave evidence to the Privy Council concerning the Gunpowder Plot. Then followed the period of his major plays: *Volpone*, acted at both the Globe and the two universities, 1605–6; *Epicene, or The Silent Woman*, 1609–10; *The Alchemist*, 1610; and *Bartholomew Fair*, 1614. In 1612–13 he was in France as tutor to *Ralegh's son, and in 1618–19 journeyed on foot to Scotland, where he stayed with *Drummond of Hawthornden, who recorded their conversation.

Though not formally appointed the first poet laureate, the essentials of the position were conferred on Jonson in 1616, when a pension was granted to him by James I. In the same year he published a folio edition of his *Works*, which raised the drama to a new level of literary respectability, and received an honorary MA from the University of Oxford. After *The Devil is an Ass* (1616), he abandoned the public stage for ten years, and his later plays. *The Staple of News* (1626), *The New Inn* (1629), *The Magnetic Lady* (1631), and *A Tale of a Tub* (1633), show a relatively unsuccessful reliance on allegory and symbolism. From 1605 onwards Jonson was constantly producing masques for the court, with scenery by I. *Jones. This form of entertainment reached its highest elaboration in Jonson's hands. He introduced into it the 'antimasque', an antithetical, usually disorderly, prelude to the main action which served to highlight by contrast the central theme of political and social harmony. There are examples of this in *The Masque of Queens* (1609), *Love Restored*

(1612), *Mercury Vindicated from the Alchemists in Court* (1616), *Pleasure Reconciled to Virtue* (1618, which gave Milton his idea for *Comus), and Neptune's Triumph for the Return of Albion* (1624). After *Chloridia* (1631), his collaboration with Jones ended with a famous quarrel, which Jonson treated in several vituperative poems, concerning the relative priority of verbal and thematic content and spectacle. His non-dramatic verse includes *Epigrams* and *The Forest*, printed in the folio of 1616, and *The Underwood* and a translation of *Horace's Ars Poetica, printed in 1640. His chief prose works are The English Grammar* and *Timber, or Discoveries, printed in 1640.

He presided over a literary circle which met at the *Mermaid Tavern. His friends included Shakespeare, *Donne, F. *Bacon, George *Chapman, *Beaumont, *Fletcher, *Cotton, and *Selden, and among the younger writers (who styled themselves the 'sons' or 'tribe of Ben') R. *Brome, *Carew, *Cartwright, Sir K. *Digby, Lord *Falkland, *Herrick, Nabbes, *Randolph, and *Suckling. His chief patrons were the *Sidney family, the earl of Pembroke, the countess of Bedford, and the duke and duchess of Newcastle. He was buried in Westminster Abbey under a tombstone bearing the inscription 'O rare Ben Johnson' and celebrated in a collection of elegies entitled *Jonsonus Virbius* (1638). During the reign of James I, Jonson's literary prestige and influence were unrivalled; his reputation declined sharply from about 1700, as Shakespeare's increased, but in this century it has revived.

Jonsonus Virbius, see JONSON, B.

JORDAN, Dorothy, *née* Phillips (1761–1816), actress, appeared from 1782 to 1815 in many leading roles, and was much praised by *Hazlitt, *Lamb, Leigh *Hunt, etc. She was for long mistress of the duke of Clarence (William IV), and bore him ten children.

Jorkins, see SPENLOW AND JORKINS.

Jorrocks, Mr, see SURTEES, R. S.

Joseph Andrews, *The History of the Adventures of, and of his Friend Mr Abraham Adams,* a novel by H. *Fielding, published 1742.

The novel was a major innovation in form and style. In an important Preface Fielding relates his book to classical forms; he describes it as a 'comic romance', and outlines his purpose in devising 'this kind of writing, which I do not remember to have seen hitherto attempted in our language'. His declared object is to defend what is good by displaying the Ridiculous, which he believes arises from Affectation, and ultimately from Vanity and Hyprocrisy.

This was the first of Fielding's novels and was begun as a skit on Richardson's *Pamela*. As the latter had related the efforts of Pamela Andrews, the serving-maid, to escape the attentions of her master, so here her brother Joseph, also in service, is exposed to attacks on his virtue. Mr B. of *Pamela* becomes young Squire Booby, and mild fun is made of Pamela herself. But presently the satire is in the main dropped, Joseph sinks rather into the background, and the real hero of the remainder of the novel is Parson Adams, the simple, good-hearted, slightly ridiculous but lovable curate in Sir Thomas Booby's family.

Joseph of Arimathea. For the legend of Joseph and the Holy Grail, see GRAIL and GLASTONBURY. According to fable, St Philip sent twelve disciples into Britain to preach Christianity, of whom Joseph of Arimathea was the leader. They founded at Glastonbury the first primitive church, which subsequently was developed into Glastonbury Abbey. Here Joseph was buried. His staff, planted in the ground, became the famous Glastonbury Thorn, which flowered at Christmas (*William of Malmesbury, *De Antiquitate Glastoniensis Ecclesiae*). The fullest version of the Joseph Grail story is Robert de *Boron's *Joseph d'Arimathie*.

JOSEPHUS, Flavius (AD 37–c.98), a Jewish statesman and soldier. He came to Rome with Titus, was honoured with Roman citizenship, and devoted himself to study. He wrote in Greek a *History of the Jewish War* and *Jewish Antiquities*, which is a history of the Jews down to AD 66.

Joseph Vance, see DE MORGAN, W.

JOSH BILLINGS, see SHAW, H. W.

Journal of a Disappointed Man, The, see CUMMINGS, B. F.

Journal of a Tour to the Hebrides, The, by *Boswell, published 1785. It is a narrative of the journey taken by Boswell and Dr *Johnson in Scotland and the Hebrides in 1773. Boswell's manuscript, which Johnson and others read, was discovered at Malahide Castle with other private papers and published in 1936, ed. F. A. Pottle and C. H. Bennett; it is longer by about a third than the earlier publication.

Journal of a Voyage to Lisbon, The, a work by H. *Fielding, published posthumously 1755.

When he set out for Portugal in 1754, in the vain hope of recovering his health, Fielding was already gravely ill. He writes of the daily events of the difficult voyage, the eccentricities of Captain Veal, the abuses suffered by the sailors, the devotion of his wife and daughter, the terror of storms, a sunset and moonrise at sea, and the details of his food and drink. He describes the

Journal as 'possibly the production of the most disagreeable hours which ever haunted the author'; he had prepared it for the press before he died in Lisbon in October.

Journal of the Plague Year, A, see PLAGUE YEAR.

Journey from this World to the Next, A, the second volume of *Miscellanies* by H. *Fielding, published 1743.

After a lively satirical account by the author of his spirit's journey, in company with those of other persons recently dead, in a stage-coach to Elysium, we have a long discourse by the spirit of Julian the Apostate. This is followed by a fragment containing a similar narrative by the spirit of Anne Boleyn.

'Journey of the Magi, The', a poem by T. S. *Eliot.

Journey's End, see SHERRIFF, R. C.

Journey to London, The, see PROVOK'D HUSBAND, THE.

Journey to the Western Islands of Scotland, A, by Dr *Johnson, published 1775. It is a narrative of the tour undertaken by *Boswell and Johnson in 1773 in Scotland and the Hebrides. (For Boswell's account, see JOURNAL OF A TOUR TO THE HEBRIDES.) It describes Johnson's response to Scottish history, culture, and landscape, and on publication aroused the wrath of *Macpherson because of its sceptical comments on the authenticity of 'Ossian'.

Joviall Crew, A, or *The Merry Beggars*, a romantic comedy by R. *Brome, produced 1641. The play is remarkable for its sympathetic portrayal of the vagabond life through the character of Springlove, steward of kindly Squire Oldrents, who each spring is seized with a longing to take to the open road. He is joined by Oldrents's own daughters, who run off for a frolic, thus fulfilling a gypsy's prediction that they must become beggars: but all ends happily.

JOWETT, Benjamin (1817–93), one of the legendary figures of late Victorian Oxford, was professor of Greek from 1855 and master of Balliol College from 1870. A Broad Churchman in the tradition of T. *Arnold, he outraged the Tractarians with the common sense of his *Epistles of Paul* (1855), came near to being charged with heresy before the vice-chancellor because of his contribution to *Essays and Reviews* (1860), and was successful in promoting the Act that abolished religious tests for university degrees (1871). His translations of *Plato (1871), *Thucydides (1881), and Aristotle's *Poetics* (1885), criticized by scholars, charmed the public.

JOYCE, James Augustine Aloysius (1882–1941), novelist, born at Rathgar, Dublin, educated at University College, Dublin, where *Gogarty was a fellow student. Early influences included Gerhard Hauptmann, *Dante, G. *Moore, *Ibsen, and *Yeats. Joyce went to Paris for a year in 1902, where he lived in poverty, wrote verse, and discovered Dujardin's novel *Les Lauriers sont coupés* (1888), which he was to credit as the source of his own use of interior monologue (see STREAM OF CONSCIOUSNESS). He returned to Dublin for his mother's death, then left Ireland more or less for good with Nora Barnacle, the woman with whom he spent the rest of his life. They lived at Trieste and Zurich, and settled finally after the war in Paris. His first published work was a volume of verse, *Chamber Music* (1907), followed by *Dubliners* (1914), a volume of short stories published after great delays and difficulties; they were greeted with enthusiasm by *Pound, whose friendship and support greatly encouraged Joyce's career and reputation. Joyce's play *Exiles* was published in 1918 and staged unsuccessfully in the same year in Munich, then first performed in London in 1926. *A Portrait of the Artist as a Young Man* was published serially in *The Egoist*, 1914–15 (part of a first draft, *Stephen Hero*, appeared in 1944). With strong backing from Yeats and Pound, Joyce received a grant from the *Royal Literary Fund in 1915, and shortly after a grant from the civil list.

His famous novel *Ulysses* (1922, Paris; 1936, England) was received as a work of genius by writers as varied as T. S. *Eliot, *Hemingway, and Arnold *Bennett. This work, together with *Finnegans Wake* (1939), revolutionized the form and structure of the novel, decisively influenced the development of the 'stream of consciousness' or 'interior monologue' (see also RICHARDSON, D.), and pushed language and linguistic experiment (particularly in the latter work) to the extreme limits of communication. (See MODERNISM.)

JOYCE, Patrick Weston (1827–1914), was author, among other works, of *A Grammar of the Irish Language* (1878), *Old Celtic Romances* (1879, 1894), *Irish Peasant Songs* (1906), and a *Social History of Ireland* (1903–20), all highly influential in the *Irish revival.

Joyous Gard, the castle of Launcelot in Arthurian legend. *Malory says it has been variously identified as Alnwick or Bamburgh (near Berwick-on-Tweed).

Juan, Don, see DON JUAN.

Jubilate Agno, see SMART, C.

'Judas', the oldest *ballad in *Child's collection, recorded in a manuscript of *c.*1300, deals with the betrayal of Christ.

Jude the Obscure, a novel by T. *Hardy, originally printed in abridged form in *Harper's New

Monthly Magazine (1894–5, as *Hearts Insurgent*), then in the 1895 edition of his works.

In the author's words, it is a story 'of a deadly war waged between flesh and spirit'. Jude Fawley, a young Wessex villager of exceptional intellectual promise, is encouraged by the schoolmaster Phillotson. He is trapped into marriage by the barmaid Arabella Donn, who shortly afterwards deserts him. He moves to Christminster (which represents Oxford), hoping one day to be admitted to the university. He meets his cousin, Sue Bridehead, an unconventional, hypersensitive young woman who works in a shop selling ecclesiastical ornaments: they fall in love. Sue, in what appears to be a fit of desperate masochism, suddenly marries Phillotson. She is driven from him by physical revulsion, and flies to Jude; they live together but do not consummate their love until Arabella reappears on the scene. Jude, who had been planning to enter the priesthood as a licentiate, as a substitute for his thwarted intellectual ambitions, is now doubly defeated. He and Sue become free to marry, but Sue shrinks from the step.

Under the pressure of poverty and social disapproval their relationship deteriorates, and tragedy overtakes them in the death of their children: the eldest, 'Old Father Time', son of Jude and Arabella, hangs the two babies and himself, leaving a note saying, 'Done because we are too menny.' In an agony of remorse and self-abasement, Sue returns to Phillotson and the church, and Jude, deeply shocked by her abandoning of her free-thinking principles, begins drinking heavily and is inveigled back by Arabella. He dies wretchedly.

Judith, a 350-line poem in Old English, fragmentary at the beginning, found in the *Beowulf* manuscript (ASPR 4), probably dating from the late 9th cent. The poem tells the story of the Apocryphal Book of Judith, and the surviving sections correspond to about the last quarter of the biblical book.

Julia, in Shakespeare's *The Two Gentlemen of Verona*, the faithful lover of Proteus.

Julia, Donna, in Byron's *Don Juan*, a lady of Seville, whose love for the hero is the first incident in his career.

Julia Melville, a character in Sheridan's *The Rivals*.

Julian, Count, see COUNT JULIAN.

'Julian and Maddalo, A Conversation', a poem partly in dialogue form by P. B. *Shelley, published 1824.

Julian (Shelley) and Count Maddalo (*Byron) ride and boat through 'bright Venice', discussing problems of free will, progress, and religious belief. They visit a 'Maniac' (partly based on *Tasso and partly on Shelley himself), confined in an island asylum in the Venetian lagoon. His presence, like the uncensored outpourings of the Freudian unconscious, deepens and darkens the terms of the debate: he provides 'the text of every heart'. A little child, based on Claire Clairmont's baby Allegra, is also introduced to show the powers of innocence and good. This is one of Shelley's most subtle studies of human affections and hopes. It is composed in fluent couplets, with evocations of the deserted Venetian lido and twinkling lagoon. It powerfully influenced Browning's *dramatic monologues.

JULIAN OF NORWICH (*c.* 1342–after 1416), a recluse in a cell attached to the church of St Julian at Norwich. She wrote *Sixteen Revelations of Divine Love* which describes visions revealed to her during her illness in 1373 and her reflections on them. She is well known now because of the quotation from the *Revelations* in T. S. *Eliot's 'Little Gidding': 'Sin is behovely; but all shall be well and all shall be well and all manner of thing shall be well.'

Julie, the heroine of *La Nouvelle Héloïse* of *Rousseau, loved by Saint-Preux.

Juliet, (1) the heroine of Shakespeare's *Romeo and Juliet*; (2) the lover of *Claudio in his *Measure for Measure*.

Julius Caesar, a Roman tragedy by *Shakespeare first printed in the First *Folio of 1623, probably written and performed 1599. Its major source is *North's translation of *Plutarch's *Lives*.

It begins with the events of the year 44 BC, after Caesar, already endowed with the dictatorship, had returned to Rome from a successful campaign in Spain, and when there are fears that he will allow himself to be crowned king. Distrust of Caesar's ambition gives rise to a conspiracy against him among Roman lovers of freedom, notably Cassius and Casca; they win over to their cause Brutus, who reluctantly joins them from a sense of duty to the republic. Caesar is slain by the conspirators in the Senate house. Antony, Caesar's friend, stirs the people to fury against the conspirators by a skilful speech at Caesar's funeral. Octavius, nephew of Julius Caesar, Antony, and Lepidus, united as triumvirs, oppose the forces raised by Brutus and Cassius. The quarrel and reconciliation of Brutus and Cassius, with the news of the death of Portia, wife of Brutus, provide one of the finest scenes in the play. Brutus and Cassius are defeated at the battle of Philippi (42 BC), and kill themselves.

Jumpers, a comedy by T. *Stoppard performed and published 1972.

The play's central character is a professor of moral philosophy, George Moore, who shares with G. E. *Moore his intuitionist ethics. The physical acrobatics of the jumpers parallel the 'verbal gymnastics' of Moore's lengthy speeches, which are brilliantly witty parodies of academic philosophy.

JUNG, Carl Gustav (1875–1961), Swiss psychiatrist. He collaborated with *Freud 1907–13, but then parted with him to found his own school of 'Analytical Psychology'. Jung introduced into psychology the terms 'complex', 'collective unconscious', 'extrovert'–'introvert', *'archetype', and 'individuation'. His notion of the mind as a self-regulating system is in line with modern ideas on cybernetics. In emphasizing the importance of man's search for meaning in life, he anticipated *Existentialism. The central theme of his work is the idea that mental illness is characterized by disunity of the personality, while mental health is manifested by unity, towards which the personality is striving.

Jung's influence has been felt in many fields outside psychiatry. J. B. *Priestley made use of his ideas in *Literature and Western Man*; the title of Maud Bodkin's *Archetypal Patterns in Poetry* (1934) is directly derived from Jung. Alex Aronson's *Psyche and Symbol in Shakespeare* (1972) is an interpretation of Shakespearian drama in terms of Jungian psychology, and Jung himself wrote an essay on Joyce's *Ulysses*.

Jungle, The, a novel by U. *Sinclair.

Jungle Book, The (1894), and *The Second Jungle Book* (1895), stories by *Kipling, which tell how the child Mowgli was brought up by wolves and was taught by Baloo, the bear, and Bagheera, the black panther, the law and business of the jungle.

JUNIUS, the pseudonymous author of a series of letters that appeared in the *Public Advertiser*, Jan. 1769–Jan. 1772, attacking, with bitter scorn and invective, among others, the duke of Grafton, Lord Mansfield, and George III himself. Junius also takes an active part on behalf of *Wilkes. Though personal invective is the cheap weapon of Junius, his political arguments, written from the Whig standpoint, are shrewd and lucidly expressed, and he shows himself well read in *Hobbes and *Locke. The identity of Junius has never been definitely established. He is now generally thought to have been Sir Philip *Francis.

JUNIUS, Francis, or **DU JON,** François (1589–1677), philologist and antiquary, librarian and tutor in the household of Thomas Howard, earl of Arundel. His *Etymologicum Anglicanum* (1743) was used by Dr *Johnson. He gave Anglo-Saxon manuscripts to the Bodleian Library (see LIBRARIES), and to the *Oxford University Press materials for printing in Gothic, Runic, Anglo-Saxon, and Roman founts. He published an edition of *Caedmon in 1655.

Junius Manuscript, The, one of the four major manuscripts containing Old English poetry, named after the editor (above) who first printed it at Amsterdam in 1655, calling it 'Caedmon the monk's poetical paraphrase of Genesis, etc.' The biblical poetry in the manuscript (*Genesis A and B, Exodus, Daniel,* and *Christ and Satan*) continued to be associated with *Caedmon for some time, but it is clear that they are unconnected with him.

Juno and the Paycock, see O'CASEY, S.

Jupe, Cissy, a character in Dickens's *Hard Times*.

JUVENAL (Decimus Junius Juvenalis) (*c.* AD 60–*c.* 136), Roman satirist, whose 16 satires are exercises in rhetorical indignation against the vices of his age. Imitations of his work are found in J. *Hall, *Jonson, *Oldham, and Dr *Johnson. *Dryden edited and wrote in part a translation of Juvenal's Satires to which he prefixed his long discourse on Satire (1693). The references to 'the English Juvenal' in Scott's *Waverley* and to 'the British Juvenal' in *The Heart of Midlothian* are to *Crabbe. The former title has also been applied to Oldham.

K

KAFKA, Franz (1883–1924), German-speaking Jewish novelist, born in Prague, whose works (most of them published posthumously) had an immense influence on European and American literature. They include *The Trial* (1925), *The Castle* (1926), and the short story 'The Metamorphosis' (1915). They portray an uncertain, troubled, surreal world, in which lonely individuals are threatened by incomprehensible events and processes: the mood, recurring situations, and disturbing narrative style of these fictions have given rise to the widely used adjective 'Kafkaesque'.

Kailyard School, from 'Kail-yard' (cabbage patch), a term applied to a group of Scottish writers who exploited a sentimental and romantic image of small town life in Scotland, with much use of the vernacular; the vogue lasted from 1888 to 1896. Leading writers in this vein were J. M. *Barrie, 'Ian Maclaren' (John Watson, 1850–1907), and S. R. Crockett (1860–1914). These false notions of Scottish life were shattered by G. *Douglas in *The House with the Green Shutters* (1901).

Kalevala, 'Land of Heroes', the national epic poem of Finland, transmitted orally until 1822, when a collection was published by Zacharius Topelius. The myths it contains are of great antiquity, possibly dating from the time when the Finns and Hungarians were still one people.

Kama Sutra, see BURTON, SIR R.

KAMES, Lord, see HOME, H.

Kangaroo (1923), a novel by D. H. *Lawrence, based on the Lawrences' visit to Australia in 1922. The book mingles political outbursts and meditations with observant evocation of Australian life and landscape.

KANT, Immanuel (1724–1804), German philosopher. He published his first considerable work, *A General Natural History of the Heavens*, in 1755. His *Critique of Pure Reason* appeared in 1781 (second edition in 1787), *Prolegomena to any future Metaphysics* in 1783, *Fundamental Principles of the Metaphysic of Ethics* in 1785, *Metaphysical Rudiments of Natural Philosophy* in 1786, *Critique of Practical Reason* in 1788, *Critique of Judgement* in 1790, and *Religion within the Boundaries of Pure Reason* in 1793.

In Kant's philosophy, knowledge is the outcome of two factors, the senses and the understanding. Space and time are essential conditions of knowledge, although they exist only as forms of our consciousness. These forms, continuous and infinite, provide the possibility of unifying our individual perceptions, and the unification is effected by the understanding. This act of synthesis Kant analyses into twelve principles or 'categories', or laws of thought. The categories are to the understanding very much what time and space are to the consciousness. They include such notions as quality, quantity, and, notably, causation. The external world is thus the product of sensations conditioned by the forms of consciousness and linked by thought according to its own laws.

Where metaphysics fails us, practical reason comes to our aid. The moral consciousness assents to certain 'categorical imperatives', such as 'do not lie'. Interpreted as a practical rule of conduct, the moral law bids you do all in your power to promote the highest good of all human beings. This is not realizable unless the course of the world is itself guided by moral law, by a moral Master of the universe, whose existence we are driven to assume. But metaphysics places religion and morality outside the province of knowledge, and in the region of faith.

Kant's philosophy was developed and profoundly modified by Fichte, *Schelling, and *Hegel. In Britain, *Coleridge and *Carlyle valued Kant's criticism of the empirical philosophy (and the atheism) of the 18th cent., particularly that of *Hume.

Kastril, the rustic lad in Jonson's *The Alchemist.

Katharina, the 'shrew', in Shakespeare's *The Taming of the Shrew.

Katharine, (1) a character in Shakespeare's *Love's Labour's Lost*; (2) in his *Henry V, the daughter of the king of France.

KATHARINE OF ARAGON, Queen, the wife of Henry VIII, whose divorce is one of the principal incidents in Shakespeare's *Henry VIII.

Katherine, St, see KATHERINE GROUP, THE.

Katherine Group, The, the name given to five Middle English works of devotional prose found together in the manuscript Bodley 34, dating from *c.*1190–1225: *Seinte Marherete, Seinte Iuliene, Seinte Katerine, *Sawles Warde*, and **Hali Meiðhad*. They come from Herefordshire, and are written in a distinctive and interesting language from a transitional period of English, in a lively, often colloquial style, with vivid details of illustration. The three saints' lives are all concerned with heroic virgins who were frequently exalted in medieval writings: St Katherine of Alexandria, St Juliana of Nicomedia, and St Margaret of Antioch.

KAVANAGH, Patrick (1905–67), Irish poet. His works include *Ploughman and other Poems* (1936), *A Soul for Sale* (1947), *Tarry Flynn* (1948, a novel set on a small farm in his home county), and *Collected Poems* (1964). *The Great Hunger* (1942) is a long poem contrasting the realities of life for an archetypal peasant, Patrick Maguire, with the more conventional idealized peasant of the *Irish revival. Much of Kavanagh's work is concerned with the relationship between Irish archetype and stereotype.

KAVANAGH, P(atrick) J(oseph) (1931–), poet, editor, and novelist, whose works reflect a religious feeling rooted in the natural world: these include *Selected Poems* (1982) and the novels *A Song and Dance* (1968) and *People and Weather* (1979). *The Perfect Stranger* (1966) is a prose memoir.

Kay, Sir, in the Arthurian legend (as in Malory's **Morte D'Arthur*), Arthur's steward, a brave but churlish knight. He was the son of Sir *Ector.

KEAN, Edmund (1787/90–1833), a great tragic actor who first achieved fame in 1814 as Shylock in * The Merchant of Venice*. His son, Charles John Kean (1811–68), was also an actor, and manager of the Princess's Theatre, 1851–9.

KEATS, John (1795–1821), the son of the manager of a livery stables in Moorfields. He was apprenticed to an apothecary-surgeon, but cancelled his fifth year of apprenticeship and became a student at Guy's Hospital; in 1816 he was licensed to practise as an apothecary, but he abandoned the profession for poetry. To this period belong 'Ode to Apollo' and 'Hymn to Apollo'. He met Leigh *Hunt, who in 1816 published in * The Examiner* Keats's poem, 'O Solitude'. Keats met *Shelley and *Haydon, and in 1817 his first volume of poems was published; it included among sonnets, epistles, and miscellaneous poems, 'I stood tip-toe upon a little hill' and 'Sleep and Poetry'. In the autumn came the first of *Lockhart's harsh attacks in *Blackwood's*, labelling Keats and his associates as members of the so-called *Cockney school. During the winter of 1817–18 Keats saw something of *Wordsworth and *Hazlitt, both of whom much

influenced his thought and practice. *Endymion*, dedicated to *Chatterton, published in the spring of 1818, was savagely attacked by Lockhart in *Blackwood's*; and Keats finished *'Isabella, or the Pot of Basil' in May. With his friend Charles Armitage Brown (1786–1842) Keats then visited the Lakes, Scotland, and Northern Ireland. In December 1817, Keats moved into Brown's house in Hampstead, now known as Keats House. There he met Fanny *Brawne, with whom he fell deeply in love. September 1818 marked the beginning of what is sometimes referred to as the Great Year; he began *Hyperion* in its first version, abandoning it a year later; he wrote, consecutively, *'The Eve of St Agnes', 'The Eve of St Mark', the 'Ode to Psyche', *'La Belle Dame sans Merci', *'Ode to a Nightingale', and probably at about the same time the *'Ode on a Grecian Urn', 'Ode on Melancholy', and 'Ode on Indolence'; *'Lamia Part I', 'Otho the Great' (in collaboration with Brown); the second version of *Hyperion*, called *The Fall of Hyperion*, *'To Autumn', and 'Lamia Part II'. During this year he was beset with financial problems. In the winter of 1819, he had become increasingly ill with tuberculosis and his great creative work was now over. His second volume of poems, *Lamia, Isabella, The Eve of St Agnes, and other Poems*, was published in July 1820, and included, as well as the title poems, five odes, *Hyperion*, 'Fancy', and other works. Shelley invited Keats to Italy and in September Keats set off with his friend *Severn. They did not go to the Shelleys but settled in Rome, where Keats died the following February.

Keats has always been regarded as one of the principal figures in the *Romantic movement, and his stature as a poet has grown steadily through all changes of fashion. *Tennyson considered him the greatest poet of the 19th cent., and M. *Arnold commended his 'intellectual and spiritual passion' for beauty.

His letters, published in 1848 and 1878, have come to be regarded with almost the admiration given to his poetry; T. S. *Eliot described them as certainly the most notable and most important ever written by any English poet.

KEBLE, John (1792–1866), became fellow and tutor at Oriel College (where *Newman and *Pusey were also fellows) and professor of poetry at Oxford, 1831–41. His sermon on national apostasy in 1833 was considered the start of the *Oxford Movement, which he also supported by nine of the *Tracts for the Times*. His volume of sacred verse *The Christian Year* (1827), intended as a guide to devotion and a commentary on the Book of Common Prayer, shows the influence of G. *Herbert and, in its feeling for the natural world, of *Wordsworth. Keble also edited *Hooker (1836), helped Newman with *Froude's *Remains*, and contributed to

*Lyra Apostolica. Keble College, Oxford, was founded in his memory in 1870.

Keep the Aspidistra Flying, see ORWELL, G.

Kehama, The Curse of, see CURSE OF KEHAMA, THE.

Kells, Book of, an 8th- to 9th-cent. manuscript of the four Gospels, with Prefaces, Summaries and Canon Tables; seven charters of the abbey of Kells have been added on blank pages. It is written in Irish majuscule and has magnificent illustrations consisting of intricate patterns made up of abstract and animal forms. It was probably written at Kells in Co. Meath, the headquarters of the Columban community after the sack of Iona in 806. It was collated by *Ussher in 1621 and presented to Trinity College, Dublin, after the Restoration.

KELLY, Hugh (1739–77), an Irishman who came to London in 1760. His False Delicacy, produced by *Garrick in 1768, is a *sentimental comedy with a triple plot in which the mistakes arise from excessive tact or delicacy. Kelly also wrote A Word to the Wise (1770) and The School for Wives (1773).

Kelmscott Press, see MORRIS, W.

KELVIN, Lord, see THOMSON, SIR W.

KEMBLE, Charles (1775–1854), son of a strolling actor-manager, Roger Kemble (1721–1802), brother of Sarah *Siddons and J. P. *Kemble; father of Fanny *Kemble and J. M. *Kemble. A leading actor for some 25 years, his range was considerable in comedy and romance, but he did not often attempt tragedy.

KEMBLE, Fanny (Frances Anne) (1809–93), daughter of Charles *Kemble, a very beautiful and accomplished actress. She played comedy and tragedy with equal success. She published a volume of poems in 1844 and Records of a Later Life in 1882.

KEMBLE, John Mitchell (1807–57), historian and philologist, elder son of Charles *Kemble. He was educated at Trinity College, Cambridge, where he was a member of the *Apostles. He later studied in Germany and became a close friend of *Grimm; he was converted to the new continental philology and his text of *Beowulf (1833) was dedicated to Grimm.

KEMBLE, John Philip (1757–1823), eldest brother of Charles *Kemble. He achieved success as a formal tragic actor.

KEMBLE, Sarah, see SIDDONS, S.

KEMP, William (fl. 1600), a comic actor and dancer, who acted in plays by Shakespeare and *Jonson. He danced a morris-dance from London to Norwich, recorded in his Kemps Nine Daies Wonder (1600).

KEMPE, Margery (c.1373–c.1439), a mystic, travelled widely on pilgrimage: to Jerusalem, Rome, Compostella, and Wilsnack in Poland. She dictated, probably in the late 1420s, her Book of Margery Kempe which recounts her visions and experiences of a more general kind: her temptations to lechery, her travels, and her trial for heresy.

KEMPIS, Thomas À, see THOMAS À KEMPIS.

Kenilworth, a novel by Sir W. *Scott, published 1821.

The novel is based on the tradition of the tragic fate of the beautiful Amy Robsart, daughter of Sir John Robsart (called Sir Hugh in the novel). She has been enticed, by the designs of the villainous Richard Varney, into a secret marriage with his patron the earl of Leicester, Queen Elizabeth's favourite, rejecting the worthy Edmund Tressilian. Varney, by misrepresenting the relations of Amy and Tressilian, has induced Leicester to believe her guilty of infidelity to him and Leicester has ordered Varney to remove Amy to Cumnor Place and kill her. Leicester learns too late that Varney's accusations are false and Tressilian arrives at Cumnor only to find that Amy, by Varney's machinations, has fallen through a trap-door and perished.

Among the many interesting features in the novel are the glimpses of the court of Elizabeth, where the young Ralegh is just coming into favour; the descriptions of the revels at Kenilworth (see under LANEHAM); and the adaptations of the legend of Wayland Smith, the skilful farrier and physician, who aids Tressilian in his attempts to recover Amy. Dickie Sludge, or Flibbertigibbet, the impish friend of Wayland Smith, also deserves mention.

Kennedy, Lady Laura, a character in A. Trollope's novels *Phineas Finn and *Phineas Redux.

KENNEDY, Margaret Moore (1896–1967), novelist, is remembered principally for her highly-praised best-seller The Constant Nymph (1924), which was dramatized (1926) and filmed several times.

KENNEDY, Walter (?1460–?1508), a Scottish poet, the rival of *Dunbar in 'The Flyting of Dunbar and Kennedy' (1508), of whose poems only a few survive.

Kenneth, Sir, or the Knight of the Leopard, the hero of Scott's *The Talisman.

Kent, earl of, in Shakespeare's *King Lear a loyal follower of the king.

Kenwigs, Mr and Mrs, a genteel couple in Dickens's *Nicholas Nickleby.*

KER, William Paton (1855–1923), became professor of poetry at Oxford in 1920, having previously held other important university posts. He is celebrated for the width of his humane criticism in English, Norse, and Scottish literature. His *Collected Essays* were edited by C. Whibley and published in 1925. His other most admired works are *Epic and Romance* (1897) and *The Dark Ages* (1904).

KEROUAC, Jack (1922–69), American novelist, became a spokesman for the *Beat generation, and is best known in Britain for his semi-autobiographical novel *On the Road* (1957), which describes the wanderings across America of Sal Paradise, a young writer, and his friend and hero, Dean Moriarty. Kerouac's other works include *The Dharma Bums* (1958) and *The Subterraneans* (1958).

Kew, countess of, a character in Thackeray's *The Newcomes.*

KEYES, Sidney Arthur Kilworth (1922–43), poet. He edited, with Michael Meyer, *Eight Oxford Poets* (1941), which contains some of his own work. His first collection, *The Iron Laurel* (1942), appeared in the year he joined the army. His second, *The Cruel Solstice*, appeared in 1943, after his presumed death in Tunisia. His *Collected Poems*, with a Memoir by M. Meyer, appeared in 1945. H. *Read described his characteristic note as 'elegiac'.

KEYNES, Sir Geoffrey Langdon (1887–1982), scholar and bibliographer, brother of J. M. *Keynes. His works include bibliographies of *Donne, *Evelyn, and *Blake (1921, 1953); his editions of Blake (1925–66, and various studies) were a major contribution towards the 20th-cent. reappraisal of Blake's work.

KEYNES, John Maynard, first baron Keynes of Tilton (1883–1946), economist, whose book *A General Theory of Employment, Interest, and Money* (1936) revolutionized economic theory by showing how unemployment could occur 'involuntarily'. For 30 years after the Second World War governments of western nations pursued 'Keynesian' full-employment policies. Keynes was a member of the *Bloomsbury Group and a noted patron of the arts. He became the first chairman of the *Arts Council of Great Britain in 1945. His portraits of President Woodrow Wilson, Georges Clemenceau, and Lloyd George (the first two of which appeared in his book *The Economic Consequences of the Peace*, 1919) are justly famous. His essay 'Dr Melchior: A Defeated Enemy', together with 'My Early Beliefs', was published posthumously in 1949.

KID, Thomas, see KYD.

Kidnapped and *Catriona*, a novel and its sequel by R. L. *Stevenson, published in 1886 and 1893.

The central incident in the story is the murder of Colin Campbell, the 'Red Fox' of Glenure, the king's factor on the forfeited estate of Ardshiel: this is a historical event. The young David Balfour, left in poverty on the death of his father, goes for assistance to his uncle Ebenezer, a miserly old villain who has illegally taken control of the Balfour estate. Having failed to effect the death of David, Ebenezer has him kidnapped on a ship to be carried off to the Carolinas. On the voyage Alan Breck is picked up from a sinking boat. He is a Jacobite who 'wearies for the heather and the deer'. The ship is wrecked on the coast of Mull, and David and Alan journey together. They are witnesses of the murder of Colin Campbell, and suspicion falls on them. After a perilous journey across the Highlands they escape across the Forth, and the first novel ends with the discomfiture of Ebenezer and David's recovery of his rights.

Catriona is principally occupied with the unsuccessful attempt of David Balfour to secure, at the risk of his own life and freedom, the acquittal of James Stewart of the Glens, who is falsely accused, from political motives, of the murder of Colin Campbell; with the escape of Alan Breck to the Continent; and with David's love affair with Catriona Drummond, the daughter of the renegade James More.

KIERKEGAARD, Søren Aabye (1813–55), Danish philosopher and theologian. He is now chiefly remembered as having initiated much that is characteristic of existentialist trends in modern philosophy (e.g. *Concluding Unscientific Postscript*, trans. W. Lowrie and D. F. Swenson, 1941). He was also the author of works whose themes were primarily religious, psychological, or literary (e.g. *The Concept of Dread and Fear and Trembling*, both trans. W. Lowrie, 1944); moreover, his satirical gifts made him a formidable social critic, witness his essay on *The Present Age* (trans. A. Dru, 1962). Yet, for all their diversity of subject, his writings have certain distinctive common features: a distrust of abstract dogma and a correlative emphasis upon the particular case or concrete example; an acute and imaginative concern with the forms under which human character and motivation may manifest themselves; and a passionate belief in the value of individual choice and judgement as contrasted with tame acquiescence in established opinions and norms. It was precisely his insistence upon the importance of personal decision, direct and unmediated by artifical ratiocination, that lay at the root of his rejection of *Hegel. Kierkegaard opposed the conception of authentic choice, the explicit self-commitment of a person who stakes his whole being and future upon a belief which he cannot prove but which he maintains in the face of all intellectual doubt and uncertainty. Some of Kierkegaard's most penetrating psychological observations occur in his description of the 'leap of faith' and in his analyses of the state of 'dread' (*Angst*) which precedes and accompanies it. The stress upon freedom in his sense, as an inescapable condition of life and action and as something which both fascinates and repels the choosing individual, represents perhaps the clearest link between his philosophical ideas and the doctrines of his existentialist successors. (See EXISTENTIALISM.)

Killigrew, Mrs Anne, To the pious Memory of, see DRYDEN.

KILLIGREW, Henry (1613–1700), brother of T. *Killigrew the elder, master of the Savoy in 1663, and author of one play, *The Conspiracy* (1638). He was the father of Anne Killigrew (1660–85; see DRYDEN).

KILLIGREW, Thomas, the elder (1612–83), was page to Charles I and groom of the bedchamber and a favourite companion of Charles II. With *D'Avenant he held the monopoly of acting in Restoration London. He built a playhouse on the site of the present Drury Lane Theatre in 1663. His most popular play, *The Parson's Wedding,* a bawdy farcical comedy, was first performed 1640/1, printed in 1664.

KILLIGREW, Thomas, the younger (1657–1719), son of T. *Killigrew the elder, and gentleman of the bedchamber to George II when prince of Wales. He was the author of *Chit Chat,* a comedy acted in 1719.

KILLIGREW, Sir William (?1606–95), brother of T. *Killigrew the elder and author of the tragi-comedy *Selindra*; the comedy *Pandora,* published 1664; and other dramatic works.

Killing No Murder, a pamphlet ironically dedicated to *Cromwell, which advocates his assassination. It was written by the Leveller Edward Sexby (d. 1658) and printed in 1657 in Holland.

KILVERT, (Robert) Francis (1840–79), became vicar of Bredwardine in 1876. He is remembered for his diary (3 vols, 1938–40, ed. W. *Plomer), kept from 1870 until his death. It provides a full portrait of the author and the remote and beautiful region of the Welsh borders where he lived and worked. He records the landscape, the distresses of his parishioners, the life of the gentry, and the beauty of girls from early childhood to young womanhood.

Kim, a novel by *Kipling, published 1901.
    Kimball O'Hara, the orphaned son of a sergeant in an Irish regiment, spends his childhood as a vagabond in Lahore, until he meets an old lama from Tibet and accompanies him in his travels. He falls into the hands of his father's old regiment, is adopted, and sent to school, resuming his wanderings in his holidays. Colonel Creighton of the Ethnological Survey remarks his aptitude for secret service ('the Great Game'), and on this he embarks under the directions of the native agent Hurree Babu. The book presents a vivid picture of India, its teeming populations, religions, and superstitions, and the life of the bazaars and the road.

Kind Harts Dreame, see CHETTLE.

Kind of Loving, A, a novel by S. *Barstow.

KING, Francis Henry (1923–), novelist, short-story writer, and critic, worked abroad for the British Council (1949–63); several of his novels have foreign settings, notably Japan and Greece. They include *To the Dark Tower* (1946), *The Dividing Stream* (1951), *The Widow* (1957), *The Custom House* (1961), *Flights* (1973), and *The Action* (1979), and are marked by a cool and ironic detachment, close analysis of human motivation, and an unobtrusive technical elegance. *Act of Darkness* (1983) is a psychological thriller, set largely in India. Volumes of short stories include *The Brighton Belle and other stories* (1968) and *Hard Feelings and other stories* (1976).

KING, Henry (1592–1669), became bishop of Chichester and was the friend of *Donne and I. *Walton. He published poems sacred and profane, the best-known of which is 'An Exequy to his Matchless never to be forgotten Friend', written for his wife.

KING, William (1663–1712), a writer of burlesques, satires, and light verse, much of which was published anonymously. In his *Dialogues of the Dead* (1699) he joined Charles Boyle in the attack on *Bentley. (See BATTLE OF THE BOOKS.)

King Alisaunder, an early 14th-cent. romance, probably from London, in 8,034 lines of short couplets. It is based on a legend according to which Alexander the Great was not the son of Philip of Macedon but of the Egyptian king Nectanabus, who tricked Philip's wife by magic into sleeping with him. The poem deals with the birth and youth of Alexander, his succession to Philip's throne, his conquest of Carthage and other cities, and his wars with Darius. The latter parts of the poem deal with his perils and conquests in the Far East, his seduction by Candace, and his death by poison.

King and No King, A, a tragi-comedy by *Beaumont and *Fletcher, performed 1611, printed 1619.

Its complex plot describes the military and sexual rivalry of two kings, Arbaces of Iberia and Tigranes of Armenia, both of whom fall in love with Arbaces' supposed sister Panthea. It is revealed that Arbaces is a changeling and therefore 'no king': he marries Panthea, the true queen, and Tigranes returns to his former love Spaconia. Comic relief is provided by Bessus, a *'miles gloriosus'.

King Charles's head, a phrase taken from Mr Dick's obsession in *David Copperfield*, and thence used to describe any recurrent and irrational obsession.

King Horn, the earliest surviving English verse romance, of about 1,500 lines, dating from about 1225. The story is substantially the same as that of *Horn Childe*, concerning Horn, the son of the king and queen of Suddene, who is turned adrift by invading Saracens and falls in love with Rymenhild, the daughter of the king of Westernesse. Horn's companion Fikenhild betrays the lovers, has Horn banished to Ireland, and marries Rymenhild. After spectacular deeds of prowess in Ireland, Horn returns to Westernesse in disguise and makes himself known to Rymenhild. Then, having recovered his land of Suddene, he kills Fikenhild and marries Rymenhild who becomes his queen.

Kingis Quair, The, 'The King's Book', a poem of 379 lines of rhyme-royal written by *James I of Scotland while he was a prisoner in England and about the time of his marriage (c. 1424) to Lady Jane Beaufort, the poem's heroine. It was discovered and printed by Lord Woodhouselee in 1783. It is one of the works traditionally described as 'Scottish *Chaucerian', and it does show the influence of Chaucer. C. S. *Lewis calls it the first poem in celebration of married love.

King John, a historical drama written in a first version before 1536, by *Bale.

King John, *The Life and Death of,* a historical play by *Shakespeare, probably largely based on an earlier anonymous play, *The Troublesome Raigne of John King of England* (1591). It was first printed in the *Folio of 1623.

The play, with some departures from historical accuracy, deals with various events in King John's reign, and principally with the tragedy of young Arthur. It ends with the death of John at Swinstead abbey. It is striking that no mention of Magna Carta appears in it. The tragic quality of the play, the poignant grief of Constance, Arthur's mother, and the political complications depicted, are relieved by the wit, humour, and gallantry of the Bastard, supposed son of Faulconbridge, actually the son of Richard Cœur de Lion.

KINGLAKE, Alexander William (1809–91), published anonymously in 1844 *Eōthen: or traces of travel brought home from the East,* an account of a journey taken some ten years earlier which is regarded as a classic of its genre; it is a lively description of his travels, giving his own reactions to, for example, the desert, the relics of the Holy Land, an encounter with Lady Hester *Stanhope, and the plague in Cairo. He devoted many years to an exhaustive history of the Crimean war (1863–87) which shows his great admiration for Lord Raglan.

King Lear, a tragedy by Shakespeare, dating from 1604–5, performed 1606. The play appeared in quarto in 1608 (reprinted 1619), and in a different form in the First *Folio (1623). The play's sources include a chronical play, *King Leir* (perf. 1594, printed 1605), the chronicles of *Holinshed, and the *Mirror for Magistrates*. The Gloucester sub-plot derives from Sidney's *Arcadia*.

Lear, king of Britain, a petulant and unwise old man, has three daughters: Goneril, wife of the duke of Albany; Regan, wife of the duke of Cornwall; and Cordelia, for whom the king of France and duke of Burgundy are suitors. Intending to divide his kingdom among his daughters according to their affection for him, he bids them say which loves him most. Goneril and Regan make profession of extreme affection, and each receives one-third of the kingdom. Cordelia, self-willed, and disgusted with their hollow flattery, says she loves him according to her duty, not more nor less. Infuriated with this reply, Lear divides her portion between his other daughters, with the condition that himself with 100 knights shall be maintained by each daughter in turn. Burgundy withdraws his suit for Cordelia, and the king of France accepts her without dowry. The earl of Kent, taking her part, is banished. Goneril and Regan reveal their heartless character by grudging their father the maintenance that he had stipulated for, and finally turning him out of doors in a storm. The earl of Gloucester shows pity for the old king, and is suspected of complicity with the French, who have landed in England. His eyes are put out by Cornwall, who receives a death-wound in the affray. Gloucester's son Edgar, who has been traduced to his father by his bastard brother Edmund, takes the disguise of a lunatic beggar, and tends his father till the latter's death. Lear, whom rage and ill-treatment have deprived of his wits, is conveyed to Dover by the faithful Kent in disguise, where Cordelia receives him. Meanwhile Goneril and Regan have both turned their affections to Edmund. Embittered by this rivalry, Goneril poisons Regan, and takes her own life. The English forces under Edmund and Albany defeat the French, and Lear and Cordelia are imprisoned; by Edmund's order Cordelia is hanged, and Lear dies from grief. The treachery of Edmund is proved by his brother Edgar. Albany, who has not abetted Goneril in her cruel treatment of Lear, takes over the kingdom.

KINGSLEY, Charles (1819–75), rector of Eversley in Hampshire. He was professor of modern history at Cambridge (1860–9) and canon of Chester and Westminster. His blank verse drama *The Saint's Tragedy* (1848) deals with the conflict between natural affections and asceticism, and its introduction attacking celibacy strikes an anti-Tractarian note that recurs throughout his work. At this period he was much influenced by F. D. *Maurice and *Carlyle. He contributed, over the signature 'Parson Lot', to *Politics for the People* (1848) and to its successor, *The Christian Socialist* (1850–1).

In 1850 he published his first novel, *Yeast* (serialized in *Fraser's Magazine*, 1848), and *Alton Locke*. Both are reforming novels, showing his concern with the sufferings of the working classes. A visit to Germany in 1851 inspired his first historical novel, *Hypatia, or New Foes with Old Faces* (1853), set in 5th-cent. Alexandria, published in *Fraser's* in 1851. *Newman's *Callista* was written in part to correct its hostile portrait of the early Church. His next novel, *Westward Ho!* (1855), was set in the Elizabethan period; its hero, Devonshire seaman Amyas Leigh, wages war against the Armada and the Spanish captain Don Guzman, his rival in love. *Two Years Ago* (1857) returns to the theme of social reform; and *Hereward the Wake* (1866) is a historical novel based on the exploits of the legendary outlaw.

Kingsley's other works include *The Heroes* (1856) and *The Water-Babies* (1863). The latter displays his interest in underwater and seashore life, as does his earlier work *Glaucus: or the Wonders of the Shore* (1855). Many of his songs and ballads remain popular; these include 'Airly Beacon' and 'The Sands of Dee', and many of his lines, such as 'Be Good, sweet maid, and let who will be clever' (quoted in *Two Years Ago*) and 'For men must work and women must weep', from 'The Three Fishers', have become proverbial. Kingsley also wrote tracts on many topics, published lectures and sermons, and his *At Last* (1871) is a record of a long-desired visit to the West Indies.

Kingsley seems to represent some of the central paradoxes of his age. A keen sportsman who was tender to animals, a champion of the working man who despised Negroes, a muscular Christian who wrote much (like his friend T. *Hughes) of the virtues of 'manliness' and who nevertheless held an unusually explicit passion for his wife, he was both Philistine and artist; his strong didacticism, while it mars many of his works, is inseparable from them.

KINGSLEY, Henry (1830–76), younger brother of C. *Kingsley. From 1853 to 1858 he was in Australia, at the gold-diggings and as a trooper in the Sydney Mounted Police, experiences which provided the basis for two of his best novels, *Geoffrey Hamlyn* (1859) and *The Hillyers and the Burtons* (1865), which have been influential in Australian literary history. For a time he was editor of the *Edinburgh Daily Review*, and was its correspondent at the Franco-Prussian War.

Ravenshoe (1862), the best-known of his 21 books, is a story of inheritance intrigues in a Roman Catholic landed family in Devonshire, and includes Crimean War scenes. Kingsley's best novels are distinguished for admirable descriptions of landscape in England and Australia, for engrossing accounts of storms and cyclones, attacks and alarms, and for humorous and well-observed character sketches.

KINGSMILL, Hugh (Hugh Kingsmill Lunn) (1889–1949), anthologist, biographer, literary critic, novelist, and parodist, whose lives of M. *Arnold (1928), *Dickens (1935), and D. H. *Lawrence (1938) gave him a reputation for iconoclasm. His other works include *The Return of William Shakespeare* (1929, a fictional fantasy) and *The Progress of a Biographer* (1949, collected literary criticism).

King's, or **Queen's, Printer,** the printer of royal proclamations, etc., appointed under royal patent. The earliest known patent was granted in 1530. At the present day the controller of the Stationery Office (under Letters Patent) is the Queen's Printer of Acts of Parliament, and in him is vested the copyright in all government publications. Messrs Eyre & Spottiswoode are also termed the Queen's Printers; their privilege is the printing of the Bible and Prayer Book, a privilege shared with the University Presses of Oxford and Cambridge.

KINGSTON, W(illiam) H(enry) G(iles) (1814–80), writer of stories for boys, covering adventures in all continents, at sea, in history, at school, and elsewhere.

'Kinmont Willie', a ballad included in Scott's *Minstrelsy of the Scottish Border.* (See ARMSTRONG, J.)

KIPLING, Rudyard (1865–1936), born in Bombay, son of John Lockwood Kipling, author and illustrator of *Beast and Man in India* (1891). He was brought to England in 1871, where he spent five years at boarding school separated from his parents, a period recalled with bitterness in his short story 'Baa, Baa, Black Sheep' (1888) and his novel *The Light that Failed* (1890). From 1878 to 1882 he attended the United Services College, Westward Ho!, later depicted in his schoolboy tales *Stalky & Co.* (1899). From 1882 to 1889 he worked as a journalist in India; many of his early poems and stories were later collected under various titles, which include *Departmental Ditties* (1886), *Plain Tales from the Hills* (1888), *Soldiers Three* (1890), and *Wee Willie Winkie* (1890). In 1889 he came to London, where he achieved instant literary celebrity, aided by *Henley's publication in his *Scots Observer* of many of the poems ('Danny Deever', 'Mandalay', etc.) later collected as *Barrack-Room Ballads* (1892). In 1892 he married Caroline Balestier, sister of his American agent Charles Wolcott Balestier (1861–91; with whom he had written *The Naulahka*, 1892). Widely regarded as unofficial poet laureate, he was in 1907 the first English writer to receive the *Nobel Prize.

Kipling's early tales of the Raj were praised for their cynical realism, but his growing reputation as the poet of Empire cut both ways. His poem 'Recessional', written for Jubilee Day 1897, was acclaimed for catching the mood of the moment, but the mood changed. His verse has added many phrases to the language (including, significantly, 'the white man's burden'), but he was increasingly accused of vulgarity and jingoism in aesthetic and anti-imperialist circles. His most uncontroversial and durable achievements are perhaps his tales for children (principally *The Jungle Book*, 1894; *Just So Stories*, 1902; *Puck of Pook's Hill*, 1906; and *Rewards and Fairies*, 1910), and his picaresque novel of India, *Kim*, is generally considered his masterpiece. His autobiographical fragment *Something of Myself* was published in 1937.

Kipps, a novel by H. G. *Wells.

KIRKE, Edward (1553–1613), a friend of *Spenser. He probably wrote the preface, the arguments, and a verbal commentary to Spenser's *Shepheardes Calendar*, under the initials 'E.K.' (1579).

Kirkrapine, in Spenser's *Faerie Queene* (I. iii), 'a stout and sturdie thiefe' of the church, who is destroyed by Una's lion.

KIRKUP, James (1923–), poet, translator, and travel writer. His volumes of poetry include *A Correct Compassion* (1952), *The Descent into the Cave* (1957), *Paper Windows* (1968), and *A Bewick Bestiary* (1971). In 1977 his poem 'The love that dares to speak its name' (which deals with the homosexual love of one of the Roman centurions for Christ) became the subject of the first prosecution for blasphemous libel for over 50 years; as a result, the editor of *Gay News*, the periodical which published the poem, was fined and given a suspended prison sentence. Kirkup's autobiographical *The Only Child* (1957) is an evocative account of a working-class northern childhood, and he has also published many books on Japan.

Kit-Cat Club, founded in the early part of the 18th cent. by leading Whigs, including (according to *Pope) *Steele, *Addison, *Congreve, *Garth, and *Vanbrugh. *Tonson was for many years its secretary and moving spirit. The club met at the house of Christopher Cat (or Kat), a pastry cook, in Shire Lane and subsequently at Tonson's house at Barn Elms.

Kitchen Sink Drama, a term applied in the late 1950s to the plays of writers such as *Wesker, S. *Delaney, and J. *Osborne, which portrayed working-class or lower-middle-class life, with an emphasis on domestic realism.

Kite, Sergeant, one of the chief characters in Farquhar's *The Recruiting Officer*. One of his songs is the well known 'Over the hills and far away'.

Kitely, the jealous husband of Jonson's *Every Man in his Humour*.

Kit Nubbles, a character in Dickens's *The Old Curiosity Shop*.

Knag, Miss, in Dickens's *Nicholas Nickleby*, Madame Mantalini's forewoman.

KNICKERBOCKER, Diedrich, the pseudonym under which W. *Irving wrote his *History of New York*, and other sketches.

Knickerbocker Magazine, The (1833–65), founded in New York City. Its contributors included W. *Irving, H. W. *Longfellow, W. C. *Bryant, O. W. *Holmes, J. R. *Lowell, H. *Greeley, and J. F. *Cooper.

KNIGHT, G(eorge Richard) Wilson (1897–), Shakespeare scholar and critic. His poetic and symbolic approach to Shakespeare is perhaps seen at its best in *The Wheel of Fire* (1930), *The Starlit Dome* (1941), and *The Crown of Life* (1947), among many other publications.

KNIGHT, William Payne, see PICTURESQUE.

Knightley, George, and John, his brother, characters in J. Austen's *Emma*.

Knight of the Burning Pestle, The, a comedy probably entirely by *Beaumont, formerly generally attributed to Beaumont and *Fletcher, probably performed 1607–8, printed (anonymously) 1613. The most successful of Beaumont's plays, it is a high-spirited comedy of manners, and a burlesque of knight-errantry, satirizing the middle-class taste for such popular and improbable romances as *Palmerin of England*.

It takes the form of a play-within-a-play: a grocer and his wife, members of an audience about to watch a drama called 'The London Merchant', interrupt the prologue to insist that their apprentice, Rafe, have a part. He therefore becomes a Grocer Errant, with a Burning Pestle portrayed on his shield, and undertakes various absurd adventures. These are interspersed with the real plot, in which Jasper, a merchant's apprentice, woos, and after much opposition wins, his master's daughter Luce.

Knight of the Leopard, Sir Kenneth of Scotland, hero of Scott's *The Talisman*.

Knight of the Swan, see LOHENGRIN.

KNIGHTS, L(ionel) C(harles) (1906–), Shakespeare critic. His longer books include *Drama and Society in the Age of Jonson* (1937) and *Some Shakespearean Themes* (1959). One of his best-known essays is 'How many children had Lady Macbeth?' (1933), a celebrated attack on the style of criticism represented by A. C. *Bradley.

Knights of the Round Table, see ROUND TABLE.

'Knight's Tale, The', see CANTERBURY TALES, 1.

KNOLLES, Richard (?1550–1610), author of *The Generall Historie of the Turkes* (1603), admired by Dr *Johnson (who took from it the plot of his *Irene*), and by *Byron, who credited it with inspiring the 'oriental colouring' of his poetry.

Knowell, in Johnson's *Every Man in his Humour*, Edward's over-solicitous father.

KNOWLES, James Sheridan (1784–1862), dramatist. His *Virginius* was produced at Covent Garden with C. *Kemble and *Macready in 1820; *Caius Gracchus* in 1823 (1815, Belfast); *William Tell* in 1825. His greatest success was *The Hunchback*, produced in 1832. *The Wife*, with Prologue and Epilogue by *Lamb, followed in 1833, and in 1837 *The Love Chase*. His friend *Hazlitt described Knowles as 'the first tragic writer of his time', and he was the recipient of many of the letters in Hazlitt's *Liber Amoris*.

KNOX, John (c.1513–72), began preaching for the reformed religion in 1547 and became chaplain to Edward VI in 1551. He went abroad at the accession of Mary Tudor, wrote his 'Epistle on Justification by Faith' in 1548, met *Calvin at Geneva in 1554, was pastor of the English congregation at Frankfurt am Main, 1554–5, and from 1556 to 1558 lived at Geneva. Thence he addressed epistles to his brethren in England suffering under the rule of Mary

Tudor, and in Scotland under the regency of Mary of Lorraine. It was this situation which led to the publication of his *First Blast of the Trumpet against the Monstrous Regiment of Women* (1558) of which the title, *Saintsbury remarks, was the best part. (See also PAMPHLETEERING, ORIGINS OF.) In 1559 appeared the *First Book of Discipline*, of which Knox was part-author, advocating a national system of education. His *Treatise on Predestination* was published in 1560. In 1572 he was appointed minister at Edinburgh, where he died. His *History of the Reformation of Religioun within the realme of Scotland* (1587) contains, in its fourth book, the notable account of the return of Mary Stuart to Scotland, of Knox's interviews with her, and his fierce denunciations from the pulpit of St Giles.

KNOX, the Rt Revd Monsignor Ronald Arbuthnott (1888–1957). His autobiographical *A Spiritual Aeneid* (1918) describes his conversion to Roman Catholicism. Knox wrote many theological works, published a new translation of the Bible, based on the *Vulgate (1945–9), and acquired a wide reputation as journalist and broadcaster. He also wrote six detective stories, and was well known for his light verse. *Let Dons Delight* (1939) describes, through conversations in an Oxford senior common room at 50-year intervals, the process of specialization that leads to the loss of a common culture. His brother, E. G. V. Knox (1881–1971), was as 'Evoe' a well-known humorist and editor (1932–49) of *Punch.

KNYVETT, Thomas (1596–1658), a royalist in sympathy during the Civil War. His letters to his wife throw an interesting light on the life of the period.

KOESTLER, Arthur (1905–83), author, born in Budapest, worked as foreign correspondent in the Middle East, Paris, and Berlin. In 1932 he joined the Communist Party and travelled in the USSR; he was imprisoned under Franco during the Spanish Civil War and broke from the Party in 1938. In 1940 he came to England, adopting the language with his first book written in English, *Scum of the Earth* (1941). His publications manifest a wide range of political, scientific, and literary interests, and include *Darkness at Noon* (1940), *Arrival and Departure* (1943), and *Thieves in the Night* (1946). Non-fiction includes *The Yogi and the Commissar and Other Essays* (1945), *The Trail of the Dinosaur and Other Essays* (1955), and *The Act of Creation* (1964). *The Roots of Coincidence* (1972) reflects his interest in parapsychology. He was one of the contributors to *The God that Failed: six studies in communism* (1950). He died by suicide, having frequently expressed a belief in the right to euthanasia.

'Kraken, The', a short poem by *Tennyson, published in *Poems, Chiefly Lyrical* (1830). It describes the mythical sea-monster mentioned by Pontoppidan, sleeping in the depths of the sea 'his ancient, dreamless, uninvaded sleep', and waiting only to rise and die.

Krook, a character in Dickens's *Bleak House.*

'Kubla Khan; a Vision in a Dream', a poem by S. T. *Coleridge, published 1816.

In 1797, while living near the *Wordsworths in Somerset, Coleridge took opium and fell asleep when reading a passage in *Purchas his Pilgrimage* (see PURCHAS), relating to the Khan Kubla and the palace that he commanded to be built. On awaking he was conscious of having composed in his sleep two or three hundred lines on this theme, and eagerly set down the lines that form this fragment. He was then interrupted by 'a person . . . from Porlock', and, on returning to his task an hour later, found that almost the entire remainder of the poem had slipped from his memory. The poem consists of a series of visionary images, suggesting themes of eternity and change. Alph, the sacred river, flung up in a tremendous fountain, connects Khan's 'stately pleasure-dome', great caverns, and the 'sunless sea'. Within the gardens of the pleasure-dome is growth and sunlight and colour. There are hints of death and war, the vision of a damsel with a dulcimer, and of the frenzy of the poet who has drunk 'the milk of Paradise'. *Lowes, in *The Road to Xanadu* (1927), traces the varied sources of Coleridge's imagery.

Kurtz, a character in Conrad's *'Heart of Darkness' whose epitaph, 'Mistah Kurtz—he dead', provides the epigraph for T. S. *Eliot's 'The Hollow Men'.

KYD, or **KID,** Thomas (1558–94), dramatist, seems to have been closely associated with *Marlowe, whose 'atheistical' writings led to Kyd's suffering a period of torture and imprisonment. His *Spanish Tragedy* was published anonymously in 1592. *Cornelia* (1594) was re-issued in 1595 as *Pompey the Great, his faire Corneliaes Tragedie. The First Part of Jeronimo* (1605) is a fore-piece to *The Spanish Tragedy*, but probably not the work of Kyd. Other works Kyd may have written are *The Tragedye of Solyman and Perseda* (1592) and a lost pre-Shakespearian play on the subject of Hamlet.

KYRLE, John, The Man of Ross (1637–1724), lived very simply upon his estates at Ross and devoted his surplus income to charity. *Pope celebrated him in his *Epistle to Bathurst* (see MORAL ESSAYS).

L

'La Belle Dame san Merci', a ballad by
*Keats, written 1819, published 1820, which
describes a knight fatally enthralled by an elfin
woman. The ballad was much admired by the
*Pre-Raphaelites and W. *Morris asserted that
'it was the germ from which all the poetry of his
group had sprung'. *La Belle Dame sans mercy* is
also the title of a poem translated from Alain
Chartier, attributed at one time to *Chaucer.

La Creevy, Miss, the cheerful little miniature-
painter in Dickens's *Nicholas Nickleby*.

Ladislaw, Will, a character in G. Eliot's
Middlemarch.

Lady Audley's Secret, see BRADDON, M. E.

Lady Chatterley's Lover, a novel by *D. H.
Lawrence (privately printed, Florence 1928;
expurgated version, London 1932; full text,
London 1960).
    Constance Chatterley is married to Sir Clif-
ford, writer, intellectual, and landowner, of
Wragby Hall in the Midlands. He is confined to a
wheelchair through injuries from the First
World War. She has an unsatisfying affair with a
successful playwright, Michaelis, followed by a
passionate love relationship with gamekeeper
Oliver Mellors. She becomes pregnant by him,
goes to Venice with her sister Hilda partly to
obscure the baby's parentage, but returns and
tells her husband the truth, spurred on by the
knowledge that Mellors's estranged wife Bertha
has been stirring scandal in an effort to reclaim
him. The novel ends with the temporary separation of the lovers, as they hopefully await
divorce and a new life together.
    Lawrence's detailed and poetic descriptions of
sexual union, and his uncompromising use of
four-letter words, caused the book to be
unpublishable in full in England until 1960 when
*Penguin Books produced a complete text.
They were prosecuted under the Obscene Publications Act 1959, and acquitted after a celebrated
trial during which many eminent authors
(including E. M. *Forster and R. *Hoggart)
appeared as witnesses for the defence, a victory
which had a profound effect on both writing and
publishing in subsequent decades.

Lady of May, The, a short pastoral entertainment by P. *Sidney, performed ?1578/9. It consists of a dispute between a shepherd and a
forester for the hand of the rustic May Lady.

Lady of Pleasure, The, a comedy by J. *Shirley,
acted 1635, printed 1637.
    In the central plot Lady Bornwell is cured of
her desire to live a life of thoughtless pleasure,
partly by the discovery of the worthlessness of
her foppish suitors and partly by her husband's
pretence that he too means to live extravagantly.
The relationship between Sir Thomas and Lady
Bornwell may, according to G. E. Bentley, have
influenced Sheridan's portrayal of the Teazles in
The School for Scandal.

'Lady of Shalott, The', a poem by *Tennyson,
published 1832, much revised for the 1842
Poems. The story bears little resemblance to his
subsequent treatment of it in 'Lancelot and
Elaine' of the *Idylls of the King*. The Lady, like
*Mariana, was one of several enchanted or
imprisoned maidens to capture the Victorian
imagination, and was the subject of many
illustrations, including a notable one by Holman
*Hunt.

Lady of the Idle Lake, see PHAEDRIA.

Lady of the Lake, in the Arthurian legends, a
rather shifting supernatural character. In
Malory's *Morte d'Arthur* she gives Arthur the
sword Excalibur, but when she asks for the head
of Balyn as payment Balyn strikes off her head.
Also called the Lady of the Lake (in Malory) is
Nimiane (Nimue, and probably by scribal mis-
reading, Vivien), the wife of Pelleas, who loves
Merlin whom she tricks into revealing his magic
arts and then imprisons in a tower of air in the
forest of *Broceliande from which he never
escapes. In Malory she is said to have
accompanied the three queens who bore Arthur
away by ship after his death. In Celtic origin she
may derive from Morgan, the archetypal lake
lady.

Lady of the Lake, The, a poem in six cantos by
Sir W. *Scott, published 1810.
    A knight, who gives his name as James Fitz-
James, receives hospitality in the home on Loch
Katrine of Roderick Dhu, the fierce Highland
chief, where he falls in love with Ellen, daughter
of the outlawed Lord James of Douglas.
Roderick himself and the young Malcolm
Graeme are also suitors for her hand, and Ellen
loves Malcolm. Under threat of an attack by the
royal forces, Roderick summons his clans.
Douglas, regarding himself as the cause of the

attack, sets out for Stirling to surrender himself to the king. Meanwhile James Fitz-James returns and proposes to carry Ellen off to safety. She refuses, confessing her love for another. Fitz-James generously withdraws, giving her a signet ring which will enable her to obtain from the king any boon. On his way back to Stirling he falls in with Roderick. A fierce quarrel springs up between them and they fight. Fitz-James's skill prevails, and the wounded Roderick is carried prisoner to Stirling. Ellen appears, at the king's court, presents her signet ring, asks for her father's pardon, and discovers that Fitz-James is the king himself. The king and Douglas are reconciled, Roderick dies of his wounds, and Ellen marries Malcolm Graeme. The poem includes the beautiful *coronach* 'He is gone on the mountain', and Ellen's song 'Soldier, rest, thy warfare o'er'. The king is as much drawn from James V as from anyone.

Lady Susan, a novel by J. *Austen, written probably 1793–4, published 1871, from an untitled manuscript dated 1805.

The story consists of letters, written chiefly between the kindly Mrs Vernon and her mother Lady de Courcy, and between the unscrupulous, beautiful Lady Susan (the widow of Mr Vernon's brother) and her London friend Mrs Johnson. The events occur mainly at Churchill, the country house of the Vernons.

Laertes, in Shakespeare's *Hamlet*, the brother of Ophelia.

Lafeu, in Shakespeare's *All's Well that Ends Well*, an old lord.

La Fleur, Yorick's French servant in Sterne's *A Sentimental Journey*.

LAFORGUE, Jules (1860–87), French poet, and a leading exponent of *vers libre*: he is notable in a foreign context as an important influence on T. S. *Eliot and *Pound.

LAȜAMON (*fl.* late 12th cent.), according to his own testimony a priest of Ernley (Arley Regis in Worcestershire), he wrote the *Brut*, a history of England from the arrival of the legendary Brutus to Cadwallader (AD 689), based mostly on Wace's French version of *Geoffrey of Monmouth's *Historia Regum Britanniae* with additions from other sources. The *Brut* gives for the first time in English not only the story of Arthur but also those of Lear, Cymbeline, and other figures prominent in later English literature. The poem employs some of the epic formulas and other stylistic features of Old English, which contribute to the poem's energy and vigour. It is in some ways a transitional work, and one of the earliest major works in Middle English. (See BRUT.)

Lagado, see GULLIVER'S TRAVELS.

Lake Poets, Lake School, terms applied to *Coleridge, *Southey, *Wordsworth, and sometimes to *De Quincey, who lived in the Lake District. The expression 'Lake School' seems first to appear in the *Edinburgh Review* of August 1817. In his *Recollections of the Lake Poets*, De Quincey denies the existence of any such 'school'.

Lallans, see SCOTS.

Lalla Rookh, a series of *oriental tales in verse connected by a story in prose, by T. *Moore, published 1817.

The frame story tells of the journey of Lalla Rookh, the daughter of the emperor, from Delhi to Kashmir, to be married to the king of Bucharia. On the way she and her train are diverted by four verse tales told by Feramorz, a young Kashmiri poet, with whom she falls in love and who turns out, on her arrival, to be the king of Bucharia himself. A series of accidents on the way throws the pompous chamberlain Fadladeen into a bad temper, which he vents in pungent criticisms of the young man's verse, in the style of the *Edinburgh Review*.

The first of the tales is written in heroic couplets, the others in stanzas of varied metre.

'L'Allegro', a poem by *Milton, written ?1631, printed 1645. The Italian title means 'the cheerful man', and this idyll is an invocation to the goddess Mirth to allow the poet to live with her, first amid the delights of pastoral scenes, then amid those of 'towered cities' and the 'busy hum of men'. It is a companion piece to *'Il Penseroso'.

LAMB, Lady Caroline (1785–1828), daughter of the third earl of Bessborough, married William Lamb, afterwards second Viscount Melbourne. In 1812, shortly after her marriage, she became infatuated with *Byron, and about the same time began to show signs of mental instability. Her first novel, *Glenarvon* (1816), is a wild *Gothic extravaganza, in which she is cast as the dashing Calantha and Byron as the fated Glenarvon.

LAMB, Charles (1775–1834), was born in London. His father, the Lovel of 'The Old Benchers of the Inner Temple' in *Essays of Elia*, was the clerk to Samuel Salt, a lawyer, whose house in Crown Office Row was Lamb's birthplace and his home during his youth. He was educated at Christ's Hospital, where he formed an enduring admiration for S. T. *Coleridge. After a few months at the South Sea House he obtained at 17 an appointment in the East India House, where he remained until his retirement in 1825. For a short time in 1795–6 he was mentally deranged, and the threat of madness became a shadow on his life. In 1796 his sister Mary, in a fit of insanity, killed their mother. Lamb undertook the charge of his sister, who remained liable to periodic breakdowns, and she repaid him with sympathy, and affection. Four sonnets by Lamb appeared in 1796 in a volume of poems by Coleridge. In 1798 appeared *Blank Verse* by Charles Lloyd and Charles Lamb, which included the poem 'The Old Familiar Faces'. In the same year appeared the *Tale of Rosamund Gray and Old Blind Margaret*, a melodramatic, sentimental village tragedy. In 1802 Lamb published *John Woodvil* (at first called *Pride's Cure*), a tragedy in the Elizabethan style; and in 1806 his farce *Mr H* proved a failure at Drury Lane. With his sister he wrote *Tales from Shakespear* (1807), designed to make Shakespeare's plays familiar to the young; *The Adventures of Ulysses* (1808); and *Mrs Leicester's School* (1809), a collection of stories. In 1808 he published *Specimens of English Dramatic Poets who lived about the time of Shakespeare*. He wrote for Leigh Hunt's *Reflector* and for the *Examiner*, and in 1814 contributed to the *Quarterly Review* an article (much altered by *Gifford, the editor) on Wordsworth's *The Excursion*. A collection of his miscellaneous writings in prose and verse appeared in 1818. From 1820 to 1823 Lamb was a regular contributor to the *London Magazine*, in which appeared the first series of essays known as *Essays of Elia*, published in a collected volume in 1823. The second series was published in 1833.

Lamb's literary criticism is scattered and small in volume. He had no interest in critical theory and a poor sense of structure, but his sympathies were wide and his sensitivity acute. His *Letters* have been edited by E. W. Marrs (3 vols, 1975–8).

LAMB, Mary Ann (1764–1847), sister of Charles *Lamb, with whom she wrote *Tales from Shakespear* (1807); and she wrote the greater part of *Mrs Leicester's School* (1809). For details of her life, see under LAMB, C.

Lambert, General, Mrs Theo, and Hetty, characters in Thackeray's *The Virginians*.

Lambeth Books, a name sometimes given to the symbolic poems which *Blake wrote and etched while living at Lambeth (1790–1800). They include *America*, *Europe*, and *The Song of Los*.

Lament of Tasso, The, a poem by Lord *Byron, published 1817.

The poem tells the story of the tragic love of the imprisoned *Tasso for Leonora d'Este, and of the writing of his *Jerusalem Delivered*.

'Lamia', a narrative poem by *Keats, written 1819, published 1820.

The story was taken from Burton's *Anatomy of Melancholy*, there quoted from Philostratus. Lamia, a sorceress, is transformed by Hermes from a serpent into a beautiful woman. She loves the young Corinthian Lycius, and he, spell-bound by her beauty, falls in love with her. They retire to a secret palace in Corinth. Here Lycius orders a bridal feast and summons his friends. Among them comes his old guide and mentor, the sage Apollonius, who pierces Lamia's disguise and calls her by her name. Her beauty withers, with a frightful scream she vanishes, and Lycius dies in a frenzy of grief.

Lammle, Alfred and Sophronia, in Dickens's *Our Mutual Friend*.

Lamorak de Galis (of Wales), Sir, in Malory's *Morte D'Arthur*, the son of Pellinore. He is slain by the four sons of King Lot because of his adultery with Arthur's sister Morgawse, the wife of King Lot.

Lancelot, see LAUNCELOT OF THE LAKE.

Lancelot du Lake, Sir, a ballad included in Percy's *Reliques*, recounting the adventure of Lancelot with Tarquin. Falstaff sings a snatch from this ballad in Shakespeare's 2 *Henry IV* (II. iv).

Landeval, Sir, see SIR LAUNFAL.

Landless, Neville and Helena, characters in Dickens's *Edwin Drood*.

LANDON, Letitia Elizabeth (1802–38), wrote under the initials L.E.L. She published between 1824 and her death a number of volumes of poetry, contributed to periodicals, and wrote several novels, of which the best is *Ethel Churchill* (1837). Her unprotected position as a woman in the literary world gave rise to various vague scandals linking her name to *Maginn and, less certainly, to *Bulwer-Lytton, who appears with his wife Rosina in her novel *Romance and Reality* (1831).

LANDOR, Robert Eyres (1781–1869), youngest brother of W. S. *Landor, was the author of five tragedies, including *The Count of Arezzi* (1823), which was attributed to *Byron; a poem, *The Impious Feast* (1828); and other works.

LANDOR, Walter Savage (1775–1864), was educated at Rugby and at Trinity College, Oxford, where he was rusticated. An intractable temper involved him in trouble throughout his life. In 1795 he published *Poems*, and in 1798 an epic poem in seven books, *Gebir*. His collection of poems *Simonidea* (1806) included *'Rose Aylmer'. A dramatic tragedy, *Count Julian, followed in 1812. In the same year Landor's intemperate 'Commentary on the Memoirs of Mr Fox' had to be suppressed. He lived in Italy (1815–35) and separated from his wife in 1835. The *Imaginary Conversations of literary men and statesmen* appeared in 1824–9, and in 1853 his *Imaginary Conversations of Greeks and Romans*. His *Pericles and Aspasia* appeared in 1836; *The Pentameron* in 1837; the trilogy *Andrea of Hungary, Giovanna of Naples*, and *Fra Rupert* in 1839–40; and *The Hellenics*, a re-telling in verse of various Greek myths, was completed in 1847. His work was much admired by R. *Browning and many others, but has not recently enjoyed any great esteem. Boythorn in Dickens's *Bleak House* is a genial caricature of Landor.

'Land o' the Leal, The' (the land of the blessed departed), the title of a song by Lady *Nairne.

LANE, Allen (1902–70), publisher, became a pioneer in the paperback revolution in publishing with the foundation in 1935 of the *Penguin series.

LANE, Edward William (1801–76), Arabic scholar, published in 1836 *An Account of the Manners and Customs of the Modern Egyptians* and in 1838–40 an expurgated but scholarly translation of *The Thousand and One Nights* (see ARABIAN NIGHTS ENTERTAINMENTS).

LANE, John (1854–1925), *fin-de-siècle* publisher who, with Charles Elkin Mathews, established The Bodley Head in 1887. Authors who appeared under its imprint included *Davidson, *Dowson, *Le Gallienne, J. A. *Symonds, and *Wilde; as publishers of *The Yellow Book* it became the centre of ferment in art and letters in the 'nineties'.

LANEHAM, or **LANGHAM,** Robert, the name attributed to the author of the letter describing some of the entertainments put on by the earl of *Leicester for the queen's visit to Kenilworth in 1575. The pamphlet is probably in fact by William Patten. The list of Captain Cox's books which 'Laneham' gives is an important source for the titles of ballads, romances, and other popular literature still read at this time.

LANFRANC (*c.*1015–89), archbishop of Canterbury from 1070 to his death. He was a celebrated teacher and a man of wide secular and classical learning who worked successfully with William the Conquerer and rebuilt the cathedral at Canterbury which had been burnt down in 1067.

LANG, Andrew (1844–1912), born at Selkirk, was educated at St Andrews University and became a fellow of Merton College, Oxford. In 1875 he settled in London, becoming one of the most prolific and versatile writers of his day.

His first book of verse, *Ballads and Lyrics of Old France* (1872), was followed by several others, including *Ballades in Blue China* (1880, 1881). Many of his poems were written in the old French forms of *rondeau, *triolet, etc. Discouraged by the poor reception of his ambitious narrative poem *Helen of Troy* (1882), his verse became increasingly lightweight. His *Collected Poems* (4 vols) was published in 1923. Lang appears to have valued himself most as an anthropologist, and he published various volumes on mythology and folklore.

As a Greek scholar Lang devoted himself largely to *Homer. He was one of the joint authors (with S. H. Butcher) of prose versions of the *Odyssey* (1879, preceded by his well-known sonnet, 'The Odyssey'), and (with W. Leaf and E. Myers) of the *Iliad* (1883). He wrote three books on the Homeric question, arguing the unity of Homer. He also took part in the *Baconian controversy in *Shakespeare, Bacon and the Great Unknown* (1912).

His many works of *belles-lettres* and reminiscences are now largely forgotten as are his melodramatic novels, which include *The Mark of Cain* (1886). As a critic he showed a distinct preference for romantic and adventurous works such as those of *Haggard, A. Hope (*Hawkins), and A. C. *Doyle.

He is now perhaps best remembered for his own fairy-tales, which include *The Gold of Fairnilee* (1888, set in Scotland), and *Prince Prigio* (1889, set in Pantouflia), and for his collections of fairy-tales, each volume named after a different colour; the first was *The Blue Fairy Book* (1889).

LANGHORNE, John (1735–79), was from 1772 a justice of the peace, and is remembered as a poet for his poem of rural life and suffering, *The Country Justice* (1774).

LANGLAND, William (perhaps *c.*1330–*c.*1386), the author of *Piers Plowman*, of whose identity and life very little is known for certain. It seems that Langland lived in London, but that he had lived in the Malvern district of the West Midlands. No other poem is now attributed to him, although *Skeat's parallel-text edition of the poem is still printed with *Richard the Redeless*, which is part of *Mum and the Sothsegger*.

Langue d'oïl, the language of the north of France during the medieval period, so called to distinguish it from the *langue d'oc* (see PROVENÇAL), the distinction being based on the particle of affirmation: late Latin 'hoc ille' for 'yes' became 'o'ïl' in the North and 'oc' in the South. The distinction of language corresponded to a difference of culture and literature, the *langue d'oïl* being the literary medium of the *trouvères, the langue d'oc, or Provençal, that of the *troubadours.

Languish, Lydia, the heroine of Sheridan's *The Rivals*.

LANIER, Emilia, *née* Bassano (1569–1645). Her collection of religious poems, *Salve Deus Rex Iudaeorum* (1611), was edited by *Rowse under the title *The Poems of Shakespeare's Dark Lady* (1978). There is no documentary proof that she and Shakespeare knew each other.

Laodicean, A, a novel by T. *Hardy, published 1881.

'Laon and Cythna', see REVOLT OF ISLAM, THE.

Laputa, see GULLIVER'S TRAVELS.

Lara, a poem by Lord *Byron, published 1814.
Lara is Conrad of *The Corsair* returned to his domains in Spain accompanied by his page Kaled, who is Gulnare in disguise. Lara lives, like other *'Byronic' heroes, aloof and alien, shrouded in mystery. He is, however, recognized as Conrad, and becomes involved in a feud in which he is finally killed, dying in the arms of Kaled.

LARKIN, Philip Arthur (1922–1985), poet and novelist. From 1943 he worked in various libraries before becoming librarian of the Brynmor Jones Library in Hull. Larkin's early poems appeared in an anthology, *Poetry from Oxford in Wartime* (1944), and a collection, *The North Ship* (1945), much influenced by *Yeats. He then published *Jill* (1946), set in wartime Oxford, a novel which describes the undergraduate career of John Kemp, a working-class boy from Lancashire; 'Jill' is the fantasy sister he creates, who is transformed into a teasing reality. A second novel, *A Girl in Winter* (1947), relates a day in the life of refugee librarian Katherine Lind, working in a drab English provincial town. Larkin's own poetic voice became distinct in *The Less Deceived* (1955), where the colloquial bravura of a poem like 'Toads' is offset by the half-tones and somewhat bitter lyricism of other pieces; his name was at this time associated with the *Movement, and his work appeared in *New Lines (1956). The Whitsun Weddings* (1964) adds a range of melancholy urban and suburban provincial landscapes. Many of the poems in *High Windows* (1974), notably 'The Old Fools', show a preoccupation with death and transience. Throughout his work, the adaptation of contemporary speech rhythms and vocabulary to an unobtrusive metrical elegance is highly distinctive. Larkin edited *The Oxford Book of Twentieth Century English Verse* (1973). A volume of essays, *Required Writing*, was published in 1983.

Lark Rise to Candleford, see THOMPSON, FLORA.

La Saisiaz and **The Two Poets of Croisic,** two long poems by R. *Browning, published 1878.
La Saisiaz is a philosophical elegy prompted by the sudden death of a close friend of Browning's, with whom he had been holidaying in a chalet called 'La Saisiaz' (the sun) near Geneva. It deals with the central religious question 'Does the soul survive the body? Is there God's self, no or yes?' *The Two Poets of Croisic,* less solemn in tone, tells the stories of two obscure poets associated with the small village of Croisic in Brittany, illustrating, in comic and grotesque vein, the folly of human (and specifically poetic) aspiration.

LASSALLE, Ferdinand, see TRAGIC COMEDIANS, THE.

Last Chronicle of Barset, The, a novel by A. *Trollope, published 1867, the last of the *'Barsetshire' series.
The Revd Josiah Crawley is accused of fraudulently acquiring a cheque for £20. He cannot remember the exact origin of the cheque and is thus committed for trial. Even before the sessions come on the autocratic Mrs Proudie pre-judges his case, and attempts to oust Crawley from his church. Matters are not finally cleared up in Crawley's favour until Dean Arabin's family are recalled from the Continent, whereupon Mrs Arabin explains her part in the muddle. At the close of the novel Mr Crawley is presented with the fatter living of St Ewold's, and the archdeacon finally removes his opposition to the marriage of Grace Crawley and his son, Major Grantly.
Interleaved with the theme of Crawley's cheque is the London life of Johnny Eames and his continuing love for Lily Dale and the deaths of Mrs Proudie and Mr Harding, once warden of Hiram's Hospital.

Last Days of Pompeii, The, a novel by *Bulwer-Lytton.

Last Man, The, (1) a collection of poems by T. *Campbell and T. *Hood; (2) a novel by M. *Shelley.

Last of the Barons, The, a historical novel by *Bulwer-Lytton.

Last of the Mohicans, The, a novel by J. F. *Cooper.

Last Tycoon, The, a novel by F. S. *Fitzgerald.

LATIMER, Hugh (?1492–1555), took priest's orders and became known as a preacher. He was accused of heresy, brought before convocation, and absolved on making a complete submission,

1532. He was appointed bishop of Worcester in 1535, but resigned his bishopric. His famous sermon 'of the plough' was preached in 1548. Latimer was committed to the Tower on Mary's accession, 1553; he was condemned as a heretic and burnt at Oxford with *Ridley on 16 Oct. 1555. His extant writings are notable for a simple vernacular style and for their graphic and vivid illustrations.

Latter-Day Pamphlets, see CARLYLE, T.

LAUD, William (1573–1645), became archbishop of Canterbury (1633). He supported the king in his struggle with the Commons and adopted the policy of enforcing uniformity in the Church of England. He was impeached of high treason by the Long Parliament in 1640, committed to the Tower in 1641, tried in 1644, condemned, and beheaded. A few of his sermons were published in 1651, and a collected edition of his works in 1696–1700. Laud gave some 1,300 manuscripts in 18 different languages, and his collection of coins, to the Bodleian Library, Oxford.

LAUDER, William (d. 1771), literary forger, a good classical scholar, was proved to have interpolated in the works of Masenius and Staphorstius (17th-cent. Latin poets) extracts from a Latin verse rendering of *Paradise Lost*. Incidentally he proved that *Milton had deeply studied the works of modern Latin poets.

Launce, in Shakespeare's *Two Gentlemen of Verona*, the clownish servant to Proteus.

Launcelot Gobbo, see GOBBO, LAUNCELOT.

Launcelot Greaves, see SIR LAUNCELOT GREAVES.

Launcelot of the Lake, Sir, the greatest and most romantic of the knights of the Round Table, son of King *Ban of Benwick in Brittany, father of *Galahad by *Elaine Sans Pere (daughter of King *Pelles) and the lover of Guinevere. He is a relatively late development in the English Arthurian tradition, not appearing at length before the 14th cent., although the story of his love for Guinevere is the subject of *Chrétien de Troyes' *Lancelot* (c. 1170s) and of the early 13th-cent. French prose 'Vulgate' *Lancelot*. His name, which probably has Welsh etymological connections, refers to a tradition that he was·abducted at birth and brought up by a lake-lady, before being brought by a hermit to Arthur's court. Chrétien's romance is concerned exclusively with the love of Launcelot and Guinevere, presented faithfully as a *Courtly Love affair. The main elements of the Launcelot story are found in the three romances of the French prose cycle: *Lancelot*; the *Queste del Saint Graal*; and the *Mort Artu*. In Malory's *Morte D'Arthur* Launcelot's love for the queen is again central; it is strained by his relations with Elaine the Fair Maid of Astolot whose death ends Guinevere's jealousy. Their love is betrayed by Agravain; the lovers flee to Launcelot's castle of *Joyous Gard and, after a siege, the queen is restored to Arthur. Launcelot withdraws to Brittany where he is pursued by Arthur and Gawain; in the ensuing clash Launcelot injures Gawain. Arthur returns to Dover to fight the usurping *Modred and Gawain is killed. Launcelot comes back to help the king, but arrives too late for the final battle in Cornwall in which both Arthur and Modred die. He finds that Guinevere has become a nun, so he becomes a priest. On his death he is carried to Joyous Gard where visions suggest that he is taken to heaven. Malory stresses the tragedy of his imperfection (his courtly amour with the queen) which prevents his full achievement of the *Grail.

Launfal, Sir, see SIR LAUNFAL.

Laura, (1) see PETRARCH; (2) the wife of Beppo in Byron's poem *Beppo*.

Laurence, Friar, in Shakespeare's *Romeo and Juliet*, counsellor and confessor to the lovers.

LAURIE, Annie (1682–1764), the subject of the famous Scottish song that bears her name. The song was written by her rejected lover William Douglas. It was revised and set to music by Lady John Scott in 1835.

LAVATER, Johann Kaspar (1741–1801), Swiss theologian and poet, is chiefly remembered as the inventor of the so-called science of phrenology (or Physiognomy, as he called it).

Lavengro, The Scholar—The Gypsy—The Priest, a narrative by G. *Borrow, published 1851. 'Lavengro', in gypsy language, means 'philologist'. The name was supplied to Borrow in his youth by Ambrose Smith, who figures in this work as Jasper Petulengro.

This work purports to be the story of Borrow's own wandering, restless life, but in it, as in his other works, fact is mingled with fiction. The son of a professional soldier, he had followed his parents while they moved from station to station around England, Scotland, and Ireland, visiting strange places and striking up unusual friendships on his travels—he became attached to a family of gypsies and met tinkers, including the Flaming Tinman, with whom he had a memorable fight, horse-copers, an old apple-woman (also a receiver of stolen goods), and a brace of future murderers. He tells the reader much of his comparative study of languages (though his scholarship is often suspect); he had violent prejudices, including a savage hatred of the

Roman Catholic Church, that frequently over-flow into his books. The book closes in the midst of the romantic episode with Belle Berners, an Amazonian vagrant, which is resumed in *The Romany Rye*.

Lavinia, in Shakespeare's *Titus Andronicus*, Titus' daughter.

LAW, William (1686–1761), was elected a fellow of Emmanuel College, Cambridge, but, declining to take the oath of allegiance to George I, lost his fellowship. Edward Gibbon made him the tutor of his son, the father of the historian *Gibbon, in c.1727, and he remained as an honoured friend of the family in their Putney home until 1740, when he became the centre of a small spiritual community at King's Cliffe (his birthplace) near Stamford.

He is chiefly remembered for his treatises of practical morality, *A Practical Treatise on Christian Perfection* (1726), and more particularly *A Serious Call to a Devout and Holy Life* (1728). This work is addressed to believers, and urges them to a simple and pious way of life, with emphasis on private rather than public prayer; it is enlivened with many satiric character portraits. This work greatly influenced Dr *Johnson and Law's friend J. *Wesley. See also BYROM for other aspects of his personality.

In later life Law became increasingly interested in mysticism and in the writings of Boehme; some critics have seen in *The Spirit of Prayer* (1749–50) and *The Spirit of Love* (1752–4) a foreshadowing of *Blake's attacks on materialism and reason.

LAWES, Henry (1596–1662), and William (1602–1645), English composers. Henry's 430-odd songs include settings of *Carew (38), *Waller (16), *Herrick (14), *Suckling, *Lovelace, and, notably, of his friend *Milton; he arranged the original performances of *Arcades (c.1630) and *Comus (1634), for both of which he wrote the songs. William composed much of the music for Shirley's *The Triumph of Peace* (1634) and the incidental music for several of *D'Avenant's masques and plays.

LAWLESS, Emily (1845–1913), author of the successful Irish novels *Hurrish* (1886) and *Grania* (1892), and of other works.

LAWRENCE, D(avid) H(erbert) (1885–1930), born at Eastwood, Nottinghamshire, one of five children of a miner and an ex-schoolteacher. He grew up in considerable poverty and his ill-suited parents quarrelled continually. At 15 Lawrence was forced to give up his education and take a job for a short time as a clerk. He then became a pupil teacher, and subsequently took up a scholarship at Nottingham University College to study for a teacher's certificate.

His first novel, *The White Peacock* (1911), was followed by *The Trespasser* (1912). After the death of his mother he became seriously ill and gave up teaching. *Sons and Lovers* (1913) is a faithful autobiographical account of these early years. In 1912 he met Frieda Weekley (née von Richthofen), wife of his old professor at Nottingham; she was six years older than Lawrence and mother of three children. They fell in love and eloped to Germany; their life together was passionate and stormy. He spent the war years in England and formed friendships with A. *Huxley, D. *Garnett, Lady O. *Morrell, J. M. *Murry, K. *Mansfield, *Aldington, and B. *Russell (with whom he was later to quarrel bitterly). His next novel, *The Rainbow* (1915), was seized by the police and declared obscene; his frankness about sex, and his use of four-letter words, was to keep him in constant trouble with the law. In 1917 he published a volume of poems, *Look! We Have Come Through!*, and in 1919 he and Frieda left for Italy. He had finished his novel *Women in Love* in 1916 but was unable to find a publisher until 1920 in New York, where an action against it failed, and 1921 in London. In 1920 *The Lost Girl* (begun before the war) won the James Tait Black Memorial Prize. *Aaron's Rod* (1922), which shows the influence of *Nietzshe, followed and the same year he began his serious travels, to Ceylon and Australia and finally to America, Australia (where he wrote *Kangaroo*, 1923), and Mexico, where he began *The Plumed Serpent* (1926). While on a visit to Old Mexico he was told that he was in an advanced state of tuberculosis. With Frieda he returned to Italy, settling finally near Florence at the Villa Mirenda where he finished *Lady Chatterley's Lover*. It was privately printed in Florence in 1928 and was finally published in unexpurgated editions in the United States and England over 30 years later.

Lawrence was a moralist, believing that modern man was in danger of losing his ability to experience the quality of life. Passionately involved with his characters and the physical world of nature, he wrote of them with a fresh immediacy and vividness. His reputation as a short story writer has always been high, many stories appearing first in small collections (*The Prussian Officer*, 1914; *England, My England*, 1922; *The Woman Who Rode Away*, 1928) and in a complete edition in 3 vols, 1955. His travel books are *Twilight in Italy* (1916), *Sea and Sardinia* (1921), *Mornings in Mexico* (1927), and *Etruscan Palaces* (1932).

In his poems Lawrence wanted to be free of the weight of formalism but not, as he said, to 'dish up the fragments as a new substance'. His volumes include *Love Poems* (1913), *Amores* (1916), *Look! We Have Come Through!* (1917), *Birds, Beasts and Flowers* (1923), *Pansies* (1929), *Complete Poems* (3 vols, 1957). Other non-fiction works include *Movements in*

European History (1921), *Psychoanalysis and the Unconscious* (1921), *Fantasia of the Unconscious* (1922), *Studies in Classic American Literature* (1923), and *Apocalypse* (1931). A first collection of *The Letters of D. H. Lawrence* (1932) was edited by A. *Huxley. A new edition, ed. J. T. Boulton, began to appear in 1979 (vol. I; vol. II, 1982).

LAWRENCE, George Alfred (1827–76), achieved immediate success with his first novel, *Guy Livingstone* (1857); as an example of 'muscular blackguardism' the novel showed a revolt against the 'muscular Christianity' of the time, and set a fashion in literature and even in the mode of dress and behaviour of the young men of the period. He produced many more novels, including *Sword and Gown* (1859) and *Border and Bastille* (1863).

LAWRENCE, T(homas) E(dward) (1888–1933), was educated at Oxford. He studied Arabic, read *Doughty, and from 1910 to 1914 worked on the excavation of Carchemish, on the banks of the Euphrates. He became involved with British Intelligence, and his daring exploits during the First World War won him the confidence of the Arabs, and later made him, as 'Lawrence of Arabia', a mythical figure in his own country. He entered Damascus in 1918 with the Arab forces after the defeat of the Turks, and after the war spent some time as adviser to the Colonial Office, resigning in 1922. He enlisted in the RAF in 1922 as an aircraft hand under the name of John Hume Ross, and a year later joined the tank corps as T. E. Shaw. He later returned to the RAF. He was killed in a motor-cycle accident near his home at Clouds Hill, Dorset.

He began writing *The Seven Pillars of Wisdom*, his account of the Arab Revolt and his own part in it, shortly after the war; he was greatly encouraged by E. M. *Forster and G. B. *Shaw. It was printed for private circulation in a limited edition in 1926 (published 1935). It has been described as the last great romantic war book. Meanwhile Lawrence was working on a documentary account of army life, subsequently published posthumously in 1936 (NY) and 1955 (England) as *The Mint*, by '352087 A/C Ross'.

Lawrence's complex personality and multiple roles as man of action, poet, ascetic, and neurotic fascinated friends, writers, and the general public, and his many biographers have suggested various explanations for both his masochism and his heroism. *Auden based *The Ascent of F6* in part on the Lawrence legend. He appeared, complete with motor cycle, as Private Meek in Shaw's *Too True to be Good* (performed 1932); in *Rattigan's play *Ross* (1960); and as the hero of the popular film *Lawrence of Arabia* (1962). Robert *Graves wrote the first authorized life (1927); *Aldington's in 1955

caused an outrage by its iconoclastic portrayal of him as a hysterical homosexual. His *Letters* (1938) were edited by D. *Garnett.

Laws of Ecclesiastical Politie, *Of the*, by R. *Hooker, a philosophical and theological treatise of which four books appeared in 1593, the fifth in 1597. The sixth and eighth appeared in 1648, the seventh was first included in Gauden's edition of 1661–2. These last three books, as we have them, do not represent work prepared by Hooker for the press. The whole was reissued with a life of Hooker by I. *Walton in 1666.

The work is a defence, written in a dignified and harmonious prose, of the position of the Anglican Church against the attacks of the Puritans. The principal characteristics of the work are its breadth of outlook and tolerant spirit, and its advocacy of intellectual liberty against the dogmatism of *Calvin and the ecclesiastical despotism recommended in the *Admonition to Parliament*, a statement of the Puritan case by John Field and Thomas Wilcox (1572).

Lay, a short lyric or narrative poem intended to be sung; originally applied specifically to the poems, usually dealing with matter of history or romantic adventure, which were sung by minstrels.

Lay of the Last Minstrel, The, a poem in six cantos by Sir W. *Scott, published in 1805. It is a metrical romance in irregular stanzas, put in the mouth of an ancient minstrel, the last of his race, based on an old Border legend. The period of the tale is the middle of the 16th cent.

The lady of Branksome Hall, the seat of the Buccleuchs, has lost her husband in an affray in which Lord Cranstoun was one of his opponents. Lord Cranstoun and Margaret, the lady's daughter, are in love, but the feud renders their passion hopeless. The lady commissions Sir William Deloraine to recover from the tomb of the wizard Michael Scott in Melrose Abbey the magic book which is to help her in her vengeance. As Deloraine returns, he encounters Lord Cranstoun and is wounded by him. At Lord Cranstoun's bidding, his elfin page carries the wounded man to Branksome Hall, and lures away the lady's little son, the heir of the house, who falls into the hands of her English enemy, Lord Dacre. The latter, with Lord William Howard, intends to storm Branksome, alleging Deloraine's misdeeds as a Border thief. The Scots army is on its way to relieve Branksome. A single combat is suggested between Sir William Deloraine, now lying wounded, and Sir Richard Musgrave, whose lands Deloraine has harried; the lady's little son to be the prize. The challenge is accepted and Musgrave defeated. It is discovered that the victor is Lord Cranstoun, who with his page's assistance has assumed the form and arms of Deloraine. The service rendered to the house of Buccleuch heals the feud, and Lord Cranstoun marries Margaret.

Lays of Ancient Rome, a collection of poems by *Macaulay, published 1842, in which Macaulay deals with episodes from traditional Roman history (some taken from *Livy), such as the defence of the bridge leading to Rome against the Tuscans ('Horatius'); 'The Battle of Lake Regillus'; and 'Virginia' (see VIRGINIA).

Lazarillo de Tormes, see PICARESQUE.

LEACOCK, Stephen Butler (1869–1944), Canadian political economist and humorist. He wrote many volumes of collected humorous essays and stories, including *Literary Lapses* (1910) and *Nonsense Novels* (1911).

Leader, The, a weekly periodical started in 1850 by *Lewes and Thornton Leigh Hunt, to which Lewes contributed satirical pieces and lively theatre reviews under the pseudonym of 'Vivian'. The staff included *Spencer and *Kinglake. It ran until 1866, in its later issues as *Saturday Analyst and Leader*.

Leander, see HERO AND LEANDER.

LEAR, Edward (1812–88), worked as a zoological draughtsman until he came under the patronage of the earl of Derby, for whose grandchildren he wrote *A Book of Nonsense* (1845), with his own *limericks and illustrations. He travelled widely, and published accounts of Italy (1846), Albania and Illyria (1851), Calabria (1852), and Corsica (1870). His posthumous reputation as a water-colourist has risen steadily and as a writer he is remembered for his nonsense verses, with their linguistic fantasies and their occasional touches of underlying melancholy. Later volumes were *Nonsense Songs, Stories, Botany and Alphabets* (1871), which contains 'The Owl and the Pussy-Cat' and 'The Jumblies'; *More Nonsense, Pictures, Rhymes, Botany etc.* (1871); and *Laughable Lyrics* (1877), with the Dong, the Yonghy-Bonghy-Bò, and the Pobble who has no toes.

Lear, King, see KING LEAR.

Leatherstocking, see COOPER, J. F.

Leaves of Grass, see WHITMAN, W.

LEAVIS, F(rank) R(aymond) (1895–1978), critic, was Cambridge born, bred, and educated. He read history, then English, at Emmanuel College, was appointed probationary lecturer 1927–31, and a college lecturer at Downing in 1935. He continued to teach in Cambridge until 1964, establishing a new critical approach that largely superseded the historical and narrative type of literary history favoured by Émile Legouis, Oliver Elton, and *Saintsbury. As a young man he attended and contributed to the Practical Criticism courses of I. A. *Richards, which encouraged close attention to the text. In 1929 he married Q. D. Leavis (1906–81), whose study of the relationship between literature and literacy, *Fiction and the Reading Public* (1932), originated as a thesis under Richards's supervision. From 1932 to 1953 he was chief editor of *Scrutiny*, a periodical which was a vehicle for the new Cambridge criticism, upholding rigorous intellectual standards and attacking the dilettante élitism which he believed to characterize the *Bloomsbury Group. *For Continuity* (1933), *Culture and Environment* (1933, with Denys Thompson), followed by *Education and the University* (1943) stress the importance of creating within universities, and particularly within English departments, an informed, discriminating, and highly-trained intellectual élite whose task it would be to preserve the cultural continuity of English life and literature, a continuity he believed to be threatened by mass media, technology, and advertising. *New Bearings in English Poetry* (1932) attacked Tennysonian and Swinburnian 'late Victorian poetastry' and Georgian poetry, presenting in their place the claims of E. *Thomas, T. S. *Eliot, *Pound, and (with qualifications) *Yeats: he also made an important reassessment of G. M. *Hopkins. *Revaluation* (1936) continued to reshape the main line of English poetry, tracing it through *Donne, *Pope, and Dr *Johnson to Hopkins and Eliot, and producing iconoclastic attacks on *Spenser, *Milton, and *Shelley. In 1948 he turned his attention to fiction in *The Great Tradition*; he traced this tradition through J. *Austen, G. *Eliot, H. *James, and *Conrad, dismissing other major authors (e.g. *Sterne and *Hardy). In later years he changed his position on *Dickens, whose *Hard Times* was the only novel to win unqualified admiration in this volume. (See *Dickens the Novelist*, with Q. D. Leavis, 1970.) *D. H. Lawrence: Novelist* (1955) presented the claims of *Lawrence, then much underrated, as a great English writer and moralist.

Leavis in his writing thus radically altered the literary map of the past and laid out new patterns for the future; but perhaps his most vital contribution lay not in his assessment of individual authors, but in his introduction of a new seriousness into English studies. His vehement dismissal of opposing views earned him much hostility, notably on the occasion of his response to C. P. Snow's Rede Lecture on *'The Two Cultures': *Two Cultures?: The Significance of C. P. Snow* (1962), but he also inspired deep devotion. See also NEW CRITICISM.

LE CARRÉ, John, pseudonym of David John Moore Cornwell (1931–), whose first novel,

Call for the Dead (1961), introduced the mild-mannered mastermind and secret agent George Smiley, who appears in many of his later books. The Spy Who Came in from the Cold (1963), a cold-war thriller inspired by the Berlin Wall, brought Le Carré immediate fame. Its successors, The Looking Glass War (1965), A Small Town in Germany (1968), Tinker, Tailor, Soldier, Spy (1974), The Honourable Schoolboy (1977), and Smiley's People (1980), confirmed his reputation as a story-teller who mixes grim and realistic detail with Byzantine elaboration of plot. The Little Drummer Girl (1983) was followed by The Perfect Spy (1986).

LECKY, William Edward Hartpole (1838–1903), published anonymously The Religious Tendencies of the Age (1860) and Leaders of Public Opinion in Ireland (1861). He won fame with his History of the Rise and Influence of Rationalism in Europe (1865), in which he traced the progress of the spirit of rationalism from religious dogmatism and persecution to tolerance. His History of European Morals from Augustus to Charlemagne (1869) discussed the relationship of morality and theology; and his History of England in the Eighteenth Century (1878–92) was concerned primarily with the history of political ideas and institutions, and social and economic history. He published several other historical studies, but devoted his last years to politics, as MP for Dublin University from 1895 to 1902.

Lectures on the English Poets, by W. *Hazlitt, published 1818.

LEDGWIDGE, Francis (1891–1917), Irish poet, was encouraged by *Dunsany, who wrote introductions for his three volumes of poetry, Songs of the Fields (1916), Songs of the Peace (1917), and Last Songs (1918). The poems are chiefly lyrics of the countryside, and some deal with Irish mythology and folklore, reminiscent of the *Celtic Twilight period of *Yeats. Ledgwidge was killed in action in Flanders.

LEE, Harriet (1757–1851), ran a private school in Bath with her sister Sophia *Lee. Her *epistolary novel Errors of Innocence appeared in 1786; Clare Lennox in 1797. Her successful Canterbury Tales (in part a collaboration with Sophia) appeared in 1798, with three further volumes in 1805; the twelve stories of the Tales, told by travellers, include 'Kruitzner' on which Byron based his poetic drama Werner (1802).

LEE, Sir Henry (1531–1611), master of the armoury and ranger of Woodstock, was closely involved in much Elizabethan pageantry and probably initiated around 1570 the celebration of the queen's accession day (17 Nov.) with tilts and allegorical devices: some of these are reflected in Sidney's revised *Arcadia. He played a part

in the Woodstock entertainments of 1575 and 1592, and his own retirement as queen's champion in 1590, when what has been claimed as his own poem, 'His Golden lockes, | Time hath to Silver turn'd', was sung, was commemorated by G. Peele in his *Polyhymnia. He appears in Scott's *Woodstock.

LEE, Laurie (1914–), writer. His volumes of poetry (The Sun my Monument, 1944; The Bloom of Candles, 1947; My Many-Coated Man, 1955) show a rich sensuous apprehension of the natural world, as does his best-known work Cider with Rosie (1959), a highly evocative and nostalgic account of his country boyhood in a secluded Cotswold valley. It describes a vanished rural world of home-made wine, village school, church outings. The 'Rosie' of the title is a village girl who 'baptized [him] with her cidrous kisses' behind a haycock. A second autobiographical volume, As I Walked Out One Midsummer Morning (1969), describes his departure from Stroud, his walk to London, and his months in Spain on the eve of the Spanish Civil War.

LEE, Nathaniel (?1649–92), a failed actor turned playwright, whose tragedies, marked by extravagance and passion, were long popular. They include Nero (1675), Sophonisba and Gloriana (1676), all in heroics; and his best-known tragedy, The Rival Queens (1677), in blank verse based on the Cassandre of La Calprenède. He collaborated with *Dryden in Oedipus (1679) and The Duke of Guise (1682). He lost his reason, and was confined to Bedlam 1684–9. (See HEROIC DRAMA.)

LEE, Sir Sidney (1859–1926), a member of the editorial staff of the DNB from the beginning, joint editor in 1890, and sole editor from 1891. His publications include Stratford-on-Avon from the Earliest Times to the Death of Shakespeare (1885, new edn 1906), Life of William Shakespeare (1898, rev. edn 1925), Great Englishmen of the 16th Century (1904), etc.

LEE, Sophia (1750–1824), daughter of an actor, sister of Harriet *Lee. Her play The Chapter of Accidents (1780) was frequently staged; and her first novel, The Recess (1783–5), a form of early historical novel, was translated into French; a verse tragedy, Almeyda, Queen of Grenada, with *Kemble and Mrs *Siddons, was staged in 1796.

LEE, Vernon, pseudonym of Violet Paget (1856–1935), essayist and novelist, who published some 45 volumes, including essays on Italian history, art, aesthetics, and travel.

LEECH, John (1817–64), caricaturist and illustrator, a friend of *Thackeray and of *Dickens, whose *A Christmas Carol and other Christmas books he illustrated. From 1841 until his death he contributed to *Punch political cartoons and scenes of everyday middle-class life. He illustrated the work of *Surtees.

LE FANU (pron. Léff-anew), J(oseph) S(heridan) (1814–73). By 1840 he had published a dozen or so stories (including 'A Strange Event in the Life of Schalken the Painter') in the *Dublin University Magazine*. Thereafter, he became increasingly involved in Irish journalism as editor of *The Warden* and owner or part-owner of that and other papers. His first two novels, *The Cock and Anchor* (1845) and *Torlogh O'Brien* (1847), were in the tradition of Sir W. *Scott and *Ainsworth; and it was not until 1861 that his main output began with the serialization in the *Dublin University Magazine*, which he acquired in that year, of *The House by the Churchyard*. There followed *Wylder's Hand* (1864), *Uncle Silas* (1864), *Guy Deverell* (1865), *The Tenants of Malory* (1867), *A Lost Name* (1868), *The Wyvern Mystery* (1869), *Checkmate* (1871), *The Rose and the Key* (1871), and *Willing to Die* (1873). In 1872 appeared the remarkable collection of stories entitled *In a Glass Darkly*.

This century's revival of interest dates from the publication in 1923 of *Madam Crowl's Ghost and Other Tales of Mystery*, a collection of forgotten tales by Le Fanu edited by M. R. *James, who considered that Le Fanu 'stands absolutely in the first rank as a writer of ghost stories'.

Le Fever, and his son, the subjects of a story related in Sterne's *Tristram Shandy*.

Left Book Club, a publishing venture founded by V. *Gollancz in 1936, in association with John Strachey and Harold Laski; its educational aim was to resist the rise of Fascism and Nazism. It flourished as a movement, circulating political books to some 50,000 members. The best-known title today is *Orwell's *The Road to Wigan Pier* (1937). The Club was dissolved in 1948.

LE GALLIENNE, Richard (1866–1947), of Channel Islands descent, became attached to the *fin-de-siècle* group which centred on *Beardsley; he was an original member of the *Rhymers' Club with *Yeats, *Wilde, L. *Johnson, and others. He contributed to *The Yellow Book, throughout the nineties wrote verse and literary criticism, and published a romantic novel, *The Quest for the Golden Girl* (1896).

Legend, Valentine, the hero of Congreve's *Love for Love*, and Sir Sampson, his father.

Legenda Aurea, see GOLDEN LEGEND.

Legend of Good Women, The, written by *Chaucer between 1372 and 1386, is based on such works as *Ovid's *Heroides*, and *Boccac-

cio's *De Claris Mulieribus* and *Vitae Virorum et Feminarum Illustrium*. The Prologue is more admired than the stories which make up the body of the poem. This Prologue occurs in two forms, the dates and order of precedence of which have been disputed. It opens with some famous lines in praise of the daisy (conforming to the tradition of 'Marguerite' poems in French) and continues with a description of the rebuking of the sleeping narrator by the god of love because of the things he had written in dispraise of women. Chaucer vows to make amends by composing this work in praise of women celebrated for their fidelity in love, as directed by the queen of love, Alceste. The poem (which is unfinished) contains nine stories of famous women: Cleopatra, Thisbe, Dido, Hypsipyle and Medea, Lucrece, Ariadne, Philomela, Phyllis, and Hypermnestra. The poem is significant, as well as for the charm of its Prologue, for the fact that it is the first attested use of the heroic couplet in Chaucer (and, as far as is known, in English poetry).

Legend of Montrose, A, a novel by Sir W. *Scott, published 1819, in *Tales of My Landlord*, 3rd series.

It is the story of the campaign of 1644, in which the Highland clans, having risen in favour of Charles I and against the Scottish Covenanters, inflicted a succession of defeats on their opponents, thanks in great measure to the skilful generalship of their great commander, the earl of *Montrose, whose character the author strongly contrasts with that of his rival, the marquess of *Argyle.

Legree, Simon, see SIMON LEGREE.

LEHMANN, (Rudolph) John (Frederick) (1907–), poet, publisher, brother of Rosamond *Lehmann, editor of *New Lines and the *London Magazine. He was associated with the *Hogarth Press, of which he became a partner in 1938. It published his first book of poems, *A Garden Revisited* (1931). His works include *Collected Poems 1930–63* (1963); three volumes of autobiography record a life rich in literary friendships and activity, as do his several volumes of reminiscence and biography, which include works on the *Sitwells (1968), the *Woolfs, and R. *Brooke (1980).

LEHMANN, Rosamond Nina (1901–), novelist, sister of John *Lehmann, educated at Cambridge, achieved a *succès de scandale* with her first novel, *Dusty Answer* (1927), which describes the awakening into womanhood of 18-year-old Judith Earle. *A Note in Music* (1930), also created a stir with its frank treatment of homosexuality. *Invitation to the Waltz* (1932) describes the impact on innocent 17-year-old Olivia Curtis of her first dance; its sequel, *The Weather in the Streets*

(1936), shocked some readers by taking Olivia through a failed marriage, an adulterous love affair, and an abortion. *The Ballad and the Source* (1944) is a child's-eye view of adult passion. *The Echoing Grove* (1953), a novel about the relationship of two sisters, was followed by *The Swan in the Evening: Fragments of an Inner Life* (1967), a short autobiographical work, and *A Sea-Grape Tree* (1976).

The new wave of *feminist criticism inspired many reprints of Rosamond Lehmann's novels in the 1980s.

LEIBNIZ, Gottfried Wilhelm (1646–1716), German philosopher and mathematician, and one of the chief forces leading to the German *Enlightenment. He is chiefly remembered in a literary context for parodies of his 'optimistic' philosophy of eternal harmony, most notably by *Voltaire (in the Dr Pangloss of *Candide*), and in the works of English satirists such as *Fielding.

LEICESTER, Robert Dudley, earl of (?1532–88), the favourite of *Elizabeth I, figures in Scott's *Kenilworth* as the husband of the unfortunate Amy Robsart.

LEIGH, Augusta (1784–1851), half-sister of Lord *Byron, daughter of his father by the latter's earlier marriage to Lady Carmarthen. Augusta's relations with Byron have been the subject of much speculation, and it is probable that he was the father of her daughter, Elizabeth Medora, born in 1814.

Leila, (1) in Byron's *Don Juan*, the Muslim child whom Juan rescues at the siege of Ismail; (2) in his *The Giaour*, the unfortunate heroine.

Leinster, Book of, an Irish MS of the 12th cent., containing stories of Gaelic mythology, in particular the feats of *Cuchulain.

L.E.L., see LANDON, L. E.

LELAND, John (c.1503–52), the earliest of modern English antiquaries. He studied at Paris, took holy orders, and by 1530 was involved with the royal libraries. He made a tour through England in 1535–43, intending his researches to be the basis of a great work on the 'History and Antiquities of this Nation', but he left merely a mass of undigested notes. *Leland's Intinerary* was first published at Oxford, in nine volumes, by *Hearne in 1710–12; and his *Collectanea* in six (1715).

LEMON, Mark (1809–70), a founder and first editor of *Punch*, from 1841 until his death. He wrote prolifically for the stage, and collaborated with *Dickens in *Mr Nightingale's Diary* (1851), a one-act farce with both authors in the cast.

LENNOX, Charlotte (1720–1804), is remembered for her novel *The Female Quixote* (1752).

Her other works include *Shakespear Illustrated* (1753–4); *Henrietta* (1758), a novel; and a comedy, *The Sister*, performed in 1769. Dr *Johnson, a friend and admirer of her work, cited her under 'Talent' in his *Dictionary*.

'Lenore' (1774), a celebrated ballad by the German poet Gottfried August Bürger (1747–94), based on the Scottish ballad 'Sweet William's Ghost'. Lenore is carried off on horseback by the spectre of her lover after his death and married by him at the graveside. It was translated first by W. *Taylor, whose version circulated in manuscript and was published in 1797. *Scott's version appeared also in 1797, anonymously, as 'William and Helen' in *The Chase and William and Helen*. The two poets corresponded about their versions.

Leodegrance ('Leodegan' elsewhere in the Arthurian cycles), in Malory's *Morte D'Arthur*, king of Cameliard and father of *Guinevere.

Leo Hunter, Mrs, a character in Dickens's *Pickwick Papers*.

Leonato, in Shakespeare's *Much Ado about Nothing*, the father of Hero and uncle of Beatrice.

Leonatus, Posthumus, see POSTHUMUS LEONATUS.

Leonine verse, a kind of Latin verse much used in the Middle Ages, consisting of hexameters, or alternate hexameters and pentameters, in which the last word rhymes with that preceding the caesura; for instance:

His replicans clare tres causas explico quare
More Leonino dicere metra sino.

The term is applied to English verse of which the middle and last syllables rhyme.

Leontes, in Shakespeare's *The Winter's Tale*, the husband of Hermione.

Lêr, or Lir, in Gaelic mythology, the sea-god, one of the *Tuatha Dé Danann; perhaps to be identified with the British sea-god Llyr. He was the father of *Manannán.

LESAGE, Alain-René (1668–1747), French novelist and playwright. He specialized in picaresque narratives: *Le Diable boiteux* (1707) and his masterpiece *Gil Blas* (1715–35) are notable for their narrative brio and their shrewd, good-humoured presentation of human nature. *Gil Blas* was translated by *Smollett in 1749: with *Don Quixote* and *Rabelais, it can be considered the greatest foreign influence on 18th-cent. English comic fiction.

LESSING, Doris May, *née* Tayler (1919–), novelist and short story writer, left Southern

Rhodesia in 1949 with the manuscript of her first novel to be published, *The Grass is Singing* (1950). Her quintet *Children of Violence* is a *Bildungsroman*, tracing the history of Martha Quest from her childhood in Rhodesia, through post-war Britain, to an apocalyptic ending in AD 2000 (*Martha Quest*, 1952; *A Proper Marriage*, 1954; *A Ripple From the Storm*, 1958; *Landlocked*, 1965; and *The Four-Gated City*, 1969). *The Golden Notebook* (1962) is a lengthy and ambitious novel which was hailed as a landmark by the Women's Movement: sections of conventional narrative ironically entitled 'Free Women' enclose and intersperse the four experimental notebooks of writer Anna Wulf who is struggling with crises in her domestic and political life, and with a writer's block. The novel ends, after a period of breakdown, with release, union, and renewed creativity. Later novels, *Briefing for a Descent into Hell* (1971) and *Memoirs of a Survivor* (1975), enter the realm of 'inner space fiction', exploring mental breakdown and the break-down of society. The sequence collectively entitled *Canopus in Argus Archives* (1975–83, 5 vols) marks a complete break with traditional realism, describing the epic and mythic events of a fictional universe with a remarkable freedom of invention. She has written many other works of fiction and non-fiction, displaying her concern with politics, with the changing destiny of women, with a fear of technological disaster. Her *Collected Stories* (2 vols, 1978) shows a similarly broad range of interests.

L'ESTRANGE, Sir Roger (1616–1704), journalist and pamphleteer, and an active royalist. He issued *The News* and *The Intelligencer* (1663–6), which were ousted by *The London Gazette* of *Muddiman, and many political pamphlets. In his periodical *The Observator* (1681–7) he attacked the Whigs, *Oates, and Dissenters. His prose is colloquial, forceful, and controversial. He was knighted by James II in 1685, but after the revolution was regarded by the Whigs as a grave threat to liberty, and was several times imprisoned.

Letter on the Spirit of Patriotism, A, see BOLINGBROKE, H. ST J.

Letters on a Regicide Peace, see REGICIDE PEACE.

Letters on the Study and Use of History, see BOLINGBROKE, H. ST J.

Letter to a Noble Lord on the attacks made upon him and his pension in the House of Lords by the Duke of Bedford and the Earl of Lauderdale, by E. *Burke, published 1796.

Burke retired from Parliament in 1794 and received a pension from the government of Pitt. This grant was criticized in the House of Lords, principally by the peers above named, as excess-ive in amount and inconsistent with Burke's own principles of economical reform. Burke replied in one of the greatest masterpieces of irony and feeling in the English language, comparing his own services to the State with those rendered by the duke of Bedford and his house, which had been the recipient of enormous grants from the Crown.

Letter to Sir William Wyndham, A, see BOLINGBROKE, H. ST J.

Letter to the Sheriffs of Bristol, A, by E. *Burke, published 1777.

The American war had at this time followed its disastrous course for two years. In this letter Burke protests against Parliament's treatment of the rebels, and argues that the scheme of taxing America is incompatible with his concept of the supremacy of Parliament and an appropriate imperial policy. Burke has consequently voted for the pacification of 1766, and even for the surrender of the right of taxation.

LEVER, Charles (1806–72), novelist born in Dublin, qualified as an MD. His first novels, *Harry Lorrequer* (1839), *Charles O'Malley* (1841), and *Jack Hinton the Guardsman* (1843), were extremely popular. In 1842 he became editor of the *Dublin University Magazine*. *Tom Burke of Ours* (1844) and *The Knight of Gwynne* (1847) were notable among the stream of his racy, anecdotal works. In 1845 he left Ireland and eventually settled in Italy. His other novels include *The Dodd Family Abroad* (1852–4), *Sir Jasper Crew* (1855), *The Fortunes of Glencore* (1857), and *Lord Kilgobbin* (1872).

LEVERSON, Ada (1862–1933), novelist, is chiefly remembered for her association with *Wilde, who named her 'The Sphinx'. For some years she held a salon frequented by the *Sitwells, *Beerbohm, the novelist G. *Moore, and H. *Acton. Her novels, which enjoyed a belated vogue in the 1960s, are set in fashionable London society; they include *Love's Shadow* (1908), *Tenterhooks* (1912), and *Love at Second Sight* (1916), all of which feature Edith Ottley as protagonist.

LEVI, Peter Chad Tigar (1931–   ), poet, translator, classical scholar, travel writer, and archaeologist, became professor of poetry at Oxford, 1984. He was a Jesuit priest from 1964 to 1977, when he resigned the priesthood. His first volume of poetry, *The Gravel Ponds* (1960), was followed by several others, including a *Collected Poems 1955–1975* (1976); his poems mingle imagery and themes from classical antiquity, British history and prehistory, Christianity, and domestic life.

Leviathan, The, or the Matter, Form, and Power of a Commonwealth, Ecclesiastical and Civil, a treatise of political philosophy by *Hobbes, published 1651, Latin text 1668.

By 'The Leviathan' the author signified sovereign power. The basis of his political philosophy is that man is not, as *Aristotle held, naturally a social being, recognizing the claims of the community upon him and sharing in its prosperity, but a purely selfish creature, seeking only his own advantage. The state of nature is one of general war, and 'the life of man [is] solitary, poore, nasty, brutish and short.' To escape these conditions man has adopted certain 'articles of peace', those 'Laws of Nature', by which a man is forbidden to do 'that which is destructive of his life'. The first law of nature is, 'that every man ought to endeavour Peace'. The second is, 'That a man be willing, when others are so too . . . to lay down his right to all things; and be contented with so much liberty against other men, as he would allow other men against himselfe.' The third is, 'that men performe their Covenants made'.

To enforce these covenants it is necessary to establish an external power, which shall punish their infraction; accordingly all individuals must enter into a contract 'to conferre all their power and strength upon one Man, or upon one Assembly of men'. 'This done, the Multitude so united in one Person, is called a Common-Wealth.' This representative person is sovereign. Hobbes is careful to repudiate the rival claim of the Church to control over the citizen. He accordingly makes the Church subordinate to the State.

The absolute power thus given to the sovereign is, however, subject to certain limits. There is liberty to refuse obedience if the command of the sovereign frustrates the end for which the sovereignty was ordained.

LEWES, G(eorge) H(enry) (1817–78), a versatile writer, was author of plays, essays (notably on *Comte and *Hegel), *Ranthorpe* (1847), a novel in imitation of *Goethe, and a popular history of philosophy from F. *Bacon to Comte (*Biographical History of Philosophy*, 1845–6). His liaison with George *Eliot, dating from 1854, could not be regularized because he had condoned the adultery of his wife Agnes with Thorton Leigh Hunt, son of Leigh *Hunt. By the time he met George Eliot, he was estranged from Agnes, but unable to obtain a divorce.

Lewes's most distinguished work is his still valuable *Life of Goethe* (1855). Lewes turned his attention increasingly to science: his later works range from biological works like *Seaside Studies* (1858) and *The Physiology of Common Life* (1859) to his ambitious attempt at psychology, *Problems of Life and Mind* (1873–9).

Lewesdon Hill, a *topographical poem by William Crowe (1745–1829), published 1788, in the style of James *Thomson.

LEWIS, Alun (1915–44), Welsh poet. His first volume of poems, *Raiders' Dawn*, appeared in 1942, and in 1943 a volume of stories, *The Last Inspection*, most of which deal with army life in England, as does his most anthologized poem, 'All Day it has Rained . . .', first published in 1941. Lewis was killed in Burma. Letters and stories were collected in *In the Green Tree* (1948), and *Selected Poetry and Prose* appeared in 1966. Many of Lewis's poems show a recurring obsession with the themes of isolation and death, and a debt to E. *Thomas, to whom one of his best poems is addressed.

LEWIS, Cecil Day, see DAY-LEWIS, C.

LEWIS, C(live) S(taples) (1898–1963), literary scholar, critic, and novelist, fellow of Magdalen College, Oxford, 1925–54, and afterwards professor of Medieval and Renaissance English at Cambridge. His critical works include *The Allegory of Love* (1936) and *English Literature in the Sixteenth Century* (vol. 3 in the *Oxford History of English Literature*, 1954). He is more widely known for his popular religious and moral writings, such as *The Problem of Pain* (1940), *The Screwtape Letters* (1940), and *The Four Loves* (1960). *Out of the Silent Planet* (1938) is the first of three science fiction novels. With *The Lion, The Witch, and The Wardrobe* (1950) he began a series of seven 'Narnia' stories for children. *Surprised by Joy* (1955) is his spiritual autobiography. *'The Inklings', a group of his friends, met in his Oxford rooms for many years to talk and read aloud their compositions.

LEWIS, M(atthew) G(regory) (1775–1818), is remembered as the author of *The Monk* (1796), a representative *Gothic novel, from which his nickname 'Monk' Lewis was derived. Lewis was greatly influenced by German Romanticism, and wrote numerous dramas. His verses (of which 'Alonzo the Brave and the Fair Imogine', appears in *The Monk*) had some influence on Sir W. *Scott's early poetry.

LEWIS, (Harry) Sinclair (1885–1951), American novelist, achieved success with his novel *Main Street* (1920), which describes with realism and satire the dullness of life in a small midwestern town. He strengthened his reputation with *Babbitt* (1922), the story of George Babbitt, a prosperous and self-satisfied house-agent in the mid-western town of Zenith; *Arrowsmith* (1925); *Elmer Gantry* (1927), a satiric view of midwestern religious evangelism; and *Dodsworth* (1929). Lewis was awarded the *Nobel Prize in 1930.

LEWIS, (Percy) Wyndham (1882–1957), artist, novelist, and critic. He was a leader of the *Vorticist movement and, with *Pound, edited *Blast, the Review of the Great English Vortex*

(1914–15). His novels include *Tarr* (1918), *The Apes of God* (1930), *The Revenge for Love* (1937), and *Self Condemned* (1957); his projected four-part work *The Human Age* (*The Childermass*, 1928; *Monstre Gai* and *Malign Fiesta*, both 1955) remained unfinished. Essays and criticism include *The Lion and the Fox: the Role of Hero in the Plays of Shakespeare* (1927) and *The Writer and the Absolute* (1952). *Blasting and Bombardiering* (1937) and *Rude Assignment* (1950) are autobiographies. His savage satirical attacks on his contemporaries (particularly the *Bloomsbury Group), his association with the British Fascist party, and his praise of Hitler alienated him from the literary world. Lewis's little magazine *The Enemy*, which appeared in three book-length issues, 1927–9, written largely by himself (with poems by L. *Riding and R. *Campbell), contained the text of the volume published as *Time and Western Man* (1927) and three of his most important essays, 'Paleface', 'The Diabolical Principle', and 'The Revolutionary Simpleton'.

Lewis and Short, Latin–English dictionary, by Charlton T. Lewis and Charles Short, first published in 1879, and frequently revised.

Lewis Baboon, see JOHN BULL.

LEYDEN, John (1775–1811), Scottish antiquarian, physician, poet, and orientalist, assisted Sir W. *Scott in *Minstrelsy of the Scottish Border* and contributed to M. G. *Lewis's *Tales of Wonder* (1801). Scott mourned his 'bright and brief career' in *The Lord of the Isles* (Canto IV. xi) and contributed a Memoir to the *Edinburgh Annual Register*. This was reproduced with Leyden's *Poems and Ballads* (1858, 1875).

Libeaus Desconus (a corruption of *le bel inconnu*, the fair unknown), a late 14th-cent. romance in 2,250 lines previously attributed to Thomas Chestre (see SIR LAUNFAL). Gingelein, the son of Gawain and Dame Ragnell, asks Arthur for knighthood and, since his name is unknown, he is knighted as *Li Beaus Desconus*. The poem is concerned with his adventures in rescuing the imprisoned Lady of Sinadoune. In *Chaucer's 'Sir Thopas' the knight's name is given simply as 'Sir Lybeux'.

Libelle of Englyshe Polycye, The ('the Little Book of English Policy'), a political poem written *c.*1436, in which the author exhorts his countrymen to regard the sea as the source of national strength, discusses commercial relations with other countries, and urges the importance of retaining Ireland, Calais, and Wales. The poem was included by *Hakluyt, and it has been doubtfully attributed to Adam Moleyns or Molyneaux (d. 1450).

Liberal, The (1822–4), a magazine of four issues only, conceived by *Shelley, but carried out after his death by *Byron and Leigh *Hunt from Pisa. In its pages appeared Byron's *The Vision of Judgement* and his *Heaven and Earth*, and work by Shelley, Hunt, *Hazlitt, J. *Hogg, and others.

Liber Amoris, by W. *Hazlitt, published 1823. This fevered piece of autobiography describes the author's obsessive and almost insane love for a simple girl, Sarah Walker. The book takes the form of letters and conversations between Hazlitt and Sarah, and of intimate letters to two friends, J. S. *Knowles and Peter Patmore.

Liberty, On, an essay by *J. S. Mill, published 1859. In this work Mill examines the proper relations of society to the individual. In his view, 'the sole end for which mankind are warranted, individually or collectively, in interfering with liberty of action of any of their number, is self-protection.' The only part of the conduct of anyone, for which he is amenable to society, is that which concerns others.

Liberty of Prophesying, The, see TAYLOR, JEREMY.

Libraries: a listing of major university libraries and national collections in England, Ireland, Scotland, and Wales, with some details of holdings.

    Aberdeen University Library. A 12th-cent. bestiary, Jacobite literature, extensive minor literature of the 18th and 19th cents.

    Ashley Library. Private library collected by *Wise. First editions from *Jonson onwards. Acquired by the British Museum in 1937.

    Bodleian Library, Oxford. Founded by Sir T. *Bodley. In 1610 the *Stationer's Company undertook to give the library a copy of every book printed in England. It received also important gifts of books and MSS from *Laud, *Cromwell, F. *Junius, and Robert *Burton. Other considerable accessions included *Selden's library, in 1659, the Tanner, Rawlinson, Gough, Malone, and Douce collections of MSS, and many of the MSS of *Locke in 1947. Copyright library.

    British Library. The national library for the United Kingdom, established in 1973 under Act of Parliament by the amalgamation of the library departments of the *British Museum and other organizations, as the national centre for reference, lending, bibliographical, and other information services. Copyright library.

    Cambridge University Library. The Royal (Bishop Moore's) Library, presented by King George I; the Bradshaw Collection of Irish Books; Taylor-Schechter collection of Hebraica; papers of C. *Darwin. Incunables include a *Gutenberg Bible and unique *Caxton items. Copyright library.

    Durham University Library. Middle English

MSS; letters of G. M. *Hopkins, the *Rossettis, E. *Thomas; MSS of *Plomer, and letters to him from *Britten, E. M. *Forster, etc. Printed books 16th–18th cent.

Glasgow University Library. 1.3 million volumes, including 350 medieval MSS, 1,100 incunabula. Research collections include: *emblem literature, Sir T. *Browne's works, broadside ballads, Scottish theatre archives, 19th-cent. art and literature.

National Library of Scotland, Edinburgh. Founded by Sir George Mackenzie of Rosehaugh (1636–91) as library of the Faculty of Advocates, opened in 1689. Became the National Library of Scotland in 1925. Four million printed items, one million maps, and 34,000 MSS, mainly of Scottish interest. Also modern foreign literature. Copyright library.

National Library of Wales, Aberystwyth. Manuscripts, books, maps, prints, and drawings relating to Wales and the Celtic peoples. Copyright library.

Queen's University of Belfast, The. University library. Hibernica Collection (Irish literature and history), Macdouall Collection (philology), Hamilton Harty Collection (music), and Thomas Percy Library.

St Andrews University Library, Scotland. First four Shakespeare Folios on permanent loan from the Folger Library; Bibles; first editions of Galileo.

Trinity College Library, University of Dublin. Largest research library in Ireland. Important collection of manuscripts, including Book of *Kells.

Libraries, Circulating, libraries from which, for a fee, books were borrowed by the public. The first appears to have been A. *Ramsay's founded in Edinburgh in 1726, and the system flourished for over two centuries. It greatly stimulated the production of books, particularly of novels, but there was also a strong link between Dissent, the self-education of the lower classes, and the circulating library, as J. *Priestley noted. The great new libraries of the 19th cent., *Mudie's, W. H. *Smith's, and *Boots, exercised a powerful censorship. The three-volume novel of the middle and late 19th cent. was largely supported by these libraries, and died out at the end of the century when they no longer wanted it. The chief circulating libraries of this century were closed by 1970, and replaced by the system of Book Clubs.

Libraries, Public. The first British public libraries were established under the Museum Act, in Canterbury (1847), Warrington (1848), and Salford (1850). The 1850 Public Libraries Act, piloted by William Ewart against stiff opposition, empowered borough councils in England and Wales (extended to Scotland in 1853) with a population of 10,000 plus to spend a halfpenny rate on libraries and museums. By 1866 the population limit was removed, and by the turn of the century some 400 libraries had been set up.

By 1913 the American philanthropist *Carnegie had given £2m for public libraries and John Passmore Edwards supported 24 libraries. After the First World War, the Public Libraries Act of 1919 removed the rate limitation and extended library powers to the counties. By 1928, with the help of the Carnegie Trust, most counties had started a library service. The Mitchell Report of 1924 and the Kenyon Report of 1927 reflected an increasing interest in library development, and marked a stage in the development of libraries for all. The Public Library service continued to grow despite being set back by the depression of 1931–3, helped by the overall increase of local government spending on libraries between 1928 and 1939. The growth of the county library service was a notable feature of the post-war years, until it was arrested by the recession of the early 1980s.

Library, The, a magazine of bibliography and literature, published from 1889 to 1898 as the organ of the Library Association, and from 1899 to 1918 as an independent journal. In 1920 it was merged with the *Transactions* of the *Bibliographical Society.

Libretto, the Italian word for the 'little book' in which the text of an opera (or oratorio) was printed, and hence the text itself. A few composers have written their own librettos, but the majority have used a poet or professional librettist.

A libretto must provide the composer with three elements: a core of character, situation, and plot; a framework of words laid out for musical treatment; and language that will stimulate the creative imagination. Few writers have succeeded in satisfying all the requirements though there are exceptions such as Hofmannsthal's librettos for Strauss, Boito's for Verdi's *Falstaff*, or *Auden's for Stravinsky's *The Rake's Progress*. *Tate's libretto for *Purcell's *Dido and Aeneas* has been much attacked on literary grounds. Tate was not the first English librettist: he is generally held to have been preceded by *D'Avenant with *The Siege of Rhodes*.

In the 18th cent. the taste for Italian music gained ground in England, and with *Handel's arrival in London in 1710 the fate of English opera was sealed. Only in the lighter field did the English libretto survive; the *ballad operas which followed Gay's *The Beggar's Opera* were effectively straight plays interspersed with music. It was not until 1871 that the first of the *Gilbert and Sullivan operas introduced a new and invigorating talent. Many 20th-cent. composers have taken an active part in the preparation of their own librettos, and the professional librettist has disappeared: in his place names like *Hardy, *Synge, A. P. *Herbert, Clifford Bax, J. B. *Priestley, and *Plomer have been found in the opera programmes. Auden, in his librettos for Britten, Stravinsky, and Henze, established himself as the most important writer in the form in the last few decades.

LIDDELL, Henry George (1811–98), head-master of Westminster School (1846) and dean of Christ Church, Oxford (1855). He compiled with Robert Scott (1811–87) the famous Greek lexicon, which, repeatedly revised, is still in use today. He is chiefly remembered now as the father of the little girl who served Lewis Carroll (C. L. *Dodgson) as a model for Alice.

Life and Adventures of Sir Launcelot Greaves, The, see SIR LAUNCELOT GREAVES, THE LIFE AND ADVENTURES OF.

Life and Death of Jason, The, a poem in heroic couplets by W. *Morris.

Life and Labour of the People in London, see BOOTH, C.

Life and Letters, a literary monthly periodical founded and edited from 1928 to 1933 by D. *MacCarthy. It subsequently continued as *Life and Letters Today,* and in 1939 absorbed the *London Mercury* and *Bookman,* reverting from 1945 to 1950 to its original title. Early contributors included *Beerbohm, A. *Huxley, C. *Bell, V. *Woolf, and C. *Connolly; poetry was better represented in its later years by G. *Barker, V. *Watkins, and others.

Life in London, see EGAN P.

Life of Samuel Johnson, The, see JOHNSON, THE LIFE OF SAMUEL.

Life on the Mississippi, an autobiographical account by Mark *Twain.

Light, Christina, a character in H. James's *Roderick Hudson* and *The Princess Casamassima.*

Light of Asia, The, see ARNOLD, SIR E.

Light Shining in Buckinghamshire, the title of an anonymous pamphlet issued by the Levellers in 1648, attacking monarchy and calling for equality of property.

Light That Failed, The, a novel by R. *Kipling.

LILBURNE, John (c.1614–57), pamphleteer, political agitator, and Leveller, was brought before the Star Chamber in 1638 for printing an unlicensed book, and imprisoned; *The Work of the Beast* (1638) gives an account of his barbarous

treatment. He published pamphlets jointly with *Overton and *Walwyn.

'Lilli-Burlero Bullen-a-la!' 'said to have been the words of distinction used among the Irish Papists in their massacre of the Protestants in 1641' (*Percy). They were made the refrain of a song, attributed to Lord Wharton, satirizing the earl of Tyrconnel on the occasion of his going to Ireland in Jan. 1686–7 as James II's papist lieutenant. The song is given in Percy's *Reliques.

Lilliput, see GULLIVER'S TRAVELS.

LILLO, George (1693–1739), was the author of the famous prose domestic tragedy *The London Merchant, or the History of *George Barnwell,* produced in 1731. His other plays include *The Christian Hero* (produced 1735), and *The Fatal Curiosity* (1736). Lillo's introduction of middle-class domestic tragedy had an influence which extended beyond English literature, notably to G. E. Lessing and *Diderot.

LILLY, William (1602–81), a noted astrologer, patronized by *Ashmole. He published almanacs yearly from 1644 until his death (issued from 1647 under the title *Merlini Anglici Aphemeris*). His *Christian Astrology* (1647) was the standard guide to the subject. He is thought to have been in part the model for Sidrophel in *Hudibras. The case-books recording his consultations survive in the Ashmole MSS of the Bodleian library, and his autobiography appears with Ashmole's *Memoirs,* in the 1774 edition. (See ALMANACS.)

Lillyvick, Mr, a character in Dickens's *Nicholas Nickleby.*

LILY, William (c.1468–1522), friend of *Colet and Sir T. *More, grandfather of J. *Lyly, and a leader of the revival of Greek studies in England. He was made a high master of St Paul's School, and was partly responsible for *Lily's Grammar,* which was long familiar to English schoolboys; cf. the Latin lesson in *The Merry Wives of Windsor,* IV. i.

Limberham, central character in Dryden's *Mr Limberham.*

Limerick, a form of facetious jingle, of which the first instances occur in *The History of Sixteen Wonderful Old Women* (1820) and *Anecdotes and Adventures of Fifteen Gentlemen* (c.1821), subsequently popularized by *Lear in his *Book of Nonsense.*

In the older form of limerick, as written by Lear, D. G. *Rossetti, and others, the first and last lines usually ended with the same word, but in more recent examples, such as those written by W. H. *Auden, G. *Ewart, O. *Nash, N.

*Douglas, R. *Conquest, and others, a third rhyming word is supplied.

LINACRE, Thomas (?1460–1524), was Latin tutor to the Princess Mary, for whom he composed a Latin grammar, *Rudimenta Grammatices.* He wrote grammatical and medical works, and translated from the Greek, mainly from *Galen.

Lindisfarne Gospels, a manuscript of the four Gospels in the *Vulgate text, probably written in honour of the canonization of St *Cuthbert (698). The script is Anglo-Saxon majuscule and there are magnificent illuminations and decorative capitals. An Anglo-Saxon gloss was added in the late 10th cent. in Northumbrian dialect with a colophon stating that the text was written by Eadfrith, bishop of Lindisfarne 698–721. The manuscript is in the Cottonian collection in the *British Museum.

LINDSAY, Lady Anne (1750–1825), daughter of the fifth earl of Balcarres, wrote in 1771 the popular ballad 'Auld Robin Gray'. She became by marriage Lady Anne Barnard, and accompanied her husband to South Africa, where she wrote the journals *Lady Anne Barnard at the Cape, 1797–1802.* After the death of her husband she established with her sister a literary salon in London.

LINDSAY, or **LYNDSAY,** Sir David (c. 1486–1555), Scottish poet and Lyon king-of-arms; usher to Prince James (afterwards James V). His first poem, 'The Dreme', written in 1528, is an allegorical lament on the misgovernment of the realm, followed by a vigorous exhortation to the king. In 1529 he wrote the *Complaynt to the King*, in octosyllabic couplets, commenting on the improved social condition of the realm except as regards the Church. The *Testament, and Complaynt, of our Soverane Lordis Papyngo* (finished 1530, printed 1538) combines advice to the king, put in the mouth of his parrot, with a warning to courtiers drawn from the examples of Scottish history. Lindsay's principal poem, *Ane *Pleasant Satyre of the Thrie Estaitis*, a morality, was produced in 1540 before the king and court. The *Historie of Squyer Meldrum* (first extant edition of 1582) is a spirited verse romance on the career and exploits of a Scottish laird.

LINGARD, John (1771–1851), a Roman Catholic priest, author of *The Antiquities of the Anglo-Saxon Church* (1806); and of a *History of England* (1819–30), the principal object of which is to emphasize the disastrous effects of the Reformation. His idealized portrait of the Middle Ages had considerable influence, notably on W. *Morris and the founders of the *Oxford Movement.

Linguistics (also 'Theoretical' or 'General' linguistics), a term used to characterize the study of language in the 20th cent. owing much to the Swiss linguist *Saussure; it distinguishes itself from earlier language study by concentrating on the language at a particular time ('synchronic') rather than the history of language and languages ('diachronic'). For major practitioners, see SAUSSURE; BLOOMFIELD, L.; CHOMSKY; and JACOBSON.

Linkinwater, Tim, in Dickens's *Nicholas Nickleby*, a clerk to the brothers Cheeryble.

LINKLATER, Eric (1899–1974), novelist. As a Commonwealth fellow in the US (1928–30), he gathered material for *Juan in America* (1930), a satirical novel which brought him immediate fame. Other works include *The Men of Ness* (1932); *Magnus Merriman* (1934); *Private Angelo* (1946), describing the campaign in Italy; and *The Wind on the Moon* (1944), his most successful children's book. *The Man on My Back* (1941) and *A Year of Space* (1953) were autobiographical.

LINNAEUS, Latinized form of LINNÉ, Carl (1707–78), Swedish naturalist and founder of the internationally used binomial system for scientifically naming animals and plants. His most important publications were *Species Plantarum* (1753) and *Systema Naturae*, 10th edn, vol. 1 (1758), both in Latin, but in Sweden he is more esteemed for the Swedish accounts of his travels in Lapland, Oland, and Gotland. In 1783 James Edward Smith bought his collections and in 1788 was one of the founders of the Linnean Society of London.

Linnean Society, see LINNAEUS.

Linton, Edgar, Isabella, and Catherine, characters in E. Brontë's *Wuthering Heights.*

LINTON, Eliza Lynn, *née* Lynn (1822–98), began her literary career with two historical novels (*Azeth the Egyptian*, 1846; *Amymone*, 1848), which she followed with many more successful novels of contemporary life, such as *Rebel of the Family* (1880). She offended many of her female contemporaries by her essays attacking feminism and the *New Woman, some of which were collected from the *Saturday Review as *The Girl of the Period* (1883). Her posthumously published memoir *My Literary Life* (1899) contains a notably hostile portrait of G. *Eliot.

LINTOT, or **LINTOTT,** Barnaby Bernard (1675–1736), bookseller and printer, published a *Miscellaneous Poems and Translations by several hands* (1712), which contained the first version of *The Rape of the Lock*. He published other works by *Pope (who compared his uncouth appearance to that of a dabchick in the *Dunciad*, ii. 63), and poems and plays by *Gay, *Farquhar, *Steele, *Rowe, and others.

Lir, see LÊR.

Lisle Letters, a collection of some 3,000 letters written to and from Arthur Plantagenet, Viscount Lisle (an illegitimate son of Edward IV), his family and household, while he was lord deputy of Calais from 1533 to 1540. They give a vivid picture of the political and domestic life of the time.

Lismahago, Obadiah, a character in Smollett's *Humphry Clinker.*

Listener, The, a BBC weekly magazine, of which the first number appeared on 16 Jan. 1929; it publishes reviews, broadcasts, essays, poetry, etc. Its literary editor from 1935 to 1959 was J. B. *Ackerley, who attracted work from many distinguished writers.

LISTER, Thomas Henry (1800–42), the first registrar-general of England and Wales, was an accomplished novelist, much influenced by J. *Austen. His novels include *Granby* (1826), *Herbert Lacy* (1828), and *Arlington* (1832), which describe with an ironic eye the aristocratic and upper-middle-class society of the time.

Literary Anecdotes *of the Eighteenth Century*, see NICHOLS, J.

Literary Club, see CLUB, THE.

Literary Gazette, The (1817–62), a journal founded by *Colburn, aimed at a wide coverage of books, fine arts, and sciences. Early contributors included *Crabbe, M. R. *Mitford, *Cornwall, and L. E. *Landon.

Literary Magazine, The: or *Universal Review* (1756–8), a periodical conducted largely by Dr *Johnson, who contributed many articles.

Literati, a term introduced by Robert *Burton to refer to the literate class in China, and later applied to the writers and readers of fashionable literature in other communities, often by contrast with the practical scientists, or virtuosi. The term is now frequently used to identify those who frequented the literary clubs of 18th-cent. Edinburgh, and the bookshops of *Ramsay, Creech, and Kincaid, but it is more particularly applied to a group of professional men, mostly lawyers and clergy, and mostly supporters of or supported by the Moderate party in the Scottish church; at a time when vernacular writing was in decline, they self-consciously cultivated an English writing style, both to make a cultural impact on London society and to cement the political union with England. They included H. *Home, *Monboddo, Adam *Smith, *Hume, H. *Blair, A. *Ferguson, J. *Home, W. *Robertson, and *Wilkie. Although their writings were primarily on history, philosophy, and the theory of criticism, many of them also supported the legalization and revival of the legitimate theatre, against fierce Calvinist opposition. Hume in 1752 and *Beattie in 1779 assisted the movement for stylistic improvement by publishing collections of unacceptable 'Scotticisms'; and Thomas Sheridan, father of the dramatist, lectured to men's and women's classes on English elocution in 1761 under the auspices in the *Select Society. (See also SCOTTISH ENLIGHTENMENT.)

Litotes, a figure of speech in which an affirmative is expressed by the negative of the contrary, e.g. 'a citizen of no mean city'; an ironical understatement.

Littimer, in Dickens's *David Copperfield*, Steerforth's hypocritical valet.

Little, Thomas, see MOORE, T.

Little Billee, a humorous ballad of three sailors of Bristol, of whom Little Billee is the youngest. *Thackeray wrote a version of the ballad. 'Little Billee' was the nickname of the hero of Du Maurier's *Trilby.

Little Dorrit, a novel by *Dickens, published in monthly parts, 1855–7.

William Dorrit has been so long in the Marshalsea prison for debtors that he has become the 'Father of the Marshalsea'. He has had the misfortune to be responsible for an uncompleted contract with the Circumlocution Office (a satirical portrait of the government departments of the day, with their incompetent and obstructive officials typified in the Barnacles). His lot is alleviated by the devotion of Amy, his youngest daughter, 'Little Dorrit'. Amy has a snobbish sister Fanny, a theatrical dancer, and a scapegrace brother, Tip. Old Dorrit and Amy are befriended by Arthur Clennam, the middle-aged hero, for whom Little Dorrit conceives a deep passion, at first unrequited. The unexpected discovery that William Dorrit is heir to a fortune raises the family to affluence. Except Little Dorrit, they become arrogant and purse-proud. Clennam, on the other hand, owing to an unfortunate speculation, is brought in turn to the debtor's prison, and is found in the Marshalsea, sick and despairing, by Little Dorrit, who tenderly nurses him and consoles him. He has meanwhile learnt the value of her love, but her fortune stands in the way of his asking her to marry him. The loss of it makes their union possible, on Clennam's release.

With this main theme is wound the thread of an elaborate mystery. Clennam has long suspected that his mother, a grim old puritanical paralysed woman, living in a gloomy house with a former attendant and present partner,

Flintwinch, has done some wrong to Little Dorrit. Through the agency of a stagy villain, Rigaud, alias Blandois, this is brought to light, and it appears that Mrs Clennam is not Arthur's mother, and that she has suppressed a codicil in a will that benefited the Dorrit family.

There are a host of minor characters in the work, of whom the most notable are the worthy Pancks, rent-collector to the humbug Casby; Merdle, the swindling financier, and Mrs Merdle, who 'piques herself on being society'; Affery, the villain Flintwinch's wife; 'Young John' Chivery, the son of the Marshalsea warder; and the Meagles and Gowan households.

Little Eva, the saintly child Evangeline St Clair in H. B. *Stowe's *Uncle Tom's Cabin* whose deathbed scene rivals in sentiment the death of Little Nell in *The Old Curosity Shop*.

Little Gidding, a manor in Huntingdonshire where N. *Ferrar and his family established, 1625–46, a religious community of some forty members, following a systematic rule of private devotion, public charity, and study. The house was visited by Charles I, *Crashaw, and G. *Herbert, and *Shorthouse's novel *John Inglesant* (1881) portrays its life vividly. It was raided by Cromwell's soldiers in 1646, and the community dispersed. T. S. Eliot celebrates it in 'Little Gidding', one of the *Four Quartets*, and its activities are recorded in *The Little Gidding Story Books*, part of which was printed in 1899, ed. E. C. Sharland.

Little John, one of the companions of *Robin Hood in the legends relating to that outlaw. He was a sturdy yeoman and a skilled archer, originally called John Little. He figures in Sir W. Scott's *Ivanhoe*.

LITTLEJOHN, Hugh, John Hugh Lockhart, the grandson of Sir W. *Scott, to whom *The Tales of a Grandfather* are dedicated.

Little Lord Fauntleroy, see BURNETT, F. H.

Little Magazines, a term used to describe minority literary and artistic periodicals, possibly derived from one of the better known of such publications, the *Little Review*. English 'little magazines' include *The Savoy, *Rhythm, Blast, *New Verse, *The Review* and its successor *The New Review, *Stand, Ambit,* and *Agenda*.

Little Musgrave and Lady Barnard, an ancient ballad, given in Percy's *Reliques*, which tells how Lady Barnard, loving Little Musgrave, passes the night with him in her bower at Bucklesford-Bury. The lovers are overheard by a foot-page who tells Lord Barnard: he kills Musgrave, then his wife, and is afterwards filled with remorse.

Musgrave is referred to in Beaumont and Fletcher's *The Knight of the Burning Pestle*, Act V, and in D'Avenant's *The Wits*, III. iii.

Little Nell (Trent), the heroine of Dickens's *The Old Curiosity Shop*.

Little Review, The (1914–29), an American monthly magazine founded in Chicago. In 1916 it came under the influence of *Pound, who was foreign editor from 1917 to 1919; it published *Yeats, W. *Lewis, T. S. *Eliot, F. M. *Ford, and, notably, from 1918, chapters of Joyce's *Ulysses*. It later became a quarterly published from Paris (1924–9), including work by *Hemingway, *Cummings, H. *Crane, etc.

Little Women, by L. M. *Alcott, published 1868–9. The story concerns the daily lives of four girls—Jo March, who aspires to be a writer, and her sisters Meg, Beth, and Amy—in a New England family in the mid-19th cent.

Liverpool Poets, the name given to a group of three poets, Adrian *Henri, Roger *McGough, and Brian Patten (1946–   ), who came together in the 1960s in the period of the Liverpool euphoria generated partly by the success of the *Beatles. Their anthologies include *The Mersey Sound* (1967), *The Liverpool Scene* (1967), and *New Volume* (1983). The combined tone of their work was pop, 'underground', urban, anti-academic, good-humoured, and vocal: poetry was conceived by them as a medium for public rather than private consumption, a performance art.

Lives of the English Poets, The, by Dr *Johnson, published 1779–81.

Johnson was invited in 1777 by a deputation of London booksellers to provide biographical prefaces for an edition of the works of selected English poets, from the period of *Milton onwards. The final total was 52, including 4 minor poets suggested by Johnson himself. When the work was completed the prefaces were issued without the texts as *Lives of the Poets*. The *Lives* contain much interesting biographical matter, but are not always trustworthy. The criticism has been considered unequal, particularly in respect of its strictures on Milton's *Lycidas, *Gray's Odes, and its evident prejudice against *Swift; Johnson's hostile analysis of the *metaphysical style, in his life of *Cowley, became notorious. But the work remains a classic, important both as a landmark in the history of critical taste and judgement, and for its own insights.

Lives of the Poets, see LIVES OF THE ENGLISH POETS, THE.

Living, a novel by H. *Green.

LIVINGSTONE, David (1813–73), Scottish missionary and explorer, embarked for the Cape of Good Hope in 1840. He travelled across more than one-third of the African continent gathering important information about the country. His many geographical discoveries included Lake Ngami, Lake Nyasa, and the Victoria Falls. His expeditions are described in *Missionary Travels and Researches in South Africa* (1857) and *Narrative of an Expedition to the Zambesi and its Tributaries and the discovery of the Lakes of Shirwa and Nyassa* (1865, in collaboration with his brother Charles). During his final expedition, to discover the sources of the Nile, he was rescued, almost dying, by H. M. *Stanley in Ujiji in 1871; he resumed his explorations but never recovered his health. His *Last Journals* appeared posthumously in 1874.

LIVY (Titus Livius) (59 BC–?AD 17), Roman historian. His great work related the history of Rome from its beginnings to 9 BC. Of its 142 books only 35 have survived, the best-known of which give us the legendary history of early Rome and the second Punic War. His stories of Rome's beginnings provided material for Painter's *Palace of Pleasure* (1566–7), for Shakespeare's *Rape of Lucrece* (1594), and for Macaulay's *Lays of Ancient Rome* (1842).

Lizzie Hexam, a character in Dickens's *Our Mutual Friend.*

LLANDAFF, bishop of, see WATSON, R.

Llangollen, The Ladies of, were Lady Eleanor Butler (?1739–1829) and Miss Sarah Ponsonby (?1735–1831), two devoted friends who left their families (against strong opposition) to set up a lifelong residence together in Plas Newydd in Llangollen Vale. Their house, adorned in the *Gothic style, was visited by distinguished guests, including *Wordsworth (who wrote them a sonnet), A. *Seward (who commemorated them in her poem 'Llangollen Vale', 1795), *Burke, and Mme de Genlis.

Llyr, see MABINOGION. Perhaps to be identified with Lir (see LÊR).

Lochinvar, the hero of a ballad included in the fifth canto of Scott's *Marmion.*

LOCKE, John (1632–1704), held various academic posts at Oxford, and became physician to the first earl of *Shaftesbury in 1667. He held official positions and subsequently lived at Oxford, then fled to Holland in 1683. In 1687 he joined William of Orange at Rotterdam; on his return to England he became commissioner of appeals and member of the council of trade.

Locke's principal philosophical work is the *Essay concerning Human Understanding* (1690), a work which led J. S. *Mill to call him the 'unquestioned founder of the analytic philo-

sophy of mind'. His defence of simple biblical religion in *The Reasonableness of Christianity* (1695), without resort to creed or tradition, led to a charge of *Socinianism, which Locke replied to in two *Vindications* (1695, 1697).

Locke published in 1690 two *Treatises of Government,* designed to combat the theory of the divine right of kings and finding the origin of the civil state in a contract. Throughout, Locke in his theory of the 'Original Contract' opposes absolutism. Although in his early manuscripts he was closer to *Hobbes's authoritarianism and continues to share with Hobbes the view that civil obligations are founded in contract, he strongly rejected Hobbes's view that the sovereign is above the law and no party to the contract. He published a volume on education in 1693, and on the rate of interest and the value of money in 1692 and 1695.

Locke's writings had an immense influence on the literature of succeeding generations, perhaps notably on *Sterne and *Addison, and his distinctions between 'wit' and 'judgement' were much discussed in the *Augustan age.

LOCKER-LAMPSON, Frederick (1821–95), born Locker, is remembered for his light verse, included in *London Lyrics* (1857), *Lyra Elegantiarum* (1867, an anthology, which, in its preface, offers a description of *vers de société*), and *Patchwork* (1879), a miscellany of prose and verse.

Locket's, a fashionable ordinary, or tavern, in Charing Cross, frequently alluded to in the drama of the 17th–18th cents, so named from Adam Locket, the landlord.

LOCKHART, John Gibson (1794–1854), became one of the principal contributors to *Blackwood's Magazine.* In 1817 he began a long series of attacks on, in particular, Leigh *Hunt, *Keats, and *Hazlitt, castigating them as the low-born *'Cockney School of Poetry'. He did, however, support *Wordsworth and *Coleridge. In 1818 he translated F. von *Schlegel's *Geschichte der alten und neuen Literatur* as *Lectures on the History of Literature, Ancient and Modern,* and he contributed several important articles on German literature to *Blackwood's* during the 1820s. He was editor of *The Quarterly Review* (1825–53) and his ferocity as a critic was well reflected in his chosen nickname, 'The Scorpion'. He published a wide range of books: *Peter's Letters to his Kinsfolk* (1819), containing spirited sketches of life in Edinburgh and Glasgow; *Valerius* (1821), a simple tale of Rome under Trajan; his novel *Some Passages in the Life of Adam Blair* (1822), a dark and disquieting story of a Scots minister; *Reginald Dalton* (1823), a popular romance; and translations of *Ancient Spanish Ballads* (1823). His *Life of Burns* appeared in 1828, and in 1837–8 his *Memoirs of the Life of Sir Walter Scott* (his father-in-law).

Lockit, and his daughter Lucy, characters in Gay's *The Beggar's Opera.*

Locksley, the name under which *Robin Hood figures in Scott's *Ivanhoe.*

Locksley Hall, a poem in trochaics by *Tennyson, published 1842. It consists of a monologue spoken by a disappointed lover, revisiting the desolate moorland home by the sea where he had been brought up by an unsympathetic uncle, and where he fell in love with his cousin Amy; she returned his love, but, through family pressure, accepted another suitor. The narrator proceeds to rail against the modern world of steamship and railway, and ends with an ambiguous acceptance of 'the ringing grooves of change'—a phrase that the notoriously poor-sighted Tennyson wrote while under the impression that the new railways ran in grooves, not on rails.

Lockwood, the narrator of E. Brontë's *Wuthering Heights.*

Locrine, or **Logrin,** according to *Geoffrey of Monmouth's *History*, the eldest son of Brutus (*Brut) and *Ignoge. He rules over Loegria (*Logres). He married Gwendolen but abandoned her for *Estrildis and was the father of her daughter Sabrina. He is mentioned by Spenser in *The Faerie Queene* and is the subject of Swinburne's play *Locrine* (1887).

Locrine, The Lamentable Tragedie of, a play of unknown authorship published 1595, and included in the third Shakespeare folio. It deals with the legend of *Locrine.

LODGE, David John (1935–   ), critic and novelist, became professor of modern English literature at the University of Birmingham in 1976. His critical works (*The Novelist at the Crossroads*, 1971; *The Modes of Modern Writing*, 1977; *Working with Structuralism*, 1981) display his gift for lucid exposition, and he has done much to introduce and explain continental literary theory in Britain. His novels include *The British Museum is Falling Down* (1965); *Changing Places* (1975; a satirical 'two-*campus novel' about a transatlantic academic exchange); and *How Far Can You Go?* (1980). *Small World* (1984) re-introduces the American academic Morris Zapp and the English professor Philip Swallow from *Changing Places*, in a jet-set world of international conferences, academic gamesmanship, and romantic pursuits.

LODGE, Thomas (1558–1625), was a student of Lincoln's Inn in 1578. In 1579–80 he published an anonymous *Defence of Poetry, Music and Stage Plays*, a reply to *Gosson's *Schoole of Abuse*, and in 1584 *An Alarum against Usurers* (dedicated to Sir P. *Sidney), to which was appended a prose

romance *Forbonius and Prisceria. Scillaes Metamorphosis* (1589), reissued as *Glaucus and Scilla* (1610), is the earliest of many Ovidian epyllia in the Elizabethan period; it bears both a generic and a specific relationship to Shakespeare's *Venus and Adonis.* In about 1586 Lodge sailed on a privateering expedition to the Terceras and the Canaries, and in 1591–3 to South America. On the earlier voyage he wrote his best-known romance *Rosalynde* (1590). He published *Phillis: Honoured with Pastorall Sonnets, Elegies, and amorous delights* (1593), including many poems adapted from Italian and French models, to which was appended 'The complaynt of Elstred', the story of the unhappy mistress of King *Locrine. *A fig for Momus* (1595) was a miscellaneous collection of satirical poems including epistles addressed to S. *Daniel and M. *Drayton. *A Margarite of America* (1596) was a remarkable romance written during his second voyage, under Thomas Cavendish, while they were near the Magellan Straits. He completed two major works of translation: *The Famous and Memorable Workes of Josephus* (1602) and *The Workes of Lucius Annaeus Seneca* (1614). Lodge is now mainly remembered for *Rosalynde* and for the lyrics scattered throughout his romances.

Loegria, see LOGRES.

LOFTING, Hugh, see CHILDREN'S LITERATURE.

Logic, A System of ratiocinative and inductive, a treatise by J. S. *Mill, published 1843, revised and enlarged in the editions of 1850 and 1872.

The importance of Mill's *Logic* lies in the fact that it supplied, to use the author's own words (*Autobiography*), 'a text-book of the opposite doctrine [to the *a priori* view of human knowledge put forward by the German school]—that which derives all knowledge from experience, and all moral and intellectual qualities principally from the direction given to the associations'. In this work Mill stressed the importance of inductive methods, while, unlike F. *Bacon, giving its proper share to deduction.

In attributing to experience and association our belief in mathematical and physical laws, he came into conflict with the intuitional philosophers, and gave his own explanation 'of that peculiar character of what are called necessary truths, which is adduced as proof that their evidence must come from a deeper source than experience'. This conflict with the intuitional school is further developed in Mill's *Examination of Sir William Hamilton's Philosophy.*

Logres, according to *Geoffrey of Monmouth's *History* (where it is called Loegria), the part of Brutus's kingdom assigned to his eldest son *Locrine, i.e. England. It is the usual term for Arthur's kingdom in medieval romance from

*Chrétien de Troyes onwards. Spenser calls it 'Logris' (*Faerie Queene*).

Logrin, see LOCRINE.

Logris, or Loegria, see LOGRES.

Lohengrin, the son of *Perceval. According to legend he is summoned from the temple of the *Grail at Montsalvatsch and borne in a swan-boat to Antwerp. He saves Princess Elsa of Brabant from Frederick of Telramund who wants to marry her against her wishes. Lohengrin will marry Elsa if she does not ask what his race is; but she does, and the swan-boat carries him back to the Grail castle. The story is the subject of *Wagner's opera (1850). In early forms of the legend the Knight of the Swan is called Helias (Helis in Icelandic).

Lolita, a novel by V. *Nabokov.

Lollards, from Dutch *lollaerd,* 'mumbler', applied to a heretical sect devoted to piety, implying pretentions to great virtue; it was borrowed in late 14th-cent. English to apply with the same connotations to the Wyclifites. See WYCLIF and OLDCASTLE.

LOLLIUS, an unknown author mentioned three times by Chaucer in connection with the Trojan War (*Troilus and Criseyde,* I. 394, v. 1,653, and *The House of Fame,* 1,468).

LOMBARD, Peter, see PETER LOMBARD.

London, a poem by Dr *Johnson, published anonymously 1738, in imitation of the Third Satire of *Juvenal. Thales (perhaps *Savage), disgusted with London, and about to leave for Wales, reflects on London's vices and affectations, and on the oppression of the poor—'All crimes are safe, but hated poverty.' Johnson attacks Sir R. *Walpole's administration and the poem's success was in part political.

LONDON, Jack (John) Griffith (1876–1916), American novelist. He grew up in poverty, scratching a living in various legal and illegal ways and taking part in the Klondike gold rush of 1897. His experiences provided the material for his works, and made him a socialist. *The Son of the Wolf* (1900), the first of his many collections of tales, is based upon life in the Far North, as is the book that brought him recognition, *The Call of the Wild* (1903), which tells the story of the dog Buck, who, after his master's death, is lured back to the primitive world to lead a wolf pack. Many other novels followed, including *The People of the Abyss* (1903), *The Sea-Wolf* (1904), *White Fang* (1906), *The Iron Heel* (1908), *South Sea Tales* (1911), *The Valley of the Moon* (1913), and *Jerry of the South Seas* (1917). The semi-

autobiographical *Martin Eden* (1909) describes the struggles of the protagonist, a sailor and labourer, to acquire education and to become a writer: he succeeds, spectacularly, only to find himself disillusioned with the world he has entered, and he drowns himself on the way to the South Seas. *John Barleycorn* (1913) is a record of London's own struggle against alcohol. He also wrote socialist treatises, autobiographical essays, and a good deal of journalism.

London, *Survey of,* see STOW.

London Cuckolds, The, a rollicking farce by Edward Ravenscroft (*fl.* 1671–97), which was produced in 1682 and annually revived on Lord Mayor's Day for nearly a century.

London Gazette, see under OXFORD GAZETTE.

London Library, The, was founded in 1840, largely at the instance of *Carlyle, with the support and encouragement of many eminent men of letters of the day, including *Gladstone, *Grote, H. *Hallam, and Mazzini. It opened on 3 May 1841, in two rooms in Pall Mall, and moved to its present premises in St James's Square in 1845.

London Magazine, The, (1) a periodical (1732–85) founded in opposition to the *Gentleman's Magazine*; (2) a magazine of great brilliance (1820–9), established under the editorship of John *Scott; it was non-political and gave a large proportion of its space to writers and books. Scott championed the work of the younger writers, including *Wordsworth, *Lamb, *De Quincey, *Clare, *Hood, *Carlyle, and in particular the *'Cockney School', *Keats, Leigh *Hunt, and *Hazlitt. But he was soon provoked into attacks on *Blackwood's,* and he was killed in a duel by a representative of that magazine. John *Taylor succeeded as editor with the assistance of Hood; (3) a monthly literary magazine founded in 1954 by J. *Lehmann, and edited by him until 1961. It was welcomed in its first issue by T. S. *Eliot as a non-university-based periodical that would 'boldly assume the existence of a public interested in serious literature'. Its distinguished contributors have included *MacNeice, E. *Waugh, R. *Fuller, *Auden, C. *Causley, D. *Walcott, G. *Ewart.

London Merchant, The, or *The History of George Barnwell,* see GEORGE BARNWELL.

London Mercury, The, a monthly literary periodical founded in 1919 by J. C. *Squire, who edited it until 1934, and used it in its early days as a vehicle to condemn *Modernism. Contributors included *de la Mare, *Chesterton, *Belloc, W. H. *Davies, *Yeats, and D. H. *Lawrence. In 1939 it was incorporated in *Life and Letters.

London Prodigal, The, a comedy published in 1605, attributed to Shakespeare in the title of the quarto edition of that year and included in the 3rd and 4th folios, but undoubtedly by some other hand.

The play is a comedy of London manners, and deals with the reclaiming of the prodigal young Flowerdale by the fidelity of his wife.

London Review of Books, a literary and cultural review founded in 1979 and edited by Karl Miller (1931–), in conscious emulation of the *New York Review of Books* (founded 1963). It has published critical essays and articles by many prominent critics and scholars, including Christopher Ricks, John Bayley, Frank Kermode, A. J. P. *Taylor, D. *Lodge, Sir Peter *Medawar, and Dan Jacobson, and has also published poetry and fiction.

Loneliness of the Long Distance Runner, The, a novella by A. *Sillitoe.

Longaville, in Shakespeare's *Love Labour's Lost,* one of the three lords attending on the king of Navarre.

Long Day's Journey into Night, see O'NEILL, E.

Longest Journey, The (1907), a novel by E. M. *Forster.

It describes the short, frustrated life of Rickie Elliot, born lame, a schoolmaster and an aspiring writer; the plot centres on his relationship with his healthy 'pagan' half-brother, Stephen Wonham. Rickie dies while saving Stephen's life.

LONGFELLOW, Henry Wadsworth (1807–82), American poet. In 1836 he began his many influential years of teaching at Harvard.

His prose romance *Hyperion* (1839), a product of his bereavement after the death of his first wife in 1835, is the tale of a young man who seeks to forget sorrow in travel; *Voices of the Night* (1839) includes his didactic pieces 'A Psalm of Life', 'Footsteps of Angels', and 'The Reaper and the Flowers'; *Ballads and other Poems* (1841) contains such well-known pieces as 'The Wreck of the Hesperus' and 'The Village Blacksmith'. In 1842 he met *Dickens in America, and visited him in London later in the same year; on his voyage home he wrote his *Poems on Slavery* (1842). In 1843 he married Frances Appleton. Subsequent volumes confirmed his reputation in the English-speaking world as second only to that of *Tennyson in popularity; these include *The Belfry of Bruges and other Poems* (1847); *Evangeline* (1849); *The Song of *Hiawatha* (1858); and *The Courtship of Miles Standish* (1858). *Tales of a Wayside Inn* (1863, first series; with the rousing 'Paul Revere's Ride' and 'The Song of King Olaf') follows the form of the *Canterbury Tales* and the *Decameron. An increased sombreness

may be seen in his translation of *Dante (1867) and his trilogy *Christus* (1872; incorporating the earlier *Golden Legend* of 1851), which he considered his masterpiece. Other 'Tales of a Wayside Inn' followed in 1872 (in *Three Books of Song*) and in 1874 (in *Aftermath*). His last volumes, *The Masque of Pandora* (1875), *Ultima Thule* (1880), and *In the Harbor* (1882) contain some poignant autumnal reflections on old age.

LONGFORD, Elizabeth, countess of (Elizabeth Pakenham, *née* Harman) (1906–), historian and biographer, educated at Oxford, whose works include *Victoria RI* (1964), *Wellington* (2 vols; 1969, 1972), a life of Wilfred Scawen *Blunt (1979), and biographies of Queen Elizabeth, the Queen Mother (1981), and Queen Elizabeth II (1983).

LONGINUS, the name bestowed by a scribe's error on the author of the Greek critical treatise περι υψους (On the Sublime) written probably in the 1st cent. AD. It locates the sources of poetic excellence in the profundity of the writer's emotions and the seriousness of his thought. The first English translation, by John Hall, appeared in 1652, but it was not until the appearance of *Boileau's French version (1674) and its influence on *Dryden that the concept of creative fire became popular. 'Longinus' had a marked effect on 18th-cent. critics and aestheticians. *Dennis, *Shaftesbury, and even *Pope were influenced by him. The cult of the *Sublime did much to prepare the way for *Romanticism.

Longinus ('Longeus' in Malory's *Morte D'Arthur*), the traditional name of the Roman soldier who pierced with his spear the side of Christ at the Crucifixion.

Long John Silver, a character in Stevenson's *Treasure Island.*

LONGMAN, Thomas (1699–1755), established the family firm of publishers still in existence as the Longman Group. The original Thomas had a share in the publication of *Johnson's Dictionary.*

Longman's Magazine (1882–1905), a family magazine, a successor to *Fraser's,* published short stories and serialized novels, poetry, and reviews. Contributors included A. *Dobson, G. *Allen, *Kipling, Mrs *Oliphant, *Newbolt, and *Hardy.

LONSDALE, Frederick (1881–1954), playwright, born Lionel Frederick Leonard, in St Helier, Jersey. His many witty and light-hearted drawing-room comedies include *Aren't We All?* (perf. 1923), *The Last of Mrs Cheyney* (1925), and *On Approval* (1927).

Look Back in Anger, a play by J. *Osborne, first produced by the *English Stage Company at the Royal Court Theatre on 8 May 1956, published 1957. It proved a landmark in the history of the theatre, a focus for reaction against a previous generation (see KITCHEN SINK DRAMA), and a decisive contribution to the corporate image of the *Angry Young Man.

The action takes place in a midlands town, in the one-room flat of Jimmy and Alison Porter, and centres on their marital conflicts, which appear to arise largely from Jimmy's sense of their social incompatibility: he is a jazz-playing ex-student from a 'white tile' university, she is a colonel's daughter. He is by turns violent, sentimental, maudlin, self-pitying, and sadistic, and has a fine line in rhetoric. The first act opens as Alison stands ironing the clothes of Jimmy and their lodger Cliff. In the second act Alison's friend Helena attempts to rescue her from her disastrous marriage; Alison departs with her father, and Helena falls into Jimmy's arms. The third act opens with Helena at the ironing board; Alison returns, having lost the baby she was expecting, and she and Jimmy find a manner of reconciliation through humiliation and games-playing fantasy.

Lord Jim, a novel by J. *Conrad, published 1900.

Jim is chief mate on board the *Patna*, an ill-manned ship carrying a party of pilgrims in Eastern waters. He is young, idealistic, and a dreamer of heroic deeds. When the *Patna* threatens to sink and the cowardly officers escape in the few lifeboats, Jim despises them, but dazed by the horror of the moment he joins them. The *Patna* does not sink and the pilgrims are rescued. What happens to Jim thereafter is related by an observer, Marlow. Jim, alone among the crew, remains to face the court of enquiry. Condemned by the court, he tries to disappear. Through Marlow's intervention Jim is sent to a remote trading station in Patusan. His efforts create order and well-being in a previously chaotic community and he wins the respect and affection of the people for whom he becomes Tuan—or Lord Jim. When Gentleman Brown and his gang of thieves arrive to plunder the village Jim begs the chiefs to spare them, pledging his own life against their departure. But Brown behaves treacherously and a massacre takes place. Jim feels he has only one course of action; rejecting the idea of flight he delivers himself up to Chief Doramin whose son was a victim of the massacre. Doramin shoots him and Jim willingly accepts this honourable death.

Lord of the Flies (1954), a novel by W. *Golding.

An aeroplane carrying a party of schoolboys crashes on a desert island. The boys' attempts, led by Ralph and Piggy, to set up a democrati-cally run society quickly fail. Terror rules under the dictator Jack, and two boys are killed; it is only with the arrival of a shocked rescue officer that a mask of civilization returns.

Lord of the Isles, The, a poem in six cantos by Sir W. *Scott, published 1815.

The poem, founded on the chronicles of the Bruce, deals with the return of Robert Bruce in 1307 to Scotland, and the period of his subsequent struggle against the English, culminating in the battle of Bannockburn.

Lord of the Rings, The, see TOLKIEN, J. R. R.

Lord Ormont and his Aminta, a novel by G. *Meredith, published 1894.

Lord Strutt, see JOHN BULL.

'Lord Ullin's Daughter', a ballad by T. *Campbell.

Lorenzo, (1) son of the duke of Castile in Kyd's *The Spanish Tragedy*; (2) the lover of *Jessica in Shakespeare's *The Merchant of Venice*.

Lorna Doone, a novel by R. D. *Blackmore, published 1869.

This celebrated story is set in the later 17th cent. on Exmoor, where an outlawed family, the Doones, and their retainers terrorize the surrounding countryside. They murder a farmer, father of the novel's hero, John Ridd. He secretly discovers the child Lorna, who has been kidnapped by the Doones, and they grow up to love each other. John Ridd, by now a giant in height and strength, is involved in adventures with the highwayman Tom Faggus, and in a rivalry with the villainous Carver Doone, from whom he rescues Lorna during a superbly described blizzard. The Doones are eventually destroyed, Lorna turns out not to be a Doone but an heiress of noble family, and she and John are married; but Carver Doone shoots her at the altar. John avenges her, she recovers, and the story ends happily. The infamous Judge Jeffreys plays a part in the action, and John Ridd and Tom Faggus are also based on historical characters.

LORRIS, Guillaume de, see ROMAN DE LA ROSE.

Lorry, Jarvis, a character in Dickens's *A Tale of Two Cities*.

Los, one of the principal characters in the symbolic books of *Blake, a complex and ambiguous figure, described in the opening of *The Song of Los* (1795) as 'the Eternal Prophet'. He is usually portrayed as the antagonist of *Urizen; in his role as blacksmith he is portrayed in *The Book of Los* (1795) binding Urizen in iron links forged in his glowing furnace, and in earlier poems of the cycle (and also in *The Four Zoas*) he binds his own son, the rebellious *Orc. He represents the artist, and also Time; his female counterpart is *Enitharmon (Inspiration, and Space); his periods of estrangement from her spell disaster for the universe. His character changes during the evolution of Blake's mythology, and he finally becomes in *Jerusalem a great heroic force of energy, while remaining morally ambiguous.

'Lost Leader, The', a poem by R. *Browning (1845) deploring *Wordsworth's political change of heart, and suggesting that he abandoned his radical views 'just for a handful of silver' and 'just for a riband to stick in his coat'.

Lot, king of Orkney in the Arthurian legends, the husband of Arthur's sister or half-sister *Morgawse. Their sons are *Gawain, Agravain, *Gareth, and *Gaheris, as well as *Modred in the earlier versions. (See PELLINORE.)

Lot, Parson, the pseudonym of C. *Kingsley.

Lothair, a novel by B. *Disraeli, published 1870.

Lothario, (1) the heartless libertine (proverbial as 'the Gay Lothario') in Rowe's *The Fair Penitent; (2) a character in the episode of The Curious Impertinent in *Don Quixote; (3) a character in *Goethe's *Wilhelm Meister.

Lousiad, The, a heroic-comic poem by J. *Wolcot (Peter Pindar), published 1785–95.

LOVE, Nicholas (fl. 1410), author before 1410 of *The Mirrour of the Blessed Lyf of Iesu Christ,* an accomplished prose translation of the Meditationes Vitae Christi attributed to Bonaventura.

Love à la Mode, a comedy by *Macklin, produced 1759.

Four suitors, an Englishman, an Irishman, a Scot, and a Jew, are rivals for the hand of the heroine. Their quality is tested by the pretence that she has lost her fortune. The play is famous for the characters of Sir Archy MacSarcasm and Sir Callaghan O'Brallaghan.

Loveday, John and Bob, brothers in Hardy's *The Trumpet Major.

Loved One, The, a novel by E. *Waugh.

Love for Love, a comedy by *Congreve, performed 1695.

Sir Sampson Legend offers his extravagant son Valentine £4,000 (only enough to pay his debts) if he will sign over his inheritance to his younger brother Ben. Valentine signs the bond. He is in love with Angelica, who possesses a fortune of her own. Sir Sampson has arranged a match between Ben, who is at sea, and Miss Prue, an awkward country girl, the daughter of Foresight, a superstitious old fool who claims to be an astrologer. Valentine pretends to be mad and unable to sign the final deed of conveyance to his brother. Finally Angelica intervenes. She induces Sir Sampson to propose marriage to her, and gets possession of Valentine's bond. Valentine, finding that Angelica is about to marry his father, generously declares himself ready to sign the conveyance in order to make her happy. She reveals the plot, tears up the bond, and declares her love for Valentine.

Love in a Tub, see COMICAL REVENGE, THE.

Lovel, (1) the name assumed by the hero in Scott's *The Antiquary; (2) the principal character in Townley's *High Life below Stairs.

Lovel the Widower, a story by *Thackeray, published in the *Cornhill Magazine, 1860.

LOVELACE, Richard (1618–57/8), heir to great estates in Kent, was a courtier, and served in the Scottish expeditions of 1639. Having presented a 'Kentish Petition' to the House of Commons in 1642, he was thrown into the Gatehouse prison, where he is supposed to have written the song 'To Althea'. He rejoined Charles I in 1645, and served with the French king in 1646. According to A. *Wood, his betrothed Lucy Sacheverell married another on a false report of his death. He was imprisoned again in 1648 and in prison prepared for the press his *Lucasta; Epodes, Odes, Sonnets, Songs etc.* which includes the well-known lyric 'On going to the wars'. He died in extreme poverty. Percy reprinted two of his lyrics in his *Reliques (1765), since when his reputation as a *Cavalier poet has steadily increased.

Lovelace, Robert, a character in Richardson's *Clarissa.

Lovell, Lord, a character in Massinger's *A New Way to pay Old Debts.

Love on the Dole, a novel by W. *Greenwood.

LOVER, Samuel (1797–1868), Irish painter, novelist, song-writer, is chiefly remembered for his ballad 'Rory O'More' and the novel developed from it in 1837 (later dramatized), which relates the tragic events in Ireland in 1798; for his Songs and Ballads (1839); his comic novel Handy Andy (1842); and Lyrics of Ireland (1858).

'Lover's Complaint, A', a poem in rhyme-royal appended to Shakespeare's *Sonnets (1609).

Lover's Melancholy, The, a romantic comedy by J. *Ford, printed 1629.

The conventional romantic plot is the framework for Ford's analysis of love melancholy, strongly influenced by Burton's *Anatomy of Melancholy*. The play contains some of Ford's purest poetry ('Minutes are numbered by the fall of sands, | As by an hourglass').

Lovers' Progress, The, a romantic drama by J. *Fletcher, produced 1623, revised 1634 as *The Wandering Lovers* by *Massinger, printed 1647.

Lovers' Vows, a play by Mrs *Inchbald, adapted from *Das Kind der Liebe* by Kotzebue, acted 1798. The play is chiefly of interest because of the place it occupies in the story of J. Austen's *Mansfield Park*.

Love's Labour's Lost, a comedy by *Shakespeare, probably written and performed about 1595, printed in quarto 1598. No major sources for it have been identified. It has often been felt to contain topical references (see SCHOOL OF NIGHT).

The king of Navarre and three of his lords have sworn for three years to keep from the sight of woman and to live studying and fasting. The arrival of the princess of France on an embassy, with her attendant ladies, obliges them 'of mere necessity' to disregard their vows. The king is soon in love with the princess, his lords with her ladies, and the courting proceeds amidst disguises and merriment, to which the other characters contribute: Don Adriano de Armado, the Spaniard, a master of extravagant language, Holofernes the schoolmaster, Dull the constable, Sir Nathaniel the curate, and Costard the clown. News of the death of the princess's father interrupts the wooing, and the ladies impose a year's ordeal on their lovers. The play ends with the beautiful owl and cuckoo song, 'When icicles hang by the wall'.

Loves of the Angels, The, a poem by T. *Moore, published 1823.

The poem, founded on the *oriental tale of Harût and Marût and certain rabbinical fictions, recounts the loves of three fallen angels for mortal women, and illustrates the decline of the soul from purity.

This was Moore's last long poem, and it enjoyed great popularity as well as provoking much stricture.

Loves of the Plants, The, see DARWIN, E.

'Loves of the Triangles, The', a clever parody by G. *Canning and J. H. *Frere in *The Anti-Jacobin* in 1798 of E. *Darwin's The Loves of the Plants.

Love's Sacrifice, a tragedy by J. *Ford, printed 1633.

Loving, a novel by H. *Green.

LOWELL, Amy Lawrence (1874–1925), American poet, took up *Imagism and in 1913 and 1914 visited England, where she met *Pound, D. H. *Lawrence, and 'H.D.' (Hilda *Doolittle). Her volumes of verse, which include *Sword Blades and Poppy Seed* (1914), *Men, Women and Ghosts* (1916), and *Can Grande's Castle* (1918), show her experiments in what she called 'polyphonic prose'. She became well known as a public figure, vast and cigar-smoking, through her lectures and readings in America.

LOWELL, James Russell (1819–91), born in Cambridge, Massachusetts, was American minister in Spain, 1877–80, and in England, 1880–5. He was editor of the *Atlantic Monthly* in 1857. His works include several volumes of verse, the satirical *Biglow Papers* (1848 and 1867, prose and verse), and memorial odes after the Civil War; and various volumes of essays.

LOWELL, Robert Traill Spence (1917–77), American poet, became a fanatical convert to Roman Catholicism: his first volume of verse, *Land of Unlikeness* (1944), betrays the conflict of Catholicism and his Boston ancestry. His second volume, *Lord Weary's Castle* (1946), which contains 'The Quaker Graveyard in Nantucket' and 'Mr Edwards and the Spider', was hailed in extravagant terms. *The Mills of the Kavanaughs* (1951) has as its title poem a meditation by a Catholic widow, Anne Kavanaugh, reflecting on the past in her ancestral home in Maine; this was followed by *Life Studies* (1959), *For the Union Dead* (1964), *Near the Ocean* (1967), and volumes of translation, plays, etc. He reached the height of his public fame during his opposition to the Vietnam war, but he had long been suffering bouts of manic illness and heavy drinking, and a visit to Britain in 1970 increased the disorder of his private life. His highly personal, confessional volume of poetry *The Dolphin* (1973) caused scandal with its revelations of marital anguish and discord. (Lowell had married three times.) *Day by Day*, a last collection, was published just before his death.

LOWES, John L(ivingstone) (1867–1945), is best known for three of his books: *Convention and Revolt in Poetry* (1919); his brilliant study of *Coleridge, *The Road to Xanadu* (1927); and *The Art of Geoffrey Chaucer* (1931). He is a greatly admired critic of 14th-cent. English, especially *Chaucer.

LOWRY, (Clarence) Malcolm (1909–57), novelist. Under the influence of *Melville, *O'Neill, *Conrad, and Jack *London he went to sea on leaving school, travelling to the Far East, then returned to take a degree at Cambridge. In 1933 he published *Ultramarine*, which shows a considerable debt to *Blue Voyage* by his friend *Aiken, in whose autobiography *Ushant* (1952) he was to appear as Hambro. He travelled widely in Europe and the US, settling in Mexico where he worked on *Under the Volcano* (1947). He was a chronic alcoholic, as are many of his characters. His posthumous publications include: *Hear Us O Lord from Heaven Thy Dwelling Place* (1961), *Selected Poems*, ed. Earle Birney and M. B. Lowry (1962), *Dark as the Grave Wherein my Friend is Laid* (1968), and *October Ferry to Gabriola* (1970).

Loyal Subject, The, a drama by J. *Fletcher, produced 1618.

LUBBOCK, Percy (1879–1965), critic and biographer, whose works include *Earlham* (1922), an account of his own Norfolk childhood holidays; *Roman Pictures* (1923), which describes an English tourist's responses to Rome; *Shades of Eton* (1923), recollections of his schooldays; and *Portrait of Edith Wharton* (1947). He edited a selection of H. *James's letters (1920); also a selection from A. C. *Benson's diary (1926). His *The Craft of Fiction* (1921) analyses the techniques of *Tolstoy, *Flaubert, James, etc.

LUCAN (Marcus Annaeus Lucanus) (AD 39–65), a Roman poet of Spanish origin, the nephew of *Seneca. His only surviving work is the *Pharsalia* (or the *Bellum Civile*), a historical epic in 10 books about the Civil Wars, which shows a remarkable skill in the depiction of character and a mastery of epigram, but he set no limits on his unruly imagination and liking for bombast. The worst features of his style had an influence on the so-called Senecan drama of the 16th cent. There are important translations by A. *Gorges, T. *May, and N. *Rowe.

LUCAS, E(dward) V(errall) (1868–1938), journalist and essayist. His works include biographies, novels, and romances (such as *Over Bemerton's*, 1908, set over an antiquarian bookshop); he edited the works and letters of Charles and Mary *Lamb (1903–35) and many popular anthologies, contributed to *Punch, and was a member of its staff for some time.

LUCAS, F(rank) L(aurence) (1894–1967), scholar, critic, and poet. His critical works include *Tragedy in Relation to Aristotle's Poetics* (1927) and *The Decline and Fall of the Romantic Ideal* (1936), and he edited an edition of J. *Webster (4 vols, 1927). He also published several volumes of verse and translations from the classics, and edited various anthologies.

Lucasta, see LOVELACE, R.

Lucentio, in Shakespeare's *The Taming of the Shrew*, the successful suitor of *Bianca.

LUCIAN OF SAMOSATA (AD *c.*125–*c.*200), Greek writer of prose satires. Many of his works

are dialogues where mythical or historical figures are placed in ridiculous situations, and the contrast between their traditional dignity and what they are made to say or do becomes a fruitful source of irony. His most influential work was *The True History* which claimed to describe a visit to the moon and inspired a long series of imaginary voyages from J. *Hall's *Mundus alter et idem* (1605) to S. Butler's *Erewhon* (1872), Swift's *Gulliver's Travels* being the most eminent example of the genre.

Lucifera, in Spenser's *Faerie Queene* (I. iv. 12), the symbol of baseless pride and worldliness.

Lucius, (1) a mythical king of Britain, supposed to have been the first to receive Christianity: see Spenser, *The Faerie Queene* (II. x. 53); (2) Lucius (Iberius) is the Roman Emperor who demands tribute from King Arthur who makes war on Rome; in Malory's *Morte D'Arthur* he is slain by Arthur, in other versions by Gawain. In *Geoffrey of Monmouth's *History* he is slain by an unknown hand. (3) Brutus's page in Shakespeare's *Julius Caesar*; (4) a character in his *Timon of Athens*; (5) a character in his *Titus Andronicus*; (6) in his *Cymbeline*, Caius Lucius is 'General of the Roman Forces'.

Luck of Barry Lyndon, The, a satirical novel by *Thackeray, published in *Fraser's Magazine* 1844, republished under the title *The Memoirs of Barry Lyndon, Esquire, by Himself* (1852, New York).

Redmond Barry flees from Ireland after a duel, wrongly believing he has killed his opponent. He serves in the Seven Years War, first in the English, then in the Prussian, army. He is set to spy upon the Chevalier de Balibari, who turns out to be his uncle Cornelius Barry. The two set up as card-sharpers, and Barry becomes a successful gambler and man of fashion. He marries the wealthy countess of Lyndon, and takes her name. He spends her fortune and ill-treats her and her son, showing affection only to his old mother and his own son Bryan, whom he indulges until the boy is killed in a riding accident. Finally the countess, with the help of her son Viscount Bullingdon, is released from Barry's hold over her. Barry is left penniless after the countess's death and ends his life miserably in the Fleet Prison.

Lucky Jim, a novel by K. *Amis.

Lucrece, *The Rape of,* see RAPE OF LUCRECE, THE.

Lucretia, or **Lucrece,** a celebrated Roman lady, daughter of Lucretius and wife of Tarquinius Collatinus, whose beauty inflamed the passion of Sextus (son of Tarquin, king of Rome), which he used threats and violence to satisfy. Lucretia, after informing her father and husband of what had passed, took her own life. The outrage committed by Sextus, coupled with the oppression of the king, led to the expulsion of the Tarquins from Rome, and the introduction of republican government. See also RAPE OF LUCRECE.

LUCRETIUS, Titus Lucretius Carus (probably *c.*99–55 BC), Roman poet. His chief work is a philosophical poem in hexameters, in six books, *De Reum Naturâ.* He adopts the atomic theory of the universe of *Epicurus, and seeks to show that the course of the world can be explained without resorting to divine intervention, his object being to free mankind from terror of the gods. The work is marked by passages of great poetical beauty. Echoes of Lucretius can be found in *Spenser, *Hobbes, *Dryden, and *Shelley; but the only major poem inspired by his work is *Tennyson's 'Lucretius' (1869).

Lucy and Colin, a *ballad by T. *Tickell.

Lucy Poems, The, name given to a group of poems by *Wordsworth. 'She dwelt among the untrodden ways', 'Strange fits of passion have I known', 'A slumber did my spirit seal', 'Three years she grew in sun and shower', were published in the *Lyrical Ballads of 1800. A fifth poem, 'I travelled among unknown men', was published in 1807. The poems are remarkable for their lyric intensity and purity, and the identity of Lucy has aroused much speculation.

Lucy Snowe, the narrator of *Villette.*

Lud, a mythical king of Britain, according to *Geoffrey of Monmouth's *History,* eldest brother of *Cassivelaunus. He built walls around the city of Brutus (Trinovantum) and renamed it Caerlud (Lud's city) from which derives its modern name London.

Luddites, a band of English craftsmen and labourers, organized 1811–16, who felt their livelihoods threatened by machinery and set about its destruction. The name is said to have come from Ned Ludd, who lived about 1779. Luddites appear in *Shirley by C. Brontë, and *Byron wrote 'A Song for the Luddites'. The term is now commonly applied to any person who resists technological change.

Ludus Coventriae, see MYSTERY PLAYS.

Lugh, see TUATHA DÉ DANANN.

LUKÁCS, Georg (1885–1971), Hungarian Marxist philosopher and literary critic. Lukács's critical works include the early, pre-Marxist *The Theory of the Novel* (1920, trans. 1971), in which he describes the novel as a 'bourgeois epic' in which the alienated, solitary hero is in constant conflict with his environment; *History and Class Consciousness* (1923; English trans. 1971), his major Marxist theoretical work; *The Historical Novel* (written 1936–7, first published in Russian, English trans. 1962), which analyses the growth of historical awareness in the novelist, relating it to the change in European consciousness that followed the French revolution (with particular emphasis on Sir W. *Scott); and *The Meaning of Contemporary Realism* (1958, trans. 1969), in which Lukács attempts to account for the Modernists (*Joyce, *Kafka, *Beckett, etc.) and argues that the artist has a duty to do more than mirror the despair and futility of bourgeois society. His large output also includes works on *Hegel, *Goethe, Russian and German Realism, aesthetics, etc. Despite ideological shifts, Lukács's emphasis is throughout on the ethical rather than the formal properties of literature; his admiration for the great 19th-cent. masters (*Balzac, Stendahl, *Tolstoy) leads him to see them as writers who transcend their class bias to produce works of art which are a harmonious totality, reconciling all contradictions. It also leads him to reject experimentalism, in conformity with the doctrine of *socialist realism.

Lumpkin, Tony, a character in Goldsmith's *She Stoops to Conquer.*

Luria, a tragedy in blank verse by R. *Browning, published 1846, together with *A Soul's Tragedy,* as no. VIII of *Bells and Pomegranates.* It is set in the 15th cent. during the conflict between Florence and Pisa, though the actual episode is unhistorical.

LURIE, Alison (1926–   ), American novelist. Her sharply satiric and observant novels include *Love and Friendship* (1962); *Imaginary Friends* (1967); *The War Between the Tates* (1974), a *campus novel; and *Foreign Affairs* (1984), which is set in England, seen through American eyes.

Lussurioso, a character in *The Revenger's Tragedy.*

LUTHER, Martin (1483–1546), the leader of the Reformation in Germany, entered the Augustinian order. As a monk he visited Rome and his experience of the corruption in high ecclesiastical places influenced his future career. He attacked the principle of papal indulgences by nailing his famous Theses to the door of the church at Wittenberg, and as a consequence the papal ban was pronounced on him (1521) at the Diet of Worms. He left the monastic order and married, and devoted himself to forming the League of Protestantism. His chief literary work, apart from polemical treatises, was his translation into German of the Old and New

Testaments, known as the Lutheran Bible (1534; portions had appeared earlier).

Luther's power lay in his hymns of joy and strength and in his revival of the doctrine of justification by the faith of the individual, implying religious liberty and attacking the scandal of indulgences.

He is the subject of a play by J. *Osborne, *Luther* (1961).

LUTTRELL, Henry (?1765–1851), wit and member of the *Holland House circle, was author of clever and lively verses, including *Advice to Julia*, admired by *Byron.

Luve Ron, or 'the Love Song', traditionally but wrongly called 'the Love Rune', a mystical love-poem in 210 lines by the Franciscan Thomas de Hales, written probably in the second quarter of the 13th cent. It describes to a young woman novice the love of Christ and the joy of mystical union with him.

LYALL, Edna, the pseudonym of Ada Ellen Bayly (1857–1903), novelist and supporter of political liberal causes including women's emancipation. She admired *Bradlaugh, whose life is vaguely reflected in her first success, *We Two* (1884), the sequel to *Donovan* (1882). Her other novels include *In the Golden Days* (1885), which was the last book to be read to *Ruskin on his deathbed, and *Doreen* (1895), which strongly states the case for Home Rule for Ireland.

Lycidas, a poem by *Milton, written 1637, published 1638. It is a pastoral elegy on the death of Edward King, a fellow student of Christ's College, Cambridge, though not, it would appear, a close friend of Milton. Like Milton himself, he had aspirations as a poet and as a clergyman. He was drowned while crossing from Chester Bay to Dublin, his ship having struck a rock and foundered in calm weather. Milton, in lamenting his premature death and the uncertainty of life, suggests deep anxieties about his own ambitions and unfulfilled promise. It is one of the finest elegies in the English language, and a work of great originality.

LYDGATE, John (?1370–1449), spent nearly all his life in the monastery at Bury. He is one of the most voluminous of all English poets. Of his more readable poems, most were written in the first decade of the 15th cent. in a Chaucerian vein: *The Complaint of the Black Knight* (originally called *A Complaynt of a Loveres Lyfe* and modelled on Chaucer's *The Book of the Duchess*); *The Temple of Glas* (indebted to *The House of Fame*); *The Floure of Curtesy* (a Valentine's Day poem); and the allegorical *Reason and Sensuality*. As he grew older his poems became longer. His bulkiest works are his *Troy Book* (1412–20), a 30,000-line translation of *Guido

delle Colonne; *The Siege of Thebes* (1420–2), translated from a French prose redaction of the *Roman de Thebes*; *The Pilgrimage of Man* (1426–30), translated from Deguileville; and *The Fall of Princes* (1431–8), a translation of a French version of *Boccaccio's *De Casibus Virorum Illustrium*. He was almost invariably coupled for praise with *Chaucer and *Gower up to the 17th cent.

Lydgate, Tertius, a character in G. Eliot's *Middlemarch*.

Lyle, Annot, a character in Scott's *A Legend of Montrose*.

LYLY, John (?1554–1606), grandson of W. *Lily. He was MP successively for Hindon, Aylesbury, and Appleby (1598–1601), and supported the cause of the bishops in the *Martin Marprelate controversy in a satirical pamphlet, *Pappe with an Hatchet* (1589). The first part of his *Euphues. The Anatomy of Wit appeared in 1578, and the second part, *Euphues and his England*, in 1580. Its peculiar style came to be known as 'Euphuism'. Among Lyly's plays are *Alexander, Campaspe and Diogenes* (see under CAMPASPE); *Sapho and Phao* (1584); *Endimion* (1591); *Midas* (1592); *Mother Bombie* (1594, see under BUMBY). The attractive songs in the plays were first printed in Blount's collected edition of 1632.

LYNDSAY, Sir David, see LINDSAY, SIR D.

Lynet (also Linet, Lunet, or the *Saveage Damsel*), in Malory's *Morte D'Arthur*, the sister of the lady *Lyones who brings Gareth to fight Ironsyde, liberating Lyones who marries Gareth. See GARETH AND LYNETTE.

Lyones (also Liones and, in Malory's *Morte D'Arthur*, Lyonesse), (1) the sister of *Lynet, imprisoned by Ironsyde in the Castle Perilous and freed by *Gareth whom she marries; (2) in Malory, the region of origin of Tristram; *Tennyson makes it the place of the last battle between Arthur and Mordred. It is traditionally said to be a tract of land between the Isles of Scilly and Land's End, now submerged.

Lyra Apostolica, a collection of 179 sacred poems, published 1836, contributed originally to the *British Magazine*. The poems appeared anonymously; the six authors, all associated with the *Oxford Movement, were each designated by a Greek letter: J. W. Bowden (α), R. H. *Froude (β), *Keble (γ), *Newman (δ), R. I. Wilberforce (ε), and I. *Williams (ζ).

Lyric, Lyric Poetry, derived from the name given in ancient Greece to verses sung to a lyre, whether as a solo performance (*Sappho) or by a choir (*Pindar). The Greek lyrists were then imitated in Latin at an artistic level by *Catullus and *Horace. The tradition of popular song which existed both in Rome and among the German tribes was important for the development of the genre, which continued to flourish and produced in all the medieval literatures of Western Europe a lyric harvest that ranged from hymns to bawdy drinking songs. In England lyric poems flourished in the Middle English period (in such manuscript collections as the *Harley Lyrics), and in the 16th cent. this lyric tradition was enriched by the direct imitation of ancient models and reached perfection in the song-books and plays of the Elizabethan age. During the next 200 years the link between poetry and music was gradually broken, and the term 'lyric' came to be applied to short poems expressive of a poet's thoughts or feelings and as such reached the high point of its popularity in the Romantic period.

Lyrical Ballads, *with a few other Poems,* a collection of poems by *Wordsworth and *Coleridge, of which the first edition appeared 1798, the second with new poems and a preface (known as the 1800 edition) Jan. 1801, and a third 1802.

The book was a landmark of English *Romanticism and the beginning of a new age. Coleridge's contributions to the first edition were *The Rime of the *Ancient Mariner*, 'The Foster-Mother's Tale', 'The Nightingale', and 'The Dungeon'; Wordsworth's include ballads and narratives such as 'The Thorn', *'The Idiot Boy', and 'Simon Lee, the old Huntsman', and more personal poems such as 'Lines written in early spring' and 'Lines written a few miles above *Tintern Abbey'. They appeared with a brief 'Advertisement' by Wordsworth, stating his theory of *poetic diction and attacking the 'gaudy and inane phraseology of many modern writers'; his views were much expanded in his important Preface to the second edition, and enlarged again in 1802. The poems themselves, with their 'low' subjects and language and their alleged banality and repetitions, were subjected to much ridicule. The second volume of the second edition added many of Wordsworth's most characteristic works, including the so-called *'Lucy poems', 'The Old Cumberland Beggar', and *'Michael, a Pastoral'.

Lysander, a character in Shakespeare's *A Midsummer Night's Dream.

LYTTELTON, George, first baron Lyttelton (1709–73), a prominent politician, and an opponent of Sir R. *Walpole, was also a friend of *Pope, *Shenstone, and *Fielding, and a liberal patron of literature. It is he whom Thomson addresses in *The Seasons and who procured the poet a pension. He published, among numerous works, Dialogues of the Dead (1760), and a history of Henry II (1767–71). Of the Dialogues, the last three were by Mrs *Montagu. He was caricatured by Smollett as Scragg in *Peregrine Pickle.

LYTTON, Edward Earle Lytton Bulwer-, see BULWER-LYTTON.

LYTTON, Edward Robert Bulwer, first earl of Lytton (1831–91), son of E. *Bulwer-Lytton, became viceroy of India (1876–80), where his 'Forward' policy aroused much opposition. He published several volumes of verse, at first under the pseudonym 'Owen Meredith'. Clytemnestra, The Earl's Return, The Artist and other Poems (1855) was followed by The Wanderer (1858). His later volumes, which include King Poppy (1875), are marred by prolixity and facile versification.

M

Mab, Queen, see QUEEN MAB.

MABBE, James (1572–?1642), is remembered for his translations of Fernando de Rojas's *Celestina* and of *The Spanish Ladye*, one of *Cervantes's 'Exemplary Novels'. Mabbe Hispanicized his name as 'Puedeser' (may-be).

Mabinogion, The, strictly, the first four Welsh tales contained in the collection of Lady Charlotte Guest, made in 1838–49. The four are preserved in two Welsh manuscripts: The White Book of Rhydderch (1300–25) and The Red Book of Hergest (1375–1425). Their subjects are (1) Pwyll, the father of Pryderi; (2) Branwen, the daughter of Llyr; (3) Manawyddan, the son of Llyr; (4) the death of Pryderi in battle with the nephews of Math. There is no mention of *Arthur in these four branches of the Mabinogion proper; but five of the other seven tales published by Guest from The Red Book of Hergest deal indirectly with him: 'The Lady of the Fountain'; 'Peredur'; 'Gereint', three romances from French originals; 'Culhwch and Olwen'; and 'The Dream of Rhonabwy'.

Macabre, Dance, see DANCE OF DEATH.

Macaronic verse, a burlesque form of verse in which vernacular words are introduced into a Latin context with Latin terminations and in Latin constructions . . . and *loosely*, any form of verse in which two or more languages are mingled together.

M'Aulay, Angus and Allan, characters in Scott's *A Legend of Montrose*.

MACAULAY, Dame (Emilie) Rose (1881–1958), novelist, essayist, and travel writer, whose many works include *Potterism* (1920), *They were Defeated* (1932), both fiction, and *Pleasures of Ruins* (1953). Her best-known novels, *The World my Wilderness* (1950) and *The Towers of Trebizond* (1956), appeared after a decade in which she wrote no fiction, and followed her return to the Anglican faith.

MACAULAY, Thomas Babington (1800–59), politician and historian, son of the noted philanthropist and reformer Zachary Macaulay. His essay on *Milton for the *Edinburgh Review* in August 1825 brought him instant fame, and for the next 20 years he wrote numerous articles on

historical and literary topics for the *Review*, becoming one of the acknowledged intellectual pundits of the age (see ESSAYS CONTRIBUTED TO THE EDINBURGH REVIEW). In 1830 he became a Whig Member of Parliament and took an active part in the passing of the Reform Bill. But in 1834 he accepted a place on the Supreme Council of India, where his famous Minutes on Law and Education had a decisive influence on the development of the subcontinent. On his return in 1838 he was a secretary at war, 1839–41, and paymaster-general, 1846–7. He published *Lays of Ancient Rome* (1842), which like *Essays Critical and Historical* (1834) sold steadily down the century. His *History of England* (vols 1–2, 1849; vols 3–4, 1855) was deeply researched; its purpose was to demonstrate that revolution on the continental model was unnecessary in England because of the statesmanlike precautions taken in 1688. He used a wide range of manuscript sources with great skill; it is still the most detailed factual account, for instance, of the reign of James II. He also affected an interest in social history, though this was focused on his superficial and discredited Chapter III, on 'The Condition of England in 1685'. He acknowledged a great debt to Sir W. *Scott. His descriptive power was one of his great assets; another was the narrative momentum he was able to achieve. The *History* brought him great wealth, and a peerage.

He was the subject of one of the best Victorian biographies, by his nephew, Sir G. O. *Trevelyan (1876). His letters have been edited by Thomas Pinney (5 vols, 1974–80).

Macaulay's History of England, see under MACAULAY, T. B.

Macbeth, a tragedy by *Shakespeare, first printed in the First *Folio of 1623, probably written and first performed in 1606. The text has often been thought to contain some non-Shakespearian material, possibly by *Middleton. Two songs certainly by him were added to the play.

Macbeth and Banquo, generals of Duncan, king of Scotland, returning from a victorious campaign against rebels, encounter three weird sisters, or witches, upon a heath, who prophesy that Macbeth shall be thane of Cawdor, and king hereafter, and that Banquo shall beget kings though he be none. Immediately afterwards comes the news that the king had created Macbeth thane of Cawdor. Stimulated by the prophecy, and spurred on by Lady Macbeth, Macbeth murders Duncan, who is on a visit to his castle. Duncan's sons, Malcolm and Donalbain, escape, and Macbeth assumes the crown. To defeat the prophecy of the witches regarding Banquo, he orders the murder of Banquo and his son Fleance, but the latter escapes. Haunted by the ghost of Banquo, Macbeth consults the weird sisters, and is told to beware of Macduff, the thane of Fife; that none born of woman has power to harm Macbeth; and that he never will be vanquished till Birnam Wood shall come to Dunsinane. Learning that Macduff has joined Malcolm, who is gathering an army in England, he surprises the castle of Macduff and causes Lady Macduff and her children to be slaughtered. Lady Macbeth goes mad and dies. The army of Malcolm and Macduff attacks Macbeth; passing through Birnam Wood every man cuts a bough and under these 'leavy screens' marches on Dunsinane. Macduff, who was 'from his mother's womb | Untimely ripp'd', kills Macbeth. Malcolm is hailed king of Scotland.

Macbeth, Lady, ambitious wife of Macbeth in Shakespeare's play; L. C. *Knights's essay 'How many children had Lady Macbeth?' (1933) is a teasing riposte to the sort of biographical speculation favoured by A. C. *Bradley.

MacBETH, George Mann (1932–), poet, was a member of the *Group during the 1950s and in the 1960s was associated with the vogue for poetry in performance. His early work was experimental and at times macabre and violent in its preoccupations; later collections show (in his own words) fewer 'comic and performance and experimental elements' (foreword to *Poems from Oby*, 1982). His works include *A Form of Words* (1954), *The Colour of Blood* (1967), and *Collected Poems 1958–1970* (1971).

MacCAIG, Norman Alexander (1910–), Scottish poet. His first volume of poetry, *Far Cry* (1943), was followed by many others which include *Measures* (1965), *Rings on a Tree* (1968), and *A Man in My Position* (1969). His *Selected Poems* appeared in 1971, and he also edited two anthologies of Scottish poetry. Much of his own poetry is inspired by the landscapes of the West Highlands and the life of Edinburgh.

MacCARTHY, Sir (Charles Otto) Desmond (1877–1952), journalist, editor, and associate of the *Bloomsbury Group, is remembered largely for his perceptive theatre criticism, some of it collected in *The Court Theatre, 1904–7* (1907), *Drama* (1940), and *Shaw* (1951).

McCARTHY, Mary (1912–), American novelist, short story writer, and critic; orphaned at the age of six, she was raised by various relatives of Catholic, Jewish, and Protestant backgrounds, a mixture that she describes in *Memoirs of a Catholic Girlhood* (1957). Her first novel, *The Company she Keeps* (1942), is a portrait of a Bohemian intellectual; *The Groves of Academe* (1952) is a satirical *campus novel set in the McCarthy period; and *The Oasis* (1949, London 1950, as *A Source of Embarrassment*) describes the failure of a New England Utopia. *Cast a Cold Eye* (1950, short stories) and *A Charmed Life* (1955, novel) were followed by *The Group* (1963), a study of the lives and careers of eight Vassar girls, which caused some stir when published in England because of its frank and amusing descriptions of contraception, breast-feeding, and other gynaecological matters. Two volumes of reportage, *Vietnam* (1967) and *Hanoi* (1968), protesting against American involvement in Vietnam, were followed by two novels, *Birds of America* (1971) and *Cannibals and Missionaries* (1980). She has also published several volumes of essays and criticism. Her second husband was Edmund *Wilson.

McCULLERS, Carson Smith (1917–67), American novelist and short story writer. Her works include *The Heart is a Lonely Hunter* (1940), *Reflections in a Golden Eye* (1941), *The Member of the Wedding* (1946, dramatized by the author, 1950), and a collection, *The Ballad of the Sad Café* (1941). Her work is frequently tinged with the macabre.

MacDIARMID, Hugh, the pseudonym of Christopher Murray Grieve (1892–1978), poet and critic, was a founder (in 1928) of the National Party of Scotland, but was expelled in 1933; he joined (1934) the Communist party from which he was expelled in 1938. In 1922, influenced by *Ulysses, he began to write lyrics in a Synthetic Scots that drew on various dialects and fortified the oral idiom with archaisms. His masterpiece, *A Drunk Man Looks at the Thistle* (1926), presents a vision that remakes Scotland in the MacDiarmidian image; a drunk man comes to consciousness on a hillside and has to contend with the huge thistle that confronts him symbolically in the moonlight; the alcoholic spirit wears off and is replaced by a spiritual awareness of what Scotland can be. MacDiarmid's Scots literary renaissance of the 1920s was followed by his political poetry of the 1930s; in 1931 he published his *First Hymn to Lenin* and thereby initiated the leftist verse of the decade. His autobiography *Lucky Poet* (1943) deeply offended the officials of his native Langholm. MacDiarmid scored some of his greatest poetic triumphs in English, albeit a Synthetic English. His long meditative poem 'On a Raised Beach', from *Stony Limits* (1934), is a subtle statement of the MacDiarmidian metaphysic: 'I will have nothing interposed | Between my sensitiveness and the barren but beautiful reality.' His later work comprises a series of long, linguistically dense poems amounting to a modern epic of the Celtic consciousness. MacDiarmid's *Complete Poems 1920–1976*, edited by Michael Grieve and W. R. Aitken, appeared (posthumously) in 1978 and his letters were edited (1984) by A. Bold. (See also SCOTS.)

MacDONALD, George (1824–1905), was, in his own day, celebrated chiefly as poet, preacher, and lecturer, and as the author of numerous novels, including *David Elginbrod* (1863), *Alec Forbes of Howglen* (1865), and *Robert Falconer* (1868), often with banal melodramatic plots and cardboard villains, but illuminated by compassionate affection for humanity and nature. The Scottish setting of his best novels helped to found the *'Kailyard School' of fiction. MacDonald is now best known for his children's stories, including *At the Back of the North Wind* (1871) and *The Princess and the Goblin* (1872), and for his two allegorical fantasies for adults, *Phantastes* (1858) and *Lilith* (1895).

Macduff and Lady Macduff, characters in Shakespeare's *Macbeth*.

MacFlecknoe, or *A Satyr upon the True-Blew-Protestant Poet, T. S.*, a poem by *Dryden (1682; definitive edn, 1684).

The outcome of a series of disagreements, between Dryden and *Shadwell, the poem represents the latter as heir to the kingdom of poetic dullness, currently governed by the minor writer *Flecknoe. It brilliantly exploits the crudity of Shadwell's farces (notably *The Virtuoso*) and critical writings; while the range of its allusions to 17th-cent. theatre demonstrates the complexity of Dryden's critical thought and, since he satirizes his own work (notably *Tyrannick Love*) as well as Shadwell's, his humility towards the tradition in which he was working.

McGONAGALL, William (1825 or 1830–1902), the son of an Irish weaver, attracted a certain following in Edinburgh with his readings in public houses and his broadsheets of topical verse. His naïve and unscanned doggerel continues to entertain, and he now enjoys a reputation as the world's worst poet.

McGOUGH, Roger (1937–), poet and songwriter, and a member of the group known as the *Liverpool poets. His publications include *Watchwords* (1969), *Gig* (1972), and *Sky in the Pie* (1983).

Macgregor, Rob Roy and Helen, see ROB ROY.

MACHAUT, Guillaume de, see GUILLAUME DE MACHAUT.

Macheath, Captain, the hero of Gay's *The Beggar's Opera*.

MACHEN, Arthur Llewellyn (1863–1947), son of a Welsh clergyman, was deeply influenced by the Welsh landscape, and local folklore. He translated *The Heptameron* (1886) and *The Memoirs of Casanova* (1894) and began writing the mystic, supernatural tales of evil and horror for which he is best remembered. They include *The Great God Pan* (1894), *The Hill of Dreams* (1907), and *The Three Impostors* (1895). Other works include *Hieroglyphics* (1902, criticism); and *Far off Things* (1922) and *Things Near and Far* (1923), both autobiographical.

MACHEREY, Pierre, see MARXIST LITERARY CRITICISM.

MACHIAVELLI, Niccolò (1469–1527), a Florentine statesman and political theorist. After holding office in the restored Florentine republic and discharging various missions abroad, he was exiled on suspicion of conspiracy against the Medici, but was subsequently restored to some degree of favour. He turned his experience to advantage in his writings, which include *Arte della guerra* (*The art of war*, written 1517–20, English trans. 1560–2) and a history of Florence (*Storie Fiorentine*, 1520–5, trans. 1595). His comedy *Mandragola*, probably written in 1518, is a powerful satire. His best-known work was *Il Principe* (*The Prince*, written in 1513), a treatise on statecraft by an acute observer of the contemporary political scene with an idealistic vision of an Italian saviour who should expel all foreign usurpers. He teaches that the lessons of the past (of Roman history in particular) should be applied to the present, and that the acquisition and effective use of power may necessitate unethical methods not in themselves desirable. The first public translation was that of Edward Dacres in 1640. *Il Principe* influenced the policy of Thomas *Cromwell, Cecil, and Leicester. It was appreciated critically by F. *Bacon; exploited intelligently by *Marlowe; used guardedly in the Maxims of State attributed to *Ralegh, and published posthumously in 1658 as *The Cabinet-Council*.

In Elizabethan and Jacobean drama, Machiavellian villains and anti-heroes abound, appearing in many guises, as pandar, atheist, poisoner, politician, miser, and revenger, and the name of Machiavelli himself is frequently invoked: for example by Gloucester, who resolved in *3 *Henry VI* 'to set the murtherous Machiavel to school' (III. iii. 193), by Flamineo in *The White Devil*, who rejoices in 'the rare tricks of a Machivillian' (v. iii. 196), and in the prologue to *The Jew of Malta* by the spirit of Machiavelli himself. There is a sketch of his character in G. Eliot's *Romola. The New Machiavelli* (1911) is a novel by H. G. *Wells.

MacINNES, Colin (1914–76), novelist, son of the novelist Angela Thirkell (1890–1961). His is best remembered for his novels of teenage and black immigrant culture *City of Spades* (1957) and *Absolute Beginners* (1957), which described the new Bohemian underworld of Notting Hill, coffee bars, jazz clubs, drugs, drink, and homosexuality.

M'Intyre, Captain Hector and Maria, in Scott's *The Antiquary*, nephew and niece of Jonathan Oldbuck.

Mac-Ivor, Fergus, of Glennaquoich, otherwise known as Vich Ian Vohr, a character in Scott's *Waverley*.

MACKENZIE, Sir (Edward Morgan) Compton (1883–1972), a prolific writer, who produced books of travel, biography, essays, poems, and much journalism, as well as the novels for which he is best remembered. The most notable of these include *Carnival* (1912); *Sinister Street* (2 vols; 1913, 1914), which presents a semi-autobiographical figure Michael Fane, 'handicapped by a public school and university education'; *Vestal Fire* (1927); and *Extraordinary Women* (1928). He published two volumes of war memoirs, *Gallipoli Memories* (1929) and *Greek Memories* (1932). During 1937–45 appeared the six volumes of *The Four Winds of Love*, tracing the life of John Ogilvie, a pensive and individualistic Scot, from the time of the Boer War to the emergence of Scottish nationalism in 1945. *Whisky Galore* (1947) was made into a successful film. *Thin Ice* (1956) is a perceptive story of two homosexuals. In 1963–71 he published the ten 'Octaves' of *My Life and Times*.

MACKENZIE, Henry (1745–1831), author of the influential novel, *The Man of Feeling* (1771). In 1773 he published *The Man of the World*, in which the protagonist is a villain; and in 1777 *Julia de Roubigné*, a novel in the manner of Richardson's *Clarissa*. Mackenzie was chairman of the committee that investigated *Macpherson's 'Ossian'. He has been referred to as 'the Addison of the North'. (See SENTIMENT, NOVEL OF.)

McKERROW, Ronald Brunlees (1872–1940), bibliographer and editor, co-founder of the *Malone Society, 1906, became joint secretary of the *Bibliographical Society, 1912, and in 1925 founded the *Review of English Studies*. His best-known works were an important edition of the works of T. *Nashe (1904–10) and *An Introduction to Bibliography for Literary Students* (1927).

MACKINTOSH, Sir James (1765–1832), author of *Vindiciae Gallicae* (1791), a reasoned defence of the French revolution. Mackintosh later recanted his views. He published a *Dissertation on the Progress of Ethical Philosophy* (1830) and wrote the first three volumes of a *History of England* (1830–1) for Lardner's *Cabinet Cyclopaedia*, as well as an unfinished *History of the Revolution in England in 1688* (1834).

MACKLIN, Charles (MacLaughlin) (?1699–1797), an Irish-born actor who made his reputation by his impersonation of Shylock. He wrote several plays, of which the most successful were *Love à la Mode*, performed 1759, and *The Man of the World*, performed 1781.

MACLAREN, Ian, see KAILYARD SCHOOL.

MACLEAN, Sorley (Somhairle Macgill-Eain) (1911–   ), Gaelic poet, one of the leading writers in Gaelic of the 20th-cent. Scottish Renaissance.

MacLEISH, Archibald (1892–1982), American poet and dramatist. He was one of the American expatriates in Paris in the 1920s, and was strongly influenced by *Pound and T. S. *Eliot. His volumes of verse include *The Pot of Earth* (1924); *The Hamlet of A. MacLeish* (1928); *New Found Land* (1930); the narrative poem *Conquistador* (1932); and his *Collected Poems, 1917–1933* (1933). Among his verse dramas are *Panic* (1935), the anti-totalitarian *The Fall of the City* (1937), and the successfully staged *J.B.* (1958), an updating of the trials of Job.

MACLEOD, Fiona, see SHARP, W.

McLUHAN, (Herbert) Marshall (1911–80), Canadian scholar whose studies of the media of communication and of the role of technology in society were highly influential. They include *The Mechanical Bride* (1951), *The Gutenberg Galaxy* (1962, the work which introduced the concept of the 'global village' created by electronic interdependence), and *Understanding Media* (1964), which explored the proposal that 'The Medium is the Message'.

Macmillan's Magazine, a periodical founded in 1859, and edited successively by D. *Masson (1859–68), George Grove (1868–83), J. *Morley (1883–85), and Mowbray Morris (1885–1907). It was one of the first magazines to use signed articles only. Contributors included *Tennyson, Thomas *Hughes, *Milnes, and F. D. *Maurice.

Macmorris, Captain, in Shakespeare's *Henry V*, the only Irishman presented in Shakespeare's plays.

MacNEICE, (Frederick) Louis (1907–63), poet, born in Belfast, educated at Merton College, Oxford, where he made the acquaintance of *Auden and *Spender, and published a book of poems, *Blind Fireworks* (1929). He became known as a poet through his contributions to *New Verse* and his *Poems* (1935). *Letters from Iceland* (1937) was written in collaboration with Auden. Subsequent volumes of poetry include *The Earth Compels* (1938); *Autumn Journal* (1938), a long personal and political meditation on the events leading up to Munich; *Plant and Phantom* (1941); *Springboard* (1944); *Holes in the Sky* (1948); *Autumn Sequel* (1954); and *The Burning Perch* (1963).

His early work revealed a technical virtuosity, a painter's eye for an image, humour, and an impulse towards making sense of what he later called the 'drunkenness of things being various'. He used most of the classic verse forms, but his distinctive contribution was his deployment of assonanace, internal rhymes, and half rhymes, and ballad-like repetitions that he had absorbed from the Irishry of his childhood. He was also renowned as an outstanding writer of radio documentaries and radio parable plays; these include *Christopher Columbus* (1944) and his most powerful dramatic work, *The Dark Tower* (1947). Among his other works are a translation of an abridged version of *Goethe's *Faust* (1951), and *Varieties of Parable* (from the 1963 Clark lectures) and a volume of autobiography, *The Strings are False* (both in 1965). His *Collected Poems*, edited by E. R. Dodds, appeared in 1966.

MACPHERSON, James (1736–96), met John *Home in 1759, for whom he produced his first 'Ossianic' fragment 'The Death of Oscar'; encouraged by Home and Hugh *Blair he then produced *Fragments of Ancient Poetry, Collected in the Highlands of Scotland, and Translated from the Galic or Erse Language* (1760). Interest in *Primitivism was at this period considerable; pressed on by his admirers, Macpherson travelled round Scotland collecting the materials for *Fingal, an Ancient Epic Poem, in Six Books* (1762). It purported to be Macpherson's faithful translation of an epic by Ossian, the son of Finn (or, in this version, Fingal), dating from some vague but remote period of early Scottish history. A second epic, *Temora* (1763), followed with suspicious speed. These works created a great sensation among patriotic Scots. *Hume and Adam *Smith were at first convinced by them: Home and Blair remained so. Ossian's fame spread to the Continent; *Goethe quoted Ossian at length in *The Sorrows of Young Werther*. At home doubts of the poems' authenticity sprang up almost at once, with Dr *Johnson as the most formidable of sceptics. Macpherson, when called upon to produce his originals, was obliged to fabricate them. A committee appointed after his death, chaired by Henry *Mackenzie, investigated the mystery and reported in 1805 that Macpherson had liberally edited Gaelic poems and inserted passages of his own. The immense popularity of the poetry survived the exposure of its origins.

MACREADY, William Charles (1793–1873), a great tragic actor, was, by 1819, an established rival of *Kean. He was manager of Covent Garden and Drury Lane theatres at various times, where he made many reforms in both acting and the texts. In 1837 he appeared in *Strafford*, which Browning had written for him.

Macro, in Jonson's *Sejanus*, the evil agent of Tiberius.

Macro Plays, The, three Morality plays (*The Castle of Perseverance, *Mankind, and *Wisdom), named after their 18th-cent. owner.

MacSarcasm, Sir Archy, a character in Macklin's *Love à la Mode*.

MacStinger, Mrs, in Dickens's *Dombey and Son*, Captain Cuttle's termagant landlady.

MADGE, Charles Henry (1912–   ), poet and sociologist, whose left-wing sympathies were manifeted in his poetry (his first volume was *The Disappearing Castle*, 1937) and other work and writings. In 1937 with H. Jennings and T. Harrison he founded Mass Observation. His first wife was Kathleen *Raine.

Madge Wildfire, see MURDOCKSON.

Madoc, a narrative poem by *Southey, published 1805.

Madrigal, originally a short lyrical poem of amatory character, a type of part-song, or short polyphonic composition to secular words and usually without instrumental accompaniment. The madrigal originated in Italy; it reached England from Europe in the 1530s but developed its own native style in the 1580s with the poetic experiments of the *Golden age. Its most famous English exponents were T. *Morley, *Weelkes, and *Wilbye.

Mad World, My Masters, A, a comedy by T. *Middleton, written 1604–7, printed 1608.

The principal characters are young Follywit, who seeks to rob his grandfather Sir Bounteous Progress, and Penitent Brothel, who seeks to seduce the wife of the jealous Hairbrain: Sir Bounteous's mistress, Gullman, plays a part in both actions, and gulls Follywit into marriage.

Maeve, or **Medb** (pron. Maeve), in the Ulster cycle, queen of Connaught. See under CUCHULAIN and TAIN-BO-CUAILGNE.

Maeviad, The, see GIFFORD, W.

'Maga, The', see BLACKWOOD'S MAGAZINE.

Magic Realism, a term coined by Franz Roh (1925), to describe tendencies in the work of certain German artists of the *neue Sachlichkeit* (new objectivity), characterized by clear, cool, static, thinly-painted, sharp-focus images, frequently portraying the imaginary, the improbable, or the fantastic in a realistic or rational manner. The term was adopted in the United States with the 1943 exhibition at the New York Museum of Modern Art, entitled 'American Realists and Magic Realists'. The term has subsequently been used to describe the works of such Latin American authors as *Borges, *García Márquez, and Alejo Carpentier (1904–), and elements of it have been noted in Günter Grass (1927–), Italo Calvino (1923–85), *Fowles, and other European writers. In the 1970s and 1980s it was adopted in Britain by several of the most original of younger fiction writers, including, notably, Emma Tennant (1938– ; titles include *Hotel de Dream*, 1976; *Wild Nights*, 1979); Angela Carter (1940– ; *The Infernal Desire Machines of Doctor Hoffman*, 1972; the remarkable *Nights at the Circus*, 1984); and Salman Rushdie (1947– ; *Midnight's Children*, 1981; *Shame*, 1983). Magic realist novels and stories have, typically, a strong narrative drive, in which the recognizably realistic mingles with the unexpected and the inexplicable, and in which elements of dream, fairy-story, or mythology combine with the everyday, often in a mosaic or kaleidoscopic pattern of refraction and recurrence. English Magic Realism also has some affinity with the neo-*Gothic.

MAGINN, William (1793–1842), wrote under various pseudonyms including 'Ensign Morgan O'Doherty', in whose persona he produced memoirs, anecdotes, and verses in English, Latin, and Greek for the *Literary Gazette* and other journals. He was a prolific contributor to *Blackwood's*, notably to the *Noctes Ambrosianae*. In 1830 he helped in the establishing of *Fraser's Magazine*, in which much of his best work, including *Homeric Ballads* and *A Gallery of Literary Characters*, appeared. His wit and learning are evident in his parodies of Sir W. *Scott, *Coleridge, T. *Moore, La Rochefoucauld, *Disraeli, *Carlyle, and many others. He was the original of Captain Shadow in Thackeray's *Pendennis*.

Magnet, The, see HAMILTON, C.

Magnetic, Lady, The, or *Humours Reconciled*, a comedy by *Jonson, performed 1632, printed 1641.

Magnus, Mr Peter, a character in Dickens's *Pickwick Papers*.

Magnyfycence, a morality play by *Skelton.

Magus, The, see FOWLES, J.

Magwitch, Abel, a character in Dickens's *Great Expectations*.

MAHONY, Francis Sylvester (1804–66), best known by his pseudonym Father Prout, a Jesuit priest who left the order for a career as a journalist and poet. He contributed many lively papers and poems to *Fraser's Magazine* (later collected as *The Reliques of Father Prout*, 1836) and *Bentley's Miscellany*. These included translations from *Horace, Béranger, *Hugo, etc., and, interspersed amongst them, mystifications in the form of invented 'originals' in French, Latin, and Greek for well known poems by T. *Moore, C. *Wolfe, and others.

Maid Marian, a female personage in the May-game (see MAY DAY) and *Morris dance. In the later forms of the story of *Robin Hood she appears as the companion of the outlaw.

Maid Marian, a medieval romance by *Peacock, published in 1822. It features *Robin Hood, *Maid Marian, *Friar Tuck, and Prince John, while lampooning institutions such as the monarchy and the church in the post-Napoleonic era. The book was later adapted as a popular operetta.

'Maid of Athens', a poem by Lord *Byron, written 1810.

The 'Maid' is said to have been the 12-year-old daughter of Mrs Macri, a widow whose husband had been vice-consul in Athens.

Maid of Honour, The, a romantic drama by *Massinger, acted about 1621–2, published 1632. It is based on a story by *Boccaccio. The play contains some of Massinger's finest scenes, and Camiola, 'the maid of honour', is his best female character.

Maid of Norway, see SIR PATRICK SPENS.

Maid's Tragedy, The, a tragedy by *Beaumont and *Fletcher, published 1619.

Amintor, a gentleman of Rhodes, breaks his engagement to Aspatia at the king's request and marries Evadne, sister to his friend Melantius. On their wedding night, Evadne reveals that she is the king's mistress and refuses to sleep with him. Amintor initially agrees to conceal the position but later he reveals the truth to Melantius, who passionately reproaches the by now penitent Evadne, and persuades her to murder the king. Meanwhile the desolate Aspatia laments her loss in some of the finest verse in the play. Aspatia later takes action by disguising herself as her brother and provoking the reluctant Amintor to a duel. He wounds her; as she lies dying Evadne arrives, fresh from the king's murder, hoping to be pardoned by Amintor. He rejects her; she commits suicide; Aspatia reveals herself and dies; Amintor takes his own life. (See HEROIC DRAMA.)

MAILER, Norman (1923–), American novelist and essayist, whose naturalistic first novel *The Naked and the Dead* (1948) was based on his experiences with the army in the Pacific. It was followed by other novels, including *Barbary Shore* (1951), *The Deer Park* (1955), and *An American Dream* (1965). Most of his work is of a more unorthodox genre, mixing journalism, autobiography, political commentary, and fictional passages in a wide range of styles (notably *Advertisements for Myself*, 1959; *The Presidential Papers*, 1963; and *The Armies of the Night*, 1968). *The Executioner's Song* (1979) is a lengthy non-fiction account of a murder. (See also FACTION.) His novel *Ancient Evenings* (1983) is set in ancient Egypt (1290–1100 BC).

MAIMONIDES (1135–1204), a Jew of Cordoba whose chief work was *The Guide for the Perplexed*, which influenced *Aquinas and other *Scholastic theologians; its endeavour was to reconcile Talmudic scripture with the philosophy of *Artistotle.

Main Street, a novel by S. *Lewis.

MAITLAND, Frederic William (1850–1906), was elected reader in English law at Cambridge, and in 1888 Downing professor. His first important work was *Bracton's Note-Book* (1887), followed by *The History of English Law before the time of Edward I* (with Sir F. Pollock, 1895) and *Roman Canon Law in the Church of England* (1898), both tracing the Roman influence on English law, essays on *Domesday Book and Beyond* (1897), his Ford lectures on *Township and Borough* (1898), his Rede lecture on *English Law and the Renaissance* (1901); and his 1887 lectures on *The Constitutional History of England* (posthumously, 1908).

Maitland Club, a club founded at Glasgow in 1828 for the publication of works on the literature and antiquities of Scotland.

MAJOR, or **MAIR,** John (*c.*1467–1550), 'the last of the schoolmen'. He studied at Cambridge and Paris, where he became a doctor of theology. He lectured on scholastic logic and theology at Glasgow and St Andrews, 1518–25, then returned to Paris, where he was regarded as the most eminent exponent of medieval learning. He published between 1509 and 1517 a Latin *Commentary on the Sentences of Peter Lombard*, and a Latin *History of Greater Britain, both England and Scotland* (1521) in which he showed himself in advance of his times by advocating the union of the two kingdoms.

Major Barbara, a play by Bernard *Shaw, performed 1905, published 1907.

It portrays the conflict between spiritual and worldly power embodied in Barbara, a major in the Salvation Army, and her Machiavellian father, millionaire armaments manufacturer Andrew Undershaft. While visiting her East End shelter for the poor, he reveals that the shelter's benefactor, Lord Saxmundham, made his money through 'Bodgers' whisky', and she suffers a crisis of faith; the next day, visiting his factory with her mother Lady Britomart and her fiancé, classical scholar Adolphus Cusins, she is further shaken to discover her father is a model employer. Cusins enters the debate, reveals that he is technically a foundling and therefore eligible to inherit the Undershaft empire (as Undershaft's own children are not), strikes a hard bargain with his prospective father-in-law, and agrees to enter the business, partly persuaded by Undershaft's quoting of *Plato to the effect that 'society cannot be saved until either the Professors of Greek take to making gunpowder, or else the makers of gunpowder become Professors of Greek.' Barbara, recovering her spirits, embraces this synthesis as a possibility of hope for the future. The portrait of Cusins is based on G. *Murray.

Malagrowther, (1) Malachi, the pseudonym under which Sir W. *Scott addressed three letters in 1826, on the question of the Scottish paper currency, to the *Edinburgh Weekly Journal*; (2) Sir Mungo, a character in Scott's *The Fortunes of Nigel*.

MALAMUD, Bernard (1914–86), American novelist, best known for his novel *The Fixer* (1967), the story of a Jewish handyman or 'fixer' in Tsarist Russia just before the First World War, who is falsely accused of murder and turned into a scapegoat for anti-Semitic feeling. Other works include *A New Life* (1961), *The Tenants* (1971), *Dubin's Lives* (1979), *God's Grace* (1982), and volumes of short stories.

Malaprop, Mrs, in Sheridan's *The Rivals*, the aunt and guardian of Lydia Languish, noted for her aptitude in misapplying words; for instance 'as headstrong as an allegory on the banks of the Nile' or 'He is the very pineapple of politeness.' Her solecisms have given the word 'Malapropism' to the language.

Malbecco, in Spenser's *Faerie Queene* (III. ix, x), a 'cancred crabbed Carle', jealous and avaricious, married to the lovely Hellenore. *Paridell elopes with her, and Malbecco, unable to escape from his jealous thoughts, throws himself from a rock.

Malcontent, The, a tragi-comedy by *Marston, published 1604 (with additions by *Webster).

The central character is Altofronto, banished Duke of Genoa, disguised as the malcontent Malevole; in this role he reveals to his successor Pietro that he is being deceived by his wife Aurelia, and watches over the attempts of the Machiavellian Mendoza to supplant Pietro, to banish Aurelia, and to marry Altofronto's own wife, Maria. After much intrigue Altofronto reveals himself to the by now penitent Pietro, and the two expose Mendoza's villainy and regain their own wives. The exposure of court corruption, lust, and greed is harshly satiric.

Maldon, Battle of, a 325-line poem in Old English, incomplete at the beginning and the end, probably written c.1000, dealing with the battle fought in 991 at Maldon in Essex against Danish raiders. The Danes are drawn up on the shore of the river Pant (Blackwater), opposed by Byrhtnoth (c.926–91), ealdorman of Essex since 956, who rejects the demand for tribute by the Danes. In the fight Byrhtnoth is killed and the English are defeated. The second half of the poem, concerned with the loyalty of the followers of Byrhtnoth to their dead leader, is a powerful statement of fidelity and determination to avenge his death.

Maldon, Jack, in Dickens's *David Copperfield*, the scapegrace cousin of Mrs Strong.

Malecasta, 'unchaste', in Spenser's *Faerie Queene* (III. i), the lady of Castle Joyeous.

Maleger, in Spenser's *Faerie Queene* (II. xi), the captain of twelve troops, the seven deadly sins and the evil passions that assail the five senses.

Malengin, in Spenser's *Faerie Queene* (V. ix), the personification of guile.

MALLETT, or **MALLOCH,** David (?1705–65), Scottish author, who wrote the well-known ballad *'William and Margaret', The Excursion* (1728, a poem), and various tragedies, including *Elvira* (1763). He collaborated with *Thomson in the masque of *Alfred* (1740), wrote a *Life of Francis Bacon* (1740), and edited *Bolingbroke's *Works* (5 vols, 1754).

Malleus Maleficarum, or *Hexenhammer*, the 'Hammer of Witches', published 1484 by Jakob Sprenger and Heinrich Krämer. It was the textbook of the day on witchcraft, setting out how it may be discovered and how it should be punished.

MALLOCH, David, see MALLET, D.

MALLOCK, William Hurrell (1849–1923), is best known as author of *The New Republic: or culture, faith and philosophy in an English country house* (1877), a lively satire on English society and ideas, in which *Ruskin figures as Mr Herbert, and *Jowett, M. *Arnold, *Pater, T. H. *Huxley, and *Tyndall appear under thin disguises. He published various other works, including poems, novels, and memoirs; a High Anglican Tory, he attacked socialism and the *Fabian Society in several studies of social and economic science.

MALMESBURY, William of, see WILLIAM OF MALMESBURY.

MALONE, Edmond (1741–1812), literary critic and Shakespearian scholar, published in 1778 his *An attempt to ascertain the order in which the plays attributed to Shakespeare were written*, and edited the works of *Goldsmith (1780), Reynolds (1791), and the prose works of *Dryden (1800). He was a friend of *Boswell, and a member of the *Club, and gave great assistance with Boswell's *Life of Samuel *Johnson* (1791). He exposed the forgeries of *Chatterton and *Ireland. His new edition of Shakespeare was issued posthumously in 1821 in 21 vols by James Boswell the younger.

Malone Society, The, was founded by *Greg in 1906 for the purpose of making accessible materials for the study of early English drama, by printing dramatic texts and documents. Its name is taken from E. *Malone.

MALORY, Sir Thomas (d. 1471), author of *Le *Morte D'Arthur*, is identified by his editor Vinaver as Sir Thomas Malory of Newbold Revel, Warwickshire, who was a knight before 1442. The *Morte D'Arthur* was written in prison and we know that Malory of Newbolt Revel was charged with crimes of violence, theft, and rape after 1450. The fact that much of the work was translated from a 'French book' has led to a proposed identification as a hostage held in France during the French wars. But the identity remains a matter of conjecture.

MALTHUS, Thomas Robert (1766–1834), became curate of Albury in Surrey in 1798. In that year, provoked by *Godwin's *Political Justice* (1793), he published *An Essay on the Principle of Population*, in which he argued that population (growing geometrically) would soon increase beyond the means of subsistence (which grew only arithmetically), and that checks in the form of poverty, disease, and starvation were necessary. After collecting further information from northern Europe, he recast the *Essay* in a second edition of 1803; modifying his conclusions, Malthus suggested that the regulation of greed and sexual activity would act as more acceptable checks on population growth. His work was attacked by Godwin, *Cobbett, and *Hazlitt but it exerted a powerful influence on social thought in the 19th cent. C. *Darwin declared in his *Life* that Malthus's *Essay* helped to point him towards his own theory of evolution.

Malvolio, in Shakespeare's *Twelfth Night*, the joyless steward.

Mammon, Sir Epicure, in Jonson's *The Alchemist*, a voluptuous, gourmandizing knight, one of Jonson's greatest characters.

Mammon, The Cave of, described in Spenser's *Faerie Queene* (II. vii), is the treasure-house of the god of wealth, visited by Sir Guyon.

Man and Superman: *A Comedy and a Philosophy*, a play by Bernard *Shaw, first published 1903, first performed (without Act 3) in 1905 by the Stage Society at the Court Theatre.

The play is Shaw's paradoxical version of the *Don Juan story, in which his hero, John Tanner (Don Juan Tenorio), witty ideologue and author of the *Revolutionist's Handbook* (a work which appears in full as an appendix to the play), is relentlessly if obliquely pursued by Ann White-field, who is more interested in him as a potential husband than she is in his political theories. Ann has been entrusted as ward by her dead father jointly to Tanner and to the elderly respectable Ramsden, who expects her to marry the devoted and poetic Octavius. Tanner is made aware of Ann's intentions by his chauffeur, Straker (the New Man of the polytechnic revolution), and flees to Spain whither he is pursued by Ann and her entourage, which includes her mother and Octavius's sister Violet, who demonstrates, through a matrimonial subplot, the superior force of women. Act Three consists of a dream sequence set in hell in which Tanner, captured by the brigand Mendoza, becomes his ancestor Don Juan, Mendoza the Devil, Ramsden 'the Statue', and Ann becomes Ana: in one of Shaw's most characteristic 'Shavio-Socratic' debates, the four characters discuss the nature of prog-ress, evolution, and the Life Force, the Devil arguing powerfully that man is essentially destructive, and Don Juan arguing for the saving power of ideas and rational effort, for the philo-sopher as 'nature's pilot'. In the last act Ann achieves her object; the play ends with the announcement of their impending marriage and Tanner's submission to the Life Force.

The concept of the Life Force bears some similarity to *Bergon's 'élan vital', although Shaw was not at the time familiar with Berg-son's work: the echo in his 'Superman' of *Nietzsche's 'Übermensch' (*Also sprach Zarathustra*) is, however, deliberate.

Manannán, the son of *Lêr, a highly popular god of the old Gaelic pantheon, the subject of many legends and the patron of sailors and merchants. The Isle of Man is said to take its name from him. There he has degenerated into a legendary giant, with three legs (seen revolving in the coat of arms of the island).

Manawyddan, see MABINOGION.

Manchester Guardian, The, founded in 1821 as a weekly, and in 1855 as a daily paper; the principal Liberal organ outside London. Its title was changed to *The Guardian* in 1959; since 1961 it has been published from London.

Manchester School, the name first applied by *Disraeli to the political party, led by Cobden and Bright, who advocated the principles of free trade. It was afterwards extended to the party who supported those leaders on other questions of policy. 'Manchester policy' was used derisively to signify a policy of *laissez-faire* and self-interest. The 'Manchester School' of drama refers loosely to the playwrights associated with Miss *Horniman's repertory seasons at the Gaiety Theatre, Manchester, 1907–14, including Harold Brighouse (1882–1958), W. S. *Hough-ton, and Allan Monkhouse (1858–1936). (1858–1936).

'Manciple's Tale, The', see CANTERBURY TALES, 23.

Mandarin, used as an adjective to describe esoteric, highly decorative, or highbrow prose.

MANDEVILLE, Bernard de (1670–1733), published *A Treatise of the Hypochondriack and Hysterick Passions* (1711, expanded into three dialogues, 1730). His other prose works include *The Virgin Unmasked* (1709, 1714), arguing for a better status and better education for women; *Free Thoughts on Religion, the Church and National Happiness* (1720), a defence of *Deism and an attack on clericalism; *A Modest Defence of Public Stews* (1724), recommending governmental regulation of bawdy-houses; and *An Enquiry into the Origin of Honour* (1732), distinguishing self-esteem from self-love. Of his moral and satirical verse the best known is 'The Grumbling Hive, or Knaves turn'd Honest' (1705), which was incorporated with various prose supplements into *The Fable of the Bees, or Private Vices, Public Benefits* (1714, 1723). Mandeville here rejects the optimistic view of benevolent human nature put forward by *Shaftesbury, and argues that the mutual help on which society thrives like a colony of bees is due to personal acquisitiveness and the love of luxury. He was attacked by W. *Law, *Dennis, *Hutcheson, *Watts, and G. *Berkeley, and he was a literary target in Pope's *Dunciad and Fielding's *Amelia.

MANDEVILLE, Sir John, the ostensible author of the famous travel book which is found in many European languages after its first appearance in Anglo-Norman French in 1356–7, the first English manuscript probably coming from Lincolnshire *c.*1375. Until J. W. Bennett's *The Rediscovery of Sir John Mandeville* (1954), Jean d'Outremeuse, a historian from Liège, was believed to be the writer of the work. The book purports to be an account of the author's journeys in the East, but it is really a compila-tion, drawn especially from William of Bolden-sele and Friar Odoric of Pordenone, and from the *Speculum Majus* of *Vincent of Beauvais. It claims to be a guide, both geographical and ethical, for pilgrims to the Holy Land, but it carries the reader far off course, to Turkey, Tartary, Persia, Egypt, and India. It is a highly entertaining work, combining geography and natural history with romance and marvels, such as the fountain of youth and the ant-hills of gold-dust. It was an important influence on subsequent English writers from *Chaucer to Shakespeare, and was the prototype in English of the popular genre of the fabulous travel book.

Manette, Dr and Lucie, characters in Dickens's *A Tale of Two Cities.

Manfred, a poetic drama by Lord *Byron, published 1817.

Manfred, a Faustian figure, 'half-dust, half deity', lives as an outcast in a castle in the Alps, and is tortured by guilt for 'some half-maddening sin'. He summons the spirits of the universe, who offer him everything except the oblivion he seeks. Eventually, overcoming his terror of death, he tries to hurl himself from an alpine crag, but is dragged back by a hunter. He invokes the Witch of the Alps and reveals his sin—his incestuous love for his sister Astarte. He descends to the underworld, the Hall of Arimanes, and encounters a vision of Astarte, who promises him death on the morrow. Back in his castle an abbot begs him to repent, but he cannot. He denies the power of the demons who summon him, and when they vanish he dies.

MANGAN, James Clarence (1803–49), Irish poet, published under various pseudonyms prose and verse in newspapers and periodicals and is chiefly remembered for a few powerful ballads and songs including 'Dark Rosaleen' and 'The Nameless One' ('Roll forth, my song, like the rushing river'). He died of malnutrition in extreme destitution. His tragic career suggested part of the theme of B. *Moore's *The Mangan Inheritance* (1979).

Manichaeism, a religion of Persian origin, spread to China in the east and to North Africa in the west. Its founder, Mani, began preaching in Ctesiphon, AD 242. His success provoked persecution and led to his martyrdom AD c.276. Mani made use of a mythology borrowed from *Gnosticism. He pictured a universe divided initially between the kingdoms of Light and Darkness, between the Spiritual and the Material. The Manichaeans advocated complete simplicity of life, were vegetarians, and were bound to abstain from harming man or beast. They did not care to acquire wealth and, since they despised ceremony and luxury, had little respect for authorities of Church and State. In the West Manichaeism adapted itself to Christianity; its followers worshipped Jesus as a spirit but they denied his humanity.

Manichaean proselytizing lost its impetus after the 6th cent. The fascination of Manichaeism, which persisted in its various modes for over a thousand years, as well as the savagery of its persecutors, are matters that have still to be explained.

Mankind, a Morality play in 914 lines from East Anglia, dating from c.1465, one of the group called *Macro plays after their 18th-cent. owner (the others are *Wisdom and *The Castle of Perseverance). Its principal theme is Sloth (*Accidia), and it is written in the Low Style with much employment of obscenity.

MANLEY, Mrs (Mary?) Delarivière (1663–1724), had a colourful life, which included a bigamous marriage with her cousin John Manley, and some years as mistress of the warden of the Fleet Prison, John Tilly. She published several novels and memoirs, including The New Atalantis (1709), a *roman à clef (published with a Key to its characters) in which she attacked various Whigs and people of note. She also wrote several plays. In 1711 she succeeded *Swift as editor of *The Examiner.

Manly, (1) a character in Wycherley's *The Plain-Dealer; (2) a character in Vanbrugh and Cibber's *The Provok'd Husband.

MANNING, Henry Edward (1808–92), succeeded *Newman as one of the leaders of the *Oxford Movement. He became archbishop of Westminster in 1865 and cardinal in 1875. He published many religious and polemical works, and was a great preacher and a subtle controversialist. He is one of the subjects of L. *Strachey's Eminent Victorians.

MANNING, Olivia (1908–80), novelist. Her first novel, The Wind Changes (1937), was set in Dublin. In 1939 she married R. D. Smith, then a British Council lecturer, subsequently a BBC producer, and at the outbreak of war travelled with him to Bucharest. Her experiences there, and later in Greece, Egypt, and Jerusalem, inspired the works for which she is best remembered, the Balkan Trilogy (The Great Fortune, 1960; The Spoilt City, 1962; Friends and Heroes, 1965) and The Levant Trilogy (The Danger Tree, 1977; The Battle Lost and Won, 1978; and The Sum of Things, 1980). This sequence opens with the experiences of the newly-married Guy and Harriet Pringle in rumour-filled Roumania, surrounded by a crowd of vividly drawn minor characters and hangers-on. Harriet spends much of her time trying to protect Guy and herself from Guy's impulsive generosity. As the German army advances the couple flee to Athens, and the second trilogy finds them in Egypt. Olivia Manning wrote other novels and two volumes of short stories (Growing Up, 1948; A Romantic Hero, 1966).

MANNYNG, Robert of Brunne (Bourne) in Lincolnshire (*fl.* 1288–1338), is known only from what he tells us of himself in the Prologues to his two works, his verse *Chronicle of England* (finished 1338) and **Handlyng Synne.*

Man of Feeling, The, a novel by H. *Mackenzie, published 1771.

The work is generally considered to have been the most influential 'Novel of *Sentiment'. The author deliberately fragments the story and explains that the MS has been mutilated; the effect is of a series of abrupt concentrated episodes. Harley is the hero, whose unwavering benevolence and acute sensibility are demonstrated through various scenes in which he assists the down-trodden, loses his love, and fails to achieve worldly success.

'Man of Law's Tale, The', see CANTERBURY TALES, 5.

Man of Mode, The, the last and finest comedy of *Etherege, first performed at court 1676. It was an immediate success, and remains a classic of the *Restoration period.

There are two main plots, neatly interwoven. Dorimant rids himself of his mistress Mrs Loveit, with the aid of faint-hearted Bellinda whom he seduces in the process. In doing so he meets the heiress Harriet Woodvil, with whom he appears to fall in love. She is wise enough to keep him at arm's length until he proposes marriage, and even then requires him to follow her into the country, there to receive her answer after the play is ended. In counterpoint, Young Bellair has been ordered by his father to marry Harriet; but he loves Emilia, who with the help of his aunt Lady Towneley enables him to outwit the old man, who has fallen for Emilia. The revelation of his own dotage induces Old Bellair to give his blessing to his son's marriage.

Etherege sustains interest through his unsentimental views, eloquent dialogue, and telling social detail. Dorimant was said to be drawn after *Rochester and Sir Fopling Flutter, 'the prince of fops', is the title character.

Man of Ross, The, see KYRLE, J.

Man of the World, The, (1) a novel by H. *Mackenzie; (2) a comedy by *Macklin, performed 1781.

MANSFIELD, Katherine, pseudonym of Kathleen Mansfield Beauchamp (1888–1923), was born in Wellington, New Zealand, but educated largely in London. In 1909 she married, but left her husband after a few days; she became pregnant by another man and gave birth to a stillborn child in Bavaria, an experience that formed the background to her first collection of stories *In a German Pension* (1911), most of which were previously published in *Orage's *New Age*. In 1911 she met John Middleton *Murry, whom she was to marry in 1918; he was editing **Rhythm*, to which, and to its successor *The Blue Review*, she also contributed stories, many based on her New Zealand childhood. In 1918 'Prelude' was published by the *Hogarth Press, and later in a collection, *Bliss, and other stories* (1920). She was increasingly recognized as an original and experimental writer, whose stories were the first in English to show the influence of *Chekhov. She had for some time been suffering from tuberculosis. *The Garden Party and other stories* (1922) was the third and last collection to be published in her lifetime: in that year she entered the institute run by *Gurdjieff near Fontainebleau, hoping to regain spiritual and physical health, and died the following January. Her stories vary greatly in length and tone, from long, impressionistic, delicate evocations of family life ('At the Bay', 'Prelude') to short, sharp sketches such as 'Miss Brill'. Two collections were published posthumously (*The Dove's Nest*, 1923; *Something Childish*, 1924) as well as various collections of letters, extracts from her journal, etc. Her *Collected Letters*, vol. i. ed. V. O'Sullivan and M. Scott appeared in 1984.

Mansfield Park, a novel by J. Austen, begun 1811, published 1814.

Sir Thomas Bertram of Mansfield Park, a stern but kind-hearted man, has two sons, Tom and Edmund, and two daughters, Maria and Julia. His wife, a charming, indolent woman, has two sisters: Mrs Norris, a near neighbour, who is spiteful and selfish, and Mrs Price, the wife of an impecunious officer of marines, with a large family of young children. In order to assist the Prices, Sir Thomas undertakes the charge of their eldest daughter Fanny, a timid child of nine. In spite of her humble situation and the cruelty of Mrs Norris, Fanny becomes an indispensable part of the household. The strength and earnestness of her character is particularly shown during Sir Thomas's absence in the West Indies, when family discipline is relaxed, forbidden private theatricals are mounted, and an unseemly flirtation begins between Maria Bertram, who is already engaged to marry Mr Rushworth, and Henry Crawford, the attractive, worldly brother-in-law of the parson of Mansfield. Against all this Fanny resolutely sets her face. Loving her cousin Edmund, she grieves to see him fascinated by the frivolous Mary Crawford, sister of Henry. Maria having become Mrs Rushworth, Henry turns his attention to Fanny, falls in love with her, and proposes. Fanny unhesitatingly rejects him, incurring the grave displeasure of Sir Thomas for what he regards as a piece of ungrateful perversity. During a visit paid by Fanny to her own home, matters come to a crisis. Henry, accidentally encountering Maria Rushworth again, runs away with her; and Julia elopes with an unsuitable suitor, Mr Yates. Mary Crawford's failure to condemn her brother's conduct, together with her aversion to marrying a clergyman (for Edmund has by now taken orders) finally opens Edmund's eyes to her true character. He turns for comfort to Fanny, falls in love, and they are married.

Mansoul, (1) see HOLY WAR; (2) a poem by *Doughty.

Mantalini, Madame, in Dickens's *Nicholas Nickleby*, a fashionable dressmaker. Her husband, Mr Mantalini, a selfish, affected fop, lives on her earnings and ruins her.

MANTUAN, or **MANTUANUS** (1448–1516), Johannes Baptista Spagnolo, a Carmelite of Mantua who wrote Latin eclogues. These had a considerable vogue in England and influenced the pastorals of *Barclay and *Spenser. He is the 'good old Mantuan' quoted by Holofernes in *Love's Labour's Lost* (IV. i).

MAP, Walter (*c.* 1140–*c.* 1209), a Welshman, archdeacon of Oxford, and the author between 1181 and 1192 of a satirical and entertaining miscellany *De Nugis Curialium*, 'Courtiers' Trifles', referred to by Chaucer in the 'Prologue to the Wife of Bath's Tale' (*Canterbury Tales*, 6). Some goliardic poems have been doubtfully attributed to him, as well as a lost Latin original of the prose *Lancelot*. He used to be identified as *Golias and hence the author of all the goliardic poems. (See also ANGLO-LATIN LITERATURE.)

MARANA, Giovanni Paolo, see TURKISH SPY.

Marble Faun, The, a novel by *Hawthorne, published 1860 (in England as *Transformation*).
   The scene is laid in Rome. Donatello is in love with the liberated young American art student Miriam, who is being persecuted by a mysterious stranger with whom she has some guilty connection. Roused to fury when encountering her with him on a moonlight expedition, Donatello murders him, with her unspoken assent, thus binding them together in a relationship 'cemented by blood'. A sub-plot describes the relationship of a sculptor, Kenyon, and Miriam's art student friend Hilda, 'the Dove'; Hilda, although herself totally innocent, feels herself under a 'mysterious shadow of guilt', by connection with Miriam.

Marchioness, The, a character in Dickens's *The Old Curiosity Shop*.

MARCIAN, see MARTIANUS CAPELLA.

MARCUS AURELIUS ANTONINUS (AD 121–80), Roman emperor 161–80 and Stoic philosopher, was the author of twelve books of 'Meditations'. For his philosophy, see STOICISM.

Margaret, (1) in Shakespeare's *Much Ado about Nothing*, a gentlewoman attendant on Hero; (2) in Goethe's *Faust*, the principal female character.

Margarete, St, see KATHERINE GROUP, THE.

MARGARET OF ANJOU (1430–82), the 'She-wolf of France', daughter of Reignier, king of Naples, who is a dominant character in Shakespeare's *1, 2,* and *3 *Henry VI* and *Richard III*. The historical Margaret remained in France after her defeat at the battle of Tewkesbury. She figures also in Scott's *Anne of Geierstein*.

Margarite of America, A, a prose romance by T. *Lodge, published 1596. It describes the tragic love of Margarite, daughter of the king of Muscovy, for the treacherous and violent Arsadachus, son of the emperor of Cusco, who eventually kills her, together with his wife Diana and their child. It is notable for its variety of visual spectacle and pageantry, its highly patterned poems and songs, and the unsparing savagery of many of the incidents.

Marguerite of Navarre, see HEPTAMERON.

Maria, (1) one of the ladies attending the princess in Shakespeare's *Love's Labour's Lost*; (2) Olivia's waiting woman in his *Twelfth Night*; (3) a character in Sterne's *Tristram Shandy* (vol. vii) and *A Sentimental Journey*; (4) a character in Sheridan's *The School for Scandal*.

Marian, Maid, see MAID MARIAN.

Mariana, (1) Diana's friend in Shakespeare's *All's Well that Ends Well*; (2) in his *Measure for Measure*, a lady betrothed to Angelo.

'Mariana' (1830) and **'Mariana in the South'** (1832), two poems by *Tennyson, suggested by Shakespeare's Mariana of 'the moated grange' in *Measure for Measure*. Both describe women waiting hopelessly and in desolate loneliness for their lovers.

MARIE DE CHAMPAGNE, daughter of *Eleanor of Aquitaine and Louis VII of France. She set up at Troyes from the 1160s a cultural centre modelled on that of her mother at Poitiers. Her most famous protégé was *Chrétien de Troyes.

MARIE DE FRANCE (*fl.* 1160–90), a French poet of whom little certain in known. She appears to have done much or all of her literary work in England. She is the author of twelve *Lais* (See BRETON LAYS), a series of apparently

Celtic stories told in Anglo-Norman couplets. She also wrote a French version of the Latin *St Patrick's Purgatory* and a collection of *Aesop's Fables called *Isopet*.

Marina, in Shakespeare's *Pericles*, the daughter of Pericles.

Marinell, see FLORIMELL.

MARINO, Giambattista (1569–1625), Neapolitan poet, best known for his *Adone* (1623), a long poem on the love of Venus and Adonis. The term *marinismo* (or sometimes *secentismo*) denotes the flamboyant style of Marino and his 17th-cent. imitators, with its extravagant imagery, excessive ornamentation, and verbal conceits. *Crashaw was profoundly influenced by Marino.

***Marino Faliero,* Doge of Venice,** a poetic drama by Lord *Byron, published 1821, produced in the same year at Drury Lane, against Byron's wish.

Marino Faliero was elected doge of Venice in 1354 and the events of Byron's play, based on historical facts, occur in 1355. The conspiracy of the doge was also the subject of a tragedy by *Swinburne, *Marino Faliero* (1885).

***Marius the Epicurean,* a philosophical romance by *Pater, published 1885.

Pater describes the boyhood, education, and young manhood of Marius, a serious young Roman imbued with a 'morbid religious idealism'. With his friend Flavian he discovers the 'jewelled' delights of *Apuleius, in particular of the story of *Cupid and Psyche*, then progresses through the philosophies of *Heraclitus, Aristippus, and *Marcus Aurelius to Christianity. He dies more or less a martyr to save a Christian friend. The work is a vehicle for Pater's own reflections on pagan and Christian art and religion.

Mark, King, in Arthurian legend, the king of Cornwall and the husband of Isoud of Ireland, who is brought to Mark by her lover *Tristram; various Tristram stories represent the king as nobly trusting, or as a treacherous coward. See TRISTRAM AND ISOUD.

MARKANDAYA, Kamala (1923–   ), British novelist, born and educated in India. *Nectar in a Sieve* (1954) established her as the first notable woman novelist from the Indian subcontinent. The impact of new economic and political ideas on traditional Indian society is Markandaya's main theme in *A Silence of Desire* (1960), *Possession* (1963), *A Handful of Rice* (1966), and *The Coffer Dams* (1969). Other novels include *The Nowhere Man* (1972); *Two Virgins* (1973), which marks a radical change, showing a more

experimental style and a more positive view of modernization; *The Golden Honeycomb* (1977); and *Pleasure City* (1982).

MARKHAM, Gervase (1568–1637), wrote on country pursuits, the art of war, and horsemanship; also plays and poems. R. *Gittings, in *Shakespeare's Rival* (1960), argues (after Fleay: see *DNB*) that he was the rival poet of the sonnets, and that Armado in *Love's Labour's Lost* was based on him.

Markleham, Mrs, in Dickens's *David Copperfield*, familiarly known as the 'Old Soldier'.

Mark Tapley, in Dickens's *Martin Chuzzlewit*, servant at the Dragon Inn, who leaves it to find some position in which it will be a credit to show his indomitable good humour. He becomes the devoted attendant of Martin during his American tour, and finally marries the hostess of the Dragon.

MARK TWAIN, see TWAIN, M.

Marley, Jacob, in Dickens's *A Christmas Carol*, Scrooge's late partner, whose ghost appears.

Marlow, (1) a character in and part-narrator of several of the works of J. *Conrad, including *Lord Jim*, *Heart of Darkness*, *Youth*, and *Chance*; (2) Sir Charles and his son, characters in Goldsmith's *She Stoops to Conquer*.

MARLOWE, Christopher (1564–93). In 1589 he was involved in a street fight in which the poet T. *Watson killed a man. Early in 1592 he was deported from the Netherlands for attempting to issue forged gold coins. On 30 May 1593 he was killed by Ingram Frizer in a Deptford tavern after a quarrel over a bill; Marlowe was at the time under warrant to appear before the Privy Council on unknown charges. *Kyd and another friend, Richard Baines, testified after his death to his blasphemy and outrageous beliefs.

He wrote The Tragedie of *Dido, Queene of Carthage* (1594) in collaboration with *Nashe; *Tamburlaine* was published in 1590. The next plays may have been *The Jew of Malta*, not published until 1633, and *Edward II*, published in 1594. The highly topical *Massacre at Paris*, which survives only in a fragmentary and undated text, and *Dr Faustus*, published 1604, may both belong to the last year of Marlowe's life. At various times he translated *Ovid's *Amores*, published without date as *All Ovids Elegies*, together with some of Sir John *Davies's 'Epigrammes'; wrote two books of an erotic narrative poem *Hero and Leander* (1598), which was completed by G. *Chapman; made a fine blank verse rendering of *Lucans First Booke*, Book I of *Lucan's *Pharsalia*; and wrote the song 'Come live with me and be my love', published in *The Passionate Pilgrim* (1599) and *England's Helicon* (1600), with a reply by *Ralegh. In spite of his violent life Marlowe was an admired and highly influential figure. Shakespeare's early histories are strongly influenced by Marlowe, and he paid tribute to him in *As You Like It* as the 'dead shepherd'. *Jonson referred to '*Marlowes* mighty line'.

MARMION, Shackerley (1603–39), wrote three plays, *Hollands Leaguer* (1632), *A Fine Companion* (1633), and, his best, *The Antiquary* (performed ?1635, printed 1641). He also wrote a long verse narrative in heoric couplets, *Cupid and Psyche* (1637), and contributed verse to the *Annalia Dubrensia* (see COTSWOLD OLIMPICK GAMES).

Marmion: A Tale of Flodden Field, a poem by Sir W. *Scott, published 1808.

The story is set in 1513. Lord Marmion, a fictitious character, a favourite of Henry VIII and a mixture of villainy and nobility, has tired of Constance de Beverley, a perjured nun who has followed him disguised as a page, and seeks to marry the wealthy Lady Clare, who is betrothed to Sir Ralph de Wilton. He accuses de Wilton of treason, proving it by a forged letter; he is helped by Constance, who hopes to regain her hold over him. She, however, is betrayed to her convent and walled up alive. Meanwhile Marmion and de Wilton have fought in the lists, and the latter has been left for dead. Lady Clare goes to a convent to escape Marmion. He, while in Scotland, unknowingly encounters de Wilton, who has survived and is disguised as a palmer. The abbess of St Hilda, who has received from Constance the proofs of Marmion's crime, entrusts them to the palmer; having revealed himself to Clare, who is in attendance on the abbess, he escapes to the English camp. Marmion, with Clare in his train, joins the English forces at *Flodden, where he is killed. De Wilton and Clare are finally united.

The poem contains the two well-known songs 'Where shall the lover rest' and 'Lochinvar'.

Marney, Lord, in *Sybil* by B. Disraeli.

Maro, see VIRGIL.

Marplot, a character in Mrs Centlivre's *The Busie Body*.

Marprelate Controversy, see MARTIN MARPRELATE.

Marriage, a novel by S. *Ferrier, published 1818. The novel, which Sir W. *Scott greatly admired, is clearly intended to commend prudent marriage.

Marriage-à-la-Mode, a tragi-comedy by *Dryden produced 1672, published 1673.

The main plot concerns a usurper's discovery that his daughter and his (lawful) predecessor's son have been secretly reared together in rural seclusion, and have fallen idealistically in love. The comic plot is a double intrigue involving two friends and their pursuit respectively of the wife of the one and the betrothed of the other. The counterpointing of these contrasting plots is striking, as each ends anti-climactically, the lawful heir being restored to his throne and the adulterous lovers failing to consummate their affairs. The play contains some of Dryden's finest songs.

Marriage of Heaven and Hell, The, a prose work by W. *Blake, etched c.1790–3, introduced by a short poem. It consists of a sequence of paradoxical aphorisms in which Blake turns conventional morality on its head, claiming that man does not consist of the duality of Soul=Reason and Body=Evil, but that 'Man has no Body distinct from his Soul . . . Energy is the only life, and is from the Body . . . Energy is Eternal Delight.' He proceeds to claim that *Milton's Satan was truly his Messiah, and that Milton 'was a true Poet and of the Devil's party without knowing it', and to produce a series of 'Proverbs of Hell' ('Sooner murder an infant in its cradle than nurse unacted desires' being one of the most notorious), which also celebrate the holiness of the natural world. He then moves to a sequence of visionary encounters with angels and prophets, in the course of which he dismisses the writings of *Swedenborg (whom he had greatly admired), accusing him of not having conversed sufficiently with Devils but only with Angels, and ends with an evocation of an Angel turned Devil. G. B. *Shaw, who greatly admired Blake, was much influenced by his doctrine of contraries.

Marrow of Modern Divinity, The, a book advocating Calvinistic views, written by E.F. (unidentified) in 1645, the condemnation of which in 1720 by the general assembly of the church of Scotland gave rise to the prolonged 'Marrow Controversy'.

MARRYAT, Captain Frederick (1792–1848), naval captain and FRS. He wrote several novels of sea-life including *The Naval Officer: or Scenes and Adventures in the Life of Frank Mildmay* (1829), *Peter Simple* (1834), *Jacob Faithful* (1834), and *Mr *Midshipman Easy* (1836). He followed these with *Japhet in Search of a Father* (1836), the story of the struggles of a foundling; *Snarleyyow* (1837), the tale of an indestructible dog; *The Phantom Ship* (1839); and *Poor Jack* (1840). With *Masterman Ready* (1841) he turned his attention to children's books, and it is chiefly for these he is remembered. *The Settlers in Canada* (1844) was followed by *Children of the New Forest* (1847).

MARSH, Sir Edward Howard (1872–1953), classicist, scholar. Between 1912 and 1922 he edited five highly influential volumes of *Georgian Poetry*. He was a friend and executor of R. *Brooke whose *Collected Poems* (1918) he edited. He made many translations of classical and French authors; and in 1939 published *A Number of People*, reminiscences of his many friends in the literary and political worlds.

MARSH, Dame Ngaio (pron. Ny-o) Edith (1899–1982), writer of *detective fiction, born at Christchurch, New Zealand. Her hero, Chief Detective Inspector Roderick Alleyn, first appears in *A Man Lay Dead* (1934); other titles include *Vintage Murder* (1937), *Surfeit of Lampreys* (1941), *Died in the Wool* (1945), and *Final Curtain* (1947).

MARSTON, John (?1575–1634), dramatist. His *The Metamorphosis of Pigmalion's Image and certaine satyres* and *The Scourge of Villanie* (both 1598) were published under the pseudonym Kinsayder, under which name he figures in *The Returne from Parnassus* (see PARNASSUS PLAYS). Some of these satires were directed against literary rivals, including Bishop J. *Hall, and were burned by order of the archbishop of Canterbury in 1599. Marston's quarrel with *Jonson resulted in his portrayal as Crispinus in *The Poetaster*, but the two became friends again. His dramatic works were printed as follows: *The History of *Antonio and Mellida* (1602), of which *Antonio's Revenge* is the second part; *The Malcontent* (1604), with additions by *Webster; *Eastward hoe* (1605), a comedy, written with Jonson and *Chapman; *The Dutch Courtezan* (1605), *The Parasitaster* or *The Fawn*, a comedy, and *Sophonisba*, a tragedy (both 1606); *What you Will* (1607), a comedy; and *The Insatiate Countess* (1613), a tragedy (possibly completed by William Barksted).

MARSTON, John Westland (1819–90), dramatic poet and critic, who contributed to the *Athenaeum*, wrote several critical works, and more than a dozen plays, including the successful *The Patrician's Daughter*, performed in 1842. His son, Philip Bourke Marston (1850–87), blinded in infancy, published several volumes of poems and short stories (*Collected Poems*, 1892).

Martext, Sir Oliver, in Shakespeare's *As You Like It*, the vicar of a country parish.

MARTIAL (Marcus Valerius Martialis) (*c.* AD 40–104) Roman epigrammatist of Spanish origin. His 1,500 epigrams, mostly satirical and often coarse, are very witty and have a great formal perfection. He found a translator in *May (1613) and was popular throughout the 17th cent. He influenced T. *Campion, *Jonson, *Herrick, and *Cowley. More recently he has been translated by P. *Porter (*After Martial*, 1972).

MARTIANUS CAPELLA (Marcian) (*fl.* 410–39), a North African writer, celebrated in the Middle Ages. He was the author of *De Nuptiis Philologiae et Mercurii* in nine books of prose and verse. The first two deal with the wooing (in a wide, metaphorical sense) of Philology by Mercury, and the last seven are an allegorical encyclopaedia of the Seven Liberal Arts (see QUADRIVIUM and TRIVIUM). Marcian is referred to by Chaucer in 'The Merchant's Tale' (*Canterbury Tales*, 10) and in *The House of Fame*.

Martin, (1) in Dryden's *The Hind and the Panther*, symbolizes the Lutheran party; (2) in Swift's *A Tale of a Tub*, the Anglican Church, the allusion being to Martin Luther.

MARTIN, Sir Theodore (1816–1909), contributed, under the pseudonym *'Bon Gaultier', to *Tait's Magazine* and *Fraser's Magazine*, and collaborated with W. E. *Aytoun in the writing of the 'Bon Gaultier ballads' (1845).

Martin Chuzzlewit, The Life and Adventures of, a novel by *Dickens, published 1843–4.

Martin, the hero, is the grandson of old Martin Chuzzlewit, a wealthy gentleman made misanthropical by the greed of his family. The old man has reared Mary Graham, a young orphan, to look after him. Young Martin is in love with Mary; but the grandfather, mistrusting his selfish character, repudiates him and gets him dismissed from his position as pupil to his cousin Mr Pecksniff, architect and arch-hypocrite. Martin, accompanied by the indomitably cheerful Mark Tapley as his servant, sails for America to seek his fortune. He goes as an architect to the fraudulent Eden Land Corporation, where he loses his money and nearly dies of fever. (This part gave great offence in the US.) He then returns to England, his experiences having reformed his selfish attitudes. His grandfather has meanwhile established himself and Mary in Pecksniff's household and pretended to place himself under his direction, thus satisfying himself of Pecksniff's meanness and treachery. (Pecksniff tries to inveigle and bully Mary into marrying him.) He exposes the hypocrite, restores his grandson to favour, and gives him Mary's hand.

A sub-plot concerns the villainous Jonas Chuzzlewit, the son of old Martin's brother. He murders his father (in intention if not in fact); marries Mercy Pecksniff and treats her with the utmost brutality; murders the director of a bogus insurance company, by whom he has been taken in and blackmailed; is detected; and finally poisons himself.

The book contains many pleasant minor characters: Tom Pinch, Pecksniff's gentle loyal assistant, and his sister Ruth; Pecksniff's daughters Charity and Mercy (Cherry and Merry); and Mrs Gamp, the disreputable old nurse; while 'Todgers's' is an eccentric London boarding-house.

MARTINEAU, Harriet (1802–76), was a devout Unitarian in youth. Her first published work was *Devotional Exercises* (1823). Between 1832 and 1834 she published a series of stories, *Illustrations of Political Economy*, revealing both her passion for social reform and the influence of *Bentham and J. S. *Mill. In 1834 she travelled in America, and supported the abolitionists at some personal risk. *Society in America* appeared in 1837, and her first novel, *Deerbrook*, in 1839. *The Hour and the Man* (1840) was a biography of Toussaint L'Ouverture; *The Playfellow* (1841), a volume of children's stories. In 1845 she settled in the Lake District and became a friend of the *Wordsworths. She had by now repudiated all religious belief. Her radical *History of the Thirty Years' Peace* was published in 1849, and her anti-theological *Laws of Man's Social Nature* in 1851. Her translation and condensation of *Comte, *The Philosophy of Comte*, appeared in 1853. *An Autobiographical Memoir* published posthumously contained many observations on public and literary figures of her day.

MARTINEAU, James (1805–1900), brother of Harriet *Martineau. After working as a Unitarian minister at Dublin and Liverpool, he was appointed professor of moral philosophy in 1840 at Manchester New College and principal from 1869 to 1885. He was an ardent upholder of the theist position, a powerful critic of materialism and naturalism, and was prompt to recognize the claims of the Darwinian philosophy of evolution. His chief books, mainly philosophical religious works, were mostly published after his 80th year. These include *Types of Ethical Theory* (1885), *A Study in Religion* (1887), and *The Seat of Authority in Religion* (1890). (See UNITARIANISM.)

MARTIN MARPRELATE, the name assumed by the authors of a number of anonymous pamphlets (seven are extant) issued in 1588–9 from a secret press, containing attacks in a railing, rollicking style on the bishops, and defending the Presbyterian system of discipline. They were stimulated by Archbishop Whitgift's attempts to impose uniformity in liturgical practice and to promote royal supremacy and the authority of the Articles.

The Marprelate tracts are among the best prose satires of the Elizabethan age. As well as ballads, rhymes, and plays, they provoked replies from such noted writers as *Lyly and *Nashe; Richard and Gabriel *Harvey later became involved in the controversy. *Hooker's work eventually settled the matter for the Church. The suspected authors, a Welshman named Penry and a clergyman named Udall, were arrested. The latter died in prison, the former was executed. Their collaborator, Job Throckmorton, denied his complicity at the trial of Penry, and escaped punishment.

***Martinus Scriblerus,** Memoirs of*, a satirical work, directed against 'false tastes in learning', initiated by the *Scriblerus Club and written mainly by *Arbuthnot. It was printed in the second volume of *Pope's prose works in 1741.

The name 'Martin Scriblerus' was occasionally used by Pope as a pseudonym, and by *Crabbe in some of his earlier poems.

MARTYN, Edward (1859–1923), one of the founders of the *Irish Literary Theatre. His best-known plays are *The Heather Field* (1899) and *Maeve* (1899). He is caricatured as 'dear Edward' in G. A. *Moore's *Hail and Farewell*.

MARVELL, Andrew (1621–78), was educated at Hull Grammar school and Trinity College, Cambridge. He travelled for four years (1643–7) in Holland, France, Italy, and Spain. On his return he apparently moved in literary circles and had friends among Royalists. His poems to *Lovelace ('his Noble Friend') and on the death of Lord Hastings were published in 1649. In 1650 he wrote 'An Horatian Ode upon Cromwell's Return from Ireland', perhaps the greatest political poem in English.

From 1650 to 1652 Marvell tutored the daughter of Lord Fairfax at Nun Appleton in Yorkshire, when, it is usually assumed, he wrote 'Upon Appleton House' and lyrics such as 'The Garden' and the Mower poems. In 1653 he became tutor to Cromwell's ward William Dutton, and moved to John Oxenbridge's house at Eton, where he probably wrote 'Bermudas'. In 1654 with 'The First Anniversary' (1655) he began his career as unofficial laureate to *Cromwell, and was appointed in 1657 Latin secretary to the Council of State (a post previously occupied by his friend and sponsor *Milton, now blind). He mourned Cromwell in 'Upon the Death of His late Highness the Lord Protector' (1658). The following year he was elected MP for Hull; at the Restoration his influence secured Milton's release from prison.

During 1662–3 Marvell was in Holland on unknown political business, possibly espionage, and in 1663 he travelled with the earl of Carlisle as private secretary on his embassy to Russia, Sweden, and Denmark. His satires against *Clarendon were written and published in 1667. Later that year he composed his finest satire 'Last Instructions to a Painter', attacking financial and sexual corruption at Court and in Parliament, and took part in the impeachment of Clarendon. *The Rehearsal Transpros'd* (1672, Part II 1673) was a controversial prose work advocating toleration for Dissenters, which set new standards of irony and urbanity. Gilbert *Burnet called these 'the wittiest books that have appeared in this age'. The second edition of *Paradise Lost* contained a commendatory poem by Marvell, and in his prose works he continued to wage war against arbitrary royal power. *Mr Smirk, Or the Divine in Mode* and *A Short Historical Essay Concerning General Councils* (both 1676), and *An Account of the Growth of Popery and Arbitrary Government in England* (1677), were all Marvell's though prudently published anonymously. His *Miscellaneous Poems* (1681) were printed from papers found in his rooms by his housekeeper Mary Palmer. The satires (the authorship of some of which is still disputed) appeared in *Poems on Affairs of State* (1689–97).

Famed in his day as patriot, satirist, and foe to tyranny, he was virtually unknown as a lyric poet. It was not until after the First World War, with *Grierson's Metaphysical Lyrics* and T. S. *Eliot's 'Andrew Marvell', that the modern high estimation of his poetry began to prevail. His oblique, ironic, and finally enigmatic way of treating what are often quite conventional poetic materials (as in 'The Nymph Complaining for the death of her Faun' or 'To his Coy Mistress') has especially intrigued the modern mind. (See METAPHYSICAL POETS.)

Marwood, Mrs, a character in Congreve's *The Way of the World.*

MARX, Karl (1818–83), born in Rhenish Prussia, of Jewish descent, was editor of the *Rheinische Zeitung* at Cologne in 1842. His extreme radical views led to the suppression of the paper, and Marx went to Paris, where he met *Engels and collaborated with him in works of political philosophy. He was expelled from Paris, moved to Brussels, and at the time of the revolutionary movement of 1848 returned to Cologne. He was again expelled, and settled in London. He and Engels wrote about contemporary politics and society in England, finding in *Carlyle's works, particularly *Latter-Day Pamphlets* (1850), the only example of proper concern on the part of a British writer for the social condition of workers.

In 1867 appeared the first volume of Marx's treatise *Das Kapital*, in which he propounded his theory of political economy. After the death of Marx this was completed by Engels. It is a criticism of the capitalistic system under which, according to Marx, a diminishing number of capitalists appropriate the benefits of improved industrial methods, while the labouring classes are left in increasing dependency and misery. The remedy for this state of things Marx finds in the total abolition of private property, effected by the class war.

Marxist Literary Criticism, a term used to cover a wide variety of interpretations of and attitudes towards literature, but always involving the recognition that literature, in both form and content, is profoundly influenced by historical, economic, and social forces. *Marx and *Engels themselves did not develop a systematic aesthetic theory. Subsequently a large body of work has arisen which seeks to develop a Marxist aesthetic, and which uses the work of later Marxist writers (Lenin, Trotsky, Gramsci, the French philosopher Louis Althusser, 1918–) and related intellectual influences (*Freudian criticism, *Structuralism). The dominant figure is *Lukács, whose concept of 'critical realism' argued that the work of avowedly non-Socialist writers (e.g. *Balzac, Sir W. *Scott) could transcend the writers' own ideological limitations and reveal the fundamental tensions of their times. Since Lukács, nearly all Marxist criticism has been Western European (e.g. Walter Benjamin, 1892–1940; Lucien Goldmann, 1913–70; Pierre Macherey). Eastern European critics have been prescriptive rather than analytic, concerned to foster *Socialist Realism. The first English Marxist critic of note is C. *Caudwell. In post-war years the most significant figure is R. *Williams. Terry Eagleton (1943–) has assimilated influences from continental writers and critics (e.g. Macherey; Michael Foucault, 1926–84; Jacques Lacan, 1901–81; Jacques Derrida, 1930–) to a greater extent than Williams. *Steiner says, 'The Marxist sensibility has contributed a sociological awareness to the best of modern criticism', and notes in support the illumination shed by *Trilling on *Dostoevsky, by L. C. *Knights on Elizabethan drama, and by Q. D. *Leavis on the reading public.

Mary, in Dickens's *Pickwick Papers*, Mr Nupkins's pretty housemaid.

Mary Barton, A Tale of Manchester Life, a novel by Mrs *Gaskell, published 1848.

The entirely working-class cast of characters in this novel was then an innovation. The background of the story is Manchester in the 'hungry forties' and the acute poverty of the unemployed mill-hands. Mary Barton is the daughter of an active and embittered worker and trade unionist, John Barton. She has attracted Henry Carson, son of one of the employers, and, flattered by his attentions and the hope of a grand marriage, has repulsed her faithful admirer Jem Wilson, a young engineering worker. A group of workmen, exasperated by the failure of the employers to consider their grievances, decide to kill young Carson, and the lot falls on Barton to do the deed. When Carson is shot dead suspicion falls on Jem Wilson. Mary, by now realizing that it is Jem whom she loves, discovers that her father is the murderer. Jem is tried for his life, and is saved by Mary's frantic efforts to prove his innocence without betraying her father. John Barton confesses to the fiercely vindictive old father of Henry Carson, and wins his forgiveness as he dies.

Mary Graham, a character in Dickens's *Martin Chuzzlewit*.

Mary Magdalene, *Play of,* the only surviving play in late medieval English drama which is based on the legend of a saint, presenting events in the saint's life both before the Resurrection and during her subsequent legendary residence in Provence. It is a very long play, in the Digby set, in two parts, 52 scenes and 2,144 lines.

'Mary Morison', a lyric by *Burns, published 1786, possibly addressed to Alison Begbie, one of his youthful loves.

MARY QUEEN OF SCOTS (Mary Stuart) (1542–87), daughter of James V of Scotland, married Francis II of France (1558), Lord Darnley (1565), and *Bothwell (1567). She was imprisoned by *Elizabeth I and finally beheaded on a charge of conspiring against the latter's life. She figures in Scott's *The Abbot, and is the subject of a tragedy by *Schiller, of a trilogy of plays by *Swinburne, and of the novel *The Queen's Quair* by M. *Hewlett; she also figures in *Baring's *In My End is My Beginning* (1931).

MASEFIELD, John Edward (1878–1967), trained for the merchant navy and sailed for Chile in 1894. He sailed again across the Atlantic, but at the age of 17 deserted ship and became a vagrant in America. Back in England he began his prolific writing career, which was eventually to compass some 50 volumes of verse, over 20 novels, eight plays, and much miscellaneous work. His first published book was *Salt-Water Ballads* (1902, which included 'I must go down to the sea again'). Masefield joined the *Manchester Guardian* in 1907. *Ballads and Poems* (1910), which contained 'Cargoes', was followed by the first of many narrative poems, *The Everlasting Mercy* (1911), an account of the conversion of the rough Saul Kane; *The Widow in the bye street* (1912); and *Reynard the Fox* (1919), a rattling verse tale set in the rural world of Masefield's childhood. His *Collected Poems* (1923) sold in great numbers, as did the novels *Sard Harker* (1924), *Odtaa* (1926), *The Bird of Dawning* (1933), and his story for children *The Midnight Folk* (1927). In 1930 Masefield became poet laureate. He produced more volumes of poetry, the sea-novels *Dead Ned* (1938) and *Live and Kicking Ned* (1939), and the autobiographical *So Long to Learn* (1952). A final luminous fragment of autobiography, describing his country childhood, appeared in 1966 as *Grace before Ploughing*.

Mask of Anarchy, The, a poem of protest by P. B. *Shelley, published 1832, written in response to the 'Peterloo Massacre'. It uses the popular ballad form with immense power and sometimes surreal effect. The 'mask' is a pageant, or masquerade, of British political leaders—Castlereagh, Eldon, Sidmouth—whom Shelley blames not only for the killing and wounding of some 500 people at a public demonstration for parliamentary reform, but also for the general conditions of harshness and oppression in England. The poem ends with a celebration of freedom, and Shelley's historic appeal for non-violent mass political protest in a great assembly of working people: 'Rise like lions after slumber | In unvanquishable number.'

Masks, see MASQUES.

Maskwell, the *'Double Dealer' in Congreve's comedy of that name, 'a sedate, thinking villain, whose black blood runs temperately bad'.

MASON, A(lfred) E(dward) W(oodley) (1865–1948), novelist, is best remembered for *The Four Feathers* (1902, film version, 1939), the story of Harry Feversham's heroism in redeeming himself from the accusation of cowardice in the eyes of three fellow officers and his beloved, Ethne Eustace. His many other popular works include the series featuring Inspector Hanaud, which began with *At the Villa Rose* (1910).

Mason, Mary, Lady, the principal character in A. Trollope's novel *Orley Farm.

MASON, William (1725–97), poet, and friend of T. *Gray and Horace *Walpole. His work includes the tragedies *Elfrida* (1751) and *Caractacus* (1759); the latter clearly shows the influence of Gray in its Pindaric odes and its chorus of bards. He also wrote a long blank verse poem on landscape gardening, *The English Garden* (4 books, 1771–81).

Masques, or **Masks,** dramatic entertainments involving dances and disguises, in which the spectacular and musical elements predominated over plot and character. They were acted indoors by amateurs, and were designed to include their spectators in the action. As they were usually performed at court, many have political overtones. They were perhaps of Italian origin, but assumed a distinctive character in England in the 16th and 17th cents. Many of the great poets and dramatists, S. *Daniel, T. *Campion, G. *Chapman, and T. *Middleton, wrote masques, and they reached their highest degree of elaboration in the hands of *Jonson who introduced the 'anti-masque' as a comic and grotesque foil to the main spectacle. The great architect Inigo *Jones designed the machinery or decoration for some of them. Jonson's *The Sad Shepherd*, Milton's *A Maske, better known as *Comus, and other such works often called masques are closer to *pastoral dramas.

Massacre at Paris, The, a play by *Marlowe written *c.*1592.

The play deals with the massacre of Protestants in Paris on St Bartholomew's day, 24 August 1572. Its most memorable character is the Machiavellian duke of Guise, whose high aspiring language seems to have influenced Shakespeare in his early history plays. The massacre is depicted in a series of short episodes, a notable one being that in which the rhetorician *Ramus is killed after a verbal onslaught by the Guise on his emendations of Aristotle. The Guise himself is eventually murdered at the behest of Henry III. Leaping over 17 years, the play concludes with the murder of Henry III and the succession of the (then) Protestant Henry of Navarre.

MASSINGER, Philip (1583–1640). His father was the trusted agent of the Herbert family, to members of which the playwright addressed various dedications and poems. He became the chief collaborator of J. *Fletcher after the withdrawal of *Beaumont and shared with Fletcher the writing of 16 plays; with Fletcher and others *The Bloody Brother* (c.1616). With *Dekker he shared the writing of a religious play, *The Virgin Martyr* (printed 1622), a work uncharacteristic of both men; and with N. *Field he wrote *The Fatal Dowry* (acted 1617–19, printed 1632), in which his high romantic seriousness blends strikingly with Field's satire.

He wrote only two social comedies, *A New Way to Pay Old Debts* (acted c.1625–6) and *The City Madam* (acted 1632). *A New Way* was the mainstay of the English stage in the late 18th and early 19th cents, with the villainous Sir Giles Overreach providing a vehicle for the talents of a long line of actors including *Kemble and *Kean. Both plays are inspired by his patrician contempt for the ambitions and affectations of the rising mercantile classes in the city.

His tragedies include *The Duke of Milan* (printed 1623), a tragedy of jealousy; *The Roman Actor* (acted 1626, printed 1629), which makes remarkable use of plays-within-the-play, and in which, in the person of Paris the actor, he was able to show something of his own prolonged difficulties with political censorship; and *Believe as You List* (acted 1631, printed 1849), perhaps his greatest tragedy, which is a powerful story of a returned nationalist leader failing to get support and being hounded by the imperial authorities.

The remainder of his plays, in the Fletcherian vein of tragi-comedy, include *The Maid of Honour* (acted c.1621–2, printed 1632), *The Bondman* (acted 1623, published 1624) and *The Great Duke of Florence* (perf. 1627, printed 1636).

The equable and lucid verse of Massinger's plays, once a big point in their favour, went out of fashion when *Webster and *Tourneur became better known, and it may well be that a lack of interest in the linguistic texture of his plays is the reason for the present comparative neglect of one of the most serious professional dramatists of the post-Shakespearian period.

MASSINGHAM, H(enry) W(illiam) (1860–1924), described by his friend G. B. *Shaw as 'the perfect master journalist' was the influential editor of *The Nation* from 1907 to 1923, when he resigned in response to a change in its political intentions.

MASSON, David (1822–1907), biographer, critic, journalist, was successively professor of English literature at University College London (1853) and Edinburgh University (1865). He is remembered for his standard *Life of Milton* (7 vols, 1859–94), now superseded. He became the founder and editor of *Macmillan's Magazine* (1859). His other works include biographies of *Drummond of Hawthornden (1873) and *De Quincey (1881), and editions of *Milton, *Goldsmith, and De Quincey.

Master Humphrey's Clock, a weekly founded by *Dickens in 1840, originally intended as a miscellany which would contain a continuous narrative (*The Old Curiosity Shop*) linked by the reminiscences of the narrator, Master Humphrey. This device was soon dropped, as was the periodical's title after the publication in weekly numbers of *Barnaby Rudge (1841).

MASTERMAN, C(harles) F(rederick) G(urney) (1874–1927), Liberal politician, whose writings describe the changing social conditions of England. *From the Abyss* (1902) is an impressionistic collection of essays about slum life; *In Peril of Change* (1905) collects essays on literary and social topics, including the telling piece 'In Dejection near Tooting', in which he reflects on the ravaged landscape and hideous architecture of London's dumping ground; *The Condition of England* (1909) laments a 'land of radiant beauty' and expresses fears for a nation acquiring social improvements without spiritual renewal.

Master of Ballantrae, The: A Winter's Tale, a novel by R. L. *Stevenson, published 1889.

It is the story of the lifelong feud between the Master of Ballantrae, violent, unscrupulous, elegant, and courageous, and his younger brother Henry, at the outset a quiet, dull, honest fellow. The Master joins Prince Charles Edward in the '45 rebellion, disappears after Culloden, and is believed dead. After many adventures the Master returns, with a price on his head, to find that Henry has succeeded to his place and the woman whom he was to have married. Embittered by misfortune, he embarks on a course of persecution, first in Scotland, then in America, which brings both brothers to an untimely grave in the Adirondacks. The story is narrated by the dour but loyal Ephraim Mackellar.

Master of the Sentences, SEE PETER LOMBARD.

'Matter of Britain, The', the term used by Jean Bodel (late 12th–early 13th cent.) in a French verse romance about *Charlemagne to describe the subject-matter of the romances concerned with the Arthurian legends, as distinct from those concerned with classical stories (the *matter of Rome), or with Charlemagne and his circle (the *matter of France). The 'matter of Britain' was a source of inspiration in the 20th cent. for D. *Jones and C. *Williams.

'Matter of England, The', a term sometimes used by 20th-cent. scholars to refer to romances concerned with English heroes or localized in England (such as *King Horn or *Havelok the Dane).

'Matter of France, The', the term used by Jean Bodel, a late 12th-cent. romance writer, to refer to the romances based on stories about *Charlemagne and his circle.

'Matter of Rome, The', the term used by Jean Bodel, a late 12th-cent. French romance writer, to refer to those romances concerned with classical stories.

MATTHEW PARIS, see PARIS, M.

Matty, Miss (Matilda Jenkyns), the principal character in Mrs Gaskell's *Cranford.

MATURIN, Charles Robert (1782–1824), was one of the principal writers of the *'Gothic' novel. He published The Fatal Revenge (1807), The Wild Irish Boy (1808), and The Milesian Chief (1811). In 1816 his tragedy Bertram was produced by *Kean at Drury Lane, on the recommendation of Sir W. *Scott and *Byron, with great success. His most memorable work was *Melmoth the Wanderer (1820).

Maud, a poem by *Tennyson, published 1855. The poem is a monodrama in sections of different metres, in which the narrator, a man of morbid temperament, describes the progress of his emotions: first describing his father's death and his family's ruin, both contrived by the old lord of the Hall; then expressing his growing love for Maud, the old lord's daughter, and the scorn of her brother, who wishes her to marry a vapid 'new-made' lord; his triumph at winning Maud; their surprisal and her brother's death in a duel; his own flight abroad and ensuing madness; and his final re-awakening to hope in the service of his country. The poem contains several of Tennyson's best lyrics ('I have led her home', 'Come into the garden, Maud'), but some contemporary critics found it obscure or morbid.

MAUGHAM, W(illiam) Somerset (1874–1965), novelist and playwright, trained as a doctor in London. His first novel, Liza of Lambeth (1897), drew on his experiences of slums and Cockney life as an obstetric clerk. He achieved fame with the production of Lady Frederick (1907), a comedy of marriage and money. In 1908 he had four plays running simultaneously in London.

In 1911 he met Syrie Wellcome, daughter of Dr Barnardo, whom he married in 1917; they spent most of their time apart. In 1914 he met Gerald Haxton, who was 18 years younger than Maugham and who became his secretary and companion. In 1916 they set out on the first of many journeys together, this time to the South Seas. Further travels to China, south-east Asia, and Mexico followed. In 1926 Maugham brought a house at Cap Ferrat on the French Riviera, which was his home until his death.

Among Maugham's plays should be mentioned Our Betters (1917), a satire on title-hunting Americans; The Circle (1921); East of Suez (1922); The Constant Wife (1926); and For Services Rendered (1932), an anti-war play. His best-known novel is a thinly disguised autobiography, Of Human Bondage (1915), which describes Philip Carey's lonely boyhood and his subsequent adventures. The Moon and Sixpence (1919) recounts the life of Charles Strickland, a Gauginesque artist who neglects duty for art. Cakes and Ale (1930), his most genial book, is a comedy about the good-natured Rosie Driffield, the wife of a Grand Old Man of Letters, whom most took to be based on *Hardy; Alroy Kear, a self-promoting writer, was recognized as Hugh *Walpole. Maugham's last important novel, The Razor's Edge (1944), takes a mystical turn; its American hero Larry Darrell goes to India, stays in an ashram, and learns the value of non-attachment. A Writer's Notebook (1949) consists of extracts from the 15 large volumes of notes that Maugham kept from the age of 18 and shows him at his best.

Of his short stories, particular mention should be made of 'Rain' (in The Trembling of a Leaf, 1921), which relates the conflict between a life-affirming American prostitute, Sadie Thompson, and a repressed Scottish missionary, Davidson. It ends with Davidson's suicide. It is characteristic of Maugham's work in its remarkable and economical evocation of the atmosphere of hot, wet, tropical Samoa, and its neat twist of plot; it was staged successfully and it has been filmed three times.

Despite his worldly success and great popularity as a writer, Maugham felt he was not considered seriously, and the view expressed in his autobiography The Summing Up (1938), that he stood 'in the very first row of the second-raters', has been largely endorsed by literary critics.

Maule, Matthew, a character in Hawthorne's *The House of the Seven Gables.

MAURICE, (John) F(rederick) D(enison) (1805–72), joined the Church of England in 1830 and was ordained in 1834. His *The Kingdom of Christ* (1838) was a plea for Christian unity. In 1840 he became professor of English literature and history at King's College, London. He became a leader of the Christian Socialist movement which brought him into close contact with C. *Kingsley. His *Theological Essays* (1835) presented his unorthodox views on Eternal Punishment and caused his dismissal from King's College. In 1854 he founded a Working Men's College, and was its first principal. In 1866 he became professor of moral philosophy at Cambridge.

Mause Headrigg, in Scott's *Old Mortality*, the zealous covenanting mother of Cuddie, the ploughman.

Maw-worm, see BICKERSTAFFE.

Maximin, a character in Dryden's *Tyrannick Love*.

MAX MÜLLER, Friedrich (1823–1900), came to England in 1846 and became a British subject. He was commissioned by the East India Company to bring out an edition of the Sanskrit *Rigveda* which was published in 1849–73. He was Taylorian professor of modern European languages at Oxford (1854–68) and of comparative philology (1868–1900); and one of the curators of the Bodleian Library, 1856–63 and 1881–94. Max Müller delivered two remarkable courses of lectures on 'The Science of Languages' at the Royal Institution in 1861–4.

MAY, Thomas (1595–1650), adopted the parliamentary cause and was secretary for the Parliament (1646). He was author of two narrative poems on the reigns of Edward III and Henry II, a history of the Long Parliament (1647), two comedies, and three tragedies on classical subjects. He also wrote translations of *Virgil's The Georgics* and *Lucan's Pharsalia* (which were praised by *Jonson).

MAYAKOVSKY, Vladimir Vladimirovich, see FUTURISM.

May Day, 1 May, celebrated with garlands and dancing, the choice of a queen of the May, the erection of a Maypole to dance round, etc. Perhaps derived from the Roman *Floralia*. The May-game was a set performance in the May-day festivities, in which *Robin Hood and *Maid Marian figured. May Day was adopted in 1889 as the international Labour day holiday.

MAYHEW, Henry (1812–87), a co-founder and briefly joint editor of *Punch*. The first of his many plays was *The Wandering Minstrel* (1834). He wrote novels, books on science, religion, education, and travel, and *The Boyhood of Martin

Luther (1865). But he is chiefly remembered for his *London Labour and the London Poor* (1851), an investigation into the plight of the London poor which revealed the extent to which starvation, disease, and transportation were daily horrors. He performed similar work on the subject of prisons.

Maylie, Mrs and Harry, characters in Dickens's *Oliver Twist*.

Mayor of Casterbridge, The, *a Story of Character*, a novel by T. *Hardy, published 1886.

Michael Henchard, a hay-trusser, gets drunk at a fair and sells his wife and child for five guineas to a sailor, Newson. When sober again he takes a solemn vow not to touch alcohol for 20 years. By his energy and acumen he becomes rich, respected, and eventually the mayor of Casterbridge. After 18 years his wife returns, supposing Newson dead, and is reunited with her husband. She brings with her her daughter Elizabeth-Jane, and Henchard believes she is his child, whereas she is in fact Newson's. Through a combination of unhappy circumstances, troubles accumulate. Henchard quarrels with his capable young assistant Donald Farfrae; Mrs Henchard dies and Henchard learns the truth about the girl; Farfrae marries Lucetta, whom Henchard had hoped to win. Soon Henchard's business is ruined, the story of the sale of his wife is revealed, and he takes again to heavy drinking. Farfrae now has Henchard's business, his house, and Lucetta, while Henchard works as a labourer in his yard. Eventually Farfrae becomes mayor. Henchard's stepdaughter is his only comfort, then Newson returns and claims her and after Lucetta's death Farfrae marries her. Henchard becomes lonelier and more desolate, and dies wretchedly in a hut on Egdon Heath.

Mazarin Bible, The, the first printed bible, and probably the first book to be printed with movable type, *c.*1455, probably by *Gutenberg in association with *Fust and Schöffer. The first known copy was discovered in the Mazarine Library in Paris. It is also known as the 'forty-two line Bible' from the number of lines to the column.

Mazeppa, a poem by Lord *Byron, published 1819.

The poem is founded on a passage in *Voltaire's *Charles XII*. While Charles, the king of Sweden, and his men rest after their defeat at Pultowa, one of the king's officers, Mazeppa, tells a tale of his early life. Being detected in an intrigue, he had been bound naked on to the back of a wild horse from the Ukraine, which was then loosed and lashed into madness. The horse galloped off, through forest and river, carrying its fainting rider, and never stopped until it reached the plains of the Ukraine, where it fell dead. Mazeppa, at the point of death, was rescued by Cossack peasants.

Meagles, Mr, Mrs, and their daughter Pet, characters in Dickens's *Little Dorrit*.

Measure for Measure, a tragi-comedy by *Shakespeare, first printed in the First *Folio of 1623, written probably in 1604. Its chief source is *Whetstone's play *Promos and Cassandra*, based on a story in Cinthio's *Hecatommithi*. It has often been categorized as a 'problem play' because of the unpleasantness of its subject matter and the complexity of its plot and themes.

The duke of Vienna, on the pretext of a journey to Poland, hands over the government to his virtuous-seeming deputy Angelo, who enforces strict laws against sexual licence which for the past 14 years had been neglected. Angelo at once sentences to death Claudio, a young gentleman who has got his betrothed Julietta with child. Claudio's sister Isabella, who is a novice in a sisterhood of nuns, pleads with Angelo for her brother's life, urged on by Claudio's friend Lucio. In response to her repeated pleas, Angelo offers to spare Claudio's life if she will consent to be his mistress. Isabella refuses, and will not be persuaded even by the desperate entreaties of Claudio in prison. The duke, disguised as a friar, has made a visit of spiritual comfort to Claudio, and now devises a way of saving his life. Isabella is to agree to a midnight assignation with Angelo, but her place is to be taken by Mariana, who was betrothed to Angelo and still loves him. Mariana is first seen (IV. i) listening to the song 'Take, O, take those lips away'. This scheme is successful, but Angelo still proceeds with the order for Claudio's execution, though unknown to Isabella Claudio is saved by the substitution of the head of Ragozine, a pirate, who has died that night in the same prison. The duke lays by his disguise, simulates a return to Vienna, and pretends to disbelieve the complaints of Isabella and suit of Mariana, in favour of Angelo's hypocritical denial. When Angelo is forced to confess, both Mariana and Isabella plead for his life; Mariana is married to Angelo, Lucio to a whore, and at the end of a baffling final speech the duke appears to propose marriage to the novice Isabella.

Medall, The, a poem by *Dryden (1682).

The earl of *Shaftesbury was acquitted of charges of high treason in 1681, and a medal was struck to commemorate the event. Dryden's response includes savage attacks on Shaftesbury himself, the City, and the Commons. It predicts with some accuracy the constitutional instability which was to beset the country in the ensuing 30 years.

MEDAWAR, Sir Peter (Brian) (1915–), medical scientist and zoologist, educated at Oxford: he was awarded the Nobel Prize for Medicine in 1960. His reflective and speculative writings have reached a wide public; his works include *The Future of Man* (1960), *The Art of the Soluble* (1967), *The Hope of Progress* (1972), and *The Limits of Science* (1984).

Medina, in Spenser's *Faerie Queene* (II. ii), represents the golden mean of sensibility, her sisters *Elissa and Perissa representing its extremes.

Medmenham Abbey, a ruined Cistercian abbey on the Thames near Marlow, rebuilt as a residence and notorious in the 18th cent. as the meeting-place of a convival club known as the Franciscans or the Hell-fire Club. This was founded by Sir Francis Dashwood, and *Wilkes and *Dodgington were among its members. There is a good deal about it in *Johnstone's *Chrysal, or the Adventures of a Guinea* (III. ii, chs 17 et seq.).

MEDWALL, Henry, see FULGENS AND LUCRECE.

Megatherium, The, a club mentioned in several of Thackeray's novels, e.g. *The New-comes* (v), *The Adventures of Philip* (v. ix).

Meg Merrilies, see MERRILIES.

Meg Murdockson, see MURDOCKSON.

MEHTA, Ved Parkash (1934–), Indian writer and journalist (now an American citizen), educated at Balliol College, Oxford, and Harvard. His works include several studies of Indian life and autobiographical and biographical memoirs, including *Face to Face* (1957); *Daddyji* (1972); *Mamaji* (1979); and *Vedi; My early education in an Indian orphanage for the blind* (1982).

Meiosis, an understatement, sometimes ironical or humorous and intended to emphasize the size, importance, etc., of what is belittled. Except in *litotes, which is a form of meiosis, the use of meiosis is chiefly colloquial; e.g. 'He's doing all right out of it'; 'That must be worth a few bob.'

Meistersinger, a title taken in the 15th cent. by certain professional German poets of high skill and culture, to distinguish themselves from the wandering gleeman. They were often craftsmen in their ordinary avocations. They represent a phase of the development of German verse from the minnesang (see MINNESINGERS). The Meister-sang and singer were governed by an elaborate set of rules and organization, which are depicted in Wagner's opera *Die Meistersinger von Nürnberg*, produced in 1868.

Melantius, a character in Beaumont and Fletcher's *The Maid's Tragedy*.

Melbury, Grace, a character in Hardy's *The Woodlanders*.

Meleagant (Mellyagaunce, Mellygaunt, etc., in Malory's *Morte D'Arthur*), in the Arthurian legends, the evil son of the good king Bademagus (Baudemagus) of Gorre. He abducts Guinevere after winning her by a trick at Arthur's court and is pursued by Arthur's knights. Their conflict is the central story in the *Lancelot* of *Chrétien de Troyes.

'Melibeus, The Tale of', see CANTERBURY TALES, 18.

Melincourt, or *Sir Oran Haut-ton*, a satire by *Peacock, published 1817.

One of the longest and most ambitious of Peacock's books, it features the wooing by various suitors of a rich young heiress, Anthelia Melincourt, her abduction by a villainous peer, Lord Anophel Achthar, and his friend, the Revd Mr Grovelgrub, and her rescue when she is about to be raped by Lord Anophel. Anthelia is ultimately rescued by a humorous variant on the Noble Savage, Sir Oran Haut-ton (see MONBODDO), an orang-utan whom the hero, Mr Sylvan Forester, has educated to everything except speech, and for whom he has bought a seat in Parliament. Sir Oran's virtues show up the corruptions of 'advanced' society. Forester, an idealistic primitivist, debates with Mr Fax, a Malthusian economist, such causes as rotten boroughs, paper currency, slavery, and the recent conservatism of the Lake Poets. Provoked by an article by *Southey in the *Quarterly Review*, vol. xvi (1816), Peacock censures Southey himself (Mr Feathernest), *Coleridge (Mr Mystic), *Wordsworth (Mr Paperstamp), and *Gifford (Mr Vamp), as a group of political renegades.

Mell, Mr, in Dickens's *David Copperfield*, the poor usher at Creakle's school.

Mellefont, a character in Congreve's *The Double Dealer*.

Melmoth the Wanderer, a novel by C. R. *Maturin, published 1820.

This was one of the most effective of the *'Gothic' novels. Melmoth, who has sold his soul for the promise of prolonged life, offers relief from suffering to each of the characters, whose terrible stories succeed one another, if they will take over his bargain with the Devil.

After his trial *Wilde adopted the name Sebastian Melmoth.

Melmotte, Augustus, a financial speculator, one of the principal characters in A. Trollope's novel *The Way We Live Now*.

Melodrama, in early 19th-cent. use, a stage play (usually romantic and sensational in plot and incident) in which songs and music were interspersed. In later use the musical element diminished and the name now denotes a dramatic piece characterized by sensational incident and violent appeals to the emotions, but with a happy ending [*OED*].

MELVILLE, Herman (1819–91), American novelist and poet. After sailing as a 'boy' on a packet to Liverpool in 1839, Melville shipped in 1841 on the whaler *Acushnet* for the South Seas, where he jumped ship, joined the US Navy, and finally returned three years later to begin writing.

The fictionalized travel narrative of *Typee or a Peep at Polynesian Life* (1846) was Melville's most popular book during his lifetime. After a well-received sequel, *Omoo: A Narrative of Adventures in the South Seas* (1847), the perfunctorily plotted *Mardi and a Voyage Thither* (1849) fared less well.

Melville wrote the realistic sea stories *Redburn: His First Voyage* (1849) and *White-Jacket; or The World in a Man-of-War* (1850), which he considered pot-boilers. His masterpiece was *Moby-Dick, or, The Whale* (1851), whose brilliance was noted by some critics and very few readers.

After the critical disaster of *Pierre, or the Ambiguities* (1852), a *Gothic romance, Melville wrote anonymous magazine stories, among them 'Bartleby the Scrivener' and 'Benito Cereno', which were collected in *The Piazza Tales* (1856), and the historical novel *Israel Potter: His Fifty Years of Exile* (1855) about a neglected hero of the American revolution.

His other works include *The Confidence-Man: His Masquerade* (1857), his last novel, a mordantly nihilistic satire of human gullibility set on the ironically named Mississippi steamboat *Fiddle*; *Battle-Pieces and Aspects of the War* (1865); *John Marr and Other Sailors* (1888); and *Timoleon* (1891). Melville died virtually forgotten, with *Billy Budd, Foretopman* still in manuscript: contemporary misunderstanding, censorship, and neglect, and the subsequent revision of Melville's reputation since the 1920s, have made him a classic case of the artist as reviled Titan. *Moby-Dick* is the closest approach the United States has had to a national prose epic.

Memoir-novel, an early form of the novel, purporting to be true autobiographical history, often including diaries and journals, but in fact largely or wholly fictitious. The form arose in 17th-cent. France, and *Defoe, with *Robinson Crusoe* (1719) and *Moll Flanders* (1722), was the first English master. During the 18th cent. the author's claim to be presenting a genuine memoir dwindled to a literary convention; Smollett's *Roderick Random*, Goldsmith's *The Vicar of Wakefield*, Mackenzie's *The Man of Feeling*, M. Edgeworth's *Castle Rackrent*, and many others were presented as memoirs under only the thinnest disguise. The popularity of the form declined sharply in the 19th cent., but Hogg's *Private Memoirs and Confessions of a Justified Sinner*, Dickens's *David Copperfield*, Melville's *Moby-Dick*, C. Brontë's *Jane Eyre*, and several novels of Thackeray (notably *The History of Henry Esmond*) are outstanding examples. (See also NOVEL, RISE OF THE.)

Memoirs of a Cavalier, a historical romance attributed with good reason to *Defoe, published 1724.

The pretended author, 'Col. Andrew Newport', a young English gentleman born in 1608, travels on the Continent, starting in 1630, goes to Vienna, and accompanies the army of the emperor, being present at the siege and sack of Magdeburg, which is vividly presented. He then joins the army of Gustavus Adolphus. After his return to England he joins the king's army, first against the Scots, then against the forces of Parliament.

Memoirs of a Woman of Pleasure, often known as *Fanny Hill*, a work by J. *Cleland, published 1748–9.

Cleland employs Fanny Hill as a vehicle for his absorbed examination of sexuality in its many varieties and in minute physiological detail.

Memoirs of Captain Carleton, a narrative published 1728 as *The Memoirs of an English Officer*, by Capt. George Carleton. Its authorship has been contested and, although it is now almost universally agreed to be by *Defoe, it was at one time attributed to *Swift. Captain Carleton, who unquestionably existed, is the subject of an attractive tale of soldierly adventure. Sir W. *Scott, who regarded the Memoirs as Carleton's own work, brought out a new edition in 1808.

Menaechmi, see PLAUTUS.

MENANDER (c. 342–292 BC), an Athenian dramatic poet, was the most distinguished writer of New Comedy, which, with its trend towards realistic fiction based on contemporary life, gave a pattern for much light drama from the Renaissance onwards, making its influence felt through Latin adaptations by *Plautus and *Terence, at least eight from Menander himself. No play survived the Dark Ages; but *Dyskolos* (or *Misanthrope*), a lighthearted early play, and large parts of others have been recovered from papyri in the 20th cent.

Men and Women, a collection of 51 poems by R. *Browning, published in two vols, 1855. The poems date from the period after Browning's marriage in 1846. They show Browning's mind at its most multitudinous and eclectic, ranging over history, art, philosophy, and religion; they include many of his finest dramatic monologues, such as 'Fra Lippo Lippi', 'Bishop Blougram's Apology', 'Andrea del Sarto', and 'Cleon'. The collection also includes Browning's most famous love-poem, 'Love Among the Ruins', and the problematic *'Childe Roland to the Dark Tower Came'.

Menaphon, a prose romance with interludes of verse by R. *Greene, published 1589. The romance tells the adventures of the princess Sephestia, shipwrecked on the coast of Arcadia. Sephestia, disguised as Samela, is wooed simultaneously by her father and her teenage son, while herself carrying on a love affair with her (disguised) husband. Her fourth lover is the shepherd Menaphon of the title. Among the charming lyrics is the cradle-song 'Weepe not my wanton, smile upon my knee'.

MENCKEN, H(enry) L(ouis) (1880–1956), American journalist and critic, who as literary editor from 1908, then as co-editor, 1914–23 (with G. J. *Nathan), of *The Smart Set* exercised a great influence on American taste, upholding the iconoclasm of writers as diverse as G. B. *Shaw, *Ibsen, *Nietzsche, *Zola, and Mark *Twain. In 1924 he founded with Nathan the *American Mercury* in which he continued to satirize and goad his countrymen.

Men's Wives, stories by *Thackeray, which appeared in *Fraser's Magazine*, 1843. They are concerned with different kinds of unhappy marriage, and the exploitation of one partner by the other.

Mephistopheles, a word of unknown origin, which appears first in the German *Faustbuch* of 1587 as 'Mephostophiles'. It is the name of the evil spirit to whom *Faust was said in the German legend to have sold his soul. Shakespeare, in *The Merry Wives of Windsor* (I, i), mentions 'Mephostophilus'.

Mercator, a trade journal edited by *Defoe. It succeeded *The Review* in 1713 and continued till the following year.

MERCER, David (1928–80), playwright, achieved recognition with his trilogy of television plays *Where the Difference Begins* (1961), *A Climate of Fear* (1962), and *The Birth of a Private Man* (1963), published together as *The Generations* in 1964. Mental disturbance, alienation, class conflict, generation conflict (particularly between working-class father and educated son), and the meaning of Marxism, are recurrent themes in many subsequent works for stage, screen, and television, which include *A Suitable Case for Treatment* (TV 1962, published in *Three TV Comedies*, 1966, filmed as *Morgan*, 1965); *After Haggerty*, staged and published in 1970; and

Shooting the Chandelier (TV 1977, pub. 1978). Mercer was one of the first playwrights to appreciate the possibilities of television as a writer's medium.

Merchant of Venice, The, a comedy by Shakespeare written between 1596 and 1598, printed in 1600, and reprinted in the First *Folio (1623). Its chief source is the first story of the fourth day in *Il Pecorone*, Giovanni Fiorentino's collection of *novelle*. Other sources include *Munday's *Zelauto* and the *Gesta Romanorum*.

Bassanio, a noble but poor Venetian, asks his friend Antonio, a rich merchant, for 3,000 ducats to enable him to prosecute fittingly his suit of the rich heiress Portia at Belmont. Antonio, whose money is all employed in foreign ventures, undertakes to borrow the sum from Shylock, a Jewish usurer, whom he has been wont to upbraid for his extortions. Shylock consents to lend the money against a bond by which, if the sum is not repaid at the appointed day, Antonio shall forfeit a pound of flesh. By her father's will Portia is to marry that suitor who selects of three caskets (one of gold, one of silver, one of lead) that which contains her portrait. Bassanio makes the right choice—the leaden casket—and is wedded to Portia, and his friend Gratiano to her maid Nerissa. News comes that Antonio's ships have been wrecked, that the debt has not been repaid when due, and that Shylock claims his pound of flesh. The matter is brought before the duke. Portia disguises herself as an advocate, Balthazar, and Nerissa as her clerk, and they come to the court to defend Antonio, unknown to their husbands. Failing in her appeal to Shylock for mercy, Portia admits the validity of his claim, but warns him that his life is forfeit if he spills one drop of blood, since his bond gives him right to nothing beyond the flesh. Pursuing her advantage, she argues that Shylock's life is forfeit for having conspired against the life of a Venetian citizen. The duke grants Shylock his life, but gives half his wealth to Antonio, half to the State. Antonio surrenders his claim if Shylock will turn Christian and make over his property on his death to his daughter Jessica, who has run away and married a Christian and been disinherited; to which Shylock agrees. Portia and Nerissa ask as rewards from Bassanio and Gratiano the rings that their wives have given them, which they have promised never to part with. Reluctantly they give them up, and are taken to task accordingly on their return home. The play ends with news of the safe arrival of Antonio's ships.

'Merchant's Tale, The', see CANTERBURY TALES, 10.

Mercilla, in Spenser's *Faerie Queene* (v. viii), 'a mayden Queene of high renowne' (Queen Elizabeth).

Mercutio, in Shakespeare's *Romeo and Juliet*, the lively, cynical friend of Romeo.

Mercy, in the second part of Bunyan's *Pilgrim's Progress*, a companion of Christiana.

Merdle and Mrs Merdle, characters in Dickens's *Little Dorrit*.

MEREDITH, George (1828–1909), had a precarious childhood in Portsmouth as the son of an indigent tailor who was early a widower. In 1849 he married Mary Ellen Nicholls, the widowed daughter of T. L. *Peacock, and in 1851 published his own *Poems*. His series of eastern fantasies *The Shaving of Shagpat* (1856) was well received by the critics. In 1857 his wife left him for Henry Wallis, the painter. His first major novel, *The Ordeal of Richard Feverel* (1859), caused much scandal, but it brought praise from reviewers and the friendship of *Carlyle and the *Pre-Raphaelites.

Meredith was now contributing to many periodicals, including the *Fortnightly Review, in which *Evan Harrington* began to appear in 1860; in the same year he became reader for *Chapman and Hall (a post he retained until 1894). *Modern Love* and *Poems of the Roadside* appeared in 1862; *Emilia in England* in 1864, retitled *Sandra Belloni* in 1886; *Rhoda Fleming* in 1865; and *Vittoria (a sequel to *Sandra Belloni*) began to appear in 1866 before its publication in book form in 1867. Meredith's reputation was growing steadily with the discerning public. He married Marie Vulliamy in 1864. *The Adventures of Harry Richmond* (1871) brought him the friendship of *Milnes. A political novel, *Beauchamp's Career*, followed in 1876. The novel for which he is chiefly celebrated, *The Egoist*, appeared in 1879; *The Tragic Comedians* in 1880; *Diana of the Crossways* in 1885; *One of our Conquerors* in 1891; *Lord Ormont and his Aminta* in 1894; and *The Amazing Marriage* in 1895. A collection of short stories, including the celebrated 'The Case of General Ople and Lady Camper', appeared in 1898. Further volumes of verse include *Poems and Lyrics of the Joy of Earth* (1883, containing 'Love in a Valley'); *Ballads . . . of Tragic Life* (1887); *A Reading of Earth* (1888, containing 'Hymn to Colour'); and *Last Poems* (1909).

Meredith's reputation stood very high well into this century, with his perceptive portrayal of women, his narrative skill, and his incisive dialogue receiving most praise; but the deliberate intricacy of much of his prose defeats many modern readers.

MEREDITH, Owen, see LYTTON, E. R. B.

MERES, Francis (1565–1647), was author of *Palladis Tamia, Wits Treasury* (1598), containing quotations and maxims from various writers, reviewing literary effort from the time of

*Chaucer to his own day, contrasting each English author with a writer of like character in Latin, Greek, or Italian; his list of Shakespeare's works with his commendation of the dramatist's 'fine filed phrase' and his account of *Marlowe's death are notable elements in English literary history.

Merion, Diana, the heroine of Meredith's *Diana of the Crossways.

Merle, Madame, a character in H. James's *The Portrait of a Lady.

Merlin, the magician who guides the destinies of *Arthur and his predecessor *Uther. His story is first set out by *Geoffrey of Monmouth in his *Vita Merlini* (c. 1150), which draws on the story of Ambrosius told by *Nennius. Merlin is born of a devil and a virtuous maiden. He is superhumanly precocious and hairy but, although wilful, not malevolent as his diabolical father intended. He grows infatuated with Nimiane (Nimue or Vivien: see LADY OF THE LAKE), who imprisons him in a forest of air in Broceliande where he dies. He predicts to *Vortigern the triumph of the Britons over the Saxons, as a gloss on the killing of a white dragon by a red one after the two creatures are released by the digging of the foundations of a citadel from which Vortigern is to fight the Saxons. In Geoffrey of Monmouth's *Historia Regum Britanniae* he aids Uther in the deceit by which he marries Igraine (Ygerna) and fathers Arthur, and he helps by magic to bring the great stones of Stonehenge from Naas in Ireland. The Arthurian stories connected with him form a very important part of the whole tradition in French in the Middle Ages, particularly as transmitted by the (fragmentary) stories of Merlin by Robert de *Boron, c.1200, the prose Vulgate *Merlin* and the *Suite du Merlin* (*Huth Merlin*).

'Merlin and Vivien', one of Tennyson's *Idylls of the King*, published 1859 as 'Vivien', retitled 1870. The wily Vivien, filled with hatred for Arthur and his court, seduces the aged Merlin and imprisons him forever in an old oak.

Mermaid Series, The, a series of unexpurgated reprints of early English dramatists, published originally by *Vizetelly, at the suggestion of Havelock *Ellis. It became in 1964 the New Mermaid Series. The series now includes English plays from the late medieval period up to the time of *Synge and *Wilde.

Mermaid Tavern, a tavern that stood in Bread Street (with an entrance in Friday Street), London. One of the earliest of English clubs, the Friday Street Club, started by Sir W. *Ralegh, met there and was frequented by Shakespeare,

*Selden, *Donne, *Beaumont, and J. *Fletcher. It is celebrated by Beaumont in 'Master Francis Beaumont to Ben Jonson'. *Keats also wrote 'Lines on the Mermaid Tavern' beginning: 'Souls of poets dead and gone'.

Merrilies, Meg, the old gypsy woman in Scott's *Guy Mannering*. She is the subject of a poem by *Keats, 'Old Meg she was a gipsy'.

MERRY, Robert, see DELLA CRUSCANS.

Merry Devil of Edmonton, The, a romantic comedy published 1608, authorship unknown. C. *Lamb, who praised it highly, suggested *Drayton as the possible author.

Merry Wives of Windsor, The, a romantic comedy by *Shakespeare printed in a 'bad' quarto (1602); the *Folio text (1623) is twice as long. The tradition that it was written at the request of *Elizabeth I for a play showing *Falstaff in love is documented no earlier than 1702 (by J. *Dennis).

Falstaff, who is 'out at heels', determines to make love to the wives of Ford and Page, two gentlemen dwelling at Windsor, because they have the rule of their husband's purses. Nym and Pistol, the discarded followers of Falstaff, warn the husbands. Falstaff sends identical love-letters to Mrs Ford and Mrs Page, who contrive the discomfiture of the knight. At a first assignation at Ford's house, on the arrival of the husband, they hide Falstaff in a basket, cover him with foul linen, and have him tipped into a muddy ditch. At a second assignation, they disguise him as the 'fat woman of Brainford', in which character he is soundly beaten by Ford. The jealous husband having also been twice fooled, the plot is now revealed to him, and a final assignation is given to Falstaff in Windsor Forest at Herne's oak (see HERNE THE HUNTER), where he is beset and pinched by mock fairies and finally seized and exposed by Ford and Page.

The sub-plot is concerned with the wooing of Anne, the daughter of Page, by three suitors: Doctor Caius, a French physician, Slender, the foolish cousin of Justice Shallow, and Fenton, a wild young gentleman, whom Anne loves. Mistress Quickly, servant to Dr Caius, acts as go-between for all three suitors, and encourages them all impartially. Fenton, after much interference and plotting on behalf of the suitors, finally runs away with Anne and marries her.

Merygreeke, Mathewe, a character in Udall's *Ralph Roister Doister.

Messiah, (1) a famous oratorio by *Handel; (2) a sacred eclogue by *Pope published in *The Spectator* in May 1712, embodying in verse the Messianic prophecies of Isaiah.

Messianic Eclogue, see VIRGIL'S FOURTH OR MESSIANIC ECLOGUE.

Metamorphoses, see APULEIUS and OVID.

Metaphor, the transfer of a name or descriptive term to an object different from, but analogous to, that to which it is properly applicable, e.g. 'abysmal ignorance'. Mixed Metaphor is the application of two inconsistent metaphors to one object.

*Empson defines metaphor as the first of his *Seven Types of Ambiguity*.

Metaphysical Poets. Poets generally grouped under this label include *Donne (who is regarded as founder of the 'school'), G. *Herbert, *Crashaw, H. *Vaughan, *Marvell, and *Traherne, together with lesser figures like *Benlowes, *Herbert of Cherbury, H. *King, A. *Cowley, and *Cleveland. The label was first used (disparagingly) by Dr *Johnson in his 'Life of Cowley' (written in 1777). *Dryden had complained that Donne 'affects the metaphysics', perplexing the minds of the fair sex with 'nice speculations of philosophy'. Earlier still W. *Drummond censored poetic innovators who employed 'Metaphysical Ideas and Scholastical Quiddities'. The label is misleading, since none of these poets is seriously interested in metaphysics (except Herbert of Cherbury, and even he excludes the interest from his poetry). Further, these poets have in reality little in common: the features their work is generally taken to display are sustained dialectic, paradox, novelty, incongruity, 'muscular' rhythms, giving the effect of a 'speaking voice', and the use of 'conceits', or comparisons in which tenor and vehicle can be related only by ingenious pseudo-logic.

With the new taste for clarity and the impatience with figurative language that prevailed after the *Restoration, their reputation dwindled. Their revival was delayed until after the First World War when the revaluation of metaphysical poetry, and the related downgrading of *Romanticism and *Milton, was the major feature of the rewriting of English literary history in the first half of the 20th cent. Key documents in the revival were H. J. C. *Grierson's *Metaphysical Lyrics and Poems of the Seventeenth Century* (1921) and T. S. *Eliot's essay 'Metaphysical Poets', which first appeared as a review of Grierson's collection (*TLS*, 20 Oct. 1921). According to Eliot these poets had the advantage of writing at a time when thought and feeling were closely fused, before the *'dissociation of sensibility' set in about the time of Milton. Their virtues of difficulty and tough newness were felt to relate them closely to the modernists—*Pound, *Yeats, and Eliot himself.

Metaphysical Society, The, founded 1869 by Sir J. T. Knowles. It lasted until 1880 and brought together most of the leaders of English thought of the period, including T. H. *Huxley, *Tyndall, *Manning, *Gladstone, and *Tennyson.

Metathesis, the transposition of letters or sounds in a word. When the transposition is between the letters or sounds of two words, it is popularly known as a 'Spoonerism', of which a well-known specimen, attributed to the Revd W. A. Spooner (1844–1930), warden of New College, Oxford, is 'Kinquering congs their titles take'.

Metre. The sound patterns on whose recurrence rhythm depends were formed in antiquity by arrangements of long and short syllables. Lines of verse consisted of 'feet', the commonest being the iambus ($\cup-$), trochee ($-\cup$), anapaest ($\cup\cup-$), dactyl ($-\cup\cup$), spondee ($--$). The pyrrhic ($\cup\cup$), tribrach ($\cup\cup\cup$), amphibrach ($\cup-\cup$), cretic ($-\cup-$), paeon ($-\cup\cup\cup$), bacchius ($\cup--$), ionic a minore ($\cup\cup--$), and choriamb ($-\cup\cup-$) featured mainly in lyric poems. The most popular ancient measure was the *hexameter; it was divided by a *caesura usually in the third foot. Elegiac couplets linked the hexameter with a pentameter which consisted of two feet (dactyls or spondees) and a single long syllable before the caesura followed by two dactyls and a single syllable, always end-stopped. Dramatists used the iambic trimeter because of its closeness to common speech. This comprised six feet arranged in pairs (hence 'trimeter') where the iamb could be replaced by other feet according to strict rules. There were also numerous lyric metres. Alcaics, Sapphics, and Asclepiads organized trochees, dactyls, and spondees in various patterns, and trochaic *hendecasyllabics flourished in satire.

The 5th cent. AD brought, however, the beginnings of a radical change. The shape of the classical feet was retained, but stress became their determining feature, so that a trochee was an accented followed by an unaccented syllable. The trochaic tetrameter catalectic, which was divided by a caesura after the fourth trochee, the second half consisting of three trochees and a single syllable, provided the basis for most medieval hymns.

English prosody is similarly based on stress. The earliest measures to develop were trochaic, but soon iambic couplets of four or five feet linked by rhyme became more popular. In the four-foot couplet we find extensive modulation: often the first foot has only one syllable, and the final syllable in the fifth foot is dropped. The five-foot couplet had a strict form, end-stopped with a marked middle break, but also a form that allowed overflow from one line to the next and substitution of different two- or even three-syllable feet for the iamb. But it is not in the couplet that the five-foot iambic line (iambic pentameter) attained greatest importance. Introduced into poetic drama in 1562, it had a distinguished history as *'blank verse', with more modulations than in the couplet and the final foot often replaced by an amphibrach. When blank verse was used later in epic by *Milton, the modulations, if more controlled, were also more frequent and the use of overflow developed into paragraph construction. Five-foot lines were also built into stanzas with a variety of rhyme schemes: rhyme-royal (or rime royal, seven lines rhymed ababbcc), used for narrative from *Chaucer to W. *Morris; the nine-line *Spenserian stanza, ababbcbcc; and, principally, the *sonnet introduced by *Wyatt and used since by every major English poet. (Wyatt copied *Petrarch, dividing the sonnet into an octave rhymed abba, abba, and a sestet ccd, ccd or cde, cde; but Shakespeare preferred three quatrains ending with a couplet.) Other popular iambic metres include in Tudor times the awkward *Poulter's Measure, a rhymed couplet where the first line had twelve, the second fourteen syllables. Broken by pause and internal rhyme, this makes a stanza 3343 which has been widely used by hymn writers. Fourteeners appear unresolved in *Chapman's *Homer*, but provide, when divided 4343 and rhymed, the buoyant and well-known ballad stanza. Trochaic, anapaestic, and dactylic metres, though they figure in many poems, have not been as popular as the iambic.

Metroland, Margot (originally Margot Beste-Chetwynde), a character in E. Waugh's *Decline and Fall, Vile Bodies, *Scoop*, and other novels.

MEUN, Jean de, see ROMAN DE LA ROSE.

MEW, Charlotte Mary (1869–1928), poet and short story writer. Her short story 'Passed' appeared in *The Yellow Book* in 1894, but she did not become well known until her first volume of poetry, *The Farmer's Bride* (1915). Her second volume, *The Rambling Sailor*, appeared posthumously in 1929. Her poems are notable for a restraint of expression combined with a powerful and passionate content which distinguish her from many of her Georgian contemporaries. She died by suicide.

MEYNELL, Alice, née Thompson (1847–1922), poet and essayist. Her first volume of poetry, *Preludes* (1875), attracted the attention of Wilfrid Meynell (1852–1948), author and editor, whom she married in 1877. Her several volumes of verse won her a considerable reputation; many of her most successful poems deal with the theme of religious mystery. She is perhaps now more admired for her essays, introductions, and anthologies, which manifest independence and sensitivity of critical judgement; these were collected under various titles, which include *The Rhythm of Life* (1893), *The Colour of Life* (1896), and *The Spirit of Place* (1899).

Micawber, Wilkins and Mrs, characters in Dickens's *David Copperfield*.

'Michael', a pastoral poem by *Wordsworth, written and published 1800. The poem is a narrative in blank verse, describing, with a moving strength and simplicity, the lonely life in Grasmere of the old shepherd Michael, his wife, and his beloved son Luke. Because of family misfortune Luke is sent away to a dissolute city, where he disgraces himself; he eventually disappears abroad. Michael dies in grief and the cottage and pasture become a ruin.

Michael Angelo Titmarsh, see TITMARSH, M. A.

Michaelmas Terme, see MIDDLETON, T.

Microcosm of London, The, see ACKERMANN, R.

Microcosmographie, see EARLE, J.

Midas, a prose play by *Lyly, published 1592, on the legend of Midas, king of Phrygia.

Middle Ages, the period from the Roman decadence (AD 5th cent.) to the Renaissance (about 1500), to designate the period between the end of classical culture proper and its revival at the Renaissance. The high point of its culture is the 12th and 13th cents. The earliest use of 'Middle Age' in this sense yet discovered is in one of *Donne's sermons (1621), but the corresponding Latin terms, *medium aevum, media aetas*, etc., are found in the 16th cent. The term is sometimes restricted to the 11th–15th cents, the earlier part of the period being called the Dark Ages.

Middle English, see ENGLISH.

Middlemarch, *A Study of Provincial Life*, a novel by G. *Eliot, published 1871–2.
   The scene is laid in the provincial town of Middlemarch, Loamshire, during the years immediately preceding the first *Reform Bill. It has a multiple plot, with several interlocking sets of characters. Dorothea Brooke, an ardent, intelligent, idealistic young woman, marries the elderly pedant Mr Casaubon, despite the doubts of her sister Celia, her neighbour and suitor Sir James Chettam (who later marries Celia), and Mrs Cadwallader, the rector's outspoken wife. The marriage proves intensely unhappy; Dorothea realizes during a disastrous honeymoon in Rome that Casaubon's scholarly plans to write a great work, a 'Key to all Mythologies', are doomed, as are her own aspirations to share her husband's intellectual life, and her respect for him gradually turns to pity. She is sustained by the friendship of Casaubon's young cousin, Will Ladislaw, a

lively young man detested by Casaubon, who begins to suspect Dorothea's feelings for Ladislaw. Shortly before he dies, with characteristic meanness, he adds a codicil to his will by which Dorothea forfeits her fortune if she marries Ladislaw.

Meanwhile we follow the fortunes of Fred and Rosamund Vincy, son and daughter of the mayor of Middlemarch; the extrovert Fred is in love with his childhood sweetheart Mary Garth, daughter of Caleb Garth, a land agent. Mary will not pledge herself to Fred unless he abandons his father's plan for him to enter the Church and proves himself stable and self-sufficient. Rosamund, the town's beauty, sets herself to capture the ambitious, idealistic, and well-connected doctor Tertius Lydgate: she succeeds, but their marriage is wrecked by her selfishness and materialism. Lydgate, heavily in debt, borrows money from Mr Bulstrode, the mayor's brother-in-law; Lydgate's career is ruined by his involvement in a scandal concerning the death of Raffles, an unwelcome visitor from Bulstrode's shady past. Only Dorothea maintains faith in him, but she is severely shocked to find Ladislaw and Rosamund together in apparently compromising circumstances. Rosamund finally reveals that Ladislaw has remained faithful to the memory of Dorothea. Dorothea and Ladislaw at last confess their love to one another; she renounces Casaubon's fortune and marries him. Fred marries Mary. Lydgate dies at 50, his ambitions frustrated.

Middleton, Clara and Dr, characters in Meredith's *The Egoist.*

MIDDLETON, Conyers (1683–1750), wrote *Letter from Rome* (1729), and a life of Cicero (1741). His *A Free Inquiry into the Miraculous Powers which are supposed to have subsisted in the Christian Church* (1749), which attacked the authenticity of post-apostolic miracles, caused much controversy.

MIDDLETON, Thomas (1580–1627), collaborated with J. *Webster, *Dekker, *Rowley, *Munday, and others, and wrote many successful comedies of city life, including *The Roaring Girle* (with Dekker, 1611), *Michaelmas Terme* (1607), *A Mad World, My Masters* (1608), *A Chaste mayd in Cheap-side* (1630), and *A Fair Quarrel*, a tragi-comedy written with Rowley (1617). *The Spanish Gipsy*, also with Rowley (and possibly *Ford, 1625) is a romantic comedy based on two plots from *Cervantes. Other plays include *The Witch* (written 1609–16, published 1778); *The Widow* (with *Jonson? and *Fletcher?, written 1615–17, published 1652), and *Anything for a Quiet Life* (with Webster?, written c.1620–2, published 1662).

A writer of great versatility, Middleton also wrote many pageants and masques for city occasions, and was appointed city chronologer in 1620. His political satire *A Game at Chesse* (1625) created a furore, and caused him and the actors to be summoned before the Privy Council. Middleton is now best known for his two great tragedies, *The Changeling* (with Rowley, written 1622, published 1653) and *Women beware Women* (written 1620–7, published 1657), both of which were highly praised by T. S. *Eliot in his influential essay on Middleton (1927). Many scholars now consider that *The Revenger's Tragedy* (1607) is by Middleton. He probably collaborated with *Shakespeare in *Macbeth and *Timon of Athens.

Midshipman Easy, Mr, a novel by F. *Marryat, published 1836.

Jack Easy is the son of a wealthy gentleman who brings his boy up to believe that all men are equal, a notion which causes considerable problems to Jack as a midshipman. But he is heir to a fortune and this, together with his cheerful honesty and the aid of his Ashanti friend Mesty, help him through many clashes, encounters, and adventures. Hawkins, the bellicose chaplain, Mr Biggs the boatswain, and Mr Pottyfar, the lieutenant who kills himself with his own universal medicine, are notable among the ship's company.

Midsummer Night's Dream, A, a comedy by *Shakespeare, written probably about 1595 or 1596, printed in quarto in 1600 and 1619. It has no single major source, but Shakespeare drew, among other authors, on *Chaucer, *Golding's translation of *Ovid, and Apuleius' *Golden Ass.

Hermia, ordered by her father Egeus to marry Demetrius, refuses, because she loves Lysander, while Demetrius has formerly professed love for her friend Helena, and Helena loves Demetrius. Under the law of Athens, Theseus, the duke, gives Hermia four days in which to obey her father; else she must suffer death or enter a nunnery. Hermia and Lysander agree to leave Athens secretly in order to be married where the Athenian law cannot pursue them, and to meet in a wood a few miles from the city. Hermia tells Helena of the project, and the latter tells Demetrius. Demetrius pursues Hermia to the wood, and Helena Demetrius, so that all four are that night in the wood. This wood is the favourite haunt of the fairies.

Oberon and Titania, king and queen of the fairies, have quarrelled, because Titania refuses to give up to him a little changeling boy for a page. Oberon tells Puck, a mischievous sprite, to fetch him a certain magic flower, of which he will press the juice on the eyes of Titania while she sleeps, so that she may fall in love with what she first sees when she wakes. Overhearing Demetrius in the wood reproaching Helena for following him, and desirous to reconcile them, Oberon orders Puck to place some of the love-juice on Demetrius' eyes, but so that Helena shall be near him when he does it. Puck, mistaking Lysander for Demetrius, applies the charm to him, and as Helena is the first person Lysander sees he at once woos her, enraging her because she thinks she is being made a jest of. Oberon, discovering Puck's mistake, now places some of the juice on Demetrius' eyes; he on waking also first sees Helena, so that both Lysander and Demetrius are now wooing her. The ladies begin to abuse one another and the men go off to fight for Helena.

Meanwhile Oberon has placed the love-juice on Titania's eyelids, who wakes to find Bottom the weaver near her, wearing an ass's head (Bottom and a company of Athenian tradesmen are in the wood to rehearse a play for the duke's wedding, and Puck has put an ass's head on Bottom); Titania at once becomes enamoured of him, and toys with his 'amiable cheeks' and 'fair large ears'. Oberon, finding them together, reproaches Titania for bestowing her love on an ass, and again demands the changeling boy, whom she in her confusion surrenders; whereupon Oberon releases her from the charm. Puck at Oberon's orders throws a thick fog about the human lovers, and brings them all together, unknown to one another, and they fall asleep. He applies a remedy to their eyes, so that when they awake they return to their former loves. Theseus and Egeus appear on the scene, the runaways are forgiven, and the couples married. The play ends with the 'play' of 'Pyramus and Thisbe', comically acted by Bottom and his fellow tradesmen, to grace these nuptials and those of Theseus and Hippolyta.

Miggs, Miss, in Dickens's *Barnaby Rudge*, the shrewish maidservant of Mrs Varden.

Miles gloriosus, the braggart soldier, a stock character in Greek and Roman comedy, and also the title of a play by *Plautus, which contains a prototype of the role in its protagonist, Pyrgopolynices. Elements of the miles gloriosus may be found in Shakespeare's *Parolles, *Pistol, and *Falstaff, in Jonson's Captain *Bobadill, and in Beaumont and Fletcher's *Bessus.

Milesians, the people of Miledh, a fabulous Spanish king, whose sons are said to have invaded Ireland about 1300 BC. They represent probably the first Gaelic invaders of the country. See FIR BOLGS.

Milesian Tales, a collection, now lost, of short Greek stories of love and adventure, of a generally licentious character, by Aristides of Miletus of the 2nd cent. BC.

MILL, James (1773–1836), was educated for the ministry, but came to London in 1802 and took up journalism. He published in 1817 a *History of British India* which obtained him a high post in the East India Company's service. He was closely associated with *Bentham and *Ricardo, whose views in philosophy and political economy, respectively, he adopted. He published *Elements of Political Economy* (1821) and *Analysis of the Phenomena of the Human Mind* (1829), in which he provided, by an elaboration of *Hartley's theory of association, a psychological basis for Bentham's utilitarianism. He also endeavoured to found on the association of ultimate sensations a theory of knowledge and reality. The *Fragment on Mackintosh* (1835) is a rejoinder to the attack on the utilitarians contained in the *Dissertation on the Progress of Ethical Philosophy* of *Mackintosh. Mill helped to found and contributed to the *Westminster Review*.

MILL, John Stuart (1806–73), son of James *Mill, formed the Utilitarian Society, which met during 1823–6 to read essays and discuss them, and in 1825 he edited *Bentham's *Treatise upon Evidence*. In 1831 he met Harriet Taylor, who was, in his view, the chief inspiration of his philosophy; after her husband's death they married in 1851. His divergence from strict Benthamite doctrine is shown in his essays on 'Bentham' and 'Coleridge' (1838, 1840, *London and Westminster Review*) whom he describes as 'the two great seminal minds of England in this age'; and, later, in *Utilitarianism* (1861). In 1843 he published his *System of *Logic* and in 1848 *Principles of Political Economy*. In 1859 appeared his essay on *Liberty* and two volumes of *Dissertations and Discussions*, and in 1865 his *Examination of Sir William Hamilton's Philosophy*. Among other works may be mentioned *Thoughts on Parliamentary Reform* (1859), *Representative Government* (1861), *Auguste Comte and Positivism* (1865), his *Inaugural Address* on being installed rector of the University of St Andrews in 1867, and *The Subjection of Women* (1869). His *Autobiography* (1873), a classic of its genre, describes his intellectual and moral development from his earliest years to his maturity.

Millamant, the heroine of Congreve's *The Way of the World*, a witty coquette, who is at the same time a lady of fashion, the author's most vivid creation.

MILLAY, Edna St Vincent (1892–1950), American poet. *A Few Figs from Thistles* (1920) established her persona as a reckless, romantic, cynical, 'naughty' New Woman with such poems as 'The Penitent' and 'My Candle Burns at Both Ends'. Other volumes followed, including dramatic pieces and her *Collected Poems* (1956).

MILLER, Arthur (1915–), American playwright, made his name with *All My Sons* (1947) and established himself as a leading dramatist with *Death of a Salesman* (1949), in which a travelling salesman, Willie Loman, is brought to disaster by accepting the false values of contemporary society. This was followed by other plays including *The Crucible* (1952); *A View from the Bridge* (1955); *The Misfits* (1961), a screenplay written for his then wife, Marilyn Monroe; *After the Fall* (1964); and *The Price* (1968). Miller has also published short stories and essays, and adapted *Ibsen's *An Enemy of the People* (1951). Although most of Miller's plays are set in contemporary America, and on the whole offer a realistic portrayal of life and society, the overtones from Ibsen and Greek tragedy are frequently conspicuous, and the theme of self-knowledge and self-realization is recurrent.

MILLER, Henry Valentine (1891–1980), American novelist and essayist. He left America for Europe in 1930, and his autobiographical novel *Tropic of Cancer* (1934, Paris) is a frank and lively account of an American artist's adventures in Paris, and was banned for decades (as were many of his works) in Britain and the US. This was followed by many other works which mingled metaphysical speculation (he was interested in both theosophy and astrology) with sexually explicit scenes, surreal passages, and scenes of grotesque comedy; they include *Tropic of Capricorn* (France, 1939; US 1962), *The Colossus of Maroussi* (1941), *The Air-Conditioned Nightmare* (1945, reflections on a return to America), and a sequence of three works, *Sexus* (1949), *Plexus* (1953), and *Nexus* (1960), known together as *The Rosy Crucifixion*. In 1944 he settled in California. He gradually became accepted as a major figure in the fight for literary and personal freedom, and a spiritual sage who greatly influenced the *Beat generation in its search for salvation through extremes of experience.

MILLER, Hugh (1802–56), born in Cromarty, began to write poetry while working as a stonemason, but made a more lasting mark as a journalist and self-educated palaeontologist. His *The Old Red Sandstone, or New Walks in an Old Field* (1841), a vivid account of his sense of excitement and discovery when, as a young man, he learned to look for fossils in the sandstone quarries, became a Victorian classic. His other works include his autobiographical *My Schools and Schoolmasters* (1854); and *The Footprints of the Creator* (1849), an attack on R. *Chambers's *The Vestiges of Creation*, in which Miller expounded his own God-centred and pre-Darwinian views of evolution.

'Miller of Dee, The', see BICKERSTAFFE.

'Miller's Tale, The', see CANTERBURY TALES, 2.

Mill on the Floss, The, a novel by G. *Eliot, published 1860.

Tom and Maggie, the principal characters, are the children of the honest but ignorant and obstinate Mr Tulliver, the miller of Dorlcote Mill on the Floss. Tom is a prosaic youth, narrow of imagination and intellect; Maggie in contrast is highly strung, intelligent, and emotional. Her deep love of her brother is thwarted by his lack of understanding, and she turns to Philip Wakem, the deformed son of a neighbouring lawyer, for intellectual and emotional companionship. Unfortunately lawyer Wakem is the object of Mr Tulliver's suspicion and dislike, which develop into hatred when Tulliver is made bankrupt as a result of litigation in which Wakem is on the other side. Tom, loyal to his father, discovers the secret friendship of Maggie and Philip, and forbids their meetings: Maggie reluctantly complies. After Mr Tulliver's death, Maggie visits St Ogg's, where her cousin Lucy Deane is to marry the handsome and agreeble Stephen Guest. Stephen is attracted by Maggie, and she by him. A boating expedition on the river leads to Maggie's being irremediably compromised; Stephen implores her to marry him, but she refuses. Her brother turns her out of the house, and the society of St Ogg's ostracizes her. She and her mother take refuge with the loyal friend of her childhood, the packman Bob Jakins. In the last chapter a great flood descends upon the town, and Maggie courageously rescues her brother from the mill. There is a moment of reconciliation before the boat overturns, and both are drowned.

Mills, Miss, in Dickens's *David Copperfield*, Dora's friend.

Mills and Boon, a publishing company founded in 1908; its early authors included P. G. *Wodehouse and Jack *London, and it launched the career of Georgette *Heyer. Its name has since become almost synonymous with popular romantic fiction.

MILMAN, Henry Hart (1791–1868), professor of poetry at Oxford (1821–31) and dean of St Paul's (1849). He wrote a number of verse dramas including *Fazio* (1815); a Miltonic epic, *Samor* (1818); and various historical works.

MILNE, A(lan) A(lexander) (1882–1956), a prolific author of plays, novels, poetry, short stories, and essays, all of which have been overshadowed by his children's books. His plays include *Mr Pim Passes By* (1919; pub. 1921), *The Truth about Blayds* (1921; pub. 1922), *The Dover Road* (1921; pub. 1922), and *Toad of Toad Hall* (1929; a dramatization of *Grahame's *The Wind in the Willows*). His books of children's stories include *When We Were Very Young* (1924), *Winnie-the-Pooh* (1926), *Now We Are Six* (1927), and *The House at Pooh Corner* (1928). (See CHILDREN'S LITERATURE.)

MILNES, (Richard) Monckton (1809–85), later Baron Houghton, was educated at Trinity College, Cambridge, where he became the friend of *Tennyson, A. H. *Hallam, and *Thackeray, the first of many close literary friendships, which included *Swinburne (whom he greatly assisted). In 1837 he became an MP and worked for various reforming causes, including the Copyright Act and the establishment of Mechanics' Institutes. He published his first volume of verse in 1838 and *Palm Leaves* in 1844, following these with works of biography, history, sociology, and Boswelliana. His major work was probably his *Life and Letters of Keats* (1848). He also did much to enhance the reputation of *Blake, and in 1875 edited the works of T. L. *Peacock. His own collected *Poetical Works* appeared in 1876. His large collection of erotic books included the first serious collection of de Sade.

Milton, a poem in two books by W. *Blake, written and etched 1804–8, one of his longest and most complex mythological works, which is prefaced by his well-known lines 'And did those feet in ancient time', commonly known as 'Jerusalem'. It uses the mythological and allegorical framework of his earlier poems and also develops Blake's own extremely powerful and personal response to *Paradise Lost* and its author, which had affected and perplexed his imagination for years (see also under MARRIAGE OF HEAVEN AND HELL, THE).

MILTON, John (1608–74), son of John Milton the elder, a scrivener and composer of music. He was educated at St Paul's School and Christ's College, Cambridge, where he wrote poetry in Latin, Italian, and English, on both sacred and secular themes. His first known attempts at English verse, 'On the Death of a Fair Infant' and 'At a Vacation Exercise', were probably written in 1628. His first distinctively Miltonic work, 'On the Morning of Christs Nativity', written in 1629, shows a growing mastery of stanza and structure, an exuberant and at times baroque use of imagery, and the love of resounding proper names so marked in his later work. His fragmentary 'The Passion' and the *'Arcades' were probably written in 1630. 'On Shakespeare', his two epitaphs for *Hobson, the unversity carrier, and 'An Epitaph on the Marchioness of Winchester' belong to 1631. His twin poems, *'L'Allegro' and *'Il Penseroso', may also have been written at Cambridge. On leaving Cambridge he embarked on an ambitious course of private study at his father's home in preparation for a future as poet or clergyman; his Latin poem 'Ad Patrem' (?1634) appears to be an attempt to persuade his father that the two pursuits were reconcilable. His 'masque' *Comus was published anonymously in 1637, in which year he wrote *Lycidas, an elegy. During the 20 years

that elapsed between this and his composition of *Paradise Lost, Milton wrote no poetry, apart from some Latin and Italian pieces, and some sonnets, of which the most notable are those 'On the late Massacre in Piedmont', on his blindness, on his deceased wife, his addresses to *Cromwell, Fairfax, and Vane, and those to *Lawes (with whom he had collaborated on the 'Arcades' and *Comus*) and to his young friends and students Edward Lawrence and Cyriack Skinner. From 1637 to 1639 Milton travelled abroad, chiefly in Italy; he met Grotius in Paris and *Galileo. His Latin epitaph on his friend *Diodati, *Epitaphium Damonis*, written in 1639, is his finest Latin poem.

His attentions were now diverted by historical events to many years of pamphleteering and political activity, and to a tireless defence of religious, civil, and domestic liberties. In 1641 he published a series of five pamphlets against episcopacy, engaging in controversy with bishops *Hall and *Ussher, and displaying from the first (*Of Reformation in England and the Causes that Hitherto Have Hindered it*) a vigorous, colourful Ciceronian prose, and a keenly polemic spirit which could yet rise to visions of apocalyptic grandeur. *The Reason of Church Government* (1642) was followed by *An Apology against a Pamphlet . . . against *Smectymnuus* (1642), which contains interesting autobiographical details. In June 1942 Milton married Mary Powell, daughter of royalist parents; he was 33, she 17. Within six weeks he consented to her going home to her parents near Oxford on condition that she returned by Michaelmas. She did not do so, for reasons perhaps connected with the outbreak of the Civil War. *The Doctrine and Discipline of Divorce* (1643) argues among other points that a true marriage was of mind as well as of body. This pamphlet made him notorious, but he pursued his arguments in three more on the subject of divorce in 1644–5, including *Tetrachordon. Of Education, and *Areopagitica, his great defence of the liberty of the press, both appeared in 1644. At this time he became aware of his growing blindness; by 1651 he was to be totally blind.

After the execution of Charles I, Milton published *The Tenure of Kings and Magistrates* (1649). He was appointed Latin secretary to the newly formed Council of State, retaining the post until the Restoration. The State papers he wrote include an interesting series of dispatches (1655–8) on the subject of the expulsion and massacre of the Protestant Vaudois. He replied officially to *Eikon Basilike in *Eikonoklastes* (i.e. Imagebreaker, 1649), and to the *Defensio Regia* of Salmasius in *Pro Populo Anglicano Defensio* (1651), a work which created a furore on the Continent and was publicly burned in Paris and Toulouse; also to Du Moulin's *Clamor* in *Defensio Secunda* (1654). He was now assisted in his secretarial duties successively by G. R. Weckherlin, Philip Meadows, and *Marvell. His first wife (having rejoined him in 1645) died in 1652, three days after the birth of their third daughter, and in 1656 he married Katherine Woodcock, then aged 28, who died in 1658. On the eve of the Restoration, he boldly published *The Ready and Easy Way to Establish a Free Commonwealth* (1660), a last-minute attempt to defend the 'Good old Cause' of republicanism. At the Restoration he went into hiding briefly, then was arrested, fined, and released: *D'Avenant and Marvell are said to have interceded on his behalf. He now returned to poetry and set about the composition of *Paradise Lost* (1667). In 1663 he married his third wife, Elizabeth Minshull (who survived him). *Paradise Regained* was published in 1671 with *Samson Agonistes*. In these later years he also published a *History of Britain* (1670), and a compendium of *Ramus's *Logic* (1672). In 1673 appeared a second edition of his *Poems* originally published in 1645, including most of his minor verse.

Milton died from 'gout struck in' and was buried beside his father in St Giles', Cripplegate. There are full biographies by D. *Masson (1859–94) and W. R. Parker (1968). Milton's towering stature as a writer was recognized early. Although appreciated as a master of polemical prose as well as of subtle lyric harmony, his reputation rests largely on *Paradise Lost*, which *Dryden (who made a rhymed version of it) was describing by 1677 as 'one of the greatest, most noble and sublime poems which either this age or nation has produced'. Poets and critics in the 18th cent. were profoundly influenced by Milton's use of blank verse (previously confined largely to drama) and his treatment of the *Sublime, and he inspired many serious and burlesque imitations and adaptations.

Mime, in modern usage, a term used to describe a kind of theatrical performance without words, in which meaning is conveyed by gesture and movement. As an art form it flourishes more on the Continent, in the work of such performers and writer-performers as Marcel Marceau (1923–) and Dario Fo (1926–) than in England.

The earliest form of mimes were the dramatic scenes from middle-class life, realistic and often obscene, first composed in the 5th cent. BC by the Athenian Sophron. The only known surviving Greek mimes (by *Theocritus and Herodas) date from two centuries later. Later still, in Rome, sketches of low life performed by several actors with masks and scenic effects became very popular. After an interlude in the Middle Ages, the genre flourished again in the 16th cent. with the *commedia dell'arte*, in which the actors relied mainly on dumb-show. Divertissements with music, dancing, and mime were also much in fashion from the Renaissance onwards and con-

tributed to the development of ballet, opera, and the English *pantomime.

Mimesis, see POETICS, THE.

Minnehaha, see HIAWATHA.

Minnesingers, German lyric poets of the late 12th to the 14th cent., so called because love (*Minne*) was the principal subject of their poetry. They corresponded to the Provençal *troubadours (who influenced them) and the Northern French *trouvères. The *Minnesang* flourished at its best in the Blütezeit period (*c.*1200). Some of the greatest Minnesingers were also writers of epic, such as *Wolfram von Eschenbach.

MINOT, Laurence, probably a soldier, the author of a series of spirited and patriotic war-songs, written about 1352, concerning events of the period 1333–52 in the English wars against the Scots and French.

Minstrel, The, see BEATTIE, J.

Minstrelsy of the Scottish Border (3 vols, 1802–3), a collection of *ballads compiled by Sir W. *Scott, who divided them into three sections, Historical Ballads, Romantic Ballads, and Imitations of the Ancient Ballad. He was aided by various friends and advisers, who included *Leyden, J. *Hogg, R. *Surtees, and many old women (including Hogg's mother) who kept alive the oral traditions. The extent to which Scott himself altered and improved on the texts has been much discussed. In his introduction Scott stated a patriotic intention: 'By such efforts, feeble as they are, I may contribute somewhat to the history of my native country; the peculiar features of whose manners and character are daily melting and dissolving into those of her sister and ally.' According to *Motherwell, Scott later in life regretted the extent of his editorial work. The volumes contain many well-known ballads, including 'The Wife of Usher's Well' (its first printing) and 'The Twa Corbies', in a version that M. J. C. Hodgart (*The Ballads*, 1950) claims is 'largely of Scott's making'.

Mirabell, (1) the hero of J. Fletcher's *Wilde Goose Chase*; (2) in Congreve's *The Way of the World*, the lover of Millamant.

Miracle Plays, see MYSTERY PLAYS.

Miranda, in Shakespeare's *The Tempest*, the daughter of Prospero.

Mirobolant, Monsieur, a character in Thackeray's *Pendennis*.

Mirour de l'Omme (*Speculum Meditantis*), see GOWER, J.

Mirror (mirour), as a literary term, based on the Medieval Latin use of the word *speculum* to mean a true reflection or description of a particular subject, hence compendium. Thus there are titles such as the *Mirror of Fools* (translation of the late 12th-cent. *Speculum Stultorum* by *Wireker) and, in the Renaissance, *A Mirror for Magistrates*.

Mirror for Magistrates, A, a work planned by George Ferrers, Master of the King's Pastimes in the reign of Henry VIII, and William Baldwin of Oxford. In it various famous men and women, most of them characters in English history, recount their downfall in verse. The book was originally begun as a continuation of *Lydgate's *The Fall of Princes*, itself based on *Boccaccio's *De Casibus*. After a suppressed edition of 1555 it first appeared in 1559, containing 20 tragedies by various authors. In the enlarged edition of 1563 T. *Sackville contributed the 'Induction' and the 'Complaint of Buckingham'.

The *Mirror* was one of the major achievements of what C. S. Lewis called the *'Drab Age', and provided source material for many major writers, including *Spenser, Shakespeare, *Daniel, and *Drayton.

Mirror of Fools (*Speculum Stultorum*), see WIREKER.

Misfortunes of Elphin, The, a satirical romance by *Peacock, published 1829.

It is an ingenious blend of Welsh Arthurian legend and current political debate about reform. Elphin is king of Ceredigion in western Wales, but the bulk of his territory has been engulfed by the sea, owing to the drunkenness of Seithenyn, who was in charge of the embankment to keep out the waves. In Seithenyn the book contains what is perhaps Peacock's finest political parody, the celebrated drunken speech about the wall ('the parts that are rotten give elasticity to those that are sound'), which imitates a speech made by *Canning in 1822 in defence of the existing Constitution. The book contains the celebrated 'War Song of Dinas Vawr', in context a sly comment on political opportunism, and a clever bardic contest in which the current Romantic fashion for escapist themes is gently mocked.

Misrule, King, Lord, or **Abbot of,** at the end of the 15th and beginning of the 16th cents an officer appointed at court to superintend the Christmas revels. At the Scottish court he was called the 'Abbot of Unreason'. Lords of Misrule were also appointed in some of the university colleges and inns of court.

MITCHELL, Adrian (1932–), poet, novelist, and playwright, was associated with the pacifism, social protest, and free verse forms of

*Underground poetry; his collections of verse include *Out Loud* (1969), *Ride the Nightmare* (1971), and *For Beauty Douglas; Collected Poems and Songs* (1981). His many plays and stage adaptations, which make considerable use of songs and lyrics, include an adaptation of Peter Weiss's *Marat/Sade* (1966) and *Tyger* (1971), based on the life and work of *Blake.

MITCHELL, James Leslie, see GIBBON, L. G.

MITCHELL, Julian (1935–), novelist and playwright. His novels include *Imaginary Toys* (1961), *The White Father* (1964, set in Africa), and the more experimental *The Undiscovered Country* (1968). Mitchell then turned to the theatre and television, adapting the novels of I. *Compton-Burnett for the stage and achieving success with *Half-Life* (1977), a play about an ageing archaeologist, and *Another Country* (1981, pub. 1982), set in the 1930s in a public school.

MITCHELL, Margaret (1900–49), American novelist, whose one novel was the best-selling *Gone with the Wind* (1936, Pulitzer Prize); the equally popular film was released in 1939. Set in Georgia at the time of the Civil War, it is the story of headstrong Scarlett O'Hara, her three marriages, and her determination to keep her father's property of Tara, despite the vicissitudes of war and passion.

MITCHISON, Naomi Mary Margaret (1897–), novelist and sister of J. B. S. *Haldane. Her many works of fiction include *The Corn King and the Spring Queen* (1931), a historical novel, *The Blood of the Martyrs* (1939), and *The Big House* (1950). Her non-fiction works, including three volumes of autobiography (1973–9), illustrate her commitment to the progressive political and social causes of the intellectual circles in which she moved.

MITFORD, Mary Russell (1787–1855), published several volumes of poems. Her dramas include *Julian* (1823), *Foscari* (1826), and *Rienzi* (1828). She is best remembered for the series of sketches and stories which made up *Our Village* (1832), based on Three Mile Cross, near Reading. This was followed by *Belford Regis* (1835), a portrait of Reading; *Country Stories* (1837); *Recollections of a Literary Life* (1852); and *Atherton, and other Tales* (1854), a novel. Her fluent letters, to *Lamb, *Haydon, *Horne, *Ruskin, Elizabeth Barrett (*Browning), W. S. *Landor, and others were published in a selection ed. A. G. L'Estrange (3 vols, 1870) and in *Letters of M. R. Mitford, 2nd Series*, ed. H. Chorley (2 vols, 1872).

MITFORD, Nancy Freeman (1904–73), writer, daughter of the second Lord Redesdale, who appears in many of her novels as the eccentric

'Uncle Matthew'. She achieved success with *The Pursuit of Love* (1945), in which the sensible Fanny, daughter of the irresponsible Bolter, describes the affairs of her six Radlett cousins. Subsequent works (*Love in a Cold Climate*, 1949; *The Blessing*, 1951; *Don't Tell Alfred*, 1960) accompany the family and its associates through various social and amatory trials and triumphs; the appeal of the novels lies in the reckless upper-class Bohemianism of many of the characters, and in Nancy Mitford's sharp ear for dialogue. *Noblesse Oblige: an enquiry into the identifiable characteristics of the English aristocracy* (1956, with A. S. C. Ross *et al.*), provoked a debate on 'U' and 'Non-U', vocabulary, terms she herself promoted in *Encounter* (1955). She also wrote several historical biographies. Her sister Jessica Mitford (1917–) has written a vivid account of Mitford family life, *Hons and Rebels* (1960).

Moby-Dick, *or, the Whale* (1851), a novel by H. *Melville.

Captain Ahab seeks revenge on the white whale that has bitten off his leg. 'Call me Ishmael', is the striking opening phrase of a story that takes the young narrator to sea on the doomed whaler *Pequod*. Both Ahab and Ishmael seek knowledge, but while Ishmael learns love and humanity 'monomaniacal Ahab' pursues a demonic God behind the 'hooded phantom' or 'unreasoning mask' of the symbolic whale. Melville interrupts the narrative with facts, tales, and soliloquies, including Father Mapple's sermon on the Leviathan, the Townho's story, a dissertation on whales ('Cetology'), and a metaphysical dissertation on the ambiguous 'whiteness of the whale'. After a fierce three-day chase Moby-Dick destroys the *Pequod*. Ishmael survives the vortex: 'And only I am escaped alone to tell thee', begins his epilogue, citing the Book of Job.

Modern Comedy, A, see GALSWORTHY, J.

Modernism, an omnibus term for a number of tendencies in the arts which were prominent in the first half of the 20th cent.; in English literature it is particularly associated with the writings of T. S. *Eliot, *Pound, *Joyce, V. *Woolf, W. B. *Yeats, F. M. *Ford, and *Conrad. Broadly, Modernism reflects the impact upon literature of the psychology of *Freud and the anthropology of Sir J. *Frazer, as expressed in *The Golden Bough* (1890–1915). A sense of cultural relativism is pervasive in much modernist writing, as is an awareness of the irrational and the workings of the unconsious mind. Technically it was marked by a persistent experimentalism. It rejected the traditional (Victorian and Edwardian) framework of narrative, description, and rational exposition in poetry and prose, in favour of a *stream-of-consciousness presentation of personality, a dependence on the poetic image as the essential vehicle of aesthetic communication, and upon myth (see ULYSSES) as a characteristic structural principle. Modernist literature is a literature of discontinuity, both historically, being based upon a sharp rejection of the procedures and values of the immediate past, to which it adopts an adversary stance; and aesthetically.

Modern Love, a poem by G. *Meredith, published 1862. A work of 50 poems, each of 16 lines; spoken by a narrator, the verses unfold the disillusionment of passionate married love slowly giving place to discord, jealousy, and intense unhappiness.

Modern Painters, by *Ruskin, a work of encyclopaedic range in four volumes: I, 1843; II, 1846, III and IV, 1856; V, 1860.

It began as a defence of contemporary landscape artists, especially *Turner. Volume I deals with the true. Turner had been accused of defying nature. For Ruskin he was the first painter in history to have given 'an entire transcript of the whole system of nature'.

In vol II the logical framework of ideas was rapidly constructed. Beauty is perceived by the 'theoretic', i.e. contemplative faculty (as opposed to the aesthetic, which is sensual and base). It consists of the varied manifestations, in natural forms, of the attributes of God. But Ruskin now wanted to write of the functions of all art. Two years' study of old art brought revelations: Tuscan painting and sculpture of the 13th and 14th cents, Venetian Gothic architecture, and oil painting of the Renaissance. The outcome was that *Modern Painters* II belies its title and exalts the 'great men of old time'.

In the third and subsequent volumes the earlier systematic treatment gives way to a looser structure. An unrelentingly detailed analysis of mountain beauty takes up most of *Modern Painters* IV, to Ruskin 'the beginning and the end of all natural scenery'. Part of Turner's greatness lies in his representation of the gloom and glory of mountains to express the wrath of God.

Modern Painters V is the work of a man embarking on a vital old age. The volume reflects a new interest in myth as a source of wisdom and instrument of interpretation. Turner's greatness is finally revealed in his mythological paintings, which express despair at the triumph of mortifying labour over beauty.

Modest Proposal, A, . . . (1729), a pamphlet by *Swift in which he suggests that the children of the poor should be fattened to feed the rich, an offer he describes as 'innocent, cheap, easy and effectual'. It is one of his most savage and powerful tracts, a masterpiece of ironic logic.

Modred, in the Arthurian legends, the nephew of King *Arthur. *Geoffrey of Monmouth makes him the son of Arthur and his sister by an illicit union. During Arthur's absence on a Roman war he treacherously seizes the queen and the kingdom. In the final battle in Cornwall he is slain by Arthur but deals the king his death blow. The form of his name from *Malory to *Tennyson is Mordred.

MOIR, David Macbeth (1798–1851), a Scottish doctor, who signed himself Δ, Delta, is chiefly remembered as the author of *Mansie Wauch, Tailor in Dalkeith* (1828), which is an imaginary autobiography, in the manner of Moir's friend, *Galt, revealing a comically parochial view of the world, and satirizing the rising fashion for autobiography.

MOLESWORTH, Mary Louisa, *née* Stewart (1839–1921), wrote novels under the pseudonym Ennis Graham, but is known for her much-loved children's books, fairy-tales, including *The Cuckoo Clock* (1877) and *The Tapestry Room* (1879), and realistic studies of child psychology in everyday life such as *Carrots* (1876) and *Two Little Waifs* (1883).

MOLESWORTH, Robert, first viscount (1656–1725), Dublin-born diplomatist and political writer. His *An Account of Denmark as it was in the Year 1692* (1694), extolling the liberty of post-revolution England in comparison with political and clerical 'tyranny' in Denmark, caused a diplomatic storm. *Swift admired him as an Irish patriot and dedicated to him the fifth of *The Drapier's Letters*. As leading spokesman for the 'Old Whigs' or 'Commonwealth Men', Molesworth was the common patron of the different groups of *Shaftesbury's followers.

MOLIÈRE, pseudonym of Jean-Baptiste Poquelin (1622–73), French comic playwright and actor, and the creator of French classical comedy. His major plays include *L'Avare* (1669), *Le Tartuffe* (1664), *Les Femmes savantes* (1672), *Le Misanthrope* (1666), and *Le Bourgeois Gentilhomme* (1660). His influence on English *Restoration comedy exceeded that of *Jonson; dramatists like *D'Avenant, *Dryden, *Wycherley, *Vanbrugh, and *Shadwell quarried his plays for characters and situations.

Moll Flanders, The Fortunes and Misfortunes of the famous, a romance by *Defoe, published 1722.
This purports to be the autobiography of the daughter of a woman who had been transported to Virginia for theft soon after her child's birth. The story relates her seduction, her subsequent marriages and liaisons, and her visit to Virginia, where she finds her mother and discovers that she has unwittingly married her own brother. After leaving him and returning to England, she becomes an extremely successful pickpocket and thief, but is presently detected and transported to Virginia in company with one of her former husbands, a highwayman. With the funds that each has amassed they set up as planters, and spend their declining years in an atmosphere of penitence and prosperity.

Molly Mog, or the Fair Maid of the Inn, a *crambo ballad probably by *Gay, with *Pope and *Swift possibly as part authors. It first appeared in 1726.

Moloch, or **Molech,** the name of a Canaanite idol, to whom children were sacrificed as burnt offerings (Lev. 18: 21 and 2 Kings 23: 10), represented by Milton (*Paradise Lost*, i. 392) as one of the chief of the fallen angels.

Monastery, The, a novel by Sir W. *Scott, published 1820.
The story centres in the monastery of Kennaquhair, of which the prototype is Melrose Abbey on the Tweed, in the reign of Elizabeth, when the reformed doctrines were first making their way in Scotland and raising troubles for the religious community that gives its title to the work.

MONBODDO, James Burnett, Lord (1714–99), a Scottish judge and pioneer in anthropology, who published *Of the Origin and Progress of Language* (1773–92) and *Antient Metaphysics* (1779–99). The orang-utan for which he is remembered figures in both these works as an example of 'the infantine state of our species', who was gentle, sociable, and intelligent, could play the flute, but never learned to speak; he suggested to *Peacock the character of Sir Oran Haut-ton in *Melincourt*. (See also PRIMITIVISM.)

Money, a comedy by *Bulwer-Lytton, produced 1840.

Monimia, the heroine of Otway's *The Orphan*.

Monk, The, a novel by M. G. *Lewis, published 1796.
Ambrosio, the worthy superior of the Capuchins of Madrid, falls to the temptations of Matilda, a fiend-inspired wanton who, disguised as a boy, has entered his monastery as a novice. Now utterly depraved, Ambrosio falls in love with one of his penitents, pursues the girl with the help of magic and murder, and finally kills her in an effort to escape detection. But he is discovered, tortured by the Inquisition, and sentenced to death, finally compounding with the Devil for escape from burning, only to be hurled by him to destruction and damnation. Although extravagant in its mixture of the supernatural, the terrible, and the indecent, the book contains scenes of great effect. It enjoyed a considerable contemporary vogue.

Monkbarns, Laird of, Jonathan Oldbuck, the principal character in Scott's *The Antiquary*.

'Monk' Lewis, the soubriquet of M. G. *Lewis, author of *The Monk*.

Monks, a character in Dickens's *Oliver Twist*.

'Monk's Tale, The', see CANTERBURY TALES, 19.

MONRO, H(arold) E(dward) (1879–1932), is chiefly remembered for his Poetry Bookshop which he founded in 1913 to publish poetry, to encourage its sale, and to promote poetry-readings; and for publishing the series *Georgian Poetry*, edited by E. *Marsh. He founded and edited the *Poetry Review*. His *Collected Poems*, introduced by T. S. *Eliot, appeared in 1933.

MONROE, Harriet, see POETRY: A MAGAZINE OF VERSE.

MONSARRAT, Nicholas John Turney (1910–79), novelist, best remembered for his highly successful novel *The Cruel Sea* (1951), based on his wartime experiences at sea.

Monsieur D'Olive, a comedy by *Chapman, published 1606, acted a few years before.

MONTAGU, Basil (1770–1851), a friend of *Wordsworth, *Coleridge, and *Godwin; his young son (also Basil) lived with the Wordsworths during their West Country period. He became a successful barrister and author; published many legal and political works; edited F. *Bacon (1825–37); and in 1846 published a little volume of mock-heroic couplets, *Railroad Eclogues*.

MONTAGU, Mrs (Elizabeth) (1720–1800), a celebrated member of the *Blue Stocking Circle. Dr *Johnson was amazed by her 'radiations of intellectual excellence' and dubbed her 'Queen of the Blues'. Many young authors, such as *Beattie and R. *Price, were befriended by her hospitality, encouragement, and gifts of money. She wrote the first three of George Lyttelton's *Dialogues of the Dead* (1760) and an *Essay on the Writings and Genius of Shakespeare* (1769) refuting the strictures of *Voltaire.

MONTAGU, Lady Mary Wortley, *née* Pierrepont (1689–1762), daughter of the fifth earl and first duke of Kingston, secretly married Edward Wortley Montagu in 1712, and accompanied him in 1716 when he went to Constantinople as ambassador. She wrote there her celebrated 'Turkish Letters' (1763), and introduced into England on her return in 1718 the practice of inoculation against smallpox, an illness from which she had suffered. For the next two decades

she was a leading member of society, famed for her wit. In 1716 *Curll piratically published some of her *Town Eclogues* and *Court Poems*. In 1737–8 she wrote an anonymous periodical, *The Nonsense of Common-Sense*, and in 1739 left England and her husband to live abroad for nearly 23 years in France and Italy; during this period she wrote many letters (mostly to her daughter, Lady Bute), for which she is principally remembered. She is also known for her quarrels with *Pope.

MONTAGUE, C(harles) E(dward) (1867–1928), became assistant editor of the *Manchester Guardian*. He earned a considerable reputation as a reviewer and dramatic critic, and wrote several novels. *Disenchantment* (1922) is his bitter account of the First World War in which he served as a private soldier.

MONTAGUE, John Patrick (1929–), Irish poet. His volumes of poetry include *Forms of Exile* (1958), *Poisoned Lands* (1961), *Tides* (1970), *The Great Cloak* (1978), and *Selected Poems* (1982). Many of his short, intense lyrics evoke the landscapes and heritage of rural Ireland, in a fine, spare diction. He has also edited various anthologies of Irish literature, and published short stories and a play.

Montagues, the, in Shakespeare's *Romeo and Juliet*, see under CAPULETS.

MONTAIGNE, Michel Eyquem de (1533–92), French moralist and essayist. He is generally regarded as the inventor of the modern 'essay', a genre which he fashioned out of the late medieval 'compilation', transforming it into a personal test of ideas and experience. The first two books of his *Essais* appeared in 1580, the fifth edition, containing the third book, in 1588, and a posthumous edition in 1595. The first English translator was *Florio (1603). His influence on European thought and literature was considerable (on writers such as *Descartes, F. *Bacon, T. *Browne, *Swift, and *Peacock): his essay 'Des Cannibales' (I. 31) was a source, via Florio, of Shakespeare's *The Tempest*.

MONTEMAYOR, Jorge de (1519–61), a Portuguese poet and author who wrote in Spanish. His chief work is *Diana* (?1559), a prose pastoral interspersed with verses, in which he transferred Arcadia to the heart of Spain. It was extremely popular and was translated into French, German, and English. The English translation was by Bartholomew Yonge (1598); the episode of Felix and Felismena in Yonge's version is almost certainly the direct source of much of the plot of Shakespeare's *The Two Gentlemen of Verona*. The scene is laid at the foot of the mountains of Leon and the pastoral is occupied with the misfortunes of Sereno and Sylvanus, two shepherd lovers of the fair Diana, a shepherdess; and the loves, transfers of affection, and disguises of various other shepherds and shepherdesses. Happiness is finally restored by the agency of enchanted potions.

MONTGOMERIE, Alexander (c.1545–c.1598), a Scottish poet, who held office in the Scottish court in 1578. He left to travel abroad in 1586, having got into trouble. His principal work is *The Cherry and the Slae* (1597), a long allegorical poem. He also wrote a *Flyting of Montgomerie and Polwart* (published 1621), sonnets, and miscellaneous poems.

Monthly Magazine, The, a radical publication founded in 1796. Contributors included *Godwin, *Malthus, *Hazlitt, *Southey, and W. *Taylor. The magazine covered literature, science, politics, philosophy, etc. Its first editor was Dr J. *Aikin; its last (in 1825) was *Thelwall.

Monthly Review, The (1749–1845), founded by the bookseller Ralph Griffiths. It was liberal in outlook and its contributors included *Sheridan, Dr C. *Burney, *Goldsmith, and others. The term 'autobiography' seems first to have appeared in its columns, in Dec. 1797.

MONTROSE, James Graham, fifth earl and first marquis of (1612–50), royalist and general, is remembered as a poet for a few songs and epigrams (printed in Mark Napier's *Memoirs of Montrose,* 1856, and since much anthologized), including 'My dear and only love'.

Montsurry, see BUSSY D'AMBOIS.

MOODY and SANKEY, Dwight Lyman Moody (1837–99) and Ira David Sankey (1840–1908), American evangelists. With Sankey as singer and organist, they carried on a revival campaign in America and England. The compilation of the *Sankey and Moody Hymn Book* (1873) was due to Sankey.

Moonstone, The, a novel by Wilkie *Collins, published 1868.
The moonstone, an enormous diamond originally stolen from an Indian shrine, is given to an English girl, Rachel Verrinder, on her eighteenth birthday, but disappears the same night. Under suspicion of stealing it are Rosanna Spearman, a hunchbacked housemaid, formerly a thief; a troop of Indian jugglers; Franklin Blake, Rachel's cousin; and Rachel herself. A detective, Sergeant Cuff, is called in to solve the mystery, and is aided by the house steward Gabriel Betteredge, principal narrator of the story, but thwarted by Rachel's reticence and by the tragic suicide of Rosanna. It is eventually discovered that Franklin Blake was seen by Rachel to take the diamond, that at the time he was sleep-walking under the influence of opium, that it was taken from him by Rachel's other suitor, Godfrey Ablewhite, a sanctimonious hypocrite, and finally secured (by the murder of Ablewhite) and returned to the shrine by the Indian jugglers, who were high-caste Brahmins in disguise.

MOORCOCK, Michael (1939–), one of the most prominent of the 'New Wave' *Science Fiction writers of the 1960s, part of whose aim was to invest the genre with literary merit. He edited *New Worlds* from 1964 to 1971, and has also edited many collections of short stories, etc.; his own works include the novels *The Final Programme* (1968), *A Cure for Cancer* (1971), and *The English Assassin* (1972).

MOORE, Brian (1921–), novelist, born and educated in Belfast, who emigrated in 1948 to Canada and subsequently moved to the USA. His novels include *Judith Hearne* (1955; pub. in the USA as *The Lonely Passion of Judith Hearne,* 1956), a poignant story of a lonely Belfast spinster who takes refuge in alcohol; *The Luck of Ginger Coffey* (1960); *I am Mary Dunne* (1968); *Catholics* (1972); and *The Mangan Inheritance* (1979, about an American journalist in search of his Irish heritage and the *poète maudit* J. C. *Mangan).

MOORE, Edward (1712–57), wrote poems and fables but is best remembered as a dramatist. His first comedy, *The Foundling* (1748), may owe something to Richardson's *Pamela; Gil Blas* (1751) is a lively comedy of intrigue, the plot of which is taken from *Lesage's Gil Blas of Santillane* (IV. iii. *et seq.*). His most successful play was a domestic prose tragedy, *The Gamester* (1753), an exposure of the vice of gambling, through which the weak creature Beverley is lured to ruin and death by the villain Stukeley. It was adapted by *Diderot.

MOORE, Francis, see OLD MOORE.

MOORE, George Augustus (1852–1933), Anglo-Irish novelist. He studied painting in Paris and the knowledge of French writing he gained there stood him in good stead when, returning to England c.1880, he set about revitalizing the Victorian novel with naturalistic and, later, realistic techniques borrowed from *Balzac, *Zola, and the Goncourts. His first novel, *A Modern Lover* (1883), set in artistic Bohemian society, was banned by the circulating *libraries, a circumstance which confirmed Moore in his outspoken battle against prudery and censorship. It was followed by *A Mummer's Wife* (1885, set in the Potteries, which influenced Arnold *Bennett); *Esther Waters* (1894), his most successful novel; *Evelyn Innes* (1898) and its sequel *Sister Teresa* (1901). *The Untilled Field* (1903) is a collection of short stories strongly influenced by *Turgenev and *Dostoevsky. In his later novels, e.g. *The Brook Kerith* (1916) and *Heloïse and Abelard* (1921), he aimed at epic effect. *Confessions of a Young Man* (1888), *Memoirs of my dead life* (1906), and *Hail and Farewell* (3 vols, 1911–14) are all autobiographical; the last is an important though unreliable source for the history of the *Irish revival. Moore collaborated in the planning of the Irish National Theatre (see ABBEY THEATRE). His collection of short stories *Celibate Lives* (1927) shows the influence of *Flaubert. The Ebury edition of Moore's works (20 vols, 1936–8) owes its name to 121 Ebury Street where he lived from 1911 until his death.

MOORE, G(eorge) E(dward) (1873–1958), brother of T. Sturge *Moore, was professor of philosophy in the University of Cambridge, 1925–39, and an influential *Apostle. His *Principia Ethica* (1903) inaugurated a new era in British moral philosophy, and had great influence on the *Bloomsbury Group, who adopted its emphasis on 'the pleasures of human intercourse and the enjoyment of beautiful objects'. His other writings include *Philosophical Studies* (1922) and *Some Main Problems of Philosophy* (1953).

MOORE, John (1729–1802), practised as a surgeon until 1772. He then travelled in Europe for several years, publishing accounts of his journeys in 1779, 1781, and 1793. His novels include *Zeluco* (1786), *Edward* (1796), and *Mordaunt* (1800).

MOORE, Marianne Craig (1887–1972), American poet, was editor (1925–9) of *The Dial*. Her first volume, *Poems* (1921), was followed by *Observations* (1924), *Selected Poems* (1935), *The Pangolin, and Other Verse* (1936), and *Collected Poems* (1951). Her tone is characteristically urbane, sophisticated, and conversational, her observations detailed and precise, and her poems are composed for the page with a strong sense of visual effect.

MOORE, Thomas (1779–1852), born in Dublin, published *The Poetical Works of the late Thomas Little* (1801), under which pseudonym Byron refers to him in *English Bards and Scotch Reviewers*. From 1808 to 1834 Moore continued to add to his *Irish Melodies*, which established him as the national bard of Ireland. He was a good musician and a skilful writer of patriotic and often nostalgic songs, which he set to Irish tunes, mainly of the 18th cent. Among his more famous songs are 'The Harp that once through Tara's Halls', 'The Minstrel Boy', and 'The Last Rose of Summer'. *The Twopenny Post Bag* (1813) is a collection of satires directed against the

prince regent. He acquired fame and a European reputation with the publication of *Lalla Rookh* (1817). In 1818 appeared the satirical and entertaining *The Fudge Family in Paris*. *The Loves of the Angels* (1823) enjoyed a considerable vogue and caused some scandal. In 1824 he was prevailed upon to permit the burning of *Byron's *Memoirs*, which Byron (a close friend) had given to him. Among his other works may be mentioned his life of Sheridan (1825); *The Epicurean* (1827), a novel about a Greek philosopher; a life of Byron (1830); and a *Life of Lord Edward Fitzgerald* (1831).

MOORE, T(homas) Sturge (1870–1944), poet, wood-engraver, and illustrator, brother of G. E. *Moore; he was a friend of *Yeats, his correspondence with whom was published in 1953, and for whom he designed several books. His first volume of verse, *The Vinedresser and other poems* (1899), was followed by several others, and by various verse dramas, including *Tragic Mothers: Medea, Niobe, Tyrfing* (1920).

Mopsa, a character in Sidney's *Arcadia*.

Moral and Political Philosophy, *Principles of*, see PALEY, W.

Moral Essays, four ethical poems by *Pope, published 1731–5.

They were inspired by *Bolingbroke and take the form of four Epistles. Epistle I, addressed to Viscount Cobham, deals with the knowledge and characters of men; it sets forth the difficulties in judging a man's character and finds their solution in the discovery of the ruling passion, which 'clue once found unravels all the rest'. Epistle II, addressed to Martha *Blount, deals with the characters of women. Atossa was intended either for Sarah, duchess of Marlborough, or for Katherine, duchess of Buckinghamshire; *Chloe for Lady Suffolk; Philomodé for Henrietta, duchess of Marlborough. Epistle III, to Lord Bathurst, deals with the use of riches. The Epistle contains the famous characters of the 'Man of Ross' (see KYRLE) and 'Sir *Balaam'. Epistle IV, to Lord Burlington, deals with the same subject as Epistle III, giving instances of the tasteless use of wealth, particularly in architecture and gardening, where nature should be followed, and ending with advice on the proper use of wealth.

Morality Plays, medieval allegorical plays in which personified human qualities acted and disputed, mostly coming from the 15th cent. They developed into the *Interludes, and hence had a considerable influence on the development of Elizabethan drama. They lost popularity with the development of naturalistic drama, but interest in them has revived in the 20th cent., prompted by a new interest in more mannered, pageant-like theatre, such as the Japanese *Nōh theatre and the plays of *Yeats and *Brecht. Among the most celebrated English examples are *Everyman; *Ane Pleasant Satyre of the Thrie Estaitis by Sir D. Lindsay; Magnyfycence by *Skelton; King John by *Bale; *Mankind; *The Castle of Perseverance. See P. Happé ed., Four Morality Plays (1979); G. Wickham ed., English Moral Interludes (1976).

Moral Ode, The, see POEMA MORALE.

Moral Sentiments, The Theory of, see THEORY OF MORAL SENTIMENTS, THE.

Mordaunt, a novel by J. *Moore, published 1800.

Morddure, in Spenser's Faerie Queene (II. viii. 20–1), the name of the sword made by Merlin for Prince Arthur. Its more general name is *Excalibur.

Mordern, Colonel, a character in Richardson's *Clarissa.

Mordred, see MODRED.

MORE, Hannah (1745–1833), an eminent member of the *Blue Stocking Circle. She published in 1773 The Search for Happiness, a pastoral play for schools, and came to London in 1774, where she became a friend of *Garrick and his wife and of *Burke, Dr *Johnson, S. *Richardson, and *Percy. She was greatly esteemed by Horace *Walpole, who honoured her by printing her Bishop Bonner's Ghost (1781) on his press at *Strawberry Hill. Her tragedy Percy, produced by Garrick in 1777, established her as a literary success. It was followed by another tragedy, The Fatal Falsehood (1779). Her poem Bas Bleu (1786) vividly describes the charm of Blue Stocking society. Meanwhile she had begun to write tracts directed towards the reform of the conditions of the poor; Village Politics (1793) and Cheap Repository Tracts (1795–8, of which the best-known is The Shepherd of Salisbury Plain). In 1809 she published her successful novel *Coelebs in Search of a Wife. Her letters give a full and entertaining picture of the intellectual and social world she frequented.

MORE, Henry, see CAMBRIDGE PLATONISTS.

MORE, Sir Thomas (St) (?1477–1535), educated at Canterbury College, Oxford. He was for a time in youth in the household of Cardinal Morton, and it was probably from Morton's information that he derived his account of Richard III's murder of the princes, etc. He was called to the bar, where he was brilliantly successful. He devoted his leisure to literature, becoming intimate with *Colet, *Lily, and, in 1499, *Erasmus. He entered Parliament in 1504. During an absence as envoy to Flanders he sketched his description (in Latin) of the imaginary island of *Utopia (1516). He completed his Dialogue, his first controversial book in English (directed mainly against *Tyndale's writings), in 1528. He succeeded Wolsey as lord chancellor in 1529, but resigned in 1532.

Although willing to swear fidelity to the new Act of Succession, More refused to take any oath that should impugn the pope's authority, and was therefore committed to the Tower of London with John *Fisher, bishop of Rochester. During the first days of his imprisonment he prepared a Dialoge of Comfort agaynst Trybulacion and treatises on Christ's passion. He was indicted of high treason, found guilty, and beheaded in 1535.

More was a critic and a patron of art, and *Holbein is said to have stayed in his house at Chelsea, and painted portraits of More and his family. More's other chief English works are his Lyfe of Johan Picus erle of Mirandula (printed by John *Rastell, c.1510), his History of Richard III (printed imperfectly in Grafton's Chronicle, 1543, used by *Hall, and printed fully by William Rastell in 1557), Supplycacyon of Soulys (1529), Confutacyon of Tyndales Answere (1532), and The Apology of Syr Thomas More (1533). His English works were collected in 1557. His Latin publications (collected 1563, etc.) included, besides the Utopia, four dialogues of *Lucian, epigrams, and controversial tracts in divinity. He was beatified by the Church of Rome in 1886, and canonized in 1935. *Bolt's play about More, A Man for All Seasons (1960), was also made into a successful film.

More, Sir Thomas, a play based on *Hall's Chronicle and biographies of *More, surviving in an incomplete transcript with additions in various hands which was submitted to Sir Edmund Tilney, Master of the Revels, probably about 1593. The scribe, *Munday, is likely to have been at least part-author of the original play. Tilney required major changes before granting permission to perform. The revisions (which may date from 1593–5 or 1601–3) are in five different hands, probably including those of *Chettle, *Heywood, *Dekker, and a playhouse scribe known to have worked for the Admiral's Men. The fifth ('Hand D') has been claimed, with strong support, as Shakespeare's. If so, this is his only surviving literary manuscript. A scene of three pages, it depicts More, as sheriff of London, pacifying apprentices in a May-Day rebellion against foreigners. More was first printed in 1844. The first known professional performance was in London in 1954.

Morgan, (1) a character in Thackeray's *Pendennis, Major Pendennis's valet; (2) a character in Smollett's *Roderick Random.

MORGAN, Charles Langbridge (1894–1958), novelist and dramatist, dramatic critic of *The Times* (1926–39). His novels include *The Fountain* (1932), *Sparkenbroke* (1936), *The Judge's Story* (1947), and *The River Line* (1949, dramatized 1952). Morgan's status as a writer has been and remains significantly higher in France than in Britain.

MORGAN, Edwin George (1920–   ), Scottish poet and translator, professor of English at the University of Glasgow from 1975. He has published several volumes of poetry, from *The Vision of Cathkin Braes* (1952) onwards, in which he mingles traditional forms with experimental and *concrete poems; many of his poems, such as *Glasgow Sonnets* (1972), evoke Scottish urban landscape. He has also translated the poetry of Montale, Mayakovsky, Neruda, and others.

MORGAN, William De, see DE MORGAN, W.

Morgan le Fay, queen of *Avalon, the half-sister of King Arthur; she is derived from a figure in Welsh and Irish mythology. In Malory's *Morte D'Arthur* she attempts to kill Arthur, but she is also the leader of the queens who carry him away to cure his wounds. See MORGAWSE.

MORGANN, Maurice (1726–1802), is remembered chiefly as the author of an *Essay on the Dramatic Character of Sir John Falstaff* (1777) in which he defends *Falstaff from the charge of cowardice.

Morgawse, or **Morcades,** in Malory's *Morte D'Arthur*, half-sister of Arthur, the wife of King Lot of Orkney, and mother of *Modred, Gawain, Agravain, Gareth, and Gaheris. She seems to be in some ways identical in origin with *Morgan le Fay; in later versions Arthur sleeps with her in disguise, thus begetting Modred.

Morgiana, in *Ali Baba and the Forty Thieves*, Ali Baba's servant.

Morglay, the name of the sword of *Bevis of Hampton, sometimes used allusively for a sword in general.

Moriarty, Professor, the enemy of Sherlock *Holmes, a character created by A. C. *Doyle.

MORIER, James Justinian (?1780–1849), became attached to Sir Harford Jones's mission to Persia; his account of these travels appeared in *A Journey through Persia, Armenia and Asia Minor to Constantinople in the years 1808–1809* (1812); *A Second Journey through Persia* appeared in 1818. He published a number of *oriental romances including the popular *The Adventures of Hajji Baba of Ispahan* (1824), a picaresque tale (the hero undergoes amusing vicissitudes, becoming successively barber, doctor, and assistant executioner) which gives a colourful and accurate presentation of life in Persia during the early 19th cent. His *Ayesha* (1834) introduced the Turkish word 'bosh' into the English language.

Morland, Catherine, a character in J. Austen's *Northanger Abbey*.

MORLEY, Henry (1822–94), joined the staff of *Household Words* at Dickens's invitation, edited *The Examiner*, and devoted his long academic career to the development of English literature as an academic subject. He wrote *A First Sketch of English Literature* (1873), 11 volumes of *English Writers* (1887–95), and edited cheap editions of English classics in Morley's Universal Library (1883–8) and Cassell's National Library (1886–92).

MORLEY, Henry Parker, Lord (1476–1556), was a successful courtier and diplomat under Henry VIII. His *Exposition and Declaration* of Psalm 94 was really a defence of Henry's position as head of the Church of England; better known now is his other published work, a translation of *Petrarch's *Trionfi* (c.1553).

MORLEY, John, first viscount Morley of Blackburn (1838–1923), was chief secretary for Ireland (1886 and 1892–5), secretary of state for India (1905–10), and lord president of the Council (1910–14). He was editor of the *Fortnightly Review* (1867–82) and the *Pall Mall Gazette* (1881–3). Many of his essays on historical and literary subjects are collected in *Critical Miscellanies* (1871–7). His literary achievements, chiefly biographical, include *Edmund Burke; an historical study* (1867), *Voltaire* (1872), *Rousseau* (1873), *On Compromise* (1874), *Burke* (1879), *The Life of Richard Cobden* (1881), *Oliver Cromwell* (1900), *Life of Gladstone* (1903), and he edited the English Men of Letters series.

Morley, Stephen, in *Sybil* by B. Disraeli.

MORLEY, Thomas (1557/8–1602), English composer, organist, and writer. His treatise *A Plaine and Easie Introduction to Practicall Musicke* (1597) is the first work of its kind in the English language.

His historical importance as a composer stemmed from his championship of the Italian *madrigal, and his development of its English counterpart. His first two publications, the *Canzonets, or Little Short Songs to Three Voyces* (1594) and the first book of *Madrigalls to Foure Voyces* (1594), contain the best of his own work in this form. The two volumes of *Balletts* and *Canzonets* (1595) were largely free transcriptions of contemporary Italian pieces. As publisher he was the moving spirit behind *The Triumphes of Oriana*

(1601), a collection of madrigals by 21 English composers in honour of Queen *Elizabeth I. His book *Ayres . . . to the Lute* (1600) contains a setting of 'It was a lover and his lass', which is apparently the earliest Shakespeare setting to survive.

Morning Chronicle, The (1769–1862), a Whig journal, rose to importance when James Perry became chief proprietor and editor in 1789. Its staff then included *Sheridan, *Lamb, T. *Campbell, Sir J. *Mackintosh, *Brougham, T. *Moore, and *Ricardo. Perry was succeeded by John Black (1783–1855). Among his contributors were James and J. S. *Mill; *Dickens was one of his reporters, and *Thackeray his art critic.

Morning Post, The, a London daily newspaper founded in 1772. Under the management of D. *Stuart, Sir J. *Mackintosh and S. T. *Coleridge were enlisted in its service, and *Southey, *Wordsworth, and A. *Young were also contributors. It was amalgamated with the *Daily Telegraph* in 1937.

Morose, in Jonson's *Epicene*, a crabbed old bachelor who hates noise.

MORRELL, Lady Ottoline (1873–1938), patron of the arts and hostess. From 1908 she entertained a wide circle of political and literary celebrities at her Thursday evening gatherings at 44 Bedford Square, and then at Garsington Manor, Oxfordshire (1915–27). Her friends and guests included Asquith, H. *James, L. *Strachey, B. *Russell, V. *Woolf, T. S. *Eliot, *Yeats, D. H. *Lawrence, and A. *Huxley. She appeared as a character in several works of fiction by her protégés, most memorably in Lawrence's *Women in Love* and Huxley's *Crome Yellow*. Both portraits caused considerable offence. Her Memoirs, edited by Robert Gathorne-Hardy, appeared in 2 volumes in 1963 and 1974.

Morris, Dinah, a character in G. Eliot's *Adam Bede*.

MORRIS, Sir Lewis (1833–1907), contributed actively to the establishment of the University of Wales. He published several volumes of mediocre verse, imitative of *Tennyson; the most popular were *Songs of Two Worlds* (1871) and *The Epic of Hades* (1876–7).

MORRIS, William (1834–96), was articled to the architect G. E. Street, and in 1858 worked with *Rossetti, Burne-Jones, and others on the frescoes in the Oxford Union. He was one of the originators of the *Oxford and Cambridge Magazine* (1856). In 1858 he published *The Defence of Guenevere and other poems*, which

includes 'The Haystack in the Floods', 'Concerning Geffray Teste Noire', 'Shameful Death', and 'Golden Wings', poems marked by a striking mixture of beauty and brutality, all with medieval settings. In 1859 he married Jane Burden, one of the most painted Pre-Raphaelite 'stunners'; their home, Red House at Bexley, was designed by Philip Webb, and was an important landmark in domestic architecture. The failure to find suitable furniture for it strengthened Morris's growing hatred of industrial 'shoddy', and led to the founding, together with Rossetti, Burne-Jones, Webb, Madox Brown, and others, of the firm of Morris, Marshall, Faulkener and Co. This firm produced furniture, printed textiles, tapestries, wallpapers, and stained glass; its designs brought about a complete revolution in public taste. In 1867 he published *The Life and Death of Jason*, a poem in heroic couplets, and in 1868–70 appeared *The Earthly Paradise*, which established him as one of the most popular poets of the day. In 1871 he took a joint tenancy of Kelmscott Manor with Rossetti, wrote the peom *Love is Enough* (1872), and visited Iceland, which stimulated his interest in the heroic themes of Icelandic literature. His epic *Sigurd the Volsung* appeared in 1876.

From this time on he turned increasingly towards political activity; in 1883 he joined the Social Democratic Federation, the doctrine of which, largely under his leadership, developed into Socialism. On its disruption in 1884 he became head of the seceders, who organized themselves as the Socialist League. His later works, with the exception of *Poems by the Way* (1891) and *Chants for Socialists* (1884–5), were mainly in prose, and most remarkable among them were *A Dream of John Ball* (1888) and *News from Nowhere* (1891), both socialist fantasies cast in a dream setting. He also wrote several historical romances set in the distant past of northern Europe. These include *The House of the Wolfings* (1889), *The Roots of the Mountains* (1890), *The Story of the Glittering Plain* (1890), *The Wood beyond the World* (1894), and *The Sundering Flood* (1898). All were published by the Kelmscott Press, which he had founded at Hammersmith in 1890, and for which he designed founts of type and ornamental letters and borders. The Press also published other works by Morris, reprints of English classics (including *Caxton's *The Golden Legend* and the Kelmscott *Chaucer), and various smaller books by other authors. Morris's view that 'the true incentive to useful and happy labour is, and must be, pleasure in the work itself' links his political and artistic aspirations, both of which have remained profoundly influential. Morris published many other works, including translations of the *Aeneid* (1875) and the *Odyssey* (1887); he collaborated with E. Magnusson in translations from the Icelandic. His letters were edited by P. Henderson (1950).

Morris Dance, a series of folk-dance pageants, performed at various seasons of the year since the 15th cent. at least, and found in many places throughout England. The most important recurrent subjects are the characters of the *Robin Hood legends in the Spring play (especially Friar Tuck and Maid Marian, who often appears as Queen of the May), 'harvest home', dances in the autumn, and year-ending plays for Christmas such as the *Revesby Play.

MORRISON, Arthur (1863–1945), novelist, whose 'realist' tales of East End life in London were first published in *Macmillan's Magazine* and later collected as *Tales of Mean Streets* (1894). He is chiefly remembered for his novel *A Child of the Jago* (1896) which describes the boyhood of Dick Perrott in an East End slum and gives a vivid account of the violent crime of the neighbourhood. His father is hanged for murder and Dick dies in a street fight aged 17.

Morte Arthure, *The Alliterative,* a 14th-cent. poem of 'The *Alliterative Revival' in 4,346 alliterative long lines. Its material corresponds roughly to Malory's first, second, and eighth romances (in Vinaver's numbering): the early exploits of Arthur, his European ventures, and the final battle with Modred. It was used as a source by *Malory and possibly by *Wace and is considered to be one of the most important and influential Middle English poems, the influence of which has been detected in Malory, *Cleanness, *The Awntyrs of Arthur, *Henry the Minstrel's *Wallace,* and elsewhere.

Morte Arthur, Le (The Stanzaic Morte Arthur), a late 14th-cent. poem from the North-West Midlands in 3,834 lines of eight-lined rhyming stanzas, surviving in one manuscript, and the source (directly or indirectly) for the sections in *Malory leading up to and dealing with the death of Arthur. It deals with Launcelot's love affairs with Guinevere and the Maid of Astolat, with Arthur's last battles, and with the king's being borne away to Avalon.

Morte D'Arthur, Le, the title generally given to the lengthy cycle of Arthurian legends by *Malory, finished in 1470 and printed by *Caxton in 1485, divided into 21 books. But in 1934 W. F. Oakeshott discovered in Winchester College Library a manuscript of the same period as Caxton's but without his division into 21 books. This superior manuscript, dividing the whole into eight parts, was used by Vinaver as the basis of his new standard edition of Malory. Though Malory refers throughout to a 'French book' as his source, it is clear that his sources were more various. Vinaver divides the cycle into eight *Works* to be treated as separate romances: (1) The Tale of Arthur and Lucius, based principally on the Alliterative English *Morte Arthure; (2) The

Book of King Arthur, based largely on the *Suite du Merlin* (Huth Merlin) (see MERLIN); (3) The Tale of Sir Launcelot du Lake, mostly from two sections of the prose *Lancelot* in the Vulgate cycle; (4) Sir Gareth of Orkney; (5) Tristram de Lyones, thought to be a translation of part of a lost 13th-cent. prose *Tristan* in French; (6) The quest of the Holy Grail, principally from the prose Vulgate *Queste del Saint Graal* (see GRAIL); (7) Launcelot and Guinevere; and (8) The Morte Arthur, both based to a considerable degree on the French Vulgate *Mort Artu,* and the 15th-cent. English stanzaic *Le Morte Arthur* (above). Since the publication of Vinaver's 3-vol. edition in 1947 criticism of Malory has concentrated on whether his work is to be regarded as a single 'whole Book' or as eight Works (Vinaver). The traditional view of Malory as a single whole, compounded of disparate parts, now prevails.

'Morte d'Arthur', a poem by *Tennyson, written 1833–4, published 1842, subsequently incorporated in 'The Passing of Arthur' (1869), preceded by 169 lines and followed by 29, where it formed one of the *Idylls of the King. It describes the last moments of Arthur after the battle with Mordred's forces, and includes his elegy on the Round Table, delivered to Sir Bedivere: 'The old order changeth, yielding place to new . . .'

Mortimer, a character in Marlowe's *Edward II.

MORTIMER, John Clifford (1923–), novelist, barrister, and playwright, was formerly married to Penelope *Mortimer. He is well known for his stand against censorship, and as the author of many successful television plays, including his series about an eccentric barrister, Rumpole of the Bailey. His plays include *The Dock Brief* (produced for both radio and television in 1957, pub. 1958) and the autobiographical *A Voyage Round my Father* (perf. 1970, pub. 1971).

MORTIMER, Penelope Ruth, *née* Fletcher (1918–), novelist, whose works, with their emphasis on frankness about female experience, contributed to the development of the woman's novel in the 1960s. They include *The Pumpkin Eater* (1962), *The House* (1971), and *Long Distance* (1974).

Mortimer his Fall, fragments of a tragedy by *Jonson, printed in 1640, concerning the earl of Mortimer, the murderer of Edward II.

Morton, Henry, of Milnwood, the hero of Scott's *Old Mortality.

MORTON, John Maddison (1811–91), son of T. *Morton, wrote farces and showed a special gift for adaptations from the French. His most successful piece was *Box and Cox* (1847).

MORTON, Thomas (?1764–1838), was the author of three successful comedies, *The Way to get Married* (1796), *A Cure for Heartache* (1797), and *Speed the Plough* (1798). The last of these introduced the name and character of 'Mrs Grundy', and the conception of Grundyism as the extreme of moral rigidity.

Mosca, Volpone's parasite in Jonson's *Volpone*.

MOSCHUS (*fl. c.*150 BC), a pastoral poet of Syracuse. The beautiful *Lament for Bion*, doubtfully attributed to Moschus, is a dirge for the author's friend and teacher. There is an echo of it in Milton's *Lycidas*, in Shelley's *Adonais*, and in M. Arnold's *'Thyrsis'*.

MOSLEY, Nicholas, 3rd Baron Ravensdale (1923–), novelist and biographer. His highly intellectual, experimental, and metaphysical novels include *Accident* (1964) and *Impossible Object* (1968), both of which were filmed; *Natalie Natalia* (1971); and *Catastrophe Practice* (1979). His biographies include a two-volume study of his father, *Rules of the Game: Sir Oswald and Lady Cynthia Mosley 1896–1933* (1982) and *Beyond the Pale: Sir Oswald Mosley 1933–1980* (1983).

Mosses from an Old Manse, published 1846, a collection of tales and sketches by N. *Hawthorne.

Moth, (1) in Shakespeare's *Love's Labour's Lost*, Armado's page; (2) in his *A Midsummer Night's Dream*, one of the fairies.

Mother Hubbard, the subject of a nursery rhyme attributed to Sarah Catherine Martin (1768–1826) and published in 1805, but probably based on oral tradition.

'Mother Hubberds Tale', or '*Prosopopoia*', a satire in rhymed couplets, by *Spenser, included in the volume of *Complaints* published in 1591. The ape and the fox, 'disliking of their evill | And hard estate', determine to seek their fortunes abroad, and assume the disguises first of an old soldier and his dog, then of a parish priest and his clerk, then of a courtier and his groom; their knaveries in these characters are recounted. The poem is a satire on the abuses of the church and the evils of the court.

MOTHERWELL, William (1797–1835), published a collection of ballads, *Minstrelsy ancient and modern* (1827), and *Poems narrative and lyrical* (1832), of which the best-known and least characteristic is 'Jeannie Morrison'. With *Hogg he issued an edition of *Burns's works in 1834–5.

Motion, the name given to puppet-plays in the 16th and 17th cents. These dealt originally with scriptural subjects, but their scope was afterwards extended. Shakespeare in *The Winter's Tale* (IV. iii) refers to a 'motion of the Prodigal Son', and there are references to 'motions' in Jonson's *Bartholomew Fair*, *A Tale of a Tub, and *Every Man out of his Humour*.

MOTLEY, John Lothrop (1814–77), was American minister to Austria, 1861–7, and to Great Britain, 1869–70. He is chiefly remembered as a historian and author of *The Rise of the Dutch Republic* (1855). This was followed by the *History of the United Netherlands* (1860–7) and *The Life and Death of John Barneveld* (1874).

MOTTEUX, Peter Anthony (1660–1718), edited and wrote much of *The Gentleman's Journal*, and completed Sir T. *Urquhart's translation of Rabelais (1693–4).

MOTTLEY, John (1692–1750), is remembered as having published *Joe Miller's jests: or the wit's vade-mecum* (1739).

MOTTRAM, R(alph) H(ale) (1883–1971), novelist, is principally remembered for *The Spanish Farm Trilogy* (1927), which consists of *The Spanish Farm* (1924), *Sixty-four, Ninety-four* (1925), and *The Crime at Vanderlynden's* (1926); it is set in northern France and based on his own experience in France and Flanders during the First World War.

Mouldy, Ralph, in Shakespeare's 2 *Henry IV (III. ii), one of Falstaff's recruits.

Mourning Becomes Electra, see O'NEILL, E.

Mourning Bride, The, a tragedy by *Congreve, produced 1697. This was the author's only attempt at tragedy, and was received with enthusiasm. The play contains lines that are widely known, such as the first in the play:

Music has charms to soothe a savage breast,

and those which close the third act:

Heaven has no rage, like love to hatred turned,
Nor hell a fury, like a woman scorned.

The plot concerns the secret marriage of Almeria and Alphonso, and the unsuccessful attempts of Almeria's father the king of Granada to part and punish the lovers.

Movement, The, a term coined by J. D. Scott, literary editor of the *Spectator, in 1954 to describe a group of writers including *Amis, *Larkin, *Davie, *Enright, *Wain, E. *Jennings, and *Conquest. Two anthologies (Enright's *Poets of the 1950s*, 1955, and Conquest's *New Lines*, 1956) illustrate the Movement's predominantly anti-romantic, witty, rational, sardonic tone; its fictional heroes tended to be lower-middle-class scholarship boys. Definitions of its aims were negative and by 1957 its members began to disown it, claiming, in Wain's words, 'its work is done'.

Mowcher, Miss, in Dickens's *David Copperfield*, a humorous and good-hearted dwarf.

Mowgli, the child in R. Kipling's *The Jungle Book*.

MOXON, Edward (1801–58), publisher and a close friend of *Lamb whose 'adopted' daughter, Emma Isola, he married. Among his list of authors were *Shelley, *Clare, *Wordsworth, *Coleridge, Lamb, *Hunt, *Keats, *Southey, R. *Browning, *Patmore, *Longfellow, and *Tennyson, whose close friend he became. In 1831 he established the *Englishman's Magazine*.

MOXON, Joseph (1627–91), maker of gloves and mathematical instruments, printer and typefounder, wrote *Mechanick Exercises; Or the Doctrine of Hand-Works applied to the Art of Printing* (1683–4), the first manual of printing and typefounding in any language.

Mr B, the hero of Richardson's *Pamela*.

'Mr Gilfil's Love-Story', see SCENES OF CLERICAL LIFE.

Mr Limberham, *or the Kind Keeper*, a comedy by *Dryden, produced 1679, published 1680.
  The play was banned by royal decree after three performances. The title character, an impotent masochist and cuckold, is possibly based on *Shaftesbury. By implication the play attacks the patriarchism of a sexually corrupt court, the blind hedonism of the nobility, and the hypocrisy of Dissenters.

Mr Norris Changes Trains, a novel by C. *Isherwood.

Mr Polly, *The History of*, a novel by H. G. *Wells.

Mr Scarborough's Family, a novel by A. *Trollope, published 1883.

Mrs Caudle's Curtain Lectures, see JERROLD, D. W.

Mrs Dalloway, a novel by V. *Woolf, published 1925.
  The action is restricted to the events of one day in central London, punctuated by the chimes of Big Ben; it opens on a June morning in Westminster as Clarissa Dalloway, wife of Richard Dalloway MP, sets off to buy flowers for her party that evening, the party which provides the culmination and ending of the book. Her

interior monologue (see STREAM OF CONSCIOUSNESS), interwoven with the sights and sounds of the urban scene, is handled with a technical confidence and bravura that herald a new phase in Woolf's mastery of the novel. Clarissa herself is captured in her many shifting moods and recollections, and contrasted with and seen through the eyes of many other characters. Her day is also contrasted with that of the shell-shocked Septimus Warren Smith, who hears the sparrows sing in Greek in Regent's Park, and who at the end of the day commits suicide by hurling himself from a window; news of his death intrudes upon Clarissa's party, brought by the Harley Street doctor whom he had uselessly consulted. Woolf insisted upon the mutual dependence of these two characters, noting in her workbook, 'Mrs D. seeing the truth. SS seeing the insane truth.'

Mrs Lirriper's Lodgings and **Mrs Lirriper's Legacy,** Christmas stories by *Dickens, which appeared in *All the Year Round*, 1863 and 1864. Mrs Lirriper lets lodgings in Norfolk Street, Strand, and her lodgers and past lodgers tell their stories.

'Mr Sludge, the "Medium" ', a poem by R. *Browning, included in *Dramatis Personae*.

Mucedorus, *A Comedie of*, a play of uncertain authorship, published 1598, and included in the Shakespeare apocrypha.

Much, in the *Robin Hood legend, a miller's son, one of the outlaw's companions.

Much Ado About Nothing, a comedy by *Shakespeare, written probably 1598–9, first printed 1600. Its chief sources are a novella by *Bandello and an episode in Ariosto's *Orlando Furioso*.
  The prince of Arragon, with Claudio and Benedick in his suite, visits Leonato, duke of Messina, father of Hero and uncle of Beatrice. The sprightly Beatrice has a teasing relationship with the sworn bachelor Benedick. Beatrice and Benedick are each tricked into believing the other in love, and this brings about a genuine sympathy between them. Meanwhile Don John, the malcontented brother of the prince, thwarts Claudio's marriage by arranging for him to see Hero apparently wooed by his friend Borachio on her balcony—it is really her maidservant Margaret in disguise. Hero is publicly denounced by Claudio on her wedding day, falls into a swoon, and apparently dies. Benedick proves his love for Beatrice by challenging Claudio to a duel. The plot by Don John and Borachio is unmasked by the 'shallow fools' Dogberry and Verges, the local constables. Claudio promises to make Leonato amends for his daughter's death, and is asked to marry a

cousin of Hero's; the veiled lady turns out to be Hero herself. Benedick asks to be married at the same time; Beatrice, 'upon great persuasion; and partly to save your life, for I was told you were in a consumption', agrees, and the play ends with a dance.

MUDDIMAN, Henry (b. 1629), was authorized as a journalist by the Rump Parliament in 1659, in which year he started *The Parliamentary Intelligencer* and *Mercurius Publicus*. He became the most famous of the 17th-cent. journalists, and his *newsletters in manuscript were an important political feature of the day. One of his principal rivals was *L'Estrange, whose papers, however, he drove from the field. In 1665 he started *The Oxford Gazette*. (See also GAZETTE and NEWSPAPERS, ORIGINS OF.)

MUDIE, Charles Edward (1818–90), the founder of Mudie's Lending Library (see LIBRARIES, CIRCULATING). He opened premises in Oxford Street in 1852, where the business prospered for many years, despite frequent complaints about Mudie's moral scruples in selecting his stock, which amounted, some claimed, to a form of censorship.

Muggletonians, a sect founded *c.*1651 by Lodowicke Muggleton, a tailor (1609–98), and his cousin John Reeve (1608–58), who claimed to be the 'two witnesses' of Rev. II: 3–6. They denied the doctrine of the Trinity, and taught that matter was eternal and reason the creation of the devil.

Muiopotmos, or *The Fate of the Butterflie,* a mythological poem by *Spenser published among his *Complaints* (1591). It describes the destruction of the butterfly Clarion by the jealous spider Aragnoll.

MUIR, Edwin (1887–1959), poet, born in Orkney. He turned to Socialism (through the writings of *Blatchford) and to the works of *Nietzsche. He became assistant to *Orage, and contributed to *New Age*. Muir married Willa Anderson (1890–1970) in 1919 and in 1921 they went to Prague and remained in Europe for four years, a period that later produced their collaborative translations from the German (notably of *Kafka, 1930–49). More importantly, it freed Muir's imagination as a poet. *First Poems* (1925) was followed by several other collections, including *Chorus of the newly dead* (1926), *The Labyrinth* (1949), and *Collected Poems 1921–1951* (1952). Muir's poetry is traditional in form, and much of his imagery is rooted in the landscapes of his childhood. A sense of subdued menace lies beneath many of his quiet and orderly poems, which sometimes (as in his well known piece 'The Horses') achieve the *apocalyptic. Muir also published three novels, a num-

ber of critical works, and a highly evocative autobiography published in 1940 as *The Story and the Fable* and revised as *An Autobiography* in 1954.

MULCASTER, Richard (*c.*1530–1611), the first headmaster of Merchant Taylors' School, London, and later high master of St Paul's. He wrote two books on education, *Positions* (1581), dedicated to *Elizabeth I, and *The Elementarie* (1582). Both books show his humanist interests and ideals and enlightened views on education. He also published Latin and English verses on the queen's death (1603), and helped devise City shows and pageants.

MULGRAVE, earl of, see SHEFFIELD, J.

Mulla, frequently referred to in *Spenser's poems, is the river Mulla or Awbeg, a tributary of the Blackwater in Ireland, near which stood Kilcolman Castle, his residence when he composed much of *The Faerie Queene*.

Mulliner, Mr, (1) in Mrs Gaskell's *Cranford*; (2) the teller of some of the stories by P. G. *Wodehouse.

MULOCK, Dinah Maria, see CRAIK, MRS.

Mum and the Sothsegger, an alliterative poem of *c.*1403–6, bewailing the follies of Richard II and offering advice to Henry IV. Two sections survive: the first of 857 lines previously called *Richard the Redeless* and edited by *Skeat with *Piers Plowman*; the second of 1,751 lines. Skeat and Jusserand believed, probably wrongly, that the poem was by *Langland.

MUMBY, Frank A. (1872–1954), journalist and historian of the British book trade, whose *Romance of Bookselling* (1910) was the basis of *Publishing and Bookselling: A History from the Earliest Times to the Present Day* (1930); it was revised by Ian Norrie, who added a second section, 1870–1970, which was itself revised as *Mumby's Publishing and Bookselling in the Twentieth Century*.

Mummers' Play, or St George Play, a folk-play evolved from the *sword-dance, widespread through England, Scotland, Ireland, and Wales. The play, in its characters and detailed action, varies in different localities, but the main lines are as follows. The principal characters are St George (Sir George, King George, Prince George), the Turkish knight, Captain Slasher, and the Doctor. After a brief prologue, the fighting characters advance and introduce themselves, or are introduced, in vaunting rhymes. A duel or several duels follow, and one or other of the combatants is killed. The Doctor then enters, boasts his skill, and resuscitates the slain.

Supernumerary grotesque characters are then presented, and a collection is made. The central incident of the play is doubtless connected with the celebration of the death of the year and its resurrection in the spring.

MUNBY, Arthur Joseph (1828–1910), is now chiefly remembered for diaries and notebooks, used by Derek Hudson as the basis of his *Munby: Man of Two Worlds* (1972). These give an interesting picture of Victorian literary and social life; they also reveal Munby's obsession with working women and the story of his secret marriage to a maidservant, Hannah, which explain some of the allusions in his poems, of which he published various volumes.

MUNDAY, Anthony (1560–1633), hackwriter, wrote or collaborated in a number of plays, and was ridiculed by *Jonson as Antonio Balladino in *The Case is Altered*. Munday wrote ballads, and as 'Shepheard Tonie' contributed several poems to *Englands Helicon* (1600). He also translated popular romances, including the *Palmerin cycle (1581–95), *Palladine of England* (1588), and *Amadis of Gaul* (?1590), and wrote City pageants from 1605.

Mundungus, the ill-tempered author (possibly Dr Sharp) of a travel-book satirized by Sterne in *A Sentimental Journey*.

Munera, The Lady, in Spenser's *Faerie Queene* (v. ii), the daughter of the Saracen Pollente, the personification of ill-gotten wealth.

Munera Pulveris, see RUSKIN, J.

Mungo, see BICKERSTAFFE, I.

MUNRO, H(ector) H(ugh), see SAKI.

Murder in the Cathedral, a play by T. S. *Eliot.

Murder on the Orient Express, a detective story by A. *Christie.

'Murders in the Rue Morgue, The', see POE, E. A.

MURDOCH, Iris Jean (1919–), novelist and philosopher. Her works on philosophy include *Sartre, Romantic Rationalist* (1953) and *The Sovereignty of Good* (1970). In 1956 she married the literary critic John Bayley. Her first novel, *Under the Net* (1954), a first-person male narration, was followed by many other successful works, including *The Bell* (1958, set in a lay community in a country house); *A Severed Head* (1961, dramatized 1963 by J. B. *Priestley); *The Red and the Green* (1965); *The Time of the Angels* (1968); *Bruno's Dream* (1969); *The Black Prince* (1973); *A Word Child* (1975); *The Sea, The Sea*

(1978, a novel about a theatre director and his childhood love, which won the *Booker Prize); *The Philosopher's Pupil* (1983); and *The Good Apprentice* (1986). She has also written three plays. Her novels, which have been described as psychological detective stories, portray complicated and sophisticated sexual relationships and her plots have an operatic quality, combining comic, bizarre, and macabre incidents in a highly patterned symbolic structure. Though clearly not intended as strictly realistic, her portrayal of 20th-cent. middle-class and intellectual life shows acute observation as well as a wealth of invention, and has baffled critics by its evasion of recognized fictional genres.

Murdockson, Meg, and her daughter Magdalen, called 'Madge Wildfire', characters in Scott's *The Heart of Midlothian*.

Murdstone, Edward and Jane, characters in Dickens's *David Copperfield*.

MURPHY, Arthur (1727–1805), playwright, wrote over 20 farces, comedies, and tragedies, including adaptations of *Molière and *Voltaire; his better-known pieces include *The Way to Keep Him* (1760), *Three Weeks after Marriage* (1764), and *Know Your Own Mind* (1777). He also wrote lives of *Fielding (1762), Dr *Johnson (1792), and *Garrick (1801).

MURPHY, Richard (1927–), Irish poet. Much of his poetry portrays the landscapes and seascapes of Ireland; his publications include *The Archeology of Love* (1955), *Sailing to an Island* (1963, which contains his long narrative poem about a fishing tragedy, 'The Cleggan Disaster', and other sea tales), *The Battle of Aughrim* (1968), and *Selected Poems* (1979).

MURRAY, (George) Gilbert (Aimé) (1866–1957), a brilliant Greek scholar; born in Sydney, Australia, he was Regius professor of Greek at Oxford 1908–36. His claim to brilliance lay in his ability to make the ancient world sensitively real to his contemporaries; and while he produced influential studies in Greek epic and drama, he is best remembered for his translations of *Euripides. He was the model for Adolphus Cusins in Shaw's *Major Barbara. Murray was an eloquent champion of women's rights and other liberal causes, and as chairman of the League of Nations Union (1922–38) he struggled without much hope to save Europe from war.

MURRAY, Sir James Augustus Henry (1837–1915), acquired his great philological and antiquarian knowledge largely through his own studies. He made the acquaintance of many scholars with similar preoccupations, including *Skeat, *Sweet, and *Furnivall; he became a member of the *Philological Society, to which he delivered in 1868 papers later printed as *The Dialect of the Southern Counties of Scotland* (1873). In 1879, after lengthy negotiation and much hesitation, he was appointed editor of the *Oxford English Dictionary*, a monumental work which was to occupy the rest of his life. He laid down the lines on which the work was to be compiled, and persevered through many difficulties.

MURRAY, John (1778–1843), the son of John Murray I (1745–93), who founded the publishing house still in existence. The second John Murray was one of those who, together with the reviews such as the *Edinburgh* and the *Quarterly*, began to substitute for the dying system of personal patronage his own personal encouragement and commercial expertise. He was one of the first publishers, according to T. *Dibdin, who treated authors 'with the respect due to gentlemen'. His publishing house became a social meeting-place for many of the literary figures of his time, and it is probable that the plan for the founding of the *Athenaeum club was devised in his rooms. With the help and encouragement of Sir W. *Scott he established the Tory *Quarterly Review* in 1809. He gave up the London agency of *Blackwood*'s in protest at its attacks on the *Cockney school. He was the friend and publisher of *Byron, who was his single most important author. Murray bought Byron's memoirs of 1818–21 from T. *Moore, and reluctantly consented to having them burned in his grate at Albemarle Street. His other authors included J. *Austen, *Crabbe, *Coleridge, *Southey, Leigh *Hunt, and *Borrow.

The John Murray succession, and the firm's independence, has continued to the present day.

MURRAY, Lindley (1745–1826), published an English Grammar in 1795, a Reader in 1799, and a Spelling Book in 1804, which earned him the title of 'the father of English grammar'.

MURRY, John Middleton (1889–1957), editor of the *modernist periodical *Rhythm* (1911–13), through which he met in 1912 Katherine *Mansfield, whom he was later (in 1918) to marry. In 1914 he met D. H. *Lawrence, who greatly influenced him; the relationship of the Lawrences and the Murrys was intense and tempestuous, and is reflected in *Women in Love*. From 1919 to 1921 Murry was editor of the *Athenaeum, in which he published an impressive range of writers, including V. *Woolf, T. S. *Eliot, and Valéry, and in which he himself attacked *Georgian poetry. In 1923, the year of his wife's death, he founded *The Adelphi; although he was to marry again three times, he continued to dwell on her memory, editing her works, publishing reminiscences, letters, etc. His many critical works include *Dostoevsky*

(1916), *The Problem of Style* (1922), *Countries of the Mind* (1922, 1931), *Keats and Shakespeare* (1925), and *Son of Woman, the Story of D. H. Lawrence* (1931). Throughout his turbulent emotional and professional life he was attracted to the extreme and the romantic, seeing life as a spiritual search. See his autobiography, *Between Two Worlds* (1935).

MUSAEUS, (1) a legendary Greek poet, said to have been a pupil of *Orpheus; (2) a Greek poet, who perhaps lived about AD 500, the author of a poem on the story of *Hero and Leander which provided the groundwork for *Marlowe's poem.

Muse's Looking-Glasse, The, a defence of the drama, in the form of a play, by *Randolph, printed 1638.

Musgrave, (1) Little, see LITTLE MUSGRAVE AND LADY BARNARD; (2) Sir Richard, a character in Scott's *The Lay of the Last Minstrel*.

Musgrove, Mr and Mrs, their son Charles and his wife Mary (*née* Elliot), and their daughters Henrietta and Louisa, characters in J. Austen's *Persuasion*.

Musidorus ('gifted by the Muses'), the young duke of Thessalia in Sidney's *Arcadia*.

'Musophilus, or A Generall defence of learning', a verse dialogue in six- and eight-lined stanzas by S. *Daniel, dedicated to his friend Fulke *Greville, published 1599.

Musophilus defends the claims of culture against the worldly arts practised by Philocosmus, the unlettered man of action. The poem shows at its best Daniel's gift for moral reflection in dignified but plain language, and his faith in a poetic vocation independent of worldly recognition.

Mustapha, (1) a tragedy (1609) by Sir F. *Greville; (2) a *heroic drama (1665) by R. *Boyle.

'Mutabilitie Cantos', name given to the fragmentary 'Book VII' of Spenser's *Faerie Queene*: two cantos only, first published with the folio edition of The Faerie Queene in 1609. They describe the challenge of the Titaness Mutabilitie to the cosmic government of Jove. The Cantos can be seen as an epilogue to The Faerie Queene.

MYERS, F(rederic) W(illiam) H(enry) (1843–1901), poet and inspector of schools, published several volumes of poetry and critical essays; his essay on G. *Eliot, first published in the *Century Magazine* in 1881 (and reprinted in *Essays Classical and Modern*, 1883), describes the celebrated incident in which she spoke to him of 'God,

Immortality, Duty', and declared 'how inconceivable was the *first*, how unbelievable the *second*, and yet how peremptory and absolute the *third*'. Myers was a founder of the *Society for Psychical Research; he was joint author (with E. Gurney and F. Podmore) of *Phantasms of the Living* (1886), a two-volume work dealing largely with telepathy.

MYERS, L(eopold) H(amilton) (1881–1944), novelist, the son of F. W. H. *Myers. His novels are concerned with the problem of how human beings can live rightly in society if they exclude spirituality. In his troubled personal life he failed to reconcile the flesh and the spirit. He was in violent opposition to humanism and to the values of the *Bloomsbury group, and after trying several political solutions he became a Communist. Apart from the *Orissers* (1922), *The 'Clio'* (1925), and *Strange Glory* (1936), the novels are set in an imaginary 16th-cent. India: *The Near and the Far* (1929), *Prince Jali* (1931), *The Root and the Flower* (1935), and *The Pool of Vishnu* (1940); all collected under the title *The Near and the Far* (1943). He died from an overdose of veronal.

'My Mind to me a Kingdom is', the first line of a poem on contentment which was first printed in William Byrd's *Psalmes, Sonets, & Songs* (1588). It was frequently referred to in the 16th and 17th cents, and often attributed to Sir E. *Dyer. It is more probably by the earl of *Oxford.

Mysteries of Udolpho, The, a novel by A. *Radcliffe (1794).

The orphaned Emily St Aubert is carried off by her aunt's villainous husband Montoni to a remote castle in the Apennines, where her life, honour, and fortune are threatened and she is surrounded by apparently supernatural terrors. These are later explained as due to human agency and Emily escapes, returns to France, and, after further mysteries and misunderstandings, is reunited with her lover Valancourt. The book plays an important part in J. Austen's *Northanger Abbey*.

Mysterious Mother, The, a tragedy in blank verse by Horace *Walpole, printed at *Strawberry Hill in 1768.

It deals with the remorse of a mother (the countess of Narbonne) for an act of incest committed many years before. The theme shocked many of his admirers but greatly interested *Byron, who described the play as 'a tragedy of the highest order, and not a puling love-play'.

Mystery Plays, biblical dramas popular in England from the 13th to the later 16th cent., take their name from the *mestier* (métier or trade) of their performers; they were previously called 'Miracle Plays' which, strictly, are enactments of the miracles performed by the saints. The Mysteries enact the events of the Bible from the Creation to the Ascension (and in some cases later). Their origin is much disputed; one of the earliest is the Anglo-Norman *Jeu d'Adam* (see ADAM), and there were cycles in many countries: France, Italy, Ireland, and Germany (surviving in the Oberammergau Passion Play). Though it is clear from their archives that many English towns had them, only four complete cycles survive: York, Chester, Wakefield (also called Towneley from the owners of the manuscript), and the *Ludus Coventriae*, also called the Hegge cycle, and N-town because it is not known where it comes from. They are connected with the feast day of Corpus Christi. The various pageants were each assigned to a particular trade-guild, often with a humorous or macabre connection between the métier and the play. Their great popularity in England from the time of *Chaucer to Shakespeare is repeatedly attested by those writers, among others. Their end was no doubt mainly caused by Reformation distate for idols and religious pageantry. Their great interest is as an early, popular form of theatre, manifesting energy, humour, and seriousness; it is not accurate to think of their composers as unlearned, as is clear from the group of six plays in the Towneley cycle assigned to a presumed author known as 'the Wakefield Master'.

Mystic, Mr, a character in Peacock's *Melincourt*, a caricature of *Coleridge.

N

NABOKOV, Vladimir Vladimirovich (1899–1977), Russian novelist, poet, and literary scholar. After studying French and Russian literature at Trinity College, Cambridge (1919–23), Nabokov lived in Berlin (1923–37) and Paris (1937–40), writing mainly in Russian under the pseudonym 'Sirin'. In 1940 he moved to the USA, and became professor of Russian literature at Cornell University (1948–59). From then on all his novels were written in English. From 1959 he lived in Montreux, in Switzerland, where he died.

Nabokov's reputation as one of the major, most original prose writers of the 20th cent., a stylist with extraordinary narrative and descriptive skill and a wonderful linguistic inventiveness in two languages, is based on his achievement in the novels *Mary* (1926), *King, Queen, Knave* (1928), *The Eye* (1930), *The Defence* (1930), *Glory* (1932), *Laughter in the Dark* (1932), *Despair* (1936), *Invitation to a Beheading* (1938), *The Gift* (1938), *The Real Life of Sebastian Knight* (1941), *Bend Sinister* (1947), *Lolita* (1955), *Pnin* (1957), *Pale Fire* (1962), *Ada* (1969), *Transparent Things* (1972), and *Look at the Harlequins!* (1974), and on several volumes of short stories. Nabokov's admiration for *Dickens, R. L. *Stevenson, and *Joyce, among English writers and his unease with J. *Austen, can be seen in his *Lectures on Literature (1980)*.

NAIPAUL, V(idiadhar) S(urajprasad) (1932–), novelist, born in Trinidad, educated at University College, Oxford. He settled in England, married in 1955, and embarked on a career of literary journalism. His first three books, *The Mystic Masseur* (1957), *The Suffrage of Elvira* (1958), and *Miguel Street* (short stories, 1959), are comedies of manners, all set in Trinidad. His next novel, *A House for Mr Biswas* (1961), also set in Trinidad, traces the fortunes of its mild hero as he progresses from sign-writer to journalist, is trapped into marriage and almost absorbed by his wife's vast family, the Tulsis, but continues to bid for independence, symbolized by the house which he acquires shortly before his death. *Mr Stone and the Knights Companion* (1963) was followed by *The Mimic Men* (1967). From this time Naipaul's work becomes more overtly political and pessimistic. *In a Free State* (1971, *Booker Prize) explores problems of nationality and identity through three linked narratives, all describing displaced characters. *Guerrillas* (1975) is a portrait of political and sexual violence in the Caribbean; *A Bend in the River* (1979) is an equally horrifying portrait of emergent Africa. His travel books include *The Middle Passage* (1962), on the Caribbean; *An Area of Darkness* (1964), his highly controversial and critical account of India; *The Return of Eva Peron; with The Killings in Trinidad* (1980); and *Among the Believers: an Islamic Journey* (1981). His brother Shiva Naipaul (1945–85), whose novels include *Fireflies* (1970) and *The Hot Country* (1983), was also a writer of distinction.

NAIRNE, Carolina, Baroness, *née* Oliphant (1766–1845), was the author of many spirited Jacobite songs, including 'Will ye no come back again?' and 'Charlie is my darling'; also of humorous and pathetic ballads, such as 'The Land o' the Leal'. Her poems were collected in *Lays from Strathearn* (1846).

Namancos, in Milton's *Lycidas, a place in Gallicia, near Cape Finisterre, shown in Mercator's Atlas of 1623. The castle of Bayona is shown near it.

Namby-Pamby, see PHILIPS, A.

NAMIER, Sir Lewis Bernstein (1888–1960), historian, born in Poland, educated at the London School of Economics and Balliol College, Oxford, became a British subject in 1913. His major works include *The Structure of Politics at the Accession of George III* (1929) and *England in the Age of the American Revolution* (1930). During the 1930s he became deeply involved with the plight of Jewish refugees and with Zionism.

Nancy, in Dickens's *Oliver Twist, the fancy woman of Bill Sikes.

Nandy, John Edward, in Dickens's *Little Dorrit, the father of Mrs Plornish.

NAPIER, Sir William Francis Patrick (1785–1860), served in Sir John Moore's campaign in Spain (1808) and in the subsequent war in the Peninsula. His *History of the War in the Peninsula* (1828–40) has placed him high among historical writers.

NARAYAN, R(asipuram) K(rishnaswami) (1906–), Indian novelist writing in English. In his first novel, *Swami and Friends* (1935), he created the imaginary small town of Malgudi, which he was to map out and populate in several succeeding novels, including *The Bachelor of Arts* (1937), *The English Teacher* (1945), *Mr Sampath* (1949), *The Financial Expert* (1952), *The Vendor of Sweets* (1967), and *The Painter of Signs* (1977). His fictional world is peopled with characters portrayed with a gentle irony as they struggle to accommodate tradition with Western attitudes inherited from the British. Narayan's other publications include volumes of short stories and a memoir, *My Days* (1975).

Narcissa, (1) in Pope's *Moral Essays* is Anne *Oldfield; (2) Roderick's love in Smollett's *Roderick Random; (3) one of the persons mourned in Young's *Night Thoughts.

Narrenschiff, see SHIP OF FOOLS.

NASH, Ogden (1902–71), American writer of sophisticated light verse, renowned for his puns, epigrams, elaborate rhymes, elaborate lack of rhymes, wildly asymmetrical lines, and other verbal fancies.

NASH, Richard, 'Beau' (1674–1761), went to Bath in 1705, where he established the Assembly Rooms, drew up a code of etiquette and dress, and became unquestioned autocrat of society. The gambling laws of 1740–5 deprived him of his source of income, and his popularity waned after 1745. *Goldsmith wrote a life of Nash, published 1762.

NASHE, Thomas (1567–1601). His first publication was a preface to Greene's *Menaphon (1589), surveying the follies of contemporary literature; he expanded this theme in *The Anatomie of Absurditie* (1589). His hatred of Puritanism drew him into the *Martin Marprelate controversy. In 1592 Nashe replied to the savage denunciations of Richard Harvey, astrologer and brother of Gabriel *Harvey, with *Pierce Pennilesse his Supplication to the Divell*. He avenged Gabriel Harvey's attack on R. *Greene with *Strange Newes, of the Intercepting certaine Letters* (1592). A florid religious meditation, *Christs Teares over Jerusalem* (1593), was dedicated to Lady Elizabeth Carey, and *The Terrors of the Night* (1594), a discourse on dreams and nightmares, was dedicated to her daughter. He published *The Unfortunate Traveller. Or The life of Jacke Wilton* (1594) and returned to satire with *Have with you to Saffron-walden. Or, Gabriell Harveys Hunt is up* (1596), to which Harvey replied; in 1599 Archbishop Whitgift ordered that the works of both writers should be suppressed. Nashe's lost satirical comedy *The Isle of Dogs* also led to trouble with the authorities. He published *Nashes Lenten Stuffe* (1599), a mock encomium of the red herring (or kipper) which includes a burlesque version of the story of *Hero and Leander; and *Summers Last Will and Testament* (1600). Nashe had a share in Marlowe's *Dido, Queene of Carthage. He was amusingly satirized as 'Ingenioso' in the three *Parnassus Plays (1598–1606).

NASO, see OVID.

NATHAN, George Jean (1882–1958), American essayist, drama critic, and polemicist, co-founder in 1924 (with H. L. *Mencken) and editor of *The American Mercury*. He published many collections of theatrical reviews and essays, including *The Popular Theatre* (1918), *The Critic and the Drama* (1922), and *Art of the Night* (1938).

Nathaniel, Sir, in Shakespeare's *Love's Labour's Lost*, a curate and friend to Holofernes.

National Anthem, The. The first recorded public performance of 'God save the King' took place at Drury Lane Theatre on 28 Sept. 1745, during the excitement and alarm caused by the Jacobite invasion of that year. The score used on this occasion was prepared by *Arne. It became customary about 1747 or 1748 to greet the king with it when he entered a place of public entertainment. The description of it as 'National Anthem' appears to have been adopted early in the 19th cent.

The remoter origin of 'God save the King' is obscure; words and tune, with slight differences, had appeared in *Thesaurus Musicus*, a song collection published in 1744. There is good evidence that the song was originally written in favour of James II in 1688 or possibly Charles II in 1681; but the author is unknown. As regards the melody, the closest resemblance is that of a galliard composed by Dr Bull in the early 17th cent. But this may be the keyboard setting of some folk-tune or other well-known air of the time, and the tune of 'God save the King' may have been drawn directly from that original.

National Biography, *Dictionary of,* see DICTIONARY OF NATIONAL BIOGRAPHY.

National Book League, an independent charitable organization founded in 1925 as the National Book Council by the Society of Bookmen (Harold Macmillan, *Galsworthy, Stanley Unwin, Maurice Marston, and others); its function is to promote the use and enjoyment of books by working with all branches of the book world (booksellers, publishers, authors, printers, librarians, teachers, etc.). The Council was renamed The National Book League in 1945.

National Library of Scotland, see under LIBRARIES.

Natty Bumppo, the hero of the 'Leatherstocking' novels of J. F. *Cooper.

Naturalism, as a term of literary history, primarily a French movement in prose fiction and (to a lesser extent) the drama during the final third of the 19th cent., although it is also applied to similar movements or groups of writers in other countries (e.g. Germany, the USA) in the latter decades of the 19th and early years of the 20th cents. In France *Zola was the dominant practitioner and the chief exponent of its doctrines. His novel *Thérèse Raquin* (1867), together with the Goncourts' *Germinie Lacerteux* (1865), are considered as marking the beginnings of the movement. Other writers who shared the ideas and aims of Naturalism are Daudet, Maupassant, and, in his early fiction, Huysmans.

Broadly speaking, Naturalism is characterized by a refusal to idealize experience and by the persuasion that human life is strictly subject to natural laws. The Naturalists shared with the earlier Realists the conviction that the everyday life of the middle and lower classes of their own day provided subjects worthy of serious literary treatment. These were to be rendered so far as possible without artificiality of plot and with scrupulous care for authenticity and accuracy of detail, thus investing the novel with the value of social history.

In Germany, the movement flourished from *c*.1885 until the 1890s, largely in the theatre, influenced both by *Ibsen and by the Théâtre Libre, which visited Berlin in 1889; one of its principal exponents was Gerhart Hauptmann. See also REALISM.

Nature and Art, a romance by Mrs *Inchbald, published 1796.

NAYLER, James (1616/17–60), a Quaker and brilliant preacher. He attracted a following of fervent devotees who encouraged him to ride in triumph on a donkey into Bristol in 1656; he was charged with blasphemy, cruelly punished, and imprisoned. He subsequently repented of his excesses and wrote movingly of his new spirit of humility and endurance.

NEALE, J(ohn) M(ason) (1818–66), educated founder of the Cambridge *Camden Society. He was author of *The History of the Holy Eastern Church* (1847–73), and many hymns (some of them translations from Greek, medieval Latin, and Eastern sources) including 'O happy band of pilgrims', 'Art thou weary', and 'Jerusalem the Golden'; *Hymns Ancient and Modern* owes much to his inspiration.

Neckett, Mr, the sheriff's officer in Dickens's *Bleak House*, generally referred to as Coavinses, the name of the sponging-house which he keeps. He has three children, Tom, Emma, and Charlotte.

NED, the 'New English Dictionary', now called the *Oxford English Dictionary*.

NEDHAM, or **NEEDHAM,** Marchamont (1620–78), journalist and pamphleteer, and chief author of *Mercurius Britanicus* (1643–6), the arch enemy of the royalist *Mercurius Aulicus* of *Berkenhead. His subsequent professional career showed shifting loyalties, and he was several times imprisoned. He exerted considerable power as editor of *Mercurius Politicus*. (See also NEWSPAPERS, ORIGINS OF.)

Negative capability, a phrase coined by *Keats to describe his conception of the receptivity necessary to the process of poetic creativity. He defined his new concept in a letter (22 Dec. 1817): 'Negative Capability, that is when man is capable of being in uncertainties, Mysteries, doubts, without any irritable reaching after fact and reason—.' Keats regarded Shakespeare as the prime example of negative capability, attributing to him the ability to identify completely with his characters, and to write about them with empathy and understanding; he contrasts this with the partisan approach of *Milton and the 'wordsworthian or egotistical sublime' (Letter to Woodhouse, 27 Oct. 1818) of *Wordsworth.

Nekayah, in Johnson's *Rasselas*, the sister of the hero.

Nelly Dean, a character in E. Brontë's *Wuthering Heights*.

Nemesis of Faith, The, a novel by J. A. *Froude.

Nemo, the law-writer in Dickens's *Bleak House*.

NENNIUS (*fl. c.*830), the author or reviser of the *Historia Britonum*, the 33 surviving manuscripts of which enshrine several versions. It is a collection of notes, drawn from various sources including *Gildas and (perhaps indirectly) *Bede, and is a mixture of legend and history characterized by pride in the Celtic people of Britain and interest in its topography; it is interesting for the account it purports to give of the historical *Arthur who, as *dux bellorum*, after Hengist's death led the Britons against the Saxons in twelve battles (including Mount Badon) which Nennius enumerates. It is one of the sources on which *Geoffrey of Monmouth drew for his *Historia Regum Britanniae*.

Neo-classicism, in literature, the habit of imitating the great authors of antiquity as a matter of aesthetic principle. Medieval writers had often used classical works for models, but *Petrarch in the 14th cent. was the first to do so because he considered it the only way to produce great literature. The epic, eclogue, elegy, ode, satire, tragedy, comedy, and epigram of ancient times all found imitators, first in Latin, then in the vernaculars. At the beginning of the 16th cent. the recovery of the previously neglected *Poetics of Aristotle provoked an attempt to establish rules for the use of the ancient genres. The *Poetics* itself was repeatedly edited, translated, and supplied with commentaries, notably by *Castelvetro (1570), and a number of treatises on poetry appeared, culminating in J. C. *Scaliger's controversial *Poëtice* (1561). These theoreticians imprisoned imitation within a rigid framework of rules. The most famous of their inventions was the observance of the dramatic *unities of time, place, and action, which won great support in France in the 1620s where a new generation was eager to attract a more educated public. A noisy battle over *Corneille's popular tragi-comedy Le Cid (1637), which was blamed for breaking the rules, ended in an acceptance of the unities, and during the next 30 years a succession of critics, the best-known of whom was *Boileau, extended the scope of their prescriptions from drama to all other major genres.

Up to the last quarter of the 17th cent. neo-classicism had little influence in England and, except for *Jonson, no important writer paid strict attention to the rules. But at that point playwrights responded to the urgings of *Rymer and began to take neo-classical theories more seriously. Dryden produced *All for Love (1677) and Addison his *Cato (1713), which has been called the only correct neo-classical tragedy in English; but the fashion was not to last.

The usual excuse for the rules was that they helped writers to be true to nature. *Pope wrote: 'Those RULES of old discover'd not devis'd, | Are Nature still, but Nature methodiz'd', and implicit in his view was the assumption that 'nature' consisted in what was generally true. *Cervantes in the early 17th cent. had argued for the representation of true facts of an exceptional nature, and a hundred years later it had become clear to everybody that extraordinary phenomena furnished literary material of considerable value. The scope of what could be regarded as natural was steadily growing, and simultaneously the difficulty *Homer's readers experienced in appreciating his poems made them aware of the fact that behaviour usual in one age could prove unacceptable in another. What undermined neo-classicism most decisively in the 18th cent. was the changing view of the goal of literary creation provoked by Boileau's translation (1674) of the pseudo-Longinian treatise of the *Sublime. A cult of Sublimity replaced the wish to produce a just representation of general Reality, and the way to *Romanticism lay open.

Neoplatonism, a philosophical and religious system, combining Platonic ideas with oriental mysticism, which originated at Alexandria in the 3rd cent. and is especially represented in the writings of *Plotinus, Porphyry, and Proclus. This system of thought, through *Augustine, left a deep mark on Christianity, combined in the 5th and 6th cents AD with survivals of *Gnosticism and persisted in this form through the Middle Ages. It experienced a notable revival in the 15th cent., associated with Ficino, *Pico della Mirandola, Agrippa, and *Paracelsus. The conglomeration of ideas found in the works of these writers extends well beyond Neoplatonism, but is often given that name, and it influenced literature in a number of distinct ways. (1) The 'Neoplatonic' theory of love rested on the beliefs that earthly beauty was an image of absolute beauty and that spiritual graces in a beloved were even more important than bodily ones. These beliefs find frequent expression in the poetry of the Renaissance and recur in *Shelley. (2) Belief in the existence of airy creatures that could be invisible, and that served or crossed mankind, appears in Dr *Dee's familiar, Prospero's Ariel in *The Tempest, or on a humorous level the sylphs of *The Rape of the Lock. (3) The attempt to bring together all systems of belief—Christian, Neoplatonist, Cabbalistic—that maintained the power of spirit over matter appears in poets like T. *Vaughan and in the writings of the *Cambridge Platonists. (4) There was the view that both Art and Nature are copies of the same supersensuous reality and that Art could be the better copy, a view that appealed to *Sidney and *Spenser.

Nerissa, in Shakespeare's *The Merchant of Venice, Portia's waiting-woman.

NESBIT, E(dith) (1858–1924), wife of Hubert Bland, a Fabian founder member, is remembered for her children's books, tales of everyday family life sometimes mingled with magic. In 1898 her first stories about the young Bastables appeared with such success that she published three 'Bastable' novels in quick succession: The Story of the Treasure-Seekers (1899), The Wouldbe-goods (1901), and The New Treasure-Seekers (1904). Other well-known titles with a lasting appeal include Five Children and It (1902), The Phoenix and the Carpet (1904), The Railway Children (1906), and The Enchanted Castle (1907).

Neville, Miss, a character in Goldsmith's *She Stoops to Conquer.

New Age, The, see ORAGE, A. R.

New Apocalypse, The, a group of writers who flourished briefly as a movement in the 1940s, united by a romantic reaction against what they saw as the 'classicism' of *Auden; it expressed itself in wild, turbulent, and at times surreal imagery. Their work appeared in three anthologies, The New Apocalypse: an anthology of criticism, poems and stories (1940), edited by James

Findlay Hendry (1912–); *The White Horseman: prose and verse of the New Apocalypse* (1941), edited by Hendry and Henry Treece (1911–66), with an introduction by George Sutherland Fraser (1915–80), and *The Crown and the Sickle* (1945), also edited by Hendry and Treece. They described themselves as 'anticerebral', claimed a 'large, accepting attitude to life', invoked the name of D. H. *Lawrence, and approved of Dylan *Thomas; G. *Barker and V. *Watkins also were associated with the movement.

New Atalantis, The, see MANLEY, MRS.

New Atlantis, The, a treatise of political philosophy in the form of a fable, by F. *Bacon (1627).

It is an account of a visit to an imaginary island of Bensalem in the Pacific and of the social conditions prevailing there; and also of 'Solomon's House', a college of natural philosophy 'dedicated to the study of the works and creatures of God'.

NEWBERY, John (1713–67), publisher and bookseller, who established himself in 1744 in St Paul's Churchyard, and was one of the earliest and best-known publishers of children's books. He produced and partly wrote many books of riddles, fables, stories, etc. *Goldsmith was one of his authors and may have written *Goody Two-Shoes* for him: he contributed his *Chinese Letters* (later *The Citizen of the World*) to Newbery's *The Public Ledger*. He was a friend of Dr *Jonson and appears as 'Jack Whirler' in *The Idler*, and as 'the philanthropic bookseller' in *The Vicar of Wakefield*.

NEWBOLT, Sir Henry John (1862–1938), is remembered principally for his rousing patriotic nautical ballads, which include 'Drake's Drum', published in *Admirals All and Other Verses* (1897).

NEWCASTLE, Margaret, duchess of (1623–73), second wife of William Cavendish, 1st duke of *Newcastle. Her works include a volume of verse, *Poems and Fancies* (1653), plays, letters, and a biography of her husband (1667). Much of her prose has an engaging directness, but she was in her lifetime mocked for her eccentricities and her intellectual pursuits.

NEWCASTLE, William Cavendish, 1st duke of (1592–1676), husband of Margaret Cavendish (above), supported the king generously during the Civil War, and lived abroad from 1644 until the Restoration.

He was the author of several poems and plays, collaborating in the latter with *Shirley, whose patron he was, and with *Dryden and *Shadwell.

Newcomes, The, a novel by *Thackeray, published in numbers 1853–5.

The story, told by Arthur Pendennis, is concerned with the descendants of a self-made man, Thomas Newcome. His eldest son, Colonel Thomas Newcome, is a simple, unworldly soldier, who has lived most of his life in India. In contrast, his half-brothers Hobson and Brian are wealthy and pretentious. Colonel Newcome is a widower, and his only son Clive is sent home to England to be educated. When Clive is almost grown up, his father returns from India. Clive loves his cousin Ethel, daughter of Sir Brian Newcome, but Ethel's brother Barnes and her grandmother Lady Kew intend her to make a grand marriage. Ethel allows herself to become engaged first to her cousin, Lord Kew, and then to Lord Farintosh. The disastrously unhappy marriage of Barnes, who treats his wife so badly that she runs away with a former admirer, Jack Belsize, makes Ethel decide that she will not marry at all, but will devote herself to her brother's children. Meanwhile Clive has been manœuvred into marriage to a pretty, superficial girl, Rosey Mackenzie. When Colonel Newcome's fortune is lost, Clive and Rosey are reduced to extreme poverty, and Rosey's mother makes life so intolerable for the Colonel that he finally takes refuge from her by becoming a pensioner in the Grey Friars almshouse, where he dies. Rosey has also died, and Thackeray allows the reader to assume that Clive and Ethel will get married.

New Country, an anthology of prose and verse published 1933, edited by M. *Roberts, with contributions by *Auden, *Spender, *Day-Lewis, *Empson, *Isherwood, *Upward, and R. *Warner. Its tone was highly political, verging on the revolutionary. A collection with many of the same contributors, *New Signatures*, also edited by Roberts, had appeared in 1932.

New Criticism, a term adopted after the publication of *Ransom's *The New Criticism* (1941), and applied to various tendencies in modern critical practice and theory. Ransom's book was a discussion of I. A. *Richards, T. S. *Eliot, *Empson, *Winters, and others; other practitioners (some of whom resisted the label) included Cleanth Brooks, R. P. *Warren, A. *Tate, and R. P. Blackmur (all, significantly, Americans) and, in England, in some respects, F. R. *Leavis. These critics differ so much that it is impossible to generalize about their aims, but it could be claimed that the New Criticism insisted on close reading of the text and awareness of verbal nuance and thematic (rather than narrative) organization; inquiries into the writer's personality or motivation were considered largely illegitimate or irrelevant. The New Criticism thus did much to weaken the tradition of old-fashioned 'literary history', in which literature was seen as a succession of dates and influences, accompanied by broad generalizations; and schools of criticism which diverge sharply in theory (see MARXIST LITERARY CRITICISM, FREUDIAN CRITICISM) nevertheless owe much to its techniques.

New Departures, see UNDERGROUND POETRY.

NEWDIGATE, Sir Roger (1719–1806), MP successively for Middlesex and Oxford University, was founder of the Newdigate Prize at Oxford for English verse (1805).

New English Dictionary, The, now called the *Oxford English Dictionary*.

Newgate Calendar, The, was published about 1773 in 5 vols, and recorded notorious crimes from 1700 to that date. Similar compilations appeared in the next 50 years under varying titles, including *The Malefactor's Register* (1779); Andrew Knapp and William Baldwin, attorneys-at-law, issued *Criminal Chronology* (1809), *The Newgate Calendar* (1824–6), and *The New Newgate Calendar* (1826). All the Newgate Calendars began in 1700 and they continued until before or a little after 1820. Plots derived from Newgate Calendars appear in novels by *Ainsworth (Jack Sheppard* and *Rookwood),* *Bulwer-Lytton (*Pelham* and *Eugene Aram),* *Fielding (*Jonathan Wild),* *Godwin (*Caleb Williams),* and in *Hood's poem 'The Dream of Eugene Aram'. See also Thackeray's *Catherine* and Dickens's *Oliver Twist. Celebrated Trials,* attributed to *Borrow, is a selection of trials from about 1413 to 1825.

New Grub Street, a novel by *Gissing, published 1891.

In this work Gissing depicts the struggle for life, the jealousies, and intrigues of the literary world of his time, and the blighting effect of poverty on artistic endeavour. It contrasts the careers of the facile, clever, and unscrupulous Jasper Milvain with that of the struggling writer Edwin Reardon, who is driven to an early grave by failure and his wife's desertion. Jasper marries Edwin's widow, and self-advertisement triumphs over artistic conscience.

New Inn, The, or *The Light Heart,* a comedy by *Jonson, performed in 1629 by the King's Men, printed 1631.

New Lines, (1956), an anthology edited by R. *Conquest, containing work by himself, E. *Jennings, John Holloway (1920–), *Larkin, *Gunn, *Amis, *Enright, *Davie, and J. *Wain, poets associated with the *Movement. In his introduction Conquest attacked obscure and over-metaphorical poetry, presenting the claims of 'rational structure and comprehensible language'. *New Lines Volume II* (1963) added other poets including *Thwaite, *Scannell, and G. *MacBeth.

NEWMAN, John Henry (1801–90), became a fellow of Oriel College, Oxford, where he came in contact with *Keble and *Pusey and later with R. H. *Froude. In 1832 he went to the south of Europe with Froude, and with him in Rome wrote much of the *Lyra Apostolica,* which included 'Lead, kindly Light'. In the same year he resolved with William Palmer (1803–85), Froude, and A. P. Perceval (1799–1853) to fight for the doctrine of apostolic succession and the integrity of the Prayer Book, and began *Tracts for the Times* (see OXFORD MOVEMENT). He was moving slowly towards the Roman Catholic Church, and in 1841 his celebrated *Tract XC,* on the compatibility of the Articles with Catholic theology, brought the Tractarians under official ban. He joined the Church of Rome in 1845, a move which profoundly shocked many of his fellow Tractarians, and caused a rift with Keble and Pusey. He was ordained in Rome in 1846; on his return in 1847 he established the Oratory in Birmingham. He was rector of the new Catholic University in Dublin, 1854–8; his lectures and essays on university eduation appeared in various forms from 1852, and finally as *The Idea of a University Defined and Illustrated* (1873). In these he maintained that the duty of a university is instruction rather than research, and to train the mind rather than to diffuse useful knowledge. In 1864 appeared his *Apologia pro Vita Sua,* in answer to C. *Kingsley, who had remarked in *Macmillan's Magazine,* misrepresenting Newman, that Newman did not consider truth a necessary virtue. It is an exposition of his spiritual history, written with much sincerity and feeling, and is now recognized as a literary masterpiece. His poem *The Dream of Gerontius* (later set to music by *Elgar) appeared in 1866. In 1870 Newman published *The Grammar of Assent,* an examination of the nature of belief, which argues that we reach certainties not through logic but through intuitive perception. In 1879 he was created a cardinal.

Newman also published two novels, both anonymously. *Loss and Gain* (1848) gives a vivid portrait of the religious ferment of Oxford at the period of the Oxford Movement; *Callista* (1856) describes the persecution and martyrdom of a Christian convert, the sculptor Callista, in the 3rd cent.

New Monthly Magazine, The (1814–84), a periodical founded by *Colburn in opposition to the *Jacobin *Monthly Magazine.* Under T. *Campbell, who became editor in 1821, much literary work of distinction appeared; among other distinguished editors were *Bulwer-Lytton, *Hood, and *Ainsworth.

NEWNES, Sir George (1851–1910), publisher and magazine proprietor, who founded *Tit-Bits* in 1881, and in 1890, with W. T. *Stead, *The Review of Reviews.* Stead took over the latter, and

Newnes proceeded to found the *Strand Magazine* and other publications.

New Republic, The, see MALLOCK, W. H.

New Review, The, (1) a literary review edited by Archibald Grove (1889–94) and by W. E. *Henley (1895–7), who serialized H. G. *Wells's *The Time Machine* (1895), and H. James's *What Maisie Knew* (1897), and published poetry by Verlaine, *Kipling, R. L. *Stevenson, and others. (2) the successor to the *Review*, edited from 1974 to 1979 by Ian Hamilton.

Newbooks, or Diurnalls, the successors of the *corantos in the evolution of the newspaper. Newsbooks consisting of one printed sheet (8 pages) and later of two printed sheets (16 pages), were issued during the period 1641–54, then gave place to the *Oxford (later *London) Gazette. (See also GAZETTE; NEWSPAPERS, ORIGINS OF; BERKENHEAD; MUDDIMAN; and NEDHAM.)

News Chronicle, see DAILY NEWS, THE.

News from Nowhere, a Utopian socialist fantasy by W. *Morris, published 1891.

The narrator falls asleep in the 'shabby London suburb' of Chiswick, after an evening at the Socialist League spent discussing the Morrow of the Revolution, and wakes in the future, to find London and its surroundings transformed into a communist paradise where men and women are free, healthy, and equal, the countryside reclaimed from industrial squalor, and money, prisons, formal education, and central government abolished. At the close he fades back into the past, inspired by the vision of what he has seen and the need to work for its fulfilment. *News from Nowhere* was in part a critical response to *Bellamy's *Looking Backward*.

Newsletters, a term specially applied to the manuscript records of parliamentary and court news, sent twice a week to subscribers from the London office of *Muddiman in the second half of the 17th cent.

New Society, a weekly periodical founded in 1962. It covers the social sciences and the arts, and reviews books of a wide range of interest.

Newsome, Chad, a leading character in H. James's *The Ambassadors*.

Newspapers, origins of. The direct ancestors of newspapers devoted to English news were the Dutch *corantos, newsbooks dealing with foreign events. The first to appear in English was a single-sheet publication, known as the *Corrant out of Italy, Germany &c*, printed in 1620 in Amsterdam. The first English weekly of home news appeared in Nov. 1641 (*The Heads of Severall Proceedings In This Present Parliament*), shortly followed by various other publications, mostly eight pages, e.g. Samuel Pecke's *A Perfect Diurnall*, Colling's *The Kingdomes Weekly Intelligencer*, *Berkenhead's *Mercurius Aulicus*, and *Mercurius Britanicus*, edited by Thomas Audley and *Nedham. Decreasingly efficient censorship and the stirring political climate stimulated demand for news, and by 1645 fourteen papers were on sale in English in London, including Dillingham's *Moderate Intelligencer*. In 1647 appeared the pro-royalist *Mercurius Pragmaticus*, edited by Nedham, *Cleveland, and Samuel Sheppard: in 1648 *The Moderate*, edited by chief censor Gilbert Mabbott, became the first paper consistently to preach a radical programme. This period also saw the birth of many unlicensed, short-lived, and counterfeit newsbooks, and the publication of numerous pamphlets (see PAMPHLETEERING). The thirst for information introduced many new readers to familiarity with the printed word, and introduced many of the ingredients of modern journalism. This vigorous proliferation came to a sudden end in Sept. 1649 when Parliament, irritated by the onslaughts of both radical pamphleteers and royalist mercuries, and anxious about public reaction to the massacre at Drogheda, passed a stringent printing law with heavy fines which effectively silenced all the licensed weeklies, while authorizing two new papers, one to deal with army news, the other with news from Westminster. Nedham was left with a virtual monopoly of information in his official 16-page *Mercurius Politicus* and its close relation *The Publick Intelligencer* (1650–60): Nedham, having offended various shades of political opinion, fled to Holland in 1660. His place was taken by *Muddiman, who started his career as spokesman for the revived monarchy in 1659 with the *Parliamentary Intelligencer*, later *Kingdomes Intelligencer*. In 1665 he founded the *Oxford Gazette*, the first real newspaper. (See GAZETTE, also L'ESTRANGE.)

New Statesman, The, a weekly journal of politics, art, and letters, originally planned as an organ of the *Fabian Society. It was first published in 1913 with Clifford Sharp as editor, J. C. *Squire as literary editor, and the *Webbs and G. B. *Shaw as regular contributors; Kingsley Martin was editor 1931–60. It has maintained its policy of 'dissent, of scepticism, of inquiry, of nonconformity'. Among other writers connected with the journal have been J. M. *Keynes, L. *Woolf, G. D. H. *Cole, J. B. *Priestley, and V. S. *Pritchett.

New Timon, The, a satirical poem by *Bulwer-Lytton, published 1846, in which he sketches various celebrities of the day.

NEWTON, Sir Isaac (1642–1727), was attached to Trinity College, Cambridge (1661–96); the rest of his life was spent in London as master of the mint and president of the *Royal Society, being knighted in 1705. Modern scholarship has not seriously affected his stature in the fields of mathematics, dynamics, celestial mechanics, astronomy, optics, natural philosophy, or cosmology. We now appreciate more fully the extent of his dedication to theology, biblical chronology, prophecy, and alchemy. In these latter spheres, Newton relates to the *Cambridge Platonists, especially More and Cudworth. Newtonianism was based on his three major works. *Philosophiae naturalis principia mathematica* (1687), the *Opticks* (1704), and *Arithmetica universalis* (1707). It was the dominant philosophy of the *Enlightenment, influencing all fields of science, and finding its way into the poetry of *Pope, J. *Thomson, and E. *Young, but eventually producing a reaction from *Goethe and *Blake. F. *Bacon and Newton were fused together to become the twin deity of English science in the 19th cent. under the banner 'inductive philosophy'.

NEWTON, John (1725–1807), an evangelical minister who went to sea as a boy and worked in the slave trade. His *An Authentic Narrative* (1764) gives a vivid picture of his ordeals. He became curate of Olney in 1764 and with *Cowper wrote *Olney Hymns* (1779).

New Verse, a little magazine edited 1933–9 by its founder G. *Grigson. It included work by *Auden, *MacNeice, G. *Barker, *Empson, R. *Fuller, and the young *Ewart, among others, and attacked, among other objects, the drowsy poeticism of the preceding century and the 'self-righteous' *Scrutiny.

New Way to pay Old Debts, A, a comedy by *Massinger, acted probably in 1625–6, published 1633.

The cruel and rapacious Sir Giles Overreach, having got possession of the property of his prodigal nephew Frank Wellborn and reduced him to utter poverty, treats him contemptuously. Lady Allworth, a rich widow, to whose husband Wellborn had rendered important services, agrees to help him by pretending she is about to marry him. Overreach, deceived, changes his attitude and helps Wellborn. Tom Allworth, Lady Allworth's stepson and page to Lord Lovell, is in love with Overreach's daughter Margaret. Overreach is determined that his daughter shall marry Lord Lovell and become 'right honourable'. Lovell consents to help Allworth to win Margaret, and a trick is played on Overreach by which he helps the marriage along, thinking that Lord Lovell is to be the bridegroom. Overreach goes mad on discovering the deceit and on finding that his

claim to Wellborn's property cannot be maintained; he is sent to Bedlam. Wellborn receives a company in Lord Lovell's regiment, and Lovell marries Lady Allworth.

New Woman, a phrase said to have been coined by Sarah *Grand in 1894 in the *North American Review* to describe a new generation of women, influenced by J. S. *Mill and other campaigners for women's rights, who believed in *Women's Suffrage, abolition of the double standard in sexual matters, Rational Dress, educational opportunities for women, etc. New Women appear in the works of *Ibsen, G. B. *Shaw, *Wells, O. *Schreiner, Rebecca *West, *Gissing, G. *Allen, and G. *Egerton, among many others.

New Writing, a book-periodical edited by J. *Lehmann, first published in 1936 and at approximately half-yearly intervals until 1940. It published imaginative writing, mainly by young authors (including *Spender, *Auden, *Isherwood, *Upward, *Anand, *Pritchett), and particularly those whose work was too unorthodox for the established magazines. New contributors were recruited from Europe, India, New Zealand, South Africa, China, and Russia. In 1940 it came out as *Folios of New Writing*; it became *New Writing and Daylight* in 1942 and this lasted until 1946. Meanwhile *Penguin New Writing* appeared in 1940, first as a monthly paperback and then in 1942 as a quarterly.

New Yorker, The, an American weekly magazine founded in 1925 by Harold Ross (1892–1951). Although famed for its humour it has also published distinguished articles of reportage, such as, notably, 'Hiroshima' by John Hersey (1914–), which occupied an entire issue in 1946. Writers and cartoonists associated with the magazine include *Thurber, O. *Nash, Charles Addams, Saul Steinberg, *O'Hara, S. J. Perelman (1904–79), and *Updike.

NGUGI, James, see THIONG'O, NGUGI WA.

Niamh, in the second or southern cycle of Irish mythology, the daughter of *Manannán, the sea-god. She fell in love with *Oisin, the son of *Finn.

Nibelung, Niblung, or **Niebelung,** in the Norse *sagas and German *Nibelungenlied, a mythical king of a race of dwarfs, the Nibelungs, who dwelt in Norway. The Nibelung kings and people also figure in W. Morris's *Sigurd the Volsung*.

Nibelungenlied, a German poem of the 13th cent. embodying a story found in primitive shape in both forms of the *Edda. In these the story is substantially as told by W. Morris in

*Sigurd the Volsung, Sigurd being the Siegfried of the German poem.

In the *Nibelungenlied*, Siegfried, son of Siegmund and Sieglind, king and queen of the Netherlands, having got possession of the Nibelung hoard guarded by Alberich, rides to woo Kriemhild, a Burgundian princess, sister of Gunther, Gernot, and Giselher. Hagen, their grim retainer, warns them against Siegfried, but the match is arranged, and the hoard is given to Kriemhild as marriage portion. Siegfried undertakes to help Gunther to win Brunhild, queen of Issland, by defeating her in trials of skill and strength. The double marriage takes place, but Brunhild remains suspicious and ill-humoured, and Siegfried, called in by Gunther to subdue her, does so in Gunther's semblance and takes away her ring and girdle, which he gives to Kriemhild. The two queens quarrel, and Kriemhild reveals to Brunhild the trick that has been played on her. Hagen, who thinks his master's honour injured by Siegfried, treacherously kills the latter at a hunt.

Kriemhild later marries Etzel (Attila), king of the Huns, and in order to avenge her husband and secure the hoard, which her brothers have seized and sunk in the Rhine, persuades them to visit Etzel's court. There they are set upon and overcome, but refuse to betray the hiding-place of the hoard, and are slain. Hagen, the last survivor of the party who knows the secret, is killed by Kriemhild with Siegfried's sword; and Kriemhild herself is slain by Hildebrand, a knight of Dietrich of Bern. Wagner's series of four musical dramas *Ring des Nibelungen* was composed 1853–70 (produced 1869–76).

Nice, Sir Courtly, see SIR COURTLY NICE.

Nicholas Nickleby, a novel by *Dickens, published 1838–9.

Nicholas, a generous, high-spirited lad of nineteen, his mother, and his gentle sister Kate are left penniless on the death of his father. They appeal for assistance to his uncle, Ralph Nickleby, a griping usurer, of whom Nicholas at once makes an enemy by his independent bearing. He is sent as usher to Dotheboys Hall, where Wackford Squeers starves and maltreats forty urchins under pretence of education. His special cruelty is expended on Smike, a half-witted lad left on his hands and employed as a drudge. Nicholas, infuriated, thrashes Squeers and escapes with Smike. For a time he supports himself and Smike as an actor in the provincial company of Vincent Crummles; he then enters the service of the brothers Cheeryble, whose benevolence and good humour spread happiness. Meanwhile Kate, apprenticed to Madame Mantalini, dressmaker, is by her uncle's designs exposed to the gross insults of Sir Mulberry Hawk, one of his associates. From this persecution she is released by Nicholas, who breaks Sir

Mulberry's head and makes a home for his mother and sister. Nicholas himself falls in love with Madeline Bray, the support of a selfish father and the object of a conspiracy of Ralph Nickleby and another revolting old usurer, Gride, to marry her to the latter. Ralph, whose hatred for Nicholas has been intensified by the failure of his plans, knowing Nicholas's affection for Smike, conspires to remove the latter from him; his plots are thwarted with the help of Newman Noggs, his eccentric clerk, but nevertheless Smike falls a victim to consumption, and eventually dies in the arms of Nicholas. Confronted with ruin and exposure, and finally shattered by the discovery that Smike was his own son, Ralph hangs himself. Nicholas, befriended by the Cheerybles, marries Madeline, and Kate marries the Cheerybles' nephew, Frank. Squeers is transported, and Gride is murdered.

NICHOLS, John (1745–1826), printer, author, and antiquarian, was manager and editor of the *Gentleman's Magazine* from 1792 until his death. In the pages of the *Magazine* he built up his digressive, disordered, but invaluable work, *Literary Anecdotes of the Eighteenth Century* (published as a collection 1812–16); and *Illustrations of the Literary History of the Eighteenth Century* (1817–58), continued after his death by his son.

NICHOLS, Peter Richard (1927–), playwright. His works include *A Day in the Death of Joe Egg* (1967), in which schoolteacher Bri and his wife Sheila struggle to share the burden of their handicapped daughter, Joe; *The National Health* (1969, pub. 1970); *Forget-me-not-Lane* (1971); and *Passion Play* (1980, pub. 1981).

NICHOLS, Robert Malise Bowyer (1893–1944), poet. His volumes of poems include *Invocation* (1915), *Ardours and Endurances* (1917), and *Aurelia* (1920); some of his work appeared in *Georgian Poetry*. He later turned to drama, but met with little success.

Nicolette, see AUCASSIN AND NICOLETTE.

NICOLSON, Sir Harold George (1886–1968), published critical and biographical works (on Verlaine, 1921; *Swinburne, 1926; Constant, 1945; King George V, 1952; and others), books on diplomacy, travel, etc., and some fiction: *Some People* (1927), is a series of nine closely observed, semi-fictitious, semi-autobiographical sketches. He married V. *Sackville-West in 1913, and his diaries were edited (3 vols, 1966–8) by his son Nigel Nicolson.

Niebelung, see NIBELUNG.

NIETZSCHE, Friedrich Wilhelm (1844–1900), German philosopher and poet. His first work,

Die Geburt der Tragödie (*The Birth of Tragedy*, 1872), was of revolutionary importance, challenging the accepted tradition of classical scholarship; it argued against the 'Apollonian' views associated with Winckelmann in favour of a 'Dionysiac' interpretation which allowed for pessimism and passion as central features of Greek literature. His most important works were *Also sprach Zarathustra* (*Thus Spake Zarathustra*, 1883–92), *Jenseits von Gut und Böse* (*Beyond Good and Evil*, 1886), and *Der Wille zur Macht* (*The Will to Power*) (published posthumously from fragments). His basic ideas are the affirmation of the Superman, the rejection of Christian morality as the morality of the slave, the doctrine of power, and the 'revision of all values'. D. H. *Lawrence's works show the influence of Nietzsche's thought. A version of Nietzsche's 'Übermensch' (from *Also sprach Zarathustra*) appears in Shaw's *Man and Superman*.

Nigger of the 'Narcissus', The, a novel by J. *Conrad, published 1897.

The voyage of the *Narcissus* from Bombay to London is disrupted by two new hands, James Wait, the 'nigger', and Donkin, a compulsive troublemaker. During a ferocious gale Wait has to be rescued from his sickbed; and in the ensuing calm Donkin tries unsuccessfully to incite the crew to mutiny. Finally, as predicted by Singleton, 'the oldest able seaman in the ship', Wait dies, the wind rises, and the *Narcissus* is able to dock in London.

Night and Day, (1) a novel by V. *Woolf; (2) a weekly periodical which ran from July to Dec. 1937, edited by John Marks and G. *Greene, with contributions by *Betjeman, E. *Bowen, *Kingsmill, E. *Waugh, H. *Read, and others; (3) a play by T. *Stoppard.

Nightmare Abbey, a satire by *Peacock, published 1818.

The most literary of Peacock's satires, it mocks the modish gloom infecting contemporary literature: *Coleridge's German transcendentalism is the prime example, but *Byron's self-dramatizing and *Shelley's esotericism are also ridiculed. In imitation of the opening of *Godwin's novel *Mandeville* (1817), Mr Glowry's isolated house is staffed by servants with long faces and names like Diggory Deathshead. He gives a house party attended by Mr Toobad, the millenarian pessimist, Mr Flosky (Coleridge), Mr Cypress (Byron), and Mr Listless, the common reader, who is currently immersed in the blue devils. Two guests remain unfashionably cheerful, Mr Asterias the scientist and Mr Hilary, whose literary tastes come from the Greeks. Scythrop Glowry, the son of the house, a young writer who resembles Shelley, cannot decide between his frivolous cousin Marionetta and Mr Toobad's sibylline daughter Stella. In a classic comic denouement, in which the ladies are discovered to one another, Scythrop loses both.

Night Thoughts on Life, Death, and Immortality, *The Complaint or,* a didactic and reflective poem of some 10,000 lines of blank verse, in nine books, by E. *Young, published 1742–5.

It is a long and somewhat rambling meditation on life's vicissitudes, death, and immortality, and includes lines which have become proverbial, such as 'Procrastination is the thief of time'. The poet deplores the deaths of Lucia, Narcissa, and Philander, loosely identified as his wife, his stepdaughter, and her husband; he also addresses much reproof and exhortation to the worldly and infidel young Lorenzo. Thus a certain narrative and autobiographical interest is added to his evocations of 'delightful gloom' and the 'populous grave'.

Nihilism (Latin *nihil*, nothing), originally a movement in Russia repudiating the customary social institutions, such as marriage and parental authority. The term was introduced by *Turgenev. It was extended to a secret revolutionary movement, social and political, which developed in the middle of the 19th cent.

Nimphidia, a fairy poem by *Drayton (1627).

Nimphidia, attendant on Queen Mab, reports to the poet the affairs and jealousies of Mab, Oberon, Puck, and Pigwiggin, with a wealth of minutely observed miniature detail of the natural world.

Nimue (Nimiane or Vivien), see LADY OF THE LAKE.

Nineteen Eighty-four, a novel by G. *Orwell, published 1949.

It is a nightmare story of totalitarianism of the future and one man's hopeless struggle against it and final defeat by acceptance. Winston Smith, the hero, has no heroic qualities, only a wistful longing for truth and decency. But in a social system where there is no privacy and to have unorthodox ideas incurs the death penalty he knows that there is no hope for him. His brief love affair ends in arrest by the Thought Police, and when, after months of torture and brainwashing, he is released, he makes his final submission of his own accord. The book is a warning of the possibilities of the police state brought to perfection, where power is the only thing that counts, where the official language, 'Newspeak', progressively narrows the range of ideas and independent thought, and where Doublethink becomes a necessary habit of mind. It is a society dominated by slogans and controlled by compulsory worship of the head of the

Party, *Big Brother. The novel had an extra-ordinary impact, and many of its phrases and coinages (including its title) passed into the common language.

Nineteenth Century, The, a monthly review founded in 1877 by J. T. *Knowles, which brought together in its pages the most eminent advocates of conflicting views. Among its contributors were T. H. *Huxley, *Gladstone, *Ruskin, B. *Webb, W. *Morris, *Ouida, and *Wilde. *Tennyson provided a prefatory sonnet for the first issue. When the century of the title ended, the review added to its old title 'And After', and changed the whole title to *The Twentieth Century* in 1951.

Nine Worthies, The, see WORTHIES OF THE WORLD.

Nipper, Susan, a character in Dickens's *Dombey and Son.

Nobel Prizes were established under the will of Alfred Bernhard Nobel (1833–96), a Swedish chemist distinguished in the development of explosives, by which the interest on the greater part of his large fortune is distributed in annual prizes for the most important discoveries in physics, chemistry, and physiology or medicine respectively, to the person who shall have most promoted 'the fraternity of nations' (the Nobel Peace Prize), and to the 'person who shall have produced in the field of literature the most outstanding work of an idealistic tendency'.

Noble Savage, see PRIMITIVISM.

Noctes Ambrosianae, a series of dialogues, which appeared in *Blackwood's Edinburgh Magazine* 1822–35. The series was devised by J. G. *Lockhart. The conversations take place at Ambrose's Tavern between various friends, largely based on real people, such as the 'Shepherd' (J. *Hogg) and 'Christopher North' (John *Wilson). Wilson wrote more than half the 71 dialogues, but Lockhart, Hogg, and *Maginn also contributed. The conversations cover a wide range of subjects, and present a romanticized and whimsical view of Scotland.

Noggs, Newman, in Dickens's *Nicholas Nickleby*, Ralph Nickleby's clerk.

Nōh Plays, form of traditional, ceremonial, or ritualistic drama peculiar to Japan, symbolical and spiritual in character. It was evolved from religious rites of Shinto worship, was perfected in the 15th cent., and flourished during the Tokugawa period (1652–1868). Both *Pound and *Yeats were much influenced by the ritual, simplicity, and stylization of the Nōh theatre, and it has had a considerable impact on 20th-cent. European drama.

Nominalism (as opposed to *Realism), the view of those Scholastics and later philosophers who regarded universals or abstract conceptions as a 'flatus vocis', mere names without any corresponding reality.

Nonesuch Press, a publishing firm established in 1923 by Francis Meynell (1891–1975, book designer, publisher, and journalist, son of Wilfrid and Alice *Meynell), Vera Mendel, and D. *Garnett, for the production of books of high quality of content and presentation, at a moderate price. Not strictly a *private press, it shared many of the aims of private presses.

NOONAN, Robert, see under TRESSELL, R.

Norris, Mrs, a character in J. Austen's *Mansfield Park.

NORRIS, Frank (Benjamin Franklin Norris) (1870–1902), American novelist. The influence of *Zola and *Naturalism is seen in his best works, which include *McTeague* (1899), a tragic account of violence, greed, and treachery in San Francisco; and in his unfinished trilogy *The Epic of the Wheat*: the masterly first two volumes, *The Octopus* (1901) and *The Pit* (1903), describe the raising of wheat in California and speculation on the Chicago wheat exchange.

NORRIS, John (1657–1711), poet and philosopher, is considered as the last of the *Cambridge Platonists, and is remembered for his *An Essay towards the Theory of the Ideal or Intelligible World* (1701–4), in which he shows himself a supporter of Malebranche's development of the theories of *Descartes.

NORTH, Christopher, a pseudonym used by John *Wilson (1785–1854).

NORTH, Roger (1653–1734), youngest son of Dudley, fourth Baron North, and great-great nephew of Sir T. *North, is remembered as the author of interesting biographies, published in 1742–4, of three of his brothers, Francis North, Lord Guildford, keeper of the Great Seal; Dudley North, the great Turkey merchant; and John North, master of Trinity College, Cambridge.

NORTH, Sir Thomas (?1535–?1601), is famous for his translations, which include the *Diall of Princes* from Guevara's *El Relox de Principes* with *The Famous Booke of Marcus Aurelius, The Morall Philosophie of Doni*, from the Italian (1570), and *Plutarch's *Lives* from the French of Amyot (1579), to which he made additions from other authors in 1595 and 1603. His Plutarch, written in a noble and vivid English, formed Shakespeare's chief storehouse of classical history and exerted a powerful influence on Elizabethan prose.

North American Review, The (1815–1939), a Boston quarterly, later monthly, review and one of the most distinguished of American periodicals. Its editors included C. E. *Norton, J. R. *Lowell, and H. *Adams, and its contributors ranged from *Emerson, W. *Irving, *Parkman, and *Longfellow to H. *James, *Wells, and *Twain. It then declined, and was revived again as a quarterly in 1963.

North and South, a novel by Mrs *Gaskell, published serially in *Household Words 1854–5, in volume form 1855.

This novel is a study of the contrast between the values and habits of rural southern England and industrial northern England. The heroine, Margaret Hale, is the daughter of a parson whose religious doubts force him to resign his Hampshire living and to move to a sooty cotton-spinning northern city. Here, at a moment of conflict between workers and employers, Margaret meets the grim intolerant Mrs Thornton and her son, an able, stubborn manufacturer, whose lack of sympathy for the workers Margaret at first finds unattractive. When she endangers herself to protect him from a mob of strikers he misunderstands her motives and offers marriage, which she refuses. But when he suspects her of an intrigue with another man (in fact her brother, whom she has to shield as he is in danger of arrest), she realizes she loves him. After a series of deaths and other misfortunes Margaret and Thornton are finally united, and Margaret comes to respect both mill-hands and mill-owners.

Northanger Abbey, a novel by J. Austen, begun 1798, published posthumously in 1818 with *Persuasion.

The purpose of the novel is to ridicule the popular tales of romance and terror, such as Mrs Radcliffe's *Mysteries of Udolpho, and to contrast with these the normal realities of life. Catherine Morland, the daughter of a well-to-do clergyman, is taken to Bath for the season by her friends, Mr and Mrs Allen. Here she meets Henry Tilney (son of the eccentric General Tilney) and his pleasant sister, Eleanor. Catherine falls in love with Henry, and has the good fortune to gain his father's approval, which is founded upon the exaggerated report of her parents' wealth given him by the foolish young John Thorpe, brother of Catherine's friend Isabella. Catherine is invited to Northanger Abbey, the medieval seat of the Tilneys. Somewhat unbalanced by a too assiduous reading of Mrs Radcliffe's novels, Catherine imagines a mystery in which General Tilney is criminally involved, and suffers severe mortification when her suspicions are discovered. General Tilney, having now received a second report from John Thorpe representing Catherine's parents as extremely humble, packs

her off back to her family. Henry, disobeying his father, follows Catherine to her home, proposes, and is accepted. General Tilney's consent is obtained when he discovers the true financial position of Catherine's family.

Interwoven with the main plot is the flirtation of Captain Tilney, Henry's elder brother, and the vulgar Isabella Thorpe, who is engaged to Catherine's brother; the consequent breaking of the engagement, and the rupture of the friendship between Catherine and Isabella; and Isabella's failure to secure Captain Tilney.

North Briton, The, a weekly political periodical founded in 1762 by *Wilkes, in opposition to The Briton, which *Smollett was conducting in the interests of Lord Bute. In this venture Wilkes was assisted by Charles *Churchill, the author of The Rosciad. Wilkes's attacks on the government grew bolder, and in No. 45 he exposed himself to prosecution for libel. Though Wilkes was discharged on the ground of privilege, The North Briton was suppressed.

NORTHCLIFFE, Viscount, see HARMS-WORTH, A. C. W.

Northern Lass, The (printed 1632), a comedy by *Brome.

Northward Hoe, a comedy by *Webster and *Dekker, printed 1607. The play was a good-humoured retort to the *Eastward hoe of Chapman, Jonson, and Marston. Like *Westward Hoe it presents a curious picture of the manners of the day.

Norton, The Hon. Mrs, see DIANA OF THE CROSSWAYS.

NORTON, Charles Eliot (1827–1908), born in Cambridge, Massachusetts, was professor of fine arts at Harvard (1873–98) and an intellectual leader of great influence. His aim was, in his own words, to arouse in his countrymen 'the sense of connection with the past and gratitude for the efforts and labours of other nations and former generations'. He was a frequent contributor to the *Atlantic Monthly, joint editor of the *North American Review (1864–8), and founder and co-editor of The Nation (1865).

NOSTRADAMUS (1503–66), French astrologer and physician, whose enigmatic prophecies, cast in the form of rhymed quatrains grouped in sets of 100 and published under the title Centuries (1556, English trans. 1672), enjoyed widespread popularity during the Renaissance.

Nostromo, a novel by J. *Conrad, published 1904.

In an imaginary South American country,

Costaguana, Charles Gould runs a silver mine of national importance in the province of Sulaco. He is married to Emilia, a woman of charm and intelligence, whose arrival has been of great benefit to the local people. In a time of political unrest and revolution, when the silver from the mine is in danger of being seized by the rebel forces, Gould becomes obsessed with the idea of saving it. He enlists the help of Decoud, the cynical, Paris-influenced journalist and of an older man, Dr Monygham, and together they appeal to Nostromo, an Italian sailor, now Capataz de Cargadores, a hero to all. With great daring Decoud and Nostromo sail off to a nearby island where they bury the treasure. Decoud is left alone to guard the silver on the deserted island; he loses his mind and, after shooting himself, drowns, his body weighted with silver. The common assumption is that the silver was lost at sea and the temptation proves too much for Nostromo, who decides to steal it. His old friend Viola, an ex-Garibaldino, is appointed lighthouse keeper on the island and, unwittingly, guard for the silver. Nostromo trifles with Viola's two infatuated daughters, grows rich as he gradually pilfers the silver, and is finally shot when mistaken for an intruder. Mortally wounded, he sends for Emilia, and confesses his crime in the hope of absolution, but dies without revealing the whereabouts of the treasure.

Notes and Queries, a periodical founded in 1849 by *Thoms, designed to furnish a means for the interchange of thought and information among those engaged in literature, art, and science. Its motto was (until 1923) Captain Cuttle's 'When found, make a note of' (see DOMBEY AND SON).

Nouveau Roman ('New Novel'), a term applied to the work of a wide range of modern French novelists, including Nathalie Sarraute (1902–　), Claude Simon (1913–　), Marguerite Duras (1914–　), Alain Robbe-Grillet (1922–　), and Michel Butor (1926–　). These writers reacted against the illusion of order in the traditional novel, and experimented with techniques that were intended to dispel the collective significance of events and to question the omniscience of narrator and author.

Nouvelle Héloïse, La, see ROUSSEAU.

Novel, rise of the. The word 'novellae' was employed in the 16th cent. to describe the short tales of the *Decameron and the *Heptameron, and others. Used in a modern sense, the word 'novel' appears in England in the mid-17th cent., when it was chiefly associated with romances of illicit love. For this reason the word 'history' was more often favoured to describe the long prose fictions of the 18th cent. which were the precursors of the modern novel. The novel form devel-oped through the memoir-novel and the epistolary novel of the 16th and 17th cents to the novel of the omniscient third-person narrator, which has dominated from the late 18th cent. to the present time. The chief novelists of the 18th cent. (*Defoe, *Richardson, *Fielding, *Smollett, and *Sterne) so greatly and rapidly developed the form that by the early 19th cent. J. *Austen could write (albeit with a hint of irony) in *Northanger Abbey, that in the novel 'the greatest powers of the mind' are displayed'. Form, style, and subject matter varied considerably, but by 1824 Sir W. *Scott could confidently define the novel as 'a fictitious narrative . . . accommodated to the ordinary train of human events', a definition which may be allowed to stand today. (See also EPISTOLARY NOVEL; FASHIONABLE NOVEL; HISTORICAL NOVEL; MEMOIR-NOVEL; ORIENTAL NOVEL; SENTIMENT, NOVEL OF.)

Novum Organum, a philosophical treatise in Latin by F. *Bacon, published 1620, in two books.

The *Novum Organum* outlines the method by which the new science was to be discovered. The purpose of the first book was both to destroy men's confidence in the earlier methods of enquiry and at the same time to encourage the hope that some better procedure lay ready to be discovered and put to use. The received view of science was that it proceeded by syllogistic deduction, but syllogisms cannot bring certainty when the words of which they are composed are the marks of confused and hastily abstracted concepts. The remedy is to employ induction and to rise by a gradual ascent to axioms of successively greater generality. First, the mind must be cleansed from its intellectual defects. Under the name of 'Idols of the Mind' Bacon distinguished four distinct types of inducement to error: (1) 'Idols of the Tribe' (*Idola tribus*), which originate in human nature, and are common to all men; (2) 'Idols of the Cave' (*Idola specus*), which arises from the peculiar constitution and circumstances of each individual; (3) 'Idols of the Market Place' (*Idola fori*), which result from man's need to communicate by the treacherous medium of language; (4) 'Idols of the Theatre' (*Idola theatri*), which arise from the hold on men's minds of false philosophical systems which, in Bacon's view like so many stage plays, represent imaginary worlds of their own manufacture.

The second book contains an exposition of Bacon's new method and an illustration of its use in practice in an investigation of the nature (in Bacon's words the 'form') of heat. The procedure is to prepare a natural and experimental history of the phenomenon, and then to draw up three tables, or lists: (1) of instances when the phenomenon under investigation is present; (2) of instances as similar as possible to those in the first list where the phenomenon is absent; and (3) of instances where the phenomenon is observed to increase or decrease in intensity, or vary in some other way. From these tables, in a manner never made adequately clear, the nature of the phenomenon is discovered by a procedure of eliminative induction.

NOYES, Alfred (1880–1959), poet, playwright, novelist, and anthologist, who held violently anti-*Modernist views on literature; his own collections of verse (many of them about seafaring) include *Drake* (1908), an epic, and *Tales of the Mermaid Tavern* (1913). His anecdotal autobiography, *Two Worlds for Memory*, appeared in 1953.

Nubbles, Mrs and Kit, characters in Dickens's *The Old Curiosity Shop*.

'Nun's Priest's Tale, The', see CANTERBURY TALES, 20.

Nupkins, Mr, a character in Dickens's *Pickwick Papers*.

Nurse, in Shakespeare's *Romeo and Juliet*, the loquacious and humorous attendant of *Juliet.

'Nut-Brown Maid, The', a 15th-cent. poem in praise of woman's fidelity, included in Percy's *Reliques*. It is the foundation of *Prior's 'Henry and Emma'.

Nym, Corporal, appears in Shakespeare's *Merry Wives of Windsor* and *Henry V* as a follower of *Falstaff.

Nymphidia, see NIMPHIDIA.

Nymphs, see PARACELSUS.

NYREN, John (1764–1837), a famous early cricketer and cricket chronicler. His recollections were published in *The Young Cricketer's Tutor* (1833, edited by C. C. *Clarke).

O

Oak, Gabriel, a character in Hardy's *Far from the Madding Crowd*.

OATES, Joyce Carol (1938–), American novelist and short story writer. Her novels, many of which portray extremes of human passion and violence, are predominantly naturalistic, with suggestions of the neo-*Gothic; they include *A Garden of Earthly Delights* (1967), *them* (1969), *Wonderland* (1971), and *A Bloodsmoor Romance* (1982). She has also published many collections of short stories.

OATES, Titus (1649–1705), the fabricator of the *Popish Plot (1678), is the 'Corah' of Dryden's *Absalom and Achitophel*.

Obadiah, the manservant of the Shandy family in Sterne's *Tristram Shandy*.

Oberon, in Shakespeare's *A Midsummer Night's Dream*, the king of the fairies and husband of Titania. He also appears in R. Greene's play *James the Fourth* and is the eponymous hero of Weber's opera.

Objective correlative, a term used by T. S. *Eliot in his essay 'Hamlet and his Problems' (1919; included in *The Sacred Wood*, 1920). Eliot ascribes the alleged 'artistic failure' of the play *Hamlet* to the fact that Hamlet himself is 'dominated by an emotion which is inexpressible, because it is in *excess* of the facts as they appear . . . The only way of expressing emotion in the form of art is by finding an "objective correlative"; in other words, a set of objects, a situation, a chain of events which shall be the formula of that *particular* emotion.' This phrase, like *'dissociation of sensibility', became very fashionable, and was doubtless one of those to which Eliot referred in the lecture in 1956 ('The Frontiers of Criticism') when he spoke of 'a few notorious phrases which have had a truly embarrassing success in the world'.

O'BRIEN, Edna (1932–), Irish novelist and short story writer. Her novels include *The Country Girls* (1960); *The Lonely Girl* (1962); *Girls in their Married Bliss* (1963); *August is a Wicked Month* (1964); *A Pagan Place* (1971, an evocation of rural Ireland); *Night* (1972); and *Johnny I hardly knew you* (1977). Her themes are female sensuality, male treachery, Irish nostalgia, and celebration of the intermittent 'good times', and her lyrical descriptive powers and lack of inhibition have led to comparisons with Colette.

O'BRIEN, Flann, pseudonym of Brian O'Nolan or O Nuallain (1911–66), contributed for many years a satiric weekly column under the name 'Myles na Gopaleen' to the *Irish Times*. His first novel, *At Swim-Two-Birds* (1939), is an exuberant work, operating on several levels of invention, much influenced by *Joyce. O'Brien's second novel, *An Béal Bocht* (1941), was written in Gaelic, translated into English in 1973 as *The Poor Mouth*. The best-known of his other works is *The Third Policeman* (written 1940, pub. 1967).

Obscurorum Virorum, *Epistolae*, see EPISTOLAE OBSCURORUM VIRORUM.

Observations on the Present State of the Nation, see PRESENT STATE OF THE NATION.

Observator, The, see L'ESTRANGE, R.

Observer, The, Britain's oldest national Sunday paper, founded in 1791.

O'CASEY, Sean (John Casey) (1880–1964), Irish playwright, began to publish articles, songs, and broadsheets under the name of Sean O Cathasaigh; his first plays were rejected by the *Abbey Theatre, but he received encouragement from Lady *Gregory and Lennox *Robinson, and *The Shadow of a Gunman* was performed in 1923, followed by *Juno and the Paycock* in 1924; they were published together as *Two Plays* (1925). *The Plough and the Stars* provoked nationalist riots at the Abbey in 1926. These plays are tragi-comedies dealing realistically with the rhetoric and dangers of Irish patriotism, with tenement life, self-deception, and survival. O'Casey moved to England in 1926; his alienation from Ireland was confirmed by a rift with *Yeats and the Abbey over its rejection of *The Silver Tassie* (1928), an experimental anti-war play about an injured footballer, which introduced the symbolic *Expressionist techniques employed in his later works. These include *Within the Gates* (1933), *Red Roses for Me* (1942), *Cock-a-Doodle Dandy* (1949), and *The Bishop's Bonfire* (1955). He also published a much-praised series of autobiographies, in six volumes (1939–54).

OCCAM

OCCAM, and **Occam's Razor,** see OCKHAM.

OCCLEVE, see HOCCLEVE.

Oceana, see COMMONWEALTH OF OCEANA, THE.

Ochiltree, Edie, a character in Scott's *The Antiquary.*

OCKHAM, William of (1285–1349), joined the Franciscans and studied at Oxford where he wrote a Commentary on the *Sentences* of *Peter Lombard. In 1324 he was summoned by the pope to Avignon to answer charges of unorthodoxy, and several of his writings were condemned in 1326. In 1328 he fled from Avignon, having taken the side of the Spiritual Franciscans in their dispute with Pope John XXII. Thereafter he remained with the emperor, Louis of Bavaria, concerned with the question of papal power. His importance is as a theologian with a strongly developed interest in logical method, whose approach was critical rather than system-building. The logical axiom associated with him is Ockham's 'Razor', that 'entities (*entia*) must not be unnecessarily multiplied', an attack on the postulation of Universals by the *Realists. The logical precision of his theory of language has been much admired (and, to some extent, copied) by 20th-cent. theoretical linguists and linguistic philosophers. His importance for literature in the century of *Langland lies in his stress on the Augustinian/Franciscan pre-eminence of Faith and the relative relegation of philosophical 'Reason', founded on Aristotle.

O'CONNOR, Flannery (1925–64), American novelist and short story writer, born in Georgia, whose works may be described as examples of Southern *Gothic. They include *Wise Blood* (1952), *The Violent Bear It Away* (1960), and *The Complete Stories* (1971).

O'CONNOR, Frank, pseudonym of Michael Francis O'Donovan (1903–66), born in Cork; his work includes two novels, translations from the Irish, literary criticism, and dramatizations, but he is best known for his short stories. Collections include *Bones of Contention* (1936), *Crab Apple Jelly* (1944), *Traveller's Samples* (1951), and *Domestic Relations* (1957). Realistic and closely observed, they offer a full portrait of the middle and lower classes of Ireland. He also wrote two volumes of autobiography, *An Only Child* (1961) and *My Father's Son* (1969).

O'CONNOR, Thomas Power (1848–1929), politician, supporter of *Parnell. His life of Lord Beaconsfield (1879) attracted much attention for its unsparing attack on *Disraeli. He was founder of the *Star* (1887), the *Sun* (1893), and *T.P.'s Weekly* (1902–16), a penny literary paper of some merit.

Octavia, the sister of Octavian (Augustus) and Mark Antony's wife, figures in Shakespeare's *Antony and Cleopatra* and Dryden's *All for Love.*

Octosyllabics, consisting of eight syllables, usually applied to the eight-syllabled rhyming iambic metre of, e.g. Milton's *'Il Penseroso'.

Odd Women, The, a novel by G. *Gissing.

Ode, in ancient literature, a poem intended or adapted to be sung; in modern use, a rhymed (rarely unrhymed) lyric, often in the form of an address, generally dignified or exalted in subject, feeling, and style, but sometimes (in earlier use) simple and familiar (though less so than a song) [OED].

'Ode on a Grecian Urn', a poem by *Keats, written 1819, published 1820.
While he describes the various pastoral scenes of love, beauty, and joy illustrated on the urn, the poet reflects on the eternal quality of art and the fleeting nature of human love and happiness. The last two lines are particularly well known and their meaning much debated:

'Beauty is truth, truth beauty,'—that is all
Ye know on earth, and all ye need to know.

'Ode to a Nightingale', a poem by *Keats, written 1819, published 1820.
Keats's friend Charles Brown relates that a nightingale had nested near his house in Hampstead (now known as Keats House), and that one morning Keats sat under a plum-tree in the garden composing his Ode. The poem is a meditation on the immortal beauty of the nightingale's song and the sadness of the observer, who must in the end accept sorrow and mortality.

'Ode to Autumn', see TO AUTUMN.

'Ode to the West Wind', a poem by P. B. *Shelley, published 1820.
The Ode is a passionate invocation to the spirit of the West Wind, both 'Destroyer and Preserver'. It is composed in five sweeping stanzaic movements, each taking the form of a sonnet, but with complex musical patterns of internal rhyme and run-on lines, culminating in a breathless series of cries or questions. Shelley's minute observations of wind, water, wood, cloud, and sky, combine imagery which is simultaneously scientific, mythical, and even biblical. The total effect is one of transcendent hope and energy, achieved through suffering and despair.

ODETS, Clifford (1906–63), American dramatist, was a founder member in 1931 of the Group Theatre, which followed the naturalistic methods of the Moscow Art Theatre, and his reputation was made when it performed his short play *Waiting for Lefty* (1935), about a taxi-drivers' strike. This was followed in the same year by two other dramas of social conflict, *Till the Day I Die*, and *Awake and Sing!* Later works include *Clash By Night* (1941); *The Big Knife* (1948); and *The Country Girl* (1950, first known in Britain as *Winter Journey*), about an alcoholic actor's marriage.

O'Dowd, Major and Mrs, characters in Thackeray's **Vanity Fair*.

Odyssey, The, a Greek epic poem attributed to *Homer describing the adventures of Odysseus in the course of his return from the Trojan War to his kingdom of Ithaca.

OED, see OXFORD ENGLISH DICTIONARY, THE.

Oedipus, see SOPHOCLES.

O'FAOLAIN, Sean (1900–), Irish novelist and short story writer, born in Cork, is best known for his short stories. His first collection, *Midsummer Night Madness and other stories* (1932), was followed by other collections, by three novels (*A Nest of Simple Folk*, 1934; *Bird Alone*, 1936; and *Come back to Erin*, 1940), several biographies, and a study of the Irish people, *The Irish* (1947). His autobiography *Vive-moi!* was published in 1964, and his *Collected Stories* in 1981. Many of his stories evoke frustrated lives, missed opportunities, and characters limited by their environment, which clearly demonstrate O'Faolain's allegiance to *Chekhov; later stories (*The Heat of the Sun; stories and tales*, 1966; *The Talking Trees*, 1971) tend to be drier, more amusing, and more resilient in tone.

Of Dramatick Poesy: an Essay by *Dryden, published 1668.

The essay is in the form of a dialogue between Eugenius (C. *Sackville). Crites (Sir Robert Howard), Lisideius (*Sedley), and Neander (Dryden himself), who take a boat on the Thames on the day of the battle between the English and Dutch navies in June 1665, and subsequently discuss the comparative merits of English and French drama, and of the old and new in English drama. The essay is largely concerned with justifying Dryden's current practice as a playwright. It also contains admirable appreciations of Shakespeare, J. *Fletcher, and *Jonson.

O'FLAHERTY, Liam (1897–1984), Irish novelist and short story writer. His novels include *The Neighbour's Wife* (1923), *The Informer* (1925), *The Puritan* (1931), and *Famine* (1937), but he is best known for his short stories, published in several volumes including *Spring*

Sowing (1924), *The Tent* (1926), *Two Lovely Beasts* (1948), etc. Characteristic stories are those which deal unsentimentally with life, or more often death, from an animal's point of view.

Og, Dryden's name for *Shadwell in *The Second Part of *Absalom and Achitophel*.

Ogham, or **Ogam,** an alphabet of twenty characters used by the ancient British and Irish, consisting of conjunctions of upright and sloping strokes, and dots.

Ogier the Dane, a hero of the *Charlemagne romances, identified with a Frankish warrior, Autgarius, who fought against Charlemagne and then submitted to him. There are a number of legends about him, some of them including him as one of the *Paladins. As Holger Danske he became the subject of Danish folk-song, and identified as a national hero.

O'HARA, John (Henry) (1905–70), American writer. More than 200 of his sharp, satiric short stories were published in the *New Yorker*. His novels, which gained wide popularity with their toughness, frankness, and sophistication, include *Appointment in Samarra* (1934); *BUtterfield 8* (1935); *Pal Joey* (1940, later a musical), told in the form of letters from a nightclub singer; *A Rage to Live* (1949), and many others.

O. HENRY, see HENRY, O.

Oisin, a legendary Gaelic warrior and bard, known also as Ossian (see MACPHERSON and FINGAL). In *The Wanderings of Oisin* (1889), a narrative poem by *Yeats, the bard tells Saint Patrick the story of his love for *Niamh, the daughter of the sea-god Manannán.

O'KEEFFE, John (1747–1833), Irish actor and dramatist, wrote some 50 farces and musical pieces of which the best known are *The Castle of Andalusia* (1782); *The Poor Soldier* (1783); and his highly skilful and witty *Wild Oats* (1791), successfully revived in London in the late 1970s. O'Keeffe was the author of the song 'I am a friar of orders grey' (from his opera *Merry Sherwood*).

Old Bachelor, The, the first comedy of *Congreve, produced 1693.

Heartwell, a 'surly old pretended woman-hater' falls in love with Silvia, not knowing her to be the forsaken mistress of Vainlove, and is inveigled into marrying her, only discovering her true character afterwards. But the marriage proves to have been a pretence conducted by Bellmour, disguised as a parson in order to carry on an intrigue with the young wife of old Fondlewife.

Oldbuck, Jonathan, Laird of Monkbarns, the principal character in Scott's **The Antiquary*. Miss Griselda ('Grizzy') Oldbuck is his sister.

Oldcastle, The First Part of Sir John, a play of unknown authorship, published in 1619 as Shakespeare's, and included in the Third and Fourth Folios of his plays. The historical John Oldcastle seems to have been Shakespeare's original model for *Falstaff.

The play deals with the proceedings in Henry V's reign against Oldcastle as the chief supporter of the Lollards.

Old Curiosity Shop, The, a novel by *Dickens, published 1841. It was originally intended to be fitted into the framework of *Master Humphrey's Clock* (1840–1), and Master Humphrey is, in fact, the narrator of the first few chapters, but this idea was soon abandoned.

Little Nell Trent lives in the gloomy atmosphere of the old curiosity shop kept by her grandfather. Reduced to poverty by a spendthrift son-in-law, and his remaining means drained by Nell's profligate brother Fred, he has borrowed money from Daniel Quilp, a hideous dwarf and a monster of iniquity, and this money he secretly expends in gambling, in the vain hope of retrieving his fortunes, for Little Nell's sake. Quilp, who believes him a rich miser, at last discovers where the borrowed money has gone, and seizes the shop. The old man and the child flee and wander about the country, suffering great hardships and haunted by the fear of being discovered by Quilp, who pursues them with unremitting hatred. They at last find a haven in a cottage by a country church, which they are appointed to look after. The grandfather's brother, returning from abroad, and anxious to relieve their needs, has great difficulty in tracing them. At last he finds them, but Nell, worn out with her troubles, has just died, and the grandfather soon follows her.

The novel contains a number of well-known characters: Quilp's associates, the attorney Sampson Brass and his grim sister Sally; the honest lad Kit Nubbles, devoted to Little Nell; Mr and Mrs Garland, the kindly old couple who befriend Kit; Dick Swiveller, the disreputable facetious friend of Fred Trent; 'the Marchioness', the half-starved drudge in the Brass household (she marries Dick in the end); Codlin and Short, the Punch and Judy men; and Mrs Jarley, of the waxworks.

Old English, see ENGLISH.

OLDFIELD, Anne (1683–1730), an actress who excelled in both tragedy and comedy. She is the 'Narcissa' of Pope's *Moral Essays.

Old Fortunatus, a comedy by *Dekker, published 1600.

The beggar Fortunatus, encountering Fortune, is offered the choice between wisdom, strength, health, beauty, long life, and riches, and chooses the last. He receives a purse from which he can at any time draw ten pieces of gold. He goes on his travels, in the course of which he secures the marvellous hat of the Soldan of Turkey, which transports the wearer wherever he wishes to go. But at the height of his success Fortune steps in and puts an end to his life. His son Andelocia, refusing to take warning by his father's fate and equipped with the purse and hat, goes through a series of adventures at the court of Athelstane, is finally deprived of his talismans, and meets a miserable death.

OLDHAM, John (1653–83), is chiefly remembered for his ironical *Satire against Virtue* (1679) and *Satires upon the Jesuits* (1681). His *Poems and Translations* appeared in 1683. *Dryden commemorated him and his verse in the well-known lines beginning 'Farewell, too little and too lately known'.

OLDMIXON, John (?1673–1742), Whig historian and pamphleteer. His works include *The British Empire in America* (1708), *The Secret History of Europe* (1712–15, anonymous), various histories of England, poems, plays, and pastorals. By his 'Essay on Criticism', prefixed to the third edition (1728) of his *Critical History of England* (1724–6) he incurred the hostility of *Pope, who pilloried him in *The Dunciad and Peri Bathous.

OLD MOORE, Francis Moore (1657–1714), astrologer and licensed physician. His *Vox Stellarum, an Almanac for 1701 with astrological observations* appeared in 1700. *Old Moore's Almanac* still thrives thanks to its reputation for sensationalism and prophecy. (See also ALMANACS.)

Old Mortality, a novel by Sir W. *Scott, published in 1816 in *Tales of my Landlord*, 1st series.

The title is taken from the nickname of a certain Robert Paterson, who towards the end of the 18th cent. wandered about Scotland cleaning and repairing the tombs of the Cameronians. The story is supposed to be based on the anecdotes told by this supporter of their cause, and covers the period from the military operations undertaken against them in 1679 to the more peaceful days of religious toleration introduced by William III. It is particularly concerned with the fortunes of Henry Morton of Milnwood, a young man of courage and high character and a moderate Presbyterian, who, at the outset of the tale, is arrested by the dragoons of John Grahame of Claverhouse for having harboured an old friend of his father, the fanatical Covenanter, John Balfour of Burley. Morton narrowly escapes immediate execution, and this act of oppression, coupled with a sense of his countrymen's sufferings, induces him to throw in his lot with the Covenanters. He accordingly becomes one of their leaders. This brings him into violent antagonism with Lady Margaret Bellenden, the Royalist owner of Tillietudlem Castle, with whose granddaughter Edith he is in love. The final defeat of the Covenanters at Bothwell Bridge, and his own capture and banishment, sever him for years from Edith, who believes him dead; and she is on the point of yielding to the patient suit of Lord Evandale, when Morton, after the accession of William III, returns to England. Evandale is killed in a skirmish with a few fanatics, and Morton marries Edith.

Old Possum's Book of Practical Cats, a volume of verse for children, by T. S. *Eliot.

Old Uncle Tom Cobbleigh, and all, see WIDDICOMBE FAIR.

Old Vic Theatre (previously the Royal Victoria), a theatre in the Waterloo Road, London, famous for its notable productions of Shakespeare's plays under the management of Lilian Baylis (1874–1937), who took it over in 1912.

Old Wives' Tale, The, a play in prose by *Peele, published 1595.

The play is a satire on the romantic dramas of the time, the first English work of this kind. Two brothers are searching for their sister Delia, who is held captive by the magician Sacrapant. The brothers also fall into his hands. They are all rescued by the knight Eumenides aided by Jack's ghost, who is impelled by motives of gratitude, because the knight had borne the expense of Jack's funeral. The play is rich in songs and magical invocations such as: 'Gently dippe, but not too deepe, | For feare thou make the goulden beard to weep.'

Old Wives' Tale, The, a novel by Arnold *Bennett, published 1908.

It is the long chronicle of the lives of two sisters, Constance and Sophia Baines, daughters of a draper of Bursley (Burslem, one of the *Five Towns) from their ardent girlhood, through disillusionment, to death. The drab life of the draper's shop, its trivial incidents, are made interesting and important. Constance, a staid and sensible young woman, marries the superficially insignificant Samuel Povey, the chief assistant in the shop, and spends all her life in Bursley. The more passionate and imaginative Sophia elopes with Gerald Scales, a commercial traveller who has come into a fortune. He is an unprincipled blackguard, has to be forced to marry her, carries her to Paris, where she is exposed to indignities, and finally deserts her. She struggles to success as a lodging-house keeper in Paris, where she lives through the siege of 1870. The sisters are reunited, and spend their last years together in Bursley.

OLDYS, William (1696–1761), antiquary, and editor of the *Harleian Miscellany. His *Life of Sir Walter Raleigh* was prefixed to the 1736 edition of *Ralegh's *History of the World*. He was general editor of and contributed to the *Biographia Britannica* (6 vols, 1747–66). He also wrote the poem 'Busy, curious, thirsty fly' (1732).

OLIPHANT, Laurence (1829–88), published *A Journey to Khatmandu* (1852) and *The Russian Shores of the Black Sea* (1853–4), accounts of some of his early adventures. He acted as *The Times correspondent in Circassia during the Crimean war and again during the Franco-Prussian war. He is then heard of as plotting with Garibaldi in Italy, as secretary of a legation in Japan, and in other parts of the world. His novel *Piccadilly* (1870) is a satirical exposure of the venal side of London society. He was an MP during 1865–7, but by 1867 he had come under the influence of the spurious American 'prophet' Thomas Lake Harris, joined his Brotherhood of New Life in New York State, and surrendered to him most of his property. Later Oliphant and his wife founded a community for Jewish immigrants in Haifa. There he wrote his second novel, *Altiora Peto* (1883), and the strange *Sympneumata* (1885) which was dictated by his wife as if possessed by a spirit.

OLIPHANT, Margaret (M.O.W.), *née* Wilson (1828–97), a prolific Scots writer, she published *Passages in the Life of Mrs Margaret Maitland* (1849), a tale of Scotland; *Caleb Field* (1851); and *The Athelings* (1857), one of her many domestic romances. She produced biographies of Edward Irving (1862) and Laurence *Oliphant (1891) (no relation). She is best remembered for her 'Chronicles of Carlingford' series (the most notable of which are *Salem Chapel*, 1863; *The Perpetual Curate*, 1864; *Miss Marjoribanks*, 1866; and *Phoebe Junior*, 1876), set among the aristocracy, professional families, and tradesmen of the town. Another interesting group, *Stories of the Seen and Unseen*, all connected in some way with death and the experience of the soul, began with *A Beleaguered City* (1880) which was followed by *A Little Pilgrim* (1882) and others.

Olivant, the ivory horn (from *Oliphaunt*) of *Roland.

Oliver, in the *Charlemagne cycle of legends, one of Charlemagne's *Paladins. He is the close friend of *Roland, with whom he has a prolonged and undecided single combat (the origin of their comradeship). At the battle of Roncesvalles he urged Roland to summon help by sounding his horn, but Roland postpones doing so till too late.

Oliver de Boys, in Shakespeare's *As You Like It, Orlando's elder brother.

Oliver Twist, a novel by *Dickens, published 1837–8.

Oliver Twist is the name given to a child of unknown parentage born in a workhouse and brought up under the cruel conditions to which pauper children were formerly exposed, the tyrant at whose hands he especially suffers being Bumble, the parish beadle. After experience of an unhappy apprenticeship, he runs away, reaches London, and falls into the hands of a gang of thieves, at the head of which is the old Jew Fagin, and whose other chief members are the burglar Bill Sikes, his mistress Nancy, and 'the Artful Dodger', an impudent young pickpocket. Every effort is made to convert Oliver into a thief. He is temporarily rescued by the benevolent Mr Brownlow, but kidnapped by the gang, whose interest in his retention has been increased by the offers of a sinister person named Monks, who has a special interest in Oliver's perversion. Oliver is now made to accompany Bill Sikes on a burgling expedition, in the course of which he receives a gun-shot wound, and comes into the hands of Mrs Maylie and her protégée Rose, by whom he is kindly treated and brought up. After a time, Nancy, who develops some redeeming traits, reveals to Rose that Monks is aware of Oliver's parentage, and wishes all proof of it destroyed; also that there is some relationship between Oliver and Rose herself. Inquiry is set on foot. In the course of it Nancy's action is discovered by the gang, and she is brutally murdered by Bill Sikes. A hue and cry is raised; Sikes, trying to escape, accidentally hangs himself, and the rest of the gang are secured and Fagin executed. Monks, found and threatened with exposure, confesses what remains unknown. He is the half-brother of Oliver, and has pursued his ruin, animated by hatred and the desire to retain the whole of his father's property. Rose is the sister of Oliver's unfortunate mother. Oliver is adopted by Mr Brownlow. Monks emigrates and dies in prison. Bumble ends his career in the workhouse over which he formerly ruled.

Olivia, (1) the wealthy Illyrian countess in Shakespeare's *Twelfth Night*; (2) a character in Wycherley's *The Plain Dealer*; (3) the elder daughter of Dr Primrose, in Goldsmith's *The Vicar of Wakefield*.

Olney Hymns, see COWPER, W., and NEWTON, J.

Olympian Odes, The, see PINDAR.

Omar Khayyám, The Rubáiyát of, a translation by E. *FitzGerald of the *rubais* or quatrains of the 12th-cent. Persian poet, first published anonymously in 1859; FitzGerald produced further editions, revised and with added quatrains, in 1868, 1872, and 1879. FitzGerald's translation preserved the stanza form of the original, but adapted the quatrains into a connected theme, sceptical of divine providence, mocking the transience of human grandeur, and concentrating on the pleasures of the fleeting moment. The felicitously phrased aphorisms of this cynical yet genial poetic sequence are among the most frequently quoted lines in English poetry.

Omnium, duke and duchess of (Plantagenet Palliser and Lady Glencora), leading characters in the *'Palliser' novels of A. Trollope.

Omoo (1847), a romance by H. *Melville, a sequel to *Typee*.

'O my luve's like a red, red rose', a lyric by *Burns, published in *The Scots Musical Museum* (1787–1803).

O'NEILL, Eugene (1888–1953), American dramatist. His first big success was the full-length naturalistic drama *Beyond the Horizon* (1920), which was followed in the same year by his expressionistic *The Emperor Jones,* a tragedy, and *Anna Christie* (1921), a naturalistic study of a prostitute on the New York waterfront. Among other important plays of this period were *The Hairy Ape* (1922), *All God's Chillun Got Wings* (1924), and *Desire under the Elms* (1924). He experimented with a *stream-of-consciousness technique in *Strange Interlude* (1928), and adapted the theme of the *Oresteia to the aftermath of the American Civil War in his trilogy *Mourning Becomes Electra* (1931). *Ah! Wilderness* (1932) and *Days without End* (1934) were followed by a long absence from the stage during which he was awarded the *Nobel Prize (1936). *The Iceman Cometh* (1946) is a lengthy naturalistic tragedy set in Harry Hope's Bowery Saloon, where a collection of down-and-out alcoholics nourish their illusions ('pipe dreams') with the aid of an extrovert salesman, Hickey. His masterpiece, *Long Day's Journey into Night* (1956), was written in 1940–1; it is a semi-autobiographical family tragedy, portraying the mutually destructive relationships of drug-addicted Mary Tyrone, her ex-actor husband James, and their two sons, hard-drinking Jamie and intellectual Edmund. His last play was *A Moon for the Misbegotten* (1947). O'Neill transcends his debt to *Ibsen and *Strindberg, producing an *œuvre* in which the struggle between self-destruction, self-deception, and redemption is presented as essentially dramatic in nature.

One of our Conquerors, a novel by G. *Meredith, published 1891.

ONIONS, C(harles) T(albut) (1873–1965), grammarian and lexicographer, co-editor of the *Oxford English Dictionary* and its original *Supplement,* 1914–33; editor of *A Shakespeare Glossary* (1911), *The Shorter Oxford English Dictionary*

(1932), *The Oxford Dictionary of English Etymology* (1966); author of *An Advanced English Syntax* (1904: rev. edn, *Modern English Syntax*, 1971).

ONIONS, George Oliver (1873–1961), novelist and short story writer born in Bradford, whose works include *The Compleat Bachelor* (1900), *Widdershins* (1911, tales of the uncanny), and *The Story of Ragged Robyn* (1945). He changed his name by deed poll in 1918 to George Oliver. He was married to the romantic novelist Berta Ruck (1878–1978), whose name appeared inadvertently in V. *Woolf's *Jacob's Room*, thus occasioning first a dispute, then an acquaintance between the two women.

Onomatopoeia, the formation of a word by an imitation of the sound associated with the object or action designated: as 'hurlyburly', 'buzz', 'creak'. The term is also applied to the use of a combination of words to evoke by sound a certain image or mood, the most frequently quoted example being *Tennyson's 'murmuring of innumerable bees'.

Opera, a dramatic performance in which music forms an essential part, consisting of recitatives, arias, and choruses, with orchestral accompaniment and scenery; also, a dramatic or musical composition intended for this, a libretto or score [OED]. It is the integration of music into the substance of the drama that differentiates opera from the *masque. The first operas developed out of the experiments in the *stile recitativo* (the 'reciting style') made by a group of cultured intellectuals at the Medici court in Florence towards the end of the 16th cent.

In England opera never established itself as an indigenous form in the way that it did in Italy, France, and Germany, although there are isolated exceptions such as *Purcell in the 17th cent. or *Britten in the 20th. The first English work that is normally regarded as an opera is *The Siege of Rhodes* (1656), of which the text was by *D'Avenant and the music, now lost, a collective effort by several composers. The first English example of which the music has survived is John Blow's *Venus and Adonis* (c.1684), which preceded Purcell's *Dido and Aeneas* by some five years. See also LIBRETTO.

Ophelia, in Shakespeare's *Hamlet*, the daughter of Polonius.

OPIE, Mrs Amelia (1769–1853), wife of John Opie the painter, and friend of Sydney *Smith, *Sheridan, and Mme de Staël. She was a copious novelist and poet, and was satirized by T. L. Peacock in *Headlong Hall* as Miss Poppyseed, 'an indefatigable compounder of novels'.

OPIE, Peter Mason (1918–82), author and folklorist, and his wife Iona Margaret Balfour Opie (1923–), produced the *Oxford Dictionary of Nursery Rhymes* (1951), *The Lore and Language of Schoolchildren* (1959), and *Children's Games in Street and Playground* (1969). They also edited various anthologies, including *The Oxford Book of Children's Verse* (1973).

Opium Eater, *Confessions of an English*, see CONFESSIONS OF AN ENGLISH OPIUM EATER.

ORAGE, Alfred Richard (1875–1934), joined the *Fabian Society, and was active in a wide range of artistic, political, and intellectual activities. Partly financed by G. B. *Shaw and assisted initially by Holbrook Jackson (1874–1948), he edited *The New Age*, a periodical which acquired during this period much political and literary prestige. His contributors included both the established (Shaw, Arnold *Bennett, *Wells, and others) and the as yet unknown (including *Pound, K. *Mansfield, *Aldington, and T. E. *Hulme). After leaving the *New Age* in 1922 he went to Fontainebleau, then New York, as a *Gurdjieff disciple, returning to England in 1931 to found the *New English Weekly*, which he edited until his death.

Oran Haut-ton, see HAUT-TON.

Orc, (1) a mythical sea-monster mentioned by *Ariosto, *Drayton, *Milton, and others, from the Latin 'orca', a kind of whale; (2) in the Prophetic Books of *Blake, the symbol of rebellion and anarchy, the son of *Los and *Enitharmon, who is chained, like *Prometheus, to a rock in *The Book of *Urizen*, and who bursts his bonds in *America: A Prophecy* to fight and defeat Albion's Angel; (3) in the personal mythology of J. R. R. *Tolkien, Orcs are the evil and hideous creations of the rebellious Vala, Melkor.

Orcades, the Orkney Islands.

ORCZY, Baronness (Mrs Montague Barstow) (1865–1947), Hungarian-born novelist who lived from the age of 15 in London. She achieved fame with her romantic novel *The Scarlet Pimpernel* (1905), the story of the League of the Scarlet Pimpernel, a band of Englishmen pledged to rescue the innocent victims of the Reign of Terror in Paris. Its leader, Sir Percy Blakeney, outwits his opponents—in particular the wily Chauvelin—by means of his courage and ingenious diguises, at the same time concealing his identity from his friends in England. The novel was first successful in a dramatized version (1903).

Ordeal of Gilbert Pinfold, The, see WAUGH, E.

Ordeal of Richard Feverel, The, a novel by G. *Meredith, published 1859.

Sir Austin Feverel's wife has run off with a poet, leaving him with their son Richard. Sir Austin devises a 'System' for Richard's education, which consists in keeping the boy at home and in trusting to authoritarian parental vigilance. Richard's struggle for freedom and knowledge forms the underlying theme of the book. Richard and Lucy Desborough, a neighbouring farmer's niece, fall in love and an idyllic courtship ends in the discovery of their attachment. Lucy has not the birth Sir Austin requires for his son. His attempts to break their relationship result in their secret marriage, but Sir Austin cruelly ensures the separation of the young couple by playing on Richard's love and duty. Ordered to await his father in London, Richard earnestly sets about the redemption of ladies of pleasure, succeeding only in falling a temporary victim to the beautiful Bella Mount. Initially Bella has acted at the instigation of the predatory Lord Mountfalcon, who has plans to ensnare Lucy. Richard becomes increasingly overwhelmed with shame at his treatment of his wife, then hears that he is a father and that Lucy and Sir Austin are reconciled. But as soon as he returns to her he learns of the designs of Lord Mountfalcon; he furiously challenges him to a duel and is seriously wounded. In the succeeding fever his confusions are stripped away and he is finally freed of his devouring father. But the shock of events proves overwhelming for Lucy, who loses her mind and eventually dies.

ORDERICUS VITALIS (1075–1142/3), a monk of St Évroul in Normandy. He wrote between 1114 and 1141 his *Ecclesiastical History of England and Normandy* in Latin, covering events from the beginning of the Christian era down to 1141, one of the standard authorities for the Norman period.

Oresteia, The, a trilogy of plays by *Aeschylus.
Agamemnon describes the return to Argos after the Trojan war of the victorious Agamemnon, brother of Helen's husband Menelaus, and his murder by his wife Clytemnestra foretold by his captive, the prophet Cassandra, daughter of King Priam of Troy. The *Choephoroe* (or *The Libation Bearers*) portrays the vengeance of the son and daughter of Agamemnon, Orestes and Electra: Orestes murders Clytemnestra and her lover Aegisthus, and is himself pursued by the Eumenides, or Furies. The *Eumenides* shows the Furies in pursuit of Orestes, who is protected by the younger god Apollo. Orestes is tried, Athena, goddess of wisdom, delivers her casting vote on his behalf, and he goes free, released from the ancient blood vengeance: Athena reconciles the Furies to the new Law, and they are transformed into the Kindly Ones, who bless the city of Athens and the land.
Other versions of the story appear in the works of *Sophocles (who wrote *Electra*) and *Euripides, and it reappears in many forms throughout

Western literature; there are notable 20th-cent. dramatic versions by T. S. *Eliot (*The Family Reunion*, 1939), *O'Neill (*Mourning Becomes Electra*, 1931), and *Sartre (*Les Mouches*, 1942).

Orfeo, Sir, a metrical romance of the early 14th cent. in about 600 lines (in three varying manuscript versions), identified in its prologue as a *Breton lay. It represents the story of Orpheus and Eurydice (see ORPHEUS) in a Celtic guise and with a happy ending, for the return of Queen Heurodys is permanent. The poem is one of the most charming and interesting of Middle English romances.

Orgilus, a character in Ford's *The Broken Heart.*

Orgoglio (Ital., signifying haughtiness), in Spenser's *Faerie Queene* (I. vii, viii), captures the *Redcrosse Knight, and is slain by Prince Arthur.

Oriana, (1) a name frequently applied by poets to *Elizabeth I, as in T. *Morley's collection of madrigals *The Triumphes of Oriana* (1601); (2) the heroine of J. *Fletcher's *The Wild-Goose Chase*; (3) the subject of an early ballad by *Tennyson.

Oriental (or **Eastern**) **novel** (or **tale**), a class of story exotically set in the Middle or Far East, and varying greatly in tone, from Johnson's *Rasselas to Beckford's *Vathek and Byron's *The Corsair and *The Giaour. Many of the tales (such as those of *Hawkesworth, J. *Ridley, and F. *Sheridan) relate the flamboyant adventures of well-defined heroes and villains, often with the intervention of the supernatural; others (such as *Southey's poem *The Curse of Kehema* or Moore's *Lalla Rookh) are more complex. These tales enjoyed great popularity in the second half of the 18th cent. and the early part of the 19th cents. Public interest in the Orient was no doubt greatly stimulated by the translation into English in 1705–8 of the *Arabian Nights; by *Knolles's history of the Turks (much admired by both Dr Johnson and *Byron); and by the translations of Sir W. *Jones.

ORIGEN (c.185–c.253), a great Christian thinker and scholar in the Alexandrian school, the author of many theological works and compiler of the Hexapla versions of the OT (from Greek translations of the 2nd cent. AD collected in parallel columns together with the current Hebrew texts and a revised text of the *Septuagint). He studied under Ammonius, sometimes regarded as the founder of *Neoplatonism, and he is of great importance as the introducer of Neoplatonic elements into Christianity. His *Principles* were rejected by Church orthodoxy. He influenced the allegorical method of literary criticism developed by *Augustine.

Origin of Species, On the, the great work of C. *Darwin, published 1859.

Orinda, The Matchless, see PHILIPS, K.

Orion, see HORNE, R. H.

Orlando, (1) the Italian form of *Roland, a hero of the *Charlemagne romances (see also ORLANDO FURIOSO and ORLANDO INNAMORATO); (2) in Shakespeare's *As You Like It, the lover of Rosalind; (3) the title of a novel by V. *Woolf.

Orlando Furioso, a poem by *Ariosto, published 1532. It continues the story of Orlando's love for Angelica begun by Boiardo in *Orlando Innamorato.

The main theme of the poem is this: Saracens and Christians, in the days of *Charlemagne, are at war for the possession of Europe. The Saracens under Agramant, king of Africa, are besieging Charlemagne in Paris with the help of Marsilio, the Moorish king of Spain, and two mighty warriors, Rodomont and Mandricardo. Christendom is imperilled. Orlando, chief of the Paladins, a perfect knight, is lured by Angelica's beauty to forget his duty and pursue her. Angelica meets with various adventures, finally coming upon the wounded Moorish youth Medoro, whom she tends, falls in love with, and marries. Orlando, learning of their story, is seized with a furious and grotesque madness, runs naked through the country, destroying everything in his path, and at last returns to Charlemagne's camp, where he is finally cured of his madness and his love and in a great conclusive battle kills Agramant.

Although the madness of Orlando gives the poem its name, a not less important theme in it is the love of Rogero for Bradamante, a maiden warrior, sister of Rinaldo, and the many adventures and vicissitudes that interrupt the course of true love. Other notable episodes in the work are the voyage of Astolfo on the hippogriff to the moon, whence he brings back the lost wits of Orlando; and the self-immolation of Isabella, the widow of the Scottish prince Zerbino, to escape the attentions of the pagan king, Rodomont. Orlando's horse is Brigliandoro; his sword Durindana.

Spenser, in *The Faerie Queene, owes much to it for his characters and form of narration. The first complete English version 'in English Heroical Verse' is that of Sir J. *Harington (1591; ed. R. McNulty, 1972).

Orlando Innamorato, a poem by *Boiardo published 1487, on the subject of the falling in love of Orlando (the Roland of the *Charlemagne cycle) with Angelica, daughter of Galafron, king of Cathay. She arrives at the court of Charlemagne, under false pretences, to carry off the Christian knights to her father's country. Several knights attempt to win her, the chief among them being Astolfo, Ferrau, Rinaldo, and Orlando. Her brother Argalia is slain and Angelica flees, but, drinking of an enchanted fountain, falls in love with Rinaldo, who, drinking of another enchanted fountain, conceives a violent aversion to her. He runs away, pursued by her, and they reach her father's country, where she is besieged in the capital, Albracca, by Agrican, king of Tartary, to whom her hand had been promised (an incident to which Milton refers in *Paradise Regained, iii. 337 ff.). Orlando slays Agrican, and carries Angelica off to France whither he had been summoned to assist Charlemagne against Agramant, king of the Moors. Owing once more to enchanted waters, Rinaldo this time falls in love with Angelica, and Angelica into hatred of him. A fierce combat ensues between Orlando and Rinaldo, suppressed by Charlemagne, who entrusts Angelica to Namo, duke of Bavaria.

Orley Farm, a novel by A. *Trollope, published 1862.

While Joseph Mason of Groby Park inherits the bulk of his father's property, the small estate at Orley Farm goes unexpectedly to Lucius Mason, the old man's son by his second marriage. The will is unsuccessfully contested. Samuel Dockwrath, formerly a tenant at Orley Farm, discovers important irregularities in the evidence brought before the court. The suspicion grows that the codicil attached to Sir Joseph's will was forged by Lucius's mother, Lady Mason. The case is re-opened, and though the verdict is in Lady Mason's favour, this is largely due to the professional skill of the lawyers who represent her, including the indefatigable Chaffanbrass. Lady Mason confesses her guilt, and surrenders the property.

Ormond, a novel by M. *Edgeworth, published 1817.

This is largely a tale of life in Ireland, but also of fashionable Paris society in the 18th cent.

Ormulum, The, a Middle English poem of which about 20,000 short lines survive, written in the East Midlands in the late 12th cent. by an Augustinian canon called Orm. It purports to consist of paraphrases of the gospels for the year as arranged in the Mass book, supplemented by a homily on each; but in fact it is a series of sermons arranged chronologically around the Gospel versions of the life of Christ. The writer's ambitious scheme is only about an eighth complete. It is of great linguistic interest, particularly for the semi-phonetic spelling system devised by the writer.

Oroonoko, or the History of the Royal Slave, a novel by A. *Behn (c.1688), adapted for the stage by *Southerne (1695).

Oroonoko, grandson and heir of an African king, loves and wins Imoinda, daughter of the king's general. The king, who also loves her, is enraged and orders her to be sold as a slave. Oroonoko himself is trapped by the captain of an English slave-trading ship and carried off to Surinam, then an English colony, where he is reunited with Imoinda and renamed Caesar by his owners. He rouses his fellow slaves to revolt, is deceived into surrender by deputy-governor Byam (a historical figure), and brutally whipped. Oroonoko, determined on revenge but not hoping for victory, kills Imoinda, who dies willingly. He is discovered by her dead body and cruelly executed.

The novel is remarkable as an early protest against the slave-trade. The author comments on the superior simplicity and morality of both African slaves and the indigenous Indians, whose Christian oppressors are shown as treacherous and hypocritical. Afra Behn's memories of her own visit to Surinam in 1663 provide a vivid background. Southerne's tragedy follows the broad lines of the novel, with alterations which decrease the violence of the story and increase its intended pathos.

OROSIUS (*fl.* early 5th cent.), a priest of Tarragona in Spain, disciple of St *Augustine and friend of St *Jerome, author of the *Historia Adversus Paganos*, a universal history and geography which was translated by the circle of King *Alfred in the 890s.

Orphan, The, a tragedy in blank verse by *Otway, produced 1680.

Castalio and Polydore, twin sons of Acasto, have been brought up with the orphan Monimia with whom they have both fallen in love. Monimia returns the love of Castalio who feigns indifference for her. Chamont, an honest but rough and tactless soldier, brother of Monimia, visits Acasto's house; he suspects that Monimia has been wronged by one of the twins and annoys her with his questions. Castalio and Monimia thereupon are secretly married. Polydore, ignorant of this and overhearing them arranging a meeting in the night, takes Castalio's place, and is not detected. Castalio, coming later, is shut out, and curses his wife for what he supposes to be her heartless and rebellious conduct. The truth is discovered through Chamont. The brothers in despair kill themselves, and Monimia takes poison.

Monimia was one of Mrs *Barry's most celebrated parts.

Orpheus, a legendary Greek hero, son of Apollo by the Muse Callipe, was renowned as a musician, a religious leader, and a seer. He was reputed to have made trees and rocks follow his singing, been one of the Argonauts, visited Egypt, and founded mystery cults in several parts of Greece. He was eventually torn to pieces by Maenads (frenzied votaresses of Dionysus); and his head and lyre, thrown into the river Hebrus, drifted to Lesbos where the head became an oracle, while Apollo placed the lyre among the stars. The relationship of Orpheus to Dionysus remains puzzling. The Maenads are said to have attacked him because as a priest of Apollo he censured their orgiastic rites. Orphic beliefs seem however to have been rooted in the assumption that 'the body is the tomb of the soul', so that one's aim in life must be to free oneself from an endless series of reincarnations, not only by moral and physical purity, but also through certain rites which involved eating the flesh of a sacrifice that represented the god; and on such occasions the god in question was always Dionysus.

The legend which found most favour in later literature was the story of Orpheus going down into hell, persuading Hades to let him have back his wife Eurydice, and then losing her because he disregarded the instruction not to look back before they reached the light of day. The popularity of this legend was due perhaps to its presence in poems that were widely read in the Middle Ages: *Virgil, *Georgics*, IV. 454–527, *Ovid, *Metamorphoses*, X. 1–85, and especially *Boethius, *De Consolatione Philosophiae*, III. 12, so that it appears in the English *Sir *Orfeo*, and in the 14th-cent. *King Orfew*. Opera has been the genre that has made most use of the Orpheus story in modern times.

ORRERY, earls of, see BOYLE.

Orsino, the duke of Illyria in Shakespeare's *Twelfth Night*, whose words 'If music be the food of love, play on' begin the play.

Orson, see VALENTINE AND ORSON.

ORTON, Joe (1933–67), playwright, whose comedies include *Entertaining Mr Sloane* (1964), *Loot* (1965), and the posthumously performed *What the Butler Saw* (1969). They are black, stylish, and violent, and their emphasis on corruption and sexual perversion made them a *succès de scandale*.

Orville, Lord, the hero of F. Burney's *Evelina*.

ORWELL, George, pen-name of Eric Arthur Blair (1903–50), born in Bengal, educated in England. He served with the Indian Imperial Police in Burma, 1922–7, and his experiences are reflected in his first novel, *Burmese Days* (1934). He returned to Europe, where he worked in Paris and London in a series of ill-paid jobs, reflected in *Down and Out in Paris and London* (1933). His novels include *A Clergyman's Daughter* (1935) and *Keep the Aspidistra Flying* (1936), which recounts the literary aspirations, financial humiliations, and shotgun wedding of Gordon Comstock, bookseller's assistant. *The Road to Wigan Pier* (1937) is an impassioned documentary of unemployment and proletarian life. The Spanish Civil War (in which he fought for the Republicans and was wounded) produced *Homage to Catalonia* (1938). The threat of the coming war hung over his next novel, *Coming up for Air* (1939). By this stage Orwell saw himself primarily as a political writer, a democratic socialist who avoided party labels, hated totalitarianism, and was to become progressively disillusioned with the methods of Communism; his plain, colloquial style made him highly effective as pamphleteer and journalist. His collections of essays include *Inside the Whale* (1940), *Critical Essays* (1946), and *Shooting an Elephant* (1950). But his most popular works were undoubtedly his political satires *Animal Farm* (1945) and *Nineteen Eighty-four* (1949). His *Collected Essays, Journalism and Letters* (4 vols, ed. S. Orwell and I. Angus) appeared in 1968.

Osbaldistone, Mr, Francis, Rashleigh, and Sir Hildebrand, characters in Scott's *Rob Roy.*

Osborne, Mr, his son George, and Maria and Jane, his daughters, characters in Thackeray's *Vanity Fair.*

OSBORNE, Dorothy (1627–95), married William *Temple in 1654. Her letters to him during the period 1652–4 were published in an edition by Parry (1888), followed by G. C. Moore-Smith's more scholarly edition in 1928. The letters provide an intimate picture of the life, manners, and reading habits of the times, and particularly of a woman's attitudes to marriage and filial duty.

OSBORNE, John James (1929–), playwright, who made his name with *Look Back in Anger* (1956, pub. 1957), which was followed by *Epitaph for George Dillon* (1957, pub. 1958; written in the mid-1950s in collaboration with Anthony Creighton); *The Entertainer* (1957, which starred Laurence Olivier as Archie Rice, a faded survivor of the great days of music hall); *Luther* (1961, based on the life of Martin *Luther); *Inadmissible Evidence* (1964, the tragedy of a down-at-heel solicitor, Bill Maitland, plunging rhetorically towards self-destruction); and *A Patriot for Me* (1965, set in Vienna, based on the rise and fall of Redl, a homosexual officer in the Austro-Hungarian army). His later works (which include *West of Suez*, 1971; *A Sense of Detachment*, 1972; *Watch it Come Down*, 1976) have become increasingly vituperative in tone; his outbursts of rage against contemporary society are frequently exhilarating, for the anger that made him known as an *'Angry Young Man' remains one of his strongest theatrical weapons, but he also expresses from time to

time an ambivalent nostalgia for the past that his own work did so much to alter. His autobiography *A Better Class of Person* appeared in 1981. (See also KITCHEN SINK.)

O'SHAUGHNESSY, Arthur William Edgar (1844–81), poet and friend of D. G. *Rossetti. He published several volumes of poetry, his best known, 'Ode' ('We are the music-makers'), appeared in *Music and Moonlight* (1874) and has been noted as a characteristic example of Victorian escapist verse.

Osric, in Shakespeare's *Hamlet*, an affected courtier.

Ossian, the name commonly given to *Oisin, a legendary Gaelic warrior and bard. See MACPHERSON and FINGAL.

OSWALD, St (d. 992), one of the three leading figures (along with *Dunstan and *Æthelwold) in the 10th-cent. Benedictine Revival in England. On Dunstan's initiative he was appointed bishop of Worcester in 961. He founded monasteries at Westbury, Worcester, Winchcombe, and on the Isle of Ramsey. In 972 he was made archbishop of York.

Othello, *The Moor of Venice*, a tragedy by *Shakespeare, written between 1602 and 1604, performed 1604, first printed in quarto in 1622, and in a different version in the *Folio of 1623. The story is taken from Cinthio, which Shakespeare could have read in Italian or French.

The play's first act (which Verdi's opera *Otello* omits) is set in Venice. Desdemona, the daughter of Brabantio, a Venetian senator, has secretly married Othello, a Moor in the service of the state. Accused before the duke and senators of having stolen Brabantio's daughter, Othello explains and justifies his conduct, and is asked by the Senate to lead the Venetian forces against the Turks who are about to attack Cyprus.

In the middle of a storm which disperses the Turkish fleet, Othello lands on Cyprus with Desdemona, Cassio, a young Florentine, who helped him court his wife and whom he has now promoted to be his lieutenant, and Iago, an older soldier, bitterly resentful of being passed over for promotion, who now plans his revenge. Iago uses Roderigo, 'a gull'd Gentlemen' in love with Desdemona, to fight with Cassio after he has got him drunk, so that Othello deprives him of his new rank. He then persuades Cassio to ask Desdemona to plead in his favour with Othello, which she warmly does. At the same time he suggests to Othello that Cassio is, and has been, Desdemona's lover, finally arranging through his wife Emilia, who is Desdemona's waiting-woman, that Othello should see Cassio in possession of a handkerchief which he had given to

his bride. Othello is taken in by Iago's promptings and in frenzied jealousy smothers
Desdemona in her bed. Iago sets Roderigo to
murder Cassio, but when Roderigo fails to do
this Iago kills him and Emilia as well, after she
has proved Desdemona's innocence to Othello.
Emilia's evidence and letters found on Roderigo
prove Iago's guilt; he is arrested, and Othello,
having tried to stab him, kills himself.

Otho the Great: A Tragedy in Five Acts, a play
written by *Keats in 1819, in collaboration with
his friend Charles Brown, who planned its
construction.

O'Trigger, Sir Lucius, a character in Sheridan's
*The Rivals.

Ottava rima, an Italian stanza of eight 11-sylla-
bled lines, rhyming a b a b a b c c, employed by
*Tasso, *Ariosto, etc. It was introduced into
England by *Wyatt, and used to great effect by
Byron in *Don Juan, with a 10-syllable iambic
line.

Otter, Captain Thomas and Mistress, the ill-
matched husband and wife in Jonson's *Epicene.

Otterbourne, The Battle of, one of the earliest of
English ballads, included in Percy's *Reliques.

Otuel, Sir, a pagan knight, miraculously con-
verted, who became one of *Charlemagne's
*Paladins. He is killed in combat by *Roland.
The Otuel story is told in three English
Romances.

OTWAY, Thomas (1652–85), playwright. Of
his three great tragedies, *Don Carlos, in rhymed
verse, was produced in 1676; *The Orphan, in
blank verse, in 1680; and *Venice Preserv'd, also
in blank verse, in 1682. Of his other plays
Alcibiades, a tragedy, was produced in 1675 (and
provided Mrs *Barry, for whom Otway
cherished an unrequited passion, with her first
successful part). He also wrote prologues, epilogues, and a few poems. He died in destitution
at the early age of 33.

OUIDA, pen-name of Marie Louise de la
Ramée (1839–1908), began her career contributing stories to *Bentley's Miscellany (1858–60),
encouraged by its editor *Ainsworth. Her first
real success was Held in Bondage (1863). She
spent much time in Italy from 1860 and in 1874
settled in Florence. Her 45 novels include Under
Two Flags (1867), Folle-Farine (1871), Two Little
Wooden Shoes (1874), and Moths (1880). They are
often set in a fashionable world far removed
from reality and show a spirit of rebellion against
the moral ideals reflected in much of the fiction
of the time. She suffered frequent ridicule for her
extravagantly portrayed heroes and for her inac-
curacies, but her faults were redeemed by her
narrative power and emotional energy.

Our Man in Havana, see GREENE, G.

Our Mutual Friend, a novel by *Dickens,
published in monthly parts between May 1864
and Nov. 1865.

John Harmon returns from the exile to which
he has been sent by a harsh father, a rich dust-
contractor; he expects to receive the inheritance
to which his father has attached the condition
that he shall marry a certain girl, Bella Wilfer.
Bella is unknown to him, and he confides to a
mate of the ship which is bringing him home
his intention of concealing his identity until
he has formed some judgement of his allotted
wife. The mate lures him to a riverside haunt,
attempts to murder him, throws his body into
the river, and is in turn murdered and his body
likewise thrown into the river. Harmon recovers
and escapes; the mate's body is found after some
days, and, owing to Harmon's papers found
upon it, it is taken to be that of Harmon.
Harmon's intention of remaining unknown is
thus facilitated; he assumes the name of John
Rokesmith and becomes the secretary of the
kindly, disinterested Mr Boffin, old Harmon's
foreman, who, in default of young Harmon,
inherits the property. He is thrown into close
contact with Bella, a flighty minx, who is adopted by Boffin and who is turned by her first taste
of wealth into an arrogant, mercenary jade.
Rokesmith nevertheless falls in love with her and
is contemptuously rejected. Harmon's identity
is now discovered by the amiable Mrs Boffin,
and the Boffins, devoted to their old master's son
and convinced of Bella's soundness of heart,
contrive a plot to prove her. Boffin pretends to
be transformed by his wealth into a hard and
griping miser, and heaps indignities on Harmon,
who is finally dismissed with contumely. Bella,
awakened to the evils of wealth and to the merits
of Rokesmith, flies from the Boffins and marries
her suitor. His identity presently comes to light,
and with his assistance the scheme of a one-
legged old villain, Silas Wegg, to blackmail
Boffin is exposed.

Concurrently with this main theme runs the
story of the love of Eugene Wrayburn, a careless, insolent young barrister, for Lizzy Hexam,
daughter of a disreputable boatman. His rival for
her affections, Bradley Headstone, a schoolmaster, attempts to murder Wrayburn. The latter is
saved by Lizzy and marries her. Among the
notable characters in the book are the Veneer-
ings, types of social parvenus; the good Jew
Riah; the blackmailing waterside villain Rogue
Riderhood; Jenny Wren, the dolls' dressmaker;
Bella Wilfer's grotesque father, mother, and
sister; and the spirited Betty Higden, an old
woman with a haunting dread of the
workhouse.

Our Village: sketches of rural life, character, and scenery, by M. R. *Mitford, published 1832.

Outsider, The, (1) a novel by American author R. *Wright, published 1953; (2) a study by C. *Wilson published 1956.

OVERBURY, Sir Thomas (1581–1613), opposed the marriage of his patron Robert Carr (afterwards earl of Somerset) with the divorced countess of Essex, and on the pretext of his refusal of diplomatic employment was sent to the Tower, where he was slowly poisoned by the agents of Lady Essex. Four of these were hanged; Somerset and his wife were convicted and pardoned. The prosecution was conducted by F. *Bacon. Overbury is chiefly remembered for his Theophrastian 'Characters' which appeared with the second edition of his poem *A Wife* (1st edn 1614). Later editions added new characters, some by J. *Webster and some by *Dekker. *Earle responded to their harsh and anti-scholastic tone in his own *Microcosmographie.* (See CHARACTER-WRITING.)

Overdo, Justice Adam, the busy seeker-out of 'enormities' in Jonson's *Bartholomew Fair.*

Overreach, Sir Giles, a character in Massinger's *A New Way to pay Old Debts.*

OVERTON, Richard (*fl.* 1646), leader of the Leveller movement, was a forceful pamphleteer, much of whose work was published anonymously, some under the pseudonym of Martin Marpriest. A tract on the immortality of the soul, *Man's Mortality* (1643), aroused much controversy, and he was imprisoned many times for his unorthodox religious and radical political views.

OVID (Publius Ovidius Naso) (43 BC–AD 18), Roman writer of love elegies (*Amores*), who then experimented with the imaginary letter (*Heroides*), mock didactic verse (*Ars Amatoria*), 'collective' narrative relating disconnected stories inside a large historical (*Metamorphoses*) or chronological (*Fasti*) frame, and finally with elegies of nostalgic complaint (*Tristia, Epistulae ex Ponto*). Ovid continued in favour with writers and public so long as Rome was pagan, but the Christian Church disapproved of his immorality. Interest revived with the 11th cent. and during the Renaissance Ovid enjoyed great favour. *Chaucer and *Gower both borrowed his stories. But the late 16th and early 17th cents were England's Ovidian Age when *Lodge, *Marlowe, *Spenser, *Shakespeare, G. *Chapman, *Drayton, T. *Heywood, were all indebted to him directly or through A. *Golding's translation of the *Metamorphoses* (1565–7). By the middle of the 17th cent. his popularity was in decline, athough echoes of his lines can be found in *Milton. With the growth of Puritan seriousness, the mixture of wit and sensuality that Ovid offered no longer had an immediate appeal. Themes from the *Metamorphoses* were handled by W. *King ('Orpheus and Eurydice', 1704), Swift (*Baucis and Philemon*), *Prior ('Daphne and Apollo', 1740), *Shelley (*Arethusa,* 1820), Morris ('Pygmalion' in *The Earthly Paradise,* 1868–70), Swinburne (*Atalanta in Calydon,* 1865), and Shaw (*Pygmalion,* 1916), but they stray very far from their originals.

Ovide Moralisé, a French work which influenced *Chaucer. It moralizes 15 books of the *Metamorphoses* and is highly significant in the development of late medieval and Renaissance literature by bringing secular literature into the official canon. Cf. *Fulgentius Metaforalis* by Ridewall (*c.* 1330) for the practice of allegorizing the stories of classical authors.

OWEN, Robert (1771–1858), socialist and philanthropist, became the wealthy owner of cotton-spinning mills in Manchester. In 1799 he purchased the New Lanark mills in Scotland, and set up there his model community, organized on principles of mutual co-operation. He was largely instrumental in bringing about the Factory Act of 1819. He published *A New View of Society* in 1813 and *The Revolution in Mind and Practice of the Human Race* in 1849. (See also SOCIALISM.)

OWEN, Wilfred (1893–1918), joined the army in 1915; he was invalided to hospital in Edinburgh, where he was greatly encouraged in his writing by *Sassoon. He returned to France in 1918, won the MC, and was killed a week before the Armistice. He found his own voice as a poet in the trenches. Only five of his poems were published in his lifetime, but his reputation slowly grew, greatly assisted by *Blunden's edition of his poems, with a Memoir, in 1931, and he is now generally regarded as a war poet of the first rank. His bleak realism, his energy and indignation, and his mastery of metrical variety and assonance are evident in most of his work. His poems were chosen by *Britten for the *War Requiem.* The poems were collected again in 1963, edited by *Day-Lewis.

Owl and the Nightingale, The, an early Middle English poem of 1,794 lines of octosyllabic couplets, probably from the beginning of the 13th cent. It is a debate between the grave owl and the gay nightingale as to the benefits each confers on mankind. It touches with light, scholastic legalism on many matters of serious contemporary interest: foreknowledge, music, Confession, papal missions, and so on. It is a learned work, highly accomplished in its style and in its humorous tone, which reaches no definite conclusion. The debate is to be submitted at the end to the judgement of one Nicholas of Guildford (probably the author); a certain John of Guildford (fl. c.1255) has also been proposed as author.

OXFORD, Edward De Vere, 17th earl of (1550–1604), married Lord Burleigh's daughter, and high hopes were placed on him as a courtier and patron, but they were dissipated by his capricious and quarrelsome temperament. His most famous quarrel was with *Sidney, whom, according to *Greville, he addressed as 'puppy' in a dispute at the tennis court in 1579. One of the 15 or so surviving poems attributed to him is entitled 'Love compared to a tennis playe'. T. J. Looney identified him in 1920 as the author of Shakespeare's plays, and a sizeable body of 'Oxfordians' have since built on this claim.

OXFORD, Robert, 1st earl of, see HARLEY, R.

Oxford and Cambridge Magazine, The, a periodical of the year 1856, of which twelve monthly numbers appeared, financed mainly by W. *Morris. Among its (anonymous) contributors were Morris and Burne-Jones (of Oxford), and Henry Lushington (1812–55) of Cambridge, and by invitation D. G. *Rossetti.

Oxford English Dictionary, The. The scheme of 'a completely new English Dictionary' was conceived in 1858, chiefly as the result of the reading of two papers 'On some Deficiencies in our English Dictionaries' by Dr R. C. *Trench to the *Philological Society in 1857. Herbert Coleridge (1830–61), and after him Dr F. J. *Furnivall, were the first editors. Their work consisted mainly in the collection of materials, and it was not until Dr J. A. H. *Murray took the matter up in 1878 that the preparation of the Dictionary began to take active form. The first part (A–Ant) was published in 1884 and it was finished in 1928, 70 years from the inception of the undertaking. At Murray's death, T had been reached. His co-editors were Dr H. *Bradley (from 1888), Dr W. A. *Craigie (from 1901), and Dr C. T. *Onions (from 1914).

The essential feature of the Dictionary is its historical method, by which the meaning and form of the words are traced from their earliest appearance on the basis of an immense number of quotations, collected by more than 800 voluntary workers. The Dictionary contains a record of 414,825 words, whose history is illustrated by 1,827,306 quotations. A supplement of 876 pages appeared in 1933. In 1957 work began, under the editorship of R. W. *Burchfield, on the new supplement, superseding that of 1933: *A Supplement to the Oxford English Dictionary* contains a record of approximately 120,000 words. Its four volumes appeared in 1972, 1976, 1982, and 1986. The original title of the main work was 'A New English Dictionary on Historical Principles' (abbreviated as *NED*). The title *The Oxford English Dictionary* first appeared in the reprint of 1933.

Oxford Gazette, The, was the first real newspaper, other than a newsletter, to be published in England. It appeared in Nov. 1665, and was started by H. *Muddiman. It became the *London Gazette* in 1666. It survives now as a record of official appointments, notices of bankruptcy, etc., having passed in 1923 into the keeping of the Stationery Office.

Oxford Movement, or Tractarian Movement, a movement of thought and doctrine within the Church of England, centred at Oxford, the impulse of which was the Assize Sermon on National Apostasy preached by *Keble in 1833. This criticized the prevalent Erastian and latitudinarian tendencies of the Anglican church, and generated an investigation into the nature of the church. The movement aimed to defend the Church of England as a divine institution with an independent spiritual status, and to revive the High Church traditions of the 17th cent. Keble's sermon inspired *Newman, R. H. *Froude, and others to launch their series *Tracts for the Times* in 1833 (which gave the Tractarian movement its name); the series attracted the influential support of *Pusey. It was Newman's famous Tract XC (1841) on the compatibility of the Thirty-nine Articles with Roman Catholic theology that brought the Tractarians under official ban, but hostility had already been aroused by the publication of the first volumes of Froude's *Literary Remains* in 1838, with its strictures on the Reformation. W. G. *Ward's *The Ideal of a Christian Church* (1844), with its praise of the Roman Catholic church, intensified hostility, and led to suspicions that the Tractarians (and principally Newman) were subversively leading their followers towards Rome. Newman himself became a Roman Catholic in 1845, a decision which dealt a severe blow to the unity of the movement. There is a remarkable history of the movement by R. W. *Church (1891); see also Newman's *Apologia pro Vita Sua* (1864) and the autobiography of I. *Williams.

The impact of the Tractarians on intellectual, religious, and cultural life was immense. In literary terms, the revival of interest in the medieval and 17th-cent. church influenced *Tennyson, W. *Morris and the *Pre-Raphaelites, C. *Rossetti and C. M. *Yonge, among others; it also added strength to the revival of *Gothic architecture associated with *Pugin.

Oxford University Press, a publishing and printing business owned by the University and directed by its Delegates of the Press, of whom the Vice-Chancellor is *ex officio* chairman. Its aims are to produce books of religious, scholarly, and educational value, and, its surplus profits being devoted to financing the editing and production of unremunerative works of this kind, its status is that of a charity.

Printing in Oxford by independent craftsmen began in the 15th cent. (see UNIVERSITY PRESSES), and in 1584 one of these was appointed 'Printer to the University'. This title was borne by a succession of printers in the 17th cent. and was revived in 1925 for the head of the printing department of the Press. One press at Oxford was excepted from the prohibition of printing outside London by a decree of the Star Chamber in 1586, and in 1632 a royal charter allowed the University three presses and to print and sell 'all manner of books'. *Laud in 1634 bound the University to provide itself with a printing house; but a press under its immediate control did not come into being until 1690. In the meantime *Fell had won an international reputation for Oxford books by his exercise of the University's privilege of printing, let to him in 1672.

Since then the Press has produced such famous books as *Clarendon's *History* (1702), the Revised Version of the English Bible (1885), and *The Oxford English Dictionary*, completed in 1928.

The copyright in Clarendon's works, once very profitable, is secured to the University in perpetuity, and in his honour the building to which the Press moved in 1829 was named 'The Clarendon Press'. This is the imprint given to learned books published under the supervision of the Secretary to the Delegates at Oxford.

Oxford Sausage, The, see WARTON, T.

Oxymoron, from two Greek words meaning 'sharp', 'dull', a rhetorical figure by which two incongruous or contradictory terms are united in an expression so as to give it point; e.g. 'Faith unfaithful kept him falsely true' (Tennyson, *Idylls of the King*).

P

Pacchiarotto *and How He Worked in Distemper: with other poems,* a collection of 19 poems, in various metres, by R. *Browning, published 1876.

Padlock, The, a comic opera by *Bickerstaffe, with music by *Dibdin, performed with much success in 1768.

It recounts the unsuccessful efforts of elderly Don Diego to protect his young prospective bride from the attentions of other suitors; the most notable character is the Negro servant, Mungo, the first black-faced comedian of the London stage, a part originally played by Dibdin himself.

Paean, a song of thanksgiving for deliverance from evil or danger, addressed usually to Apollo who, as god of healing, was given the name Paean. Later the word is used for a shout or song of triumph.

Paeon, see METRE.

Page, Mrs Page, and Anne Page, their daughter, characters in Shakespeare's *The Merry Wives of Windsor*.

PAGET, Violet, see LEE, V.

PAINE, Thomas (1737–1809), son of a Quaker staymaker of Thetford. He was dismissed as an exciseman in 1774 for agitating for an increase in excisemen's pay. He sailed for America, where he published his pamphlet *Common Sense* (1776) and a series of pamphlets, *The Crisis* (1776–83), encouraging American independence and resistance to England, he also wrote against slavery and in favour of the emancipation of women. In 1787 he returned to England (via France), and published in 1791 the first part of *The Rights of Man* in reply to Burke's *Reflections on the *Revolution in France*; the second part appeared in 1792. Paine left for France, to avoid arrest, where he was warmly received and elected a member of the Convention. However, he opposed the execution of Louis XVI, was imprisoned for nearly a year, and narrowly escaped the guillotine. *The Age of Reason* (1793) greatly increased the violent hatred with which he was regarded in England. He returned to America in 1802, where his views on religion and his opposition to Washington had made him unpopular. His writings became a textbook for the radical party in England; his connection with the American struggle and the French revolution gave him a unique position as an upholder of the politics of the *Enlightenment.

PAINTER, George, see BIOGRAPHY.

PAINTER, William, see PALACE OF PLEASURE.

Pair of Blue Eyes, A, a novel by T. *Hardy, published 1873.

The scene is the northern coast of Cornwall. Stephen Smith, a young architect, comes to Endelstow to restore the church tower and falls in love with Elfride Swancourt, the blue-eyed daughter of the vicar. Her father is incensed that someone of Stephen's humble origin should claim his daughter. Elfride and Stephen run away together, but Elfride vacillates over marriage, and Stephen, hoping to better himself, accepts a post in India. Henry Knight, Stephen's friend and patron, then meets Elfride, and after she has saved his life on a cliff they become engaged. However, Knight is horrified to hear of Elfride's truancy with Stephen. He harshly breaks off the engagement. Eventually he and Stephen meet; Stephen learns that Elfride is still unmarried and Knight learns the innocent facts of her past escapade with Stephen. But the train which carries them both to Cornwall is also carrying Elfride's dead body. They learn when they arrive at Endelstow that she has died, and that she had recently married Lord Luxellian.

Palace of Pleasure, a collection of translations into English of 'Pleasant Histories and excellent Novelles . . . out of divers good and commendable Authors', made by William Painter (*c.* 1525–95), Clerk of the Ordnance, and published in 1566, 1567, and 1575. Many of the translations are from *Boccaccio, Bandello, and Marguerite of Navarre (see HEPTAMERON), but Painter also drew on *Herodotus, *Livy, and *Gellius. The book provided a storehouse of plots for Elizabethan writers, especially dramatists.

Paladins, The, in the cycle of *Charlemagne legends, the twelve peers who accompanied the king. The origin of the conception is seen in the *Chanson de Roland* (see ROLAND), where the twelve peers are merely an association of particularly brave warriors, under the leadership of Roland and *Oliver, who all perish at Roncesvalles. From the Spanish war the idea was transported by later writers to other parts of the cycle, and Charlemagne is found always surrounded by twelve peers. The names of the twelve are differently stated by different authors; but Roland and Oliver figure in all the enumerations. Among the best known are *Otuel, Fierabras or *Ferumbras, and *Ogier the Dane. Since the 16th cent. the word is applied to any great knightly champion (cf. word 'Peer').

Palamon and Arcite, the two Theban princes whose love for Emelye is the subject of Chaucer's 'The Knight's Tale' (see CANTERBURY TALES, 1), following the *Teseida* of *Boccaccio. The tale was paraphrased in heroic couplets by *Dryden under the title 'Palamon and Arcite'. It is also the subject of *The Two Noble Kinsmen.

PALEY, William (1743–1805), one of the principal exponents of theological utilitarianism of which his *Moral and Political Philosophy* (1785), is the textbook; an attack on private property in Book III, drawing an analogy between human greed and the behaviour of a flock of pigeons, gave him his nickname 'Pigeon' Paley. In *Evidences of Christianity* (1794) and *Natural Theology* (1802) he finds proof of the existence of God in the design apparent in natural phenomena, and particularly in the mechanisms of the human body.

PALGRAVE, Francis Turner (1824–97), professor of poetry at Oxford, 1885–95. He is chiefly remembered for his anthology *The Golden Treasury of best songs and Lyrical poems in the English language* (1861; second series, 1897). In the selection for the first edition Palgrave was advised by his close friend *Tennyson; it contained no work by living poets, and is a reflection of the taste of the age (e.g. no *Donne and no *Blake, though work by these poets and later writings was added to subsequent editions). Palgrave compiled other anthologies and selections, and published several volumes of his own verse.

Palimpsest, from παλιν 'again', and ψηστός 'rubbed smooth', a manuscript in which a later writing is superimposed on an effaced earlier writing. Of frequent occurrence in the early Middle Ages because of the cost of parchment.

Palindrome, from παλίνδρομος, 'running back again', a word, verse, or sentence that reads the same forward or backwards, e.g.:

> Lewd did I live & evil I did dwel
> (Phillips, 1706)

and the Latin line descriptive of moths:

> In girum imus noctes et consumimur igni.

Palinode, from παλινωδία 'singing over again', a recantation. 'Palinode' is the name of the Catholic shepherd in the fifth eclogue of Spenser's *The Shepheardes Calender.

Palinurus, see CONNOLLY, C.

Palladis Tamia, see MERES, F.

Palliser Novels, The, a term used to describe the political novels of A. *Trollope, which are: *Can You Forgive Her?, *Phineas Finn, *The Eustace Diamonds, *Phineas Redux, The Prime Minister, and The Duke's Children.

Pall Mall Gazette, The, was founded in 1865 by Frederick Greenwood (1830–1909) and George *Smith to combine the features of a newspaper with the literary features of the *Spectator and the *Sunday Review. Its name was taken from Thackeray's *Pendennis, where Captain Shandon in the Marshalsea prepares the prospectus of 'The Pall Mall Gazette', 'written by gentlemen for gentlemen'. Its early contributors included *Trollope, Sir J. F. *Stephen, L. *Stephen, and M. *Arnold. J. *Morley took over as editor, to be succeeded (1883–9) by W. T. *Stead, whose sensational journalism altered the character of the paper.

Palmerin of England (Palmerin de Inglaterra), a chivalric romance attributed to the 16th-cent. Portuguese writer Francisco de Moraes.

The 'Palmerins' consist of eight books dealing with the exploits and loves of Palmerin d'Oliva, emperor of Constantinople, and his various descendants, of which Palmerin of England is the subject of the sixth. *Munday translated the Palmerin cycle into English (through a French intermediary), 1581–95. It was highly popular with the Elizabethan middle classes, and there are many references to Palmerin in the plays of the time (e.g. *The Knight of the Burning Pestle, where the vogue for such chivalric fantasies is mocked). A revised translation by *Southey appeared in 1807.

Palmerin of England and *Amadis of Gaul* were two romances of chivalry specially excepted from the holocaust of such works carried out by the curate and the barber in *Don Quixote.

Palomydes the Saracen, in Malory's *Morte D'Arthur, a prominent knight and great fighter who follows the *Questing Beast and who once abducts Iseult, for whom he entertains an unrequited and mostly selfless passion. He is the great friend of Tristram who has him christened at the end.

PALTOCK, Robert, author of *Peter Wilkins.

Pamela, the heir to the dukedom of Arcadia in the romance of *Sidney. Richardson took her name for the heroine of his first novel (below).

Pamela, or Virtue Rewarded, a novel by S. *Richardson (1740–1).

The first of Richardson's three novels, *Pamela*

consists, like them, entirely of letters and journals, of which Richardson presents himself as the 'editor'. He raised the *epistolary form of novel to a level hitherto unknown, and transformed it to display his own particular skills.

There are six correspondents in *Pamela*, but Pamela Andrews, the heroine, herself provides most of the letters and journals, with the 'hero', Mr B., having only two. Pamela is a young maidservant, whose mistress has just died when the story opens. The lady's son, Mr B., becomes enamoured of Pamela, and, taking a dishonourable advantage of her position, pursues her with his advances. She indignantly repels them, leaves the house, is pursued by B., and shows considerable astuteness in defending herself. Finally B., being much in love with her, comes to terms and decides to marry her.

Because of the success of *Pamela* and because of the number of forged continuations that began to appear, *Pamela, Part II* appeared in 1741. Here Pamela is exhibited, through various small and separate instances, as the perfect wife, patiently leading her profligate husband to reform; a devoted mother who brings about the penitence of the wicked. Much space is given over to discussion of moral, domestic, and general subjects.

Shamela (1741, almost certainly by *Fielding) vigorously mocked what the author regarded as the hypocritical morality of *Pamela*; and Fielding's *Joseph Andrews*, which begins as a parody of *Pamela*, appeared in 1742.

Pamphleteering, origins of. The word 'pamphlet' appears to derive, curiously, from the generalized use of the title of a popular 12th-cent. Latin love poem called *Pamphilus, seu de Amore*, which was adapted to 'Pamphilet'. *Orwell, in his introduction to *British Pamphleteers* (Vol. I, 1948), describes a pamphlet as 'a short piece of Polemical writing, printed in the form of a booklet and aimed at a large public', usually of 5,000–10,000 words, and without hard covers. Pamphleteering may be said to have started with the Reformation, and during the 16th cent. became widespread (see NASHE, DEKKER, and MARTIN MARPRELATE); J. *Knox's *First Blast of the Trumpet against the Monstrous Regiment* (i.e. 'government') *of Women* (1588) was perhaps the first British political pamphlet. In the 17th cent. the religious and political ferment that gave rise to the Civil War produced many thousands of pamphlets, some of high literary quality; *Milton's are perhaps the best known, but see also WINSTANLEY, OVERTON, WALWYN, CLARKSON, COPPE, LILBURNE, NEDHAM, and BERKENHEAD. *Tyranipocrit Discovered* and *Light Shining in Buckinghamshire* (1648) were both anonymous as were many others. These writers played an important part in the transition from the learned, allusive prose of men like *Donne, *Andrewes, and Sir T.

*Browne to the plain, clear, and colloquial style recommended by the *Royal Society. In the 18th cent., though important works in pamphlet form were produced by writers as considerable as *Defoe and *Swift, the rise of weekly periodicals tended to reduce the demand for this form of communication. The form was revived in the 19th cent. by the 'tracts' of the *Oxford Movement and the *Fabian Society.

Pancks, a character in Dickens's *Little Dorrit*.

Pandarus, in classical legend, a son of Lycaon who assisted the Trojans in their war against the Greeks. The role that he plays in *Chaucer's and Shakespeare's stories of Troilus and Criseyde (Cressida) was the invention of *Boccaccio in his *Filostrato* (where he is called Pandaro). In Boccaccio he is the cousin of Cressida. Chaucer changes him from her cousin to her uncle and guardian, increasing the sense of irresponsibility towards her in arranging the love affair. His role plays a striking part in the atmosphere of sourness in which the events of Shakespeare's play occur. The word 'pander' (as Shakespeare says: v. x. 34) derives from his role as go-between for Troilus and Criseyde.

Pandemonium, a word coined by *Milton, the abode of all the demons; a place represented by Milton (*Paradise Lost*, i. 756) as the capital of Hell, containing the council-chamber of the Evil Spirits.

Pandosto, or *The triumph of time*, a prose romance by R. *Greene published 1588. It is now best known as the source for *The Winter's Tale*.

Pandulph, Cardinal, in Shakespeare's *King John*, the papal legate.

Pangloss, Dr, (1) in *The Heir-at-Law* by G. *Colman the younger, a pompous pedant; (2) in *Voltaire's *Candide* he is a philosopher (based on *Leibniz) ridiculed for his optimism.

PANIZZI, Antonio (later Sir Anthony) (1797–1879), born in Italy, fled to England as a political exile in 1823. He became in 1856 principal librarian at the British Museum and was responsible for the preparation of a new catalogue and for the plans of the celebrated circular domed Reading Room which he opened personally in 1857.

PANKHURST, Emmeline and Christabel, see WOMEN'S SUFFRAGE.

Pantagruel, the second book (in chronological order of the narrative) of *Rabelais's great work, but the first to be written and published (1532). Pantagruel is presented as the son of *Gargantua and Badebec, daughter of the king of Amaurotes of Utopia (a reference to Sir T. *More's work). The book tells of his birth, education, and life, satirizing the pious advice with burlesque. The narrative, which is continued in three further books, provides occasion for abundant satire directed against monks and schoolmen, the papacy, and the magistrature.

Pantaloon, adapted from the Italian *Pantalone,* 'a kind of mask on the Italian stage, representing the Venetian'. The Venetian character in the *commedia dell'arte* was represented as a lean and foolish old man, wearing slippers, pantaloons, and spectacles. In the Victorian pantomime or harlequinade he was represented as a foolish and vicious old man, the butt of the clown's jokes, and his abettor in his tricks [OED].

Pantisocracy, see COLERIDGE, S. T.

Pantomime, (1) originally a Roman actor, who performed in dumb show, representing by mimicry various characters and scenes; (2) an English dramatic performance, originally consisting of action without speech, but in its further development consisting of a dramatized traditional fairy-tale, with singing, dancing, acrobatics, clowning, topical jokes, a transformation scene, and certain stock roles, especially the 'principal boy' (i.e. hero) acted by a woman and the 'dame' acted by a man. (See MIME.)

Paolo and Francesca. Francesca, daughter of Giovanni da Polenta, count of Ravenna, was given in marriage by him to Giovanni Malatesta, of Rimini. She fell in love with Paolo, her husband's brother, and, their relations being discovered, the two lovers were put to death in 1289. *Dante, at the end of the fifth canto of the *Inferno,* relates his conversation with Francesca. The story was the subject of Leigh Hunt's poem *The Story of Rimini* and of Tchaikovsky's symphonic fantasy *Francesca da Rimini.*

Paper Money Lyrics, burlesque poems by *Peacock, ridiculing political economists and bankers, published 1837.

Pappe with an hatchet, the title of a tract contributed in 1589 by *Lyly to the Marprelate controversy (see MARTIN MARPRELATE) on the side of the bishops; it is a mixture of abuse and ribaldry.

PARACELSUS (Theophrast Bombast Von Hohenheim) (1493–1541). Swiss-born physician. He was attracted to alchemy, astrology, and mysticism, and flouted the traditional methods of *Avicenna and *Galen. Although frequently labelled a charlatan, he had many followers and exerted considerable influence, particularly through the *Rosicrucian move-

ment. He believed in the divine alchemy of the Creation, in which God (the Divine Artificer) separated by chemical process the elements from the primal matter, the Mysterium Magnum: he supported the notion of the four Aristotelian elements (earth, air, fire, water), and added the concept of the 'three principles' of sulphur, mercury, and salt. The elements were inhabited by spirits—the air by sylphs, the water by nymphs or undines, the earth by gnomes, the fire by salamanders—and by many other spiritual or supernatural beings, such as syrens, nenuphar, lorins, etc. (Paracelsus: *De Nymphis, Pygmiis, Salamandris, De Homonculis et Monstris,* etc., *Works,* 1658). This mythological machinery was borrowed by Pope, via the Rosicrucians, in *The Rape of the Lock.* Paracelsus was the subject of a poem by *Browning (below).

Paracelsus, a dramatic poem in blank verse by R. *Browning, published 1835. The career of the historical *Paracelsus serves Browning, despite his claim to the contrary, as a stalking-horse for his own exploration of the processes of the creative imagination, in particular the conflict between 'Love' (self-forgetting) and 'Knowledge' (self-assertion) in the mind of the artist.

Parade's End, a tetralogy by F. M. *Ford, now known under this collective title, but originally published as *Some Do Not . . .* (1924), *No More Parades* (1925), *A Man Could Stand Up* (1926), and *Last Post* (1928).

The hero is Christopher Tietjens of Groby, a Tory Yorkshire squire married to the neurotic, beautiful, tormenting, unfaithful Catholic, Sylvia. In the first volume Christopher agrees to take back his wife and to conceal her adultery; meanwhile he himself falls in love with a young suffragette schoolteacher, Valentine Wannop. The next two volumes cover his wartime experiences and his resolution, on Armistice Day, to leave Sylvia and make Valentine his mistress. In *Last Post* Valentine is pregnant, Christopher is making his living by restoring antiques, and his older brother Mark is dying; Sylvia eventually agrees to divorce Christopher. The subject of the novel appears to be the breakdown of the accepted standards of the old world and the necessary emergence of a new order.

Paradise Lost, an epic poem in blank verse by *Milton, originally in ten books, subsequently rearranged in twelve, first printed 1667.

Milton formed the intention of writing a great epic poem, as he tells us, as early as 1639. A list of possible subjects, some of them scriptural, some from British history, written in his own hand about 1640–1, still exists, with drafts of the scheme of a poem on 'Paradise Lost'. The work was not, however, begun in earnest until 1658, and it was finished according to *Aubrey, in 1663.

Book I. The poet, invoking the 'Heav'nly Muse', states his theme, the Fall of Man through disobedience, and his aim, which is no less than to 'justifie the wayes of God to men'. He then presents the defeated archangel Satan, with *Beelzebub, his second-in-command, and his rebellious angels, lying on the burning lake of hell. Satan awakens his legions, rouses their spirits, and summons a council. The palace of Satan, *Pandemonium, is built.

Book II. The council debates whether another battle for the recovery of Heaven be hazarded. Satan undertakes to visit it alone, and passes through Hell-gates, guarded by Sin and Death, and passes upward through the realm of Chaos.

Book III. Milton invokes celestial light to illumine the 'ever-during dark' of his own blindness, then describes God, who sees Satan's flight towards our world, and foretells his success and the fall and punishment of man. The Son of God offers himself as a ransom, is accepted, and exalted as the Saviour. Satan alights on the outer convex of our universe, 'a Limbo large and broad, since call'd | The Paradise of Fools'. He finds the stairs leading up to Heaven, descends to the Sun, disguises himself as 'a stripling Cherube', and in this shape is directed to Earth by Uriel, where he alights on Mount Niphates in Armenia.

Book IV. Satan journeys on towards the Garden of Eden, where he first sees Adam and Eve 'in naked Majestie', and overhears their discourse about the forbidden Tree of Knowledge. He resolved to tempt them to disobey the prohibition but is discovered by the guardian angels and expelled from the garden by their commander, Gabriel.

Book V. Eve relates to Adam the disquieting dream of temptation which Satan had inspired. Raphael, sent by God, comes to Paradise, warns Adam, and enjoins obedience. Raphael, at Adam's request, relates how Satan, inspired by hatred and envy of the newly anointed Messiah, inspired his legions to revolt.

Book VI. Raphael continues his narrative, telling how Michael and Gabriel were sent to fight against Satan. After indecisive battles the Son of God himself, alone, attacked the hosts of Satan, and, driving them to the verge of Heaven, forced them to leap down through Chaos into the deep.

Book VII. Raphael gives an account of God's decision to send his Son to create another world from the vast abyss. He describes the six days of creation, ending with the creation of man.

Book VIII. Adam inquires concerning the motions of the heavenly bodies, and is answered 'doubtfully'. (The controversy regarding the Ptolemaic and Copernican systems was at its height when *Paradise Lost* was written, and Milton was unable to decide between them, as seen in Bk X, 668 ff.) Adam relates what he remembers since his own creation and with Raphael talks of the relations between the sexes, then, with a final warning to 'take heed least Passion sway | Thy Judgment', Raphael departs.

Book IX. Milton describes Satan's entry into the body of the serpent, in which form he finds Eve, she having insisted, despite Adam's warnings, on pursuing her labours alone. He persuades her to eat of the Tree of Knowledge. Eve relates to Adam what has passed and brings him of the fruit. Adam, recognizing that she is doomed, resolves to perish with her and eats the fruit, and after initial intoxication in their lost innocence, they cover their nakedness and fall to mutual accusation.

Book X. God sends his Son to judge the transgressors and he pronounces his sentence. Sin and Death resolve to come to this world, and make a broad highway thither from Hell. Satan returns to Hell and announces his victory, whereupon he and his angels are temporarily transformed into serpents. Adam at first reproaches Eve, but then, reconciled, they together resolve to seek mercy from the Son of God.

Book XI. The Son of God, seeing their penitence, intercedes. God decrees that they must leave Paradise, and sends down Michael to carry out his command. Eve laments; Adam pleads not to be banished but Michael reassures him that God is omnipresent, then unfolds to him the future, revealing to him the consequences of his original sin in the death of Abel and the future miseries of mankind, ending with the Flood and the new Covenant.

Book XII. Michael relates the subsequent history of the Old Testament, then describes the coming of the Messiah, his incarnation, death, resurrection, and ascension, which leads Adam to rejoice over so much good sprung from his own sin. Michael also foretells the corrupt state of the Church until the Second Coming. Resolved on obedience and submission, and assured that they may possess 'a Paradise within', they are led out of the Garden.

Paradise Regained, an epic poem in four books by *Milton, published 1671.

It is a sequel to *Paradise Lost*, and deals exclusively with the temptation of Christ in the wilderness. According to the poet's conception, whereas Paradise was lost by the yielding of Adam and Eve to Satan's temptation, so it was regained by the resistance of the Son of God to the temptation of the same spirit. Satan is here represented not in the majestic lineaments of *Paradise Lost*, but as a cunning, smooth, and dissembling creature, a 'Spirit unfortunate', as he describes himself. There is a comparative scarcity of similes and ornament, and only a vivid and ingenious expansion of the biblical texts.

Paradiso, of Dante, see DIVINA COMMEDIA.

Paradyse of Dainty Devises, The, a collection of works by minor poets of the 1560s and 70s compiled by R. *Edwards, published 1576. They include Lord *Vaux, the earl of *Oxford, *Churchyard, and William Hunnis.

Parasitaster, The, or *The Fawn,* a comedy by J. *Marston, published 1606.

Hercules, the widowed duke of Ferrara, wishes his son Tiberio to marry Dulcimel, the daughter of a neighbouring prince. To defeat his unwillingness he declares that he will marry Dulcimel himself. He sends Tiberio to negotiate the marriage: Dulcimel falls in love with Tiberio and wins him.

Pardiggle, Mrs, in Dickens's *Bleak House,* a lady 'distinguished for rapacious benevolence'.

'Pardoner's Tale, The', see CANTERBURY TALES, 14.

Paridell, in Spenser's *Faerie Queene,* a false and libertine knight (Bks III. viii, ix, x, and IV. i, ii) who consorts with *Duessa and elopes with Hellenore, the wife of *Malbecco.

Paris, Count, in Shakespeare's *Romeo and Juliet* a *Capulet and suitor of *Juliet.

PARIS, Matthew (d. 1259), monk and historian, entered the monastery of St Albans in 1217, succeeding *Roger of Wendover as chronicler, and compiling the *Chronica Majora,* his greatest work, there from 1235 to 1259. He extends the range of the chronicle to include foreign events; the work is outstanding for its expressive liveliness and its great historical value. He also wrote the *Historia Minor* (or *Historia Anglorum*), a summary of events in England from 1200 to 1250, and the *Vitae Abbatum S. Albani,* the lives of the first 23 abbots up to 1255, the last two or three of which were composed by him.

'Parish Register, The', a poem by *Crabbe, published in 1807. It relates the memories of a country parson and includes the terrible account, written in stanzas (and possibly under the influence of opium) in 'Sir Eustace Grey', of a patient in a madhouse.

Parisina, a poem by *Byron, published 1816.

Paris Sketch Book, The, *Thackeray's first full-length book, published 1840, a collection of articles and stories.

PARK, Mungo (1771–1806), explored the course of the Niger and became famous by his vivid account of his travels, *Travels in the Interior District of Africa . . . in the Years 1795, 1796 and 1797* (1799). He perished at Boussa in a conflict with the natives.

PARKER, Dorothy (Rothschild) (1893–1967), American humorist and journalist, legendary for her instant wit and for her satirical verses; she wrote sketches and short stories, many of them published in the *New Yorker* and various collections.

PARKER, Matthew (1504–75), was in 1544 elected master of Corpus Christi College, Cambridge, where he reformed the library, to which he was to bequeath his fine manuscripts. He fled to Frankfurt-on-Main during Queen Mary's reign and reluctantly accepted the archbishopric of Canterbury on Elizabeth's accession. He identified himself with the party (afterwards known as the Anglican party) which sought to establish a *via media* between Romanism and Puritanism. From 1563 to 1568 he was occupied with the production of the Bishop's Bible (see BIBLE, THE ENGLISH), his most distinguished service to the theological studies of the day. To his efforts we are indebted for the earliest editions of *Asser, *Ælfric, the *Flores Historiarum* of Matthew of Westminster, *Paris, and other early chroniclers.

PARKINSON, John (1567–1650), king's herbalist, author of *Paradisi in sole Paradisus terrestris* (1629), with woodcuts; also of a great herbal, *Theatrum botanicum* (1640).

PARKMAN, Francis (1823–93), American historian, travelled in Europe, then journeyed out to Wyoming to study Indian life, giving an account of his journey in *The Oregon Trail* (1849). His history of the struggle of the English and French for dominion in North America was published in a series of studies, beginning with his *History of the Conspiracy of the Pontiac* (1851) and continuing through several volumes, concluding with *A Half-Century of Conflict* (1892).

Parleyings With Certain People of Importance in Their Day, a volume of poems in blank verse by R. *Browning, published 1887. The phrase 'certain people of importance' derives from a passage in *Dante's *Vita Nuova,* Browning refers to a number of obscure historical figures whose works he has studied in his youth. Each of these figures is matched by a contemporary of Browning's, and Browning 'parleys' with them in a renewed consideration of the central topics of art and life. The collection is of unique value to an understanding both of the sources of Browning's art and of the mature processes of that art.

Parliament of Bees, The, see DAY, J.

Parliament of Fowls, The, a dream-poem by *Chaucer in 699 lines of rhyme-royal, possibly written between 1372 and 1386. It centres on a conference of birds to choose their mates on St Valentine's Day.

The poet falls asleep after a prologue in which he makes the Boethian lament that he has not what he wants, and has what he does not want. He then has a vision of a garden of the kind which is the setting for the *Roman de la Rose* and in which the goddess Nature presides over the choosing of mates. Three tercel eagles pay court to a beautiful 'formel' (female) and there follows a long dispute about the criteria for success in a love suit, the argument of which centres on the opposition between the courtly love approach of the noble eagles and the pragmatism of the duck (whose worldly advice has been called 'bourgeois'). The debate is unresolved, and the birds agree to assemble again a year later to decide. The poem has rightly been called one of the finest occasional poems in the language.

Parnassians, a group of French poets, headed by Leconte de Lisle, who sought restraint, precision, and objectivity in poetry, in reaction to the emotional extravagances of Romanticism. Their name derives from the three collections of their work published under the title *Le Parnasse contemporain*, in 1866, 1871, and 1876.

Parnassus Plays, The, the name given to a trilogy produced between 1598 and 1602 by students of St John's College, Cambridge, consisting of *The Pilgrimage to Parnassus* and *The Returne from Parnassus*, the latter apparently in two parts. Authorship has not been established; they have been attributed to J. *Day and, more recently, to John Weever of Queen's and J. *Hall. They treat amusingly of the attempts of a group of young men (one apparently modelled on *Nashe) to resist temptation and to gain preferment or at least a livelihood, and are full of allusions to contemporary literature. In the third more satirical section the students are shown on their way to London, learning how to catch a patron or cheat a tradesman, and following menial occupations, which they finally abandon in discouragement and 'returne' to Cambridge. They were first published as a whole in the edition by J. B. Leishman (1949).

PARNELL, Thomas (1679–1718), was archdeacon of Clogher and a friend of *Swift and *Pope (to whose *Iliad* he contributed an introductory essay). He was a member of the *Scriblerus Club. His 'Hymn to Contentment' was published in *Steele's *Poetical Miscellanies* (1714) and his mock-heroic *Homer's Battle of the Frogs and Mice with the Remarks of Zoilus* in 1717 (see BATRACHOMYOMACHIA), but most of his work was published posthumously by Pope in 1721. His poems include 'The Hermit', a moral narrative in heroic couplets, and 'Night-Piece on Death', in fluent octosyllabics, perhaps the first

of the 18th-cent. *graveyard poems which in *Goldsmith's view inspired 'all those night-pieces and churchyard scenes that have since appeared' (Goldsmith's *Life of Parnell*, 1770).

Parody, a form of literary composition in which an author's characteristics are ridiculed by imitation and exaggeration. True parody, it has been said, implies a sound and valid criticism of the original. *Swinburne, for example, was able to parody effectively his own excessive use of alliteration. Famous English parodists have been Horace and James Smith in their *Rejected Addresses*; C. S. *Calverley, and Sir J. *Squire.

Parolles, in Shakespeare's *All's Well That Ends Well*, the cowardly follower of Bertram.

Paronomasia, a play on words, a kind of *pun.

PARR, Samuel (1747–1825), a fine Latin scholar, excelled as a writer of Latin epitaphs, and wrote that on Dr *Johnson in St Paul's.

PARRY, Sir William Edward (1790–1855), Arctic explorer, whose expeditions, undertaken between 1819 and 1825, are described in his three *Journals* of voyages for the discovery of a North-West Passage (pub. 1821, 1824, 1826) and in his *Narrative of an attempt to reach the North Pole, 1827* (1828).

Parsifal, see PERCEVAL.

Parson Lot, see KINGSLEY, C.

'Parson's Tale, The', see CANTERBURY TALES, 24.

Parthenophil and Parthenope, see BARNES, B.

PARTINGTON, Mrs, referred to by Sydney *Smith in his speech on the rejection of the *Reform Bill. He compares the attempts of the House of Lords to stop the progress of reform to the efforts of a Mrs Partington to keep out the Atlantic with a mop, during a great storm at Sidmouth in 1824.

B. P. Shillaber (1814–90), American humorist, published in 1854 the *Life and Sayings of Mrs Partington*, a benevolent village gossip reminiscent of an American Mrs *Malaprop.

Partlet, the hen in the tale of *Reynard the Fox and in Chaucer's 'The Nun's Priest's Tale' (*Canterbury Tales*, 20) as Pertelote. 'Sister Partlet with her hooded head' in Dryden's *The Hind and the Panther* stands for Catholic nuns.

Partridge, a character in Fielding's *Tom Jones*.

PARTRIDGE, John (1644–1715), the victim of a mystification by *Swift. See BICKERSTAFF and ALMANACS.

Parzifal, an epic by *Wolfram von Eschenbach, composed early in the 13th cent. on the subject of the legend of *Perceval and the Holy *Grail. (See also TITUREL.)

Pasquil, Pasquin. 'Pasquino' or 'Pasquillo' was the name popularly given to a mutilated statue disinterred at Rome in 1501, and set up by Cardinal Caraffa at the corner of his palace near the Piazza Navona. It became the custom to salute Pasquin on St Mark's day in Latin verses. In process of time these *pasquinate* or pasquinades tended to become satirical, and the term began to be applied, not only in Rome but in other countries, to satirical compositions and lampoons, political, ecclesiastical, or personal.

PASQUIN, Anthony, see WILLIAMS, J.

Passage to India, A, a novel by E. M. *Forster, published 1924.

The story is told in three parts, I, *Mosque,* II, *Caves,* III, *Temple,* and concerns Aziz, a young Muslim doctor, whose friendliness and enthusiasm for the British turn to bitterness and disillusionment when his pride is injured. A sympathy springs up between him and the elderly Mrs Moore, who has come to visit her son, the City Magistrate. Accompanying her is Adela Quested, young, earnest, and charmless, who longs to know the 'real' India and tries to disregard the taboos and snobberies of the British circle. Aziz organizes an expedition for the visitors to the famous Caves of Marabar, where an unforeseen development plunges him into disgrace and rouses deep antagonism between the two races. Adela accuses him of insulting her in the Caves, he is committed to prison and stands trial. Adela withdraws her charge, but Aziz turns furiously away from the British, towards a Hindu–Muslim entente. In the third part of the book he has moved to a post in a native state, and is bringing up his family in peace, writing poetry and reading Persian. He is visited by his friend Mr Fielding, the former Principal of the Government College, an intelligent, hard-bitten man. They discuss the future of India, and Aziz prophesies that only when the British are driven out can he and Fielding really be friends. Among the many characters is Professor Godbole, the detached and saintly Brahmin who is the innocent cause of the contretemps, and who makes his final appearance in supreme tranquillity at the festival of the Hindu temple.

Passetyme of Pleasure, or *The Historie of Graunde Amoure and La Bell Pucel,* an allegorical poem in rhyme-royal and decasyllabic couplets by *Hawes, printed by *Wynkyn de Worde in 1509. It is an allegory of life in the form of a romance of chivalry. It contains a well-known couplet in perhaps its original form:

For though the day be never so longe,
At last the belles ryngeth to evensonge.

'Passing of Arthur, The', see MORTE D'ARTHUR.

Passionate Pilgrim, The, an unauthorized anthology of poems by various authors, published by *Jaggard in 1599, and attributed on the title-page to Shakespeare, but containing only a few authentic poems by him.

Past and Present, see CARLYLE, T.

PASTERNAK, Boris Leonidovich (1890–1960), Russian poet and prose writer. His worldwide fame is based on his novel *Doctor Zhivago* (1957), a work which he intended to be his testament, a witness to the experience of the Russian intelligentsia before, during, and after the Revolution. *Doctor Zhivago* was not officially published in the USSR until 1987. Pasternak was awarded the *Nobel Prize for literature in 1958.

Pastiche, a literary composition made up from various authors or sources, or in imitation of the style of another author; or a picture made up of fragments pieced together or copied with modification from an original, or in professed imitation of the style of another artist: the imitative intention is now the most usual meaning.

Paston Letters, The, a collection of letters preserved by the Pastons, a well-to-do Norfolk family, written between *c.*1420 and 1504. They concern three generations of the family, and most were written in the reigns of Henry VI, Edward IV, and Richard III. They are unique as historical material, showing the violence and anarchy of 15th-cent. England and the domestic conditions in which a family of this class lived and are of great value for the evidence they give of the language of their time.

Pastoral, a form of escape literature concerned with country pleasures, which is found in poetry, drama, and prose fiction. Its earliest examples appear in the *Idylls* of *Theocritus in which shepherds lead a sunlit, idealized existence of love and song. The eclogues of *Virgil and Longus' romance *Daphnis and Chloe blended the idealization with a more authentic picture of country life, and Virgil added an important new feature to the tradition in making his poems a vehicle for social comment. Neglected during the Middle Ages, the pastoral reappeared during the Renaissance when *Petrarch and his imitators composed eclogues in Latin and in the vernaculars. It was with the prose romance (*Sannazar, *Cervantes, *Sidney, D'Urfé), and the drama that pastoral attained its peak of popularity: *Tasso's *Aminto* (1581), *Guarini's *Il Pastor Fido* (1590, which served as a model for

Fletcher's *The Faithful Shepherdess*), Lodge's *Rosalynde* (the chief source of *As You Like It*), Jonson's *The Sad Shepherd*, and Milton's *Comus*. In the 17th cent. the Theocritean vision gave place to a more realistic dream of enjoying a rural retreat. Poets like James *Thomson extolled country pleasures and represented rural trades as enjoyable, until *Crabbe showed that their descriptions were divorced from reality, and *Wordsworth taught men to seek comfort in a Nature endowed with visionary power. The pastoral in its traditional form died with the rise of *Romanticism.

Pastorella, in Spenser's *Faerie Queene* (VI. ix–xii), a shepherdess, loved by Coridon the shepherd and by Sir Calidore.

PATER, Walter Horatio (1839–94), educated at The Queen's College, Oxford, he became a fellow of Brasenose in 1864 and lived with his unmarried sisters first at Oxford, then in London, in a style much influenced by the *Pre-Raphaelites: among his friends were *Swinburne, *Rosetti, the Humphry *Wards, and the Mark *Pattisons. He achieved recognitions through *Studies in the History of the Renaissance* (1873), which included essays on Winckelmann and the then neglected Botticelli, and his celebrated evocation of the Mona Lisa in his essay describing her as one 'who has learned the secrets of the grave'. The volume had a profound influence on the undergraduates of the day and was acclaimed by *Wilde as 'the holy writ of beauty'. *Marius the Epicurean* (1885), a fictional biography set in the days of Marcus Aurelius, reflected his responses to paganism, Christianity, and Rome. *Imaginary Portraits*, historical fantasies on a favourite theme of early promise and early death, appeared in 1887, and with *Appreciations: with an Essay on Style* (1889) Pater was widely acknowledged as a master of English prose. *Plato and Platonism* (1893) collected his earlier lectures. His lecture on Mérimée (1890), his two short historical romances, 'Emerald Uthwart' (1892) and 'Apollo in Picardy' (1893), and his unfinished *Gaston de Latour* (1896), clearly reveal a preoccupation with the cruelty, beauty, and religious sensibility of a largely imaginary 'impassioned past'. (See also ART FOR ART'S SAKE.)

Pathetic fallacy, a phrase coined by *Ruskin in 'Of the Pathetic Fallacy' (*Modern Painters*, III, 1856, ch. 12), indicating the tendency of writers and artists to ascribe human emotions and sympathies to nature. The technique was extensively used in the late 18th and 19th cents by *Goethe, *Gray, *Collins, *Cowper, *Wordsworth, and *Shelley, and *Tennyson.

Pathfinder, The, see COOPER, J. F.

Path to Rome, The, see BELLOC, H.

Patience, an alliterative poem in 531 lines from the second half of the 14th cent., the only manuscript of which is the famous Cotton Nero A x (see PEARL). It tells in a vigorous and humorous way the story of Jonah and his trials sent by God.

Patience, an opera by *Gilbert and *Sullivan produced in 1881, a deliberate satire on the *Aesthetic Movement, in which *Bunthorne is said to be modelled on *Wilde and Grosvenor on *Swinburne.

Patient Grissil, a comedy by *Dekker in collaboration with *Chettle and Haughton, printed 1603.
The marquess of Salucia, smitten with the beauty of Grissil, the virtuous daughter of a poor basket-maker, makes her his bride. Wishing to try her patience, he subjects her to a series of humiliations and cruelties. The play contains the well-known songs 'Art thou poore yet hast thou golden slumbers, | O sweet content' and 'Golden slumbers kisse your eyes'.
The same subject is treated in Chaucer's 'Clerk's Tale' (see CANTERBURY TALES, 9). It was taken originally from the *Decameron* (Day 10, Tale 10).

PATMORE, Coventry Kersey Dighton (1823–96), published his first volume, *Poems*, in 1844. His work was much admired by the *Pre-Raphaelites, and he contributed to *The Germ*. In 1847 he married his first wife, Emily, who inspired his sequence of poems *The Angel in the House* (1854–63); together the Patmores represented an image of the ideal Victorian couple, and in this role entertained many eminent literary figures. Emily died in 1862. In 1864 he travelled to Rome, where he met his second wife Marianne, a Roman Catholic, and was himself converted to Catholicism. *The Unknown Eros* (1877) contains odes marked by an erotic mysticism, but also some more autobiographical pieces (now the most anthologized), including 'The Azalea', 'Departure', and 'A Farewell', directly inspired by Emily's illness and death. Subsequent volumes included *Amelia, Tamerton church-tower, etc.* (1878) and *The Rod, The Root and The Flower* (1895), chiefly meditations on religious subjects.

PATON, Alan, see CRY, THE BELOVED COUNTRY.

PATRICK, St (*c*.389–*c*.461), the patron saint of Ireland, the son of a Roman decurion, was probably born in Scotland (or Wales). He was taken captive to Ireland when he was a child, and returned there voluntarily to preach the Gospel in 432. He journeyed through the whole of Ireland. Many stories, legends, and purported writings of his are current in Ireland.

Patriot King, The Idea of a, see BOLINGBROKE, H. ST J.

Patronage, Literary, traditionally, individual patronage, in the form of financial help, payment in kind, or more indirect assistance, exercised by royalty and the wealthy in return for dedications, entertainment, and prestige (as well as sometimes for more altruistic motives). Among innumerable examples, *Chaucer was assisted by *John of Gaunt, *Shakespeare by the earl of Southampton, *Donne by Sir Robert Drury, Dr *Johnson (belatedly) by the earl of *Chesterfield, *Wordsworth by Sir G. *Beaumont. The relationship was not always happy, as Johnson's definition of a patron as 'a wretch who supports with insolence and is paid with flattery' suggests, but it also directly inspired many fine works, such as *Jonson's tribute to the *Sidneys in his 'country house poem', 'To Penshurst' (see PENSHURST PLACE).

Patronage was also exercised through the gift of clerical livings; *Crabbe, befriended by the duke of Rutland, wrote of the possible misfortunes of such an experience in 'The Patron' (1812). Another indirect form of patronage was through subscription publishing (see PUBLISHING, SUBSCRIPTION).

Early in the 18th cent. new sources of support for authors began to develop. The circulating *libraries offered new openings for sales, and the rising success of *periodicals provided more work until well into the 20th cent. Patronage thus passed largely from men of individual wealth to men of professional power or commercial interest, such as literary editors and library owners and suppliers.

In 1790 the *Royal Literary Fund was founded and in 1837 the Civil List Act permitted the Treasury to assist authors by the grant of pensions (and by the occasional gift of a 'bounty'), provided they could demonstrate 'desert and distress'. Over 750 authors (and their dependants) have benefited, including *Wordsworth, *Tennyson, M. *Arnold, W. H. *Hudson, W. B. *Yeats, and T. F. *Powys. Pensions are awarded on the recommendation of the Royal Literary Fund, the *Society of Authors, the *Poetry Society, and other bodies. The *Arts Council also has provided grants to individual writers, as well as assisting literature in more indirect ways.

PATTEN, Brian, see LIVERPOOL POETS.

Patterne, Sir Willoughby, Eleanor and Isabel, Lieutenant, and Crossjay, characters in Meredith's *The Egoist.*

Pattieson, Peter, a schoolmaster, the imaginery author of *Tales of My Landlord* by Sir W. Scott.

PATTISON, Mark (1813–84), supporter of *Newman and the *Oxford Movement until Newman's departure for Rome. He was ordained priest in 1843 and became successively fellow, tutor, and rector of Lincoln College, Oxford. He was keenly interested in university reform, and travelled to Germany to study continental systems of education. His ideas on education can be found in *Oxford Studies* (1855) and *Suggestions on Academical Organisation* (1868). His best-known work was his classic biography *Isaac Casaubon 1559–1614* (1875). In 1861 he married Emilia Francis Strong (later Lady *Dilke) who was 27 years his junior; this, and the fact that both parties remained apart as far as convention would allow, gave rise to the famous theory that Mr and Mrs Pattison were the originals of Casaubon and Dorothea in G. Eliot's *Middlemarch.* His *Memoirs* (1885) are an important study of 19th-cent. Oxford.

Paul Emmanuel, a character in *Villette* by C. Brontë.

Paul Ferroll, see CLIVE, MRS C. A.

Paulina, in Shakespeare's *The Winter's Tale,* the wife of Antigonus.

Pauline, a poem in blank verse, the first poem to be published by R. *Browning; it appeared anonymously in 1833.

Paul's, Children of, a company of boy actors, recruited from the choristers of St Paul's Cathedral, whose performances enjoyed great popularity at the end of the 16th and beginning of the 17th cents. The Children of the Chapel, recruited from the choristers of the Chapel Royal, was another company enjoying popular favour at the same time. Their rivalry with men actors is alluded to in *Hamlet* (II. ii).

Paul's Letters to his Kinsfolk, a series of letters by Sir W. *Scott, published in 1816, describing his visit to Brussels, Waterloo, and Paris a few weeks after the battle of Waterloo. The account of the battle is interesting for the details it contains, some of them obtained from Napoleon's Belgian guide.

PAUL THE DEACON (Paulus Diaconus) (c.725–97), a Lombard who is one of the best chroniclers of the Dark Ages, author of the *Historia Lombardorum,* and an important figure in the Carolingian Renaissance.

PAYNE, John Howard (1791–1852), American actor, playwright, and song-writer, famous as author of the popular song 'Home, Sweet Home'.

PEACHAM, Henry (?1576–?1643), is remembered for *The Compleat Gentleman* (1622). Dr

*Johnson drew all the heraldic definitions in his dictionary from the 1661 edition.

Peachum, and his daughter Polly, characters in Gay's *The Beggar's Opera*.

PEACOCK, Thomas Love (1785–1866), satirist, essayist, and poet, was the son of a London glass merchant. He became a close friend of *Shelley and his *Memoirs of Shelley* appeared in 1858. Peacock's prose satires, *Headlong Hall* (1816), *Melincourt* (1817), and *Nightmare Abbey* (1818), survey the contemporary political and cultural scene from a Radical viewpoint. Many of Peacock's convivial arguments take place over a dinner table. The satiric debate is diversified by a romantic love-plot, increasingly important in *Crotchet Castle* (1831) and *Gryll Grange* (1860–1), and by amusing, clever song. Peacock assembles his characters in English country houses, and sends them on excursions into mountain and forest scenery. In *Maid Marian* (1822) and *The Misfortunes of Elphin* (1829) he varies his format by employing a historical setting. *Rhododaphne* (1818) is a fine and historically important poem; Peacock also wrote some touching lyrics, especially 'Long Night Succeeds thy little Day' (1826) and 'Newark Abbey' (1842). Of his satirical poems and squibs, *The Paper Money Lyrics* (1837) lampoon the dogmas of political economists and the malpractices of bankers. Peacock's sceptical attitude to the fashionable cult of the arts is apparent in his two most sustained critical essays, 'Essay on Fashionable Literature' (a fragment, written 1818) and *'The Four Ages of Poetry' (1820), to which Shelley's *Defence of Poetry* is a reply. In 1819 Peacock married Jane Gryffydh, the 'White Snowdonian antelope' of Shelley's 'Letter to Maria Gisborne'. His eldest daughter Mary Ellen became the first wife of G. *Meredith. Peacock entered the East India Company's service in 1819 and worked immediately under J. *Mill until the latter's death in 1836, when he succeeded to the responsible position of examiner.

PEAKE, Mervyn Laurence (1911–68), novelist, poet, and artist. He was commissioned as a war artist and visited Belsen in 1945 on a journalistic expedition for *The Leader*, an experience which profoundly affected him. His novel *Titus Groan* (1946) was followed by *Gormenghast* (1950) and *Titus Alone* (1959), which as a trilogy form the work for which Peake is best remembered, a creation of grotesque yet precise Gothic fantasy, recounting the life of Titus, 77th earl of Groan, in his crumbling castle of Gormenghast, surrounded by a cast of characters which includes the colourful Fuchsia, Dr Prunesquallor, and the melancholy Muzzlehatch. Peake's poetry includes *The Glassblowers* (1950) and *The Rhyme of the Flying Bomb* (1962), a ballad of the blitz; he illustrated most of his own work, and also produced memorable drawings for *The Rime of the *Ancient Mariner* (1943), *Treasure Island* (1949), and other works. A lighter side of his prolific imagination is seen in his posthumous *A Book of Nonsense* (1972).

PEARCE, Philippa A., see CHILDREN'S LITERATURE.

Pearl, an alliterative poem in 1,212 lines of twelve-lined octosyllabic stanzas from the second half of the 14th cent., the only manuscript of which is the famous Cotton Nero A x which is also the sole manuscript of *Patience, *Cleanness, and Sir *Gawain and the Green Knight and which comes from the North-West Midlands. Modern critical practice treats the four poems in the manuscript as the work of a single author. Pearl was the author's daughter and only child, who had died before she was two years old. Wandering in misery, in the garden where she is buried, he has a vision of a river beyond which lies Paradise. Here he sees a maiden seated whom he recognizes as his daughter. She chides him for his excessive grief and describes her blessed state. He argues with her about the justice that makes her queen of Heaven when she died so young. Convinced by her, he plunges into the river in an attempt to join her, and awakes, comforted and reassured of his faith in God. The form and language of the poem are extremely brilliant.

PEARSON, (Edward) Hesketh (Gibbons) (1887–1964), actor and biographer, whose first book *Modern Men and Mummers* (1921), contained portraits of many of the theatre personalities of the time. His other works include *The Whispering Gallery* (1926) and many lively biographies, of (for example) *Hazlitt (1934), Sydney *Smith (*The Smith of Smiths*, 1934), G. B. *Shaw (1942), *Wilde (1946), and Beerbohm Tree (1956).

PEARSON, John (1613–86), one of the most erudite theologians of his age, became bishop of Chester in 1673. His series of lectures was published as his classic *Exposition of the Creed* (1659), the notes of which are a rich mine of patristic learning.

Pecksniff, Mr, a character in Dickens's *Martin Chuzzlewit*.

PECOCK, Reginald (1395–c.1460), a Welshman who became bishop successively of St Asaph and Chichester. Most of his writings employ the syllogistic logic of the Scholastics, and many were directed against the *Lollards, notably his *Repressor of over much Blaming of the Clergy* (1455), a monument of 15th-cent. English prose of considerable eloquence and lexical variety. His *Book of Faith* was issued in 1456, and in his *Donet* and the *Folewer to the Donet* he sought to define a body of faith acceptable to all. He alienated by his writings all sections of theological opinion in England, was arraigned before the archbishop of Canterbury, and obliged to resign his bishopric and recant his opinions (1458). His work has considerable importance for its development of the English vocabulary, which he added to, both by loan-translations and by borrowings.

Pedro, Don, in Shakespeare's *Much Ado About Nothing*, the prince of Aragon.

PEEL, John (1776–1854), the hero of the well-known hunting song 'D'ye ken John Peel?', was born at Caldbeck, Cumberland, and for over 40 years ran the famous pack of hounds that bore his name. The words of the song were composed by his friend John Woodcock Graves.

PEELE, George (1556–96). From about 1581 he pursued an active and varied literary career. He was an associate of many other writers of the period, such as T. *Watson and R. *Greene. His works fall into three main categories: plays, pageants, and 'gratulatory' and miscellaneous verse. His surviving plays are *The Araygnement of Paris* (1584); *Edward I* (1593); *The Battle of Alcazar* (1594); *The Old Wives' Tale* (1595); and *David and Fair Bethsabe* (1599). His miscellaneous verse includes *Polyhymnia* (1590) and *The Honour of the Garter* (1593), a gratulatory poem to the Earl of Northumberland. Peele's work is dominated by courtly and patriotic themes, and his technical achievements include extending the range of non-dramatic blank verse.

Peggotty, Daniel, Clara, and Ham, characters in Dickens's *David Copperfield*.

Pegler, Mrs, in Dickens's *Hard Times*, Bounderby's mother.

Peg Woffington, a novel by C. *Reade, based on an episode in the life of Peg *Woffington, and adapted from his play *Masks and Faces*.

Pelagian, derived from **Pelagius**, the latinized form of the name of a British monk, Morgan, of the 4th and 5th cents. The Pelagians denied the doctrine of Original Sin, asserting that Adam's fall did not involve his posterity, and maintained that the human will is itself capable of good without the assistance of divine grace. Their beliefs died slowly and were only finally defeated, by the Augustinian view that grace is God-given, at the Council of Orange (529). The voluntarist tendency of Pelagianism revived in the Middle Ages.

Pelham: or The Adventures of a Gentleman, a novel by *Bulwer-Lytton, published 1828.

It recounts the adventures of Henry Pelham, a young dandy, wit, and aspiring politician, who falls in love with Ellen, sister of his old friend from Eton days, Reginald Glanville. The latter is falsely suspected of a murder, and tells his story to Pelham, who unearths the real murderer, Thornton, a character drawn from the well-known murderer Thurtell. But the interest of the novel lies in its lively portrayal of fashionable society, and in such minor characters as Lady Frances, Pelham's worldly mother, and Lord Vincent, whose conversation is laced with puns, largely in Latin. Bulwer-Lytton mocks the genre of the *Fashionable novel even while employing it, which adds to the tone of sparkling cynicism which captivated contemporary readers and made his hero's name a catch-phrase.

Pell, Solomon, in Dickens's *Pickwick Papers*, an attorney in the Insolvent Court.

Pellam, King, 'The Maimed King', in Arthurian legend, father of the Grail King, *Pelles. Wounded by Balyn's *'Dolorous Stroke', he is healed by his great-grandson Galahad in the Grail quest.

Pelleas, Sir, 'The Noble Knight', in Arthurian legend the lover of Ettarde. After her death he marries Nimue, the *Lady of the Lake.

'Pelleas and Ettarre', one of Tennyson's *Idylls of the King*, published 1869. Pelleas woos the heartless Ettarre, is tricked by Gawain, learns of the adultery of Lancelot and Guinevere, and vows to avenge the treasons of the Round Table.

Pelles, King, 'The Grail King', in Malory's *Morte D'Arthur*, one of the Fisher Kings and said to be 'cousin nigh unto Joseph of Arimathie'. Founded perhaps on *Pwyll of Welsh mythology, he was the father of Elaine who was the mother of Galahad by Launcelot.

Pellinore, King, 'The King of the Waste Lands', in Malory's *Morte D'Arthur* the father of Sir Lamorak, Sir Perceval, and Sir Torre, and the brother of King *Pelles. The rivalry between his family and King *Lot's is a running theme in Malory.

PEMBROKE, Mary Herbert, countess of (1561–1621), was the younger sister of P. *Sidney, whose first version of the *Arcadia was written for her at Wilton. After her brother's death in 1586 she became in effect his literary executrix, overseeing the publication of the *Arcadia* and the rest of his works for the editions of 1593 and 1598. She completed the *Psalms*, of which Sidney had translated only the first 42, rendering them in a very wide variety of English verse forms; they were not published as a whole until the edition of J. C. A. Rathmell (1963). She translated several works including *Petrarch's *Trionfo della morte*. Her reputation as a patroness perhaps outstripped her specific achievements. The epitaph on her by W. *Browne was popular throughout the 17th cent.

PEN, an international association of Poets, Playwrights, Editors, Essayists, and Novelists founded in 1921 by Mrs Dawson-Scott, under the presidency of J. *Galsworthy.

Pendennis, The History of, a novel by *Thackeray, published in numbers 1848–50.

A *Bildungsroman* in which the main character, Arthur Pendennis, is the only son of a devoted and unworldly widow, Helen. As a very young man he falls in love with an actress, Emily Costigan ('Miss Fotheringay'), and is only rescued from an unsuitable marriage by the tactful intervention of his uncle, Major Pendennis, who persuades her disreputable old father, Captain Costigan, that Arthur has no money of his own. Pendennis then goes to the university of Oxbridge, where he runs up bills and has to be rescued by a loan from Helen's adopted daughter, Laura Bell. Helen hopes that Laura and her son will marry, but Pendennis's next entanglement is with Blanche Amory, an affected and hard-hearted girl, the daughter of the rich, vulgar Lady Clavering by her first husband. Major Pendennis encourages a match between his nephew and Blanche, although he is secretly aware that Blanche's father is an escaped convict who is still alive and is blackmailing Sir Francis Clavering.

Pendennis goes to London and is supposed to be reading for the bar. He shares chambers with George Warrington, who starts him on a literary career by introducing him to Captain Shandon, a debt-ridden Irish journalist who is editing a new magazine, the 'Pall Mall Gazette', from prison. Pendennis has a mild flirtation with a working-class girl, Fanny Bolton, and, when he falls ill, Fanny nurses him devotedly. Helen Pendennis jumps to the false conclusion that Fanny is Pendennis's mistress, and treats the girl very unkindly. Pendennis is so indignant that he threatens to marry Fanny, but is dissuaded by Warrington. Fanny soon finds consolation with Sam Huxter, a medical student, but Blanche is harder to shake off. After the exposure of the existence of her villainous father, Pendennis feels obliged to go through with an engagement to her. Fortunately Blanche decides in favour of Harry Foker, heir to a brewing fortune, and Pendennis and Laura finally marry, after Helen's death.

Pendragon, a title given to an ancient British or Welsh chief holding or claiming supreme power. In English chiefly known as the title of *Uther Pendragon, father of King *Arthur.

Penguin Books, the name first given to a series of paperback books published in 1935 by A.

*Lane, and established as a publishing company in 1936. The first ten titles, which sold for sixpence each, included *Ariel* by Maurois (No. 1), and fiction by A. *Christie, *Hemingway, D. L. *Sayers, and M. *Webb. In 1937 the non-fiction Pelican series was launched and Puffin Picture Books for children followed in 1940. Other notable ventures include the Penguin Classics, edited for many years by E. V. Rieu (1887–1972), whose own translation of the *Odyssey* (1946) was its first and best-selling volume; and the first unexpurgated edition of *Lady Chatterley's Lover* (1960), which led to a celebrated trial and acquittal at the Old Bailey.

PENN, William (1644–1718), a Quaker and founder of Pennsylvania, was committed to the Tower in 1668 for publishing *The Sandy Foundation Shaken* (an attack on orthodox doctrines of the Trinity and the Atonement, and on the Calvinist theory of justification) and there wrote *No Cross, No Crown* (1669), an eloquent and learned dissertation on Christian duty and a Quaker classic. He suffered frequent persecutions, and looked to America as a refuge for his faith; in 1682 he obtained grants of East New Jersey and Pennsylvania, and framed, possibly in concert with A. *Sidney, a new constitution for the colony by which religious toleration would be secured.

PENNANT, Thomas (1726–98), naturalist, antiquarian, zoologist, and traveller, published *A Tour in Scotland* in 1771, *A Tour in Wales* in 1778–81, *A Tour in Scotland and Voyage to the Hebrides* in 1774–6, and *The Journey from Chester to London* in 1782. He figures in G. *White's *Selborne* as one of the author's correspondents.

'Penseroso, Il', see IL PENSEROSO.

Penshurst Place, in Kent, has been in the possession of the Sidney family since 1552, and was the birthplace of Sir P. *Sidney. Many writers enjoyed its hospitality, including *Jonson, who paid a graceful tribute in 'To Penshurst' (*The Forest*, 1616). (See also PATRONAGE.)

Pentameron, The, a prose work by W. S. *Landor, published 1837. The book consists of imaginary conversations between *Petrarch and *Boccaccio.

Pentameter, in Greek and Latin prosody, a form of dactylic verse of which each half consists of two feet and a long syllable. In English literature, a line of verse of five feet, e.g. the English 'heroic' or iambic verse of ten syllables, as used in *Paradise Lost*. (See METRE.)

Penthea, a character in Ford's *The Broken Heart*.

PEPYS (pron. peeps or peppis), Samuel (1633–1703), son of John Pepys, a London tailor, entered the household of Sir Edward Montagu (afterwards first earl of Sandwich) in 1656; his subsequent successful career was largely due to Montagu's patronage. His famous *Diary* opens on 1 Jan. 1660, when Pepys was living in Axe Yard, Westminster, and was very poor. Soon after this he was appointed 'clerk of the King's ships' and clerk of the privy seal. In 1665 he became surveyor-general of the victualling office. Owing to an unfounded fear of failing eyesight he closed his diary on 31 May 1669, and in the same year his wife died. In 1672 he was appointed secretary to the Admiralty. In 1679 he was committed to the Tower for a short time on a charge of complicity in the *'Popish Plot' and deprived of his office. In 1683 he was sent to Tangier with Lord Dartmouth and wrote an interesting diary while there. In 1684 he was reappointed, and laboured hard to provide the country with an efficient fleet. At the revolution he was deprived of his appointment and afterwards lived in retirement. His *Diary* remained in cipher (a system of shorthand) at Magdalene College, Cambridge, until 1825, when it was deciphered by John Smith and edited by Lord Braybrooke. On his death his friend *Evelyn remembered Pepys as 'a very worthy, industrious and curious person, none in England exceeding him in knowledge of the navy . . . universally beloved, hospitable, generous, learned in many things, skilled in music, a very great cherisher of learned men'. (See also RESTORATION.)

Perceforest, a vast French prose romance of the 14th cent., in which the author seeks to link the legends of *Alexander and *Arthur. Alexander, after the conquest of India, is driven by a storm on the coast of England, and makes one of his followers (called Perceforest because he has killed a magician in an impenetrable forest) king of the land. Under the latter's grandson the *Grail is brought to England.

Perceval, Sir, probably to be identified with Peredur of the *Mabinogion, is a legendary figure of great antiquity, first found in the *Perceval, ou Le Conte du Graal* of *Chrétien de Troyes (c.1182) and the German *Parzival* (c.1205) of *Wolfram von Eschenbach (which was the inspiration for *Wagner's *Parsifal). In English he appears in *Sir Perceval of Galles*, a romance from the 15th cent. and in Malory's *Morte D'Arthur. The former tells of the childhood of Perceval and his being knighted by Arthur, without any allusion to the *Grail. Malory makes him a son of King *Pellinore, describing his success in the Quest for the Grail with Galahad and Bors.

PERCY, Thomas, born Piercy (1729–1811), published in 1761 a translation (from the Portuguese) of the first Chinese novel to appear in English, *Hau Kiou Choaan*, and in 1763 his *Five Pieces of Runic Poetry Translated from the Islandic Language*, which considerably influenced the study of ancient Norse in England. Percy also published poetry (including his ballad *The Hermit of Warkworth*, 1771), translated from the Hebrew and Spanish, and wrote a *Memoir of Goldsmith* (1801). He is best known for his celebrated collection *Reliques of Ancient English Poetry* (3 vols, 1765), which contributed greatly to the understanding of the older English poetry. (See also PERCY FOLIO and BALLAD.)

Percy Folio, The, a manuscript in mid-17th-cent. handwriting, the most important source of our *ballad literature and the basis of *Child's collection. From it T. *Percy drew the ballads included in his *Reliques. The Percy Folio was printed in its entirety by Hales and *Furnivall in 1867–8.

Percy Society, The, founded 1840 by T. C. *Croker, *Dyce, *Halliwell-Phillipps, and J. P. *Collier, for the purpose of publishing old English lyrics and ballads. It was named in honour of T. *Percy.

Percy's Reliques, see RELIQUES OF ANCIENT ENGLISH POETRY.

Perdita, in Shakespeare's *The Winter's Tale*, the daughter of Hermione and Leontes.

Peredur, the Arthurian subject of one of the seven tales added by Lady Charlotte Guest to the *Mabinogion proper and now normally included in it. The story corresponds closely to the *Perceval of *Chrétien de Troyes, and to a number of other Arthurian texts.

Peregrine Pickle, The Adventures of, a novel by T. *Smollett (1751, revised edn 1758).
   The hero is a scoundrel and a swashbuckler, with little to his credit except wit and courage; and the book is mainly occupied with his adventures in England and on the Continent, many of them of an amatory character. In the course of these he visits Paris, is imprisoned in the Bastille, visits the Netherlands, hoaxes the physicians of Bath, sets up as a magician, endeavours to enter Parliament, is confined in the Fleet and released on inheriting his father's property, finally marrying Emilia Gauntlet, a young lady whom he has from the outset of the story intermittently pursued with his attentions.
   The novel contained many savage caricatures of, for instance, *Fielding as Mr Spondy, *Garrick as Marmozet, and *Akenside as the Doctor.

Peri Bathous, or the Art of Sinking in Poetry (1727), a treatise by *Pope.

Pericles and Aspasia, a prose work by W. S. *Landor, published 1836.
   The book consists of imaginary letters mainly between Aspasia and Cleone. Others are

between Pericles and Aspasia, and some are between Pericles and prominent figures of the time. The letters include discussions of artistic, literary, political, religious, and philosophical subjects, and they end with the death of Pericles.

Pericles, Prince of Tyre, a romantic drama by *Shakespeare, the first two acts probably written with a collaborator. It was composed between 1606 and 1608 and a textually corrupt quarto appeared in 1609. It was included in the second issue of the third Folio of 1664. The play is based on the story of Apollonius of Tyre in *Gower's *Confessio Amantis* and a prose version, *The Patterne of Painefull Adventures*.

The play is presented by Gower, who acts as Chorus throughout, and tells how having solved the riddle set by King Antiochus and discovered his incestuous relationship with his daughter, Pericles, prince of Tyre, finds his life in danger. He leaves his government in the hands of his honest minister, Helicanus, and sails from Tyre to Tarsus where he relieves a famine. Off the coast of Pentapolis Pericles alone survives the wreck of his ship, and in a tournament defeats the suitors for the hand of Thaisa, daughter of King Simonides, whom he marries.

Hearing that Antiochus has died, Pericles sets sail for Tyre, and during a storm on the voyage Thaisa gives birth to a daughter, Marina, and faints. Apparently dead, Thaisa is buried at sea in a chest, which is cast ashore at Ephesus, where Cerimon, a physician, opens it and restores Thaisa to life. She, thinking her husband drowned, becomes a priestess in the temple of Diana. Pericles takes Marina to Tarsus, where he leaves her with its Governor Cleon and his wife Dionyza.

When the child grows up Dionyza, jealous of her being more favoured than her own daughter, seeks to kill her; but Marina is carried off by pirates and sold in Mytilene to a brothel, where her purity and piety win the admiration of Lysimachus, the governor of the city, and the respect of the brothel-keeper's servant, Boult, and secure her release. In a vision Pericles is shown Marina's tomb, deceivingly erected by Cleon and Dionyza. He puts to sea again and lands at Mytilene, where through Lysimachus and to his intense joy Pericles discovers his daughter. In a second vision, Diana directs him to go to her temple at Ephesus and there recount the story of his life. In doing this, the priestess Thaisa, his lost wife, recognizes him, and is reunited with her husband and daughter. At the end of the play the Chorus tells how Cleon and Dionyza are burnt by the citizens of Tarsus as a penalty for their wickedness.

Perilous Chair, the 'Siege Perilous' at the *Round Table.

Periodical, Literary, a term here taken to describe any repeating series of literary journal, magazine, or review. From the beginning of the 18th cent. until the beginning of the Second World War the literary periodical flourished, and contributed greatly to the development of creative writing and criticism. The *Mercurius Librarius* of 1668 was the first periodical to catalogue books, and the *Universal Historical Bibliotheque* of 1687 the first publication to invite contributions and include rudimentary comments on essays and other recent writings. At about this time periodical publications began to divide into two main types; the first to become established was the magazine miscellany of which *The Gentleman's Journal* of 1692 is generally held to be the first established ancestor. Subsequent examples followed including the *Tatler* of *Addison and *Steele, *Cave's *Gentleman's Magazine, the *Analytical Review, the 19th-cent. *Blackwood's Magazine, the *London Magazine, and *Bentley's Miscellany; and the 20th-cent. Monthly Review (1900–7), John O'London's (1919–54), and the *London Mercury.

The second type of periodical was the review, with which may be grouped the weekly journal of original, critical, and general literary work. The *Monthly Review, Smollett's *Critical Review, and the Analytical Review established a form which culminated in the influential reviews of the 19th cent.—the *Edinburgh Review, the *Quarterly Review, the *Examiner, the *Westminster Review, the *Athenaeum, the *Cornhill Magazine, the *Fortnightly Review, and others, including the notorious *Yellow Book. These led directly to the significant periodicals of this century, such as the Bookman (1891–1934), the *English Review, the *Times Literary Supplement, the *Criterion, *Horizon, *Encounter, and London Magazine (1954–   ). Specialist reviews, such as *Scrutiny, designed for the more academic reader, have exerted great critical influence.

The single-essay (or serial-essay) publication, best represented by Steele's *Spectator and Johnson's *Rambler, had immeasurable literary influence until the end of the 18th cent.

For almost a century before 1800 the periodical had encouraged many talents, including those of *Defoe, *Swift, *Fielding, *Smollett, and *Goldsmith. By the beginning of the 19th cent., the dying system of personal *patronage was largely replaced by the support of the literary periodicals and their editors (such as Leigh *Hunt and John *Scott). The work of the *Romantics, and of the Victorian poets and novelists, was greatly encouraged and widely published. For the first part of the 20th cent. new weeklies and periodicals joined others living on from the 19th cent. in supporting a wide range of new writers. But economic problems have compelled the closure of many periodicals.

Peripeteia, see POETICS, THE.

Perissa, in Spenser's *Faerie Queene, see MEDINA.

Perker, Mr, in Dickens's *Pickwick Papers*.

Perkin Warbeck, a historical play by J. *Ford, printed 1634.

PERRAULT, Charles (1628–1703), French raconteur, is remembered today for a collection of fairy-tales published under the name of his son Pierre: *Histoires et contes du temps passé* (1697), subtitled 'Contes de ma Mère l'Oye'. These tales, based on French popular tradition, were translated into English as 'Mother Goose Tales' by Robert Samber in 1729.

PERSIUS (Aulus Persius Flaccus) (AD 34–62), Roman satirist, author of six satires, which show the influence of *Horace and of *Stoicism and which were all translated by *Dryden (1692).

Persuasion, a novel by J. *Austen, written 1815–16, published posthumously 1818.

Sir Walter Elliot, a spendthrift baronet and widower, with a swollen sense of his social importance and personal elegance, is obliged to retrench and let his seat, Kellynch Hall. His eldest daughter, Elizabeth, haughty and unmarried, is now twenty-nine; the second, Anne, who is pretty, intelligent, and amiable, had some years before been engaged to a young naval officer, Frederick Wentworth, but had been persuaded by her trusted friend Lady Russell to break off the engagement, because of his lack of fortune and a misunderstanding of his easy nature. The breach had brought great unhappiness to Anne, and caused indignation in Wentworth. When the story opens Anne is twenty-seven, and the bloom of her youth is gone. Captain Wentworth, who has had a successful career and is now prosperous, is thrown again into Anne's society by the letting of Kellynch to Admiral and Mrs Croft, his sister and brother-in-law. Sir Walter's youngest daughter, Mary, is married to Charles Musgrove, the heir of a neighbouring landowner. Wentworth is attracted by Charles's sisters, Louisa and Henrietta, and in time becomes involved with Louisa. During a visit of the party to Lyme Regis, Louisa, being 'jumped down' from the Cobb by Wentworth, falls and is badly injured. Wentworth's partial responsibility for the accident makes him feel an increased obligation to Louisa at the very time that his feelings are being drawn back to Anne. However, during her convalescence Louisa becomes engaged to Captain Benwick, another naval officer, and Wentworth is free to proceed with his courtship. He goes to Bath, where Sir Walter is now established with his two elder daughters and Elizabeth's companion, Mrs Clay, an artful woman with matrimonial designs on Sir Walter. There Wentworth finds another suitor for Anne's hand, her cousin William Elliot, the heir to the Kellynch estate, who is also indulging in an intrigue with Mrs Clay, in order to detach her from Sir Walter, Anne has remained unshaken in her love for Wentworth and moreover learns about the duplicity of William Elliot. Accidentally made aware of Anne's constancy, Wentworth renews his offer of marriage and is accepted.

In this, Jane Austen's last completed work, satire and ridicule take a milder form, and the tone is more grave and tender.

Pertelote, the hen in Chaucer's 'Nun's Priest's Tale' (see CANTERBURY TALES, 20); also the wife of Chanticleer in the tale of *Reynard the Fox (see PARTLET). The word in Old French was a female proper name. Its later equivalent, used as the proper name of a hen, is Partlet.

Peter Bell, a poem by *Wordsworth, published with a dedication to *Southey 1819.

Peter Bell is a potter, a lawless, roving man, insensible to the beauty of nature. Coming to the edge of the Swale he sees a solitary ass and hopes to steal it. The ass is gazing into the water at some object, which turns out to be the dead body of its owner. After a series of supernatural events Peter mounts the ass, which eventually leads him to the cottage of the drowned man's widow. Peter's spiritual and supernatural experiences on this ride make him a reformed man. The ludicrous nature of part of the poem made it the subject of many parodies, including Shelley's *Peter Bell The Third.

Peter Bell The Third, a satirical poem by P. B. *Shelley published 1839.

It is a demonic parody of *Wordsworth's poem (above). Shelley uses inventive doggerel, outrageous rhymes, and effervescent social satire to mock Wordsworth's 'defection' from the radical cause. He follows Peter's progress through a black, comic underworld, described in seven sections: 'Death', 'The Devil', 'Hell', 'Sin', 'Grace', 'Damnation', and 'Double Damnation'. Part III begins with the celebrated, 'Hell is a city much like London'; while Part V draws a surprisingly sympathetic cartoon of Peter the poet, who remembered 'Many a ditch and quick-set fence; | Of Lakes he had intelligence'.

Peterborough Chronicle, The, the last part of the Laud manuscript of the *Anglo-Saxon Chronicle, written in Peterborough between 1121 and 1154, the date of its last annal. It extends beyond 1080, and is of great linguistic interest in exemplifying the developments between Old and Middle English. The 12th-cent. entries, which describe the disasters and hardships of Stephen's reign, have a vigour and circumstantiality far beyond the earlier parts of the Chronicle.

'Peter Grimes', one of the tales in Crabbe's *The Borough. It tells the story of a fisherman who, having ill-treated his apprentices, has become a recluse, tormented by guilt and imagined terrors. He is the principal figure in *Britten's opera *Peter Grimes*.

PETER LOMBARD (*c.*1100–60), *Magister Sententiarum*, or Master of the Sentences, became professor of theology and, in 1159, bishop of Paris. His *Sententiae*, written between 1145 and 1150, are a collection of opinions on the Church Fathers, dealing with God, the Creation, the Redemption, and the nature of the Sacraments. It became the standard theological textbook of the 13th cent.

PETER MARTYR (1500–62), Pietro Vermigli, born in Florence, an Augustinian monk, who accepted the Reformed faith, fled from Italy in 1542 to Switzerland, and subsequently to England, and became Regius professor of divinity at Oxford (1548). He helped *Cranmer in the preparation of the second *Book of *Common Prayer*.

PETER OF BLOIS, see ANGLO-LATIN LITERATURE.

Peter Pan, see BARRIE, J. M.

PETER PINDAR, see WOLCOT, J.

Peter Porcupine, see COBBETT, W.

Peter Wilkins, A Cornishman, The Life and Adventures of (1751), a romance by Robert Paltock (1697–1767), an attorney of Clement's Inn.

This is the tale of the mariner Wilkins, shipwrecked in the Antarctic region, who reaches a land where the inhabitants can fly. One of them, Youwarkee, falls outside his hut and he tends her and eventually marries her. The work was much admired by *Coleridge, *Shelley, *Scott, and other writers of the Romantic period.

PETHICK-LAWRENCE, E., see WOMEN'S SUFFRAGE.

Peto, in Shakespeare's 1 and 2 *Henry IV*, a crony of *Falstaff's.

Petowker, Henrietta, a character in Dickens's *Nicholas Nickleby*. She marries Mr Lillyvick.

PETRARCH (Francesco Petrarca) (1304–74), Italian poet and humanist, the most popular Italian poet of the English Renaissance. In 1312 he migrated to Avignon, where in 1327 he first saw the woman who inspired his love poetry. He calls her Laura; her true identity is unknown. Until 1353 Petrarch's life was centred in Provence, but he made extended visits to Italy, on the first of which, in 1341, he was crowned poet

laureate in Rome. From 1353 onwards he resided in Italy.

Today Petrarch is best known for his 'Rime Sparse', the collection of Italian lyrics which includes the long series of poems in praise of Laura; but to his contemporaries and the generations that immediately succeeded him he was best known as a devoted student of classical antiquity, and he wrote the majority of his works in Latin.

Petrarch is justly regarded as the father of Italian humanism and the initiator of the revived study of Greek and Latin literature, but for English writers his chief inspiration was to the early sonneteers; he was imitated and translated by *Surrey, *Wyatt, T. *Watson, and, later, by *Drummond of Hawthornden. *Sidney bears witness to his powerful and persuasive influence. Henry Parker, Lord Morley (1476–1556), translated at some point before 1546 his *Trionfi* as *The Tryumphes of Fraunces Petrarcke* (?1555; ed. D. D. Carnicelli, 1971), and the countess of *Pembroke translated the *Trionfo della Morte* into *terza rima*.

PETRONIUS, traditionally identified with the Gaius Petronius Arbiter who, having been one of Nero's favourites, was forced to commit suicide AD 65. He was the author of the *Satyricon*, a realistic novel of low life, pornographic but written in a pure and elegant Latin interspersed with verses and containing much parody; only excerpts have survived, the most striking of which are the description of a dinner given by a rich freedman (*Cena Trimalchionis*), a poem on the Civil War, and a story, *The Matron of Ephesus*.

Petruchio, in Shakespeare's *The Taming of the Shrew*, suitor to *Katharina.

PETTIE, George (*c.*1548–89), author of *A petite Pallace of Pettie his pleasure* (1576), a collection of twelve 'pretie Hystories' concerning lovers, and all but one deriving from classical sources. Their style to some extent anticipates *Lyly's euphuism. This work follows on from Painter's *Palace of Pleasure* from which Pettie derived his title, and his translation of most of Guazzo's *Civile Conversation* (1581) contributed to the Elizabethan vogue for *courtesy literature and fiction.

PETTY, Sir William (1623–76), published economic treatises, the principal of which was entitled *Political Arithmetic* (1690), a term signifying that which we now call statistics. In this he examined, by the quantitative method, the current allegations of national decay and traced the sources of wealth to labour and land. He was knighted and made an original member of the *Royal Society in 1662.

Petulengro, Jasper, the principal gypsy character in Borrow's *Lavengro* and *The Romany

Rye, founded upon the Norfolk gypsy Ambrose Smith, with whom Borrow was acquainted in his youth. 'Petulengro' means 'shoeing smith'.

Peveril of the Peak, a novel by Sir W. *Scott, published 1823.

The story is in the main concerned with the times of the pretended *'Popish Plot', though it is only in the 14th chapter that the principal theme is reached.

The author draws elaborate portraits of Charles II and Buckingham, and gives glimpses of such historical characters as Titus Oates, Colonel Blood (the impudent revolutionary who tried to steal the crown jewels), and Sir Geoffrey Hudson (Henrietta Maria's dwarf).

PEVSNER, Sir Nikolaus Bernhard Leon (1902–83), art historian, born in Germany. He became, in 1941, associated with *Penguin Books, as editor of King Penguins and of his celebrated county-by-county series *The Buildings of England* (1951–74). His many works on art, design, and architecture include *Pioneers of the Modern Movement, from William Morris to Walter Gropius* (1936), · *High Victorian Design* (1951), and *The Englishness of English Art* (1956).

Pew, the blind buccaneer in Stevenson's *Treasure Island*.

Phaedra, a daughter of Minos and Pasiphaë, and wife of Theseus. She became enamoured of Hippolytus, the son of Theseus by the Amazon Hippolyta. Her advances being rejected, she accused Hippolytus to Theseus of attempts upon her virtue and caused his death. This story is the subject of tragedies by *Euripides, *Seneca, and *Racine.

Phaedria, in Spenser's *Faerie Queene* (II. vi), the Lady of the Idle Lake, symbolizing immodest mirth.

Phalaris, *Epistles of*, were letters attributed to Phalaris, a tyrant of Acragas in Sicily (6th cent. BC). They were edited by Charles Boyle, fourth earl of Orrery (1676–1731) in 1695; R. *Bentley proved that they were spurious and dated from perhaps the 2nd cent. AD. There is an echo of the controversy in Swift's *The Battle of the Books*.

Phaon, (1) in Spenser's *Faerie Queene* (II. iv), is the unfortunate squire who slays Claribel and poisons Philemon; (2) in classical mythology, the boatsman with whom *Sappho is said to have fallen in love. *Lyly wrote a play on the subject (*Sapho and Phao*).

Pharonnida, see CHAMBERLAYNE, W.

Pharsalia, see LUCAN.

Phebe, in Shakespeare's *As You Like It*, a shepherdess.

Philaster, or *Love lies a-Bleeding*, a romantic tragi-comedy by *Beaumont and *Fletcher, printed 1620.

The King of Calabria has usurped the crown of Sicily. The rightful heir, Philaster, loves and is loved by Arethusa, daughter of the usurper, but the latter intends to marry her to Pharamond, prince of Spain. To maintain contact with her, Philaster places his page, Bellario, in her service. Arethusa reveals to the king that Pharamond has embarked on an affair with Megra, a lady of the court; Megra in turn accuses Arethusa of misconduct with the handsome young Bellario. After various pastoral pursuits and disasters, it is revealed that Bellario is in fact Euphrasia, daughter of a Sicilian lord, in love with Philaster. Reassured thus of Arethusa's virtue, Philaster regains both his loved one and his kingdom, whereas Bellario is left with their gratitude, to devote herself to a life of chastity.

Philip, see ADVENTURES OF PHILIP, THE.

Philippics, see CICERO and DEMOSTHENES.

Philip Quarll, *The Adventures of*, an adventure story originally published as *The Hermit* (1727) by 'Edward Dorrington', but generally attributed to Peter Longueville, though some authorities ascribe it to Alexander Bicknell. A derivative of *Robinson Crusoe*, it describes Quarll's fifty years of solitude and suffering on a South Sea Island.

PHILIPS, Ambrose (1674–1749), poet, is remembered chiefly for his quarrel with *Pope over the relative merits of their pastorals. Pope drew, in the *Guardian* (No. 40, 1713), 'a comparison of Philips's performance with his own, in which, with an unexampled and unequalled artifice of irony . . . he gives the preference to Philips' (Johnson, *Lives of the English Poets*). Philips's 'Epistle to the Earl of Dorset' (1709) memorably evokes the frozen landscape of Denmark. His infantile trochaics addressed to children earned him the nickname of 'Namby Pamby'.

PHILIPS, John (1676–1709), the author of *The Splendid Shilling* (unauthorized 1701, authorized 1705), a burlesque in Miltonic blank verse, in which Philips contrasts the happy possessor of the splendid shilling with the poor poet in his garret. In 1705 he published *Blenheim*, written at the suggestion of *Harley and *Bolingbroke, as a Tory counterpart to *The Campaign* of *Addison. *Cyder* (1708), a poem in blank verse written in imitation of *Virgil's *Georgics*, celebrates the cultivation, manufacture, and virtues of cider; it provided a model for later blank verse georgics.

PHILIPS, Katherine (1631–64), *née* Fowler, known as the 'Matchless Orinda'. Her earliest

verses were prefixed (1651) to the *Poems* of H.
*Vaughan. Her collected poems (which had
appeared unauthorized in 1664) were published
in 1667. They indicate the existence of some kind
of Platonic 'Society of Friendship', but the only
known member is Mrs Anne Owen, 'Lucasia',
to whom she addressed almost half her verses,
and the notion of a literary salon appears to have
been given currency by *Gosse. Her death was
mourned in elegies by *Cowley and Sir W.
*Temple.

Philip Sparrow, see PHYLLYP SPAROWE.

Philistine, the name of an alien warlike people
who in early biblical times constantly harassed
the Israelites. The name is applied, (1)
humorously or otherwise to persons regarded as
'the enemy' into whose hands one may fall,
bailiffs, literary critics, etc.; (2) to persons defi-
cient in liberal culture and enlightenment, in
which sense the word was introduced into
English by M. *Arnold ('Heine', *Essays in
Criticism*).

PHILLIPS, Edward (1630–?96), brother of
John *Phillips and nephew of *Milton, was tutor
to Philip Herbert, afterwards 7th earl of Pembroke. His various literary works include a
popular philological dictionary called *The New
World of English Words* (1658).

PHILLIPS, John (1631–1706), younger brother
of Edward *Phillips and nephew of *Milton,
wrote a scathing attack on Puritanism in his
poem *A Satyr against Hypocrites* (1655), supported Charles II and *Oates, and worked as
translator and hack-writer.

PHILLIPS, Stephen (1864–1915), published a
successful volume *Poems* (1898) and wrote
several poetic dramas, including *Francesca* (pub.
1900, perf. 1902), *Herod* (1901), *Ulysses* (1902),
and *Nero* (1906), which were all well received.

Phillotson, Richard, a character in Hardy's
Jude the Obscure.

PHILLPOTTS, Eden (1862–1960), prolific
and popular novelist, playwright, and poet,
most of whose many novels are set in Dartmoor.
He collaborated as playwright with Arnold
*Bennett and J. K. *Jerome.

Philoclea, younger sister of Pamela in Sidney's
Arcadia.

Philological Society, The, was founded in its
present form in 1842 to investigate and to promote the study and knowledge of the structure,
the affinities, and the history of language. Active
in its formation were *Thirlwell, A. P. *Stanley,
and T. *Arnold; prominent members were to
include *Furnivall, *Trench, and James *Murray, all of whom were involved in the creation of
the *Oxford English Dictionary*.

Philosophical Enquiry *into the Origin of our Ideas
of the Sublime and Beautiful*, see SUBLIME AND
BEAUTIFUL.

Philosophical View of Reform, A, a political
essay by P. B. *Shelley, written 1820, not
published until 1920. Intended as an 'instructive
and readable' octavo booklet, this was Shelley's
most mature political statement about Liberty,
Revolution, and Reform; it confirms his position
as a Radical (rather than a liberal)—but not a
revolutionary.

Philotas, a Senecan tragedy in blank verse by S.
*Daniel, published 1605.

Phineas Finn, *The Irish Member*, a novel by A.
*Trollope, published 1869, the second of the
*'Palliser' series.
   Phineas Finn, a young Irish barrister, catches
the eye of Lord Tulla and is elected to Parliament
for the family seat of Loughshane. In London
Phineas is admitted to high society, and falls in
love with the politically-minded Lady Laura
Standish. Lady Laura's personal fortune is considerably diminished after paying the debts of
her brother Lord Chiltern, and she feels she must
marry money, in the person of Mr Kennedy.
Phineas turns for consolation elsewhere. He first
pursues Violet Effingham, Lord Chiltern's
childhood sweetheart, but after a brief quarrel
between the two suitors (featuring a duel fought
in Belgium), Violet settles for Chiltern.
Madame Max Goesler, the rich widow of a
Viennese banker, is Phineas's next favourite.
Phineas had lost his government salary by stick-
ing to his principles over the issue of Irish Tenant
Right. Madame Max offers him her hand in
marriage and her fortune to finance a fresh political career. This he is too scrupulous to accept in
view of his prior engagement to a pretty Irish
girl, Mary Flood-Jones, and he returns to
Ireland.

Phineas Redux, a novel by A. *Trollope,
published 1874, the fourth in the *'Palliser'
series.
   Phineas Finn returns to politics and earnestly
hopes for office under Mr Gresham's government. Unhappily a series of quarrels makes his
progress anything but smooth. First Mr Kennedy, outraged at Phineas's visit to his wife Lady
Laura in her Dresden exile, unsuccessfully tries
to shoot him. Then Phineas exchanges heated
words with the president of the Board of Trade,
Mr Bonteen, and when, later that night, Bonteen is murdered, the burden of circumstantial
evidence against Phineas is very strong. He is
arrested and remanded for trial, and only the

spirited efforts of Madame Max (see PHINEAS FINN) in discovering the true culprit, and a brilliant courtroom performance by Chaffanbrass, succeed in getting him off. Towards the end of the novel Phineas rallies, returns to politics, and marries Madame Max. Bonteen's murderer turns out to have been the Revd Mr Emilius, the converted Jew who married Lizzie Eustace. Emilius, who has a previous wife still living at Prague, is convicted of bigamy and imprisoned, but there is insufficient evidence to hang him.

In this novel the old duke of Omnium dies, and Plantagenet and Lady Glencora become duke and duchess.

Phiz, see BROWNE, H. K.

Phoenix, The, an Old English poem of 677 lines, in the *Exeter Book, possibly written in the later 9th cent. It is a beast allegory of the kind found in the *bestiaries. The poem is admired for the vividness of its imagery and the accomplishment of its syntax.

'Phoenix and the Turtle, The', an allegorical elegy ascribed to *Shakespeare included in Robert Chester's collection *Love's Martyr* (1601).

Phoenix Nest, The, a poetic miscellany published 1593. It includes poems by *Ralegh, *Lodge, and *Breton, and opens with three elegies on *Sidney, the 'Phoenix' of the title.

Phunky, Mr in Dickens's *Pickwick Papers, Serjeant Snubbin's junior in the case of Bardell v. Pickwick.

Phyllyp Sparowe, a poem by *Skelton.

'Physician's Tale, The', see CANTERBURY TALES, 13.

Physiologus, see BESTIARIES.

Picaresque, from the Spanish *pícaro,* a wily trickster; the form of novel accurately described as 'picaresque' first appeared in 16th-cent. Spain with the anonymous *Lazarillo de Tormes* (1553) and Alemán's *Guzmán de Alfarache* (1599–1604), which relate the histories of ingenious rogues, the servants of several masters, who eventually repent the error of their ways; examples of their descendants in English would be *Moll Flanders, *Roderick Random, and *Tom Jones. The term was apparently first used in England in the 19th cent. Nowadays it is commonly, and loosely, applied to episodic novels, especially those of *Fielding, *Smollet, and others of the 18th cent. which describe the adventures of a lively and resourceful hero on a journey. *The Golden Ass of Apuleius is regarded as a forerunner of the picaresque novel.

PICCOLOMINI, Aeneas Silvius (1405–64), Pope Pius II from 1458, was a patron of letters

and author of a romance, *Eurialus and Lucretia,* of treatises on many subjects, and of commentaries on his times. His secular works include the *Miseriae Curialium,* which provided one of the models for the *Eclogues of A. *Barclay. He visited Scotland in 1435, and wrote a somewhat hostile report of its poverty-stricken condition.

Pickwick Papers (*The Posthumous Papers of the Pickwick Club*), a novel by *Dickens, first issued in 20 monthly parts April 1836–Nov. 1837, and as a volume in 1837.

Mr Samuel Pickwick, general chairman of the Pickwick Club which he has founded, Messrs Tracy Tupman, Augustus Snodgrass, and Nathaniel Winkle, members of the club, are constituted a Corresponding Society of the Club to report to it their journeys and adventures, and observations of characters and manners. This is the basis on which the novel is constructed, and the club serves to link a series of detached incidents and changing characters, without elaborate plot. The principal elements in the story are: (1) the visit of Pickwick and his friends to Rochester and their falling in with the specious rascal Jingle, who gets Winkle involved in the prospect of a duel (fortunately averted). (2) The visit to Dingley Dell, the home of the hospitable Mr Wardle; the elopement of Jingle with Wardle's sister, their pursuit by Wardle and Pickwick, and the recovery of the lady; followed by the engagement of Sam Weller as Pickwick's servant. (3) The visit to Eatanswill, where a parliamentary election is in progress. (4) The visit to Bury St Edmunds, where Mr Pickwick and Sam Weller are fooled by Jingle and his servant, Job Trotter. (5) The pursuit of Jingle to Ipswich, where Mr Pickwick inadvertently enters the bedroom of a middle-aged lady at night. (6) The Christmas festivities at Dingley Dell. (7) The misapprehension of Mrs Bardell, Mr Pickwick's landlady, regarding her lodger's intentions, which leads to the famous action of Bardell v. Pickwick for breach of promise of marriage. (8) The visit to Bath, in which Winkle figures prominently in his courtship of Arabella Allen. (9) The period of Mr Pickwick's imprisonment in the Fleet in consequence of his refusal to pay the damages and costs of his action; and the discovery of Jingle and Job Trotter in that prison, and their relief by Mr Pickwick. (10) The Affairs of Tony Weller (Sam's father) and the second Mrs Weller, ending in the death of the latter and the discomfiture of the pious humbug and greedy drunkard Stiggins, deputy shepherd in the Ebenezer Temperance Association. (11) The affairs of Bob Sawyer and Benjamin Allen, medical students and subsequently struggling practitioners. The novel ends with the happy marriage of Emily Wardle and Augustus Snodgrass.

PICO DELLA MIRANDOLA, Giovanni (1463–94), an Italian humanist and philosopher, spent part of his life at Florence in the circle of Lorenzo de' Medici. In 1486 he published 900 theses, offering to maintain them at Rome, but some of his propositions were pronounced heretical and the public debate did not take place. The famous oration *De dignitate hominis*, with which he intended to introduce the debate, is one of the most important philosophical works of the 15th cent. Pico was a daring syncretist, who vainly tried to make a synthesis of Christianity, Platonism, Aristotelianism, and the Jewish Cabbala. His Life and some of his writings were translated by Sir T. *More.

Picturesque, a term which came into fashion in the late 18th cent., principally to describe a certain kind of scenery. Writers on the picturesque include W. *Gilpin, W. *Mason, William Payne Knight (1750–1824), who published *The Landscape* in 1794), Uvedale Price (1747–1829, who published *Essays on the Picturesque*, 1794), and the landscape gardener Humphry Repton (1752–1818). The impact of these writers on the sensibility and vocabulary of writers of the 19th cent. was considerable. The 'picturesque', as defined by Price, was a new aesthetic category, to be added to *Burke's recently established categories of the *Sublime and the Beautiful; its attributes were roughness and irregularity, and its most complete exponent in terms of painting was Salvator Rosa; Mrs *Radcliffe's works dwell frequently on the picturesque, and J. *Austen and many of her characters were familiar with the works of Gilpin. The entertaining aesthetic disputes of Price and Knight are satirized in Peacock's *Headlong Hall*, and *Combe's adventures of Dr Syntax are aimed at the movement in general and Gilpin in particular. The development of the picturesque movement into *Romanticism is a subject of much complexity and literary interest.

'Pied Piper of Hamelin, The, A Child's Story', a poem by R. Browning, included in *Dramatic Lyrics*.

Pierce Penniless, *His Supplication to the Divell*, a fantastic prose satire by T. *Nashe, 1592. The author, in the form of a humorous complaint to the Devil, discourses on the vices of the day, throwing interesting light on the customs of his time.

Pierce the Ploughman's Crede, an alliterative poem dating from the last decade of the 14th cent., influenced by *Langland, to whom it pays tribute, and attacking the friars. It contains the most effective piece of social criticism in Middle English, in its lines describing the hardships of the ploughman and his wife.

Pierre, a character in Otway's *Venice Preserv'd*.

Piers Plowman, the greatest poem of the Middle English *Alliterative Revival, by *Langland. It survives in about 50 manuscripts, in three widely varying versions, known as the A, B, and C texts. The A-text, totalling 2,567 lines in its longest version, was probably written about 1367–70; the B-text, a very considerable extension of the A-text, extends to 7,277 lines (or more), and was probably written about 1377–9; the C-text is a substantial revision of the B-text, about the same length, dating from about 1385–6. It is now generally agreed that the three versions were all the work of Langland. The principal division of the poem has been into two parts, the 'Visio' and the 'Vita', the 'Visio' comprising the Prologue and the first seven *Passus* in the B-text. This 'Visio'–'Vita' distinction has been seen to be of such importance by some critics that they have argued that they are properly to be regarded as two distinct poems, but the distinction is not found in B manuscripts. The following account follows the B-text in its division into eight separate visions.

Vision 1. While wandering on the Malvern Hills, the narrator (who, it transpires later, is called Will) falls asleep and has a vision of a Tower where Truth dwells, a deep Dungeon, and between them 'a fair feeld ful of folk' where all the order of human society can be seen about their business. The worldly values thus raised are expounded by Lady Holy Church; the theme is sustained by the analytical trial of Lady Meed which considers whether Meed (Reward or payment) is to be given to Wrong or according to Conscience and Reason.

Vision 2. The narrator observes what J. A. Burrow has shown to be an established sequence of events: Sermon (preached by Reason); Confession (by the Seven Deadly Sins); Pilgrimage (to Truth, led by Piers the Plowman who first appears as the just leader on the road to Salvation); and Pardon (a paper pardon sent to Piers by Truth, but torn up by him when its validity is questioned by a priest, who rejects it as a moral statement rather than a papal document). The conflict with the priest awakens the dreamer; this is the end of the 'Visio'.

Vision 3 shows Will turning to the faculties and sources of knowledge and understanding, as the search for Truth (now referred to as 'Dowel') becomes individualized. Will progressively consults Thought, Wit, Study, Clergy, Scripture, Ymagynatyf (Imagination—linked with Nature in an inner dream containing an inspired description of the workings of nature) and Reason.

Visions 4 and 5. The theme of these visions is Charity. Piers Plowman reappears, in a transfigured form in which his action is indistinguishable from that of Christ.

Vision 6. The Passion of Christ is described as the culmination of doing well; the death of Christ is evoked with great power, and after his death the *harrowing of Hell.

Visions 7 and 8. These *Passus* continue with the liturgical cycle begun in Lent and show the attempts to put into practice the lessons gained from observing the saving actions of Christ. The attempts to perfect the Church are still frustrated by evil-doers, as Piers Plowman had first been as he set out on his first pilgrimage, and the poem ends with Conscience setting out to find Piers, to lead the perfected search for salvation.

The strength of *Piers Plowman* does not lie in its structure or argument, both of which are often confusing and uncertain. But the passages of greatest imaginative power have a sublimity beyond the reach of any other medieval English writer.

Pierston, Jocelyn, a character in Hardy's *The Well-Beloved.*

Pilgrim's Progress, The, from this World to that which is to come, an allegory by *Bunyan (Part I 1678, Part II 1684).

The allegory takes the form of a dream by the author. In this he sees Christian, with a burden on his back and reading in a book, from which he learns that the city in which he and his family dwell will be burned with fire. On the advice of Evangelist, Christian flees from the *City of Destruction. Pt I describes his pilgrimage through the *Slough of Despond, the Interpreter's House, the House Beautiful, the *Valley of Humiliation, the *Valley of the Shadow of Death, *Vanity Fair, Doubting Castle, the Delectable Mountains, the country of *Beulah, to the Celestial City. On the way he encounters various allegorical personages, among them Mr *Worldly Wiseman, *Faithful, Hopeful, Giant Despair, Apollyon, and many others.

Pt II relates how Christian's wife Christiana, moved by a vision, sets out with her children on the same pilgrimage, accompanied by her neighbour Mercy.

The work is remarkable for the beauty and simplicity of its language (Bunyan was permeated with the English of the Bible, though he was also a master of the colloquial English of his own time), the vividness and reality of the characterization, and the author's sense of humour and feeling for the world of nature.

Pills to Purge Melancholy, see D'URFEY, T.

Pinch, Tom and Ruth, characters in Dickens's *Martin Chuzzlewit.*

Pinchwife, a character in Wycherley's *The Country Wife.*

PINDAR (*c.* 522–443 BC), Greek lyric poet, the majority of whose surviving works are the Olympian Odes celebrating victories in the games at Olympia and elsewhere. Antiquity's most notable exponent of the Greater Ode, he served as an inspiration to all subsequent poets attempting this difficult genre. His compositions

were elevated and formal, distinguished by the boldness of their metaphors and a marked reliance on myth and gnomic utterance. He used a framework of strophe, antistrophe, and epode which his imitators sought to copy, but in Pindar this framework rested on an elaborate prosodic structure that remained unknown until it was worked out by August Boeckh in his edition of the Odes (1811). The 17th- and 18th-cent. writers of Pindarics—*Cowley, *Dryden, *Pope, *Gray—employed a much looser prosodic system, so that their odes, although elevated and rich in metaphor, lack Pindar's architectural quality.

PINDAR, Peter, see WOLCOT, J.

Pindaric, see PINDAR.

PINERO, Sir Arthur Wing (1855–1934), began as an actor, and was noticed by H. *Irving who later produced some of his plays. His first one-act play, *Two Hundred a Year,* was performed in 1877. The first of his farces, *The Magistrate* (perf. 1885), brought Pinero both fame and wealth. His first serious play, on what was to be the recurrent theme of double standards for men and women, was *The Profligate* (1889). *Lady Bountiful* (1891) was the first of the 'social' plays in which Pinero was deemed to display his understanding of women. *The Second Mrs Tanqueray* (1893) was a lasting success. *Trelawny of the 'Wells'* (1898), a sentimental comedy, nostalgically recalls his own passion for the theatre. He was knighted in 1909, but in his later years became eclipsed by the rising popularity of the new theatre of *Ibsen and G. B. *Shaw.

Pinkerton, the Misses, characters in Thackeray's *Vanity Fair.*

Pinner of Wakefield, The, see GEORGE-A'-GREEN.

PINTER, Harold (1930–), poet and playwright, born in East London, the son of a Jewish tailor. His first play, *The Room* (1957), was followed by *The Birthday Party* (1958), in which Stanley, an out-of-work pianist in a seaside boarding house, is mysteriously threatened and taken over by two intruders, an Irishman and a Jew, who present him with a Kafkaesque indictment of unexplained crimes. Pinter's distinctive voice was soon recognized, and many successful plays followed including *The Caretaker* (1960), *The Lover* (1963), *The Homecoming* (1965), *Old Times* (1971), *No Man's Land* (1975), and *Betrayal* (1978). Pinter's gift for portraying, by means of dialogue which realistically produces the nuances of colloquial speech, the difficulties of communication and the many layers of meaning in language, pause, and silence, has created a style labelled by the popular imagination as 'Pinteresque'. Pinter has also written for radio and television, directed plays, and written several screenplays, which include versions of L. P. *Hartley's *The Go-Between* (1969), *A la recherche du temps perdu* (1978), and J. *Fowles's *The French Lieutenant's Woman* (1982). *Poems and Prose, 1947–1977* was published in 1978.

PIOZZI, Mrs, see THRALE, H.

Pip, in Dickens's *Great Expectations*, the name by which the hero, Philip Pirrip, is commonly known.

Pipchin, Mrs, in Dickens's *Dombey and Son,* a boarding-house keeper in Brighton.

Pippa Passes, by R. *Browning, published 1841 as no. I of the series *Bells and Pomegranates*. In its final version it consists of an 'Introduction' in verse and four parts, entitled 'Morning', 'Noon', 'Evening', and 'Night'. The first two parts and the fourth combine verse and prose, a combination which was influenced by Browning's study of Elizabethan and Jacobean drama.

The play is set in and around Asolo, a small town near Venice. The plot is a web of dramatic ironies. The Introduction shows Pippa, a young silk-worker, waking up on the morning of her annual holiday. She contrasts the life of 'Asolo's Four Happiest Ones' with her own. These four constitute an ascending scale of value, from carnal love, through married love, filial love, reaching at last for the love of God. Pippa 'passes' by each of the four main scenes in turn, singing as she goes; each song, ironically juxtaposed with the action, effects a moral revolution in the characters concerned. (The famous concluding lines of Pippa's first song, 'God's in his heaven—All's right with the world!', are often quoted out of context as evidence of Browning's own naïve optimism.) At the end of the drama we see Pippa back in her room at nightfall, unaware of the day's events.

PIRANDELLO, Luigi (1867–1936), Italian dramatist, short story writer, and novelist, who exercised a pervasive influence on European drama by challenging the conventions of *Naturalism. In his plays, which include *Sei personaggi in cerca di autore* (*Six Characters in Search of an Author*, 1921) and *Enrico IV* (*Henry IV*, 1922), he anticipated the anti-illusionist theatre of *Brecht, and he also influenced *Beckett, *O'Neill, Anouilh, Giradoux, and Genet.

Pirate, The, a novel by Sir W. *Scott, published 1821. The scene is laid principally in Zetland (Shetland) in the 17th cent.

Pisanio, in Shakespeare's *Cymbeline, the servant Posthumus leaves to Imogen's service when he is banished.

Pistol, Ancient or Ensign, in Shakespeare's 2 *Henry IV*, *Henry V*, and *The Merry Wives of Windsor*, one of Falstaff's associates.

Pistyl of Susan (or *The Pistel of Swete Susan*), meaning 'the epistle of Susanna', a northern alliterative poem, c.1350–60, in 364 lines of 13-line tail-rhyme stanzas, telling the story of Susanna and the Elders (Daniel, 13).

PITMAN, Sir Isaac (1813–97), the inventor of phonography. He published at fourpence in 1837 *Stenographic Sound-Hand*, substituting phonographic for the mainly orthographic methods adopted by former shorthand authors.

Pizarro, a tragedy adapted by *Sheridan from a German play by Kotzebue, on the Spanish conqueror of Peru (1471–1541).

Plagiary, Sir Fretful, a character in Sheridan's *The Critic, a caricature of R. *Cumberland.

Plague Year, A Journal of the, a historical fiction by *Defoe, published 1722.

It purports to be the narrative of a resident in London during 1664–5, the year of the Great Plague. It tells of the gradual spread of the plague and the terror of the inhabitants; the terrible scenes witnessed by the supposed narrator are described with extraordinary vividness. The *Journal* embodied information from various sources, including official documents; some scenes appear to have been borrowed from *Dekker's *The Wonderfull Yeare* (1603). *Hazlitt ascribed to the work 'an epic grandeur, as well as heart-breaking familiarity'.

Plain-Dealer, The, a comedy by *Wycherley, probably performed 1676, published 1677.

It is loosely based on *Molière's *Le Misanthrope*; Wycherley's hero Manly is an honest misanthropic sea-captain (from whom the playwright took the nickname 'Manly' Wycherley). Manly, returned from the Dutch Wars, has lost faith in all but Olivia, to whom he has confided his money, and his friend Vernish: he finds Olivia married to Vernish, and faithless even to him. Manly is beloved by Fidelia, a young woman who has followed him to sea in man's clothes; she intercedes with Olivia on his behalf, is discovered by Vernish, who attempts to rape her, and is finally wounded in an attempt to defend Manly from Vernish. Manly forswears Olivia and pledges himself to Fidelia. There is a subplot in which the litigious widow Blackacre, who has a passion for legal jargon, trains up her son Jerry in her footsteps, and thereby overreaches herself.

PLANCHÉ, James Robinson (1796–1880), prolific dramatist of Huguenot descent. Besides his many original pieces for the stage, mainly burlesques and extravaganzas, he made translations and adaptations from French, Spanish, and Italian authors, including fairy-tales by the Countess d'Aulnoy (1855) and by *Perrault (1858). His stage works include *The Vampyre; or the Bride of the Isles* (1820), an adaptation of a French melodrama which introduced the 'vampire' trap to the English stage. He wrote several opera librettos. His *History of British Costumes* (1834) long remained a standard work.

Plantagenet Palliser, see OMNIUM, DUKE OF.

PLATH, Sylvia (1932–63), poet and novelist, born in Boston, Massachusetts. She married Ted *Hughes in 1956. After teaching in America she and Hughes returned to England in 1959. Her first volume of poetry, *The Colossus*, appeared in 1960, and in 1963 her only novel *The Bell Jar*. Less than a month after its publication she committed suicide in London. Her best-known collection, *Ariel* (1965), established her reputation with its courageous and controlled treatment of extreme and painful states of mind. Much of her symbolism was deeply rooted in actuality; the poems on bee-keeping ('The Bee Meeting', 'The Arrival of the Bee Box', etc.), and other poems —'Elm', 'The Moon and the Yew Tree'—describe the physical surroundings of her house in Devon. Other poems refer directly to her own experiences: 'Lady Lazarus' is based on her two previous suicide attempts, 'Daddy' on the early loss of her father. Other posthumous volumes include *Crossing the Water* and *Winter Trees* (both 1971); *Johnny Panic and the Bible of Dreams* (1977, collected prose pieces); and *Collected Poems* (1981, with an introduction by T. Hughes). Although her best poems deal with suffering and death, others are exhilarating and affectionate, and her tone is frequently witty as well as disturbing.

PLATO (*c.*428/7–*c.*348/7 BC), the great Greek philosopher. Born in Athens, he was a friend and admirer of *Socrates, after whose death he went into exile; he returned to Athens in the 380s and set up a school which was then or at a later stage known as the Academy. The majority of his works are in dialogue form. The principal speaker is nearly always Socrates, but it is impossible to say how close Plato's 'Socrates' stands to the real man either in character or in his teaching. The dialogues fall roughly into three groups. About a dozen demonstrate what has been called the Socratic Method. Socrates plies his interlocutors with a chain of questions, and their replies trap them into self-contradiction; the best-known of these are the *Ion, Euthyphro, Protagoras,* and *Gorgias*. The second group includes the *Crito, Apology, Phaedo, *Symposium*; these do not employ the Socratic Method. The third group comprises the profound and technically subtle dialogues such as the *Theaetetus,*

Parmenides, Timaeus, Sophistes, Philebus. There are also two monumental treatises, *The Republic* and *The Laws*.

Plato's ideas have had a lasting appeal for philosophers. Notable among these were: (1) the Theory of Forms which is best illustrated by an example. The concept 'cat' is derived from our knowledge of particular cats. Plato held that concepts of this nature have a real existence outside the world of sense, and this belief served to reinforce men's hope that there existed an eternal order. (2) The project of establishing philosopher-kings which produced a multitude of schemes for the education of princes. (3) Platonic Love, a devotion inspired by the best qualities of the beloved and aiming at their further development, was formulated originally by Plato in the context of a homosexual relationship, but by the 16th cent. it was applied to a heterosexual love that could rise above sexual desire. Plato has played a markedly vitalizing role in the history of European thought. Through *Augustine he came to exercise a formative influence on Christianity. Through the Florentine Platonists of the 15th cent. he made a manifold impact on art and ideas in the major countries of Europe. Platonic themes appear in *Spenser, *Chapman, *Donne, *Marvell, and later *Wordsworth, and *Bridges, as well as in the work of his attested students such as the *Cambridge Platonists, *Milton, *Gray, *Shelley, E. B. *Browning, M. *Arnold, and *Pater.

Platonic Love, see PLATO.

Platonists, Cambridge, see CAMBRIDGE PLATONISTS.

PLAUTUS, Titus Maccius (*c.*254–184 BC), early Roman dramatist who adapted the Greek New Comedy for the Roman stage. The extent of his originality remains uncertain. Twenty of his plays have survived, and it was from him and from his successor *Terence that Europe learned about ancient comedy. His direct influence on English literature is slight, though Udall was indebted to him in *Ralph Roister Doister,* Shakespeare adapted his *Menaechmi* in *The Comedy of Errors, *Jonson conflated the *Captivi* and the *Aulularia* in *The Case is Altered*, and Dryden adapted his *Amphitryon*; but the tradition he represented is responsible for the form taken by English comedy up to the 19th cent.

Playboy of the Western World, The, a comedy by *Synge, performed and published 1907.

Christy Mahon, 'a slight young man, very tired and frightened', arrives at a village in Mayo. He gives out that he is a fugitive from justice, who has killed his bullying father, splitting him to the chine with a single blow. His character as a dare-devil gives him a great advantage with the women (notably Pegeen Mike and

Widow Quin). But admiration gives place to angry contempt when the father himself arrives in pursuit of the fugitive, who has merely given him a crack on the head and run away. The implication that Irish peasants would condone a murder and the frankness of some of the language caused outrage and riots when the play was first performed at the *Abbey Theatre. This play is Synge's best known effort to fuse the language of ordinary people with a dramatic rhetoric of his own making.

Pleasant Satyre of the Thrie Estaitis, Ane, *in Commendatioun of Vertew and Vituperatioun of Vyce,* a morality play by Sir D. *Lindsay, produced 1540.

Pt I represents the temptation of Rex Humanitas by Sensuality, Wantonness, Solace, and other evil companions, while Good Counsel is hustled away, Verity is put in the stocks, and Chastity is warned off. Pt II presents the Three Estates summoned before the king, and their misdeeds denounced by John the Common Weal. The Lords and Commons repent, but the clergy remain impenitent, are exposed, and the malefactors brought to the scaffold.

The play, which is extremely long and exists in three different versions, is written in various metres. As a dramatic representation, it is in advance of all contemporary English plays, and gives an interesting picture of the Scottish life of the time.

Pleasures of Hope, The, a poem by T. *Campbell published 1799.

In Pt I the poet considers the consolation and inspiration of Hope. In Pt II he reflects upon Love in combination with Hope, and on the belief in a future life.

Pleasures of Imagination, The, a philosophical poem by *Akenside, published 1744; it was completely rewritten and issed as *The Pleasures of the Imagination* in 1757.

The poem is based on the philosophical and aesthetic doctrines and distinctions of *Addison, *Shaftesbury, and *Hutcheson. It examines the primary and secondary pleasures of the imagination, the first connected with the *Sublime, the wonderful, and the beautiful, the second with passion and sense. Akenside's speculations range from Platonic theories of form and essence to I. *Newton's account of the rainbow.

Pleasures of Memory, The, see ROGERS, S.

Pléiade, La, a group of seven French writers of the 16th cent., led by Ronsard. The name had originally been applied by Alexandrian critics to a group of seven poets from the reign of Ptolemy II. The French group, inspired by a common interest in the literatures of antiquity and of the Italian Renaissance, sought to promote the claims of the French language to a comparably dignified status as a medium for literary expression, and their aims were set forth in *du Bellay's *Deffence et illustration de la langue françoyse* of 1549. The Pléiade were largely responsible for the acclimatization of the sonnet form in France, and for the establishment of the alexandrine as the dominant metrical form for much later French poetry. Their inauguration sonnet stimulated the interest in England of this form of verse.

Pliable, in Bunyan's *Pilgrim's Progress,* one of Christian's companions, who turns back at the *Slough of Despond.

Pliant, (1) Dame, the rich widow in Jonson's *The Alchemist.

PLINY THE ELDER, (Gaius Plinius Secundus) (AD 23–79), Roman compiler of a Natural History, which was widely read in the Middle Ages; it provided a cosmology for *Du Bartas's *La Semaine, ou la création du monde* (1578), which *Sylvester's translation established for the 17th cent. as an English classic. But Pliny's direct influence in England was small. Sir T. *Browne made use of him, and so occasionally did *Milton.

PLINY THE YOUNGER, (Gaius Plinius Caecilius Secundus) (AD 62–c.112), Roman letter-writer, nephew of the above. The vogue for letter-writing in the 1690s led to the translation of some of his correspondence. Pliny is remembered mainly for his description of the eruption of Vesuvius and his official correspondence with Trajan.

PLOMER, William Charles Franklyn (1903–73), poet and novelist. Several of his works, including his first novel, the savagely satirical *Turbott Wolfe* (1926), are portraits of South African life. Plomer's experiences teaching in Japan are reflected in his poems, in *Paper Houses* (1929, stories), and *Sado* (a novel, 1931). He came to England in 1929 and settled in Bloomsbury, where he was befriended by L. and V. *Woolf. His first volume of poetry, *The Fivefold Screen* (1932), was followed by several others, and his *Collected Poems* appeared in 1973. His poems are largely satirical and urbane; many of them, like the title piece of *The Dorking Thigh* (1945), are modern ballads with a macabre touch. His edition of *Kilvert's *Diary* appeared in 3 vols, 1938–44. He wrote the librettos for several of *Britten's operas.

Plornish, Mr and Mrs, characters in Dickens's *Little Dorrit.

PLOTINUS (AD c.203–62), Greek philosopher, the chief exponent of *Neoplatonism.

His *Enneads* did much to shape Christian theology in the 4th cent. and also exercised a wide influence on Renaissance thought through *Ficino's translation (1492). They were studied by the *Cambridge Platonists. The concept of the Chain of Being which Plotinus elaborated was generally accepted until the end of the 18th cent., as was the principle, which *Sidney learnt from *Scaliger, that a poet is a second creator, Art re-ascending to the Ideas from which Nature is derived.

Plough and the Stars, The, see O'CASEY, S.

Plough Monday Play, a folk-drama of the East Midlands. Like the St George Play, the Plough Monday Play probably symbolizes in its central incident the death and resurrection of the year.

Plume, Captain, a character in Farquhar's *The Recruiting Officer*.

Plumed Serpent, The, a novel by D. H. *Lawrence, published 1926.
   Kate Leslie, an Irish widow of 40, weary of Europe, arrives in Mexico at a turning-point in her life. The theme of the novel is Kate's struggle for deliverance, for a mystical rebirth. She is drawn to General Don Cipriano Viedma, who introduces her to Don Ramón Carrasco, a mystic and revolutionary leader, reviver of the cult of the ancient god Quetzalcoatl, the plumed serpent. The book contains scenes of violent Aztec 'blood-lust'; Kate, though repelled, is fascinated by the darkness and elemental power of Mexico and its people, and herself enters the cult as the fertility goddess Malintzi and the bride of Cipriano. The novel ends with her acceptance of the subjugation and loss-of-self demanded of her by Cipriano and her hopes for fulfilment.

Plurabelle, Anna Livia, a character in Joyce's *Finnegans Wake*, and also the title of a section of the novel published as 'Work in Progress' (1928), with an introduction by P. *Colum.

PLUTARCH, (AD *c*.50–*c*.125), biographer and moralist, the most popular of Greek authors at the time of the Renaissance. His *Parallel Lives* exemplified the tradition of biography associated with the Peripatetic school, illustrating the moral character of his subjects through a series of anecdotes. Translated by T. *North (1579), they served as a source-book for Shakespeare's Roman plays and later as a model for I. *Walton's *Lives* (1670). *Dryden gave a pioneer analysis of their style and structure in his *Life of Plutarch* (1683).
   The *Moral Essays* provide a compendium of ancient wisdom on moral philosophy, religious belief, education, health, literary criticism, and social customs. Individual essays were translated

into English during the 16th cent., and material from Plutarch's Morals can be found in a number of Elizabethan authors: *Elyot, *Painter, *Lyly, Fennes, *Meres, Cornwallis, *Chapman. The first complete version in English, by *Holland, appeared in 1603. After the middle years of the 17th cent., when they were read by Jeremy *Taylor and *Milton, the popularity of the *Moral Essays* declined, by which time there were more recent examples of the genre. (See also BIOGRAPHY.)

Plymley, *Letters of Peter*, by Sydney *Smith, published 1807–8.

POCAHONTAS, or Matoaka (1595–1617), an American-Indian princess. According to Capt. John *Smith, he was rescued by her when her father was about to kill him in 1607. She became a Christian, was named Rebecca, and married a colonist, John Rolfe. She was brought to England in 1616, where she at first attracted considerable attention, but died neglected. She is introduced by Jonson in his *The Staple of News*, II. i. George Warrington in Thackeray's *The Virginians* composes a tragedy on her, and she becomes a national symbol in H. *Crane's *The Bridge* (1930).

Pocket, Herbert, a character in Dickens's *Great Expectations*.

Podsnap, Mr, a character in Dickens's *Our Mutual Friend*, a type of self-satisfaction and self-importance.

POE, Edgar Allan (1809–49), born in Boston, Massachusetts. He became an orphan in early childhood, and was taken into the household of John Allan. He came to England with the Allans (1815–20) and attended Manor House school at Stoke Newington (which he describes in his *Doppelgänger* story 'William Wilson', 1839). He published his first volume of verse, *Tamerlane and other poems* (1827, anonymously), then enlisted in the US army. He was sent to Sullivan's Island, South Carolina, which provided settings for 'The Gold Bug' (1843) and 'The Balloon Hoax' (1844). He entered West Point in 1830, having published a second volume of verse, *Al Aaraaf* (1829); he was dishonourably discharged in 1831, for intentional neglect of his duties, and published a third volume of verses *Poems* (1831, containing 'To Helen'). He worked as editor on various papers, and began to publish his stories in magazines. His first collection, *Tales of the Grotesque and Arabesque* (1839, for 1840), contains one of his most famous works, 'The Fall of the House of Usher', a *Gothic romance in which the narrator visits the crumbling mansion of his childhood companion, Roderick Usher, to find both Usher and his twin sister Madeline in the last stages of mental and physical weakness; Madeline is buried alive while in a trance, arises, and carries her brother to death, whereupon the house itself splits asunder and sinks into the tarn. The title poem of *The Raven and other Poems* (1845) brought him fame, but he and his ménage continued to suffer poverty and ill health, his wife dying in 1847. He died in Baltimore, five days after having been found semi-conscious and delirious, from alcohol, heart failure, epilepsy, or a combination of these. His posthumous reputation and influence have been great. *Freudian critics (and Freud himself) have been intrigued by the macabre and pathological elements in his work, ranging from hints of necrophilia in his poem 'Annabel Lee' (1849) to the indulgent sadism of 'The Pit and the Pendulum' (1843); *Existentialism has been detected in the motiveless obsession in such stories as 'The Cask of Amontillado' (1846). Readers have been impressed by the cryptograms and mysteries of the stories which feature Poe's detective, Dupin ('The Murders in the Rue Morgue', 1841; 'The Purloined Letter', 1845) and the morbid metaphysical speculation of 'The Facts in the Case of M. Waldemar' (1845).

Poema Morale (or 'The Moral Ode'), a Southern poem of about 400 lines dating from *c*.1175, very early in the Middle English period after the transition from Old English. It deals with themes of transience and repentance.

Poetaster, a comedy by *Jonson, performed 1601, printed 1602.

Set in the court of the Emperor Augustus, the main plot concerns the conspiracy of the poetaster Crispinus and his friend Demetrius (who represent Jonson's contemporaries *Marston and *Dekker) and a swaggering captain, Pantilius Tucca, to defame Horace, who represents Jonson. The matter is tried before Augustus, with Virgil as judge. Horace is acquitted, the 'dresser of plays' Demetrius is made to wear a fool's coat and cap, and Crispinus is given a purge of hellebore and made to vomit up his windy rhetoric. Marston and Dekker replied to the attack in *Satiromastix*, where the main characters of this play reappear.

Poetical Rhapsody, A, a collection of Elizabethan verse published by Francis Davison (?1575–?1619) and his brother Walter in 1602, 'containing divers sonnets, odes, elegies, madrigals and other Poesies'. It includes 'The Lie', attributed to *Ralegh; the song 'In praise of a Beggar's Life' quoted in *The Compleat Angler*; and poems by *Greene, *Wotton, *Sidney, *Spenser, *Donne, and others.

Poetic Diction, a term used to mean language and usage peculiar to poetry, which came into prominence with *Wordsworth's discussion in

his Preface (1800) to the *Lyrical Ballads*, in which he claims to have taken pains to avoid 'what is usually called poetic diction'. Wordsworth implies that there should be no such thing as 'language and usage peculiar to poetry', and illustrates his point by attacking a sonnet by *Gray. Gray himself had declared (1742, letter to West) that 'the language of the age is never the language of poetry'. Wordsworth's attack on *Neoclassicism, archaisms, abstractions, personifications, etc., was both forceful and revolutionary, although his views were later repudiated by *Coleridge; moreover, although poetry became less stilted in its language, its vocabulary remained on the whole distinctive throughout the Romantic and Victorian periods. *Clare is a rare and isolated example of a poet capable of resisting conventional notions of 'poetic diction'; it was not until the 20th cent. and the advent of *Modernism in the works of *Yeats, T. S. *Eliot, *Pound, and others that another major attempt to enlarge the poetic vocabulary and bring it closer to ordinary speech was made.

Poetics, The, a fragment of a treatise by *Aristotle which greatly influenced the theory of *Neo-classicism. It is the source of the principles elaborated by later critics as the *Unities, and it also introduced many much-discussed concepts related to the theory of tragedy, such as *mimesis* (imitation); *catharsis* (purification or purgation); *peripeteia* (reversal); and *hamartia* (either 'tragic flaw' or, more accurately, 'error of judgement'). *Hubris* (overweening pride or confidence) was a form of *hamartia*.

Poet Laureate, the title given to a poet who receives a stipend as an officer of the Royal Household, his duty (no longer enforced) being to write court-odes, etc.

The first poet laureate in the modern sense was *Jonson, followed by *D'Avenant, whose successor *Dryden was the first to be given the title officially. The other laureates in chronological order are: *Shadwell, *Tate, *Rowe, *Eusden, *Cibber, *Whitehead, T. *Warton, *Pye, *Southey, *Wordsworth, *Tennyson, A. *Austin, *Bridges, *Masefield, *Day-Lewis, *Betjeman, Ted *Hughes. See E. K. Broadus, *The Laureateship* (1921).

Poetry, *A Magazine of Verse* (1912–), founded at Chicago by the American poet and critic Harriet Monroe (1860–1936), who edited it until her death. In its early days it published work by E. *Pound, A. *Lowell, T. S. *Eliot, *Frost, H.D. (Hilda *Doolittle), F. M. *Ford, and others, and has continued to publish work by major American poets of the 20th cent.

Poetry Bookshop, see MONRO, H. E.

Poetry London, a bi-monthly which became the leading poetry magazine of the 1940s. It was conceived by Dylan *Thomas, James Meary Tambimuttu (1915–83), Anthony Dickins, and Keidrych Rhys, and its first fifteen issues were edited by Tambimuttu. The first issue appeared in Feb. 1939. It published work by G. *Barker, V. *Watkins, G. *Ewart, H. *Pinter, C. *Tomlinson, D. *Gascoyne, L. *Durrell, and others.

Poetry Nation, a twice-yearly poetry magazine edited by C. B. Cox and Michael Schmidt (6 issues, 1973–6). Contributors included C. *Tomlinson, P. *Porter, E. *Jennings, G. *Hill, and Douglas Dunn; D. *Davie and C. H. *Sisson became co-editors of its thrice-yearly successor, *PN Review* (1976–).

Poetry Review, see MONRO, H. E., and POETRY SOCIETY.

Poetry Society, The, a society founded in 1909 (as the Poetry Recital Society) for the promotion of poetry and the art of speaking verse, and sponsored by many literary figures including G. *Murray, A. P. *Graves, Sturge *Moore, *Gosse, *Newbolt, Arnold *Bennett, E. V. *Lucas, and A. C. *Benson. Its journal, *Poetry Review,* founded 1912, succeeded the earlier *Poetry Gazette*; its first editor was H. E. *Monro, and its contributors have included most of the notable British 20th-cent. poets.

Poets' Corner, part of the south transept of Westminster Abbey containing the tombs or monuments of *Chaucer, *Spenser, Shakespeare, *Jonson, *Milton, *Drayton, Samuel *Butler, A. *Behn, *Gay, and many later distinguished poets and authors.

Poins, in Shakespeare's 1 and 2 *Henry IV,* one of Prince Henry's companions.

Point Counter Point, see HUXLEY, A.

Poirot, Hercule, the Belgian detective in A. *Christie's murder mysteries.

Polite Learning, An Enquiry into the Present State of, see ENQUIRY INTO THE PRESENT STATE OF POLITE LEARNING.

POLITIAN, see POLIZIANO.

Political Register, The, (1802–35), a weekly newspaper founded by *Cobbett. It began as a Tory paper but by 1809 was thoroughly Radical. He continued to issue it even when committed to prison for an article condemning military flogging. His new version of the paper produced in 1816 at 2d. reached a remarkable circulation of 40,000–50,000 a week. In 1821 *Rural Rides began to appear serially. Cobbett continued the paper until his death.

Politic Would-be, Sir and Lady, the foolish traveller and his loquacious wife in Jonson's *Volpone.

Polixines, in Shakespeare's *The Winter's Tale, the king of Bohemia.

POLIZIANO, in English **POLITIAN,** Angelo (1454–94), Italian humanist. He was professor of Greek and Latin at the University of Florence, and wrote poetry in both these languages. His Italian works include *Orfeo* (1480), the first secular drama in Italian. His philological acumen made him one of the founders of modern textual criticism. *Linacre was one of his students, and G. *Chapman translated and imitated his verse.

POLLARD, A(lfred) W(illiam) (1859–1944), keeper of the Department of Printed Books at the British Museum, 1919–24. He edited several volumes of Chaucer's *Canterbury Tales (1886–7) and the 'Globe' Chaucer (1898), published other pioneering works which influenced the study of medieval literature, and also made important contributions to Shakespeare criticism. He was largely responsible for the completion of the *Short-title Catalogue of Books, printed in England, Scotland and Ireland . . . 1475–1640* (1926).

Pollente, in Spenser's *Faerie Queene (v. ii), the 'cruell Sarazin', who is slain by Sir *Artegall.

Pollexfen, Sir Hargreve, a character in Richardson's *Sir Charles Grandison.

Polly, a musical play by J. *Gay, published 1729, the sequel to *The Beggar's Opera. Its performance on stage was prohibited by the Lord Chamberlain. The principal characters are Macheath and Polly Peachum of the earlier play, transported to the West Indies.

Polly, The History of Mr, a novel by H. G. *Wells.

Polonius, in Shakespeare's *Hamlet, the lord chamberlain, father of Ophelia and Laertes.

Polychronicon, The, see HIGDEN, R.

Polydore, (1) in Shakespeare's *Cymbeline, the name borne by Guiderius while in the Welsh forest; (2) a character in Otway's *The Orphan; (3) a character in J. *Fletcher's The Mad Lover.

POLYDORE VERGIL, see VERGIL, P.

Polyglot Bible, The, edited in 1653–7 by Brian Walton (?1600–61), bishop of Chester, with the help of many scholars. It contains various oriental texts of the Bible with Latin translations, and a critical apparatus.

Polyglots, The, a novel by W. *Gerhardie.

Polyhymnia, a poem by *Peele written in 1590. It contains at the end the beautiful song 'His Golden lockes, | Time hath to Silver turn'd', made widely known by Thackeray's quotation of part of it in *The Newcomes, ch. 76.

Poly-Olbion, The (this is the spelling of the 1st edn), the most ambitious work of *Drayton. It was written between 1598 and 1622 and consists of thirty 'Songs' each of 300–500 lines, in hexameter couplets, in which the author endeavours to awaken his readers to the beauties and glories of their country.

During his travels he describes the principal topographical features of the country, interspersing in the appropriate places legends, fragments of history, catalogues of British saints and hermits, of great discoverers, of birds, fishes, and plants with their properties. The word 'poly-olbion' (from the Greek) means 'having many blessings'.

POMFRET, John (1667–1702), a Bedfordshire vicar remembered for his poem The Choice (1700), which describes the pleasures of a quiet country estate where the author 'might live genteelly, but not great'. It secured its author inclusion in Johnson's *Lives of the English Poets.

Pompey the Great, his faire Corneliaes Tragedie, see CORNELIA.

Pompey the Little, The History of, see COVENTRY, F.

PONSONBY, Sarah, see LLANGOLLEN, THE LADIES OF.

Poor Richard's Almanack, see FRANKLIN, B.

Poor Tom, a name assumed by *Edgar in Shakespeare's *King Lear (II. iii).

Pooter, the archetypally suburban protagonist of *The Diary of a Nobody by G. and W. Grossmith.

POPE, Alexander (1688–1744), was the son of a Roman Catholic linen-draper of London. His health was ruined and his growth stunted by a severe illness at the age of 12. He showed his precocious metrical skill in his 'Pastorals' (1709) written, according to himself, when he was 16. He became intimate with *Wycherley, who introduced him to London life. His *Essay on Criticism (1711) made him known to *Addison's circle, and his 'Messiah' was published in The Spectator in 1712. *The Rape of the Lock appeared in *Lintot's Miscellanies in the same year and was republished, enlarged, in 1714. *Windsor Forest (1713) appealed to the Tories by its references to the Peace of Utrecht. He drifted away from

Addison's 'little senate' and became a member of the *Scriblerus Club. His translation in heroic couplets of Homer's *Iliad (1715–20) is more *Augustan than Homeric in spirit and diction. It was supplemented in 1725–6 by a translation of the *Odyssey, in which he was assisted by William Broome and Elijah Fenton. The two translations brought him financial independence.

In 1717 had appeared a collection of his works containing two poems dealing with the passion of love. They are 'Verses to the Memory of an Unfortunate Lady', and *'Eloisa to Abelard'. About this time he became strongly attached to Martha *Blount, with whom his friendship continued throughout his life, and to Lady M. W. *Montagu, whom in later years he assailed with bitterness.

Pope assisted *Gay in writing the comedy Three Hours after Marriage (1717). In 1723, Pope's portrait of *Atticus, a satire on Addison, appeared. In the Miscellanies (1727, by Pope, *Swift, *Arbuthnot, and Gay) Pope published his prose treatise Peri Bathous, or the Art of Sinking in Poetry, ridiculing among others Ambrose *Philips, *Theobald, and J. *Dennis. In 1725 Pope published an edition of Shakespeare, the errors in which were pointed out in a pamphlet by Theobald. This led to the selection of Theobald by Pope as hero of his *Dunciad, a satire on Dullness. An additional book, The New Dunciad, was published in 1742. Influenced in part by the philosophy of his friend *Bolingbroke, Pope published a series of moral and philosophical poems, *An Essay on Man (1733–4), consisting of four Epistles; and *Moral Essays (1731–5). In 1733 Pope published the first of his miscellaneous satires, Imitations of Horace. In it he defends himself against the charge of Malignity, and professes to be inspired only by love of virtue. He inserts, however, a gross attack on Lady Mary Wortley Montagu as 'Sappho'. An Epistle to Dr Arbuthnot (1735), the prologue to the above Satires, is one of Pope's most brilliant pieces of irony and invective, mingled with autobiography. It contains the famous portraits of Addison and Lord *Hervey, and lashes at his minor critics, Dennis, Cibber, *Curll, Theobald, etc.

He was partly occupied during his later years with the publication of his earlier correspondence, which he edited and amended in such a manner as to misrepresent the literary history of the time. He also employed discreditable artifices to make it appear that it was published against his wish. Thus he procured the publication by Curll of his 'Literary Correspondence' in 1735, and then endeavoured to disavow him.

With the growth of *Romanticism Pope's poetry was increasingly seen as artificial. It was not until *Leavis and *Empson that a serious attempt was made to rediscover Pope's richness, variety, and complexity.

Popish Plot, a plot fabricated in 1678 by Titus *Oates. He deposed at the end of September before the Middlesex magistrate Sir Edmond Berry Godfrey that it was intended to murder Charles II, place James on the throne, and suppress Protestantism. Godfrey disappeared on 12 Oct. and was found murdered on 17 Oct., and many persons were falsely accused and executed.

POPPER, Sir Karl Raimund (1902–), Austrian philosopher of science. He left Vienna for New Zealand on Hitler's rise to power, and came to England in 1946, where, in 1949, he was appointed professor of logic and scientific method at the London School of Economics. His philosophy of science claims to solve the problem of induction: the problem of extrapolating from past to future, or, more precisely from limited evidence to a general conclusion. He has also contributed to political philosophy and a defence of free will and the 'self-conscious mind'. His works include *The Logic of Scientific Discovery* (*Logik der Forschung*, 1934); *The Open Society and Its Enemies* (1945), and *The Self and Its Brain* (1977, with John C. Eccles).

POPPLE, William (1701–64), dramatist, wrote two comedies, *The Lady's Revenge* (1734) and *The Double Deceit: or a cure for Jealousy* (1735), in which two young men, intended to marry two heiresses, conspire to avoid their fate by exchanging places with their valets. The ladies, apprised of the trick, exchange places with their maids, the pseudo-valets fall in love with the pseudo-maids, and all ends well.

Porretta, Clementina, a character in Richardson's *Sir Charles Grandison*.

PORSON, Richard (1759–1808), distinguished classical scholar. He edited four plays of *Euripides (most notably *Hecuba*), and advanced Greek scholarship by his elucidation of Greek idiom and usage, by his study of Greek metres, and by his emendation of texts. He is also remembered for various witticisms and for contributions to *The Gentleman's Magazine*.

Porteous, Captain John, see HEART OF MIDLOTHIAN, THE.

Porter, in Shakespeare's *Macbeth*; he lets Macduff and Lennox into Macbeth's castle (II. iii), and is the subject of *De Quincey's essay 'On the Knocking at the Gate'.

PORTER, Endymion (1587–1649), was groom of the bedchamber to Charles I, and the friend and patron of painters and poets. He was painted by Van Dyck, and *Jonson, *Herrick, *D'Avenant, and *Dekker, among others, celebrated him in verse.

PORTER, Jane (1776–1850), published the successful *Thaddeus of Warsaw* (1803), which led to friendship with one of its heroes, the Polish General Kosciuszko. She also wrote *The Scottish Chiefs* (1810), a story of William Wallace; and *The Pastor's Fireside* (1815), a story of the later Stuarts.

PORTER, Peter Neville Frederick (1929–), poet, born in Brisbane, Australia; he came to England in 1951. He was briefly associated with the *Group in the 1960s, and the work in his early collections (*Once Bitten, Twice Bitten*, 1961; *Poems, Ancient and Modern*, 1964; *The Last of England*, 1970) provides a sharply satiric portrait of London in the 'swinging sixties'. In the 1970s, his work became more meditative, complex, and allusive, though no less colloquial and urbane; its learned references to Italian baroque, classical mythology, opera, and German Romanticism add both richness and obscurity. *The Cost of Seriousness* (1978) and *English Subtitles* (1981) explore the poet's conflicting responsibilities to his art and to others. His *Collected Poems* was published in 1983.

PORTER, William Sydney, see HENRY, O.

Portia, (1) the heroine of Shakespeare's *The Merchant of Venice* ; (2) in his *Julius Caesar*, the wife of Brutus.

Portrait of a Lady, The, a novel by H. *James, published 1881.

The story centres in Isabel Archer, the 'Lady', an attractive American girl. Around her we have the placid old American banker, Mr Touchett; his hard repellent wife; his ugly, invalid, witty, charming son Ralph, whom England has thoroughly assimilated; and the crude, brilliant, indomitably American journalist Henrietta Stackpole. Isabel refuses the offer of marriage of a typical English peer, the excellent Lord Warburton, and of a bulldog-like New Englander, Caspar Goodwood, to fall a victim, under the influence of the slightly sinister Madame Merle (another cosmopolitan American), to a worthless and spiteful dilettante, Gilbert Osmond, who marries her for her fortune and ruins her life; but to whom she remains loyal in spite of her realization of his vileness.

Portrait of the Artist as a Young Dog (1940), a collection of stories by Dylan *Thomas.

Portrait of the Artist as a Young Man, A, an autobiographical novel by J. *Joyce, first published in *The Egoist*, 1914–15.

It describes the development of Stephen Dedalus (who reappears in *Ulysses* in a slightly different incarnation) from his early boyhood, through bullying at school and an adolescent crisis of faith inspired partly by the famous 'hellfire sermon' preached by Father Arnall (ch. 3) and partly by the guilt of his own precocious sexual adventures, to student days and a gradual sense of his own destiny as poet, patriot, and unbeliever.

Positivist Philosophy, see COMTE.

Posthumus Leonatus, the hero of Shakespeare's *Cymbeline* and husband of *Imogen.

'Pot of Basil, The', see ISABELLA.

Pott, Mr, in Dickens's *Pickwick Papers*, the editor of the 'Eatanswill Gazette'.

POTTER, (Helen) Beatrix (1866–1943), wrote and illustrated little story books for children. In a letter to the son of her former governess in 1893 she began *The Tale of Peter Rabbit*, which she published at her own expense in 1901; *The Tailor of Gloucester* followed in 1902, and *Squirrel Nutkin* in 1903, her first great success. *Johnny Town-Mouse* (1918) was the last of her books in the old style. *The Journal of Beatrix Potter* (1966), written in code, was transcribed by Leslie Linder.

POTTER, Dennis Christopher George (1935–), playwright, has written fiction, stage plays, screenplays, and adapted works for television, but is best known for his own television plays, which show an original and inventive use of the medium. These include two plays dealing with the career of an aspiring working-class, Oxford-educated politician, *Vote, Vote, Vote for Nigel Barton* (1965) and *Stand up, Nigel Barton* (1965), published together in 1968; *Pennies from Heaven*, a six-part serial (1978, pub. 1981); *Blue Remembered Hills* (1979, a tragic evocation of childhood); and *The Singing Detective* (1986).

POTTER, Stephen Meredith (1900–69), writer, editor, and radio producer, whose book *The Theory and Practice of Gamesmanship; or the Art of Winning Games without Actually Cheating* (1947) had a great vogue and added a new word and concept to the language; he followed it with *Some Notes on Lifemanship* (1950), *One-Upmanship* (1952), and *Supermanship* (1958).

Poulter's measure, a fanciful name for a metre consisting of lines of 12 and 14 syllables alternately. Poulter = poulterer.

'Poulter's measure, which giveth xii for one dozen, and xiiij for another'.
(Gascoigne, *The Steele Glas*).

POUND, Ezra Weston Loomis (1885–1972), American poet, came to Europe in 1908 and published his first volume of poems, *A Lume Spento* (1908). He published several other volumes of verse, including *Personae* (1909),

Canzoni (1911), *Ripostes* (1912), and *Lustra* (1916). Together with F. S. Flint, R. *Aldington, and Hilda *Doolittle he founded the *Imagist school of poets; in 1914 he edited *Des Imagistes: An Anthology*. Pound also championed the *Modernist work of avant-garde writers and artists like *Joyce, W. *Lewis, Gaudier-Brzeska, and T. S. *Eliot. Further volumes of poetry include *Quia Pauper Amavi* (1919, which contains 'Homage to Sextus Propertius') and *Hugh Selwyn Mauberley* (1920). Pound was now increasingly turning away from the constrictions of Imagism, and finding freedom partly through translations; his early volumes had contained adaptations from Provençal and early Italian, a version of the Old English *The Seafarer*, and in 1915 *Cathay*, translations from the Chinese of Li Po. Pound was thus moving towards the rich, grandly allusive, multicultural world of the *Cantos*, his most ambitious achievement; the first three Cantos appeared in 1917 in *Poetry*. In 1920 Pound left London for Paris; in 1925 he settled permanently in Rapallo. The Cantos appeared intermittently over the next decades until the appearance of the final *Drafts and Fragments of Cantos CX to CXVII* (1970).

In Italy Pound became increasingly preoccupied with economics and embraced Social Credit theories. His own interpretation of these theories led him into anti-Semitism and at least partial support for Mussolini's social programme. During the Second World War he broadcast over the Italian radio: in 1945 he was arrested at Genoa, then sent to a US Army Disciplinary Training Centre near Pisa, a period which produced the much-admired *Pisan Cantos* (1948). He was then moved to Washington, found unfit to plead, and confined to a mental institution; he was released in 1958 and returned to Italy, where he died.

Povey, Samuel, a character in Bennett's *The Old Wives' Tale*.

POWELL, Anthony Dymoke (1905–), novelist, whose initial reputation as a satirist and light comedian rests on five pre-war books, beginning with *Afternoon Men* (1931) which maps a characteristically seedy section of pleasure-loving, party-going London.

After the war he embarked on a more ambitious sequence of twelve novels, *A Dance to the Music of Time* (named after Poussin's painting). Starting with *A Question of Upbringing* (1951) and ending with *Hearing Secret Harmonies* (1975), the whole is framed and distanced through the eyes of a narrator, Nicholas Jenkins, whose generation grew up in the shadow of the First World War to find their lives dislocated by the Second. Jenkins's canvas, following the perspectives of time rather than space, is hospitable and broad, especially rich in literary and artistic hangers-on, stiffened by a solid contingent from society, politics, and the City, enlivened and sometimes convulsed by eccentrics, derelicts, and drop-outs of all classes and conditions. Against these looms Kenneth Widmerpool, one of the most memorable characters of 20th-cent. fiction, whose ruthless pursuit of power, which carries him from innately ludicrous beginnings to a position of increasingly formidable, eventually sinister, authority, is the chief of many threads binding this panoramic view of England.

Powell's memoirs, *To Keep the Ball Rolling* (4 vols, 1976–82), shed considerable light on the creation of the characters of his fictional world.

Power and the Glory, The, a novel by G. *Greene, published 1940.

Set in Mexico at a time of religious persecution in the name of revolution, it describes the desperate last wanderings of a whisky priest as outlaw in his own state, who, despite a sense of his own worthlessness, is determined to continue to function as priest until captured. He is contrasted with Padre Jose, a priest who has accepted marriage and humiliation; with 'the gringo', bank robber, murderer, and materialist, also on the run; and with the lieutenant, portrayed as an angry idealist and 'a good man', who pursues the priest and corners him when he is drawn back (by the Judas-figure of a half-caste) to offer the last rites to the dying gringo, just as he has reached safety over the border. His execution (and martyrdom?) is witnessed by the grotesque expatriate dentist Mr Tench, and the final episode indicates that the Church will survive its persecution.

POWYS, John Cowper (1872–1963), brother of Llewelyn and Theodore *Powys, was brought up in the Dorset–Somerset countryside which was to become of great importance in his later writing. He became a prolific writer of poetry and of essays on philosophy and religion, and produced a remarkable *Autobiography* (1934), but he is remembered for his novels which include *Wood and Stone* (1915, NY; 1917, London), *Rodmoor* (1916), and *Ducdame* (1925). His first major novel was *Wolf Solent* (1929), a crowded work set in the West Country. *A Glastonbury Romance* (1932, NY; 1933, London), his best-known novel, is a work on a huge scale, in which *Glastonbury and its legends exert a supernatural influence on the life of the town—on the religious revival led by Johnny Geard, on the hard commercial interests of Phil Crow, on the Communist workers, and on the complex loves, both sacred and sexual, of the town's inhabitants. *Weymouth Sands* (1934, NY) is set against a sombre background of Portland and the sea; the human struggle centres on Jobber, his love for Perdita and his hatred of Dog Cattistock, and on the final relinquishing of dream

in favour of the possible. *Maiden Castle* (1936, NY; 1937, London), set in Dorchester, follows the interlocking loves of several couples, no longer young. Most of the later novels, written after Powys had settled in Wales, share an extravagance of subject and style and strong elements of the supernatural. They include *Morwyn* (1937); *Owen Glendower* (1940, NY; 1941, London), a historical novel; *Porius* (1951); and *Atlantis* (1954), containing Powys's most extreme flights of imagination, in which Odysseus, returned from Troy, sets out again to discover the continent of America, where he settles.

POWYS, Llewelyn (1884–1939), essayist and journalist, brother of John Cowper and Theodore *Powys. His many books include *Skin For Skin* (1925), a sombre account of the course of his tuberculosis with idyllic Dorset interludes; *Apples be Ripe* (1930), a novel; *Impassioned Clay* (1931), a personal account of the human predicament; *Earth Memories* (1934) and *Dorset Essays* (1935), both volumes of essays; and *Love and Death* (1939), an eloquent 'imaginary autobiography', on the theme of his lost first love and his approaching death. *Damnable Opinions* (1935) presented many of the radical, iconoclastic views he shared with his brothers.

POWYS, T(heodore) F(rancis) (1875–1953), brother of John Cowper and Llewelyn *Powys. East Chaldon, Dorset, provided the background to most of his novels and stories. His works include *Soliloquies of a Hermit* (1916), a series of meditations; short stories, including *The Left Leg* and *Black Bryony* (both 1923), and *Mr Tasker's Gods* and *Mark Only* (both 1924); and *Innocent Birds* (1926), stories of eccentric village simpletons. He is best remembered for his novel *Mr Weston's Good Wine* (1927). In this vivid allegory Mr Weston (or God) comes to the worldly village of Folly Down, selling from his old van his vintages of Love and Death. *Fables* (1929), in which Powys's beliefs are most clearly exposed, was followed by his other major novel, *Unclay* (1931). His most complex work, it interlocks the stories of several bizarre characters, innocent, evil, and mad, whose lives and loves are altered by Death's arrival.

Poyser, Martin and Mrs, characters in G. Eliot's *Adam Bede*.

Practical Criticism, a term given currency by I. A. *Richards's experiment in *Practical Criticism: A Study in Literary Judgement* (1929) to describe a certain method of literary criticism, which was to form a quasi-scientific foundation for the *New Criticism; for an account of the experiment, see under RICHARDS, I. A. The term 'practical' was clearly chosen deliberately to distinguish this approach from the theoretical. His work became a textbook for the sharpening of critical appreciation and attention.

PRAED, Winthrop Mackworth (1802–39), was called to the bar, then went into Parliament. He is remembered principally as a humorous poet and composer of elegant *vers de société*; 'The County Ball', 'A Letter of Advice', 'Stanzas on seeing the Speaker Asleep', and 'The Vicar' are characteristic examples of his light verse. Like *Hood, with whom he is often compared, he sometimes uses humour to clothe a grim subject, as in 'The Red Fisherman'. He also wrote verse epistles, e.g. 'Sir Nicholas at Marston Moor'. His verse was published largely in periodicals and annuals, but his inoffensive satire, gentle wit, and fluent metrical variations assured him a more lasting readership. His *Poems* appeared in 1864.

Praeterita, see RUSKIN, J.

Pragmatism, in philosophy, the doctrine that the test of the value of any assertion lies in its practical consequences. See JAMES, W.

Prancing Nigger, see FIRBANK, R.

Prayer, The Book of Common, see COMMON PRAYER.

PRAZ, Mario (1896–1982), Italian critic and scholar, wrote on many aspects of English literature and the connections between the English and Italian traditions; his best-known work is *La Carne, La Morte e Il Diavolo nella Letteratura Romantica* (1930; published in a translation by Angus Davidson as *The Romantic Agony*, 1933) in which he explores the legacy of de Sade, the perverse and pathological elements in *Poe, *Swinburne, *Wilde, etc., and the cult of the Fatal Woman.

Prelude, The: or, Growth of a Poet's Mind, an autobiographical poem in blank verse by *Wordsworth, addressed to *Coleridge, and begun in 1798–9; a complete draft in 13 books was finished in 1805, but it was several times remodelled, and published posthumously in its final version in 1850. The full text, showing the work of Wordsworth on it in his later years (which increased the number of books to 14, toned down some of the earlier political views, tidied up structure, syntax, etc.) was published by de *Selincourt in 1926. The poem was originally intended as an introduction to 'The Recluse' (see EXCURSION, THE).

Although profoundly autobiographical, the poem does not proceed in terms of strict chronology; it deals with infancy, school days, Cambridge, his walking tour through the Alps, his political awakening in France, and consequent horrors, etc., but (for example) the pass-age describing the 'visionary dreariness' of a highly charged moment in his early boyhood is delayed until Book XI ('Imagination, How Impaired and Restored') and the landscape there described is immediately linked in the immediate past with his sister Dorothy and Coleridge, both of whom are intermittently addressed throughout the work. The tone is similarly flexible and variable; conversational and informal in some passages, narrative and naturalistic in others, it rises at points to an impassioned loftiness. A constant theme throughout is Wordsworth's sense of himself as a chosen being, with an overriding duty to his poetic vocation. Apart from its poetic quality, the work is remarkable for its psychological insight into the significance of childhood experience, a theme dear to *Romanticism, but rarely treated with such power and precision.

Premium, Mr, the name taken by Sir Oliver Surface in Sheridan's *The School for Scandal*.

Pre-Raphaelite Brotherhood, a group of artists, poets, and critics—John Everett Millais, D. G. *Rossetti, W. Holman *Hunt, W. M. *Rossetti, T. *Woolner, Frederic George Stephens (1828–1907), and James Collinson (1825–81)—who first met as a group, led by the first three, in 1848. The initials 'P.R.B.' first appeared on their work in the RA exhibition of 1849. As its periodical *The Germ (1850) suggests, the movement was strongly literary, and some of its most striking paintings were inspired by *Keats (see Millais's *Isabella*), *Dante, Shakespeare, and *Tennyson. Common aspirations of the group included fidelity to nature (manifested in clarity, brightness, detailed first-hand observation of flora, etc.), and moral seriousness, in some expressed in religious themes or symbolic mystical iconography. Many of the subjects were medieval as well as literary, and the movement (much influenced by *Ruskin, who became its champion) saw itself in part as a revolt against the ugliness of modern life and dress. Artists connected with the PRB include Ford Madox Brown, W. B. *Scott, William Dyce, Henry Wallis, Arthur Hughes, Burne-Jones, and *De Morgan. In literary terms, the movement's most important recruits were perhaps W. *Morris and, more indirectly, *Pater. The brotherhood dissolved in the 1850s, but its influence was enduring, and the term 'Pre-Raphaelite' has come to denote a distinctive style of appearance, décor, design, etc.

Present Discontents, Thoughts on the cause of the, a political treatise by E. *Burke, published 1770.

Burke reflects on *Wilkes's expulsion from Parliament after the Middlesex election, and expounds for the first time his constitutional creed. He attributes the convulsions in the country to the control of Parliament by the cabal known as the 'King's friends', a system of favouritism essentially at variance with the constitution. He thinks the first requirement is the restoration of the right of free election, and looks for further safeguards in the 'interposition of the body of the people itself' to secure decent attention to public interests, and in the restoration of party government.

Present State of the Nation, *Observations on a late publication intituled the*, a political treatise by E. *Burke, published 1769.

This was Burke's first controversial publication on political matters. It is a reply to an anonymous pamphlet attributed to George Grenville, in which the decision of the Grenville administration to tax America was defended on the ground that the charges left by the war had made this course necessary. Burke reviews the economic condition of England and France, and defends the repeal of the Stamp Act by the Rockingham administration for the reason that 'politics should be adjusted, not to human reasonings, but to human nature', and that 'people must be governed in a manner agreeable to their temper and disposition'.

PRESTON, Thomas (1537–98), vice-chancellor of Cambridge University, 1589–90, is thought to have been the author of *A lamentable Tragedie, mixed full of plesant mirth, containing the life of Cambises king of Percia* (1569, see CAMBYSES).

Price, Fanny, a character in J. Austen's *Mansfield Park.

PRICE, Richard (1723–91), a Dissenting minister who became, with his friend Joseph *Priestley, one of the original members of the Unitarian Society in 1791; he was from 1758 minister at Newington Green, which had been a centre of Dissent for many years, where he influenced many younger writers, including S. *Rogers and M. *Wollstonecraft. He published in 1756 his best-known work, *A Review of the Principal Questions in Morals*, in which he questions *Hutcheson's doctrine of 'moral sense'. He was a close friend of *Franklin, and supported the cause of American independence; he also supported the French revolution, and his sermon delivered on 4 Nov. 1789, celebrating 'the ardour for liberty' of the French, provoked Burke to write his *Reflections on the* **Revolution in France*.

PRICE, Uvedale, see PICTURESQUE.

Pride and Prejudice, a novel by J. *Austen, published 1813. It was originally a youthful work entitled 'First Impressions' and was refused by Cadell, a London publisher, in 1797.

Mr and Mrs Bennet live with their five daughters at Longbourn in Hertfordshire. In the absence of a male heir, the property is due to pass by entail to a cousin, William Collins, who has been presented with a living near Rosings, the Kentish seat of Lady Catherine de Bourgh. Charles Bingley, a rich young bachelor, takes Netherfield, a house near Longbourn, bringing with him his two sisters and his friend Fitzwilliam Darcy, nephew of Lady Catherine. Bingley and Jane, the eldest Bennet girl, fall in love. Darcy, though attracted to the next sister, Elizabeth, offends her by his supercilious behaviour. The aversion is intensified when Darcy and Bingley's sisters, disgusted with the vulgarity of Mrs Bennet and her two youngest daughters, effectively separate Bingley from Jane.

Meanwhile the fatuous Mr Collins, urged to marry by Lady Catherine (for whom he shows the most grovelling and obsequious respect), proposes to Elizabeth. When firmly rejected he promptly transfers his affections to Charlotte Lucas, a friend of Elizabeth's who accepts him. Staying with the newly married couple in their parsonage, Elizabeth again encounters Darcy. Captivated by her in spite of himself, Darcy proposes to her in terms which do not conceal his wounded pride. Elizabeth indignantly rejects him.

On an expedition to the north of England with her uncle and aunt, Mr and Mrs Gardiner, Elizabeth visits Pemberley, Darcy's seat in Derbyshire, believing Darcy to be absent. However Darcy appears and welcomes the visitors. His manner, though grave, is now gentle and attentive. At this point news reaches Elizabeth that her youngest sister Lydia has eloped with the unprincipled Wickham (son of the late steward of the Darcy estate). With help from Darcy, the fugitives are traced, their marriage is arranged, and (again through Darcy) they are suitably provided for. Bingley and Jane are reunited and become engaged. In spite, and indeed in consequence, of the insolent intervention of Lady Catherine, Darcy and Elizabeth also become engaged.

PRIESTLEY, J(ohn) B(oynton) (1894–1984), Bradford-born novelist, playwright, and critic. He achieved success as a novelist with *The Good Companions* (1929), an account of theatrical adventures on the road, which was followed by the grimmer novel of London life, *Angel Pavement* (1930). His many other novels, which vary greatly in scope, include *Bright Day* (1946), *Festival at Farbridge* (1951), *Lost Empires* (1965), and *The Image Men* (1968). Priestley also wrote some 50 plays and dramatic adaptations; amongst the best known are his 'Time' plays, influenced by the theories of J. W. *Dunne (*Dangerous Corner*, 1932; *I have been here before*, 1937; *Time and the Conways*, 1937), his psychological mystery drama *An Inspector Calls* (1947), and his West Riding farce *When We Are Married* (1938). He also published many miscellaneous works, ranging from *English Journey* (1934), an account of his own travels through England, to collections of his wartime broadcasts (*Britain Speaks*, 1940; *All England Listened*, 1968); from the ambitious, *Jungian Literature and Western Man* (1960) to informal social histories and commentaries. He also wrote several volumes of autobiography, including *Margin Released* (1962) and *Instead of the Trees* (1977).

PRIESTLEY, Joseph (1733–1804), became with his friend R. *Price one of the original members of the Unitarian Society in 1791. In politics he was a Radical, labelled 'Gunpowder' Priestley for his remarks about laying gunpowder 'under the old building of error and superstition'. He supported the French revolution and attacked *Burke. His *Essay on the First Principles of Government* (1768) considerably influenced *Bentham's development of the principle of Utilitarianism. He was himself influenced by *Hartley. He was the discoverer of oxygen and the author of various valuable scientific works.

Prig, Betsey, a character in Dickens's *Martin Chuzzlewit*.

Primas, the name (meaning 'first', 'chief') given to Hugh of Orleans, a canon of Orleans *c.*1140 and a *Goliardic poet who excelled in Latin lyrics which reveal both scholarship and a libertine disposition.

Prime Minister, The, a novel by A. *Trollope, published 1876, the fifth in the *'Palliser' series.

Prime of Miss Jean Brodie, The, a novel by M. *Spark, published 1961.

Set in Edinburgh during the 1930s, it describes the career of eccentric and egotistical Miss Brodie, teacher at the Marcia Blaine School for Girls, and her domination of her 'set' of 16-year-olds. With many flashes back and forward, it describes the manner in which Miss Brodie fascinates her disciples, who are particularly intrigued by her relationships with two male teachers, the married and Catholic art master, Mr Lloyd, and the bachelor Church of Scotland singing-master, Mr Lowther, who, rejected after much dalliance by Miss Brodie, in despair marries the science mistress. Sandy, one of the set, has an affair with Mr Lloyd while Miss Brodie is away in the summer of 1938 touring Hitler's Germany; the results of this are that Sandy becomes a Catholic and arranges the dismissal of Miss Brodie on the grounds of her sympathy with Fascism. Miss Brodie herself, dangerous and compelling, is the centre of the novel's considerable moral ambiguity and complexity.

Primitivism, and the cult of 'the noble savage', are associated predominantly with the 18th cent., though they are clearly in some aspects descended from the classical concept of the Golden Age, and preceded by individual works like A. Behn's *Oroonoko*. Primitivism took the form of a revolt against luxury (see Goldsmith's *The Deserted Village*), against sophistication (see Colman's *Inkle and Yarico*, Cumberland's *The West Indian*, Mrs *Inchbald's *The Child of Nature*, *Bage's *Hermsprong*, all works which stress the superiority of a simple education), and, in terms of critical theory, against *Neo-classicism. (See HURD; GRAY, T.) Primitivism proposed a belief in man's natural goodness, and in the inevitable corruptions of civilization. Interest in the educational and philosophic theories of *Rousseau was accompanied by great enthusiasm for travel writings and for real-life South Sea Islanders, Eskimos, Lapplanders, Negroes, etc. There was also much curiosity about the phenomenon of the 'wild child'. Home-grown primitives were also in demand, and 'peasant' poets such as S. *Duck and A. *Yearsley were taken up by eager patrons: the notorious fake primitives *Macpherson and *Chatterton enjoyed a considerable vogue. They in turn were stimulated by the scholarly researches of *Percy and *Ritson, who revived an interest in early English poetry. One of the most important figures in the movement was Gray, whose poems *The Bard* and *The Progress of Poesy* reflect his own interest in and feelings for the non-classical past. It was in the cause of liberty that writers such as *Cowper and T. *Day defended the Noble Savage and attacked the slave trade. The ideas embodied in Primitivism were in many ways continued in the *Romantic movement, with its stress on Nature, freedom (both political and artistic), and the natural man.

Primrose, Dr, the vicar of Wakefield in *Goldsmith's novel of that name. His family consists of his wife Deborah; daughters Olivia and Sophia; sons George and Moses; and two younger boys.

Prince, The, see MACHIAVELLI, N.

PRINCE, F(rank) T(empleton) (1912–), poet, born in South Africa. His collections of poetry include *Poems* (1938), *Soldiers Bathing and other poems* (1954), and *The Doors of Stone: Poems 1938–62* (1963); his *Collected Poems* appeared in 1979.

Prince Hohenstiel-Schwangau, *Saviour of Society*, a poem in blank verse by R. *Browning, written and published 1871. The poem, while alluding in detail to Napoleon III's career, also raises questions about truth and imagination which are central to Browning's aesthetics:

political and poetic idealism, opposed to and yet dependent on the materialism of action and language, mirror one another.

Princess, The, *A Medley*, a poem by *Tennyson, published 1847. Some of the well-known lyrics ('The splendour falls', 'Ask me no more: the moon may draw the sea') were added in the third edition of 1850, but others, including 'Tears, idle tears' (composed in 1834 at Tintern) and 'Now sleeps the crimson petal, now the white' were included in the first.

A prince has been betrothed since childhood to Princess Ida, daughter of neighbouring King Gama. She becomes a devotee of women's rights, abjures marriage, and founds a university. The prince and two companions, Cyril and Florian, gain admission to the university dressed as women, and are detected by the two tutors, Lady Psyche and Lady Blanche, who from different motives conceal their knowledge. The deceit is presently detected by Ida, but not before the prince has had occasion to rescue her from drowning. Her determination is unshaken, and a combat ensues, between fifty warriors led by the prince and fifty led by Gama's son, during which the three comrades are wounded. The university is turned into a hospital, the prince urges his suit, and he wins Ida, envisaging a future in which 'The man [may] be more of woman, she of man'. It formed the basis of the satirical *Gilbert and Sullivan opera *Princess Ida*.

Principe, Il, see MACHIAVELLI, N.

Principia Ethica, see MOORE, G. E.

Principia Mathematica, see NEWTON, I., and RUSSELL, B.

Principles of Moral and Political Philosophy, see PALEY, W.

Principles of Morals and Legislation, *An Introduction to the*, see BENTHAM, J.

Pringle, Guy and Harriet, the principal characters of O. *Manning's *Balkan Trilogy* and *Levant Trilogy*.

PRINGLE, Thomas (1789–1834), a friend of Sir W. *Scott, and for a short time editor of the *Edinburgh Monthly Magazine*. In 1809 he published his first volume of poems, which included 'The Emigrant's Farewell'. He emigrated to South Africa, and he is remembered chiefly as a poet of that country. His *Ephemerides* (1828) and *African Sketches* (1834) reveal his sympathetic interest in the native races and the wild life of Africa.

PRIOR, Matthew (1664–1721), joined with Charles Montagu (later earl of Halifax) in The

Hind and the Panther Transvers'd to the Story of the Country Mouse and the City Mouse (1687, see TOWN MOUSE AND COUNTRY MOUSE), a satire on Dryden's *The Hind and the Panther*. He was appointed secretary to the ambassador at The Hague and employed in the negotiations for the treaty of Ryswick. He joined the Tories and in 1711 was sent to Paris as a secret agent at the time of the peace negotiations, the subsequent treaty of Utrecht (1713) being popularly known as 'Matt's Peace'. He was recalled on Queen Anne's death and imprisoned for over a year. A folio edition of his poems was brought out in 1718 after his release. Prior is best remembered for his brilliant occasional verses, epigrams, and familiar pieces ('My noble, lovely, little Peggy' and 'Jinny and Just', for example, in which he combines lightness of touch with mock seriousness), but also wrote longer works in various styles. *Carmen Seculare* (1700) is an ode celebrating the arrival of William III; 'Alma; or the Progress of the Mind' (1718) is a *Hudibrastic dialogue ridiculing various systems of philosophy. 'Hans Carvel' (1701) and 'The Ladle' (1718) are narratives ending with coarse jests, whereas 'Henry and Emma' (1709) is a sentimental burlesque of an old ballad *'The Nut-Brown Maid'.

'Prioress's Tale, The', see CANTERBURY TALES, 16.

Prisoner of Chillon, The, a poem by *Byron, published 1816. The poem describes the imprisonment of a historical character, the patriot François de Bonnivard (1496–?1570), in the castle of Chillon, on the lake of Geneva.

Prisoner of Zenda, The, and its sequel *Rupert of Hentzau*, novels by Anthony Hope (*Hawkins), published 1894 and 1898.

They deal with the perilous and romantic adventures of Rudolf Rassendyll, an English gentleman, in Ruritania, where, by impersonating the king (to whom he bears a marked physical resemblance), he defeats a plot to oust him from the throne. He falls in love with the king's betrothed, Princess Flavia, and she with him, but gallantly relinquishes her to the restored king. In the sequel he defeats a plot of the villain Rupert of Hentzau against Flavia, now the unhappy wife of the king, and has another chance of taking the throne and of marrying Flavia. But he is assassinated before his decision is known.

PRITCHETT, Sir V(ictor) S(awdon) (1900–), novelist, critic, and short story writer. His first novel, *Clare Drummer* (1929), was followed by several others, but Pritchett is principally known for his short stories, the first of which appeared in the *Cornhill*, the *New Statesman*, etc., in the 1920s; his first collection, *The Spanish Virgin and other stories* (1930), was followed by many others, including *You Make Your Own Life* (1938), *When my Girl Comes Home* (1961), *The Camberwell Beauty* (1974), and two volumes of *Collected Stories* (1982, 1983). They are distinguished by their wide social range, shrewd observation of the quirks of human nature, and humane irony. Pritchett's other works include *The Living Novel* (1946), studies of *Balzac (1973) and *Turgenev (1977), two volumes of much-praised autobiography, *The Cab at the Door: Early Years* (1968) and *Midnight Oil* (1971). He also edited the *Oxford Book of Short Stories* (1981). As critic he has contributed most regularly to the *New Statesman*, of which he became a director in 1946.

Private Memoirs and Confessions of a Justified Sinner, The, a novel by J. *Hogg, published 1824.

In the first part of the book Colwan, believing himself to be one of the 'saved' (according to the Calvinist doctrine of predestination), commits a series of horrifying crimes, including the murder of his half-brother. The second section of the book purports to be a memoir written by Colwan, and discovered when his grave was opened a century after his suicide. This reveals that he also murdered his mother, a girl, and a preacher, all under the supposed auspices of divine justice, before coming eventually to believe that the stranger who haunts him is in fact the Devil. His skull, on exhumation, is found to have two horn-like protuberances.

Private Presses are distinguished by aims that are aesthetic rather than commercial and by printing for the gratification of their owners rather than to order. Many have been set up since the 17th cent. by amateurs of books or printing, such as that of Horace *Walpole at *Strawberry Hill (1757–97). At the end of the 19th cent. presses of this kind were intended as a protest against the low artistic standards and degradation of labour in the printing trade. W. *Morris set up the Kelmscott Press (1891–8) with this object. The *Cuala Press was founded in Ireland in 1902. The 1920s saw the foundation of the *Golden Cockerel Press and *Gregynog Press, and a considerable revival of interest in the art of wood engraving.

PROCTER, Adelaide Anne (1825–64), daughter of B. W. Procter (Barry *Cornwall), contributed to Dickens's *Household Words* under the pseudonym 'Mary Berwick'. She was the author of much popular sentimental (and often morbid) verse, including 'A Lost Chord' (*Legends and Lyrics*, 1858–61). Her complete works were issued in 1905 with a foreword by Dickens.

PROCTER, Brian Waller, see CORNWALL, B.

Prodigal Son, The, the general subject of a group of plays written about 1540–75, showing the influence of the continental neo-classic writers of the period. The chief of these are *Misogonus* (c.1560, author unknown), *Jacke Jugeller* (1563), and *Gascoigne's *Glasse of Government* (1575). The parable of the Prodigal Son is in Luke 15: 11–32.

Professor, The, a novel by C. *Brontë, written 1846 (before *Jane Eyre*), but not published until 1857.

The story is based, like *Villette*, on the author's experiences in Brussels, and uses much of the same material, though the two principal characters are transposed. William Crimsworth, an orphan, goes to seek his fortune in Brussels. At the girls' school where he teaches English he falls in love with Frances Henri, whose Protestant honesty and modesty are contrasted with the manipulating duplicity of the Catholic headmistress, Zoraide Reuter. Crimsworth resists Mlle Reuter's overtures, resigns his post, and, after finding a new and better one, is able to marry Frances.

Progress of Poesy, The, a Pindaric ode by T. *Gray, published 1757. Gray describes the different kinds of poetry, its varying powers, its primitive origins, and its connections with political liberty. He recounts its progress from Greece, to Italy, to Britain, paying homage to Shakespeare, *Milton, and *Dryden—a footnote singling out Dryden's *'Sublime' 'Ode on St Cecilia's Day'—and concludes that no one in his day can equal them. Dr *Johnson found the poem obscure. (See also BARD, THE.)

Prometheus (the name means 'Forethought') appears in Greek myth as a divine being, one of the Titans, descended from the original union of the Sky God with the Earth Mother. In some stories he is the creator of mankind, and he is always their champion. He is supposed to have stolen fire for them from Heaven when they were denied it by Zeus, and to have been punished by being fastened to a cliff in the Caucasus where an eagle tore daily at his liver. The fire and the skills which were his gifts to mankind were not an unmixed blessing, since they were also the source of work and war.

The modern popularity of the Promethean myth dates from the 1770s when *Goethe came to see in the Titan a symbol of man's creative striving and of his revolt against the restraints of society and life. Goethe set the pattern which the 19th cent. followed. Shelley's *Prometheus Unbound* (1820) glorified the virtues of revolt, representing authority as responsible for man's sufferings. *Coleridge wrote an essay on the *Prometheus* of Aeschylus (1825), Elizabeth Barrett (*Browning) translated the play (1833) and *Bridges wrote a version called *Prometheus the Firegiver* (1883).

Prometheus the Firegiver, a poem by *Bridges.

Prometheus Unbound, a lyrical drama in four acts by P. B. *Shelley, published 1820.

A work that orchestrates all Shelley's aspirations, and contradictions, as a poet and radical, it is partly mythical drama (or 'psychodrama') and partly political allegory. Shelley began with the idea of completing the Aeschylean story of *Prometheus the firebringer and champion of mankind, who is bound to his rock for all eternity by a jealous Jupiter. He combined this with his view of Satan as the hero of *Paradise Lost, and of God as the Oppressor. He presents a Prometheus–Lucifer figure of moral perfection and 'truest motives', who is liberated by 'alternative' and benign forces in the universe and triumphs over Tyranny in the name of all mankind. The work is executed in a bewildering variety of verse forms, some more successful than others: rhetorical soliloquies, dramatic dialogues, love-songs, dream visions, lyric choruses, and prophecies.

The sexual, scientific, and political symbolism of the drama have been variously interpreted: but the concept of liberation is central. Act II sc. 4 in which Asia (the Spirit of Love) confronts and questions Demogorgon (Fate, Historical Necessity, or perhaps 'the People-Monster') must count among Shelley's poetic masterpieces. The work has an important Preface on the role of poetry in reforming society, which links with the *Defence of Poetry.

Promos and Cassandra, see WHETSTONE, G.

PROPERTIUS, Sextus (*c.*50–*c.*16 BC), Roman elegiac poet, most of whose extant works are concerned with the sophisticated love of a certain 'Cynthia'. He employed an allusive style full of mythological references in a Hellenistic manner. Echoes of his verse can be found in B. *Barnes and T. *Campion. *Pound wrote a 'Homage to Sextus Propertius' (1919).

Prophetic Books, the name sometimes given to the symbolic and prophetic poems of *Blake, e.g. *The Book of *Urizen, The Book of *Los, *Milton,* and *Jerusalem.*

'Prosopopoia', the subtitle of Spenser's *'Mother Hubberds Tale'.

Prospero, in Shakespeare's *The Tempest, the usurped duke of Milan and father of Miranda.

Proteus, one of *The Two Gentlemen of Verona in Shakespeare's play.

Prothalamion, a 'Spousall Verse' written by *Spenser, published 1596, in celebration of the double marriage of the Lady Elizabeth and the Lady Katherine Somerset, daughters of the earl of Worcester. The name was invented by Spenser on the model of his *Epithalamion.

Proudie, Mrs, the violently Evangelical wife of the bishop of Barchester, and a leading character in the *'Barsetshire' novels of A. Trollope.

Prout, Father, see MAHONY, F. S.

Provençal, or *langue d'oc* (as distinct from the *langue d'oïl*), the language of the southern part of France, and the literary medium of the *troubadours.

Provençal literature in the medieval period consisted chiefly of the lyric poetry composed by the troubadours for the feudal courts of the Midi, northern Italy, and Spain. The *canso,* the love song in the courtly style which was the troubadours' special achievement, was known all over western Europe, and inspired the courtly poetry of northern France, the Minnesang of Germany, and the Petrarchan poetry of Italy. Provençal was considered the language *par excellence* of lyric poetry, courtly in content and very elaborate in style. This poetic flowering came to an end with the decline, after the Albigensian crusade, of the aristocratic society which had produced it.

Proverbial Philosophy, see TUPPER, M.

Proverbs of Alfred, The, an early Middle English poem, dating, in the form in which it has reached us, from the 13th cent., though probably composed about 1150–80. The poem's 600 lines begin by giving an account of Alfred and proceed to a series of 35 sayings, each beginning 'Thus quath Alfred', containing proverbial instructions. The attribution of the proverbs to Alfred is no more than traditional.

'Proverbs of Hell', see MARRIAGE OF HEAVEN AND HELL, THE.

Provok'd Husband, The, or a Journey to London, a comedy by *Vanbrugh, finished by C. *Cibber, produced 1728.

The 'provok'd husband' is Lord Townly, who, driven to desperation by the extravagance of his wife, decides to separate from her and to make his reasons public. The sentence (according to Cibber's ending) brings Lady Townly to her senses, and a reconciliation is promoted by Manly, Lord Townly's sensible friend and the successful suitor of Lady Grace, Lord Townly's exemplary sister.

Provok'd Wife, The, a comedy by *Vanbrugh, produced 1697, but possibly written before *The Relapse.

Sir John Brute, a debauched man of quality, married his wife for love, but is now disillusioned with her and with matrimony, and rails against both. Lady Brute married for money, but has remained technically faithful; she is courted by Constant, whose cynical friend Heartfree falls in love with her niece Belinda. Various intrigues and encounters ensue, in which the affected Lady Fancyfull plays a malign and interfering part, but at the end of the play the Brutes are at least temporarily reconciled, and Heartfree wins Belinda.

Provost, The, a novel by J. *Galt, published 1822. The Provost, Mr Pawkie, reflects on the arts of authority and rule, and his own successful manipulation of them throughout his life.

PRUDENTIUS (Aurelius Prudentius Clemens) (348–post 405), a Christian Latin poet born in Spain, the composer of many hymns. His *Psychomachia* (*The Battle for the Soul of Man*), written 405, was a very important influence on the development of medieval and Renaissance allegorical works.

'Prufrock, The Love Song of J. Alfred', a poem by T. S. *Eliot.

Pryderi, see MABINOGION.

Prynne, Hester, the heroine of Hawthorne's *The Scarlet Letter*.

PRYNNE, William (1600–69), Puritan pamphleteer. He wrote against *Arminianism from 1627, and endeavoured to reform the manners of his age. He published *Histriomastix* (1632), an enormous work attacking stage-plays. For a supposed aspersion on Charles I and his queen in it he was sentenced by the Star Chamber, in 1634, to be imprisoned during life, to be fined, and to lose both his ears in the pillory. He was released by the Long Parliament, and his sentences declared illegal in Nov. 1640. He continued an active paper warfare, attacking Laud, then the independents, then the army (1647), then, after being arrested by Pride, the government. In 1660 he asserted the rights of Charles II, and was thanked by him. He published his most valuable work *Brevia Parliamentaria Rediviva*, in 1662.

PSALMANAZAR, George (?1679–1763), a literary impostor, was a native of the south of France. He came to London at the end of 1703 and became a centre of interest, presenting Bishop Compton with the catechism in 'Formosan' (his invented language), and talking volubly in Latin to Archbishop Tillotson. He published in 1704 a *Description* of Formosa, with an introductory autobiography. He was unable to sustain the imposture and passed from ridicule to obscurity, although he still found patrons. He renounced his past life after a serious illness in 1728, became an accomplished Hebraist, wrote

A General History of Printing, and contributed to the *Universal History*. Psalmanazar was regarded with veneration by Dr *Johnson. In 1764 appeared posthumously his autobiographical *Memoirs*, containing an account of the imposture.

Psalms, The, the Book of Psalms, one of the books of the Old Testament. The Psalms were the basis of the medieval church services, probably the only book in the Bible on the use of which, by the laity, the medieval church imposed no veto at all. The Prayer Book version of them, attributed to *Coverdale, is one of our greatest literary inheritances. A *Metrical Version* of the Psalms was begun by *Sternhold and Hopkins (2nd edn, 1551), and continued at Geneva during Mary's reign by Protestant refugees. The complete *Old Version* (metrical) was published in 1562. The *New Version* by *Tate and Brady appeared in 1696.

PSEUDO-DIONYSIUS, see DIONYSIUS THE AREOPAGITE.

Pseudodoxia Epidemica: or, Enquiries into Very many received Tenents, And commonly presumed Truths, often referred to as *Vulgar Errors*, by Sir T. *Browne, first published 1646, revised and augmented 1650, 1658, and 1672. This is Browne's longest work, in which he examines more than 100 problems in the light of his extensive learning, the verdicts of reasoned argument, and the results of his own experiments and observations. It comprises one general book, treating of the sources and propagation of error—original sin, popular gullibility, logical fallacy, learned credulity and laziness, reverence for antiquity and authority, influential authors, and Satan—and six particular books, three on natural history—mineralogy, botany, zoology, physiology—and three on civil, ecclesiastical, and literary history—iconography, magic and folklore, chronology, historical geography, and biblical, classical, and medieval history.

Pseudo-Martyr, see DONNE, J.

PTOLEMY (Claudius Ptolemaeus), who lived at Alexandria in the 2nd cent. AD, was a celebrated mathematician, astronomer, and geographer. He devised the system of astronomy (according to which the sun, planets, and stars revolved round the earth) which was generally accepted until displaced by that of *Copernicus. Ptolemy's work on this subject is generally known by its Arabic name of *Almagest*.

Public Lending Right, a right achieved by Act of Parliament in 1979. The idea that the author of a book (in copyright) should be paid for its use by a public, commercial, or other kind of lending library was conceived by the novelist John Brophy in 1951, then formally adopted by the *Society of Authors which conducted a prolonged campaign.

PLR was finally secured, not by amendment to the Copyright Act, but by a separate statute, because of the need for reciprocal agreements with other countries, e.g. West Germany, operating comparable schemes. The scheme is financed by a central grant from the Treasury. Qualifying authors received their first cheques in 1984. See COPYRIGHT.

Publishing, subscription, a system by which the author collected a pre-publication list of buyers prepared to pay for his book in advance and usually at a reduced rate. The first book known to be published by subscription was John Minsheu's lexicographical *Guide into Tongues* of 1617, though *Caxton, in the late 15th cent., acquired promises of sales before producing his major works. The system flourished most widely in the 18th cent. Subscription publishing was still flourishing at the end of the 19th cent. and survives in a modified form in certain areas of scholarly and technical publishing.

Puck, originally an evil or malicious spirit or demon of popular superstition; from the 16th cent. the name of a mischievous or tricksy goblin or sprite. He figures in Shakespeare's *A Midsummer Night's Dream* (II. i. 40) and Drayton's *Nimphidia* (xxxvi).

Puff, Mr, a character in Sheridan's *The Critic.*

PUGIN, Augustus Welby Northmore (1812–52), architect, was the protagonist and theorist of the *Gothic Revival, and developed his thesis that Gothic was the only proper Christian architecture in *Contrasts: or, a parallel between the noble edifices of the fourteenth and fifteenth centuries and similar buildings of the present day . . .* (1836), an important work that foreshadowed *Ruskin and *Carlyle's *Past and Present.*

Pullet, Mr and Mrs, characters in G. Eliot's *The Mill on the Floss.*

Pumblechook, Mr, a character in Dickens's *Great Expectations.*

Pun, a play on words, depending on similarity of sound and difference in meaning. Shakespeare was greatly given to punning, both in comic and in serious contexts: for an example of the latter, see Sonnet 135, 'Therefore I lie with her, and she with me, | And in our faults by lies we flattered be.' The pun fell in to disrepute in the 18th and 19th cents, but was somewhat reinstated as a form of ambiguity in W. Empson's *Seven Types of Ambiguity.*

Punch, or *The London Charivari*, an illustrated weekly comic periodical, founded 1841; at first a rather strongly Radical paper, gradually becoming less political.

It appears that the idea of starting in London a comic paper first occurred to Ebenezer Landells, draughtsman and wood-engraver, who submitted it to *Mayhew. Mayhew enlisted the support of *Lemon and Joseph Stirling Coyne (1803–68), who became the first joint-editors. The first number was issued on 17 July 1841. Gilbert Abbott *À Beckett and *Jerrold were among the original staff, soon joined by *Thackeray, *Hood, *Leech, and *Tenniel, among others.

The most famous drawing for the cover, by R. *Doyle, was used from 1849 to 1956, when it was replaced by a full-colour design, different each week.

Puntarvolo, in Jonson's *Every Man out of his Humour*, a boastful, quixotic knight.

Puppet-play, see MOTION.

PURCELL, Henry (1659–95), English composer. He composed many anthems and sacred works; songs for stage works by *Dryden, *Shadwell, *D'Urfey, *Southern, and others; a celebrated opera, *Dido and Aeneas* (1689, libretto by *Tate); and music for several 'semi-operas', including *King Arthur* (1691) by Dryden, which contains 'Fairest Isle'.

PURCHAS, Samuel (?1577–1626), published in 1613 *Purchas his Pilgrimage, or Relations of the World and the Religions observed in all Ages*; in 1619 *Purchas his Pilgrim*; and in 1625 *Hakluytus Posthumus, or Purchas his Pilgrimes, contayning a History of the World in Sea Voyages and Land Travell by Englishmen and others*, which is in part based on manuscripts left by *Hakluyt. It contains accounts of voyages to India, China, Japan, Africa, and the Mediterranean and attempts to discover the North-West Passage, the Muscovy expeditions, and the explorations of the West Indies and Florida. *Coleridge was reading about Kubla Khan in Purchas when he fell into the trance that produced his own poem on the subject, and J. L. *Lowes in *The Road to Xanadu* (1927) further traces his debt. (See also ROMANTICISM.)

Purgatorio, The, of Dante, see DIVINA COMMEDIA.

Puritan, The, or the *Widow of Watling-Street*, published 1607, a farcical comedy of London manners, as 'written by W. S.' and included in the 3rd and 4th Shakespeare folios, but by some other hand, almost certainly *Middleton's.

Purley, The Diversions of, see TOOKE, J. H.

Purple Island, The, see FLETCHER, P.

PUSEY, Edward Bouverie (1800–82), was elected a fellow of Oriel College, Oxford, in

1823. In 1828 he was ordained deacon and priest, and appointed Regius professor of Hebrew. He became attached to the *Oxford Movement and contributed to *Tracts for the Times*. Pusey gave the Movement cohesion and prestige by his erudition, and in 1841 when *Newman withdrew he became its leader. His sermon 'The Holy Eucharist, a Comfort to the Penitent' (1843) caused his suspension for heresy from the office of university preacher for two years. The condemnation drew him wide publicity and attracted attention to the doctrine of the Real Presence of which he was a devoted defender. He was a principal defender of the doctrines of the High Church Movement, a passionate believer in the union of the English and Roman Churches, and endeavoured to hinder secessions to the Roman Catholic Church which prevailed at that time.

PUSHKIN, Alexander Sergeevich (1799–1837), Russia's greatest poet, whose works include lyric poems, *Byronic verse narratives, prose stories, historical dramas, and the great political poem *The Bronze Horseman* (1833). His novel in verse, *Eugene Onegin* (1823–31), is usually considered his masterpiece. He was widely read in English literature, and was frequently translated into English from 1835 onwards.

Puss in Boots, a popular tale, from the French of *Perrault, translated by Robert Samber (?1729).

A miller bequeaths to his three sons respectively, his mill, his ass, and his cat. The youngest, who inherits the cat, laments his ill-fortune. But the resourceful cat, by a series of unscrupulous ruses, in which he represents his master to the king as the wealthy marquis of Carabas, secures for him the hand of the king's daughter.

*Lang, in *Perrault's Popular Tales* (1888), discusses the origin of the story, which is found, in various forms, in several countries.

PUTTENHAM, George (c.1529–91), was almost certainly author of *The Arte of English Poesie* (1589), sometimes ascribed to his brother Richard. It is a critical treatise in three books, *Of Poets and Poesie, Of Proportion*, and *Of Ornament*, important as a record of Elizabethan taste and theory. The author's tone is personal, and he mingles anecdotes with serious appraisal. In the second book he discusses 'courtly trifles' such as anagrams, *emblems, and posies. The third book defines and illustrates various figures of speech. He attacks excessive use of foreign words, but is aware of the rapidly changing vernacular. George Puttenham may also be the author of a royal panegyric, *Partheniades*.

Pwyll, in Welsh mythology, prince of Dyfed and 'Head of Hades', the subject of the first story in the *Mabinogion*. The stories of Sir Pelleas and King *Pelles in Malory's *Morte D'Arthur* are perhaps connected with his myth.

PYE, Henry James (1745–1813), became poet laureate in 1790, and was the constant butt of contemporary ridicule.

Pyke and Pluck, in Dickens's *Nicholas Nickleby*, the toadies of Sir Mulberry Hawk.

Pygmalion, a play by Bernard *Shaw, first performed 1913 in Vienna, published and performed in London, 1916.

It describes the transformation of a Cockney flower-seller, Eliza Doolittle, into a passable imitation of a duchess by the phonetician Professor Henry Higgins (modelled in part on H. *Sweet), who undertakes this task in order to win a bet and to prove his own points about English speech and the class system: he teaches her to speak standard English and introduces her successfully to social life, thus winning his bet, but she rebels against his dictatorial and thoughtless behaviour, and 'bolts' from his tyranny. The play ends with a truce between the two of them, as Higgins acknowledges that she has achieved freedom and independence, and emerged from his treatment as a 'tower of strength: a consort battleship': in his postscript Shaw tells us that she marries the docile and devoted Freddy Eynsford Hill. *My Fair Lady*, the 1957 musical version, makes the relationship between Eliza and Higgins significantly more romantic.

Pygmalion, in classical legend, was the king of Cyprus, who fell in love with his own sculpture; Aphrodite endowed the statue with life and transformed it into the flesh-and-blood of Galatea.

Pylon School, a nickname for the group of younger left-wing poets of the 1930s, chiefly *Auden, *Day-Lewis, *MacNeice, and *Spender, alluding to the rather self-conscious use of industrial imagery in their work. Spender's poem 'The Pylons' was published in 1933.

PYM, Barbara Mary Crampton (1913–80), novelist. Her novels include *Excellent Women* (1952), *Less than Angels* (1955), *A Glass of Blessings* (1958), and *Quartet in Autumn* (1977). They are satirical tragi-comedies of middle-class life; many of the relationships described consist of a kind of celibate flirtation.

Pyncheon, Hepzibah, a character in Hawthorne's *The House of the Seven Gables*.

PYNCHON, Thomas (1937–), American novelist. His first novel *V* (1963), a complex philosophical allegory, was followed by the shorter fable *The Crying of Lot 49* (1966), and the lengthy *Gravity's Rainbow* (1973), set in the closing years of the Second World War.

Pyrochles, in Spenser's *Faerie Queene*, the brother of *Cymochles. He symbolizes rage; on his shield is a flaming fire, with the words *'Burnt I do burne'*. He is overcome by Sir **Guyon (II. v), rescued and healed by *Archimago (II. vi. 42–51), and finally killed by Prince *Arthur (II. viii).

Pyrocles, the young prince of Macedon in Sidney's **Arcadia*, who adopts a disguise as an Amazon in order to woo Philoclea.

Pyrrhic, see METRE.

Pyrrho, see SCEPTICISM.

PYTHAGORAS, the Greek philosopher, native of Samos, who lived in the second half of the 6th cent. BC. He is credited with the discovery that the square on the hypotenuse of a right-angled triangle is equal to the sum of the squares on the other two sides, the Pythagorean Theorem. He worked out a mathematical basis for music and supposed the heavenly bodies to be divided by intervals according to the laws of musical harmony, whence arose the idea of the harmony of the spheres. His religious teachings centred on the doctrine of metempsychosis, or the transmigration of souls from man to man, man to animal, or animal to man in a process of purification or punishment. There are references to this Pythagorean doctrine in the dialogue between Feste and Malvolio (**Twelfth Night*, IV. ii), in **The Merchant of Venice* (IV. i), in **As you Like It* (III. ii); and in Marlowe's **Dr Faustus* (V. ii).

Pythias, see DAMON AND PITHIAS.

Q

'Q', see JERROLD, D. W., and QUILLER-COUCH.

Quadrivium, the higher division of the Seven Liberal Arts, comprising the sciences, arithmetic, geometry, astronomy, and music (as distinct from the methodological subjects of the *Trivium, grammar, rhetoric, and logic). The Quadrivium as such originates with *Martianus Capella (early 5th cent.) followed by *Boethius and his pupil Cassiodorus.

Quakers, members of the Society of *Friends.

QUARLES, Francis (1592–1644), went abroad in the suite of the Princess Elizabeth on her marriage with the Elector Palatine. He made his reputation in the 1620s by a series of biblical paraphrases (e.g. *A Feast for Worms*, 1620), but is chiefly remembered for his *Emblems* (1635) and *Hieroglyphikes of the Life of Man* (1638). In 1639 he was appointed chronologer to the City of London. From 1640 he turned to prose, publishing pamphlets, some anonymous, holding a constitutionalist-royalist position.

Quarterly Review, The (1809–1967), was founded by John *Murray as a Tory rival to the Whig *Edinburgh Review*. Sir W. *Scott, who had been harshly reviewed in the *Edinburgh*, became an ardent supporter of the venture. The journal stood, politically, for the defence of the established order, Church, and Crown. The first editor, *Gifford, brought with him several clever writers from *The Anti-Jacobin*, including *Canning and *Frere. The *Quarterly*, unlike the *Edinburgh*, supported the *'Lake School' and *Byron, although it fiercely condemned *Keats, *Hunt, *Hazlitt, *Lamb, *Shelley, and later *Tennyson, *Macaulay, *Dickens and C. *Brontë. Two of its more famous early articles were those of Scott in praise of J. Austen's *Emma*; and a review of Keats's *'Endymion', by J. W. *Croker, which, according to the poet's friends, hastened Keats's death. Gifford was succeeded as editor in 1825 by *Lockhart, who was in his turn followed by a distinguished line, including members of the Murray family. In the second half of the 19th cent. the *Quarterly* published the work of many notable writers and critics, including *Bulwer-Lytton, *Thackeray, *Martineau, *Borrow, M. *Arnold, and *Swinburne.

Queen Mab, a visionary and ideological poem by P. B. *Shelley, published privately in 1813.

The poem is in nine cantos, using 'didactic and descriptive' blank verse. Despite its lyrical opening, invoking 'Death and his brother Sleep' and Mab the Fairy Queen in her time-chariot (Cantos I and II), the poem largely consists of attacks on Monarchy (III), War (IV), Commerce (V), and Religion (VI and VII). In place of these Shelley celebrates a future of Republicanism, Free Love, Atheism, and Vegetarianism. The verse is furious and polemical in style, with occasional passages of grandiloquent beauty. Seventeen remarkable prose *Notes* are attached as Appendices, many of them substantial essays, 'against Jesus Christ, & God the Father, & the King, & the Bishops, & Marriage, & the Devil knows what': they are often better than the poetry. The work was extremely popular among working-class radicals.

Queen Mary, a historical drama by *Tennyson published 1875, a lengthy treatment of the reign of Mary Tudor in 23 scenes.

Queen of Cornwall, *The Famous Tragedy of the,* a poetic drama by T. *Hardy, published 1923. The play is a re-telling of the old story of King Mark, the two Iseults, and Tristram.

Queen of the May, see MAY DAY.

Queen's Maries (or **Marys**), **The,** the four ladies named Mary attendant on *Mary Queen of Scots. The list is variously given, including: Mary Seton, Mary Beaton, Mary Livingstone, Mary Fleming, Mary Hamilton, and Mary Carmichael. They are frequently mentioned in Scottish ballads.

Queen's Wake, The, a poem by J. *Hogg, published 1813. Queen Mary of Scotland holds her 'wake' at Holyrood, during which 17 bards, including Rizzio, sing their songs in competition. These are verse-tales in various styles: martial, comic, horrible, or mystical.

QUENNELL, Peter (1905–), poet, historian, biographer, was editor of the *Cornhill Magazine* (1944–51) and of *History Today* (1951–79). His first volume, *Masques and Poems* (1922), was followed by many other works, including *Four Portraits* (1945; studies of *Boswell, *Gibbon, *Sterne, and *Wilkes).

Quentin Durward, a novel by Sir W. *Scott, published 1823.

The scene is laid in the 15th cent. and the principal character is Louis XI of France, crafty, cruel, and superstitious, yet prudent and capable, in contrast to his vassal and enemy, the violent and impetuous Charles the Bold of Burgundy. The story is concerned with the intrigues by which Louis attempts to procure, with the assistance of William de la Marck, the Wild Boar of the Ardennes, the revolt of Liège against Charles; with the murder of the bishop of Liège; and with the famous visit of Louis to Charles at Peronne and their temporary reconciliation. The romance of Quentin Durward (a young Scot of good family) is subordinate to these. The *Mémoires* of Phillippe de Commines (called Philip des Comines in the novel) provided the background for the plot. The well-known lyric 'County Guy' occurs in ch. iv.

Questing Beast, The, in Malory's *Morte D'Arthur*, pursued by *Palomydes the Saracen. See GLATYSAUNT BEAST.

Quickly, Mistress, in Shakespeare's *1* and *2* *Henry IV*, hostess of the Boar's Head Tavern. In *The Merry Wives of Windsor* she is housekeeper to Dr Caius. In *Henry V* she is married to Pistol.

QUILLER-COUCH, Sir Arthur Thomas (1863–1944), wrote under the pseudonym 'Q'. He was knighted in 1910 and became professor of English at Cambridge in 1912. His prolific literary career opened with the publication of a novel of adventure, *Dead Man's Rock* (1887). In 1900 he edited the first *Oxford Book of English Verse*. Two volumes of lectures, *On the Art of Writing* and *On the Art of Reading*, appeared in

1916 and 1920, and his edition of the *New Cambridge Shakespeare* began to appear in 1921. In 1928 his collected novels and stories appeared in 30 volumes.

Quilp, Daniel and Mrs, characters in Dickens's *The Old Curiosity Shop*.

QUIN, James (1693–1766), an actor who took leading parts in tragedy. He was the last of the old school of actors, which gave place to that of *Garrick.

Quinbus Flestrin, 'the Great Man-Mountain', the name by which Gulliver was known in Lilliput (*Gulliver's Travels*, ch. 2), and sometimes used as a pseudonym in magazines of the period.

Quince, Peter, in Shakespeare's *A Midsummer Night's Dream*, a carpenter, the stage-manager of the interlude 'Pyramus and Thisbe'.

QUINTILIAN (Marcus Fabius Quintilianus) (AD *c.*35–*c.*100), Roman rhetorician, educationist, and literary critic. His monumental *De Institutione Oratoria*, a treatise on rhetoric, contains in Book X a critical history of Greek and Roman literature. Jonson excerpted it in *Timber*, Milton referred to it in the *Tetrachordon* sonnet, and *Dryden cited it on a number of points.

Quinze Joyes de Mariage, Les, a French antifeminist satire, of doubtful authorship, dating from the early 15th cent. Several English versions of the work were made in the 17th and 18th cents, including one by *Dekker entitled *The Batchelars Banquet* (1603).

Quixote, see DON QUIXOTE.

R

'Rabbi Ben Ezra', a poem by R. Browning included in *Dramatis Personae*.

RABELAIS, François (*c.*1494–*c.*1553), French physician, humanist, and satirist whose great work, the satirical entertainments on the popular giants *Gargantua and *Pantagruel (*Gargantua*, 1534; *Pantagruel*, 1532 or 1533; *Tiers Livre*, 1546; *Quart Livre* 1548–52; and *Cinquième Livre*, of questionable authenticity, 1562–4) had a widespread influence on English literature, particularly on S. *Butler, *Swift, *Sterne, *Peacock, and *Joyce. *Urquhart's translation of Books I and II appeared in 1653 and Book III (together with *Motteux's translation of Books IV and V) in 1693–4.

RACINE, Jean (1639–99), French tragic dramatist whose major works include *Andromaque* (1667), *Phèdre* (1677), *Britannicus* (1669), *Bajazet* (1672), and *Athalie* (1691). The plays have been extensively translated into English since the 1670s, but the peculiar clarity and intensity of Racine's verse have defeated most efforts at adaptation.

RACKHAM, Arthur (1867–1939), children's book illustrator. Amongst his most successful works are *Fairy Tales of the Brothers Grimm* (1900), *Rip van Winkle* (1905), which established him as the fashionable illustrator of his time, and *Peter Pan in Kensington Gardens* (1906).

RADCLIFFE, Mrs Ann (1764–1823), (née Ward), a novelist who published five novels, *The Castles of Athlin and Dunbayne* (1789), *A Sicilian Romance* (1790), *The Romance of the Forest* (1791), *The Mysteries of Udolpho* (1794), and *The Italian* (1797), and various travel works. She was the leading exponent of the *Gothic novel. Her portrayals of the raptures and terrors of her characters' imagination in solitude are compelling, and she was one of the first novelists to include vivid descriptions of landscape, weather, and effects of light.

Radigund, in Spenser's *Faerie Queene* (v. iv–vii), a queen of the Amazons.

Raffles, see HORNUNG, E. W.

Ragged Trousered Philanthropists, The, see TRESSELL, R.

Rainbow, The, a novel by D. H. *Lawrence, published 1915.

It opens as a family chronicle relating the history of the long-established Brangwen family of March Farm, on the Derbyshire–Nottinghamshire border. Tom Brangwen marries the vicar's housekeeper, a Polish widow who already has a daughter, Anna, by her first marriage. Anna marries Will Brangwen, Tom's nephew, a craftsman and draughtsman at a lace factory; they produce a large family, of which the two oldest are Ursula and Gudrun of *Women in Love*. Ursula becomes the 'child of her father's heart', and the interest of the novel gradually shifts to her developing consciousness. When she is about eight her grandfather is drowned and Ursula grows close to her grandmother Lydia at the March, intrigued by her Polish heritage; she meets Anton, son of a Polish *émigré* friend of Lydia's and they fall in love, but he, a subaltern, departs for the Boer war. She then matriculates, and resolves to earn her living as a teacher. Will Brangwen is appointed Art and Handwork Instructor for the County of Nottingham, and the whole family move to Beldover. Ursula embarks on a three-year BA course. Anton returns, and they become engaged, and plan to go out to India together, but Ursula breaks away, and Anton abruptly marries his colonel's daughter. The novel ends with Ursula emerging from a spell of illness and suffering (and an implied miscarriage) to contemplate a rainbow arching symbolically over the ugly industrial landscape.

RAINE, Kathleen Jessie (1908–), poet and critic, was formerly married to Charles *Madge. She published many collections of poetry, from her first, *Stone and Flower* (1943), to her *Collected Poems* (1981), and also three volumes of autobiography. Much of her poetry is inspired by the landscapes of Scotland, and has an intense and mystic vision of the vitality of the natural world which also informs her critical work on *Blake and the *Neoplatonic tradition.

RAINOLDS, John (1549–1607), composed Latin lectures on Aristotle which contributed to the development of euphuism (see EUPHUES), and controversial works and Protestant apologetics. His part in a controversy over the lawfulness of acting plays produced his *Th'Overthrow of Stage-Playes* (1599).

Raj Quartet, The, see SCOTT, P.

Rake's Progress, The, a series of engravings by *Hogarth which inspired an opera by Stravinsky of the same title with a libretto by W. H. *Auden in collaboration with Chester Kallman.

RALEGH, Sir Walter (?1554–1618) spent four years as a volunteer with the Huguenot forces in France and was at the battle of Montcontour in 1569. He then began his long career as an explorer and colonizer. Throughout the 1580s he seems to have enjoyed royal favour. His marriage to Elizabeth Throckmorton, one of the maids of honour, led to a period of imprisonment in the summer of 1592. Through his leadership of the expedition to sack Cadiz harbour in June 1596 and his dissociation from the earl of *Essex, he maintained a strong position until the queen's death. Ralegh's trial, on largely trumped-up charges of high treason, was one of the first events of James I's reign, and from 1603 to 1616 he was imprisoned in the Tower with his wife and family. He was released to search out the gold mine he claimed to have discovered in Guiana 20 years before. On returning from this disastrous expedition, a commission of inquiry set up under Spanish pressure determined that the gold mine was a fabrication, the old charge of treason was renewed, and on 29 Oct. 1618 Ralegh was executed.

His poems are beset by uncertainties as to date and authenticity, though a few of them, including the fragmentary '21th: the last booke of the Ocean to Scinthia', survive in his own handwriting. Two well-known poems formerly attributed to him, 'The Lie' and 'The Pilgrimage', are not now thought to be his work. Among the authentic poems are his 'Epitaph of Sir Philip Sidney' and the prefatory sonnet to *The Faerie Queene. There are numerous prose works including his 'Report of the Truth of the Fight about the Isles of Açores' (1591) and *Discoverie of Guiana* (1596). *The History of the World* (1614), originally intended for Henry, prince of Wales (d. 1612), is an ambitious book, which deals with Greek, Egyptian, and biblical history up to 168 BC.

RALEIGH, Sir Walter Alexander (1861–1922), became in 1904 the first holder of the chair of English literature at Oxford. Among his works are *Style* (1897), *Milton* (1900), and *Shakespeare* (1907), but in his day he was renowned more as a lecturer than as a critic.

Ralpho, the squire in Butler's *Hudibras*. (See VAUGHAN, T.)

Ralph Roister Doister, the earliest known English comedy, by *Udall, probably performed about 1552 and printed about 1566, and perhaps played by Westminster boys while Udall was headmaster of that school. The play, in short rhymed doggerel, represents the courting of the widow Christian Custance, who is betrothed to Gawin Goodlucke, an absent merchant, by Roister, a swaggering simpleton, instigated thereto by the mischievous Mathewe Merygreeke. Roister is repulsed and beaten by Custance and her maids; and Goodlucke, after being deceived by false reports, is reconciled to her. The play shows similarity to the comedies of *Plautus and *Terence.

Rambler, The, a twice-weekly periodical in 208 numbers issued by Dr *Johnson from 20 March 1750 to 14 March 1752.

The contents are essays on all kinds of subjects, character studies, allegories, eastern fables, criticisms, etc., and were, with the exception of five, written by Johnson himself. The moral seriousness of his enterprise is indicated by the fact that he wrote a prayer on beginning the work. The other contributors were *Richardson, E. *Carter, Mrs *Chapone, and Catherine Talbot (1720–70).

RAMSAY, Allan (1686–1758), Scottish poet and a bookseller. He opened the first circulating library in Edinburgh in 1726 (see LIBRARIES, CIRCULATING). In 1718 he brought out anonymously several editions of *Christis Kirk on the Green*, with supplementary verses of his own in fake antique *Scots. A collection of his elegies and satires appeared in 1721. He issued *The Tea-Table Miscellany* (1724–37), the first of many 18th-cent. collections of songs and ballads; *The Ever Green* (1724), which contained work by the great poets of late medieval Scotland, notably *Dunbar and *Henryson, though with revisions and additions of his own, and which contributed much to the revival of vernacular Scottish poetry; and a pastoral comedy, *The Gentle Shepherd* (1725), with Scots songs.

Ramsay, Margaret, a character in Scott's *The Fortunes of Nigel*.

RAMUS, Petrus, Latin form of Pierre de la Ramée (1515–72), French philosopher and grammarian. His *Dialectique* of 1555 systematically challenged and refuted Aristotelian and *Scholastic logic. It was introduced into England in the late 16th cent. by Andrew Melville and William Temple, and obtained wide academic currency, especially at Cambridge. His followers were known as Ramists and his anti-Scholastic system of logic as Ramism.

RANDOLPH, Thomas (1605–35), educated at Trinity College, Cambridge, where he became known as a writer in English and Latin verse. His principal plays are *Amyntas*, a pastoral comedy, and *The Muse's Looking Glass*, printed 1638; and *Hey for Honesty*, printed 1651. He wrote an eclogue included in *Annalia Dubrensia* in celebration of the *Cotswold Games.

Ranger, (1) a rakish man of fashion in *Love in a Wood* by *Wycherley; (2) a character in Hoadley's *The Suspicious Husband*.

RANSOM, John Crowe (1888–1974), American poet and critic, was a professor (1937–58) at Kenyon College, Ohio, where he founded and edited the important *Kenyon Review*, a scholarly publication committed to the close textual analysis associated with the *New Criticism. His critical works include *God without Thunder* (1930) and *The New Criticism* (1941). His volumes of verse include *Chills and Fever* (1924) and *Two Gentlemen in Bonds* (1927), and he is particularly remembered for his formal, subtle, taut ballad-portraits and elegies, which include 'Captain Carpenter' and 'Bells for John Whiteside's Daughter'.

RANSOME, Arthur Michell (1884–1967), journalist and author. He went to Russia in 1913 to learn the language, covered the revolution at first hand for the *Daily News*, and published a collection of Russian legends and fairy stories, *Old Peter's Russian Tales* (1916). He is best remembered for his classic sequence of novels for children, which reflect his keen interest in sailing, fishing, and the countryside: beginning with *Swallows and Amazons* (1930) and ending with *Great Northern?* (1947), it describes the adventures of the Walker (Swallow) and Blackett (Amazon) families, and various of their friends, in the Lake District, the Norfolk Broads, and other vividly drawn locations.

RAO, Raja (1909–   ), Indian writer, whose novels include *Kanthapura* (1938) and *The Serpent and the Rope* (1960). Rao's stories have been collected in *The Cow of the Barricades* (1947) and *The Policeman and the Rose* (1978).

Rape of Lucrece, The, a poem in rhyme-royal by Shakespeare, published 1594 and dedicated to Henry Wriothesley, earl of Southampton. It is a highly rhetorical expansion of the story as told by *Livy. See LUCRETIA.

Rape of the Lock, The, a poem by *Pope, in two cantos, published in *Lintot's *Miscellany* 1712; subsequently enlarged to five cantos and thus published 1714.

Lord Petre having forcibly cut off a lock of Miss Arabella Fermor's hair, the incident gave rise to a quarrel between the families. With the idea of allaying this, Pope treated the subject in a playful mock-heroic poem, on the model of Boileau's *Le Lutrin*. He presents Belinda at her toilet, a game of ombre, the snipping of the lock while Belinda sips her coffee, the wrath of Belinda and her demand that the lock be restored, the final wafting of the lock, as a new star, to adorn the skies. The poem was published in its original form with Miss Fermor's permission. Pope then expanded the sketch by introducing the machinery of sylphs and gnomes, adapted from a light erotic French work, *Le Comte de Gabalis*, a series of five discourses by the Abbé de Montfaucon de Villars, which appeared in English in 1680; in his dedication he credits both *Gabalis* and the *Rosicrucians. (See also PARACELSUS.)

RASHDALL, Hastings (1858–1924), philosopher and theologian. His most important work, *The Theory of Good and Evil* (1907), expounds his own version of what he called 'ideal utilitarianism'. *The Universities of Europe in the Middle Ages* (1895; new edn, ed. Powicke and Emden, 1936) is a standard work.

Rasselas, Prince of Abyssinia, The History of, a didactic romance by Dr *Johnson, published 1759. It is an essay on the 'choice of life', a phrase repeated throughout the work, usually in italics. Rasselas, a son of the emperor of Abyssinia, weary of the joys of the 'happy valley' where the inhabitants know only 'the soft vicissitudes of pleasure and repose', escapes to Egypt, accompanied by his sister Nekayah, her attendant Pekuah, and the much-travelled old philosopher Imlac. Here they study the various conditions of men's lives, and after a few incidents of no great importance resolve to return to Abyssinia, in a 'conclusion, in which nothing is concluded'. The charm of the work lies in its wise and humane melancholy, stressing that happiness is unobtainable, and demonstrating that philosophers, hermits, and the wealthy all fail to achieve it.

RASTELL, John (*c.*1475–1536), brother-in-law of Sir T. *More, wrote and published an interlude (*Four Elements, c.*1520) and two comedies of *c.*1525, *Gentleness and Nobility* (which has been attributed to J. *Heywood) and *Calisto and Melebea* (see CELESTINA).

Rat, the Cat, and Lovel the dog, in the political rhyme, refers to three adherents of Richard III: Sir Richard Ratcliffe (killed at Bosworth, 1485), Sir John Catesby (d. 1486), and Francis, first Viscount Lovell (1454–?88).

RATTIGAN, Sir Terence Mervyn (1911–77), playwright. His first West End success, a comedy, *French Without Tears* (1936, pub. 1937), was followed by many other works, including *The Winslow Boy* (1946), a drama in which a father fights to clear his naval-cadet son of the accusation of petty theft; *The Browning Version* (1948); *The Deep Blue Sea* (1952); *Separate Tables* (1954, pub. 1955), two one-act plays set in a hotel, both studies of emotional failure and inadequacy; *Ross* (1960), based on the life of T. E. *Lawrence; and *Cause Célèbre* (1977, pub. 1978), based on an actual murder trial. Rattigan's *Collected Works* was published in 1953. The so-called *kitchen-sink dramatists of the 1950s and 1960s reacted against the middle-class, middle-brow nature of Rattigan's plays, but his works are still much performed.

'Raven, The', a poem by E. A. *Poe.

Ravenshoe, a novel by H. *Kingsley.

Ravenswood, Edgar, Master of, the hero of *Scott's The Bride of Lammermoor.

RAVERAT, Gwen(dolen Mary), née Darwin (1885–1957), wood-engraver and grand-daughter of C. *Darwin, born in Cambridge; her childhood is described in her autobiographical Period Piece (1952). Works illustrated by her include Spring Morning (1915) by her cousin F. *Cornford, and various anthologies in association with K. *Grahame.

READ, Sir Herbert Edward (1893–1968), served in France throughout the First World War. The first volumes of his spare, taut poems (much influenced by *Imagism) were Songs of Chaos (1915) and Naked Warriors (1919), largely based on the war; these were followed by various volumes of collected poems, a long poem, The End of a War (1933), and the final Collected Poems of 1966. His critical work includes studies of *Wordsworth, *Malory, *Sterne, and others; Form in Modern Poetry (1932), The True Voice of Feeling (1953), and Essays in Literary Criticism (1969) contain much of his most valuable work. Many publications on art include Art and Industry (1934) and Education through Art (1943). His personal prose writing includes two records of trench life, In Retreat (1925) and Ambush (1930); The Innocent Eye (1933), a brief autobiography of his Yorkshire childhood, and a full autobiography, The Contrary Experience (1963); and his only novel, The Green Child (1935).

READE, Charles (1814–84), became a fellow of Magdalen College, Oxford, with which he was long associated. He began his literary career publishing a stage version of Smollett's *Peregrine Pickle (1851); Masks and Faces (perf. 1852) became the novel Peg Woffington (1853). Christie Johnstone (1853), the first of his 'reforming' novels, was followed by It is Never Too Late to Mend (1856) and Gold! (1856), a play later converted into the novel Foul Play (1868–9). In 1854 he met the actress Mrs Seymour, with whom he lived until her death in 1879. The Autobiography of a Thief and Jack of all Trades (both 1858) were followed by his best-remembered work, *The Cloister and the Hearth (1861). Hard Cash (1863), *Griffith Gaunt (1866), and Put Yourself in his Place (1870) are all reforming novels. A long collaboration with *Boucicault produced many other plays and adaptions. After the death of Mrs Seymour he wrote little, turned to religion, and gave up theatrical management. Reade enjoyed great fame, and was accepted as the natural successor to *Dickens, but his reputation has now dimmed. His expression of sexual frustration and hatred of celibacy, a dominant theme in many of his works, was much stifled by the proprieties of the time, and his passion for realistic detail at times overwhelms his considerable narrative powers.

READE, William Winwood (1838–75), nephew of C. *Reade. His explorations in West and South-West Africa are described in Savage Africa (1863), The African Sketchbook (1873), and The Story of the Ashanti Campaign (1874). His other works include the notable The Martyrdom of Man (1872), which exposes the author's atheistical views and influenced H. G. *Wells.

Ready-to-Halt, Mr, in Bunyan's *Pilgrim's Progress, a pilgrim who follows Mr Great-heart, though upon crutches.

Realism, in *Scholastic philosophy, the doctrine that attributes objective or absolute existence to universals, the principal exponent of which was St Thomas *Aquinas. The opposite view is *Nominalism.

Realism, a literary term so widely used as to be more or less meaningless except when used in contradistinction to some other movement, e.g. *Naturalism, *Expressionism, *Surrealism. The French realist school of the mid-19th cent. (for which the novelist Champfleury, 1821–89, produced a manifesto, Le Réalisme, 1857) stressed 'sincerity' as opposed to the 'liberty' proclaimed by the Romantics; it insisted on accurate documentation and sociological insight; subjects were to be taken from everyday life, preferably from lower-class life. This emphasis clearly reflected the interests of an increasingly positivist and scientific age. *Balzac and Stendhal were seen as the great precursors of Realism; *Flaubert and the Goncourts as among its practitioners. French Realism developed into Naturalism. In England, the French realists were imitated consciously and notably by G. A. *Moore and Arnold *Bennett, but the English novel from the time of *Defoe had had its own unlabelled strain of realism, and the term is thus applied to English literature in varying senses and contexts, sometimes qualified as 'social' or 'psychological' realism etc. (See also SOCIALIST REALISM.)

Reasonableness of Christianity, see Locke's ESSAY CONCERNING HUMAN UNDERSTANDING.

Rebecca, (1) the name given (in allusion to Gen. 24: 60) to the leader, in woman's attire, of the rioters who demolished tollgates in S. Wales in 1843–4; (2) a character in Scott's *Ivanhoe; (3) a novel by D. *Du Maurier.

Rebecca and Rowena, a humorous sequel by *Thackeray to Scott's *Ivanhoe, in which Ivanhoe tires of domestic life with Rowena, and after various comic vicissitudes is reunited with Rebecca.

'Recluse, The', see EXCURSION, THE.

Recruiting Officer, The, a comedy by *Farquhar, produced 1706.

It deals with the humour of recruiting in a country town, with a vividness suggesting that the author drew on his own experience. It describes Captain Plume making love to the women in order to secure their followers as recruits; Kite, his resourceful sergeant, employing his wiles and assuming the character of an astrologer, for the same purpose; while Sylvia, daughter of Justice Ballance, who is in love with Plume but has promised not to marry him without her father's consent, runs away from home disguised as a man, gets herself arrested for scandalous conduct, is brought before her father, and delivered over by him to Capt. Plume, as a recruit. Capt. Brazen, a rival recruiting officer, who boasts of battles and friends in every quarter of the globe, endeavours to marry the rich Melinda, but finds himself fobbed off with her maid.

Red Badge of Courage, The, see CRANE, S.

Red Book of Hergest, see MABINOGION.

Red Cotton Night-Cap Country or **Turf and Towers,** a poem in blank verse by R. *Browning, published 1873. The title refers ironically to the description by Browning's friend Anne Thackeray (*Ritchie) of a district in Normandy as 'white cotton night-cap country'; Browning undertakes to show that the 'red' of passion and violence should replace the 'white'.

The story is based on a contemporary *cause célèbre*, involving the violent life and death of the wealthy heir to a Paris jewellery business, Antoine Mellerio (in the poem, Léonce Miranda). The struggle in Miranda's spirit between idealism and materialism is the real topic of the poem: Miranda is a nightmare parody of the figure of the artist in Browning.

Redcrosse Knight, The, in Bk I of Spenser's *Faerie Queene, is St George, the patron saint of England. He is the 'patron' or champion of Holiness, and represents the Anglican Church.

Redgauntlet, a novel by Sir W. *Scott, published 1824.

The story is concerned with an apocryphal return of Prince Charles Edward to England some years after 1745, to try once more his fortunes, an attempt that meets with inglorious failure. Though not generally accounted one of the three or four greatest *Waverley novels, *Redgauntlet* (written in the last years of Scott's

prosperity) contains some of his finest writing, notably in 'Wandering Willie's Tale', a perfect example of the short story.

REDGROVE, Peter William (1932–), poet and novelist, was a founder-member of the *Group, and his first volume of poetry, *The Collector and Other Poems* (1960), was followed by many others. His poetry is marked by a richness of visual imagery, a sense of physical immediacy, and a deep preoccupation with religious and sexual mysteries. His novels, which include *In the Country of the Skin* (1973) and *The Beekeepers* (1980), are written in a highly poetic prose. He has written several works in collaboration with the poet and novelist Penelope Shuttle.

Red Riding Hood, Little, a popular tale translated from the French of *Perrault by Robert Samber (?1729).

Little Red Riding Hood is sent by her mother to take a cake and a pot of butter to her sick grandmother. She loiters on the way, and gets into conversation with a wolf, who learns her errand. He hurries on, eats up the grandmother, takes her place in the bed, and impersonates her when Red Riding Hood arrives, finally devouring her. In the German variant the child is resuscitated. *Lang in *Perrault's Popular Tales* (1888), discusses the analogies of the story in other legends.

Redworth, Thomas, a character in G. Meredith's *Diana of the Crossways.

REED, Henry (1914–), poet, translator, and radio dramatist, is best known for his book of verse *A Map of Verona* (1946), which contained his much-anthologized poem, inspired by his wartime experiences in the army, 'Naming of Parts'. His plays made a notable contribution to radio drama in the 1950s, and two collections have been published.

REEVE, Clara (1729–1807), a novelist whose *The Champion of Virtue; a Gothic Story* (1777) was reprinted in 1778 as *The Old English Baron.* The author acknowledged her debt to Walpole's *The Castle of Otranto.* Her hero, the virtuous and noble Edmund, moves resolutely through many adventures of romantic horror in order to obtain his rightful heritage.

'Reeve's Tale, The', see CANTERBURY TALES, 3.

Reflections on the Revolution in France, see REVOLUTION IN FRANCE.

Reformation, The, the great religious movement of the 16th cent., aiming to reform the doctrines and practices of the Church of Rome, and ending in the establishment of the various

Reformed or Protestant churches of central and north-western Europe. Its principal leaders were *Luther in Germany, *Calvin in Geneva, *Zwingli in Zurich, and J. *Knox in Scotland.

Reformation, History of the, see KNOX, J.

Reform Bills. The Reform Bill of 1832 widened the parliamentary franchise by extending the vote to include the rich middle classes, and removed some of the inequalities in the system of representation by redistributing members of Parliament to correspond with the great centres of population. The Bill was introduced by Lord J. *Russell in 1831, and carried in 1832. The Reform Bill of 1867, which more than doubled the electorate, extended the franchise to include many male members of the industrial working class, and the Bill of 1884 took in (with the exception of certain categories, i.e. lunatics, convicted criminals, and peers) all males over 21. In 1872 voting by ballot was introduced. Women over 30 were enfranchised in 1918; and women over 21 received the vote in 1928. (See also WOMEN'S SUFFRAGE.) In 1969 an Act was passed which lowered the age of all voters to 18. The question of Reform is a principal theme in many Victorian novels, notably in G. Eliot's *Middlemarch and *Felix Holt.

Regan, in Shakespeare's *King Lear, the second of Lear's daughters.

Regicide Peace, Letters on a, by E. *Burke, the first two published 1796, the third 1797, the fourth posthumously in the collected works.
  The theme of these letters, which purport to be addressed to a Member of Parliament, is the necessity for stamping out the Jacobin government of France, that 'vast tremendous unformed spectre'; and the ability of England from an economic standpoint to carry on the struggle.

Regional Novel, a novel set in a real and well-defined locality. The first English regional novel, set in a specific and little-known locality, appears to have been M. Edgeworth's *Castle Rackrent (1800), set in Ireland. It was rapidly followed by the Irish novels of Lady Morgan and by the Scottish novels of *Galt and Sir W. *Scott. From about 1839 the localities described in regional novels were often smaller and more exact, as in the works of Mrs *Gaskell and G. *Eliot (set in the Midlands) and of the *Brontës (set in Yorkshire). Later novelists became ever more interested in precise regional attachment and description, as is shown in much of the work of C. *Kingsley and R. D. *Blackmore (Devon); *Hardy (Dorset and 'Wessex'); R. *Jefferies (Hampshire); R. L. *Stevenson (Highlands and Lowlands); J. M. *Barrie (Angus); Arnold *Bennett (Staffordshire); and D. H. *Lawrence (Nottinghamshire). The industrial or urban

novel, set in a specific town or city, flourished in the mid-19th cent., with *Disraeli's Sybil, Mrs Gaskell's *Mary Barton, Dickens's *Hard Times, and G. Eliot's *Middlemarch, and the tradition continued into this century, notably in the work of *Joyce.

Regius professorships were first founded by Henry VIII in 1540 at Cambridge (divinity, civil law, physic, Hebrew, and Greek). In 1546 five further Regius professorships were founded at Oxford (theology, medicine, civil law, Hebrew and Greek). Regius professorships of modern history at Cambridge, and of ecclesiastical history, modern history, and moral and pastoral theology at Oxford, have since been added.

Rehearsal, The (printed 1672), a farcical comedy attributed to George Villiers, 2nd duke of *Buckingham, but probably written by him in collaboration with others, among whom is mentioned S. *Butler.
  The play satirizes the heroic tragedies of the day, and consists of a series of parodies of passages from these, strung together in an absurd heroic plot. The author of the mock play is evidently a laureate (hence his name 'Bayes'), and *D'Avenant was probably intended; but there are also hits at *Dryden (particularly his Conquest of Granada) and his brothers-in-law, Edward and Robert Howard. Bayes takes two friends, Smith and Johnson, to see the rehearsal of his play, and the absurdity of this work, coupled with the comments of Bayes and his instructions to the actors, remains highly entertaining. Prince Pretty-man, Prince Volscius, and Drawcansir are among the characters. (See also HEROIC DRAMA.)

REID, Forrest (1875–1947), Ulster novelist. His fiction includes The Kingdom of Twilight (1904), The Garden God: a Tale of two boys (1905), Following Darkness (1912), and a trilogy, Uncle Stephen (1931), The Retreat (1934), and Young Tom (1944); the last three were published in one volume in 1955 as Tom Barber, with an introduction by Reid's friend E. M. *Forster. Reid's dominant subject is boyhood; he evokes a pagan, lyrical world in which hints of the supernatural are contrasted with the realities of everyday. His autobiographies, Apostate (1926) and Private Road (1940), vividly describe his sense of the numinous in nature.

REID, Thomas (1710–96), succeeded Adam *Smith as professor of moral philosophy at Glasgow in 1764, largely through the influence of his patron Henry *Home, Lord Kames. He published his first major work, An Inquiry into the Human Mind, on the Principles of Common Sense (1764), and after retiring from active teaching at Glasgow in 1780 he published his Essays on the Intellectual Powers of Man (1785) and Essays on *the Active Powers of Man* (1788). His lectures on the fine arts were first published in 1973. Reid was perhaps the most notable 18th-cent. exponent of the philosophy of common sense, by which phrase he meant both a faculty of the mind, and a set of incontrovertible beliefs implanted in the human mind by God. He also questioned the widely-held theory that the immediate objects of perception are 'ideas', arguing that we directly perceive external objects rather than mental representations of them. Aesthetic qualities he conceived either as intrinsic qualities of mind, or, derivatively, as the qualities of objects of design. He was a vigorous critic of the writings of *Hume, and, later in life, J. *Priestley, and he championed the inductive methods of F. *Bacon and I. *Newton.

Rejected Addresses, a collection of parodies by James and Horatio *Smith, published 1812.

A competition was held to find a suitable address to celebrate the opening of the new *Drury Lane Theatre in 1812. James and Horatio Smith produced a large batch of bogus entries, purporting to be by *Wordsworth, *Byron, T. *Moore, *Southey, *Coleridge, *Crabbe, Sir W. *Scott, *Cobbett, and others.

Relapse, The, or *Virtue in Danger*, the highly successful first play of *Vanbrugh, produced 1696.

It is an avowed continuation of *Love's Last Shift* by C. *Cibber. Loveless, a reformed libertine living happily in the country with his wife Amanda, is obliged to go with her to London where he suffers a relapse under the temptation of Berinthia, an unscrupulous young widow. Amanda, though bitterly resenting her husband's faithlessness, resists the overtures of Worthy, and remains firm in her virtue.

The subplot concerns Sir Novelty Fashion, now Lord Foppington, and his attempts to marry the heiress Miss Hoyden, daughter of Sir Tunbelly Clumsey, a country squire. He is fore-stalled by his younger brother, Fashion, who disguises himself and marries Hoyden in his place.

The play was adapted by *Sheridan as *A Trip to Scarborough*.

Religio Laici, a poem by *Dryden, published 1682.

Written in defence of Anglicanism against Deist, Catholic, and Dissenting arguments, *Religio Laici* combines an exalted recognition of religious sublimity with a defence of a 'layman's' reasonable and straightforward religious attitudes. Its opening lines, beginning 'Dim as the borrow'd Beams of Moon and Stars', are among the finest Dryden wrote.

Religio Medici, by Sir T. *Browne, first published in an unauthorized edition 1642,

reprinted 1643 with corrections, revisions, and additions.

The work is divided into two parts, relating broadly to God and to man. The first treats of matters of faith, the hostilities among rival sects and religions, and man as microcosm. In the second part, he expresses love for all sorts and conditions of men, English or foreign, rich or poor, learned or ignorant, friend or foe, good or bad. While based on biblical teaching, the arguments are reinforced and widened with citations of classical philosophers, historians, and poets.

Reliques of Ancient English Poetry, a collection of *ballads, sonnets, historical songs, and metrical romances by T. *Percy (1765). The majority of them were extracted from the *Percy Folio and edited and 'restored' by Percy. They were of very different periods, some of great antiquity, some as recent as the reign of Charles I.

Remorse, a tragedy by S. T. *Coleridge, written in 1797 as *Osorio*, produced at Drury Lane 1813.

The story, set in Granada at the time of the Spanish Inquisition, tells of the slow corruption of the character of Osorio, a man who is gradually led by temptations and events into guilt and evil.

Renaissance, the great flowering of art, architecture, politics, and the study of literature, usually seen as the end of the Middle Ages and the beginning of the modern world, which came about under the influence of Greek and Roman models. It began in Italy in the late 14th cent., culminated in the High Renaissance in the early 16th cent., and spread to the rest of Europe in the 15th cent. and afterwards. Its emphasis was humanist, but much of its energy also came from the *Neoplatonic tradition in writers such as *Pico della Mirandola. The Italian Renaissance is still seen as a watershed in the development of civilization, both because of its extent and because of its emphasis on the human, whether independent of or in association with the divine.

Renaud, see RINALDO.

Renault, a character in Otway's *Venice Preserv'd*.

RENAULT, Mary, pseudonym of Mary Challans (1905–83), novelist, known principally for her *historical novels, most of which are set in Ancient Greece or Asia Minor. They include *The King must Die* (1958), *The Bull from the Sea* (1962), and *The Persian Boy* (1972).

RENÉ OF PROVENCE, duc d'Anjou and comte de Provence (1408–80), known as 'le bon Roi René', son of Louis II, duke of Anjou, was titular king of Naples, the two Sicilies, and Jerusalem, 'whose large style agrees not with the leanness of his purse' (Shakespeare, 2 *Henry VI, I. i). His daughter *Margaret of Anjou was wife of Henry VI. There is a picture of his court in Sir W. *Scott's Anne of Geierstein.

Repressor of over much Blaming of the Clergy, see PEACOCK, R.

REPTON, Humphry, see PICTURESQUE.

Republic, The, one of the dialogues of *Plato, in which *Socrates is represented as eliciting, in the course of a discussion on justice, the ideal type of state. In this the perfect forms of goodness, truth, and beauty are cultivated, and everything repugnant to them excluded.

Republic of Letters, The, the collective body of those engaged in literary pursuits. The expression occurs first in *Addison's Dialogues upon Ancient Medals (i. 19).

'Resolution and Independence', a poem by *Wordsworth, written 1802, published 1807, sometimes known as 'The Leech Gatherer'.

The poet describes his own elation as he walks over the moors on a fine spring morning after a storm, and his sudden descent into apprehension and dejection, as he ponders the fate of earlier poets, such as *Chatterton. At this stage he comes upon the aged leech gatherer, whom he cross-questions about his way of life; the old man responds with cheerful dignity, and the poet resolves to remember him as an admonishment. The poem's mixture of elevated language and sentiment with prosaic detail is peculiarly Wordsworthian. Wordsworth's own comments on his use of imagery in the poem and 'the conferring, the abstracting, and the modifying powers of the Imagination' in his 1815 Preface are of great interest.

Restoration, the re-establishment of monarchy in England, with the return of Charles II (1660); also the period marked by this event of which the chief literary figures are *Dryden, *Rochester, *Bunyan, *Pepys, *Locke, and the Restoration dramatists. One of the characteristic genres of the period is Restoration comedy, or the comedy of manners, which developed upon the re-opening of the theatres. Its principal writers were *Congreve, *Etherege, *Farquhar, *Vanbrugh, and *Wycherley, and its predominant tone was witty, bawdy, cynical, and amoral. The plays were mainly in prose, with passages of verse for the more romantic moments; the plots were complex and usually double, sometimes triple, though repartee and discussions of marital behaviour provide much of the interest, reflecting the fashionable manners of the day. The playwrights came under heavy attack for frivolity, blasphemy, and immorality (see COLLIER, JEREMY): they and their subsequent admirers defended their works as serious social criticism, and mirrors to the age. During the 18th cent. the plays were presented in more 'genteel' versions, and in the 19th cent. hardly at all: the 20th cent. saw a considerable revival of interest, with such notable productions as *The Way of the World, one of the masterpieces of the period, in 1924 with Edith Evans as Millamant. (See also HEROIC DRAMA and COMEDY.)

Retaliation, an unfinished poem by *Goldsmith, published 1774, consisting of a string of humorous and critical epitaphs on *Garrick, Sir J. *Reynolds, *Burke, and other friends, in reply to their similar efforts directed against himself.

Retrospective Review, The (1820–8), founded by Henry Southern (1799–1853), its first editor, as a 'Review of past literature'. Extracts from literary works, chiefly drawn from the 16th and 17th cents, included that of Sir T. *Browne, F. *Bacon, G. *Herbert, *Vaughan, *Jonson, G. *Chapman, and others.

Return of the Druses, The, a tragedy in blank verse by R. *Browning, published 1843 as no. IV of *Bells and Pomegranates.

Return of the Native, The, a novel by T. *Hardy, published 1878.

The scene is the sombre Egdon Heath, powerfully and symbolically present throughout the novel. Damon Wildeve, engineer turned publican, dallies between the two women by whom he is loved—the gentle Thomasin Yeobright and the wild, capricious Eustacia Vye. Thomasin rejects her humble suitor Diggory Venn, a reddleman, and is eventually married to Wildeve. Thomasin's cousin Clym Yeobright, a diamond merchant in Paris, returns to Egdon intending to become a schoolmaster. He falls in love with Eustacia, and she marries him, hoping to induce him to return to Paris. But to her despair he will not return; his sight fails and he becomes a furzecutter on the heath. She becomes the cause of estrangement between Clym and his beloved mother, and unintentionally causes the mother's death. This, together with the discovery that Eustacia's relationship with Wildeve has not ceased, leads to a violent scene between Clym and his wife, and ultimately to Eustacia's flight, in the course of which both she and Wildeve are drowned. Clym, blaming himself for the death of his mother and his wife, becomes an itinerant preacher, and the widowed Thomasin marries Diggory Venn.

Revelation, Book of, see APOCALYPSE.

Revels, Master of the, an officer appointed to superintend *masques and other entertainments at court. He is first mentioned in the reign of Henry VII.

Revenge of Bussy D'Ambois, The, a tragedy by G. *Chapman, written 1610/11, printed 1613, a sequel to *Bussy D'Ambois.*

Clermont D'Ambois, brother of Bussy, is urged by Bussy's ghost to avenge his murder, but is reluctant to do so except honourably, in a duel. The anti-revenge aspects recall some elements of *Hamlet.* (See REVENGE TRAGEDY.)

Revenger's Tragedy, The, a tragedy published anonymously in 1607, and from 1656 ascribed to *Tourneur; modern scholarship attributes the play to *Middleton, though its authorship is still disputed.

It deals with the revenge of Vendice (or Vindice) for the murder of his betrothed lady by the licentious duke, and for the attempt of the duke's son, Lussurioso, to seduce Vendice's sister, the chaste Castiza. The play is marked by a tragic intensity of feeling, a powerfully satiric wit, and passages of great poetic richness. (See also REVENGE TRAGEDY.)

Revenge Tragedy, a dramatic genre that flourished in the late Elizabethan and Jacobean period, sometimes known as 'the tragedy of blood'. Kyd's *The Spanish Tragedy* (1592) helped to establish a demand for this popular form; later examples are Marlowe's *The Jew of Malta,* Shakespeare's *Titus Andronicus,* *The Revenger's Tragedy,* and, most notably, *Hamlet.* Common ingredients include: the hero's quest for vengeance, often at the prompting of the ghost of a murdered kinsman or loved one; scenes of real or feigned insanity; a play-within-a-play; scenes in graveyards; scenes of carnage and mutilation; etc. Many of these items were inherited from Senecan drama, with the difference that in revenge tragedy violence was not reported but took place on stage. The revenge code also produced counterattacks, as in *The Atheist's Tragedy,* in Chapman's *The Revenge of Bussy D'Ambois,* and again in *Hamlet,* in which the heroes refuse or hesitate to follow the convention.

Revesby Play, The, a folk-drama acted by morris-dancers at Revesby in Lincolnshire at the end of the 18th cent. The central incident no doubt symbolizes the death of the year and its resuscitation in the spring.

Review, The, (1) a thrice-weekly periodical started by *Defoe in 1704, under the title of *A Weekly Review of the Affairs of France,* which after various transformations became *A Review of the State of the British Nation* in 1707; it lasted until 1713. It was a non-partisan paper, an organ of the commercial interests of the nation and was written, practically in its entirety, by Defoe himself, who expressed in it his opinions on all current political topics, thus initiating the political leading article. It also had lighter articles on love, marriage, gambling, etc.; (2) a quarterly magazine of poetry and criticism, founded in 1962 and edited by Ian Hamilton (1938–), poet, biographer, and critic. It ran for 30 issues, and was succeeded by *The New Review,* also edited by Hamilton, which ran from 1974 to 1979. Contributors included R. *Lowell, E. *O'Brien, P. *Porter, R. *Fuller, J. *Fuller, S. *Heaney, and Douglas Dunn.

Review of English Studies, a scholarly quarterly founded by R. B. *McKerrow. The first issue appeared in Jan. 1925, and the present New Series began in 1950.

Revised Version, The, see BIBLE, THE ENGLISH.

Revolt of Islam, The, an epic political poem by P. B. *Shelley, written in 1817 (under the title 'Laon and Cythna: or The Revolution in the Golden City, A Vision of the Nineteenth Century'), published 1818.

The poem, in twelve cantos of Spenserian stanzas, is Shelley's idealized and idiosyncratic version of the French revolution, transposed to an Oriental setting. The revolt is organized by a brother and sister, Laon and Cythna, whose temporary success is celebrated in incestuous love-making (Canto VI). But the tyrants recover power, and Islam is subject to plague and famine, vividly described (Canto X). Brother and sister are burnt at the stake, but sail together with an illegitimate child to a visionary Hesperides (Canto XII). The figure of Cythna, the revolutionary feminist, is of historical interest; and the prose Preface, concerning reactions to the French revolution, is impressively argued.

Revolution in France, Reflections on the, by E. *Burke, published 1790.

This treatise was provoked by a sermon preached by R. *Price in Nov. 1789, in which he exulted in the French revolution and asserted that the king of England owes his throne to the choice of the people, who are at liberty to cashier him for misconduct. Burke repudiates this constitutional doctrine, and contrasts the inherited rights of which the English are tenacious with the 'rights of man' of the French revolutionaries, based on 'extravagant and presumptuous speculations', inconsistent with an ordered society and leading to poverty and chaos. The well-known eloquent passage on the downfall of Marie Antoinette leads to the lament that 'the age of chivalry is gone . . . All the decent drapery of life is to be rudely torn off' in deference to 'the new conquering empire of light and reason'. His general conclusion is that the defective institutions of the old régime should have been reformed, not destroyed.

Reynard the Fox, the central character in the *Roman de Renart,* a series of popular satirical fables, related to the *Bestiaries and the tradition from *Aesop's Fables, written in France at various times c.1175–1250. The first known cycle is the Latin one by Nivard of Ghent, *Ysengrimus* (c.1148), and this was followed by the Middle High German *Reinhard Fuchs* (c.1180). There is a Flemish version from c.1250; another Flemish version (now lost) was translated into English and printed by *Caxton in 1481. In these anthropomorphic stories, the fox is the man who preys on society and is brought to justice but escapes by his cunning. The most important of these is the Middle English 'The Fox and the Wolf'. Other related works in English are Chaucer's 'The Nun's Priest's Tale' (*Canterbury Tales*, 20), some of *Henryson's 'Morall Fabillis of Esope' (where the fox is called Lowrence), and J. C. *Harris's Uncle Remus stories (where the role of the fox is taken by Brer Rabbit). The principal characters in Caxton's version are: Reynard the Fox, King Noble the Lion, Isengrym the Wolf, Courtoys the Hound, Bruin the Bear, Tybert the Cat, Grymbert the Badger, Coart (or Cuwaert) the Hare, Bellyn the Ram, Martin and Dame Rukenawe the Apes, Chanticleer the Cock, Partlet the Hen. Ermeline is Reynard's wife and Malperdy (*Malpertuis*) his castle.

REYNOLDS, John Hamilton (1796–1852), poet, a close friend and correspondent of *Keats. Reynolds published *Safie* (1814), an *oriental novel reminiscent of *Byron. *The Garden of Florence* (1821) contains his most serious work. He had great skill in parody and comic verse; his parody of Wordsworth's *Peter Bell* appeared in 1819, *The Fancy* in 1820, and *Odes and Addresses* (with T. *Hood) in 1825.

REYNOLDS, Sir Joshua (1723–92), portrait painter, became first president of the Royal Academy in 1768. He was also a distinguished man of letters; it was he who suggested the idea of the *Club to his friend Dr *Johnson. He painted Johnson at least five times and wrote a Memoir of him and two Johnsonian dialogues; *Boswell dedicated his *Life of Johnson* to the painter and Goldsmith dedicated *The Deserted Village* to him in 1770. Reynold's first literary works were three essays published in the *Idler (1759). His *Discourses* (1769–90), in which he supported the traditional values of academic art, are his most significant achievement as a writer. They were fiercely criticized by *Blake, who believed 'this man was hired to depress art', and frequently attacked Reynolds.

Rhetoric, in Greek, the art of speaking so as to persuade, was from the first tied up with ethics (persuasion of what is true) and literature (use of language in order to please). It was a branch of the medieval *Trivium and therefore an important part of the school syllabus up to the 17th

cent. Literary rhetoric is concerned with the organization (*inventio* and *dispositio*) and embellishment (*elecutio*) of works. The first of these is prominent in many 18th-cent. works (*Tristram Shandy* and *A Tale of a Tub*, for instance), and the second is important in its provision of poetic 'devices' (figures and tropes) in poets from *Chaucer to the present day.

Rhoda Fleming, a novel by G. *Meredith, published 1865.

RHODES, Cecil John (1853–1902), made a fortune at the diamond fields of Kimberley, became a statesman of South Africa, and was famous for his colonizing activities in Southern Africa. He was prime minister of Cape Colony from 1890, but resigned after being pronounced guilty of grave breaches of duty arising from the unauthorized raid into the Transvaal of Dr Jameson. In his will he endowed 170 scholarships at Oxford, for students from the colonies, America, and Germany.

RHODES, William Barnes (1772–1826), translated the *Satires* of *Juvenal in 1801 and the *Epigrams* in 1803. He wrote a successful farce *Bombastes Furioso* (1810).

Rhododaphne, a narrative poem in octosyllabics by *Peacock, published 1818.

Rhyme: 'male' or 'masculine' rhymes or endings are those having a final accented syllable, as distinguished from 'female' or 'feminine' rhymes or endings in which the last syllable is unaccented.

Rhyme-royal, or Rime royal, see METRE.

Rhymers Club, a group of poets that met at the *Cheshire Cheese in Fleet Street for two or three years, from 1891, to read poetry. Members and associates included *Yeats, Ernest Rhys (1859–1946, poet and editor of the *Everyman's Library), *Le Gallienne, *Dowson, L. *Johnson, Arthur *Symons, and J. *Davidson. It published two collections of verse, 1892 and 1894.

Rhyming Poem, The, an Old English poem from the *Exeter Book and therefore not later than the 10th cent., striking for the fact that the two halves of its alliterating lines rhyme. It is a loose discussion of the vicissitudes of life, contrasting the misfortunes of a fallen king with his past glory. It has been suggested that the poem is a paraphrase of Job 29 and 30.

RHYS, Ernest, see RHYMERS CLUB and EVERYMAN'S LIBRARY.

RHYS, Jean (Ella Gwendolen Rees Williams) (?1890–1979), novelist, born in Dominica, came to England in 1907. In 1919 she left England and remained abroad for many years, living mainly in Paris, where she began to write and where much of her early work is set. Her works include *The Left Bank: Sketches and Studies of Present-Day Bohemian Paris* (1927); *Postures* (1928, reprinted 1969 as *Quartet*); *After Leaving Mr Mackenzie* (1930); *Voyage in the Dark* (1934), a first-person account of 19-year-old Anna Morgan's experiences as a chorus girl in London and on tour; and *Good Morning, Midnight* (1939). A long silence followed, during which Jean Rhys lived quietly in the West Country, until a radio adaptation of *Good Morning, Midnight* (1958) brought her back to public attention. *Wilde Sargasso Sea* (1966), set in Dominica and Jamaica during the 1830s, presents the life of the mad Mrs Rochester from *Jane Eyre*, a Creole heiress here called Antoinette Cosway. *Tigers are Better Looking* (1968) and *Sleep it Off, Lady* (1976) are collections of short stories.

Rhythm (1911–13, superseded 1913 by *The Blue Review*), a periodical edited by J. M. *Murry, with M. *Sadleir and K. *Mansfield. Murry conceived it as '*The Yellow Book* of the modern movement', and in it appeared work by D. H. *Lawrence, Mansfield, F. M. *Ford, Picasso, Gaudier-Brzeska, and others.

Riah, the Jew in Dickens's *Our Mutual Friend*.

RICARDO, David (1772–1823), English economist, who made a fortune on the London stock exchange and then, under the influence of Adam *Smith, devoted himself to the study of political economy. James *Mill became a close friend and encouraged him in the composition and publication of his chief work, *On the Principles of Political Economy and Taxation* (1817), in which he set forward his views on prices, wages, and profits, and his theory of rent. He became MP for Pontarlington in 1819. His personal and social interests and sympathies appear to have been narrow, and in many ways he represents the archetypal 'Dryasdust' economist, concerned only with facts and statistics, of *Carlyle's diatribes.

RICE, Elmer (1892–1967), American dramatist. His first major play was the expressionist drama *The Adding Machine* (1923). His plays of the 1930s (*We, the People*, 1933; *Judgment Day*, 1934; *Between Two Worlds*, 1934) are a response to the Depression and international ideological conflict. Rice was a campaigner for social justice and an outspoken critic of censorship.

RICH, Barnaby (1542–1617), fought at Le Havre, in Ireland, and in the Netherlands, and from 1574 turned to literature, writing romances in the style of Lyly's *Euphues*, pamphlets, and reminiscences. From 1587 he received a pension.

His best-known romance is *Farewell to Militarie Profession* (1581), which includes 'Apolonius and Silla', the source of Shakespeare's *Twelfth Night*.

RICH, John (?1692–1761), theatrical producer, opened the New Theatre in Lincoln's Inn Fields in 1714. In 1728 he produced Gay's *Beggar's Opera* which was popularly said to have 'made Rich gay and Gay rich'. He became manager of Covent Garden in 1732, and in 1735 founded the Sublime Society of Beef Steaks, a club which met there.

RICH, Penelope (*c.* 1562–1607), sister of Robert Devereux, earl of *Essex. In 1581 she was unhappily married to Lord Rich, and soon after provided the model for *Sidney's 'Stella'. The exact nature of their relationship can never be known, but details in some sonnets make it clear that she is the lady in question. After she had been legally separated from Lord Rich, she married Lord Mountjoy. She was a famous beauty and a good linguist, took part in masques by *Jonson and *Daniel, and was addressed by other poets besides Sidney.

RICHARD I, 'Cœur de Lion', king of England 1189–99, became a figure of romantic admiration in England (in the *Robin Hood legends, and in Scott's *The Talisman* and *Ivanhoe*). (See RICHARD COEUR DE LION.)

Richard II, King, a historical tragedy by *Shakespeare, probably written and acted 1595, printed 1597. After the death of *Elizabeth I a fourth quarto was issued in 1608, which contained the first appearance in print of the deposition scene (IV. i. 155–320). The scene was included in the text of the play printed in the First *Folio of 1623. Shakespeare's main source was the *Chronicles* of *Holinshed, but he appears to have drawn on S. Daniel's narrative poem *The Civil Wars*.

The play begins with the quarrel between Henry Bolingbroke, son of John of Gaunt, and Thomas Mowbray, duke of Norfolk, which King Richard resolves arbitrarily by exiling Mowbray for life and Bolingbroke for ten years. When 'time-honoured' John of Gaunt dies Richard confiscates his property to pay for his Irish wars, for which he leaves the country. Bolingbroke returns to claim his inheritance and takes Berkeley Castle, which the duke of York has as regent to yield him. The king returns to Wales, hears that his Welsh supporters have deserted him and that Bolingbroke has executed the king's favourites Bushy and Green; accompanied by York's son Aumerle, he withdraws to Flint Castle, where Bolingbroke accepts his surrender. The first half of the play ends with a discussion between a gardener and Richard's Queen Isabel about the government of the garden-state and the possibility of the king's deposition (III. iv).

In London Richard relinquishes his crown to Bolingbroke, who sends him to the Tower. The earl of Carlisle's and Aumerle's plot to kill Bolingbroke, who has now proclaimed himself Henry IV, is foiled by York. Richard is transferred to Pomfret Castle, where he hears of Henry's coronation and is murdered by Sir Pierce of Exton.

Richard II is written entirely in verse.

Richard III, King, a historical tragedy by *Shakespeare probably written and performed 1591. It was first published in 1597; it appeared again, in a fuller and more reliable text, in the First *Folio of 1623. The play's chief sources are the chronicles of R. *Holinshed and E. *Hall.

The play completes the tetralogy whose first three parts are the *Henry VI plays. It centres on the character of Richard of Gloucester, afterwards King Richard III, ambitious and bloody, bold and subtle, treacherous, yet brave in battle, a murderer, and usurper of the crown. The play begins with the deformed Richard's announcement: 'Now is the winter of our discontent | Made glorious summer by this sun of York', that is the king, Edward IV, who is dying. Richard is determined that he shall succeed to the crown and sets out to eliminate any opposition to this and to secure his position. He has his brother the duke of Clarence, who has been imprisoned in the Tower, murdered. As she accompanies the corpse of her dead father-in-law Henry VI, Anne, the widow of Edward, prince of Wales, is wooed by Richard, and they are later married.

When the king dies Richard begins his attack on Queen Elizabeth's family and supporters, with the help of the duke of Buckingham. Hastings, Rivers, and Grey are all executed, and Buckingham persuades the citizens of London to proclaim Richard king. After his coronation he murders his nephews, Edward V and Richard, duke of York, in the Tower, and following the death of his wife Anne, which he encourages, tries to marry his niece, Elizabeth of York. However, Buckingham rebels and goes to join Henry Tudor, earl of Richmond, who has landed in Wales at Milford Haven to claim the crown. Buckingham is captured and Richard has him executed, but he now has to face Richmond's army at Bosworth. On the night before the battle the ghosts of those whom Richard has killed appear to him and foretell his defeat. In the battle the next day he loses his horse and is killed by Richmond, who is then proclaimed Henry VII, the first of the Tudor monarchs.

Richard Cœur de Lion, a verse romance in 7,136 lines of short couplets dating from the early 14th cent. It is assumed that the source is Anglo-Norman, dating from about 1230–50. The poem describes the discomfiture of the Saracens in the course of the Third Crusade and breaks off, unfinished, when a three-year truce is arranged.

Richard Feverel, see ORDEAL OF RICHARD FEVEREL, THE.

RICHARDS, Frank, see HAMILTON, C.

RICHARDS, (Thomas Franklin) Grant (1872–1948), publisher and author. His *Memories of a Misspent Youth* (1932) and *Author Hunting* (1934) describe a life devoted to literature, and to the support of authors as diverse as A. E. *Housman, *Firbank, *Tressell, and *Dreiser. He was the founder, in 1901, of the World's Classics Series.

RICHARDS, I(vor) A(rmstrong) (1893–1979), critic and poet, became a fellow of Magdalene College, Cambridge, in 1929, then in 1931 moved to Harvard, where he devoted many years to the study of linguistics and education. He was the founder, with Charles Kay Ogden (1889–1957), of Basic English, 'an auxiliary international language comprising 850 words arranged in a system in which everything may be said for all the purposes of everyday language'; Richards and Ogden published two works together, *The Foundations of Aesthetics* (1922, with J. Wood) and *The Meaning of Meaning* (1923). In a literary context Richards is best known for his *Principles of Literary Criticism* (1924), *Science and Poetry* (1926), and above all *Practical Criticism: a study of literary judgement* (1929), a work which revolutionized the teaching and study of English. It was based on an experiment conducted by Richards in Cambridge in which he issued unsigned poems to students and asked for their written comments. Richards's attacks on vagueness, sentimentality, and laziness in poets and readers, and his praise of irony, ambiguity, complexity, and allusiveness, did much to create the climate which accepted *Modernism, and greatly influenced *Empson (his student from 1928 to 1929) and *Leavis; but perhaps his greatest contribution lay in his emphasis on the importance of close textual study and the danger of random generalization. (See NEW CRITICISM and PRACTICAL CRITICISM.) Richards also published several volumes of poetry; a collection, *Internal Colloquies: Poems and Plays*, appeared in 1972.

RICHARDSON, Dorothy Miller (1873–1957), novelist, became an intimate friend of H. G. *Wells and other avant-garde thinkers of the day who encouraged her to write. *Pointed Roofs* (1915) was the first of a sequence of highly autobiographical novels entitled *Pilgrimage*, of which the last volume is *March Moonlight* (1967). She was a pioneer of the *stream-of-consciousness technique, narrating the action through the mind of her heroine Miriam. She believed in 'unpunctuated' female prose (citing *Joyce in support), and V. *Woolf credited her with inventing 'the psychological sentence of the feminine gender'.

The formidable length of her great work deterred many readers, but interest revived in the 1960s and 1970s with the growth of *feminist criticism.

RICHARDSON, Henry Handel, the penname of Ethel Florence Lindesay Richardson (1870–1946), novelist, born in Melbourne, Australia; she studied music in Leipzig from 1888, and from 1904 she lived in England. Her novels include *Maurice Guest* (1908) a tale of *grande passion* set in Leipzig; *The Getting of Wisdom* (1910), describing her Australian schooldays in the person of Laura Rambotham, an intelligent child caught between ambition and reality; *The Fortunes of Richard Mahony*, a trilogy (*Australia Felix*, 1917; *The Way Home* 1925; and *Ultima Thule*, 1929), of which the last is rooted in the biography of her own parents. In its epic sweep it is at once the history of a man, a marriage, and a continent, capturing the landscapes, developing social attitudes, and growing prosperity and respectability of Australia. Her last novel, *The Young Cosima* (1939), is based on a life of Cosima Wagner.

RICHARDSON, Jonathan, the elder (1665–1745), British portrait painter, whose *Theory of Painting* (1715) was the first significant work on aesthetic theory by an English author; in the second edition, 1725, he added an influential essay on the *Sublime. He had a wide circle of literary friends, amongst them *Pope, *Gay, and *Prior, and himself wrote a book on *Milton.

RICHARDSON, Samuel (1689–1761), received little education owing to his father's poverty. In 1706 he was apprenticed to a printer and set up in business on his own in 1721, in which year he married Martha Wilde. He combined printing and publishing. In 1723 he took over the printing of an influential Tory Journal, the True Briton. In the 1720s and early 1730s he suffered the early deaths of all his six children, and in 1731 that of his wife; he attributed the nervous disorders of his later life to the shock of these deaths. In 1733 he married Elizabeth Leake, and four daughters of their marriage survived. His *The Apprentice's Vade Mecum* (1733) is a book of advice on morals and conduct. In 1738 he purchased in Fulham a weekend 'country' house, which he always referred to as 'North End', and which later became famous for his readings and literary parties. He published in 1739 his own version, pointedly moral, of *Aesop's Fables.*

His novel *Pamela* (1740–1) started as a series of 'familiar letters', which were published separately as *Letters . . . to and for Particular Friends* (1741). The morality and realism of *Pamela* were particularly praised, but complaints of its impropriety persuaded him to revise his second edition considerably. Imitations and forged 'continuations' persuaded Richardson to continue the story in *Pamela II* (1741); a stinging parody, *An Apology for the Life of Mrs *Shamela Andrews* (1741), appeared which Richardson believed to be by *Fielding (as it almost certainly was) and which he never forgave. Fielding's *Joseph Andrews* begins as a parody of *Pamela.*

In 1733 he had begun printing for the House of Commons and in 1742 he secured the lucrative post of printer of its Journals. *Clarissa (8 vols, 1747–9) was an undoubted success, but there were complaints about both its length and its indecency. Similar criticisms greeted *Sir Charles Grandison (7 vols, 1753–4). He became friendly with Dr *Johnson, to whose *Rambler he contributed in 1750.

Richardson is generally agreed to be one of the chief founders of the modern novel. All his novels were *epistolary, a form he took from earlier works in English and French, and which he raised to a level not attained by any of his predecessors. The 'letters', of which his novels consist, contain many long transcriptions of conversations. He was acutely aware of the problems of prolixity ('Length, is my principle Disgust') and worked hard to prune his original drafts, but his interest in minute analysis led inevitably to an expansive style.

Richard the Redeless, see MUM AND THE SOTHSEGGER.

Richard the Thirde, The History of King, by Sir T. *More, included in his *Workes* (1557). It is distinguished from earlier English chronicles by its unity of scheme and dramatic effectiveness. It was More, however, who was ultimately responsible for the image of Richard as a *Machiavellian tyrant which Shakespeare transmits in *Richard III. (See also BIOGRAPHY.)

Richland, Miss, the heroine of Goldsmith's *The Good-Natur'd Man.*

RICKETTS, Charles (1866–1931), English aesthete, illustrator, designer, and painter, whose many literary friends included *Wilde (whose works he illustrated), G. B. *Shaw, and *Yeats. He wrote a memoir, *Recollections of Oscar Wilde* (1932). With Charles Shannon, Ricketts edited *The Dial (1889–97), a lavishly illustrated literary magazine deeply influenced by the then little-known works of French and Belgian Symbolists. His Vale Press, founded in 1896, was one of the most important of the *private presses.

RICKWORD, Edgell (1898–1982), poet, critic, and radical, edited from 1925 to 1927, *The

Calendar of Modern Letters. He also edited two volumes of **Scrutiny* (1928–32), the *Left Review* (1936–8), and *Our Time* (1944–7), and edited the essays of **Caudwell* (1949). His *Collected Poems* appeared in 1976.

Ridd, John, see LORNA DOONE.

Riddle of the Sands, The, see CHILDERS, E.

Riderhood, Rogue, a character in Dickens's **Our Mutual Friend.*

RIDING, Laura (1901–   ), American poet and critic, who worked with Robert **Graves (1927–39). Her work includes *Collected Poems* (1938) and *Selected Poems* (1970); *A Survey of Modernist Poetry* (1927; with Graves) and *Contemporaries and Snobs* (1928), both critical works; *A Trojan Ending* (1937), a novel; and *Lives of Wives* (1939), on various marriages in history.

RIDLEY, James (1736–65), a cleric, remembered for his *Tales of the Genii* (1764). Many of these curious **Oriental tales are modelled on those of the **Arabian Nights.* The book enjoyed great success; it was later bowdlerized, and read by several generations of children, including the young **Dickens.

RIDLEY, Nicholas (?1500–55), became one of **Cranmer's chaplains and began gradually to reject many Roman doctrines. As bishop of London he exerted himself to propagate reformed opinions. On Edward VI's death he denounced Queen Mary and Elizabeth as illegitimate at St Paul's Cross, London. He was sent to the Tower in June 1553 and deprived of his bishopric. In September 1555 he was condemned on the charge of heresy and burnt alive with **Latimer at Oxford, 16 Oct. He wrote several theological treatises.

Rience, see RYENCE.

Rigaud, a character in Dicken's **Little Dorrit.*

Rigdum-Funnidos, see CHRONONHOTONTHO-LOGOS.

Rights of Man, The, a political treatise by T. **Paine in two parts (1791, 1792).

Pt I is in the main a reply to Burke's *Reflections on the *Revolution in France.* Paine accuses **Burke of seeking theatrical effects at the expense of truth, and of disorderly arguments. He denies that one generation can bind another as regards the form of government. He traces the incidents of the French revolution up to the adoption of the Declaration of the Rights of Man by the National Assembly. He alleges that Burke cares only for the forms of chivalry, and not for the nation. 'He pities the plumage, and forgets the dying bird.'

In Pt II Paine passes to a comparison of the new French and American constitutions with those of British institutions, to the disadvantage of the latter. The work also contains Paine's farsighted proposals for reform of taxation, family allowances, maternity grants, etc.

Rights of Woman, *Vindication of the,* see WOLL-STONECRAFT, M.

RIMBAUD, Arthur (1854–91), French poet, see SYMBOLISM.

Rime of the Ancient Mariner, The, see ANCIENT MARINER, THE RIME OF THE.

Rime royal, or rhyme-royal, see METRE.

Rimini, The Story of, see STORY OF RIMINI, THE.

Rinaldo, or **Renaud,** first figures under the latter name in the **Charlemagne cycle of legends as the eldest of the Four Sons of **Aymon, who were first the enemies of Charlemagne but later pardoned on condition that Renaud goes to Palestine to fight the Saracens and surrenders his horse Bayard. Renaud complies and becomes a hermit in Palestine; but Bayard will allow no one else to mount him. As Rinaldo, he figures in Boiardo's **Orlando Innamorato,* Ariosto's **Orlando Furioso,* and Tasso's **Gerusalemme Liberata:* in the first two as the cousin of Orlando and the suitor of Angelica; in the third as a prince of Esta, the lover of Armida and the victor in the battle for Jerusalem.

Ring and the Book, The, a poem in blank verse, in twelve books, by R. **Browning, published 1868–9.

The 'Ring' of the title is a figure for the process by which the artist transmutes the 'pure crude fact' of historical events into living forms; the 'Book' is a collection of documents relating to the Italian murder trial of the late 17th cent. on which the poem is based. Browning found the volume on a market stall in Florence.

Pietro and Violante Comparini were a middle-aged childless couple living in Rome whose income could only be secured after Pietro's death if they had a child; Violante bought the child of a prostitute. This child, Pompilia, was eventually married to Count Guido Franceschini, an impoverished nobleman from Arezzo. The marriage was unhappy, and the Comparini returned to Rome, where they sued Guido for the restoration of Pompilia's dowry on the grounds of her illegitimacy. Pompilia herself eventually fled from Arezzo in the company of a young priest, Giuseppe Caponsacchi. Guido pursued them and had them arrested on the outskirts of Rome; as a result, Caponsacchi was exiled to Civita Vecchia for three years, and Pompilia was sent to a convent while the lawsuits were decided. But then, because she was pregnant, she was released into the custody of the Comparini. A fortnight after the birth of her child, Guido and four accomplices murdered her and her putative parents. They were arrested and sentenced to death.

In Browning's poem, the story is told by a succession of speakers—citizens of Rome, the participants themselves, the lawyers, and the pope—each of whose single, insufficient perceptions combines with the others to form the 'ring' of the truth.

In its immense but ordered size and scope and in its rich evocation of time and place, the poem stands at the centre of Browning's achievement.

Ring des Nibelungen, Der, a series of four music dramas by Richard *Wagner. *Das Rheingold*; *Die Walküre* (*The Valkyrie*); *Siegfried*; and *Gotterdämmerung* (*The Twilight of the Gods*). They are indirectly based on the *Nibelungenlied*.

'Rip Van Winkle', a story by W. *Irving attributed to 'Diedrich *Knickerbocker' and included in *The Sketch Book* (1820).

Rip Van Winkle, taking rufuge from a termagant wife in a solitary ramble in the Catskill mountains, falls asleep, and awakens after twenty years, to find his wife dead, his house in ruins, and the world completely changed.

Risingham, Bertram, a character in Scott's *Rokeby*.

RITCHIE, Anne Isabella Thackeray, Lady (1837–1919), elder daughter of *Thackeray. She wrote novels of an impressionistic kind which influenced her step-niece V. *Woolf: *Old Kensington* (1873) and *Mrs Dymond* (1885) are probably the best remembered. She also wrote reminiscences of the literary figures she had known in her youth.

RITSON, Joseph (1752–1803), literary antiquarian, and a friend of Sir W. *Scott, who consulted him while working on his *Border Minstrelsy*. Riston was a man of an irritable and bitter nature, exacerbated by ill health, which expressed itself in his attacks (often justified) on the works of fellow scholars: he challenged T. *Warton's *History of English Poetry* (1782) and also Dr *Johnson's and *Steevens's edition of Shakespeare. In 1783 he published *A Select Collection of English Songs* containing strictures on Percy's *Reliques*, accusing *Percy of corrupting texts. He published *Robin Hood: a collection of all the ancient poems, songs and ballads now extant relative to that outlaw* (1795), with illustrations by *Bewick, and *Ancient English Metrical Romances* (1802), as well as several popular collections and anthologies of songs, children's verses, fairy-stories, etc. He became increasingly odd in later

life and finally insane. (See also PRIMITIVISM and BALLAD.)

Rival Queens, The: or the Death of Alexander the Great, a tragedy by N. *Lee, produced 1677.

Rivals, The, a comedy by R. B. *Sheridan, produced 1775.

This was Sheridan's first play; it is generally agreed to be one of the most engaging and accomplished of English comedies. It is set in Bath. Captain Absolute, son of Sir Anthony Absolute, is in love with Lydia Languish, the niece of Mrs *Malaprop. Lydia prefers a poor half-pay lieutenant to the heir of a baronet, so he assumes, for the purposes of courtship, the character of Ensign Beverley, and in this guise he is favourably received. But Lydia will lose half her fortune if she marries without her aunt's consent, and Mrs Malaprop will not approve of an indigent ensign. Sir Anthony arrives in Bath to propose a match between his son and Lydia Languish, a proposal welcomed by Mrs Malaprop. Captain Absolute is afraid of revealing his deception to Lydia in case he loses her; while Bob Acres, who is also Lydia's suitor and has heard of Beverley's courtship, is provoked by the fiery Irishman Sir Lucius O'Trigger to ask Captain Absolute to carry a challenge to Beverley. Sir Lucius himself, who has been deluded into thinking that some love-letters received by him from Mrs Malaprop are really from Lydia, likewise finds Captain Absolute in his path, and challenges him. But when Acres finds that Beverley is in fact his friend Absolute, he declines his duel with relief and resigns all claim to Lydia. Sir Lucius's misapprehension is removed by the arrival of Mrs Malaprop, and Lydia, after a pretty quarrel with her lover for shattering her hopes of a romantic elopement, finally forgives him. Another plot, neatly interwoven with the rest, concerns the love-affair of the perverse and jealous Faulkland with Lydia's friend Julia Melville.

'Rizpah', a poem by *Tennyson, published in *Ballads and other poems* (1880), the monologue of a mother who collects the unhallowed bones of her son night by night from the foot of the gallows and buries them secretly in the churchyard.

Road to Oxiana, The, see BYRON, R.

Road to Wigan Pier, The, see ORWELL, G., and LEFT BOOK CLUB.

Road to Xanadu, The, see LOWES, J. L.

Roaring Girle, The, or *Moll Cut-Purse*, a comedy by T. *Middleton and *Dekker, written ?1604–8, published 1611.

In this comedy there are some bustling scenes

in which the life of the London streets is vividly presented, shop-keepers selling tobacco and feathers, their wives intriguing with gallants, and Moll Cutpurse talking thieves' cant and discomfiting overbold admirers.

Robene and Makyne, a pastoral by *Henryson, on the model of the French *pastourelle* included in Percy's *Reliques*.

Robert Elsmere, see WARD, M.A.

ROBERT OF GLOUCESTER (*fl.* 1260–1300), the reputed author of a metrical Chronicle of England from Brutus to Henry III, for much of which he drew upon *Laȝamon. It is written in long lines and is not the work of a single hand. It contains a famous description of the death of Simon de Montfort at the battle of Evesham and a section in praise of England.

ROBERTS, Michael William Edward (1902–48), poet, critic, editor, and teacher of mathematics, whose anthologies *New Signatures* (1932) and *New Country* (1933), containing work by *Auden, *Day-Lewis, *Empson, *Spender, and others established him, in T. S. *Eliot's phrase, as 'expositor and interpreter of the poetry of his generation'. *The Recovery of the West* (1941) is a study of the ills of Western civilization and *The Estate of Man* (1951) shows him as a pioneer ecologist. He also edited the influential *Faber Book of Modern Verse* (1936).

ROBERTSON, T(homas) W(illiam) (1829–71), began life as an actor, then became a dramatist. His plays *Society* (1865), *Ours* (1866), *Caste* (1867), *Play* (1868), *School* (1869), and *M.P.* (1870), introduced a new and more natural type of comedy to the English stage than had been seen during the first half of the century.

ROBERTSON, William (1721–93), a Presbyterian parish minister who achieved fame on the publication of his *History of Scotland during the Reign of Queen Mary and of King James VI* (1759). He also published a history of the reign of Charles V (1769), *The History of America* (1777), and a *Disquisition concerning the knowledge which the Ancients had of India* (1791). Both in style and in scholarship his work is comparable with that of *Hume.

Robert the Devil, 6th duke of Normandy and father of William the Conqueror, a personage about whom many legends gathered in consequence of his violence and cruelty. *The Life of Robert the Devil*, a verse-tale, is a translation from the French and was printed in 1496 by *Wynkyn de Worde. T. *Lodge wrote a drama on the same subject.

'Robin Gray, Auld', see LINDSAY, LADY A

Robin Hood, a legendary outlaw. The name is part of the designation of places and plants in every part of England. The facts behind the legend are uncertain. Robin Hood is referred to in *Piers Plowman. As a historical character he appears in *Wyntoun's *The Orygynale Cronykil* (*c.*1420), and is referred to as a ballad hero by Abbot Bower (d. 1449), *Major, and *Stow. The first detailed history, *Lytell Geste of Robyn Hode* (printed *c.*1495), locates him in south-west Yorkshire; later writers place him in Sherwood and Plumpton Park (Cumberland), and finally make him earl of Huntingdon. *Ritson says he was born at Locksley in Nottinghamshire about 1160, that his true name was Robert Fitz-Ooth, and that he was commonly reputed to have been earl of Huntingdon. There is a pleasant account of the activities of his band in Drayton's *Poly-Olbion, song 26. According to Stow, there were about the year 1190 many robbers and outlaws, among whom were Robin Hood and Little John, who lived in the woods, robbing the rich, but killing only in self-defence, allowing no woman to be molested, and sparing poor men's goods. He is the centre of a whole cycle of ballads, one of the best of which is *Robin Hood and Guy of Gisborne* printed in Percy's *Reliques, and his legend shows affinity with Chaucer's 'Cook's Tale of Gamelyn' (see GAMELYN) and with the tales of other legendary outlaws such as Clym of the Clough and *Adam Bell. Popular plays embodying the legend appear to have been developed out of the village *May Day game, the king and queen of May giving place to Robin and Maid Marian. Works dealing with the same theme were written by *Munday, *Chettle, *Tennyson, and others. The *True Tale of Robin Hood* was published in 1632, *Robin Hood's Garland* in 1670, and a prose narrative in 1678. He figures in Scott's *Ivanhoe* as Locksley.

Robin Hood, A *Tale of*, sub-title of Jonson's *The Sad Shepherd*.

Robin Hood and Guy of Gisborne, one of the best known of the ballads of the *Robin Hood cycle.

Robin Oig M'Combich, the Highland drover in Scott's *'The Two Drovers'.

ROBINSON, E(dwin) A(rlington) (1869–1935), American poet. His admiration for *Hardy, *Crabbe, and R. *Browning is manifest in his many volumes of poetry about New England life, beginning with *The Torrent and the Night Before* (1896) and *The Children of the Night* (1897), which introduce, often through dramatic monologues, the population of his fictitious and representative Tilbury Town. He also wrote several long blank-verse narratives. He was introduced in England by a *Collected Poems* (1922) with an introduction by *Drinkwater.

ROBINSON, Henry Crabb (1775–1867), was a solicitor and later a barrister, but is chiefly remembered for his diaries, reading-lists, and letters, first collected in 1869, which provide valuable information about the writers and events of his time. He was the friend of *Wordsworth, *Coleridge, *Lamb, *Hazlitt, and later *Carlyle. He did much to popularize German culture in England. For many years he wrote for *The Times, at home and abroad, and he was one of the founders of both University College London, and the *Athenaeum club.

ROBINSON, (Esmé Stuart) Lennox (1886–1958), Irish dramatist, manager of the *Abbey Theatre, 1910–14 and 1919–23, when he became the director until his death. Among his best-known plays are The Clancy Name (1911); the patriotic Harvest (1911) and Patriots (1912); The Whiteheaded Boy, a comedy (1920); Crabbed Youth and Age (1924); the ambitious The Big House (1928), on the changing state of Ireland; and two successful later comedies, The Far-off Hills (1931) and Church Street (1955). He also edited the Oxford Book of Irish Verse (with D. MacDonagh, 1958) and other anthologies; and wrote The Irish Theatre (1939) and Ireland's Abbey Theatre. A History (1951).

Robinson Crusoe, The Life and strange and surprising Adventures of, a romance by *Defoe, published 1719.

The story is based on the experiences of Alexander *Selkirk on the uninhabited island of Juan Fernandez. Defoe added many incidents from his own imagination to his account of Crusoe, presenting it as a true story. The extraordinarily convincing account of the shipwrecked Crusoe's successful efforts to make himself a tolerable existence in his solitude first revealed Defoe's genius for vivid fiction; it has a claim to be the first English novel. Defoe was nearly sixty when he wrote it.

The author tells how Crusoe built himself a house, domesticated goats, and made himself a boat. He describes the perturbation of his mind caused by a visit of cannibals, his rescue from death of an indigenous native he later names Friday, and finally the coming of an English ship whose crew are in a state of mutiny, the subduing of the mutineers, and Crusoe's rescue.

Defoe followed it with The Farther Adventures of Robinson Crusoe (1719), in which with Friday he revisits his island, is attacked by a fleet of canoes on his departure, and loses Friday in the encounter.

Robot, a word coined from the Czech 'robota' (meaning drudgery). A play by the Czech novelist Karel Čapek (1890–1938) entitled R.U.R. (1920), which stands for 'Rossum's Universal Robots', was first performed in England in 1923, and the concept of the mechanical robot has opened up a whole new vein of *Science Fiction as well as adding a word to the English language.

Rob Roy, a novel by Sir W. *Scott, published 1817.

The story takes place just before the Jacobite rising of 1715. Francis Osbaldistone, the son of a rich London merchant, on refusing to adopt his father's profession, is banished to Osbaldistone Hall in the north of England, the home of his fox-hunting, hard-drinking uncle, Sir Hildebrand Osbaldistone. Here he is brought into contact with Sir Hildebrand's six boorish sons, one of whom, Rashleigh, is a malignant plotter who has been selected to occupy the place of Francis in the London counting-house, and Sir Hildebrand's niece, the high-spirited Diana Vernon. Rashleigh is deeply involved with Jacobite intrigues, has evil designs on Diana, and becomes the bitter enemy of Francis, who falls in love with Diana and is received by her with favour. The story is occupied with the attempts of Rashleigh to destroy Francis and to rob and ruin Francis's father, attempts that are defeated partly by Diana, and partly by the singular Scotsman Rob Roy Macgregor. This historical character, member of a proscribed clan, was once an honest drover; embittered by misfortune and injustice, he is now an outlaw, the ruthless and cunning opponent of the government's agents, but capable of justice and even generosity. In the outcome Rashleigh is forced to surrender the funds that he has misappropriated, and is killed by Rob Roy after having betrayed his Jacobite associates to the government. Francis is restored to his father's favour, becomes the owner of Osbaldistone Hall, and marries Diana. His rascally, sanctimonious servant Andrew Fairservice is one of Scott's great characters.

Robsart, Amy, a character in Scott's *Kenilworth. (See DUDLEY, SIR ROBERT.)

ROCHESTER, John Wilmot, second earl of (1647–80), lyric poet, satirist, and a leading member of the group of 'court wits' surrounding Charles II. He fought with conspicuous gallantry in the naval wars against the Dutch. He married the heiress, Elizabeth Malet; he also had several mistresses, including Elizabeth *Barry, and moved in fashionable London circles.

Although Dr *Johnson dismissed Rochester's lyrics, their wit and emotional complexity give him a good claim to be considered one of the last important *Metaphysical poets and he was one of the first of the *Augustans, with his social and literary verse satires. He wrote scurrilous lampoons, dramatic prologues and epilogues, 'imitations' and translations of classical authors, and several other brilliant poems such as his tough self-dramatization 'The Maimed Debauchee' and the grimly funny 'Upon Nothing'. Although his output was small he produced an important body of poems. *Marvell admired him, *Dryden, *Swift, and

*Pope were all influenced by him (he was Dryden's patron for a time), and he has made an impression on many subsequent poets.

Rochester is famous for having, in Johnson's words, 'blazed out his youth and health in lavish voluptuousness'. He became very ill in his early thirties and G. *Burnet superintended and subsequently wrote up the poet's death-bed conversion.

Rochester, Edward Fairfax, the hero of C. Brontë's *Jane Eyre.*

Roderick, *Vision of Don,* a poem by Sir W. *Scott, published in 1811.

Roderick Dhu, a character in Scott's *The Lady of the Lake.*

Roderick Hudson, the first novel of H. *James, published in book form 1876. It is the story of a young man transplanted from a lawyer's office in a Massachusetts town to a sculptor's studio in Rome. Incapable of adjustment to his environment, he fails both in art and love, and meets a tragic end in Switzerland. The leading female character, Christina Light, was taken up again by the author in a later novel, *The Princess Casamassima.*

Roderick Random, *The Adventures of,* by T. *Smollett, published 1748.

This is Smollett's first novel. In the Preface the author declares his wish to arouse 'generous indignation . . . against the vicious disposition of the world'. It is modelled on *Lesage's *Gil Blas,* and is a series of episodes, told with vigour and vividness, strung together on the life of the combative, often violent hero, who is also capable of generosity and affection. It gives an interesting picture, drawn from personal experiences, of the British navy and the British sailor of the day.

Roderick, *the last of the Goths,* a narrative poem by *Southey, published 1814.

Roderigo, Iago's gull in Shakespeare's *Othello.*

ROETHKE, Theodore (1908–63), American poet. His first book of poems, *Open House* (1941), displays characteristic imagery of vegetable growth and decay, rooted in childhood memories of the greenhouses of his father. It was followed by various volumes, including *The Lost Son* (1948), *Praise to the End* (1951), *I Am! Says the Lamb* (1961; light verse), and *The Far Field* (1964).

Roger, the name of the London cook (from Ware) in Chaucer's *Canterbury Tales.*

Roger de Coverley, Sir, see COVERLEY.

Rogero, or **Ruggiero,** the legendary ancestor of the house of Este, extolled in *Orlando Furioso.*

ROGER OF WENDOVER (d. 1236), monk and chronicler at St Albans; his *Flores Historiarum* was a history of the world from the creation to AD 1235, compiled from many different sources.

ROGERS, Samuel (1763–1855), the son of a banker and himself a banker for some years, was a highly successful poet. In *The Pleasures of Memory* (1792) the author wanders reflectively round the villages of his childhood. He published a fragmentary epic, *Columbus* (1810); *Jacqueline* (1814); *Italy* (1822–8), a collection of verse tales; and *Poems* (1832).

ROGERS, Woodes (d. 1732), commander of a privateering expedition (1708–11) in which *Dampier was pilot, and in the course of which *Selkirk was discovered on the island of Juan Fernandez. This was among the incidents described in his entertaining journal, *A Cruizing Voyage round the world.*

Roget's Thesaurus *of English Words and Phrases,* by Dr Peter Mark Roget (1779–1879), English physician and scholar, is a compilation of words classified in groups according to the ideas they express, the purpose of which is to supply a word, or words, which most aptly express a given idea. The volume, first published in 1852, has been successively revised by Roget's son, John Lewis Roget (from 1879), his grandson, Samuel Romilly Roget (from 1933) and more recently by Robert A. Dutch (from 1962) and Susan M. Lloyd (1982).

Rogue Literature, a type of underworld writing popular in the 16th and 17th cents. Its practitioners include the Kentish magistrate Thomas Harman; R. *Greene, whose pamphlets describe 'coney-catching', that is, the deception of innocents; and T. *Dekker. Rogue literature is generally vividly descriptive and often confessional, providing an important source for our knowledge of everyday common life and its language, as well as for the canting terms of thieves and beggars. It can be related to stories about *Robin Hood, *jest-book literature, and early attempts at writing fiction and autobiography.

Rokeby, a poem in six cantos by Sir W. *Scott, published 1813.

The scene is Rokeby, near Greta Bridge in Yorkshire, immediately after the battle of Marston Moor (1644). The complicated plot concerns the conspiracy of Oswald Wycliffe, lord of Barnard Castle, with the sturdy ruffian Bertram Risingham, to murder the latter's patron Philip of Mortham, in order to obtain his lands and the treasure he brought back from the Spanish main.

The poem includes the beautiful songs 'A weary lot is thine, fair maid' and 'Brignal

Banks'. Scott (in spite of the good first reception of the poem) recognized his own comparative failure as a poet, and thereupon turned to his true vocation as a novelist.

Rokesmith, John, in Dickens's *Our Mutual Friend*, the name assumed by John Harmon.

Roland, the most famous of the *Paladins of Charlemagne. According to the chronicler Einhard, his legend has the following basis of fact. In August 778 the rearguard of the French army of Charlemagne was surprised in the valley of Roncevaux by the Basque inhabitants of the mountains; the baggage was looted and all the rearguard killed, including Hrodland, count of the Breton marches. The story of this disaster was developed by the imagination of numerous poets. For the Basques were substituted the Saracens. Roland becomes the commander of the rearguard, appointed to the post at the instance of the traitor Ganelon, who is in league with the Saracen king Marsile. Oliver is introduced, Roland's companion in arms. Oliver thrice urges Roland to summon aid by sounding his horn, but Roland from excess of pride defers doing so until too late. Charlemagne returns and destroys the pagan army. Ganelon is tried and executed. The legend has been handed down in three principal forms: in the fabricated Latin chronicle of the 12th cent. erroneously attributed to Archbishop Turpin (d. *c*.800); in the *Carmen de proditione Guenonis* of the same epoch; and in the *Chanson de Roland*, in medieval French, also of the early 12th cent. It is a well-known tradition that Taillefer, a *jongleur* in the army of William the Conqueror, sang a poem on Roncesvalles at the battle of Hastings (1066), possibly an earlier version of the extant *Chanson*. Roland, as Orlando, is the hero of Boiardo's *Orlando Innamorato* and Ariosto's *Orlando Furioso*. Roland's sword was called 'Durandal' or 'Durindana', and his horn 'Olivant'. (See also OLIVER.)

Roland, Childe, see CHILDE ROLAND.

Roland de Vaux, (1) the baron of Triermain, in Sir W. *Scott's *The Bridal of Triermain*; (2) in Coleridge's *'Christabel', the estranged friend of Christabel's father.

ROLFE, Frederick William (1860–1913), who liked to call himself 'Baron Corvo', or, equally misleadingly, Fr Rolfe. His most outstanding novel, *Hadrian the Seventh* (1904), appears to be a dramatized autobiography—a self-justification and a dream of wish-fulfilment, in which Rolfe's protagonist, George Arthur Rose, is rescued from a life of literary poverty and elected pope. His other writings include *Stories Toto Told Me* (published in 1898, after first appearing in the *Yellow Book*), *Chronicles of the House of Borgia*

(1901, an eccentric historical study), and *The Desire and Pursuit of the Whole: a romance of modern Venice* (1934), in which Rolfe describes his own poverty, his homosexual fantasies, and the beauties of Venice, as well as abusing in characteristic vein many of those who had previously befriended him, including R. H. *Benson. Rolfe's style is highly ornate and idiosyncratic, and his allusions erudite. He alienated most of his admirers by his persistent paranoia and requests for financial support. The story of his unhappy life is told by A. J. A. *Symons in *The Quest for Corvo: An Experiment in Biography* (1934).

ROLLE, Richard, of Hampole (*c*.1300–49), one of the principal 14th-cent. English mystical writers, in prose and poetry. He became a hermit and lived at various places in Yorkshire, finally at Hampole near a Cistercian nunnery where he had disciples. Among these was Margaret Kirkeby who became an anchoress and to whom a number of his major English works (notably *The Forme of Perfect Living*) are addressed. The essential element in his mysticism is personal enthusiasm, rather than the rationalism of the more classical mystical writings. Among the large canon of his works are the *Meditations on the Passion*, *Ego Dormio*, and *The Commandment of Love*. (See ANGLO-LATIN LITERATURE.)

Rolliad, *Criticism on the,* a collection of Whig political satires directed against the younger Pitt and his followers after their success at the election of 1784, first published in the *Morning Herald and Daily Advertiser* during that year. The authors, members of the 'Esto Perpetua' club, are not known with certainty.

Rollo Duke of Normandy, see BLOODY BROTHER, THE.

Rolls Series, otherwise *Chronicles and Memorials of Great Britain and Ireland from the Invasion of the Romans to the Reign of Henry VIII.* Their publication was authorized by government in 1847 on the suggestion of Joseph Stevenson, the archivist, and the recommendation of Sir John Romilly, master of the rolls, and it produced texts of many of the most important literary and historical writings of the Middle Ages and Renaissance.

Roman à clef, i.e. a 'novel with a key', in which the reader (or some readers) are intended to identify real characters under fictitious names. The key is sometimes literal, sometimes figurative, and sometimes provided by the author, as in the case of Mrs *Manley's *The New Atalantis*, sometimes published separately by others, as in the case of Disraeli's *Coningsby*.

Roman Actor, The, a tragedy by *Massinger, acted 1626, printed 1629. The play is based on the life of the Emperor Domitian as told by *Suetonius and Dio Cassius.

Romance, derived from the Medieval Latin word *romanice,* 'in the Roman language'. The word *roman* in Old French was applied to the popular courtly stories in verse which dealt with three traditional subjects: the legends about Arthur, Charlemagne and his knights, and stories of classical heroes especially Alexander (see MATTER). English correspondents, almost always translations, are found from the 3th cent. onwards. Some of the most distinguished include *King Horn, *Havelok, Sir *Gawain and the Green Knight, Sir *Orfeo* (see also BRETON LAYS). They usually involve the suspension of the circumstances normally attendant on human actions (often through magic) in order to illustrate a moral point. From the 15th cent. onwards English romances are mostly in prose, and some 16th. cent. examples were the inspiration for *Spenser and Shakespeare (*Pandosto* by R. *Greene was used by Shakespeare in *The Winter's Tale*). A new interest in the medieval romance (in writers such as Sir W. *Scott and *Keats) contributed to the naming of the 19th-cent. *Romanticism, though the term was also used to embrace some sentimental novels from the 18th cent. onwards, as in the *Mills and Boon romances of the modern era.

Romance languages, the group of modern languages descended from Latin (which itself joins with them to form the branch of *Indo-European known as Italic), the chief of which are French, Italian, Spanish, Portuguese, and Romanian (and, of literary-historical importance, *Provençal).

Roman d'Alexandre, see ALEXANDER THE GREAT.

Roman de Brut and **Roman de Rou,** see WACE.

Roman de la Rose. The first 4,058 lines of this allegorical romance were written *c.*1230 by Guillaume de Lorris (*c.*1237); the remaining 17,622 lines were composed *c.*1275 by Jean de Meun. Loris's part of the poem is an allegorical presentation of *courtly love; the allegorical figures mostly embody various aspects of the lady whom the lover-narrator meets in his endeavours to reach the rose which symbolizes the lady's love. The story is set in the walled garden of the god of love, the unpleasant realities of life being depicted on the walls outside. Jean de Meun shows love in a wider context of scholarship, philosophy, and morals, shifting the work from the courtly to the encyclopaedic literary tradition, in line with the rationalist and compendious spirit of the 13th cent. The poem remained an immense literary influence all through the later Middle Ages, both inside and outside France. About one-third of the whole (ll.

1–5,154 and 10,679–12,360) is translated in the Middle English *The Romaunt of the Rose,* the first part of which may be by *Chaucer.

Roman de Renart, see REYNARD THE FOX.

Roman fleuve, the French term for a novel sequence. The practice of pursuing a family story through a number of related novels in order to render a comprehensive account of a social period ultimately derives from *Balzac and *Zola, but it reached its culmination between 1900 and 1940 in the works of Romain Rolland (1866–1944), Roger Martin du Gard (1881–1958), Georges Duhamel (1884–1966), and Jules Romains (1885–1972). Translations of these works have been popular in England, but the English version of the phenomenon, descending from *Trollope and including such novelists as *Galsworthy, C. P. *Snow, and A. *Powell, has not had the same consistency of purpose.

Romanticism (the Romantic Movement), a literary movement, and profound shift in sensibility, which took place in Britain and throughout Europe roughly between 1770 and 1848. Intellectually it marked a violent reaction to the *Enlightenment. Politically it was inspired by the revolutions in America and France and popular wars of independence in Poland, Spain, Greece, and elsewhere. Emotionally it expressed an extreme assertion of the self and the value of individual experience (the *'egotistical sublime'), together with the sense of the infinite and the transcendental. Socially it championed progressive causes, though when these were frustrated it often produced a bitter, gloomy, and despairing outlook. In Britain, Romantic writers of the first generation included *Wordsworth and *Coleridge (*Lyrical Ballads,* 1798), *Burns, and *Blake; though introspective 18th-cent. poets such as *Gray and *Cowper show pre-Romantic tendencies, as well as *Gothic novelists such as Horace *Walpole and 'Monk' *Lewis. Terror, passion, and the *Sublime are essential concepts in early Romanticism; as is the sense of primitive mystery of *Macpherson's 'Ossian', the ballads collected by *Percy, and the poetry forged by *Chatterton (whom *Southey edited) (see PRIMITIVISM). Foreign sources were also vital: *Goethe's *The Sorrows of Young Werther* (1774); the ghostly ballads of Bürger (*Lenore,* 1773); the verse dramas of *Schiller (*The Robbers,* 1781); and the philosophical criticism of A. W. *Schlegel. The tone of Romanticism was shaped by the naked emotionalism of *Rousseau's *Julie, ou la nouvelle Héloïse* (1761), and the exotic legends and mythology found in Oriental and Homeric literatures and 17th-cent. travel writers (see PURCHAS). The second generation of British Romantics—*Byron, *Shelley, and *Keats—

absorbed these influences, wrote swiftly, travelled widely (Greece, Switzerland, Italy), and died prematurely: their life-stories and letters became almost as important for Romanticism as their poetry. They in turn inspired autobiographical prose-writers such as *Hazlitt, *De Quincey, and *Lamb; while the historical imagination found a champion in Sir W. *Scott. The Romantics had a new intuition for the primal power of the wild landscape, the spiritual correspondence between Man and Nature, and the aesthetic principle of 'organic' form. In their critical writings and lectures they described poetry and drama with new psychological appreciation (the character of Hamlet, for example); they discussed dreams, dramatic illusion, Romantic sensibility, the process of creativity, the limits of Classicism and Reason, and the dynamic nature of the Imagination. Remembered childhood, unrequited love, and the exiled hero were constant themes. Romanticism expressed an unending revolt against classical form, conservative morality, and human moderation. The British Romantics had a powerful influence in France.

Romany Rye, The, a novel by *Borrow, published 1857. 'Romany Rye' in gypsy language means 'Gypsy Gentleman', a name applied to Borrow from his youth by Ambrose Smith, the Norfolk gypsy. This book is a sequel to *Lavengro, and continues the story of the author's wanderings and adventures.

Romaunt of the Rose, The, a translation into Middle English octosyllabics of about one-third of the *Roman de la Rose made in the time of *Chaucer and usually included in editions of his Works because previously attributed to him. *Skeat (in The Chaucer Canon, 1900) argued that only Part A (1–1,705, corresponding to 1–1,672 in De Lorris's French) is by Chaucer.

In this dream poem the narrator enters the Garden of Mirth where he sees various allegorized figures and falls in love with a rosebud. Parts A and B describe the dreamer's instructions by the god of love, his being befriended by Bialacoil who is imprisoned, the opposition of Daunger and other adverse figures, and the discourse of Resoun; Part C is a fragment of Jean de Meun, satirizing the hypocrisy (represented by Fals-Semblant) of religion, women, and the social order. Part A is a closer translation than the other sections.

Romeo and Juliet, Shakespeare's first romantic tragedy, probably written about 1595 and first printed in a bad quarto in 1597; a good quarto (1599) reappeared in the First *Folio of 1623. The play is based on Arthur Brooke's poem The Tragicall Historye of Romeus and Juliet (1562), a translation from the French of *Bandello's Novelle.

The Montagues and Capulets, the two chief families of Verona, are bitter enemies; Escalus, the prince, threatens anyone who disturbs the peace with death. Romeo, son of old Lord Montague, is in love with Lord Capulet's niece Rosaline. But at a feast given by Capulet, which Romeo attends disguised by a mask, he sees and falls in love with Juliet, Capulet's daughter, and she with him. After the feast he overhears, under her window, Juliet's confession of her love for him, and wins her consent to a secret marriage. With the help of Friar Laurence, they are wedded next day. Mercutio, a friend of Romeo, meets Tybalt, of the Capulet family, who is infuriated by his discovery of Romeo's presence at the feast, and they quarrel. Romeo comes on the scene, and attempts to reason with Tybalt, but Tybalt and Mercutio fight, and Mercutio falls. Then Romeo draws and Tybalt is killed. The prince, Montague, and Capulet come up, and Romeo is sentenced to banishment. Early next day, after spending the night with Juliet, he leaves Verona for Mantua, counselled by the friar, who intends to reveal Romeo's marriage at an opportune moment. Capulet proposes to marry Juliet to Count Paris, and when she seeks excuses to avoid this, peremptorily insists. Juliet consults the friar, who bids her consent to the match, but on the night before the wedding drink a potion which will render her apparently lifeless for 42 hours. He will warn Romeo, who will rescue her from the vault on her awakening and will carry her to Mantua. The friar's message to Romeo miscarries, and Romeo hears that Juliet is dead. Buying poison, he comes to the vault to have a last sight of Juliet. He chances upon Count Paris outside the vault; they fight and Paris is killed. Then Romeo, after a last kiss on Juliet's lips, drinks the poison and dies. Juliet awakes and finds Romeo dead by her side, and the cup still in his hand. Guessing what has happened, she stabs herself and dies. The story is unfolded by the friar and Count Paris's page, and Montague and Capulet, faced by the tragic results of their enmity, are reconciled.

Romford, Mr Facey, see SURTEES, R. S.

Romola, a novel by G. *Eliot, published 1863.

The background of the novel is Florence at the end of the 15th cent., the troubled period, following the expulsion of the Medici, of the expedition of Charles VIII, distracted counsels in the city, the excitement caused by the preaching of Savonarola, and acute division between the popular party and the supporters of the Medici. The story is that of the purification by trials of the noble-natured Romola, devoted daughter of an old blind scholar. Into their lives comes a clever, adaptable young Greek, Tito Melema, whose self-indulgence develops into utter perfidy. He robs, and abandons in imprisonment, the benefactor of his childhood, Baldassare. He cruelly goes through a mock marriage ceremony with the innocent little contadina Tessa. After marrying Romola he wounds her deepest feelings by betraying her father's solemn trust. He plays a double game in the political intrigues of the day. Nemesis pursues and at last overtakes him in the person of old Baldassare, who escapes from imprisonment crazed with sorrow and suffering. Romola, with her love for her husband turned to contempt and her trust in Savonarola destroyed, is left in isolation, from which she is rescued by the discovery of her duty in self-sacrifice.

Roncesvalles or **Roncevaux,** a valley in the western Pyrenees, celebrated as the scene of the defeat of the rearguard of *Charlemagne's army and the death of *Roland in 778.

Rondeau, a French verse form consisting of ten (or, in stricter sense, thirteen) lines, having only two rhymes throughout, and with the opening words used twice as a refrain. It became popular in England in the late 19th cent. and was much used by *Dobson, *Swinburne, and others. The rondel is a form of rondeau, again using two rhymes and a refrain, usually of three stanzas.

Rondel, see RONDEAU.

Room at the Top, see BRAINE, J.

Room of One's Own, A, a feminist essay by V. *Woolf, published 1929 and based on two lectures on 'Women and Fiction'.

The author describes the educational, social, and financial disadvantages and prejudices against which women have struggled throughout history, arguing that women will not be able to write well and freely until they have the privacy and independence implied by 'a room of one's own' and 'five hundred a year'. She pays tribute to women writers of the past (including A. *Behn, D. *Osborne, J. *Austen, and the *Brontës); and projects a future in which increasing equality would enable women to become not only novelists but poets. In the last chapter she discusses the concept of 'androgyny', pleading for unity and harmony rather than a rigid separation into 'male' and 'female' qualities.

Room with a View, A, a novel by E. M. *Forster, published 1908.

It opens in an English pensione in Florence with a confrontation between Lucy Honeychurch's chaperone Miss Bartlett and the upstart Mr Emerson and his son George; the two men offer to exchange rooms, in order to give the ladies a room with a view, a favour which they reluctantly accept. The novel describes the inmates of the Pensione Bertolini, among them the clergyman Mr Beebe and the 'original' lady novelist Miss Lavish and their reactions to Italy and to one another. Lucy is disturbed first by witnessing a street murder, and then by an impulsive embrace from George Emerson during an excursion to Fiesole. Miss Bartlett removes her charge from these dangers, and the two return to Surrey, where Lucy becomes engaged to a cultured dilettante, Cecil Vyse, whom Mr Beebe, who has reappeared as the local vicar, ominously describes as 'an ideal bachelor'. The Bertolini cast continues to reassemble as the Emersons take a villa in the neighbourhood. Lucy comes to realize that she loves George, but it takes her some time to extricate herself (helped, unexpectedly, by Miss Bartlett) from what she describes as 'the muddle'. The second half of the drama is played against a sharply and intimately observed background of tennis and tea parties and amateur piano recitals; it ends in the Pensione Bertolini, with George and Lucy on their honeymoon.

Roots, see WESKER TRILOGY.

ROPER, Margaret (1505–44), daughter of Sir T. *More. According to Stapleton (1535–98), she purchased the head of her dead father nearly a month after it had been exposed on London Bridge and preserved it in spices until her death. It is believed that it was buried with her. *Tennyson alludes to this:

> her, who clasped in her last trance
> Her murdered father's head.
>
> ('A Dream of Fair Women')

ROPER, William (1498–1578), married Sir T. *More's daughter Margaret (above) and wrote an early life of his father-in-law first published at Paris (1626).

ROS, Amanda McKittrick, *née* Ann Margaret McKittrick (1860–1939), Irish writer, known as 'the World's Worst Novelist', wrote *Irene Iddesleigh* (1897), *Delina Delaney* (1898), and other works, remarkable for their extraordinary and unselfconsciously colourful prose.

Rosa Bud, a character in Dickens's *Edwin Drood.*

Rosalind, (1) in Spenser's *Shepheardes Calender and *Colin Clouts come home againe,* an unknown lady celebrated by the poet as his love; (2) the heroine of Shakespeare's *As You Like It,* whose chief source was Lodge's *Rosalynde.*

Rosaline, (1) in Shakespeare's *Love's Labour's Lost,* a lady attendant on the princess of France; (2) in his *Romeo and Juliet,* Capulet's niece. She is mentioned, but does not appear in the play.

Rosalynde, Euphues Golden Legacie, a pastoral romance in the style of Lyly's *Euphues,* diversified with sonnets and eclogues, by *Lodge, published 1590.

The story is borrowed in part from *The Tale of *Gamelyn* and was dramatized by Shakespeare in *As You Like It*. Lodge's romance includes such well-known lyrics as 'Love in my bosome like a Bee | Doth sucke his sweete'.

ROSAMOND, Fair, Rosamond Clifford (d. ?1176), probably mistress of Henry II in 1174. A legend transmitted by *Stow following *Higden declares that Henry kept her in a maze-like house in Woodstock where only he could find her, but the queen, *Eleanor of Aquitaine, traced her whereabouts and 'so dealt with her that she lived not long after'. The story is told in a ballad by *Deloney included in Percy's *Reliques*; *Daniel published in 1592 'The Complaint of Rosamond', a poem in rhyme-royal; and *Addison wrote an opera, *Rosamond*, in 1707.

Rosciad, The (1761), a satire by Charles *Churchill in heroic couplets, originally 730 lines, but expanded in later editions to 1,090.

It describes the attempt to find a worthy successor to Roscius, the celebrated Roman comic actor who died *c*.62 BC. It provides satiric sketches of many famous theatrical personalities of the day, both actors and critics (including *Quin, *Foote, and *Colman the elder). But Churchill's criticism is not all negative, and his praise of *Garrick, chosen to succeed Roscius, is high.

ROSCOE, William (1753–1831), published a considerable number of works of poetry, biography, jurisprudence, botany, and arguments against the slave-trade. His principal work was his *Life of Lorenzo de' Medici* (1795). He published the *Life of Leo the Tenth* (1805), and his *The Butterfly's Ball and the Grasshopper's Feast* (1806) became a children's classic. His edition of *Pope appeared in 1824. He did much to stimulate an interest in Italy and Italian literature in England.

Rose and the Ring, The, a fairy-story written and illustrated by *Thackeray, first published 1855.

The magic rose and ring have the property of making those who have possession of them seem irresistibly attractive, which introduces comic complications into the story of Prince Giglio and Princess Rosalba. Thackeray makes gentle fun both of fairy-story conventions, and of 'improving' children's books in this 'Fireside Pantomime for Great and Small Children'.

'Rose Aylmer', a short poem by W. S. *Landor, published 1806, on the daughter of Lord Aylmer. She was an early love of Landor's, but on her mother's second marriage she was sent out to her aunt at Calcutta, where she died at the age of twenty.

ROSENBERG, Isaac (1890–1918), poet, attended the Slade School of Art. He published at his own expense a collection of poems, *Night and Day* (1912), and was encouraged by *Bottomley, *Pound, and others. In 1915 he published another volume of verse, *Youth*. In the same year he joined the army and was killed in action. His poetry is forceful, rich in its vocabulary, and starkly realistic in its attitudes to war. His poor Jewish urban background gives the poems a note not found in the work of his fellow war-poets. Bottomley edited a selection of his poems and letters, introduced by *Binyon, in 1922, but it was not until his *Collected Works* (1937) that his importance became generally accepted.

Rosencrantz and **Guildenstern,** courtiers who serve the king in Shakespeare's *Hamlet*; their view of the play is interpreted in Stoppard's *Rosencrantz and Guildenstern are Dead*.

Rosencrantz and Guildenstern are Dead, a comedy by T. *Stoppard, performed and published 1966, which places the peripheral 'attendant lords' from *Hamlet* at the centre of a drama in which they appear as bewildered witnesses and predestined victims.

Rose Tavern, in Russell Street, Covent Garden, was a favourite place of resort in the late 17th and early 18th cents. It is frequently referred to in the literature of the period, e.g. by *Pepys (18 May 1668), and by Farquhar (*The Recruiting Officer*).

Rose Theatre, on Bankside, Southwark, opened in 1592 and was managed by *Henslowe. Shakespeare acted there.

Rosicrucian, a member of a supposed society or order, 'the brethren of the Rosy Cross', reputedly founded by one Christian Rosenkreuz in 1484, but first mentioned in 1614. Its manifestos were the *Fama Fraternitatis* (1614) and the *Confessio Fraternitatis* (1615), which aroused intense interest on the Continent and in Britain. Its members were said to claim various forms of secret and magic knowledge, such as the transmutation of metals, the prolongation of life, and power over the elements and elemental spirits, and to derive much of their alchemy and mystical preoccupations from *Paracelsus. The Rosicrucian movement seems to have been rooted in some kind of anti-Jesuit Protestant alliance, with deep religious interests, as well as interests in alchemy, medicine, and the Cabbala. F. *Yates, in her study *The Rosicrucian Enlightenment* (1972), names as major figures in the English Rosicrucian movement *Dee, *Fludd, and *Ashmole; she also discusses the Rosicrucian connections of F. *Bacon, *Comenius, I. *Newton, *Leibniz, and many others.

Rosinante, or **Rozinante,** the horse of *Don Quixote.

ROSS, Alan, see LONDON MAGAZINE (3).

ROSS, Alexander (1699–1784), published a lengthy pastoral in *Scots entitled *The Fortunate Shepherdess* (1768; or *Helenore, or the fortunate shepherdess*). He is best remembered as the author of various spirited songs, including 'Woo'd and Married and a'.

ROSS, Sir James Clark (1800–62), Arctic and Antarctic explorer, nephew of Sir John *Ross; he discovered in 1831 the north magnetic pole. He was author of *A Voyage of Discovery and Research in the Southern Antarctic Regions during the years 1839–43* (1847). He commanded the first relief expedition in search of *Franklin in 1848–9.

ROSS, Sir John (1777–1856), Arctic explorer, uncle of Sir James Clark *Ross, was author of *A Voyage of Discovery inquiring into the Probability of a North-West Passage* (1819) and a *Narrative of a Second Voyage of Discovery . . . 1829–1833* (1833). He failed in his expedition to find *Franklin in 1850.

Ross, The Man of, see KYRLE, J.

ROSS, Martin, see SOMERVILLE AND ROSS.

ROSSETTI, Christina Georgina (1830–94), sister of D. G. and W. M. *Rossetti. She was a devout High Anglican, much influenced by the Tractarians (see OXFORD MOVEMENT). She contributed to *The Germ* (1850), where five of her poems appeared under the pseudonym 'Ellen Alleyn'. In 1861 *Macmillan's Magazine* published 'Up-hill' and 'A Birthday', two of her best-known poems. *Goblin market and other poems* appeared in 1862, *The prince's progress and other poems* in 1866, *Sing-Song, a nursery rhyme book* (with illustrations by Arthur Hughes) in 1872, and *A Pageant and other poems* in 1881. *Time Flies: a reading diary* (1885) consists of short passages and prose, one for each day of the year. Her *Poetical Works*, ed. W. M. Rossetti, with a memoir, was published in 1904. Her work ranges from poems of fantasy and verses for the young to ballads, love lyrics, sonnets, and religious poetry. Much of it is pervaded by a sense of melancholy, verging at times on the morbid. Her technical virtuosity was considerable, and her use of short irregularly rhymed lines is distinctive.

ROSSETTI, Dante Gabriel (1828–82), the son of Gabriele Rossetti (1783–1854), an Italian patriot who came to England in 1824. He studied painting with Millais and H. *Hunt, and in 1848, with them and four others, founded the *Pre-Raphaelite Brotherhood. Several of his poems,

including *'The Blessed Damozel' and 'My Sister's Sleep', and a prose piece, 'Hand and Soul', were published in *The Germ* (1850). In 1854 he met *Ruskin and in 1856 W. *Morris, whom he greatly influenced; he was to paint Morris's wife Jane many times. In 1860 Rossetti and Elizabeth (Lizzie) Siddal (or Siddall) married; she was by this time an invalid, and after a brief recovery of health and spirits she gave birth to a still-born child. She died in 1862, from an overdose of laudanum. Later that year he moved to 16 Cheyne Walk, Chelsea. In 1868 he showed a renewed interest in poetry, possibly inspired by renewed contact with Jane Morris; sixteen sonnets, including the 'Willowwood' sequence, were published in March 1869 in *The Fortnightly Review*. That summer he arranged the exhumation of poems buried with his wife. *Poems* (1870) contained 'Sister Helen', 'Troy Town', 'Eden Bower', *'Jenny', and the first part of his sonnet sequence *'The House of Life'. In 1871 Morris and Rossetti took a joint lease of Kelmscott Manor, where Rossetti continued his intimacy with Jane, with Morris's apparent approval. In Oct. 1871 appeared R. *Buchanan's notorious attack 'The Fleshly School of Poetry' (under the pseudonym Thomas Maitland) in *The Contemporary Review*. Rossetti's reply, 'The Stealthy School of Criticism', appeared in *The Athenaeum*, Dec. 1872. Rossetti's later years were overshadowed by ill-health and chloral, though he was recognized by a new generation of aesthetes, including *Pater and *Wilde, as a source of inspiration. *Poems* and *Ballads and Sonnets* both appeared in 1881; the first was largely rearrangements of earlier works, and the second completed 'The House of Life' with 47 new sonnets, and also contained other new work, including 'Rose Mary', 'The King's Tragedy' and 'The White Ship'.

Rossetti's poetry is marred for many readers by its vast and cloudy generalities about Life, Love, and Death, though much of it has an undeniable emotional and erotic power. His letters (ed. O. Doughty and J. R. Wahl, 4 vols, 1965–7) reveal another side of his colourful and extravagant personality; they are witty, irreverent, at times coarse. Mention should also be made of his translations from the Italian (*The Early Italian Poets together with Dante's Vita Nuova*, 1861, known later as *Dante and his Circle*, 1874), and of Villon.

The standard edition of his collected works, edited by W. M. *Rossetti, appeared in 1911.

ROSSETTI, William Michael (1829–1919), brother of D. G. *Rossetti, is remembered as a man of letters and art critic. He was a member of the *Pre-Raphaelite Brotherhood, edited *The Germ*, and wrote the sonnet that was printed on its cover. His reviews of art exhibitions for the *Spectator were published as *Fine Art: Chiefly Contemporary* (1867). He was responsible for important editions of *Blake and *Shelley. He edited *Whitman in 1868, introducing him to a British public. He translated *Dante, and was responsible for encouraging James *Thomson ('B.V.'). He also edited many of his family's papers, letters, and diaries, and wrote memoirs of his brother and his sister Christina (above). His *Some Reminiscences* (1906) is a valuable biographical source.

Rosy Cross, see ROSICRUCIAN.

Rota, The, a coffee-house academy for political discussion, one of the first of its kind in England, founded in 1659 by James *Harrington. It was attended by a wide variety of people, including *Aubrey (who left an account of it), *Pepys, soldiers, peers, etc. The club's aim was to defend the concept of a commonwealth or republic.

ROTH, Philip (1933–), novelist, born in New Jersey. His complex relationship with his Jewish background is reflected in most of his works. They include *Goodbye, Columbus* (1959, a novella with five short stories) *Letting Go* (1962), and a sequence of novels featuring Nathan Zuckerman, a Jewish novelist who has to learn to contend with success: *My Life as a Man* (1974), *The Ghost Writer* (1979), *Zuckerman Unbound* (1981), and *The Anatomy Lesson* (1983). He remains best known for *Portnoy's Complaint* (1969), a *succès de scandale* which records the intimate confessions of Alexander Portnoy to his psychiatrist.

Roundabout Papers, The, a series of discursive essays by *Thackeray, published in the *Cornhill Magazine*, 1860–3.

Round Table, The, in the Arthurian legend, the symbol of the common purpose of Arthur's court and knights. According to *Malory it was made for *Uther Pendragon who gave it to King Lodegrean (or Leodegrance), who gave it as a wedding gift, with 100 knights, to Arthur when he married Guinevere, his daughter. It would seat 150 knights, and all places round it were equal. The 'Siege Perilous' was reserved for the knight who should achieve the quest of the *Grail. In *Laȝamon's *Brut*, however, the table was made for Arthur by a crafty workman. It is first mentioned by *Wace.

ROUSSEAU, Jean-Jacques (1712–78), was born at Geneva. He resided in Switzerland, France, and Italy, and (in 1766–7) in England. He maintained himself by a succession of clerical, secretarial, and tutorial posts and by teaching and copying music. His life-long interest in music and excursions into opera and drama, a voluminous correspondence, and important and influential contributions to social and political philosophy, the novel, autobiography, moral theology, and educational theory mark him out as one of the dominant writers and thinkers of the age.

Rousseau's *Discours sur les sciences et les arts* (1750) was the first of many works in which the natural man is preferred to his civilized counterpart; he argued that the development and spread of knowledge and culture, far from improving human behaviour, had corrupted it by promoting inequality, idleness, and luxury. The *Discours sur l'origine de l'inégalité* (1755) contrasts the innocence and contentment of primitive man in a 'state of nature' with the dissatisfaction and perpetual agitation of modern social man.

A return to primitive innocence being impossible, these ills were only to be remedied, Rousseau held, by reducing the gap separating modern man from his natural archetype and by modifying existing institutions in the interest of equality and happiness. *Émile* (1762) lays down the principles for a new scheme of education in which the child is to be allowed full scope for individual development in natural surroundings, shielded from the harmful influences of civilization, in order to form an independent judgement and a stable character. *Du contrat social* (1762) is his theory of politics, in which he advocated universal justice through equality before the law, a more equitable distribution of wealth, and defined government as fundamentally a matter of contract providing for the exercise of power in accordance with the 'general will' and for the common good, by consent of the citizens as a whole, in whom sovereignty ultimately resides.

In the novel *Julie, ou la Nouvelle Héloïse* (1761), Rousseau's greatest popular success, a critical account of contemporary manners and ideas is interwoven with the story of the passionate love of the tutor St Preux and his pupil Julie, their separation, Julie's marriage to the Baron Wolmar and the dutiful, virtuous life shared by all three on the Baron's country estate.

The posthumously published autobiographical works *Les Confessions* (1781–8) and *Les Rêveries du promeneur solitaire* (1782) were written as exercises in self-justification and self-analysis. Unexampled in their time for candour, detail, and subtlety, they remain landmarks of the literature of personal revelation and reminiscence.

Roussillon, countess of, in Shakespeare's *All's Well that Ends Well*, *Bertram's mother and *Helena's guardian.

ROUTH, Martin Joseph (1755–1854), president of Magdalen College, Oxford, for 63 years, edited the *Gorgias* and *Eutheydemus* of *Plato, and *Reliquiae Sacrae* (1814–43), a collection of writings of ecclesiastical authors of the 2nd and 3rd cents. His long life and literary experience lend weight to his famous utterance: 'I think, Sir, you will find it a very good practice *always to verify your references.'*

Rover, The, a play by A. *Behn.

ROWE, Nicholas (1674–1718), became a barrister of the Middle Temple; but abandoned the legal profession for that of a playwright, and made the acquaintance of *Pope and *Addison. He produced at Lincoln's Inn Fields his tragedies *The Ambitious Stepmother* (1700), *Tamerlane* (1701), and *The Fair Penitent* (1703). His *Ulysses* was staged in 1705, *The Royal Convert* in 1707, *Jane Shore* in 1714, and *Lady Jane Grey* in 1715. He became poet laureate in 1715. His poetical works include a famous translation of *Lucan (1718). Rowe also did useful work as editor of Shakespeare's plays, dividing them into acts and scenes, supplying stage directions, and generally making the text more intelligible. As a writer he is best remembered for his 'She-Tragedies'; their tone is moral, their stress is on the suffering and penitence of victimized women.

Rowena (1) the legendary daughter of Hengist, who married the British chief *Vortigern; (2) a character in Scott's *Ivanhoe.

Rowland, Childe, see CHILDE ROLAND.

ROWLANDS, Samuel (?1570–?1630), a writer of satirical tracts, epigrams, jests, etc., mainly in verse. His works include a satire on the manners of Londoners, *The Letting of Humors Blood in the Head-Vaine* (1600); '*Tis Merrie when Gossips Meete* (1602), a vivid and dramatic character sketch of a widow, a wife, and a maid who meet in a tavern and converse; and *Greene's Ghost* (1602), on the subject of 'coney-catchers' (see GREENE, R.).

ROWLANDSON, Thomas (1756–1827), caricaturist and painter of humorous low life scenes. Among his illustrations were those for the 'Dr Syntax' series of *Combe, which, like many of his other works, were published by *Ackermann.

ROWLEY, Thomas, a fictitious 15th-cent. poet invented by *Chatterton.

ROWLEY, William (?1585–1626), dramatist and actor. His most notable partnership was with *Middleton with whom he wrote *A Fair Quarrel* (1615–16, printed 1617) and *The Changeling* (1622, printed 1653). He also assisted in *The Witch of Edmonton* (1621, printed 1658) with *Dekker and *Ford; and *A Cure for a Cuckold* (1624–5, printed 1661), with *Webster. Rowley's tragedy *All's Lost by Lust* (c.1619, printed 1633) remained popular throughout the 17th cent.

Rowley Poems, see CHATTERTON, T.

ROWSE, A(lfred) L(eslie) (1903–   ), poet, biographer, and Tudor historian. Cornwall forms

the setting for many of his poems and works of history and autobiography, including *A Cornish Childhood* (1942). He has published several books on Shakespeare (1963, 1973, and 1977), and argued that Emilia *Lanier was the 'dark lady' of Shakespeare's *Sonnets.

Roxana, or *the Fortunate Mistress,* a romance by *Defoe, published 1724.

This purports to be the autobiography of Mlle Beleau, the beautiful daughter of French Protestant refugees, brought up in England and married to a London brewer, who, having squandered his property, deserts her and her five children. She enters upon a career of prosperous wickedness, passing from one protector to another in England, France, and Holland, amassing much wealth, and receiving the name Roxana by accident, in consequence of a dance that she performs.

ROXBURGHE, John Ker, 3rd duke of (1740–1804), an ardent bibliophile. His splendid library was dispersed in 1812. The chief bibliophiles of the day inaugurated the Roxburghe Club, the first of the 'book-clubs', consisting of 25 members, with T. F. *Dibdin as its first secretary. The Club, at first rather convivial in character, began its valuable literary work with the printing of the metrical romance of *Havelok the Dane (1828).

Roxburghe Club, see ROXBURGHE, J.K.

Royal Academy of Arts was founded under the patronage of George III in 1768, for the annual exhibition of works of contemporary artists and for the establishment of a school of art. Sir Joshua *Reynolds was its first president. Since 1870 the Academy has also held important loan exhibitions.

Royal Court Theatre, see ENGLISH STAGE COMPANY.

Royal Historical Society, The, was founded in 1868 and took the title 'Royal' in 1887; its papers are published annually as *Transactions.* In 1897 the *Camden Society was amalgamated with the Royal Historical Society, which now publishes the Camden Series.

Royal Literary Fund, a benevolent society to aid authors and their dependants in distress, founded in 1790 as the Literary Fund Society at the instigation of the Revd David Williams, a Dissenting minister. In 1818 it was granted a Royal Charter, and was permitted to add 'Royal' to its title in 1845. The Fund receives no government subsidy and depends on gifts, subscriptions, and legacies.

Royal Society, The, more correctly The Royal Society of London for the Improving of Natural

Knowledge, obtained its Royal charters in 1662 and 1663. The prehistory of the Society extends back to a variety of scientific meetings held in London and Oxford from 1645 onwards. F. *Bacon provided the major philosophical inspiration for the Society. Its founders and early members included *Boyle, *Petty, and John Ray. Among more literary figures, *Ashmole, *Aubrey, *Cowley, *Dryden, *Evelyn, and *Waller were members. The Society featured prominently in Dryden's *Annus Mirabilis. Its Philosophical Transactions (1665–   ), first edited by Henry Oldenburg, is the first permanent scientific journal.

Royal Society of Edinburgh, The, was established in 1783 for 'the cultivation of every branch of science, erudition, and taste'. The membership was originally divided into the Physical Class and a larger Literary Class, the latter including A. *Alison, *Beattie, H. *Blair, *Burke, A. *Carlyle, A. *Ferguson, A. *Gerard, J. *Home, *Jamieson, H. *Mackenzie, T. *Reid, W. *Robertson (who was instrumental in the Society's creation), and Sir W. *Scott (president 1820–32). *Tennyson (1864) and T. *Carlyle (1866) had honorary membership.

Royal Society of Literature was founded in 1823. The Associates were elected by the council of the Society (*Malthus and S. T. *Coleridge were among the first ten). The Society published papers read to it under the title Transactions; publication was suspended during the First World War and was resumed in 1921 as Essays by Divers Hands. The Society has Members, Fellows, and since 1961, Companions; recipients of the title of Companion have included *Betjeman, *Koestler, E. M. *Forster, and Angus *Wilson.

Royns, see RYENCE.

Rubáiyát of Omar Khayyám, The, see OMAR KHAYYÁM.

RUDKIN, David (1936–   ), playwright, made his name with a powerful drama set in a rural district of the Black Country, Afore Night Come (1962, published in Penguin's New English Dramatists 7, 1963); subsequent works include Ashes (1974, pub. 1977), and Penda's Fen (TV 1974, pub. 1975).

'Rugby Chapel', a poem by M. *Arnold.

Rugby School, founded by Laurence Sheriff in 1567. T. *Arnold was its headmaster from 1828 to 1842. A vivid picture of school life at Rugby in his time is given in Tom Brown's Schooldays by Thomas *Hughes.

RUGGLE, George, see IGNORAMUS.

'Ruin The', a 45-line poem in Old English in the *Exeter Book. The poem describes the result of the devastation of a city, possibly Bath which was a ruin in Anglo-Saxon times.

'Ruined Cottage, The', or 'The Story of Margaret', a poem by *Wordsworth, written in 1797, and subsequently embodied in Bk I of *The Excursion.
    It is a harrowing tale of misfortune befalling a cottager and his wife. The husband leaves his home and joins a troop of soldiers going to a distant land. The wife stays on, pining for his return in increasing wretchedness, until she dies and the cottage falls into ruin.

'Ruines of Time, The', a poem by *Spenser, included in the Complaints published in 1591. It is an allegorical elegy on the death of Sir P. *Sidney (see ASTROPHEL). The poet passes to a lament on the decline of patronage and neglect of literature, with allusion to his own case. It is dedicated to the countess of *Pembroke, Sidney's sister.

Rule a Wife and Have a Wife, a comedy by J. *Fletcher, performed 1624.
    The play recounts the humbling of Margarita, who has married only for convenience, by her apparently docile husband Leon, who tames her and wins her affection.

'Rule, Britannia'; for the words see THOMSON, J. The air was composed by *Arne for Thomson and *Mallet's masque Alfred.

Rune, a letter or character of the earliest surviving Germanic script, most extensively used in inscriptions on wood or stone by the Scandinavians and Anglo-Saxons. The earliest runic alphabet seems to date from about the 3rd cent. AD, and is formed by modifying the letters of the Greek and Roman alphabets. Magical and mysterious powers were associated with runes from the Anglo-Saxon period, perhaps because of their employment in riddles, as in the Rune Poem, a 94-line piece illustrating the runes of the Anglo-Saxon Runic alphabet, the *Futhorc.

Rupert of Hentzau, see PRISONER OF ZENDA, THE.

Rural Rides, a collection of essays by W. *Cobbett, published 1830. A committee in 1821 had proposed certain remedies for the agricultural distress that followed the war. Cobbett disapproved of these and 'made up his mind to see for himself'. The result was this series of lively, opinionated accounts of his travels on horseback between Sept. 1822 and Oct. 1826, largely in the south and east of England. (Later journeys, in the midlands and the north, were added in subsequent editions.) He rails against tax-collectors, 'tax-eaters', landlords, gamekeepers, stock-jobbers, and excisemen, and against the monstrous swelling of the 'Great Wen' of London; but the whole work is also informed with his own knowledge of and love of the land in all its minutely observed variety.

Ruritania, an imaginary kingdom in central Europe, the scene of *The Prisoner of Zenda* by Anthony Hope (*Hawkins). The name connotes more generally a world of make-believe romance, chivalry, and intrigue.

RUSHDIE, Salman, see MAGIC REALISM.

RUSKIN, John (1819–1900), the only child of John James Ruskin, a partner in a successful wine business. Among his earliest publications were poems and stories written for Christmas annuals. He also devoted time to drawing; and with the first of the five volumes of *Modern Painters* (1834) he became the public champion of Turner and other contemporary artists.

Seven months' work in Italy in preparation for *Modern Painters II* (1846) confirmed Ruskin in his 'function as interpreter'. They also compelled him to write of the medieval buildings of Europe before they should be destroyed by neglect, restoration, industrialization, and revolutions. *Modern Painters III* and *IV* appeared in 1856; vol. *V* in 1860, *The Seven Lamps of Architecture* (1849) and *The Stones of Venice* (1851–3) were written during the period of his marriage to Euphemia Chalmers Gray, for whom the lastingly popular *The King of the Golden River* (1851) had been a gift. In 1854, after seven years of marriage, she divorced him on grounds of impotence, and soon afterwards married Millais. Ruskin had defended Millais and the *Pre-Raphaelites in letters to *The Times* and the pamphlet *Pre-Raphaelitism* (1851). He continued to notice their work in *Notes on the Royal Academy* (1855–9 and 1875).

Ruskin wrote for the Arundel Society (*Giotto and his Works in Padua*, 1853–4, 1860), taught at the Working Men's College in Red Lion Square, produced drawing manuals, helped with plans for the Oxford Museum of Natural History building, arranged for the National Gallery the drawings of the Turner bequest, tried to guide the work of individual artists (D. G. *Rossetti, J. Inchbold, J. W. Brett). Some of his addresses appeared in *Lectures on Architecture and Painting* (1854) and *The Two Paths* (1859). Speaking in Manchester on *The Political Economy of Art* (1857), Ruskin challenged economic laws affecting matters in which he had a standing. In the final volume of *Modern Painters* (1860) he denounced greed as the deadly principle guiding English life. In attacking the 'pseudo-science' of J. S. *Mill and *Ricardo in *Unto this Last* (1860) and *Essays on Political Economy* (1862–3; later *Munera Pulveris*, 1872), Ruskin declared open warfare against the spirit of science of his times.

This fight, against competition and self-interest, for the recovery of heroic, feudal, and Christian social ideals was to occupy Ruskin for the rest of his life. It is expressed in considerations of engraving or Greek myth (*The Cestus of Aglaia*, 1865–6; *The Queen of the Air*, 1869), geology lectures for children (*The Ethics of the Dust*, 1866), as essays on the respective duties of men and women (*Sesame and Lilies*, 1865, 1871), lectures on war, work, and trade (*The Crown of Wild Olives*, 1866, 1873), or letters to a workman (*Time and Tide, by Weare and Tyne*, 1867). In *Fors Clavigera* (1871–8) he found a serial form well suited to his public teaching and to the diversity of his interests, which also expressed themselves during the 1870s and 1880s in a multitude of writings on natural history, travel, painting, etc., and in practical projects, many associated with the Guild of St George, a Utopian society founded by Ruskin under his own mastership in 1871.

In 1870 Ruskin was elected first Slade professor of art at Oxford. He started a drawing school, arranged art collections of his own gift, and seven volumes of his lectures were published. Ruskin's 'own peculiar opinions' alarmed senior members of the university and he resigned in 1878; he returned in 1883 but his statements were even more startling than before, and he resigned once more in 1885.

The isolation of his later years was barely mitigated by the loyalty of his disciples. Older friends, such as Sir Henry Acland and *Carlyle, remained doubtful about the schemes, the vehemence and the frequent obscurity of his later pronouncements. In middle and old age he made many young girls the objects of his affection. Rose La Touche, an Anglo-Irish girl, was 11 when Ruskin met her and 18 when he proposed in 1866. But he could not share her Evangelical religious views, and she died, mad, in 1875. He often wrote for her and, indirectly, of her, in later life, and in *Praeterita*, the uncompleted autobiography on which he worked between 1885 and 1889. After 1889 Ruskin wrote nothing and spoke rarely, but was cared for by his cousin, Joan Severn, at his house on Coniston Water.

Russell, Lady, a character in J. Austen's *Persuasion*.

RUSSELL, Bertrand Arthur William, 3rd Earl Russell (1872–1970), wrote voluminously on philosophy, logic, education, economics, and politics, and throughout his life was the champion of advanced political and social causes. While much of his writing was relatively practical and ephemeral in intent, he also contributed work of lasting importance in some of the most technical fields of philosophy and logic. He was the inventor of the Theory of Descriptions. *The Principles of Mathematics* (1903) and *Principia Mathematica* (the latter in collaboration with A. N. *Whitehead, 1910) quickly became classics of mathematical logic. Other important philosophical works include *The Analysis of Mind* (1921), *An Inquiry into Meaning and Truth* (1940), and *Human Knowledge, its Scope and Limits* (1948). Russell was awarded the *Nobel Prize for literature in 1950.

RUSSELL, George William (Æ) (1867–1935), Irish poet and dramatist, published *Homeward* (1894), his first volume of mystical verses, with the encouragement of *Yeats. His poetic drama *Deirdre* was performed in 1902 at the Irish National Theatre (later the *Abbey), which he helped to found. Other volumes of verse include *The Divine Vision* (1904), *Gods of War* (1915), *The Interpreters* (1922), and *Midsummer Eve* (1928). He edited *The Irish Statesman* (1923–30). In 1934 he published an ambitious poem of Celtic mythology, *The House of the Titans*, and in 1935 his *Selected Poems*.

RUSSELL, Lord John, 1st Earl Russell (1792–1878), entered Parliament in 1813; he proposed the *Reform Bill of 1832. In 1845 he announced his support for the repeal of the Corn Laws, which led to Peel's resignation and Russell's elevation to prime minister, 1846–52; he was again prime minister on the death of Palmerston (1865–6); and foreign secretary in 1852–3 under Aberdeen and in 1859–65. He published a *Life of William Lord Russell* (1819), Memoirs of C. J. *Fox and of T. *Moore, and other works. He was often caricatured in *Punch.

Ruth, a novel by Mrs *Gaskell, published 1853.
 Ruth Hilton, a 15-year-old orphan apprenticed to a dressmaker, is seduced and then deserted by the wealthy young Henry Bellingham. She is rescued from suicide by Thurston Benson, a Dissenting minister, who takes her into his own house. She bears Bellingham's son. Later she is employed as a governess in the family of the tyrannical and pharisaical Mr Bradshaw, where she is discovered by Bellingham, whose offer of marriage she rejects. Bradshaw, learning the truth,

brutally dismisses her. Ruth regains esteem by becoming a heroic hospital nurse during a cholera epidemic, and dies after nursing Bellingham to recovery. Mrs Gaskell's purpose in this novel was to arouse more sympathy for 'fallen women' who had been unprotected victims of seduction, but she shocked many contemporary readers.

RUTHERFORD, Mark, see WHITE, W.H.

Ruthwell Cross, a stone monument in the parish church at Ruthwell, Dumfriesshire, dating perhaps from the 8th cent. on which are inscribed in *runes some alliterating phrases closely corresponding to parts of the Old English poem *The Dream of the Rood.

Ryecroft, The Private Papers of Henry, see GISSING, G.

Ryence (Rion, Rience or **Royns)**, King, a British or Celtic king (usually of Ireland but of North Wales in Malory's *Morte D'Arthur*) who sent an arrogant message to Arthur demanding his beard to make up a set of twelve taken from his vanquished enemies.

RYLE, Gilbert (1900–76), Waynflete professor of metaphysical philosophy in the University of Oxford (1945–68). He is best known for his attack on the traditional metaphysical dualism of mind and body, which he calls the 'dogma of the ghost in the machine'. His works include *The Concept of Mind* (1949) and *Dilemmas* (1954).

RYMER, Thomas (1641–1713), is chiefly remembered for his valuable collection of historical records, *Foedera* (1704–35). He is known as a critic of considerable learning but dogmatic views, who supported the ancients in the battle between them and the moderns (see BATTLE OF THE BOOKS). *The Tragedies of the Last Age Considered* (1678) was a critical attack on Elizabethan drama, continued in his *A Short View of Tragedy* (1692), which contains his famous condemnation of *Othello as 'a bloody farce'.

S

Sabrina, a poetic name for the river Severn (see under ESTRILDIS). In Milton's *Comus*, Sabrina is the nymph of the Severn.

Sacharissa, see WALLER, E.

SACKVILLE, Charles, Lord Buckhurst, and later 6th earl of Dorset (1638–1706), a friend and patron of poets. His poems, which appeared with those of *Sedley in 1701, include some biting satires and the ballad 'To all you Ladies now at Land'. He has been identified with Eugenius in Dryden's *Of Dramatick Poesy.

SACKVILLE, Thomas, 1st earl of Dorset and Baron Buckhurst (1536–1608), was raised to the peerage in 1567, and held a number of high official positions. He wrote the Induction and 'The Complaint of Buckingham' for *A Mirror for Magistrates, and collaborated with Thomas Norton in the tragedy of *Gorboduc.

SACKVILLE-WEST, Hon. Victoria Mary ('Vita'), CH (1892–1962), poet and novelist, was born at Knole, Kent, about which she wrote *Knole and the Sackvilles* (1922). In 1913 she married Harold *Nicolson, with whom she travelled widely before settling at Sissinghurst, Kent, where she devoted much time to gardening. In 1922 she met Virginia *Woolf, whose *Orlando* (1928) was inspired by their close friendship. Her other works include a pastoral poem, *The Land* (1926, Hawthornden Prize), *All Passion Spent* (1931, novel), *Collected Poems* (1933), and many works on travel, gardening, and literary topics. Her unorthodox marriage was described by her son Nigel Nicolson in *Portrait of a Marriage* (1973).

Sacripant, (1) in *Orlando Innamorato* and *Orlando Furioso*, the king of Circassia and a lover of *Angelica; (2) Sacrapant, a magician in Peele's *The Old Wives' Tale*. In modern French *sacripant* is a rascal or blackguard.

SADLEIR, Michael (formerly Sadler) (1888–1957), bibliographer and novelist. His works include *Excursions in Victorian Bibliography* (1922) and *Nineteenth Century Fiction* (2 vols, 1951). His best-known novel, *Fanny by Gaslight* (1940), has been made into a film.

Sad Shepherd, The, or *A Tale of Robin Hood*, an unfinished pastoral tragi-comedy by *Jonson,

written *c.*1635, printed 1641.

Robin has invited the shepherds and shepherdesses of the Vale of Belvoir to a feast in Sherwood Forest. Aeglamour, the Sad Shepherd, relates the loss of his beloved Earine, believed drowned in the Trent. In reality she has been shut up in an oak tree by the witch Maudlin as prey for her son Lorel, a swineherd. The witch, in the form of Maid Marian, abuses Robin Hood and throws his guests into confusion, but her wiles are detected and Robin's huntsmen pursue her.

Saga, an Old Norse word meaning 'story', applied to narrative compositions from Iceland and Norway in the Middle Ages. There are three main types of saga: family sagas, dealing with the first settlers of Iceland and their descendants; kings' sagas, historical works about the kings of Norway; and legendary or heroic sagas, fantastic adventure stories about legendary heroes. The most celebrated of the family sagas is *Njáls saga*, a long but tightly structured narrative about Gunnarr, a brave and worthy man who married the beautiful but morally flawed Hallgerðr; she sets in motion a series of feuds which culminates first in her husband's heroic last stand and death, and then in the burning of Gunnarr's friend Njall, a wise and peaceable lawyer who accepts his fate with Christian resignation. The main concerns of the saga (the growth of social stability, legal and political, among the settlers of a new community, and the part played by human emotions) are characteristic of the other family sagas. *Eyrbyggja saga* is especially concerned with the emergence of a politically stable community, though it also recounts some bizarre supernatural incidents. *Laxdaela saga* deals with the theme of a tragic love triangle and the fortunes of one of Iceland's most powerful families at that time. *Grettis saga* tells, with remarkable psychological depth and sublety, the story of a famous Icelandic outlaw; Grettir's fights with the monstrous walking corpse Glámr and with a troll woman are analogous to Beowulf's fight with Grendel and Grendel's mother (see BEOWULF). Snorri Sturluson's *Heimskringla* comprises a history of the kings of Norway; *Vǫlsunga saga* is notable amongst the legendary ones and recounts the legends of the Goths and Burgundians which underlie *Wagner's *Ring* cycle. *Sturlunga saga* is unique in being a compilation of sagas about figures almost contemporary with their 13th-cent.

authors. W. *Morris did much to popularize Icelandic literature in England. (See SIGURD THE VOLSUNG.)

St Cleeve, Swithin, a character in Hardy's *Two on a Tower*.

ST JOHN, Henry, see BOLINGBROKE, H. ST J.

ST JOHN SPRIGG, Christopher, see CAUDWELL, C.

SAINT-PIERRE, Jacques-Henri Bernardin de (1734–1814), French natural philosopher and novelist, and author of the immensely influential *Paul et Virginie* (1788), a pastoral romance set on a tropical island, describing the idyllic childhood and upbringing of two French children. It ends tragically: Virginie drowns and Paul dies of grief. Saint-Pierre was a follower of *Rousseau and his works offer a French version of *Primitivism.

St Ronan's Well, a novel by Sir W. *Scott, published 1823.

In this work the author for once chose a contemporary scene, in the Scottish spa of St Ronan's Well, whose idle fashionable society is satirically described.

SAINTSBURY, George Edward Bateman (1845–1933), became professor of English literature and rhetoric at Edinburgh in 1895, a post he held for 20 years. He contributed numerous articles to the *Fortnightly Review, *Pall Mall Gazette, and other journals, and introduced many editions of prose and poetry. His larger works include *A History of Nineteenth Century Literature* (1896), *A Short History of English Literature* (1898, reprinted 1960), *The History of Criticism and Literary Taste in Europe* (1900–4), *A History of English Prosody* (1906–10), and books on *Sir Walter Scott* (1897), *Matthew Arnold* (1898), and *A History of the French Novel* (1917–19). Saintsbury was a connoisseur of wine and the success of his *Notes on a Cellarbook* (1920) led to the founding of the Saintsbury Club. He remains a doyen of Victorian taste in literature, but his hedonistic approach to literary criticism, based on style rather than on content, is no longer in favour.

Saint's Everlasting Rest, The, see BAXTER, R.

Saint Valentine's Day, see FAIR MAID OF PERTH, THE.

SAKI, pseudonym of Hector Hugh Munro (1870–1916), known principally for his short stories. Between 1902 and 1908 he was correspondent for the *Morning Post in Poland, Russia, and Paris. His first characteristic volume of short stories, *Reginald,* was published under the

pseudonym Saki (of uncertain origin) in 1904, followed by *Reginald in Russia* (1910), *The Chronicles of Clovis* (1911), *Beasts and Super-Beasts* (1914), *The Toys of Peace* (1919), and *The Square Egg* (1924). *The Unbearable Bassington* (1912) and *When William Came* (1913) are both novels. In 1914 he enlisted as a trooper and he was killed in France. His stories include the satiric, the comic, the macabre, and the supernatural, and show a marked interest in the use of animals as agents of revenge upon mankind.

SALA, George Augustus (1828–95), journalist and illustrator, became a regular contributor to *Household Words* (1851–6); he was sent by *Dickens to Russia as correspondent at the end of the Crimean war and subsequently wrote for the *Daily Telegraph. He published books of travel and novels.

SALADIN (Salah-ed-Din Yusuf ibn Ayub) (c.1138–93), a Kurd, the founder of the Ayubite dynasty in Egypt. He was established as Caliph there in 1171, and he took possession of southern Syria and Damascus on the death of Noureddin in 1174. He defeated the Christians at the battle of Tiberias in 1187. He then besieged and captured Acre and Jerusalem (1187). He is traditionally represented as chivalrous, loyal, and magnanimous: by Boccaccio in the *Decameron; by *Dante who places him in the Limbo of heroes (*Inferno*, iv. 129); and by English writers such as Scott in *The Talisman.

Salamander, see PARACELSUS.

Salanio and **Salarino,** in Shakespeare's *The Merchant of Venice,* friends of Antonio and Bassanio.

Salathiel, a novel on the theme of the *Wandering Jew by G. *Croly.

SALINGER, J(erome) D(avid) (1919–), American novelist and short story writer, is best known for his novel *The Catcher in the Rye* (1951), the story of adolescent Holden Caulfield who runs away from boarding-school in Pennsylvania to New York, where he preserves his innocence despite various attempts to lose it. Salinger's other works include *Franny and Zooey* (1961), two stories about two members of the eccentric Glass family; and two stories narrated by Buddy Glass appeared originally in the *New Yorker and were published together as *Raise High the Roof-Beam, Carpenters and Seymour: an Introduction* (1963).

SALLUST (Gaius Sallustius Crispus) (86–35 BC), Roman historian whose surviving works are two monographs on *The Conspiracy of Catiline* and *The War Against Jugurtha.* Sallust was one of Julius Caesar's henchmen and as a historian he manipulates the truth in favour of the Caesarian party. His practice of including speeches, gnomic sayings, and character sketches in his narrative was copied by *William of Malmesbury. The *Jugurtha* was translated by A. *Barclay early in the 16th cent., and T. *Heywood translated both monographs (1608).

'Sally in our Alley', a ballad by H. *Carey.

Salome, a play by O. *Wilde, which later formed the basis for the libretto of an opera by Richard Strauss.

Salvation Army, see BOOTH, WILLIAM.

Samient, in Spenser's *Faerie Queene* (v. viii), the lady sent by Queen *Mercilla to Adicia, the wife of the *Soldan, received by her with contumely, and rescued by Sir *Artegall.

Sampson, Dominie, a character in Scott's *Guy Mannering*. His favourite expression of astonishment is 'Prodigious!'

Samson Agonistes, a tragedy by *Milton, published 1671, in the same volume as *Paradise Regained*. A closet drama never intended for the stage, it is modelled on Greek tragedy. Predominantly in blank verse, it also contains passages of great metrical freedom and originality, and some rhyme. *Samson Agonistes* (i.e. Samson the Wrestler, or Champion) deals with the last phase of the life of the Samson of the Book of Judges when he is a prisoner of the Philistines and blind, a phase which many have compared to the assumed circumstances of the blind poet himself, after the collapse of the Commonwealth and his political hopes.

Samson, in prison at Gaza, is visited by friends of his tribe (the Chorus) who comfort him; then by his old father Manoa, who holds out hopes of securing his release; then by his wife Dalila (see DELILAH) who seeks pardon and reconciliation, but being repudiated shows herself 'a manifest Serpent'; then by Harapha, a strong man of Gath, who taunts Samson. He is finally summoned to provide amusement by feats of strength for the Philistines, who are celebrating a feast to *Dagon. He goes, and presently a messenger brings news of his final feat of strength in which he pulled down the pillars of the place where the assembly was gathered, destroying himself as well as the entire throng.

Sancho Panza, the squire of *Don Quixote, who accompanies him in his adventures.

SANDBURG, Carl August (1878–1967), American poet, who challenged contemporary taste by his use of colloquialism and free verse. He published *Chicago Poems* (1916), *Cornhuskers* (1918), *Smoke and Steel* (1920), *Slabs of the*

Sunburnt West (1922), *Good Morning America* (1928), and *Complete Poems* (1950). His other works include *The American Songbag* (1927; folksongs); a monumental life of Abraham Lincoln (6 vols, 1926–39); his novel *Remembrance Rock* (1948); and *Always the Young Strangers* (1953), an autobiography.

Sandford and Merton, The History of, see DAY, T.

Sanditon, an unfinished novel by J. *Austen, written 1817.

Mr Parker is obsessed with the wish to create a large and fashionable resort out of the small village of Sanditon, on the south coast. Charlotte Heywood, an attractive, alert young woman, is invited to stay with the Parkers, where she catches the fancy of Lady Denham, the local great lady. Lady Denham's nephew and niece, Sir Edward and Miss Denham, live near by, and Clara Brereton is staying with her. Edward plans to seduce Clara; but his aunt intends him to marry a West Indian heiress, under the care of a Mrs Griffiths and her entourage, whose visit to Sanditon is anticipated shortly. After a ludicrous series of complications, involving both Mrs Griffiths's party and a ladies' seminary from Camberwell, the excited inhabitants of Sanditon find the expected invasion of visitors consists merely of Mrs Griffiths and three young ladies.

This highly entertaining fragment was written early in 1817, when Jane Austen was already suffering from Addison's disease (of which she died on 18 July).

Sandra Belloni, a novel by G. *Meredith, originally published 1864 as *Emilia in England*, retitled 1886. The sequel is in the author's *Vittoria*.

SANDYS, George (1578–1644), a member of *Falkland's circle at Great Tew. His chief works were a verse translation of *Ovid's *Metamorphoses* (1621–6), a verse *Paraphrase upon the Psalmes* (1636), and *Christ's Passion, a Tragedy*, a verse translation from the Latin of Grotius (1640).

Sanglier, Sir, in Spenser's *Faerie Queene* (v. i), the wicked knight who has cut off his lady's head, and is forced by Sir *Artegall to bear the head before him, in token of his shame. He is thought to represent Shane O'Neill, second earl of Tyrone (?1530–67), a leader of the Irish, who invaded the Pale in 1566.

Sangreal, the Holy Grail, see GRAIL.

SANKEY, I. D., see MOODY AND SANKEY.

SANNAZAR (Jacopo Sannazzaro) (1458–1530), Neapolitan author and rediscoverer of the charms of nature and the rustic life, was author of an influential pastoral, in prose and verse, *Arcadia* (1504), and of Latin eclogues and other poems.

Sansfoy, Sansjoy, and **Sansloy,** three brothers in Spenser's *Faerie Queene* (I. ii. 25 et seq.). Sansfoy ('faithless') is slain by the *Redcrosse Knight, who also defeats Sansjoy ('joyless'), but the latter is saved from death by *Duessa. Sansloy ('lawless') carries off Una and kills her lion (I. iii). This incident is supposed to refer to the suppression of the Protestant religion in the reign of Queen Mary.

SANSOM, William (1912–76), short story writer, travel writer, and novelist. His first volume of stories, *Fireman Flower and other stories* (1944), reflects his experiences with the National Fire Service in wartime London. This was followed by many other collections of stories, some set in London, others making full use of backdrops from Germany, Scandinavia, and the Mediterranean. His most successful novel, *The Body* (1949), is set in London.

SANTAYANA, George (1863–1952), a Spaniard brought up in Boston and educated at Harvard, where he was professor of philosophy from 1889 to 1912; he then came to Europe. He was an eminent speculative philosopher, of a naturalist tendency and opposed to German idealism, whose views are embodied in his *The Life of Reason* (1905–6). He later modified and supplemented his philosophy in a series of four books, *Realms of Being* (1927–40). Santayana also published poetry, criticism, reviews, memoirs, etc.; his other works include *Soliloquies in England* (1922), essays on the English character; *Character and Opinion in the United States* (1920), and *Persons and Places* (3 vols, 1944–53). His only novel is *The Last Puritan* (1935). Santayana's style has been variously praised for its richness and condemned for its 'purple passages'.

SAPPER, the pseudonym of Herman Cyril McNeile (1888–1937), creator of Hugh 'Bull-dog' Drummond, the hefty and apparently brainless British ex-army officer who foils the activities of Carl Peterson, the international crook. He appears in *Bull-dog Drummond* (1920), *The Female of the Species* (1928), and many other popular thrillers; after McNeile's death the series was continued under the same pseudonym by G. T. Fairlie.

Sapphics, see METRE.

SAPPHO (b. *c.* mid-7th cent. BC), a Greek lyric poet, born in Lesbos. The story of her throwing herself into the sea in despair at her unrequited love for Phaon the boatman is mere romance. Twelve of her poems survive. Her principal subject is always love, which she expresses with great simplicity and a remarkable felicity of phrase.

Sapsea, Mr, in Dickens's *Edwin Drood,* an auctioneer and mayor of Cloisterham.

Sardanapalus, a poetic drama by Lord *Byron, published 1821.

The subject was taken from the *Bibliotheca Historica* of Siculus. Sardanapalus is represented as an effete but courageous monarch. When Beleses, a Chaldean soothsayer, and Arabaces, governor of Media, lead a revolt against him, he shakes off his slothful luxury and, urged on by Myrrha, his favourite Greek slave, fights bravely at the head of his troops. Defeated, he arranges for the safety of his queen, Zarina, and of his supporters, then prepares a funeral pyre round his throne and perishes in it with Myrrha.

Sarras, in the legend of the *Grail, the land to which *Joseph of Arimathea fled from Jerusalem.

Sartor Resartus: The Life and Opinions of Herr Teufelsdröckh, by T. *Carlyle, originally published in *Fraser's Magazine* 1833–4; first English edition 1838.

This work was written under the influence of the German Romantic school and particularly of Richter. It consists of two parts: a discourse on the philosophy of clothes (*sartor resartus* means 'the tailor re-patched') based on the speculations of an imaginary Professor Teufelsdröckh; and a biography of Teufelsdröckh himself, which is in some measure the author's autobiography.

SARTRE, Jean-Paul (1905–80), French philosopher, novelist, playwright, literary critic, and political activist. His novel *La Nausée* (1938; *Nausea,* 1949) was one of the earliest manifestations of *Existentialism, a movement in which Sartre figured prominently, and which is also expounded in his plays (*Les Mouches,* 1943, *The Flies,* 1947; and *Huis Clos,* 1945, *In Camera,* 1946) and in his philosophical writings (*L'Être et le néant,* 1943, *Being and Nothingness,* 1956).

SASSOON, Siegfried Louvain (1886–1967), began to write the poetry for which he is remembered in the trenches during the First World War; his bleak realism and his contempt for war leaders found expression in his verse. Dispatched as 'shell-shocked' to hospital, he encountered and encouraged W. *Owen, and organized a public protest against the war; his war poems appeared in *The Old Huntsman* (1917) and in *Counter-Attack* (1918). Further volumes of poetry published in the 1920s finally established a high reputation, and collections were published in 1947 and 1961. Sassoon was much influenced by G. *Herbert and *Vaughan. The spare, muted poems in *Vigils* (1935) and *Sequences* (1956) are much concerned with spiritual growth. In 1957 he became a Catholic.

Meanwhile he was also achieving success as a prose writer. His semi-autobiographical trilogy (*Memoirs of a Fox-Hunting Man*, 1928; *Memoirs of an Infantry Officer*, 1930; and *Sherston's Progress*, 1936) were published together as *The Complete Memoirs of George Sherston* (1937). Sassoon published three autobiographical works: *The Old Century and Seven More Years* (1938), *The Weald of Youth* (1942), and *Siegfried's Journey* (1945). In 1948 he published an important biography of G. *Meredith. His attachment to the countryside emerges as a major theme in his post-1918 works. His diaries 1920–2 and 1915–18, ed. R. Hart-Davis, were published 1981 and 1983.

Satanic School, the name under which R. *Southey attacks *Byron and the younger Romantics in the preface to his *A Vision of Judgement.*

Satire, from the Latin *satira*, a later form of *satura*, which means 'medley', being elliptical for *lanx satura*, 'a full dish, a hotch-potch'. The word has no connection with 'satyr', as was formerly often supposed. A 'satire' is a poem, or in modern use sometimes a prose composition, in which prevailing vices or follies are held up to ridicule [*OED*]. In English literature, satire may be held to have begun with *Chaucer, who was followed by many 15th-cent. writers, including *Dunbar. *Skelton used the octosyllabic metre, and a rough manner which was to be paralleled in later times by Butler in *Hudibras*, and by *Swift. Elizabethan satirists include *Gascoigne and *Lodge, whereas J. *Hall claimed to be the first to introduce satires based on *Juvenal to England. The great age of English satire began with *Dryden, who perfected the epigrammatic and antithetical use of the *heroic couplet for this purpose. He was followed by *Pope, Swift, *Gay, *Prior, and other satirists of the Augustan period. The same tradition was followed by Charles *Churchill, and brilliantly revived by Byron in *English Bards and Scotch Reviewers*. The Victorian age was not noted for pure satire, although the novel proved an excellent vehicle for social satire with *Dickens, *Thackeray, and others. In the early 20th cent. *Belloc, *Chesterton, and R. *Campbell (in his *Georgiad*) contributed to a moderate revival of the tradition, pursued in various verse forms by P. *Porter, J. *Fuller, Clive James, and other young writers; and prose satire continues to flourish in the works of E. *Waugh, A. *Powell, Angus *Wilson, *Amis, and others. In theatre and television the 'satire boom' of the 1960s is generally held to have been pioneered by the satirical revue *Beyond the Fringe* (1960) by Alan

*Bennett, Jonathan Miller, Peter Cook, and Dudley Moore.

Satiromastix, *or The Untrussing of the Humorous Poet*, a comedy by *Dekker, written 1601 (with John *Marston?), printed 1602.

Jonson in his *Poetaster* had satirized Dekker and Marston, under the names of Demetrius and Crispinus, while he himself figures as Horace. Dekker here retorts, bringing the same characters on the stage. Horace is discovered laboriously composing an Epithalamium and at a loss for a rhyme. Crispinus and Demetrius enter and reprove him gravely for his querulousness. Presently Captain Tucca (of the *Poetaster*) enters, and turns effectively on Horace the flow of his profanity. Horace's peculiarities of dress and appearance, his vanity and bitterness, are ridiculed; and he is finally untrussed and crowned with nettles.

The satirical part of the play uses a somewhat inappropriate romantic setting.

Saturday Night and Sunday Morning, the first novel of A. *Sillitoe, published 1958.

Its protagonist, anarchic young Arthur Seaton, lathe operator in a Nottingham bicycle factory, provided a new prototype of the working-class *Angry Young Man; rebellious, contemptuous towards authority, he unleashes his energy on drink and women, with quieter interludes spent fishing in the canal. His affair with Brenda, married to his workmate Jack, overlaps with an affair with her sister Winnie, inaugurated in the night that Brenda attempts a gin-and-hot-bath abortion recommended by his Aunt Ada; both relationships falter when he is beaten up by soldiers, one of them Winnie's husband, and he diverts his attention to young Doreen, to whom he becomes engaged (after a fashion) in the penultimate chapter. A landmark in the development of the post-war novel, with its naturalism relieved by wit, high spirits, and touches of lyricism, the novel provided the screenplay (also by Sillitoe) for Karel Reisz's 1960 film.

Saturday Review, The (1855–1938), an influential periodical. Among the many brilliant contributors of its early days were Sir J. F. *Stephen, J. R. *Green, and *Freeman; it became more literary in its interests under the editorship of F. *Harris (1894–8), publishing work by *Hardy, H. G. *Wells, *Beerbohm, Arthur *Symons, and others. G. B. *Shaw was dramatic critic from 1895 to 1898.

Saturninus, the emperor in Shakespeare's *Titus Andronicus*.

Satyrane, Sir, in Spenser's *Faerie Queene* (I. vi), a knight 'Plaine, faithfull, true, and enimy of shame'. He rescues Una from the satyrs, perhaps symbolizing the liberation of the true religion by *Luther.

Satyric Drama, a humorous piece with a chorus of satyrs that authors in the 5th and 4th cents BC were expected to append to tragic trilogies offered for competition. This practice, which had the incidental virtue of providing light relief, may have been due to the fact recorded by *Aristotle (*Poetics*, ch. 4) that Tragedy had its origin in performances by actors dressed as satyrs. The only complete extant satyric drama is *Euripides' *Cyclops*.

Satyricon, see PETRONIUS.

SAUSSURE, Ferdinand de (1857–1913), born in Geneva. In 1891 he became professor at Geneva where, between 1907 and 1911, he delivered the three courses of lectures which were reconstructed from students' notes into the *Cours de linguistique générale* (published 1915), which is the basis of 20th-cent. linguistics and of much modern literary criticism. His most important and influential idea was the conception of language as a system of signs, arbitrarily assigned and only intelligible in terms of the particular system as a whole. (This idea was applied outside language in the new science called Semiotics.) Language is a *structure* whose parts can only be understood in relation to each other; this *'structuralism' has been very influential in literary criticism and in other fields, such as sociology. Saussure's emphasis was on the value of synchronic study (with which the term 'linguistics' is sometimes used synonymously, as distinct from 'philology' for historical study), rather than the diachronic philology with which he had previously been concerned. One of the compilers of the *Cours* was Charles Bally (1865–1947), who developed the ideas of Saussure and, with other followers, is sometimes assigned to the 'Geneva School'.

SAVAGE, Richard (c.1697–1743), claimed to be the illegitimate son of the fourth Earl Rivers and Lady Macclesfield, but the story of his birth and ill treatment given by Dr *Johnson in his remarkable life (1744, reprinted in *The Lives of the English Poets*) has been largely discredited. Johnson describes Savage's career as a struggling writer, his pardon after conviction on a murder charge in 1727, and his poverty-stricken death in a Bristol gaol. Savage wrote two plays and various odes and satires, but is remembered as a poet for *The Wanderer* (1729) and 'The Bastard' (1728), a spirited attack on his 'Mother, yet no Mother'.

Savage Club, a club with strong literary and artistic connections founded in 1857; it was named after Richard *Savage. Members have included *Bridie, E. *Wallace, G. and W. *Grossmith, and Dylan *Thomas.

SAVILE, George, see HALIFAX.

SAVILE, Sir Henry (1549–1622), was secretary of the Latin tongue to *Elizabeth I, and one of the scholars commissioned to prepare the authorized translation of the Bible. He translated the *Histories* of *Tacitus (1591) and published a magnificent edition of St John *Chrysostom (1610–13) and of *Xenophon's *Cyropaedia* (1613) and assisted *Bodley in founding his library, to which he left a collection of manuscripts and printed books.

Savile Club, founded in 1868 as the Eclectic Club, renamed in 1869 the New Club, and from 1871, the Savile Club. The club has always had a strong literary tradition; members have included R. L. *Stevenson, *Hardy, *Yeats, L. *Strachey, H. *James, and S. *Potter.

SAVONAROLA, Fra Girolamo (1452–98), Dominican monk, an eloquent preacher whose sermons at Florence gave expression to the religious reaction against the artistic licence and social corruption of the Renaissance. Savonarola was leader of the democratic party in Florence after the expulsion of the Medici. His influence was gradually undermined, and he was executed as a heretic. There is a careful study of his character in G. Eliot's *Romola*.

Savoy, The, a short-lived but important periodical, edited by Arthur *Symons, of which eight issues appeared in 1896, with contributions by *Beardsley, *Conrad, *Dowson, and others.

Savoy Operas, see GILBERT AND SULLIVAN OPERAS.

Sawles Warde, an allegorical work of alliterative prose, found in three manuscripts with the saints' lives called *'The Katherine Group'. It presents a morality in which the body is the dwelling-place of the soul and comes under attack by the vices. Its prose is elegant and colloquial.

Sawyer, Bob, a character in Dickens's *The Pickwick Papers*.

SAXO GRAMMATICUS, a 13th-cent. Danish historian, author of the *Gesta Danorum*, a partly mythical Latin history of the Danes (which contains the *Hamlet story).

SAYERS, Dorothy L(eigh) (1893–1957). Her detective fiction is among the classics of the genre, being outstanding for its well-researched backgrounds, distinguished style, observant characterization, and ingenious plotting, and for its amateur detective Lord Peter Wimsey; she reached her peak with *Murder Must Advertise* (1933) and *The Nine Tailors* (1934). She also wrote religious plays, mainly for broadcasting. Her last years were devoted to a translation of Dante's *Divina Commedia*.

Scald, Scaldic verse, see SKALDIC VERSE.

Scales, Gerald, a character in Bennett's *The Old Wives' Tale*.

SCALIGER, Joseph Justus (1540–1609), the son of J. C. *Scaliger, was the greatest scholar of the Renaissance; he has been described as 'the founder of historical criticism'. He edited Manilius (1579) and issued critical editions of many classical authors.

SCALIGER, Julius Caesar (1484–1558). Besides polemical works directed against *Erasmus (1531), he wrote a long Latin treatise on poetics, scientific commentaries on botanical works, and a philosophical treatise.

SCANNELL, Vernon (1922–), poet. His first volume of verse, *Graves and Resurrections* (1948), was followed by several others including *The Masks of Love* (1960), *A Sense of Danger* (1962), *The Loving Game* (1975), and *New and Collected Poems 1950–1980* (1980). Many of the poems combine informal colloquial language and domestic subjects with a sense of underlying violence. He has also written several novels and an autobiography, *The Tiger and the Rose* (1971).

Scaramouch, adaptation of the Italian *scaramuccia*, 'skirmish', a stock character in *commedia dell'arte*, a cowardly and foolish boaster, who is constantly cudgelled by Harlequin. The character was intended in ridicule of the Spanish don, and was dressed in Spanish costume, usually black. A comedy entitled *Scaramouch*, by Edward Ravenscroft, was produced in 1677.

Scarlet, or **Scarlock,** or **Scathelocke,** Will, one of the companions of *Robin Hood.

Scarlet Letter, The, a novel by N. *Hawthorne, published 1850.

The scene of the story is the Puritan New England of the 17th cent. An aged English scholar has sent his young wife, Hester Prynne, to Boston, intending to follow her, but has been captured by the Indians and delayed for two years. He arrives to find her in the pillory, with a baby in her arms. She has refused to name her lover, and has been sentenced to this ordeal and to wear for the remainder of her life the red letter A, adulteress, upon her bosom. The husband assumes the name of Roger Chillingworth. Hester goes to live on the outskirts of the town with her child, Pearl. Her ostracism opens for her a broader view of life, she devotes herself to works of mercy, and gradually wins the respect of the townsfolk. Chillingworth, in the character of a physician, sets out to discover her paramour. Hester's lover is, in fact, Arthur Dimmesdale, a young and highly revered minister. The author traces the steps by which Chillingworth discovers him, and the cruelty with which he fastens on and tortures him. When Dimmesdale at the end of seven years is on the verge of lunacy and death, Hester proposes to him that they shall flee to Europe. But he puts the idea from him as a temptation of the Evil One, makes public confession on the pillory, and dies in her arms.

Scarlet Pimpernel, The, see ORCZY, BARONESS.

Scenes of Clerical Life, a series of three tales by G. *Eliot, published in two volumes 1858, having appeared in *Blackwood's Magazine* in the previous year.

'The Sad Fortunes of the Rev. Amos Barton' is the sketch of a commonplace clergyman, the curate of Shepperton, unpopular with his parishioners, who earns their affection by his misfortune—the death from overwork, childbearing, and general wretchedness of his beautiful gentle wife, Milly.

'Mr Gilfil's Love-Story' is the tale of a man whose nature has been warped by a tragic love experience. Maynard Gilfil was parson at Shepperton before the days of Amos Barton. He had been the ward of Sir Christopher Cheverel and his domestic chaplain, and had fallen deeply in love with Caterina Sastri (Tina), the daughter of an Italian singer, whom the Cheverels had adopted. But the shallow Capt. Anthony Wybrow, the heir of Sir Christopher, won Tina's heart; then, at his uncle's bidding, threw her over for the rich Miss Assher. The strain drove Tina to the verge of lunacy. All this Gilfil had watched with sorrow and unabated love. Tina rallied for a time under his devoted care and finally married him, but died in a few months, leaving Gilfil like a tree lopped of its best branches.

'Janet's Repentance' is the story of a conflict between religion and irreligion, and of the influence of a sympathetic human soul. The Revd Edgar Tryan, an earnest Evangelical clergyman, comes to Milby, an industrial town sunk in religious apathy. His endeavour to remedy this condition is vigorously opposed by a group of inhabitants led by Dempster, a hectoring drunken lawyer, whose brutality to his wife drives her to drink. Her husband's illtreatment causes her to appeal to Tryan for help, and under his guidance her struggle against the craving for drink begins. Dempster dies after a fall from his gig. The death of Tryan from consumption leaves her bereaved, but strengthened for a life of service.

Scepticism, a philosophical stance which questions the possibility of attaining lasting knowledge about the reality, as distinct from the appearance, of things, and which rejects all dogmatism, fanaticism, and intolerance. Scepticism had its origin in the teaching of some of the *Sophists in the 5th cent. BC. 'Pyrrhonian' scepticism, associated with Pyrrho in the following century, held that any argument supporting one side of a case could be balanced by a contrary argument of equal weight. 'Academic' scepticism, associated with the Academy of Carneades, held that although the same evidence is always compatible with two contrary conclusions, some beliefs are more reasonable than others and we can act upon the balance of probabilities. Sceptical techniques have frequently been practised by both supporters and opponents of religion to show that it rests on faith rather than reason. *Hume carried the study to new lengths in his *Treatise of Human Nature*. Since the time of *Descartes critics of scepticism, particularly in religion and morals, have tended to depict it as a form of negative dogmatism.

Scheherazade, or **Shahrazad**, in the *Arabian Nights*, the daughter of the vizier of King Shahriyar, who married the king and escaped the death that was the usual fate of his wives by telling him the tales which compose that work, interrupting each one at an interesting point, and postponing the continuation till the next night. There is a symphonic suite for orchestra (*Sheherazade*) by Rimsky-Korsakov.

SCHELLING, Friedrich Wilhelm Joseph von (1775–1854), German philosopher, whose theories considerably influenced *Coleridge's formulation of the poetic Imagination as the reconciler of opposite qualities.

SCHILLER, Johann Christoph Friedrich von (1759–1805), German dramatist and lyric poet, and one of the principal figures of the *Sturm und Drang* period and of German Romanticism in general. He was deeply influenced by Shakespeare, and greatly admired by *Hazlitt and *Coleridge. His principal plays include *Don Carlos* (1787), *Wallenstein* (1799), *Maria Stuart* (1800), and *Wilhelm Tell* (1804). His essays on aesthetics influenced the *Schlegels and Coleridge.

SCHLEGEL, August Wilhelm von (1767–1845), German Romanticist, critic, and philologist, chiefly known in England for his translation into German, with the assistance of his wife and others, of the plays of Shakespeare, and for his influence on *Coleridge.

SCHLEGEL, Friedrich von (1772–1829), younger brother of A. W. von *Schlegel, notable for his studies of the history of literature, and for his theory of 'romantic irony', or the consciousness on the part of the artist of the gap between the ideal artistic goal and the limited possibilities of achievement.

SCHOENBAUM, Samuel (1927–), American scholar. His *Shakespeare's Lives* (1970) is a history of accounts of Shakespeare's life; his *William Shakespeare: A Documentary Life* (1975) reproduces most of the relevant documents and this has been revised as *William Shakespeare: A Compact Documentary Life* (1977).

'Scholar-Gipsy, The', a poem by M. *Arnold, published 1853. The poem pastoral in setting, is based on an old legend, narrated by *Glanvill in his *The Vanity of Dogmatizing*, of an 'Oxford scholar poor', who, tired of seeking preferment, joined the gypsies to learn their lore, roamed with them, and still haunts the Oxford countryside. With this is woven a vivid evocation of the landscape and reflections on the contrasts between the single-minded faith of the scholar-gypsy and the modern world, 'the strange disease of modern life, | With its sick hurry, its divided aims'. The tone, as in many of Arnold's best works, is elegiac.

Scholasticism, the doctrines of the *Schoolmen, and the predominant theological and philosophical teachings of the period 1100–1500, mainly an attempt to reconcile *Aristotle with the Scriptures, and Reason with Faith. Its greatest monument is the *Summa Theologica* of *Aquinas. In the 14th cent., after *Ockham, Scholasticism had exhausted itself as an intellectual movement.

Scholemaster, The, see ASCHAM, R.

Schoole of Abuse, see GOSSON, S.

School for Scandal, The, a comedy by R. B. *Sheridan, produced 1777.

In this play, Sheridan's masterpiece, the author contrasts two brothers: Joseph Surface, the sanctimonious hypocrite, and Charles, the good-natured, reckless spendthrift. Charles is in love with Maria, the ward of Sir Peter Teazle, and his love is returned; Joseph is courting the same girl for her fortune, while at the same time dallying with Lady Teazle. Sir Peter, an old man who has married his young wife six months previously, is made wretched by her frivolity and the fashionable society she inhabits. This includes the scandal-mongers Sir Benjamin Backbite, Crabtree, Lady Sneerwell, and Mrs Candour. Sir Oliver Surface, the rich uncle of Joseph and Charles, returns unexpectedly from India, and decides to test the characters of his nephews before revealing his identify. He visits Charles in the guise of a money-lender, Mr Premium, and Charles cheerfully sells him the family portraits—but refuses to sell the portrait of Sir Oliver himself and thus unwittingly wins the old man's heart. Meanwhile Joseph receives a visit from Lady Teazle and attempts to seduce her. The sudden arrival of Sir Peter obliges Lady

Teazle to hide behind a screen. The arrival of Charles sends Sir Peter in turn to hide. The conversation between Charles and Joseph proves to Sir Peter that his suspicions of Charles were unfounded. When Charles flings down the screen he reveals Lady Teazle. Sir Oliver then enters in the character of a needy relative, begging for assistance. Joseph refuses, giving as his reason the avarice of his uncle, Sir Oliver, and his character now stands fully revealed. Charles is united to Maria, and Sir Peter and Lady Teazle are happily reconciled.

Schoolmen, the succession of writers, from about the 11th to the 15th cent., who treat of logic, metaphysics, and theology, as taught in the 'schools' or universities of Italy, France, Germany, and England, that is to say on the basis of *Aristotle and the Christian Fathers, whom the schoolmen endeavoured to harmonize. Among the great Schoolmen were Peter *Lombard, *Abelard, *Albertus Magnus, *Aquinas, *Duns Scotus, and *Ockham. (See SCHOLASTICISM.)

Schoolmistress, The, see SHENSTONE, W.

School of Night, a name drawn from a satirical allusion in *Love's Labour's Lost* (IV. iii. 214), and first ascribed by Arthur Acheson in 1903 (*Shakespeare and the Rival Poet*) to a supposed circle of speculative thinkers led by *Harriot and *Ralegh, and including *Marlowe, *Chapman, Lawrence Keymis, and the 'Wizard Earl' Northumberland. J. Dover *Wilson, G. B. *Harrison in his edition of *Willobie his Avisa* (1926), and M. C. *Bradbrook in *The School of Night* (1936) supported the theory that *Love's Labour's Lost* was an attack upon this coterie, which engaged in free-thinking philosophical debate (not necessarily atheistic) and dabbled in hermeticism, alchemy, and the occult. The existence of such a circle is now much disputed.

SCHOPENHAUER, Arthur (1788–1860), was the author of a pessimistic philosophy embodied in his *Die Welt als Wille und Vorstellung* (*The World as Will and Idea*, 1819), which considerably influenced *Wagner and the later Romantics.

SCHREINER, Olive Emilie Albertina (1855–1920), born in Cape Colony, the daughter of a missionary. She came to England in 1881. Her best-known novel was *The Story of an African Farm* (1883), published under the pseudonym 'Ralph Iron'. Set in the vividly evoked landscape of her childhood, it recounts the lives of two orphaned cousins. This novel won her the friendship of Havelock *Ellis. Her other novels, both with feminist themes, *From Man to Man* (1927) and *Undine* (1929), appeared posthumously, but during her lifetime she published

various other works, including collections of allegories and stories, articles on South African politics, and *Woman and Labour* (1911). Schreiner has been acknowledged as a pioneer both in her treatment of women and in her fictional use of the African landscape.

Science Fiction is the current name for a class of prose narrative which assumes an imaginary technological or scientific advance, or depends upon an imaginary and spectacular change in the human environment. Although examples exist from the time of *Lucian, and Swift's *Gulliver's Travels*, Mary Shelley's *Frankenstein*, and Bulwer-Lytton's *The Coming Race* are unmistakable precursors, it was not until the end of the 19th cent. that the form emerged as we know it today. The works of Jules Verne (1828–1905) have always been popular in this country, but the first successful English author was H. G. *Wells whose stories include several of the themes later dominant: invasion from outer space (*The War of the Worlds*, 1898), biological change or catastrophe (*The Food of the Gods*, 1904), time travel (*The Time Machine*, 1895), and air warfare (*The War in the Air*, 1908).

Since the Second World War scientific developments and their possible consequences have been reflected in fictional forms by motifs such as interplanetary travel, robots (originally introduced by the Czech dramatist Karel Capek, in the 1920s, see ROBOT), mechanical brains, and atomic hand weapons; and the destruction of the world as a result of its own technological achievements has proved a favourite theme, often carrying strong *apocalyptic undertones. The literary quality of Science Fiction is extremely variable, ranging from violent strip cartoons in pulp magazines, through the speculative works of the philosopher Olaf Stapledon (1886–1950), to the respectable domestic novels of *Wyndham and the more challenging intellectual ventures of *Ballard, *Aldiss, and *Moorcock.

Scillaes Metamorphosis, a poem by T. *Lodge, later published (1610) under the title *Glaucus and Scilla*.

SCOGAN, Henry (?1361–1407), a poet who, it is generally agreed, is the dedicatee of *Chaucer's 'Lenvoy de Chaucer a Scogan'. He is perhaps mentioned in Shakespeare's *2 Henry IV*, III. ii. 30—though the reference may be to John Scogan, below.

SCOGAN, John, a celebrated jester of Edward IV, whose exploits, real or imagined, are recorded in *The Jestes of Skogyn* (c.1570).

Scoop, a novel by E. *Waugh, published 1938.
Lord Copper, proprietor of *The Beast* (which stands for 'strong mutually antagonistic govern-

ments everywhere') is persuaded to send novelist John Boot to cover the war in Ishmaelia, but William Boot, writer of nature notes is dispatched by mistake. After many adventures he returns to find himself covered with glory, although in another case of mistaken identity John Boot has been knighted in his stead. The novel is a brilliantly comic satire of Fleet Street ethics and manners, and on the battle for readership between *The Beast* and *The Brute*.

SCOT, Michael, see SCOTT, M. (*c.*1175–*c.*1235).

SCOT, or **SCOTT,** Reginald (?1538–99), author of *The Discoverie of Witchcraft* (1584). This was written with the aim of preventing the persecution of poor, aged, and simple persons who were popularly believed to be witches, by exposing the impostures on the one hand, and the credulity on the other, that supported the belief in sorcery.

Scotist, see DUNS SCOTUS.

Scots is a historical offshoot of the Northumbrian dialect of Anglo-Saxon, sharing with Northern Middle English a strong Norse element in vocabulary and vowel and consonant developments which still mark off northern speech from Standard English. To this Gaelic, French (Norman and Parisian) and Dutch elements accrued and the political independence of Scotland gave this speech a national status. It became also the vehicle of a considerable literature in *Barbour, *Henryson, *Dunbar, *Douglas, Sir D. *Lindsay, and there was much prose translation as well, but the failure to produce a vernacular Bible at the Reformation, the Union of the Crowns in 1603, and that of the Parliaments in 1707 all helped to extend the bounds of English and prevent the evolution of an all-purpose Scots prose. The 18th-cent. literary revival of Scots under *Ramsay, *Fergusson, and *Burns, who gave it the name of 'Lallans' (Lowlands), was confined to poetry, with prose used merely to represent the colloquy of rustic characters, in Sir W. *Scott, *Hogg, *Galt, R. L. *Stevenson and the *'Kailyard School'. With the renaissance of the period 1920–50, writers like *MacDiarmid, Robert Maclellan (1907–85), S. G. *Smith, Douglas Young (1913–73), Alexander Scott (1920–), Robert Kemp (1908–), and others, attempted a re-creation of a full canon of Scots to cope with modern themes, which was also called Lallans, the name now connoting the new experimental speech rather than the old historical vernacular.

Scots Musical Museum, The (1787–1803), edited by James Johnson, an important collection of songs with music, some genuinely antique, some fake antique, and some new. *Burns made many notable contributions to the later volumes.

'Scots wha hae', a battle-song by *Burns published in *The Scots Musical Museum*.

SCOTT, Geoffrey (1883–1929), poet and biographer. His interest in architectural theory was confirmed by his friendship with *Berenson, and culminated in his study *The Architecture of Humanism* (1914). Scott's best-known book is *The Portrait of Zélide* (1925), an elegant and evocative life of Mme de Charrière. Scott was working on a biography of *Boswell and an edition of a collection of Boswell papers when he died in New York of pneumonia.

SCOTT, John (1783–1821), was the first editor, 1820–1, of the *London Magazine*; he had by then edited *The Champion*, and published *A Visit to Paris* (1814) and *Paris Revisited* (1816). He attracted a brilliant set of contributors; De Quincey's *Confessions of an Opium Eater, *Lamb's earlier 'Elia' essays, and much of *Hazlitt's *Table-Talk* first appeared in the *London Magazine*, as well as work by *Keats, *Clare, *Hood, *Darley, *Carlyle, *Cunningham, and others. He came into conflict with *Blackwood's Magazine*, detesting what he saw as its 'scurrility' and 'duplicity and treachery', and he felt obliged to defend his *'Cockney School'. His attacks on *Blackwood's*, in particular on *Lockhart, led to a series of confusions which culminated in a duel with J. H. Christie, a close friend of Lockhart, in which Scott was killed.

SCOTT, or **SCOT,** Michael (*c.*1175–*c.*1235), a Scottish scholar, studied at Oxford, Bologna, and Paris, and was attached to the court of Frederick II at Palermo, probably as official astrologer. He translated works of *Aristotle from Arabic to Latin (including *De Anima*, pre-1220), and perhaps *Averroes' great Aristotelian Commentary. He studied astronomy, and legends of his magical power served as a theme for many writers from *Dante (*Inferno*, xx. 116) to Sir W. Scott in *The Lay of the Last Minstrel*.

SCOTT, Michael (1789–1835), published in *Blackwood's Magazine*, between 1829 and 1833, the anonymous *Tom Cringle's Log*, entertaining sketches of the life he had known in the Caribbean.

SCOTT, Paul Mark (1920–78), novelist, who was an officer in the Indian army during the Second World War, and worked for many years in publishing and for a literary agency. His first novel, *Johnnie Sahib* (1952), was followed by twelve others, most of them dealing with Anglo-Indian relationships, and he is best remembered for the four novels known as the 'Raj Quartet': *The Jewel in the Crown* (1966), *The Day of the Scorpion* (1968), *The Towers of Silence* (1971), and *A Division of the Spoils* (1975). These interwoven narratives, set in India during and immediately after the Second World War, portray political, personal, racial, and religious conflicts in the period leading up to Independence and Partition, presenting events from various points of view. There are two key episodes in the first volume: the death of a missionary, Edwina Crane, who commits suicide after a violent incident in which an Indian colleague is killed, and the alleged rape in the Bibighar Gardens of Mayapore of Daphne Manners. A group of young Indians, including Daphne's friend, the English-reared and public-school-educated Hari Kumar, is accused, and all are brutally interrogated by Ronald Merrick, the district superintendent of police. The affair takes on a political aspect, and its repercussions include, in the fourth volume, Merrick's murder, Daphne having died in childbirth after refusing to implicate Kumar. Scott's last novel, *Staying On* (1977; *Booker Prize), picks up the story of two minor characters from the Quartet, Colonel 'Tusker' Smalley and his wife Lucy, social misfits who stay on after Independence and attempt to adjust to the attitudes and conditions of the new India. The Raj Quartet was televised in 1984 as *The Jewel in the Crown*.

SCOTT, Reginald, see SCOT, R.

SCOTT, Robert Falcon (1868–1912), Antarctic explorer, commanded the National Antarctic Expedition (1900–2), which he recorded in his *The Voyage of the Discovery* (1905). His notable journal, published as *Scott's Last Expedition* (1913), describes his second Antarctic expedition, the last entry of which was made as Scott lay dying, stormbound on his return from the South Pole.

SCOTT, Sir Walter (1771–1832), was educated at Edinburgh High School and University, and was called to the bar in 1792. His interest in the old Border tales and ballads was stimulated by Percy's *Reliques* and by the study of the old romantic poetry of France and Italy and of the modern German poets. He devoted much of his leisure to the exploration of the Border country. In 1797 he published anonymously in *The Chase and William and Helen*, a translation of Bürger's 'Der wilde Jäger' (*'The Wild Huntsman') and *'Lenore', and in 1799 a translation of *Goethe's *Götz von Berlichingen*. In 1797 he married Margaret Charlotte Charpentier (or Carpenter). In 1802–3 appeared the three volumes of Scott's *Minstrelsy of the Scottish Border*; and in 1805 his first considerable original work, the romantic poem *The Lay of the Last Minstrel*. He then became a partner in James *Ballantyne's printing business and published *Marmion in 1808. This was followed by *The Lady of the Lake (1810), *Rokeby and The Bridal of Triermain (1813), *The Lord of the Isles (1815), and Harold the Dauntless (1817), his last long poem. In 1811 he had pur-

chased Abbotsford on the Tweed, where he built himself a residence. Scott promoted the foundation in 1809 of the Tory *Quarterly Review—he had been a contributor to the *Edinburgh Review, but seceded from it owing to its Whig attitude. In 1813 he refused the offer of the laureateship and recommended *Southey for the honour. Eclipsed in a measure by *Byron as a poet in spite of the great popularity of his verse romances, he now turned his attention to the novel as a means of giving play to his wide erudition, his humour, and his sympathies. His novels appeared anonymously in the following order: *Waverley (1814); *Guy Mannering (1815); *The Antiquary (1816); The Black Dwarf and *Old Mortality (1816), as the first series of *Tales of My Landlord; *Rob Roy (1817); *The Heart of Midlothian (1818), the second series of Tales of My Landlord; The Bride of Lammermoor and *A Legend of Montrose (1819), the third series of Tales of My Landlord; *Ivanhoe (1819); *The Monastery (1820); *The Abbot (1820); *Kenilworth (1821); The Pirate (1821); *The Fortunes of Nigel (1822); *Peveril of the Peak (1823); *Quentin Durward (1823); St Ronan's Well (1823); *Redgauntlet (1824); The Betrothed and *The Talisman (1825), together as Tales of the Crusaders; *Woodstock (1826); Chronicles of the Canongate (1827, containing 'The Highland Widow', *'The Two Drovers', and The Surgeon's Daughter); Chronicles of the Canongate (second series): Saint Valentine's Day, or *The Fair Maid of Perth (1828); Anne of Geierstein (1829); Tales of My Landlord (fourth series): *Count Robert of Paris and Castle Dangerous (1831). Scott was created a baronet in 1820, and avowed the authorship of the novels in 1827. In 1826 James Ballantyne & Co. became involved in the bankruptcy of Constable & Co., and Scott, as partner of the former, found himself liable for a debt of about £114,000. He shouldered the whole burden himself and henceforth worked heroically, shortening his own life by his strenuous efforts, to pay off the creditors, who received full payment after his death.

Scott's dramatic work, in which he did not excel, includes Auchindrane or the Ayrshire Tragedy (1830). Scott wrote, or issued under his editorship, many important historical, literary, and antiquarian works. These include The Works of Dryden with a Life (1808); The Works of Swift with a Life (1814); *The Tales of a Grandfather (1827–30); History of Scotland (1829–30); and the *Memoirs of Captain George Carleton (1808). *Paul's Letters to his Kinsfolk appeared in 1816. Scott founded the *Bannatyne Club in 1823.

Scott's *Life by J. G. *Lockhart, published in 1837–8, has been considered one of the great biographies of English literature. Scott's Journal was published in 1890 and in subsequent editions. An edition of his letters in 12 vols was published by H. J. C. Grierson (1932–7).

Scott's influence as a novelist was incalculable;

he established the form of the *Historical novel, and, according to V. S. *Pritchett, the form of the short story (with 'The Two Drovers' and 'The Highland Widow'). He was avidly read and imitated throughout the 19th cent., after which his reputation gradually declined until there was a revival of interest from European *Marxist critics in the 1930s (see LUKÁCS), who interpreted his works in terms of historicism.

SCOTT, William Bell (1811–90), poet, artist, and art critic. He was a friend of D. G. *Rossetti and later of *Swinburne; he was associated with the birth of the *Pre-Raphaelite movement, and contributed to * The Germ. His poems and verses range from rambling Pindaric odes to sonnets and medieval-style ballads.

Scottish Chaucerians, see CHAUCERIANS, SCOTTISH.

Scottish Chiefs, The, a *historical novel by J. *Porter, published 1810.

Scottish Enlightenment, a phrase used to describe an intellectual movement originating in Glasgow in the early 18th cent. but reaching fruition mainly in Edinburgh between 1750 and 1800. Several threads are traceable in the attitudes of the scientists, philosophers and *literati associated with the movement, although no single tenet was held by all: a deep concern for the practical implications and social benefits of their enquiries (proclaimed as leading to 'improvement'), an emphasis on the interconnection between separable human practices, and an interest in the philosophical principles underlying them. Several of the group developed an interest in history, and many were at least nominal *Deists.

The main philosophers were *Hutcheson, *Hume, Adam *Smith, A. *Ferguson; for his leadership of the so-called 'common-sense' opposition, *Reid should be mentioned, and later D. *Stewart. The literary figures were often ambivalent towards the theories and practices of their scientific and speculative colleagues, and increasingly distanced themselves towards the end of the century. Sir W. *Scott is associated with its closing decades. The founding of the *Encyclopaedia Britannica was in part a product of the movement. (See also ROYAL SOCIETY OF EDINBURGH.)

Scottish Texts Society, The, founded in 1882 for the purpose of printing and editing texts illustrative of the Scottish language and literature, has issued editions of many works of general literary interest, such as * The Kingis Quair, *Barbour's Bruce, Gawin *Douglas's Eneados, and the Basilikon Doron of *James I, and the poems of *Dunbar, *Henryson, *Drummond of Hawthornden, and Sir D. *Lindsay. It

has also produced editions of later writers, including A. *Ramsay and R. *Fergusson.

SCOTUS, John Duns, see DUNS SCOTUS.

SCOTUS ERIGENA, John (John the Scot) (c.810–77), of Irish origin, was employed as teacher at the court of Charles the Bald, afterwards emperor, c.847. The leading principle of his philosophy, as expounded in his great work De Divisione Naturae, is that of the unity of nature; this proceeds from God, the first and only real being, through the Creative Ideas to the sensible Universe; everything is ultimately resolved into its First Cause (immanent, unmoving God: Nature which is not created and does not create). He was one of the originators of the Mystical thought of the Middle Ages, as well as a precursor of *Scholasticism (though with no Aristotelian elements). He translated the works of Pseudo-*Dionysius in 858, as well as of other Neoplatonists, and he wrote a Commentary on the Celestial Hierarchy of Pseudo-Dionysius. The presence of a Neoplatonic element in all medieval philosophers, including *Aquinas, owes much to his influence.

Scriblerus Club, an association of which *Swift, *Arbuthnot, T. *Parnell, *Pope, and *Gay were members, and the earl of Oxford (R. *Harley) a regularly invited associate member. The group appears to have met from January to July 1714. Its object was to ridicule 'all the false tastes in learning', but nothing was produced under the name of *Martinus Scriblerus for some years.

Scrooge, a character in Dickens's *A Christmas Carol.

Scrutiny, a Cambridge periodical which ran for 19 volumes, 1932–53, edited by L. C. *Knights, Donald Culver, Denys Thompson, D. W. Harding, and others, but dominated largely by F. R. *Leavis; a 20th issue, with a 'Retrospect' by Leavis, appeared in 1963. Its contributors include Q. D. Leavis, H. A. Mason, E. *Rickword, D. A. Traversi. It published little creative work of importance, with the exception of the posthumous poems of *Rosenberg, but was an important vehicle for the views of the new Cambridge school of criticism, and published many seminal essays, particularly in the pre-war years, on J. *Austen, Shakespeare, *Marvell, etc. Its critical standards proved less illuminating when applied to contemporary writing; it ignored most of *Orwell, dismissed G. *Greene, Dylan *Thomas, and most of V. *Woolf and in later years attacked the reputations of *Spender and *Auden, both of whom had been originally greeted as heralds of a Poetic Renascence which, by 1940, Leavis declared not to have taken place. Leavis deplored the lack of support that this indisputably important periodical had received and he blamed the British Council, the BBC, the 'intellectuals of literary journalism', etc., for its demise.

Scudamour, Sir, in Spenser's *Faerie Queene* (Bk. IV), the lover of *Amoret, who is reft from him on his wedding-day by the enchanter *Busirane.

Scythrop, a character in Peacock's *Nightmare Abbey*, a satirical portrait of the style and literary opinions of *Shelley.

Seafarer, The, an Old English poem of about 120 lines in the *Exeter Book, one of the group known as 'elegies'. The opening section of the poem ostensibly discusses the miseries and attractions of life at sea, before moving by an abrupt transition to moral reflections on the transcience of life and ending in an explicitly Christian part (the text of which is uncertain), concluding with a prayer. *Pound made a loose but highly evocative translation of the first half of the poem.

Seagrim, Molly, a character in Fielding's *Tom Jones*.

Seasons, The, a poem in blank verse, in four books and a final hymn, by J. *Thomson (1700–48), published 1726–30.

'Winter' was composed first; it describes the rage of the elements and the sufferings of men and animals; two well-known episodes are the visit of the redbreast to a family who feed him crumbs from the table, and the death of a shepherd in a snowdrift. Many of the passages are notably *Sublime.

Next came 'Summer' (1727), which sets forth the progress of a summer's day, with scenes of hay-making, sheep-shearing, and bathing, followed by a panegyric to Great Britain and her 'solid grandeur'. It also includes two narrative episodes, one of the lover Celadon whose Amelia is struck by lightning, the other of Damon who beholds Musidora bathing.

'Spring' (1728) describes the influence of the season on all the natural world, and ends with a panegyric on nuptial love.

'Autumn' (1730) gives a vivid picture of shooting and hunting, of harvesting, wine-making, etc., and ends with a panegyric to the 'pure pleasures of the rural life'. It includes the episode of Palemon who falls in love with Lavinia, a gleaner in his fields, based on the story of Ruth and Boaz.

The text of Haydn's oratorio *Die Jahreszeiten* (1801) was adapted from Thomson by Baron van Swieten.

Sebastian, (1) Viola's twin brother in Shakespeare's *Twelfth Night*; (2) in his *The Tempest*, brother to Alonso.

Second Mrs Tanqueray, The, a play by Sir A. *Pinero, first performed 1893.

Tanqueray, knowing of Paula's past reputation, still determines to marry her. Ellean, his young convent-bred daughter from a previous marriage, comes to live with him and Paula; soon Tanqueray begins to realize that Ellean, his friends, and his own suspicions are proved too powerful an opposition to his once-loving marriage. When Paula also realizes that she has lost his love, she kills herself.

'Second Nun's Tale', see CANTERBURY TALES, 21.

Secret Agent, The, a novel by *Conrad, published 1907.

A seedy shop in Soho provides cover for Verloc, the secret agent, who is working as a spy for a foreign embassy and as informer for Chief Inspector Heat of Scotland Yard. His wife Winnie has married him chiefly to provide security for her simple-minded younger brother Stevie, and is ignorant of Verloc's spying activities. The shop is a meeting place for a bunch of ill-assorted political fanatics united only in their effort to arouse some extremism in the over-moderate British. We are introduced to the Russian *agent provocateur* Vladimir; the American terrorist 'the Professor'; and Ossipon, Yundt, and Michaelis who easily accommodate their principles to their material needs. The foreign embassy is planning a series of outrages aimed at discrediting the revolutionary groups which will be held responsible. The first target is the Greenwich Observatory and an unwilling Verloc is ordered to engineer the explosion. He uses the poor innocent Stevie as an accomplice and the boy is blown to pieces while carrying the bomb. Winnie, grief-stricken, kills Verloc with a knife. Fleeing, she encounters Ossipon who flirts with her and they plan to leave the country. But when he discovers Verloc's murder he steals her money and abandons her. Winnie, alone and in terror of the gallows, throws herself overboard from the Channel ferry.

Secreta Secretorum, a compendium of pronouncements on political and ethical matters. Written in Syriac in the 8th cent. AD and claiming to be advice from Aristotle to Alexander. It reached Europe through Arabic and 12th-cent. Hispano-Arabic and influenced poets until the 16th cent.

Secret Garden, The, see BURNETT, F. H.

Sedley, Mr, Mrs, Joseph, and Amelia, characters in Thackeray's *Vanity Fair*.

SEDLEY, or **SIDLEY,** Sir Charles (?1639–1701), dramatist and poet, friend of *Rochester and *Dryden, was famous for his wit and urbanity and notorious for his profligate escapades. His tragedy *Antony and Cleopatra* (1677) was followed by two comedies, *Bellamira* (1687) and *The Mulberry Garden* (1668), which was based partly on *Molière's *L'École des maris*. His poems and songs ('Phillis is my only joy', 'Love still has something of the sea', etc.) were included with his *Miscellaneous Works* (1702). *Malone identified him as the Lisideius of Dryden's *Of Dramatick Poesie*.

SEELEY, Sir John Robert (1834–95), professor of Latin at University College London from 1863 and of modern history at Cambridge from 1869 until his death. In 1865 he published anonymously *Ecce Homo*, a survey of the life of Christ as one of the great religious reformers. His historical works, designed to promote a practical object, the training of statesmen, include: *The Expansion of England in the Eighteenth Century* (1883) and *The Growth of British Policy* (1895).

Seithenyn, a character in Peacock's *The Misfortunes of Elphin*.

Sejanus his Fall, a Roman tragedy by *Jonson, performed by the King's Men 1603, with Shakespeare and *Burbage in the cast, printed 1605.

Based mainly on *Tacitus, the play deals with the rise of Sejanus during the reign of Tiberius, his destruction of the family of Germanicus, and his poisoning of Tiberius' son Drusus. Suspecting the scope of his favourite's ambition, Tiberius leaves Rome, setting his agent Macro to spy on him. Tiberius denounces Sejanus in a letter to the senate, which condemns him to death, and the mob, stirred up by Macro, tears him to pieces.

Selborne, *Natural History and Antiquities of*, see WHITE, G.

SELDEN, John (1584–1654), historian and antiquary, became an eminent lawyer and bencher of the Inner Temple. He won fame as an orientalist with his treatise *De Diis Syris* (1617), and subsequently made a valuable collection of oriental manuscripts, most of which passed at his death to the Bodleian Library. His *Table Talk* (1689) contains reports of his utterances during the last 20 years of his life, composed by his secretary Richard Milward. His works include *Marmora Arundelliana* (1624), *Mare Clausum* (1635), translated by *Nedham, in which he maintained against the *Mare Liberum* of Grotius that the sea is capable of sovereignty, and *Illustrations* to the first 18 'songs' of Drayton's *Poly-Olbion*.

Selden Society, The, was founded in 1887 by *Maitland for the publication of ancient legal records.

Select Society, The, an association of educated Scotsmen formed in 1754, whose members met in Edinburgh to discuss philosophical questions. *Hume and W. *Robertson were among its prominent members.

Self-Help, see SMILES, S.

Selima, Horace *Walpole's cat, whose death by drowning in a bowl of goldfish was lamented in a poem by *Gray.

SELINCOURT, Ernest de (1870–1943), scholar and literary critic, professor of poetry at Oxford 1928–33. As a scholar he is remembered principally for his editions of the works of Dorothy and William *Wordsworth, which include *The Prelude* (1926); *Letters of William and Dorothy Wordsworth* (6 vols, 1935–9), William's *Poetical Works* (vols 1 and 2, 1940–4), and Dorothy's *Journals* (2 vols, 1941). He also wrote a life of Dorothy, published in 1933.

SELKIRK, Alexander (1676–1721), joined the privateering expedition of *Dampier in 1703. Having quarrelled with his captain, Thomas Stradling, he was at his own request put ashore on the uninhabited island of Juan Fernandez in 1704, and remained there until 1709 when he was rescued by W. *Rogers. *Steele published an account of his experience in *The Englishman* (3 Dec. 1713); Defoe used the story in *Robinson Crusoe* and *Cowper in his poem, 'I am monarch of all I survey'.

Semiotics, see SAUSSURE, F.

SENECA, Lucius Annaeus (*c*.4 BC–AD 65), Roman Stoic philosopher, tragic poet, and, like his father the elder Seneca, a noted rhetorician. He was appointed tutor to the young Nero and, when the latter became emperor, acted as one of his chief advisers, but, finding this position untenable, he withdrew from the court in AD 62. Three years later he was accused of being implicated in a conspiracy and was forced to commit suicide. His writings consist of tragedies in verse, dialogues, treatises, and letters in prose, which in their different ways all aim to teach *Stoicism. Most of his nine plays are on subjects drawn from Greek mythology and treated in extant Greek dramas, but his manner is very different from that of Greek tragedy. He uses an exaggerated rhetoric, dwells habitually on blood-thirsty details and introduces ghosts and magic, the plays were almost certainly not intended for performance but for reading aloud, probably by the author himself, to a select audience.

Seneca's prose writings consist of treatises, some of which are clumsily disguised as dialogues (*De Clementia*, *De Ira*, etc.) and a collection of what purport to be letters addressed to one Lucilius constituting a sort of elementary course in Stoicism. These writings were widely read in the 17th and 18th cents. *L'Estrange's digest of them (1678) reached ten editions by 1711, so that there is an undercurrent of Stoicism in much of early 18th-cent. thinking, visible not only in Addison's *Cato but also in a wide range of writers from *Pope to *Duck. (See SENECAN TRAGEDY, below.)

Senecan tragedy. The plays of *Seneca exercised great influence on medieval playwrights, who used them as models for literary imitation. They were edited by Nicholas *Trivet, and in the 15th and 16th cents there was a considerable vogue in Italy for Senecan tragedy. The plays of Giraldi (1504–73)—notably his Orbecche (1541)—and of Ludovico Dolce (1508–68) were particularly famous. The same movement in France had its effect on Buchanan's Latin plays and on the plays of Jodelle and Garnier, and both the Italian and the French fashion influenced English drama in the 16th cent.

The characteristics of the Senecan tragedy were: (1) a division into five acts with Choruses—and in the English imitations often a dumb show expressive of the action; (2) a considerable retailing of 'horrors' and violence, usually, though not always, acted off the stage and elaborately recounted; (3) a parallel violence of language and expression.

*Gorboduc is a good example of a Senecan tragedy in English. The fashion, which developed in learned rather than popular circles, was short-lived, and was displaced by a more vital and native form of tragedy. But its elements persisted in Elizabethan drama and may be traced in such plays as * Tamburlaine the Great and * Titus Andronicus. More than a century later traces of Senecan influence are apparent in *Dryden's Troilus and Cressida (1679).

Sensation, Novel of, a branch of fiction that flourished from c. 1860 onwards, depicting lurid, implausible, or sensational events, and frequently involving guilty secrets; classics of the genre include Wilkie Collins's * The Woman in White (1860); Mrs H. *Wood's East Lynne (1861); and M. E. *Braddon's Lady Audley's Secret (1862). Many of the novels of the period (e.g. those of Mrs *Gaskell and *Dickens) include sensational elements, and the genre later developed into the thriller and detective novel. (See DETECTIVE FICTION.)

Sense and Sensibility, a novel by J. Austen, which grew from a sketch entitled 'Elinor and Marianne'; revised 1797–8 and again 1809; published 1811.

Mrs Henry Dashwood and her daughters Elinor, Marianne, and Margaret are left in straitened circumstances, because her husband's estate has passed to her stepson John Dashwood. Henry Dashwood, before his death, had urgently recommended to John that he look after his stepmother and sisters, but John's selfishness defeats his father's wish. Mrs Dashwood and her daughters accordingly retire to a cottage in Devonshire, but not before Elinor and Edward Ferrers, brother of Mrs John Dashwood, have become mutually attracted. However, Edward shows a strange uneasiness in his relations with Elinor. In Devonshire Marianne is thrown into the company of John Willoughby, an attractive but impecunious and unprincipled young man, with whom she falls desperately in love. Willoughby likewise shows signs of a strong affection for her, but he suddenly departs for London, leaving Marianne in acute distress. Eventually Elinor and Marianne also go to London, on the invitation of their tactless and garrulous old friend Mrs Jennings. Here Willoughby shows complete indifference to Marianne, and finally, in a cruel and insolent letter, informs her of his approaching marriage to a rich heiress. Marianne makes no effect to hide her great grief. Meanwhile Elinor has learned, under pledge of secrecy, from Lucy Steele (a sly, self-seeking young woman) that she and Edward Ferrers have been secretly engaged for four years. Elinor, whose self-control is in strong contrast to Marianne's demonstrative emotions, conceals her distress. Edward's engagement, which had been kept secret because of his financial dependence on his mother, now becomes known to her. In her fury at Edward's refusal to break his promise to Lucy, she dismisses him from her sight, and settles on his younger brother Robert the property that would otherwise have gone to Edward. At this juncture a small living is offered to Edward, and the way seems open for his marriage with Lucy. But Robert, a fashionable young fop, falls in love with Lucy, who, seeing her best interest in a marriage with the wealthier brother, throws over Edward and marries Robert. Edward, relieved to be released from an engagement he has long and painfully regretted, proposes to Elinor and is accepted. Marianne, eventually accepts the proposal of Colonel Brandon, an old family friend, whose considerable quiet attractions had been eclipsed by his brilliant rival.

Sensibility, see SENTIMENT, NOVEL OF.

Sentiment, Sensibility, Novel of. The object of this type of novel was to illustrate the alliance of acute sensibility with true virtue. An adherence to strict morality and honour, combined with sympathy and feeling, were the marks of the man or woman of sentiment. The cult may be traced particularly to the work of Marivaux, *Richardson, and S. *Fielding; the most popular and influential novels to which they gave rise were probably H. Brooke's * The

Fool of Quality, Sterne's *A Sentimental Journey*, and Mackenzie's *The Man of Feeling*, together with the work of F. *Brooke, C. *Lennox, and F. *Sheridan. Late in the century *Lamb's *The Tale of Rosamund Gray* (1798) was in the mainstream of such novels, but the cult was then dying. The early chapters of J. Austen's *Northanger Abbey* mock the 'refined susceptibilities' of the Novel of Sentiment, and *Sense and Sensibility* was intended to demonstrate the serious consequences of following its standards. (See also NOVEL, RISE OF THE.)

Sentimental Comedy, a type of sentimental drama introduced by *Steele, a reaction from the comedy of the *Restoration. (See KELLY, H.)

Sentimental Journey, A, through France and Italy, by L. *Sterne, published 1768.
    The narrator, Parson Yorick (borrowed from *Tristram Shandy*), is a man of great charm, sensibility, and gallantry, who sets out to travel through France and Italy. He reveres 'Dear sensibility!' and is frequently moved to tears. In parodying fashionable works of travel, he contrasts his own appreciation with Smelfungus (a caricature of *Smollett) and with Mundungus (perhaps a Dr Sharp), both of whom had written disparaging travel books about Europe. The parson is as full of gaiety and irony as of tender feeling. In his travels from Calais to Amiens, Paris, the Bourbonnais, and nearly to Modane, with his servant La Fleur, he enjoys many encounters with all manner of men, from marquis to potboy, and, more especially, with pretty women, who range from ladies of wealth and elegance to chambermaids and shop girls.
    The book was no doubt based on Sterne's two journeys abroad in 1762–4 and 1765. It was well received by the public, and in 1769, after Sterne's death, was continued by a 'Eugenius', for long incorrectly assumed to be Sterne's old friend *Hall-Stevenson. *A Sentimental Journey* is probably the first English novel to survive in the handwriting of its author.

Septuagint, The (commonly designated LXX), the Greek version of the OT which derives its name from the story that it was made by 72 Palestinian Jews at the request of Ptolemy Philadelphus (285–246 BC) and completed in 72 days; or it may have been so called because it was authorized by the 70 members of the Jewish Sanhedrin (Jebb).

Serious Call, A, to a Devout and Holy Life, see LAW, W.

SERVICE, Robert William (1874–1958), poet. He emigrated to Canada in 1895 where he observed the gold rush in the Yukon; this inspired his best-known ballads, which include 'The Shooting of Dan McGrew' and 'The Cre-

mation of Sam McGee', published in *Songs of a Sourdough* (1907, Toronto; as *The Spell of the Yukon*, New York). He published other volumes of verse, collected volumes (1933, 1955, 1960), and two autobiographical works.

SERVIUS HONORATUS, Marius or Maurus (end of 4th cent. AD), Roman grammarian, whose commentary on *Virgil has survived in two versions, the longer of which was not printed till 1600. It preserved a mass of antiquarian, mythographical, and rhetorical information that has done much to forward our understanding of Latin poetry.

Sesame and Lilies, see RUSKIN, J.

Sestina, a poem of six six-line stanzas (with an envoy) in which the line-endings of the first stanza are repeated, but in different order, in the other five [*OED*].

Setebos, a god of the Patagonians, worshipped by Caliban's mother Sycorax (in Shakespeare's *The Tempest*). His purpose in creating the world is worked out by Caliban in R. *Browning's 'Caliban upon Setebos'.

SETTLE, Elkanah (1648–1724), the author of a series of bombastic oriental melodramas which threatened *Dryden's popularity and aroused his hostility. His *The Empress of Morocco* (1673) had such a vogue that Dryden, with *Crowne and *Shadwell, wrote a pamphlet of criticism of it. Dryden satirized Settle as Doeg in the second part of *Absalom and Achitophel*. Settle published *Absalom Senior or Achitophel Transpros'd* in 1682, and *Reflections on several of Mr Dryden's Plays* in 1687.

Seven Champions of Christendom, The Famous History of the, see JOHNSON, R.

Seven Deadly Sins, usually given as Pride, Envy, Anger, Sloth, Covetousness, Gluttony, and Lust; frequently personified in medieval literature, e.g. *Piers Plowman*, B. *Passus* 5; *Dunbar's 'The Dance of the Sevin Deidly Synnis'; Chaucer's 'Parson's Tale' (*Canterbury Tales*, 24); and in Spenser's *Faerie Queene*. They provide one of the organizing structures for *Dante's *Inferno* and *Purgatorio*.

Seven Lamps of Architecture, The, a treatise by *Ruskin.

Seven Liberal Arts, see QUADRIVIUM and TRIVIUM.

Seven Pillars of Wisdom, The, see LAWRENCE, T. E.

Seven Sages of Rome, The, a metrical romance of the early 14th cent., varying in length in different versions from 2,500 to 4,300 lines. In form it is a framed collection of tales, derived through Latin and French from Eastern collections, the original of which is the Indian *Book of Sindibad*, of interest as one of the earliest English instances of the form of short verse-story used by Chaucer in *The Canterbury Tales*.

Seven Types of Ambiguity, a critical work by W. *Empson, published 1930, rev. 1947, 1953; one of the most enjoyable and influential offshoots from I. A. *Richards's experiments with *Practical Criticism.

Empson uses the term ambiguity 'in an extended sense', to refer to 'any verbal nuance, however slight, which gives room for alternative reactions to the same piece of language'. The first, or simplest, type of ambiguity he defines as simple metaphor, 'a word or a grammatical construction effective in several ways at once'. The second occurs 'when two or more meanings are resolved into one' (as by 'Double Grammar' in Shakespeare); the third consists of two apparently disconnected meanings given simultaneously, as in a pun, or, by extension, in allegory or pastoral, where reference is made to more than one 'universe of discourse'; the fourth occurs when 'alternative meanings combine to make clear a complicated state of mind in the author' (with examples from Shakespeare, *Donne, and G. M. *Hopkins); the fifth consists of what Empson calls 'fortunate confusion', with examples from *Shelley and *Swinburne, suggesting the possibility that 19th-cent. technique is 'in part the metaphysical tradition dug up when rotten'; the sixth occurs when a statement in itself meaningless or contradictory forces the reader to supply interpretations; and an account of the seventh, which 'marks a division in the author's mind', is accompanied by quotations from *Freud and illustrations from *Crashaw, *Keats, Hopkins.

Seven Wonders of the World, the seven structures regarded as the most remarkable monuments of antiquity, viz. the Egyptian Pyramids, the Mausoleum at Halicarnassus, the Hanging Gardens of Babylon, the Temple of Artemis at Ephesus, the statue of Zeus by Phidias at Olympia, the Colossus at Rhodes, and the Pharos at Alexandria, or, according to another list, the walls of Babylon.

SEVERN, Joseph (1793–1879), painter and devoted friend and correspondent of *Keats. He accompanied Keats to Italy in 1820 and attended him at his death.

SEWARD, Anna (1747–1809), the 'Swan of Lichfield'. She furnished *Boswell with many details of Dr *Johnson's early life. In 1802 she wrote an admiring letter to Sir W. *Scott, who found some merit in her poetry and edited her works in 3 vols, with a memoir, in 1810, at her suggestion. Her letters were published in 1811.

SEWELL, Anna (1820–78), wrote only one book, *Black Beauty* (1877), a story for children relating the life of a black horse, which suffers much but eventually finds a happy home. The book became a children's classic.

Shabby Genteel Story, A, a story by *Thackeray, published in *Fraser's Magazine, 1840. Caroline Gann, the down-trodden daughter of a failed merchant, is tricked into a false marriage by the dashing 'George Brandon' (really Firmin). He abandons her, and her baby dies. The characters reappear in *The Adventures of Philip*.

Shadow, Simon, in Shakespeare's *2 *Henry IV*, one of Falstaff's recruits.

SHADWELL, Thomas (?1642–92), dramatist, whose first play *The Sullen Lovers* (1668) was based on *Molière's *Les Fâcheux*. He wrote some 14 comedies, including *The Squire of Alsatia* (1688), *The Virtuoso* (1676, a satire on the *Royal Society), *Epsom Wells* (1672), and *Bury Fair* (1689). He also wrote operas, adapting Shakespeare's *The Tempest* as *The Enchanted Island* (1674). A successful dramatist in his day, he has been perhaps unfairly remembered for his quarrel with *Dryden, dating from 1682. He was probably the author of *The Medal of John Bayes* (1682) and other anonymous attacks on Dryden; Dryden's counterattacks include *Mac-Flecknoe* and the second part of *Absalom and Achitophel*, where Shadwell appears as Og. Shadwell defends himself from the charge of dullness in his dedication to *Sedley of his translation of the *Tenth Satire of Juvenal* (1687). He succeeded Dryden as poet laureate in 1689.

SHAFFER, Peter Levin (1926–), playwright. His first play, *Five Finger Exercise* (1958), was followed by many other successes, including *The Royal Hunt of the Sun* (1964, pub. 1965), an epic about the conquest of Peru; *Black Comedy* (1965, pub. 1967), a farce; *Equus* (1973), a drama about an analyst's relationship with his horse-obsessed patient; and *Amadeus* (1979, pub. 1980), which deals with the nature of creativity through a portrayal of the composers Mozart and Salieri.

His twin brother Anthony Shaffer, author of *Sleuth* (1970, pub. 1971), is also a successful playwright.

SHAFTESBURY, Anthony Ashley Cooper, first Baron Ashley and 1st earl of (1621–83), a statesman prominent on the king's side in the Civil War, as leader of the parliamentary opposition to *Cromwell, after the Restoration as a member of the Cabal and chancellor. After his dismissal he was leader of the opposition, and a supporter of Monmouth. He was satirized as Achitophel in Dryden's *Absalom and Achitophel*, by Otway in *Venice Preserv'd*, and by many others.

SHAFTESBURY, Anthony Ashley Cooper, 3rd earl of (1671–1713), excluded by ill-health from active politics after 1702, devoted himself to intellectual pursuits, and in particular to moral and aesthetic philosophy. His principal writings are embodied in his *Characteristics of Men, Manners, Opinions, and Times* (1711; rev. ed, 1714). Shaftesbury was influenced by *Deism; he was at once a Platonist and a churchman, an opponent of the selfish theory of conduct advocated by *Hobbes. Man has 'affections', Shaftesbury held, not only for himself but for the creatures about him. And there is no conflict between the self-regarding and social affections; for the individual's own good is included in the good of society. Moreover, man has a capacity for distinguishing right and wrong, the beauty or ugliness of actions and affections, and this he calls the 'moral sense'. His influence is seen in the writing of *Arbuckle, *Akenside, and *Fielding, and in the philosophy of *Hutcheson and *Turnbull.

SHAFTESBURY, Anthony Ashley Cooper, 7th earl of (1801–85), philanthropist, active in many movements for the protection of the working classes and the benefit of the poor.

Shagpat, *The Shaving of*, see SHAVING OF SHAGPAT, THE.

Shahrazad, see SCHEHERAZADE.

SHAKESPEARE, William (1564–1616), was baptized in Holy Trinity Church, Stratford-upon-Avon, on 26 April 1564. His birth is traditionally celebrated on 23 April, also known to have been the date of his death. He was the eldest son of John Shakespeare, a glover and dealer in other commodities who played a prominent part in local affairs. John had married c.1557 Mary Arden, who came from a family of higher social standing. It is probable that William was educated at the local grammar school. Records indicate that in 1582 he married Anne Hathaway of Shottery, eight years his senior. A daughter, Susanna, was baptized on 26 May 1583, and twins, Hamnet and Judith, on 2 February 1585. According to *Aubrey, 'he had been in his younger yeares as Schoolmaster in the Countrey.'

Nothing is known of his beginnings as a writer, nor when or in what capacity he entered the theatre. The first printed allusion to him is from 1592, in the pamphlet *Greenes Groats-Worth of Witte*; its mention of 'an upstart Crow' who 'supposes he is well able to bombast out a blanke verse as the best of you' and who 'is in

his owne conceit the onely Shakescene in a countrey' suggests rivalry, and parody of a line from 3 *Henry VI* shows that Shakespeare was established on the London literary scene. He was a leading member of the Lord Chamberlain's Men soon after their re-foundation in 1594. With them he worked and grew prosperous for the rest of his career as they developed into London's leading company, occupying the Globe Theatre from 1599, becoming the King's Men on James I's accession in 1603, and taking over the Blackfriars as a winter house in 1608.

London became Shakespeare's professional base, but his family remained in Stratford. In August 1596 William's son Hamnet died. In October Shakespeare was lodging in Bishopsgate, London; in May 1597 he bought a substantial Stratford house, New Place, and in 1604 he lodged in London with a family called Mountjoy.

Evidence suggests that by 1608 Shakespeare was withdrawing to New Place, but his name continues to appear in London records; in March 1613 he bought a gatehouse close to the Blackfriars theatre. He died, according to the inscription on his monument, on 23 April 1616, and was buried in Holy Trinity, Stratford.

Shakespeare's only writings for the press are the narrative poems *Venus and Adonis* (1593) and *The Rape of Lucrece* (1594), both dedicated to Henry Wriothesley, earl of Southampton, and the short poem *'The Phoenix and the Turtle' (1601), published in Robert Chester's *Loves Martyr*. His *Sonnets (1609) date probably from the mid-1590s; the volume includes the poem *'A Lover's Complaint'.

Shakespeare's plays were published by being performed. Scripts of only half of them appeared in print in his lifetime, some in reported texts now known as 'bad quartos'. Dates and order of composition are often difficult to establish. The list that follows gives dates of first printing of all the plays other than those that first appeared in the 1623 *Folio.

Probably Shakespeare began to write for the stage in the late 1580s. The ambitious trilogy known as *Henry VI* Parts One, Two, and Three, and its sequel *Richard III*, are among his early works. Parts Two and Three were printed in reported texts as *The First Part of the Contention betwixt the Two Famous Houses of York and Lancaster* (1594) and *The True Tragedy of Richard, Duke of York* (1595). A bad quarto of *Richard III* appeared in 1597. Shakespeare's first Roman tragedy is *Titus Andronicus*, printed 1594, and his earliest comedies are *The Two Gentlemen of Verona*, *The Taming of the Shrew* (a derivative play, *The Taming of a Shrew*, was printed 1594), *The Comedy of Errors* (acted 1594), and *Love's Labour's Lost* (printed 1598). All these plays are thought to have been written by 1595.

King John is particularly difficult to date, but it must be from some time between 1591 and

1598. *Richard II, printed 1597, is usually dated 1595. For some years after this, Shakespeare concentrated on comedy, in *A Midsummer Night's Dream and *The Merchant of Venice (both printed 1600), *The Merry Wives of Windsor (printed in a reported text 1602), *Much Ado About Nothing (printed 1600), *As You Like It (mentioned in 1600), and *Twelfth Night, probably written in 1600, or soon afterwards. *Romeo and Juliet (ascribed to the mid-1590s) is a tragedy with strongly comic elements, and the tetralogy begun by Richard II is completed by three comical histories: *Henry IV Parts One and Two (Part One printed 1598, Part Two 1600), and *Henry V (printed 1600), almost certainly written 1599.

Late in the century Shakespeare turned again to tragedy. *Julius Caesar was performed in 1599. *Hamlet was entered in the register of the *Stationers' Company in July 1602. A play that defies easy classification is *Troilus and Cressida, probably written 1602, printed 1609. The comedy *All's Well that Ends Well and the tragicomedy *Measure for Measure are probably of this period. *Othello, performed 1604, was printed in 1622. *King Lear probably dates, in its first version, from 1605. *Timon of Athens, printed in the Folio from uncompleted papers, was probably written in collaboration with T. *Middleton. *Macbeth is generally dated 1606, *Antony and Cleopatra 1606–7, and *Coriolanus 1607–9.

Towards the end of his career Shakespeare turned to romantic tragi-comedy. *Pericles was printed in a debased text 1609; it is generally believed to be mostly by Shakespeare but it was not included in the 1623 Folio. *Cymbeline, *The Winter's Tale, and *The Tempest were performed in 1611.

The last three plays associated with Shakespeare appear to have been written in collaboration with J. *Fletcher. They are *Henry VIII, performed 1613; a lost play *Cardenio, acted 1613 and attributed to the two dramatists in a Stationers' Register entry of 1653; and *The Two Noble Kinsmen, which appears to derive in part from a 1613 masque by F. *Beaumont, and was first printed 1634. No Shakespeare play survives in authorial manuscript, though three pages of revisions to a manuscript play, Sir Thomas *More, variously dated about 1593 or 1601, are often thought to be by Shakespeare and in his hand.

*Heming and *Condell prepared the First Folio, which appeared in 1623, and which includes a dedicatory epistle to William and Philip Herbert, earls of Pembroke and Montgomery, and the substantial poem by Jonson in which he declares that Shakespeare 'was not of an age, but for all time'. Its title-page engraving, by *Droeshout, is, along with the half-length figure bust by Gheerart Janssen erected in Holy Trinity, Stratford, by 1623, the only image of Shakespeare with strong claims to authenticity.

(See FOLIOS AND QUARTOS, SHAKESPEARIAN.)

Over 200 years after Shakespeare died, doubts were raised about the authenticity of his works (see BACONIAN THEORY). They are best answered by the facts that the monument to William Shakespeare of Stratford-upon-Avon compares him with *Socrates and *Virgil, and that Jonson's verses in the Folio identify the author of that volume as the 'Sweet Swan of Avon'.

The first editor to try to bring into order the documents committed to print between 1593 and 1623, reconcile their discrepancies, and correct their errors, was the dramatist *Rowe, in 1709. His 18th-cent. successors include *Pope (1723–5), *Theobald (1733), Dr *Johnson (1765), *Capell (1767–8), and *Malone (1790; third variorum 1821 by *Boswell, out of Malone's edition). The most important 19th-cent. edition is the Cambridge Shakespeare (1863–6, rev. 1891–3), on which the Globe text (1864) was based. The American New Variorum edition, still in progress, began to appear in 1871. Early in the 20th cent. advances in textual studies transformed attitudes to the text. Subsequent editions include the Arden Shakespeare (1899–1924), *Quiller-Couch's and J. Dover *Wilson's New Shakespeare (Cambridge, 1921–66), G. L. Kittredge's (1936), Peter Alexander's (1951), the New Arden (1951–), and the Riverside (1974). The first volumes in the Oxford English Texts edition appeared in 1982, and William Shakespeare: The Complete Works, ed. Stanley Wells and Gary Taylor, was published in 1986.

Great critics who have written on Shakespeare include *Dryden, Samuel Johnson, S. T. *Coleridge, *Hazlitt, A. C. *Bradley, and (less reverently) G. B. *Shaw. The standard biographical studies are E. K. *Chambers, William Shakespeare: A Study of Facts and Problems (2 vols, 1930) and S. *Schoenbaum, William Shakespeare: A Documentary Life (1975).

Shakespearean Criticism, a two-volume collection of the lectures of S. T. *Coleridge given between 1808 and 1818, ed. T. M. Raysor, 1907.

Shakespeare–Bacon controversy, see BACONIAN THEORY.

Shallow, in Shakespeare's 2 *Henry IV a foolish country justice. He appears again in *The Merry Wives of Windsor.

'Shalott, The Lady of', see LADY OF SHALOTT, THE.

Shamela Andrews, An Apology for the Life of Mrs, a parody by H. *Fielding, published pseudonymously 1741.

Richardson's *Pamela was published in 1740, and Fielding, irritated by what he regarded as the sententious hypocrisy of the book, replied with the lively travesty *Shamela*. Events and characters remain as in *Pamela*, but all is now seen in a very different light, with Parson Williams appearing as a scheming rogue, Mr B as Mr Booby, Pamela as a calculating hussy, and morality equated with expediency throughout. Richardson was convinced the work was Fielding's and never forgave him.

Shandean, derived from 'shandy', a word of obscure origin, meaning 'crack-brained, half-crazy', now used to describe anyone or anything reminiscent of Sterne's *Tristram Shandy*.

Shandon, Captain, a character in Thackeray's *Pendennis*.

Shandy, Tristram, Walter, Mrs, and Captain Tobias (Toby), see TRISTRAM SHANDY.

SHARP, Cecil (1859–1924), English folk-music collector and editor. He transcribed during the course of his life a total of 4,977 tunes, of which he published 1,118.

Sharp, Rebecca (Becky), a leading character in Thackeray's *Vanity Fair*.

SHARP, William ('Fiona Macleod') (1855–1905), wrote under his own name essays, verse, minor novels, and Lives of *Rossetti (1882), *Shelley (1887), and R. *Browning (1890). He is chiefly remembered for his mystic Celtic tales and romances of peasant life by 'Fiona Macleod' written in the manner of the *'Celtic twilight' movement. These include *Pharais* (1893), *The Mountain Lovers* (1895), *The Sin Eater* (1895), and several plays.

Shaving of Shagpat, The, an *Arabian Entertainment*, a series of eastern fantasies by G. *Meredith, published 1856.

SHAW (George) Bernard (1856–1950), born in Dublin, came to London in 1876. After an unsuccessful career as a novelist, he wrote music, art, and book criticism for several periodicals including the *Pall Mall Gazette* (1885–8) and *The Star* (1888–90, as 'Corno di Bassetto'). His music criticism has been collected as *Shaw's Music* (3 vols, 1981; ed. Dan H. Laurence). As drama critic for *The Saturday Review* (1895–8) he produced a series of remarkable and controversial weekly articles (published as *Our Theatres in the Nineties*, 3 vols, 1932), voicing his impatience with the artificiality of the London theatre and pleading for the performance of plays dealing with contemporary social and moral problems. During these years he joined several literary and political societies, notably the *Fabian Society; he edited and contributed to *Fabian Essays in Socialism* (1889) and wrote many tracts setting down his socialist and collectivist

principles. He was a freethinker, a supporter of women's rights, and an advocate of equality of income, the abolition of private property, and a radical change in the voting system. He also campaigned for the simplification of spelling and punctuation and the reform of the English alphabet. He was well known as a journalist and public speaker when his first play, *Widowers' Houses* (pub. 1893), was produced in 1892. There followed *Arms and the Man* (1894, pub. 1898: later turned into a musical called *The Chocolate Soldier*), *The Devil's Disciple* (perf. NY 1897, pub. 1901), *You Never Can Tell* (1899, pub. 1898), *Caesar and Cleopatra* (pub. 1901, perf. Berlin 1906), *Mrs Warren's Profession* (pub. 1898, perf. 1902), and *John Bull's Other Island* (1904, pub. NY 1907), a play which, thanks to its characteristic 'Shavian' wit, brought his first popular success in London.

Shaw wrote over 50 plays, including *Man and Superman* (pub. 1903, perf. 1905), *Major Barbara* (1905, pub. 1907), *The Doctor's Dilemma* (1906, pub. Berlin 1908), *Getting Married* (1908, pub. Berlin 1910), *Androcles and the Lion* (pub. Berlin 1912, perf. Hamburg 1913), *Pygmalion* (perf. Vienna 1913, pub. Berlin 1913, later turned into a popular musical *My Fair Lady*), *Heartbreak House* (pub. 1919, perf. 1920, both NY), *Back to Methuselah* (perf. and pub. NY 1921), *Saint Joan* (perf. NY 1923, pub. 1924), *The Apple Cart* (perf. Warsaw 1929, pub. Berlin 1929), and *Too True to be Good* (perf. Boston 1932, pub. Berlin 1932).

These plays were published with lengthy prefaces in which Shaw clearly expresses his views as a non-romantic and a champion of the thinking man. The dramatic conflict in his plays is the conflict of thought and belief, not that of neurosis or physical passion. Discussion is the basis of the plays, and his great wit and intelligence won audiences over to the idea that mental and moral passion could produce absorbing dramatic material. He believed that war, disease, and the present brevity of our lifespan frustrate the 'Life Force' (see under MAN AND SUPERMAN) and that functional adaptation, a current of creative evolution activated by the power of human will, was essential to any real progress, and indeed to the survival of the species. Shaw's unorthodox views, his humour, and his love of paradox have become an institution. Amongst his other works should be mentioned *The Quintessence of Ibsenism* (1891, revised and expanded 1913), which reveals his debt to Ibsen as a playwright and presents an argument for Fabian Socialism; *The Perfect Wagnerite* (1898); *Common Sense About the War* (1914); *The Intelligent Woman's Guide to Socialism and Capitalism* (1928); and *Everybody's Political What's What* (1944). Shaw's correspondence with the actresses Ellen *Terry and Mrs Patrick Campbell and other letters have been published in volumes.

In 1898 Shaw married Charlotte Payne-

Townshend and they lived together until her death in 1943. He was a strict vegetarian and never drank spirits, coffee, or tea. He was awarded the *Nobel Prize in 1925.

SHAW, Henry Wheeler (1818–85), American comic essayist and philosopher who wrote under the pseudonym 'Josh Billings'.

SHEFFIELD, John, 3rd earl of Mulgrave and afterwards 1st duke of Buckingham and Normanby (1648–1721), a patron of *Dryden and a friend of *Pope. He wrote an *Essay upon Satire* (published anonymously, ?1680), and an *Essay upon Poetry* (1682) of no great value.

SHELLEY, Mary Wollstonecraft (1797–1851), only daughter of W. *Godwin and Mary *Wollstonecraft. In 1814 she left England with P. B. *Shelley, and married him in 1816 on the death of his wife Harriet. Only one of their children, Percy, survived infancy. She is best remembered as the author of *Frankenstein, or the Modern Prometheus* (1818), but wrote several other works. *Valperga* (1823), is a romance set in 14th-cent. Italy. *The Last Man* (1826), a novel set in the future, describes England as a republic, and the gradual destruction of the human race by plague; its narrator, Lionel Verney, finds himself as the last survivor amidst the ruined grandeurs of Rome in the year 2100, an interesting variation on the 'noble savage' motif (see PRIMITIVISM). The same motif is seen in *Lodore* (1835). She wrote other novels, biographies, and short stories, most of which were published in *The Keepsake*; some have *science fiction elements, others are *Gothic or historical, and many are continental in setting. Her *Rambles in Germany and Italy, in 1840, 1842 and 1843* (1844) was well received. She also edited her husband's poems (1830) and his essays, letters, etc. (1840).

SHELLEY, Percy Bysshe (1792–1822), born at Field Place, Sussex, and educated at University College, Oxford; his conventional upbringing made him deeply unhappy and rebellious.

In his teens he privately published a series of *Gothic-horror novelettes including *Zastrozzi* (1810). At Oxford he dressed and behaved with provoking eccentricity, and in March 1811 was summarily expelled for circulating a pamphlet, *The Necessity of *Atheism*, written with his friend T. J. *Hogg. He eloped to Scotland with 16-year-old Harriet Westbrook and they married in Edinburgh in August 1811, though Shelley disapproved of matrimony, as well as royalty, meat-eating, and religion. Three years of nomadic existence followed. In Dublin he spoke on public platforms, and published *An Address to the Irish People* (1812) and *Proposals* for reform associations. Much of his early philosophy, both in poetry and politics, is expressed in *Queen Mab* (1813), which shows Shelley as the direct heir to the French and British revolutionary intellectuals of the 1790s.

In 1814 his marriage with Harriet collapsed, despite the birth of two children and the kindly intervention of *Peacock. After suicidal scenes, Shelley eloped abroad with Mary Godwin (see above), together with her 15-year-old stepsister Jane 'Claire' Clairmont: their triangular relationship endured for the next eight years. His unfinished novella *The Assassins* (1814) reflects their dreamy travels through post-war France, Switzerland, and Germany, as does their combined journal, *History of a Six Weeks Tour* (1817). He returned to London and lived with Mary on the edge of Windsor Great Park. Here he wrote *Alastor* (1816), which first brought him general notice and reviews. The summer of 1816 was spent on Lake Geneva with *Byron, and Shelley composed two philosophic poems much influenced by *Wordsworth, the 'Hymn to Intellectual Beauty' (partly about his childhood) and 'Monte Blanc', a meditation on the nature of power in a Godless universe.

In the autumn of 1816 Harriet drowned herself in the Serpentine. Shelley immediately married Mary and began a Chancery case for the custody of his first two children, which he lost. The experience shook him deeply, and is recalled in many verse fragments, such as the 'Invocation to Misery', and the cursing 'To the Lord Chancellor' (1817—a so-called *'flyting'). However, friendships developed with Leigh *Hunt, *Keats, *Hazlitt, and others of the liberal *Examiner circle; while Peacock, now an intimate family confidant, drew a portrait of Shelley as Scythrop Glowry in *Nightmare Abbey*. In 1817 the family settled at Great Marlow where Shelley wrote his polemical 'Hermit of Marlow' pamphlets, and slowly composed 'Laon and Cythna', which was published, with alterations to avoid prosecution, as *The Revolt of Islam* (1818).

Harried by creditors, ill-health, and 'social hatred', Shelley took his household to Italy in the spring of 1818, leaving behind his sonnet 'Ozymandias'. He stayed at Lucca, where he translated Plato's *Symposium* and wrote a daring essay 'On the Manners of the Ancient Greeks'; and then at Venice and Este, where he composed *'Julian and Maddalo'.

His domestic situation was increasingly strained. His little daughter Clara had died at Venice; his favourite son William ('Willmouse') died at Rome and Mary suffered a nervous breakdown. The shaken family settled in Tuscany: first outside Livorno and finally at Pisa, which became their more or less permanent home until 1822.

The twelve months from the summer of 1819 saw Shelley's major period of activity. He completed *Prometheus Unbound* and wrote *The Mask of Anarchy*; *'Ode to the West Wind'; the satirical *Peter Bell The Third*; his long political odes, 'To Liberty' and 'To Naples'; the 'Letter to Maria Gisborne'; and the *'Witch of Atlas'. Much of this work was inspired by news of political events, which also produced 'Young Parson Richards', 'Song to the Men of England', and 'Sonnet: England 1819'. At the same time he composed several pure lyric pieces, including 'To a Skylark' and 'The Cloud', of dazzling metrical virtuosity; and completed *The Cenci.

The quieter period at Pisa which followed (1820–1), saw him at work on a number of prose pieces: *A Philosophical View of Reform (1820); the impish 'Essay on the Devil'; and his *Defence of Poetry (1821). He also wrote some of his most delicate, low-keyed, and visually suggestive short poems: 'The Two Spirits', 'To the Moon', 'The Aziola', and 'Evening: Ponte Al Mare, Pisa'.

In the spring of 1821 news of the death of Keats in Rome produced *Adonais. His platonic love-affair with Emilia Viviani, a beautiful 17-year-old heiress, resulted in *Epipsychidion (1821).

In the winter of 1821 Byron also moved to Pisa, and a raffish circle formed round the two poets, including E. J. *Trelawny, Edward and Jane Williams, and eventually Leigh Hunt. Shelley's last completed verse drama, *Hellas (1822), was inspired by the Greek war of independence.

In April 1822 he moved his household to the bay of Lerici. Here he began *The Triumph of Life, and he composed a number of short lyrics, some to Jane Williams, of striking melodic grace: 'When the lamp is shattered', and the melancholy 'Lines Written in the Bay of Lerici'. Shelley was drowned in August 1822, in his small schooner the 'Ariel', together with Edward Williams and an English boatboy, on a return trip from visiting Byron and Hunt at Livorno.

His lyric powers and romantic biography have until recently obscured Shelley's most enduring qualities as a writer: his intellectual courage and originality; his hatred of oppression and injustice; and his mischievous, sometimes macabre, sense of humour. He translated from Greek (Plato and Homer), Latin (Spinoza), Spanish (Calderón), German (Goethe), Italian (Dante), and some Arabic fragments. His essays—very few published in his lifetime—are highly intelligent, his political pamphlets both angry and idealistic.

His weaknesses as a writer have always been evident: rhetorical abstraction; intellectual arrogance; and moments of intense self-pity. Among the English Romantics, he has recovered his position as an undoubted major figure: the poet of volcanic hope for a better world, of fiery aspirations shot upwards through bitter gloom.

Shelley's Letters have been edited by F. L. Jones (2 vols, 1964); the standard Life remains that by N. O. White (2 vols, 1947).

SHENSTONE, William (1714–63), poet, essayist and landscape gardener of the Leasowes, Halesowen, published his Poems Upon Various Occasions (1737) and established his reputation with The Judgement of Hercules (1741) and The Schoolmistress (1742). His poetic works included elegies, odes, songs, ballads, and levities, the most famous being 'A Pastoral Ballad' and 'Lines written at an Inn'. From 1743 he transformed the Leasowes, a grazing farm, into a ferme ornée, an early example of a natural landscape garden. His poetry, mainly pastoral in treatment, was popular in the 18th cent.; his 'Essays on Men and Manners', in the style of La Rochefoucauld, included his views on 'landskip gardening'; his essay on elegy contributed to the development of that form.

Shepheardes Calender, The, the earliest important work of *Spenser (1579), dedicated to *Sidney. It was illustrated by woodcuts and had accompanying glosses by one 'E.K.' (see KIRKE, E.).

It consists of twelve eclogues, one for each month of the year, written in different metres, and modelled on the eclogues of *Theocritus, *Virgil, and more modern writers, such as *Mantuan and Marot. They take the form of dialogues among shepherds, except the first and last, which are complaints by 'Colin Clout', the author himself. Four of them deal with love, one is in praise of Elisa (Queen Elizabeth), one a lament for a 'mayden of greate bloud', four deal allegorically with matters of religion or conduct, one describes a singing-match, and one laments the contempt in which poetry is held.

SHEPHERD, Lord Clifford, The, Henry de Clifford, 14th Baron Clifford (?1455–1523), celebrated in *Wordsworth's 'Brougham Castle' and The White Doe of Rylstone. His father was attainted and his estates forfeited in 1461. Henry de Clifford was brought up as a shepherd, and restored to his estates and title on the accession of Henry VII.

Shepherd's Calendar, The, a volume of verse by J. *Clare.

Shepherd's Hunting, The, pastorals written by *Wither in the Marshalsea.

Shepherd's Week, The, a series of six pastorals by J. *Gay, published 1714.

They are eclogues in mock-classical style, five of them based more or less closely on *Virgil, but presenting shepherds and milkmaids not of the golden age but of the poet's day, in their earthy simplicity. They were designed to parody those of A. *Phillips. Gay portrays his rustic characters (Blouzelinda, Bowzybeus, Cloddipole, Grubbinol, etc.) at work as well as at play, and paints (in his own words) a 'lively landscape'.

SHEPPARD, John, 'Jack Sheppard' (1702–24), a notorious thief and highwayman, who, after repeated escapes from prison, was hanged at Tyburn. He was the subject of tracts by *Defoe, of many plays and ballads, and of a novel by W. H. *Ainsworth. See NEWGATE CALENDAR.

SHERIDAN, Frances (1724–66), wife of Thomas and the mother of R. B. Sheridan (below). She was greatly encouraged in her writing by *Richardson, who arranged for the publication of *The Memoirs of Miss Sydney Biddulph* ('after the manner of *Pamela*') (1761, expanded 1767). Her other works include *The Discovery* (1763), a comedy, and *The History of Nourjahad* (1767), a much admired and highly moral *Oriental novel.

SHERIDAN, Richard Brinsley (1751–1816), the son of Thomas Sheridan, an Irish actor-manager, and Mrs F. *Sheridan. He fell in love with (and in 1773 married) Eliza Linley, a beautiful and accomplished young singer, with whom he eloped to France. Very short of money, he decided to try his hand at a play, and in a very few weeks wrote *The Rivals*, produced at Covent Garden in 1775. It established Sheridan in the fashionable society he sought and was followed in the same year by the farce *St Patrick's Day* and *The Duenna*, and in 1777 by *A Trip to Scarborough*. In 1776 Sheridan, with partners, bought *Garrick's half-share in the *Drury Lane Theatre and became its manager. He was elected a member of Dr *Johnson's *Club in 1777, and *The School for Scandal* was produced in the same year. The play was universally acclaimed, but nevertheless Sheridan's financial anxieties became even more acute. In 1779 he became sole proprietor of Drury Lane and produced his new play *The Critic*. In spite of the success of his plays, Sheridan wished to shine only in politics. He became the friend and ally of *Fox and in 1780 won the seat at Stafford. In 1783 he became secretary to the Treasury and established his reputation as a brilliant orator in the House of Commons. In 1787 *Burke persuaded him into supporting the impeachment of Warren Hastings, and his eloquent speech of over five hours on the Begums of Oude ensured that he was made manager of the trial. He became a friend of the prince regent and other royal figures. Eliza died in 1792, and in the same year the Drury Lane Theatre had to be demolished. Sheridan raised £150,000 for a new theatre. In 1795 he married Esther Ogle. *Pizarro*, a historical tragedy adapted by Sheridan from Kotzebue, was performed in 1799. Sheridan's friendship with Fox was fading, and when Grenville formed the 'ministry of all the talents' in 1806 Sheridan was offered only the treasurership to the navy. In 1809 the new Drury Lane was destroyed by fire, in 1811 he lost his seat at Stafford, and in 1813 he was arrested for debt. He is remembered chiefly as the author of two superb comedies, but his speeches and letters have also been published.

***Sheriffs of Bristol,** A Letter to the,* see LETTER TO THE SHERIFFS OF BRISTOL, A.

SHERRIFF, R(obert) C(edric) (1896–1975), playwright. His best-known play was *Journey's End* (1928, pub. 1929), based on his experiences in the trenches as a captain during the First World War. Realistic and low-key, it portrays the relationships under stress of Captain Stanhope, new lieutenant Raleigh, the reliable second-in-command Osborne, the cowardly Hibbert, etc., and ends in mid-battle after the deaths of Osborne and Raleigh. Other plays include *Badger's Green* (1930); *St Helena* (1934); *Home at Seven* (1950); and *The White Carnation* (1953).

SHERWOOD, Mrs Mary Martha (1775–1851), author of numerous books of stories and tracts, many for children and young people, the best known of which is *The History of the Fairchild Family* (3 parts, 1818–47).

***She Stoops to Conquer,** or The Mistakes of a Night,* a comedy by *Goldsmith, produced 1773.

The principal characters are Hardcastle, Mrs Hardcastle, and Miss Hardcastle their daughter; Mrs Hardcastle's son by a former marriage, Tony Lumpkin, a frequenter of the Three Jolly Pigeons, idle, ignorant, cunning and mischievous, and doted on by his mother; and young Marlow. His father, Sir Charles Marlow, has proposed a match between young Marlow and Miss Hardcastle, and the young man and his friend Hastings accordingly travel down to pay the Hardcastles a visit. Losing their way they arrive at night at the Three Jolly Pigeons, where Tony Lumpkin directs them to a neighbouring inn, which is in reality the Hardcastles' house. The fun of the play arises largely from the resulting misunderstanding, Marlow treating Hardcastle as the landlord of the supposed inn, and making violent love to Miss Hardcastle, whom he takes for one of the servants. The arrival of Sir Charles Marlow clears up the misconception and all ends well.

The play was seen as a victory in the newly formulated battle against 'that monster called *Sentimental Comedy' (*London Magazine, 1773).

***She wou'd if she cou'd,** the second of the comedies by *Etherege, produced 1668.

It contrasts town and country manners in a plot which describes the adventures in London of Sir Oliver and Lady Cockwood, and Sir Joslin Jolley and his young kinswomen Ariana and Gatty.

Shimei, name for Slingsby Bethel in Dryden's *Absalom and Achitophel*.

'Shipman's Tale, The', see CANTERBURY TALES, 15.

Ship of Fools, The, an adaptation of the famous *Narrenschiff* of Sebastian Brant. The *Narrenschiff* was written in the dialect of Swabia and first published in 1494. It became extremely popular and was translated into many languages. Its theme is the shipping off of fools of all kinds from their native land to the Land of Fools.

It was translated into English 'out of Laten, Frenche, and Doche' by A. *Barclay, and published in England in 1509; the translation is not literal but is an adaptation to English conditions, and gives a picture of contemporary English life. The work is interesting as an early collection of satirical types.

Shipwreck, The, see FALCONER, W.

Shirburn Ballads, The, edited in 1907 by Andrew Clark from a manuscript of 1600–16 (a few pieces are later) at Shirburn Castle, Oxfordshire, belonging to the earl of Macclesfield. The collection contains ballads not found elsewhere, dealing with political events, with legends and fairy-tales, or with stories of domestic life. Some of them are homilies.

Shirley, a novel by C. *Brontë, published 1849.

The scene of the story is Yorkshire, and the period the latter part of the Napoleonic wars, the time of the *Luddite riots. Robert Gérard Moore, half English, a mill-owner of determined character, persists in introducing the latest labour-saving machinery, undeterred by the opposition of the workers, which culminates in an attempt first to destroy his mill, and finally to take his life. To overcome his financial difficulties he proposes to Shirley Keeldar, an heiress of independent spirit; he himself loves not her but his gentle and retiring cousin Caroline Helstone, who is pining away for love of him and through enforced idleness in the oppressive atmosphere of her uncle's rectory. Robert is indignantly rejected by Shirley, who is in fact in love with his brother Louis, a tutor in her family. The misunderstandings are resolved, and the two couples united.

This is Charlotte Brontë's most social novel, and one of its recurrent themes is its plea for more useful occupations for women, condemned by society either to matrimony or, as old maids, to a life of self-denial and acts of private charity. Charlotte told Mrs *Gaskell that Shirley was intended to be what Emily *Brontë might have been 'had she been placed in health and prosperity'.

SHIRLEY, James (1596–1666), was educated at St John's College, Oxford, and St Catherine's Hall, Cambridge. He took Anglican orders, was a schoolmaster until 1624, and then converted to Roman Catholicism. He wrote plays for the Cockpit Theatre until 1636. In the dedication to his play *The Bird in a Cage* (1632–3), he sarcastically complimented *Prynne, who was then in prison awaiting trial for writing *Histriomastix*. Perhaps because of this dedication, Shirley was made a member of Gray's Inn and invited to supply the literary part of the Inns of Court masque *The Triumph of Peace* (1634).

During the Civil War he was in the royalist army under the earl of *Newcastle, his patron. After the defeat of the royalist cause he returned to his career as a schoolmaster. His *Contention of Ajax and Ulysses* (pub. 1659), written during this period, is largely a dramatic debate interspersed with songs, one of which, 'The glories of our blood and state', was a favourite with Charles II.

Shirley wrote some forty dramas, most of which are extant, including *The Traitor* (1631), *Hyde Park* (1632), *The Gamester* (1633), *The Lady of Pleasure* (1635), and *The Cardinal* (1641). He had a considerable reputation in his lifetime and died very well off; Dryden's bracketing of him with *Heywood and *Shadwell in *Mac-Flecknoe* probably does not represent a considered judgement of his work.

SHIRLEY, John (?1366–1456), the scribe of many works of *Chaucer, *Lydgate, and others, whose attributions have been particularly important for the ascriptions to Chaucer of some of the shorter poems. He translated a number of works from French and Latin.

Shoemaker's Holiday, The, or A pleasant comedie of the Gentle Craft, a comedy by *Dekker, written 1599, published 1600.

Rowland Lacy, a kinsman of the earl of Lincoln, loves Rose, the daughter of the lord mayor of London. To prevent the match the earl sends him to France in command of a company of men. Lacy resigns his place to a friend and, disguised as a Dutch shoemaker, takes service with Simon *Eyre, who supplies the family of the lord mayor with shoes. Here he successfully pursues his suit, is married and is pardoned by the king. The most entertaining character in the play is that of Eyre, the cheery, eccentric mastershoemaker, who becomes lord mayor of London. See also DELONEY, T.

SHORE, Jane (d. ?1527), mistress of Edward IV, over whom she exercised great influence by her beauty and wit. She was accused by Richard III of sorcery, imprisoned, and made to do public penance in 1483, and she died in poverty.

She is the subject of a ballad included in Percy's *Reliques*, of *Churchyard's *Shore's Wife* in *Mirror for Magistrates*, of a remarkable passage in Sir T. *More's *History of Richard III*, of a descriptive note by *Drayton (*Englands Heroicall Epistles*), and of a tragedy by *Rowe.

Short, Codlin and, see CODLIN.

Shortest Way with the Dissenters, see DEFOE, D.

SHORTHOUSE, Joseph Henry (1834–1903), is remembered as the author of the historical novel *John Inglesant* (1881), an evocation of 17th-cent. religious intrigue and faith. Inglesant becomes a tool of the Jesuit faction, joins the court of Charles I, and after the king's death visits Italy to seek vengeance for his brother's murder; the most interesting part of the book is an account of N. *Ferrar's religious community at *Little Gidding; the novel bears witness to the religious and historical interests revived by the *Oxford Movement and the *Pre-Raphaelites.

Short-Title Catalogue, see BIBLIOGRAPHICAL SOCIETY.

Short View *of the Immorality and Profaneness of the English Stage,* see COLLIER, JEREMY.

Shropshire Lad, A, see HOUSMAN, A. E.

Shylock, in Shakespeare's *The Merchant of Venice,* the Jewish usurer.

Sibylline Leaves, a volume of poems by S. T. *Coleridge.

SIDDAL, E., see ROSSETTI, D. G.

SIDDONS, Mrs Sarah (1755–1831), sister of C. and J. P. *Kemble. In 1782 she was heralded as a tragic actress without peer. Her great roles were in tragic and heroic parts: Jane *Shore, in *Rowe's play of that name, Belvidera in Otway's *Venice Preserv'd,* Shakespearian heroines, and in particular Lady Macbeth.

SIDGWICK, Henry (1838–1900), professor of moral philosophy at Cambridge from 1883. A follower in economics and politics of J. S. *Mill, his attitude on the question of our knowledge of the external world resembles that of *Reid. His reputation rests on *The Methods of Ethics* (1874). Here he considers three 'methods' of determining the right course of action: intuitionism, according to which we have direct apprehension of moral principles; egoism, according to which an agent's own interests determine what he should do; Utilitarianism, according to which right and wrong are fixed by considerations of the interests of everyone affected by our actions.

SIDNEY, Algernon (1622–83), the grand-nephew of Sir P. *Sidney, took up arms against Charles I and was wounded at Marston Moor. He was employed on government service until the Restoration, but his firm republicanism aroused *Cromwell's hostility. At the Restoration he refused to give pledges to Charles II, and lived abroad in poverty and exile until 1677. He was imprisoned in the Tower after the discovery of the Rye House plot, and condemned to death without adequate evidence, though there was little doubt of his guilt. His *Discourses concerning Government* were published in 1698, and a treatise on *Love* in 1884.

SIDNEY, Sir Philip (1554–86), born at *Penshurst Place, eldest son of Sir Henry Sidney (who was thrice lord deputy governor of Ireland). Between 1572 and 1575 he travelled in France, where he witnessed the massacre of St Bartholomew's day in Paris, and in Germany, Austria, and Italy. After his return to England, Sidney did not achieve any official post which matched his ambitions until his appointment as governor of Flushing in 1585. His knighthood was awarded for reasons of court protocol in 1582.

Years of comparative idleness enabled him to write and revise the *Arcadia, and to complete the *Defence of Poetry, *The Lady of May,* and *Astrophel and Stella.* The first *Arcadia,* and probably other works, were composed while he was staying with his younger sister Mary, countess of *Pembroke, at Wilton. We do not know his exact relations with Penelope Devereux (later *Rich), whose father's dying wish had been that she should marry Philip Sidney. Though this did not happen (Philip in 1583 marrying Frances, daughter of Sir Francis Walsingham), verbal and heraldic references leave no room for doubt that she was the 'Stella' of Sidney's sonnet sequence. During these years Sidney also became a notable literary patron, receiving dedications from a variety of authors, the best known being that of Spenser's *The Shepheardes Calender* in 1579. Sidney was interested in experimenting with classical metres in English, but it is unlikely that his discussion of this and other matters with *Greville, *Dyer, and *Spenser (the 'Areopagus') amounted to anything so formal as an academy or learned society. The last year of his life was spent in the Netherlands, and on 22 Sept. 1586 he led an attack on a Spanish convoy bringing supplies to the fortified city of Zutphen; he died as a result of musket shot in his thigh. Sidney was buried in St Paul's Cathedral, and the almost immediate appearance of volumes of Latin elegies from Oxford, Cambridge, and the Continent testified to the great political and literary promise he had shown. Among many English elegies on him the best known, Spenser's *'Astrophel', was not printed until 1595, among his *Complaints.*

None of Sidney's works were published during his lifetime, but Greville and the countess of Pembroke seem to have taken pains to preserve the texts they thought best. Editions of the *Arcadia* from 1598 onwards included all the literary works except his version of the Psalms.

These were completed posthumously by his sister, and not printed until 1823.

SIDNEY, Sir Robert (1563–1626), the younger brother of Sir P. *Sidney. His early career closely followed that of his brother, whom he succeeded as governor of Flushing in 1588. He was created Baron Sidney by James I in 1603, Viscount Lisle in 1605, and earl of Leicester in 1618. It has been claimed that he wrote lyrics for settings by Robert Dowland, his godson. An autograph manuscript of his poems, consisting of sonnets, pastorals, songs, and epigrams, apparently written in the mid-1590s, was identified by P. J. Croft in 1973.

'Sidney's sister, Pembroke's mother', see BROWNE, W.

Siege of Corinth, The, a poem by Lord *Byron, published 1816, founded on the story of the Turkish siege of Corinth, then held by the Venetians.

Siege of Rhodes, The, one of the earliest attempts at English opera, by *D'Avenant, performed 1656.

Dramatic performances having been suppressed by the Commonwealth government, D'Avenant obtained permission in 1656 to produce at Rutland House an 'Entertainment after the manner of the ancients'; this was accompanied by vocal and instrumental music, composed by Henry *Lawes. Immediately after this prologue was given *The Siege of Rhodes* (at first in one, but in 1662 in two parts), a heroic play, the 'story sung in recitative music', which was composed by Dr Charles Coleman and George Hudson. The play deals with the siege of Rhodes by Solyman the Magnificent, and the devotion by which Ianthe, wife of the Sicilian Duke Alphonso, saves her husband and the defenders of the island.

Siege Perilous, see ROUND TABLE.

Sigismonda (Ghismonda), in Boccaccio's *Decameron* (IV. i), daughter of Tancred, prince of Salerno. Her father, having discovered her love for her squire Guiscardo, slew the latter and sent his heart in a golden cup to Sigismonda, who took poison and died. The father, repenting his cruelty, caused the pair to be buried in the same tomb. The story is the subject of *Dryden's 'Sigismunda and Guiscardo', and of Robert Wilmot's *Tancred and Gismund*. James *Thomson's *Tancred and Sigismunda* (1745) deals with a different story.

Sigmund, in the *Volsunga saga* and in W. Morris's *Sigurd the Volsung*, the son of King Volsung and the father of Sigurd.

Sigurd the Volsung and the Fall of the Niblungs, The Story of, an epic in anapaestic couplets by W.

*Morris, founded on the *Volsunga saga*, and published 1876.

It is in four books; the first, 'Sigmund', is the story of Volsung's son Sigmund and of the fatal marriage of his sister Signy to the king of the Goths; the second and third, 'Regin' and 'Brynhild', deal with Sigmund's son Sigurd, his betrothal to Brynhild, his subsequent marriage (under the influence of a magic potion) to Gudrun, the Niblung king's daughter, and the deaths of Sigurd and Brynhild; the last, 'Gudrun', tells of Gudrun's own death and the fall of the Niblungs. (See also SAGA.)

Sikes, Bill, a character in Dickens's *Oliver Twist.*

Silas Marner, a novel by G. *Eliot, published 1861.

Silas Marner, a linen-weaver, driven out of a small religious community by a false charge of theft, takes refuge in the agricultural village of Raveloe. His only consolation in his loneliness is his growing pile of gold. This is stolen from his cottage by the squire's reprobate son Dunstan Cass, who disappears. Dunstan's elder brother Godfrey is in love with Nancy Lammeter, but is secretly and unhappily married to a woman of low class in a neighbouring town. Meditating revenge for Godfrey's refusal to acknowledge her, this woman carries her child one New Year's Eve to Raveloe, intending to force her way into the Casses' house; but dies in the snow. Her child, Eppie, finds her way into Silas's cottage and is adopted by him. After many years the draining of a pond near Silas's door reveals the body of Dunstan with the gold. Moved by this revelation, Godfrey, now married to Nancy, acknowledges himself the father of Eppie and claims her, but she refuses to leave Silas.

Silence, in Shakespeare's 2 *Henry IV*, a country justice.

Silent Woman, The, see EPICENE.

SILKIN, Jon (1930–), poet. His first volume, *The Peaceable Kingdom* (1954), was followed by many others, including *Nature with Man* (1965), which contains many of his piercingly observed 'flower poems'), *Amana Grass* (1971), and *The Principle of Water* (1974); his *Selected Poems* was published in 1980. He founded the literary quarterly *Stand* in 1950.

SILLITOE, Alan (1928–), writer, whose first volume of verse, *Without Beer or Bread* (1957), was followed by his much praised first novel, *Saturday Night and Sunday Morning* (1958). The tiny story of *The Loneliness of the Long Distance Runner* (1959) is the first-person portrait of a rebellious and anarchic Borstal boy who refuses both literally and metaphorically to play the games of the establishment. Many other works followed, including the novels *The Death of William Posters* (1965); *A Tree on Fire* (1967) and *A Start in Life* (1970); the semi-autobiographical *Raw Material* (1972), a vivid evocation of his own family ancestry and working-class attitudes to the First World War and the Depression; *Men Women and Children* (1973), a collection of short stories; *Mountains and Caverns* (1975), a collection of autobiographical and critical essays; *The Widower's Son* (1976, a novel). He has also published several volumes of poetry, including *Storm and other poems* (1974) and *Barbarians and other poems* (1974), and written plays and screenplays from his own fiction.

Silver-fork school, see FASHIONABLE NOVEL.

Silvia, in Shakespeare's *The Two Gentlemen of Verona*, the duke of Milan's daughter. The famous song 'Who is Silvia?' (IV. ii) is addressed to her.

Simile, an object, scene, or action, introduced by way of comparison for explanatory, illustrative, or merely ornamental purpose, e.g. 'as strong as an ox', or more poetically, 'The moon, like a flower | In Heaven's high bower | With silent delight | Sits and smiles on the night' (Blake, 'Night', *Songs of Innocence*); or, in more *Modernist vein, 'the evening is spread out against the sky | Like a patient etherised upon a table' (T. S. *Eliot, 'The Love Song of J. Alfred Prufrock'). See also EPIC SIMILE.

SIMON EYRE, see EYRE.

Simon Legree, the brutal slave-owner in H. B. *Stowe's *Uncle Tom's Cabin*, who beats Tom to death.

Simon Pure, a character in S. Centlivre's *A Bold Stroke for a Wife*.

Simple Story, A, a romance by Mrs *Inchbald, published 1791.

Simpliciad, The, an anonymous parody of *Wordsworth, published 1808.

SIMPSON, N(orman) F(rederick) (1919–), playwright, whose surreal comedies *A Resounding Tinkle* (perf. 1957) and *One-Way Pendulum* (perf. 1959) established him as a writer of the Theatre of the *Absurd.

SINCLAIR, Catherine (1800–64), Scottish writer of travel, biography, children's books, novels, essays, and reflections. In her classic children's novel *Holiday House* (1839) she made a conscious stand against the prevailing fashion for moralizing tales for the young.

SINCLAIR, May (Mary Amelia St Clair Sinclair) (1863–1946), novelist, a supporter of *Women's Suffrage. Among the most notable of her 24 novels are *The Divine Fire* (1904), *The Three Sisters* (1914, a study in female frustration with echoes of the *Brontë story), *The Tree of Heaven* (1917), *Mary Olivier: a life* (1919), and *Life and Death of Harriett Frean* (1922). The last two are *stream-of-consciousness novels, taking a woman from girlhood to unmarried middle age, and both show themselves keenly aware (though not necessarily wholly critical) of woman's tendencies towards self-denial. Her novels had a considerable influence on R. *West and R. *Lehmann, but were largely forgotten until their revival (by Virago) in the 1980s.

SINCLAIR, Upton Beall (1878–1968), American novelist and journalist. He is best known for his novel *The Jungle* (1906), an exposé of the Chicago meat-packing industry to which the public reacted so violently that an investigation of the yards was instituted by the US government. Sinclair's many other works include *The Metropolis* (1908), *King Coal* (1917), *Oil!* (1927), and *Boston* (1928); and a series featuring Lanny Budd, illegitimate son of a munitions manufacturer, who appears in *World's End* (1940), *Dragon's Teeth* (1942), *The Return of Lanny Budd* (1953), and other works.

Sindbad of the Sea, or *Sindbad the Sailor*, one of the tales of the *Arabian Nights. Sindbad, a rich young man of Baghdad, having wasted much of his wealth in prodigal living, undertakes a number of sea voyages as a merchant and meets with various marvellous adventures. The best known are those of the Roc, a huge bird that could lift elephants in its claws, and of the Old Man of the Sea.

SINGER, Isaac Bashevis (1904–), Polish-born Yiddish author. In 1935 he emigrated to New York, in the footsteps of his brother, the novelist Israel Joshua Singer (1893–1944), and became a journalist, writing in Yiddish for the *Jewish Daily Forward*, which published most of his short stories. The first of his works to be translated into English was *The Family Moscat* (1950), which was followed by many other works including *Satan in Goray* (Yiddish, 1935; English, 1955); *The Magician of Lublin* (1960); *The Slave* (1962); *The Manor* (1967) and its sequel *The Estate* (1969). His collections of stories include *Gimpel the Fool* (1957); *The Spinoza of Market Street* (1961); *Zlateh the Goat* (1966); and *A Friend of Kafka* (1970). Singer's work portrays with a colourful intensity and much realistic detail the lives of Polish Jews of many periods of Polish history, illuminated by hints of the mystic and supernatural; many of his novels and stories describe the conflicts between traditional religion and rising scepticism, between varying forms of nationalism, and between the primitive, the exotic, and the intellectually progressive. He was awarded the *Nobel Prize for literature in 1978.

Singleton, Adventures of Captain, a romance of adventure by *Defoe, published 1720.

Sinister Street, a novel by C. *Mackenzie.

Sinners, Beware, a 13th-cent. homiletic poem in 354 lines of 6-line rhyming stanzas, concerned with the pains of Hell and the *Seven Deadly Sins.

Sir Charles Grandison, a novel by S. *Richardson, published 1754.

Richardson had been thinking of the portrayal of a 'Good Man' to balance his female creations in *Pamela and *Clarissa. The novel, again *epistolary in form, is the only one set in aristocratic and wealthy society, of which Richardson had little personal knowledge.

The beautiful and accomplished Harriet Byron comes to London, where she attracts many admirers, among them the wealthy and unscrupulous Sir Hargreve Pollexfen. When she refuses his advances he has her abducted from a masquerade, then after the failure of a secret marriage ceremony has her carried off into the country. Sir Charles, hearing her cries from the coach, rescues her and gives her into the care of his kindly married sister. He and Harriet fall in love, but on the day she learns of his love for her he has to set out for Italy. There, in the past, he has become involved with one of the noblest-born women in Europe, Clementina Porretta, but religious differences have kept them apart. Clementina's unhappiness has deranged her mind, and her parents, now prepared to accept any terms for the cure of their daughter, summon Sir Charles to Italy. As she recovers, however, Clementina reaffirms that she cannot marry a heretic, and Sir Charles, released, returns to England to marry Harriet.

Sir Courtly Nice, or It Cannot be, a comedy by *Crowne, produced 1685, founded on a comedy by the Spanish dramatist Moreto. Leonora is in love with Farewel, a young man of quality, but her brother Lord Bellguard, owing to a feud between the families, is determined she shall not marry him. Bellguard keeps Leonora under watch by her aunt and a pair of spies, Hothead and Fanatick. Crack introduces himself in an assumed character into Lord Bellguard's house and Farewel is enabled to carry off and marry Leonora; while her rival suitor Sir Courtly Nice, a fop, favoured by Lord Bellguard, is fobbed off with the aunt; and Surly, the rough ill-mannered cynic, gets no wife at all.

Sir Launcelot Greaves, The Life and Adventures of, a novel by T. *Smollett, published 1762.

Smollett's shortest novel, written in episodes (many of them while he was in prison in 1760); he describes it as 'an agreeable medley of mirth and madness', but his purpose is serious in examining various states of madness and questioning conventional definitions of sanity.

It contains the well-known words 'I think for my part one half of the nation is mad—and the other half not very sound' (spoken by Crowe).

Sir Launfal, by Thomas Chestre, a late 14th-cent. *Breton Lay. It is one of the two English versions of *Marie de France's Lanval. Launfal is a knight of the Round Table who leaves the court, affronted by tales of *Guinevere's misconduct. He falls in love with a fairy lady, Tryamour. When he returns to Arthur's court Guinevere declares her love for him, but he rejects her.

Sir Patrick Spens, an early Scottish *ballad, included in Percy's *Reliques. The subject is the dispatch of Sir Patrick to sea, on a mission for the king, in winter; his foreboding of disaster; and his destruction with his ship's company. Sir W. *Scott, in his version, makes the object of the expedition the bringing to Scotland of the Maid of Norway (1283–90), who died on her voyage to marry Edward, prince of Wales.

Sir Thomas More, see MORE, SIR THOMAS.

Sirventes, a form of poem or lay, usually satirical, employed by the *troubadours.

SISSON, C(harles) H(ubert) (1914–   ), poet and translator. His volumes of poetry include The London Zoo (1961), Numbers (1965), Metamorphoses (1968), and Anchises (1976); and In the Trojan Ditch: Collected Poems and Selected Translations (1974). Translations include works of Heine, *Catullus, *Horace, and Dante's *Divina Commedia (1980). His poetry mingles biblical and classical themes and imagery with Arthurian references drawn from his native Somerset. His Collected Poems was published in 1984.

Sister Carrie, a novel by T. *Dreiser.

SITWELL, Dame Edith Louisa (1887–1964), sister of O. and S. *Sitwell. With her brothers she actively encouraged *Modernist writers and artists; from 1916 to 1921 she edited Wheels, an anti-Georgian magazine, which first published W. *Owen. Her first volume of verse, The Mother and other poems (1915), was followed by many others, and she quickly acquired a reputation as an eccentric and controversial figure, confirmed by the first public performance, in 1923, of Façade, a highly original entertainment (with music by W. *Walton) with verses in syncopated rhythms. Gold Coast Customs (1929), a harsh and powerful work, compared modern Europe with ancient barbaric Africa. Her prose works include a study of *Pope (1930), *English Eccentrics* (1933), and *Victoria of England* (1936). Her poems of the blitz and the atom bomb (*Street Songs*, 1942; *Green Song*, 1944; *The Song of the Cold*, 1945; *The Shadow of Cain*, 1947) were highly praised, but in the 1950s her reputation began to fade, as the new austerity of the *Movement became fashionable. She remained, however, a considerable public figure, well known outside literary circles for her theatrical dress and manner and by her indignant response to real or suspected criticism.

SITWELL, Sir (Francis) Osbert (Sacheverell) (1892–1969), brother of Edith and Sacheverell *Sitwell. He reluctantly served in the First World War, and his early poetry (e.g. *The Winstonburg Line*, 1919) is sharply satirical and pacifist in tone. He produced many volumes of poetry, fiction, and autobiography, and was, with his brother and sister, an outspoken enemy of the *Georgian poets and an ardent supporter of *Pound, T. S. *Eliot, W. *Lewis, and W. *Walton (for whose *Belshazzar's Feast*, 1931, he wrote the words). His prose works include *Triple Fugue* (1924), a collection of satirical stories; *Before the Bombardment* (1926), a novel describing the shelling of Scarborough in 1914; *Winters of Content* (1932), describing travels in Italy; and *Escape with me!* (1939), describing travels in China and the Far East. His most sustained achievement was his autobiography, in five volumes (*Left Hand! Right Hand!*, 1945; *The Scarlet Tree*, 1946; *Great Morning!*, 1948; *Laughter in the Next Room*, 1949; *Noble Essences*, 1950: with a later addition, *Tales my Father Taught Me*, 1962). These are remarkable for the portrait of the eccentric, exasperating figure of his father, Sir George.

SITWELL, Sir Sacheverell (1897–), brother of Osbert and Edith (above). His volumes of verse include *The People's Palace* (1918), *Collected Poems* (1936), and *An Indian Summer* (1982). Many of his prose works combine an interest in art and travel; they include *Southern Baroque Art* (1924) and *German Baroque Art* (1927); *Conversation Pieces* (1936); *British Architects and Craftsmen* (1945); and *Bridge of the Brocade Sash* (1959), on the arts of Japan. His imaginative prose includes *The Dance of the Quick and the Dead* (1936) and *Journey to the Ends of Time* (1959), a macabre and despairing work about the condition of man.

Skaldic Verse (also 'scaldic'), a form of Old Norse poetry distinguished by its elaborate metre, alliteration, consonance, and riddling diction. Skaldic verse flourished in the 10th cent. and on into the 11th, and much of it composed to commemorate the deeds of chieftains who ruled in Norway at this time. Such verses are preserved mainly in the kings' sagas; many 'lausavísur' or occasional verses, and some love poetry are included in the narratives of family sagas (see SAGA).

SKEAT, W(alter) W(illiam) (1835–1912), was appointed to the chair of Anglo-Saxon at Cambridge in 1878. His edition of *Lancelot of the Laik* was one of the first publications of the *Early English Text Society (no. 6, 1865). He edited *Ælfric, *Barbour's *Bruce*, *Chatterton, and the Anglo-Saxon Gospels; his greatest works were the editions of Langland's *Piers Plowman* (1886) setting out in parallel the three manuscript versions, the existence of which was Skeat's discovery, and of *Chaucer (7 vols, 1894–7). He founded the English Dialect Society in 1873, which led to the appearance of Joseph *Wright's *English Dialect Dictionary* (1896–1905), and his own *Etymological Dictionary* (1879–82, revised and enlarged 1910) was begun with the object of collecting material for the *New English Dictionary* (See MURRAY, J. A. H.). He also began the systematic study of place-names in English.

SKEFFINGTON, Sir Lumley St George (1771–1850), fop and playwright, was caricatured by Gillray, and his dramatic works were described by Byron in *English Bards and Scotch Reviewers* (1809) as 'skeletons of plays'.

SKELTON, John (?1460–1529), was created 'poet-laureate' by the universities of Oxford, Louvain, and Cambridge, an academical distinction. He became tutor to Prince Henry (Henry VIII) and enjoyed court favour despite his outspokenness. He was admitted to holy orders in 1498 and became rector of Diss in Norfolk. His principal works include: *The Bowge of Courte* (c.1498, a satire on the court of Henry VII), *The Garlande of Laurell* (a self-laudatory allegorical poem, describing the crowning of the author among the great poets of the world); *Phyllyp Sparowe* (a lamentation put into the mouth of Jane Scroupe, a young lady whose sparrow has been killed by a cat); *Collyn Clout* (a complaint by a vagabond of the misdeeds of ecclesiastics), which influenced *Spenser. Not only this last poem, but also his satires 'Speke Parrot' and *Why come ye nat to Courte*, contained attacks on Cardinal Wolsey. His most vigorous poem was *The Tunnyng of Elynour Rummyng*. His play *Magnyfycence* is an example of the *Morality. Skelton's *Ballade of the Scottysshe Kynge* is a spirited celebration of the victory of *Flodden.

The verse form known as 'skeltonic verse' is derived from his favourite metre, 'a headlong voluble breathless doggrel, which rattling and clashing on through quick-recurring rhymes . . . has taken from the name of its author the title of Skeltonical verse' (J. C. *Collins). As he himself said (*Collyn Cloute*, 53–8):

For though my ryme be ragged,
Tattered and jagged,
Rudely rayne-beaten,
Rusty and mothe-eaten,
Yf ye take well therwith,
It hath in it some pyth.

Skeltonic Verse, see SKELTON, J.

Sketches by Boz, a collection of sketches of life and manners, by *Dickens, first published in various periodicals, and in book form in 1836–7 (in one volume, 1839).

Skewton, The Hon. Mrs, in Dickens's *Dombey and Son*, the mother of Edith, Dombey's second wife.

Skimpole, Harold, a character in Dickens's *Bleak House*.

Slawkenbergius, the author of a Latin treatise on noses, in Sterne's *Tristram Shandy*.

Slay-good, in Pt II of Bunyan's *Pilgrim's Progress*, a giant whom Mr Great-heart killed.

Sleary, the circus proprietor in Dickens's *Hard Times*.

Sleeping Beauty, The, a fairy-tale, translated from the French of *Perrault by Robert Samber (1729).

Seven fairies are invited to attend the baptism of the daughter of a king. An old fairy has been overlooked and comes unbidden. Six fairies bestow on the child every imaginable perfection. The old fairy spitefully pronounces that she shall wound herself with a spindle and die. The seventh fairy, who has purposely kept in the background, amends this fate, converting the death into a sleep of a hundred years, from which the princess will be awakened by a king's son. And so it falls out, and the fairy puts every one in the castle to sleep so that the princess may not wake up all alone. In due course the prince comes and wakens the princess, which causes the other sleepers to awake.

For analogous legends see A. *Lang, *Perrault's Popular Tales* (1888). It is suggested that the Sleeping Beauty represents the earth awakened from her winter sleep by the kiss of the sun.

'**Sleepy Hollow,** The Legend of', a story by W. *Irving, included in *The Sketch Book*.

Slender, Abraham, in Shakespeare's *The Merry Wives of Windsor*, a cousin of Shallow's.

Slipslop, Mrs, a character in Fielding's *Joseph Andrews*.

SLOANE, Sir Hans (1660–1753) a physician, secretary to the *Royal Society, 1693–1712, and

president of the Royal College of Physicians, 1719–35. He purchased the manor of Chelsea in 1712 and endowed the Chelsea Physic Garden. His collection (including a large number of books and manuscripts) was purchased by the nation and placed in Montague House, afterwards the British Museum; the geological and zoological specimens formed the basis of the Natural History Museum in South Kensington, opened in 1881. Sloane Square and Hans Place are named after him.

Slop, Dr, in Sterne's *Tristram Shandy*, a thoroughly incompetent and argumentative physician.

Slope, The Revd Obadiah, a character in Trollope's *The Warden* and *Barchester Towers*.

Slough of Despond, in Bunyan's *Pilgrim's Progress*, a miry place on the way from the City of Destruction to the wicket-gate.

Sludge, Dicky, or 'Flibbertigibbet', a character in Scott's *Kenilworth*.

Slumkey, The Hon. Samuel, a character in Dickens's *Pickwick Papers*.

Sly, Christopher, see TAMING OF THE SHREW, THE.

Small House At Allington, The, a novel by A. *Trollope, published 1864, the fifth in the *'Barsetshire' series.

Lily Dale becomes engaged to Adolphus Crosbie, an ambitious civil servant, but Crosbie, at a house party at Courcy Castle, proposes to Lady Alexandrina de Courcy. When the news comes back to Allington, Lily behaves well, but Johnny Eames, her childhood sweetheart, assaults Crosbie at Paddington station. Crosbie finds that he and his bride are incompatible; Lady Alexandrina returns to her family and travels to Baden. Meanwhile Eames's reputation continues to develop. He begins to spend much of his free time at Allington. There he becomes the protégé of Lord de Guest, and at the intercession of Lady Julia renews his suit to Lily. Lily, however, considers herself bound to Crosbie for life.

SMART, Christopher (1722–71) author of *Poems on Several Occasions* (1752), which included a blank-verse georgic in two books, 'The Hop-Garden', and lighter verse; and of *The Hilliad* (1753), a satire on the quack doctor John Hill, written with the help of A. *Murphy and modelled on *The Dunciad*. He spent the years 1759–63 in a private home for the insane in Bethnal Green. His derangement took the form of a compulsion to public prayer, which occasioned the famous comment of Dr *Johnson: 'I'd as lief pray with Kit Smart as anyone else.' He is remembered for *A Song to David* (1763), a song of praise to David as author of the psalms, and a celebration of the Creation and the Incarnation; the poem is built on a mathematical and mystical ordering of stanzas grouped in threes, fives, and sevens. Smart also published in these later years translations of the psalms, of *Horace, two oratorios, and poems. His work was little regarded until the 1920s, when there was a wave of biographical interest, and his reputation as a highly original poet was confirmed by the publication of his extraordinary work *Jubilate Agno* in 1939 (ed. W. F. Stead as *Rejoice in the Lamb: A Song from Bedlam*). This unfinished work, composed largely at Bethnal Green, celebrates the Creation in a verse form based on the antiphonal principles of Hebrew poetry. Its most celebrated passage is the one on Smart's cat, which begins 'For I will consider my cat Jeoffrey . . .'

Smectymnuus, the name under which five Presbyterian divines, Stephen Marshall, Edmund Calamy, Thomas Young, Matthew Newcomen, and William Spurstow, published a pamphlet in 1641 attacking episcopacy and Bishop J. *Hall. It was answered by Hall, and defended by *Milton in his *Animadversions upon the Remonstrant's Defence against Smectymnuus* (1641) and his *An Apology against a Pamphlet . . . against Smectymnuus* (1642). From 'Smectymnuus' is derived 'Legion Smec' in *Hudibras* (II. ii), signifying the Presbyterians:

New modell'd the army and cashier'd
All that to Legion Smec adher'd.

SMEDLEY, Francis Edward (1818–64), author of three high-spirited novels of sport, romance, and adventure, including the popular *Frank Fairleigh* (1850), illustrated by *Cruikshank, *Lewis Arundel* (1852), and *Harry Coverdale's Courtship* (1855).

Smelfungus, in Sterne's *A Sentimental Journey*, a caricature of *Smollett, who in 1766 had published his *Travels through France and Italy*.

Smike, a character in Dickens's *Nicholas Nickleby*.

SMILES, Samuel (1812–1904), devoted his leisure to the advocacy of political and social reform, on the lines of the *Manchester School, and to the biography of industrial leaders and humble self-taught students. He published a *Life of George Stephenson* (1875), *Lives of the Engineers* (1861–2), *Josiah Wedgwood* (1894), and many similar works, but is now principally remembered for his successful *Self-help* (1859), which preached industry, thrift, and self-improvement, and attacked 'over-government'.

SMITH, Adam (1723–90), was appointed professor of logic at Glasgow in 1751, and in 1752 of moral philosophy. He became the friend of *Hume. In 1759 he published *The Theory of Moral Sentiments*, which brought him into prominence. In 1764 he resigned his professorship and visited France, where he saw *Voltaire and was admitted into the society of the physiocrats. After his return he devoted himself to the preparation of his great work *An Inquiry into the Nature and Causes of the *Wealth of Nations* (1776). This revolutionized the economic theories of the day. Its appearance at the actual date of the 'Declaration of Independence' of the American rebels was of importance if only for the prophecy in Bk IV, 'They will be one of the foremost nations of the world.' Smith's edition of the autobiography of Hume in 1777 occasioned some controversy.

SMITH, Alexander (?1830–67), published in 1853 *Poems* (including 'A life-drama'), which were satirized, along with other works of the *Spasmodic School, in *Aytoun's *Firmilian*. He published in 1855 sonnets on the Crimean war jointly with S. T. *Dobell; and *City Poems* in 1857. His best prose is to be seen in *A Summer in Skye* (1865).

SMITH, Charlotte (1748–1806), chiefly a novelist, began her career with *Elegiac Sonnets* (1784). Her novels include *Emmeline* (1788) and *The Old Manor House* (1793), which Sir W. *Scott, and posterity, considered her best.

SMITH, George (1824–1901), in 1846 became sole head of the firm of Smith & Elder, publishers and East India agents. Under his control the business quickly grew in both the India agency and publishing directions. The chief authors whose works he published in his early career were *Ruskin, C. *Brontë, whose *Jane Eyre* he issued in 1848, and *Thackeray, whose *The History of Henry Esmond* he brought out in 1852.

In 1853 he took a partner, H. S. King, and after weathering the storm of the Indian Mutiny, founded in 1859 *The Cornhill Magazine*, with Thackeray as editor, and in 1865 (with Frederick Greenwood) he founded *The Pall Mall Gazette*. In 1868 he dissolved partnership with King and carried on the publishing branch of the business alone at 15 Waterloo Place, London. His chief authors now included R. *Browning, M. *Arnold, (Sir) L. *Stephen, and Anne Thackeray *Ritchie. He was founder (1882) and proprietor of the *Dictionary of National Biography*.

Smith (or Gow), Henry, the hero of Scott's *The Fair Maid of Perth*.

SMITH, Horatio (Horace) (1779–1849), brother of James (below), joint author, with his brother, of *Rejected Addresses* (1812), and of *Horace in London* (1813), imitations of certain

Odes of *Horace. He then turned to the writing of historical romances; his *Brambletye House* (1826), the story of a young Cavalier, was followed by many others including *The Tor Hill* (1826), as well as plays and poems and work for the *New Monthly Magazine*.

SMITH, James (1775–1839), elder brother of Horatio (above), with whom he produced *Rejected Addresses* (1812) and *Horace in London* (1813), imitations of certain Odes of *Horace.

SMITH, Captain John (1580–1631), set out with the Virginia colonists in 1606 and is said to have been rescued by *Pocahontas when taken prisoner by the Indians. He was author of *The General History of Virginia, New England, and the Summer Isles* (1624).

SMITH, John (1618–52), see CAMBRIDGE PLATONISTS.

SMITH, (Lloyd) Logan Pearsall (1865–1946), man of letters, born in Philadelphia, spent most of his life in England. He was a founder of the *Society for Pure English. His works include *Trivia* (1902), *More Trivia* (1921), and *Afterthoughts* (1931), collections of much polished observations and aphorisms; one of his more memorable, 'People say that life is the thing, but I prefer reading', indicates the nature of his success and limitations as an author.

SMITH, Stevie (Florence Margaret) (1902–71), poet and novelist, who was brought up in Palmers Green, north London, where she spent most of her adult life with an aunt. She wrote three novels, but has been more widely recognized for her witty, caustic, and enigmatic verse, much of it illustrated by her own comic drawings. Her first volume, *A Good Time was Had By All* (1937), was followed by seven others, including *Not Waving But Drowning* (1957). Her *Collected Poems* appeared in 1975.

SMITH, Sydney (1771–1845), lived for a time as a tutor in Edinburgh, where he became a friend of *Jeffrey and *Brougham with whom he founded the *Edinburgh Review* in 1802. He came to London in 1803, lectured with great success on moral philosophy at the Royal Institution, and became the wittiest and one of the most beloved of the Whig circle at *Holland House. He published *The Letters of Peter Plymley* (1807) in defence of Catholic emancipation, and a considerable number of sermons, speeches, essays, and letters. He was made a canon of St Pauls in 1831.

SMITH, Sydney Goodsir (1915–75), poet, critic, and journalist, is remembered for his part in the 20th-cent. revival of poetry in the *Scots language. His first volume, *Skail Wind* (1941),

was followed by several others, and he also edited various works on Scottish literature.

Smith, W. H., and Son, Ltd, a firm of stationers, newsagents, and booksellers, which originated in a small newsvendor's shop opened in London in Little Grosvenor Street in 1792 by Henry Walton Smith and his wife Anna. His son, William Henry Smith (1792–1865), gave the firm its name of W. H. Smith in 1828; his son, also William Henry (1825–91), became a partner in 1846 and the words 'and Son' were added. The business profited from the railway boom by opening station bookstalls throughout the country and establishing a circulating *library which lasted until 1961. The W. H. Smith Literary Award has been given annually since 1959, for a work of any genre that constitutes 'the most outstanding contribution to English literature' in the year under review. Past winners include P. *White, L. *Lee, *Gombrich, and *Heaney.

SMITH, Sir William (1813–93), editor of the *Quarterly Review* (1867–93). He is associated with the revival of classical teaching in England and among his many educational works are his *Dictionary of Greek and Roman Antiquities* (1842).

SMOLLETT, Tobias George (1721–71), attended Glasgow university. In 1741 he sailed as a surgeon's mate for the West Indies on an expedition against the Spaniards and was present at the abortive attack on Cartegena. While in Jamaica he met Anne Lassells, whom he married, probably in 1743. In 1744 he set himself up as a surgeon in London.

Smollett's first publication, in 1746, was a much-admired poem, 'The Tears of Scotland'. His novels appeared as follows: *The Adventures of *Roderick Random* (1748); *The Adventures of *Peregrine Pickle* (1751, rev. edn 1758); *The Adventures of Ferdinand Count Fathom* (1753); *The Life and Adventures of *Sir Launcelot Greaves* (1762), the story of an 18th-cent. Don Quixote; and *The Expedition of *Humphry Clinker* (1771), his most accomplished work. He may have been the author, in 1752, of the scurrilous pamphlet *The Faithful Narrative of Habbakkuk Hilding*, attacking *Fielding for plagiarism and on many other counts. He and Fielding conducted intermittent warfare, chiefly in the *Critical Review* of which he was co-founder and editor from 1756 to 1763, and the *Covent Garden Journal*.

He had long been translating *Cervantes, and in 1755 his *History and Adventures of Don Quixote* appeared. *A Compendium of Authentic and Entertaining Voyages*, an anthology of travel, appeared in 1756, and in 1757–8 he published his *Complete History of England*. The first volume of the *Continuation of the Complete History* appeared in 1760. His edition of a new translation of *The Works of . . . Voltaire* began to appear in 1761. In

1762–3 Smollett wrote and edited the Tory journal *The Briton*, which was rapidly killed by Wilkes's *The North Briton.

Smollett's health had long been deteriorating, and he left England with his wife and household for France and Italy. They returned in 1765 and in 1766 he published *Travels through France and Italy, a caustic work which earned him from *Sterne the nickname of Smelfungus. *The Present State of All Nations was published in eight volumes in 1768–9.

In 1769 appeared *The History and Adventures of an Atom*, a rancorous satire on public men and affairs which was possibly, but not certainly, by Smollett.

Smollett's avowed purpose in writing was to arouse 'generous indignation' against cruelty and injustice, but his relish in the exploits of his 'heroes' sometimes distorts his professed moral purpose. His works are often described as *picaresque.

Smorltork, Count, in Dickens's *Pickwick Papers*, 'the famous foreigner' at Mrs Leo Hunter's party.

Snagsby, Mr and Mrs, characters in Dickens's *Bleak House.

Snake, a character in Sheridan's *The School for Scandal.

Snark, see HUNTING OF THE SNARK, THE.

Sneerwell, Lady, one of the scandal-mongers in Sheridan's *The School for Scandal.

Snevellicci, Mr, Mrs, and Miss, in Dickens's *Nicholas Nickleby*, actors in Crummles's company.

Snobs of England, see BOOK OF SNOBS, THE.

Snodgrass, Augustus, a character in Dickens's *Pickwick Papers.

SNORRI STURLUSON (1178–1241), an Icelandic historian and literary antiquarian, the author of *Heimskringla*, and the Prose *Edda. Snorri is the most important figure in Old Icelandic literature; our knowledge of Norse myth and understanding of Old Norse poetry is due largely to him.

Snout, Tom, in Shakespeare's *A Midsummer Night's Dream*, an Athenian tinker. He appears as Wall in the play 'Pyramus and Thisbe'.

SNOW, C(harles) P(ercy) (Baron Snow of Leicester) (1905–80), novelist. His early career was devoted to scientific research in Cambridge; but he turned increasingly to administration, and in later life held many important public posts. His novel sequence *Strangers and Brothers* (the original title of the first volume, 1940, retitled subsequently *George Passant*), spanned 30 years of writing, and more years in the life of its narrator, Lewis Eliot, a barrister who, like Snow himself, rose from lower middle-class provincial origins to enjoy worldly success and influence. The settings of the novels (*The Light and the Dark*, 1947; *Time of Hope*, 1949; *The Masters*, 1951; *The New Men*, 1954; *Homecomings*, 1956; *The Conscience of the Rich*, 1958; *The Affair*, 1959; *Corridors of Power*, 1963; *The Sleep of Reason*, 1968; *Last Things*, 1970) are largely academic or scientific; *The Masters*, a study of the internal politics of a Cambridge college, is perhaps his best known. His interest in public affairs is reflected in his work, and his novel on Westminster life, *The Corridors of Power*, added a phrase to the language of the day, as did his Rede Lecture on *The Two Cultures and the Scientific Revolution* (1959). He published several other novels and critical works, including a critical biography of *Trollope (1975). In 1950 he married Pamela Hansford *Johnson.

Snubbin, Mr Serjeant, in Dickens's *Pickwick Papers*, counsel for the defendant in Bardell v. Pickwick.

Snug, in Shakespeare's *A Midsummer Night's Dream*, a joiner, who appears as the lion in 'Pyramus and Thisbe'.

Social Contract, The, the English title of *Du Contrat Social*, by J. J. *Rousseau.

Socialism, a theory or policy of social organization that aims at the control of the means of production, capital, land, property, etc., by the community as a whole, and their administration or distribution in the interests of all. The early history of the word is obscure, but it was claimed that it was first used in something like the modern sense in 1827 in the Owenite *Co-operative Magazine*, and it is found in the 1830s used in the sense of Owenism. (See OWEN, ROBERT.) One of the most articulate and persistent of British socialists was Bernard Shaw, who published in 1928 *The Intelligent Woman's Guide to Socialism and Capitalism.

Socialist Realism, a term used to describe the official artistic doctrine adopted at the Congress of Soviet Writers in 1934, approved by Stalin, Gorky, N. Bukharin, and A. A. Zhdanov. It required that the creative artist should serve the proletariat by being realistic, optimistic and heroic: it denigrated the bourgeois artist and all forms of experimentalism and formalism as degenerate and pessimistic. (The works of *Joyce were singled out for particular condemnation at this first Congress.) It presented problems for such Marxist critics as *Lukács, and after the hard Stalinist period the use of the term was modified to cover the works of such artistic innovators as *Brecht and Mayakovsky; but it is still seen in the Western world as an impediment to creativity and freedom of expression. 'Social Realism' is a distinct term, used loosely to describe a realistic, objective, yet socially aware and detailed method of artistic presentation. (See REALISM.)

Society for Promoting Christian Knowledge, see SPCK.

Society for Psychical Research, The, a body founded in 1882 by F. W. H. *Myers, H. *Sidgwick, and others. The Society, in a period of intense interest in spiritualism and the supernatural, investigated with high standards of scientific detachment such matters as telepathy, apparitions, etc. Its presidents have included A. J. *Balfour, W. *James, and Sir Oliver Lodge (1851–1940). Members and associates have included Ruskin, *Tennyson, *Gladstone, and A. R. *Wallace.

Society for Pure English, The, an association of writers and academics, formed in 1913, inspired by *Bridges. Its original committee included H. *Bradley, Sir W. *Raleigh, and L. P. *Smith. The name of the Society was somewhat misleading in that the founders had no objections to the entry of foreign words into English, and the writers of its tracts were not for the most part purists in the dogmatic sense. A typical tract would offer an urbane and well-researched enquiry into some question of grammar, pronunciation, etymology, or vocabulary.

Society of Authors, The, an organization founded in 1884 by W. *Besant to promote the business interests of authors and fight for their rights, especially in copyright. It conducted a successful 28-year campaign for *Public Lending Right. Its quarterly publication is *The Author*.

Society of Friends, see FRIENDS, SOCIETY OF.

Society of Jesus, see JESUITS.

Socinianism, the doctrine of Lelio Sozini (Socinus) (1525–62) and his nephew Fausto Sozzini (1539–1604) that Jesus was not God but a divine prophet of God's word, and that the sacraments had no supernatural quality. The doctrine was set forth in the Confession of Rakow (1605), and was an influence on early *Unitarianism.

SOCRATES (469–399 BC), the Greek philosopher, born near Athens. He occupied his life with oral instruction, frequenting public places and engaging in discourse designed to reveal truth and expose error. He incurred much enmity, was attacked by *Aristophanes in the *Clouds*, and was finally accused by Meletus, a leather-seller, of introducing strange gods and corrupting youth. He was sentenced to death, and thirty days later took hemlock. Socrates wrote nothing, but his teaching methods are preserved in the Dialogues of *Plato and a more homely account is to be found in *Xenophon's *Memorabilia*. The prominent features of his teaching appear to have been: the view that it is the duty of philosophy to investigate ethical questions; and the view that virtue is knowledge: no one is willingly wicked, for happiness lies in virtue; if a man is wicked, it is from ignorance. He inclined to belief in the immortality of the soul, and thought himself subject to divine promptings. (For Socratic Method see PLATO.)

'Sofa, The', see TASK, THE.

'Sohrab and Rustum', a poem by M. *Arnold, published 1853. The story is taken from *Firdausi's Persian epic. It recounts, in blank verse adorned by *epic similes, the fatal outcome of Sohrab's search for his father Rustum, the leader of the Persian forces. Rustum (who believes his own child to be a girl) accepts the challenge of Sohrab, now leader of the Tartars: the two meet in single combat, at first unaware of one another's identity, which is confirmed only when Sohrab has been mortally wounded.

Soldan (from the Arabic *sultan*). The Soldan, or Souldan, in Spenser's *Faerie Queene* (v. viii) represents Philip II of Spain.

Solinus, in Shakespeare's *The Comedy of Errors*, the duke of Ephesus.

Solmes, a character in Richardson's *Clarissa*.

Solomon Daisy, in Dickens's *Barnaby Rudge*, the parish clerk and bell-ringer at Chigwell.

SOLZHENITSYN, Alexander Isayevich (1918–), Russian prose writer. He joined the Red Army in 1941. Arrested in 1945 for remarks critical of Stalin, he was sent to a labour camp where in 1952 he developed stomach cancer. In 1953 he was released into 'administrative exile'. In 1956 he returned to Ryazan, in central Russia, to work as a teacher. His first published story, *One Day in the Life of Ivan Denisovich* (1962), caused a sensation through its honest and pioneering description of camp life. His major novels, *Cancer Ward* (1968) and *The First Circle* (1969), could only be published abroad, and in late 1969 he was expelled from the Union of Soviet Writers. In 1970 he was awarded the *Nobel Prize for literature. The appearance abroad of the first volume of *The Gulag Archipelago* (1973–5), an epic 'history and geography' of the labour camps, caused the Soviet authorities to deport Solzhenitsyn to West Germany on 13 February 1974. He settled in the United States, where he continued a series of novels begun with *August 1914* (1971), offering an alternative picture of Soviet history.

Some Experiences of an Irish R.M., a collection of stories by *Somerville and Ross, published 1899.

This exuberant and skilful series of stories is narrated by Major Yeates, the resident magistrate, whose misfortune is to attract calamity. With his gallant wife Philippa, he lives at the centre of a vigorous and wily community as the tenant of a dilapidated demesne, Shreelane, which he rents from a well-to-do rogue, Flurry Knox. The eccentricities of the populace contribute to innumerable confusions involving collapsing carts, missed meals, sinking boats, shying horses, and outraged visitors. Yet few of the stories are merely farcical, and some have a sombre echo.

SOMERVILE, William (1675–1742), a country gentleman, is remembered as the author of *The Chace* (1735), a poem in four books of Miltonic blank verse on the pleasures of hunting. In 1740 he published *Hobbinol*, a mock-heroic account of rural games in Gloucestershire (see COTSWOLD OLIMPICK GAMES).

SOMERVILLE (Edith) and ROSS (Martin). Edith Oenone Somerville (1858–1949) and Violet Martin (1862–1915), were second cousins of Irish families who separately and together wrote some 30 books, mainly set in Ireland. Their collaborations include *An Irish Cousin* (1889), *The Real Charlotte* (1894), and *The Silver Fox* (1897). Their most successful work was a skilful series of stories, **Some Experiences of an Irish R.M.** (1899), followed by *Further Experiences of an Irish R.M.* (1908), and *In Mr Knox's Country* (1915).

'Somnium Scipionis' (Dream of Scipio) is the fable with which *Cicero ends his *De Republica*. The only extant manuscript of Cicero's treatise breaks off early in the last book, and the survival of the *Somnium* is due to its being reproduced by a certain Macrobius, who in the 4th cent. AD furnished it with a *Neoplatonist commentary that interested medieval thinkers.

The fable relates how the younger Scipio saw his grandfather, the elder Scipio, in a dream and was shown the dwelling set aside in the Milky Way for those who follow virtue and especially for those who distinguish themselves in the service of their country. The *Somnium* may have inspired *Petrarch's choice of Scipio Africanus as the hero of his epic *Africa*. Chaucer gives a poetical summary of it in *The Parliament of Fowls* and mentions it in other passages.

Song of Solomon, The, otherwise 'The Song of Songs', one of the poetical books of the OT, at one time attributed to King Solomon, now considered on linguistic grounds to be of later date, perhaps of the 4th or 3rd cent. BC.

The allegorical interpretations of the work have been generally abandoned, and it is widely accepted that its original character was erotic.

'Song of the Shirt, The', a poem by T. *Hood, originally published anonymously in *Punch* in 1843. It takes the form of a passionate protest by an overworked and underpaid seamstress—'It is not linen you're wearing out | But human creatures' lives.'

Songs of Experience, see SONGS OF INNOCENCE.

Songs of Innocence, a collection of poems written and etched by W. *Blake, published 1789. Most of the poems are about childhood, some of them written, with apparent simplicity, as if by children (e.g. 'Little lamb, who made thee?' and 'The Chimney Sweeper'); others commenting on the state of infancy ('The Ecchoing Green'); and yet others introducing the prophetic tone and personal imagery of Blake's later work ('The Little Girl Lost', 'The Little Girl Found').

In 1795 Blake issued a further volume, entitled *Songs of Innocence and of Experience: Shewing the Two Contrary States of the Human Soul*, to which he added the 'Songs of Experience', some of them (e.g. 'The Chimney Sweeper' and 'Nurse's Song') bearing identical titles to poems in the first collection, but replying to them in a tone that questions and offsets their simplicities, and manifests with great poetic economy Blake's profoundly original vision of the interdependence of good and evil, of energy and restraint, of desire and frustration. They range from fairly straightforward, if highly provocative, attacks on unnatural restraint ('The Garden of Love', 'London') to the extraordinary lyric intensity of 'Infant Sorrow', 'Ah! Sun-Flower', and 'Tyger! Tyger!'

Song to David, A, see SMART, C.

Sonnet, a poem consisting of 14 lines (of 11 syllables in Italian, generally 12 in French, and 10 in English), with rhymes arranged according to one or other of certain definite schemes, of which the Petrarchan and the Elizabethan are the principal, viz.: (1) a b b a a b b a, followed by two, or three, other rhymes in the remaining six lines, with a pause in the thought after the octave (not always observed by English imitators, of whom *Milton and *Wordsworth are prominent examples); (2) a b a b c d c d e f e f g g. The *sonnets of Shakespeare are in the latter form.

The sonnet was introduced to England by *Wyatt and developed by *Surrey (see also under METRE) and was thereafter widely used, notably in the sonnet sequences of Shakespeare, *Sidney, *Daniel, *Spenser, and other poets of the *Golden period, most of which are amatory in nature, and contain a certain narrative development: later sonnet sequences on the theme of love include those of D. G. *Rossetti and E. B. *Browning. *Milton, *Donne, *Keats, and *Yeats have all used the form to great and varied effect, and it continues to flourish in the 20th cent.

Sonnets from the Portuguese, a sonnet-sequence by E. B. *Browning first published 1850; the so-called 'Reading Edition' of 1847 was a forgery by T. J. *Wise. It describes the growth and development of her love for Robert *Browning, at first hesitating to involve him in her sorrowful invalid life, then yielding to gradual conviction of his love for her, and finally rapturous in late-born happiness. The title uses a secret reference for the Brownings to his nickname for her, 'the Portuguese', based on her poem 'Catarina to Camoens'.

Sonnets of Shakespeare, The, were printed in 1609 and probably date from the 1590s. Most of them trace the course of the writer's affection for a young man of rank and beauty: the first 17 urge him to marry to reproduce his beauty. The complete sequence of 154 sonnets was issued by the publisher Thomas Thorpe in 1609 with a dedication to 'Mr W.H., the onlie begetter of these insuing sonnets'. Mr W.H. has been identi-fied as (among others) William, Lord Herbert, afterwards earl of Pembroke, or Henry Wrio-thesley, earl of Southampton, and further as the young man addressed in the sonnets. Another view argues that Mr W.H. was a friend of Thorpe, through whose good offices the manu-script had reached his hands—'begetter' being used in the sense of 'getter' or 'procurer'. Other characters are alluded to in sequence including a mistress stolen by a friend (40–2), a rival poet (78–80 and 80–6), and a dark beauty loved by the author (127–52). Numerous identifications for all the 'characters' involved in the sequence, as well as for Mr W.H., have been put forward. Perhaps the most ingenious and amusing of these is *Wilde's *The Portrait of Mr W. H.*

For the form of these poems see SONNET.

Sons and Lovers, by D. H. *Lawrence, published 1913, a closely autobiographical novel set in the Nottinghamshire coalmining village of Bestwood.

Walter Morel has married a sensitive and high-minded woman better educated than him-self. She begins to shrink from his lack of fine feeling and drunkenness. Morel, baffled and thwarted, is sometimes violent, while Mrs Morel turns all her love towards her four chil-dren, particularly her two eldest sons, William and Paul. She struggles to keep herself and her family 'respectable' and is determined that her boys will not become miners. William goes to London to work as a clerk, and Paul also gets a job as a clerk with Mr Jordan, manufacturer of surgical appliances; William develops pneumonia and dies. Mrs Morel, numbed by despair, is roused only when Paul also falls ill. She nurses him back to health, and subsequently their attachment deepens. Paul is friendly with the Leivers family of Willey Farm, and a tender-ness grows between him and the daughter Miriam, a soulful, shy girl. Mrs Morel fears that Miriam will exclude her and tries to break up their relationship, while Paul, himself sickened at heart by Miriam's romantic love and fear of physical warmth, turns away and becomes involved with Clara Dawes, a married woman, separated from her husband Baxter, and a sup-porter of Women's Rights. Paul is made an overseer at the factory and he now begins to be noticed as a painter and designer. Clara returns to her husband. Meanwhile Mrs Morel is ill with cancer. At last, unable to bear her suffering, Paul and his sister Annie put an overdose of morphia in her milk. Paul resists the urge to follow her 'into the darkness' and, with a great effort, turns towards life. *Sons and Lovers* was perhaps the first English novel with a truly working-class background.

Sophia Western, the heroine of Fielding's *Tom Jones.*

Sophism, a specious but fallacious argument, used either deliberately to mislead or to display ingenuity in reasoning.

Sophist, in ancient Greece, one who undertook to give instruction in intellectual and ethical matters in return for payment; contrasted with 'philosopher', and frequently used as a term of disparagement.

SOPHOCLES (496–406 BC), the best-liked (in his own day) of the three great Attic tragedians, and the first to increase the number of actors from two to three. Seven of his plays are extant, three of which deal with the unhappy Oedipus and his family. Sophocles has not the epic grandeur of *Aeschylus or Euripides' radical fire, but he is excellent at drawing character and evoking pathos. His view of the universe is a matter over which scholars disagree. Man's fate depends on the gods, but do the gods share man's moral insights? Though T. *Watson pro-duced a Latin translation of the *Antigone* in 1581, Milton's *Samson Agonistes* was the first work in English to bear the stamp of Sophocles, but it came before its time. *Dryden's *Oedipus* though seven years later is chiefly indebted to *Seneca. It was in the 19th cent. that Sophocles really came into favour. *Shelley read him on his last fatal sailing-trip. *Bulwer-Lytton adapted his

Oedipus the King (1846). M. *Arnold produced his Sophoclean play *Merope* (1858) and two Sophoclean fragments, an *Antigone* (1849) and a *Dejaneira* (1867). *Swinburne introduced Sophoclean touches into his *Erechtheus* (1876); and during the first decade of the 20th cent. *Freud hit on the term 'Oedipus Complex' to describe certain features of infantile sexuality. This caught the public imagination and led to numerous translations and adaptations of the Theban plays.

Sophonisba, the daughter of Hasdrubal, a Carthaginian general, who avoided captivity by taking poison at the instigation of her betrothed Masinissa, was the subject of several plays, notably by *Marston, N. *Lee, and James *Thomson. The notorious line 'Oh! Sophonisba, Sophonisba, Oh!' occurs in Thomson's version (1730), was altered to 'Oh Sophonisba, I am wholly thine' in later editions, and parodied by Fielding in *Tom Thumb* as 'O Huncamunca, Huncamunca O!'

Sophy Crewler, in Dickens's *David Copperfield*, 'the dearest girl in the world', whom Traddles marries.

SORDELLO (*c.*1200–?69), a poet born near Mantua, who spent much of his later life in Provence. He accordingly wrote 'troubadour' poetry in *Provençal and so became an important link between the love poetry of Provence and that of Italy which was descended from it. *Dante places him in the Ante-Purgatory in *Purgatorio* vii.

Sordello, a narrative poem in iambic pentameter couplets by R. *Browning, published 1840. The poem was received with incomprehension and derision by the critics and the public, and its notorious 'obscurity' caused prolonged damage to Browning's reputation. The *Pre-Raphaelites, for whom it became a cult text, were its first defenders, followed later by *Pound; it is now coming to be recognized as one of the finest long poems of the century, and of central importance in the interpretation of Browning's work, particularly its relation to the Romanticism on whose tenets it heavily relies and which, at the same time, it challenges and disputes. Its genuine difficulty springs from the swiftness and compression of the language, the convoluted time-scheme of the narrative, and the fusion of intense specificity (or historical detail, landscape, etc.) with the abstract ideas which form the core of the argument.

The narrative is set in Italy during the period of the Guelf–Ghibelline wars of the late 12th and 13th cents, and traces the 'development of a soul', that of the troubadour Sordello (above), along a path of self-realization where political, aesthetic, and metaphysical ideas reflect each other; all this in the framework of a plot strongly influenced by the elements of fairy-tale (lost heir, wicked stepmother, unattainable princess, etc.).

SORLEY, Charles Hamilton (1895–1915), poet; served in the trenches in France during the First World War where he was killed. He left only 37 complete poems; his posthumous collection, *Marlborough and Other Poems* (1916), was a popular and critical success in the 1920s, but his verse was then long neglected, despite the efforts of Robert *Graves and of *Blunden. The best known of his poems include 'The Song of the Ungirt Runners', 'Barbury Camp', and the last, bitter 'When you see millions of the mouthless dead'.

Sorrel, Hetty, a character in G. Eliot's *Adam Bede*.

Soul's Tragedy, A, a play by R. *Browning, published 1846, together with *Luria, as no. VIII of *Bells and Pomegranates*. It is a tragi-comedy in two parts, the first in verse, the second in prose: the division of verse and prose represents Browning's idiosyncratic adaptation of Elizabethan and Jacobean models.

Chiappino, the 'hero', is a discontented liberal in 16th-cent. Faenza, who, at the climax of Act One, nobly (or egotistically?) takes on himself the punishment for the supposed assassination of the tyrannical Provost by his friend Luitolfo. He expects to be lynched by the Provost's guards, but is instead acclaimed by the people as their liberator, and is unable to resist the temptation of his new-found role. The Provost turns out not to have been killed after all and, just as Chiappino is about to become the new Provost himself, he is unmasked by the papal legate Ogniben, who has sardonically played up to his self-deceiving justification for seizing power. Ogniben, who had arrived in Faenza remarking that he had seen 'three-and-twenty leaders of revolts', utters the famous line 'I have seen *four*-and-twenty leaders of revolts!' as he watches Chiappino fleeing the town after his humiliation.

Sound and the Fury, The, a novel by W. *Faulkner.

SOUTAR, William (1898–1943), Scottish poet. He published several volumes of poetry from 1923 onwards; he wrote in both *Scots and English, though his Scots work is generally considered more significant. All his poems are short; they include lyrics, epigrams, riddles, and pieces for children. Several of his poems sing the praises and frustrations of the lost heritage of 'the lawland tongue'. His *Collected Poems* (1948) has an introduction by *MacDiarmid, and his *Diaries of a Dying Man*, ed. A. Scott, were published in 1954.

SOUTHCOTT, Joanna (1750–1814), a religious fanatic and farmer's daughter who acquired a large following through her doggerel prophecies and supernatural claims.

SOUTHERNE, or **SOUTHERN,** Thomas (1659–1746), of Irish parentage, lived in London from 1680. He was a friend of *Dryden, for several of whose plays he wrote prologues and epilogues. His first tragedy, *The Loyal Brother: or the Persian Prince* (1682), was an attack on *Shaftesbury and the Whigs. He wrote several comedies, but is chiefly remembered for his two highly successful tragedies, * *The Fatal Marriage* (1694) and *Oroonoko* (1695), both founded on novels by A. *Behn. Remarkably little is known of his long and, in later years, unproductive life. Southerne is regarded as a successor to *Otway in the art of pathos, and as a link between Restoration tragedy and the sentimental tragedies of the 18th cent.

SOUTHEY, Robert (1774–1843), was expelled from Westminster School for originating a magazine, *The Flagellant*, a precocious essay against flogging, and proceeded to Balliol College, Oxford. He became friendly with S. T. *Coleridge and together they planned their Utopian Pantisocratic society. At Oxford, with Coleridge, he wrote *The Fall of Robespierre*. In 1795 he travelled to Portugal, married Elizabeth Fricker (Coleridge married her sister, Sara), and wrote *Joan of Arc* (1796). Between 1796 and 1798 he wrote many ballads, including *'The Inchcape Rock', 'The Battle of *Blenheim', and 'The Holy Tree'. In 1800 he went to Spain, and on his return settled in the Lake District where he remained for the rest of his life as one of the *'Lake Poets'. A narrative poem, *Thalaba the Destroyer*, appeared in 1801, but sold poorly. In 1803 he published a translation of *Amadis of Gaul* (revised from an older version); in 1805, *Madoc*; and in 1807, the year in which he received a government pension, appeared a version of *Palmerin of England. In 1808 he translated the *Chronicle of the Cid* and in 1809 began his long association with the *Quarterly Review. The Curse of Kehama* appeared in 1810 and *Omniana*, an original commonplace book, with contributions by Coleridge, in 1812. He was appointed in 1813 *poet laureate, a post which he came greatly to dislike, and in the same year published his short but admirable *Life of Nelson*. A narrative poem *Roderick; the Last of the Goths* appeared in 1814. In 1817 he produced an edition of *Malory and had to endure the publication, by his enemies, of his youthful and revolutionary *Wat Tyler*. The final volume of his *History of Brazil* (3 vols, 1810–19) appeared a year before his *Life of Wesley*. In 1821, to commemorate the death of George III, he wrote *A Vision of Judgement*, in the preface to which he vigorously attacked *Byron, who replied in * *The Vision of Judgement. The Book of the Church* appeared in 1824; *A Tale of Paraguay* in 1825; *Sir Thomas*

More, in which he converses with the ghost of More, in 1829; *All for Love; and The Pilgrim to Compostella* in 1829; and in 1832 *Essays Moral and Political* and the last volume of *History of the Peninsular War* (1823–32). Between 1832 and 1837 he worked on a Life and an edition of *Cowper, and on his *Lives of the British Admirals* (1833). His wife died in 1837, and in 1839 he married Caroline Bowles. *The Doctor, etc.* was begun in 1834 (7 vols, 1834–47). Southey's last years were marked by an increasing mental decline.

Many of his contemporaries, in particular *Hazlitt and Byron, felt that in accepting pensions and the laureateship, and in retracting his youthful Jacobinism, Southey was betraying principles.

South Sea Company, The, was formed in 1711 by *Harley (later earl of Oxford) to trade with Spanish America under the expected treaty with Spain. A bill was passed in 1720 by which persons to whom the nation owed money were enabled to convert their claims into shares in the Company, and the shares rose in value from £100 to £1,000. The Company shortly afterwards failed. The collapse of the South Sea scheme, and of other financial schemes which had proliferated in its wake, caused widespread ruin. The whole affair was known as the South Sea Bubble.

The South-Sea House, where the Company had its offices, is the subject of one of Lamb's *Essays of Elia.

SOUTHWELL, St Robert (?1561–95), educated by the Jesuits at Douai and Rome, took Roman orders and came to England in 1586 with Henry Garnett (who was subsequently executed for complicity in the Gunpowder Plot). He became in 1589 domestic chaplain to the countess of Arundel, was captured when going to celebrate mass in 1592, repeatedly tortured, and executed after three years' imprisonment. His poems were mainly written in prison. Of these it was his object to make spiritual love, instead of 'unworthy affections', the subject. His chief work was *St Peters Complaint* (1595), a long narrative of the closing events of the life of Christ in the mouth of the repentant Peter. He also wrote many shorter devotional poems (some of them collected under the title *Moeoniae*, 1595) of a high order, notably 'The Burning Babe'. He was beatified in 1929 and canonized in 1970.

Sowerberry, in Dickens's *Oliver Twist*, an undertaker.

SOYINKA, Wole (1934–), Nigerian dramatist. He was play reader at the Royal Court Theatre, London, where *The Swamp Dwellers* (1958), *The Lion and the Jewel* and *The Invention* (both 1959) were produced. These already demonstrated his development from simple Nigerian village comedies to a more complex and individual drama incorporating mime and dance. *A Dance of the Forest* (1960) is a half-satirical, half-fantastic celebration of Nigerian independence. Soyinka's first novel, *The Interpreters* (1965), captures the idealism of young Nigerians regarding the development of a new Africa. In prison for pro-Biafran activity during 1967–9, he produced increasingly bleak verse and prose, *Madmen and specialists* (1970), and his second novel, *Season of Anomy* (1973). A brighter period has followed. *Death and the King's Horseman* (1975), embodies his post-Biafran cultural philosophy, enunciated in *Myth, Literature and the African World* (1976), of the need for the distinct aesthetics of Africa and Europe to cross-fertilize each other. He was awarded the *Nobel Prize in 1986.

SPALDING, John (*fl.* 1650), a Scottish historian, author of a valuable history of the troubles in Scotland and England, 1624–45, first published in 1792. The Spalding Club, an antiquarian publishing society, was founded in his memory in 1839.

Spanish Bawd, The, see CELESTINA.

Spanish Curate, The, a comedy by J. *Fletcher, probably in collaboration with *Massinger, performed 1622.

Spanish Fryar, The, a tragi-comedy by *Dryden (1681).
The serious plot is characteristically about a usurpation. Torrismond, though he does not know it, is lawful heir to the throne, and secretly marries the reigning but unlawful queen, who has allowed Torrismond's father, the true king, to be murdered in prison. The sub-plot is dominated by Father Dominic, a monstrous corrupt friar, who pimps for the libertine and whiggish Lorenzo. The latter is a highly dubious character, yet ironically it is through his agency that the lawful Torrismond is rescued. The woman Lorenzo is pursuing turns out to be his sister. The play is like *Mr Limberham* in its deeply sceptical treatment of religious and political orthodoxies.

Spanish Gipsy, The, (1) a romantic comedy by T. *Middleton and others (1625); (2) a dramatic poem by G. *Eliot (1868).

Spanish Tragedy, The, a tragedy in blank verse by *Kyd, acted and printed 1592.
The political background of the play is the victory of Spain over Portugal in 1580. Lorenzo and Bel-imperia are the children of Don Cyprian, duke of Castile (brother of the king of Spain); Hieronimo is marshal of Spain and Horatio his son. Balthazar, son of the viceroy of Portugal, has been captured in the war. He courts Bel-imperia, and Lorenzo and the king of Spain favour his suit for political reasons. Lorenzo and Balthazar discover that Bel-imperia loves Horatio; they surprise the couple by night in Hieronimo's garden and hang Horatio on a tree. Hieronimo discovers his son's body and runs mad with grief. He discovers the identity of the murderers, and carries out revenge by means of a play, *Solyman and Perseda*, in which Lorenzo and Balthazar are killed, and Bel-imperia stabs herself. Hieronimo bites out his tongue before killing himself.
*Jonson is known to have been paid for additions to the play, but the additional passages in the 1602 edition do not seem Jonsonian. The play was one of Shakespeare's sources for *Hamlet* and the alternative title given to it in 1615, *Hieronimo is mad againe*, provided T. S. *Eliot with the penultimate line of *The Waste Land*.

SPARK, Muriel (1918–), author, of Scottish–Jewish descent, born and educated in Edinburgh. After spending some years in Central Africa, which was to form the setting for several of her short stories, including the title story of *The Go-Away Bird* (1958), she returned to Britain where she worked for the Foreign Office during the Second World War. She began her literary career as editor and biographer, working for the *Poetry Society and editing its *Poetry Review* from 1947 to 1949; the problems of biography and autobiography form the subject of one of her recent novels, *Loitering with Intent* (1981). Her first novel, *The Comforters* (1957), was followed by many others, including *Memento Mori* (1959), a comic and macabre study of old age; *The Ballad of Peckham Rye* (1960), a bizarre tale of the underworld, mixing shrewd social observation with hints of necromancy; perhaps her best-known work, *The Prime of Miss Jean Brodie* (1961); *The Girls of Slender Means* (1963); *The Mandelbaum Gate* (1965); *The Public Image* (1968); *The Driver's Seat* (1970), about a woman possessed by a death-wish; *The Abbess of Crewe* (1974); and *The Take Over* (1976), set in Italy, where she settled. Her novels are elegant and sophisticated, with touches of the bizarre and the perverse; many have a quality of fable or parable, and her use of narrative omniscience is highly distinctive. Her *Collected Poems* and *Collected Plays* were both published in 1967.

Sparkish, a character in Wycherley's *The Country Wife*.

Sparkler, Edmund, a character in Dickens's *Little Dorrit*.

Sparsit, Mrs, a character in Dickens's *Hard Times*.

Spasmodic School, a term applied by *Aytoun to a group of poets which included P. J. *Bailey, J. W. *Marston, S. *Dobell, and Alexander *Smith. Their works for a brief while enjoyed great esteem; this was largely destroyed by Aytoun's attacks and by his parody *Firmilian* (1854), which also satirized their critical champion, *Gilfillan. Spasmodic poems tended to describe intense interior psychological drama, were violent and verbose, and were characterized by obscurity, *pathetic fallacy, and extravagant imagery; their heroes (who owed much to *Byron and *Goethe) were lonely, aspiring, and disillusioned, and frequently poets themselves.

Specimens of English Dramatic Poets who lived about the time of Shakespeare, by C. *Lamb, published 1808; an anthology, with brief but cogent critical comments, of extracts of scenes and speeches from Elizabethan and Jacobean dramatists. They include extracts from *Beaumont and *Fletcher, *Jonson, *Marlowe, *Webster, and others. The book did much to draw the attention of Lamb's contemporaries to this then neglected period of drama.

SPCK, the Society for Promoting Christian Knowledge, was founded in 1698. One of its primary objects was the setting up of charitable schools for the instruction of poor children. The Society is also a publishing agency for the dissemination of works of a Christian character.

Spectator, The, (1) a periodical conducted by *Steele and *Addison, from 1 March 1711 to 6 Dec. 1712. It was revived by Addison in 1714, when 80 numbers (556–635) were issued. *The Spectator* which succeeded *The Tatler* appeared daily. Addison and Steele were the principal contributors; other contributors included *Pope, *Tickell, Eustace Budgell, A. *Philips, *Eusden, and Lady M. W. *Montagu.

It purported to be conducted (see the first two numbers) by a small club, including Sir Roger de *Coverley, who represents the country gentry, Sir Andrew Freeport, Captain Sentry, and Will Honeycomb, representing respectively commerce, the army, and the town. Mr Spectator himself, who writes the papers, is a man of travel and learning, who frequents London as an observer. The papers are mainly concerned with manners, morals, and literature. Their object is 'to enliven morality with wit, and to temper wit with morality'; both its style and its morals were considered exemplary by Dr *Johnson, H. *Blair, and other arbiters.

(2) a weekly periodical started in 1828 by Robert Stephen Rintoul as an organ of 'educated radicalism'. It supported Lord John Russell's *Reform Bill of 1831. R. H. Hutton was joint editor, 1861–97. John St Loe Strachey was editor and proprietor from 1898 to 1925, and his cousin Lytton *Strachey was a frequent contributor. Other notable contributors in later years include P. *Fleming, G. *Greene, E. *Waugh, L. A. G. Strong, P. *Quennell, K. *Amis.

Speculum Meditantis (Mirour de l'Omme), see GOWER, J.

Speculum Stultorum, see WIREKER, N.

SPEDDING, James (1808–81), edited *The Works of Francis Bacon* (7 vols, 1857–9). His *Evenings with a Reviewer* (1848) was a refutation of *Macaulay's 'Essay' on *Bacon which he subsequently developed in his *The Letters and Life of Francis Bacon* (1861–72).

Speed, in Shakespeare's *The Two Gentlemen of Verona*, Valentine's servant.

SPEED, John (?1552–1629), historian and cartographer, made various maps of English counties, and was encouraged by *Camden, *Cotton, and others to write his *Historie of Great Britaine* (1611). The maps were far more valuable than the history; they began about 1607, and an atlas of them appeared in 1611.

Speed the Plough, see MORTON, T.

SPEKE, John Hanning (1827–64), explorer, discovered Lake Victoria Nyanza, Lake Tanganyika, and gave information to Sir S. *Baker which led to the discovery of Lake Albert Nyanza. He published in 1863 his *Journal of the Discovery of the Source of the Nile* and in 1864 *What led to the Discovery of the Source of the Nile*.

SPENCE, Joseph (1699–1768), clergyman, anecdotist, scholar, succeeded T. *Warton as professor of poetry at Oxford in 1728. He was a close friend of *Pope, and from 1726 collected anecdotes and recorded conversations with Pope and other literary figures. These, although not published until 1820, were well known and widely quoted during the 18th cent., and were made available to and used by *Warburton and Dr *Johnson. They are usually referred to under the title *Spence's Anecdotes*.

SPENCER, Herbert (1820–1903), worked as a civil engineer for the London and Birmingham Railway Company until 1841, then turned his attention to philosophy and published *Social Statics* (1850) and *Principles of Psychology* (1855); in 1860, after reading C. *Darwin, he announced a systematic series of treatises, to the elaboration of which he devoted the remainder of his life: *First Principles* (1862), *Principles of Biology* (1864–7), *Principles of Sociology* (1876–96), and *Principles of Ethics* (1879–93). His other works include an autobiography (1904).

Spencer was the founder of evolutionary

philosophy, pursuing the unification of all knowledge on the basis of a single all-pervading principle, that of evolution, which he defines as follows: 'an integration of matter and concomitant dissipation of emotion; during which matter passes from an indefinite incoherent homogeneity to a definite coherent heterogeneity; and during which the retained motion undergoes a parallel transformation'. The process continues until equilibrium is reached, after which the action of the environment will in time bring about disintegration.

This theory of a physical system leads up to Spencer's ethical system, where he is less successful in producing a consistent whole. He was essentially an individualist, and his first ethical principle is the equal right of every individual to act as he likes, so long as he does not interfere with the liberty of others. His effort is to reconcile utilitarian with evolutionary ethics, but he had to confess that for the purpose of deducing ethical principles 'the Doctrine of Evolution has not furnished guidance to the extent that I had hoped'.

In a literary context Spencer is remembered for his friendship with G. *Eliot, whom he met in 1851.

SPENDER, Sir Stephen Harold (1909–   ), poet and critic, educated at University College, Oxford, where he became friendly with *Auden and *MacNeice and met *Isherwood. After leaving Oxford he lived in Germany for a period, an experience which sharpened his political consciousness. His *Poems* (1933) contained both personal and political poems, including 'The Landscape near an Aerodrome', and 'The Pylons', which gave the nickname of *'Pylon poets' to himself and his friends. He also published a critical work, *The Destructive Element* (1935), largely on H. *James, T. S. *Eliot, and *Yeats. During the Spanish Civil War he did propaganda work in Spain for the Republican side, a period reflected in his volume of poems *The Still Centre* (1939). A gradual shift in his political allegiances may be seen in his poetry, in his critical works (e.g. *The Creative Element*, 1953), and in his contribution to *The God That Failed*; he also gives an account of his relationship with the Communist Party in his autobiography *World Within World* (1951). His interest in the public and social role and duty of the writer has tended to obscure the essentially personal and private nature of much of his own poetry, including his elegies for his sister-in-law, in *Poems of Dedication* (1947), and many of the poems in such later volumes as *Collected Poems 1928–1953* (1955). His other works include *Trial of a Judge* (1938); many translations; and *The Thirties and After* (1978, a volume of memoirs). His *Collected Poems 1982–85* and his *Journals 1939–83* were both published in 1985.

Spenlow, Dora, in Dickens's *David Copperfield*, the hero's 'child-wife'.

Spenlow and Jorkins, in Dickens's *David Copperfield*, a firm of proctors in Doctors' Commons, to whom Copperfield is articled.

Spens, Sir Patrick, see SIR PATRICK SPENS.

SPENSER, Edmund (*c.* 1552–99), was educated at Merchant Taylors' School and Pembroke Hall, Cambridge. In 1569, while still at Cambridge, he contributed a number of 'Visions' and sonnets, from *Petrarch and *Du Bellay, to van der Noodt's *Theatre for Worldlings*. To the 'greener times' of his youth belong also the 'Hymne in Honour of Love' and that of 'Beautie' (not published until 1596), which reflect his study of *Neoplatonism. In 1579, through his college friend G. *Harvey, Spenser obtained a place in Leicester's household and became acquainted with Sir P. *Sidney, to whom he dedicated his *Shepheardes Calender* (1579). He probably married Machabyas Chylde in the same year, and began to write *The Faerie Queene*. In 1580 he was appointed secretary to Lord Grey of Wilton, then going to Ireland as lord deputy. In 1588 or 1589 he became one of the 'undertakers' for the settlement of Munster, and acquired Kilcolman Castle in Co. Cork. Here he occupied himself with literary work, writing his elegy *'Astrophel', on Sidney, and preparing *The Faerie Queene* for the press. The first three books of it were entrusted to the publisher during his visit to London in 1589. He returned reluctantly to Kilcolman, which he liked to regard as a place of exile, in 1591, recording his visit to London and return to Ireland in *Colin Clouts come home againe* (printed 1595). The success of *The Faerie Queene* led the publisher, Ponsonby, to issue his minor verse and juvenilia, in part rewritten, as *Complaints, Containing sundrie small Poemes of the Worlds Vanitie* (1591). This volume included *'The Ruines of Time', a further elegy on Sidney, dedicated to Sidney's sister, the countess of *Pembroke; *'Mother Hubberds Tale'; *'Muiopotmos'; *'The Teares of the Muses', and 'Virgils Gnat'; also in 1591 *Daphnaïda* was published. In 1594 he married Elizabeth Boyle, whom he had wooed in his *Amoretti*, and celebrated the marriage in his superb *Epithalamion*: the works were printed together in 1595. He published Books IV–VI of *The Faerie Queene* and his *Fowre Hymnes* in 1596, being in London at the house of his friend the earl of Essex, where he wrote his *Prothalamion* and also his well-informed though propagandist *View of the Present State of Ireland*. His castle of Kilcolman was burnt in October 1598, in a sudden insurrection of the natives. He died in London in distress, if not actual destitution, and was buried near his favourite *Chaucer in Westminster Abbey. His monument describes him as

'THE PRINCE OF POETS IN HIS TYME': there have been few later periods in which he has not been admired, and the poetry of both *Milton and *Keats had its origins in the reading of Spenser.

Spenserian stanza, the stanza invented by E. *Spenser, in which he wrote *The Faerie Queene. It consists of eight five-foot iambic lines, followed by an iambic line of six feet, rhyming a b a b b c b c c.

Spirit of the Age, The, essays by W. *Hazlitt, published 1825.

The essays are on the work and characters of a selection of Hazlitt's contemporaries, such as *Coleridge, *Wordsworth, and *Lamb, and of writers of the previous half-century. The essays are generally considered to represent Hazlitt at the height of his powers as writer and critic.

Spiritual Quixote, The, see GRAVES, RICHARD.

Spleen, The, (1) a poem by Anne Finch, countess of *Winchelsea (1709); (2) a poem by M. *Green (1737).

Splendid Shilling, The, see PHILIPS, J.

Spondee, see METRE.

Sponge, Mr Soapey, see SURTEES, R. S.

Spoonerism, see METATHESIS.

Sporus, the name under which *Pope satirizes Lord *Hervey in his Epistle to Dr Arbuthnot (ll. 305 ff.). The original Sporus was an effeminate favourite of the Emperor Nero.

SPRAT, Thomas (1635–1713), bishop of Rochester and dean of Westminster. As a writer he is chiefly remembered for his history of the *Royal Society (1667), of which he was one of the first members, but he was also known as a poet (The Plague of Athens, 1659, was his most popular poem) and for his life of his friend *Cowley, which was attached to Cowley's works from 1668 onwards.

Springrove, Edward, a character in Hardy's *Desperate Remedies.

Sprung rhythm (or 'abrupt' rhythm), a term invented by G. M. *Hopkins to describe his own idiosyncratic poetic metre, as opposed to normal 'running' rhythm, the regular alternation of stressed and unstressed syllables. Hopkins maintained that sprung rhythm existed, unrecognized, in Old English poetry and in Shakespeare, *Dryden, and *Milton (notably in *Samson Agonistes). It is distinguished by a metrical foot consisting of a varying number of syallables. The extra, 'slack' syllables added to

the established patterns are called 'outrides' or 'hangers'. Hopkins demonstrated the natural occurrence of this rhythm in English by pointing out that many nursery rhymes employed it, e.g.

Díng, Dóng, Béll,
Pússy's in the wéll.

He felt strongly that his poetry should be read aloud, but seems to have felt that the words themselves were not enough to suggest the intended rhythms, and frequently added various diacritical markings. Some critics have suggested that sprung rhythm is not a poetic metre at all, properly speaking, merely Hopkins's attempt to force his own personal rhythm into an existing pattern, or recognizable variation of one, and that his sprung rhythm is in fact closer to some kinds of free verse or polyphonic prose.

SPURGEON, Caroline (1886–1942), American critic, whose Shakespeare's Imagery (1935) was the first detailed study of its subject.

Square, a character in Fielding's *Tom Jones.

Squeers, Wackford, in Dickens's *Nicholas Nickleby, the headmaster of Dotheboys Hall. He has a heartless wife, a spiteful daughter, Fanny, and a spoilt son, Wackford.

SQUIRE, J(ohn) C(ollings) (1884–1958), a highly influential literary journalist and essayist, a skilful parodist, and poet. He established the *London Mercury in 1919, and as sometime literary editor of the *New Statesmen and chief literary critic of the *Observer he exercised considerable power. In the 1920s and 1930s he and his friends formed a literary establishment which was violently opposed by the *Sitwells and the *Bloomsbury group, known as 'the Squirearchy'. Squire edited several anthologies, including A Book of Women's Verse (1921) and The Comic Muse (1925), and three volumes of Selections from Modern Poets (1921–34). His Collected Poems, edited by *Betjeman, were published posthumously in 1959.

Squire of Dames, a humorous character in Spenser's *Faerie Queene (III. vii).

Squire of Low Degree, The, a metrical romance, probably mid–15th cent.

The squire declares his love to a princess, who consents to marry him when he has proved himself a distinguished knight. But he is seen in his tryst by a steward whom he kills after the steward reports to the king. The squire is imprisoned but finally released because the princess is inconsolable, whereupon he sets out on his quest, proves his worth, and marries the princess.

'Squire's Tale, The', see CANTERBURY TALES, 11.

Squyre Meldrum, The Historie of, see LINDSAY, SIR D.

STACPOOLE, H(enry) de Vere (1863–1931) is remembered for his best-selling romance *The Blue Lagoon* (1908), the story of two cousins, Dick and Emmeline, marooned at the age of eight on a tropical island; they grow up, produce a baby, and are eventually swept away across their lagoon to the ocean and the oblivion of 'the never-wake berries' which they providentially carry with them in their dinghy.

Stagirite, or **Stagyrite, The,** *Aristotle, born in Stagira in Macedon.

Stalky & Co., tales of schoolboy life, by *Kipling.

Stand, a literary quarterly founded in 1952 by J. *Silkin. It publishes poetry, fiction, and criticism and contributors have included G. *Hill, G. *MacBeth, Lorna Tracy, D. *Abse, and many others; it has also published many works in translation.

STANHOPE, Lady Hester (1776–1839), was the niece of the younger Pitt, in whose house she gained a reputation as a brilliant political hostess. In 1814 she established herself in a remote ruined convent at Djoun in the Lebanon where she lived in great magnificence among a semi-oriental retinue; she gained some political power in Syria and the desert. In later years her debts accumulated, her eccentricity increased, and she claimed to be an inspired prophetess and mistress of occult sciences. She became a legendary figure, and was visited by many distinguished European travellers, including Lamartine and *Kinglake.

Stanhope Press, an iron printing-press invented by Charles, third early Stanhope (1753–1816), the father of Lady Hester (above). He also devised a stereotyping process, and a microscopic lens which bears his name.

STANLEY, Arthur Penrhyn (1815–81), a leader of the *Broad Church movement and author of *The Life and Correspondence of Thomas Arnold* (1844).

STANLEY, Sir Henry Morton (1841–1904), explorer and journalist, joined the *New York Herald* in 1867 and in 1869 was instructed by his editor Gordon Bennett to find *Livingstone. He first travelled to Egypt, Palestine, Turkey, Persia, and India; he found Livingstone at Ujiji in 1871. *How I found Livingstone* (1872) relates his adventures. His further explorations and discoveries in Africa are described in *Through the Dark Continent* (1878) and *In Darkest Africa* (1890).

Stanzaic Life of Christ, The, a 14th cent. compilation in 10,840 lines of English quatrains, drawn from the *Polychronicon* of *Higden and the *Legend Aurea* of Jacobus de Voragine (see GOLDEN LEGEND). It was written by a monk of St Werburgh's, Chester, and it was an influence on the Chester *Mystery Plays.

STAPLEDON, Olaf, see SCIENCE FICTION.

Staple of News, The, a comedy by *Jonson, performed 1626, printed 1631, in which on the one hand he satirizes the credulity of the age, and on the other illustrates the use and abuse of riches.

Stareleigh, Mr Justice, in Dickens's *Pickwick Papers,* the judge in the case of Bardell v. Pickwick.

STARK, Freya (1893–), whose many books on her travels in Iran, Iraq, southern Arabia, and Asia Minor include *The Valleys of the Assassins* (1934), *The Southern Gates of Arabia* (1936), *Iona: A Quest* (1954), and *The Lycian Shore* (1956). Four volumes of autobiography, including *Traveller's Prelude* (1950), and six volumes of letters appeared in 1950–61 and 1974–81. She was made a DBE in 1972.

Starveling, in Shakespeare's *A Midsummer Night's Dream,* a tailor, who appears as Moonshine in the play 'Pyramus and Thisbe'.

Stationers' Company, The, was incorporated by royal charter in 1557. No one not a member of the Company might print anything for sale in the kingdom unless authorized by special privilege or patent. Moreover, by the rules of the Company, every member was required to enter in the register of the Company the name of any book that he desired to print, so that these registers furnish valuable information regarding printed matter during the latter part of the 16th cent. The Company's control of the printing trade waned during the 17th cent., to be revived in a modified form under the Copyright Act of 1709. See also COPYRIGHT.

STATIUS, Publius Papinius (AD *c.*45–96), Roman epic poet and Silver Age imitator of *Virgil. His surviving works are: *Silvae,* occasional verses which include a famous piece on sleep that inspired *Drummond of Hawthornden, an epic, *Thebais,* in 12 books, relating the bloody quarrel between the sons of Oedipus, and an unfinished epic, the *Achilleis.* Chaucer based his 'Knight's Tale' (*Canterbury Tales,* 1) on *Boccaccio, who had used the *Thebais.*

Staunton, Sir George, alias George Robertson, a character in Scott's *The Heart of Midlothian.*

Staying On, see SCOTT, P.

STEAD, Christina Ellen (1902–83), Australian novelist, came to London in 1928 and subsequently worked and travelled in Europe and America, returning to Australia in 1968. Her wandering life and her left-wing views may have contributed to the neglect of her work, which towards the end of her life received renewed attention and admiration. Her first collection of stories, The Salzbury Tales (1934), was followed by several full-length novels, which include her best-known work, The Man who loved Children (1940), a bitterly ironic view of American family life and conflict; For Love Alone (1945), Letty Fox: Her Luck (1946), and Cotter's England (1967), which presents a vivid portrait of post-war working-class Britain, centred on the extraordinary personality of chain-smoking, emotional, destructive Nellie Cook, née Cotter, a journalist working on a left-wing London paper.

STEAD, W(illiam) T(homas) (1849–1912), assistant editor of the *Pall Mall Gazette in 1880 and editor 1883–8, in which capacity he initiated new and influential political and social movements. He achieved wide notoriety for his 'Maiden Tribute of Modern Babylon' (1885) exposing sexual vice, which led to Parliament raising the age of consent to 16 years. He founded the Review of Reviews in 1890. He was drowned in the Titanic disaster.

STEELE, Sir Richard (1672–1729), was born in Dublin, in the same year as *Addison, and was educated with him at the Charterhouse. He was subsequently at Merton College, Oxford, whence he entered the army as a cadet in the Life Guards. As a result of a poem on Queen Mary's funeral dedicated to Lord Cutts, colonel of the Coldstream Guards, he became his secretary and obtained the rank of captain. He published *The Christian Hero in 1701, in which he first displayed his missionary and reforming spirit. In the same year he produced his first comedy, The Funeral. Neither this nor his two next comedies, The Lying Lover (1703) and The Tender Husband (1705), proved very successful.

In 1709 he started *The Tatler, which he conducted with the help of Addison until January 1711, and, again with Addison, he carried on *The Spectator during 1711–12. This was followed by *The Guardian. In 1713 he was elected MP for Stockbridge. In 1714 he published The Crisis, a pamphlet in favour of the Hanoverian succession, which was answered by *Swift, and led to Steele's expulsion from the House on 18 March 1714. The tide turned in his favour with the accession of George I. He was appointed supervisor of Drury Lane Theatre, and to other posts, and was knighted in 1715. His last comedy, *The Conscious Lovers, was produced in 1722. His letters to his second wife, Mary Scurlock ('dear Prue'), were printed in 1787. Less highly regarded as an essayist than Addison, his influence was nevertheless great; his attacks on *Restoration drama; his approval

of the 'sober and polite Mirth' of *Terence; his praise of tender and affectionate domestic and family life; and his own reformed and sentimental dramas did much to create an image of polite behaviour for the new century.

Steele Glas, The, a satire in verse by *Gascoigne, published 1576

The common looking-glass only shows the thing much better than it is. Looking into his 'steele glas' the poet sees himself with his faults and then successively the faults of kings; covetous lords and knights; drunken soldiers; false judges; merchants; priests; etc. Finally the ploughman is held up as a model:

> Behold him (priests) & though he stink of sweat
> Disdaine him not: for shal I tel you what?
> Such clime to heaven, before the shaven crownes.

Steerforth, James, a character in Dickens's *David Copperfield.

STEEVENS, George (1736–1800), Shakespearian commentator, who in 1766 issued in four volumes Twenty of the Plays of Shakespeare, being the whole Number printed in Quarto during his Lifetime, or before the Restoration, and in 1773 a complete annotated edition (including notes by Dr *Johnson) in ten volumes, to which a supplementary volume of poems, together with seven plays ascribed to Shakespeare, was added in 1780. He supplied to his edition a vast range of illustrative quotations from other works. He was elected a member of Johnson's *Club in 1774. He assisted *Tyrwhitt in his edition of the 'Rowley' poems of *Chatterton, but declared his disbelief in them.

STEIN, Gertude (1874–1946), American author. In 1902 she went to Paris where she settled; her home in the rue de Fleurus became a literary salon and art gallery and a home of the avant-garde. Her friend, secretary, and companion from 1907 was San Francisco-born Alice B. Toklas (1877–1967), whom she made the ostensible author of her own memoir, The Autobiography of Alice B. Toklas (1933). Her fiction includes Three Lives (1909); The Making of Americans (1925); and A Long Gay Book (1932). Tender Buttons (1914) is an example of her highly idiosyncratic poetry. Her characteristic repetitions and reprises, her flowing, unpunctuated prose, and her attempts to capture the 'living moment' owe much to William *James and to *Bergson's concept of time, and represent a personal but influential version of the *stream-of-consciousness technique.

STEINBECK, John Ernst (1902–68), American novelist. California, his native state, formed the background for his early short stories and novels. *Tortilla Flat* (1935) was his first success, and he confirmed his growing reputation with two novels about landless rural workers, *In Dubious Battle* (1936) and *Of Mice and Men* (1937), the story of two itinerant farm labourers, one of huge strength and weak mind, exploited and protected by the other. His best-known work, *The Grapes of Wrath* (1939), is an epic account of the efforts of an emigrant farming family from the dust bowl of the West to reach the 'promised land' of California. Among his later novels are *East of Eden* (1952), a family saga, and *The Winter of our Discontent* (1961). He was awarded the *Nobel Prize in 1962.

STEINER, (Francis) George (1929–   ), American critic and author. His critical works include *The Death of Tragedy* (1961); *Language and Silence* (1967); *In Bluebeard's Castle: Some Notes Towards the Re-Definition of Culture* (1971); and *After Babel: Aspects of Language and Translation* (1975). One of Steiner's recurrent themes is the way in which the 20th-cent. experiences of totalitarianism and world war, and, more specifically, of the Holocaust, have destroyed the assumption that literature is a humanizing influence. The Holocaust is the subject of his novella *The Portage to San Cristobal of A. H.* (1979; dramatized by Christopher Hampton, 1982). *Antigones* (1985) is concerned with individual resistance to oppression.

Stella, (1) the chaste lady loved by Astrophel in Sidney's sonnet sequence *Astrophel and Stella*, based on Penelope *Rich; (2) Swift's name for Esther Johnson; see SWIFT, and in particular the account there of the *Journal to Stella*.

Stephano, in Shakespeare's *The Tempest*, a drunken butler.

STEPHEN, Sir James (1789–1859), father of Sir J. F. *Stephen and Sir L. *Stephen, and professor of modern history at Cambridge (1849–59). He is remembered as author of *Essays in Ecclesiastical Biography* (1849) and *Lectures on the History of France* (1851).

STEPHEN, Sir James Fitzjames (1829–94), son of Sir J. *Stephen and brother of Sir L. *Stephen, became legal member of council in India (1869–72) and high court judge (1879–91). In 1861 he was counsel for Rowland Williams in the *Essays and Reviews* case. He was a member of the *Apostles and the *Metaphysical Society and vigorously contributed articles on social, moral, and controversial theological subjects to periodicals. Among his works were *A History of the Criminal Law in England* (1883), *Horae Sabbaticae* (1892, collected articles from the *Saturday Review*), and *Liberty, Equality, Fraternity* (1873, re-published 1967) in which he criticized J. S. *Mill's utilitarian position in his essay *On Liberty*.

STEPHEN, James Kenneth (1859–92), younger son of Sir J. F. *Stephen. He began a weekly paper, *The Reflector*, chiefly written by himself. He was author (as 'J.K.S.') of highly successful parodies and light verse, collected as *Lapsus Calami* and *Quo Musa Tendis* (both 1891). His promising career ended as a result of an accident in 1886 which slowly drove him insane, and he has been suggested as a candidate for the role of *Jack the Ripper.

STEPHEN, Sir Leslie (1832–1904), son of Sir J. *Stephen and brother of Sir J. F. *Stephen, was educated at Trinity Hall, Cambridge, where he became tutor, having taken orders. From his family he inherited a strong tradition of Evangelicalism and muscular Christianity, and he became a noted mountaineer: he edited the *Alpine Journal*, 1868–72, and the best of his Alpine essays were collected in *The Playground of Europe* (1871).

Stephen's reading of J. S. *Mill, *Comte, and *Kant inclined him to scepticism, and by 1865 he had abandoned all belief. In 1864 he came to London and embarked on a literary career of prodigious industry and output, contributing articles to many periodicals. He was editor of the *The Cornhill* (1871–82), then he became editor of the *Dictionary of National Biography. His great work, *History of English Thought in the 18th Century* (1876), reviews the Deist controversy of that age, and the intuitional and utilitarian schools of philosophy. He also contributed several biographies to the English Men of Letters series and almost 400 entries to the *DNB*. His last important volume was *English Literature and Society in the Eighteenth Century* (1904). He was one of the most prominent intellectuals of his day (portrayed by his friend *Meredith as Vernon Whitford in *The Egoist*).

Stephen's first wife was *Thackeray's daughter 'Minny', who died in 1875. His acute grief, and his second marriage to Julia Duckworth, are both recorded in his autobiographical papers, written for his children by Julia (one of whom was V. *Woolf) and step-children and published in 1977 (ed. A. Bell) as *Mausoleum Book*. V. Woolf portrays some aspects of his character in her portrait of Mr Ramsay in *To the Lighthouse* (1927).

STEPHENS, James (1882–1950), Irish poet and storywriter whose best-known work is the prose fantasy *The Crock of Gold* (1912). His volumes of verse include *Insurrections* (1909) and *Collected Poems* of 1926 and 1954. His first novel, *The Charwoman's Daughter* (1912), was followed by *The Demi-Gods* (1914) and *Deirdre* (1923). Many volumes of stories include *Irish Fairy Tales* (1920) and *Etched in Moonlight* (1928).

STERLING, John (1806–44), a leading member of the *Apostles and disciple of *Coleridge.

With *Maurice he was briefly proprietor of the *Athenaeum (1828). He was offered in 1834 the curacy of Herstmonceux by his old tutor *Hare, who was vicar, but he resigned the following year. Sterling owes his fame to his close friendship with *Carlyle whose vivid Life of Sterling (1851) reveals the tragic history of Sterling's short life, interrupted by persistent ill health. His monthly meetings of literary friends, from 1838, became known as the Sterling Club; among its members were Carlyle, Hare, J. S. *Mill, and *Tennyson. Among his few published works were a novel, Arthur Coningsby (1833), Poems (1839), and Essays and Tales (1848).

STERNE, Laurence (1713–68), educated at Jesus College, Cambridge, where he embraced the philosophy of *Locke and made a lifelong friend of *Hall-Stevenson, who was probably the model for *Eugenius. He took holy orders and obtained the living of the Yorkshire parish of Sutton-on-the-Forest in 1738. In 1741 he married Elizabeth Lumley. In 1759 he began *Tristram Shandy, Vols I and II being published in that year. This work brought him fame and success, although Dr *Johnson, *Richardson, *Goldsmith, and others criticized it on both literary and moral grounds. He went to London and he was fêted by society, had his portrait painted by *Reynolds, was invited to Court. He published The Sermons of Mr Yorick (1760), a volume whose title caused some scandal, and in 1761 four more volumes of Tristram Shandy appeared. Meanwhile Sterne's health was deteriorating steadily. In 1762 in the hope of improvement he and his wife and daughter left for France. Sterne returned alone to England in 1764, and in 1765 published Vols VII and VIII of Tristram Shandy; Vol IX appeared in 1767. In 1765 he returned to France and undertook an eight-month tour of France and Italy, which clearly provided him with much of the material for *A Sentimental Journey through France and Italy (1768). In 1766 he published two further volumes of sermons. In 1767 Sterne met and fell in love with Elizabeth *Draper, and began his Journal to *Eliza. He died of tuberculosis in London in March 1768.

A spate of forgeries appeared after Sterne's death, including another volume of Tristram Shandy, Posthumous Works, and a continuation by 'Eugenius' (an author whose identity is not known, but who was not Hall-Stevenson) of A Sentimental Journey.

Sterne is generally acknowledged as an innovator of the highest originality, and has been seen as the chief begetter of a long line of writers interested in the *'stream-of-consciousness'. He acknowledges in Tristram Shandy his own debt in this respect to *Locke. Throughout his work he parodies the developing conventions of the still-new 'novel', and its problems in presenting reality, space, and time. His sharp but often salacious wit is balanced by the affection he displays towards the delights and absurdities of life.

STERNHOLD, Thomas (d. 1549), and **HOPKINS,** John (d. 1570), joint versifiers of the Psalms. A collection of 44 of these versified Psalms appeared in 1549; music was first supplied in the Geneva edition of 1556, and by 1640 about 300 editions had been published. In 1562 The Whole Book of Psalmes, by Sternhold, Hopkins, Norton, and others, was added to the Prayer Book.

STEVENS, Wallace (1879–1955), American poet. His first volume of poems, Harmonium (1923), containing 'Thirteen Ways of Looking at a Blackbird', was followed by other collections (including Ideas of Order, 1935; The Man with the Blue Guitar and other Poems, 1937; Notes towards a Supreme Fiction, 1942; The Auroras of Autumn, 1950; Collected Poems, 1954) which slowly brought him recognition, but it was not until his last years that his enigmatic, elegant, intellectual, and occasionally startling meditations on order and the imagination, on reality, appearance, and art, gained the high reputation that they now enjoy.

STEVENSON, John Hall-, see HALL-STEVENSON, J.

STEVENSON, Robert Louis (originally Lewis) Balfour (1850–94), entered Edinburgh University to study engineering but soon abandoned this for the law. In 1875 L. *Stephen introduced him to W. E. *Henley, who became a close friend, and with whom he was to collaborate on four plays. From this time on much of his life was spent travelling in search of health; he suffered from a chronic bronchial condition (possibly tuberculosis). In France in 1876 he met Mrs Fanny Osbourne whom he married in 1880. He published An Inland Voyage (1878), describing a canoe tour in Belgium and France, and Travels with a Donkey in the Cevennes (1879), relating a tour with his donkey Modestine. He travelled to California in 1879; published The Silverado Squatters (1883); then returned to Europe, settling at Bournemouth for three years in 1884, where he consolidated a friendship with H. *James. By this time he had published widely in periodicals, and many of his short stories, essays, and travel pieces were collected in volume form. His first full-length work of fiction, *Treasure Island (1883), brought him fame, which increased with the publication of The Strange Case of Dr *Jekyll and Mr Hyde (1886). This was followed by his popular Scottish romances, *Kidnapped (1886), its sequel Catriona (1893), and *The Master of Ballantrae (1889).

In 1888 Stevenson had set out with his family entourage for the South Seas. He visited the leper colony at Molokai, which inspired his celebrated defence of the Belgian priest Father Damien (1841–89), in *Father Damien: an open letter to the Reverand Dr Hyde of Honolulu* (1890). He finally settled in Samoa at Vailima, where he gained a reputation as 'Tusitala' or 'The Story Teller'. He died there suddenly from a brain haemorrhage, while working on his unfinished masterpeice, *Weir of Hermiston* (1896).

Stevenson published many other volumes, including *The Merry Men* (1887, with 'Markheim' and his earliest Scottish story, 'Thrawn Janet'); many travel books; *Island Nights' Entertainments* (1893), which includes 'The Beach of Falesá'; and *St Ives* (1897, unfinished, completed by *Quiller-Couch). With his stepson Lloyd Osbourne he wrote *The Wrong Box* (1889), *The Wrecker* (1892), and *The Ebb-Tide* (1894). He also published volumes of poetry, including *A Child's Garden of Verses* (1885) and *Underwoods* (1887): his *Collected Poems*, ed. Janet Adam Smith appeared in 1950. In them as in many of his prose works, critics have detected beneath the lightness of touch a sense of apprehension, sin, and suffering. The theme of dualism and the *Doppelgänger* recurs in his work, as does an admiration for morally ambiguous heroes or anti-heroes. Although his more popular books have remained constantly in print, and have been frequently filmed, his critical reputation has been obscured by attention to his vivid personality and adventurous life.

STEWART, Dugald (1753–1828), professor of moral philosophy at Edinburgh from 1785 to 1810, in which post he exercised a powerful influence on Scottish thought, largely because of his brilliant pedagogy and his elegant prose. Although Stewart considered himself a disciple of T. *Reid, he was an eclectic thinker who borrowed from a wide range of sources. He was particularly indebted to the writings of Adam *Smith. In both his lectures and his publications Stewart was primarily concerned with the inculcation of virtue rather than with abstract theorizing. His works, collected by Sir W. *Hamilton (11 vols, 1854–60), include: *Elements of the Human Mind* (1792, 1814, 1827), *Outlines of Moral Philosophy* (1793), *Philosophical Essays* (1810), and *Biographical Memoirs* (1810), consisting of lives of Adam Smith, W. *Robertson, and Reid.

STEWART, J(ohn) I(nnes) M(ackintosh) (1906–), Edinburgh novelist and critic, under the pseudonym Michael Innes has written many successful works of *detective fiction beginning with *Death at the President's Lodging* (1936), which introduced his detective, John Appleby of Scotland Yard; they are rich in literary allusions and quotations. He has also published several novels as J. I. M. Stewart, and has written critical works on Shakespeare, *Joyce, *Peacock, *Kipling, *Hardy, and others.

Stewart of the Glens, James, a character in R. L. Stevenson's *Kidnapped* and *Catriona*; a real character, who was executed in 1752 for a murder which he did not commit, after trial by a jury of Campbells (the foes of his clan).

Steyne, marquis of, a character in Thackeray's *Vanity Fair*.

Stichomythia, in classical Greek drama, dialogue in alternate lines of verse, employed in sharp disputation. The form is sometimes imitated in English drama, e.g. in the dialogue between Richard III and Elizabeth in Shakespeare's *Richard III* (IV. iv).

Stiggins, Mr, a character in Dickens's *Pickwick Papers*.

Stoicism was a system of thought which originated in Athens during the 3rd cent. BC, flourished in Rome c.100 BC–c. AD 200, exercised a lasting influence on Christianity, and enjoyed a vigorous revival at the time of the Renaissance.

The Stoics' prime concern was always with ethics, but they held that right behaviour had to be grounded on a general understanding of the universe, and their theories extended to cover the nature of the physical world, the arts of discourse (under which they included logic, rhetoric, literature, and grammar), epistemology, and politics. The founders of the school insisted that the ends men usually pursue—health, wealth, success, pleasure—had no real importance. Their successors of the Middle Stoa, who came under Roman influence, looked more favourably on the qualities that promote civilized life and recommended their exercise.

Only fragments have survived of the writings of the founders of Stoicism—Zeno of Citium (336–246 BC), the pious Cleanthes (?331–?232 BC), whose 'Hymn to Zeus' has been preserved, and Chrysippus (c.280–206 BC), the group's system-builder—who all taught in Athens. Information about them comes from later writers like *Diogenes Laertius. The philosophers of the Middle Stoa, Panaetius of Rhodes (189–109 BC) and Posidonius (135–51 BC), whose works are lost, are known through their disciple *Cicero. The Stoics whose writings survive lived under the Roman Empire: *Seneca, *Epictetus, and *Marcus Aurelius. Their interests were almost exclusively ethical, so that it is as a system of morality that Stoicism was to exercise its greatest influence.

Extolling Providence, the brotherhood of men, and the need to curb natural desires, Stoicism had much in common with Christianity, and a compilation of Stoic maxims, the *Distichs* *of Cato*, was the most popular of medieval schoolbooks. In England the years 1595–1615 saw translations of *Montaigne, his disciple Charron, Epictetus, and Seneca, and the influence of Stoicism can be traced in a great number of writers from *Chapman and Sir William Cornwallis (d. ?1631) to *Addison, and, many claim, in the ethos of Victorian public schools.

STOKER, Bram (Abraham) (1847–1912), born in Dublin, was for 27 years secretary and touring manager to Sir H. *Irving, an experience that produced *Personal Reminiscences of Henry Irving* (1906). Stoker wrote a number of novels and short stories, as well as some dramatic criticism, but is chiefly remembered for *Dracula* (1897), a tale of vampirism influenced by 'Carmilla', one of the stories in Le Fanu's *In a Glass Darkly* (1872).

Stones of Venice, The, by *Ruskin, an architectural study in 3 vols, published 1851–3.

Volume I sets out first principles for discrimination between good and bad architectural features; there follows, in this and volume II, a criticism of the romantic, *Byronic vision of Venice that blinds the traveller to present misery and disorder. From the remnants of the past Ruskin creates a myth of Venice, where power is decommercialized and desecularized, and religion pre-Catholic. The famous chapter 'The Nature of Gothic' contrasts feudal relations between authority and workman with those resulting from the division of labour and mechanical mass production in English manufacturing. Volume III describes phases in Renaissance architectural history as illustrations of the gradual degradation of Europe.

STOPES, Marie Charlotte Carmichael (1880–1958), distinguished palaeobotanist, established the first birth control clinic in England in 1921, in Holloway, London. She wrote on such subjects as *Married Love* (1918), *Wise Parenthood* (1918), *Radiant Motherhood* (1920), and sexual fulfilment within marriage. She also published several volumes of plays and of poetry.

STOPPARD, Tom (1937–), dramatist, born in Czechoslovakia; his family settled in England after the war. He published a novel, *Lord Malquist and the Moon* (1965), and his play *Rosencrantz and Guildenstern are dead* (1966) attracted much attention. This was followed by many witty and inventive plays, including *The Real Inspector Hound* (1968); *Jumpers* (1972); *Travesties* (1974); *Dirty Linen* (1976, a satire of political life); *Every Good Boy Deserves Favour* (1977); *Night and Day* (1978), about the dangers of the 'closed shop' in journalism; and *The Real Thing* (1982), a marital tragi-comedy. Stoppard has also written many works for film, radio, and television, including *Professional Foul* (TV, 1977). Stoppard's work displays a metaphysical wit, a strong theatrical sense, and talent for pastiche which enables him to move from mode to mode within the same scene with great flexibility and rapidity; yet the plays appear far from frivolous in intention, increasingly posing considerable ethical problems.

STOREY, David Malcolm (1933–), novelist and playwright, the son of a Yorkshire miner; he was educated at the Slade School of Fine Art. He worked as professional footballer, teacher, farm worker, and erector of show tents, acquiring a variety of experience which is evident in his works. His first novel, *This Sporting Life* (1960), describes the ambitions and passions of a young working man, Arthur Machin, a Rugby League player who becomes emotionally involved with his landlady. This was followed by other novels including *Flight into Camden* (1960), about the unhappy affair of a miner's daughter with a married teacher; *Radcliffe* (1963), a sombre, violent, Lawrentian novel about class conflict, the Puritan legacy, and destructive homosexual passion; and *Saville* (1976, *Booker Prize), an epic set in a South Yorkshire mining village. Meanwhile Storey had also established himself as a playwright, with such works as *In Celebration* (1969); *The Contractor* (1970); *Home* (1970), set in a mental home; *The Changing Room* (1972), again using football as a setting; *Life Class* (1974), set in an art college; and *Mother's Day* (1976), a violent black comedy set on a housing estate. Both plays and novels show a preoccupation with social mobility and the mental disturbance it frequently appears to cause, and an interesting and challenging combination of documentary naturalism with a sense of the symbolic and unspoken.

Story of an African Farm, The, a novel by O. *Schreiner.

Story of my Heart, The, a discourse by R. *Jefferies, published 1883.

Story of Rimini, The, a poem by Leigh *Hunt published 1816. The work (with which Hunt had assistance from *Byron) is based on *Dante's story of Paolo and Francesca.

Francesca leaves Ravenna as a bride, and journeys in moonlight to Rimini. The events which overtake her, and the feelings which arise, lead to her adulterous love for Paolo. The lovers are discovered, and their deaths conclude the poem.

STOW, John (1525–1605), chronicler and antiquary. He began from about 1564 to collect and transcribe manuscripts and to compose historical works, the first to be based on systematic study of public records.

As well as assisting M. *Parker with editing historical texts, his chief publications were: *The Workes of Geoffrey Chaucer* (1561); *Summarie of English Chronicles* (1565), an original historical work; *The Chronicles of England* (1580), later entitled *The Annales of England*; the second edition of *Holinshed's Chronicles* (1585–7); and lastly *A Survey of London* (1598 and 1603), invaluable for the detailed information it gives about the ancient city and its customs. Modernized and annotated editions have since been published. The fullest edition of the original work was C. L. Kingsford's of 1908.

STOWE, Mrs Harriet Elizabeth Beecher (1811–96), born in Connecticut, sister of Henry Ward Beecher (1813–87, divine, religious author, and journalist), was a schoolteacher in Cincinnati before marrying in 1836 C. E. Stowe. Her anti-slavery novel *Uncle Tom's Cabin* (1852; serialized in *National Era*, 1851–2) had a sensational success and stirred up great public feeling. It describes the sufferings caused by slavery; pious old Uncle Tom, sold by his well-intentioned Kentucky owner Mr Shelby to meet his debts, is bought first by the idealistic Augustine St Clair, in whose New Orleans household he becomes the favourite of the daughter, the saintly little Eva. But both Eva and St Clair die, and Tom is sold again, this time to a brutal cotton plantation owner, Simon Legree, who finally beats the unprotesting Tom to death just before Shelby's son arrives to redeem him. A parallel plot describes the escape to freedom in Canada of Shelby's slave, the beautiful quadroon Eliza, her child, and her husband George. The sensational religiosity of the story and its dubious conclusion (in which most of the survivors, including the once-irrepressible little slave Topsy, disappear back to Africa to become missionaries) contributed to a shift of attitude which came to use the phrase 'Uncle Tom' pejoratively, to indicate a supine collaboration with the oppressor. The novel's success brought Mrs Stowe to England in 1853, 1856, and 1859, where she was honoured by Queen *Victoria, although she later alienated British opinion by her *Lady Byron Vindicated* (1870), in which she charged *Byron with incestuous relations with his half-sister. Her other works include *Dred: A Tale of the Dismal Swamp* (1856); *The Minister's Wooing* (1859); *Old Town Folks* (1869); and *Poganuc People* (1878).

STRABO, (b. *c.*63 BC), author of a history, continuing that of Polybius, which is lost, and of an important extant historical geography of the Roman Empire in 17 books.

STRACHEY, (Giles) Lytton (1880–1932), biographer and essayist, educated at Trinity College, Cambridge; he became a member of the *Apostles and a friend of G. E. *Moore, M.

*Keynes, and L. *Woolf. He was thereafter a prominent member of the *Bloomsbury Group, advocating both in words and life its faith in tolerance in personal relationships. Strachey wrote extensively for periodicals and his flamboyant *Landmarks in French Literature* appeared in 1912. His *Eminent Victorians* (1918) is a landmark in the history of *biography. This was a collection of four biographical essays, on Cardinal *Manning, Florence Nightingale, T. *Arnold, and General Gordon; Strachey's wit, iconoclasm, satiric edge, and narrative powers captured a large readership. His irreverent but affectionate life of Queen *Victoria (1921) combined careful construction, telling anecdote, and an elegant mandarin style. His last full-length work, *Elizabeth and Essex: A Tragic History* (1928), is more lurid and pictorial; its emphasis on Elizabeth's relationship with her father and its effect on her treatment of Essex shows a clear (and early) debt to *Freud. Various collections of Strachey's essays, on subjects ranging from *Voltaire to the *Muggletonians, appeared during his life and posthumously.

STRAFFORD, Sir Thomas Wentworth, first earl of (1593–1641), English statesman, and from 1639 chief adviser to Charles I. He was impeached by the Commons in 1640, and he was executed, after the king's assent, on Tower Hill. His death was the subject of many epitaphs, the best known of which (attributed to *Cleveland) contains the lines 'Strafford, who was hurried hence | Twixt Treason and Convenience'; also of a tragedy by R. *Browning (below).

Strafford, a tragedy in blank verse by R. *Browning, published 1837. It was written at the instigation of *Macready, who produced it at Covent Garden on the day of publication, with himself in the title role.

The action deals loosely with the events surrounding the impeachment of *Strafford; Browning's interest lies in the interplay of love and loyalty between Strafford and the three other main characters: King Charles I, John Pym, and Lady Carlisle.

Strand Magazine, The (1891–1950), a popular illustrated monthly founded by G. *Newnes, which included amongst its contributions fiction by A. C. *Doyle (the first appearance of Sherlock Holmes), H. G. *Wells, *Morrison, and short stories of P. G. *Wodehouse.

Strange Case of Dr Jekyll and Mr Hyde, The, see JEKYLL.

Strap, a character in Smollett's *Roderick Random*.

STRAUSS, David Friedrich (1808–74), German biblical critic, whose *Das Leben Jesu* (*The*

Life of Jesus, 1835–6) had an immense influence on 19th-cent. religious thought. It was translated by G. *Eliot (1846) and her study of it helped to confirm her break with Christianity.

Straw, Jack, see JACK STRAW.

Strawberry Hill, near Twickenham, about ten miles west of the centre of London. Horace *Walpole settled there in 1747, and with advice from his friends *Chute and Richard *Bentley transformed it into 'a little Gothic castle', housing in it his collection of articles of virtu, and establishing in 1757 a private press. (See also GOTHIC REVIVAL.)

Stream of Consciousness, a phrase coined by W. *James in his *Principles of Psychology* (1890) to describe the flow of thoughts of the waking mind, but now widely used in a literary context to describe the narrative method whereby certain novelists describe the unspoken thoughts and feelings of their characters, without resorting to objective description or conventional dialogue and often without logical sequence or syntax. *Les Lauriers sont coupés* (1888) by the minor French novelist Édouard Dujardin (1861–1949) has been credited (by *Joyce, principally) as a pioneering example of the technique, and it was adapted and developed by Joyce himself, by D. *Richardson, V. *Woolf, Proust, and others. The related phrase 'interior monologue' is also used to describe the inner movement of consciousness in a character's mind: celebrated examples are the opening pages of *Mrs Dalloway*, and Molly Bloom's reflections in the closing pages of *Ulysses*.

STREATFEILD, Noel, see CHILDREN'S LITERATURE.

Streetcar named Desire, A, a play by T. *Williams.

Strephon, the shepherd whose lament for his lost Urania forms the opening of Sidney's *Arcadia*. 'Strephon' has been adopted as a conventional name for a rustic lover.

Strether, Lewis Lambert, a character in H. James's *The Ambassadors*.

STRETTON, Hesba, the *nom de plume* of Sarah Smith (1832–1911), author of *Jessica's First Prayer* (1867), which remained popular for many years. She also wrote three long novels, which were well received.

STRINDBERG, (Johan) August (1849–1912), Swedish playwright and author. His first important play, *Master Olof* (1881), was followed by others, including *The Father* (1887), *Miss Julie* (1888), and *Creditors* (1889), works

which combine a highly aggressive and original version of *naturalism with a sense of the extreme and pathological. His later works are tense, symbolic, psychic dramas, marked by a sense of suffering and a longing for salvation and absolution; they include *To Damascus* (1898–1901; 3 parts), *The Dance of Death* (1901), *A Dream Play* (1902), and *The Ghost Sonata* (1907), all distinctive and innovative works which influenced the psychological and symbolic dramas of *O'Neill and the writers of the Theatre of the *Absurd.

Strong, Dr, in Dickens's *David Copperfield*, an amiable old schoolmaster.

Structuralism, a continental European movement in the human sciences which has had a powerful and controversial influence on literary theory and criticism in the English-speaking world since the 1960s. Its intellectual roots are in the linguistics of *Saussure, and in the work of the Russian Formalists in the Revolutionary period and of the Prague School in the 1930s—*Jakobson being a key figure in both groups. In the 1960s a brilliant generation of French, or French-based, critics, notably Roland Barthes (1915–80), Tzvetan Todorov (1940–), and Gérard Genette (1930–), elaborated and developed structuralist ideas and methods, with particularly successful results in application to narrative. The studies of myth by the anthropologist Claude Lévi-Strauss (1908–) also enhanced the prestige of structuralism at this time.

Structuralism views any cultural phenomenon, from a folk-tale to a menu or an advertisement, as the product of a 'system of signification', or code, and maintains that it is the relationships between the elements of such a system that allow it to signify, rather than the relationships between the elements and 'reality'. All codes of signification are arbitrary, and there is no way of apprehending reality without a code. In its purest form, structuralism tries to do for culture at large what grammar does for natural languages—to identify and define the rules and constraints within which and by virtue of which meaning is generated and communicated. As applied to literary criticism it calls into question the idea that a literary text reflects a reality that is already given, or that it expresses a unique authorial self, and thus challenges the empiricist and humanist assumptions of traditional literary scholarship. This challenge has become more radical in 'post-structuralist' critical theory and practice inspired by the psychoanalyst Jacques Lacan (1901–81) and the philosopher Jacques Derrida (1930–). Critical 'deconstruction', derived from the work of Derrida, aims to show that any and every text inevitably undermines its own claims to a determinate meaning, and emphasizes the role of the reader in the production of meaning.

Struldbrugs, see GULLIVER'S TRAVELS.

STRUTT, Joseph (1749–1802), author, artist, engraver, and antiquary, was author of many works valuable for their research and engravings, including a *Chronicle of England* (1777–8), *Dresses and Habits of the English People* (1796–9), and *Sports and Pastimes of the People of England* (1801). An unfinished novel by Strutt was completed by Sir W. *Scott (*Queenhoo Hall*, 1808), and suggested to him the publication of his own *Waverley*.

STUART, Daniel (1766–1846), journalist, and an early press baron, who in 1795 bought the *Morning Post* and in 1796 *The Courier*, raising both papers to importance by his management. He employed excellent writers, including *Southey, *Lamb, *Wordsworth, and *Coleridge.

STUBBES, or **STUBBS,** Philip (*fl.* 1583–91), a Puritan pamphleteer, author of *The Anatomie of Abuses* (1583), a denunciation of evil customs of the time which, in the author's opinion, needed abolition. It contains a section on stage plays and is one of the principal sources of information on the social and economic conditions of the period.

STUBBS, John (*c.*1541–90), published *The Discoverie of a Gaping Gulf whereinto England is like to be Swallowed* (1579) against the Queen's marriage to the French king's brother, François, duc d'Alençon. For this he was imprisoned and had his right hand cut off.

STUBBS, William (1825–1901), was appointed Regius professor of modern history at Oxford in 1866. He was the first substantial scholar to hold such a chair at either university. He showed supreme professional skill, acquired by the study of contemporary German academic method, in the 18 volumes of medieval texts he edited for the *Rolls Series, and this was the foundation for his great *Constitutional History of [Medieval] England* (3 vols, 1874–8), which has been described as 'one of the most astonishing achievements of the Victorian mind'. Together with his *Select Charters and other Illustrations of English Constitutional History to 1307* (1870), it imposed a pattern and a method on the teaching of history in all British universities which survived until the mid-20th cent. (in Oxford longer), though he published nothing more after his elevation to the bishopric of Chester in 1884 and subsequently (1888) Oxford.

Stukeley, a character in George Peele's *Battle of Alcazar*. The real Thomas Stukeley was said to be a natural son of *Henry VIII. An adventurer with a very varied career, he joined the king of Portugal's expedition against Morocco and was killed at the battle of Alcazar.

STUKELEY, William (1687–1765), antiquary, became secretary to the Society of Antiquaries, which he shared in founding (1718). He was particularly interested in Druidism, and his discussions of Stonehenge (*Stonehenge: a temple restor'd to the British druids*, 1740) and Avebury (*Abury*, 1743) claimed (after *Aubrey) that they had been built by the Druids. He believed that the beliefs of the Druids were 'near akin to the Christian doctrine', and defended them from attacks by *Toland. His views may have influenced *Blake's vision of *Albion, and *Wordsworth was also familiar with them. (See PRIMITIVISM.)

STURLA THORDARSON, (*c.*1214–84), Icelandic historian, author of the *Sturlunga saga*, or contemporary history of the house of Sturla, a vivid picture of old Icelandic life.

Sturm und Drang (Storm and Stress), the name (taken from the title of an absurd romantic drama of the American War of Independence by the German playwright Klinger, 1775) given to a period of literary ferment which prevailed in Germany during the latter part of the 18th cent. It was inspired by *Rousseau's fervent idealism and characterized by a revolt against literary conventions (particularly the *unities in drama), by the cult of genius, and by a return to 'nature'. The principal figures of the movement were the young *Goethe, *Herder, and *Schiller. Many of the plays were translated and adapted for the English stage during the 1790s.

Stutly, Will, one of the legendary companions of *Robin Hood.

Sublime, the, an idea associated with religious awe, vastness, natural magnificence, and strong emotion which fascinated 18th-cent. literary critics and aestheticians. Its development marks the movement away from the clarity of *Neoclassicism towards *Romanticism, with its emphasis on feeling and imagination; it was connected with the concept of original genius which soared fearlessly above the rules. Sublimity in rhetoric and poetry was first analysed in an anonymous Greek work, *On the Sublime*, attributed to *Longinus. The concept was elaborated by many writers, including *Addison, *Dennis, *Hume, *Burke, and R. *Blair and the discussion spread from literature to other areas. The most widely read work was Burke's *Philosophical Enquiry into the Origin of our Ideas of the *Sublime and Beautiful* (1757). Burke put a new emphasis on terror; he saw the sublime as a category distinct from beauty. With the former he associated obscurity, power, darkness, solitude, and vastness and with the latter smoothness, delicacy, smallness, and light. These varied ideas were brought together, and discussed with greater philosophical rigour, by

*Kant in the *Critique of Judgement* (1790). Burke's theory stimulated a passion for terror that culminated in the Gothic tales of A. *Radcliffe and the macabre paintings, crowded with monsters and ghosts, of Barry, Mortimer, and *Fuseli. The cult drew strength from *Macpherson's Ossianic poems; Ossian took his place beside *Homer and *Milton as one of the great poets of the sublime, whose works were frequently illustrated by painters. The sublime of terror kindled the enthusiasm for wild scenery and cosmic grandeur already apparent in the writings of Addison and *Shaftesbury, and of E. *Young and James *Thomson. Many writers making the *Grand Tour dwelt on the sublimity of the Alps: they contrasted them with the pictures of Salvator Rosa, whose stormy landscapes provided a pattern for 18th-cent. descriptions of savage nature. By the 1760s travellers sought out the exhilarating perils of the rushing torrent, the remote mountain peak, and the gloomy forest. Many published their impressions in 'Tours', and sublimity became a fashion, pandered to by the dramatic storms shown by de Loutherbourg's Ediophusikon, a small theatre with lantern slides, and later by John Martin's vast panoramas of cosmic disaster.

The Romantic poets rejected the categories of 18th-cent. theorists and yet these writers on the sublime were moving, albeit clumsily, towards that sense of the mystery of natural forces that is so powerful in the poetry of *Byron, *Shelley, and *Wordsworth, and in the paintings of *Turner.

Sublime, *On the*, see SUBLIME, THE, and LONGINUS.

Sublime and Beautiful, *A Philosophical Enquiry into the Origin of our Ideas of the*, a treatise by E. *Burke, published anonymously 1757, with an 'Introduction on Taste' added 1759.

Burke discusses the distinctions between the *Sublime, and the beautiful, which consists in relative smallness, smoothness, and brightness of colour. There are interesting sections on pleasure gained from distress (as in tragedy, or in the sight of a conflagration), and his descriptions of 'a sort of delightful horror, a sort of tranquillity tinged with terror' had much influence on the aesthetic theory of the later 18th cent. and in particular on G. E. Lessing. Aphorisms like 'A clear idea is another name for a little idea' mark the transition from the lucidity admired by *Pope to the sublimity of writers like T. *Gray.

Subtle, the false alchemist and astrologer of Jonson's *The Alchemist.*

SUCKLING, Sir John (1609–42), a member of *Falkland's circle at Great Tew, he was knighted in 1630. He became a leader of the royalist party in the early troubles, then fled to France and is said by *Aubrey to have committed suicide in Paris. His chief works are included in *Fragmenta Aurea* (1646) and consist of poems, plays, letters, and tracts, among them the famous 'Ballad upon a Wedding'. His 'Sessions of the Poets', in which various writers of the day, including *Jonson, *Carew, and *D'Avenant, contend for the laurel, appeared in 1637; it is interesting as an expression of contemporary opinion on these writers. Suckling's plays are chiefly valuable for their lyrics. Among these are *Aglaura* (with two fifth acts, one tragic, the other not) printed in 1638, *The Goblins* (1646), a romantic drama, and *Brennoralt* (1646), an expansion of the *Discontented Colonell* (1640), a tragedy, interesting for the light which the melancholy colonel throws on the author himself. Suckling has enjoyed a steady reputation as one of the most elegant and brilliant of the *Cavalier poets. According to Aubrey, he invented the game of cribbage.

Suddlechop, Benjamin and Dame Ursula, characters in Scott's *The Fortunes of Nigel.*

SUETONIUS, (Gaius Suetonius Tranquillus) (AD *c*.70–*c*.140), Roman biographer whose major surviving work is the *Lives of the Caesars.* His aim was to bring out the moral character of his subjects, and he paid attention to their private habits as well as to their imperial policy. His method, adopted by later Roman biographers, may be said to have paved the way for the intimate biographies that began to appear in the second half of the 17th cent. The flavour of his writing has been best caught recently by Robert *Graves in *I, Claudius* and *Claudius the God.*

SULLIVAN, Sir Arthur (1842–1900), English composer. His *Thespis* (1871), the libretto of which was by W. S. *Gilbert, was the beginning of a collaboration which produced the famous *Gilbert and Sullivan Operas. His other works, with important literary connections, included the music for *Burnand's *Cox and Box* (1866); the incidental music for *The Tempest*, written when he was nineteen, and for other Shakespeare plays (*The Merchant of Venice*, 1871; *Henry VIII*, 1877; and *Macbeth*, 1888); *Five Shakespeare Songs* (1866, which includes the famous setting of 'Orpheus with his lute'); and *The Window, or the Songs of the Wrens* (1871), a song cycle in collaboration with *Tennyson. His only attempt at serious opera was *Ivanhoe* (after Sir W. *Scott, 1891).

'Sumer is icumen in', one of the earliest known English lyrics, from the first half of the 13th cent. The music, and Latin instructions for singing it, are also in the MS. (BM MS Harley 978).

Summers last will and Testament, a play by T. *Nashe, published 1600. It is framed by the jocular comments of Will Summers, *Henry VIII's jester (who died *c*. 1560), and is an allegorical pageant in which Summer, personified as a dying old man, decides to whom to leave his riches.

Summerson, Esther, a character in Dickens's *Bleak House*, and one of the narrators of the tale.

'Summoner's Tale, The', see CANTERBURY TALES, 8.

Sunday Times, The, a Sunday paper founded in 1822 by Henry White. It grew greatly in circulation and influence from the 1930s onwards, earning a high reputation for its arts pages and, recently, for its investigative journalism. The gossip column 'Atticus' was started by T. P. *O'Connor.

Supposes, a comedy in prose, one of the earliest in English, by G. *Gascoigne, translated from *Ariosto's *I Suppositi*, performed 1566. It concerns a series of disguises and confused identities; the scenes with servants are effectively comic, especially those with the old nurse Balia.

Surface, Joseph and Charles, the two brothers in Sheridan's *The School for Scandal*.

Surgeon's Daughter, The, a novel by Sir W. *Scott, published 1827 as one of the stories in *Chronicles of the Canongate*.

Surly, the choleric gamester of Jonson's *The Alchemist*.

'Surprised by Joy—impatient as the Wind', a sonnet by *Wordsworth, first published in 1815, suggested by the death of his daughter Catherine in 1812.

Surrealism, a movement founded in Paris in 1924 with the publication of André Breton's first *Surrealist Manifesto*. It was conceived as a revolutionary mode of thought and action, concerned with politics, philosophy, and psychology as well as literature and art. The *Manifesto* attacked rationalism and narrow logical systems; drawing on *Freud's theories concerning the unconscious and its relation to dreams, it called for the exploration of hidden and neglected areas of the human psyche. The group of writers and painters that gathered round Breton experimented with automatic processes, which were considered the best means of producing the surreal poetic image: the spontaneous coupling of unrelated objects. An extended conception of poetry, which was to be part of, not separate from, life, was central to surrealism. Other writers associated with the movement included Aragon, Éluard, and René Crevel. Surrealist artists in the 1920s sought equivalents to automatic writing. In the 1930s writers and artists alike collected or fabricated surrealist objects, and Breton mixed words and images in his poem-objects. Several surrealists joined the Communist Party and theoretical texts, including Breton's *Surrealist Manifesto* of 1929, try to reconcile Freud and *Marx. Surrealism was a major intellectual force between the wars, although as it spread internationally in the 1930s interest tended to concentrate on surrealist art. In England the movement attracted some attention among literary circles, but it was only after the International Surrealist Exhibition of 1936 that a surrealist group was established, its members including D. *Gascoyne, H. *Read, Roland Penrose (1900–84), and the documentary film-maker Humphrey Jennings (1907–50).

SURREY, Henry Howard, (by courtesy) earl of (?1517–47), poet, was the son of Thomas Howard (afterwards third duke of Norfolk). He was with the army during the war with France (1544–6) and was commander of Boulogne, 1545–6. He was accused of various minor offences, but tried and executed on the charge of treasonably quartering the royal arms. His works consist of sonnets and poems in various metres notable for their elegance of construction. His sonnets were predominantly in the 'English' form (a b a b c d c d e f e f g g), later to be used by Shakespeare, which appears to have been his invention. (See SONNET.) A still more durable innovation was his use of blank verse in his translation of the *Aeneid*, Bks II and IV. Forty of his poems were printed in *Tottel's Miscellany* (1557). *Nashe and *Drayton built up a picture of Surrey as the languishing lover of 'Geraldine' (Elizabeth, daughter of the ninth earl of Kildare); but he seems to have done no more than address a single sonnet to this lady, possibly when she was as young as nine.

SURTEES, Robert (1779–1834), antiquary and topographer, the author of a *History of Durham* (1816–40). He is commemorated in the Surtees Society, which publishes original materials relating to the history of the region constituting the old kingdom of Northumbria. Sir W. Scott included in his *Minstrelsy of the Scottish Border* a spurious and spirited ballad by him, 'The Death of Featherstonhaugh'.

SURTEES, Robert Smith (1805–64), founded, with R. Ackermann the younger, the *New Sporting Magazine* in 1831, to which he contributed his comic sketches of Mr Jorrocks, the sporting Cockney grocer, later collected as *Jorrocks's Jaunts and Jollities* (1838). Jorrocks, whose adventures to some extent suggested the original idea of *Pickwick Papers*, reappears in *Handley Cross* (1843; expanded and illustrated by *Leech, 1854). His second great character, Mr Soapey Sponge, appears in *Mr Sponge's Sporting Tour*

(1853); another celebrated character was Mr Facey Romford, who appears in his last novel, *Mr Facey Romford's Hounds* (1865). His eight long novels deal mainly with the characteristic aspects of English fox-hunting society, but his vivid caricatures, the absurd scenes he describes, the convincing dialect and often repeated catch-phrases, distinguish him from other writers of this genre. The illustration of his novels by Leech, Alken, and 'Phiz' (H. K. Browne) also contributed to their success.

Survey of London, A, see STOW, J.

Suspicious Husband, The, a comedy by Dr B. *Hoadly and his brother, produced 1747.

The plot centres on the attempts of young Jacintha to escape from her jealous guardian Strictland and to elope with her admirer, Bellamy: a rope ladder is provided, but there are many mistakes and misunderstandings before the final happy outcome.

SUTCLIFF, Rosemary, see CHILDREN'S LITERATURE.

Svengali, see TRILBY.

Swan of Avon, The Sweet, see AVON, THE SWEET SWAN OF.

Swan of Lichfield, see SEWARD, A.

SWEDENBORG, Emanuel (1688–1772), born Swedberg, Swedish philosopher, scientist, and mystic, studied at Uppsala, and travelled extensively in England, where he was influenced by Henry More, J. *Locke, and I. *Newton. His theosophic system sought to demonstrate that the universe had, essentially, a spiritual structure: God, as Divine Man, is infinite love and wisdom, and from him emanate both nature and spirit. Swedenborg died in London, and his followers there organized themselves into the New Church, of which *Blake was for a while an active member. Blake was deeply influenced by Swedenborg's writings, which began to appear in English from 1750, a printing society being founded in Manchester in 1782 to propagate his works. Swedenborg also had a considerable influence on other writers, including *Strindberg and the French *Symbolists.

Sweedlepipe, Paul or Poll, in Dickens's *Martin Chuzzlewit.

Sweeney Agonistes, a poetic drama by T. S. *Eliot.

SWEET, Henry (1845–1912), a great phonetician. He is said to be the inspiration for Shaw's Henry Higgins in *Pygmalion. His works are still a staple of the study of Old English and the philology of English; the most celebrated are *History of English Sounds* (1874, 1888); *Anglo-Saxon Reader* (1876); *Anglo-Saxon Primer* (1882); *A New English Grammar* (1892, 1898); *The History of Language* (1900); and *The Sounds of English: an Introduction to Phonetics* (1908).

SWIFT, Jonathan (1667–1745), was born in Dublin and was educated with *Congreve, at Kilkenny Grammar School, then at Trinity College, Dublin. He was a cousin of *Dryden. He was admitted (1689) to the household of Sir W. *Temple, and there acted as secretary. He wrote pindarics, one of which provoked, according to Dr *Johnson, Dryden's remark, 'Cousin Swift, you will never be a poet.' He returned to Ireland, was ordained (1694), and returned to Temple at Moor Park in 1696, where he edited Temple's correspondence, and in 1697 wrote *The Battle of the Books, which was published in 1704 together with *A Tale of a Tub. At Moor Park he first met Esther Johnson ('Stella'). On the death of Temple in 1699, Swift went again to Ireland, where he was given a prebend in St Patrick's, Dublin. He wrote his *Discourse of the Contests and Dissensions between the nobles and the commons in Athens and Rome*, with reference to the impeachment of the Whig lords, in 1701. In the course of numerous visits to London he became acquainted with *Addison, *Steele, and Halifax. In 1708 he began a series of pamphlets on church questions with his ironical *Argument against Abolishing Christianity*. Amid these serious occupations, he diverted himself with the series of squibs upon the astrologer John Partridge (1708–9, see under BICKERSTAFF) and his 'Description of a City Shower' and 'Description of the Morning', poems depicting scenes of London life (1709). Disgusted at the Whig alliance with Dissent, he went over to the Tories in 1710, attacked the Whig ministers in *The Examiner, which he edited, and in 1711 wrote The Conduct of the Allies and Some Remarks on the Barrier Treaty, pamphlets written to dispose the mind of the nation to peace. He became dean of St Patrick's in 1713. He had already begun his *Journal to Stella*, a series of intimate letters (1710–13) to Esther Johnson and her companion Rebecca Dingley, who had moved to Ireland in 1700/1; it is written partly in baby language, and gives a vivid account of Swift's daily life in London. Swift's relations with Stella remain obscure; they were intimate and affectionate, and some form of marriage may have taken place. Another woman, Esther Vanhomrigh (pron. 'Vanummery'), entered his life in 1708; his poem *Cadenus and Vanessa suggests that she fell deeply in love with him ('She wished her Tutor were her Lover'). She is said to have died of shock in 1723 after his final rupture with her, inspired by her jealousy of Stella. Stella died in 1728.

In 1714 Swift joined *Pope, *Arbuthnot,

*Gay, and others in the celebrated *Scriblerus Club. He returned to Ireland in August 1714 and occupied himself with Irish affairs, and by his famous *Drapier's Letters (1724) he prevented the introduction of 'Wood's Half-pence' into Ireland. He came to England in 1726 and published *Gulliver's Travels (1726). He wrote some of his most famous tracts and characteristic poems during his last years in Ireland, The Grand Question Debated (1729); Verses on the Death of Dr Swift (1731, pub. 1739), in which with mingled pathos and humour he reviews his life and work; A Complete Collection of Polite and Ingenious *Conversation (1738); and the ironical Directions to Servants (written about 1731 and published after his death). He kept up his correspondence with *Bolingbroke, Pope, Gay, and Arbuthnot. He spent a third of his income on charities, and saved another third to found St Patrick's Hospital for Imbeciles (opened 1757). The symptoms of the illness from which he suffered for most of his life (now thought to have been Ménière's disease) became very marked in his last years, and he suffered the decay of his faculties to such a degree that many considered him insane. He was buried by the side of Stella, in St Patrick's, Dublin, his own famous epitaph 'ubi saeva indignatio ulterius cor lacerare nequit' being inscribed on his tomb. Nearly all his works were published anonymously, and for only one, Gulliver's Travels, did he receive any payment (£200). Dr Johnson, *Macaulay, and *Thackeray, among many other writers, were alienated by his ferocity and coarseness, and his works tended to be undervalued in the late 18th–19th cents. The 20th cent. has seen a revival of biographical and critical interest, stressing on the whole Swift's sanity, vigour, and satirical inventiveness rather than his alleged misanthropy.

Swift published a great number of works besides those mentioned above including political writings, notably The Importance of the Guardian considered (1713) and The Public Spirit of the Whigs (1714); pamphlets relating to Ireland, notably A Modest Proposal (1729); pamphlets on Church questions; miscellaneous verses, including *Baucis and Philemon (1709); and other writings.

SWINBURNE, Algernon Charles (1837–1909), educated at Balliol College, Oxford, where he was associated with *Rossetti and the *Pre-Raphaelite circle. *Atalanta in Calydon (1865), a drama in classical Greek form with choruses that revealed his great metrical skills, brought him celebrity. Chastelard (1865), the first of three dramas on the subject of *Mary Queen of Scots, raised doubts about the morality of Swinburne's verse, doubts reinforced by the first series of Poems and Ballads (1866), which brought down a torrent of abuse from R. *Buchanan, J. *Morley, and others. The volume contains many of his best as well as his most notorious poems (*'Dolores', 'Itylus',

'Hymn to Proserpine', 'The Triumph of Time', 'Faustine', 'Laus Veneris', etc.) which clearly demonstrate the preoccupation with de Sade, masochism, and femmes fatales, and also his outspoken repudiation of Christianity. A Song of Italy (1867) and Songs before Sunrise (1871) express his support for Mazzini in the struggle for Italian independence, and a hatred of authority which owes much to *Blake. Bothwell (1874) and a second Greek drama, Erechtheus (1876), were followed by the more subdued Poems and ballads: second series (1878), which contains 'A Forsaken Garden'. By this time Swinburne's health was seriously undermined by heavy drinking and other excesses. In 1879 he moved to Putney with his friend *Watts-Dunton, who gradually weaned him from drink and restored his health. He published many more volumes, including Mary Stuart (1881), *Tristram of Lyonesse and other poems (1882), *Marino Faliero (1885, a tragedy on the same subject as Byron's of the same title), and Poems and ballads: third series (1889), but they lack the force of his earlier work.

Swinburne commanded an impressive variety of verse forms, writing in classical metres, composing burlesques, modern and mock-antique ballads, roundels, etc.; he also translated the ballads of Villon. His influence on fellow aesthetes like *Pater and a later generation of poets was considerable. Swinburne was a critic of perception and originality; his studies of Chapman (1875), *Marlowe (1883, *Encyclopaedia Britannica), *Middleton (1887), *Tourneur (1889, E.B.), and others were the first important successors to *Lamb in the revival of interest in Elizabethan and Jacobean drama.

His letters were edited in 6 vols, 1959–62, by C. Y. Lang Many of his writings remain unpublished, presumably unpublishable.

Swing, Captain, an imaginary person to whom about 1830–3 were attributed a number of outrages against farmers who had adopted the use of agricultural machinery.

SWINNERTON, Frank (1884–1982), novelist. His novels include Nocturne (1917, his greatest success) and Harvest Comedy (1937). He was a familiar figure in the literary life of the first half of this century. His knowledge of the period provided material for his literary reminiscences, notably The Georgian Literary Scene (1935), and two autobiographical works, Swinnerton: An Autobiography (1937) and Reflections from a Village (1969). Arnold Bennett: A Last Word (1978) appeared in his 94th year. He was president of the *Royal Literary Fund (1962–6).

Swiss Family Robinson, The, the romance of a family wrecked on a desert island, written in German by Johann David Wyss (1743–1818), a Swiss pastor. It was published in two parts in

Zurich in 1812–13 and the first English translation was a year later.

Swiveller, Dick, a character in Dickens's *The Old Curiosity Shop*.

Sword-dance, a medieval folk custom, of ritual origin, probably symbolizing the death and resurrection of the year. The stock characters were the fool, dressed in the skin of an animal, and the 'Bessy', a man dressed in woman's clothes. In many of the extant dances one of the characters is surrounded with the swords of the other dancers or slain. The characters were introduced in rhymed speeches. The sword-dance is one of the origins of the *Mummers'* play and so of English drama. See also REVESBY PLAY.

Sword of Honour, a trilogy by E. *Waugh, published under this title in 1965.

Men at Arms (1952) introduces 35-year-old divorced Catholic Guy Crouchback, who after much effort succeeds in enlisting in the Royal Corps of Halberdiers just after the outbreak of the Second World War. Much of the plot revolves around his eccentric fellow-officer Apthorpe, an old Africa hand who suffers repeatedly from 'Bechuana tummy', is deeply devoted to his 'thunder box' (or chemical closet), and dies in West Africa at the end of the novel of some unspecified tropical disease, aggravated by Guy's thoughtful gift of a bottle of whisky. Other characters include Guy's ex-wife, the beautiful socialite Virginia Troy, her second husband, Tommy Blackhouse, and the ferocious one-eyed Brigadier Ritchie-Hook, who involves Guy in a near-disastrous escapade.

Officers and Gentlemen (1955) continues Waugh's semi-satiric, semi-emotional portrayal of civilian and military life with an account of Guy's training on the Hebridean island of Mugg with a Commando unit, and of the exploits of ex-hairdresser Trimmer, now Captain McTavish, which include an affair with Virginia and the blowing up of a French railway; the action moves to Alexandria, then to the withdrawal from Crete, with all but four of 'Hook-force' taken prisoner.

Unconditional Surrender (1961) opens with a frustrated and disillusioned Captain Guy Crouchback in London, working at Hazardous Offensive Operations Headquarters: he then injures himself learning to parachute, and on his sickbed is wooed by Virginia, now pregnant by Trimmer, and conscious that Guy has inherited his father's fortune. He remarries her out of a sense of chivalry and compassion, is transferred to the chaos and conflicts of Yugoslavia as a liaison officer with the Partisans, and there learns that Virginia has given birth to a son, then that she has been killed in an air raid. The baby survives, and an Epilogue informs us that Guy marries again, and has more children of his own.

Sybil, or *The Two Nations*, a novel by B. *Disraeli, published 1845.

This is the second book of the trilogy *Coningsby—Sybil—*Tancred*. It was written, like *Coningsby*, to celebrate the ideas of the 'Young England' Tories and was designed to describe 'the Condition of the People' and of the 'Two Nations of England, the Rich and the Poor'. The book points to reforms a generation before Disraeli's government was able to introduce them. Poverty and oppression are described with feeling, and in the industrial town of Mowbray aspects of the wealthy social and political world are described with irony and contempt.

The plot concerns the love of Charles Egremont for Sybil Gerard, daughter of *Chartist Walter Gerard, and Egremont's growing understanding of the Chartist cause, as he endeavours to win her affection. In a violent denouement Egremont's brother, the pitiless landowner Lord Marney, is killed by rioters, and Sybil's friend the radical Stephen Morley is shot: Egremont rescues Sybil (who has been revealed as true heir to the Marney lands) and they are married.

Sycorax, in Shakespeare's *The Tempest* a witch, the mother of Caliban; she does not appear in the play.

Syllepsis, a figure of speech by which a word, or a particular form or inflection of a word, is made to refer to two or more words in the same sentence, while properly applying to them in different senses: e.g. 'Miss Bolo . . . went home in a flood of tears and a sedan chair' (Dickens, *Pickwick Papers*, ch. 35). Cf. *zeugma.

Sylphs, see PARACELSUS.

Sylva, a book on arboriculture by J. *Evelyn.

SYLVANUS URBAN, the pseudonym of E. *Cave.

SYLVESTER, Joshua (*c.*1563–1618), a London merchant who translated into rhyming couplets *The Divine Weeks and Works* of *Du Bartas (1592–1608). The edition of 1621 contained many of Sylvester's other works, including his poems in the important collection *Lachrymae Lachrymarum* (1613). This contained elegies by John Hall and *Donne, among others, on Prince Henry, to whom Sylvester had attached himself.

Sylvia's Lovers, a novel by Mrs *Gaskell, published 1863.

The scene is the whaling port of Monkshaven (based on Whitby in Yorkshire) during the Napoleonic wars, and the plot hinges on the activities of the press-gangs whose seizure of Monkshaven men to man naval warships provokes bitter resentment. The last few chapters of the book, full of heroic rescues, improbable encounters, and death-bed reunions, are notably inferior to the earlier part of the novel, which is remarkable for its vivid reconstruction of life in the little town dominated by the whaling industry (which Mrs Gaskell carefully researched) and at the farm where quiet, unreasonable Daniel Robinson, his quiet, devoted wife, and their sturdy old servant Kester combine to cherish the much-loved and lovely but hapless Sylvia.

Symbolism, a movement associated with a group of French writers (Symbolists) *c.*1880–95. It may be seen as a reaction against dominant *realist and *naturalist tendencies in literature generally and, in the case of poetry, against the descriptive precision and 'objectivity' of the *Parnassians. The symbolists stressed the priority of suggestion and evocation over direct description and explicit analogy. Symbolist writers were particularly concerned to explore the musical properties of language, through the interplay of connotative sound relationships, but were deeply interested in all the arts and much influenced by the synthesizing ideals of *Wagner's music dramas. Other influences on the movement were the mystical writings of *Swedenborg, and the poetry of Nerval, Baudelaire, and *Poe.
 Generally associated with the symbolist movement are: the poets Mallarmé, Verlaine, Rimbaud, and Laforgue; the dramatists Villiers de l'Isle-Adam and Maeterlinck, and the novelists Huysmans and Édouard Dujardin. The movement exercised an influence on painting and on a wide range of 20th-cent. writers including *Pound, T. S. *Eliot, W. *Stevens, *Yeats, *Joyce, V. *Woolf, Claudel, Valéry, Stefan George, and Rilke. It was the subject of A. W. *Symons's *The Symbolist movement in literature* (1899) and played a part in the development of the Russian symbolist movement and of the *modernista* movement in Latin America.

Symkyn, Symond, the miller of Trumpington in *Chaucer's 'The Reeve's Tale' (see CANTER-BURY TALES, 3).

SYMONDS, John Addington (1840–93), suffered from tuberculosis, and spent much of his life in Italy and Switzerland. He was much attracted by the Hellenism of the Renaissance, and both his prose and poetry are coloured by his concept of Platonic love and his admiration for male beauty. His largest work, *Renaissance in Italy* (1875–86), is more picturesque than scholarly, but remains a valuable source of information. His works include collections of travel sketches and impressions; several volumes of verse; a translation of the autobiography of Cellini (1888); and translations of Greek and Italian poetry. He married in 1864 but acknowledged increasingly his own homosexuality, and

campaigned, albeit discreetly, for legal reform and more outspoken recognition of inversion, which he saw as a congenital condition. His privately printed pamphlets *A Problem in Greek ethics* (1883) and *A problem in modern ethics* (1891) were reproduced in part by H. *Ellis in *Sexual Inversion* (1897).

SYMONS, A(lphonse) J(ames) A(lbert) (1900–41), bibliographer, bibliophile, dandy, and epicure, who became an authority on the literature of the 1890s and published *An anthology of 'Nineties' verse* in 1928. He wrote several biographies, but is best remembered for *The Quest for Corvo: an experiment in biography* (1934), a life of F. W. *Rolfe.

SYMONS, Arthur William (1865–1945), poet and critic, became a friend of *Yeats, G. A. *Moore, and H. *Ellis, and attended the *Rhymers' Club; his early volumes of poetry (*Days and Nights,* 1889; *London Nights,* 1895) were very much of their time in their celebration of decadence and the *demi-monde* of stage, street, and *Café Royal. He was editor of *The Savoy,* 1896, and published *Beardsley, *Conrad, *Dowson, L. P. *Johnson, etc. His *The Symbolist movement in literature* (1899) was an attempt to introduce French *Symbolism to England, and he wrote critical studies of *Blake, Baudelaire, *Pater, *Wilde, and others. He is largely remembered as a leading spirit in the Decadent movement, a defender of *'Art for Art's Sake'.

Symposium, The, or 'The Banquet', the title of a dialogue in which *Plato describes a drinking party where *Socrates, *Aristophanes, and others propound their views of love and distinguish three forms of the emotion: the sensual, the altruistic, and the wisdom-oriented. Written soon after 371 BC, the dialogue appears to have had for its aim the rehabilitation of Socrates against the charge of corrupting the young, but its influence, once it had been translated into Latin by *Ficino (1482), had a far wider scope. It popularized the identification of love with a quest for the highest form of spiritual experience, and although the love discussed in Plato's dialogue was primarily a homosexual one, the exalted claims made on its behalf were easily transferred to heterosexual relationships and came to be linked with the conventions of courtly love. Another idea in the *Symposium* that gained wide currency was the fanciful notion advanced by Aristophanes in his speech that each human being is a male or female half of a whole which was originally hermaphrodite, and that every person necessarily seeks his or her lost half. The belief that every person has a single predestined mate was to become a romantic commonplace.

Synecdoche (pron. 'sinekdoki'), a figure of speech by which a more comprehensive term is used for a less comprehensive or vice versa, as whole for part or part for whole, e.g. 'There were six guns out on the moor' where 'guns' stands for shooters; and 'Oxford won the match', where 'Oxford' stands for 'the Oxford eleven'.

SYNGE, (Edmund) John Millington (1871–1909), Irish playwright. Following a suggestion from *Yeats, whom he met in Paris, Synge went to the Aran islands in order to write of Irish peasant life; his description, *The Aran Islands*, was published in 1907. His plays *In the Shadow of the Glen* (perf. 1903) and *Riders to the Sea* (perf. 1904) were published, as was *The Well of the Saints*, in 1905. His best-known play, and in its time the most controversial, * *The Playboy of the Western World*, was performed in 1907; the anticlerical *The Tinker's Wedding* was published in 1908. All except the last were performed at the *Abbey Theatre, of which Synge became a director in 1906. His *Poems and Translations* (many of which foreshadow his imminent death) appeared in 1909. He completed his last play, *Deirdre of the Sorrows* (1910), as he was dying of Hodgkin's disease. In this as in his other work, Synge uses a spare, rhythmic, lyric prose to achieve effects of great power and resonance; both tragedies and comedies display the ironic wit and realism which many of his countrymen found offensive. The *Collected Works* (4 vols, 1962–8) were edited by Robin Skelton; his *Collected Letters*, edited by Ann Saddlemyer, appeared 1983–4.

Synoptic Gospels, those of Matthew, Mark, and Luke, so called as giving an account of the events from the same point of view, or under the same general aspect.

Syntax, Dr, see COMBE, W.

T

TACITUS, Cornelius (*c.* AD 55–after 115), the greatest historian of Imperial Rome. He wrote *Dialogus de Oratoribus*, which discusses the short-comings of contemporary oratory; *Vita Agricolae*, a biography of his father-in-law Julius Agricola; and *Germania*, an ethnographical account of the German tribes which contains one of the earliest representations of the Noble Savage (see PRIMITIVISM). His fame rests on his *Annals* (18 books, of which 11 and part of a 12th survive) and his *Histories* (12 books, of which 4 and part of a 5th survive), which related events from the death of Augustus to the Flavian period. Tacitus' avowed aim was to keep alive the memory of virtuous and vicious actions so that posterity could judge them, and his great achievement was to have drawn a picture of how men must live under tyranny. Little known in the Middle Ages, Tacitus was rediscovered by *Boccaccio in the 14th`cent., but he did not become widely popular till the age of autocracy 200 years later. The *Agricola* and the *Histories* were translated into English by Sir H. *Savile (1591), the *Germania* and *Annals* by R. Greneway (1598); and after this Tacitus became in *Donne's phrase the 'Oracle of Statesmen' or at any rate the model for historians like F. *Bacon in his *History of Henry VII* (1622) and Sir John *Hayward. He was also influential as a stylist in the 17th cent., when attempts were made to imitate his concision and trenchancy.

Tadpole and **Taper,** in Disraeli's *Coningsby* and *Sybil*, typical party wire-pullers.

TAGORE, Rabindranath (1861–1941), most eminent modern Bengali poet, was also critic, essayist, composer, and author of short fiction innovative in Bengali literature. He is known outside India principally in English translation. He won the *Nobel Prize for literature in 1913, its first award to an Asian.

TAILLEFER (Incisor Ferri), a minstrel in the army of William the Conqueror who is said to have marched in front of the army at Hastings, singing of the deeds of *Roland to encourage the Normans.

Tail-rhyme, translated from the Latin *rhythmus caudatus*, the measure associated in particular with a group of Middle English romances in which a pair of rhyming lines is followed by a single line of different length and the three-line

pattern is repeated to make up a six-line stanza. Chaucer's 'Sir Thopas' (see CANTERBURY TALES, 17) is an example.

Tain-Bo-Cuailgne, the chief epic of the Ulster cycle of Irish mythology, the story of the raid of Queen *Maeve of Connaught to secure the Brown Bull of Cuailgne and her defeat by Cuchulain.

Tale of a Tub, A, a comedy by *Jonson, performed 1633, printed 1640.

It concerns the attempts, in the course of St Valentine's Day, of Squire Tub among other suitors to marry Audrey, the daughter of Toby Turf, high constable of Kentish Town.

Tale of a Tub, A, a satire in prose by *Swift, written, according to his own statement, about 1696, but not published until 1704.

The author explains in a preface that it is the practice of seamen when they meet a whale to throw out an empty tub to divert him from attacking the ship. Hence the title of the satire, which is intended to divert Hobbes's *Leviathan* and the wits of the age from picking holes in the weak sides of religion and government. The author proceeds to tell the story of a father who leaves as a legacy to his three sons Peter, Martin, and Jack a coat apiece, with directions that on no account are the coats to be altered. Peter symbolizes the Roman Church, Martin (from Martin *Luther) the Anglican, Jack (from John *Calvin) the Dissenters. The sons gradually disobey the injunction. Finally Martin and Jack quarrel with the arrogant Peter, then with each other, and separate. The narrative is freely interspersed with digressions, on critics, on the prevailing dispute as to ancient and modern learning, and on madness—this last an early example of Swift's love of paradox and of his misanthropy.

Tale of Chloe, The, a short novel by G. *Meredith published 1879.

Tale of Genji, The, a classic Japanese novel written *c.* AD 1001–15 by Lady Murasaki (?978–?1031) and translated in a slightly abridged version by A. *Waley in 6 vols (1925–33).

Tale of Two Cities, A, a novel by *Dickens, published 1859.

The 'two cities' are Paris, in the time of the

French revolution, and London. Dr Manette, a French physician, having been called in to attend a young peasant and his sister in circumstances that made him aware that the girl had been outrageously treated and the boy mortally wounded by the marquis de St Évremonde and his brother, has been confined for 18 years in the Bastille to secure his silence. He has just been released, demented, when the story opens; he is brought to England, where he gradually recovers his sanity. Charles Darnay, who conceals under the name the fact that he is a nephew of the marquis, has left France and renounced his heritage from detestation of the cruel practices of the old French nobility; he falls in love with Lucie, Dr Manette's daughter, and they are happily married. During the Terror he goes to Paris to try to save a faithful servant, who is accused of having served the emigrant nobility. He is himself arrested, condemned to death, and saved only at the last moment by Sydney Carton, a reckless wastrel of an English barrister, whose character is redeemed by his generous devotion to Lucie. Carton, who strikingly resembles Darnay in appearance, smuggles the latter out of prison, and takes his place on the scaffold.

The book gives a vivid picture (modelled on Carlyle's *The French Revolution*) of Paris at this period.

Tales of a Grandfather, The, a history of Scotland to the close of the rebellion of 1745–6, by Sir W. *Scott, published 1827–9. A later series (1831) deals with the history of France.

The 'Tales' were designed in the first instance for the author's grandson, John Hugh Lockhart ('Hugh Littlejohn').

Tales of My Landlord, four series of novels by Sir W. *Scott: *The Black Dwarf*, *Old Mortality* (1st Series); *The Heart of Midlothian* (2nd Series); *The Bride of Lammermoor*, *A Legend of Montrose* (3rd Series); *Count Robert of Paris*, *Castle Dangerous* (4th Series). Jedediah Cleishbotham, schoolmaster and parish clerk of Gandercleugh, by a fiction of Scott, sold these tales to a publisher. They were supposed to be compiled by his assistant Peter Pattieson. The title of the series is a misnomer as Scott himself admitted, for the tales were not told by the landlord; nor did the landlord have any hand in them at all.

Tales of the Crusaders, two novels by Sir W. *Scott, *The Betrothed* and *The Talisman*.

TALFOURD, Sir Thomas Noon (1795–1854), MP, literary critic and author of *Ion* (1836), *The Athenian Captive* (1838), and other lifeless tragedies. Talfourd is remembered for his editing of the letters of his friend Charles *Lamb, and for having introduced an Act securing real legal protection for authors' copyright. Dickens dedicated *Pickwick Papers* to him.

TALIESIN (*fl.* 550), a British bard, perhaps a mythic personage, first mentioned in the *Saxon Genealogies* appended to the *Historia Britonum* (*c.*690). A mass of poetry, probably of later date, has been ascribed to him, and the *Book of Taliesin* (14th cent.) is a collection of poems by different authors and of different dates. Taliesin figures prominently in Peacock's *The Misfortunes of Elphin*, and he is mentioned in Tennyson's *Idylls of the King* as one of the Round Table.

Talisman, The, a novel by Sir W. *Scott, published 1825, forming part of the *Tales of the Crusaders*.

The Crusaders, led by Richard I of England, are encamped in the Holy Land, and torn by the dissensions and jealousies of the leaders, including, besides Cœur de Lion himself, Philip of France, the duke of Austria, the marquis of Montferrat, and the Grand Master of the Templars. The army's impotence is accentuated by the illness of Richard. A poor but doughty Scottish crusader, known as Sir Kenneth or the Knight of the Leopard, on a mission far from the camp encounters a Saracen emir, with whom, after an inconclusive combat, he strikes up a friendship. This emir proves subsequently to be Saladin himself, and he presently appears in the Christian camp in the disguise of a physician sent by the Soldan to Richard, whom he quickly cures by means of an amulet, the talisman of the book's title. Meanwhile Sir Kenneth is lured from his post by Queen Berengaria, Richard's wife, who in a frolic sends him an urgent message purporting to come from Edith Plantagenet, between whom and the knight there exists a romantic attachment. During his brief absence his faithful hound is wounded, and the English flag torn down. Sir Kenneth, thus dishonoured, narrowly escapes execution at Richard's order by the intervention of the Moorish physician, who receives him as his slave. Kindly and honourably treated by Saladin, he is sent, in the disguise of a black mute attendant, to Richard, whom he saves from assassination. Richard pierces Kenneth's disguise and gives him the opportunity he desires of discovering who wounded the hound and tore down the standard. As the Christian princes and their forces file past the re-erected standard, the hound springs on Conrade of Montferrat and tears him from his horse. A trial by combat is arranged in which Sir Kenneth defeats and wounds Montferrat, and is revealed to be Prince David of Scotland. The obstacle which his supposed lowly birth presented to his union with Edith Plantagenet is thus removed.

Talus, a character in Spenser's *Faerie Queene*, who represents the executive power of government.

TAMBIMUTTU, see POETRY LONDON.

Tamburlaine the Great, a drama in blank verse by *Marlowe, written not later than 1587, published 1590. It showed an immense advance on the blank verse of *Gorboduc and was received with much popular approval.

Part I of the drama deals with the first rise to power of the Scythian shepherd-robber Tamburlaine, whose unbounded ambition and ruthless cruelty carry all before him. He conquers the Turkish emperor Bajazet and leads him about, a prisoner in a cage, goading him and his empress Zabina with cruel taunts till they dash out their brains against the bars of the cage. His ferocity is softened only by his love for his captive Zenocrate.

Part II deals with the continuation of his conquests, which extend to Babylon, whither he is drawn in a chariot dragged by the kings of Trebizond and Soria, with the kings of Anatolia and Jerusalem as relay, 'pampered Jades of Asia' (a phrase quoted by Pistol in Shakespeare, 2 *Henry IV, II, iv); it ends with the death of Zenocrate, and of Tamburlaine himself.

Tamerlane, a tragedy by *Rowe, produced 1701, of some historical interest because under the name of Tamerlane the author intended to characterize William III, while under that of Bajazet he held up Louis XIV to detestation. The play was, for more than 100 years, annually revived on 5 Nov., the date of William III's landing.

Taming of the Shrew, The, a comedy by *Shakespeare, first printed in the *Folio of 1623, probably written c.1592 and based in part on the *Supposes* adapted by G. *Gascoigne from *Ariosto.

The play begins with an induction in which Christopher Sly, a drunken Warwickshire tinker, picked up by a lord and his huntsmen on a heath, is brought to the castle, sumptuously treated, and in spite of his protestations is assured that he is a lord who has been out of his mind. He is set down to watch the play that follows, performed solely for his benefit by strolling players.

Baptista Minola of Padua has two daughters, Katherina the Shrew, who is the elder of the two, and Bianca, who has many suitors but who may not marry until a husband has been found for Katherina. Petruchio, a gentleman from Verona, undertakes to woo the shrew to gain her dowry and to help his friend Hortensio win Bianca. To tame her he pretends to find her rude behaviour courteous and gentle and humiliates her by being late for their wedding and appearing badly dressed. He takes her off to his country house and, under the pretext that nothing there is good enough for her, prevents her from eating or sleeping. By the time they return to Baptista's

house, Katherina has been successfully tamed, and Lucentio, a Pisan, has won Bianca by disguising himself as her schoolmaster, while the disappointed Hortensio has to console himself with marriage to a rich widow. At the feast which follows the three bridegrooms wager on whose wife is the most docile and submissive. Katherina argues that 'Thy husband is thy lord, thy life, thy keeper, | Thy head, thy sovereign' and Petruchio wins the bet.

Tam Lin, the subject of an old *ballad. Janet wins back to mortal life her elfin lover, Tam Lin, from the queen of the fairies.

Tamora, in Shakespeare's *Titus Andronicus, queen of the Goths.

'Tam o' Shanter', a narrative poem by *Burns, published 1791.

Tam, a farmer, spends the evening of Ayre's market-day in a snug alehouse, where he becomes tipsy and amorous ('Tam was glorious'). Riding home, he passes the Kirk of Alloway. Seeing it mysteriously lighted, he stops and looks in. Weird warlocks and witches are dancing to the sound of the bagpipes, played by Old Nick, the Devil. Roused by the sight of one 'winsome wench' among the old beldams, Tam shouts to her. At once the lights go out and the horde of witches rush out in pursuit of Tam. Terrified, he wildly spurs his grey mare, Meg, and just reaches the middle of the bridge over the Doon before the girl catches him. Once over the middle of the bridge he is out of her power, but his mare's tail is still within the witches' jurisdiction, and this the girl pulls off. The narrative is swift, and both the humour and the horror are effectively conveyed.

Tanaquil, the name used by Spenser to signify Queen Elizabeth in the introduction to Book I of *The Faerie Queene*.

Tancred, or the New Crusade, a novel by B. *Disraeli, published 1847.

This is the last of the trilogy *Coningsby—*Sybil—Tancred. Much of the novel is devoted to an attempt to resolve the antagonism between Judaism and Christianity and to establish a role for a reforming faith and revitalized church in a progressive society.

Tancred and Gismund, The Tragedie of, or Gismond of Salerne, a play by R. Wilmot (fl. c.1566–1608) and others, published 1591 but dating from 1566 or 1568. Act II is by Henry Noel, Act IV by *Hatton. The play is founded on a tale by *Boccaccio (see SIGISMONDA).

Tancred and Sigismunda, a tragedy by J. *Thomson, published 1745, produced (with *Garrick as Tancred) 1752.

Tanglewood Tales, see HAWTHORNE, N.

TANNAHILL, Robert (1774–1810), born in Paisley, became an apprenticed handloom weaver to his father. At 17 he paid homage to *Burns in Ayrshire and was inspired to write his first song 'My Ain Kind Dearie O'. From 1805 his work began to appear in newspapers and journals. He published by subscription *Poems and Songs* (1807) but, aggrieved at having a revised edition declined by a publisher, he burnt his manuscript and drowned himself in a culvert near Paisley.

TANNHÄUSER, a German *Minnesinger of the 13th cent. and the subject of the legend embodied in the 16th-cent. ballad, the *Tannhäuserlied*, in which he becomes enamoured of a beautiful woman who beckons him into the grotto of Venus in the 'Venusberg' (located in Thuringia), where he spends seven years in revelry. When he emerges he goes to Rome to seek absolution from the pope, who replies that it is as impossible for Tannhäuser to be forgiven as for his dry staff to burgeon. Tannhäuser departs in despair. After three days the pope's staff breaks into blossom, and he urgently sends for Tannhäuser, but he is not to be found, having returned to Venus. The story is the subject of an opera by *Wagner (perf. 1845), and of *Swinburne's poem 'Laus Veneris' (1866).

Tanqueray, Paula, see SECOND MRS TANQUERAY, THE.

Tapley, Mark, see MARK TAPLEY.

Tappertit, Simon, in Dickens's *Barnaby Rudge*, Gabriel Varden's apprentice.

Tarka the Otter, see WILLIAMSON, H.

TARLTON, Richard (d. 1588), actor, of humble origin and imperfect education, who was introduced to Queen Elizabeth through the earl of *Leicester. He became one of the queen's players in 1583, and attained an immense popularity by his jests, comic acting, and improvisations of doggerel verse. He led a dissipated life and died in poverty. Many fictitious anecdotes connected with him were published, notably *Tarlton's Jests* (1613, in three parts).

Tartar, Mr, a character in Dickens's *Edwin Drood*.

Tarzan, see BURROUGHS, E. R.

Task, The, a poem in six books by *Cowper, published 1785.
   Cowper's friend Lady Austen (whom he met in 1781) having suggested to him the sofa in his room as the subject of a poem in blank verse, the poet set about 'the task'. Its six books are entitled 'The Sofa', 'The Time-piece', 'The Garden', 'The Winter Evening', 'The Winter Morning Walk', and 'The Winter Walk at Noon'. Cowper opens with a mock-heroic account of the evolution of the sofa and thence digresses to description, reflection, and opinion. The poem stresses the delights of a retired life; describes the poet's own search for peace; and evokes the pleasures of gardening, winter evenings by the fire, etc. The moral passages condemn blood sports, cards, and other diversions; the poet manifests tenderness not only for his pet hare, but even for worms and snails.

TASSO, Torquato (1544–95), son of Bernardo Tasso (author of an epic on Amadis of Gaul), spent many years at the court of Ferrara. He was from early life in constant terror of persecution and adverse criticism, and his conduct made it necessary for the duke, Alphonso II of Este, to lock him up as mad from 1579 to 1586. The legend of his passion for Leonora d'Este, the duke's discovery of it, and his consequent imprisonment, is no longer credited, but was for long widely believed; *Milton refers to it (in a Latin poem), *Byron's *The Lament of Tasso* (1817) is based on it, and *Goethe's *Torquato Tasso* (1789) supports it, as does Donizetti's opera (1833) of the same title. His chief works were *Rinaldo*, a romantic epic (1562); a pastoral play, *Aminta* (1573); *Jerusalem Delivered* (1580–1); and a tragedy, *Torrismondo* (1586). He also wrote *Pindaric odes, and Spenser used his sonnets in many of his *Amoretti*. Tasso's epics and his critical works (*Discorsi dell'arte poetica, Discorsi del poema eroica*) had a great influence on English literature, displayed in the works of *Daniel, Milton, Giles and Phineas *Fletcher, *Cowley, *Dryden, and others. *Fairfax's translation of *Jerusalem Delivered* (1600) also had an influence in its own right; according to Dryden, *Waller said that he 'derived the harmony of his numbers' from it. In the following century, *Gray translated a passage (Book XIV, 32–9), and *Collins recorded ('Ode on the Popular Superstitions of the Highlands') his great admiration for both Tasso and Fairfax.

TATE, (John Orley) Allen (1899–1979), American poet and critic, born in Kentucky, began his literary career as editor of the Tennessee-based little magazine *The Fugitive*, 1922–5, which published work by J. C. *Ransom, L. *Riding, R. P. *Warren, and others. His collections include *Mr Pope and Other Poems* (1928), *Poems 1928–1931* (1932), and *Collected Poems* (1977). As a critic he is associated with the *New Criticism.

TATE, Nahum (1652–1715), playwright. His version of *King Lear* omits the Fool, makes Edgar and Cordelia lovers, and ends happily; Dr

*Johnson defended it on the grounds that the original is too painful, and the full text was not restored until the 19th cent. Tate also wrote, with *Dryden, the second part of *Absalom and Achitophel*; also the libretti of *Purcell's *Dido and Aeneas*. In 1696 he published with Nicholas Brady the well-known metrical version of the psalms that bears their name. He was appointed poet laureate in 1692 and was pilloried by Pope in *The Dunciad*.

TATE and BRADY, see TATE, N.

Tatler, The, a periodical founded by R. *Steele, of which the first issue appeared on 12 April 1709; it appeared thrice weekly until 2 Jan. 1711.

According to No. 1, it was to include 'Accounts of Gallantry, Pleasure and Entertainment . . . under the Article of White's Chocolate House'; poetry under that of Will's Coffee House; foreign and domestic news from St James's Coffee-house; learning from the Grecian; and so on. Gradually it adopted a loftier tone; the evils of duelling and gambling are denounced in some of the earlier numbers, and presently all questions of good manners are discussed from the standpoint of a more humane civilization, and a new standard of taste is established. The ideal of a gentleman is examined, and its essence is found to lie in forbearance. The author assumes the character of Swift's *Bickerstaff, the marriage of whose sister, Jenny Distaff, with Tranquillus gives occasion for treating of happy married life. The rake and the coquette are exposed, and virtue is held up to admiration in the person of Lady Elizabeth Hastings (1682–1739), somewhat inappropriately named Aspasia—'to love her is a liberal education'. Anecdotes, essays, and short stories illustrate the principles advanced.

From an early stage Steele had the collaboration of *Addison, who contributed notes, suggestions, and a number of complete papers. It was succeeded by *The Spectator*.

Tattycoram, in Dickens's *Little Dorrit*, a foundling brought up in the Meagles household.

TAUCHNITZ, Christian Berhard von (1816–95), the founder of a publishing house at Leipzig which in 1841 began to issue a series of 5,370 volumes eventually designated 'Collection of British and American Authors'. This and other textually significant English-language 'collections', though specified for sale only on the Continent, were distributed world-wide.

TAWNEY, R(ichard) H(enry) (1880–1962), educated at Rugby and Balliol College, Oxford; historian, socialist (of the *Ruskin, *Morris, and Christian Socialist tradition), and teacher and activist in the Workers' Educational Association. From 1917 he was attached to the London School of Economics, becoming professor of economic history in 1931. His works include *The Acquisitive Society* (1921) and *Religion and the Rise of Capitalism* (1926).

TAYLOR, A(lan) J(ohn) P(ercivale) (1906–), historian. His many publications include *The Habsburg Monarchy* (1941), *The Troublemakers* (1957, from his Ford lectures), *The Origins of the Second World War* (1961), a life of *Beaverbrook (1972), and an autobiography, *A Personal History* (1983). He also became widely known as a journalist and television personality.

TAYLOR, Edward (c.1644–1729), American metaphysical poet and divine. His devotional poems remained in manuscript, at his own request, and were not published until 1937, when their importance to the history of early American letters, and their own considerable quality, were at once recognized.

TAYLOR, Elizabeth (1912–75), writer. Her first novel, *At Mrs Lippincote's* (1945), was followed by many others, most of them delicate but shrewd observations of middle-class life in the stockbroker belt. They include *A Wreath of Roses* (1950) and *Mrs Palfrey at the Claremont* (1972). Her collection of stories, *Hester Lilly* (1954), *The Blush* (1958), *A Dedicated Man* (1965), and *The Devastating Boys* (1972), are much admired.

TAYLOR, Sir Henry (1800–86), held an appointment in the Colonial Office from 1824 to 1872, during which time he published a number of verse dramas. The most admired was *Philip van Artevelde* (1834), a lengthy work set in Flanders in the 14th cent. His only work with any lasting reputation is *The Statesman* (1836), an ironical exposition of the arts of succeeding as a civil servant. Taylor was a friend of *Southey and his literary executor.

TAYLOR, Jane (1783–1824) and Ann (1782–1866), authors of books for children. They published *Original Poems for Infant Minds* (1804); *Rhymes for the Nursery* (1806), which included 'Twinkle, twinkle little star'; and other volumes.

TAYLOR, Jeremy (1613–67), was chaplain to *Laud and Charles I, and was appointed rector in 1638. He was taken prisoner in the royalist defeat before Cardigan Castle in 1645, and retired to Golden Grove, Carmarthenshire, where he wrote most of his greater works. After the Restoration he was made bishop of Down and Connor, and subsequently of Dromore. He died at Lisburn and was buried in his cathedral of Dromore. His fame rests on the combined simplicity and splendour of his style, of which *The Rule and Exercise of Holy Living* (1650) and *The Rule and Exercises of Holy Dying* (1651) are perhaps the best examples. Among his other works, *The Liberty of Prophesying*, an argument for toleration, appeared in 1647; his *Eniautos*, or series of sermons for the Christian Year, in 1653; and *The Golden Grove*, a manual of daily prayers, in 1655.

TAYLOR, John (?1578–1653), the 'water-poet', became a Thames waterman, and increased his earnings by writing rollicking verse and prose; he obtained the patronage of *Jonson and others, and diverted both court and city. He accomplished several journeys, each one resulting in a booklet with an odd title. He published in 1630 a collective edition of his works, *All the Workes of John Taylor, the Water Poet*.

TAYLOR, John (1781–1864), first distinguished himself, amid much controversy, by identifying *'Junius' as Sir P. *Francis in 1813. He was editor of the *London Magazine*, 1821–4, and became a partner in the publishing firm of Taylor and Hessey. He published the work of *De Quincey, *Lamb, *Hazlitt, *Keats, *Clare, *Carey, and others.

TAYLOR, Philip Meadows (1808–76), Anglo-Indian novelist and historian, author of the successful *Confessions of a Thug* (1839), a result of his investigation into Thuggism, the secret terrorist movement in India. His reputation rests mainly on stories written after his retirement to England in 1860, notably the trilogy *Tara: a Mahratta Tale* (1843), *Ralph Darnell* (1865), and *Seeta* (1872).

TAYLOR, Thomas (1758–1835), classical scholar, mathematician, and *Neoplatonist, the friend of T. L. *Peacock. He was the first to embark on a systematic translation and exposition of Orphic and Neoplatonic literature. He published many works covering these interests.

TAYLOR, Tom (1817–80), editor of *Punch, 1874–80. He produced several successful plays (some in collaboration with C. *Reade), most of them adaptations. His comedy *Our American Cousin* (1858) contained the character of the brainless peer Lord Dundreary. He edited *Haydon's autobiography in 1853.

TAYLOR, William (1765–1836), author and translator, who did much to popularize German literature through his translations of Bürger's ballads (see LENORE) and works by G. E. Lessing and *Goethe. He was a friend and correspondent of *Southey.

'Teares of the Muses, The', a poem by *Spenser, included in the *Complaints*, published 1591. In this the poet deplores, through the mouth of several Muses, the decay of literature and learning.

Tearsheet, Doll, in Shakespeare's 2 *Henry IV*, *Falstaff's mistress.

Teazle, Sir Peter and Lady, characters in Sheridan's *The School for Scandal*.

'Te Deum', a Latin hymn of praise to God, so called from its opening words. Its authorship has been ascribed to St *Ambrose, but modern scholars attribute it to Niceta of Remesiana.

Tell, William, a legendary hero of the liberation of Switzerland from Austrian oppression. The stories concerning him differ in details, but in its generally accepted form the legend represents him as a skilled Swiss marksman who refused to do honour to the hat of Gessler, the Austrian bailiff of Uri, placed on a pole, and was in consequence arrested and required to hit with an arrow an apple placed on the head of his little son. This he successfully did, and with a second arrow shot Gessler, subsequently stirring up a rebellion against the oppressors. Swiss historians have found no evidence for the existence of a real William Tell. The story is found in writings of the 15th cent. William Tell is the subject of a play by *Schiller and an opera by Rossini.

Temora, see FINGAL.

Tempest, The, a romantic drama by *Shakespeare performed and probably written in 1611, printed in the First *Folio (1623). Although there are contemporary accounts of the shipwreck of the *Sea-Venture* in 1609 and passages from *Golding's Ovid and *Florio's Montaigne contribute details to the play, no single source for it is known.

Prospero, duke of Milan, ousted from his throne by his brother Antonio, and turned adrift on the sea with his child Miranda, has been cast upon a lonely island. This had been the place of banishment of the witch Sycorax. Prospero, by his knowledge of magic, has released various spirits (including Ariel) formerly imprisoned by the witch, and these now obey his orders. He also keeps in service the witch's son Caliban, a misshapen monster, the sole inhabitant of the island. Prospero and Miranda have lived thus for twelve years. When the play begins a ship carrying the usurper, his confederate Alonso, king of Naples, his brother Sebastian and son Ferdinand, is by the art of Prospero wrecked on the island. The passengers are saved, but Ferdinand is thought by the rest to be drowned, and he thinks this is their fate. According to Prospero's plan Ferdinand and Miranda are thrown together, fall in love, and plight their troths. Prospero appears to distrust Ferdinand and sets him to carrying logs. On another part of the island Sebastian and Antonio plot to kill Alonso and Gonzalo, 'an honest old Councellor' who had helped Prospero in his banishment. Caliban offers his services to Stephano, a drunken butler, and Trinculo, a jester, and persuades Sebastian and Antonio to try to murder Prospero. As their conspiracy nears him, Prospero breaks off the masque of Iris, Juno, and Ceres, which Ariel has presented to Ferdinand and Miranda. Caliban, Stephano and Trinculo are driven off and Ariel brings the king and his courtiers to Prospero's cell. There he greets 'My true preserver' Gonzalo, forgives his brother Antonio, on the condition that he restores his dukedom to him, and re-unites Alonso with his son Ferdinand, who is discovered playing chess with Miranda. While Alonso repents for what he has done, Antonio and Sebastian do not speak directly to Prospero, but exchange ironical and cynical comments with each other. The boatswain and master of the ship appear to say that it has been magically repaired and that the crew is safe. Before all embark for Italy Prospero frees Ariel from his service, renounces his magic, and leaves Caliban once more alone on the island.

Templars, Knights, an order founded about 1118, consisting originally of nine knights whose profession was to safeguard pilgrims to Jerusalem. Many noblemen from all parts of Christendom joined the order, and it acquired great wealth and influence in France, England, and other countries. The knights were organized in commanderies, under a preceptor in each province, and a grand master at the head of the order. From a state of poverty and humility they became so insolent that the order was crushed by the kings of Europe in their various dominions with circumstances, especially in France, of great cruelty. It was also officially suppressed by the Pope and the Council of Vienne (1312).

Temple, Miss, a character in C. Brontë's *Jane Eyre*.

TEMPLE, Sir William (1628–99), was envoy at Brussels in 1666, and visited The Hague, where he effected the triple alliance between England, Holland, and Sweden. In 1655 he married Dorothy *Osborne, whose letters to him give a vivid picture of the times. He first settled at Sheen, then at Moor Park, near Farnham, where *Swift was an inmate of his household. His principal works include *Observations upon . . . the Netherlands* (1672), an essay upon *The Advancement of Trade in Ireland* (1673), and three volumes of *Miscellanea* (1680, 1692, 1701). The second of these contains 'Of Ancient and Modern Learning', an essay which, by its uncritical praise of the spurious epistles of *Phalaris, exposed Temple to the censure of *Bentley and led to a vigorous controversy.

Tenant of Wildfell Hall, The, a novel by A. *Brontë, published 1848.

The narrator, Gilbert Markham, a young farmer, falls in love with Helen Graham, a young widow newly arrived in the neighbourhood with her son Arthur. Her youth, beauty, and seclusion, and her mysterious relationship with her landlord Lawrence, gives rise to local gossip. Markham violently assaults Lawrence, and Helen, distressed at the threatened rupture of their friendship, reveals to him that she had married Arthur Huntingdon who after a period of initial happiness had relapsed into a life of drinking, debauchery, and infidelity. She had fled, to protect her child, to Wildfell Hall, provided for her by Lawrence, who is in fact her brother. Shortly after the revelation Helen returns to nurse her husband through an illness which is fatal and the way is left clear for Markham successfully to renew his suit. In her 'Biographical Notice' (1850) Charlotte *Brontë suggested that the portrait of the dissolute Huntingdon was based on their brother Branwell.

Ten Days that Shook the World, an eye-witness account of the Russian revolution by American journalist and socialist John Reed (1887–1920), published 1919; published in England in 1926 with an introduction by Lenin.

Tender is the Night, a novel by F. S. *Fitzgerald.

TENNANT, William (1784–1848), author of a poem in six cantos, *Anster Fair* (1812), a mock-heroic description of the humours of the fair (in James V's reign) and of the courting, with fairy interposition, of Maggie Lauder by Rob the Ranter.

TENNIEL, Sir John (1820–1914), illustrator, worked for *Punch from 1850, and from 1864 became its chief cartoonist. His illustrations for *Alice's Adventures in Wonderland* (1865) and *Through the Looking Glass* (1871) are perfect examples of the integration of illustration with text.

TENNYSON, Alfred, first Baron Tennyson (1809–92), was educated at Trinity College, Cambridge, where he joined the *Apostles and became acquainted with A. H. *Hallam. In 1829 he won the chancellor's medal for English verse with 'Timbuctoo'. *Poems by Two Brothers* (1827) contains some early work as well as poems by his brothers Charles and Frederick (below). *Poems, Chiefly Lyrical* (1830, including *'Mariana') was unfavourably reviewed by *Lockhart and John *Wilson. In 1832 he travelled with Hallam on the Continent. Hallam died abroad in 1833, and in that year Tennyson began *In Memoriam*, expressive of his grief for his lost friend.

He became engaged to Emily Sellwood, to whom, however, he was not married until 1850. In Dec. 1832 he published a further volume of *Poems* (dated 1833), which included 'The Two

Voices', 'Oenone', 'The Lotos-Eaters', and 'A Dream of Fair Women'; *'Tithonus' (1860) was composed 1833–4. In 1842 appeared a selection from the previous two volumes, many of the poems much revised, with new poems, including *'Morte d'Arthur' (the germ of the *Idylls*). *'Locksley Hall', *'Ulysses', and 'St Simeon Stylites'. In 1847 he published * *The Princess* and in 1850 *In Memoriam*, and in the latter year he was appointed poet laureate in succession to *Wordsworth. He wrote his 'Ode' on the death of *Wellington in 1852 and *'The Charge of the Light Brigade' in 1854, having at this time settled in Farringford on the Isle of Wight.

Tennyson's fame was by now firmly established, and *Maud, and other Poems* (1855, see MAUD) and the first four * *Idylls of the King* (1859) sold extremely well. Among the many friends and admirers who visited Farringford were E. *FitzGerald, *Lear, *Patmore, *Clough, F. T. *Palgrave, and *Allingham. Prince Albert called in 1856, but Queen *Victoria never visited him, preferring to summon him to Osborne or Windsor. *Enoch Arden Etc.* (see ENOCH ARDEN) appeared in 1864. *The Holy Grail and Other Poems* (including 'Lucretius') in 1869 (dated 1870), 'The Last Tournament' in the *Contemporary Review* in 1871, and *Gareth and Lynette, etc.* in 1872. His dramas *Queen Mary* and *Harold* were published in 1875 and 1876, and *The Falcon*, *The Cup*, and *Becket in 1884, in which year he was made a peer. In 1880 appeared *Ballads and Other Poems*, including 'The Voyage of Maeldune', *'Rizpah', and 'The Revenge'. He published *Tiresias, and Other Poems* (see TIRESIAS) in 1885, and *The Foresters* appeared in 1892. He was buried in Westminster Abbey, and a life by his son Hallam appeared in 1897.

In his later years there were already signs that the admiration Tennyson had long enjoyed was beginning to wane. Critical opinion has tended to endorse *Auden's view that 'his genius was lyrical', and that he had little talent for the narrative, epic, and dramatic forms to which he devoted such labour. More recently there has been a revival of interest in some of the longer poems, e.g. 'Locksley Hall', *The Princess*, and 'Enoch Arden'.

TENNYSON, Frederick (1807–98), elder brother of A. *Tennyson, contributed to the *Poems by Two Brothers* (1827), and published *Days and Hours* (1854), *The Isles of Greece* (1890), and other volumes of verse.

TENNYSON TURNER, Charles (1808–79), elder brother of A. *Tennyson, contributed to *Poems by Two Brothers* (1827) and published volumes of sonnets, some of them depicting the rustic aspects of the Lincolnshire wolds.

Ten Thousand a Year, see WARREN, S.

TERENCE, (Publius Terentius Afer) (*c.*190 or *c.*180–159 BC), Roman comic poet, supposedly an African and a slave at birth. His six plays (all extant) owed a great deal to the Greek New Comedy. He was famed already in antiquity for the elegance and colloquial character of his Latin. It was as a stylist that he was studied in the Middle Ages. There is an early translation of the *Andria*, probably by J. *Rastell (*c.*1520), and an English version of all the six comedies by R. Bernard (1598). But Terence was known more through imitations than through translations. Along with Plautus, he contributed plots, characters, and tone to the mainstream of Renaissance comedy in 16th-cent. Italy, then (with original features) in the France of *Corneille and *Molière, from where it spread to Restoration London.

TERRY, Ellen Alice (1847–1928), celebrated actress. She was H. *Irving's leading lady during his brilliant management of the Lyceum Theatre.

TERTULLIAN (b. *c.*150), one of the greatest of the early Christian writers in Latin, author of the *Apologeticus* (197), an eloquent appeal to Roman governors on behalf of the Christians. He was opposed to the introduction of classical authors into Christian schools, and posed the famous question adapted by St *Jerome and *Alcuin: 'What has Athens to do with Jerusalem?' (*De Spectaculis*).

Terza rima, the measure adopted by Dante in the *Divina Commedia*, consisting of lines of five iambic feet with an extra syllable, in sets of three lines, the middle line of each rhyming with the first and third lines of the next set (a b a, b c b, c d c, etc.).

Tess of the D'Urbervilles; A Pure Woman, a novel by T. *Hardy, published 1891.

Tess Durbeyfield is the daughter of a poor villager of Blackmoor Vale, whose head is turned by learning that he is descended from the ancient family of D'Urberville. Tess is cunningly seduced by Alec, a young man of means, whose parents, with doubtful right, bear the name of D'Urberville. Tess gives birth to a child, which dies. Later, while working as a dairymaid she becomes blissfully engaged to Angel Clare, a clergyman's son. On their wedding night she confesses to him the seduction by Alec, and Angel hypocritically abandons her. Misfortunes come upon her and her family, and accident throws her once more in the path of Alec D'Urberville. He has become an itinerant preacher, but his temporary religious conversion does not prevent him from persistently pursuing her. When her pathetic appeals to her husband, now in Brazil, remain unanswered, she is driven for the sake of her family to become the mistress of Alec. Clare, returning from Brazil and repenting of his harshness, finds her living with Alec in Sandbourne. Maddened by this second wrong that has been done her by Alec, Tess stabs and kills him to liberate herself. After a brief halcyon period of concealment with Clare in the New Forest, Tess is arrested at Stonehenge, tried, and hanged.

Testament of Beauty, The, see BRIDGES, R.

Testament of Cresseid, The, a poem in 616 lines of rhyme-royal by *Henryson. The poet describes in the Prologue how he took up Chaucer's *Troilus and Criseyde* and proceeded to tell of the retribution that came upon Cresseid, who is abandoned by Diomede, then stricken with leprosy. As she sits by the roadside with her leper's cup, Troilus passes by and, not recognizing her, gives her alms. She dies after sending him a ring he had once given her.

Testament of Love, The, see USK, T.

Tetrachordon, the third of *Milton's pamphlets on divorce, published 1645. It deals with the four sets of passages on marriage and nullities in marriage from Genesis, Deuteronomy, St Matthew, and the First Epistle to the Corinthians. Milton seeks to reconcile the passages and to prove their essential harmony. (A tetrachordon was a four-stringed Greek lyre.) Milton also wrote two sonnets in defence of his views on divorce.

Teufelsdröckh, Herr Diogenes, see SARTOR RESARTUS.

THACKERAY, Anna Isabella, see RITCHIE, A. I.

THACKERAY, William Makepeace (1811–63), educated at Trinity College, Cambridge, where he became a close friend of E. *FitzGerald. He left Cambridge without taking a degree, having lost some of his inheritance through gambling. He entered the Middle Temple, but he never practised as a barrister. He began his career in journalism as proprietor of a struggling weekly paper, the *National Standard*, in 1833; it ceased publication a year later. He also studied art in London and in Paris where he lived from 1834 until 1837. He married Isabella Shawe in 1836, the year in which his first publication in volume form, *Flore et Zephyr*, appeared. The Thackerays returned to London, where their first child Anne (Anne Thackeray *Ritchie) was born in 1837. Thackeray began to contribute to *Fraser's Magazine*, the *Morning Chronicle*, the *New Monthly Magazine*, *The Times*, and many other periodicals. After the birth of their third child, Harriet Marian (later the first wife of Leslie *Stephen), in 1840 Isabella Thackeray suffered a mental breakdown which proved permanent.

Thackeray first came to the attention of the public with *The Yellowplush Papers*, which appeared in *Fraser's Magazine* in 1837–8, followed by *Catherine* (1839) and *A Shabby Genteel Story* (1840). His first full-length volume, *The Paris Sketch Book* (1840), and *The Great Hoggarty Diamond* (1841) both appeared under his most familiar pseudonym, Michael Angelo *Titmarsh. In 1842–3 he wrote, as 'George Savage *FitzBoodle', *The FitzBoodle Papers* and *Men's Wives*, and FitzBoodle is also the 'editor' of *The Luck of Barry Lyndon* (1844). The Irish Sketch Book (1843) has a preface signed, for the first time, with Thackeray's own name.

Thackeray began his association with *Punch in 1842, contributing caricatures, articles, and humorous sketches. *The Snobs of England* (later republished as *The Book of Snobs*) appeared there in 1846–7, and *Mr Punch's Prize Novelists*, parodies of the leading writers of the day, in 1847. In 1847 his first major novel, *Vanity Fair*, began to appear in monthly numbers, with illustrations by the author. *Pendennis* followed in 1848–50. His next novel, *The History of Henry Esmond* (3 vols, 1852), was followed by *The Newcomes*, published in numbers in 1853–5. Thackeray continued to produce lighter work, including a series of 'Christmas Books' which he illustrated himself. In 1851 he gave a series of lectures, *The English Humourists of the Eighteenth Century*, and in 1855–7, *The Four Georges*. He twice visited the United States to deliver his lectures, in 1851–3 and 1855–6. *The Virginians*, set in America, appeared in numbers in 1857–9. In 1860 he became the first editor of the *Cornhill Magazine*, for which he wrote his *Roundabout Papers* and in which appeared *Lovel the Widower*, *The Adventures of Philip*, and the unfinished *Denis Duval*.

Thaddeus of Warsaw, a *historical novel by J. *Porter, published 1803. It is interesting as an early example of the *historical novel, written before the form was established by Sir W. *Scott.

Thaisa, in Shakespeare's *Pericles*, the wife of Pericles.

Thalaba the Destroyer, a narrative poem by R. *Southey, published 1801.

Theatre of the Absurd, see ABSURD, THEATRE OF THE.

Thel, The Book of, see BLAKE, W.

Thenot, (1) a shepherd in Spenser's *The Shepheardes Calender*; (2) a character in Fletcher's *The Faithfull Shepherdess*.

THEOBALD, Lewis (1688–1744), Shakespearian scholar and author of poems, essays, and dramatic works. His *Shakespeare Restored*

(1726) exposed *Pope's incapacity as an editor of Shakespeare; Pope retaliated with his devastating portraits of Theobald as hero of his *Dunciad. Nevertheless Pope incorporated many of Theobald's corrections in his second edition, and Theobald's 1733–4 edition of Shakespeare surpassed that of his rival. Over 300 emendations made to the texts by Theobald are still accepted by most modern editors. *Double Falshood* (1728), a dramatization of *Cardenio, bears the inscription on the title page: 'Written Originally by W. *Shakespeare*; and now Revised and Adapted to the Stage By Mr. Theobald.' It is likely that *Double Falshood* is Theobald's attempt at establishing a vital relationship between Shakespeare and *Cervantes.

THEOCRITUS (c.308–c.240 BC), born in Sicily, was the most important of the Greek bucolic poets and the one who established for the *pastoral the formal characteristics, setting, and tone, which it was to retain for centuries. Theocritus wrote in the Doric dialect, and the difficulties this produced for his readers led to his comparative neglect during the Renaissance. Editions of his text did not appear in substantial numbers until the end of the 18th cent., and modern writers of pastoral from *Petrarch to *Pope tended rather to take *Virgil for a model. There was an anonymous translation of six of his idylls in 1588 and in 1684 Thomas Creche's English translation of all his works. *Dryden (whose preface praised Theocritus' 'tenderness and naturalness') contributed some stilted and artificial renderings to *Tonson's *Miscellany*. By the 19th cent. the vogue of the pastoral as a genre was at an end. Admirers of Theocritus were concerned merely to re-create his world of pastoral delights, and like *Tennyson in 'The Lotos-Eaters' (1833) most of them over-emphasized its sensuous aspects.

THEODORE (602–90), a native of Tarsus in Cilicia, was consecrated Archbishop of Canterbury by Pope Vitalius in 668. He imposed the Roman order and was the first archbishop to whom (according to *Bede) the whole English church agreed in submitting after the divisions leading up to the Synod of Whitby (663/4). He founded a school of learning at Canterbury, and created many new bishoprics. Theodore was author, at least in part, of the *Poenitentiale*, of considerable ecclesiastical and historical interest.

Theodoric, see DIETRICH OF BERN.

THEOPHRASTUS (c.372–287 BC), Greek philosopher, head of the Peripatetic School after *Aristotle. His interest for English literature derives from his *Characters*, brief sketches of human types embodying particular faults: the toady, the over-proud, the churlish. The popularity of Theophrastus in modern times

dates from I. *Casaubon's Latin translation of the *Characters* (1592). An English rendering by John Healey appeared in 1616, but before then J. *Hall enlarged Theophrastus' scope, in his Characters of *Virtues and Vices* (1608), and Sir T. *Overbury produced, in collaboration with J. *Webster, *Dekker, and *Donne, a volume of *Characters* (1614). (See also CHARACTER WRITING.)

Theophrastus Such, see IMPRESSIONS OF THEOPHRASTUS SUCH, THE.

Theory of Moral Sentiments, The, a philosophical work by Adam *Smith.
The author advances the view that all moral sentiments arise from sympathy. The basis of morality is pleasure in mutual sympathy, which moderates our natural egocentricity.

Theosophical Society, see BLAVATSKY.

Theosophy, from a Greek word meaning wisdom concerning God or things divine, a term applied in the 17th cent. to a kind of speculation, such as is found in the Jewish Cabbala, which sought to derive from the knowledge of God contained in secret books, or traditions mystically interpreted, a profounder knowledge and control of nature than could be obtained by the current philosophical methods. It was often applied specifically to the system of the German mystic Jacob Boehme.
In more recent times, it is more commonly applied to the movement associated with Mme *Blavatsky.

Thersites, the most querulous and ill-favoured of the Greek host in the Trojan War. He was killed by Achilles for laughing at the latter's grief over the death of Penthesilea, the queen of the Amazons. He figures in Shakespeare's *Troilus and Cressida* as a scabrous cynic.

Theseus, a son of Poseidon, or, according to later legend, of Aegeus, king of Athens. His exploits (in association with Medea, the Minotaur, Ariadne, Phaedra, etc.) form the basis of many literary works, and he appears as the duke of Athens in Shakespeare's *A Midsummer Night's Dream*, with his newly won bride *Hippolyta, and also in Fletcher's *The Two Noble Kinsmen*.

Thierry King of France, and his brother Theodoret, The Tragedy of, a play by J. *Fletcher, with the collaboration probably of *Massinger and possibly of *Beaumont, published 1621.

Things As They Are, see CALEB WILLIAMS.

THIONG'O, Ngugi Wa, formerly known as James T. Ngugi (1938–), Kenyan novelist. *Weep Not, Child* (1964), a novel of childhood that draws largely from his own upbringing and mission-school education, ends by rejecting the romantic individualism of its protagonist. Other novels include *The River Between* (1965) and *A Grain of Wheat* (1967), which blends the realism and compassion of his undergraduate short stories with the messianic political search of his first two novels. When Ngugi took to writing in his own language, Gikuyu, his government arrested him in 1977, and he wrote his first Gikuyu novel largely in prison; it was translated as *Devil on the Cross* (1982), after being published in Nairobi in 1980 in its original version. *Detained: A Prison Writer's Diary* (1981) was, however, written in English. Several extracts from works banned in Kenya have appeared in *Index on Censorship*.

Third Man, The, see GREENE, G.

THIRLWALL, Connop (1797–1875), was ordained priest in 1828. He translated Schleiermacher's *Essay on the Gospel of St Luke* (1825) and his Introduction to this work was remarkable for its acquaintance with German theology. In collaboration with *Hare he translated Niebuhr's *History of Rome* (1828–42) and edited the *Philological Museum* (1832–3), which contained Thirlwall's important essay 'The Irony of Sophocles'. His main work was the *History of Greece* (1835–44, for *Lardner's Cyclopaedia*, rev. 1847–52). He supported the admission of Jews to Parliament, the disestablishment of the Irish Church, and allowed Bishop *Colenso to preach in his diocese. These subjects and the *Essays and Reviews* controversy are dealt with in his 'Charges' (published in *Remains, Literary and Theological*, 1877–8).

This Sporting Life, see STOREY, D.

THOMAS, (Walter) Brandon, see CHARLEY'S AUNT.

THOMAS, D(onald) M(ichael) (1935–), poet, novelist, and translator. His work has been enriched by his familiarity with Russian literature, and his translations include two volumes of the poems of Akhmatova (1976, 1979) and *Pushkin's *The Bronze Horseman and other poems* (1982); his own volumes of poetry include *Two Voices* (1968), *Logan Stone* (1971), *Love and other Deaths* (1975), *The Honeymoon Voyage* (1978), *Dreaming in Bronze* (1981), and *Selected Poems* (1983). His novels include *The Flute-Player* (1979) and *Birthstone* (1980). Thomas achieved international success with his novel *The White Hotel* (1981), which combines an invented case history of one of *Freud's patients, Russian–Jewish Lisa Erdman, with her erotic and nightmare fantasies in prose and verse, a realistic account of her cure, her career as opera singer and subsequent marriage, and the steps that lead her and her stepson Kolya to her dream-foreseen death in the 1941 massacre at Babi Yar. *Ararat* (1983) shows a similar brooding on the theme of holocaust (this time of the Armenians).

THOMAS, Dylan Marlais (1914–53), poet, born in Swansea, where he worked as a journalist before moving to London in 1934; his first volume of verse, *18 Poems*, appeared in the same year. He then embarked on a Grub Street career of journalism, broadcasting, and film-making, rapidly acquiring a reputation for exuberance and flamboyance, as both poet and personality. In 1937 he married Caitlin Macnamara. Thomas's romantic, affirmative, rhetorical style gradually won a large following; it was both new and influential (and much imitated by his contemporaries of the *New Apocalypse movement), and the publication of *Deaths and Entrances* (1946), which contains some of his best-known work (including 'Fern Hill' and 'A Refusal to Mourn the Death by Fire of a Child in London') established him with a wide public: his *Collected Poems 1934–1952* (1952) sold extremely well.

Thomas also wrote a considerable amount of prose. *The Map of Love* (1939) is a collection of prose and verse; *Portrait of the Artist as a Young Dog* (1940) is a collection of largely autobiographical short stories; *Adventures in the Skin Trade* (1955) is a collection of stories; *A Prospect of the Sea* (1955) is a collection of stories and essays. Shortly before his death he took part in a reading in New York of what was to be his most famous single work, *Under Milk Wood*. His *Notebooks* (ed. R. N. Maud) were published in 1968, and a new edition of *The Poems of Dylan Thomas*, with critical notes and comments by Daniel Jones, in 1971.

THOMAS, (Philip) Edward (1878–1917), poet, and writer of many volumes of prose, much of it topographical and biographical, including a biography of R. *Jefferies (1909). With the encouragement of *Frost he turned to poetry. In 1915 Thomas enlisted in the army and was killed at Arras. Most of his poetry was published posthumously, though a few pieces appeared under the pseudonym 'Edward Eastaway' between 1915 and 1917. His *Collected Poems* (1978) was edited by R. George Thomas. His work shows a loving and accurate observation of the English pastoral scene, combined with a bleak and scrupulous honesty and clarity. Both he and Frost advocated the use of natural diction and of colloquial speech rhythms in metrical verse, and his work is now highly regarded.

THOMAS, R(onald) S(tuart) (1913–), poet and clergyman. His first volume of poems, *The Stones of the Field* (1946), was followed by many others, including *Song at the Year's Turning*

(1955), *Tares* (1961), *Pietà* (1966), *Not that he brought flowers* (1968), *Laboratories of the Spirit* (1975); and *Selected Poems 1946–68* (1973). His poetry is deeply coloured by his experience of working in remote rural communities, where life was harsh and the landscape bleak; he has created his own form of bleak Welsh pastoral, streaked with indignation over the history of Wales and the Welsh. Many of the poems unite religious and rural imagery. He had edited various works including *The Penguin Book of Religious Verse* (1963), and selections from E. *Thomas (1964), G. *Herbert (1967), and *Wordsworth (1971).

THOMAS À BECKET, see BECKET, ST THOMAS.

THOMAS À KEMPIS (Thomas Hämmerlein or Hämmerken) (1380–1471), born of humble parents at Kempen near Cologne. He became an Augustinian monk and wrote Christian mystical works, among which is probably to be included the famous *De Imitatione Christi*, which has been translated from the Latin into many languages (into English in the middle of the 15th cent.). It traces in four books the gradual progress of the soul to Christian perfection, its detachment from the world, and its union with God.

THOMAS BECKET, see BECKET, ST THOMAS.

Thomas the Rhymer, see ERCELDOUNE.

Thomist (pron. 'Tomist'), a follower of the *scholastic philosopher St Thomas *Aquinas.

THOMPSON, E(dward) P(almer (1924–   ), historian. His works include a study of W. *Morris (1955) and *The Making of the English Working Class* (1963).

THOMPSON, Flora Jane, née Timms (1876–1947), is remembered for her autobiographical trilogy *Lark Rise to Candleford* (1945), published originally as *Lark Rise* (1939), *Over to Candleford* (1941), and *Candleford Green* (1943), works which evoke through the childhood memories and youth of third-person 'Laura' a vanished world of agricultural customs and rural culture.

THOMPSON, Francis (1859–1907), after failed attempts to train for the Roman Catholic priesthood, spent three years, from 1885, of homeless and opium-addicted destitution in London, till he was rescued by Wilfred and Alice *Meynell, who secured him literary recognition. He never freed himself for long from opium which, together with tuberculosis, caused his early death. His best-known poems are 'The Hound of Heaven' and 'The Kingdom of God'; he published three volumes of verse, in 1893, 1895, and 1897, and much literary criticism in

Meynell's *Merry England*, *The Academy*, and the *Athenaeum*. His finest work conveys intense religious experience in imagery of great power; he was influenced especially by *Shelley, *De Quincey, and *Crashaw.

THOMS, William John (1803–85), antiquary, author of several works including *The Book of the Court* (1838), and editor of a number of volumes including a collection of *Early Prose Romances* (1827–8) and *The History of Reynard the Fox* (1844) for the *Percy Society. He was secretary of the *Camden Society from 1838 to 1873. In 1846, in an article in the *Athenaeum* headed 'Folk Lore' he introduced this term into the English language. Encouraged by *Dilke he founded *Notes and Queries* in 1849.

THOMSON, James (1700–48), born at Ednam on the Scottish border, came to London in 1725, and wrote 'Winter', the first of *The Seasons*, which appeared successively in 1726–30. He made the acquaintance of *Arbuthnot, *Gay, and *Pope, found patrons, and eventually, through the influence of Lord *Lyttelton received a sinecure. He published in 1735–6 his long patriotic poem *Liberty*. He produced a series of tragedies, *Sophonisba* (1730), *Agamemnon* (1738), *Edward and Eleanora* (1739); *Tancred and Sigismunda* (published 1745) and *Coriolanus* (1749) were produced after his death. In 1740 was performed the masque of *Alfred* by Thomson and Mallet, containing 'Rule, Britannia', probably written by Thomson. In 1748 he published *The Castle of Indolence*, which contains a portrait of himself ('A bard here dwelt, more fat than bard beseems') supposed to have been written by Lyttelton, the first line by J. *Armstrong, which affectionately mocks the poet's notorious love of idleness. *The Seasons*, one of the most popular of English poems, was immensely influential, offering both in style and subject a new departure from the urbanity of Pope and developing in a highly distinctive manner the range of *topographical poetry; *Wordsworth recognized Thomson as the first poet since *Milton to offer new images of 'external nature'. He contributed greatly to the vogue for the *picturesque.

THOMSON, James (1834–82), trained as an army schoolmaster, in which capacity he was sent in 1851–2 to Ireland, where he met *Bradlaugh. For his early work he used the pseudonym 'B.V.' Signs of growing alcoholism appeared in the late 1850s and in 1862 Thomson was discharged from the army, probably for drunkenness. He came to London, took various jobs and wrote for several magazines, publishing among other work 'Vane's Story', 'Sunday up the River', and 'Sunday at Hampstead'. 'Weddah' (1871), a long poem relating a tragic Arabian love-story, led to friendship with

W. M. *Rossetti. For part of 1872 Thomson was with a gold company in Colorado, and in 1873 in Spain as a war reporter; on his return he completed his best-known poem, 'The City of Dreadful Night', which appeared in Bradlaugh's *National Reformer* in 1874. This long poem, which much influenced the mood of *fin-de-siècle* poetic pessimism, is a powerful evocation of a half-ruined city, a 'Venice of the Black Sea', through which flows the River of the Suicides; the narrator, in vain search of 'dead Faith, dead Love, dead Hope' encounters tormented shades wandering in a Dantesque vision of a living hell, over which presides the sombre and sublime figure of Melancolia (based on Dürer's engraving of 1514). His first volume of verse, *The City of Dreadful Night and Other Poems* (1880), and a second volume in the same year were well received. *Essays and Phantasies* appeared in 1881; *Satires and Profanities* in 1884.

THOMSON, Sir William, first Baron Kelvin (1824–1907), became professor of natural philosophy at Glasgow. His formulation of the second law of thermodynamics, predicting that the world would sooner or later suffer a heat death as a result of entropy, contributed significantly to late 19th-cent. pessimism. The ignorance of this law displayed by most 20th-cent. literary intellectuals was used as an illustration of the gap between the *'Two Cultures' by C. P. *Snow.

'Thopas, The Tale of Sir', see CANTERBURY TALES, 17.

THOREAU, Henry David (1817–62), American author, became a follower and friend of *Emerson. He supported himself by a variety of occupations; a few of his poems were published in *The Dial*, but he made no money from literature, and published only two books in his lifetime. The first was *A Week on the Concord and Merrimack River* (1849); the second, *Walden, or Life in the Woods* (1854), attracted little attention, but has since been recognized as a literary masterpiece and as one of the seminal books of the century. It describes his two-year experiment in self-sufficiency (1845–7) when he built himself a wooden hut on the edge of Walden Pond, near Concord; he describes his domestic economy, his agricultural experiments, his visitors and neighbours, the plants and wild life, and the sense of the Indian past, with a deeply challenging directness that questions the materialism and the prevailing work ethic of the age. *Walden* is studded with apparently casual illuminations and with lines of poetic sensibility. Equally influential in future years was his essay 'Civil Disobedience' (1849; originally entitled 'Resistance to Civil Government'), in which he argues the right of the individual to refuse to pay taxes when conscience dictates and describes the technique of passive resistance later adopted by Gandhi. Thoreau has also been hailed as a pioneer ecologist. His *Journal* (14 vols) and his collected *Writings* (20 vols) were both published in 1906.

Thornberry, Job, (1) in *Endymion* by B. Disraeli; (2) in *John Bull* by *Colman the younger, an honest, kindly English tradesman, supposed to typify the national character.

Thornhill, Squire and Sir William, characters in Goldsmith's *The Vicar of Wakefield*.

Thorpe, John and Isabella, characters in J. Austen's *Northanger Abbey*.

Thoughts on the Cause of the Present Discontents, see PRESENT DISCONTENTS.

Thousand and One Nights, The, see ARABIAN NIGHTS ENTERTAINMENTS.

THRALE, Hester Lynch, Mrs, *née* Salisbury (1741–1821), was married against her inclinations in 1763 to Henry Thrale. The following year they met Dr *Johnson, who became very friendly with both, at one time becoming almost domesticated at their house in Streatham Place. Three years after Thrale's death in 1781, and amid much opposition from family and friends (including F. *Burney), she married Gabriel Piozzi, an Italian musician; this drew from Johnson a letter of anguished protest, and ended their intimacy. She published several works, including *Anecdotes of the late Samuel Johnson* (1786).

Three Clerks, The, a novel by A. *Trollope, published 1858.

Three Men in a Boat, see JEROME, J. K.

Threepenny Opera, The (*Die Dreigroschenoper*), *Brecht's updated version of *The Beggar's Opera*.

Three Weeks after Marriage, a comedy by *Murphy, performed 1764.

Thrie Estaitis, Satyre of the, see PLEASANT SATYRE OF THE THRIE ESTAITIS, ANE.

Through the Looking-Glass and *What Alice Found There*, a book for children by Lewis Carroll (see DODGSON), published 1872.

Alice (see ALICE'S ADVENTURES IN WONDERLAND) walks in a dream through the looking-glass into Looking-Glass House, where she finds that the chessmen, particularly the red and white queens, are alive; meets with Tweedledum and Tweedledee and Humpty-Dumpty; and so forth. The story ends with Alice, who has the red queen in her arms, 'shaking her into a kitten' (for she had gone to sleep playing with the black and white kittens). The well-known verses about the *Jabberwock and the Walrus and the Carpenter occur in the course of the story.

THUCYDIDES (*c*.460–*c*.395 BC), Athenian historian who left a brilliant account of the disastrous war Athens waged against Sparta. He was prepared to trace effects to rational causes; his handling of eyewitness accounts (all-important in a contemporary history) was securely scientific. Like other difficult Greek authors, Thucydides was little read before the 19th cent., although there were translations by T. Nichols (1550) and by *Hobbes (1629). S. T. Bloomfield produced an annotated translation (1829), in 1830–5 T. *Arnold published a commentary in which he tried to derive lessons for his own time from the text of Thucydides, and *Jowett's elegant translation followed in 1881.

THURBER, James Grove (1894–1961), American humorist, many of whose essays, stories, and sketches appeared in the *New Yorker*, including one of his best-known short stories, 'The Secret Life of Walter Mitty' (1932), which describes the colourful escapist fantasies of a docile husband.

Thurio, in Shakespeare's *The Two Gentleman of Verona*, Silvia's suitor.

Thwackum, a character in Fielding's *Tom Jones*.

THWAITE, Anthony Simon (1930–   ), poet and critic. His volumes of poetry include *Home Truths* (1957), *The Stones of Emptiness* (1967), and *A Portion for Foxes* (1977). Thwaite uses a wide range of theme and subject matter, ranging from the domestic to the exotic. *Victorian Voices* (1980) is a collection of 14 dramatic monologues. His collected *Poems 1953–1983* was published in 1984.

'Thyrsis, A Monody, to commemorate the author's friend, Arthur Hugh Clough, who died at Florence, 1861', a poem by M. *Arnold, published 1866. The poem is a pastoral elegy lamenting *Clough as Thyrsis, recalling his 'golden prime' in the days when he and Arnold wandered through the Oxfordshire countryside, their youthful rivalry as poets, and Clough's departure for a more troubled world. It invokes the *Scholar-Gipsy as an image of hope and perpetual quest.

Tibert, the cat in *Reynard the Fox. The name is the same as Tybalt (see the exchange between Mercutio and Tybalt in *Romeo and Juliet*, III. i. 75 ff.: 'Tybalt, you rat-catcher . . . Good King of Cats, nothing but one of your nine lives').

TIBULLUS, Albius (*c*.48–19 BC), Roman elegiac poet, noted for his gentleness and his love of country life. He wrote verses of great elegance, marked by a fastidious melancholy. Of the three books of poems that bear his name, the first two, published in his lifetime, were his work. Something of his gentleness survives in *Campion, something of his contentment with country life is met in *Herrick.

TICKELL, Thomas (1685–1740), was author of various poems including *Oxford* (1707), *On the Prospect of Peace* (1713), *Kensington Garden* (1722), and the sentimental *ballad *Lucy and Colin* (1725). But he is chiefly remembered as a friend and supporter of *Addison. He edited Addison's works (1721), publishing in the first volume an elegy on Addison's death.

Tietjens, Christopher, a character in *Parade's End*, by F. M. Ford.

Tigg, Montague, a character in Dickens's *Martin Chuzzlewit*.

Tilburina, the heroine of Mr Puff's tragedy 'The Spanish Armada' in Sheridan's *The Critic*. It is she who observes that even an oyster may be crossed in love.

Till Eulenspiegel, see EULENSPIEGEL.

TILLOTSON, John (1630–94), a latitudinarian who became archbishop of Canterbury. His sermons, which were very popular, show a marked difference from the earlier *metaphysical style of *Donne and *Andrewes; they were extolled as models of lucidity and good sense.

TILLYARD, E(ustace) M(andeville) W(etenhall) (1889–1962), scholar and critic. His works include *Milton* (1930), *Shakespeare's last plays* (1938), *Shakespeare's history plays* (1944), *Shakespeare's problem plays* (1950), and the influential short essay *The Elizabethan World Picture* (1943).

Tilney, General, his sons Henry and Frederick, and his daughter Eleanor, characters in J. Austen's *Northanger Abbey*.

Timber, or *Discoveries Made upon Men and Matter*, by *Jonson, printed in the folio of 1640, a collection of notes, extracts, and reflections on miscellaneous subjects, made in the course of the author's wide reading, mainly adapted from Latin writers.

Time and Tide: An Independent Non-Party Weekly Review (1920–77), a periodical founded by Viscountess Rhondda (Margaret Haig Thomas, 1883–1958), with the support of R. *West and others. Originally a strongly left-wing and feminist publication, it went through many shades of political opinion before its disappearance. Its contributors included D. H. *Lawrence, V. *Woolf, S. *Jameson, G. B. *Shaw, and Robert *Graves.

Time Machine, The, see WELLS, H. G.

Times, The, was founded under the name of 'The Daily Universal Register' on 1 Jan. 1785 by John Walter, the name being changed to *The Times* in 1788. It was one of the first papers to employ special foreign correspondents and war correspondents. Among notable men of letters who contributed to *The Times* in the early days were *Borrow (from Spain), Leigh *Hunt, and B. *Disraeli ('Runnymede Letters'). The most dramatic change in the appearance of the paper was the removal, on 3 May 1966, of the column marked 'Personal' from the front page, and its replacement by news. Of the three weekly supplements published by *The Times* group, *The Times Literary Supplement* was founded in 1901. *The Times Educational Supplement* in 1910, and *The Times Higher Educational Supplement* in 1971.

Times Literary Supplement, The (1902–), an influential weekly literary periodical; it first appeared with *The Times*, then in 1914 became a separate publication. The first editor, Bruce Richmond, supported and encouraged many writers of his time, including V. *Woolf, T. S. *Eliot, J. M. *Murry, E. *Blunden, the historians *Namier and E. H. Carr. Reviews continued to be anonymous until 1974.

Timias, in Spenser's *Faerie Queene*, Prince *Arthur's squire, may represent *Ralegh.

Timon, a misanthropical citizen of Athens who lived about the time of the Peloponnesian War, the subject (1) of one of *Lucian's finest Dialogues; (2) of Shakespeare's *Timon of Athens*.

Pope's Timon, in *Moral Essays* IV. 98, an example of ostentatious wealth without sense or taste, was said to be drawn from the duke of Chandos, but Pope repudiated this charge, apparently to the duke's satisfaction.

Timon of Athens, a drama by *Shakespeare, possibly in collaboration with *Middleton, written probably about 1607 and apparently left unfinished; it was printed in the First *Folio (1623). The material for the play is in *Plutarch's *Life of Antony*, Painter's *Palace of Pleasure*, *Lucian's *Timon, or the Misanthrope*, and possibly an anonymous play *Timon* among the Dyce MSS.

Timon, a rich and noble Athenian of good and gracious nature, having ruined himself by his prodigal liberality to friends, flatterers, and parasites, turns to the richest of his friends for assistance in his difficulties, and is denied it and deserted by all who had previously frequented him. He surprises these by inviting them once more to a banquet; but when the covers are removed from the dishes (Timon crying, 'Uncover, dogs, and lap', III. vi.), they are found to contain warm water, which with imprecations he throws in his guests' faces. Cursing the city, he betakes himself to a cave, where he lives solitary and misanthropical. While digging for roots he finds a hoard of gold, which has now no value for him. His embittered spirit is manifested in his talk with the exiled Alcibiades, the churlish philosopher Apemantus, the thieves and flatterers attracted by the gold, and his faithful steward Flavius. When the senators of Athens, hard pressed by the attack of Alcibiades, come to entreat him to return to the city and help them, he offers them his fig-tree, on which to hang themselves as a refuge from affliction. Soon his tomb is found by the sea-shore, with an epitaph expressing his hatred of mankind.

Tina Sastri, a character in G. Eliot's 'Mr Gilfil's Love-Story' (see SCENES OF CLERICAL LIFE).

TINDAL, William, see TYNDALE.

Tintagel, a castle on the north coast of Cornwall, of which ruins remain. It figures in Malory's *Morte D'Arthur* as the castle where *Uther Pendragon was wedded to Igraine, and subsequently as the home of King Mark of Cornwall.

'Tintern Abbey, Lines composed a few miles above, on revisiting the banks of the Wye during a tour', a poem by *Wordsworth published in the first edition of the *Lyrical Ballads*, 1798.

Wordsworth's second visit to Tintern, recorded in this work, was with his sister Dorothy, who is addressed in its closing passage. It is written in blank verse and Wordsworth referred to 'the impassioned music of the versification', which resembled the elevation of an ode. It is a central statement of Wordsworth's faith in the restorative and associative power of nature; he describes the development of his own love of nature from the 'coarser pleasures' of boyhood, through the 'aching joys' and 'dizzy raptures' of young manhood, to the more reflective, moral, philosophic pleasures of maturity informed by 'the still, sad music of humanity'.

'Tiresias', a dramatic monologue in blank verse by *Tennyson, published in 1885, but composed in 1833. The prophet Tiresias, blinded and doomed to 'speak the truth that no man may believe' as a consequence of glimpsing Athene naked, urges Menoeceus, son of Creon, to sacrifice himself for Thebes.

'Tis Pity She's a Whore, a tragedy by J. *Ford, printed 1633.

The play deals with the guilty passion of Giovanni and his sister Annabella for each other.

Being with child, Annabella marries one of her suitors, Soranzo, who discovers her condition. She refuses to name her lover, though threatened with death by Soranzo. Soranzo invites Annabella's father and the magnificoes of the city, with Giovanni, to a sumptuous feast, intending to execute his vengeance. Although warned of Soranzo's intentions, Giovanni boldly comes. He has a last meeting with Annabella just before the feast, and to forestall Soranzo's vengeance, stabs her himself. He then enters the banqueting room with her heart on his dagger, defiantly tells what he has done, fights with and kills Soranzo, and is himself killed by his servant Vasques.

'Tis Pity is an obsessive, passionate play, focusing on the sensationalist incest taboo which is portrayed, with rich symbolic imagery, as doomed but intensely beautiful. This has made it Ford's most famous play, in the study and on the stage.

Titania, in Shakespeare's *A Midsummer Night's Dream*, the queen of the fairies, and wife of Oberon.

Tit-Bits, a popular weekly magazine, founded in 1881 by G. *Newnes. The original formula included jokes, quizzes, correspondence, short stories and serialized fiction, snippets of news, etc., and such ingredients as comic strips, cartoons, and sports coverage have been added. In its early years it attracted short stories by Arnold *Bennett and *Conrad.

'Tithonus', a dramatic monologue in blank verse by *Tennyson, published in the *Cornhill in 1860, then in 1864, but composed in 1833. Tithonus is granted perpetual life but not perpetual youth by Aurora, and in a dramatic monologue he longs for death; like *In Memoriam*, the poem reflects Tennyson's anxiety about the nature of personal immortality.

Titmarsh, (1) Michael Angelo, a pseudonym used by *Thackeray for much of his early journalism. (2) Samuel, a character in his *The Great Hoggarty Diamond*.

Tito Melema, a character in G. Eliot's *Romola*.

Titurel, a German *Grail legend of the 13th cent., left incomplete by *Wolfram von Eschenbach. Titurel (the great-grandfather of Parsifal) is entrusted from Heaven with the guardianship of the Grail, and he builds a chapel at Mount Selvagge (Montsalvatsch) where he reposes it and organizes a band of defenders for it.

Titus Andronicus, a tragedy by *Shakespeare, dating possibly from 1590, published 1594, and included in the First *Folio of 1623.

Shakespeare's authorship has been questioned, but it is now generally agreed that he wrote the whole play. Sources for *Titus Andronicus* that have been put forward include the *Hecuba* of *Euripides, *Seneca's *Thyestes* and *Troades*, and *Ovid's version of 'the tragic tale of Philomel' (*Metamorphoses*, Book XIII); *Plutarch also contributed to the plot.

The first half of the play deals with the return of Titus Andronicus to Rome after his sixth victory over the Goths. He brings with him their Queen Tamora and her three sons, the eldest of whom, Alarbus, is sacrificed to avenge his own sons' deaths. Titus is offered the imperial mantle, but gives it instead to the late emperor's son Saturninus, to whose marriage with his daughter, Lavinia, Titus consents. Saturninus' brother Bassianus claims Lavinia as his own and, while taking her off, Titus kills his son Mutius, who has tried to block his way. Saturninus changes his mind, renounces Lavinia and marries Tamora, who engineers a false reconciliation between the emperor and Titus, whom she plans to destroy. She does this with the help of her lover Aaron, the Moor, who gets Tamora's sons Chiron and Demetrius to murder Bassianus, whose body is thrown into a pit, rape Lavinia, and cut off her tongue and hands. Titus' sons Quintus and Martius are then lured by Aaron to fall into the pit, where they are found and accused of Bassianus' murder. Aaron tells Titus that his sons will not be executed if he sacrifices his hand and sends it to the emperor. Titus does this, but gets it back again with the heads of his two sons.

In the second half of the play, Titus discovers who raped and mutilated his daughter, and with his brother, Marcus, and last remaining son Lucius, vows revenge. Lucius leaves Rome, but returns with an army of Goths, which captures Aaron and his child by Tamora. Tamora and her sons Demetrius and Chiron visit Titus disguised as Revenge, Rapine, and Murder and ask him to have Lucius banquet at his house, where the emperor and the empress and her sons will be brought. Titus recognizes his enemies and with the help of Lavinia slits the throats of Chiron and Demetrius and uses their flesh in a pie, some of which Tamora eats at the banquet before Titus kills her. He also stabs Lavinia, but is killed by Saturninus, who is in turn killed by Lucius. He is elected emperor and sentences Aaron to be buried breast-deep in the ground and starved to death.

(Andro*ni*cus in the play is accentuated thus, on the second syllable; in Latin it is Andro*ni*cus.)

Titus Groan, see PEAKE, M. L.

Toad of Toad Hall, a dramatic adaptation by A. A. *Milne of K. *Grahame's *The Wind in the Willows*.

'To Autumn', a poem by *Keats, written Sept. 1819, published 1820. It was his last major poem, and although usually included in a discussion of the Odes, it was not so labelled by Keats himself.

The poem, in three stanzas, is at once a celebration of the fruitfulness of autumn (lightly personified as a figure in various autumnal landscapes) and an elegy for the passing of summer and the transience of life, and its mood has been generally taken to be one of acquiescence.

Toby, Uncle, Captain Tobias Shandy, in Sterne's *Tristram Shandy*.

Todgers, Mrs, in Dickens's *Martin Chuzzlewit*.

TOKLAS, Alice B., see STEIN, G.

TOLAND, John (1670–1722), freethinker, born in Ireland. He settled in Oxford where he completed *Christianity not Mysterious* (1696), which made him notorious. It also began the Deist controversy (see DEISM) and initiated the one great epoch of Irish philosophy. He addressed to the queen of Prussia his *Letters of Serena* (1704), whose materialistic pantheism—he coined the word 'pantheist' in 1705—he flamboyantly expressed in *Pantheisticon* (1720). In 1698 he wrote a life of *Milton and edited his prose works. Toland's *Tetradymus* (1720) contains perhaps the first essay on the esoteric/exoteric distinction. *Pope ridiculed him; *Swift called him 'the great Oracle of the Anti-Christians'.

TOLKIEN, J(ohn) R(onald) R(euel) (1892–1973), Merton professor of English language and literature at Oxford, 1945–59. He published a number of philological and critical studies, such as 'Beowulf: the Monsters and the Critics' (in *Proceedings of the British Academy*, 1936), and became internationally known for two books based on a mythology of his own: *The Hobbit* (1937) and its sequel *The Lord of the Rings* (3 vols, 1954–5). *The Silmarillion* (1977), which has an earlier place in this sequence of stories, was published posthumously.

TOLSTOY, Count Lev Nikolaevich (1828–1910), Russian prose writer. His first published work was *Childhood* (1852), the first part of a remarkably perceptive trilogy on his early years completed by *Boyhood* (1854) and *Youth* (1857). His other works include *Sevastopol Sketches* (1855–6); *Family Happiness* (1859); *The Cossacks* (1863); *War and Peace* (1863–9), an epic novel of the Napoleonic invasion and the lives of three aristocratic families; and *Anna Karenina* (1873–7), the story of a married woman's passion for a young officer and her tragic fate. From about 1880 Tolstoy's constant concern with moral

questions developed into a spiritual crisis which led to radical changes in his life. The major fictional works bearing the imprint of changes in his thinking are *The Death of Ivan Illich* (1886), *The Kreutzer Sonata* (1889), *Master and Man* (1895), *Resurrection* (1899), and *Hadji Murad* (1904). His collected works were translated 1899–1902 and have been retranslated many times since. Among those who played a part in establishing his English reputation were M. *Arnold, G. B. *Shaw, *Galsworthy, E. M. *Forster, and D. H. *Lawrence.

Tom and Jerry, the two chief characters in *Egan's *Life in London*; hence used in various allusive senses, e.g. of riotous behaviour.

Tom Brown's Schooldays, see HUGHES, T.

Tom Jones, The History of, a novel by H. *Fielding, published 1749, consisting of 18 'books', each preceded by an introductory chapter in the nature of an essay on some theme more or less connected with the story, in the manner subsequently adopted by *Thackeray and George *Eliot. These essays contain some of Fielding's best prose, and the work is generally regarded as Fielding's greatest.

The plot is briefly as follows. Tom Jones is a foundling, discovered one night in the bed of the wealthy and benevolent Mr Allworthy, who gives him a home and educates him, but later repudiates him. In the first place Tom, a generous, but too human, youth, has incurred his benefactor's displeasure by his amour with Molly Seagrim, the keeper's daughter. Then he has fallen in love with the beautiful Sophia (daughter of the bluff irascible foxhunter, Squire Western). He has incurred the enmity of his tutor, the pedantic divine, Thwackum, and in a less degree, of his colleague, the hypocritical philosopher Square. And lastly he is the victim of the cunning misrepresentations of young Blifil, Squire Allworthy's nephew, who expects to marry Sophia himself, and hates Tom. Tom sets out on his travels, accompanied by the schoolmaster, Partridge, a simple lovable creature, and meets with many adventures, some of them of an amorous description. Meanwhile Sophia, who is in love with Tom and determined to escape from the marriage with Blifil to which her despotic father has condemned her, runs away from home, with Mrs Honour, her maid, to a relative in London. Finally Tom is discovered to be the son of Allworthy's sister, the machinations of Blifil are exposed, Sophia forgives Tom his infidelities, and all ends happily.

TOMKIS, Thomas (?1580–?1634), author of two university comedies, *Lingua, or the Combat of the Tongue and the five Senses for Superiority* (1607) and *Albumazar*. Albumazar (historically an Arabian astronomer, 805–85) is a rascally wizard who transforms the rustic Trincalo into the person of his master, with absurd consequences.

TOMLINSON, (Alfred) Charles (1927–), poet and artist. His aspirations as a painter are reflected in the visual qualities of his verse. His volumes of verse include *Relations and Contraries* (1951), *Seeing is Believing* (US 1958; London 1960), *The Way of the World* (1969), *Written on Water* (1972), *The Way In and Other Poems* (1974), and *The Flood* (1981).

TOMLINSON, H(enry) M(ajor) (1873–1958), novelist and journalist, the son of a foreman at the West India Dock; his early love of ships and the sea is reflected in his life and works, e.g. *The Sea and the Jungle* (1912, an account of a voyage to Brazil and up the Amazon), *London River* (1921, essays and reflections), and his first novel, *Gallions Reach* (1927).

Tom o' Bedlam, a wandering beggar. After the dissolution of the religious houses the poor wandered over the country, many assuming disguises calculated to obtain them charity. Among other disguises some affected madness, and were called Bedlam Beggars (so in *Gammer Gurtons Nedle* 'Diccon the Bedlam'). Edgar, in *King Lear*, II. iii, adopts this disguise. Some of these Bedlam beggars sang mad songs, examples of which are given in Percy's *Reliques*.

Tom Sawyer, *The Adventures of*, a novel by Mark *Twain, published 1876.

Tom, a lively and adventurous lad, lives with his priggish brother Sid and his good-hearted Aunt Polly in the quiet town of St Petersburg, Missouri. His companion is the irrepressible Huckleberry Finn, and together they embark on many exploits, during one of which they happen to observe Injun Joe stab the town doctor to death and attempt to incriminate the drunken Muff Potter; Tom is later able to absolve Potter at his trial. Tom and his sweetheart Becky Thatcher wander away from a school picnic and are lost for three days in a cave, where Tom spies Injun Joe; after the children are rescued Injun Joe is found dead and his treasure is divided between Tom and Huck. Huck's subsequent escapades become the subject of the classic sequel *The Adventures of *Huckleberry Finn.

Tom's Coffee House, named after Thomas West, its landlord, was situated in Russell Street, Covent Garden, and frequented by the best company after the play; its patrons include Dr *Johnson, *Goldsmith, and *Garrick. It became a subscription club *c*.1768.

Tom Thumb, *a Tragedy*, a farce by H. *Fielding, performed and published 1730, and published in a different version 1731 under the title of *The Tragedy of Tragedies, or, The Life and Death of Tom Thumb the Great*. This is an exuberant farce in the mock-heroic manner, ridiculing the 'Bombastic Greatness' of the fashionable grandiose tragedies of authors such as N. *Lee and J. *Thomson, and similar in form to Buckingham's *The Rehearsal*. It was published with a frontispiece by *Hogarth. (See HEROIC DRAMA.)

Tono-Bungay, see WELLS, H. G.

TONSON, Jacob (1656–1737), publisher and bookseller who published the foremost poets and playwrights of the age; his long association with *Dryden began in 1679, with the publication of his version of *Troilus and Cressida*, and his other writers included A. *Behn, *Otway, *Cowley, *Rowe, *Addison, and *Pope; he also acquired the profitable copyright of *Paradise Lost*. He was well known for his *Miscellanies* (1684–1709) in six parts, of which the earliest were edited and largely written by Dryden; they contained translations from *Horace, *Ovid, *Lucretius, *Virgil, etc., as well as original work by *Pope, A. *Philips, *Swift, and others. He was secretary of the *Kit-Cat Club and the butt of satire from Dryden (who mocked his 'two left legs') and Pope, who took up the theme of his ungainly legs in the *Dunciad*. The firm was continued by his nephew and great-nephew who bore the same name.

Tony Lumpkin, a character in Goldsmith's *She Stoops to Conquer*.

Toodle, Polly and Robin ('Rob the Grinder'), her son, characters in Dickens's *Dombey and Son*. Polly was Paul Dombey's foster-mother.

TOOKE, John Horne (1736–1812), radical politician who vigorously supported *Wilkes in connection with the Middlesex election. His principal work, Ἔπεα πτερόεντα, *or the Diversions of Purley* (1786–1805, two volumes of a planned three), established his reputation as a philologist; but its philosophical approach to language and grammar, and its wildly speculative etymologies, delayed for decades, it has been alleged, the introduction of the new and sounder philology from the Continent.

Toots, Mr, a character in Dickens's *Dombey and Son*.

TOPLADY, Augustus Montague (1740–78), is remembered for his hymns, especially 'Rock of Ages', published in the *Gospel Magazine* in 1775.

Topographical Poetry, described by Dr *Johnson as 'local poetry, of which the fundamental object is some particular landscape . . . with the addition of . . . historical retrospection or incidental meditation'. *Cooper's Hill* (1642) by *Denham is an early example of a genre that flourished principally in the 18th cent.: see DYER, GARTH, JAGO, THOMSON, J., for example. Many topographical poems are also 'prospect poems', i.e. written from a high point, surveying a large view, and many were written in praise of particular parks, estates, and gardens, evidently in the hope of patronage. The genre had a renewed vogue in the late 20th cent., when the emphasis has been less on the country estate, more on the vanishing rural scene.

Topsy, the lively little slave girl in H. B. *Stowe's *Uncle Tom's Cabin*.

Torre, Sir, in Malory's **Morte D'Arthur*, the illegitimate son of a cowherd's wife and King *Pellinore.

Torrismond, hero of Dryden's **The Spanish Fryar*.

To the Lighthouse, a novel by V. *Woolf, published 1927, which draws powerfully on the author's recollections of family holidays at St Ives, Cornwall, although the setting is ostensibly the Hebrides; her parents, as she acknowledged, provided the inspiration for the maternal, managing, gracious, much-admired Mrs Ramsay, and the self-centred, self-pitying, poetry-reciting, absurd, and tragic figure of the philosopher, Mr Ramsay, who become the focus of one of her most profound explorations of the conflict between the male and female principles.

The novel is in three sections. The first, 'The Window', describes a summer day, with the Ramsays on holiday with their eight children and assorted guests, who include the plump and lethargic elderly poet Augustus Carmichael; the painter Lily Briscoe and the graceless lower-middle-class academic Charles Tansley. Family tension centres on the desire of the youngest child, James, to visit the lighthouse, and his father's apparent desire to thwart him. The second section, 'Time Passes', records with laconic brevity the death of Mrs Ramsay and of her son Andrew, killed in the war, and dwells with a desolate lyricism on the abandoning of the family home, and its gradual post-war re-awakening; it ends with the arrival of Lily Briscoe and Mr Carmichael. The last section, 'The Lighthouse', describes the exhausting but finally successful efforts of Lily, through her painting, to recapture the revelation of shape-in-chaos which she owes to the vanished Mrs Ramsay, and the parallel efforts of Mr Ramsay, Camilla, and James to reach the lighthouse, which they also accomplish.

TOTTEL, Richard (*c.*1530–94), a publisher chiefly known as the compiler (with *Grimald)

of *Songs and Sonnets*, known as *Tottel's Miscellany* (1557), comprising the chief works of *Wyatt and *Surrey. He also published, besides law-books, Sir T. *More's *Dialogue of Comfort* (1553) and Surrey's *Aeneid* (1557).

Touchett, Mr, Mrs, and Ralph, characters in H. James's **The Portrait of a Lady*.

Touchstone, in Shakespeare's **As You Like It*, the jester to the exiled Duke Frederick's court.

Touchwood, Lord, a character in Congreve's **The Double Dealer*.

TOURNEUR, Cyril (?1575–1626), dramatist. Practically nothing is known of his life. His small known output includes **The Atheist's Tragedy* (1611) and an elegy on the death of Prince Henry (1613). **The Revenger's Tragedy*, printed anonymously in 1607, was first ascribed to him in 1656 by Edward Archer, and generally accepted as his until the end of the 19th cent., when *Middleton was proposed as the author. Since then there has been prolonged debate over attribution, with Middleton gradually emerging as the most likely candidate.

Towneley Plays, see under MYSTERY PLAYS.

TOWNLEY, Revd James (1714–78), was a friend of *Garrick, and author of the successful farce **High Life below Stairs* (1759).

Town Mouse and Country Mouse, a fable told by *Horace (*Sat.* II. vi) and by La Fontaine (though the latter substitutes rats for mice). The city mouse, contemptuous of the country mouse's cave and humble fare, invites it to a sumptuous supper in its palace. But the feast is disturbed by an alarm, and the mice scurry away. The country mouse concludes that it prefers its safe wood and cave and its homely fare.

M. *Prior was part-author of *The Hind and the Panther Transvers'd to the Story of the Country Mouse and the City Mouse*.

TOWNSHEND, Aurelian (?1583–?1643), travelled in France and Italy, then appears in 1632 as a writer of court *masques. He seems to have collaborated with I. *Jones in *Albion's Triumph* and to have contributed verses for the queen's masque of *Tempe Restored*. He enjoyed favour at the court of Charles I, as his lyric 'On his hearing Her Majesty sing' records. His poems were not collected, but scattered through various miscellanies, until E. K. *Chambers's edition, *Poems and Masks* (1912).

Tow-wouse, Mr and Mrs, characters in Fielding's **Joseph Andrews*.

Toxophilus, see ASCHAM, R.

TOYNBEE, Arnold Joseph (1889–1975), historian. His great work *A Study of History* (10 vols, 1934–54) is a survey of the chief civilizations of the world, and an enquiry into cycles of creativity and decay. His view that the fragmentation and waning of Western civilization could already be detected, and that hope lay in a new universal religion which would recapture 'spiritual initiative', aroused much controversy. His other works include *Civilization on Trial* (1948) and *The World and the West* (1953). His son Philip Toynbee (1916–81) was a critic and novelist.

T.P.'s Weekly, see O'CONNOR, T. P.

Tractarian Movement, *Tracts for the Times,* see OXFORD MOVEMENT.

Traddles, a character in Dickens's **David Copperfield.*

TRADESCANT, John (d. ?1637), traveller, naturalist, and gardener, probably author of *A voiag of ambasad* (1618), containing the earliest known account of Russian plants. His son John Tradescant (1608–63) was likewise a traveller and gardener. He published *Museum Tradescantianum* in 1656, and gave his collection to *Ashmole. Both Tradescants held the appointment of gardener to Charles I.

Tragedy, a word of uncertain derivation, applied, broadly, to dramatic (or, by extension, other) works in which events move to a fatal or disastrous conclusion. Aristotle's **Poetics* was the first attempt to define the characteristics of tragedy and its effect upon the spectator, and it profoundly influenced the neo-classic concept of tragedy in France and England. Shakespeare and other English dramatists of the Elizabethan period evolved new tragic conventions (see REVENGE TRAGEDY), partly derived from *Seneca, and the genre continued to flourish in the Jacobean period (see WEBSTER, J.; MIDDLETON, T.; BEAUMONT, F.; FLETCHER, J.). A period of predominantly dull and frigid *neo-classicism followed, and tragedy as a form, with odd exceptions, did not seriously revive until the 20th cent., when the works of *Ibsen, *Strindberg, *O'Neil, A. *Miller, T. *Williams, and S. *Beckett brought it a new seriousness, relevance, and urgency.

Tragedy of Tragedies, see TOM THUMB.

Tragic Comedians, The, a novel by G. *Meredith, published 1880. The story is based on the account given by Helène von Dönniges of her love-affair with Ferdinand Lassalle (1825–64), the German socialist.

TRAHERNE, Thomas (1637–74), was educated at Brasenose College, Oxford. In 1657 he was appointed rector of Credenhill, Hereford-shire, and he was ordained in 1660. At Credenhill he joined the religious circle centring on Susanna Hopton at Kington, for whom he was to write the *Centuries.* The *Centuries* and many of his poems were discovered in a notebook (now in the Bodleian) which was picked up for a few pence on a London bookstall in 1896–7 by W. T. Brooke. Bertram Dobell identified Traherne as the author, and edited the *Poetical Works* (1903) and the *Centuries of Meditation* (1908). More poems, prepared for publication by Traherne's brother Philip as 'Poems of Felicity', were discovered in a British Museum manuscript and published by H. I. Bell in 1910. A further manuscript of *Select Meditations* has since come to light. In his lifetime Traherne published *Roman Forgeries* (1673), which exposes the falsifying of ecclesiastical documents by the church of Rome, concentrating in the mid-9th-cent. collection known as 'False Decretals'. His *Christian Ethicks* (1675) was prepared for the press before he died. But his major achievement comprises the *Centuries*, the poems, and the Thanksgivings, written in exuberant, unconventional verse, which appeared in 1699. He expresses a rapturous joy in creation, and his memories, in the *Centuries*, of his own early intuitions are the first convincing depiction of childhood experience in English literature. He is also among the first English writers to respond imaginatively to new ideas about infinite space, and at times virtually equates infinite space with God. In both, his thought is influenced by *Neoplatonism, especially by the Hermetic books.

Traitor, The, a tragedy by J. *Shirley, acted 1631, printed 1635. It is based on the assassination of the Florentine Duke Alessandro de' Medici by his kinsman Lorenzo.

Tranio, in Shakespeare's **The Taming of the Shrew,* *Lucentio's servant.

Transatlantic Review, a literary periodical edited from Paris by F. M. *Ford, from Jan. 1924 to Jan. 1925, in which he published *Joyce, E. E. *Cummings, and others. The title was revived in 1959 by J. McCrindle: the new *Transatlantic Review* publishes fiction, poetry, interviews, etc., and contributors have included W. *Trevor, I. *Murdoch, J. G. *Ballard, A. *Burgess, D. M. *Thomas, and J. *Arden.

Transcendental, a word that signifies, in the philosophy of *Kant, not derived from experience but concerned with the presuppositions of experience; pertaining to the general theory of the nature of experience or knowledge.

Transcendental Club, a group of American intellectuals who met informally for philosophical discussion at *Emerson's house and elsewhere during some years from 1836, the embodiment of a movement of thought, philosophical, religious, social, and economic, produced in New England between 1830 and 1850 by the spirit of revolutionary Europe, German philosophy, and *Wordsworth, *Coleridge, and *Carlyle. The philosophical views of this Transcendentalism may be gathered from Emerson's short treatise *Nature* (1836). Its literary organ was *The Dial.

Its social and economic aspects took form in the Brook Farm Institute (1841-7) of George Ripley, a self-supporting group of men and women, who shared in manual labour and intellectual pursuits.

transition: *an international quarterly for creative experiment*, a periodical founded in 1927 in Paris by Eugène and Maria Jolas. It published new and experimental work by *Joyce, G. *Stein, Dylan *Thomas, *Durrell, *Beckett, etc.

Transome, Harold, a character in G. Eliot's *Felix Holt.

Trapbois, and his daughter Martha, characters in Scott's *The Fortunes of Nigel.

Traveller, The, *or a Prospect of Society*, a poem by *Goldsmith, published 1764, and the first production under his own name. It is dedicated and addressed to his brother, a country clergyman.

The poet as traveller, from a vantage point in the Alps, surveys and compares the social, political, and economic conditions of the various countries spread before his eyes and his imagination, and endeavours to illustrate that (in the words of his preface) 'there may be equal happiness in states, that are differently governed from our own.' The vividly drawn landscapes of Italy, the Loire valley, and the 'slow canals' of Holland are clearly based on Goldsmith's own continental tour in 1755. The poem ends with a lament for rural decay in the face of growing commerce that foreshadows the theme of *The Deserted Village. Dr *Johnson, who greatly admired the poem, contributed nine lines to it, ll. 420, 429-34, 437-8.

Travels in France, a record of travel in that country during the years 1787-90, by A. *Young, published 1792. Visiting France shortly before and during the revolution, Young draws attention to the defective social and economic conditions of the *ancien régime*. The work contains the famous phrase, 'The magic of property turns sand into gold.'

Travels through France and Italy, a work by *Smollett, published 1766.

The book covers the period of Smollett's main sojourn abroad, between mid-1763 and mid-1765. It is sharply observant, prejudiced and idiosyncratic, often highly entertaining, and

almost universally derogatory about all levels of French and Italian society. Smollett's attitude induced *Sterne to describe him in *A Sentimental Journey* as 'the learned Smelfungus'.

Travels with a Donkey, see STEVENSON, R. L.

TRAVEN, B. (?1882-1969), novelist and short story writer, whose first stories (*The Cottonpickers*) appeared in German in Berlin in 1925. His successful novel *The Death Ship* (1925) recounts the wanderings of an American seaman after the First World War, bereft of passport and nationality. Traven, whose identity remained for many years shrouded in mystery, went to Mexico in the 1920s, whence appeared some 12 novels and collections of stories, including *The Treasure of Sierra Madre* (1934) filmed by John Huston in 1947. *The Man who was B. Traven* (1980) by W. Wyatt established that he was Albert Otto Max Feige, later known as Ret Marut, born in Swiebodzin, a Polish town then in Germany.

TRAVERS, Ben (1886-1980), novelist and playwright, chiefly known for his 'Aldwych farces' of the 1920s, which include *A Cuckoo in the Nest* and *Rookery Nook* (both produced in 1926) and *Thark* (1927).

Travesties, a comedy by T. *Stoppard, performed 1974, published 1975.

The play is largely set, with various time shifts, in Zurich during the First World War, where Lenin, *Joyce, and Tristan Tzara happened to be residing; they appear as characters, as does the marginally historical figure of Henry Carr (1894-1962), through whose memories much of the action is portrayed. Stoppard produces from a minor incident from *Ellman's life of Joyce a theatrical, informative, and witty commentary on the birth of *Dada, the writing of *Ulysses, and the genesis of the doctrine of *socialist realism, and on the nature of the artist as revolutionary or conformist.

Treasure Island, a romance by R. L. *Stevenson, published in book form 1883.

The narrator is Jim Hawkins, whose mother keeps the Admiral Benbow inn somewhere on the coast in the west of England in the 18th cent. An old buccaneer takes up his quarters at the inn. He has in his chest information, in the shape of a manuscript map, as to the whereabouts of Capt. Flint's treasure. Of this his former confederates are determined to obtain possession, and a body of them, led by the sinister blind pirate Pew, makes a descent on the inn. But Jim Hawkins outwits them, secures the map, and delivers it to Squire Trelawney. The squire and his friend Dr Livesey set off for Treasure Island in the schooner *Hispaniola* taking Jim with them. Some of the crew are the squire's faithful dependants, but the majority are old buccaneers recruited by

Long John Silver. Their design to seize the ship and kill the squire's party is discovered by Jim, and after a series of thrilling fights and adventures is completely thwarted; and the squire, with the help of the marooned pirate Ben Gunn, secures the treasure.

Treatise of Human Nature, A, a philosophical work by *Hume, written in France 1734–7, published in three volumes in London 1739–40. The work was recast as three separate and simpler works published between 1748 and 1757: *An Enquiry* (originally *Philosophical Essays*) *concerning Human Understanding*, *An Enquiry concerning the Principles of Morals*, and *A Dissertation on the Passions*.

Hume's work has been traditionally depicted as the culmination of one of two philosophical traditions. His contemporary critic T. *Reid established the common view that Hume was heir to a tradition set by *Locke and *Berkeley, whereas Kemp Smith (1941) saw him as heir to *Hutcheson. Current research emphasizes his debt to *Cicero, *Descartes, and *Boyle.

Hume saw the disputes of philosophers as centred upon the conflicting roles of reason and instinct or sentiment, and tried to define these roles for metaphysics in Book I of the *Treatise* and for the passions and morals in Books II–III. He agreed with Locke, against Descartes, that there are no innate ideas, and that all the data of reason stem from experience, and derived from Descartes the thesis that whatever may be conceived distinctly may be distinct. He argued that reason has insufficient data in experience to form adequate ideas of the external world, distance, bodily identity, causality, the self, and other minds, and that any beliefs we form about these must fall short of knowledge.

Compensating for the inadequate data of experience and unaided reason are certain 'natural instincts' by which the imagination forges its own links between distinct ideas. Through association we project on to the world a sense of the continuity and externality of bodies and of cause and effect. 'Philosophical decisions' are the reflections of common life, corrected by reason, sense, and natural instinct. In regard to morals, Hume again argued for an accommodation between reason and experience on the one hand and sentiment on the other (in so far as moral distinctions are felt, not judged). In so far as there is a common structure of human nature, there is general consensus as to the motives and acts that are accounted morally virtuous and vicious.

Trelawney, see HAWKER, R. S.

TRELAWNY, Edward John (1792–1881), a friend of *Shelley who was present at Leghorn when Shelley was drowned, was author of the notable *Adventures of a Younger Son* (1831) and of *Records of Shelley, Byron, and the Author* (1858).

Tremendous Adventures of Major Gahagan, The, a story by *Thackeray, published in the *New Monthly Magazine*, 1838–9. The Major is an Irish Munchausen whose adventures as an officer in the Indian Army burlesque military memoirs.

TRENCH, Frederic Herbert (1865–1923), author of several plays. Of his various poetic works, the most interesting is 'Apollo and the seaman' (1907), a haunting narrative poem with echoes of the *Ancient Mariner*, in which Apollo and the seaman debate the sinking of the great ship, Lost Immortality, and the future of the soul.

TRENCH, Richard Chenevix (1807–86), dean of Westminster and archbishop of Dublin. He was the author of works dealing with history and literature, poetry, divinity, and philology. His *On the Study of Words* (1851) and *English Past and Present* (1855) popularized the scientific study of language. The scheme of the *Oxford English Dictionary* originated in a resolution passed at his suggestion in 1858 by the *Philological Society. His anthology *Sacred Latin Poetry, chiefly lyrical* (1849) drew attention to the masterpieces of Latin hymnody.

Trent, the detective in E. C. *Bentley's *Trent's Last Case* (1913).

Trent, Fred, a character in Dickens's *The Old Curiosity Shop*. His sister is 'Little Nell'.

TRESSELL, Robert, the pen-name of Robert Noonan (?1870–1911), a house-painter of Irish extraction, is remembered for his posthumously published novel *The Ragged Trousered Philanthropists*, which first appeared in 1914, edited from a manuscript left in the care of his daughter. An abridged edition appeared in 1918, but on the discovery of the original handwritten manuscript in 1946 it became clear that the author's intentions had been widely altered, and it reappeared, ed. by F. C. Ball, in 1955.

The action takes place during one year in the lives of a group of working men in the town of Mugsborough, and the novel is a bitter but spirited attack on the greed, dishonesty, and gullibility of employers and workers alike, and on the social conditions that gave rise to these vices. Debates on socialism, competition, employment, and capitalism are skilfully interwoven with a realistic and knowledgeable portrayal of skilled and unskilled labour in the decorating and undertaking business, and with the human stories of the families of the workers. Noonan's coining of names for local worthies—Sweater, Didlum, Grinder, Botchit, etc.—indicates his attitude towards the widespread corruption and hypocrisy that he exposes, and the book has become a classic text of the Labour movement. The ironically named 'philanthropists' of the title are the workers who toiled for pitiful wages while making no effort to understand or better their lot.

Tressilian, Edmund, a character in Scott's *Kenilworth*.

TREVELYAN, G(eorge) M(acaulay) (1876–1962), historian, son of Sir G. O. *Trevelyan, was educated at Harrow and Trinity College, Cambridge, where he became a member of the *Apostles. He was appointed Regius professor of modern history at Cambridge in 1927, and master of Trinity in 1940. He was author of three remarkable works on Garibaldi, *Garibaldi's Defence of the Roman Republic* (1907), *Garibaldi and the Thousand* (1909), and *Garibaldi and the Making of Italy* (1911). His many other works include his popular and nostalgic *English Social History* (1944).

TREVELYAN, Sir George Otto (1838–1928), nephew of *Macaulay, entered Parliament as a Liberal in 1865 and held several important offices. He published several volumes of humorous writings. The first of his great works, *The Life and Letters of Lord Macaulay* (1876), was followed by *The Early History of George the Third and Charles Fox* (1912–14).

TREVISA, John of (?1340–1402), translated the *Polychronicon* of *Higden in 1387, adding a short continuation and an introduction; part of this has become famous as an account of the state of the English language in its time. His principles of translation are declared in two short essays prefixed to the *Polychronicon*.

TREVOR, William (William Trevor Cox) (1928–   ), Anglo-Irish novelist and short story writer. His novels include *The Old Boys* (1964), *Mrs Eckdorf in O'Neill's Hotel* (1969), and *Fools of Fortune* (1983); collections of short stories include *The Day We Got Drunk on Cake* (1969), *Angels at the Ritz* (1975), and *Beyond the Pale* (1981). The title story of *The Ballroom of Romance* (1972) is a characteristically low-key, poignant evocation of a rural Ireland where men drink and women wait. Trevor writes with insight of the elderly, the lonely, and the unsuccessful, and his more recent works show an increasing preoccupation with the effects of terrorism in Northern Ireland.

Triamond, in Spenser's *Faerie Queene* (IV. iii. iv), the Knight of Friendship. He marries Canacee, Cambello's sister. (See CAMBELL.)

Tribrach, see METRE.

Tribulation Wholesome, the fanatical Puritan elder in Jonson's *The Alchemist*.

Trilby, a novel written and illustrated by George *du Maurier, published 1894.

The setting of the story reflects the writer's years as an art student in Paris. The charming Trilby O'Ferrall, an artist's model, slowly falls under the spell of Svengali, a German–Polish musician, who establishes her as a famous singer. His power over her is such that when he dies her voice collapses, she loses her eminence, languishes, and finally dies herself. Trilby's hat is the origin of the 'trilby'.

TRILLING, Lionel (1905–75), American critic, whose many works include *The Liberal Imagination* (1950), *The Opposing Self* (1955), and *Sincerity and Authenticity* (1972). His works are written from the standpoint of liberal humanism and manifest an admiration for *Freud. He also wrote one novel, *The Middle of the Journey* (1947).

Trilogy, in Greek antiquity, a series of three tragedies (originally connected in subject) performed at Athens at the festival of Dionysus. Hence any series of three related dramatic or other literary works.

Trim, Corporal, the devoted servant of Toby in Sterne's *Tristram Shandy*.

Trimalchio, see PETRONIUS.

Trimeter, see METRE.

Trimmer, originally applied to one who trims between opposing parties in politics; hence, one who inclines as his interest dictates. But *Halifax in his *Character of a Trimmer* (1682) accepted the nickname in the sense of 'one who keeps even the ship of state'.

Trimmer, Character of a, see HALIFAX.

TRIMMER, Mrs Sarah, *née* Kirby (1741–1810), known as 'Good Mrs Trimmer', was the author of the popular children's book *The History of the Robins*, originally entitled *Fabulous Histories* (1786). In her periodical *The Guardian of Education* (1802–6) she attacked traditional children's literature and fairy-stories, describing *Cinderella as a tale inculcating 'envy, jealousy, a dislike for mothers-in-law and half-sisters, vanity, a love of dress'.

Trinculo, in Shakespeare's *The Tempest*, companion to Stephano.

Triolet, a poem of eight lines, with two rhymes, in which the first line is repeated as the fourth and seventh, and the second as the eighth.

Triplet, three successive lines of verse rhyming together, occasionally introduced among heroic couplets, e.g. by *Dryden.

Trip to Scarborough, A, a musical play by R. B. *Sheridan, produced 1777. The play is based on Vanbrugh's *The Relapse* with considerable modifications and with music and songs added.

Trismegistus, see HERMES TRISMEGISTUS.

'Tristram and Iseult', a poem in three parts by M. *Arnold, published 1852. This is the first modern version of the story that was made familiar by *Wagner and *Tennyson; it deals with the death of Tristram (Tristan, in earlier editions of the same work), who lies dying, watched over by Iseult of Brittany, and dreaming in his fever of his love for Iseult of Ireland, the wife of Marc. She arrives, and after a brief passionate dialogue he dies. In Part III Iseult of Brittany tells her children the story of Merlin, entranced by Vivian.

Tristram and Isoud (*Tristan and Isolde*); the long story of Tristram de Lyones is the fifth of Vinaver's eight *Works* of *Malory. The love of Tristram and Isoud is much older than the corresponding Arthurian story of the love of Launcelot and Guinevere, and it was incorporated into the Arthurian legends only at a late stage. It is thought likely that there was a *Tristan* romance (since lost) by *Chrefien de Troyes in the 1170s, and it is possible that there was an early Provençal *Tristan*. There are three versions surviving from the 12th cent. The first English version is *Sir Tristrem*, a northern 3,344-line romance in 11-line stanzas dating from *c.*1300 (unpersuasively attributed to Thomas of *Erceldoune). In Malory, Tristram is the child of Meliodas, king of Lyonesse, and Elizabeth, the sister of King Mark of Cornwall, who dies soon after his sorrowful birth. The sad child is brought up at the court of King Mark whose attitude to the boy varies in different versions from great affection to jealousy. Tristram defeats and kills Sir Marhalt (Marhaus), the brother of Isoud, queen of Ireland. Tristram is sent to Ireland to be cured of his wounds by Isoud the queen, and he falls in love with her daughter Isoud; when the queen discovers that this knight (whom she too holds in special esteem) is the slayer of her brother, Tristram returns to Cornwall. Later King Mark sends Tristram as ambassador in seeking for him the hand of the younger Isoud. The princess and her maid Brangwayn return by ship to Cornwall; Brangwayn has been given a love-potion by Queen Isoud to be given on their wedding-night to Isoud and King Mark, which will bind them in unending love. By mistake the love-potion is drunk by Tristram and Isoud who are bound thereafter in endless passion, though Isoud has to marry Mark. The rest of the story is concerned with the fated love of Tristram and Isoud and the subterfuges which the lovers have to adopt. Tristram leaves Mark's court and, while fighting for Howel of Brittany, falls in love with and marries a third Isoud (Isolde of the White Hands). But, on the invitation of Isoud of Ireland, he returns to Cornwall where he is killed by Mark while playing his harp before Isoud. In some versions his death is not mentioned at all; in the most celebrated (adopted by *Wagner) Tristram sends for Isoud while he lies dying in Brittany. If she is on the ship when it returns, a white flag is to be flown; if not, a black one. The flag is white, but Isoud of the White Hands tells Tristram it is black, whereupon he dies. When Isoud comes to his bedside, she dies too. The story is the classic of medieval romance and of medieval love poetry.

Tristram of Lyonesse, a poem in heroic couplets by *Swinburne, published 1882, which tells the story of Tristram's love for Queen Iseult, his marriage to Iseult of Brittany, and his death.

Tristram Shandy, The Life and Opinions of, by L. *Sterne, published 1759–67.

This unique work, although itself the culmination of experiments by lesser authors, is generally regarded as the progenitor of the 20th-cent. *stream-of-consciousness novel. It owes much to *Rabelais, to Robert *Burton, and to Locke's *Essay concerning Human Understanding*. The word 'shandy', of obscure origin, means 'crack-brained, half-crazy', and Tristram in Volume VI of his book declares that he is writing a 'civil, nonsensical, good humoured Shandean book'.

In spite of the title, the book gives us very little of the life, and nothing of the opinions, of the nominal hero, who gets born only in Vol. IV, and breeched in Vol. VI, and then disappears from the story. Instead we have a group of humorous figures: Walter Shandy of Shandy Hall, Tristram's father; 'my Uncle Toby', his brother, wounded in the groin at the siege of Namur, whose hobby is the science of attacking fortified towns; Corporal Trim, his servant, wounded in the knee at Landen, devoted to his master. Behind these three major figures, the minor characters, Yorick the parson, Dr Slop, Mrs Shandy, and the widow Wadman, play more elusive parts.

Triumph of Life, The, an unfinished visionary poem by P. B. *Shelley, published from rough drafts 1824.

Composed in *terza rima, the poem is strongly influenced by *Dante's *Inferno*, *Petrarch's *Trionfi*, and the carvings of Roman triumphal processions Shelley had seen in the Forum. The 'triumph' or masquerade (as the *'Mask of Anarchy') belongs to the cruel Chariot of Life, here shown as one of Shelley's Tyrant-figures. Life appears to vanquish the hope and ideals of all men, dragging in its train even the greatest, like Plato, Alexander, or

Napoleon. Only the 'sacred few', like Jesus and Socrates, who early 'Fled back like eagles to their native noon', escape compromise and captivity.

The poet is conducted by the spirit of *Rousseau (as Dante is led through Hell by Virgil); he observes that most men do not know themselves truly, and are destroyed by 'the mutiny within'. The atmosphere of the poem, full of images drawn from the sea is darkly hypnotic.

Triumph of Peace, The, a masque by J. *Shirley, acted and printed 1634.

This was the best known of all 17th-cent. *masques, mainly because of the spectacular torchlight procession (or 'triumph') of the masquers, from Holborn to Whitehall, which preceded the masque proper. It was an expression of loyalty to the Crown on the part of the four Inns of Court, after *Prynne had published his *Histriomastix* (1633) with a dedication to his fellow-benchers at Lincoln's Inn. The masque was designed by I. *Jones, and its score (by W. *Lawes and Simon Ives) is among the few examples of masque music that have survived.

TRIVET, Nicholas (*c.*1258–?1334), a Dominican who is most celebrated as the writer of three histories in the 1320s: his Anglo-Norman Chronicle, extending from the Creation to 1285, containing the tale of Constance, told by *Gower in *Confessio Amantis* and by Chaucer's Man of Law (*Canterbury Tales*, 5); *Annals of Six Kings of England 1136–1307*; and the *Historia ab orbe Condita* (1327–9).

Trivia, or *The Art of Walking the Streets of London*, a poem by J. *Gay in three books, published 1716. It is a town eclogue, owing 'some hints' to *Swift, whose 'City Shower' (1710) is in the same vein. Gay conducts the reader through the streets of London, by day and then by night. It is a lively, affectionate, and entertaining piece, and a mine of information. 'Trivia' means 'streets', from the root meaning of 'road junction', and Gay, who invokes Trivia as a goddess of the highways, also refers to the murder of Laius by Oedipus at the crossroads in Book 3, l. 217.

Trivium, the lower divisions of the Seven Liberal Arts, consisting of the methodological subjects Grammar, Rhetoric, and Logic, as distinct from the mathematically based sciences of the *Quadrivium.

Trochee, see METRE.

Troilus and Cressida, a tragedy by *Shakespeare probably written 1602, printed 1609, included in the First *Folio of 1623. As well as *Homer's and *Chaucer's handling of material concerning the lovers and the siege of Troy, Shakespeare knew of Henryson's *Testament of Cresseid*, *Caxton's *Recuyell of the Historyes of Troye*, and *Lydgate's *Troy Book*, and drew on *Ovid's *Metamorphoses* Books XI and XII and R. *Greene's *Euphues his Censure to Philautus* (1587).

Shakespeare's treatment of the love of Troilus and Cressida and its betrayal, against the setting of the siege of Troy by the Greeks, is conventional. The play contains much formal debate, and takes the story up to the death of Hector at the hands of Achilles: Troilus fails to kill his rival Diomedes, and the cynically railing Thersites escapes death.

Troilus and Criseyde, *Chaucer's longest complete poem, in 8,239 lines of rhyme-royal probably written in the second half of the 1380s. Chaucer takes his story from *Boccaccio's *Il Filostrato*, adapting its eight books to five and changing the characters of Criseyde and *Pandarus. In Boccaccio Troilo falls in love with Criseida whose cousin, Troilo's friend Pandaro, persuades her to become Troilo's lover. In the end Criseida has to leave the Trojan camp to join her father who had defected to the Greeks; in the Greek camp she betrays Troilo by falling in love with Diomede. Chaucer deepens the sense of seriousness in his story by making Pandaro Criseida's uncle and guardian, by showing her deliberating at more length (this series of exchanges between uncle and niece in Book II is one of the most admired and anthologized parts of the poem), and by introducing deliberative material, principally from *Boethius, calling into question the lovers' freedom of action. The poem ends with an adjuration to the young to repair home from worldly vanity and to place their trust, not in unstable fortune as Troilus did, but in God. Discussion of the poem has centred largely on the appropriateness of the epilogue to the preceding action, on the attitudes to love (*courtly love in particular) in the poem, and on the personality of the narrator and his effect on the narrative. The love story is the invention of *Benoît de Saint-Maure in his *Roman de Troie*, which was based on the pretended histories of Troy by *Dares Phrygius and *Dictys Cretensis. Boccaccio's intermediate source was *Guido delle Colonne. After Chaucer, the story was treated by Henryson in *The Testament of Cresseid* and by Shakespeare in *Troilus and Cressida*.

TROLLOPE, Anthony (1815–82), became a junior clerk in the General Post Office in London in 1834, but only began to make any professional progress when transferred to Ireland in 1841. He married Rose Heseltine in Ireland in 1844. Trollope did not return permanently to England until 1859, although he travelled extensively on Post Office business. By the end of his professional career he had become a successful and important civil servant. Among his achievements is the introduction in Great Britain of the pillar-box for letters. He resigned from the Post Office in 1867, and stood unsuccessfully for Parliament as a Liberal in 1868. He edited the *St Paul's Magazine*, 1867–70.

His literary career began with *The Macdermots of Ballycloran* (1847) but not until his fourth novel, *The Warden* (1855), did he establish the manner and material by which he is best known. This, the first of the 'Barsetshire' series, was followed by *Barchester Towers* (1857), *Doctor Thorne* (1858), *Framley Parsonage* (1861), *The Small House at Allington* (1864), and *The Last Chronicle of Barset* (1867). The action of these novels is for the most part set in the imaginary west country county of Barset and its chief town, Barchester. The Barset novels are interconnected by characters who appear in more than one of them, and Trollope developed this technique in his second series, known as the 'Political' novels or—perhaps more appropriately—as the 'Palliser' novels, after Plantagenet Palliser, who appears in all of them. This series began with *Can you Forgive Her?* (1864) and continued with *Phineas Finn* (1869), *The Eustace Diamonds* (1873), *Phineas Redux* (1876), *The Prime Minister* (1876), and *The Duke's Children* (1880). Trollope established the novel-sequence in English fiction.

Trollope attributed his remarkable output, which included 47 novels, several travel books, and biographies, as well as collections of short stories and sketches, to a disciplined regularity of composition, producing a given number of words an hour in the early morning before going off to his post office duties. He was more concerned with character than with plot. In his *Autobiography* (1883; written 1875–7) Trollope writes eloquently of the novelist's need to live with his creatures 'in the full reality of established intimacy'. He also stresses the importance of recording change and the effects of time.

Trollope's other principal novels include: *The Three Clerks* (1857), *The Bertrams* (1859), *Orley Farm* (1862), *The Belton Estate* (1866), *The Claverings* (1867), *He Knew He Was Right* (1869), *The Vicar of Bullhampton* (1870), *The Way we Live Now* (1875), *The American Senator* (1877), *Doctor Wortle's School* (1881), *Ayala's Angel* (1881), *Mr Scarborough's Family* (1883). Trollope became a popular figure in London and literary society in his later years. He greatly admired *Thackeray, of whom he nevertheless wrote a clear-sighted study (1879), and was a close friend of G. *Eliot and G. H. *Lewes.

TROLLOPE, Frances (1780–1863), mother of A. *Trollope. When her family was reduced to poverty she supported them by her writing. After the failure of their farm at Harrow (later to appear in her son Anthony's *Orley Farm*), she went to America and later published her caustic *Domestic Manners of the Americans* (1832). She lived for the next few years on the Continent and produced *Paris and the Parisians* (1835); *Vienna*

and the Austrians (1838); and *A Visit to Italy* (1842). Meanwhile she was writing a long sequence of popular (though little remembered) novels.

Trompart, in Spenser's *Faerie Queene* (II. iii), attends Braggadochio as his squire, and with him is finally exposed and beaten out of court.

Trotter, Job, in Dickens's *Pickwick Papers*, Jingle's servant.

Trotwood, Betsey, a character in Dickens's *David Copperfield*.

Troubadours, poets composing in Provençal during the 12th and early 13th cents, famous for the complexity of their verse forms in the lyric, and for the conception of *Courtly Love which is founded to an important degree in their poems. Guilhem IX (1071–1127), count of Poitiers and duke of Aquitaine, is the first known troubadour; Jaufre Rudel (d. before 1167) developed the theme of 'amor de lonh', love from afar. The best admired troubadour love poets are Bernart de Ventadorn (*fl.* 1140–75), Raimbaut d'Aurenga (*c.*1144–73), Guiraut de Borneil (*c.*1165–1212), and Arnaut Daniel (*fl.* 1180–1200). The troubadours flourished in the courts of Spain, Italy and northern France, as well as in the south of France, and courtly poetry in Provençal was being written and cultivated in Italy in the later 13th cent. (See SORDELLO and DANTE.) Through their influence on the Northern French poets (such as *Chrétien, and the writers of the *Roman de la Rose*) and on the German poets of the *Minnesang* (see MINNESINGERS) they had a major effect on all the subsequent development of European lyric poetry.

Trouvères, poets composing narrative, dramatic, satyric, comic, and especially lyric verse in the north of France during the late 12th and 13th cents. They were either professional entertainers (overlapping with *jongleurs*), *clercs*, or feudal lords composing fashionable verse. *Chrétien de Troyes was a *clerc*; other prominent trouvères were Conon de Béthune (d. *c.*1224), Gâce Brulé (d. *c.*1220), *Blondel de Nesle (late 12th cent.), and Thibaut de Champagne, count of Champagne and king of Navarre. Their poetry was much influenced by that of the Provençal *troubadours, one of whom, Bernart de Ventadorn, came north to the court of *Eleanor of Aquitaine.

Troy, Sergeant, a character in Hardy's *Far from the Madding Crowd*.

True Law of Free Monarchies, a political treatise attributed to James I, published 1598, and written to combat the Calvinist theory of government advocated by G. *Buchanan in his *De Jure*

Regni (1579). It sets forth the doctrine of the divine right of kings and of the king's responsibility to God alone.

Truewit, the gallant and chief wit of Jonson's *Epicene*, a model for the wits of *Restoration comedy.

Trumpet Major, The, a novel by T. *Hardy, published 1882. The story is set during the Napoleonic wars. It tells of the wooing of Anne Garland, whose mother is tenant of a part of Overcombe Mill, where the dragoons come down from the nearby camp to water their horses. One of these dragoons is John Loveday, the trumpet-major, the son of the miller. He loves Anne Garland, but has a rival in his brother Bob, a lighthearted sailor. Her third suitor is the boorish yeoman Festus Derriman. The story ends with the discomfiture of Festus and the success of Bob's courtship, while John marches off with his dragoons, to die on a battlefield in Spain.

Tryamour, see SIR LAUNFAL.

Tryan, the Revd Edgar, a character in G. Eliot's 'Janet's Repentance' (see SCENES OF CLERICAL LIFE).

Tuatha Dé Danann, in Gaelic mythology, the gods, the 'Folk of the goddess Danu', the enemies of the *Fomors. They are represented as invaders of Ireland, subsequent to the Fomors and the *Fir Bolgs. They rout the Fomors at the battle of Moytura, and are ousted in their turn by the *Milesians. Conspicuous among the Tuatha Dé Danann are Lugh, the Gaelic sun-god, their leader; and *Lêr, the god of the sea.

Tucca, Captain Pantilius, the swaggering bully of Jonson's *Poetaster*, who reappears in Dekker and Marston's *Satiromastix*.

Tuck, Friar, see FRIAR TUCK.

TUCKER, Abraham (1705–74), one of the first writers of the utilitarian school of philosophy. In his great work *The Light of Nature Pursued* (6 vols, 1768–78) he rejects the moral sense theory of *Shaftesbury and *Hutcheson and finds the criterion of moral conduct in general happiness, and the motive of the individual in his own happiness. There comes a point where virtue requires a self-sacrifice that prudential motives do not justify. Here Tucker finds the place for religion and its promise of a future life.

Tulkinghorn, a character in Dickens's *Bleak House*.

Tulliver, Mr and Mrs, Tom and Maggie the principal characters in G. Eliot's *The Mill on the Floss*.

Tully, see CICERO.

Tunnyng of Elynour Rummyng, The, a poem by *Skelton, is a vigorous Hogarthian description of contemporary low life. Elinour Rumming is an alewife who dwells beside Leatherhead and brews 'noppy ale', and the poem, coarse but full of humour and life, describes the mixed company who throng to drink it.

Tupman, Tracy, a character in Dickens's *Pickwick Papers*.

TUPPER, Martin Farquhar (1810–89), prolific writer of verse and prose. His *Proverbial Philosophy* (1838–76, 4 series), presenting maxims and reflections couched in vaguely rhythmical form, became the favourite of millions who knew nothing about poetry.

TURBERVILLE, George (c.1544–c.1597), published *Epitaphes, Epigrams, Songs and Sonets* (1567); *The Books of Faulconrie* (1575), and various translations from *Ovid and *Mantuan, including Mantuan's eclogues (1567). *The Noble Art of Venerie or Hunting* (1575) is also attributed to him (reprinted 1908). His poems reflect the use of Italian models and show the influence of *Wyatt and *Surrey.

TURGENEV, Ivan Sergeevich (1818–83), Russian novelist and playwright and the first Russian writer to find success in Europe. His novels include *A Nest of Gentlefolk* (1859), *On the Eve* (1860), *Fathers and Sons* (1862), in which, in Bazarov, he created a *Nihilist hero, *Smoke* (1867), and *Virgin Soil* (1877). His greatest short stories are 'Asya' (1858), 'First Love' (1860), and 'Torrents of Spring' (1870). His best play is *A Month in the Country* (1850).

He lived for many years in Western Europe, and visited England many times: he was acquainted with *Dickens, G. *Eliot, *Browning, and many other literary figures. He was one of the earliest admirers of H. *James, on whom he had substantial influence. Perhaps the greatest English debt to him is owed by G. A. *Moore, whose whole mature career was given shape by the discovery of Turgenev's artistry. By 1890 most of Turgenev's major work had appeared in English. The most complete early translation is C. *Garnett's *Turgenev—The Novels and Tales* (1894–9), the edition through which he exerted his influence on such writers as *Galsworthy, *Conrad, and V. *Woolf.

Turkish Spy, *Letters written by a,* eight vols, published ?1687–94. The first is a translation of 'L'Espion du Grand Seigneur' by Giovanni Paolo Marana, a Genoese residing in Paris, published in French in 1684–6, partly itself a translation from an Italian version. The work inaugurated a new genre in European literature, the pseudo-foreign letter, of which the *Lettres persanes* of Montesquieu is the chief example.

A continuation to the *Letters*, probably by *Defoe, was published in England in 1718.

TURNBULL, George (1698–1748), was an early member of the Rankenian club in Edinburgh, and his published lectures (*Principles of Moral and Christian Philosophy*, 2 vols, 1740) and surviving correspondence show him as an ardent follower of *Shaftesbury in his advocacy of civic virtue and educational reform, and the prominence he attached to the sense of beauty. His *Treatise on Ancient Painting* (1739), which figures in a caricature by *Hogarth, discusses the place of the fine arts in education.

TURNER, J(oseph) M(allord) W(illiam) (1775–1851), major English landscape painter, whose mature works convey a profoundly Romantic vision of the magnificence of nature and the violence of the elements. His works were frequently inspired by poetry, and many of his paintings were accompanied by quotations (notably from James *Thomson); he also wrote poems himself, besides the drawings in his sketch-books, and to accompany his larger works. In the 1830s Turner did many designs for book illustrations, amongst them charming and highly successful vignettes for *Rogers's *Italy* (1830) and *Poems* (1834). He also illustrated works by *Milton, *Byron, Sir W. *Scott, and T. *Campbell. His great works exerted a major influence on the Romantic imagination (see ROMANTICISM), and he was passionately admired by *Ruskin, who devoted the first volume of *Modern Painters* (1843) to his defence.

Turn of the Screw, The, a ghost story by H. *James, published 1898.

The narrator is a young governess, sent off to a country house, Bly, to take charge of two orphaned children. She has been engaged by their uncle, a handsome man to whom she feels attracted. She finds a pleasant house and a comfortable housekeeper, Mrs Grose, while the children, Miles and Flora, are unusually beautiful and charming. But she soon begins to feel the presence of intense evil, and sees the figure of the ex-valet Peter Quint and that of her own predecessor Miss Jessel. In fact they are both dead, and she learns of the guilty liaison that existed between them. She becomes convinced that, despite their denials, Miles and Flora are communicating with them. These terrible figures have returned to draw the children into their web of sin and evil, and the governess is determined to exorcize them. After a dramatic scene by the pond, where the narrator believes that Flora is meeting Miss Jessel, the little girl is taken off to safety by the housekeeper, and Miles, left with the governess, dies in her arms as she battles for his soul with the apparition of

Peter Quint. It is left to the reader to decide whether these ghosts exist for anyone else in the story, or whether they are simply the hysterical fantasies of the young governess. James himself described this story as 'a trap for the unwary'.

Turveydrop, father and son, characters in Dickens's *Bleak House*.

TUSSER, Thomas (?1524–80), agricultural writer and poet, published his *Hundreth good pointes of husbandrie* in 1557 (amplified in later editions) in verse of quaint and pointed expression, many proverbs being traceable to this work. It is a collection of instructions on farming, gardening, and housekeeping, together with humorous and wise maxims on conduct in general.

'Twa Dogs, The', a poem by *Burns, published 1786.

TWAIN, Mark, pseudonym of Samuel Langhorne Clemens (1835–1910), American writer. He was a pilot on the Mississippi (1857–61) and from 1862 worked as a newspaper correspondent, adopting the pseudonym 'Mark Twain', familiar to him as the leadsman's call on the Mississippi. Under this name he published his first successful story, 'Jim Smiley and his Jumping Frog', in 1865 in the New York *Saturday Press*. This comic version of an old folktale became the title story of *The Celebrated Jumping Frog of Calaveras County, and other Sketches* (1867), which established him as a leading humorist, a reputation consolidated by *The Innocents Abroad* (1869), an account of a voyage through the Mediterranean. *Roughing It* (1872) is an account of his adventures as miner and journalist in Nevada. England provided the background for his democratic historical fantasy *The Prince and the Pauper* (1882), in which Edward VI as a boy changes places with Tom Canty, a beggar, and for *A Connecticut Yankee in King Arthur's Court* (1889). Meanwhile appeared his most famous works, *The Adventures of *Tom Sawyer* (1876) and its sequel *The Adventures of *Huckleberry Finn* (1885), which paint an unforgettable picture of Mississippi frontier life.

In his later years, which were beset by financial anxieties, he wrote some memorable if sombre works, including *The Man that Corrupted Hadleyburg* (1900), a fable about the venality of a smug small town, and *The Mysterious Stranger* (published posthumously in 1916, in a much-edited version), an extraordinary tale set in 16th-cent. Austria.

Twelfth Night, Or *What You Will*, a comedy by *Shakespeare probably written 1601, performed 1602, and printed in the *Folio of 1623. Shakespeare's immediate source for the main plot was 'The History of Apolonius and Silla' in

B. *Rich's *Riche his Farewell to Militarie Profession* (1581).

Sebastian and Viola, twin brothers and sister and closely resembling one another, are separated in a shipwreck off the coast of Illyria. Viola, brought to shore in a boat, disguises herself as a youth, Cesario, and takes service as page with Duke Orsino, who is in love with the lady Olivia. She rejects the duke's suit and will not meet him. Orsino makes a confidant of Cesario and sends her to press his suit on Olivia, much to the distress of Cesario, who has fallen in love with Orsino. Olivia in turn falls in love with Cesario. Sebastian and Antonio, captain of the ship that has rescued Sebastian, now arrive in Illyria. Cesario, challenged to a duel by Sir Andrew Aguecheek, a rejected suitor of Olivia, is rescued from her predicament by Antonio, who takes her for Sebastian. Antonio, being arrested at that moment for an old offence, claims from Cesario a purse that he had entrusted to Sebastian, is denied it, and hauled off to prison. Olivia coming upon the true Sebastian, takes him for Cesario, invites him to her house, and marries him out of hand. Orsino comes to visit Olivia. Antonio, brought before him, claims Cesario as the youth he had rescued from the sea; while Olivia claims Cesario as her husband. The duke, deeply wounded, is bidding farewell to Olivia and the 'dissembling cub' Cesario, when the arrival of the true Sebastian clears up the confusion. The duke, having lost Olivia and becoming conscious of the love that Viola has betrayed, turns his affection to her, and they are married.

Much of the play's comedy comes from the sub-plot dealing with the members of Olivia's household: Sir Toby Belch, her uncle, Sir Andrew Aguecheek, his friend, Malvolio, her pompous steward, Maria, her waiting-gentle-woman, and her clown Feste. Exasperated by Malvolio's officiousness, the other members of the household make him believe that Olivia is in love with him and that he must return her affection. In courting her he behaves so outrage-ously that he is imprisoned as a madman. Olivia has him released and the joke against him is explained, but he is not amused by it, threaten-ing, 'I'll be reveng'd on the whole pack of you.' The play's gentle melancholy and lyrical atmosphere are captured in Feste's beautiful song 'Come away, come away, death.'

Twentieth Century, The, see NINETEENTH CENTURY.

Twitcher, Jemmy, in Gay's *The Beggar's Opera*, one of Captain Macheath's associates, who betrays him. The nickname was given to the fourth earl of Sandwich (1718–92), who had been associated with *Wilkes in the *Medmen-ham 'brotherhood'.

Two Cultures *and the Scientific Revolution, The.* 'The Two Cultures' is a phrase coined by C. P. *Snow in the Rede Lecture delivered at Cam-bridge in 1959 and published the same year. In it, he contrasts the culture of 'literary intellectuals' and that of 'scientists, and as the most represen-tative, physical scientists', claiming that 30 years earlier the two sides could at least manage 'a frozen smile' but are now incapable of com-munication. His analysis of the educational attitudes that produced this situation and his recommendations for change were strongly attacked by *Leavis. (See also THOMSON, SIR W.)

'Two Drovers, The', a short story by Sir W. *Scott, one of the *Chronicles of the Canongate*, published 1827.

It tells of the conflict between two drovers, the Highlander Robin Oig M'Combich and the Yorkshireman Henry Wakefield. Wakefield insults Robin's patriotism and picks a fight: Robin kills Wakefield, then surrenders himself to justice.

Two Foscari, The, a poetic drama by *Byron, published 1821.

Jacopo, son of the doge of Venice, Francesco Foscari, has twice been exiled. He has been brought back from exile on a charge of treason-able correspondence, and the play opens with his examination on the rack. The dogs, broken-hearted at his disgrace, signs the sentence for his third perpetual exile. But Jacopo dies with hor-ror at the prospect of another banishment. The Council of Ten meanwhile require the abdica-tion of the old doge. He at once leaves the palace, and as he descends the steps he falls and dies.

Two Gentlemen of Verona, The, a comedy by *Shakespeare, probably written about 1592–3, first printed in the *Folio of 1623. The play's main source is the story of Felix and Felismena in the *Diana* of *Montemayor.

The two gentlemen of Verona are the friends Valentine and Proteus. Proteus is in love with Julia, who returns his affection. Valentine leaves Verona for Milan 'to see the wonders of the world abroad', and there falls in love with Silvia, the duke of Milan's daughter. Presently Proteus is sent also on his travels, and exchanges vows of constancy with Julia before starting. But arriv-ing at Milan, Proteus is at once captivated by Silvia, and, betraying both his friend and his former love, reveals to the duke the intention of Valentine to carry off Silvia. Valentine is banished and becomes a captain of outlaws and Proteus continues his courting of Silvia. Mean-while Julia, pining for Proteus, comes to Milan dressed as a boy and takes service as Proteus' page, unrecognized by him. Silvia, to escape marriage with Thurio, her father's choice, leaves Milan to rejoin Valentine, is captured by outlaws and rescued from them by Proteus. Proteus is violently pressing his suit on Silvia when Valentine comes on the scene. Proteus is struck with remorse, and his contrition is such that Valentine is impelled to surrender Silvia to him, to the dismay of Proteus' page, the disguised Julia. She swoons, and is then recognized by Proteus, and the discovery of her constancy wins back his love. The duke and Thurio arrive. Thurio shows cowardice in face of Valentine's determined attitude, and the duke, approving Valentine's spirit, accords him Silvia and pardons the outlaws. Launce, the clownish servant of Proteus, and his dog Crab, 'the sourest-natured dog that lives', provide much humour.

Two Nations, The, see Disraeli's *Sybil.*

Two Noble Kinsmen, The, a tragi-comedy attributed to J. *Fletcher and Shakespeare, published 1634. Recent studies of the play suggest that it is probably a genuine work of collaboration between Fletcher and Shakespeare, written in about 1613.

The play is closely based on Chaucer's 'Knight's Tale' (*Canterbury Tales*, 1), which Shakespeare had drawn on before in *A Midsummer Night's Dream*. The overall tone is considerably lighter than in Chaucer's poem, the play being diversified with songs and lyrical passages.

Two on a Tower, a novel by T. *Hardy, published 1882.

Lady Constantine, whose disagreeable husband is away, falls in love with Swithin St Cleeve, an astronomer, younger than herself, who works at the top of a tower, where many of the scenes of the novel occur. Hearing her husband has died, Lady Constantine secretly marries Swithin, but later learns that by so doing she had deprived him of a legacy; and that her husband, though now dead, was alive when she married Swithin. Thus their marriage is void, and she nobly insists on his leaving her, to take up employment abroad. She then finds she is pregnant by him; she accepts an offer of marriage from Bishop Helmsdale and a son is born. Swithin returns after the bishop's death, and is appalled that she is no longer a young woman. Eventually he offers to marry her, but the joy is too great and she falls dead in his arms.

Two Poets of Croisic, The, see LA SAISIAZ.

Two Years Ago, a novel by C. *Kingsley, published 1857.

In the last of his reforming novels, Kingsley describes the descent of cholera upon the little West Country fishing village of Aberalva, attacks the poor sanitary conditions and public apathy that allowed it to take hold, and praises the gallantry and dedication of various of the inhabitants. A secondary plot involves a denunciation of slavery in the United States, influenced by H. B. *Stowe's Uncle Tom's Cabin.

Tybalt, in Shakespeare's *Romeo and Juliet*, a Capulet. For the allusion in the play to cats in connection with his name, see TIBERT.

TYLER, Wat (d. 1381), the leader of the peasants' revolt of 1381. He is the subject of a drama by *Southey.

TYNAN, Katharine (1861–1931), poet and novelist, born in Dublin, is now remembered principally for her association with the *Irish revival and as a friend of *Yeats. Yeats's *Letters to Katharine Tynan*, ed. R. McHugh, was published in 1953.

TYNAN, Kenneth Peacock (1927–80), dramatic critic, wrote most influentially for the *Observer* (1954–63), and championed the plays of *Osborne, *Wesker, S. *Delaney, N. F. *Simpson, *Beckett, and others, playing a leading role in the shift of taste from drawing-room comedy and the poetic drama of T. S. *Eliot and C. *Fry to naturalism and 'working class drama'. (See KITCHEN SINK DRAMA.) He also vigorously attacked theatre censorship. His various collections of reviews and essays include *Curtains* (1967), *The Sound of Two Hands Clapping* (1975), and *A View of the English Stage* (1976).

TYNDALE, William (c. 1495–1536), the translator of the *Bible. About 1522 he formed the project of translating the Scriptures into the vernacular, but finding difficulties in England went to Hamburg for the purpose. He visited *Luther at Wittenberg, and commenced printing his translation of the New Testament at Cologne in 1525. He completed the work at Worms and introduced copies into England, which were denounced by the bishops and destroyed. He was arrested for heresy, imprisoned at Vilvorde in 1535, and strangled and burnt at the stake there, in spite of Cromwell's intercession. Tyndale was one of the most remarkable of the *Reformation leaders; his original writings show sound scholarship, but his translation of the Bible—consisting of the New Testament (1525), Pentateuch (1530), and Jonah (1531)—the accuracy of which has been endorsed by the translators of the Authorized Version, is his surest title to fame.

TYNDALL, John (1820–93), professor of natural history at the Royal Institution in 1853, did much in his writings and lectures to popularize science. His famous address to the British Association in Belfast in 1874, on the relation between science and theology, gave rise to acute controversy.

Typee, or a Peep at Polynesian Life, a novel by H. *Melville, published 1846.

'Typhoon', a story by J. *Conrad, published 1903.

The unimaginative and imperturbable Captain MacWhirr pilots his steamer *Nan-Shan* through a typhoon of such violence that even he is moved to doubt the possibility of survival. Nevertheless, to avoid trouble between decks, he sends his appalled chief mate Mr Jukes down to confiscate the money of his 200 Chinese passengers. Later, the money redistributed and the ship safe in Fu-chau harbour, Jukes is forced to conclude that MacWhirr 'got out of it very well for a stupid man'.

Tyranipocrit Discovered, one of the best-written of the radical pamphlets of the Commonwealth, published anonymously in Rotterdam, 1649. The writer attacks the 'White Devil' of hypocrisy, which cloaks tyrannical power, idleness, and greed with Christian piety, finding it yet more pernicious than the 'Black Devil' of undisguised oppression, or the petty crimes of the poor. It is an eloquent plea for equality.

Tyrannick Love, or the Royal Martyr, a heroic play by *Dryden (1669).

Based on the legend of the martyrdom of St Catharine by the Roman emperor Maximin, it contains some of Dryden's most extravagant heroic verse. It was ridiculed in *The Rehearsal*, and by *Shadwell. Dryden himself satirizes its excesses in *MacFlecknoe.

TYRWHITT, Thomas (1730–86), is remembered partly for his edition and exposure of *Chatterton's Rowley poems which he published in 1777 and in an appendix in 1778 stated authoritatively that they were modern, not ancient, a view he elaborated in his *Vindication* (1782). His *Observations and Conjectures upon Some Passages of Shakespeare* (1765, dated 1766) criticized Dr *Johnson's edition for its lack of attention to the early texts. His edition of Chaucer's *Canterbury Tales* (4 vols, 1775, vol. 5 with Glossary, 1778), expounded *Chaucer's versification and helped to establish the canon.

U

Ubi sunt, derived from the opening words of a type of Medieval Latin poem ('Where are they?'), taken up in Old English poems such as *Beowulf* and particularly *The Wanderer* (ll. 92–3) and in many Middle English lyrics (especially the one beginning 'Where beth they, beforen us weren', *c*.1300). Many later medieval French poems use the theme, most famously Villon's 'Ballade des Dames du Temps Jadis' with its refrain, 'Mais où sont les neiges d'antan?' —'Where are the snows of yesteryear?'

UDALL, or **UVEDALE,** Nicholas (1504–56), dramatist and scholar, successively headmaster of Eton and Westminster. He was author of *Ralph Roister Doister*, the earliest known English comedy. He translated selections from *Terence and other works, and wrote Latin plays on sacred subjects.

Udolpho, *The Mysteries of*, see MYSTERIES OF UDOLPHO, THE.

ULFILAS, or **WULFILA** (AD 311–81), a Christian of Cappadocian origin, was consecrated bishop of the Arian Visigoths in 341. He translated the Bible into Gothic from the Greek, inventing, it is said, an alphabet for the purpose. Fragments of this translation survive, and are of great value to the philological science of the Germanic languages.

'Ulysses', a poem by *Tennyson, composed 1833, published 1842. In a dramatic monologue Ulysses describes how he plans to set forth again from Ithaca after his safe return from his wanderings after the Trojan war, 'to sail beyond the sunset'. The episode is based on *Dante (*Inferno*, xxvi). It expresses the poet's sense of 'the need of going forward and braving the struggle of life' after the death of A. H. *Hallam.

Ulysses, a novel by J. *Joyce, serialized in the *Little Review* from 1918, published in Paris 1922. Copies of the first English edition were burned by the New York post office authorities, and the Folkestone Customs authorities seized the second edition in 1923. Various later editions appeared abroad and after the United States District Court found the book not obscene in 1933, the first English edition appeared in 1936, and the first unlimited edition in America and England in 1937.

The novel deals with the events of one day in Dublin, 16 June 1904 (the anniversary of Joyce's first walk with Nora Barnacle, who became his wife), now known as 'Bloomsday'.

The principle characters are Stephen Dedalus (the hero of Joyce's earlier *A Portrait of the Artist as a Young Man*); Leopold Bloom, a Jewish advertisement canvasser; and his wife Molly. The plot follows the wanderings of Stephen and Bloom through Dublin, and their eventual meeting. The last chapter is a monologue by Molly Bloom. The various chapters roughly correspond to the episodes of Homer's *Odyssey*: Stephen representing Telemachus, Bloom Odysseus, and Molly Penelope. In the course of the story a public bath, a funeral, a newspaper office, a library, public houses, a maternity hospital, and a brothel are visited. The style is highly allusive and employs a variety of techniques, especially those of the *stream of consciousness and of parody, and ranges from extreme realism to fantasy.

Ulysses, in Shakespeare's *Troilus and Cressida*, a Greek commander.

Umbriel, 'a dusky melancholy sprite' in Pope's *The Rape of the Lock*.

Una, in Bk I of Spenser's *Faerie Queene*, typifies singleness of the true religion. (See REDCROSSE KNIGHT.)

Uncle Remus, see HARRIS, J. C.

Uncle Silas, a novel by J. S. *Le Fanu, published 1864.

Silas Ruthyn is suspected of the murder of a wealthy gambler who has been found dead at Bartram-Haugh, Silas's Derbyshire home. Believing in Silas's innocence, his brother Austin at his death leaves a will designed to demonstrate his confidence in his brother: Silas is made guardian to Austin's daughter, Maud, and her entire fortune is to go to him if she dies under age. Uncle Silas, who is heavily in debt, summons Maud to Bartram-Haugh, where he attempts to marry her to his boorish son Dudley (who is already secretly married). When she refuses, he pretends to send her to school in France; but when, after two days' travel, she wakes up believing she is in Dover, she finds herself a prisoner back at Bartram-Haugh, where Silas and Dudley, aided by a sinister French governess, Mme de la Rougierre, attempt to murder her. The plot miscarries and the governess is horribly murdered by Dudley in mistake for Maud, who escapes.

Uncle Toby, see TOBY, UNCLE.

Uncle Tom's Cabin, a novel by Mrs H. E. B. *Stowe.

UNDERDOWNE, Thomas (*fl.* 1566–87), translated the *Aethiopica* of Heliodorus under the title *An Aethiopian Historie* (?1569).

Underground Poetry, a phrase used to describe the work of a number of writer-performers active in Britain between the late 1950s and mid-1970s, including A. *Mitchell, Jeff Nuttall (1933–), Tom Pickard (1946–), Alexander Trocchi (1925–84), Heathcote Williams (1941–), and the *Liverpool poets. The open forms and protest or folk-song bias of this poetry reflected the experimental anti-war aspirations of the 'alternative society' of the 1960s, and found its public largely through readings, events, and little magazine publications. Michael Horovitz's populist magazine *New Departures,* founded in 1959, and his Penguin anthology *Children of Albion* (1969) record the mood of the movement.

Under Milk Wood, a radio drama by Dylan *Thomas, first broadcast by the BBC on 25 Jan. 1954 and subsequently adapted for the stage; the published version was completed shortly before his death in 1953.

Set in the small Welsh seaside town of Llareggub, it evokes the lives of the inhabitants—Myfanwy Price the dressmaker, and her lover Mog Edwards the draper; twice-widowed Mrs Ogmore-Pritchard; Butcher Beynon and his daughter Gossamer; the Reverend Eli Jenkins; the romantic and prolific Polly Garter; nostalgic Captain Cat, dreaming of lost loves; and many others. The poetic, alliterative prose is interspersed with songs and ballads.

Under the Greenwood Tree, a novel by T. *Hardy, published 1872.

This is a gentle, humorous novel, skilfully interweaving the love story of Dick Dewy and Fancy Day with the fortunes and misfortunes of a group of villagers, many of whom are musicians and singers in Mellstock church. The novel marks the first appearance of Hardy's village rustics, who drew much critical comment, both favourable and unfavourable, and who were to reappear frequently in later novels.

Under the Volcano, a novel by M. *Lowry, published 1947, considered his masterpiece.

It opens in Quauhnahuac, Mexico, on the Day of the Dead, Nov. 1939, as film-maker Jacques Laruelle looks back on the dramatic events of the same day in the preceding year, which occupy with many flashbacks, and shifts of time sequence the main action of the book. The characters are the British ex-consul Geoffrey Firmin, an alcoholic, his wife Yvonne, an ex-film star who has returned after a year's estrangement, Laruelle, with whom she has had an affair, and the consul's half-brother Hugh, an anti-Fascist journalist much preoccupied by the Spanish Civil War. The theme of self-destruction is linked with the menace to Western civilization, and the mood grows increasingly sombre, ending with the consul's death. The Mexican landscape, over which brood the two volcanoes Popocatapetl and Ixtaccihuatl, is described with much vividness.

Under Western Eyes, a novel by J. *Conrad.

Underwood, The, or *Underwoods,* a collection of poems by *Jonson, printed in the folio of 1640. It includes 'A Celebration of Charis', 'An Ode to Himself', 'An execration upon Vulcan' (concerning the fire in Jonson's library in 1623), 'An Epigram on the Court Pucelle', and the ode to Sir Lucius Cary and Sir Henry Morison.

Unfortunate Traveller, The, or *The life of Jacke Wilton,* a prose tale of adventure by T. *Nashe, published 1594, the earliest picaresque romance in English, and the most remarkable work of the kind before *Defoe.

Jack Wilton is 'a certain kind of an appendix or page' attending on the court of Henry VIII, who lives by his wits, playing tricks on a niggardly old victualler and other gullible occupants of the camp, and gets whipped for his pains. Subsequent travels take him to Italy (as page to the earl of *Surrey), and to Wittenberg, where he hears *Luther's disputations. The book includes much literary parody and pastiche.

Unitarianism, a Christian body which rejects the Trinity and the divinity of Christ in favour of the single personality of the Godhead. In England John Biddle (1615–62) published Unitarian tracts in 1652–4 and from 1652 his followers (Biddelians, *Socinians, or 'Unitarians') began regular Sunday worship. More than 100 years later Joseph *Priestley in his *Appeal to the Serious and Candid Professors of Christianity* (1770) defended Unitarian principles, and in 1773 Theophilus Lindsey (1723–1808) formed the first Unitarian denomination, opening in 1774 Essex Chapel in London. In the 18th cent. Dissenting congregations, including the English Presbyterians, turned to Unitarian views. Later in the 19th cent. J. *Martineau influenced the organization of the Unitarian body in England and Ireland and led the advance from biblical to rational Unitarianism.

Unities, The, principles of dramatic composition supposedly derived from Aristotle's

Poetics. Aristotle states that a play should have the unity of a living organism, and that the action it represents should last, if possible, no longer than a single revolution of the sun. It was from these hints that 16th-cent. critics, most notably *Castelvetro, developed the rule of the three unities: action, time, and place. The exclusion of sub-plots became the rule in France only after the controversy over *Corneille's *Le Cid* (1637). The time allowed for the action of a tragedy was extended by common consent to 24 hours. The place the stage represented was allowed to shift from one point to another within a larger area: a palace or even a city. Moreover, dramatists learnt to circumvent the limitations of the unities by avoiding the mention of specific times and places. The impact of *neo-classicism on English tragedy was delayed by the disturbances connected with the Civil War and was weakened by the taste for exciting action that was a legacy from the Jacobean stage. Dryden's essay *Of Dramatick Poesy* (1668) offers the unities only half-hearted support, and in spite of the efforts of French-inspired critics like *Rymer and *Dennis, and the success of Addison's *Cato* (1713), neo-classical drama never took firm root in England.

University Wits, name given by *Saintsbury to a group of Elizabethan playwrights and pamphleteers, of whom *Nashe, R. *Greene, *Lyly, and T. *Lodge were the chief.

Unquiet Grave, The, (1) a ballad included in *Child's collection, in which a lover laments his dead love for a twelvemonth and a day; from the grave she asks him to content himself and let her sleep; (2) see CONNOLLY, C.

Unreason, Abbot of, see MISRULE.

Unto this Last, see RUSKIN, J.

UPDIKE, John Hoyer (1932–), American novelist, short story writer, and poet. His novels include the trilogy *Rabbit Run* (1960), *Rabbit Redux* (1971), and *Rabbit is Rich* (1981), a small-town domestic tragi-comedy which traces the career of ex-basketball champion Harry Angstrom; *The Centaur* (1963); and *Couples* (1968), a portrait of sexual passion and realignment amongst a group of young surburban married couples in Tarbox, Mass. Updike's characteristic preoccupations are with the erotic, with the pain and striving implicit in human relationships, and with the sacred in daily life; these are conveyed in highly charged prose. His volumes of short stories include *Pigeon Feathers and other stories* (1962), *Museums and Women* (1972), and *Problems and other stories* (1979).

UPWARD, Edward Falaise (1903–), novelist, educated at Corpus Christi College, with *Isherwood, whose lifelong friend he became. His works include *Journey to the Border* (1938); *The Railway Accident and other stories* (1969); his trilogy *In the Thirties* (1962), *The Rotten Elements* (1969), and *No Home but the Struggle* (1977), published together in 1977 as *The Spiral Ascent*, describing the alternating political and artistic conflicts in the life of Marxist poet and schoolmaster Alan Sebriel. Upward was for some years a member of the Communist Party.

URBAN, Sylvanus, the pseudonym of E. *Cave and, by succession, of the later editors of the *Gentleman's Magazine*.

Urizen, a principal character in the symbolic books of *Blake, represented as God of Reason and law-maker. *The Book of Urizen* (1794) is Blake's version of the myth of Genesis, describing the creation of the material world by Urizen from the 'abominable void', from which is engendered Urizen's opponent, *Los, and Pity, the first female form, who is named *Enitharmon. The spirit of the book is of anguish, revolt, and suffering, and Urizen, after long struggles with Los, surveys his creation in a sorrow that engenders a web, 'The Net of Religion'.

Urn Burial, see HYDRIOTAPHIA.

URQUHART, Sir Thomas (1611–60), followed Prince Charles to Worcester, where many of his manuscripts were lost, was imprisoned 1651–2, and died abroad. His best-known work is a translation of the first three books of *Rabelais, the first two 1653, the third 1693 (completed by *Motteux). He wrote a number of curious treatises on mathematics, linguistics, etc.; among them is *Ekskubalauron* (1651, known as 'The Jewel'), which contains in his 'Vindication of the Honour of Scotland' the story of the 'Admirable' *Crichton.

Ursula, (1) the pig-woman in Jonson's *Bartholomew Fair*; (2) Hero's maidservant in Shakespeare's *Much Ado About Nothing*; (3) one of the Brangwen sisters in D. H. Lawrence's *The Rainbow* and *Women in Love*.

'Usher, Fall of the House of', see POE, E. A.

USK, Thomas (d. 1388), the author of *The Testament of Love*, formerly ascribed to *Chaucer. He was under-sheriff of London in 1387, by the mandate of Richard II, and he was proceeded against and executed by the 'Merciless Parliament' in 1388. *The Testament of Love* is an allegorical prose-work perhaps written by Usk in prison to elicit sympathy; it is sometimes (though unreliably) dated 1385. Skeat noticed that the first letters of the sections formed an acrostic reading 'Margaret of virtu have merci on 'TSKNVI', and Henry Bradley rearranged the text so that the last letters read THINUSK, i.e. 'thine Usk'. This crypticism is typical of the allusiveness of the poem, part of which is now impenetrable.

Usnach, The Sons of, see DEIRDRE.

USSHER, James (1581–1656), became archbishop of Armagh in 1625. His chief work is the *Annales Veteris et Novi Testamenti*, a chronological summary in Latin of the history of the world from the Creation to the dispersion of the Jews under Vespasian, said to be the source of the dates later inserted in the margins of the Authorized Version of the Bible, which fixed the Creation at 23 Oct. 4004 BC.

Uther Pendragon, in the Arthurian legend, king of the Britons and father of *Arthur. Pendragon means 'chief dragon', and Uther has been variously explained. After he became king of the Britons, he lusted after Ygerna, wife of Gorlois, duke of Cornwall. He picked a quarrel with Gorlois, and was transformed by Merlin's magic into his shape, whereupon he slept with Ygerna. After the death of Gorlois he married Ygerna who bore him two children, Arthur and Anna. (See IGRAINE.)

Utilitarianism, an essay by J. S. *Mill, first published in a series of articles in *Fraser's Magazine* in 1861, in book form 1863. The term 'utilitarian' was first adopted by Mill in 1823, from Galt's *Annals of the Parish*. In this work, Mill, while accepting the Benthamite principle (see BENTHAM) that Utility, or the greatest happiness of the greatest number, is the foundation of morals, departs from it by maintaining that pleasures differ in kind or quality as well as in quantity, 'that some *kinds* of pleasure are more desirable and more valuable than others'; also by recognizing in 'the conscientious feelings of mankind' an 'internal sanction' to be added to Bentham's 'external sanctions'. 'The social feelings of mankind, the desire to be in unity with our fellow creatures' constitute 'the ultimate sanction of the greatest happiness, morality'.

Utopia, the principal literary work of Sir T. *More, is a speculative political essay written in Latin, published 1516. The subject is the search for the best possible form of government. More meets at Antwerp a traveller, one Raphael *Hythloday, who has discovered 'Utopia', 'Nowhere land'. Communism is there the general law, a national system of education is extended to men and women alike, and the freest toleration of religion is recognized. The work at once became popular, and was translated by Ralph Robinson into English in 1551, and into French (in 1550), German, Italian, and Spanish.

The name 'Utopia' ('no place'), coined by More, passed into general usage, and has been used to describe, retrospectively, Plato's *Republic*, and many subsequent fictions, fantasies, and blueprints for the future, including Bacon's *New Atlantis*, Harrington's *The Commonwealth of Oceana*, Morris's *News from Nowhere*, and *Bellamy's Looking Backward*. Satirical Utopias include Swift's *Gulliver's Travels* and Samuel Butler's *Erewhon*. Many works of *Science Fiction use the Utopian form.

UTTLEY, Alison (1884–1976), is best remembered for her 'Little Grey Rabbit' series (of which the first was published in 1929) and for her 'Sam Pig' series (1940 onwards). (See CHILDREN'S LITERATURE.)

V

Vainlove, a character in Congreve's *The Old Bachelor*.

Vala, see FOUR ZOAS, THE.

Valentine, (1) one of *The Two Gentlemen of Verona* in Shakespeare's play; (2) one of *Orsino's court in his *Twelfth Night*.

Valentine and Orson, the subject of an early French romance. Bellisant, sister of King Pepin, is married to Alexander, emperor of Constantinople. The archpriest treacherously accuses Bellisant to her husband and she is banished. A bear carries away one of her children (Orson), who is reared as a wild man. The other (Valentine) is found by Pepin and brought up as a knight. Valentine meets Orson, conquers him, brings him to the court, and tames him. Numerous adventures follow.

The story appeared in English about 1550. A ballad in Percy's *Reliques* deals with it.

Valentinian, *The Tragedy of,* a play by J. *Fletcher, performed between 1610 and 1614, published 1647.

Valerian, the husband of St Cecilia, whose story is told in Chaucer's 'The Second Nun's Tale' (*Canterbury Tales*, 21).

Valley of Humiliation, in Bunyan's *Pilgrim's Progress*, the place where *Christian encounters Apollyon.

Valley of the Shadow of Death, see Psalm 23: 4. Christian, in Bunyan's *Pilgrim's Progress*, passed through it.

VALLON, Annette, see WORDSWORTH, W.

Valmouth, see FIRBANK, R.

VANBRUGH, Sir John (1664–1726), dramatist and architect. He produced *The Relapse, or Virtue in Danger* (1696), with immense success, and *The Provok'd Wife* (1697). His other principal comedies are *The Confederacy* (1705), and *The Provok'd Husband,* which he left unfinished and C. *Cibber completed and brought out in 1728. He, together with *Congreve, was specially attacked by Jeremy *Collier in his *Short View*.

Vanbrugh's first building was Castle Howard,

1699–1726. This already shows the grandeur and dramatic quality of his style, which reaches its climax in Blenheim Palace.

VAN DER POST, Sir Laurens Jan (1906–   ), writer, whose many works of travel, anthropology, and adventure (much influenced by *Jung) include *The Lost World of the Kalahari* (1958), *The Heart of the Hunter* (1961), *A Story like the Wind* (1972), and *A Far-Off Place* (1974).

Vanessa, *Swift's name for Esther Vanhomrigh.

VANHOMRIGH, Esther, see SWIFT, J.

Vanity Fair, in Bunyan's *Pilgrim's Progress*, a fair set up by *Beelzebub, Apollyon, and Legion in the town Vanity, through which pilgrims passed on their way to the Eternal City.

Vanity Fair, a novel by *Thackeray, published in numbers 1847–8, illustrated by the author.

The story follows the fortunes of two sharply contrasted characters, Rebecca (Becky) Sharp, the penniless orphaned daughter of an artist and a French opera dancer, and Amelia Sedley, the sheltered child of a rich City merchant. The two girls have been educated at Miss Pinkerton's Academy. Becky, having failed to capture Amelia's elephantine brother Jos, becomes governess to the children of Sir Pitt Crawley, a coarse old man who bullies his fading second wife. Becky charms the Crawley family, and becomes a favourite of Miss Crawley, Sir Pitt's rich sister. When his wife dies Sir Pitt proposes to Becky, but she has to confess that she is already married, to his younger son Rawdon. The young couple abruptly fall from favour with Miss Crawley, and have to live on Becky's wits.

Meanwhile Amelia's father has lost all his money and her engagement to George Osborne, the vain and shallow son of another City magnate, has been broken off in consequence. William Dobbin, George's awkward, loyal friend, who is secretly in love with Amelia, persuades George to defy his father and go on with the marriage, and Mr Osborne disinherits his son.

George, Rawdon, and Dobbin are all in the army, and Amelia and Becky accompany their husbands to Belgium, where Becky carries on an intrigue with George Osborne. George is killed at Waterloo, and Amelia, with her baby son Georgy, goes to live in poverty with her parents, while Becky and Rawdon manage to make a brilliant display in London society on 'nothing a year'. Amelia is finally forced by poverty to part with Georgy to his grandfather. Dobbin, despairing of ever winning Amelia's love, has spent ten years in India. Becky and Rawdon part, after Rawdon has discovered his wife in a compromising situation with Lord Steyne. Becky leads an increasingly disreputable life on the Continent. Rawdon, who has become governor of Coventry Island, dies of fever. Amelia steadfastly refuses to marry Dobbin, until Becky tells her of George Osborne's infidelity. Disillusioned, she marries Dobbin, but by then his love for her has lost much of its intensity.

Vanity of Human Wishes, The, a poem by Dr *Johnson, published 1749, in imitation of the Tenth Satire of *Juvenal. It owes its success to its moral seriousness and to its weighty but well-illustrated generalizations. Johnson comments on the vanities of various ambitions and cites the examples of Wolsey, *Clarendon, *Laud, and others. This was the first work to which he put his name.

VANSITTART, Peter (1920–), was a schoolteacher for 25 years before becoming a full-time writer. His novels range from experimental historical narratives (*Passtimes of a Red Summer*, 1969; *Lancelot*, 1978) to portraits of contemporary life, which include *Landlord* (1970) and *Quintet* (1976).

Varden, Gabriel, a character in Dickens's *Barnaby Rudge*, father of Dolly Varden.

Variorum, or **Variorum Editions,** an edition, especially of the complete works of a classical author, containing the notes of various editors or commentators [*OED*].

Varney, Richard, a character in Scott's *Kenilworth*.

VASARI, Giorgio (1511–74), Italian painter, architect, and author of *The Lives of the most excellent Italian Architects, Painters and Sculptors* (1550 and 1568), for generations the main source for the history of Italian art. A selection translated by G. Bull appeared in 1965.

Vathek, An Arabian Tale, written in French by W. *Beckford, published in English 1786. It was one of the most successful of the *oriental tales then in fashion.

The cruel and sensual Caliph Vathek, whose eye can kill with a glance, is compelled, by the influence of his sorceress mother and by the unbridled pride of his own nature, to become a servant of Eblis, the Devil. He makes a sacrifice

of fifty children, and sets off from his capital, Samarah, to the ruined city of Istakar, where he is promised the sight of the treasures of the pre-Adamite sultans. On the way he falls in love with Nouronihar, the exquisite daughter of one of his emirs, who accompanies him on his journey. After various exotic and terrifying incidents, he obtains admission to the great subterranean halls of Eblis, only to discover the sickening worthlessness of the riches that he sees there, and to receive the penalty of his sin, when his own heart and the hearts of all the damned burst into flame in their living bodies.

Vaudeville, a light popular song or a stage performance of a light and amusing character interspersed with songs, from *vau de vire*, in full *chanson du Vau de Vire*, a song of the Valley of the Vire (in Calvados, Normandy).

'**Vaudracour and Julia**', see WORDSWORTH, W.

VAUGHAN, Henry (1621–95), twin brother of Thomas *Vaughan, was born at Newton-upon-Usk, Breconshire. His wooing of his first wife Catherine is apparently recalled in the poem 'Upon the Priory Grove' printed in *Poems with the Tenth Satire of Juvenal Englished* (1646), his first collection. His second, *Olor Iscanus* ('The Swan of Usk'), has a dedication bearing the date 1647, but was not published till 1651. The poems in these two volumes are almost wholly secular and there is little in them that anticipates the great religious poetry of Vaughan's next volume, *Silex Scintillans* (1650). Further devotional works followed: *The Mount of Olives, or Solitary Devotions* (1652), *Flores Solitudinis* (1654), and the second edition (with a second part) of *Silex Scintillans* (1655), in which he acknowledges his debt to G. *Herbert. Vaughan's first wife having died, he married her younger sister Elizabeth, probably in 1655. According to a letter he sent to *Aubrey in 1673 he had by that date been practising physic 'for many years with good success'. In 1678 *Thalia Rediviva*, containing poems by both twins, was published.

Vaughan's religious poetry is uneven, but its best moments, like the start of 'The World' ('I saw Eternity the other night'), are wholly distinctive, and have prevailed with critics to class him as a 'mystic'. He was seized with the idea of childish innocence, and the child's recollections of prenatal glory. He writes, in 'The Retreat', of his own 'Angel-infancy', when he would muse on clouds and flowers and see in them 'Some shadows of eternity'. Vaughan's fascination with hermeticism, and particularly with the idea of sympathetic bonds uniting microcosm and macrocosm, is clear in his poems.

VAUGHAN, Thomas (1621–66), twin brother of Henry *Vaughan, a disciple of Cornelius

*Agrippa, published various treatises on alchemy, magic, and mysticism, and a Preface to a *Rosicrucian work, *The Fame and Confession of the Fraternity of R.C., commonly, of the Rosie Cross* (1652). Most of his works were published under the pseudonym of 'Eugenius Philalethes'. He was satirized by S. *Butler in his 'Character of a Hermetic Philosopher' (published posthumously) and is said to have suggested some aspects of Ralpho in *Hudibras.

VAUGHAN WILLIAMS, Ralph (1872–1958), English composer who was deeply interested in the folk-song tradition. Among his many settings in English were 'Linden Lea' (1901), to words by W. *Barnes; 'Silent Noon', from D. G. *Rossetti's *The House of Life*; *Songs of Travel* from R. L. *Stevenson; the *Houseman cycle, *On Wenlock Edge* (1909); and *Five Mystical Songs* to poems by G. *Herbert. He also made settings of *Chaucer, Shakespeare, *Whitman, and the *Ten Blake Songs* (1957). In *An Oxford Elegy* (1949; words from Arnold's *'The Scholar-Gipsy' and *'Thyrsis') he combines speaker, chorus and orchestra. Vaughan Williams contributed to the liberation of English opera in *Hugh the Drover* (1924), much influenced by folk-song; *Riders to the Sea* (1937) is a setting of *Synge's tragedy; and *The Pilgrim's Progress* (1951) is based on *Bunyan.

Vaux, (1) Roland de, the baron of Triermain, in *Scott's *The Bridal of Triermain*; (2) Roland of, in Coleridge's *'Christabel', the estranged friend of the heroine's father.

VAUX, Thomas, second Baron Vaux of Harrowden (1509–56), a contributor to *Tottel's *Miscellany* and *The Paradyse of Dainty Devises*. He is chiefly remembered now as the author of 'The aged Lover renounceth Love', the song mumbled by the grave-digger in *Hamlet*, v. i.

Veal, (1) Captain, the ship's captain in Fielding's *Journal of a Voyage to Lisbon*; (2) Mrs, see DEFOE, D.

Vendice, or **Vindice,** see REVENGER'S TRAGEDY, THE.

Veneering, Mr and Mrs, in Dickens's *Our Mutual Friend*, types of flashy social parvenus.

Venetia, a novel by B. *Disraeli, published 1837. The novel celebrates, in the author's words, 'two of the most renowned and refined spirits', *Byron as Carducis and *Shelley as Herbert; but the parallels are only intermittent.

Venice Preserv'd, or a Plot Discovered, a tragedy in blank verse by *Otway, produced 1682.
    Jaffeir, a noble Venetian youth, has secretly married Belvidera, daughter of a proud senator, Priuli, who has repudiated her. Jaffeir, reduced to poverty, begs Priuli for assistance, but is met with insults. Pierre, a foreign soldier with a grievance against the Venetian republic, stimulates Jaffeir's desire for revenge, confides in him a plot that is hatching against the State, and introduces him to the conspirators. As a pledge of his loyalty to them Jaffeir places Belvidera in the charge of their leader, Renault, but without explaining the reason. Renault tries to rape her in the night. She escapes to her husband, who in spite of his pledge to the contrary, makes known to her the conspiracy. To save her father, who as one of the senators is to be killed, she persuades Jaffeir to reveal the plot to the Senate, but to claim as reward the lives of the conspirators. These are arrested. Jaffeir, loaded by them with insults, is overwhelmed with remorse. The senators, in spite of their promise, condemn the conspirators to death. Jaffeir threatens to kill Belvidera unless she secures their pardon from her father. She succeeds, but Priuli's intervention is too late. Belvidera goes mad. Jaffeir stabs his friend Pierre on the scaffold and then himself, and Belvidera dies broken-hearted.

Venn, Diggory, a character in Hardy's *The Return of the Native*.

Ventidius, (1) in Shakespeare's *Timon of Athens*, one of the faithless friends of Timon; (2) in his *Antony and Cleopatra* and in Dryden's *All for Love*, one of Antony's generals.

Venus, Mr, a character in Dickens's *Our Mutual Friend*.

Venus and Adonis, an Ovidian poem by *Shakespeare, published 1593, and written in *sestra rima* (i.e. a quatrain followed by a couplet). It was dedicated to Henry Wriothesley, earl of Southampton, who has been connected with the *Sonnets. The poem was probably Shakespeare's first publication, and was first printed by Richard Field in 1593.
    Venus, in love with the youth Adonis, detains him from the chase and woos him, but cannot win his love. She begs him to meet her the next day, but he is then to hunt the boar. She tries in vain to dissuade him. When the morning comes she hears his hounds at bay; filled with terror she goes to look for him and finds him killed by the boar.

Vercelli Book, The, an Old English manuscript, made in England before the year 1000, now in the possession of the chapter of Vercelli in North Italy. It contains prose sermons and about 3,500 lines of Old English poetry; its most distinguished contents are the poems *The Dream of the Rood* and *Andreas*, and two of the four signed poems of *Cynewulf: *Elene* and *The Fates of the Apostles*.

Verdant Green, The Adventures of, see BRADLEY, E.

VERE, Edward de, see OXFORD.

Verges, in Shakespeare's *Much Ado About Nothing,* head borough or petty constable to Dogberry's constable.

VERGIL, the Roman poet, see VIRGIL.

VERGIL, Polydore (?1470–?1555), a native of Urbino, who came to England in 1502; he was archdeacon of Wells 1508–54. He was a friend of Sir T. *More and other English humanists. He published his *Anglicae Historiae Libri XXVI* in 1534–55, a chronicle of special value for the reign of Henry VII. He was also author of a *Proverbiorum Libellus* (Venice, 1498) anticipating the *Adagia* of *Erasmus.

Verisopht, Lord Frederick, a character in Dickens's *Nicholas Nickleby.*

VERLAINE, Paul (1844–96), French poet. (See SYMBOLISM.)

Verloc, a character in Conrad's *The Secret Agent.*

VERNE, Jules (1828–1905), French novelist whose books, combining adventure and popular science, include *Voyage au centre de la terre* (1864), *Vingt mille lieues sous les mers* (1869, the adventures of Captain Nemo and his crew aboard the submarine *Nautilus*), and *Le tour du monde en quatre-vingts jours* (1873, recounting the travels of the Englishman Phileas Fogg and his valet Passepartout). (See SCIENCE FICTION).

Vernon, Diana, the heroine of Scott's *Rob Roy.*

Vers de société, a term applied to a form of light verse dealing with events in polite society, usually in a satiric or playful tone, sometimes conversational, sometimes employing intricate forms such as the *villanelle or the *rondeau. English writers noted for their *vers de société* include *Prior, *Goldsmith, *Praed, *Calverley, *Dobson, and *Locker-Lampson.

Vers libre, a term used to describe many forms of irregular, syllabic, or unrhymed verse, in which the ordinary rules of prosody are disregarded. *Whitman pioneered a form of *vers libre* in America, and its independent evolution in France and Belgium (in the works of Laforgue, Maeterlinck, and others in the 1890s) had a great influence on the early *Modernists such as T. S. *Eliot and *Pound.

VERTUE, George (1684–1756), engraver and antiquary. His notebooks were sold to Horace

*Walpole, who used them as a basis for his *Anecdotes of Painting in England.*

Verver, Adam and his daughter Maggie, characters in *The Golden Bowl* by H. James.

VESEY, Mrs Elizabeth (?1715–91), an Irish woman, the first of the *Blue Stocking hostesses. In the early 1750s she determined to open her doors to literary and fashionable society for an entirely new kind of evening party. She set the pattern of Blue Stocking evenings for the next 50 years.

Vholes, a lawyer in Dickens's *Bleak House.*

'Vicar of Bray, The', a well-known song of unknown authorship, dating from the 18th cent. The subject is a time-serving parson, who boasts that he has accommodated himself to the religious views of the reigns of Charles, James, William, Anne, and George, and that 'whatsoever king may reign' he will remain vicar of Bray.

Vicar of Bullhampton, The, a novel by A. *Trollope, published 1870.

Vicar of Wakefield, The, a novel by *Goldsmith, published 1766.

The story is told by the Revd Dr Primrose, the Vicar, kindly, charitable, and devoid of worldly wisdom. His wife Deborah is proud of her housekeeping and her six children, two girls, Olivia and Sophia, and four boys. The Vicar loses his independent fortune through the bankruptcy of a merchant. They move to a new living under the patronage of a certain Squire Thornhill. Thornhill, who is an unprincipled ruffian, seduces Olivia after a mock ceremony of marriage, and deserts her. She is discovered by her father and brought home, but his humble vicarage is destroyed by fire. He himself is thrown into prison for debt at the suit of Thornhill; and George Primrose, who challenges the latter to a duel to avenge his sister, is overpowered by ruffians and likewise sent to prison. The Vicar's second daughter, Sophia, is forcibly carried off in a postchaise by an unknown villain, and Olivia, who has been pining away since her desertion, is reported to the Vicar to be dead. All these misfortunes he bears with fortitude and resignation.

On their removal to their new vicarage the Primrose family had made the acquaintance of a certain Mr Burchell, who appears to be a broken-down gentleman, kind-hearted but somewhat eccentric. By good fortune he is now the means of rescuing Sophia. It thereupon appears that he is in reality the benevolent Sir William Thornhill, the squire's uncle. The squire's villainy is now exposed, and at last all ends happily. Sir William marries Sophia. Olivia is found not to be dead, and her marriage to the squire is shown to have been, contrary to his intentions, legal. The Vicar's fortune is restored to him, and George marries the young lady of his heart.

The well-known poems 'The Hermit', and 'Elegy on the Death of a Mad Dog', and 'When lovely woman stoops to folly' are placed at three turning-points of the story.

Vice, The, a fool or buffoon introduced into some of the *interludes and later Moralities as a figure of evil. The descent of the figure from characters in *Mystery cycles and *Morality Plays (such as 'The Vices', the *Seven Deadly Sins) is likely, though they are related too to the mischievous devil figure Titivil (or Tutivillus).

VICTORIA (1819–1901), queen of England from 1837, wrote innumerable letters and accumulated over 100 volumes of diaries and journals, kept from the age of 13 until shortly before her death. Her early writings published in her lifetime were *Leaves from a Journal of our Life in the Highlands 1848–61* (1868) and *More Leaves* (1883), covering the years 1862–3. The queen's lively and heavily underlined letters to her eldest daughter, Vicky, have been published. Queen Victoria took an interest in the novelists of her own reign but she preferred poetry ('in all shapes'), a preference which led to her friendship with *Tennyson, whom she regarded as the perfect poet of 'love and loss'. Their correspondence has been published. Among many biographical studies, mention may be made of L. *Strachey's highly unauthorized Life (1921) and E. *Longford's authorized version (1964).

Vignette, an ornamental design on a blank space in a book, especially at the beginning or end of a chapter, of small size, and unenclosed in a border. The word is a diminutive of the Fr. *vigne*, a vine; originally meaning an ornament of leaves and tendrils. It is now, by extension, used for any miniature work, visual, verbal, or musical.

Village, The, a poem by *Crabbe, published 1783.

The poet contrasts the cruel realities of country life with the Arcadian pastoral favoured by poets. He was assisted in the writing of the work (which Dr *Johnson found 'original, vigorous, and elegant') both by his patron *Burke and by Johnson. The poem established Crabbe's reputation as a writer.

'Village Blacksmith, The', a poem by *Longfellow.

Villanelle, a poem, usually of a pastoral or lyrical nature, consisting normally of five three-lined stanzas and a final quatrain, with only two

rhymes throughout. The first and third lines of the first stanza are repeated alternatively in the succeeding stanzas as a refrain, and form a final couplet in the quatrain [OED]. The form has been much employed in light verse and *vers de société* by A. *Lang, A. *Dobson, and others, and in the 20th cent. was used to more serious purpose by *Auden, *Empson ('Slowly the poison the whole blood stream fills'), Dylan *Thomas ('Do not go gentle into that good night'), and others.

Villette, a novel by C. *Brontë, published 1853.

The novel, like its predecessor *The Professor* (then unpublished), is based on the author's experiences in Brussels, here renamed Villette, and also has as its centre a pupil–teacher relationship. The narrator, Lucy Snowe, poor, plain, and friendless, finds herself a post as teacher in a girls' school in Villette, where she wins the respect of the capable, if unscrupulous headmistress, Madame Beck. She becomes deeply attached to the handsome John Bretton, the school's English doctor, whom she recognizes as a childhood acquaintance; she represses her unreturned passion for him, and gradually falls in love with the waspish, despotic, but good-hearted little professor, M. Paul Emmanuel, Mme Beck's cousin. His generosity leaves her mistress of her own school when he is called away on business to the West Indies; the ending is ambiguous, and the reader is left to decide whether he returns to marry her or is drowned on his way home. The novel combines a masterly portrayal of Belgian daily life with a highly personal use of the elements of *Gothic fiction. In Paul Emmanuel the author successfully creates an unromatic hero very far removed from the *Byronic Rochester of *Jane Eyre.

Vincentio, (1) Lucentio's father in Shakespeare's *The Taming of the Shrew*; (2) the duke in his *Measure for Measure*.

VINCENT OF BEAUVAIS, the Dominican author of *Speculum Naturale, Historiale, Doctrinale* (c.1250), an enormous compilation of all the knowledge known at the time. He is mentioned by Chaucer in one version of the Prologue to *The Legend of Good Women*.

Vincy, Fred and Rosamond, characters in G. Eliot's *Middlemarch*.

Vindication of a Natural Society, A, a treatise by E. *Burke, published anonymously 1756, his first substantial work. It is an ironical answer to *Bolingbroke's indictment of revealed religion, in imitation of his style and in the form of a *reductio ad absurdum*; it was so successful a parody that even *Warburton was deceived by it, and in 1765 Burke published another edition with a preface explaining his ironical stance. Bolingbroke had exalted the claims of natural religion by pointing to the unfortunate results of religious creeds; Burke points to the evil results of artificial society and the artificial division of rich and poor, but expects his exposition to reinforce 'the necessity of political institutions, weak and wicked as they are'.

Vindication of the Rights of Woman, A, by M. *Wollstonecraft, published 1792.

In this work the author attacks the educational restrictions and 'mistaken notions of female excellence' that keep women in a state of 'ignorance and slavish dependence'. The work was much acclaimed, but also inevitably attracted hostility; Horace *Walpole referred to its author as 'a hyena in petticoats'.

Vindice, SEE REVENGER'S TRAGEDY, THE.

Vinegar, Captain Hercules and family, introduced by Fielding in *The Champion.

Vinegar Bible, The, an edition of the Bible printed by *Baskett at Oxford in 1716–17, so called from the substitution or misprint of the word 'vinegar' for 'vineyard' in the heading of Luke 20.

Violenta, one of the dramatis personae of Shakespeare's *All's Well that Ends Well who appears only once (III. v) in the play and does not speak; sometimes referred to as a typical nonentity.

Virago Press, see FEMINIST CRITICISM.

Virelay, a song or short lyric piece, of a type originating in France in the 14th cent., usually consisting of short lines arranged in stanzas with only two rhymes, the end-rhyme of one stanza being the chief one of the next [OED].

Virgidemiarum, Sex Libri, by J. *Hall, two volumes of English satire, 1597 and 1598. The first volume, called 'Toothless', treats mildly certain literary conventions in the spirit of *Martial and *Horace; the second volume, Juvenalian in character, 'bites' fiercely into such ills as sexual promiscuity, ostentatious piety, impostures in astrology and genealogy, economic injustices, etc. The title means 'a sheaf of rods', with which the satirist delivers his blows.

VIRGIL (Publius Vergilius Maro) (70–19 BC), the greatest of Roman poets. He imitated successively the pastorals of *Theocritus, the didactic poems of *Hesiod and Aratus, and the epics of *Homer, making original contributions to all three genres. In his Eclogues he added a new level of meaning to the pastoral's idealization of country life by alluding to topics of contemporary interest; in the Georgics he transformed the bald didacticism of his models into a panegyric of Italy and the traditional way of rural life; and in the Aeneid he committed the epic to the presentation of a major patriotic theme. He began by working within the conventions of *Hellenistic poetry, but later, helped by the patronage of Augustus, widened his stylistic range and created a diction and a manner of presentation that were all his own.

Many generations found in him their main gateway to the *Sublime. In the Middle Ages he was regarded as a seer and a magician, and the 'Messianic Eclogue' (below) led *Dante to choose him as a guide through Hell and Purgatory. His Aeneid served as a model for all the Latin epics of the medieval period and then for the new classical epic of the Renaissance. There are Virgilian similes in *Spenser, Virgilian motifs in Shakespeare's *Rape of Lucrece and Milton's *Paradise Lost. The Georgics came into their own in the 18th cent., when they provided a model for descriptive poets like J. *Thomson. In the 19th cent. came *Wordsworth's 'Laodamia' and *Tennyson's avowal in 'To Virgil' of indebtedness beyond the obvious. *Dryden's version of his works (1697) remains probably the finest. Gavin *Douglas, writing in Scots, produced a vivid Aeneid (1513) and W. *Morris a ponderously medieval one (1885). Recently there have been interesting translations by C. *Day-Lewis of the Georgics (1940) and the Aeneid (1952).

Virgilia, in Shakespeare's *Coriolanus, the wife of Coriolanus.

Virgil's Fourth (or **Messianic**) **Eclogue,** written 40 BC, celebrated the coming birth of a child who would bring back the Golden Age. This was taken in the Middle Ages to be a prophecy of the birth of Christ, and the interpretation appeared the more plausible because the poem contains imagery reminiscent of the Bible. The voluminous literature provoked by this work has focused on two problems: the first, the identity of the child (Augustus'? Antony's?); the second, the puzzle of the language. A plausible explanation advanced recently is that Virgil's source was not the Bible, but Sibylline writings originating in a South Italian culture that had come under Phoenician influence.

'Virgils Gnat', a poem by *Spenser, published 1591, and adapted from the Culex attributed to *Virgil.

Virginia, a daughter of the centurion Lucius Virginius. Appius Claudius, the decemvir, became enamoured of her and sought to get possession of her. For this purpose she was claimed by one of his favourites as daughter of a slave, and Appius in the capacity of a judge gave sentence in his favour and delivered her into the hands of his friend. Virginius, informed of these proceedings, arrived from the camp, and plunged a dagger into his daughter's breast to save her from the tyrant. He then rushed to the camp with the bloody knife in his hand. The soldiers, incensed against Appius Claudius, marched to Rome and seized him. But he destroyed himself in prison. The story (in *Livy, iii. 44 *et seq.*) is the basis of two plays called *Appius and Virginia*, one by *Webster and/or *Heywood (perf. ?1603–34), one by *Dennis (1709); of *Knowles's tragedy *Virginius*; and of *Macaulay's lay 'Virginia'.

Virginians, The, a novel by *Thackeray, published in numbers, 1857–9.

The novel takes up the story of the Esmond family of *The History of Henry Esmond*, and mainly concerns the fortunes of Esmond's twin grandsons, George and Harry Warrington, in America and England. Their mother is Esmond's only daughter Rachel. When George disappears in a military expedition against the French and is presumed dead, Harry, now the heir, visits England, and meets his Castlewood relations. Under their influence Harry plunges into gambling and dissipation, and is inveigled into an engagement to his much older cousin, Maria. He is arrested for debt and imprisoned in a spunging-house. He is rescued by the sudden reappearance of George, who has escaped from the French. Maria releases Harry from his engagement, since he is no longer heir to a fortune. But when George falls in love with and marries Theo, the daughter of a poor soldier, General Lambert, rather than an American heiress, his mother cuts off his allowance, and he is only saved from penury by becoming the heir of Sir Miles Warrington, of the English branch of the family. Harry has become a favourite of the rakish old Baroness Bernstein, the former Beatrix Esmond, and she leaves money to him in her will. Harry joins the army, and is with Wolfe at the capture of Quebec. He falls in love with Fanny Mountain, the daughter of his mother's housekeeper, and marries her rather than Hetty Lambert, Theo's sister, who is in love with him. When the War of Independence breaks out, Harry joins Washington, and George, who is in the British army, resigns his commission rather than run the risk of fighting against his brother. He settles on the Warrington estates in England, and gives up the Virginian property to Harry.

Virgin Martyr, The, a tragedy by *Massinger and *Dekker, printed 1622. It is based on the story of St *Dorothea, who, with her lover Antoninus, is martyred for her faith during the reign of Diocletian, after converting the daughters of the zealous persecutor Theophilus: Theophilus is also converted in the last act, and is himself tortured to death. The same story has been treated in poems by *Swinburne and G. M. *Hopkins.

Virgin Queen, a name for Queen *Elizabeth I.

Virtuosi, see LITERATI.

Vision of Judgement, A, a poem in hexameters by R. *Southey, published 1821, at the time when Southey was poet laureate.

The preface, written in defence of this metrical innovation, contains, in a digression, a violent attack on the works of *Byron; Byron retorted with his parody *The Vision of Judgement* (below).

The poet in a trance sees George III (who had died in 1820) rise from the tomb and, after receiving from the shade of Perceval news of affairs in England, proceed to the gates of Heaven. The Devil, accompanied by *Wilkes, comes forward to arraign him, but retires discomfited, and the king, after receiving a eulogy from Washington, is admitted to Paradise, where he is greeted by previous English sovereigns, the worthies of England, and finally by his family.

Vision of Judgement, The, a satirical poem by Lord *Byron, published in *The Liberal*, 1822.

In 1821 Southey's *A Vision of Judgement* appeared containing in the Preface a violent attack on Byron's works, and describing Byron as the leader of the 'Satanic school' of poetry. Byron replied with a travesty of Southey's poem. George III, at the celestial gate on his way to Heaven, is hindered by Satan's claim to his soul. Byron, attacking the pomposity and sycophancy of Southey, gives Satan and his witnesses a formidable indictment of the king's reign. Southey is swept up from the Lake District by one of the devils and offers to write Satan's biography. When he attempts to read aloud his own 'Vision' he is knocked back down to his Lakes, and George slips into Heaven.

'Vision of Mirzah, The', an allegory by *Addison, published in *The Spectator* (No. 159). Mirzah has a vision of human life as a bridge over which multitudes are passing, some dropping through concealed trap-doors into the flood beneath.

Vita Nuova, see DANTE.

VITRUVIUS POLLIO (*fl.* 40 BC), Roman architect and author of *De architectura*, the only surviving classical treatise on architecture.

Vittoria, a novel by G. *Meredith, published 1867. The continuation of Meredith's novel *Sandra Belloni*, it is set in northern Italy during the failed revolution of 1848–9, led by Mazzini, who appears as a heroic figure.

Vittoria Corombona, see WHITE DEVIL, THE.

Vivian Grey, a novel by B. *Disraeli, published 1826, with a continuation in 1827.

Vivian, a brilliant and difficult boy, is expelled from school, and discovers that by clever manipulation of his charm and social skills he can advance himself in the world of politics. He becomes the protégé of the marquis of Carabas, a powerful but disappointed politician, and by cynically playing on the follies of various discontented peers and MPs builds a faction round the marquis. His secret efforts to create a new party are exposed by the tempestuous Mrs Lorraine (a reminiscence of Lady Caroline *Lamb). Vivian is challenged to a duel by the outraged Cleveland, leader-designate of the party, whom Vivian kills. All hopes destroyed, the young man leaves England and begins a desultory life of intrigue, adventure, and lost love among German princelings and principalities. The last four Books were added by popular demand in 1827.

VIZETELLY, Henry (1820–94), engraver, publisher, journalist and editor, whose defiance of censorship and policy of issuing cheap reprints had a considerable impact on the literary scene. In 1885 he published with G. A. *Moore a cheap one-volume edition of *A Mummer's Wife*, an act which did much to break the power of the circulating *libraries and the three-decker novel; in 1886 with H. *Ellis he founded the *Mermaid Series. He also published translations, including 17 novels by *Zola; it was his publication of Zola's *La Terre* that led to his three-month imprisonment in 1888 on an obscenity charge. This bankrupted his publishing company. His memoirs, *Glances Back through Seventy Years* (1893), give a lively portrait of 19th-cent. Bohemia.

Volpone, or *The Fox*, a comedy by *Jonson, performed 1605–6, printed 1607.

Volpone, a rich Venetian without children, feigns that he is dying, in order to draw gifts from his would-be heirs. Mosca, his parasite and confederate, persuades each of these in turn that he is to be the heir, and thus extracts costly presents from them. One of them, Corvino, even attempts to sacrifice his wife to Volpone in hope of the inheritance. Finally Volpone, to enjoy the discomfiture of the vultures who are awaiting his death, makes over his property by will to Mosca and pretends to be dead. Mosca takes advantage of the situation to blackmail Volpone, but rather than be thus defeated Volpone chooses to reveal all to the authorities. They direct that Volpone shall be cast in irons, Mosca whipped and confined to the galleys, Corvino made to parade in ass's ears, and his wife be returned to her family with a trebled dowry. A secondary plot involves Sir Politic Would-be, an English traveller who has absurd schemes for improving trade and curing diseases, and his Lady. The names of the principal characters, Volpone (the Fox), Mosca (the fly), Voltore (the vulture), Corbaccio (the crow), Corvino (the raven), indicate their roles and natures.

Vǫlsunga saga, a prose version of a lost cycle of heroic songs of which fragments survive in the poetic *Edda, dealing with the families of the Volsungs and the Niblungs. For the treatment in it of the story of Sigurd and Brunhild, see SIGURD THE VOLSUNG.

VOLTAIRE, pseudonym of François-Marie Arouet (1694–1778), French satirist, novelist, historian, poet, dramatist, polemicist, moralist, critic, and correspondent. Voltaire was the universal genius of the *Enlightenment. Welcomed in the free-thinking circles of Parisian society, he was committed to the Bastille for his satires in 1717–18, and again exiled to England in 1726–9. The remainder of his life was divided between long periods of retreat in the provinces and brief returns to metropolitan centres (Paris, Versailles, Berlin). His literary principles as manifested in his epic poem *La Henriade* (1723 and 1728), and his heroic tragedies, notably *Zaire* (1732), were fundamentally *neo-classical. His political principles were essentially liberal. The *Lettres philosophiques* (1734, English version 1733), inspired by his residence in England, attack the abuses of the *ancien régime* in the name of tolerance and liberty, while his history *Le Siècle de Louis XIV* (1751) disregards providence as an explanatory principle, seeking instead evidence of social and moral progress. His most characteristic works, however, were his philosophical tales, notably *Zadig* (1747) and *Candide* (1759).

Volumnia, in Shakespeare's *Coriolanus*, the mother of Coriolanus.

VON ARNIM, Elizabeth (1866–1941), novelist and cousin of K. *Mansfield, was born Mary Annette Beauchamp in Sydney, Australia. Her best-known work, *Elizabeth and her German Garden* (1898, anonymous), describes her family life and the garden she created at Nassenheide in Pomerania. She published several novels, including *Pastor's Wife* (1912) and *Vera* (1921).

VONNEGUT, Kurt (1922–), American novelist and short story writer, whose works mingle realism, *Science Fiction, fantasy, and satire. They include *Player Piano* (1952), *Cat's Cradle* (1963), and *Slaughterhouse-Five; or The Children's Crusade* (1969).

VORAGINE, Jacobus de, see GOLDEN LEGEND.

Vorticism, an aggressive literary and artistic movement that flourished 1912–15; it attacked the sentimentality of 19th-cent. art and celebrated violence, energy, and the machine. The Vorticists, dominated by W. *Lewis, included *Pound, Gaudier-Brzeska, the painters C. R. Nevison and Edward Wadsworth; they were associated with T. E. *Hulme, F. M. *Ford, and the sculptor Jacob Epstein. In the visual arts this revolutionary fervour was expressed in abstract compositions of bold lines, sharp angles, and planes. *Blast: the Review of the Great English Vortex* (1914), edited by Lewis, was an ambitious attempt to establish in England a magazine dedicated to the modern movement and to draw together artists and writers of the avant-garde. Its long lists of the blasted and blessed, its mixture of flippancy and rhetoric, and its provocative title and typography were designed to jolt the English out of their complacent insularity.

Vortigern, a legendary 5th-cent. king of Britain who is reputed to have enlisted Hengist and Horsa against his former allies the Picts, thus causing the transfer of Britain to the Anglo-Saxons. He marries Renwein (Rowena), the daughter of Hengist. After a lifetime of feuds and alliances with the Germanic invaders, he is burnt alive in the tower in Wales to which he had retired. The story is told in *Geoffrey of Monmouth's *History* and in *Laȝamon's *Brut*.

Vortigern and Rowena, see IRELAND, W. H.

Voss, a novel by P. *White.

Vox Clamantis, see GOWER, J.

VOYNICH, Ethel Lillian, *née* Boole (1864–1960), novelist, remembered (largely in the Soviet Union) for her revolutionary novel *The Gadfly* (1897), set in pre-1848 Italy.

Vril, see COMING RACE, THE.

Vulgar Errors, see PSEUDODOXIA EPIDEMICA.

Vulgate, The, a term applied to St *Jerome's Latin version of the Bible completed in *c.*404. The Clementine text of this, a recension made by order of Clement VIII (1592–1605), is the authorized Latin text of the Roman Catholic Church. See BIBLE.

Vulgate Cycle, The, a group of Arthurian romances in French prose, dating from 1215–30. It comprises the three romances which make up the Prose *Lancelot* (*Lancelot* itself, the *Queste del Saint Graal*, and *Mort Artu*) and two others: the *Estoire del Saint Graal*, and a version of Robert de *Boron's partially surviving *Merlin*. The group is the most influential version of the Arthurian legends between *Geoffrey of Monmouth and *Malory.

Vye, Eustacia, a character in Hardy's *The Return of the Native*.

W

WACE (c.1100–after 1171), wrote in French verse of 15,000 short couplets the *Roman de Brut* (or *Geste des Bretons*), completed 1155 and dedicated to *Eleanor of Aquitaine, which is based on *Geoffrey of Monmouth's *Historia Regum Britanniae*. This work was the principal source of *Laȝamon's *Brut*. He also wrote a *Roman de Rou* (i.e. Rollo) (or *Geste des Normands*) a history of the dukes of Normandy in the course of which he provided some apparently autobiographical information. He was made a canon of Bayeux by Henry II.

Wackles, Mrs and the Misses Melissa, Sophy, and Jane, in Dickens's *The Old Curiosity Shop*, kept a 'Ladies' Seminary' at Chelsea.

WADDELL, Helen Jane (1889–1965), medieval scholar and translator, is remembered for her popular study of the 'vagantes' of the Middle Ages, *The Wandering Scholars* (1927), for her anthology of translations from their works in her *Medieval Latin Lyrics* (1929), and for her novel *Peter Abelard* (1933), based on the life of *Abelard.

Wade, Miss, a character in Dickens's *Little Dorrit*.

Wade's boat in *Chaucer's 'The Merchant's Tale' (*Canterbury Tales*, 10). According to *Skeat's note, Wade was a famous hero of antiquity who is mentioned in various poems and in *Malory. The 'tale of Wade' is also mentioned in *Troilus and Criseyde*, iii. 614. Wade (mentioned in the Old English *Widsith*, 22) was the father of Wayland, who in Norse legend built a famous boat to escape his pursuers.

Wadman, Widow, or Mrs, in Sterne's *Tristram Shandy*.

Wagg, Mr, in Thackeray's *Vanity Fair* and *Pendennis*, a parasitical journalist and diner-out, based on T. *Hook.

Waggoner, The, a poem by *Wordsworth, composed 1805, published 1819 with a dedication to Charles *Lamb.

Wagner, the attendant of Faust in Marlow's *Dr Faustus* and in *Goethe's *Faust*.

WAGNER, Richard (1813–83), German composer, dramatist, and writer, whose theories and works were the subject of vigorous controversy. A revolutionary in 1848–9, he later came under the influence of *Schopenhauer. His ideas were on the grandest scale; *Der *Ring des Nibelungen* (based on the *Nibelungenlied*) required four separate evenings for its performance. His first champion in England was G. B. *Shaw; later Ernest Newman wrote a Life (4 vols, 1933–47). *Swinburne wrote an elegy, 'The Death of Richard Wagner'; much of D. H. *Lawrence's later work is Wagnerian in its symbolism. G. A. *More and C. *Morgan make substantial reference to Wagner and it is evident in *The Waste Land*, *Ulysses*, and *Finnegans Wake*. Wolfram von Eschenbach's *Parzival* inspired Wagner's opera *Parsifal* (1882). (See also TANNHÄUSER, LOHENGRIN, MEISTERSINGER.)

WAIN, John Barrington (1925–), poet, critic, and novelist. His first novel, *Hurry On Down* (1953), is an episodic and picaresque account of the career of Charles Lumley, who, on leaving university, rejects his lower-middle-class origins by working as a window-cleaner, crook, hospital orderly, chauffeur, and bouncer. It has been seen as a manifestation of the spirit of the *'angry young men' of the 1950s. Other novels include *The Contenders* (1958), *A Travelling Woman* (1959), *Strike The Father Dead* (1962), *The Young Visitors* (1965), *The Pardoner's Tale* (1978), and *Young Shoulders* (1982). As a poet Wain was associated with the *Movement and contributed to *New Lines. He published several volumes of verse, collected in *Poems 1949–79* (1981), a volume of autobiography, *Sprightly Running* (1962), and a biography of Dr *Johnson (1974).

Waiting for Godot, the first stage play of S. *Beckett, published in French as *En attendant Godot*, 1952, staged in French in Paris, 1953, first staged in English in Cambridge, 1955.

One of the most influential plays of the post-war period, it portrays two tramps, Estragon and Vladimir, trapped in an endless waiting for the arrival of a mysterious personage named Godot. They amuse themselves meanwhile with various bouts of repartee and word-play, and are for a while diverted by the arrival of whip-cracking Pozzo, driving the oppressed and burdened Lucky on the end of a rope. Towards the end of each of the two acts, a boy arrives, heralding Godot's imminent appearance, but he does not come; each act ends with the interchange between the two tramps, 'Well, shall we go?' 'Yes, let's go', and the stage direction, 'They do not move.' There are strong biblical references throughout, but Beckett's powerful and symbolic portrayal of the human condition as one of ignorance, delusion, paralysis, and intermittent flashes of human sympathy, hope, and wit has been subjected to many varying interpretations. (See also ABSURD, THEATRE OF THE.)

Wakefield, Harry, the English drover in Scott's *The Two Drovers*.

Wakefield Master, Wakefield (or Towneley) **Plays,** see MYSTERY PLAYS.

Wakem, Mr and Philip, characters in G. Eliot's *The Mill on the Floss*.

WALCOTT, Derek Alton (1930–   ), poet and playwright, born in St Lucia. His plays include *Dream on Monkey Mountain* (1967, pub. 1971), *The Joker of Seville* (1974, pub. 1978; based on Tirso da Molina's *El Burlador de Sevilla*), and *O Babylon!* (1976, pub. 1978; set amongst a Rastafarian community in Kingston, Jamaica). His collections of poetry include *In a Green Night: Poems 1948–60* (1962), *The Castaway and other Poems* (1965), *Sea Grapes* (1976), and *The Fortunate Traveller* (1982). Both plays and poetry show a preoccupation with the national identity of the West Indies and their literature, and with the conflict between the heritage of European and West Indian culture.

Walden, or Life in the Woods, see THOREAU, H. D.

Waldenses, or **Waldensians** (in French, *Vaudois*), the adherents of a religious sect which originated in the south of France about 1170 through the preaching of Peter Waldo, a rich merchant of Lyons. They rejected the authority of the pope and various rites, and were excommunicated in 1184 and subjected to persecution. But they survived, became a separately organized church, which associated itself with the Protestant Reformation of the 16th cent. and still exists, chiefly in northern Italy and the adjacent regions. Their persecution by the duchess-regent of Savoy in 1655 led to *Milton's sonnet, 'Avenge, O Lord, thy slaughtered saints'.

'Waldhere', the name given to two short fragments of an Old English poem in a manuscript of the late 10th cent., totalling 63 lines, possibly from an epic of considerable length. The manuscript is in the Royal Library at Copenhagen. We know from other sources that Waldhere was the son of a king of Aquitaine, who was given up to Attila the Hun and became one of his generals. He escapes with Hiltgund, a Burgundian

princess to whom he had been betrothed as a child. In the course of their flight they are attacked, and Waldhere, after slaying his assailants in a fist fight, is ambushed and wounded the next day. But they are able to continue the journey and are finally married.

WALEY, Arthur David (1889–1966), poet and authority on Chinese and Japanese literature. He published *A hundred and seventy Chinese poems* (1918). His translations are unrhymed, elegant, and lucid; his use of stressed and unstressed syllables had, he believed, something in common with G. M. Hopkins's *Sprung Rhythm. His other translations in prose and verse include *The Tale of Genji* (1925–33), *The Pillow-book of Sei Shonagon* (1928, from the diary of a 10th-cent. Japanese court lady), and *Monkey* (1942, translation of a 16th-cent. Chinese novel). He was on friendly terms with many of the *Bloomsbury Group and the *Vorticists.

WALLACE, Alfred Russel (1823–1913), accompanied the naturalist Henry Walter Bates on a trip to the Amazon in 1848, an expedition described in Wallace's *Travels on the Amazon and Rio Negro* (1853). A further voyage to the Malay archipelago is described in *The Malay Archipelago* (1869). In 1858, during an attack of fever at Ternate in the Moluccas, the idea of natural selection as the solution to the problem of evolution flashed upon him, and he at once communicated it to C. *Darwin. The outcome, a testimony to the generosity of both, was the famous joint communication to the Linnean Society on the theory of evolution. He published numerous other works and scientific papers and in 1905 his autobiography, *My Life*.

WALLACE, (Richard Horatio) Edgar (1875–1932), a prolific writer of thrillers, which include *The Four Just Men* (1905), *The Crimson Circle* (1922), and *The Green Archer* (1923).

WALLACE, Sir William (?1272–1305), Scottish patriot of the time of Edward I, devoted his life to resistance to the English and is the subject of a long poem by *Henry the Minstrel.

WALLER, Edmund (1606–87), entered Parliament early and was at first an active member of the opposition. Later he became a royalist, and in 1643 was leader in a plot to seize London for Charles I. For this he was imprisoned, fined, and banished. He made his peace with *Cromwell in 1651, returned to England, and was restored to favour at the Restoration. After the death of his first wife he unsuccessfully courted Lady Dorothy Sidney, the 'Sacharissa' of his poems. Waller was a precocious poet; he wrote, probably in 1625, the complimentary piece *His Majesty's Escape at St Andere* in heroic couplets, one of the first examples of the form. His verse is of a polished simplicity; *Dryden described him as 'the father of our English numbers', linking his name with *Denham's as poets who brought in the *Augustan age. His early poems include 'On a Girdle' and 'Go, lovely rose'; his later *Instructions to a Painter* (1666) and 'Of the Last Verses in the Book'. His *Poems* first appeared in 1645, *Divine Poems* in 1685.

WALPOLE, Horace, fourth earl of Orford (1717–97), fourth son of Sir Robert *Walpole, travelled in France and Italy with *Gray during 1739–41, and met in Florence Sir Horace Mann, who became one of his most valued correspondents. Walpole was MP successively for Callington, Castle Rising, and Lynn, 1741–67. In 1747, supported by various sinecures, he settled in Twickenham in the house he made known as *Strawberry Hill: he made it into 'a little Gothic castle', aided by his fellow enthusiasts *Chute and R. *Bentley (the younger), collected in it articles of virtue, and in 1757 established there his own printing press. His first publication was Gray's Pindaric odes. In 1758 he printed several minor poems, essays, etc., as *Fugitive Pieces in verse and prose*, and in 1762 his *Anecdotes of Painting in England*. His Gothic novel *The Castle of Otranto* (1764) appeared at first pseudonymously, purporting to be a translation from an Italian work of 1529. In 1765 he paid the first of several visits to Paris, where he met Mme du Deffand, with whom he formed a lasting friendship; he was less enchanted (though not himself religious) with the prevailing atmosphere of rationalism and freethinking. In 1768 he published *Historic Doubts on the Life and Reign of King Richard the Third*, in which he attempted to acquit Richard of the crimes imputed to him by history, and in the same year appeared his tragedy *The Mysterious Mother*. In 1787/8 he met the sisters Agnes and Mary Berry, who became intimate friends of his last years; in 1791 they settled at Little Strawberry Hill.

Walpole left his Memoirs ready for publication in a sealed chest, which was opened in 1818. *Memoires of the last ten years of the Reign of George II* was edited by Lord Holland, 2 vols, 1822, and *Memoirs of the Reign of King George the Third* by D. Le Marchant, 4 vols, 1845. His literary reputation rests largely on his letters which are remarkable for their charm, their wit, and their autobiographical, political, and social interest. His model was Mme de Sévigné, whose letters he greatly admired, and he clearly wrote for posterity as well as for his correspondents. His letters to Mme du Deffand were destroyed at his own wish; hers to him were edited by Mrs Paget Toynbee in 1912. Later editions of his correspondence, with recent biographies (e.g. R. W. Ketton-Cremer, *Horace Walpole*, 1946) have done much to dispel the 19th-cent. image of Walpole, inspired by *Macaulay's famous attack

in the *Edinburgh Review*, 1833, as a malicious and affected gossip, though even Macaulay had allowed that he possessed 'irresistible charm'. His name has also been cleared of the accusation that he hastened *Chatterton's suicide by his neglect.

WALPOLE, Sir Hugh Seymour (1884–1941), novelist, was born in New Zealand and came to England aged five. His short experience of teaching is reflected in his third novel, *Mr Perrin and Mr Traill* (1911), which set a vogue for novels and plays about schoolmasters. Other works include the *Herries Chronicle*, a historical sequence set in Cumberland consisting of *Rogue Herries* (1930), *Judith Paris* (1931), *The Fortress* (1932), and *Vanessa* (1933). Although proud of his popularity, he worried that his work was 'old-fashioned' and expressed envy of the *modernism of his friend and correspondent V. *Woolf.

WALPOLE, Sir Robert, first earl of Orford (1676–1745), father of Horace *Walpole, and the leader of the Whig party, was prime minister and chancellor of the exchequer 1715–17, and again 1721–42. His longstanding relationship with his mistress Maria Skerrett (whom he married on his wife's death in 1737) is satirized in Gay's *The Beggar's Opera*. In 1737, provoked by this and other satirical attacks in the threatre (by *Fielding in particular), he introduced the Licensing Act, which has been blamed for the decline of the drama in the 18th cent.

WALTON, Izaak (1593–1683), was a friend of *Donne and *Wotton and of bishops Morley, Sanderson, and *King. His biographies of Donne (1640), Wotton (1651), *Hooker (1665), G. *Herbert (1670), and Sanderson (1678) are gentle and admiring in tone. He is chiefly known for *The Compleat Angler*, first published 1653, and largely re-written for the second edition (1655). (See also COTTON.)

WALTON, Sir William Turner (1902–83), English composer, whose early association with the *Sitwell family was the background to his 'entertainment' *Façade* (1922), for reciter with six instrumental soloists; twenty-one of Edith Sitwell's poems were accompanied by a score skilfully adapted to the rhythms, sounds, and allusions of the words. Osbert Sitwell contributed, from biblical sources, the score of Walton's dramatic cantata, *Belshazzar's Feast* (1931). The choral work *In Honour of the City of London* (1937) is a setting of *Dunbar, and Walton's opera *Troilus and Cressida* (1954) is adapted from *Chaucer. Walton also wrote the incidental music for Laurence Olivier's three Shakespeare films (*Henry V*, 1944; *Hamlet*, 1947; and *Richard III*, 1955), and the score for a stage production of *Macbeth* (1941).

WALWYN, William (*fl.* 1649), pamphleteer and a leader of the Leveller movement. He was imprisoned in 1649 with *Lilburne, *Overton, and T. Prince as one of the authors of *England's New Chains discovered*, and was accused of communism and atheism. He was released later that year, after the publication of *Walwyn's Just Defence*.

Wamba, in Scott's *Ivanhoe*, the heroic jester of Cedric the Saxon.

Wanderer, The, an Old English poem of 115 lines in the *Exeter Book, telling of the hardships of a man who has lost his lord. It is a plangent lament for the transience of life, culminating towards its end in a powerful *'ubi sunt' passage. It begins and ends with a brief and bald statement of Christian consolation. It is paralleled in spirit and structure by the *Seafarer. The poem was admired by *Auden, among other modern poets, and he translated it loosely.

Wanderer, The, a poem in five cantos by R. *Savage (1729).

Wandering Jew, The, a Jew condemned to wander about the world until Christ's second coming because, according to the legend, as Christ bore the cross to Calvary the Jew chid him, and urged him to go faster.

A pamphlet was published in Leyden in 1602, relating that Paulus von Eizen, bishop of Schleswig, had in 1542 met a man named Ahasuerus, who declared that he was the Jew in question. The story, which had previously flourished in Spain and Italy, became popular, and many instances of the Wandering Jew are recorded from the 16th to the 19th cents.

But a somewhat similar story is told much earlier by *Roger of Wendover, in his *Flores Historiarum*. An Armenian archbishop visited England in 1228, and, while being entertained at St Albans, was asked if he had ever seen or heard of Joseph, who was present at the Crucifixion, and was said to be still alive, as a testimony to the Christian faith. The prelate replied that the man had recently dined at his own table. He had been Pontius Pilate's porter, by name Cartaphilus, who, when they were dragging Jesus from the Judgement Hall, had struck him on the back, saying, 'Go faster, Jesus, why dost thou linger?', to which Jesus replied, 'I indeed am going, but thou shalt tarry till I come.' This man had been converted soon after and named Joseph. He lived for ever, and was now a very grave and holy person.

The legend of the Wandering Jew has been the subject of many German works; *Goethe contemplated (but did not write) a poem on the subject of a meeting of Ahasuerus and Spinoza. There are elements of the story in Lewis's *The Monk* and Maturin's *Melmoth the Wanderer*, a ballad on the subject is in Percy's *Reliques, and *Croly wrote a version called *Salathiel: a story of the past, the present and the future* (1828), in which the Wanderer takes on a tragic nationalist grandeur.

Wandering Willie, (1) Willie Steenson, the blind fiddler in Scott's *Redgauntlet; (2) the name of a song by *Burns.

WANLEY, Humfrey (1672–1726), an assistant in the Bodleian Library in 1696. He displayed remarkable skill in palaeography and produced in 1705 a catalogue of Anglo-Saxon manuscripts, which is still the standard work. He began the catalogue of the *Harleian MSS, a work on which he was engaged when he died.

WANLEY, Nathaniel (1634–80), divine and father of Humfrey *Wanley. He published *The Wonders of the Little World* (1678), a collection of tales and superstitions in which R. *Browning found the story of the 'Pied Piper of Hamelin' and other oddities.

WARBURTON, Eliot (Bartholomew Eliott George) (1810–52), is remembered for his account of an eastern tour, *The Crescent and the Cross: or romance and realities of Eastern travel* (1845), a highly successful work which covered much the same ground as his friend *Kinglake's *Eothen*. He also wrote two historical novels, *Reginald Hastings* (1850) and *Darien* (1852).

WARBURTON, John (1682–1759), herald and antiquary, an indefatigable collector of rare manuscripts. Most of the rare Elizabethan and Jacobean plays in his possession were through his own 'carelessness and the ignorance' of Betsy Baker, his servant, 'unluckily burned or put under pye bottoms'.

WARBURTON, William (1698–1779), rose to be bishop of Gloucester in 1759. He was much engaged in theological controversy, writing with vigour and arrogance. He was author of *The Divine Legation of Moses* (1738–41), *A View of Lord Bolingbroke's Philosophy* (1754), attacking *Bolingbroke's views on natural religion, and *The Doctrine of Grace* (1762), attacking the 'enthusiasm' of *Wesley. He brought out in 1747 an edition of Shakespeare in 8 volumes which was sharply criticized as unscholarly, and in 1751 an edition of *Pope's works. He was Pope's literary executor, and is said to have encouraged him in the composition of *The New Dunciad*.

WARD, Artemus, see BROWNE, C. F.

WARD, Edward ('Ned') (1667–1731), tavern keeper and writer of *Hudibrastic sketches of London life. Some of the best of these are contained in *The London-Spy* (1698–1709). His

Hudibras Redivivus, a burlesque poem, was published in 1705-7.

WARD, Mary Augusta, better known as Mrs Humphry Ward (1851-1920), was grand-daughter of T. *Arnold of Rugby. In 1872 she married Thomas Humphry Ward. Her most famous novel, *Robert Elsmere* (1888), is in part a vivid evocation of the Oxford of *Pater, *Pattison, and T. H. *Green, and of the many varieties of religious faith and doubt which succeeded the ferment of the *Oxford Movement. Its protagonist, an earnest but questioning clergyman, resigns his orders for a life of social service in the East End, to the distress of his devout wife Catherine. The novel was reviewed by *Gladstone and initiated much debate. Most of her other novels deal with social and religious themes, frequently contrasting traditional belief with the values of progress and intellectual freedom; they include *The History of David Grieve* (1892) and *The Marriage of William Ashe* (1905). She supported the movement for higher education for women, but opposed women's suffrage on the grounds that women's influence was stronger in the home than in public life. Her *A Writer's Recollections* (1918) draws a striking picture of Oxford life and of the domestic influence of W. *Morris, Burne-Jones, and Liberty prints.

WARD, Plumer (formerly Robert) (1765-1846), a lawyer and MP. When he was sixty he became, somewhat eccentrically, an exponent of the *Fashionable novel with the publication of his first novel, *Tremaine, or a Man of Refinement* (1825). In 1827 appeared *De Vere, or the Man of Independence* and in 1841 *De Clifford, or the Constant Man*. All are lengthy, ponderous works, in which (to use the author's own words of *Tremaine*) 'variety and incident are equally wanting'.

WARD, William George (1812-82), theologian, fellow of Balliol College, Oxford, and a follower of *Newman. In 1844 he published *The Ideal of a Christian Church* in praise of the Roman Catholic Church from which he gained the title 'Ideal' Ward. He was subsequently deprived of his degrees for heresy, and in 1845 joined the Roman Catholic Church. (See OXFORD MOVEMENT.)

Warden, The, a novel by A. *Trollope, published in 1855, and the first in the *'Barsetshire' series.

The income of Hiram's Hospital, a charitable institution, has grown in real terms down the centuries, but the twelve old bedesmen have not benefited. The surplus has created a pleasant sinecure for the mild-mannered old Warden, the Revd Septimus Harding, a fact which John Bold, a local surgeon with a passion for causes,

makes known to the national press. Harding finds himself the object of unpleasant publicity, and his son-in-law, the combative Archdeacon Grantly, bullies him to dispute the case along party lines. But Harding with considerable personal courage resigns. The novel ends with Bold withdrawing his accusations and marrying the Warden's daughter Eleanor, and Harding receiving a new preferment in the Cathedral Close.

Warden, Henry, in Scott's *The Monastery* and *The Abbot*, an earnest Protestant divine.

Wardle, Mr, a character in Dickens's *Pickwick Papers*.

Wardour, Sir Arthur, and his son and daughter Captain Reginald and Isabella, characters in Scott's *The Antiquary*.

WARNER, Rex (1905-86), poet, novelist, and translator, educated at Wadham College, Oxford, where he was a close friend of *Auden and *Day-Lewis. His first volume of poetry, *Poems* (1937), shares their Messianic revolutionary fervour. Warner's early novels, which include *The Wild Goose Chase* (1937), *The Professor* (1938), and *The Aerodrome* (1941), are more sombre, Kafkaesque political parables, which reflect the gathering gloom of the 1930s. His later fiction is based largely on Greek or Roman historical subjects, and he also translated the *Medea* (1944), *Hippolytus* (1950), and *Helen* (1951) of *Euripides, and the *Prometheus Bound* (1947) of *Aeschylus.

WARNER, Sylvia Townsend (1893-1978), novelist and poet. Her first volume of verse, *The Espalier* (1925), was followed by several others, including *Whether a Dove or a Seagull* (1933), written in collaboration with her friend and companion Valentine Ackland; the posthumous *Twelve Poems* (1980); and *Collected Poems* (1982). Her original voice is heard more strongly in her novels, which include *Lolly Willowes* (1926), a tale of the supernatural; *Mr Fortune's Maggot* (1927), which describes the visit of ex-clerk missionary Timothy Fortune to the remote South Sea island of Fanua, where he makes only one doubtful convert and in the process loses his own faith through his love of the islanders; and *The True Heart* (1929), which retells the story of *Cupid and Psyche through the medium of a Victorian orphan, Sukey Bond. Her later works include a biography of T. H. *White (1967), and various collections of short stories.

WARNER, William (c.1558-1609), published *Pan his Syrinx*, seven prose tales (1584). His chief work was *Albions England*, a metrical British history, with mythical and fictitious episodes, extending in the first edition (1586) from Noah to the Norman Conquest. It was brought up to Elizabeth's reign in 1592; and a complete edition, reaching James I, was published posthumously (1612). *Meres, in his *Palladis Tamia* (1598), claimed to have heard Warner called 'our English *Homer*', and *Drayton praised him in his elegy *To Henery Reynolds*.

War of the Worlds, The, a *Science Fiction fantasy by H. G. *Wells, published 1898. It describes the arrival of the Martians in Woking, driven from their own planet by its progressive cooling to take refuge in a warmer world. In a letter Wells described his plan for the work, in which: 'I completely wreck and sack Woking —killing my neighbours in painful and eccentric ways—then proceed via Kingston and Richmond to London, selecting South Kensington for feats of peculiar atrocity'; much of the novel's power depends on the contrast between the familiar stupid bourgeois complacent reactions of the humans and the terrifying destructive intelligence of the Martians, which consist of round bodies, each about 4 feet in diameter, each body containing a huge brain. They live by the injection into themselves of the fresh living blood of other creatures, mostly of human beings, and they devastate the country before eventually falling victims to terrestrial bacteria. A broadcast by Orson Welles of a dramatization of the novel in the US on 30 Oct. 1938 caused a furore, many of its millions of listeners taking it for a factual report of the invasion by Martians of New Jersey.

WARREN, Robert Penn (1905–   ), American poet, novelist, and critic. His novels include *All the King's Men* (1946), a study of a power-crazed, corrupt Southern politician, Willie Stark, and his volumes of poetry include *Selected Poems 1923– 43* (1944) and *Promises* (1957). His critical works are associated with the *New Criticism, and include two anthologies-with-commentaries, compiled in collaboration with Cleanth Brooks, *Understanding Poetry* (1938) and *Understanding Fiction* (1943).

WARREN, Samuel (1807–77), studied medicine and became successively barrister, recorder of Hull, MP for Midhurst, and master of lunacy. From early youth he aimed for literary fame. His *Passages from the Diary of a Late Physician* (1832–8) provoked criticism from the *Lancet* for revealing professional secrets. Warren is chiefly remembered as the author of the sensationally popular *Ten Thousand a Year* (1840–1), a story of greed and imposture concerning Mr Titlebat Titmouse, a draper's assistant who inherits a vast fortune by way of documents forged by the lawyers Quirk, Gammon, and Snap.

Warrington, George, a character in Thackeray's *Pendennis*, and *The Newcomes*. He is a

descendant of the Warringtons in *The Virginians*.

Wart, Thomas, in Shakespeare's 2 *Henry IV*, one of the recruits for Falstaff's force.

WARTON, Joseph (1722–1800), brother of Thomas *Warton the younger, held various livings and was a conspicuously unsuccessful headmaster of Winchester (1766–93). He is better remembered as a critic of wide knowledge and independent judgement. His *An Essay on the Writings and Genius of Pope* (1756, 1782) distinguishes between the poets of 'the sublime and pathetic' (see SUBLIME) and the 'men of wit and sense'. He was elected a member of the *Club in 1777 at Dr *Johnson's request.

WARTON, Thomas (c.1688–1745), father of Joseph and Thomas *Warton, was from 1718 to 1728 professor of poetry at Oxford; his poems, including some 'runic odes', were published posthumously in 1748, edited by his son Thomas.

WARTON, Thomas (1728–90), brother of Joseph *Warton, was professor of poetry at Oxford (1757–67), and became poet laureate in 1785, an appointment celebrated in the *Probationary Odes* (see ROLLIAD). His many poetic works included odes, sonnets (a form then unfashionable, which he did much to revive), and light verse; he edited the early poems of *Milton (1785), He also edited *The Oxford Sausage* (1764), a celebrated miscellany of university verse. He was elected to Dr Johnson's *Club in 1782. He is best remembered for his valuable work *The History of English Poetry* (3 vols, 1774–81), the first literary history of any real scope, which throws much light on the taste of the time and the interest in *primitivism, and has been seen as an important stage in the transition towards *Romanticism.

Warwick, Mrs, the heroine of Meredith's *Diana of the Crossways*.

Washington Square, a novel by H. *James, published 1881.
   Catherine Sloper lives in Washington Square with her widowed father, a rich physician. She is plain, without social graces or conversation. Dr Sloper is disappointed that she has nothing of her dead mother's beauty and wit. When the handsome, but penniless and indolent, Morris Townsend begins to court her, he casts him as a fortune-hunter. Both Catherine's romantic hopes and Morris's pecuniary ones are encouraged by the girl's silly aunt, Lavinia Penniman. Dr Sloper will disinherit Catherine if she marries Morris, and he jilts her. Catherine, despised by her father, pitied by her aunt, refuses later chances of a suitable match and withdraws into a

lonely humdrum life. After her father's death (cautiously, he has largely disinherited her in any case) Morris reappears to try his luck again. His continued lack of success has made him less ambitious. But Catherine finds no charm in this balding middle-aged stranger. With some bitter reminders of his past cruelty, she turns him away. This novel has been filmed and re-entitled *The Heiress*.

Waste Land, The, a poem by T. S. *Eliot, first published 1922 in *The Criterion*.

It consists of five sections, 'The Burial of the Dead', 'A Game of Chess', 'The Fire Sermon', 'Death by Water', and 'What the Thunder Said', together with Eliots own 'Notes' which explain his many varied and multicultural allusions, quotations, and half-quotations (from *Webster, *Dante, Verlaine, *Kyd, etc.), and express a general indebtedness to the *Grail legend and to the vegetation ceremonies in *Frazer's *The Golden Bough*. The poem was rapidly acclaimed as a statement of the post-war sense of depression and futility; it was seriously praised by I. A. *Richards as 'a perfect emotive description of a state of mind which is probably inevitable for a while to all meditative people' (*Science and Poetry*, 1926), and less seriously but significantly chanted as a kind of protest against the older generation by the undergraduates of the day. Complex, erudite, cryptic, satiric, spiritually earnest, and occasionally lyrical, it became one of the most recognizable landmarks of *modernism, an original voice speaking through many echoes and parodies of echoes. Eliot himself remarked that the poem could be seen not so much as 'an important bit of social criticism', but as 'the relief of a personal and wholly insignificant grouse against life; it is just a piece of rhythmical grumbling.'

Watchman, The (1796), a political and literary journal, of ten issues only, produced by *Coleridge.

Water-Babies, The: *A Fairy Tale for a Land-Baby*, by C. *Kingsley, published 1863 (serialized in *Macmillan's Magazine* 1862–3).

The story tells of the adventures of Tom, the chimney-sweep, employed by the bully Mr Grimes. Tom stumbles down a chimney into the bedroom of a little girl, Ellie, and for the first time he becomes aware of his own grimy body; he runs away, hounded by the household, falls into a river, and is transformed into a water-baby. In his underwater life he makes the acquaintance of many vividly realized creatures, from caddis flies to salmon, and also of Mrs Doasyouwouldbedoneby and Mrs Bedonebyasyoudid, who play a large part in the moral re-education which finally unites him with Ellie. The story remains popular with children today, though it also provides rich opport-

unities for psychoanalytic interpretation, much of it based on Kingsley's obsession with water, washing, and the public-school cold bath.

WATERHOUSE, Keith Spencer (1929–), journalist, novelist, and dramatist, had considerable success with his second novel, *Billy Liar*, a regional comedy about a youth who attempts to escape his dull family life through fantasy, which he adapted for the stage in collaboration with W. *Hall (1960). Waterhouse and Hall subsequently worked together on many stage, screen, and television plays, adaptations, and musicals.

Waterloo, see WELLINGTON.

Water-Poet, The, see TAYLOR, JOHN.

WATKINS, Vernon Phillips (1906–67), poet, lived most of his life in and near Swansea and was for many years a friend of Dylan *Thomas. His first volume demonstrated his range; the title poem of *Ballad of the Mari Lwyd* (1941) is a long, rhetorical piece rooted in Welsh folklore and mythology, whereas 'The Collier' and other poems are marked by simplicity and a restrained compassion. Watkins's lyric gift was developed in many subsequent volumes, including *The Lamp and the Veil* (1945), *Cypress and Acacia* (1959), and *Fidelities* (1968), and his *Selected Poems 1930–60* appeared in 1967. He translated, and was influenced by, German and French poetry.

Watson, Dr, companion of Sherlock *Holmes, a character created by A. C. *Doyle.

WATSON, John, see KAILYARD SCHOOL.

WATSON, Richard (1737–1816), from 1782 bishop of Llandaff, wrote a notable *Apology for Christianity* (1776) and an *Apology for the Bible* (1796). *Wordsworth's *Letter to the Bishop of Llandaff*, not published until 1876, was a reply to Watson's sermon on 'The Wisdom and Goodness of God in having made both Rich and Poor'.

WATSON, Thomas (*c*.1557–92), published a Latin version of the *Antigone* of *Sophocles, with an appendix of Latin allegorical poems and experiments in classical metres (1581). His most important work was The Ἑκατομπα Θια or *Passionate Centurie of Love* (1582), 18-line poems, called sonnets, often based on classical, French, and Italian sources, and accompanied by learned explanatory notes. He published a Latin version of *Tasso's *Aminta* (1585) and *The first Sett of Italian Madrigalls Englished* (1590), which were set to music by William Byrd. A few of his previously unpublished poems were included in *The Phoenix Nest* and *Englands Helicon*. His 'sonnets', among the earliest in English, were an influence on Shakespeare and others.

Watsons, The, an unfinished novel by J. *Austen, written some time between 1804 and 1807.

The story largely concerns the unremitting efforts of Emma Watson's three sisters to get themselves married. Emma, a pretty, sensible girl, has been brought up by a well-to-do aunt. She returns to her family, who live in genteel poverty in a Surrey village, where she is surrounded by people in every way inferior to herself. Even her good-natured sister Elizabeth is as intent on a good match as her unpleasant sisters Margaret and Penelope. The other principal characters are Lady Osborne, handsome and dignified; her son, Lord Osborne, a fine but cold young man; Mr Howard, a gentlemanly clergyman; and Tom Musgrave, a cruel and hardened flirt. The author left no hint as to the future course of events.

WATT, Robert (1774–1819), Scottish bibliographer, is remembered for his remarkable *Bibliotheca Britannica, or a general Index to British and Foreign Literature,* published in 1824.

WATTS, Isaac (1674–1748), became a minister, but was forced into early retirement by ill health. He published four collections of verse, *Horae Lyricae* (1706), *Hymns and Spiritual Songs* (1707), *Divine Songs for the Use of Children* (1715), and *The Psalms of David Imitated* (1719). He is chiefly remembered for his hymns, which include 'O God, our help in ages past' and 'When I survey the wondrous Cross', and for his songs for children ('How doth the little busy bee'), some of which foreshadow those of *Blake. But he was also the author of Pindaric Odes, blank verse, and of daring technical experiments such as his alarming 'The Day of Judgement' (1706), in English Sapphics. He was included in *The Lives of the English Poets* at Johnson's own suggestion.

WATTS-DUNTON, (Walter) Theodore (1832–1914), gave up his profession as solicitor to devote himself to literature. He reviewed for the *Examiner, then from 1876 to 1902 was an influential writer for the *Athenaeum, and as its chief poetry reviewer he supported the work of his friends in the *Pre-Raphaelite movement. Like *Borrow, whom he met in 1872, he was much interested in the gypsies and uses gypsy settings in his novel *Aylwin* (1898), a curious work which recounts the love of Henry Aylwin for a Welsh girl, Winifred, his separation from her through a Gnostic curse, and his pursuit of her until their final reunion. His other works include sketches of *Rossetti, *Tennyson, etc., collected as *Old Familiar Faces* (1916), and an essay, 'The Renascence of Wonder in English Poetry' (in Chambers's *Cyclopaedia of English Literature,* Vol. iii, 1901), in which he strongly defends the Romantic movement. He is prob-

ably best remembered, however, for his loyal support of *Swinburne, who lived with him from 1879 until his death at The Pines, Putney.

WAUGH, Alec (Alexander Raban) (1898–1981), novelist and travel writer, brother of Evelyn *Waugh. His first novel, *The Loom of Youth* (1917), became a *succès de scandale* through its colourful suggestions of public-school homosexuality. It was followed by many others, including *Island in the Sun* (1956), and several autobiographical volumes.

WAUGH, Evelyn Arthur St John (1903–66), novelist, educated at Hertford College, Oxford. He worked for some years (unhappily) as assistant schoolmaster in various posts which provided material for *Decline and Fall* (1928), his first and immensely successful novel, which followed the publication of an essay on the *Pre-Raphaelites (1926). In 1928 he was received into the Roman Catholic Church. His career as a novelist prospered, with *Vile Bodies* (1930, set in Mayfair), *Black Mischief* (1932, set in Africa), *A Handful of Dust* (1934), and *Scoop* (1938), works of high comedy and social satire which capture the brittle, cynical, determined frivolity of the post-war generation. He also established himself as journalist and travel writer with accounts of a journey through Africa (*Remote People,* 1931), a journey through South America (*Ninety-two Days,* 1934), and Mussolini's invasion of Abyssinia (*Waugh in Abyssinia,* 1936).

Put Out More Flags (1942) was written while he was serving in the Royal Marines, and his wartime experiences in Crete and Yugoslavia appear in his trilogy *Sword of Honour* (1965), originally published as *Men at Arms* (1952), *Officers and Gentlemen* (1955), and *Unconditional Surrender* (1961). In the interim appeared *Brideshead Revisited* (1945), and a macabre comedy about Californian funeral practices, *The Loved One* (1948). *The Ordeal of Gilbert Pinfold* (1957) is a bizarre novel about a famous 50-year-old Roman Catholic novelist who sets off on a cruise to Ceylon to escape growing hallucinations, but becomes increasingly paranoid, imagining himself accused of being homosexual, Jewish, Fascist, alcoholic, a social climber, etc.; it is a self-caricature which ends in salvation. He casts an equally cold eye on himself in his revealing *Diaries* (1976, ed. M. Davie).

Waverley, the first of the novels of Sir W. *Scott, published 1814.

Edward Waverley, a romantic young man, has been brought up in part by his father, a Hanoverian in politics, in part by his uncle Sir Everard Waverley, a rich landowner of Jacobite leanings. Obtaining a commission in the army in 1745, he joins his regiment in Scotland, and there, while on leave, visits his uncle's friend, the baron of Bradwardine, a kind-hearted but pedantic old Jacobite, and attracts the favourable notice of the gentle Rose, his daughter. Impelled by curiosity, he visits Donald Bean Lean, a Highland freebooter, in his lair, and Fergus Mac-Ivor Vich Ian Vohr of Glennaquoich, a young Highland chieftain, active in the Jacobite interest. He falls in love with Fergus's sister Flora. These visits, injudicious in an officer of the British army at a time of acute political tension, compromise Edward with his colonel. He moreover falls a victim to Jacobite intrigues, finds himself accused of fomenting mutiny in his regiment, and is finally cashiered and arrested. Rescued by the action of the devoted Rose, and under the influence of a sense of unjust treatment, Flora's enthusiasm, and a gratifying reception by Prince Charles Edward, he joins the Jacobite forces. At the battle of Prestonpans he has the good fortune to save from death Colonel Talbot, a distinguished English officer and friend of his family, and the latter, after the final defeat and dispersal of the Pretender's Army, secures Edward's pardon and the rehabilitation of the baron. Meanwhile Edward has been decisively rejected by the spirited Flora, and has turned his affections to Rose, to whom in due course he is married. Fergus is convicted of high treason and bravely meets his end, and Flora retires to a convent.

Among the minor characters may be mentioned Davie Gellatley, the 'innocent', the mouthpiece of some of Scott's most beautiful lyrics; and Colonel Gardiner, Edward Waverley's commanding officer (see DODDRIDGE).

Waves, The, a novel by V. *Woolf, published 1931, and regarded by many as her masterpiece.

It traces the lives of a group of friends (Bernard, Susan, Rhoda, Neville, Jinny, and Louis) from childhood to late middle age, evoking their personalities through their reflections on themselves and on one another. Their individuality is presented through a highly patterned sequence of recurring phrases and images, and what we learn of their daily lives (that Susan marries a farmer, that Bernard's ambitions as a writer are disappointed, that Louis becomes a man of power and wealth) we learn obliquely. The main text is introduced and divided by sections of lyrical prose describing the rising and sinking of the sun over a seascape of waves and shore. There is one additional character, Percival: his death in India, half-way through the novel, becomes the focus for fears and defiance of death and mortality. One of the dominant images of the novel, used by phrasemaker Bernard, is that of a fin breaking from the water; this was, as Woolf's diary reveals, her starting-point for the work.

Way of All Flesh, The, a novel by S. *Butler, published posthumously 1903.

In this study of four generations, dissecting the stultifying effects of inherited family traits and attitudes, many experiences of Butler's life are clearly visible. The story (narrated by a family friend, Overton) was originally called *Ernest Pontifex*; Ernest is the awkward and unhappy great-grandson of John Pontifex, a village carpenter, whose natural instinctive character he comes to revere. His own father, Theo, is a tyrannical, canting parent, repeating the attitudes of Ernest's grandfather, George. After his ordination the inept Ernest, taking a respectable woman for a prostitute, is sentenced to prison, where he tries to free himself from his immediate forbears and return to the simplicity of Old Pontifex. On his release he plunges into a disastrous union with Ellen, a drunken maidservant. Fortunately she turns out to be already married, and Ernest's beloved aunt Alethea leaves him sufficient money to devote himself to literature.

Way of the World, The, a comedy by *Congreve, produced 1700. This is the most finished of Congreve's comedies, but it was not very well received.

Mirabell is in love with Millamant, a niece of Lady Wishfort, and has pretended to make love to the aunt in order to conceal his suit of the niece. The deceit has been revealed to Lady Wishfort by Mrs Marwood to revenge herself on Mirabell, who has rejected her advances. Lady Wishfort determines to disinherit her niece if she marries Mirabell. Mirabell contrives an elaborate plot to trick Lady Wishfort into consent to his marriage: the counterplots of Mrs Marwood (who threatens to reveal Mirabell's past intrigues with Lady Wishfort's daughter Mrs Fainall) at first prevail, but eventually her own intrigue with Fainall is exposed, and Mirabell is forgiven.

Congreve enlivens the action with a fine gallery of fools, including Sir Wilfull Witwoud, Lady Wishfort's boisterous and good-natured country nephew; they serve to highlight the central contrast between the passionate and grasping relationship of Fainall and Mrs Marwood and the delicate process by which Mirabell persuades Millamant that even in such a mercenary society, love can survive into marriage. The dialogue is exceptionally brilliant, and many critics also consider the play a study of the battle between good and evil, rather than of the characteristically *Restoration conflict between the witty and the foolish.

Way We Live Now, The, a novel by A. *Trollope, published 1875.

Augustus Melmotte has the reputation of a great financier. Yet no one thinks to examine the nature of the Melmotte millions until he is caught forging the title deeds to one of the estates he is buying up. Subsequent inquiries into Melmotte's prize speculation, a Central American railway, prove it to be a gigantic confidence trick, and when it becomes clear that he has tampered with his daughter's trust fund, his disgrace is absolute. After a drunken appearance in the House of Commons he commits suicide. The sordidness of Melmotte's career is matched by his daughter Marie's experiences in the marriage-mart. She is treated as a commodity by the cautious Lord Nidderdale, and when the dissipated Carbury entices her to elope with him she steals the money necessary for the elopement, but Carbury does not keep his appointment, having gambled the money away. At the end of the novel she marries Hamilton K. Fisker, a leading promoter of the American railway scheme.

Weak ending, the occurrence of an unstressed or proclitic monosyllable (such as a preposition, conjunction, or auxiliary verb) in the normally stressed place at the end of an iambic line.

Wealth of Nations, Inquiry into the Nature and Causes of the, a treatise on political economy by Adam *Smith, published 1776.

Smith's work is the first comprehensive treatment of the whole subject of political economy, and is remarkable for its breadth of view. The work sets out with the doctrine that the labour of the nation is the source of its means of life. In a more advanced state of society three elements enter into price—wages, profit, and rent—and these elements are discussed separately.

The second book deals with capital, its nature, accumulation, and employment. Smith's political economy is essentially individualistic; self-interest is the proper criterion of economic action. But the universal pursuit of one's own advantage contributes, in his view, to the public interest.

WEBB, Beatrice, *née* Potter (1858–1943), married Sidney Webb (1859–1947), the son of a London shopkeeper, in 1892. Both were leading spirits in the *Fabian Society, and they produced jointly numerous works on social history, served on many royal commissions, and helped to found the London School of Economics. Beatrice also wrote two autobiographical works (*My Apprenticeship,* 1926; *Our Partnership,* 1948), and kept a remarkable diary of which selections were published in 1952 and 1956, ed. M. Cole; the first volume of a fuller four-volume edition, ed. N. and J. Mackenzie, appeared in 1982. These show the width of her human and intellectual interests and considerable literary skill, and are a valuable record of social life and progressive thought of the period.

WEBB, (Gladys) Mary *née* Meredith (1881–1927), novelist. Her works include *The Golden Arrow* (1916), *Gone to Earth* (1917), and *The House in Dormer Forest* (1920). They are tales of rustic life, romantic, passionate, morbid, and frequently naïve, written in a fervid prose easily ridiculed by Stella Gibbons in *Cold Comfort Farm,* but they nevertheless retain a certain emotional power. Stanley Baldwin wrote an introduction (1928) to a reprint of *Precious Bane* (1924), her most famous novel, praising her lyrical intensity, and her evocation of the Shropshire landscape.

WEBB, Sidney, see WEBB, BEATRICE.

WEBSTER, John (*c.*1578–*c.*1632), combined the careers of coachmaker and playwright. He wrote several plays in collaboration with other dramatists; these include *Westward Hoe* and *Northward Hoe,* with *Dekker (both printed 1607); and *A Cure for a Cuckold* (printed 1661), probably with *Rowley (and possibly *Heywood). He expanded Marston's *The Malcontent* for the *King's Men in 1604, and published elegies on Prince Henry in 1613 with Heywood and *Tourneur. His great reputation rests on his two major works, *The White Devil* (pub. 1612) and *The Duchess of Malfi* (pub. 1623). With these two tragedies Webster has achieved a reputation second only to Shakespeare's. The 20th cent. has seen a strong revival of interest in the plays as drama, and in Webster as a satirist and moralist.

WEBSTER, Noah (1758–1843), American lexicographer and philologist, is remembered for his great and scholarly *An American Dictionary of the English Language* (2 vols, 1828). (See also DICTIONARY.)

WEDGWOOD, Dame (Cicely) Veronica (1910–   ), historian. Her publications include *Strafford* (1935), *The Thirty Years' War* (1938), *Oliver Cromwell* (1939, rev. 1973), *The King's Peace* (1955), *The King's War* (1958), and *The Great Rebellion* (1966).

WEELKES, Thomas (?1576–1623), English composer. With *Wilbye, he was the most important of the English madrigalists who followed the lead given by *Morley in 1593 and 1594. He published several volumes of *madrigals and contributed one of the finest madrigals to *The Triumphes of Oriana* in 1601. Weelkes is one of the composers whose imagination is most evidently fired by the bold and vivid imagery of the age of *Donne.

'Wee Willie Winkie', a short story by Rudyard *Kipling.

Wegg, Silas, in Dickens's *Our Mutual Friend,* a one-legged impudent old rascal.

Weir of Hermiston, an unfinished novel by R. L. *Stevenson, published 1896.

Archie Weir is the only child of Adam Weir, Lord Hermiston, the lord justice clerk, a formidable 'hanging judge', based on the character of Robert Macqueen, Lord Braxfield (1722–99), known as 'the Jeffrey of Scotland'. His mother, a pale, ineffectual, religious woman, dies young, leaving Archie to the care of a father he dreads and dislikes. The conflict between the two comes to a head when Archie witnesses his father hounding a wretched criminal to death at a trial with sadistic glee; he publicly confronts his father, speaking out against capital punishment, and is banished to Hermiston, a remote Lowland village. There he lives as a recluse with Kirstie, his devoted housekeeper and distant relative, who is aunt to four notable brothers, the 'Black Elliotts', famed for hunting down their father's murderer. Archie falls in love with their sister, and Kirstie's niece, Christina. The novel ends as Archie, warned by the jealous Kirstie, tells Christina that their secret meetings must end. We know from Stevenson's notes that the novel was to end with another confrontation between father and son, in which Archie is on trial for his life for the alleged murder of Christina's seducer, Frank Innes. Archie and Christina escape to America, but the old man dies of shock. Critics agree that it promised to be the most ambitious and profound of his works.

WELCH, (Maurice) Denton (1915–48), writer. He intended to be a painter, but in 1935 was severely injured in a bicycle accident; he was an invalid for the rest of his life. A volume of autobiography, *Maiden Voyage* (1943), was followed by a novel about adolescence, *In Youth is Pleasure* (1944), and a volume of short stories, *Brave and cruel, and other stories* (1949). His unfinished, autobiographical *A Voice Through a Cloud* (1950) is a vivid, heightened, and at times painfully sensitive account of accident and illness.

WELDON, Fay, *née* Birkinshaw (1933–), novelist, dramatist, and television screenwriter. Her novels, which express the rising feminist consciousness of the 1970s, include *The Fat Woman's Joke* (1967), *Down Among the Women* (1971), *Female Friends* (1975), *Praxis* (1978), and *Puffball* (1980). Her gift for realistic dialogue is manifested both in her fiction and in her many plays for television.

Well-Beloved, The, a novel by T. *Hardy, published serially 1892, revised and reissued 1897.

The central figure is Jocelyn Pierston, a sculptor of the Isle of Slingers (i.e. Portland) who falls in love successively with three generations of island women; Avice Caro, her daughter, and her granddaughter, all of the same name. He is seeking in each the perfect form in woman, as he seeks it in stone. Perversity of circumstances,

and the varying natures of the women, prevent him from marrying any of them. He eventually marries an elderly widow, Marcia, when both he and she have been, like the rock of Portland, subjected to the raspings and chisellings of time.

Wellborn, Frank, a character in Massinger's *A New Way to pay Old Debts.*

Weller, Samuel, in Dickens's *Pickwick Papers*, Mr Pickwick's devoted servant, and his father Tony, a coach driver.

WELLESLEY, Arthur, see WELLINGTON.

WELLINGTON, Arthur Wellesley, first duke of (1769–1852), soldier and statesman, who fought in the Indian Campaign (1799–1803), the Peninsular Campaign (1808–14), and was the hero of the battle of Waterloo (18 June 1815) at which Napoleon was decisively defeated. He first became a national figure with the victory of Talavera in 1809, and was created marquess of Douro and duke of Wellington in 1814. He was prime minister 1828–30, and secretary of state for foreign affairs 1834–5. Known as the 'Iron Duke', or, more familiarly, as 'Old Nosey', he was much portrayed by caricaturists. Although a less romantic figure than Napoleon, his exploits and his phlegmatic utterances (e.g. 'Publish and be damned', attributed to him) caught the imagination of contemporary and later writers: the battle of Waterloo is depicted in Byron's *Childe Harold's Pilgrimage* (Canto 3, xxi, 'There was a sound of revelry by night') and in *Vanity Fair*; he inspired much of the Juvenilia of C. *Brontë; and he appears in historical novels by A. C. *Doyle, *Henty, and others. By the queen's wishes he was given the most magnificent state funeral ever accorded to a subject, a pageant commemorated in *Tennyson's 'Ode on the Death of the Duke of Wellington' (1852).

Well of Loneliness, The, see HALL, R.

WELLS, Charles Jeremiah (1800–79), author (under the pseudonym of H. L. Howard) of *Joseph and his Brethren: a Scriptural Drama* (1824), a verse play much admired by *Rossetti, republished in 1876 with an essay by *Swinburne.

WELLS, H(erbert) G(eorge) (1866–1946), the son of an unsuccessful small tradesman, was apprenticed to a draper in early life, a period reflected in several of his novels. For some years, in poor health, he struggled as a teacher, studying and writing articles in his spare time. In 1903 he joined the *Fabian Society, but was soon at odds with it, his sponsor G. B. *Shaw, and Sidney and Beatrice *Webb. His literary output was vast and extremely varied. As a novelist he is perhaps best remembered for his scientific romances, among the earliest products of the new genre of *science fiction. The first, *The Time Machine* (1895), is a social allegory set in the year 802701, describing a society divided into two classes, the subterranean workers, called Morlocks, and the decadent Eloi. This was followed by *The Wonderful Visit* (1895), *The Island of Doctor Moreau* (1896), *The Invisible Man* (1897), *The War of the Worlds* (1898, a powerful and apocalyptic vision of the world invaded by Martians), *When the Sleeper Wakes* (1899), *The First Men in the Moon* (1901), *Men Like Gods* (1923), and others. Another group of novels evokes in comic and realistic style the lower-middle-class world of his youth. *Love and Mr Lewisham* (1900) tells the story of a struggling teacher; *Kipps* (1905) that of an aspiring draper's assistant; *The History of Mr Polly* (1910) recounts the adventures of an inefficient shopkeeper who liberates himself by burning down his own shop and bolting for freedom, which he discovers as man-of-all-work at the Potwell Inn.

Among his other novels, *Ann Veronica* (1909) is a feminist tract about a girl who defies her father and conventional morality by running off with the man she loves. *Tono-Bungay* (1909) is a picture of English society in dissolution, and of the advent of a new class of rich, embodied in Uncle Ponderevo, an entrepreneur intent on peddling a worthless patent medicine. *The Country of the Blind, and other stories* (1911), his fifth collection of short stories, contains the memorable 'The Door in the Wall'. *The New Machiavelli* (1911), about a politician involved in sexual scandal, was seen to mark a decline in his creative power, evident in later novels, which include *Mr Britling Sees It Through* (1916) and *The World of William Clissold* (1926). He continued to reach a huge audience, with his massive *The Outline of History* (1920) and its shorter offspring *A Short History of the World* (1922), and with many works of scientific and political speculation (including *The Shape of Things to Come*, 1933); the dark pessimism of his last prediction, *Mind at the End of its Tether* (1945), may be seen in the context of his own ill health and the course of the Second World War.

His *Experiment in Autobiography* (1934) is a striking portrait of himself, his contemporaries (including Arnold *Bennett, *Gissing, and the Fabians), and their times.

WELSH, Jane, see CARLYLE, J. B. W.

Wemmick, in Dickens's *Great Expectations*, clerk to Mr Jaggers the lawyer.

Wentworth, Captain, a character in J. Austen's *Persuasion*.

WENTWORTH, Sir Thomas, see STRAFFORD.

Werner, a poetic drama by Lord *Byron, published 1822, founded on 'The German's Tale' in Sophia and Harriet *Lee's *Canterbury Tales*.

Wertherism, a cultural phenomenon resulting from the fame throughout Europe of *Goethe's early novel *Die Leiden des jungen Werthers* (*The Sorrows of Young Werther*, 1774). This was a semi-autobiographical work about a sensitive artist, melancholy, at odds with society, and hopelessly in love with a girl, Charlotte, who was engaged to someone else. Its combination of the hero's 'Weltschmerz' (sense of ill-ease with the world) and 'Ichschmerz' (dissatisfaction with self), together with the scandalous suicide of Werther, made the work a huge success throughout Europe. Young men wore blue coats and yellow breeches in imitation of Werther, china tea-sets were produced with scenes from the novel depicted on them, and perfumes named after Werther were sold. Goethe was later much embarrassed by this early work and by the assumption that it was autobiographical. *Thackeray wrote a well-known sardonic poem about Werther and Charlotte, and the term 'Wertherism' became current in English to describe a man's early self-indulgent moods of melancholy.

WESKER, Arnold (1932–   ), playwright, born in Stepney of Jewish immigrant parents, and educated in Hackney. He worked at various jobs (including furniture-maker's apprentice and pastry cook) before making his name as a playwright. His early work was closely associated with the *English Stage Company. His three plays, *Chicken Soup with Barley* (1958), *Roots* (1959), and *I'm Talking about Jerusalem* (1960), are now grouped together as the Wesker Trilogy (see below). *The Kitchen* (1959) shows the stresses and conflicts of life behind the scenes in a restaurant, which culminate in tragedy; its use of the rhythms of working life was highly innovative and did much to stimulate the growth of what was to be known (though in a slightly different sense) as *kitchen sink drama. His subsequent plays include *Chips with Everything* (1962), a study of class attitudes in the RAF during National Service; *The Four Seasons* (1965); *Their Very Own and Golden City* (1966); *The Friends* (1970); *The Merchant* (1977); and *Caritas* (1981). Wesker has also published essays, screenplays, and volumes of short stories; the title story of *Love Letters on Blue Paper* (1974) was televised and adapted (1978) for the stage.

Wesker Trilogy, The, the name given to three plays by A. *Wesker, directed as a sequence for the first time by the *English Stage Company in 1960.

Chicken Soup with Barley (1958) introduces the Kahn family in their East London home in 1936; Sarah Kahn, a warm-hearted Communist Jewish matriarch, energetically supports Socialist opposition to the Fascist marches, but her weak husband Harry is less enthusiastic. Harry becomes enfeebled by successive strokes, but Sarah battles for her ideals, manifested in her daughter Ada and her emotional and volatile son Ronnie.

Roots (1959), set in Norfolk, portrays the effects of Ronnie's infectious idealism in his fiancée, Beatie Bryant, daughter of an agricultural labourer; she returns to her family for a visit, full of his praises and his notions. In the last act Beatie is playfully trying to stir her family to some intellectual exertion while awaiting Ronnie's visit, when a letter arrives from him breaking off their engagement; after her initial despair, Beatie finds her own voice as she attacks her family for its acceptance of the third-rate and the dull, and realizes triumphantly that she is no longer quoting Ronnie.

I'm Talking about Jerusalem (1960) opens in 1946 in Norfolk, as newly-demobbed Dave, and Ada, helped by Sarah and Ronnie, move into their new home, where they hope to create a William Morris oasis of independence, with Dave working as a craftsman-carpenter, but over the next two acts they are defeated by economic and social reality.

WESLEY, Charles (1707–88), brother of John *Wesley, also an active member of the Oxford Methodists. He remained faithful to the Anglican church and regretted his brother's departure from it. He composed many thousands of hymns, including such favourites as 'Jesu, lover of my soul'.

WESLEY, John (1703–91), was the centre of a group of devout Christians in Oxford (including his brother Charles, above, and *Whitefield); they practised severe self-discipline and self-examination, and were nicknamed the 'Holy Club' or 'Methodists'. He became a member of the Moravian society at Fetter Lane. He visited the Moravian colony at Herrnhut in 1738, and appointed his first lay preacher in the same year. He opened a Methodist chapel at Bristol, and for the rest of his life conducted his ministry with extraordinary energy, preaching 40,000 sermons, and travelling thousands of miles a year, mainly on horseback. His literary output was also prodigious. He published from 1737 many collections of hymns; the singing of hymns to familiar tunes by the whole congregation was a new practice and contributed greatly to the fervent Methodist spirit. He wrote educational works, practical treatises, edited *Thomas à Kempis (1735), published selections from W. *Law, by whom he was deeply influenced, and kept a *Journal* (standard edn ed. N. Curnock, 1909–11) remarkable not only as a record of his spiritual life, but for its pathos and humour. Wesley's impact on public and private life, notably in his concern for the illiterate industrial poor, was enormous.

Wessex, the name used by *Hardy to designate the south-west counties, principally Dorset, which form the setting of many of his works.

WEST, Nathanael, the pseudonym of Nathan Wallenstein Weinstein (1903–40), American novelist, is known principally for two macabre and tragic novels, *Miss Lonelyhearts* (1933), the story of a heavy-drinking agony columnist, and *The Day of the Locust* (1939), a satire of Hollywood life.

WEST, Dame Rebecca, the adopted name of Cecily Isabel Fairfield (1892–1983), trained briefly for the stage in London, then became a feminist and journalist, much influenced at this stage by the Pankhursts (see WOMEN'S SUFFRAGE); from 1911 she wrote for *The Freewoman, The New Freewoman*, and *The Clarion*. Many of her shrewd, witty, and combative pieces have been collected and reprinted as *The Young Rebecca* (1982, ed. Jane Marcus); this includes her outspoken review of H. G. *Wells's *Marriage* (1912), which led to a ten-year love affair and the birth of a son, Anthony West. Her first novel, *The Return of the Soldier* (1918), which describes the return home of a shell-shocked soldier, was followed by *The Judge* (1922), *The Strange Necessity* (1928), *Harriet Hume* (1929), *The Thinking Reed* (1936), *The Fountain Overflows* (1956), and *The Birds Fall Down* (1966). *Black Lamb and Grey Falcon* (1941) is a two-volume study of the Yugoslav nation. She was present at the Nuremberg trials, and *The Meaning of Treason* (1949) grew out of articles originally commissioned by the *New Yorker*. The reputation of her novels tends to have been eclipsed by the panache of her reportage and journalism, but feminist re-assessments in the 1980s have admired her strong and unconventional heroines, and her fine craftsmanship.

WEST, Richard (1716–42), son of a lawyer, became at Eton a close friend of T. *Gray and Horace *Walpole. Gray wrote a moving sonnet on his early death, 'In vain to me the smileing Mornings shine', first printed in 1775, which *Wordsworth used to illustrate his views on poetic diction in the *Preface* of 1800 to the *Lyrical Ballads*.

Western, Squire, and Sophia, characters in Fielding's *Tom Jones*.

West Indian, The, a comedy by R. *Cumberland, produced 1771. It contrasts the generosity and simplicity of young Belcour, a Rousseauesque child of nature brought up in the West Indies, with the civilized decadence of London. (See PRIMITIVISM.)

Westlock, John, a character in Dickens's *Martin Chuzzlewit*, at one time pupil of Mr Pecksniff.

'**Westminster Bridge,** Composed upon', a sonnet by *Wordsworth ('Earth hath not anything to show more fair'), written 1802, published 1807.

Westminster Review, The (1824–1914), was established by J. *Mill, an ardent supporter of *Bentham, as the journal of the 'philosophical radicals', in opposition to the *Edinburgh Review* and the *Quarterly Review*. *Byron, *Coleridge, *Tennyson, and *Carlyle were among the literary figures it supported. The journal survived several changes of name and ownership, and under the editorship of John *Chapman from 1851 published *Froude, *Pattison, *Pater, George *Eliot, and others. In this century it dropped its literary interests.

Westward for Smelts, a collection of tales borrowed from *The Decameron* and similar sources, recounted by seven fishwives who embark after selling their fish in London; by 'Kinde-Kit of Kingston' (?1603, 1620).

Westward Ho!, see KINGSLEY, C.

Westward Hoe, a comedy by *Webster and *Dekker, printed 1607.

WEYMAN, Stanley John (1855–1928), author of historic novels. These include *A Gentleman of France* (1893), *The Red Cockade* (1895), *Under the Red Robe* (1896), *Count Hannibal* (1901), and *Chippinge* (1906).

Weymouth Sands, a novel by J. C. *Powys.

WHARTON, Edith, *née* Newbold Jones (1862–1937), American novelist and short story writer. She devoted her considerable energy to a cosmopolitan social life, which included a close friendship with H. *James, and to a literary career. Her first volume of short stories, *The Greater Inclination* (1899), was followed by a novella, *The Touchstone* (1900), but it was *The House of Mirth* (1905), the tragedy of failed social climber Lily Bart, which established her as a leading novelist. Many other works followed, including *Ethan Frome* (1911), a grim and ironic tale of passion and vengeance on a poor New England farm; *The Custom of the Country* (1913), which wittily recounts a poor, provincial girl's ascent of the social ladder via a succession of marriages; *The Age of Innocence* (1920), which describes the frustrated love of a New York lawyer, Newland Archer, for Ellen Olenska, the separated wife of a dissolute Polish count; *The Mother's Recompense* (1925); and *Hudson River Bracketed* (1929), contrasting Middle West with New York society. She published many volumes of short stories, various travel books, and an autobiography, *A Backward Glance* (1934). Her observant, satiric, witty portrayal of social

nuance, both in America and Europe, shows her keen interest in what she called the 'tribal behaviour' of various groups.

WHATELY, Richard (1787–1863), professor of political economy at Oxford (1829–31), then archbishop of Dublin. He involved himself in educational reform and published works on philosophy and religion, supporting *Broad Church views, but his reputation rested largely on his *Logic* (1826) and *Rhetoric* (1828).

What Maisie Knew, a novel by H. *James, published 1897.

With insight and humour James takes us into the world of Maisie, the child of divorced parents. Her father, Beale Farrange, marries Maisie's governess, Miss Overmore, while her mother marries a handsome, weak, and younger man, Sir Claude, to whom Maisie becomes devoted. These new marriages collapse, the step-parents become lovers, and her parents enter into new amorous entanglements. A new governess, Mrs Wix, appears to offer support, but also becomes infatuated with Sir Claude. Maisie is used as a pawn in the power games of the adults who surround her; her perception of their corrupt lives leads her to an odd and disconcerting maturity, yet she is not of their world and retains a fundamental honesty and innocence.

What You Will, the sub-title of Shakespeare's *Twelfth Night*; its meaning is 'whatever you want to call it'. It is clearly connected, in some way, with *Marston's *What You Will* which probably appeared in 1601.

WHEATLEY, Dennis Yates (1897–1977), novelist of the occult, whose Satanic thrillers and romances (*The Devil Rides Out*, 1935; *To the Devil—a Daughter*, 1953, etc.), were extremely popular.

'**When lovely woman stoops to folly**', a poem by Goldsmith, from *The Vicar of Wakefield*.

Where Angels Fear to Tread, E. M. *Forster's first novel, published 1905.

It is a tragi-comedy describing the consequences of the marriage of Lilia Herriton, an impulsive young widow, to the son of an Italian dentist, Gino Carella. Lilia dies in childbirth: Philip Herriton is dispatched by her ex-mother-in-law to rescue the baby, but falls under the spell of Italy, as Caroline Abbott, Lilia's chaperone, has fallen under the spell of Gino. The baby is killed in a characteristic Forsterian 'muddle' and the two English characters return home empty-handed.

WHETSTONE, George (1550–87), author of miscellaneous verse, especially elegies, and prose tales, is principally remembered for his *Promos and Cassandra* (1578), a play in rhymed verse (based on a tale in Cinthio's *Hecatommithi*), which provided the plot for Shakespeare's **Measure for Measure* and is an early example of English romantic comedy.

WHEWELL, William (1794–1866), professor of moral philosophy at Cambridge (1838–55) and master of Trinity College from 1841 till his death. His principal works were *The History* (1837) and *The Philosophy* (1840) *of the Inductive Sciences* and *Astronomy and Physics in reference to Natural Philosophy* (1833). He published and edited many other works in natural and mathematical science, philosophy, and theology.

WHICHCOTE, Benjamin, see CAMBRIDGE PLATONISTS.

Whig Examiner, The, a literary and political periodical published by *Addison. Five numbers appeared, Sept.-Oct. 1710.

Whiskerandos, Don Ferolo, a character in Sheridan's **The Critic.*

WHISTLER, James Abbott McNeill (1834–1903), an American painter, who moved between Paris and London; his art and ideas were an important link between the two capitals. He mixed in *Pre-Raphaelite circles, discussed his ideas on art with *Swinburne, and was at the centre of the Aesthetic Movement. In 1877 *Ruskin attacked him for 'flinging a pot of paint into the public's face'; Whistler sued him, won, and was awarded a farthing damages. The trial stimulated Whistler's gifts as a polemicist; he wrote a series of pamphlets and vituperative letters to the press, later published together in *The Gentle Art of Making Enemies* (1890). Whistler's influence is evident in *Wilde's lectures in America (1882) and in 'The Decay of Lying' and 'The Critic as Artist'. Whistler was to accuse him of plagiarism.

WHITAKER, Joseph (1820–95), founded the *Educational Register* (1850), *Whitaker's Clergyman's Diary* (1850), *The Artist* (1855), *The Bookseller* (1858), and *Whitaker's Almanack* (1868), a compendium of general information regarding the government, finances, population, and commerce of the world, with special reference to the British Commonwealth and the United States. (See ALMANACS.)

Whitaker's Almanack, see WHITAKER, J.

WHITE, Antonia (1899–1979), novelist and translator. Her convent childhood is described in her first auobiographical novel, *Frost in May* (1933). The heroine Nanda Grey becomes Clara Batchelor in her three subsequent novels, also largely autobiographical, *The Lost Traveller* (1950), *The Sugar House* (1952), and *Beyond the Glass* (1954); these give a vivid account of her experiences as an actress in provincial repertory, her struggles as a freelance copy-writer, her complex relationship with her possessive father, and her descent into mental illness and confinement in an asylum. Antonia White also translated many of the novels of Colette and published an account of her reconversion to Catholicism, *The Hound and the Falcon* (1966).

WHITE, Gilbert (1720–93), spent most of his life as curate of Selborne. He began in 1751 to keep a 'Garden Kalendar' and later a 'Naturalist's Journal'. He made the acquaintance of two distinguished naturalists, Thomas *Pennant and Daines *Barrington, with whom he carried on a correspondence from 1767 which formed the basis of his classic *Natural History and Antiquities of Selborne* (pub. Dec. 1788, title page 1789), a work which displays his affectionate and detailed observations of wild life and nature, and his love of the *picturesque in landscape.

WHITE, Henry Kirke (1785–1806). His volume of verses in 1803 attracted the attention of *Southey, who assisted him. Southey collected his works, with a memoir, and published them in 1807. Little is remembered of his work except a few hymns, such as 'Oft in danger, oft in woe'.

WHITE, Joseph Blanco (1775–1841), born in Seville, a Catholic priest. He abandoned the priesthood and came to England in 1810. He studied at Oxford and became an Anglican cleric, and the friend of *Whately, *Newman, *Pusey, and *Froude. His publications include various ecclesiastical works, and translations of *Paley's *Evidences.* *Coleridge declared his sonnet 'Night and Death' (1828) 'the finest . . . sonnet in our language'.

WHITE, Patrick Victor Martindale (1912–), Australian novelist, educated in England. He settled in London, served in the RAF during the war, and returned after the war to Australia. His first published novel, *Happy Valley* (1939), set in New South Wales, was followed by *The Living and the Dead* (1941), set in pre-war London, and *The Aunt's Story* (1948). *The Tree of Man* (1955) is an epic account of a young farmer, Stan Parker, at the beginning of the 20th cent., and his struggles to build himself a life and a family in the Australian wilderness; the epic theme was continued in *Voss* (1957), which returns to the heroic Australian past in its description of the doomed attempt of a Nietzschean German visionary and aspiring hero, Johann Voss, to lead an expedition across the continent in 1845. He is bound in a form of mystic communion with Laura Trevelyan, who, at home in Sydney, suffers with him and is released from fever at the moment when, already *in extremis*, he is decapitated by the aboriginal boy Jackie. Voss lives on as an increasingly legendary, martyred figure. White strengthened his reputation with several subsequent works, including *Riders in the Chariot* (1961); *The Solid Mandala* (1966); *The Vivisector* (1970); *The Eye of the Storm* (1973); *A Fringe of Leaves* (1976); and *The Twyborn Affair* (1979), a baroque novel with an international canvas, which ends apocalyptically in the London blitz; he has also published *Four Plays* (1965), volumes of short stories, and a frank self-portrait. *Flaws in the Glass* (1981). White was awarded the *Nobel Prize for literature in 1973.

WHITE, T(erence) H(anbury) (1906–64), is best known for his novels on the Arthurian legend, published under the title *The Once and Future King* (1958); the first in this sequence, *The Sword in the Stone* (1937), is a classic children's novel, as is *Mistress Masham's Repose* (1947). He also wrote several adult novels, *The Goshawk* (1951), and *The Book of Beasts* (1954), a translation from a 12th-cent. Latin *bestiary.

WHITE, William Hale (1831–1913), known as a writer under the pseudonym of 'Mark Rutherford', entered the Civil Service in 1854. He supplemented his income by parliamentary and literary journalism, and in 1881 published *The autobiography of Mark Rutherford, dissenting minister*: Rutherford, born in a small Midlands town, attends a Dissenting college and then becomes a minister, but is beset both by theological doubts and by distress at the narrowness and hypocrisy of his colleagues and congregations. Loneliness makes him an easy prey to melancholy, and he gradually loses his faith. It is a compact and powerful account of the progress of 19th-cent. doubt. Other imaginative works followed, including *Mark Rutherford's Deliverance* (1885), *The Revolution in Tanner's Lane* (1887), *Miriam's Schooling and other Papers* (1893), *Catherine Furze* (1893), and *Clara Hopgood* (1896). His other pseudonymous works include *Pages from a Journal* (1900, essays and stories), *More Pages from a Journal* (1910), and *Last Pages from a Journal* (1915); works published under his own name include a life of *Bunyan (1905).

White Devil, The (*The White Divel: or the tragedy of . . . Brachiano, with the life and death of Vittoria Corombona*), a tragedy by *Webster, published 1612.

The duke of Brachiano, husband of Isabella, the sister of Francisco, duke of Florence, is weary of her and in love with Vittoria, wife of Camillo. The *Machiavellian Flamineo, Vittoria's brother, helps Brachiano to seduce her, and contrives (at her suggestion, delivered indirectly in a dream) the death of Camillo: Brachiano causes Isabella to be poisoned. Vittoria is tried for adultery and murder in the celebrated central arraignment scene (III. ii), and defends herself with great spirit. She is sentenced to confinement in 'a house of penitent whores', whence she is carried off by Brachiano, who marries her. Flamineo quarrels with his younger brother, the virtuous Marcello, and kills him; he dies in the arms of their mother Cornelia, who later, driven out of her wits by grief, sings the dirge 'Call for the robin redbreast, and the wren', a scene which elicits from Flamineo a speech of remorse. Meanwhile Francisco, at the prompting of Isabella's ghost (see REVENGE TRAGEDY) avenges her death by poisoning Brachiano, and Vittoria and Flamineo, both of whom die Stoic deaths, are murdered by his dependants.

WHITEFIELD, George (1714–70), the popular evangelical preacher, came under the influence of John and Charles *Wesley while at Oxford. He attracted much attention by his fervent and emotional sermons. His views diverged from those of the Wesleys, as he became increasingly Calvinistic. He became domestic chaplain to Lady *Huntingdon and through her patronage opened a Tabernacle in Tottenham Court Road. Whitefield died near Boston on the last of several evangelical visits to America. His Journals were published in 7 parts, 1738–41, and *Hymns for Social Worship* in 1753.

WHITEHEAD, A(lfred) N(orth) (1861–1947), professor of philosophy at Harvard University (1924–36) and the author of many important philosophical and mathematical works, including *Principia Mathematica* (with B. *Russell, 1910), *Science and the Modern World* (1925), *Symbolism* (1927), *Adventures of Ideas* (1933).

WHITEHEAD, William (1715–85), was best known in his day for his successful *neo-classical tragedy *The Roman Father* (1750), a version of *Corneille's *Horace*. In 1757 he was appointed poet laureate, an elevation which caused much satiric comment, notably from Charles *Churchill. His *Plays and Poems* were collected in 1774, and a complete edition of his poems appeared in 1788.

White Hotel, The, a novel by D. M. *Thomas.

White Lady of Avenel, The, a supernatural being introduced by Scott in *The Monastery*.

White's, a chocolate-house in St James's Street, London, started in 1697 by Francis White. The first number of *The Tatler* announced that accounts of gallantry, pleasure, and entertainment would emanate from White's Chocolate House. It was converted into a club, which became a celebrated gaming centre. The present clubhouse dates from 1755.

Whitford, Vernon, a character in Meredith's *The Egoist*.

WHITING, John (1917–63), playwright, whose plays marked a historic break from the prevailing vogue for drawing-room comedy. They include *A Penny for a Song* (1956, pub. 1969), *Saint's Day* (perf. and pub. 1951), *Marching Song* (perf. and pub. 1954), and *The Gates of Summer* (1956, pub. 1969). He first achieved popular success with *The Devils*, adapted from *The Devils of Loudun* by A. *Huxley, performed in 1961; influenced by *Brecht, it deals with a case of hysterical demonic possession in a French nunnery.

WHITMAN, Walt (1819–92), American poet, had little formal education, and started work as an office boy; he subsequently worked as printer, wandering schoolteacher, and contributor to and editor of various magazines and newspapers, entering politics as a Democrat, and travelling in 1848 to New Orleans. He returned to New York via St Louis and Chicago, and the experience of the frontier merged with his admiration for *Emerson to produce the first edition of *Leaves of Grass* (1855), 12 poems. The second edition (1856) added 21 poems, and the third edition (1860) 122, including the group entitled 'Calamus', which has been taken as a reflection of the poet's homosexuality. The six further editions that appeared in his lifetime were revised or added to, the work enlarging as the poet developed. During the Civil War Whitman worked as a clerk in Washington, but his real business was as a volunteer hospital visitor among the wounded, an experience reflected in his prose *Memoranda during the War* (1875) and in the poems published under the title of *Drum-Taps* in 1865. In the *Sequel* to these poems (1865–6) appeared the great elegy on Lincoln, 'When Lilacs Last in the Dooryard Bloom'd'. In spite of his achievement Whitman was disregarded by the public at large. His reputation began to rise after recognition in England by W. M. *Rossetti, *Swinburne (who compared him to *Blake), Mrs *Gilchrist, and E. *Carpenter. The free, vigorous sweep of his verse conveys subjects at once national ('Pioneers! O Pioneers!', 1865), mystically sexual ('I sing the body electric', 1855), and deeply personal ('Out of the Cradle Endlessly Rocking', 1860), and his work proved a liberating force for many of his successors, including H. *Miller, D. H. *Lawrence, H. *Crane, and the poets of the *Beat Generation.

WHITNEY, Geoffrey, see EMBLEM BOOKS.

WHITTIER, John Greenleaf (1807–92), American poet. He became an ardent Abolitionist; his poems on slavery were collected as *Voices of Freedom* (1846). He was a regular contributor to the *Atlantic Monthly*, which he helped to found. He wrote in many genres; his first book, *Legends of New-England in Prose and Verse* (1831), was

followed by many volumes of verse on political and rural themes, by verse narratives, sonnets, and ballads.

WHITTINGTON, Richard (d. 1423), rose to be lord mayor of London, 1397–8, 1406–7 (a year of plague), and 1419–20. He was a liberal benefactor of the city. The popular legend of Whittington and his cat, the germ of which is probably of very remote origin, is not known to have been narrated before 1605.

Whole Duty of Man, The, a devotional work published 1658, in which man's duties in respect of God and his fellow men are analysed and discussed in detail. The book, by internal evidence, is the work of a practised divine, perhaps Richard Allestree (1619–81), chaplain in ordinary to the king.

Who's Who, an annual biographical dictionary of contemporary men and women, first issued in 1849 but taking its present form in 1897. The first *Who Was Who 1897–1916* appeared in 1920, and the seventh (1971–80) in 1981.

WHYTE-MELVILLE, George John (1821–78), was an authority on field sports. Most of his literary works were novels, sometimes historical, and hunting figures largely in many of them. His first *Digby Grand*, was published in 1853; *Galsworthy, at Oxford, fell under the spell of the 'Bright Things' in Whyte-Melville's novels and Digby Grand was Jolyon's (in *The Forsyte Saga*) first idol. His other novels include *Holmby House* (1859), a historical romance describing the Civil War; *Market Harborough* (1861); and *The Gladiators* (1863). He also published his *Songs and Verse* (1869), and *Riding Recollections* (1879) was a notable book on horsemanship. He was killed in a hunting accident.

WHYTHORNE, Thomas (1528–96). After three years as 'servant and scholar' in the household of J. *Heywood he became a teacher of music and composer of madrigals. His autobiography, *A Book of Songs and Sonetts*, discovered in manuscript in 1955 (ed. James M. Osborn, 1961) is not only an interesting document of Tudor life, poetry, and music, but also, because Whythorne wrote in his own phonetic system, a key to the pronunciation of his day.

Wickfield, Mr and Agnes, characters in Dickens's *David Copperfield*.

WICKHAM, Anna, pseudonym of Edith Alice Mary Harper (1884–1947), poet, whose publications include *The Contemplative Quarry* (1915), *The Little Old House* (1921), and *Thirty-Six New Poems* (1936); a collection, *The Writings of Anna Wickham* (1984), was edited by R. D. Smith. More popular in the US and France than at home, she was an original and copious poet; in imagery and subject matter in advance of her time, she charted the struggle of a woman artist to achieve freedom to work as well as to fulfil herself as wife and mother.

'Widdicombe Fair', the title of a popular song which has become the accepted Devonshire song. The date of words and tune is probably the end of the 18th cent.

Tom Pearse lends his grey mare to carry a party (including Old Uncle Tom Cobbleigh) to Widdicombe Fair, but the mare takes sick and dies, and is still to be seen haunting the moor at night.

Widmerpool, a character in A. *Powell's *A Dance to the Music of Time.*

Widowers' Houses, a play by Bernard *Shaw, first performed 1892, published 1893. It is designed to show the manner in which the capitalist system perverts and corrupts human behaviour and relationships.

Dr Harry Trench, on a Rhine holiday, meets Blanche Sartorius, travelling with her wealthy father, and proposes marriage to her: Sartorius is willing to permit the match if Trench's family (including his aunt Lady Roxdale) agrees to accept her as an equal. All seems well, until it is revealed in Act II that Sartorius is a slum landlord. Trench is horrified, refuses to accept Sartorius's money, suggests that he and Blanche should live on his £700 a year, and is even more horrified when Sartorius points out that this income is derived from a mortgage of Sartorius's property, and that he himself and his miserable rent collector Lickcheese are merely intermediaries: 'You are the principal.' Blanche, revealing a passionate and violent nature, rejects Trench for his hesitations. In the third act Lickcheese, himself now rich through dubious dealings in the property market, approaches Sartorius with an apparently philanthropic but in fact remunerative proposition, which involves Lady Roxdale as ground landlord and Trench as mortgagee. Trench, now considerably more cynical, accepts the deal, and he and Blanche are reunited.

Widsith, a poem of 143 lines in Old English, named from its opening word, in the *Exeter Book. It is constructed around three 'thulas' (i.e. mnemonic name-lists), connected by the ostensible experience of the eponymous minstrel: the first names great rulers; the second lists the tribes among whom the minstrel claims to have travelled; and the third speaks of people that the minstrel sought out. The poem is thought to date substantially from the 7th cent. and thus to be the earliest poem in the language. There are important editions by R. W. Chambers (1912) and K. Malone (1962).

Wife of Bath, see CANTERBURY TALES, 6.

WILBERFORCE, William (1759–1833), MP for Yorkshire, devoted himself to the abolition of the slave-trade and to other philanthropic projects. He published in 1797 *A Practical View of the Prevailing Religious System of Professed Christians,* a work which was influential. He was the leading layman of the evangelical *'Clapham Sect'.

WILBUR, Richard Purdy (1921–), American poet. His elegant, urbane, and witty poetry appears in several collections, from *Ceremony* (1950) to *Seven Poems* (1981).

WILBYE, John (1574–1638), English composer, with *Weelkes, the most important of the English madrigalists who followed the lead given by *Morley in 1593 and 1594. He published two sets of *madrigals (1598, 1609) and contributed one madrigal to *The Triumphes of Oriana* in 1601.

WILCOX, Ella Wheeler (1850–1919), American poet whose many volumes of romantic, sentimental, and mildly erotic verse (with titles such as *Poems of Passion* and *Poems of Cheer*) brought her a vast readership.

WILD, Jonathan (?1682–1725), worked as a buckle-maker in London. He became head of a large corporation of thieves, gained notoriety as a thief-taker, and was ultimately hanged at Tyburn. His 'Life and Actions' were related by *Defoe (1725). For Fielding's satire, see JONATHAN WILD THE GREAT.

Wildair, Sir Harry, a character in Farquhar's *The Constant Couple* and in its sequel, *Sir Harry Wildair.*

WILDE, Oscar Fingal O'Flahertie Wills (1854–1900), studied at Trinity College, Dublin, then at Magdalen College, Oxford, where in 1878 he won the Newdigate Prize for his poem 'Ravenna'. His flamboyant aestheticism attracted attention, much of it hostile; he proclaimed himself a disciple of *Pater and the cult of *'Art for Art's sake' mocked in *Gilbert and Sullivan's *Patience* (1881). Wilde undertook a lecture tour of the United States in 1882, after the publication of his first volume of verse, *Poems* (1881). In 1884 he married, and in 1888 published a volume of fairy-stories, *The Happy Prince and other tales,* written for his sons. In 1891 followed *Lord Arthur Savile's Crime, and other stories* and his only novel, *The Picture of Dorian Gray,* a Gothic melodrama. Wilde claimed in his preface, 'There is no such thing as a moral or an immoral book. Books are well written or badly written. That is all.' He published *A House of Pomegranates* (1891), fairy-stories; and *The Duchess of Padua*

(1891), a dull verse tragedy. He achieved theatrical success with his comedies *Lady Windermere's Fan* (1892); *A Woman of No Importance* (1893); *An Ideal Husband* (1895); and his masterpiece *The Importance of Being Earnest* (1895). *Salomé* (now known chiefly by Richard Strauss's opera), written in French, was refused a licence, but performed in Paris in 1896 and published in 1894 in an English translation by Lord Alfred *Douglas with illustrations by *Beardsley. Lord Alfred's father, the marquess of Queensberry, disapproved of his son's friendship with Wilde and publicly insulted the playwright. This started a chain of events which led to Wilde's imprisonment for homosexual offences in 1895. He was declared bankrupt while in prison and wrote a letter of bitter reproach to Lord Alfred, published in part in 1905 as *De Profundis*. He was released in 1897 and went to France where he wrote *The Ballad of Reading Gaol* (1898), inspired by his prison experience. In exile he adopted the name Sebastian Melmoth, after the romance by *Maturin. He died in Paris. His other writings include critical dialogues ('The Decay of Lying' and 'The Critic as Artist', 1891) and *The Soul of Man under Socialism*, a plea for individualism and artistic freedom, first published in the *Fortnightly Review* in 1891.

A volume of letters, ed. R. Hart-Davis, appeared in 1962.

Wilde-Goose Chase, The, a comedy by J. *Fletcher, acted 1621, printed 1652.

Mirabell, the 'wild goose', a boastful Don Juan with an aversion to marriage, is 'chased' by Oriana, his betrothed, who tries various wiles to bring him to the altar. She feigns madness for love of him, but he sees through the pretence, and she finally traps him in the disguise of a rich Italian lady.

WILDER, Thornton Niven (1897–1975), American novelist and dramatist. His novels include *The Bridge of San Luis Rey* (1927) and *The Ides of March* (1948). He scored considerable success in the theatre with *Our Town* (1938), *The Skin of Our Teeth* (1942), and *The Merchant of Yonkers* (1938), a comedy which was revised as *The Matchmaker* (1954) and adapted as the musical comedy *Hello, Dolly!* (1963).

Wildeve, Damon, a character in Hardy's *The Return of the Native*.

Wildfell Hall, see TENANT OF WILDFELL HALL, THE.

Wildfire, Madge, see MURDOCKSON.

Wild Huntsman, The, a spectral huntsman of German folklore, the subject of a ballad ('Der wilde Jäger') by Gottfried August Bürger (1747–94), imitated by Sir W. *Scott.

Wild Oats, a play by J. *O'Keeffe.

Wildrake, Roger, a character in Scott's *Woodstock*.

Wilfer Family, characters in Dickens's *Our Mutual Friend*.

WILKES, John (1727–97), led a life of dissipation and became a member of the *Medmenham Abbey fraternity. He was elected MP for Aylesbury in 1757 and in 1762 founded *The North Briton* in which, aided by his friend Charles *Churchill, he attacked Bute's government. In the notorious No. 45 he denounced the King's Speech, and was arrested for libel on a general warrant, but released; he was then expelled from Parliament for publishing an obscene libel, the *Essay on Woman* (a parody of *Pope), and retired to Paris. He returned in 1768 and took his seat unopposed as MP for Middlesex in 1774, in which year he was also lord mayor of London.

A man of wit, learning, and ability, and a popular hero in the cause of liberty, he secured important legal rights, including the illegality of general warrants, the freedom of choice of the electorate, and the freedom of the press.

WILKIE, William (1721–72), author of *The Epigoniad*, an epic poem in nine books modelled on *Homer (1757, 1759). Wilkie never fully mastered literary English, but was a skilled classicist and mathematician. He was a member of the *Select Society.

Wilkins, Peter, see PETER WILKINS.

Willet, John, in Dickens's *Barnaby Rudge*, the host of the Maypole Inn, and Joe his son.

'William and Margaret', a ballad by *Mallet, published 1724 in A. *Hill's *Plain Dealer*; in Percy's *Reliques* it appears as 'Margaret's Ghost'. Margaret's 'grimly ghost' visits her faithless lover William and summons him to her grave; he lays his cheek upon her grave 'and word spake never more'.

William of Cloudesley, see ADAM BELL.

WILLIAM OF MALMESBURY (*c.*1095–1143), the first full-scale writer of history in England after *Bede. His major works were the *Gesta Regum Anglorum*, a history of England from 449 to 1120 which includes two stories about *Arthur; the *Gesta Pontificum Anglorum*, an ecclesiastical history of England from 597 to 1125; the *Historia Novella*, the sequel to the *Gesta Regum*, dealing with 1128 to 1142 and left unfinished; *De Antiquitate Glastoniensis Ecclesiae* (a work which has led to the speculation that he may have lived at Glastonbury, written between

1129 and 1139); and the *Life of St Dunstan*, a hagiographical work. As well as being an authoritative and serious historian, William was a picturesque and circumstantial writer who enlivened his narrative with topographical observation, anecdote, reminiscence, and comment.

WILLIAM OF NEWBURGH (1135/6–?98), author of *Historia Rerum Anglicarum*, suddenly abandoned in 1198, presumably at his death. The work deals with events from 1066 to 1198, especially the reigns of Stephen and Henry II; it exposes the *Historia* of *Geoffrey of Monmouth as legend rather than fact.

William of Palerne, one of the earliest of the 14th-cent. English romances of the *Alliterative Revival, of 5,540 lines in a West Midland dialect. It was based on the late 12th-cent. French *Roman de Guillaume de Palerne*, and tells the story of a prince saved by a werewolf, who turns out to be another prince, under the spell of a wicked stepmother.

WILLIAM OF WYKEHAM (1324–1404), bishop of Wincheter and chancellor of England, founder of New College, Oxford (1379), and Winchester College (1382). He was one of the leaders of the bishops who opposed *John of Gaunt, and he was a lifelong opponent of Wyclifitism.

WILLIAMS, Charles Walter Stansby (1886–1945), poet, novelist, and theological writer. His novels, which have been described as supernatural thrillers, include *War in Heaven* (1930), *Descent into Hell* (1937), and *All Hallows Eve* (1944). Of his theological writings the most important was *The Descent of the Dove* (1939). His literary criticism included a study of *Dante, *The Figure of Beatrice* (1943). He wrote several verse plays on religious themes, but his most original poetic achievement is perhaps his cycle on the Arthurian legend. *Taliessin through Logres* (1938), and *The Region of the Summer Stars* (1944), afterwards reissued in one volume (1974) together with *Arthurian Torso*, a study of Williams's poetry by his friend C. S. *Lewis.

WILLIAMS, Helen Maria (1762–1827), published her first poem, a ballad, *Edwin and Eltruda* in 1782, and travelled in 1788 to Paris. She became friendly with the leading Girondists, and made the acquaintance of M. *Wollstonecraft; her *Letters* (1790–5) contain interesting information on the state of Paris and France just before and during the Revolution.

WILLIAMS, Isaac (1802–65), was influenced by *Keble, participated in the *Oxford Movement, and contributed to *Tracts for the Times*. He was author of poems in *Lyra Apostolica* and

other poetical works including *The Cathedral* (1838) and *The Baptistery* (1842). His autobiography (edited by Sir G. Prevost, 1892) is an interesting record of the days of the Oxford Movement.

WILLIAMS, John, known as Anthony Pasquin (1761–1818), was a voluminous satirist and miscellaneous writer, often threatened with prosecution for libel. *The Children of Thespis* (1786–8) was his most successful poem.

WILLIAMS, Raymond Henry (1921–   ), critic and novelist. His novels include *Border Country* (1960) and *Second Generation* (1964), and his critical works, which explore the relationship of literature and society from an increasingly Marxist viewpoint, include *Culture and Society 1780–1950* (1958), *The Long Revolution* (1961), *Modern Tragedy* (1966), and *The Country and the City* (1973). (See also MARXIST LITERARY CRITICISM.)

WILLIAMS, Tennessee (Thomas Lanier Williams) (1911–83), American dramatist, achieved success with the semi-autobiographical *The Glass Menagerie* (1944, pub. 1945), a poignant and painful family drama set in St Louis, in which a frigid and frustrated mother's dreams of her glamorous past as a Southern belle conflict with the grimness of her reduced circumstances. His next big success was *A Streetcar named Desire* (1947), a study of sexual frustration, violence, and aberration, set in New Orleans, in which Blanche Dubois' fantasies of refinement and grandeur are brutally destroyed by her brother-in-law, Stanely Kowalski. Williams continued to write prolifically, largely in a Gothic and macabre vein, but with insight into human passion and its perversions; his other works include *The Rose Tattoo* (1950); *Camino Real* (1953); *Cat on a Hot Tin Roof* (1955), a Freudian family drama which takes place at wealthy cotton planter Big Daddy's 65th birthday, while his daughter-in-law Maggie fights to save her marriage to the alcoholic and despairing Brick; *Suddenly Last Summer* (1958); *Sweet Bird of Youth* (1959); *The Night of the Iguana* (1962); and a novella, *The Roman Spring of Mrs Stone* (1950).

WILLIAMS, William Carlos (1883–1963), American poet, novelist, short story writer, and, for many years, a paediatrician. In his student days he was a friend of *Pound and H. *Doolittle, and some early poems (*Poems*, 1909; *The Tempers*, 1913) are Imagist, although he was to move from *Imagism to what he called Objectivism. His poems range from the minimal eight-line, sixteen-word 'The Red Wheelbarrow' (1923) to his most ambitious production, *Paterson* (1946–58), a long, five-part, free-verse, collage-mixed evocation of a characteristic industrial city, with the mystic motif, 'man is himself a city'. The title of his last collection, *Pictures from Brueghel* (1963), suggests the plain, poverty-stricken subjects of some of his verse and prose; and his skill at painting the ordinary with freshness and compassion is manifested in his short stories, collected as *The Farmers' Daughters* (1961). Other prose works include *In the American Grain* (1925), an important series of essays exploring the nature of American literature and the influence of Puritanism in American culture. Williams's work was more or less disregarded in Britain until the 1950s. Recently interest has increased considerably, and he is now established as one of the masters of *Modernism.

WILLIAMSON, Henry (1895–1977), writer. He served in the First World War, then worked briefly in Fleet Street while writing his first novel, *The Beautiful Years* (1921: Vol. I of *The Flax of Dream* quartet). In 1921 he moved to North Devon, and embarked on a modest country life (much influenced by R. *Jefferies) which produced his most widely known work, *Tarka the Otter* (1927), which remains a popular classic. This was followed by other tales of wildlife including *Salar the Salmon* (1935). In the 1930s Williamson became an admirer of Hitler and Sir Oswald Mosley, addressing Hitler in a notorious foreword to *The Flax of Dream* (1936) as 'the great man across the Rhine, whose life symbol is the happy child'. This led, in the short term, to a brief internment at the outbreak of the Second World War, and possibly to the neglect of his most ambitious work, a series of fifteen novels known under the collective title *A Chronicle of Ancient Sunlight*, a panoramic survey which opens in the mid-1890s with *The Dark Lantern* (1951) and closes with *The Gale of the World* (1969). This traces the career of Phillip Maddison, writer, from birth to the aftermath of the Second World War. *A Patriot's Progress* (1930) is a devastating account of trench warfare seen through the eyes of a naïve, suffering Everyman, City clerk John Bullock. Williamson wrote about his friendship and correspondence with T. E. *Lawrence in *Genius of Friendship* (1941).

Willobie his Avisa (1594), one of the books which, with G. *Harvey's and T. *Nashe's satirical works, was called in by the High Commission in 1599. The poem consists of 74 songs and a few poems by Henry Willoby (?1574–?96). They narrate the unsuccessful courting of Avisa, a country inn-keeper's wife, by a nobleman before her marriage, and by four foreign suitors after it. The last of these has a 'familiar friend W.S.' as a companion; he has been identified with Shakespeare, who is also mentioned as author of *The Rape of Lucrece* in prefatory verses.

Willoughby, (1) Sir Clement, a character in F. Burney's *Evelina*; (2) John, a character in J. Austen's *Sense and Sensibility*.

WILLS, W(illiam) G(orman) (1828–91), an Irish verse dramatist. A long succession of popular plays, including *A Man and his Shadow* (1865), led to his appointment as 'Dramatist to the Lyceum', for which he wrote many historical dramas, including *Charles I* (1872, with H. *Irving). He produced a version of *Faust in 1885, and a long poem, *Melchior* (1885), dedicated to R. *Browning. His chief interest, however, was in portrait painting, at which he was also eminently successful.

Will's Coffee House was at No. 1, Bow Street, at the corner of Russell Street. It was frequented in the 17th and 18th cents by authors (notably by *Wycherley, *Addison, *Pope, and *Congreve), wits, and gamblers, and is particularly associated with *Dryden; Dr Johnson in his *Lives of the English Poets* recalls that at Will's, Dryden presided over all literary disputes. The first number of the *The Tatler* announced that all poetry appearing in it would be under the article of Will's Coffee House.

WILMOT, John, see ROCHESTER.

WILMOT, Robert, see TANGRED AND GISMUND.

WILSON, Sir Angus Frank Johnstone (1913–). His novels include *Hemlock and After* (1952), about the doomed attempts of a middle-aged novelist, Bernard Sands, to establish a writer's centre in a country house; *Anglo-Saxon Attitudes* (1956), which also has a middle-aged protagonist, historian Gerald Middleton, who tries to reconstruct and understand the past, including the mystery of a possible archaeological forgery; *The Middle Age of Mrs Eliot* (1958), about the reversed fortunes of Meg Eliot, who finds herself suddenly widowed in reduced circumstances; *The Old Men at the Zoo* (1961), which reflects Wilson's concern with conflicts between the wild and the tame, the disciplined and the free, and ends with a portrayal of Europe at war; *Late Call* (1964), set in a New Town; *No Laughing Matter* (1967), a family saga covering some fifty years in the history of the Matthews family, which marks a departure from the realism of earlier works, mingling parody and dramatization with direct narration in a rich and complex evocation of family politics and neuroses; *As if by Magic* (1973); and *Setting the World on Fire* (1980). *The Wrong Set* (1949), *Such Darling Dodos* (1950), and *A Bit off the Map* (1957) are volumes of short stories. Wilson has also written on *Zola (1950), *Dickens (1970), and *Kipling (1977), and an interesting account of his own sources and creative processes, *The Wild Garden* (1963). His works display a brilliant satiric wit, acute social observation, and a love of the macabre and the farcical, combined with humanity.

WILSON, Colin Henry (1931–), was brought up in Leicester, and left school at sixteen. *The Outsider* (1956) describes the sense of alienation of the man of genius, using a mixture of texts, from Barbusse, *Camus, *Sartre, T. E. *Lawrence, Hesse, etc. and did much to popularize a version of *Existentialism in Britain. It earned him the label of *Angry Young Man. Wilson has since written many works on mysticism, existentialism, the occult, etc., and published many novels in various genres.

WILSON, Edmund (1895–1972), American author. He served abroad during the First World War, an experience which inspired verse and short stories published in *The Undertaker's Garland* (1922, with J. P. Bishop). He published the novel *I Thought of Daisy* (1929, rev. 1967) and short stories, *Memoirs of Hecate County* (1946). He is principally known for his influential, wide-ranging, and independent works of literary and social criticism, which include *Axel's Castle* (1931), a study of *Symbolist literature; *The Triple Thinkers* (1938); *To the Finland Station* (1940), a study of socialist theory; *The Wound and the Bow* (1941), a series of studies with a *Freudian angle; and *Patriotic Gore: Studies in the Literature of the American Civil War* (1962), a comprehensive survey of the period and the war's roots in the national psyche. His third wife was the novelist Mary *McCarthy.

WILSON, Harriette, *née* Dubochet (1786–1846), courtesan, who left a spirited account of her adventures and amours in the fashionable Regency world in *Memoirs of Harriette Wilson, written by herself* (1825), which describes her impressions of and friendships with *Brummell, Prince Esterhazy, the dukes of *Wellington, Argyle, Beaufort, Leinster, etc.

WILSON, John (?1627–96), became recorder of Londonderry. His two principal plays, *The Cheats* (1663) and *The Projectors* (printed 1665), are Jonsonian satires in which sharks, gulls, usurers, and astrologers are vigorously and effectively displayed.

WILSON, John (1785–1854), joined the editorial staff of *Blackwood's* to which he contributed; he provided more than half the series *Noctes Ambrosianae*, in which he appears as 'Christopher North'. He was part-author of the notorious *Chaldee MS*; he wrote a ferocious attack on Coleridge's *Biographia Literaria*; and joined in *Lockhart's prolonged onslaught on the *Cockney school. He wrote some poetry and three sentimental novels of Scottish life.

WILSON, John Dover (1881–1969), Shakespearian scholar and editor. He was responsible for editing most of the plays in the New Cambridge Shakespeare series. Among other scholarly works are his influential 'biographical adventure' *The Essential Shakespeare* (1932), *What Happens in Hamlet* (1935), and *The Fortunes of Falstaff* (1943).

WILSON, Thomas (*c.*1525–81), privy councillor and secretary of state in 1578. He published *The Rule of Reason*, a work on logic (1551); and the *Arte of Rhetorique* (1553; rev. and improved, 1560) a notable landmark in the history of English prose. Wilson provides interesting examples of epistles and orations in a variety of English styles, one of the most amusing of which is the famous *'ink-horn' letter from a Lincolnshire clergyman seeking preferment, which exhibits the worst excesses of Latinism and affectation. *The Arte of Rhetorique* was edited by G. H. Mair (1909).

Wilton, Jacke, see UNFORTUNATE TRAVELLER, THE.

Wilton House, in Wiltshire, seat of the earls of Pembroke, is associated with Sir P. *Sidney, who is said to have written much of the first version of the *Arcadia there while staying with his sister Mary, countess of *Pembroke. According to *Aubrey, 'In her time Wilton house was like a College, there were so many learned and ingeniose persons.'

Wimble, Will, in *The Spectator*, a friend of Sir Roger de *Coverley.

Wimsey, Lord Peter, the detective hero of most stories by D. L. *Sayers.

WINCHILSEA, Anne Finch, countess of, *née* Kingsmill (1661–1720), poet, was a friend of *Pope, *Swift, *Gay, and *Rowe. Her *Miscellany poems on several occasions* appeared in 1713; they were admired by *Wordsworth, who chose a selection for an album (1819). Her best-known poem is *The Spleen*; her couplet about the jonquil and 'aromatic pain' was echoed by Pope in his *Essay on Man*.

Wind in the Willows, The, see GRAHAME, K.

Windsor Forest, a *topographical poem by *Pope in the genre of *Cooper's Hill* by *Denham, published 1713, to celebrate the Peace of Utrecht; it combines description of landscape with historical, literary, and political reflections.

WING, Donald Goddard (1904–), American scholar, librarian, and bibliographer, who was responsible for compiling the *Short-Title Catalogue of Books Printed in England, Scotland, Ireland, Wales and British America, and of English Books Printed in Other Countries 1641–1700*, published in 1945 (rev. and enlarged 1972).

Wings of the Dove, The, a novel by H. *James published 1902.

The handsome and clever Kate Croy allows herself to be taken up by her rich aunt, Maud Lowder; she is as determined to feather her nest as she is genuinely in love with Merton Densher, a journalist without bright financial prospects. While on a visit to New York Densher meets Milly Theale, an orphaned, gentle girl who is immensely rich. Her wings are weighted with gold. Milly travels to Europe with her friend Susan Stringham, and in London she is gathered into Mrs Lowder's circle. She is anxious to meet Densher again and is disturbed to learn, from a disapproving Mrs Lowder, of his interest in Kate. While in London she learns that she is doomed and is advised by the sympathetic doctor Sir Luke Strett to seize what joy she can from life. She instals herself in a palazzo in Venice, and with their varying motives her friends gather round her. Kate and Densher become lovers. The predatory Kate persuades a reluctant Densher to make a show of love for Milly in the hope that, dying, she will provide for him—and for them. After Milly's death Densher does indeed discover that she has done so, but he finds himself unable to accept the money, and Kate. Their very success in this dreadful game has brought about the death of their relationship.

Winkle, Nathaniel, a character in Dickens's *Pickwick Papers.*

'Winkle, Rip Van', see RIP VAN WINKLE.

Winner and Waster, see WYNNERE AND WASTOUR.

Winnie-the-Pooh, the bear of very little brain, and friend of Piglet, Eeyore, and others, in the popular stories of A. A. *Milne.

WINSTANLEY, Gerrard (*c.* 1609–76), radical pamphleteer and leader of the Diggers, or True Levellers. In 1649 with a group of comrades he started digging and planting crops on St George's Hill, in Surrey, in a bold but short-lived attempt to claim the common land for 'the common people of England'; the failure of this experiment is expressed in *The Law of Freedom, in a Platform* (1652). His first Digger manifesto, *The True Levellers' Standard Advanced* dated 20 April 1649, was followed by others including *A Watchword to the City of London, and the Army* (1649) and *Fire in the Bush* (1650). His prose is powerful and lucid; many of his metaphors are drawn from daily life, but he can also express himself with poetic intensity, and with a personal and inventive use of biblical imagery that prefigures *Blake. His contribution to literature and political thought was neglected until the 20th cent., but he is now acclaimed by many as one of the most original and prophetic writers of his time.

Winterborne, Giles, a character in Hardy's *The Woodlanders.*

WINTERS, (Arthur) Yvor (1900–68), American poet and critic, whose own poems exemplify his critical doctrine of classicism, restraint, moral judgement, and 'cold certitude'. (See NEW CRITICISM.) His *In Defense of Reason* (1947) contains three earlier works, *Primitivism and Decadence* (1937), *Maule's Curse* (1938), and *The Anatomy of Nonsense* (1943), all of which attack obscurantism and *Romanticism.

Winter's Tale, The, a play by *Shakespeare written in 1610 or 1611, performed 1611, first printed in the *Folio of 1623. Its main source is *Greene's *Pandosto.*

Leontes, king of Sicily, and Hermione, his virtuous wife, are visited by Leontes' childhood friend Polixenes, king of Bohemia. Leontes presently convinces himself that Hermione and Polixenes are lovers, attempts to procure the death of the latter by poison, and on his escape imprisons Hermione, who in prison gives birth to a daughter. Paulina, wife of Antigonus, a Sicilian lord, tries to move the king's compassion by bringing the baby to him, but in vain. He orders Antigonus to leave the child on a desert shore to perish. He disregards a Delphian oracle declaring Hermione innocent. He soon learns that his son Mamillius has died of sorrow for Hermione's treatment, and shortly after that Hermione herself is dead, and is filled with remorse. Meanwhile Antigonus leaves the baby girl, Perdita, on the shore of Bohemia, and is himself killed by a bear. Perdita is found and brought up by a shepherd. Sixteen years pass. When she grows up, Florizel, son of King Polixenes, falls in love with her, and his love is returned. This is discovered by Polixenes, to avoid whose anger Florizel, Perdita, and the old shepherd flee from Bohemia to the court of Leontes, where the identity of Perdita is discovered, to Leontes' great joy, and the revival of his grief for the loss of Hermione. Paulina offers to show him a statue that perfectly resembles Hermione, and when the king's grief is intensified by the sight of this, the statue comes to life and reveals itself as the living Hermione, whose death Paulina falsely reported in order to save her life. Polixenes is reconciled to the marriage of his son with Perdita, on finding that the shepherd-girl is really the daughter of his former friend Leontes. The rogueries of Autolycus, the pedlar and 'snapper-up of unconsidered trifles', add amusement to the later scenes of the play; and his songs 'When daffodils begin to peer' and 'Jog on, jog on, the footpath way' are famous.

WIREKER, Nigel (*fl.* 1190), author of *Burnellus* or *Speculum Stultorum,* a satire on monks recounting the adventures of *Burnell the ass. (See also ANGLO-LATIN LITERATURE.)

Wisden, *A Cricketer's Almanac,* first published under this title by John Wisden and Co. in 1870 (previously known, 1864–9, as *The Cricketer's Almanac*). The publication remains the cricket enthusiast's vade-mecum.

Wisdom (also *Mind, Will and Understanding* or *Wisdom, who is Christ*), a *Morality play from *c.*1460, one of the group called *Macro plays, describing the seduction by Lucifer of Mind, Will, and Understanding in a series of dances.

Wisdom of Solomon, one of the books of the *Apocrypha, attributed by tradition to Solomon's authorship, but probably from a Greek original of a period little anterior to Christianity.

WISE, Thomas James (1859–1937), bibliographer, collector, and editor who formed the Ashley Library (see LIBRARIES). The publication of *An enquiry into the nature of certain 19th-century pamphlets* (1934), by J. Carter and G. Pollard, proved that many rare pamphlets whose authenticity depended on Wise's statements were in fact forgeries, notably an edition of E. B. Browning's *Sonnets from the Portuguese* said to have been published in Reading in 1847.

WISHART, William (*c.*1692–1753), Scots cleric and controversialist, and co-founder of the Rankenian club. He was an energetic exponent of the moral sense philosophy of *Shaftesbury and *Hutcheson. In addition to sermons, he published anonymous satires on *Berkeley's *Alciphron* in 1734 and *Doddridge's *Life of Col. Gardiner* in 1747.

Wishfort, Lady, a character in Congreve's *The Way of the World*.

Witch, The, a play by T. *Middleton, written before 1616, not printed until 1778.

The plot concerns the revenge of Rosamund upon her husband Alboin, king of the Lombards, who has forced her to drink from a cup made from her father's skull. She calls on the assistance of Hecate. Part of the interest of the play lies in the comparison between Middleton's Hecate and the witches in Shakespeare's *Macbeth*. *Lamb in his *Specimens* indicated the difference between them.

Witchcraft, *The Discoverie of,* see SCOT, R.

'Witch of Atlas, The', a fantasy poem, in *ottava rima*, by P. B. *Shelley, published 1824.

The beautiful Witch is the daughter of Apollo, and the spirit of mischief and poetry. She besports herself amid pyrotechnic imagery of magic boats, airships, storms, and fireballs. Her mysterious companion is the Hermaphrodite, and together they circle the globe, weaving spells over recalcitrant kings, priests, soldiers, and young lovers.

Witch of Edmonton, The, a tragi-comedy by *Dekker, *Ford, *Rowley, 'etc.' (possibly *Webster?), first performed probably 1621, not published until 1658. It is partly based on the story of Elizabeth Sawyer, who was hanged as a witch in April 1621.

Frank Thorney marries his fellow servant Winifred. To save himself from being disinherited, at his father's bidding he also marries Susan Carter, and to extract himself from his embarrassment, murders her, but is discovered and in due course executed.

The old woman of Edmonton is persecuted by her neighbours and to revenge herself she sells her soul to the devil, who appears to her in the form of a dog. Her character is notable for the characteristic sympathy shown by Dekker for the poor outcast. Both plots reflect the theme of revenge, but are otherwise little connected. The play has been successfully staged several times in recent decades.

WITHER, George (1588–1667), poet and pamphleteer. His satires *Abuses stript and whipt*, published 1613, in spite of the innocuous character of their denunciations of Avarice, Gluttony, and so forth, earned him imprisonment in the Marshalsea. There he wrote five pastorals under the title of *The Shepheards Hunting*, a continuation of *The Shepheard's Pipe*, which he had written in conjunction with William *Browne, the 'Willie' of these verses. His *Fidelia* appeared in 1617 and again, with the famous song 'Shall I, wasting in despair', in 1619; it was this song, printed by Percy in his *Reliques*, that was to rescue Wither's reputation from a century of neglect.

In 1622 appeared *Faire-Virtue, the mistresse of Phil'arete*, a long sequence of poems in various verse forms in praise of his semi-allegorical mistress. From this time Wither's poetry became increasingly religious and satirical in tone, which led to accusations that he was a Puritan, and his portrayal as 'Chronomastix' in *Jonson's masque *Time Vindicated* (1623). He published *The hymnes and songs of the Church* in 1623, a poem on the plague in 1628, a book of *emblems in 1634–5, and *Heleluiah* in 1641.

Witterly, Mr and Mrs, in Dickens's *Nicholas Nickleby*, typical snobs.

Wits, The, a comedy by *D'Avenant, published 1636, revised by him after the Restoration, and generally considered his best comedy.

It concerns the love of the spendthrift young wit Pallatine for Lucy, who is thrown out by her cruel aunt for selling her jewels to help him. After many intrigues and adventures the young couple are provided for by Pallatine's at first reluctant elder brother, who is trapped into generosity.

WITTGENSTEIN, Ludwig Josef Johann (1889–1951), born in Vienna, came to England in 1908; he lived most of his adult life in Cambridge, where he was professor of philosophy (1939–47). He came to philosophy through the study of the philosophy of mathematics with B. *Russell. He himself published only the *Tractatus Logico-Philosophicus* (1922); in this aphoristic and difficult book he presents the view that the only meaningful use of language is as a picture of empirical, scientific fact; otherwise language will be tautological, as in logic and mathematics, or nonsensical, as in metaphysics and judgements of value. About 1930 he began to doubt the correctness of this approach; he gradually developed the view that language had a vast multiplicity of uses, which he likened to the multiplicity of tools in a carpenter's toolbag, and that the traditional problems of philosophy arose from a misunderstanding of the use of those concepts in terms of which the problems arose; this misunderstanding he likened to mental cramp or bewilderment, and held that the problems could be dissolved by carefully bringing out the true character of the language in which they were framed. Thus there were no philosophical results, in the form of answers to questions, but only the growth and dissolution of philosophical puzzlement.

Witwoud, and his half-brother Sir Wilfull Witwoud, characters in Congreve's * *The Way of the World*.

Wives and Daughters, the last and unfinished novel of E. *Gaskell, published in the *Cornhill Magazine*, 1864–6, and in volume form 1866.

This novel, Mrs Gaskell's masterpiece, centres on two families, the Gibsons and the Hamleys. Mr Gibson, surgeon in the little country town of Hollingford, is a widower with one daughter, Molly. As she grows up her father feels he ought to marry again for her sake. He marries a widow, Mrs Kirkpatrick, formerly governess in the family of Lord Cumnor, the local magnate. Molly is made unhappy by her graceful stepmother's shallow selfishness, but her lot is improved when her stepmother's daughter by her previous marriage, Cynthia, joins the household. Cynthia is a fascinating beauty, more sincere than her mother, but with few moral principles.

The Hamleys are an ancient county family—the proud and hot-tempered Squire, his invalid wife, their elder son Osborne who is handsome and clever, and a young son, Roger, sturdy, honest, and a late developer. Molly Gibson often stays with the Hamleys, and discovers that Osborne is secretly married to a French

nursery-maid. Molly has begun to love and admire Roger, but he becomes engaged to Cynthia, and, being by now a successful scientist, goes on an expedition to Africa. Cynthia is in fact already secretly engaged to Preston, Lord Cumnor's ill-bred agent, and she enlists Molly's help in extricating herself from this entanglement, thus compromising Molly's reputation. The secret of Osborne Hamley's marriage comes out, causing a bitter estrangement with his father, but when Osborne dies Squire Hamley, deeply repentent, adopts Osborne's baby son. Cynthia throws over Roger Hamley and marries a man more suited to her, and when Roger returns he has realized that it is Molly whom he really loves.

WODEHOUSE, Sir P(elham) G(renville) (1881–1975), began by writing short stories for boys' magazines, and later published extensively in the *Strand Magazine*, *Punch*, etc., establishing himself as one of the most widely read humorists of his day. His prolific output, of over 120 volumes, included *The Man with Two Left Feet* (1917), the collection of stories which first introduced *Jeeves and Bertie *Wooster; a series of Jeeves volumes (*My Man Jeeves*, 1919; *The Inimitable Jeeves*, 1923; *Carry On, Jeeves*, 1925, etc.); and other works featuring such favourite characters as Lord Emsworth (and his prize sow, the Empress of Blandings), Mr Mulliner, Psmith, several redoubtable aunts, and many patrons of the Drones Club. Wodehouse's amiable career also embraced successes in musical comedy, the theatre, and Hollywood. After the Second World War he settled in America (where he had previously lived for some years), taking American citizenship in 1955.

WOFFINGTON, Peg (Margaret) (c.1714–60), the celebrated actress. She had many lovers, and lived for some time with *Garrick. She is the subject of *Masks and Faces* (1852), a play by C. *Reade and Tom *Taylor, on which Reade based his novel *Peg Woffington* (1853).

WOLCOT, John (1738–1819), 'Peter Pindar', author of vigorous and witty satirical verses. Among these were *Lyric Odes to the Royal Academicians* (1782–5); a mock-heroic poem, *The Lousiad* (1785–95), and various other satires on George III. *Bozzy and Piozzi*, in which *Boswell and Mrs *Thrale set forth their reminiscences of Dr *Johnson, appeared in 1786, as did his *Poetical and Congratulatory Epistle to James Boswell*.

WOLFE, Charles (1791–1823), was author of the well-known lines on 'The Burial of Sir John Moore', his only poem of note, apparently based on *Southey's narrative in the *Annual Register*, and first published in the *Newry Telegraph* in 1817. His *Poems* was published in 1903.

WOLFE, Reyner or Reginald (d. 1573), bookseller and printer, who came from Strasburg, was the first printer in England to possess a large stock of Greek type of good quality, and he printed in 1543, with Greek and Latin text, the *Homilies* of *Chrysostom, edited by *Cheke, the first Greek book printed in this country. In 1547 he was appointed King's Printer in Latin, Greek, and Hebrew.

WOLFE, Thomas Clayton (1900–38), American novelist, made his name with his vast autobiographical novel *Look Homeward, Angel* (1929), which describes the adolescence of Eugene Gant; this was followed by a sequel, *Of Time and the River* (1935), and various posthumous works, which include *The Web and the Rock* (1939) and its sequel *You Can't Go Home Again* (1940). Wolfe's undisciplined work owed much in its published form to editorial assistance, but its emotional power won many readers.

WOLFRAM VON ESCHENBACH (*fl. c.*1200–20), a great German epic poet, whose principal works were the epics *Parzifal* and *Willehalm*. He also composed fragments of *Titurel*. Wolfram appears as a character in *Wagner's *Tannhäuser*. (See MINNESINGERS.)

WOLLSTONECRAFT, Mary (1759–97), opened a school at Newington Green in 1784 with her sister Eliza and a friend; there she made the acquaintance of R. *Price and other eminent Dissenters. She was the author of *Thoughts on the Education of Daughters* (1787); *Mary* (1788), a novel; and *A Vindication of the Rights of Men* (1790, a reply to *Burke). Her most famous work was **A Vindication of the Rights of Woman* (1792). In 1792 she went to Paris, where she met Gilbert Imlay, an American writer, by whom she had a daughter, Fanny, in 1794; in the same year she published her 'View' of the French revolution. In 1797 she married W. *Godwin, and she died from septicaemia shortly after the birth of her daughter, the future Mary *Shelley. Godwin published a memoir in 1798, edited her *Posthumous Works* in the same year, and portrayed her in his novel *St Leon* (1799).

Wolsey, The Life and Death of Cardinal, see CAVENDISH, G.

Woman in the Moone, The, a prose play by *Lyly, published 1597.

Woman in White, The, a novel by Wilkie *Collins, published 1860.

The narrative, related in succession by Walter Hartright and other characters in the story, starts with his midnight encounter on a lonely road with a mysterious and agitated woman dressed entirely in white, whom he helps to escape from pursuers. When working as a drawing-master in the family of Mr Fairlie, a selfish valetudinarian,

he falls in love with his niece Laura, who strikingly resembles the woman in white. She returns his love, but is engaged to Sir Percival Glyde, whom she marries. It comes to light that Sir Percival has married Laura to get possession of her wealth, that he was responsible for the confinement of the woman in white, Anne Catherick, in an asylum, and that Anne Catherick and her mother know a secret concerning Sir Percival. Unable to obtain Laura's signature to the surrender of her money, Sir Percival and his friend Count Fosco (a fat, smooth villain, admirably conceived) contrive to get Laura confined in an asylum as Anne Catherick, while Anne Catherick, who dies, is buried as Laura Glyde. The device is discovered by Marian Halcombe, Laura's half-sister, and Laura is rescued. Hartright takes Laura and Marian under his care, and discovers Sir Percival's secret (that he was born out of wedlock and has no right to the title). Sir Percival is burnt to death while tampering with a parish register. Fosco is forced to supply the information which restores Laura to her identity, and is killed by a member of an Italian secret society which he has betrayed.

Woman Killed with Kindness, A, a domestic tragedy by T. *Heywood, acted about 1603, printed 1607.

Frankford, a country gentleman, is the husband of Anne, a 'perfect' wife. But his happiness is ruined by the treachery of Wendoll, a guest to whom Frankford has shown every kindness and hospitality. Frankford discovers Anne in the arms of Wendoll, but instead of taking immediate vengeance on her, he determines to 'kill her even with kindness'. He sends her to live in comfort in a lonely manorhouse, only prohibiting her from seeing him or her children again. She dies from remorse, after having sent for Frankford to ask forgiveness on her deathbed and received it.

The sub-plot, in which Susan Mountford is used as a pawn to redeem her bankrupt brother from prison, but finds herself loved by her new husband, offers interesting perspectives on the main plot. The play is one of the most successful examples of English domestic tragedy.

Woman's Prize, The, or the Tamer Tamed, a comedy by J. *Fletcher, printed 1647. It shows the second marriage of Petruchio, from Shakespeare's *The Taming of the Shrew*.

Woman Who Did, The, see ALLEN, G.

Women Beware Women, a tragedy by T. *Middleton, published posthumously in 1657.

Set in Florence, the action involves two interwoven plots. The sub-plot is concerned with the guilty love of Hippolito for his niece Isabella. The main plot is loosely based on the life of the historical Bianca Cappello, who became the mistress, and then the consort, of Francesco de' Medici (1541–87). In Middleton's version, she is at the opening of the play innocently but secretly married to Leantio, a merchant's clerk. The duke sees her at a window and falls in love with her: in Act II, ii, while Livia outwits Leantio's mother at chess (a scene invoked by T. S. Eliot in *The Waste Land*), the duke gains access to Bianca and seduces her. Thereafter both she and Leantio are plunged into the corruption of the court. Bianca becomes the duke's mistress: the duke, reproved by the cardinal, his brother, for his sin, contrives the death of Leantio, who has sworn everlasting enmity to Bianca, and accepted both financial and amorous compensation for her loss. These various crimes, in the last act, meet with retribution in a wholesale massacre of the characters, through the theatrical medium of a masque accompanied by poisoned incense: Bianca destroys herself by drinking deliberately from a poisoned cup.

Women in Love, a novel by D. H. *Lawrence, published in London 1921.

The sisters Ursula and Gudrun Brangwen (who first appeared in *The Rainbow*) live in Beldover, a Midlands colliery town. Ursula has been teaching at the Grammar School and Gudrun has just returned from art school in London. Ursula is in love with Rupert Birkin (a self-portrait of Lawrence), a school-inspector involved in an unsatisfactory affair with Hermione Roddice, an eccentric and dominating literary hostess. Gudrun meets Gerald Crich, friend of Birkin and son of the local colliery owner. As a boy Gerald has accidentally killed his brother and now he feels responsible when his sister Diana is drowned. His father, Walter, is dying and he takes over management of the mine; Birkin breaks free from Hermione and hopes to find with Ursula the complete union between man and woman. Gerald suffers in his relationship with Gudrun, his mixture of violence and weakness arousing a destructive demon in her. Birkin offers Gerald love and friendship to be based on a new intimacy between men, but Gerald is unable to accept. Ursula and Birkin are married. Both couples take a trip to the Alps where they meet the corrupt sculptor Loerke, the 'wizard rat', with whom Gudrun flirts. While Ursula and Birkin move towards a real tenderness, Gudrun and Gerald become purely destructive until finally, in despair, Gerald wanders off into the snow and dies.

Women's Press, The, see FEMINIST CRITICISM.

Women's Suffrage. The campaign for women's suffrage began in 1866 when a group of women presented a petition to J. S. *Mill requesting female enfranchisement. Mill moved an amendment to the *Reform Act of 1867 to include women, which was defeated. Thereafter organizations sprang up all over the country and joined forces to form the National Union of Women's Suffrage Societies (NUWSS). By the end of the century a majority of MPs had pledged themselves to vote for women's suffrage bills, which passed their second readings three times only to be blocked by governments.

To invigorate the campaign Mrs Emmeline Pankhurst (1858–1928) founded in 1903 the Women's Social and Political Union (WSPU), and her daughter Christabel (1880–1958) in 1905 initiated mildly militant tactics, designed to make the incoming Liberals take the women's demand seriously. Because of their youthfulness militants were known as suffragettes, and members of the NUWSS, led by Millicent Garrett Fawcett (1847–1929), as suffragists.

In 1912, when other means were failing to break Asquith's resistance, the Pankhursts resorted to destruction of empty property on a massive scale. The war brought the campaign virtually to an end; women's patriotism (coupled with a fear of renewed militancy) induced Parliament in 1918 to enfranchise women over 30, provided they occupied or were the wives of occupiers of premises of not less than £5 annual value.

The campaign was supported by many writers; in 1908 the Women Writers Suffrage League was founded by Cicely Hamilton (1872–1952), journalist, playwright, and novelist, and journalist Bessie Hatton. Its president was Elizabeth Robins (1862–1952); her play Votes for Women (1907) was highly influential. Other supporters included O. *Schreiner, M. *Sinclair, A. *Meynell, S. *Grand, R. *West, and V. *Hunt. Suffragists and suffragettes were widely portrayed in the literature of the period: see V. *Woolf's Night and Day, H. G. *Wells's Ann Veronica, G. B. *Shaw's Press Cuttings. Accounts of the movement were also written by leading feminists, including the Pankhursts and E. Pethick-Lawrence (1867–1954). It produced many periodicals, including Women's Suffrage Journal, The Common Cause, Votes for Women, and Women's Dreadnought.

WOOD, Anthony, or, as he latterly called himself, Anthony à Wood (1632–95), historian and antiquary. He prepared a treatise on the history of the University of Oxford, which was translated into Latin and edited (with alterations) by *Fell and published as Historia et Antiquitates Univ. Oxon. (1674). Wood published Athenae Oxonienses (1691–2), a biographical dictionary of Oxford writers and bishops, containing severe judgements on some of these, and was expelled from the University in 1693 at the instance of Henry Hyde, for a libel which the work contained on his father, the first earl of *Clarendon.

WOOD, Ellen, *née* Price, better known as Mrs Henry Wood (1814–87), married Henry Wood, a banker, in 1836. She had an immense success with her first novel *East Lynne* (1861). She subsequently owned and edited the magazine *The Argosy*, and wrote nearly 40 novels, among the best of which are *Mrs Halliburton's Troubles* (1862), *The Channings* (1862), and *The Shadow of Ashlydyat* (1863). Her ingenious plots about murders, thefts, and forgeries, her numerous court scenes and well-planted clues, make her in such novels as *Lord Oakburn's Daughters* (1864), *Elster's Folly* (1866), and *Roland Yorke* (1869) one of the forerunners of the modern *detective story. The sensational, and occasionally supernatural, events in her novels are presented in solidly detailed settings of middle-class country-town communities.

Woodall, the hero of Dryden's *Mr Limberham*.

Woodcourt, Allan, a character in Dickens's *Bleak House*.

WOODFORDE, the Revd James (1740–1803), is remembered as the author of *The Diary of a Country Parson* (5 vols, ed. J. Beresford, 1924–31), which covers the period of the American War of Independence and the French revolution; but in the main the life he describes is concerned with daily events, minor travels, and his love of food and drink recorded in frequent descriptions of meals. The popularity of the work is due more to its social interest and period charm than to its literary qualities.

Woodhouse, Mr, the heroine's father in J. Austen's *Emma*.

Woodlanders, The, a novel by T. *Hardy, published 1887.

The scene is set in Little Hintock, a village deep in the woods of Dorset. In this luxuriant woodland country live a group of native woodlanders. Giles Winterbourne, who tends trees and travels in the autumn with his cider-press, loves and is betrothed to Grace Melbury, daughter of a well-to-do Hintock timber merchant. But when she returns from her finishing school she appears as the social superior of Giles. At about the same time Giles suffers financial misfortune. Grace's father brings the engagement to an end and presses his daughter into marriage with Edred Fitzpiers, a handsome young doctor. Meanwhile Marty South, a village girl who had always loved Giles, has to sell her splendid hair to help herself and her sick father to live. Fitzpiers is soon lured away from Grace by a wealthy widow, Felice Charmond. The hope of divorce brings Grace and the faithful Giles together again. When Fitzpiers returns from his travels with Mrs Charmond, Grace flies for refuge to Giles's cottage in the woods. Giles, although ill, makes for himself a shelter of hurdles, where a few days later he dies. The loving, faithful Marty meets Grace by Giles's deathbed, and together they regularly visit his burial-place. With Mrs Charmond's death Grace and Fitzpiers are reconciled, and Marty is left alone to tend Giles's grave.

Wood's half-pence, SEE DRAPIER'S LETTERS, THE.

Woodstock; or, The Cavalier. A tale of the year 1651, a novel by Sir W. *Scott, published 1826. The work was written when misfortunes were heaping themselves upon the author: his financial ruin, the death of his wife, and the serious illness of his beloved grandson.

The period is that of the Civil War, and the story centres in the escape of Charles II from England after the battle of Worcester. The scene is the royal lodge and park of Woodstock, near Oxford.

The portrait of Cromwell has been criticized; the author makes, it is said, the mistake of representing Oliver as being in supreme power before he became lord protector in 1653. But the work gives a vivid picture of a reckless cavalier, Roger Wildrake; of the Revd Nehemiah Holdenough, Presbyterian minister of the town of Woodstock; of Puritan soldiers and preachers (including Joseph Tomkins, the steward of the parliamentary commissioners, a mixture of hypocrisy and enthusiasm); and of plotters and spies on both sides.

WOOLF, Leonard Sidney (1880–1969), author, Fabian, and social reformer, educated at Trinity College, Cambridge, where he became a member of the *Apostles. He entered the colonial service and in 1904 went to Ceylon, which was to form the background for his first novel, *The Village in the Jungle* (1913); it was followed by *The Wise Virgins* (1914). Woolf left the colonial service in 1912 to marry Virginia Stephen (see below); he and his wife shared a close intellectual comradeship and a commitment to the *Hogarth Press. He wrote on the Co-operative Movement, Socialism, imperialism, the League of Nations, and international affairs, was literary editor of the *Nation* (1923–30), and co-founder and joint editor of the *Political Quarterly* (1931–59). *After the Deluge* (2 vols, 1931 and 1939) and *Principia Politica* (1953) were his most concerted attempt to formulate a political philosophy, but the five volumes of his autobiography, written after his wife's death, have reached a much wider audience: *Sowing* (1960), *Growing* (1961), *Beginning Again* (1964), *Downhill All the Way* (1967), and *The Journey not the Arrival Matters* (1969) together constitute a clear-sighted view of a life devoted to social progress and rich in intellectual friendships

WOOLF, (Adeline) Virginia (1882–1941), daughter of Leslie *Stephen and Julia Duckworth (1847–95), was born at Hyde Park Gate, where she lived with her sister Vanessa (later Vanessa Bell) and her brothers until her father's death in 1904. The Stephen children then moved to Bloomsbury, where they formed the nucleus of the *Bloomsbury Group. In 1905 she began to write for the *Times Literary Supplement, a connection which lasted almost until her death. In 1912 she married Leonard *Woolf; she was already working on her first novel, The Voyage Out (1915). She had meanwhile experienced one of the bouts of acute mental disturbance from which she had suffered since her mother's death, and it was partly as therapy for her that she and Leonard founded, in 1917, the *Hogarth Press; its first production was Two Stories, one by each of them. Her second novel, Night and Day (1919), set in London, centres on Katherine Hilbery, daughter of a famous literary family (modelled on Vanessa), whose pursuits are contrasted with her friend Mary's involvement with *Women's Suffrage. Jacob's Room (1922), a novel evoking the life and death (in the First World War) of Jacob Flanders (clearly related to the death of her brother Thoby in 1906) was recognized as a new development in the art of fiction, in its indirect narration and poetic impressionism. Shortly afterwards she published one of her important statements on modern fiction, 'Mr Bennett and Mrs Brown', in the Nation and Athenaeum, 1 Dec. 1923, which attacked the realism of Arnold *Bennett and advocated a more fluid, internal approach to the problem of characterization, etc. From this time onwards she was regarded as one of the principal exponents of *Modernism, and her subsequent major novels, *Mrs Dalloway (1925), *To the Lighthouse (1927), and *The Waves (1931), established her reputation securely. Orlando (1928) is a fantastic biography inspired by her friend V. *Sackville-West, which traces the history of the youthful, beautiful, and aristocratic Orlando through four centuries and both male and female manifestations; Flush (1933), a slighter work, is the 'biography' of E. B. *Browning's spaniel. *The Years (1937) is in form a more conventional novel, whereas her last work, *Between the Acts (1941), is highly experimental. Shortly after finishing it she drowned herself in the Ouse, near her home at Rodmell, Sussex.

Virginia Woolf is now acclaimed as one of the great innovative novelists of the 20th cent., many of whose experimental techniques (such as the use of the *stream of consciousness) have been absorbed into the mainstream of fiction; her novels have been particularly highly regarded from the 1970s onwards by the new school of *feminist criticism. She was also a literary critic and journalist of distinction. *A Room of One's Own (1929) is a classic of the feminist movement; a sequel, Three Guineas, appeared in 1938. Her critical essays were published in several collections, including *The Common Reader (1925; Second Series, 1932), The Death of the Moth (1942), The Captain's Death Bed (1950), and Granite and Rainbow (1958). A volume of short stories, A Haunted House (1943), collects earlier stories and some not previously published. Her letters (ed. Nigel Nicolson and J. Trautmann, 6 vols, 1975–80) are a dazzling, at times malicious evocation of a world of literary and social friendships and intrigues, with a cast list that includes *Strachey, the *Sitwells, Ottoline *Morrell, R. *Fry, and many others; her diaries (5 vols, ed. Anne Olivier Bell and A. McNeillie, 1977–84) are a unique record of the joys and pains of the creative process.

WOOLNER, Thomas (1825–92), poet and sculptor, one of the original *Pre-Raphaelite brethren, who contributed to *The Germ two cantos of what was to become My Beautiful Lady (1863). He became a prosperous portrait sculptor, doing busts and statues of (among many others), *Tennyson, *Newman, C. *Kingsley, and J. S. *Mill. His other poems include the blank verse Pygmalion (1881). 'The Piping Shepherd', which appears as a frontispiece to Palgrave's Golden Treasury, is by him.

Wooster, Bertram (familiarly known as 'Bertie'), an amiable, vacuous young man-about-town in the stories of P. G. *Wodehouse; the employer of *Jeeves.

Wopsle, Mr, a character in Dickens's *Great Expectations.

WORDE, Winkyn de, see WYNKYN DE WORDE.

WORDSWORTH, Dorothy (1771–1855), was the sister of William *Wordsworth. She settled with William in 1795, and from that time they lived together, through William's marriage until his death. After a short time in Dorset they moved to Alfoxden in Somerset, where she, William, and *Coleridge walked and talked, as Coleridge wrote, 'as three persons with one soul'. There she began her Alfoxden Journal, of which only the months Jan.–April 1798 remain. Her Grasmere Journal, covering the years 1800–3, demonstrates her skill with words in the precise descriptions of the Lake District and of the daily events of life in Dove Cottage.

Dorothy kept several other journals of travels and expeditions including Journal of a Tour on the Continent 1820; Journal of a Second Tour of Scotland (1822); and a Journal of a Tour in the Isle of Man (1828).

It is clear from passages in his notes and from certain of his poems (for instance, the untitled 'Daffodils') that Wordsworth made use of his sister's journals, and several of his poems, as well as the famous closing lines of *'Tintern Abbey', are addressed to Dorothy. In his Life (1933) her editor de *Selincourt finds her 'probably . . . the most distinguished of English writers who never wrote a line for the general public'. Her *Journals* were edited by W. Knight, 1896 and 1904.

WORDSWORTH, William (1770–1850), educated at Hawkshead Grammar School. His mother died in 1778, his father in 1783, losses recorded in *The Prelude*. He attended St John's College, Cambridge, but disliked the academic course. In 1790 he went on a walking tour of France, the Alps, and Italy, and returned to France late in 1791, to spend a year there; during this period he fell in love with the daughter of a surgeon at Blois, Annette Vallon, who bore him a daughter. (This love affair is reflected in 'Vaudracour and Julia', composed ?1804, pub. 1820.) After his return to England he published in 1793 two poems in heroic couplets, *An Evening Walk* and *Descriptive Sketches*, both conventional attempts at the *picturesque and the *sublime. In this year he also wrote (but did not publish) a *Letter to the Bishop of Llandaff* (see WATSON, R.) in support of the French Republic. England's declaration of war against France shocked him deeply, but the institution of the Terror marked the beginning of his disillusion with the French revolution, a period of depression reflected in his verse drama *The Borderers* composed 1796–7, pub. 1842). In 1795 he received a legacy of £900 from his friend Raisley Calvert, which allowed him to pursue his vocation as a poet, and to be reunited with his sister Dorothy (above); they settled first at Racedown in Dorset, then at Alfoxden in Somerset, to be near *Coleridge, then living at Nether Stowey, whom Wordsworth had met in 1795. This was a period of intense creativity for both poets, which produced the *Lyrical Ballads* (1798), a landmark in the history of English *Romanticism. (See ANCIENT MARINER, IDIOT BOY, TINTERN ABBEY.) The winter of 1798–9 was spent in Goslar in Germany, where Wordsworth wrote the enigmatic *'Lucy' poems. In 1799 he and Dorothy settled in Dove Cottage, Grasmere; to the next year belong 'The Recluse', Book I (later *The Excursion*), 'The Brothers', *'Michael', and many of the poems included in the 1800 edition of the *Lyrical Ballads* (which, with its provocative Preface on *poetic diction, aroused much criticism). In 1802 Wordsworth married Mary Hutchinson. In the same year he composed *'Resolution and Independence', and began his ode on *'Intimations of Immortality from Recollections of Early Childhood', both of which appeared in *Poems in Two Volumes* (1807), along with many of his most celebrated lyrics. To the same period belong the birth of five children, travels with Dorothy and Coleridge, and new friendships, notably with Sir W. *Scott, Sir G. Beaumont, and *De Quincey. Wordsworth's domestic happiness was overcast by the death of his sailor brother John in 1805

(which inspired several poems, including 'Elegiac Stanzas suggested by a Picture of Peele Castle', 1807), the early deaths of two of his children (one of which inspired his sonnet 'Surprised by joy', 1815), and the physical deterioration of Coleridge, from whom he was for some time estranged, and with whom he was never entirely reconciled. But his productivity continued, and his popularity gradually increased. *The Excursion* was published in 1814, *The White Doe of Rylstone* in 1815, two volumes of *Miscellaneous Poems* in 1815, and *Peter Bell* and *The Waggoner* in 1819. Wordsworth slowly settled into the role of patriotic, conservative public man, abandoning the radical politics and idealism of his youth. Much of the best of his later work was mildly topographical, inspired by his love of travel. In 1843 he succeeded *Southey as poet laureate. He died in Rydal Mount, Ambleside (where he had lived since 1813) after the publication of a finally revised text of his works (6 vols, 1849–50). *The Prelude* was published posthumously in 1850.

De Quincey wrote of Wordsworth in 1835, 'Up to 1820 the name of Wordsworth was trampled underfoot; from 1820 to 1830 it was militant; from 1830 to 1835 it has been triumphant.' Early attacks in the *Edinburgh Review* were followed by criticism and satire by the second generation of Romantics; *Byron and *Shelley mocked him as 'simple' and 'dull', *Keats distrusted what he called the *'egotistical sublime', and *Hazlitt and later *Browning, deplored him as *'The Lost Leader', who had abandoned his early radical faith. But these doubts were counterbalanced by the enormous and lasting popularity of much of his work, which was regarded by writers such as M. *Arnold and J. S. *Mill with almost religious veneration, as an expression in an age of doubt of the transcendent in nature and the good in man. His biography by M. Moorman was published in 1968 (2 vols), and a long-lost collection of letters between Mary and William appeared in *The Love Letters of William and Mary Wordsworth*, ed. B. Darlington (1982).

Worldly Wiseman, Mr, in Bunyan's *Pilgrim's Progress*, an inhabitant of the town of Carnal Policy, who tries to dissuade Christian from going on his pilgrimage.

Worthies of England, The History of the, by T. *Fuller (1662).

The work is a kind of gazetteer of England, in which the author takes the counties one by one, describes their physical characteristics, natural commodities, and manufactures, with quaint comments on each, some of his own aphorisms, some proverbial. After these come short biographies of the local saints, Protestant martyrs, prelates, statesmen, writers, etc., and lists of the gentry and sheriffs.

Worthies of the World, The Nine, were 'three Paynims, three Jews, and three Christian men', viz. Hector of Troy, Alexander the Great, and Julius Caesar; Joshua, David, and Judas Maccabaeus; Arthur, Charlemagne, and Godefroi de Bouillon. (Caxton, Preface to Le *Morte D'Arthur*). The list of worthies in Shakespeare's *Love's Labour's Lost*, v. ii. is not quite the same, for it includes Pompey and Hercules.

WOTTON, Sir Henry (1568–1639), became agent and secretary to the earl of Essex, 1595, and was employed by him in collecting foreign intelligence. He was employed on various other diplomatic missions from 1604 to 1624. A collection of his poetical and other writings appeared under the title *Reliquiae Wottonianae*, containing his famous 'Character of a Happy Life' and 'On his Mistress, the Queen of Bohemia' ('You meaner beauties of the night') in 1651. His *Life* was written by his friend Izaak *Walton (1651).

Would-be, Sir Politic and Lady, characters in Jonson's *Volpone*.

Wrayburn, Eugene, a character in Dickens's *Our Mutual Friend*.

'Wreck of the Deutschland, The', see HOPKINS, G. M.

'Wreck of the Hesperus, The', a poem by *Longfellow.

Wren, Jenny, the business name of the doll's dressmaker in Dickens's *Our Mutual Friend*. Her real name was Fanny Cleaver.

WREN, P(ercival) C(hristopher) (1885–1941), novelist, who achieved popular success with *Beau Geste* (1924), the first of his Foreign Legion novels, a romantic adventure story which became a best-seller, and which was followed by *Beau Sabreur* (1926), *Beau Ideal* (1928), etc.

WRIGHT, Joseph (1855–1930), lexicographer and philologist, editor (1891–1905) of the *English Dialect Dictionary* and author of the *English Dialect Grammar* (1905) and several primers and grammars of Old and Middle English, Old and Middle German, and Gothic.

WRIGHT, Richard (1908–60), black American writer; he joined the Communist Party in the 1930s, but left in the 1940s, as he records in *The God that Failed* (1950). His best-known novels are the powerful and violent *Native Son* (1940) and *The Outsider* (1953), both of which deal with tragedy in the lives of black victims of poverty and politics.

'Wulf and Eadwacer', an Old English poem in 19 lines from the *Exeter Book. Its theme seems to be the separation of lovers, but it is very unclear, despite its powerfully suggestive atmosphere.

WULFILA, see ULFILAS.

WULFSTAN (d. 1023), author of homilies in English including the famous 'Address to the English', *Sermo Lupi ad Anglos*, in which he describes the desolation of the country brought about by the Danish raids and castigates the vices and demoralization of the people. He held the sees of Worcester and York simultaneously from 1002 to his death; this pluralism is possibly the reason why he is called *reprobus* and *impius* by some contemporary commentators. He had contacts with *Ælfric, with whom he shares a distinction as a writer of sermons in rhythmical, alliterative prose. He drafted codes of Laws for Ethelred from 1008 to 1015, and for Cnut (*Canute), despite his earlier deploring of the Danish raids.

Wuthering Heights, a novel by E. *Brontë, published 1847.

The story is narrated by Lockwood, temporary tenant of Thrushcross Grange, who has stumbled into the violent world of Wuthering Heights, the home of his landlord Heathcliff. The narration is taken up by the housekeeper, Nelly Dean, who had been witness of the interlocked destinies of the original owners of the Heights, the Earnshaw family, and of the Grange, the Linton family. Events are set in motion by the arrival at the Heights of Heathcliff, picked up as a waif of unknown parentage in the streets of Liverpool by the elder Earnshaw, who brings him home to rear as one of his own children. Bullied and humiliated after Earnshaw's death by his son Hindley, Heathcliff's passionate and ferocious nature finds its complement in Earnshaw's daughter Catherine, but Heathcliff, overhearing Catherine tell Nelly that she cannot marry him because it would degrade her, and failing to stay to hear her declare her passion for him, leaves the house. He returns three years later, mysteriously enriched, to find Catherine married to the insignificant Edgar Linton. Heathcliff is welcomed by Hindley, by now widowed with a son, Hareton. Heathcliff marries Edgar's sister Isabella and cruelly ill-treats her, hastens Catherine's death by his passion as she is about to give birth to a daughter, Cathy, and brings Hareton and Hindley under his power, brutalizing the latter in revenge for Hindley's treatment of himself as a child. Edgar Linton dies. Heathcliff forces a marriage between Cathy and his son, the young Linton, in order to secure the Linton property. Young Linton also dies, and an affection springs up between her and the ignorant Hareton, whom she does her best to educate. Heathcliff now longs for the death that will reunite him with

Catherine; at his death there is a promise that the two contrasting worlds and moral orders represented by the Heights and the Grange will be united in the next generation, in the union of Cathy and Hareton.

WYATT, Sir Thomas (1503–42), held various diplomatic posts in the service of *Henry VIII in France, Italy, Spain, and the Netherlands. His first visit to Italy in 1527 probably stimulated him to translate and imitate the poems of *Petrarch. In the same year he made a version of a *Plutarch essay, based on Budé's French translation, *The Quyete of Mynde*, which he dedicated to the queen (Catherine of Aragon) whom the king was in the process of divorcing. He was certainly closely acquainted with Henry VIII's next bride, Anne Boleyn, before her marriage and, according to three 16th-cent. accounts, confessed to the king that she had been his mistress and was not fit to be a royal consort. Possibly this frankness explains why Wyatt was not executed, along with Anne's other lovers, in 1536, suffering only a period of imprisonment in the Tower. He subsequently became a sheriff of Kent, and in 1537–9 was ambassador to Charles V's court in Spain. He celebrated his departure from Spain in the epigram 'Tagus, farewell'. In 1540 the tide of Wyatt's fortunes turned, with the execution of his friend and patron Thomas *Cromwell, which is probably referred to in the sonnet (based on Petrarch) 'The piller pearisht is whereto I lent'. Wyatt himself was arrested, on charges of treason, in July 1541; though released two months later he never fully regained favour.

Wyatt's poetry is beset by problems in three main areas; authorship, biographical relevance, and artistic aims. Though the canon of Wyatt's poems is generally taken to include all the poems in the Egerton manuscript, even this cannot be proved with certainty. The authenticated poems and translations include sonnets, rondeaux, epigrams, satires, lute songs, and a version (based on Aretino) of the seven Penitential Psalms. *Tottel in his *Songes and Sonettes* (1557) adapted many of Wyatt's poems to conventional iambic stress, including 'They fle from me that sometyme did me seke'. Critical estimates of Wyatt's poetry in the 20th cent. have varied widely. C. S. *Lewis called him 'the father of the Drab Age', but others have viewed him as a complex and original writer whose love poems anticipate those of *Donne.

WYCHERLEY, William (1641–1715), dramatist, whose first play, *Love in a Wood, or, St James's Park*, a comedy of intrigue, was probably acted in 1671, and published in 1672. His second play, *The Gentleman Dancing-Master*, was probably acted 1671, published 1673; *The Country Wife* was published and probably first acted 1675; his last play, *The Plain-Dealer*, was probably acted 1676, published 1677. His *Miscellany*

Poems (1704) led to a friendship with *Pope, who revised many of his writings.

Wycherley's plays, admired by *Lamb but condemned by *Macaulay as licentious and indecent, are highly regarded for their acute social criticism, particularly of sexual morality and the marriage conventions; his characterization and thematic organization are also strong, and his last two plays have been successfully revived many times. (See also RESTORATION.)

WYCLIF, John (c. 1330–84), probably born at Hipswell (near Wycliffe), a village near Richmond in North Yorkshire. He was connected with Merton, Balliol, and The Queen's colleges, Oxford, during 1354 to 1381. He was a protégé of *John of Gaunt, and he preached against *William of Wykeham and the Good Parliament in 1376. He was a trained scholastic who lectured and wrote on logic, 1361–72. He was an extreme exponent of *Realism, and his attacks on the authority and abuses in the Church, and ultimately his denial of Transubstantiation, led to repeated attempts to condemn him from at least 1378 onwards; he was finally condemned in 1380. His followers were known as *Lollards. His great significance lies in the Bible translations which he instigated. The earliest versions of these come from the 1380s. (See also BIBLE, THE ENGLISH.)

WYKEHAM, William of, see WILLIAM OF WYKEHAM.

WYNDHAM, John, the best-known pseudonym of John Wyndham Parkes Lucas Beynon Harris (1903–69), a successful writer principally of *Science Fiction. Works in this genre included *The Day of the Triffids* (1951), *The Kraken Wakes* (1953), *The Chrysalids* (1955), and *The Midwich Cuckoos* (1957). Most of his works are distinguished by the contrast between a comfortable English background and the sudden invasion of catastrophe, usually of a fantastic or metaphysical nature.

The word 'triffid' has passed into the language to describe almost any kind of imaginary hostile and dangerous plant: Wyndham's species, lethal and mobile monsters, were so called because of their three-pronged roots, on which they propelled themselves.

WYNKYN DE WORDE (d. 1535), printer from Wörth in Alsace, came to London in 1476. He was Caxton's principal assistant until his death in 1491/2 whereupon Wynkyn succeeded to the printing business. He printed many important literary works in the 1490s, and the catalogue of his works is evidence of bibliographical demand between 1490 and 1535.

Wynnere and Wastour, an alliterative dream-poem of about 500 lines in a North-West Midland dialect, based on events of 1352–3 and thought to have been written shortly after that, discussing the economic problems of the day. In its concerns and methods, the poem has often been compared to, and said to be an influence on, *Piers Plowman.*

WYNTOUN, Andrew of (*c.*1350–*c.*1425), a canon regular of St Andrews and author of *The Orygynale Cronykil* (*c.*1420), first published in 1795, a metrical history of Scotland in octosyllabics, from the beginning of the world to the accession of James I. Among his stories is that of Macbeth and the witches, and of Macduff and Malcolm.

X

Xanadu, in Coleridge's *'Kubla Khan', the place where the Khan decreed 'a stately pleasure-dome'.

XAVIER, St Francis (1506–52), a Spaniard, one of the founders of the Society of Jesus. (See JESUITS.)

XENOPHON (*c*.430–352 BC), Athenian writer who may fairly be called the world's earliest journalist. He left an account of a military expedition in which he participated (*Anabasis*), a history of his own times (*Hellenica*), a panegyric on a contemporary monarch (*Agesilaus*), memoirs about *Socrates (*Memorabilia, Symposium*), and treatises on domestic economy, horsemanship, and hunting. His most popular work was the *Cyropedia*, a fictionalized biography of the Persian king Cyrus. This created a vogue for such biographies in which the fictional element became progressively greater until the world saw the emergence of a new genre—the novel. The *Cyropedia* was translated into English by W. Baker, *c*.1560, and contributed a story to Painter's *Palace of Pleasure* (1566). *Milton spoke highly of the *Memorabilia*, whose account of Socrates he placed on a level with *Plato's.

Ximena (in French Chimène), the wife of the *Cid. C. *Cibber wrote an adaptation of *Corneille's *Le Cid*, called *Ximena, or the heroick daughter* (1712).

Y

Yahoo, see GULLIVER'S TRAVELS.

'Yardley-Oak', a poem by *Cowper.

Yarico, see INKLE AND YARICO.

YATES, Dornford, the pseudonym of Cecil William Mercer (1885–1960), whose sequence of stories about 'Berry' Pleydell and his family includes *The Brother of Daphne* (1914), *Berry and Co.* (1920), and *The House that Berry Built* (1945). These and his 'Chandos' thrillers (*Blind Corner*, 1927, etc.) were much influenced by Anthony Hope (*Hawkins); both reflect a world of wealth and idleness.

YATES, Dame Frances Amelia (1899–1981), Renaissance scholar. Some of her most important work was on *Neoplatonism and the *Rosicrucian tradition in Renaissance thought, and their connections with literature and the drama: *The Rosicrucian Enlightenment* (1972) and *Elizabethan Neoplatonism Reconsidered* (1977).

Year at Hartlebury, A, or the Election, a novel by Sarah and Benjamin *Disraeli, published in 1834 under the pseudonyms 'Cherry' and 'Fair Star'. This hitherto anonymous and unattributed novel was discovered in 1979 by the Disraeli Project in Kingston, Ontario, to be by the Disraelis.

Year Books, reports of English common law cases for the period 1292–1534, of great historical and legal interest. They were succeeded by the law 'Reports'. F. W. *Maitland began editing them, and the work continues.

Years, The, a novel by V. *Woolf, published 1937.
  The novel traces the history of a family, opening in 1880 as the children of Colonel and Mrs Pargiter, living in a large Victorian London house (later described by one of them as 'Hell'), wait for their mother's death and the freedom it will bring; it takes them through several carefully dated and documented sections to the 'Present Day' of 1936, and a large family reunion, where two generations gather.

YEARSLEY, Ann, *née* Cromartie (1752–1806), the daughter of a dairywoman, pursued her mother's trade. She published three collections of poems (*Poems, on several occasions*, 1785;

Poems on various subjects, 1787; *The Rural Lyre*, 1796), a play, *Earl Goodwin* (1791), and a *Gothic historical novel, *The Royal Captives* (1795), based on the story of the Man in the Iron Mask. See also PRIMITIVISM.

Yeast, a novel by C. *Kingsley, published in *Fraser's Magazine* 1848, in volume form 1851.
  This was the first of Kingsley's novels and is crude as a literary work. It deals with some of the social and religious problems of the day (the miserable conditions of the rustic labourer, the game laws, and Tractarianism: see OXFORD MOVEMENT), largely by means of dialogues between the hero and various other characters.

YEATS, William Butler (1865–1939), born in Dublin, the eldest son of J. B. Yeats and brother of Jack Yeats, both celebrated painters. He studied at the School of Art in Dublin, where with a fellow student, G. *Russell (Æ), he developed an interest in mystic religion and the supernatural. At 21 he abandoned art in favour of literature, writing *John Sherman and Dhoya* (1891) and editing *The Poems of William Blake* (1893), *The Works of William Blake* (with F. J. Ellis, 3 vols, 1893), and *Poems of Spenser* (1906). A nationalist, he applied himself to the creation of an Irish national theatre, an achievement which, with the help of Lady *Gregory and others, was partly realized in 1899 when his play *The Countess Cathleen* (1892) was acted in Dublin. The English actors engaged by the *Irish Literary Theatre gave place in 1902 to an Irish amateur company, which produced Yeats's *Cathleen ni Houlihan* in that year. The Irish National Theatre Company was thereafter created, and, with the help of Miss A. E. *Horniman, acquired the *Abbey Theatre in Dublin. Yeats's early study of Irish lore and legends resulted in *Fairy and Folk Tales of the Irish Peasantry* (1888), *The Celtic Twilight* (1893), and *The Secret Rose* (1897). Irish traditional and nationalist themes and the poet's unrequited love for Maude Gonne, a beautiful and ardent revolutionary, provided much of the subject matter for *The Wanderings of Oisin and other Poems* (1889), *The Land of Heart's Desire* (1894), *The Wind among the Reeds* (1899), *The Shadowy Waters* (1900), and such of his later plays as *On Baile's Strand* (1904) and *Deirdre* (1907).
  With each succeeding collection of poems Yeats moved further from the elaborate, *Pre-Raphaelite style of the 1890s. *In the Seven Woods*

(1903) was followed by *The Green Helmet and Other Poems* (1910), *Poems Written in Discouragement* (1913), *Responsibilities: Poems and a Play* (1914), and *The Wild Swans at Coole* (1917). In 1917 he married Georgie Hyde-Lees, who on their honeymoon attempted automatic writing, an event that exercised a profound effect on his life and work. His wife's 'communicators' ultimately provided him with the system of symbolism described in *A Vision* (1925) and underlying many of the poems in *Michael Robartes and the Dancer* (1921), *Seven Poems and a Fragment* (1922), *The Cat and the Moon and Certain Poems* (1924), *October Blast* (1927), *The Tower* (1928), *The Winding Stair* (1929), *Words for Music Perhaps and Other Poems* (1932), *Wheels and Butterflies* (1934), *The King of the Great Clock Tower* (1934), *A Full Moon in March* (1935), *New Poems* (1938), and *Last Poems and Two Plays* (1939). In the poems and plays written after his marriage he achieved a spare, colloquial lyricism wholly unlike his earlier manner.

Yeats served as a senator of the Irish Free State from 1922 to 1928, and in 1923 he received the *Nobel Prize for literature. Yeats also published collections of essays and edited many books including *The Oxford Book of Modern Verse* (1936), a somewhat eccentric and personal selection. He wrote good letters and five major collections have been made. Posthumous publications include *Collected Poems* (1950), *Collected Plays* (1952), *Autobiographies* (1955), *The Variorum Edition of the Poems* (1957), *Mythologies* (1959), *Essays and Introductions* (1961), *The Senate Speeches of W. B. Yeats* (1961), and *Explorations* (1962).

'Ye Banks and Braes', a lyric by *Burns.

Yellow-backs, cheap editions of novels, so called from being bound in yellow boards. They were the ordinary 'railway novels' of the 1870s and 1880s.

Yellow Book, The (1894–7), an illustrated quarterly, devoted to literature and art. Published by J. *Lane and edited by H. *Harland, with the initial assistance of *Beardsley as art editor, its first issue (which included *Beerbohm's essay 'A Defence of Cosmetics') provoked a public storm which did not subside during the three years of the *Book*'s life. Writers and artists published included H. *James, *Gosse, *Le Gallienne, Arnold *Bennett, *Dowson, Beardsley, Walter Sickert, and Wilson Steer.

Yellowplush Papers, The, sketches by *Thackeray, published in *Fraser's Magazine* in 1837–8. The narrator is a footman who observes and comments on the lives of his employers and their friends in a comic mixture of malapropisms and misspellings.

Yeobright, Clym, Thomasin, and Mrs, characters in Hardy's *The Return of the Native*.

'Yeoman's Tale, The', see CANTERBURY TALES, 22.

YONGE, Charlotte M(ary) (1823–1901), came under the influence of *Keble, and absorbed the Tractarian religious views which thereafter coloured all her writings. Her best-known novel is *The Heir of Redclyffe* (1853); her other novels of contemporary life include *Heartsease* (1854), *The Daisy Chain* (1856), *Dynevor Terrace* (1857), *Hopes and Fears* (1860), *The Trial* (1864), *The Clever Woman of the Family* (1865), *The Pillars of the House* (1873), and *Magnum Bonum* (1879). She also wrote many historical romances for children (including *The Little Duke*, 1854; *The Dove in the Eagle's Nest*, 1866; and *The Chaplet of Pearls*, 1868). Her chief excellence as a novelist was her loving depiction of life in large families, particularly sibling relationships, presented with convincing dialogue and unstinted incident.

Yorick, (1) in Shakespeare's *Hamlet* (v. i), the king's jester, whose skull the grave-diggers throw up when digging Ophelia's grave; (2) in Sterne's *Tristram Shandy*, 'the lively, witty, sensible, and heedless parson', of Danish extraction, and probably a descendant of Hamlet's Yorick. Sterne adopted 'Yorick' as a pseudonym in his *Sentimental Journey*.

Yorick to Eliza, Letters from, by *Sterne, published 1773. A collection of ten brief letters from Sterne to Mrs E. *Draper.

York Plays, see MYSTERY PLAYS.

Yorkshire Tragedy, A, a play published 1608, stated in the title to be by Shakespeare, but internal evidence and the late date make it extremely improbable that he had any part in its authorship. The play is based on certain murders actually committed on 1605.

YOUNG, Andrew John (1885–1971), born in Scotland, ordained a minister of the Free Church in 1912; in 1939 he was ordained in the Church of England. In 1910 his father paid for the publication of his *Songs of Night*, the first of many slim volumes of poetry. The first *Collected Poems* appeared in 1936 and the verse-play *Nicodemus* in 1937. *The Green Man* (1947) is sometimes considered his best collection. In 1952 he published a long, disturbing poem, 'Into Hades', which was later combined with the visionary 'A Traveller in Time' to create *Out of the World and Back* (1958), his most ambitious work. His lifelong interest in botany was reflected in a prose account of his travels and searches, *A Prospect of Flowers* (1945), but also in many lyrics. His spare line, sharp specific imagery, and skill with conceit, brought him much critical and public admiration. The *Complete Poems* was revised in 1974.

YOUNG, Arthur (1741–1820), became well known as an agricultural theorist; he wrote a large number of works on agricultural subjects and edited the periodical *The Annals of Agriculture* (1784–1809). His power of political and social observation is shown by his *Political Arithmetic* (1774) and his *Tour in Ireland* (1780), but his fame rests chiefly on *Travels in France (1792). Young was connected with the *Burneys, and his country house, Bradfield Hall, Suffolk, is described in Fanny Burney's *Camilla.

YOUNG, Edward (1683–1765). His early works include the tragedies *Busiris*, produced in 1719, and *The Revenge*, produced in 1721. In 1725–8 he published a series of satires under the title *The Universal Passion* (the love of fame). He took orders and became rector of Welwyn in 1730, where he spent the remainder of his life. Young's most celebrated poem, *The Complaint, or Night Thoughts on Life, Death and Immortality* (1742–5, see NIGHT THOUGHTS) is a noted example of the *graveyard genre. *The Brothers*, a tragedy written decades earlier, was performed and published in 1753, and *Resignation*, his last considerable poem, with a preface to Mrs *Boscawen, appeared in 1762.

YOUNG, Francis Brett (1884–1954), novelist, short story writer, poet, and doctor, is remembered largely for his solid, traditional novels of the West Midlands, which include *Portrait of Clare* (1927) and *My Brother Jonathan* (1928), but he also wrote novels based on his African experiences, including *Jim Redlake* (1930) and *They seek a Country* (1937). His volumes of verse include *Poems 1916–1918* (1919) and *The Island* (1944), a history of England employing the verse forms of succeeding periods in strict chronological sequence.

YOUNG, G(eorge) M(alcolm) (1882–1959), historian, educated at Balliol College, Oxford, is remembered principally for his *Victorian England, Portrait of an Age* (1936), a broad study which reached a popular readership, based on the notion that 'history is not what happened, but what people felt about it when it was happening . . . the conversation of the people who counted.' Other works include studies of *Gibbon (1932) and Baldwin (1952), and collections of essays and reviews.

Young Duke, The, a novel by B. *Disraeli, published 1831.

Younger Son, The Adventures of a, see ADVENTURES OF A YOUNGER SON, THE.

Ywain and Gawain, a northern romance from the first half of the 14th cent. of 4,032 lines. The poem is principally concerned with Ywain, being a translation (with variations) from *Yvain* by *Chrétien de Troyes. The English translation (which is about 150 years later than the original) has some elements in common with other versions of the Ywain story.

Ywain kills the knight of a castle who seems to have magical connections with the weather, and, aided by her serving-lady Lunet, marries his widow Alundyne (Lunete and Laudine in Chrétien). Gawain persuades him to go, assisted by a lion, in search of adventure, abandoning his lady. The two knights have many adventures, ending by fighting each other incognito; but they recognize each other and are reconciled. At the end, Ywain is reconciled to Alundyne, again by the skills of Lunet.

Z

ZAMYATIN, Evgeny Ivanovich (1884–1937), Russian prose writer, critic, and playwright. He is best known for his anti-Utopian novel *We* (1920–1), which was influenced by H. G. *Wells and in turn influenced *Orwell. Zamyatin introduced many English writers to the Soviet Union, but eventually emigrated to Paris, partly as a result of the vicious campaign against him occasioned by the publication (abroad) of *We* in the late 1920s.

ZANGWILL, Israel (1864–1926), a noted Jewish spokesman, writer, and translator. The popular novel *Children of the Ghetto* (1892) established his reputation by its realistic and sympathetically critical portrayal of London's poor Jews. *Ghetto Tragedies* (1899), *Ghetto Comedies* (1907), and *The King of Schnorrers* (1894), a *jeu d'esprit*, contain vignettes of Jewish life. The historical *Dreamers of the Ghetto* (1898) testifies both to Judaism's inner strength and to its role in civilization. *The War for the World* (1916) and *The Voice of Jerusalem* (1920) combine apologia with polemic. His plays are vehicles for ideas, notably *The Melting Pot* (1909), which coined the phrase.

Zapolya, a 'dramatic poem . . . in humble imitation of "The Winter's Tale" of Shakespeare', by S. T. *Coleridge, published 1817.

Zastrozzi, see SHELLEY, P.B.

Zeal-of-the-land Busy, in Jonson's *Bartholomew Fair*, a canting, gluttonous Puritan.

Zeitgeist, German, the spirit of genius which marks the thought or feeling of a period.

Zelmane, in Sidney's *Arcadia*, the name assumed by Pyrocles when disguised as a woman.

Zeluco, a novel by Dr J. *Moore, published 1786.

ZENO (1) of Citium (336–c.264 BC), see STOICISM; (2) of Elia (early 5th cent. BC), a monistic philosopher famous for his paradoxes which were intended to discredit belief in the multiplicity of entities.

Zenobia, a character in Hawthorne's *The Blithedale Romance*.

Zenocrate, the wife of Tamburlaine, in *Marlowe's play of that name.

Zeugma, a figure of speech by which a single word is made to refer to two or more words in a sentence, when properly applying in sense to only one of them; e.g. 'See Pan with flocks, with fruits Pomona crowned'. Cf. SYLLEPSIS.

Zimri, name for the duke of *Buckingham in Dryden's *Absalom and Achitophel*.

ZOILUS, a grammarian of Amphipolis, of the period of Philip of Macedon. His name became proverbial as that of a carping critic, on account of his strictures on *Homer, *Plato, and Isocrates.

ZOLA, Émile (1840–1902), the leading figure in the French school of *naturalistic fiction, of which *Thérèse Raquin* (1867) is his earliest example. The first volume (*La Fortune des Rougòn*) of his principal work, *Les Rougon-Macquart*, which he termed the 'natural and social history of a family under the Second Empire', appeared in 1871; in 19 more volumes (including *L'Assommoir*, 1877; *Germinal*, 1885; *La Terre*, 1887; *La Bête humaine*, 1890; *La Débâcle*, 1892), Zola produces an extraordinary panorama of mid-19th-cent. misery, poverty, and the violence of human instinct. Zola spent 11 months in exile in England (1898–9) as a result of his support of Dreyfus. His works were widely read in this country, but heavily censored, and his publisher *Vizetelly was imprisoned in 1888 for publishing *La Terre*. He considerably influenced G. A. *Moore, *Bennett, and other realist writers.

Zuleika, the heroine of Byron's *The Bride of Abydos*.

Zuleika Dobson, the eponymous heroine of *Beerbohm's novel, a great beauty who pays a fatal visit to her uncle, the warden of Judas College, Oxford, in Eights Week. All the young men fall madly in love with her and, when rejected, they rush 'like lemmings' and drown themselves in the Isis. The only survivor is the less agile Noaks, who trips on the way.

ZWINGLI, Ulrich (1485–1531), a famous Swiss leader of the Reformation. He first found his inspiration in *Erasmus and *Luther, but soon drew away from the latter, and by 1525 had rejected the mass altogether; this split Switzerland into Catholic and Protestant cantons. To Zwingli the Eucharist was purely symbolic; there was no 'real presence' at all, not even in the (later) Calvinistic sense, still less in the Lutheran sense of 'consubstantiation'. The conflict ended in civil war, in which Zwingli was killed in battle.

W9-ACJ-658

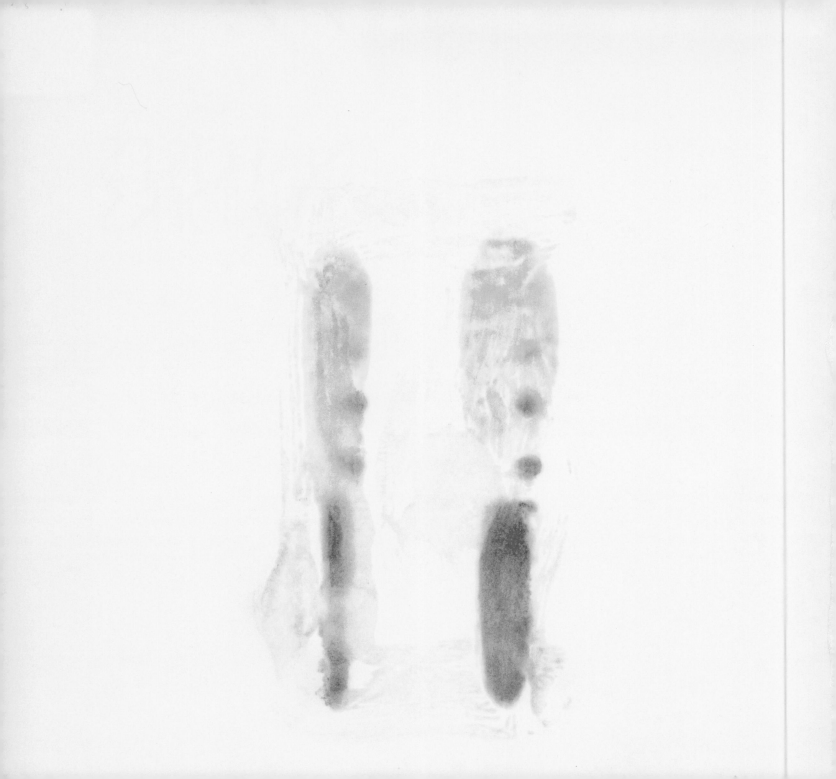

NATURE'S PRETENDERS

NATURE'S PRETENDERS

by ALICE L. HOPF

G. P. Putnam's Sons
New York

PHOTO CREDITS

Thomas Eisner: 83
Museum of Comparative Zoology, Harvard
University,
    photo by Turid Holldobler: 78
Leonard Lee Rue III: 2, 31, 37, 40, 41, 43, 70, 73
San Diego Zoological Society; 46, 47
The Natural History Photographic Agency, Kent,
England,
    photo by Arthur Butler: 34
    photos by Stephen Dalton: 14, 20, 23, 52
    photo by Laurence E. Perkins: 27
    photo by Gordon F. Woods: 87
USDA: 8, 15, 56

Copyright © 1979 by Alice L. Hopf
All rights reserved. Published simultaneously
in Canada by Longman Canada Limited, Toronto.
Printed in the United States of America.
Library of Congress Cataloging in Publication Data
Hopf, Alice Lightner
Nature's pretenders.
Bibliography: p.
Includes index.
SUMMARY: Discusses the defenses and deceptions in
appearance and behavior developed by animals to
facilitate their survival.
1. Animal defenses—Juvenile literature.
2. Camouflage (Biology)—Juvenile literature.
3. Predation—Juvenile literature. [1. Animal
defenses. 2. Camouflage (Biology) 3. Predatory
animals] I. Title.
QL759.H63   591.5'7   78-31560
ISBN 0-399-20671-X
Design by Diane Zuromskis

For Mary . . . . . .

with love

Contents

1 · The Eternal Struggle

All nature's children are engaged in a constant struggle: to eat or to escape being eaten; to live or to die. This is the eternal war for survival. Some scientists refer to it as the Great Chain of Life, in which the majority of individuals are sacrificed so that others may grow and live. Thus, plant-eating animals devour plants. Meat-eating animals kill and eat the plant-eating animals—and often other meat eaters. This struggle goes on from the smallest, microscopic creatures all the way up to elephants and tigers and, of course, ourselves. In the process, some extraordinary deceptions and defenses have been developed by various creatures. Long before human hunters thought of disguising themselves in buffalo skins to creep nearer to the herd, or Malcolm told his soldiers to cut branches from Birnam Wood in order to conceal their numbers as they advanced upon Macbeth's castle, nature's many children were doing much the same thing.

The cock grouse finds a special log, where he struts about, displaying his feathers to the female and making a loud, drumming noise to warn other males away.

We must not think that the ground-nesting grouse says to itself, "I need a set of speckled feathers to keep me hidden among the leaves." Or that the Arctic fox changes to a white winter coat because it knows it will be invisible in the snow. But over the thousands and millions of years that plants and animals have been living and growing on our earth, the plant or animal that happened to develop a slightly better defense or disguise was the one that escaped being eaten; or, conversely, was able to catch a better meal and so survived. And therefore, its offspring were the ones that were born and survived. Its inheritance (or genes) went into building the species, and if its offspring were still better at that defense or deception, they survived even longer. That is what we call evolution.

This is true even of plants, many of which have developed thorns and tough branches to discourage the leaf eaters. On the other hand, an animal such as the giraffe has developed tough skin in its mouth and tongue so that the thorns do not bother it, and it seems to relish the roughest vegetation.

Perhaps the greater number of deceptions are developed in the interest of self-defense. But a sizable number have come about to help the aggressor—a manner of hiding so as to jump out and seize the unsuspecting prey. And some very strange deceptions have developed for quite different reasons: to achieve fertilization on the part of a plant, or merely to provide a safe haven against the rigorous climate.

Whatever brilliant innovations we humans may think up with our superior brains, in all probability it has already been done by the children of Nature through the long-term methods of evolution. Sometimes it is merely a case of being colored like the surroundings: green, if the habitat is vegetation; yellow, if the creature lives in the sandy desert; or speckled like the grouse that nests among brown leaves or grass. In other cases, the animal has grown to look like some particular part of its environment, such as the insect that so resembles a stick or leaf that it is almost impossible to recognize it. This is called protective resemblance by the scientists.

But there is another kind of resemblance, called mimicry, in which one creature manages to look almost exactly like another as a means of protection. In this case, we have first an animal that has managed to build up a degree of protection against predators. It may be a moth or butterfly that has a bad taste—or even a poison—and thus is avoided by birds (the chief predators). Or it may be a wasp or bee, protected against would-be predators by a painful sting. Or it may be a snake, carrying deadly poison in its fangs. Such creatures are usually brightly colored as a warning for enemies to beware. We often find living in the same area another creature of the same kind, but quite unrelated to the "protected species" that looks almost exactly like it. This creature has no sting or poison to protect it, but because it looks like the deadly or unpalatable animal, it, too, is avoided by predators.

In this kind of mimicry, there are always more of the protected creatures—known as the models—than of the harmless, unprotected ones. Otherwise, the birds would catch more of the harmless variety and would not learn to avoid the protected ones. This type of protection, which is visual and usually colorful, is good only against predators that see well and have color vision. These include the birds, some reptiles and amphibians and a few mammals, such as ourselves.

Predators, also, have taken to disguising themselves. The spider may be colored to match the flower! There it waits for the fly or other insect that may come in search of nectar. In the ocean, many predators have managed to look like something else, in an effort to lure prey close enough for catching. Even flowers have taken to disguising themselves so as to attract the right pollinator.

More remarkable are the behavior disguises. In these cases, the animal pretends to be something else in the way it acts. Such a one is the spider that runs with the ants, using only six of its eight legs so that it will seem more antlike. Other animals pretend to be hurt or to be dead, and this pretense may be used either as a defense or as a disguise for the hunter.

In the case of behavior disguises, it almost seems as though the creature must know what it is doing. And yet science tells us that this behavior also is an inherited instinct; just as is the coloring of camouflage. The spider runs like the ants because this behavior is built into its genes. The possum falls down and plays dead for a like reason. There may be some question about the fox that rolls in the grass to attract a curious duck, for we know that members of the wild-dog family teach their offspring how to hunt and that a pup raised in captivity, without the benefit of a mother to teach it, will have a hard time feeding itself if returned to the wild.

In the majority of cases, however, Nature's children have acquired their remarkable ways of pretending to be something that they are not along with the genes that give them smell and sight and hearing and all the ways of adapting to the world into which they have been born.

2 · The Beautiful Creatures

Perhaps the greatest amount of pretending can be found in the insect communities. Among them, the most obvious are the butterflies and moths—Lepidoptera, as the scientists call them.

Some of these insects find protection with simple camouflage, looking as much as possible like their surroundings. Mostly these are the forest-dwelling members of the group and are clothed in browns or grays with shadings and mottlings that allow them to blend with their backgrounds. One of the most famous of these is the peppered moth *(Biston betularia)* in England, which makes a habit of settling on the trunks of birch and other trees. Originally, these trees were light in color and dappled with pale gray lichens, and the majority of the moths were a light gray, peppered with dark spots, making them almost invisible when perched on the gray, mottled bark. There was an occasional dark moth; but

The caterpillar of the spicebush swallowtail butterfly looks like a little snake with a baleful eye. It has made a nest by folding over the leaf and has just come out to feed.

these were quickly picked off by the birds, so that the dark form was a rarity.

However, when England became industrialized, with more and more smokestacks belching black smoke into the atmosphere, the lichens were killed by the soot and the trees gradually darkened. Now the light-gray moths showed up easily on the darker tree trunks, an obvious invitation to the birds, whereas the occasional dark-gray or black individual was concealed. The birds ate the light-colored moths, and the dark ones were left to perpetuate the species. In a remarkably short span of time, the peppered moth had changed its coloring from light to dark.

Another kind of pretense has been developed among the Lepidoptera. Many of them are brightly colored and fly in the open where they are readily seen. The defense they have developed is to have various colorful eyespots on their wings. Butterflies settle to rest with their wings folded erect above their bodies. Thus their eyespots are often found on the undersides of their wings. Moths, on the other hand, settle

down with their wings spread out flat, and so the eyespots are displayed on the tops of their wings. There is a whole group of moths, known as the underwing moths, having dull, drab front wings which spread out to cover the hind wings when they are at rest. But the rear (or under) wings have bright flash colors and sometimes elaborate eyespots in reds and yellows. When a predator approaches, the moth quickly moves the upper wings aside, displaying the brilliant "eyes" staring at the intruder.

For a long time, many naturalists refused to believe that this pretense would be enough to frighten away a hungry bird. They argued that what looks like a frightening eye to a human might not be so interpreted by a bird. But more recently, scientists have experimented with birds and various kinds of signs and decorations.

In 1957, A. D. Blest performed a number of experiments with captive birds. He found that the bird would draw back when a moth or butterfly suddenly displayed the eyespots on its wings. Blest went even further with his experiments, using a variety of designs from circles to crosses. These he projected on the feeding tray alongside a mealworm, just as the bird was about to pick it up. In most cases, the birds paid no attention to cross designs. But when it was a simple circle, the bird would draw back, and the more nearly the circle design resembled an eye,

This "wasp" might frighten you, but it cannot sting.
It is really a beetle.

the more startled the bird seemed to be. Furthermore, if the scientist removed the eyespots from the wings of a live butterfly by scraping off the colored scales, the birds did not react to the insect's signal but quickly gobbled it up.

These methods of defense are all employed by the adult insect. But what about the young, growing insects? Many insects go through several stages of growth before they become adult. First there is the egg, laid—in the case of Lepidoptera—on the plant that the emerging baby insect must eat. In many cases, the young, or larvae (popularly known as caterpillars), eat only a certain species of plant. In others, they will eat a great variety. Eggs are usually laid on the underside of the leaf to hide them from birds and other predators. Butterflies are inclined to lay one egg at a time, while moths may lay a number of eggs in a group.

Eggs are in many sizes, shapes and colors. But the real camouflage comes with the emerging larvae. Insects grow by shedding their skins as each new skin is filled out and becomes too tight. There are usually four or five of such sheddings before the insect reaches its full growth and enters the pupal stage. Many caterpillars are armed with stinging hairs, spines and bristles to make them less palatable to the birds. But others rely on disguise and they may change that disguise each time they change their skins. A favorite disguise is to look like a bird dropping. A bird is not likely to eat its own excrement, and a number of caterpillars do look just like that.

When this moth is at rest, only the brown upper wings can be seen. But if something disturbs it, it whisks them up, displaying the bright, menacing eyespots on the hindwings.

One of the best imitations of bird droppings is put on by the larva of our spicebush swallowtail (*Papilio troilus*). In the early stages it looks very much like something left on the leaf by a bird. However, it does not confine itself to this disguise. In later stages, the larva begins to form a "head" at the front end and takes on the appearance of a tiny snake or reptile. This false head is not really the insect's head, which is confined to a small point at the very front and is usually curled under so that the swelling behind it makes it look like a different creature. In the last stages, beautiful blue and green eyespots appear on the caterpillar, giving it an even more "frightening" look. The spicebush swallowtail has other defense mechanisms, one being to build a hiding place by folding over the leaf, where it rests when not eating. It also, like all swallowtails, has a pair of orange scent glands, located just behind the head. When disturbed, it shoots out these glands, expelling an unpleasant smell at its attacker.

Butterflies are usually brightly colored insects, and in nature bright colors are often used to signal danger. So we find that many of these brilliantly colored species are unpleasant in taste or even poisonous. There are other species that are not so protected, but by looking as much as possible like the poisonous ones, they are avoided by the birds. This kind of mimicry is found among butterflies all over the world. But one of the most obvious cases is that of our monarch butterfly and the viceroy butterfly that mimics it.

The monarch butterfly (*Danaus plexippus*) is perhaps the most famous American butterfly, and there are many remarkable things about its life history. It is a big, orange-red butterfly with black markings and white spots. You can hardly miss it if it makes a visit to your garden. But it will not stay around very long as other butterflies do. The monarch is forever going somewhere. In the spring it is flying north and in the fall it is flying south. It is the butterfly that copies the birds in their seasonal migrations and it is often seen migrating with them by birdwatchers at such points as Hawk Mountain in Pennsylvania.

How does it manage to do this, since birds are the great predators of butterflies? The fact is that the monarch is a protected butterfly. It lays its eggs solely on milkweed plants and the larvae will eat nothing but milkweed. Milkweed has an unpleasant taste, which is then imparted to the caterpillar and eventually to the butterfly. Some species of milkweed are even highly poisonous, and one investigator reports that it carries enough of a heart poison to kill a cat.

So the lordly monarch flies along among the birds unafraid. Its bright colors and markings give warning, and once a bird has tasted one, it will seldom try another. Monarchs cover vast distances in their migrations. A program of tagging has revealed that they often fly over a thousand miles, wintering in Mexico and traveling up into Canada in the summer, laying their eggs on the milkweed that they pass along the way.

The viceroy (*Limenitis archippus*) belongs to an entirely different family of butterflies, and yet it looks almost exactly like the monarch. It is slightly smaller than its model, but has the same orange-red coloring with black markings and white spots. The chief difference is a black horizontal line across the hind wings. This distinction would hardly be noticed by a bird, so that the viceroy must derive a good deal of protection from looking like the protected monarch.

The viceroy butterfly lays its eggs on innocuous plants like willow, poplar and cherry, which do not endow it with a bad taste or harmful poison. The caterpillars look quite unlike the monarch larvae; and when fall comes, the insect prepares for winter by hibernating, which it does as a half-grown larva. It spends its life in one area and does not migrate like the monarch. And yet it looks so much like that butterfly that it takes a keen-eyed naturalist to tell them apart while in flight.

One way to do so is by watching their manner of flying. The monarch flies in long, lazy swoops, soaring up and down on the air currents. It is unhurried, but it can fly fast when necessary and disappears very quickly if alarmed. The viceroy, on the other hand, flits about, up and down, from flower to flower. It seldom flies as high as the monarch does.

I, myself, have been completely taken in by the viceroy's disguise. Many years ago, when I was looking for monarch eggs and larvae to raise for the tagging program, I drove past a little grove of trees and saw there (I thought) several monarchs. This was unusual, for monarchs do not go in groups except on the big fall migrations. I hastened home to get my net. The butterflies were still there when I returned, and I wondered why, since I saw no milkweed in the grove. I found out as soon as I had one in my net, and laughed at myself for having been fooled so completely.

In our southern states, like Florida, there is a close relative of the monarch, popularly called the queen (*Danaus gilippus*). This butterfly is marked like the monarch, but the background coloring is a darker shade, more like a reddish brown than an orange red. The queen lays her eggs on milkweed also, and so is a protected species. And just as there is a viceroy mimic in the north,

there is one in the south, known as the southern or Florida viceroy (*Limenitis archippus floridensis*). This viceroy is colored like the queen and can be identified by the same row of dots on the hind wings. However, the southern queen does not migrate as does the monarch.

The monarch's migration routes take it down into Florida, where at some times it must be flying with its relative. Why does the monarch make these long, yearly flights, which have helped to spread it around the world, wherever there is milkweed, and the queen stay at home in the warm South? This is a question that will probably never be answered; but scientists can speculate.

One scientist, Professor Lincoln P. Brower, has suggested that perhaps these migrations came about because the queen larvae are cannibalistic. The monarch and the queen lay their eggs on the same plants; and it has been found that if there are two queen eggs on the same leaf, the first one to hatch will eat the other. Many larvae make a practice of eating the eggshell after it has hatched, so perhaps the queen's cannibalistic tendencies developed from this. The female butterfly usually lays its eggs well apart, on different leaves if not on different plants. But as long as the monarch stayed at home in the South with the queen, there were more eggs being laid on milkweed and more chance that some would be eaten.

I discovered this situation to my cost when collecting queen eggs in Florida. I went home with about ten eggs in a covered container, and when I got there found I had only two. The first two had hatched in transit and had eaten the other eggs!

The monarch is a tropical insect. It has not built up any means of surviving the northern winters, but must fly south at the first breath of autumn. Other butterflies have learned to hibernate through the cold months. Some hibernate as butterflies, some as pupae. Some do it in the egg and some even as larvae. The viceroy butterfly, which moved north with the monarch and stayed there, has learned to do this. But not the monarch. When the great Ice Ages came to an end and the ice retreated northward, the plant and animal life that had been pushed to the south began to move northward, too. And the monarch followed the spreading milkweed all the way up into Canada. But every fall it must fly south again, over the long, long trails that lead back to Florida and Mexico and its original tropical home-lands.

3 · The Pesky Flies

Everyone knows what a fly looks like. But are you sure? The familiar housefly is easy enough to identify. But flies, or the order Diptera, as arranged by the scientists, are two-winged insects. This includes the mosquitoes, crane flies, blackflies, horseflies, the pesky gnats and many others. Somewhere on the long road of evolution, all these insects lost the hind pair of wings. Remnants of those wings have been retained as little knobbed organs, called halteres. They act as gyroscopic stabilizers in flight.

Anyone who has seen clouds of midges or mosquitoes will know that there are untold billions of flies in the world. But even so, you may not realize how many kinds of flies there are. A conservative estimate is 80,000 species, and there are many more waiting to be discovered and described by science. However, ordinary citizens should be able to recognize a housefly or a gnat or a mosquito or most of the others—shouldn't they?

The answer is no. For there are certain flies that have taken on an appearance and coloring that make them look like very different insects; like bees and wasps and, in the larval form, even like ants. The family Syrphidae, popularly known as hover flies, is particularly adept at this. It is one of the largest of the fly families. As long ago as 1952, an estimated 4,600 species had been described in the scientific literature—939 from the United States. Many of these look so much like bees or wasps that for a long time they went unrecognized and were believed to be rare insects; whereas all the time they were feeding at garden flowers, along with the real bees and wasps, unnoticed by the gardener or the scientist.

Like most insects, flies go through four stages of growth: the egg, the larva, the pupa and the adult, flying insect. The larva grows by molting its skin several times. In some species this period is compressed, the larva going through some of its molts while still in the egg or making the last molt after it has become a pupa. Some flies even skip the egg period; the ova remain inside the female where they hatch, and she then lays living larvae, which are often called maggots. One

Hoverflies look like wasps or bees. Although they have no sting, birds and humans are afraid of them.

group, known as flesh flies (*Sarcophaga*), deposits its tiny larvae upon meat; if chased away from its objective, the female can drop them while flying past, from as much as two feet above. The larvae are so small as to be unnoticeable.

Flies are some of the greatest enemies of humans because they are serious carriers of disease. One individual housefly may harbor thirty-three million bacteria in its intestines, and on its legs and body surfaces there may lurk another five hundred million.

However, all flies are not as deadly as the common housefly, and the great pretenders of the order, the hover flies, lead a much more exemplary life. Flies lay their eggs and pass their larval stage in almost every environment that our world provides. Some do this in water and some on land, some in mud and muck, some in decaying flesh or vegetable matter. There is hardly any sphere offering nutrition that flies have not exploited for the rearing of their young.

Adult hover flies would seem to lead blameless lives. They do not bite and they cannot sting. They are not parasites, laying their eggs in or on other creatures. They do not pollute our food, but feed on the nectar of flowers and spend much of their time hovering over the colorful blooms. Their only problem is that they look so much like bees or wasps that they often bring down upon themselves the wrath of observing humans in the form of a hasty swat with some handy weapon.

These flies may be fat and hairy, like bees, or thin and small-waisted, like wasps. They are brightly colored in black and yellow or black and orange, and the designs often copy those of a certain wasp or bee. And they make a loud buzzing sound, much like a bee, thus warning intruders away. They can continue to buzz even while at rest, so it would seem that the sound is not made by the wings. It is thought that the noise comes from rhythmical contractions of the thorax (the chest part of an insect) or possibly by vibrating the halteres (the remains of the discarded rear wings).

Hover flies have brought the act of hovering to a high art. It is believed that originally hovering was used by male insects to attract the females. But with the hover flies, both sexes do it. They hover in front of a flower while searching for nectar and also hover when not feeding, but merely sunning themselves or observing their surroundings. Like the bees and wasps that they mimic, they are valuable pollinators and therefore very useful insects.

While hover flies live on nectar and sweet juices during their adult lives, many flies store up the protein needed for their very active adult stages by a carnivorous larval period. One such fly, popularly called the drone fly (*Eristalis tenax*) because it looks so much like a bumblebee, has a most ingenious method of larval feeding. It lives in the mud of stagnant ponds and pools and walks along the bottom, filtering out the food from the murky waters by means of a sievelike organ not unlike the filters used by giant whales when feeding on plankton. In order to obtain

oxygen in the murky depths, the drone fly larva breathes through its tail, which is so long that the creature is often called the rat-tailed larva. This tail is in three segments that work like a telescope and can adjust to a short or a long distance from the bottom of the pool to the fresh air above.

Other hover-fly larvae feed on aphids or on the stems and leaves of plants. Some make their way into the nests of bumblebees and wasps, where they eat the larvae, and others invade the ant cities for the same reason. Some use cow manure as a source of nourishment, or the sap flowing from diseased trees. One fly larva (*Eumerus strigatus*) has acquired a taste for onions and flower bulbs, and is a pest to the gardener. It is thought that these larvae originally fed on rotting vegetable matter, since that is the food of related species. Somewhere in the course of evolution, they discovered the delights of eating onions!

All the hover flies look like bees or wasps, but some species seem to be copying one specific species of bee or wasp. However, we find that these flies do not usually invade the nests of the model they are mimicking to deposit their eggs, but rather a different bee or wasp. Remember that inside the invaded nests there is complete darkness, and so the appearance of these flies and their larvae is unimportant there. The benefit of the disguise is probably the protection it offers the flies against predators such as birds and amphibians. Once such a predator has snapped up a stinging bee, it is unlikely to try again with a look-alike fly.

4 · Sticks That Walk

Some of the most expert pretenders in the insect world are the walkingsticks, or leaf insects. These creatures copy the vegetation on which they live so closely that they are almost invisible to our eyes. In the process of evolution, their bodies and even their heads have become so long and thin that one wonders where there is room for the ordinary life functions. Their legs, too, are long, thin and sticklike and help them blend into the background of leaves and twigs. In spite of, or perhaps because of this attenuation, walking-sticks include the longest insects in the world, a foot or more for some Asiatic species, and those in the United States are among our largest.

Only one of our species, a resident of Florida, has wings. But in the tropics these creatures are usually winged. Some females have lost the hind wings, but they still use their fore wings as part of their camouflage. In many of the tropical species the bodies have become flattened, and the wings and body have scalloped edges and brown or yellow patches among the green, thus perfecting the image of a leaf.

The walkingsticks and leaf insects belong to the family Phasmidae, which comes from a Greek word meaning apparition. And one can understand why that name was chosen when we see the many strange and weird forms that they have assumed. All these insects are so hard to see in their natural environment that they seem to be quite rare to the casual observer. Even the best scientist or naturalist must train the eye well to be able to pick them out among the trees and bushes. Yet walkingsticks are quite common. It is simply a case of their being almost invisible. In some years, they have become pests to the forester, defoliating large tracts of trees. The "stick" eats the whole leaf, leaving only the stiff midrib. In 1972, sixteen thousand acres of the Ozark National Forest in Arkansas were stripped of leaves, and twenty-five thousand acres in Oklahoma and Arkansas suffered a like attack. It is said that at such times, when the walkingsticks are so numerous, the sound of their eggs falling to the forest floor is like raindrops spattering on the leaves. However, in certain cases, the voracious walkingsticks may be useful. On the plains of Texas, a huge population of sticks began feeding on mesquite, a brushy plant, of no value for grazing animals. The insects did not eat the grasses that make for good pasturage, and by removing the mesquite they enlarged the area of good grazing land.

Unlike many insects, which go to great trouble when laying their eggs, depositing them on just the right leaf, or injecting them inside a stem, the walkingstick female simply drops her eggs wherever she happens to be. There they lie and pass the winter among the dead leaves and grass. In the northern regions, they remain there for a whole year and do not hatch until the second spring after they were laid. Thus, there are alternate broods in the north, but in the south all eggs hatch the following spring.

Our most common species of walkingstick (*Diapheromera femorata*) emerges from the egg in May or June. When fully grown, the female is about six inches long. The males are apt to be smaller. The young nymphs climb upon low plants like strawberry and rose bushes. After several molts, when they are bigger, they move up into the trees. They especially like wild cherry, black oak and basswood, but may feed on others if these are not available. They very rarely eat pines or firs, and box elder and maples are not to their taste.

There are two walking-stick insects in this picture. Can you see both of them?

By late July and August they have become adult and mating begins. A few days later, the females start to drop their eggs. Each female lays about three eggs a day until she has exhausted her supply of one hundred fifty or until cold weather intervenes. In years when there has been a walkingstick infestation, as many as a hundred eggs have been found on a square foot of ground.

With their long, thin legs, walkingsticks somewhat resemble grasshoppers, and were originally classed with them by the scientists. But they cannot jump, as do grasshoppers, and more recently they have been put in an order of their own, the Phasmida. Besides their remarkable likeness to sticks and leaves, they also use color as camouflage. The very young ones are usually green, imitating the young, small leaves on which they feed. The larger insects may be brown or tan and sometimes speckled, matching the colors of forest trees. Some species even change their colors with the changing light, being light in the daytime and dark at night. They move very slowly, for any sudden move would betray their presence. They will even stay still when being picked off a leaf. A few species are said to emit a bad smell as a form of defense.

There are about two thousand species of stick-leaf insects around the world, the majority of them in the tropics, and some have unusual abilities. Many can escape from a predator by breaking off a leg, which later grows back again, leaving the predator with only a thin, brittle, inedible appendage for its meal. Some species can reproduce parthenogenetically. That is, the female can lay fertile eggs without the assistance of a male. In the species *Carausius morosus*, there is but one male for every thousand females.

Walkingsticks have enemies besides the hungry birds. Some tiny midges have been found to suck blood from the larger individuals, and some species of wasps parasitize their eggs. However, the stick insects are harmless to humans; they eat only vegetation and they are very interesting creatures. For these reasons, they have become popular as laboratory animals and as pets for the terrarium.

5 · Magician of the Deep

One of the most versatile pretenders in the ocean is the octopus. There have been so many tall tales about this creature that people think of it as a menacing monster. For this reason you might believe that its protective devices are used primarily in catching its prey and that it should be listed with the aggressors. But this is far from the case. The average cephalopod is a very timid creature. Its pretenses are those of defense.

The *Cephalopoda*—the group of sea animals that includes the octopus and the squid—are related to oysters. They are shellfish that have discarded the shell. Somewhere in the distant past oysters and octopuses must have had a common ancestor, but that time is very distant. The fossil record for the cephalopods goes back four hundred million years.

There are around one hundred fifty species of octopuses and they vary in size from little ones, two inches across, to great giants with a thirty-five-foot spread. Most of this great size is in the length of the arms, the head being only about two feet across. The giants live in the ocean depths and are seldom seen by humans. And even they are more defensive than aggressive, for they are the food of the sperm whales. The great whales dive into the depths to catch their prey; and while many whales are found with large suction marks on their skin, indicating a battle of giants, the octopus usually ends up in the whale's stomach. (Now that humans have hunted the sperm whale almost to extinction, the big octopuses may grow even larger!)

Octopuses are usually fairly small. It's a lucky individual that lives to attain its full growth, for they are the food and prey of many sea creatures—as well as of humans. Even a large octopus is no threat to swimmers, unless one should get a firm hold and cause the swimmer to drown. But such accidents are rare. The only other really dangerous octopus is a small blue one (*Octopus maculosus*), found in the waters of Australia, that is highly poisonous.

The octopus has no bones. It has a head and body, joined without a neck, and eight long arms (the squids have ten or more), covered with sucking discs. The number of these discs varies with the species. The common octopus *(Octopus vulgaris)* has 240 suckers on each arm. The animal moves through the water by jet propulsion—a method we have only recently perfected for travel. It shoots water out of a siphon and moves rapidly in the opposite direction. It can also walk on the sea bottom, using its arms as legs, and can drift down upon its smaller prey, using its arms and mantle like a parachute.

With all the world trying to make a meal of octopus, these remarkable creatures have evolved a number of pretenses that help them to escape. To begin with, they are very adept at changing color. The octopus can change color faster and for a greater range than any known animal. Even inside the egg the tiny creatures can be seen flashing from one color to another. When an octopus is angry, it becomes a dark red. When it is frightened, it loses its color and becomes almost white. It can adjust its coloring to match the spot where it is hiding: yellowish for sand; splotchy gray for rocks; green or brown, according to the seaweed.

Another form of defense the octopus has developed is the ability to shoot a black fluid from its syphon; the fluid is called ink and is made into a kind of ink known as sepia, often used by artists. But the octopus uses its ink as a smoke screen. When attacked by an enemy such as the moray eel (which likes nothing better than octopus for a meal) it throws out its inky smoke screen, often shaped very much like itself. At the same time, it changes color, becoming almost white—a ghost octopus—and shoots off in the opposite direction. The moray chases the smoke-screen octopus, and by the time it discovers its mistake the real octopus is well hidden in some distant crevice.

Still another defense of the octopus is its ability to break off an arm without any permanent injury. If the octopus's great enemy, the moray eel, seizes hold of its arm, this breaks off. The cephalopod makes good its escape, while the eel is left with only the leathery appendage for a meal. The octopus finds a safe haven and later grows another arm to take the place of the one lost to the moray.

The octopus is a solitary animal and it is always looking for a hiding place from its enemies. Caves and crevices in the rocks are favorites; but often there are not enough to go around, and an octopus will hide in any old can or bottle that may be lying on the ocean floor. For this reason, fishermen going after a catch of octopus lower an empty jar to the sea bottom. When they pull the jar to the surface after a suitable wait, it often holds an octopus.

The octopus's method of mating is one of the strangest in the animal world. One arm of the male develops into a special sperm-carrying organ (the hectocotylus). In the common oc-

The octopus is an escape artist. It can squeeze through tiny holes. It can change color and hide behind its smoke screen.

topus, this is the third right arm, but it varies with the species. The male inserts this into the female's mantle—the bag of skin that covers head and body. After she has thus received the sperm, her eggs are fertilized as they develop. Octopus eggs are shaped something like a grain of rice. They range in size from one thirtieth of an inch to about one and three-quarter inches. Those of the common octopus are one-eighth inch long. Usually eggs are laid in clusters, but the pearly nautilus, which lays the largest eggs, is said to lay them singly. The mother attaches her eggs to rocks, seaweed or ocean debris. The number produced by an individual octopus is astonishing. One scientist reported in 1959 that a captive octopus had laid 328,000 eggs, and this is by no means the record.

When a mother octopus gets ready to lay her eggs, she finds the safest cave or hole that she can. The smaller the opening the better, for this will keep out predators; and an octopus, having no bones, can squeeze into very small holes. Sometimes she piles up stones around the entrance to make the opening smaller. The eggs are laid in long ribbons which she fastens to the roof or sides of the cave. The mother stays in the cave with her eggs, rarely going outside. She stops eating and gives her entire attention to her eggs. She shoots water over them from her syphon, thus keeping them clean of fungus or any dirt. If a predator approaches the entrance, she rushes out to the attack.

Incubation takes about fifty days. After hatching, the tiny octopuses leave the cave and are on their own, for the mother often dies soon after. In some species, the babies swim to the surface of the sea, where they find food among the plankton and other tiny creatures. Other species sink to the bottom and spend their early life on the sea floor. In any case, the vast majority become food for other sea creatures, which is why such vast numbers of eggs are needed to ensure the survival of the species.

Since octopuses evolved from shellfish, we might expect them to have a low grade of intelligence, if any. But this is not the case. Laboratory studies of these creatures have shown them to have a remarkably high animal IQ. An octopus can remember for a fair length of time. In one experiment, an octopus was offered food on a white plate that was wired for electricity. Each time the creature tried to take the food, it received a mild shock. It soon learned to avoid that plate and to accept food only when the white plate was not around. In another experiment, an octopus quickly learned to pull the plug from a bottle in order to reach the meal of crab inside.

So in addition to its defensive pretense of fast color changes and its smoke screen of squirted ink, the octopus manages to elude its enemies with a quick, receptive brain.

6 · Even the Lowly Snake

There is hardly a group of animals on the planet that has not produced at least one, if not many, species with some kind of definite display of pretense, usually as a defense mechanism. Among the reptiles, our hog-nosed snake *(Heterodon platyrhinos)* is famous. This is the eastern species, but there are also related species in our South and West.

Hog-nosed snakes are fairly small, averaging twenty to thirty-three inches. They are quite harmless as they have no fangs or poison or ability to strangle prey. Nevertheless, when approached by an intruder, this snake puts on a great show of aggressive behavior. It rears up as though preparing to strike, while its head and neck are flattened threateningly. Its tail is coiled and the hood spread, making it appear to be twice its size, and all the while it hisses viciously. It opens its mouth to bite and may even try to strike, but pulls back before a strike is completed.

This display is all bluff, for the snake is really timid and has no desire to fight. If the intruder continues to attack, it tries another ruse. Suddenly it falls limply to the ground, goes into convulsions, and then rolls over on its back with its mouth hanging open. It gives every indication of being dead. But if the observer picks it up and turns it into the proper position, back upward and stomach on the ground, the snake comes to life for the few seconds it takes it to roll over, belly up, and relaxes once more with its mouth open. Apparently it considers this the only good position for simulating death.

Scientists, of course, do not believe that the snake thinks about its actions. Death-feigning is believed to be a physical reaction to danger and the fear that is building inside the creature. We can understand how this works when we think of how we ourselves react to great fear. Adrenaline pours into our systems, our hearts beat faster; yet sometimes we are so frozen by fear that we cannot act or run, even though we realize that we should do so. Perhaps fear has this effect on the many creatures that play dead. Yet why does the hog-nosed snake turn over to lie on its back, thus ruining an otherwise perfect act of death-feigning?

In many parts of the country, this snake's aggressive display is taken quite seriously. Some people don't wait to see the death-feigning act! This is especially true in the South, where the snake has been given such fearsome names as blowing viper, puff adder and checkered adder. But if kept in captivity, the snake soon gives up its playacting. It learns that it is safe and will be treated with kindness and there is no need for it to act aggressive—or dead. And, of course, there is nothing to frighten it and start its glands working.

The hog-nosed snake likes to live in sandy places. There it catches and eats such creatures as toads, frogs and lizards. The young ones catch crickets and other insects. Their color varies from yellow, gray and olive to orange, red and brown. In the eastern species, the underside of the tail is lighter than the rest of the underbody. In the southern species, this entire area is the same color. And in the western species, the underparts are covered with dark blotches.

Like most snakes, the hog-nosed lays eggs. Mating occurs in April or May, and eggs are laid in June or July. The female may lay from eight to forty eggs, and when the young hatch they are from six and a quarter to ten inches long. As is the custom with snakes, they are on their own from that moment onwards.

The remarkable death-feigning display or pre-

tense has been evolved by a snake that is otherwise quite defenseless. What is even more surprising is to find almost the same masquerade being practiced by one of the deadly snakes, a spitting cobra from South Africa.

The cobra is one of the most poisonous snakes. Its venom is used both for defense and in the killing of its prey. However, the spitting cobras use their unique method of delivering the venom only as a means of defense. These snakes have fangs specially adapted for spitting, so that the venom shoots both outward and upward. The snake aims for the attacker's eyes, often with uncanny accuracy. As the venom comes out of the glands into the fangs, the snake emits a blast of air from its lungs, shooting out a spray of poison for a distance of five to seven feet. The venom is harmless to the unbroken skin, but can be disastrous if it reaches the eyes. It is very painful and must be washed out immediately, or permanent injury and even blindness will result.

One would think that this method of defense should be sufficient for any snake, but one of the two South African species of spitting cobras has still another trick to fall back on. This snake, known as the ringhals (*Haemachates haemachatus*), has evolved the practice of shamming death to escape from an enemy. At first the snake rears up, spreads it hood, hisses and prepares to attack. But if the spray of venom fails to discour-

The hog-nosed snake in attack position. It is not as dangerous as it looks.

age an attacker, the snake suddenly goes limp and rolls onto its back with jaws agape. In this condition, it can be picked up and thrown about. However, it keeps an eye open for any chance of making a quick escape.

The ringhals is common in most of South Africa, from the coastal plains up into the high mountains. It averages three and a half to four feet in length when grown, with five feet about the largest. It varies in color, being dark brown to black above, with irregular crossbars of yellow or creamy white. The underparts are dark brown or black, and there are one or two pale crossbars on the neck. Old snakes may be all black.

These snakes do not see well and rely on their sense of smell to find their prey. Their food consists of rodents, toads, lizards and even other snakes.

All the true cobras lay eggs, but the ringhals differs in this respect. The female retains the eggs inside her body until they have hatched. Then she produces fifteen to sixty live babies. Thus she is said to be ovoviviparous. This is obviously an advantage to the snake, for she does not need to guard her eggs or leave them where, no matter how well hidden, some predator might find and eat them. She takes her offspring with her until they are able to fend for themselves. By retaining the eggs inside her, the mother snake can also regulate their temperature so that they are not subjected to the changes of heat and cold in the outside world. Quite a few snakes have developed this habit of retaining their eggs until they can produce live young. Usually this practice is found among species that have expanded their range to northern regions or to high altitudes where colder weather can be expected.

The young of the ringhals are about seven inches long at birth and can rear up, expand their hoods and bite almost immediately. Their poison glands are active and they go through their first shedding of skin within an hour after birth.

Cobras are usually found in pairs, especially at mating time. They have an elaborate courtship in which the male sidles up to the female, rubbing and nudging her with his head. He crawls over her back and investigates her with his sensitive, flickering tongue. When they are ready to mate, the male coils his tail around hers and the two snakes lie fully extended and close together while mating takes place. This can last for five hours or, with interruptions, may continue for several days. While involved in the business of mating, cobras will not spread their hoods.

7 · The Feathered Actors

Birds have many expert "pretenders" among their ranks. Almost all birds use camouflage and many of them practice some sort of behavioral pretense, from fluffing up their feathers in order to appear bigger than they are to genuine acting out of an injury in an effort to lead an enemy away from the eggs or chicks. These injury displays are usually found among the ground-nesting birds, for their nests are the most vulnerable. If a powerful enemy discovers the nest, there is little the mother can do to defend it. Birds that nest in trees or holes have a certain amount of for-tresslike defense. Their nests are harder to reach and less open to detection and attack.

One of the best-known ground-nesting birds is the grouse. These are small, chickenlike birds, about the size of a bantam, and they are circumpolar in their range. That is, they are found in all the countries surrounding the North Pole. There are many species of grouse, and they have been given different names by the peoples among whom they live. Such names include ptarmigan (in the far north), prairie chicken and capercaillie

(in Europe). But they are all related species, living north of twenty-six degrees north latitude and usually preferring a forest habitat. They are good to eat and consequently have been heavily hunted, in some cases to extinction. The heath hen is an example of a bird that American settlers exterminated, the last one dying at Martha's Vineyard in 1931.

Grouse are generally mottled brown in color to blend with the leaves on the forest floor. The northern ptarmigan changes its color to white in the winter. They usually have feathered legs and in winter grow a mat of stiff feathers on the toes which serve as snowshoes, allowing the bird to run on the top of the snow. This is especially true of the ptarmigan. Grouse do not have spurs, as do many chickenlike birds.

Grouse are not true migratory birds; but they do make some seasonal movements, from summer to winter quarters. The ptarmigan and blue grouse make long journeys on foot, and the sage grouse has been known to move as far as one hundred miles to find winter food.

One of the best-known American species is the ruffed grouse (*Bonasa umbellus*). It ranges throughout the United States and into Canada and Alaska. In some parts of its original range, such as Iowa, Nebraska and Kansas, it has been exterminated by hunting.

The courtship display of the ruffed grouse has been a subject of argument since colonial times. In fall and spring, the cock bird seeks out a suitable log where he struts and expands his feathers to attract the females and to warn other males away from his territory. The climax of this display is a drumming sound which can be heard from almost a mile away and is one of the memorable sounds of the New England woods. What has mystified naturalists for centuries is how the bird produces this sound. At first it was supposed that he did this by clapping his wings against his sides, and in 1755 a naturalist by the name of John Bartram described the action. An even earlier observer, in 1703, said that the bird flaps one wing against the other. Another opinion suggested that the birds beat the air with their wings; and in 1905 a naturalist reported that the Indians called the grouse the carpenter bird, because it beats upon the log with its wings. It was not until the invention of the motion-picture camera that this argument was settled. In the spring of 1929, near Ithaca, New York, a bird was photographed with a very fast film, and the resulting pictures proved that it is the outward

Sitting on her nest, the female grouse is almost invisible.

and upward motions of the wings striking the air that cause the famous drumming sound.

The grouse's nest is no more than a little hollow scraped in the ground, lined with leaves and a few feathers. The hen makes her nest alone, lays between nine and twelve eggs and does all the work of incubation. The nest is usually at the base of a tree or between two rocks. The chicks are precocial, which means that they are able to run about and look for food almost as soon as they are out of the shell and dry. However, they are still vulnerable to cold and damp weather, typical of spring in northern climes. The hen broods them under her wings to keep them warm and dry.

Once the eggs are laid, the mother grouse becomes a furious engine of defense for her nest and later for her chicks. While she is sitting on the eggs she usually depends on camouflage until the last minute; but when the enemy is very near, she flies up with such a fluttering of wings that the surrounding leaves are blown over her eggs.

Sometimes she scuttles away close to the ground, dragging a wing. This display becomes more frantic if the chicks have hatched. The bird flutters along the ground, uttering cries of distress and giving every indication of being a seriously injured bird. But once she has lured the predator away she flies up into a tree and waits for the danger to pass. Some hens will even attack an intruder. A shrill cry signals the babies to hide, while the mother rushes out in a raging flurry of puffed-out feathers and spreading tail. Many hunters are so startled by her appearance that they forget about the chicks, which are soon well hidden, impossible to find.

Grouse eat mainly vegetable matter, but the young especially consume a lot of insects. Adults prefer nuts and seeds, such as acorns and hazelnuts and the seeds of hemlock, maple, blackberry and sedges; also buds of trees and fruit of roses, grapes, dogwood and even poison ivy. People have been poisoned by eating birds that have fed on poisonous plants. In winter, when much of their food is snow-covered, the grouse fly up into the trees to find buds and berries and even leaves that are still green. Farmers have accused them of eating the buds off their apple trees; but careful observation has found that this pruning is a help to the tree, resulting in more and better apples in the fall.

A very different type of bird that uses the broken-wing pretense is the stilt. Stilts are shore birds. This kind of bird also nests on the ground and so has developed the deceiving displays to lure predators away from their eggs and young. They are medium-sized birds with very long legs and long, narrow beaks. Their legs are longer in proportion to their bodies than those of any other birds, with the exception of flamingos. They are colored in striking patterns of black and white. As they wade in shallow water, often up to their body feathers, or in soft mud, they snap up insects from floating plants or from the water itself.

The black-necked stilt (*Himantopus mexicanus*) is one species found in the United States, as well as Central and South America. In winter it stays south in Florida, Texas, sometimes Louisiana and lower California. But in summer it migrates through New Mexico and Arizona as far north as Oregon and Utah. It is found wading in salt marshes in the Florida Keys; but it is also at home in fresh water, and has flocked to irrigated areas, once desert, in Southern California.

Unlike the grouse, which nests alone, the stilts nest in colonies and move about in flocks. They are noisy, aggressive birds, and build a much more elaborate nest than does the grouse. Because they nest so close to water, they sometimes build little mounds to support their nests and keep the eggs safe from floods. Observers have watched nesting stilts that anxiously thrust sticks and leaves underneath their nests in an effort to save them from the rising water. Often when a bird leaves her nest, she picks up any loose material lying about and tosses it over her back, to be near the nest for future use. Of course, such nests can hardly be concealed from view; one bird was seen sitting on a pillar of vegetation eight inches high.

Since stilts nest in groups, the collective instinct may help in choosing the proper site: not too far from water and not too near. But there have been occasional small groups that could not discern the difference between a permanent lake or pond and an irrigated area, soon to dry up.

The black-necked stilt puts on a convincing broken-leg act, while trying to lure enemies away from her nest.

Such unfortunates may have to abandon their nests and eggs and start all over again in a better location.

Stilts make little effort at camouflage and seem to rely on the screaming attacks of the flock to ward off predators. In fact, they are far from timorous birds, often nesting in a swampy meadow under the feet of a herd of cows. Apparently, a sudden scolding from the sitting bird or a sharp jab from the long beak is enough to move the cow away from a collision course.

Because of their long legs, baby stilts are slower at learning to run than are baby grouse, which can do so as soon as they are dry. Stilt chicks are able to crawl into the underbrush within an hour after hatching; but it takes several more hours for them to learn how to handle their long legs, and they are still unsteady for another day. When disturbed, the chicks try to hide by squatting with their long necks stretched out along the ground. But while the young freeze into immobility, the adults immediately put on a show of great motion, jumping into the air, fluttering with dangling legs, beating their wings and performing any kind of acrobatics that might distract the invader and draw attention to themselves. And all the while, the colony is in an uproar of screeching birds.

This is when the stilt's true acting ability as a decoy comes to light, for the bird whose nest is closest to danger will put on the broken-leg act. Suddenly collapsing to the ground, she flutters about as though those delicate legs had mysteriously snapped in half. As the bird moves just beyond reach, she repeats this performance, falling down in a flutter every few steps. If all this fails to have the desired effect, she takes to fluttering her wings, as though to show that this is what is really broken. She has a technique of holding up one wing at a time and letting the wind ruffle the feathers, giving a most realistic picture of a broken wing.

By late summer, the young have all grown their flight feathers and they join the adults to form flocks. They feed and fly together in preparation for their migration to the warmer parts of their range, where they spend the winter months. As they take off on their journey, their long legs are held stiffly horizontal and extend well beyond their tails, so that the Spaniards have christened them "little storks."

8 · Playing Possum

Of all Nature's pretenders, the opossum (*Didelphis virginiana*) is probably the best known. The expression "playing possum" has become a popular synonym for feigning death. And the possom (or opossum, as it is also called) does this so well that it has deceived countless people as well as many wild predators.

The common opossum, as our North American species is called, is also found throughout much of Central and South America. South America is the home of a great variety of unusual pouched animals called marsupials. They evolved and multiplied in the southern continent during the long millennia when it was cut off from North America and was a kind of island continent, like Australia. When the land now known as Central America rose out of the sea and connected the two continents, the common opossum was the only one of these strange creatures that made its way northward across the land bridge and survived to the present. It has been expanding its range ever since. Although it is usually associated with our southern states, in recent years it has ranged as far north as the Hudson River and the Great Lakes, and even occasionally into Canada.

The opossum is a marsupial, which means that its young are born when they are still in a very early stage of development. They are blind and hairless, and their limbs have hardly begun to develop. But the mother has an outside pouch which contains the teats where the young can suck milk. In some miraculous way, the newborn babies crawl over the mother's abdomen and into her pouch, where each fastens its mouth on a teat and holds on tenaciously. Here they stay, safe and warm and well fed, until they have grown big enough to face the outside world. This is how our American possum raises her young. The pouch of the opossum has a vertical opening, unlike those of the kangaroos, which open horizontally. In South America there are many more species of opossums, and some of them don't even have a pouch! The young are carried in a kind of bunch between the hind legs or on the mother's back. The babies of the mouse opossum are no larger than a grain of rice when they are born. One

39

species, known as the water opossum or yapok, swims underwater when searching for food, and observers have wondered how the babies keep from drowning. But in this case the pouch opening is at the rear of the female, and a strong muscle closes it tightly when the mother is swimming and diving. The young are safe in an air-filled cradle.

The American opossum was the first marsupial known to Western science. Long before Australia was explored and settled and its fantastic fauna of marsupials discovered, the possum had been brought to Europe from America. A Spaniard named Pinzón brought the first specimen back to his homeland in the early 1500s and Ferdinand and Isabella, the monarchs who had financed the exploration of the New World, were astonished by this animal with a pouch full of babies.

Possums are believed to be among the oldest forms of the marsupials. The fossil record shows that they go back seventy million years, to the Age of Dinosaurs. Scientists have speculated that perhaps their penchant for eating eggs may have led to the extinction of those animals. And the possum has changed little in all that time. Whereas the more "modern" marsupials of Australia developed grinding molar teeth for eating grass, and long legs with only two very strong

(Left) Mother possums have large litters, which they carry about on their backs.
(Right) Sometimes baby possums are left at home in their hollow log or tree.

toes for running and jumping, the opossum still has fifty sharp, primitive teeth and five fingers and toes on each of its four paws. There is a definite thumb on the hind paws which helps in holding onto branches when climbing. All the toes have claws except the two thumbs. The possum is also blessed with a prehensile tail. That is, it can wrap it around branches and hold on. Although it is not as dextrous with its tail as some monkeys, it is known to use the tail for carrying things such as nesting materials.

Possums are colorful animals. Their long outer hairs may be of different colors, producing animals in a variety of shades: all the way from white and yellow to brown and black and sometimes even spotted coloring. They often have an unkempt appearance because of the sparse, long outer hairs and the naked tail and ears. The possum folds its ears when asleep, giving them a crumpled look. In northern regions, the winter cold often causes them to lose their ears and part of their tails from frostbite; but they seem to survive well enough without them.

The possum's vision and sense of smell are only passable, but its hearing is very keen. Even the slightest sound causes the animal to become excited. The sound of mealworms crawling on a piece of paper has drawn a reaction from captive animals, and the slightest sound of an approaching enemy can warn the possum in the wild.

Although the possum has adapted to changing conditions over the millennia, it has not enlarged the size of its brain. The animal is about the size of a cat, some twenty inches long and eight to fifteen pounds in weight. But its brain is only one fifth the mass of the cat's brain. In comparison with wild animals, it is almost the same size as the raccoon; but with a much smaller brain, it has only half that animal's life span. The raccoon can live for fourteen years, but the possum (with its small brain) is old at seven.

And yet the species has lived on the planet much longer than many large-brained animals. Perhaps some of its built-in defenses have ensured its survival. For one thing, the animal is said to have a bad smell. Olfactory defenses have worked for many creatures, from the tortoise to the skunk. It is also said to taste bad, so that it is not a favorite food for many predators. However, in some of our southern states, roast possum is considered a great delicacy!

Possums are also hard to kill. The bones of museum specimens show many serious breaks that have healed successfully; injuries that other animals could hardly have survived. And of course, there is the famous "playing possum" caper. When chased by hunters and dogs, the possum takes to a tree and climbs as high as possible. But if the tree is shaken and the animal falls out, it lies on the ground with every appearance of death. The eyes are closed, the tongue hangs out of the open mouth; it is stiff and lifeless. It can be thrown about and swung by its

When "playing possum," this animal looks very dead. But if left undisturbed, the possum will soon jump up and run away.

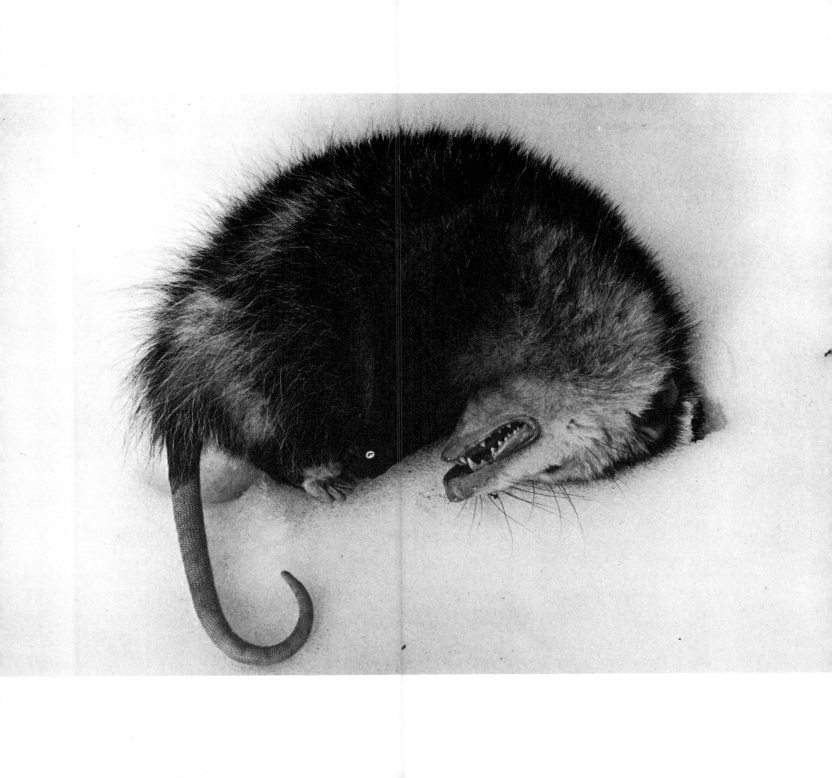

tail. But the canny hunter simply picks it up and puts it in a bag. If left alone for a short time, it will suddenly come to life and escape into hiding.

Another characteristic that has kept the possum going through the ages is that it is not particular about what it eats. It likes berries and fruit and plant roots, but it is also a meat eater, catching mice, beetles and snails. It is fond of birds' eggs and will raid the hen house for both the eggs and the chickens. They are also scavengers, and a family of possums was once seen dining on a dead horse. However, they are clean little animals. After eating, they wash themselves as does a cat.

In my part of the country, the Northeast, possums are the most frequent animals seen dead along the highway. Possibly the death-feigning act is a hazard in the age of the automobile. For possums are nocturnal and usually go about at night. The sight of the bright headlights coming at him must terrify the animal so that he falls over, feigning death—right in the path of the oncoming car.

Baby possums stay in the mother's womb for only thirteen days. When the mother feels that birth is imminent, she looks for a nest. Somebody else's nest. She does not care about digging her own, but takes over one deserted by another animal, any hole in the ground or a hollow tree. An average of twenty fetuslike young are born, hardly larger than a navy bean. As there are but thirteen nipples in the female's pouch, only the strongest can survive. By the time they are as large as mice, the pouch is too full and they move out to their mother's back. At three months they are weaned, and begin to eat such food as roots and insects. And when they are about a year old, they start to wander off and take up the life of solitary animals.

Possum pelts are used in the fur industry and over two million are caught for this purpose every year. But although the animals are considered to be stupid, they do sometimes escape from traps. Like the coyotes, they will chew off the part that is held by the trap. Agnes Akin Atkinson, who fed and observed possums for many years, reports that three-footed and three-legged possums sometimes came to dinner.

In recent years, these animals have been used in scientific research in the laboratory. Scientists studying the growth of embryos no longer have to remove them surgically from an animal, thus killing the specimen and perhaps the mother as well. They need only reach inside the pouch of a possum and bring out a baby that is really still a fetus. Female possums make good laboratory animals, adjusting to life there as they have adjusted to changing conditions on the planet for over seventy million years.

44

9 · Sound and Fury

The mountain gorilla (*Gorilla gorilla*) was the last of the great apes—the animal group closest to humans—to be discovered by Western science. That was in 1902. The lowland gorilla was discovered in 1847, but it was not until some time later that Europeans saw their first gorilla.

This is the largest of the apes, and while it is not quite as tall as a human, it is much heavier and much, much stronger. A grown male stands five and a half feet when upright and weighs over four hundred pounds. Females are considerably smaller. But even a female, when grown, is much too strong for a person to control, and those who have raised and loved them as pets eventually must put them in a zoo.

Because of its size and rather horrifying appearance, the gorilla has always been considered a monster and assumed to be aggressive and menacing. But this is very far from the truth. With its great strength it can do a lot of damage if aroused. But fundamentally the gorilla is a peaceful, rather placid animal. Like the elephant, another very large and strong beast, it is more sinned against than sinning. Its aggressiveness is shown only in defense of itself and its family. Even among themselves, gorillas are not fighters.

These largest of the apes are entirely herbivorous, or plant-eating. They live in small groups of one or more silver-backed males (the leaders), a few black-backed males (the younger ones), a number of females and their offspring of various ages. They spend their time moving slowly through the forest, eating as they go. They do not specialize in flowers and fruit, as do some apes, but eat leaves and stems. Their food includes wild celery, bedstraw and even nettles. They select what they want from the bounty spread around them, and when their leader feels the urge to move to greener pastures, they all gradually follow along.

George B. Schaller, the scientist who made the first serious study of gorillas in the wild, found that there were a number of such groups sharing the same large area. They usually managed to stay away from each other, but there was no defending of territories as with many other social

animals. When two groups met, they simply passed each other by, each group filtering through the other's ranks as they fed along the way. On occasion, an individual would drop out of one group and attach itself to the other. No notice was taken of this change of allegiance.

Gorillas are not as arboreal as other primates because they are so heavy when grown. But the young ones climb trees readily and even build nests there for sleeping. Adults usually build their nests on the ground. Although the silver-backed males are the strongest and the leaders, they do little to assert their supremacy. Occasionally, one will push a smaller animal out of the way or administer a slap; but even in the matter of sex—the area most apt to be preempted by the dominant males of other species—the gorilla is tolerant. In the two matings that Schaller was able to observe, the male was not the dominant animal of the group, and the leader paid no attention to what was going on.

Whereas men are often proud of the amount of hair on their chests, with the gorilla, the situation is reversed. They have hair almost everywhere except in that area. The excited males make a resonant, far-carrying sound by slapping their chests. The gorilla male is famous for this agressive action, which is called a "display" and it is one of the things that has led to its reputation as a

(Left) In the wild, mother gorillas take good care of their babies.
(Right) A young gorilla, practicing its famous "display" of aggression.

vicious, frightening animal. Schaller noted nine parts to this display, in pretty much the following order: hooting, placing a leaf between the lips in symbolic feeding, rising up on the hind legs, throwing leaves into the air, beating the chest (which marks the climax), leg kicking, running sidewise, tearing up the vegetation and, finally, thumping the ground.

All or part of this display may be given when an individual male wants to impress his group or another male, and young males sometimes practice bits of the display. A dominant male, however, will go through the whole sequence when he feels disturbed or threatened or just wants to assert his authority.

It was this display, accompanied by fearsome roars and the baring of fangs, that so impressed and alarmed the early explorers. But it is all a pretense—an act on the part of the gorilla. A display designed to frighten away the intruder. And in performing this way, the animal presented a perfect target for the guns. While other animals ran away in fear, the hunter stood and shot, and that was the end of the gorilla.

It was not until 1959 and 1960, when Schaller made the first studies of the wild gorilla, that it was learned how much of a pretense this display really is. Schaller refused to take a gun with him as he watched the animals. Soon he gave up all efforts to hide himself, but walked out into plain sight of a feeding group and stood quietly, being careful to make no frightening movements. At first the gorillas all ran away, although the leader usually stopped long enough to roar and beat his chest. Eventually, the gorillas became used to him, and Schaller was able to approach them more closely and to sit on the branch of a tree near where they were feeding. Sometimes a curious youngster would climb up and sit on the branch beside him. He even took to spending the night with the wild gorillas and never experienced any threat or reason for fear.

On one occasion he saw a female come out of the bushes, carrying a newborn baby. She approached the big male gorilla and leaned against him, and he reached over and fondled the infant in the gentlest manner. In fact, the life-style of the gorillas seems to be based on gentleness and tolerance. The menacing display is kept for dangerous intruders and is not as fearful as it seems.

Another student of gorilla behavior, Dian Fossey, describes the creatures as "the gentlest and shiest of animals." Her one alarming encounter occurred when she was working in the same area as Schaller, but a few years later. She followed his example of bringing no guns and trying not to alarm the animals. But once, for no apparent reason, a group of five large males rushed at her, roaring loudly. This must have been a very frightening experience; but the courageous scientist stood her ground, and when they were only a few feet away she spread out her arms and yelled as loudly as she could, "Whoa!" The gorillas stopped at once and then went back to their previous occupations.

Schaller says that with most animals, staring is a threatening action, and so he refrained from doing this with the gorillas. But in one instance, he saw how the animals use this threat with each other. It was the only time he ever saw a serious confrontation between two big male gorillas. In this case, two groups of the animals were passing each other slowly through the forest, individuals sitting and eating peacefully. There was one silver-backed male in each group, and for some reason they seemed to resent each other. One began to display, beating his chest and throwing leaves about. He climbed upon a log and jumped down with a crash. He beat the ground with the palm of his hand. The other male, who had been sitting on the ground staring at nothing as though in deep thought, got up and walked toward him until the two were only a foot apart. There they stood, staring into each other's eyes. When neither could stare the other down, the second male went back to his seat. Twice again he returned to the "attack" and tried by staring to make the other male back down. At last he reared to his full height, threw a few leaves into the air and raced at the other male until their faces were within an inch of each other. But since the other male was just as stubborn and would not give in, they presently went back to feeding. There was no real battle and none of the other gorillas in the two groups paid any attention to the confrontation between the two leaders.

Schaller says that he never got used to the male gorilla's roar, even when he knew that it was coming. It is so loud and ferocious that it never fails to start the adrenaline of fear running in the hearer. Even the other gorillas are startled, the scientist observed. But it is all a pretense, a big bluff. The gorilla does not want to fight anyone. He only wants to be allowed to live in peace in his forest.

10 · The Hidden Monsters

Although most of the elaborate pretenses and disguises evolved by Nature's children have been developed as a protection against enemies, the predators, too, have taken up the practice. These are the creatures that eat meat and every day must catch their food. Their food is not simply waiting there for them in the form of vegetation. They must run after it or wait and pounce on it, and all too often their dinner gets away and they are left hungry. So every time one of the prey animals develops a good protective device, the predators must do something to outwit it. And just as the prey species have become adept at looking like something else, the predators, in many cases, have done likewise.

In the insect world, the biggest, most ferocious meat eaters are found among the mantids. The praying mantis, often seen in gardens in late summer, is a large insect, colored green or brown and winged as an adult. There are some eighteen hundred species distributed around the world in the tropics and the temperate regions. Most of the native American mantids are rather small; but

three large species have been introduced, one from Europe and two from the Far East. They are larger than many of our native mantids, the European being two to two and a half inches long and the Oriental species reaching four inches. They have become well established in many parts of our country.

Mantids belong to the order Orthoptera, which includes grasshoppers, crickets, katydids, walkingsticks and cockroaches. The mantids differ from their relatives in that they have gone on a completely carnivorous diet. Their front legs are greatly elongated and very strong and armed with rows of teeth. They can close at the joints, snapping shut like a jackknife. Once the prey insect is caught in this trap, it cannot escape.

The mantis can turn its head more freely than other insects. The head is triangular and perched on a long neck. The mouth is at the bottom of the triangle, and at the upper corners are two large eyes made up of several hundred tiny facets. There are also three simple eyes across the top of the head. All this gives the mantis a keen sense of vision. Unlike the grasshoppers and crickets, which have ears near the front knees, the mantids have no ears at all. However, at the base of each antenna they have a group of sensory cells, known as Johnston's organ, which is believed to receive vibrations and act like an ear.

The mantis's method of hunting is to sit perfectly still, looking as much like its surroundings as possible, and let the prey come to it. It sits in an erect position on its four rear legs and holds its two front legs in front of it with the first joints crooked and the lower part hanging down. This looks so much like a praying human that people all over the world have given it similar popular names: praying mantis, *prégadiou* (in France), *louva dios* (in Spain), *Gottesanbeterin* (in Germany)—and the scientific name is *Mantis religiosa*. The word "mantis," given by the great scientist, Linnaeus, is Greek and means soothsayer or prophet.

From this you can see that people have been aware of the mantis since very ancient times and have felt that there must be something supernatural about it. The Moslems think that the insects always pray properly, facing toward Mecca. And in Africa it is believed to be related to gods and demons.

The mantis, especially the female, has an insatiable appetite and will eat anything it can catch. Once an insect is seized by those scissorlike front legs, there is no escape, and the mantis bites off pieces until it has devoured all edible parts. Wings and legs are usually allowed to fall to the ground. Large mantids have even been known to catch and eat lizards, frogs and young birds. They are famous for their cannibalistic tendencies and for this reason cannot be reared together—each little mantis must have its own cage. Much has been written about the horrifying sight of a female mantis devouring her mate. This often happens with captive mantids during mating. The male is perched on the female's back, and she can move around with him there. Sometimes she turns her head and begins to eat him from the head downwards, not in the least interrupting his work of pumping sperm into her at the other end. However, these reports are usually about captive mantids. In most instances in the wild, the male manages to make his escape before he is eaten.

There seems to be no limit to the amount a female mantis will eat. It is because of her great need for protein in order to produce the many eggs that she will soon be laying. She reaches her adulthood late in summer and then has only a few weeks in which to lay her eggs before she dies. She may lay well over a thousand eggs, and they are deposited, about a hundred at a time, each group in an egg capsule which she attaches to some low vegetation. Each species of mantis has a differently shaped egg capsule and they are made in a remarkable manner. The female pumps from her abdomen a frothy liquid which soon hardens. While she is making this nest, she is also laying the eggs inside it. The eggs are arranged in rows and layers, and there is a hatching area on the surface of the case opposite the side fastened

to the support. Through this the young mantids find their way to the outside world in the spring. How the mother mantis achieves all this simply by the sense of touch and the way she moves her abdomen and ovipositor about in the frothy mass is a wonder of nature.

The young mantids in our area hatch in May or June. They emerge through the hatching area and are tiny, limp, yellow nymphs, in shape much like the adults, but without wings. In a few hours their soft tissues harden, and they become gray in color. In the next three months they molt their skins six to nine times as they grow to adulthood, the last time appearing with wings. But when they are first hatched, the little mantids are very vulnerable. All kinds of predators hasten to the spot to make a meal. Birds and ants are two of the many enemies; and if the little mantids don't soon disperse, they may start eating each other!

There are other dangers that beset the mantid tribe, for even the greatest predator cannot escape other predators and parasites. Of course, a bird is not averse to snapping up a big fat mantis, if it can find one. But the mantis's camouflage works both ways: to hide it from its enemies as well as from its prey. Such animals as mice, rats, skunks and possums have been known to eat mantids. When confronted by such enemies, the mantis has another pretense. It stands erect and

The praying mantis looks like part of the bush it is sitting on.

spreads its wings in a menacing manner. This makes it look much larger and fiercer and may well frighten some attackers away.

There are other, more subtle enemies. Some small flies and wasps manage to lay their eggs inside the mantid nest where the larvae or grubs can feed on the mantid eggs. In France, there is a tiny wasp that fastens itself to the adult mantis and rides about with it. It holds on near the base of the wings or on the underside of the abdomen. When the female mantis makes her nest and deposits her eggs, the wasp leaves her, after laying her own eggs in the egg mass, where the wasp larvae will feed on the mantid eggs.

Our mantids achieve their camouflage by simply standing still for long periods among the leaves and grasses and letting their green or brown coloring merge with the vegetation. But in the tropics, many mantids have developed bizarre forms in order to look like their surroundings. Some species have become flattened and have grown extensions on their legs that make them look like leaves. Others are brilliantly colored and look very much like the flowers among which they hide. It is probable that this bright, flowerlike appearance even attracts nectar-seeking insects, which the mantis promptly catches and eats.

Mantids are considered useful insects because of the many pest insects that they catch and eat. Some gardeners collect the egg cases in the fall and put them out among their plants in the spring as a protection against invading insect pests. But the mantis is indiscriminate in its eating habits. It will eat beneficial insects, like bees, as well as the injurious ones. A garden cannot get along without bees to pollinate its flowers. And many of the mantis's victims may be insects that also war on agricultural pests.

People who have kept mantids for study or as pets report that they exhibit great individuality. Some adjust easily to captivity, eating and drinking whatever is offered. They will drink water from a spoon and accept chopped meat when it is held out to them in tweezers. But others refuse such food and will starve rather than eat meat they have not caught themselves.

Observers report that some mantids take great care in the capture of stinging wasps and bees, holding them away from their bodies and beginning to eat at the head. If stung, they sometimes drop the prey and lick the wound. One mantis that was offered a scorpion seized it in such a way that the tail was confined and unable to sting, and the mantis ate it without difficulty. But another did not get a good hold on her scorpion, which swung its tail around and stung the mantis on the head. The injured mantis released the scorpion and would not go near it again. She seemed to be affected by the venom, for she had difficulty eating; and when she made her egg case a week later, it was misshapen. Ten days after being stung by the scorpion, the mantis died.

11 · The Luring Lights

Fireflies, of course, are not really flies. They are beetles. The more than fifteen hundred species are found all over the world, the most spectacular being in the tropics. Among our North American species, both the males and the females usually have lights. But in other species, especially those in England, northern Europe and our Far West, only the females and sometimes the larvae light up. In many cases, the females do not fly and often they have no wings, but sit on the ground, a blade of grass or a bush, and signal the males to come to them.

Each species has its own code for flashing so that there is no chance of the wrong male and female getting together. The female also answers in code. If the female of *Photinus pyralis*—our common firefly— answers two seconds after the male has signaled, he flies toward her. When the male alights near the female, he brushes her with his antennae to be sure that she has the right smell. Sometimes she tests him also before mating takes place. It is possible to stand in a field or garden at night with a small flashlight and, by copying the rhythm of the flashing beetles, induce them to come to you.

Adult fireflies feed on nectar and pollen, if they eat at all. Some species never eat in the adult stage. They have no special protection nor do they conceal themselves as predators. So where is the pretense? As far as we know, there is only one species of firefly that disguises itself, the North American firefly *(Photuris pennsylvanica)*. The disguise is very ingenious. As with humans, when a good thing had been discovered and developed, there are always some among nature's children that take advantage of it for their own benefit.

This firefly may be found from Massachusetts to Panama, and it is the female that has become the pretender. Somehow she has learned to reply in code to the males of other species; and when the brightly signaling male comes down to her, she grabs him and proceeds to eat him! The males that are thus preyed upon are usually *Photinus scintillans*, but sometimes our common firefly *(Phontinus pyralis)* is taken.

The "fireflies" that light up the summer fields at night are actually beetles.

Pennsylvanica uses a single, fairly dim light when replying to the flashing signals. If the flying beetle gives two to five sharp, greenish-yellow bursts of light, she knows that her mate is on the way. But if the flares are very short and orange-colored, with five to ten seconds between, she can tell that they come from a male of another species, and she prepares to seize and eat him. Some scientists believe that the cannibalistic female may have already mated before she begins luring the males to their death. Possibly she needs to store up extra protein for the eggs she is about to lay, and so is impelled to continue the carnivorous diet she followed as a larva. When we consider the remarkable evolution of the fireflies' codes, designed to keep the species separate when mating, this breaking of the code by a different species for a very different purpose is extraordinary.

Scientists have long wondered at and studied the firefly's marvelous light. It is different from all our methods of lighting, because it is a cold light. Therefore, very little energy is wasted. Only three percent of the energy of the average electric light bulb goes into light; the rest is wasted in heat. The firefly's light would not be satisfactory for human use because colors do not look natural in its glow. But we hope that by studying how the insects make light, we may be able to develop a chemical light that will be useful.

The light-making organs of the firefly are located in its abdomen. They are groups of cells that store up two substances, known as luciferin and luciferase. When these combine with oxygen, they produce the firefly's cold light. Many experiments have been made to duplicate this light in the laboratory, but so far the results are much too expensive to compete with our hot lighting. If in the future chemists are able to manufacture luciferin and luciferase cheaply, it may revolutionize our methods of making light. Recently these firefly substances have been used by scientists in cancer research.

Beetles belong to the groups of insects known as the higher insects. They have a complete metamorphosis. That means that they go through four stages of growth and in the early stages they are quite unlike the adult beetle. They begin as an egg; and even in this very early stage luminosity is usually visible. Eggs are laid underground sometime between June and August, depending on the species. The incubation period lasts between thirteen and eighteen days, also depending on the species and the temperature.

Our *Photinus* fireflies lay their eggs in moist meadows, where the male flies about displaying his flashing signals. Although she also has wings, the female does not fly, but sits on a blade of grass and signals her mate to come to her. Neither the male nor the female of this species eats in the adult stage. The cannibalistic female of *Photurus pennsylvanica*, on the other hand, does use her wings to fly. She frequents the edges of woodlands and also deposits her eggs underground or among the roots of grass.

Firefly larvae stay underground during the day but come to the surface at night. They also have luminous organs and they are hungry little creatures. The larvae of both *Phontinus* and *Photurus* are carnivorous and attack and eat animals much larger than themselves, such as snails and earthworms. They inject a substance that paralyzes and then liquifies their victims so that the food can be easily sucked up. They spend at least two years in the larval stage, passing the winter in little underground cells that they make for themselves. Some individuals even take three years to reach maturity, so that the broods have an uneven development. This works in favor of the species. For if one group pupates and emerges in a year of harsh weather, they may all die before reproducing. But there will still be the late developers to emerge the following season and carry on the species.

The larvae pupate underground in the spring. This period is quite brief, after which the adult beetle emerges and within a few days is ready to start its short life of mating and egg laying.

It may seem astonishing that all stages of our fireflies have the wonderful ability to make light. Since this is used as a mating device by the adults, we can wonder why the early stages should also have it. Scientists theorize that luminosity was originally developed by the insect in all stages, and only much later was it put to use as a courtship and mating device.

Like all living creatures, fireflies have their enemies; and while some predators may not like the taste of the beetles with the chemical lights, frogs seem to be quite fond of them. A frog that has eaten a quantity of fireflies will show a distinct light glowing in its stomach!

In the tropics, fireflies are even more spectacular than ours. They often congregate in a certain bush or tree where they all flash in unison, as though an electric switch were turning off and on the lights of a Christmas tree. Such displays have been reported for over two hundred years from localities in Southeast Asia and India. How thousands of fireflies can time themselves exactly to the same rhythm is a mystery. But some observers speculate that it may start with one male answering a female and then another and another tuning in until there is a mass signaling. If they are all of the same species, they would all use the same code.

Fireflies are not the only luminous beetles. In the South American tropics there is a very large fire beetle called *Pyrophorus*. Four or five of these can make a light strong enough to ready by. Girls sometimes put them in their hair for decoration or fasten them by a thread to their dresses—without harming the insect. Like our fireflies, these beetles can be attracted to a collector by flashing the female's code with a flashlight. One scientist, collecting in Jamaica, says that he always flinched when the big, fast-flying male beetle zoomed in at him.

12 · The Weapon-Slinging Spider

Like many of the insects, spiders—which are not classed as insects, but as arachnids, because they have eight instead of six legs—are blessed with the ability to produce silk. Many use this silk to make elaborate webs in which they trap their insect prey. But some species have not developed the web-making technique. They use the silk for other purposes, such as lining a nest or cementing a trapdoor for their hidden hole in the ground.

A few have found even more bizarre uses for their silken threads, and one of these is the bolas spider (*Mastophora*). These spiders, which inhabit many regions of the Americas and have close relatives in Africa and Australia, belong to the large family of orb weavers. Orb weavers are responsible for the many elaborate and beautifully symmetrical webs that have made the weaving of spiders famous. However, this one little group of orb weavers, at some time in the distant past, gave up the practice of spinning webs in favor of a unique method of hunting. They make a small blob of sticky silk at the end of a short line

and then sling it at any moth or other insect that comes within range. Because this action seems to resemble the hunting technique of South American gauchos (cowboys), the spider has been named after their famous missile weapon. The bolas is made of several stones or metal balls, each fastened to a cord, with the cords tied together. When the bolas is thrown at the legs of fleeing animals, it wraps around them and brings the creatures to the ground.

The bolas spider is quite common in our country, but it is seldom noticed because it has abandoned the making of large and striking webs, easily detected in the garden. Instead, the female spider perches on a branch of a tree or bush, often several feet above the ground. The males of most species are so much smaller than their mates that they are hardly noticeable and usually do not make webs or hurl bolas. The female is the aggressive hunter and the male must be careful lest he also become the prey.

Mastophora, however, is quite timid during the daytime. There she sits on her perch, looking very much like a bird dropping or perhaps like a bud of the tree or a snail. For she is a fat spider with many odd bumps and markings on her back. If picked up, she curls in her legs and plays dead very convincingly. She can be turned over and upside down without moving or giving a sign of life.

But when night comes, if undisturbed on her perch, she shows a different character. Her web arrangements are very simple compared to the expert weavings of her relatives. First she fastens a line of silk to a point on the branch or twig. Then, holding it away from the stick, she crawls along for several inches, pulling out the silk as she goes and fastening it at a further point along the branch. Her line now hangs loosely, much like a trapeze, and after she has strengthened it along the length of the stick, she moves down to the lowest point on her thread.

Now the spider pulls out a new thread from her spinnerets. Holding it taut, she proceeds to comb out onto this line a quantity of sticky silk until she has a droplet as large as a seed pearl. She does this with her hind legs, each taking a turn at pulling out the sticky silk. She then pulls out a bit more of her line, until the tiny ball is hanging free. Then using the claw of one hind leg, she cuts the line close to the droplet so that it swings free with the droplet at the end. Quickly she turns around on her trapeze and grasps the swinging line with one of her front legs. She holds on to her trapeze with the three hindmost legs on the other side of her body. This is her hunting position, and now

she waits patiently for an insect to come within reach of her missile.

Spiders have notoriously poor eyesight, and *Mastophora* hunts in the dark; so how does she aim her missile? Web spiders know when a victim has stumbled into their webs by feeling the vibrations, and it is believed that some similar sense must warn the bolas spider of the approach of prey. Her usual victims are moths, and it is possible that the beating of their wings causes a vibration in the air, or even in the spider's trapezelike line. At any rate, she seems to know when prey is coming, for she adjusts her body and line as though getting ready for her throw, and when the moth comes within range, she swings her line in its direction.

When the spider's bolas connects, usually with the moth's wing, the prey is well caught, and no amount of fluttering can free it from the sticky missile. The spider quickly climbs down to it, bites and paralyzes it with her venom, and then either eats it on the spot or rolls it up in silk for a future meal. Sometimes the spider will have several of these rolled-up victims hanging alongside her perch. When she has sucked them dry, she cuts the threads that are holding them and lets the remains fall to the ground.

Naturalists have been studying the bolas spider since the beginning of this century, and many wondered at the patience of this spider that could wait until the prey just happened to come within reach of her swinging missile. It was noted that the moth often seemed to come back again and again, if the spider missed with its first throw. There were many guesses about why this happens, but only very recently has the reason come to light. William G. Eberhard, of the Smithsonian Tropical Research Institute, has described this remarkable behavior in the publication *Science.*

It has been found that not only does *Mastophora* protect herself by feigning death and disguising herself as a bird dropping, but she has an even more subtle pretense that helps her in her hunting. She emits an odor that copies the smell given off by the females of certain noctuid moths to attract the males of the species. Thus male noctuids are lured within reach of the spider's missile. This explains the remarkable behavior of the moth in returning again and again to the spider's reach. In mimicking the female moth's odor (or pheromone, as the scientists call this sex attractant), the spider has developed a unique kind of pretense.

Professor Eberhard and his co-workers base their proof on several observations and experiments. For one thing, the moth always approaches the spider from downwind. If it escapes in the first pass, it circles about and again comes in from downwind. The spider also seems to expect the moth to come from that direction; and when in the hunting position its abdomen points downwind, suggesting that the counterfeit pheromone is released in that direction.

Some naturalists have suggested that perhaps the moth is attracted to the "bolas" itself, that it may shine in a way to attract moths. To test this, the experimenters removed the bolas from the end of a spider's line—which did not deter the hunting spider—and found that the moth came to the spider nevertheless. The moth was found to approach the spider only when she was in her hunting position, leading to the belief that it is then that she releases her luring smell.

Since the spider has her underside (ventral) facing the direction from which the moth will come, and her eyes are on her back (dorsal) side, there is no chance that she can see her approaching prey. The scientists, however, noted that she extended her legs toward the moth when it was approaching; and if they made little humming noises, she responded with this same action. This suggests that she uses sound to sense the approach of prey.

Other interesting discoveries included the fact that all the 165 moths captured by one spider were males of two species of noctuid moths. The scientists placed sticky traps in the vicinity of their observed spiders and captured a great variety of other insects, such as flies and beetles, but only one moth like those being caught by the spiders. Presumably, all others were lured to the spiders' traps.

The bolas spiders live for only one season in our climate. When cold weather comes, the female dies. But before this, she has mated and laid her eggs. She constructs a strong and durable cradle to keep her babies safe through the winter. This egg sac is, of course, made of silk. Usually, she makes several of them and hangs them from the vegetation near her hunting grounds. Building the egg sac and laying the eggs is an exhausting job, and she usually rests for a week between each one and the next. The sacs are about the same size as the spider. The silk soon hardens, and the little nests look like nuts or other plant fruits. They are fastened to twigs or leaves by a long stem drawn off from the base of the sac. Each species has a distinctive way of building the sac, with different shades of light and dark silk. One is a bell-shaped sac, and another is attached to the twig at the base, while the stem hangs free. There may be one hundred fifty eggs in a sac, and the spider may lay up to seven hundred eggs before she is done.

In the spring, the eggs hatch inside the sac, and the baby spiders emerge from the nest. They squeeze out of a little hole near the base of the stem, appearing one after the other, and their first instinct is to climb up the bush or tree. As they go higher, they let out little lines of silk, which in time are caught by the wind. Then the spiderlings go ballooning away across the country. In this manner, they become widely separated, so that each will have its own hunting territory. However, as with most creatures of the wild, only a few will grow to adulthood to carry on the species. No doubt baby spiders are on the menu of many birds and animals.

The male spiders can be distinguished from the females when they first emerge from the sac. At this point, they are all the same size; but the males have a reddish coloring and their tiny palpi are rounded and swollen at the ends. These are their secondary sex organs, and the males are already adult when they leave the nest. They will hardly grow any larger than their one sixteenth of an inch. But the females will grow to ten times that size in the few months before they reach adulthood.

In a warm climate, like California, some egg sacs may disgorge their babies in the fall, in which case there will be adult females in the vicinity with whom the newly emerged adult males can mate. But in colder regions, the spiderlings must wait until spring to venture out into their world. In that case, the males will have to wait several months before the females are mature and ready for mating. How the little creatures survive for that period is still not known to science.

13 · The Fish That Goes Fishing

In early spring, as soon as the season opens, there is a rush of anglers to our streams and rivers, all hoping to make an early catch. Fishing has been a sport and a way of life since earliest times. But few realize that the fish have gone afishing for millions of years—long before a human being hung hook and line in the water.

There are 225 known species of anglerfish in the seas, living in tropical, subtropical and temperate waters. Scientists have divided them into three general types. The so-called goosefish, the largest of all, lives in shallow waters near the shore where it hides among the rocks and seaweed. The frogfish and batfish are much smaller and are apt to be found in warmer waters. The deep-sea anglerfish, the most startling in appearance, have taken to living at the bottom of the deepest parts of the ocean. For this reason, they are seldom seen or captured, and in some cases only one specimen of the species has been seen and described. Undoubtedly, there are many more down there; but fishingnets have only recently been developed to go that deep, and fish must be widely dispersed at such great depths.

What all anglerfish have in common is some kind of appendage or long feeler, usually extending from the top of the head and protruding out in front of the mouth. Often there is a fleshy blob at the end of this "line," which the fish can wiggle about, simulating a nice, fat worm. When another fish or ocean dweller approaches, attracted by the fake worm, the anglerfish simply opens its mouth and sucks in the water; the victim is swept into the jaws, where it is quickly hooked on a variety of sharp teeth and pulled down through the gullet and into the stomach. Many of the teeth point backwards, so that once the victim is caught, it cannot wiggle back out and escape.

Anglerfish usually have very large mouths, and the jaws are hinged in such a way that they can swallow victims that are larger than themselves. This often works to the disadvantage of the angler, for it is unable to release the captive once it is caught on those backward-pointing teeth. In such cases, both fish eventually die.

Some of the specimens that have been studied by scientists were caught because the dead fish floated to the surface of the sea and were picked up by some astonished fisherman.

The remarkable fishing apparatus of the anglerfish has evolved from dorsal (top of the back) fins. Often just one spine has been modified into a long ray, and in some cases the fish can move it forward and backward to entice the prey nearer to its mouth. The deep-sea anglers not only have their fishing apparatus attached to their heads—and some of it is extremely grotesque—they may also have weird appendages hanging down from the lower jaw. These fish seem to be all head and jaws. They have lost the slim, graceful, vertical look of dwellers near the surface. The great weight of water under which they live has had a flattening effect and given them a squat appearance. Their fins have shrunken into little-used appendages, for these fish move very slowly, if at all. They are content to sit on the bottom and wait for the food to come to them. In color, they are dark brown or black and their skin is usually without scales, but covered with warts, furrows and folds. And as they live in complete darkness, many of them have developed some kind of luminosity. Their eyes are small in relation to their bodies, for they have little use for sight at those black depths. Many of their angling lures have some kind of light, since sea creatures seem to be as easily attracted to light as are moths and other insects on land. One amazing anglerfish (*Galatheathauma*) has its lighted "bait" hanging inside its jaws from the roof of its mouth!

On the whole, these deep-sea anglers are quite small, for there is not much food to be found at the bottom of the sea. They have to rely on dead or dying animals and plants that drift downward in the water. Or perhaps they may be able to catch some deep-sea creature that makes periodic trips in seach of food to the upper layers of the ocean. But in spite of their small size, anglerfish manage to look dangerous and fearsome with their sharp teeth and fantastic protuberances.

These anglerfish, some of the ugliest in the ocean, are all females! Like the Bolas spider, only the females have developed these remarkable hunting techniques. For many years, scientists sought in vain for the males and did not recognize them when they saw them. For the males are tiny little creatures, a fraction of the size of the females, and they are usually found securely fastened to their mates, acting much like a parasite.

It is believed that the anglerfish female spawns her eggs in the deep sea, and that they float up toward the surface. There, where there is light and food, they hatch, and the babies live on the tiny sea creatures that inhabit the surface waters. At this time, males and females look much alike, except that the beginning of the fishing-line spines can be seen on the heads of the females. These little fish have eyes of a normal size, but the eyes never grow larger, so that they seem tiny on the adult female fish.

While they are in this larval stage, the little

anglers have a transparent envelope of gelatin beneath their colorless skin. The scientists believe that this unusual device may help them to float in the upper layers of the ocean and keep them from sinking too soon into the abyss. It may also protect them from enemies by making them seem larger than they are to the predators in their area.

Larval life continues for about two months, and as the tiny fish grow, the differences between male and female become apparent. The females grow rounder and fatter, the males slimmer. The females begin to develop their fishing apparatus, while the males grow buck teeth, which they will later use to grab hold of a female. In time, they all sink down into the abyss of the ocean, which becomes their permanent home.

Again as with the spiders, the males mature much faster than the females and are ready to mate sooner. Unlike the eyes of the females, which remain the same size throughout life, those of the males continue to grow. They become tubular in shape and point upward toward the light. The males also possess a keen sense of smell, having the largest olfactory organs, in proportion to their size, of any vertebrate. These highly developed senses of sight and smell are very important to the little fish, which must now swim swiftly through the vast ocean depths in search of an adult female. Such females are rare, moving slowly, if at all, along the bottom of the sea. But it is presumed that they must leave some kind of aromatic trail behind them for the male to follow. Finding her is of the utmost necessity, for if he does not do so within a few months, he dies.

Once a female is located, it is imperative that he never lose her again, so he swims to her and seizes hold with his sharp, prominent teeth. It is a grip that will never be broken. It does not seem to be important where he takes his hold. Males have been found clinging to the head, stomach and gill covers of the females. As he clings to his bride, extraordinary changes develop in his body and the two become practically one. The skin of his mouth fuses with hers, leaving only two small openings for water for his breathing purposes. His eyes and gut organs degenerate, and all his nourishment now comes from her bloodstream. He is practically a parasite on his mate, nothing more than a reproductive organ for the female, always ready to supply sperm to fertilize her eggs. Although he may grow after joining the female, it is never as much as she does. The largest male angler found so far was only one third the size of the female.

The species of anglerfish that live nearer the surface are larger than the bottom-dwelling kind. The largest of all is the goosefish, so called because it is believed capable of swallowing such a bird. This may seem a bit of exaggeration for a fish that grows no bigger than four or five feet long. But there are definite, confirmed reports of such fish being captured with a duck or a seagull lodged in their throats. Like its relatives of the deep, the goosefish seems to be all mouth, with a long, dangling appendage jutting out from the head to bob enticingly in front of the jaws.

This fish frequents shallow waters along our coasts, where it lies on the bottom, well hidden among the rocks and seaweed. Its fishing line, poking out from the bottom debris and wiggling like a worm, may well attract a variety of sea creatures to their doom. Perhaps even a duck, diving for choice morsels, may grab hold of it and be snared. However, in at least one of the reported cases of bird swallowing, the victim seems to have been asleep on the surface when the fish decided that it would make a good meal. Fish and bird were captured by some New Jersey duck hunters, who were in a boat five miles offshore, and when the gull was finally freed from the fish's mouth, it was found to have its head under one wing.

This, the largest of the anglerfish, and the one most often seen by land creatures like ourselves since it lives in the upper regions of the ocean, commonly feeds on twenty-seven varieties of fish. But when one particularly hungry individual manages to catch (and choke on) a duck, cormorant, loon or gull—that's news! From such extraordinary circumstances do species acquire their popular names.

14 · Doctors and Deceivers

The ocean is full of masquerades put on by some of the best pretenders in Nature's galaxy of strange creatures. One of the most subtle bits of work is that developed by a group of little fish known as blennies. To understand what they are doing, we must first consider a remarkable activity that has been going on among the reefs and coastal waters, as far as we know, for thousands of years, but was only recently discovered and observed by scientists.

When two species live together amicably for the mutual benefit of each, the condition is known as symbiosis, and this is what has been happening among the fishes of tropical reefs around the world. It was first observed by a scientist called de Beaufort, who saw a small wrasse in the Amsterdam Aquarium cleaning the mouths and gill openings of much larger fish. But it was not until the 1950s, when scuba diving became common, that it was realized how widespread this behavior is. Then for the first time, scientists could go down underwater for extended periods of time and watch the activities of fish in their natural habitat. What they observed astonished them.

Some twenty-six species of fish have been seen to clean parasites from larger fish, as well as six shrimps and one crab species. The best known and most often observed is a little wrasse (*Labroides dimidiatus*). This little fish is brightly marked, blue with a striking black stripe along its length. Others of its relatives may have different color schemes, but all have the distinctive stripes, which seem to advertise their intentions to the bigger fish that might otherwise snap them up for food.

Some of the cleaner fish move about the reef, looking for customers that need cleaning. But others set up a kind of station in one place and stay there, letting the big fish come to them. And that they do. Often there are lines of fish patiently waiting their turn in what some observers have compared to a barbershop or a doctor's office. A great variety of fish come to these stations to be cleaned: sea bass, jacks, parrot fish, squirrel fish, groupers, vicious moray eels and even poisonous scorpion fish. In other parts of the reef, these fish are enemies and ready to fight and eat each other. But here they wait quietly with no signs of discord.

The little cleaner fish (sometimes there may be two servicing the same station) take care of the big fish, one after the other. They swim all over them, biting off the tiny crustaceans and other parasites or bits of dead skin. The big fish hold their mouths open and the little cleaners swim right in unafraid. They do the same with the gill openings, and the big fish seem to stop breathing so that the cleaners can do a good job.

This symbiotic activity is achieved by the proper signaling on both sides. In addition to their striking colors which mark them as cleaner fish, the wrasses often do a little dance to advertise their intentions. The big fish also have ways of signaling their desires and need to be cleaned. Some of them change colors. The spotted goatfish blushes red. Others stand on their heads or tails, or may roll from side to side. Some simply spread out their fins. But all wait patiently until their turn comes and the little wrasses have cleaned and groomed them.

The fish that come to these cleaning stations often are not regular inhabitants of the reef, but may come from the deep ocean. Experimenters have found that if the cleaner fish are removed from the station, the other fish quickly disappear and the unusual gathering of visitors soon disperses. One observer counted as many as three hundred fish being cleaned at one station in a period of six hours. It is believed that the cleaner fish provide a vital medical service to the other fish on the reef. Fish everywhere suffer from infections spread by parasites that become attached to their bodies or invade their mouths and gills. So it seems that these little cleaner fish perform a much-needed function in keeping the fish population healthy. In fact, when the cleaners were experimentally removed from one area, the remaining fish developed sores and swellings due to parasitic infections.

As is often the way in nature, when a good thing has been established there are some individuals that will use it for their own advantage. And that is what the masquerading blennies (*Aspidontus taeniatus*) have done with the cleaner wrasses. Known as the saber-toothed blenny, *Aspidontus* looks deceptively like the wrasse. It is about the same size, has the same coloring and the same black stripe. It even performs the same little dance as it approaches a big fish and advertises itself as a cleaner. But it has far different intentions. When the big fish settles down, expecting a helpful grooming, the blenny swims along its back and takes a quick bite out of its tail or fin! When the client fish swirls about, looking for its attacker, it sees only a little cleaner fish quietly going about its business.

This kind of treatment naturally discourages the big fish, and it may go away and not patronize that station again. However, older fish are said to catch on to this subterfuge. The blennies are most successful with younger fish. The older ones learn to tell the difference and to avoid or even to chase away the pretending blennies. Wrasses from different areas or islands may have different markings, and the blennies in those areas have mimicked the markings. In one island reef, the cleaner wrasses have orange-red spots on their sides. The false cleaner blennies have also developed the red spots.

The sex life of the wrasse is hardly less remarkable than its cleaning activities. The males set up individual territories and defend their females against other males. Each male is surrounded by a group of females, the oldest and largest living nearest to the male. The male goes around among his females, displaying to them, keeping himself available for spawning time. But if the male dies—or is removed by an experimenter—the oldest female takes his place. She takes on the behavior of the male, displaying aggressively to the other females. Within a few days, she has become a male, has developed his sexual characteristics and is ready to fertilize the eggs of the other females when they spawn.

15 · The Quick Red Fox

Since earliest times, the fox has been considered a very smart animal. The word "foxy" means sly and tricky—a first-class deceiver. The great storyteller of ancient Greece, Aesop, a slave who lived around 550 B.C., made great use of the fox in his fables. One of the best-known stories concerned a fox that saw a crow flying off with a piece of cheese. The fox wanted the cheese, and so he sat beneath the tree where the crow had perched and began to flatter her, telling her what a beautiful singing voice she had. "The best of all the birds," said the fox. And so, in order to display her singing abilities, the crow began to caw, the cheese fell to the ground, and the fox snapped it up and ran off with it.

This story was not original with Aesop, for it goes back to an earlier version from India. And it was retold throughout the Middle Ages in all the European countries, showing how universally accepted was the idea of the fox as a great

The red fox has a bag of tricks to help it catch a meal or avoid an enemy.

deceiver. Of course, this kind of story is what we now call anthropomorphic: the imputing of human thought and morals to the animal world. Nevertheless, there is a good basis in fact for the general belief that the fox is a smart and wily animal, expert at stealing the best hen from the chicken coop and evading all the farmer's efforts to destroy it. As long ago as the beginnings of agriculture in ancient India, the farmers must have suffered from the depradations of the red fox.

The red fox (*Vulpes vulpes*) is found throughout most of the northern hemisphere, in Eurasia and North America and even in a bit of North Africa. When it was introduced into Australia in the nineteenth century, it adjusted easily to the new land and spread throughout much of that continent. The fox is an animal that has adapted itself to people. Far from being pushed aside by the advance of civilization, as are many animals, the fox fits right in and flourishes. For people bring food for foxes along with them. There are rats and mice and other rodents that gather around human habitations. They eat the farmer's grain and plunder the food supplies in the big cities. And of course, there have always been the farmer's eggs and chickens, food most appropriate to foxes. So as the dwellings of humans have spread across the continents, the red fox has spread with them.

The red fox does not fear winter and can endure bitter cold, as is demonstrated by the successful fox populations in Siberia and Alaska. But it does not thrive in the tropics and prefers somewhat open country to dense forests. It is not found in South America or Mexico, where its place is taken by quite different native foxes. There is a second fox species in North America, called the gray fox (*Urocyon cinereoargenteus*). It ventures no farther north than southern Canada, but extends its range through Mexico and Central America to the top of South America. It is easy to understand the difference in ranges of these two foxes, for the gray fox likes dense woods and forests and shuns farmlands and cities. It is the only canine that is adept at climbing trees, and will hide in the treetops to escape pursuit. The red fox, on the other hand, takes to flight when being hunted, which has made it the favorite quarry of that ancient and perhaps decadent sport known as riding to hounds. The red fox is a master at leading dogs astray and has developed such tricks as walking up a stream to cover its trail, or running along the railroad tracks to jump off just in front of a train, leaving the dog to its death. When pursued, it can run up to forty-five miles an hour.

In pre-Columbian times, there were no red foxes along our eastern seaboard, for the land was heavily forested and the fox native to that environment was the gray. But as colonists settled, cut down the trees and developed farming communities, the gray fox disappeared and the red fox took its place. This change was helped along by the settlers, who made several importations of foxes from England. Today, where many New England farms have been abandoned and the forests are returning, the gray fox is once again replacing the red.

Whether or not we believe in the thinking capacity of animals, this ability to adapt to changing conditions and to make use of new developments in its environment points to a keen and active brain in the fox. Long ago these animals developed a method of hunting called tolling, which human hunters have copied. In this, the fox puts on a show—a pretense—for some game that is beyond its reach. Usually it is birds that would otherwise keep well out of the way. A fox, seeing a flock of ducks on a lake or stream, will lie down near the water's edge and indulge in a number of crazy antics, rolling on its back with its legs in the air or throwing a stick about. Ducks are curious creatures and will often come up on shore to see what is going on, at which point the fox jumps up and grabs the nearest. Hunters have copied this technique by training small dogs to perform similar tricks and lure the ducks inshore for a better shot by the hunters. Only yellow dogs are used, because they are thought to resemble foxes.

The well-known naturalist, Ronald Rood, writes that he once observed a group of pigeons in a field near the road, flying and circling over something on the ground. Rood stopped his car to watch but could not make out what the object was. So he got out of the car to sneak up on the group. But at the first sound of his approach, the object leaped into the air, snapped at the nearest bird and ran off into the woods. It was a red fox, tolling for its dinner, and Mr. Rood had unwittingly interrupted the act. The naturalist also tells me that he has watched an apparently lame fox trying to lure him away from the vicinity of its den. The amusing thing about this performance was that the five fox pups forgot to hide, but sat at the mouth of their den watching the antics of their mother.

Just as the lion is the most "doglike" of the felines, living and hunting in social prides, so the fox is considered the most "catlike" of the canines. It is, on the whole, a solitary animal. There is some difference of opinion among observers as to how much, if at all, the male helps with the raising of the young. It has not even been established whether the fox is monogamous or polygamous. Roger Burrows, who has studied foxes in England, thinks that it all depends on territory. He says that the male establishes a territory and will then mate with any females that have dens in that area. Thus one fox may father several litters. This would account for the fact that

Baby foxes must learn from their parents how to hunt and defend themselves.

Burrows saw only one fox at the various dens he watched. A single male would find it hard to supply meat to several vixens and their litters, and this scientist does not believe they even try.

However, there is a different story from observers on the American continent. The eminent scientist, Adolph Murie, watched foxes in Mt. McKinley National Park in Alaska and noted that a female with five pups was actively assisted by her mate. And the writer-photographer, Leonard Lee Rue, has described the enthusiastic affection with which a vixen welcomed her mate each time he returned to the den with food. In captivity, male foxes are sometimes seen giving food to females and even carrying it into the den for the pups.

We can only infer that fox fathers, like human fathers, differ greatly in their behavior. There is no doubt that on the whole the fox is a solitary animal and does not form packs as do wolves and other canines. By the age of four months the pups are learning to hunt for themselves, and soon after, the family group breaks up. The parents separate until the next mating season, and the pups wander away to find territories of their own. Some of them travel long distances, and it is doubtless this habit that has helped to spread the red fox over such vast areas of the earth's surface. They can withstand the sub-zero winters of the far north as easily as the more equable temperatures of the temperate regions. In the north, the fox grows an extremely thick coat under its long guard hairs, and its long, bushy tail is an added protection against the cold. When sleeping, the fox curls its tail across its feet and nose to keep those extremities warm.

The red fox comes in a variety of colors: black, blue or silver, even albino. Sometimes the red phase is so light that it appears yellow. People once thought these were different species or subspecies, but it is now known that they are different color phases of the same animal, and there may be a variety of colors in the same litter.

The red fox is said to eat almost anything, and its diet certainly covers a wide range of edibles. Rodents and insects lie easily within its reach. But in winter, when many of its prey animals, such as marmots and ground squirrels, hibernate, the fox must give more time to stalking such birds as the ptarmigan. Even earthworms and slugs, reptiles and amphibians are eaten by the fox, and fruits and vegetables are relished. (Another famous Aesop fable concerned a fox and some grapes.) Blueberries are favorites in season, but the fox will also eat pears, plums and apples, picking up the early fruits as soon as they begin to fall to the ground. They also eat grain, clover, acorns and just plain grass.

Foxes are often scavengers and will dine off any kills left by larger predators. In our few national parks where wolves still exist, foxes have been seen to take advantage of a moose killed by its larger relative. In urban areas, the fox has always preyed on domestic animals, especially chickens and ducks. In recent years, large-scale raising of poultry has been moved indoors and out of the fox's reach, so that now the city-oriented fox must content itself with raiding the garbage dumps or cans. It is said to have become quite adept at getting into the latter.

The life of the fox is full of danger, and few live more than a year or two. Tagged foxes in New York and Michigan have been found to live an average of only 178 and 187 days after release. A fox that is both smart and lucky may live about ten years in the wild, but that is unusual. In captivity, the record is eighteen years. The chief reason for this is, of course, hunting. Human beings are the greatest predator of the fox. In England and parts of the United States, fox hunting with horses and hounds is an established sport. Some fifty thousand foxes are killed yearly in the British Isles. But even more lethal is the trapping for pelts. This death toll varies with people's fashions. When furs are out of style, the price goes down and there is less demand for fox pelts and less trapping and shooting. When furs are again in style, the price goes up and so does the death toll of the animals.

Foxes are useful creatures. They are a great help in keeping down the rodent population, which, in spite of all our efforts, continues to deplete our food supplies.

In the wild, the fox may be preyed upon by the larger predators. The lynx, which eats much the same prey as the fox, will sometimes hunt the smaller predator if the winter is hard and other food not available. On bare ground, the fox can easily outrun the lynx, but in deep snow the lynx has an advantage. Its huge feet act like snowshoes to support its weight, whereas the fox flounders in the snow. In such a situation, the fox may well become the hunted and the prey.

Another enemy of the fox is the grizzly bear. While this huge predator would have small chance of harming an adult fox, it often tries to dig out the dens to eat the pups. In such a contingency, the male fox becomes a veritable hero. Writing in *Outdoor Life* J. S. Crawford describes how he watched such a scene in Alaska. He says that the vixen stayed with the pups, while the male fox went out to meet the bear. The grizzly was still seventy-five yards from the den and may not yet have scented it. The fox circled the bear, an opponent that could easily kill him with one swipe of its paw. He made quick, feinting rushes at the animal, dashing in to nip the bear's rump when an opening offered and leaping aside to avoid the counterattack from the huge paw. Thus, circling, bluffing and teasing, he lured the great predator away from the den and his babies.

Perhaps it is no wonder that an animal as intelligent, courageous and adaptable as the red fox has spread all over the world in its chosen range and is the most widely distributed of all the canines.

16 · Intruders and Looters

While most acts of pretense in the natural world have evolved either for reasons of defense or as hunting and aggressive techniques, there are some unusual cases that don't seem to fit into either category. Foremost among these are the many creatures known as ant mimics and ant guests. Ants are among the most successful life forms on the planet. They are very old. Their ancestry has been traced back two hundred million years, and they are found all over the world except in the polar regions, where they were annihilated by the Ice Ages. Until recently, there were no ants in Iceland or Greenland, as the creatures had no way of returning there when those areas became somewhat warmer. But today, with our modern packaging and shipment of vegetable products, they have found their way back to those cold regions and are busily populating them.

Ants are social insects, and most species live in large colonies with hundreds of thousands of individuals. The different species have developed many varied ways of living, mostly underground. Some ants are almost blind and live entirely underground. Others build large "cities" in the earth with big cones of dirt and pine needles piled above, and spend the day foraging for food on the ground above. Some excavate their homes in trees or other wood, and still others build their nests of leaves, sewing them together with the silk derived from their grubs or larvae. And then there are the army ants of the tropics, which don't make a nest at all. They march at night in huge columns and camp during the day in some sheltered spot, where the whole group of ants clings together, making a nest of their bodies, with the queens and brood in the center.

Any creatures that are as successful as the ants in providing food and shelter for themselves and their young are bound to attract other creatures that want to share in this bonanza. And that is what has happened with the ants. Their ability to work together as a social whole has enabled them to build shelters that protect them against adverse weather and climates, to overcome and kill insects and other creatures much larger than themselves, to develop a way of life that is comparable to human agriculture. All this has not been overlooked by a myriad of creatures that are unable to do these things for themselves.

There are some fifteen thousand ant species so far known to science, and their many different homes (even the army ants are not immune) have been found to harbor some five thousand species of insects and other small creatures that in one way or another live off the ants' bounty. Ants are quick to protect their homes. When an invader threatens, they rush out in a frantic horde, biting and spraying formic acid, according to the defenses developed by the species. Thus, any insect wanting to get into the nest must develop some kind of ruse to sneak past the guards. Ants, moreover, are distasteful to most birds and other predators because many of them are endowed with formic acid, providing a very bad taste. A few animals in the tropics—the anteaters—have developed a special taste for ants. And the honey-barrel ants, which store their nectar food in the crops of certain members of the colony, are relished for their sweet taste by many creatures—including humans. But aside from these few exceptions, ants seem to have a built-in protection against many predators.

Therefore, just looking like an ant is a helpful defense, and a great variety of creatures have come to mimic the ants for this reason. Spiders are some of the best mimics. Two species copy the army ants. They are colored like them and run in the same manner, holding up two of their eight legs so that they run on six, like the ants. They have acquired the ants' smell, and so are tolerated by them, and they feed on the insects and other creatures that the foraging ants stir up along the way.

Many other creatures have learned to invade ant cities. Some get only as far as the front door and must be satisfied with feeding outside on the ants' refuse dump. A strange little wasplike insect, called *Gonatopus* manages to live just inside the entrance of *Formica* and *Myrmica* nests. It has not been able to copy more than the rudiments of the ants' language of pheromones, and so is not allowed farther into the nest. But it enjoys this much shelter and protection and rushes out to attack and eat any small bugs that may pass by.

Other mimics are allowed into the outer rooms of the nest and are fed by the ants themselves. And still others are able to penetrate to the inner areas of the city, where they feed on the ant brood and even lay their own eggs there so that their grubs can live on the ant eggs or larvae. To our eyes, the mimics that live outside the ant nest, moving about with the ants on top of the nest or in the entrances, may seem to have achieved the best act of mimicry. Some of them so closely resemble the host ants that it is almost impossible to tell them apart. Because they live in the light where visual recognition is the norm, they must look like their hosts. This is especially true of the species that live with the army ants, which never

After being fed by the deceived ants, this beetle defends itself by pulling in its legs and using passive resistance.

go underground. But then army ants are blind, so this protection must be against birds and other predators rather than against their hosts. Then why don't the army ants eat these hangers-on, as they do every other creature that comes across their path? Undoubtedly, there is another form of pretense operating here.

Communication in the insect world is primarily achieved by smell. Each insect gives off its own peculiar odor; often different odors, which mean different things. When a colony of bees is threatened, the workers give off a certain odor that summons all the hive to attack the enemy.

When a female moth is ready for mating, she gives off the special smell that attracts the male moth to her. These chemical odors of insect communication are called pheromones. The creatures that invade the camps of the army ants have copied the pheromones of those ants. They might be said to have learned the ants' language. And so they are accepted, just as though they were other ants, and they move among the colony unmolested.

In the big ant cities, other intruders have managed to learn the language of the colonies and by acquiring the smell of these particular ants to find food and shelter in their nests. As these invaders spend most of their time inside the nests, where it is completely dark, they do not mimic the ants as closely in appearance as the outside mimics. But they must have a close resemblance in odor to the inhabitants, or they would at once be killed and thrown out of the nest. They also must copy the ants in their behavior, stroking with their antennae in just the right manner so that the ants accept them and even feed them with regurgitated food. In America there are four species of crickets that invade ants' nests. They are the smallest of their kind, and while they have lost their wings in the process of learning to live with the ants, they still have their strong jumping legs. They have adapted so well to living with ants that their hosts accept them and feed them as they do each other.

Some of the most remarkable ant mimics are beetles. In Europe there is a beetle called *Atemeles* that spends most of its life in ant nests. But it has not confined its attentions to one species of ant, as is usually the case. Instead, it spends the summer with one species and in the fall moves into the nest of a different species. These ants live in quite different habitats. *Formica polyctena* is a wood ant that builds a mound of twigs or pine needles above its home. It lives in forests and wooded areas. It is in such nests that the larvae of *Atemeles* grow to adulthood. But for the winter the beetle moves to a nest of *Myrmica* ants, which inhabit grasslands outside the woods.

The larva of the *Atemeles* beetle has certain glands that emit an odor that attracts the *Formica* ants. It is believed to be similar to the odor or pheromone emitted by the ant larvae to encourage the adult ants to feed them. When an ant encounters a beetle larva outside the nest, it begins to lick it all over and soon picks it up and carries it into the nest. Scientists have learned these details by various experiments. Through radioactive tracers, they have demonstrated that substances passed from the larva to the ant that licked it. And when a larva was covered with shellac, so that the chemical substance could not leak out, and was then placed at the entrance to the ants' nest, the ants ignored it or else carried it to their garbage dump. If the larva was not painted with shellac, it was carried into the nest. Even bits of filter paper, soaked in the secretions of the larvae, were carried into the nest.

Once inside the nest, the beetle larva begins to beg for food. It does this in the same way that the ant larvae do. When the ant touches the larva with its mouth, the larva rears up and tries to reach the ant's head with its mouth. If contact is made, the ant regurgitates a drop of food into the larva's mouth. The ant carries the beetle larva to the brood chamber and puts it down among its own larvae. But the beetle larvae are much more energetic about begging for food, and so they get a greater share of attention and food. The ant children get less.

The beetle larvae are also predacious. They are not satisfied with the food brought to them by the brood-tending ants. They eat the ant babies that are all around them in the chamber. We might think that a few of these beetles could thus destroy the ant colony, but this is not so. The reason is that the beetle larvae are also cannibalistic. They don't confine themselves to eating the ant larvae: they eat each other. Investigators looking into the brood chambers of a *Formica* nest find that the ant larvae are clustered in little groups whereas the *Atemeles* beetle larvae are found individually. The one larva has eaten its relatives as well as a number of the ant larvae.

The beetle larvae stay in the *Formica* nest until they have attained their full growth and pupated. But once they have emerged from the pupal stage and become beetles, they leave their summer home. It is now fall and they go in search of a winter home. They find this with the *Myrmica* ants. At this point, the beetles are not sexually mature and they will need food during the winter so that they can grow into fully developed beetles. In the *Formica* nest, the raising of brood is discontinued during the winter and the ants go into a kind of hibernation. But in the *Myrmica* nest, activity continues all winter. The brood is maintained and food is available. There is no hibernation or winter starvation in the *Myrmica* nest.

Bert Hölldobler, writing in *Scientific American*, tells us how the *Atemeles* beetle finds its way from a *Formica* nest in the woods to a *Myrmica* nest out in a field. It would seem to be an impossible task, but the beetle simply moves toward the light and after a period of wandering finds itself out in the field. It locates the *Myrmica* nest by its odor. The smell comes to the beetle on the wind. Hölldobler says that it cannot find its way if the air is completely still, and that it is sensitive to this smell for only two weeks after leaving the *Formica* nest. Presumably, if it does not find a nest within that time, it will be without a home for the winter.

When a *Myrmica* nest is located, the beetle approaches one of the ants. It taps it with its antennae and raises its abdomen with the tip pointing toward the ant, and the ant responds by licking the secretions from the tip. The beetle's glands that release this secretion are called by Hölldobler the "appeasement glands." They seem to discourage any aggression on the part of the ant. There are other glands along the sides of the beetle's abdomen, which Hölldobler calls the "adoption glands." The ant proceeds to lick up the secretion oozing from them. Probably the odor from this secretion mimics the smell of the ant's nest. The ant is now convinced that the beetle is a friend and should be welcomed into the nest. When the beetle lowers its abdomen, the ant seizes it by the bristles that grow along its side and carries it into the nest: right into the brood chamber where it will be assured of good food and care throughout the winter.

Many beetles and other creatures have learned to copy the pheromones and thus speak the language of the ants of one species or another. But *Atemeles* is remarkable in having learned the secret of two such languages and to have put them to such good seasonal use.

17 · The Wolf in Sheep's Clothing

Deceiving the ants seems to be an activity quite common in the insect world; but I doubt that any are more original than the larvae of the green lacewing fly (*Chrysopa slossonae*). Lacewings are not really flies. They have received that popular name simply because they flit about. They belong to the order Neuroptera and at first glance might seem to resemble dragonflies or damselflies, but are not as energetic fliers. As adults, they seem quite harmless, but the larvae are insect predators and voracious eaters. Another member of the order is the ant lion, famous as the doodlebug which digs inverted conical pits in sandy soil to trap ants and other insects that may stumble into them. The ant lion lies in wait, hidden at the bottom of the pit, and catches and eats any insect unfortunate enough to fall into it.

The young of the green lacewing fly are equally voracious, but their food is aphids. The female lays her eggs in groups on alder leaves. Each egg is on a little stalk, raising it above the leaf. This is because the larvae might eat each other or the unhatched eggs if not so protected. However, the mother has laid her eggs close to a colony of alder aphids, so that the young larvae soon find their natural food.

Aphids are tiny insects, the bane of gardeners, who call them greenfly. They spend their lives sucking the juices out of plants and they are very prolific. A pair of aphids can become a whole colony in hardly any time at all. In fact, it doesn't take a pair, for the females often reproduce without help from the males. In order to reproduce at this rate, the aphids need abundant nitrogenous food. They get this by pumping quantities of plant juices through their bodies; but in so doing, they acquire unwanted carbohydrates which they expel with their excreta as a sweet fluid known as honeydew.

This honeydew is not entirely wasted by the aphids, for it is highly attractive to ants. Aphids are very vulnerable creatures, hardly moving about at all. They stay attached to the stem or leaf and suck the juice out, making no effort whatever to escape a hungry predator. And there are plenty of those in the insect world. Birds, too, relish aphids. But the aphids have powerful protectors in the ants. Ants are very fond of honeydew, as they are of any sweet liquid, and many ant species have formed the habit of collecting aphids and herding them, much as humans herd domestic cattle. In fact, aphids are often referred to as "ant cows." In some cases, the ants take them to their nests for protection or move them about from one desirable location to another. Some species of ants even build little shelters over their aphids, very like cowsheds.

Other ants simply milk the aphids of their honeydew right on the plants where they are feeding. They walk about over the colony, stroking them with their antennae. And the aphids in response give out a drop of honeydew which the ant quickly laps up and stores in its crop, to be taken back to its nest as food. The ants are very protective of their aphids, and any predator that approaches is promptly attacked and chased away or killed.

The story of the woolly alder aphid is told in the journal, *Science*, by three scientists: Thomas Eisner, Karen Hicks, and Maria Eisner. This aphid *(Prociphilus tesselatus)* appears to be covered with fluffy white wool. This is really a covering of dense tufts of waxy filament, and the shining white aphids are easily noticed on the dark branches of alder bushes. Three species of formicine ants have been observed to guard them, but only one species is found at a single colony. If the flock of aphids is small, there will only be a few ants moving about among them.

But if the colony numbers in the hundreds, there will be dozens of ants. Observers found that if they disturbed the aphids, poking them with a finger or a pencil, the ants immediately attacked and tried to bite. However, ants that were not with the flock, but merely running about the alder branches, did not offer resistance.

The lacewing larvae feed on the aphids by piercing them with their sickle-shaped mouth parts and sucking out the juices. When one aphid is sucked dry, it is thrown aside and the larva goes on to the next. The larvae are not easily seen among the aphid flock, for they are also white and approximately the same size and shape as the aphids. The observing scientists soon discovered the reason. The larvae are covered with the same waxy "wool" as the aphids!

The larvae of some related species of aphids are known to pile bits of vegetable matter and debris upon their backs as a kind of protection against predators; but this is the first known instance of an insect's using the covering of its prey. The predator in this instance has become an almost exact mimic of its prey. Birds are believed to avoid woolly aphids—perhaps the waxy wool is distasteful—and so they must also refuse the woolly larvae.

The larva has the white wax only on its dorsal (top) surface, but this white, waxy shield easily

This ant recognizes the larva that is feeding on the aphids, because the white, wooly covering has been scraped off. The ant is rushing to attack.

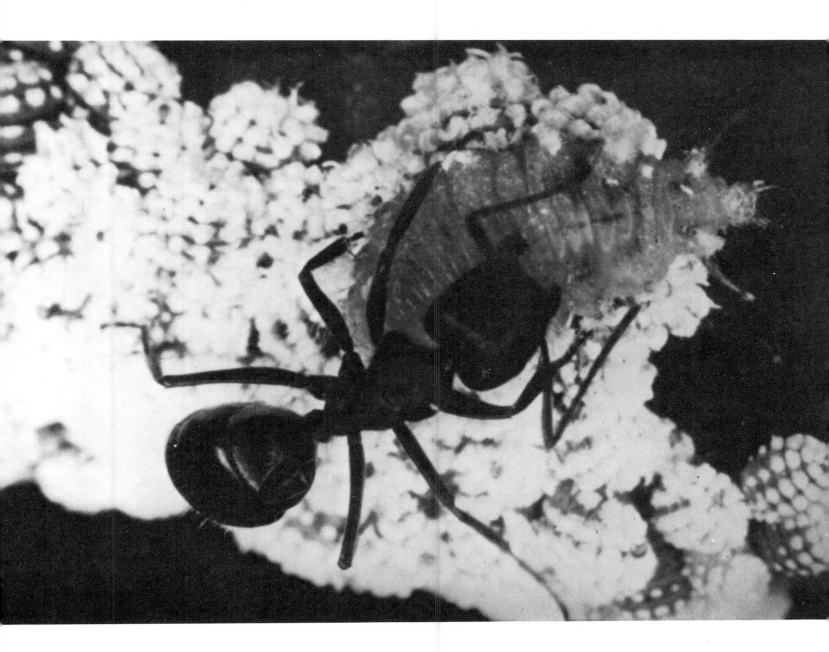

conceals it from above. The "wool" sticks to the bristles on the larva's back. The scientists found that it was easily pulled off with tweezers. Then they watched as the larva hastened to recover itself. It thrust its head into the wool of the nearest aphid and, grabbing hold of the strands of wax with its mouth, pulled the stuff away from the aphid, which reacted only with a slight twitch. The larva then reared up and pushed its head backward so that it could deposit the "wool" onto its own back, at the same time arching its back to receive the new pile of wax. It took about twenty minutes for a larva to recover itself completely.

Without its shield of protective "wool," the larva was open to attack by the ants, which immediately recognized it as an enemy. The scientists watched to see what happened to these denuded predators, and they saw that the guardian ants were not slow in rushing to the attack. Very few larvae were able to escape to an unguarded part of the aphid colony. Most were immediately bitten by the attacking ants, which seized them in their mouths and pulled them away from the alder twig or leaf. Once the larva had lost its hold, the ant dropped it to the ground. In some cases, the ant carried the larva down to the ground, and once or twice ant and larva fell to the ground together.

The bodies of these larvae have a rubbery consistency that offers a certain resistance to the ants, but when the ant's biting did pierce the skin and the ant stopped to feed on the liquid that oozed out, the larva soon died.

The scientists also released twenty-three larvae among the ants, still with their woolly shields intact. Only eight were bitten by attacking ants, and then the story was quite different. The ant quickly gave up and backed away, its mouth full of the waxy strands from the larva's back. It spent some time cleaning itself before it returned to its job of guarding the aphids. Some ants only inspected the wax-covered larvae and then left them alone, and the larvae then found suitable niches among the aphids and settled down to the business of feeding. They had passed inspection with the ants and were accepted as part of the aphid herd.

The scientists note that the ants in this instance recognized the larvae as part of the aphid herd by touching and by contamination with the waxy covering. But they feel that there must also be a visual recognition. These ants have good eyes and undoubtedly recognize the white covering on both aphids and larvae. The pretense must also be a good protection against birds. The "wolf in sheep's clothing" act pays off for these little pretenders on several fronts.

18 · Don't Forget the Plants

Over the millennia, all kinds of animals have evolved ways of fooling other creatures for their own benefit. Some of the very best pretenders are the insects. But sometimes the tables are turned and the plants deceive the insects!

You may think of orchids as being rare and unusual plants, growing in tropical forests and being sold as expensive corsages for beautiful women. But this is far from the truth. Orchids comprise the largest family of flowering plants and account for ten percent of all species. Their flowers may be tiny or large and showy, and they run the gamut of colors. There are over twenty-five thousand species of wild orchids that flourish on every continent except Antarctica, as well as many hybrids created by orchid growers. Far from being confined to tropical jungles, they are found in the woods and meadows, bogs and marshes of the temperate regions, in deserts and on snowy mountains. Species like our lady's slipper grow low on the ground, while others attach themselves to trees or rocks and are called epiphytes or air plants. They are not parasites.

They do not get nourishment from the tree itself, but somehow derive it from nutrients in the moist air and from rainwater trapped in the rough bark of trees. In Australia there are even orchids that live underground and flower beneath the soil.

Perhaps it is not surprising that such versatile plants should work out methods of fooling the insects. Insects and plants evolved together. Their symbiotic relationship goes back millions of years to the Age of the Dinosaurs. Some scientists believe that the insects made the flowers. Certainly, they are still dependent on each other today and could hardly exist separately. The insects derive their food of nectar and pollen from flowers, and the immature insects feed on the leaves. The plants have become dependent on the insects for pollination: the spreading of the male sperm in the form of pollen from flower to flower. True, there are still some plants—mostly trees—that still rely on the wind to spread their pollen. But the flowers and fruits and many of the plants that feed us could not flourish without the insects.

Plants have developed many subterfuges to attract insects and spread their pollen. They produce flowers with brilliant colors, calculated to catch the eye. The beautiful markings and designs that we admire—dots and lines—are no more than guidelines to direct the insect to the nectar and at the same time to the male anthers, heavy with pollen. And the myriad shapes of flowers have evolved as a way of attracting, even of trapping, insects. Some flowers have little landing platforms, encouraging the insect to alight and find its way to the nectar. Others have traps that close and will not release the pollinator until she has squeezed past the anthers. And most plants give out an attractive smell, beckoning the insects from afar. Usually this is a sweet, pleasant smell. But a few plants that rely on flies for pollination give out a smell like rotting meat, attractive to most flies.

While these interrelationships have been known and studied for many years, it is only recently that naturalists observed and unraveled an incredible mystery among the orchids. The plant in question is not one of the spectacular tropical varieties. It is a small terrestrial species, growing in southern Europe and North Africa, with the scientific name, *Ophrys speculum*. It got its name because the lip of the flower is a shining, metallic blue that suggests a mirror, and speculum is the Latin word for mirror. *O. speculum* does not produce any nectar, so how does it attract insect pollinators? After careful study by scientists, it has been shown that the

Ophrys orchids have a very special relationship with certain wasps and bees. They do not offer food, but something just as attractive. What they offer is sex. The blossoms, arranged upward on a single stalk, bear a striking resemblance to a female wasp or bee.

With these insects, the males emerge earlier in the spring than the females, and the mimicking orchids open their flowers at the same time. The male wasp, flying about in search of a female, sees what looks like a prospective mate, lands on the orchid's lip and tries to copulate with it. In the case of *O. speculum*, the shining blue lip looks very much like the crossed wings of a resting female wasp *(Scolia ciliata)*. The fringe of red hairs on the orchid blossom suggests the hairs on the body of the wasp, and the dark, threadlike upper petals of the flower are remarkably like the insect's antennae.

Different members of the *Ophrys* clan seem to mimic different flying insects; to our eyes they may not all be equally successful, but they are all sufficiently artful to insure pollination. For we must not forget that the great language of the insect world is odor—the pheromones. On further investigation, it has been found that this is undoubtedly the strongest part of the orchid's pretense. Each orchid emits a fragrance like that of the female wasp or bee it is mimicking. When the male arrives, lured by this sexual odor, he sees what looks like a female and at once begins the act of mating.

Orchids distribute their sperm in a different

manner from other flowers. Instead of showering out the pollen when the anther is touched or shaken, the pollen of orchids is glued together in little clumps, called pollinia. When the wasp or bee tries to mate with the blossom that looks like his female, he slides down the slippery surface past the pollinia, several of which stick to his body. When he continues his search for a mate and again tries to copulate with another blossom, the pollinia are transferred to that flower and pollination is accomplished. However, this act is a little different from the usual story. The bee looking for nectar goes headfirst into a flower and comes out with pollen all over its head and shoulders. In the case of *Ophrys*, the wasp is using its rear end, and that is where the pollinia adhere and are carried to the next bloom.

In Australia, an entirely different orchid has been found to achieve pollination in a similar way. Four species of the orchid *Crystostylis* have slender flowers that mimic a small ichneumon wasp *(Lissopimpla semipunctata)*. The antennae and ovipositor of the female wasp are well imitated and even the white spots on her abdomen are copied.

Scientists have experimented with the *Ophrys* mimics by cutting off the small blooms and attaching them to some of the nectar-bearing flowers most favored by bees. It was found that

This orchid looks and smells like a certain female fly. The male fly will try to mate with it, and in so doing, will pollinate the orchid.

bees then avoided these blossoms. Bees and bumblebees naturally shun flowers already occupied by other large insects, and it appears that in this case they take the orchid blossoms for the wasp they mimic. *Ophrys* designs its act for one particular male wasp or bee, each species of orchid having its own particular attractant. But other insects are inclined to leave the blossoms alone, seeing them as a wasp or bee already in residence.

Other orchids have varied their pretense. Instead of mimicking a female wasp or bee, they have copied the prey of certain wasps. Thus, the little spots on the flower look like tiny spiders, and the spider-hunting wasps dive down upon the flowers, trying to sting their prey. In this case, it is the female wasp that pollinates the orchid, and she departs from this foray with the flower's pollinia attached to her rear, ready to be deposited on the next orchid that seems to be offering her a spider. Another orchid from Australia is popularly known as a beardie because of the hairs on its petals. These are designed to look like the hairs of a caterpillar, the prey of a certain species of wasp, which obliges by stinging the make-believe prey and so helping to pollinate the flower.

Orchids count their seeds in the thousands and millions. Whereas each plant may produce many blossoms, only a few seedpods develop, showing that in spite of their many attractants to pollinators the desired result is not always accomplished. But the plant gets around this prob-lem by having extremely small, fine seeds, packed in myriad numbers into the few seedpods. One Venezuelan orchid has been found to carry four million seeds in a capsule.

Orchids are chiefly used by people for decorative purposes and are economically important to the flower industry. However, there is one orchid that is essential to the art of cooking. *Vanilla planifolia*, a native of Mexico, is one significant species. When the conquering Spaniards arrived at the Aztec capital 450 years ago, they found the native Americans putting bits of orchid seedpods into their cocoa. Thus vanilla was introduced into Europe and thence around the world and it is now widely cultivated in the tropics.

The seedpods are ground up to make our delightful flavoring; but growers of these exotic vines are faced with the problem that orchids do not normally produce many pods. Consequently, plantation owners hire workers to do the job that insects must do in the wild. Workers go from flower to flower, using a pointed stick to press the anther (male) and stigma (female) together, accomplishing what they call marrying the orchid. This assures a large crop of long podlike capsules and a good supply of vanilla for the kitchens of the world.

Orchids were known and studied by the ancient Greeks, who gave them the name, orchis, which means testicle. This is because the orchids of the temperate regions (which include Greece) are all terrestrial and have tuberose roots. While the shapes may vary, there are usually two for each plant, arranged among the roots on each side of the stem. These tubers play an important role for the plant, storing food and moisture underground where they are protected against winter's cold, and insuring new growth in the spring. But the arrangement of these tubers reminded the Greeks of the male genitalia, and so the plants got their name.

Of course, this comparison with human sex guaranteed the development of many myths over the millennia. For centuries the ground-up tubers were used as a love potion and later as a relief for croup and diarrhea. With the advent of modern medicine, these doubtful remedies have been discarded. But orchids are still favored in human courtship rituals, and florists continue to claim that "When you send your Valentine orchids, wonderful things happen!"

In the immense variety of flora and fauna that our world supports, there are many opportunities for one species to gain protection or some other advantage by copying another. Usually it is the appearance that is copied, but in some cases the scent, the signals or other behavior are mimicked by the pretender. (We call these pretenders the mimics, and the species being copied, the models.) In all cases, there must be more models—those mimicked—than mimics in the area; they must cover a wider range and be active over a longer period of time than the mimics. As scientists continue to study our environment, they are finding more and more remarkable cases of this kind of behavior.

An unusual bit of pretending, discovered within the last few years and reported by Raymond B. Huey and Eric R. Pianka in *Science* (January 14, 1977), concerns a lizard that mimics a beetle. These very different creatures live in the Kalahari Desert of southern Africa. We might expect to find a beetle trying to look like a lizard, but the actual situation is just the reverse. For the beetles, known locally as oogpister beetles (*Anthia*), belong to a protected species. They are armed with an acidic fluid, made up of formic acid and several other noxious acids. They not only have a very nasty taste, but they can squirt this fluid at birds and other predators.

Oogpister beetles (their native name means "eye squirter") are black with some white lines on their wings and bodies, and they run about energetically, looking for food. Adult lizards of the species *Eremias lugubris* are pale reddish tan, a color that blends well with their sandy environment. They run close to the ground in the undulating, sidewise manner of most lizards. But the baby *lugubris* are quite different. They are jet black with white stripes, a color that stands out against the desert sand. Moreover, they do not slither across the sand, as do the adults. Instead, they hunch their bodies up in the middle and run with a stiff, jerky motion. The greater part of their long tails, which might mark them as being something other than a beetle, are sandy colored and scarcely noticed against their natural background. In fact, the pretense is so good that the scientists admit to having been fooled several times by the young lizards.

This remarkable disguise lasts only while the lizard is as small as the beetle. By the time it has grown to be larger than its model, it has shed its skin and changed to adult coloration, which blends with the sandy habitat. At this time, it also ceases to run in its hunched, jerky manner, but reverts to the normal lizard's undulating dashes.

In an effort to learn how successful this pretense is against predators, the scientists counted the numbers of broken tails found among *E. lugubris,* as compared with other species. Breaka-ble tails are the lizards' chief defense against attack, for if the predator seizes one by the tail, the creature can often get away, leaving that appendage behind. Huey and Pianka found that the juveniles of *E. lugubris* have far fewer broken tails than lizards of related species. This would seem to prove that the mimicry is quite successful.

This is probably the first known case of a terrestrial vertebrate that mimics an invertebrate or insect. In the future, even more extraordinary examples may be brought to light, as scientists continue to probe into the mysteries of nature.

Bibliography

Atkinson, Agnes Akin. "Br'er Possum, Hermit of the Lowlands." *National Geographic*, March 1953.

Bent, Arthur Cleveland. *Life Histories of North American Gallinaceous Birds*. New York: Dover Publications, 1963.

————. *Life Histories of North American Shore Birds*. New York: Dover Publications, 1962.

Bueler, Lois E. *Wild Dogs of the World*. Philadelphia & New York: Stein & Day, 1975.

Crawford, J. S. "North Country Red." *Outdoor Life,* July 1971.

Eisner, Thomas; Hicks, Karen; and Eisner, Maria. "Wolf-in-Sheep's-Clothing Strategy of A Predaceous Insect Larva," *Science,* February 17, 1978.

Faulkner, Douglas. "Finned Doctors of the Deep." *National Geographic,* December 1965.

Fichter, George S. "Cleaning Up the Big Guys." *International Wildlife,* January/February 1977.

Fossey, Dian. "More Years with Mountain Gorillas." *National Geographic,* October 1971.

Gertsch, Willis J. "Spiders That Lasso Their Prey." *Natural History,* April 1947.

Grzimek, Bernhard. *Animal Life Encyclopedia*, vols. 2, 4, 5, 6, 7, 8, 10. New York: Van Nostrand Reinhold Co., 1972, 1973, 1974, 1975.

Gudger, E. W. "Wide-Gab, The Angler Fish." *Natural History,* March/April 1929.

Gurney, Ashley B. *Praying Mantids of the United States*. Washington, D.C.: Smithsonian Institution, 1951.

Heald, Weldon F. "Snakes Are Interesting." *Audubon,* July/August 1963.

Hölldobler, Bert. "Communication Between Ants and Their Guests." *Scientific American,* March 1971.

Huey, Raymond B., and Pianka, Eric R. "Natural Selection for Juvenile Lizards Mimicking Noxious Beetles." *Science,* January 14, 1977.

Idyll, C. P. *Abyss*. New York: Thomas Y. Crowell Co., 1964.

Klots, Alexander B., and Klots, Elsie B. *Living Insects of the World.* Garden City, N.Y.: Doubleday & Co., 1975.

Lane, Frank W. *Kingdom of the Octopus.* New York: Sheridan House, 1960.

Marden, Luis. "The Exquisite Orchids." *National Geographic,* April 1971.

Meeuse, B. J. *The Story of Pollination.* New York: Ronald Press, 1961.

Oldroyd, Harold. *The Natural History of Flies.* New York: W. W. Norton Co., 1964.

Parker, Hampton Wildman. *Snakes of the World.* New York: Dover Publications, 1963.

Rogers, Charlie E. "Walkingsticks—Insects or Twigs?" *Insect World Digest,* March/April 1975.

Schaller, George B. *The Year of the Gorilla.* Chicago: University of Chicago Press, 1964.

Simon, Hilda. *The Private Lives of Orchids.* Philadelphia: J. B. Lippincott Co., 1975.

Vosburgh, Frederick G. "Torchbearers of the Twilight." *National Geographic,* May 1951.

Wickler, Wolfgang. *Mimicry in Plants and Animals.* New York: McGraw-Hill Book Co., 1968.

Index